Child Development

A Topical Approach

Robert S. Feldman

University of Massachusetts Amherst

PEARSON

Boston   Columbus   Indianapolis   New York   San Francisco   Upper Saddle River
Amsterdam   Cape Town   Dubai   London   Madrid   Milan   Munich   Paris   Montréal   Toronto
Delhi   Mexico City   São Paulo   Sydney   Hong Kong   Seoul   Singapore   Taipei   Tokyo

To Alex and Miles

Executive Editor: Erin Mitchell
Editorial Project Manager: Diane Szulecki
Editorial Assistant: Sarah Henrich
Director of Marketing: Brandy Dawson
Marketing Manager: Jeremy Intal
Managing Editor: Linda Behrens
Senior Production Project Manager: Annemarie Franklin
Operations Specialist: Diane Peirano
Senior Art Director: Leslie Osher
Interior Designer: Ximena Tamvakopoulos

Cover Photo: © olly/Fotolia
Cover Designer: Wanda España
Senior Digital Media Editor: David Alick
Director of Media Development: Brian Hyland
Media Project Manager, Production: Caitlin Smith
Full-Service Project Management: Revathi Viswanathan/PreMediaGlobal
Composition: PreMediaGlobal
Printer/Binder: LSC Communications
Cover Printer: LSC Communications
Text Font: 10/12 Times Lt Std Roman

Credits and acknowledgments borrowed from other sources and reproduced, with permission, in this textbook appear on the appropriate page within text.

Library of Congress Cataloging-in-Publication Data

Feldman, Robert S. (Robert Stephen)
  Child development: a topical approach / Robert S. Feldman, University of Massachusetts Amherst.
    pages cm
  Revised edition of the author's Child development, 6th ed., published in 2012.
  Includes bibliographical references and index.
  ISBN-13: 978-0-205-92349-6
  ISBN-10: 0-205-92349-6
  1. Child development. 2. Child psychology. 3. Adolescence. 4. Adolescent psychology.
I. Title.
  HQ767.9.F43 2014
  305.231—dc23

                                  2013015514

11 17

ISBN 10:   0-205-92349-6
ISBN 13: 978-0-205-92349-6

Book a la carte Edition
ISBN 10:   0-205-94768-9
ISBN 13: 978-0-205-94768-3

Brief Contents

CHAPTER **1** An Introduction to Child Development 2

CHAPTER **2** Theoretical Perspectives and Research 20

CHAPTER **3** The Start of Life: Genetics and Prenatal Development 56

CHAPTER **4** Birth and the Newborn Infant 94

CHAPTER **5** Physical Growth and Health 124

CHAPTER **6** Cognitive Development: Piaget and Vygotsky 160

CHAPTER **7** Cognitive Development: Information Processing 190

CHAPTER **8** Language Development 218

CHAPTER **9** Intelligence 244

CHAPTER **10** Social and Emotional Development 272

CHAPTER **11** Development of the Self 304

CHAPTER **12** Gender and Sexuality 326

CHAPTER **13** Moral Development and Aggression 350

CHAPTER **14** Friends and Family 380

CHAPTER **15** Schooling, Culture, and Society: Living in a Multicultural World 418

Contents

Preface   xii
About the Author   xix

1 An Introduction to Child Development   2

PROLOGUE: Conceptions, Old and New   3

● MODULE 1.1: **An Orientation to Child Development**   4

Characterizing Child Development: The Scope of the Field   5
Topical Areas in Child Development   5
Age Ranges and Individual Differences   6
The Links between Topics and Ages   7
Cohort Influences on Development: Developing with Others in a Social World   9
Review, Check, and Apply   10

● MODULE 1.2: **Children: Past, Present, and Future**   10

Early Views of Children   11
Philosophers' Perspectives on Children   11
Baby Biographies   11
Focus on Childhood   11
The 20th Century: Child Development as a Discipline   11
Contributions of Women   12
Today's Key Issues and Questions: Child Development's Underlying Themes   12
Continuous Change versus Discontinuous Change   12
Critical and Sensitive Periods: Gauging the Impact of Environmental Events   13
Life Span Approaches versus a Focus on Particular Periods   14
The Relative Influence of Nature and Nurture on Development   14
Implications for Child Rearing and Social Policy   14
The Future of Child Development   15
Review, Check, and Apply   17
The Case of . . . Too Many Choices   18
Looking Back   18
Key Terms and Concepts   19
Epilogue   19

2 Theoretical Perspectives and Research   20

PROLOGUE: The Unasked Questions   21

● MODULE 2.1: **Perspectives on Children**   22

The Psychodynamic Perspective: Focusing on Internal Forces   23
Freud's Psychoanalytic Theory   23
Erikson's Psychosocial Theory   24
Assessing the Psychodynamic Perspective   25
The Behavioral Perspective: Focusing on External Forces   25
Classical Conditioning: Stimulus Substitution   26
Operant Conditioning   26
Social-Cognitive Learning Theory: Learning through Imitation   27
Assessing the Behavioral Perspective   27
The Cognitive Perspective: Examining the Roots of Understanding   27
Piaget's Theory of Cognitive Development   28
Assessing Piaget's Theory   29
Information Processing Approaches   29
Assessing Information Processing Approaches   30
Cognitive Neuroscience Approaches   30
Assessing Cognitive Neuroscience Approaches   30
The Contextual Perspective: Taking a Broad Approach to Development   31
The Bioecological Approach to Development   31
The Influence of Culture   32
Assessing the Bioecological Approach   32
Vygotsky's Sociocultural Theory   32
Assessing Vygotsky's Theory   33
Evolutionary Perspectives: Our Ancestors' Contributions to Behavior   34
Assessing the Evolutionary Perspective   34
Why "Which Perspective Is Right?" Is the Wrong Question   35
Review, Check, and Apply   36

● MODULE 2.2: **The Scientific Method and Research**   37

Theories and Hypotheses: Posing Developmental Questions   37
Theories: Framing Broad Explanations   38
Hypotheses: Specifying Testable Predictions   38
Choosing a Research Strategy: Answering Questions   38

Correlational Studies   39
The Correlation Coefficient   40
Types of Correlational Studies   41
Experiments: Determining Cause and Effect   42
Designing an Experiment   43
Random Assignment   43
Choosing a Research Setting   44
Review, Check, and Apply   46

● MODULE 2.3: **Research Strategies and Challenges   47**

Theoretical and Applied Research: Complementary Approaches   47
Measuring Developmental Change   47
Longitudinal Studies: Measuring Individual Change   48
Cross-Sectional Studies   49
Sequential Studies   50
Ethics and Research   50
Review, Check, and Apply   52
The Case of . . . a Study in Violence   53
Looking Back   53
Key Terms and Concepts   54
Epilogue   54

3 The Start of Life: Genetics and Prenatal Development   56

PROLOGUE: An Agonizing Choice   57

● MODULE 3.1 **Earliest Development   58**

Genes and Chromosomes: The Code of Life   58
Multiple Births: Two—or More—for the Genetic Price of One   59
Boy or Girl? Establishing the Sex of the Child   59
The Basics of Genetics: The Mixing and Matching of Traits   60
Transmission of Genetic Information   61
Polygenic Traits   62
The Human Genome and Behavioral Genetics: Cracking the Genetic Code   63
Inherited and Genetic Disorders: When Development Goes Awry   63
Genetic Counseling: Predicting the Future from the Genes of the Present   66
Prenatal Testing   66
Screening for Future Problems   67
Review, Check, and Apply   69

● MODULE 3.2: **The Interaction of Heredity and Environment   70**

The Role of the Environment in Determining the Expression of Genes: From Genotypes to Phenotypes   70
Interaction of Factors   70

Studying Development: How Much Is Nature? How Much Is Nurture?   71
Nonhuman Animal Studies: Controlling Both Genetics and Environment   72
Contrasting Relatedness and Behavior: Adoption, Twin, and Family Studies   72
Physical Traits: Family Resemblances   73
Intelligence: More Research, More Controversy   73
Genetic and Environmental Influences on Personality: Born to Be Outgoing?   74
Psychological Disorders: The Role of Genetics and Environment   77
Can Genes Influence the Environment?   78
Review, Check, and Apply   78

● MODULE 3.3: **Prenatal Growth and Change   79**

Fertilization: The Moment of Conception   80
The Stages of the Prenatal Period: The Onset of Development   80
The Germinal Stage: Fertilization to 2 Weeks   80
The Embryonic Stage: 2 Weeks to 8 Weeks   81
The Fetal Stage: 8 Weeks to Birth   82
Pregnancy Problems   83
Infertility   83
Ethical Issues   84
Miscarriage and Abortion   84
The Prenatal Environment: Threats to Development   84
Mother's Diet   86
Mother's Age   86
Mother's Prenatal Support   86
Mother's Health   87
Mothers' Drug Use   88
Mothers' Use of Alcohol and Tobacco   88
Do Fathers Affect the Prenatal Environment?   89
Review, Check, and Apply   90
The Case of . . . The Genetic Finger of Fate   91
Looking Back   92
Key Terms and Concepts   93
Epilogue   93

4 Birth and the Newborn Infant   94

PROLOGUE: Smaller than a Soda Can   95

● MODULE 4.1: **Birth   96**

Labor: The Process of Birth Begins   96
Birth: From Fetus to Neonate   98
The Apgar Scale   98
Physical Appearance and Initial Encounters   99
Approaches to Childbirth: Where Medicine and Attitudes Meet   99
Alternative Birthing Procedures   100
Childbirth attendants: Who delivers?   101

Pain and Childbirth   102
Use of Anesthesia and Pain-Reducing Drugs   102
Postdelivery Hospital Stay: Deliver, Then Depart?   102
Newborn Medical Screening   103
Review, Check, and Apply   105

● **MODULE 4.2:** **Birth Complications**   106

Preterm Infants: Too Soon, Too Small   106
Very-Low-Birthweight Infants: The Smallest of the Small   107
What Causes Preterm and Low-Birthweight Deliveries?   108
Postmature Babies: Too Late, Too Large   109
Cesarean Delivery: Intervening in the Process of Birth   110
Infant Mortality and Stillbirth: The Tragedy of Premature Death   111
Postpartum Depression: Moving from the Heights of Joy to the Depths of Despair   114
Review, Check, and Apply   114

● **MODULE 4.3:** **The Competent Newborn**   115

Physical Competence: Meeting the Demands of a New Environment   116
Sensory Capabilities: Experiencing the World   117
Early Learning Capabilities   117
Classical Conditioning   118
Operant Conditioning   118
Habituation   119
Social Competence: Responding to Others   119
Review, Check, and Apply   121
The Case of . . . No Place Like Home?   121
Looking Back   122
Key Terms and Concepts   123
Epilogue   123

5 Physical Growth and Health   124

PROLOGUE: Waiting for Allan's First Steps   125

● **MODULE 5.1:** **Physical Growth and Change**   126

The Growing Body   126
Height and Weight   126
Four Principles of Growth   127
Individual Differences in Height and Weight   128
Changes in Body Shape and Structure   128
Cultural Patterns of Growth   129
The Growing Brain   130
Brain Growth during Childhood and Adolescence   130
Lateralization   131
Gross Motor Development   133
Development of Gross Motor Skills   133
The Preschool Years   134
Middle Childhood   135
Fine Motor Development   136
Infancy   136
The Preschool Years   136

Middle Childhood   137
Handedness: Separating Righties from Lefties   137
Art: The Picture of Development   138
Puberty: The Start of Sexual Maturation   138
Review, Check, and Apply   140

● **MODULE 5.2:** **The Development of the Senses**   141

First Looks: Visual Perception in Infancy   142
First Sounds: Auditory Perception in Infancy   143
Smell and Taste in Infancy   145
Infants' Sensitivity to Pain and Touch   145
Contemporary Views on Infant Pain   145
Responding to Touch   146
Multimodal Perception: Combining Individual Sensory Inputs   146
Sensory Development beyond Infancy   148
Review, Check, and Apply   148

● **MODULE 5.3:** **Nutrition and Health**   149

Nutrition: Links to Overall Functioning   149
Malnutrition   150
Childhood Obesity: Genetic and Social Factors   151
Dealing with Obesity   153
Health and Wellness   153
Serious Childhood Illnesses   154
Asthma   154
Injury   155
Sleep   156
Review, Check, and Apply   156
The Case of . . . Girls Don't   157
Looking Back   157
Key Terms and Concepts   158
Epilogue   159

6 Cognitive Development: Piaget and Vygotsky   160

PROLOGUE: Jared   161

● **MODULE 6.1:** **Piaget's Approach to Cognitive Development**   162

Piaget: The Master Observer of Children   162
Key Elements of Piaget's Theory   163
Cognitive Development in Infancy   164
The Sensorimotor Period: The Earliest Stage of Cognitive Growth (Birth to 2 Years)   164
Cognitive Development in the Preschool Years   168
Piaget's Stage of Preoperational Thinking (Ages 2 to 7)   169
The Relation between Language and Thought   169
Centration: What You See Is What You Think   169
Conservation: Learning That Appearances Are Deceiving   170

Incomplete Understanding of Transformation 171
Egocentrism: The Inability to Take Others' Perspectives 172
The Emergence of Intuitive Thought 172
Cognitive Development in the School Years and
  Adolescence 174
The Rise of Concrete Operational Thought (Ages 7 to 12) 174
Piaget's Formal Operational Stage (Ages 12 to 15) 175
Using Formal Operations to Solve Problems 175
The Consequences of Adolescents' Use of Formal Operations 177
Review, Check, and Apply 177

● **MODULE 6.2: Appraising Piaget: Support and
Challenges 178**

Piaget's Contributions to Developmental Science 179
The Critics Weigh In 179
A Final Summation 181
Review, Check, and Apply 182

● **MODULE 6.3: Vygotsky's View of Cognitive
Development: Taking Culture into Account 182**

The Importance of Culture 183
The Zone of Proximal Development 183
Cultural Tools 185
Evaluating Vygotsky's Contributions 185
Review, Check, and Apply 187
The Case of . . . the Risky Bet 187
Looking Back 188
Key Terms and Concepts 189
Epilogue 189

**7 Cognitive Development: Information
Processing 190**

PROLOGUE: Forgotten Memories 191

● **MODULE 7.1: The Basics of Information
Processing 192**

Encoding, Storage, and Retrieval: The Foundations of
  Information Processing 192
Automatization 193
Early Abilities 193
Information-Processing Perspectives: Gradual Transformations
  in Abilities 194
Cognitive Growth during the School Years 194
Explaining the Teenage (Mental) Growth Spurt 194
Egocentrism in Thinking: Adolescents' Self-Absorption 195
Academic Performance and Stereotype Threat 197
Review, Check, and Apply 198

● **MODULE 7.2: Memory and Attention 199**

The Three-System Approach to Memory 199
Memory During Infancy: They Must Remember This . . . 199

The Duration of Memories 200
Memory in Early Childhood 201
Preschoolers' Understanding of Numbers 201
Memory: Recalling the Past 201
Memory Development in the School Years 202
Improving Memory 203
The Cognitive Neuroscience of Memory 203
Attention 204
Attention: The First Step in Information Processing 204
Review, Check, and Apply 208

● **MODULE 7.3: Applying Information Processing
Approaches 209**

Forensic Developmental Psychology: Bringing Child
  Development to the Courtroom 209
Information Processing Contributions to the Classroom 211
How Should We Teach Reading? 211
Teaching Critical Thinking 212
Information Processing Approaches in Perspective 213
Review, Check, and Apply 214
The Case of . . . the Frustrated Fantasy 215
Looking Back 215
Key Terms and Concepts 217
Epilogue 217

8 Language Development 218

PROLOGUE: The First Word Spoken 219

● **MODULE 8.1 The Course of Language
Development 220**

The Fundamentals of Language: From Sounds to
  Symbols 220
Early Sounds and Communication 220
First Words 222
First Sentences 223
Language Advances During the Preschool Years 225
Private Speech and Social Speech 226
Language Development during Middle Childhood: Mastering
  Language 226
Mastering the Mechanics of Language 226
Metalinguistic Awareness 227
How Language Promotes Self-Control 227
Review, Check, and Apply 228

● **MODULE 8.2: The Origins of Language
Development 229**

Language Acquisition 230
Learning Theory Approaches: Language as a Learned Skill 230
Nativist Approaches: Language as an Innate Skill 230
The Interactionist Approaches 231
How Are Language and Thought Related? 231
Review, Check, and Apply 233

● MODULE 8.3: Children's Conversations: Speaking to and With Children   234

The Language of Infant-Directed Speech   234

Gender Differences in Speech Directed toward Children   236

The Links between Language Development and Poverty   236

Bilingualism: Speaking in Many Tongues   237

Review, Check, and Apply   239

The Case of . . . the Deedio Mystery   240

Looking Back   241

Key Terms and Concepts   242

Epilogue   242

9 Intelligence   244

PROLOGUE: The Exceptional Daniel Skandera   245

● MODULE 9.1 Intelligence: Determining Individual Strengths   246

Intelligence Benchmarks: Differentiating the Intelligent from the Unintelligent   247

Binet's Test   247

Measuring IQ: Present-Day Approaches to Intelligence   248

Fairness in IQ Testing   249

Reliability and Validity   249

The Meaning of IQ Scores   251

What IQ Tests Don't Tell: Alternative Conceptions of Intelligence   252

Smart Thinking: The Triarchic Theory of Intelligence   253

Emotional Intelligence   254

Review, Check, and Apply   255

● MODULE 9.2: Controversies Involving Intelligence   256

Individual Differences in Intelligence: Is One Infant Smarter Than Another?   256

What Is Infant Intelligence?   257

Developmental Scales   257

Information-Processing Approaches to Infant Intelligence   258

Group Differences in IQ   259

Explaining Racial Differences in IQ   260

The Bell Curve Controversy   260

Review, Check, and Apply   262

● MODULE 9.3: Intellectual Deficits and the Intellectually Gifted   263

The Least Restrictive Environment   263

Below the Norm: Intellectual Disability   265

Degrees of Intellectual Disability   265

Above the Norm: The Gifted and Talented   266

Educating the Gifted and Talented   266

Review, Check, and Apply   268

The Case of . . . the Worried Eighth-Grade Teacher   269

Looking Back   269

Key Terms and Concepts   270

Epilogue   270

10 Social and Emotional Development   272

PROLOGUE: The Child-Proof Bin   273

● MODULE 10.1 Forming the Roots of Sociability   274

Attachment: Forming Social Bonds   274

The Ainsworth Strange Situation and Patterns of Attachment   275

Producing Attachment: The Roles of the Mother and Father   277

Mothers and Attachment   277

Fathers and Attachment   278

Are There Differences in Attachment to Mothers and Fathers?   278

Infant Interactions: Developing a Working Relationship   279

Infants' Sociability with Their Peers: Infant–Infant Interaction   281

Review, Check, and Apply   282

● MODULE 10.2: Emotional Development   283

Emotions in Infancy: Do Infants Experience Emotional Highs and Lows?   283

Experiencing Emotions   284

Stranger Anxiety and Separation Anxiety   285

Smiling   286

Decoding Others' Facial and Vocal Expressions   286

Social Referencing: Feeling What Others Feel   287

Two Explanations of Social Referencing   288

Theory of Mind: Infants' Perspectives on the Mental Lives of Others—and Themselves   288

Understanding What Others Are Thinking   289

Emotional Development in Middle Childhood   289

Emotional Development in Adolescence   290

The Instability of Emotions in Adolescence   290

The Neurological Basis of Emotion   291

Emotional Self-Regulation   291

Emotional Difficulties in Adolescence: Depression and Suicide   292

Adolescent Depression   292

Adolescent Suicide   293

Review, Check, and Apply   295

● MODULE 10.3: Personality Development   296

Temperament: Stabilities in Infant Behavior   296

Categorizing Temperament: Easy, Difficult, and Slow-to-Warm Babies   297

The Consequences of Temperament: Does Temperament Matter?   298

The Biological Basis of Temperament   298

Erikson's Theory of Psychosocial Development   299

Psychosocial Development During Middle Childhood and Adolescence   300

Review, Check, and Apply   300
The Case of . . . the Long Good-bye   301
Looking Back   301
Key Terms and Concepts   302
Epilogue   303

11 Development of the Self   304

PROLOGUE: Who Is Karl Haglund?   305

● MODULE 11.1 The Development of the Self   306

The Roots of Self-Awareness: Do Infants Know
  Who They Are?   306
Self-Concept in the Preschool Years: Thinking about
  the Self   307
Culture and Self-Concept   307
Understanding One's Self in Middle Childhood   308
The Shift in Self-Understanding from the Physical to the
  Psychological   309
Review, Check, and Apply   309

● MODULE 11.2: Adolescence: The Search for Identity   311

Self-Concept: What Am I Like?   311
Identity Formation: Change or Crisis?   312
Societal Pressures and Reliance on Friends and Peers   312
Psychological Moratorium   313
Limitations of Erikson's Theory   313
Marcia's Approach to Identity Development: Updating
  Erikson   313
Identity, Race, and Ethnicity   314
Review, Check, and Apply   316

● MODULE 11.3: Evaluating the Self   317

Self-Esteem: Developing a Positive—or Negative—View of
  Oneself   317
Change and Stability in Self-Esteem   318
Parenting Styles and Self-Esteem   319
Self-Esteem in Adolescence: How Do I Like Myself?   320
Socioeconomic Status and Race Differences in Self-Esteem   320
Social Identity Theory   321
Social Comparison   322
Downward Social Comparison   322
Social Comparison in Adolescence: The Importance of Peer
  Groups   322
Reference Groups   322
Review, Check, and Apply   323
The Case of . . . the Failed Star   323
Looking Back   324
Key Terms and Concepts   325
Epilogue   325

12 Gender and Sexuality   326

PROLOGUE: Rules of the Game   327

● MODULE 12.1 Gender: Why Do Boys Wear Blue and Girls Wear Pink?   328

Gender Differences   328
Gender Roles   329
Gender Identity: Developing Femaleness and Maleness   329
Explaining Gender Differences   331
Biological Perspectives on Gender   331
Psychoanalytic Perspectives   332
Social Learning Approaches   332
Cognitive Approaches   333
Review, Check, and Apply   334

● MODULE 12.2: Gender and Social Relationships   335

Gender and Friendships: The Sex Segregation of Middle
  Childhood   335
Gender Relations in Adolescence   336
Gender Expectations and Self-Esteem in Adolescence   337
Dating: Close Relationships in the 21st Century   338
The Functions of Dating   338
Dating, Race, and Ethnicity   339
Review, Check, and Apply   339

● MODULE 12.3: Sexual Behavior and Teenage Pregnancy   340

Becoming Sexual   340
Masturbation   340
Sexual Intercourse   341
Sexual Orientation: Heterosexuality, Homosexuality,
  and Bisexuality   342
Teenage Pregnancies   344
The Challenges of Teenage Pregnancy   344
Virginity Pledges   345
Review, Check, and Apply   346
The Case of . . . the Wrong Role Models?   347
Looking Back   347
Key Terms and Concepts   348
Epilogue   349

13 Moral Development and Aggression   350

PROLOGUE: Jesse's Dilemma   351

● MODULE 13.1 Developing Morality: Following Society's Rights and Wrongs   352

Piaget's View of Moral Development   352
Evaluating Piaget's Approach to Moral Development   353

Social Learning Approaches to Morality   354

Empathy and Moral Behavior   354

Effective Parenting: Teaching Desired Behavior   355

Cultural Differences in Childrearing Practices   357

Review, Check, and Apply   358

● **MODULE 13.2: Moral Reasoning and Prosocial Behavior   359**

Kohlberg's Approach to Moral Development   360

Gilligan's Approach to Moral Development: Gender and Morality   362

Moral Behavior and Moral Reasoning: Why the Disconnect?   363

Prosocial Reasoning and Prosocial Behavior: The Other Side of the Coin   364

Gender and Cultural Differences in Prosocial Behavior   365

Review, Check, and Apply   365

● **MODULE 13.3: Aggression and Violence   366**

Aggression and Violence in Preschoolers: Sources and Consequences   366

Roots of Aggression   367

Social Learning Approaches to Aggression   368

Viewing Violence on TV: Does It Matter?   368

Cognitive Approaches to Aggression: The Thoughts Behind Violence   370

School Violence   371

Schoolyard—and Cyber-Yard—Bullies   373

Bullies and Their Victims   374

The Lingering Stress of Being Bullied   374

Juvenile Delinquency: The Crimes of Adolescence   375

Review, Check, and Apply   376

The Case of . . . the Turncoat Friend   376

Looking Back   377

Key Terms and Concepts   378

Epilogue   378

14   Friends and Family   380

PROLOGUE: Rewriting the Rules   381

● **MODULE 14.1 Friendships in Preschool and Middle Childhood   382**

Preschoolers' Friendships   382

Playing by the Rules: The Work of Play   382

Categorizing Play   383

The Social Aspects of Play   383

How Preschoolers' Theory of Mind Affects Play   385

Building Friendships In Middle Childhood   385

Stages of Friendship: Changing Views of Friends   386

Individual Differences in Friendship: What Makes a Child Popular?   387

What Makes Children Popular?   387

The Social Benefits of Physical Competence   388

Social Problem-Solving Abilities   388

Teaching Social Competence   389

Review, Check, and Apply   390

● **MODULE 14.2: The Role of Peers in Adolescence   391**

Peer Relationships in Adolescence: The Importance of Belonging   391

Cliques and Crowds   392

Online Social Networks: Cyberspace Peers   392

Popularity: Who's In, Who's Out?   394

Personal Qualities and Popularity   394

Popularity and Rejection   394

Conformity: Peer Pressure in Adolescence   396

Review, Check, and Apply   397

● **MODULE 14.3: Family Relationships   397**

Family Life   397

Preschoolers' Family Lives   398

Family Life in Middle Childhood   398

Changing Family Relations and the Quest for Autonomy in Adolescence   398

Culture and Autonomy   399

The Myth of the Generation Gap   400

Conflicts with Parents   401

Cultural Differences in Parent–Child Conflicts During Adolescence   402

Family Constellations: The Array of Possibilities   402

The Changing Home Environment   403

When Both Parents Work Outside the Home: How Do Children Fare?   403

Home and Alone: What Do Children Do?   404

The Impact of Divorce on Children   404

Blended Families   405

Single-Parent Families   406

Multigenerational Families   406

Families with Gay and Lesbian Parents   407

Race and Family Life   407

Poverty and Family Life   407

Group Care: Orphanages in the 21st Century   408

Child Abuse and Psychological Maltreatment: The Grim Side of Family Life   410

Physical Abuse   410

Psychological Maltreatment   412

Review, Check, and Apply   413

The Case of . . . Too Much of a Good Thing   414

Looking Back   415

Key Terms and Concepts   416

Epilogue   416

15 Schooling, Culture, and Society: Living in a Multicultural World   418

PROLOGUE: First Day   419

● MODULE 15.1 **Getting a Start on Schooling**   420

Early Childhood Education: Taking the Pre- Out of Preschool   420
The Varieties of Early Education   421
The Effectiveness of Child Care   422
The Quality of Child Care   422
Does Head Start Truly Provide a Head Start?   424
Are We Pushing Children Too Hard and Too Fast?   424
Learning from the Media   425
Television: Controlling Exposure   426
Sesame Street: A Teacher in Every Home?   426
Media and Technology Use by Children and Adolescents   427
Viewing Television   428
Computers and the Internet: Living in a Virtual World   428
Review, Check, and Apply   429

● MODULE 15.2: **Sociocultural Aspects of Schooling**   430

Schooling Around the World: Who Gets Educated?   430
What Makes Children Ready for School?   430
Educational Trends: Beyond the Three *R*s   431
The Transition from Elementary to Middle School   432
Homeschooling: An Alternative to Traditional Schools   434
School Performance in Adolescence   435
Socioeconomic Status and School Performance   436
Ethnic and Racial Differences in School Achievement   436
Review, Check, and Apply   437

● MODULE 15.3: **Living in a Multicultural World**   438

How Culture Defines Us   438
Acculturation: When Cultures Collide   439
Developing an Ethnic Identity   440
Achieving Ethnic Identity   441
Multicultural Education   441
Cultural Assimilation or Pluralistic Society?   442
Fostering a Bicultural Identity   442
The Impact of Socioeconomic Status and Poverty on Children and Adolescents   443
Prejudice and Discrimination   444
Prejudice, Stereotypes, and Discrimination: The Foundations of Hate   444
The Roots of Prejudice   445
Review, Check, and Apply   448
The Case of . . . the Secret Reader   449
Looking Back   449
Key Terms and Concepts   451
Epilogue   451

References   452
Credits   567
Name Index   570
Subject Index   581

Preface

Child development is a unique field of study. Unlike other disciplines, each of us has experience with its subject matter in personal ways. It is a discipline that deals not just with ideas and concepts and theories, but one that above all has at its heart the forces that have made each of us who we are.

This text, *Child Development: A Topical Approach,* seeks to capture the discipline in a way that sparks and nurtures students' inherent interest in the field. It is meant to excite readers about the field, to draw them into its way of looking at the world, and to shape their understanding of developmental issues. By exposing students to both the current content and the promise inherent in child development, the text is designed to keep interest in the discipline alive long after their formal study of the field has ended.

Child Development: A Topical Approach also addresses two common concerns of course instructors. First, the field of child development is so vast that it is difficult to cover within the confines of a traditional college term. Consequently, many instructors see most child development texts as too long. Second, and more critical, many instructors express the concern that traditional, chronologically based child development books are arranged in a way that made it difficult for students to understand the scope of development within particular topical areas (such as social or personality development across childhood) without skipping from one chapter to another.

Child Development: A Topical Approach addresses both of these concerns. This book is shorter than traditional child development books, and it is arranged in a way that helps students to see the "big picture" of development across the entire span of childhood and adolescence within a specific topical area.

Child Development: A Topical Approach is rich in examples and illustrates the applications that can be derived from the research and theory of child developmentalists. It pays particular attention to the applications that can be drawn from theory and research in the field.

To optimize student learning and to provide instructors with maximum flexibility, the book uses a modular approach. Each chapter is divided into three modules focusing on particular subtopics. Consequently, rather than facing long, potentially daunting chapters, students encounter material that is divided into smaller, more manageable chunks, representing a structure that research long ago found to be optimum for promoting learning.

The modular approach has another advantage: It allows instructors to customize instruction by assigning only those modules that fit their course. Because the modules are self-contained, instructors can pick and choose which modules best contribute to their course. This flexibility allows instructors who wish to highlight a particular topic to do so easily and—equally important—have the option of not including specific modules.

Overview of *Child Development: A Topical Approach*

Child Development: A Topical Approach provides a broad overview of the field of child development. It covers major topics such as physical development, cognitive development, and social and personality development. In addition, separate chapters focus on language development, intelligence, development of the self, moral development and aggression, gender, relationships, and living in a multicultural world.

The book seeks to accomplish the following four major goals:

- First, the book is designed to provide a broad, balanced overview of the field of child development. It introduces readers to the theories, research, and applications that constitute the discipline, examining both the traditional areas of the field as well as more recent innovations. It pays particular attention to the applications developed by child development specialists, demonstrating how child developmentalists use theory, research, and applications to help solve significant social problems.

- The second goal of the text is to explicitly tie development to students' lives. Findings from the study of child development have a significant degree of relevance to students, and this text illustrates how these findings can be applied in a meaningful, practical sense. Applications are presented in a contemporaneous framework, including current news items, timely world events, and contemporary uses of child development that draw readers into the field. Numerous descriptive scenarios and vignettes reflect everyday situations in children's and adolescents' lives, explaining how they relate to the field.

- The third goal is to highlight both the commonalities and diversity of today's multicultural society. Consequently, the book incorporates material relevant to diversity in all its forms—racial, ethnic, gender, sexual orientation, religion, and cultural diversity—throughout every chapter. In addition, every chapter has at least one "Developmental Diversity and Your Life" section. These features explicitly consider how cultural factors relevant to development both unite and diversify our contemporary, global society.

- Finally, the fourth goal is one that is implicit in the other three: making the field of child development engaging, accessible, and interesting to students. Child development is a joy both to study and teach, because so much of it has direct, immediate meaning to our lives. Because all of us are involved in our own developmental paths, we are tied in personal ways to the content areas covered by the book. *Child Development: A Topical Approach,* then, is meant to engage and nurture this interest, planting a seed that will develop and flourish throughout readers' lifetimes.

In accomplishing these goals, the book strives to be user-friendly. Written in a direct, conversational voice, it duplicates as much as possible a dialogue between author and student. The text is meant to be understood and mastered on its own by students of every level of interest and motivation. To that end, it includes a variety of pedagogical features that promote mastery of the material and encourage critical thinking.

Child Development: A Topical Approach is meant to be a book that readers will want to keep in their personal libraries, one that they will take off the shelf when considering problems related to that most intriguing of questions: How do children and adolescents come to be the way they are?

Features of *Child Development: A Topical Approach*

In addition to its modular structure, *Child Development: A Topical Approach* includes features designed to engage students and help them learn the material effectively. These include:

CHAPTER-OPENING PROLOGUES
Each chapter begins with a short vignette, describing an individual or situation that is relevant to the basic developmental issues being addressed in the chapter.

LOOKING AHEAD SECTIONS
These opening sections orient readers to the topics to be covered, bridging the opening prologue with the remainder of the chapter and providing orienting questions.

LEARNING OBJECTIVES
Every chapter includes sequentially numbered learning objectives, stated as engaging questions and based on Bloom's taxonomy. They allow students to understand clearly what they are expected to learn. The learning objectives are tied to the Looking Back summary at the end of each chapter and are also keyed to test bank items.

FROM RESEARCH TO PRACTICE
Each chapter includes a box that describes current developmental research or research issues, applied to everyday problems.

DEVELOPMENTAL DIVERSITY AND YOUR LIFE

Every chapter has at least one "Developmental Diversity and Your Life" section incorporated into the text. These sections highlight issues relevant to today's multicultural society.

ARE YOU AN INFORMED CONSUMER OF DEVELOPMENT?

Every chapter includes information on specific uses that can be derived from research conducted by developmental investigators.

NEUROSCIENCE AND DEVELOPMENT

To illustrate the influence of neuroscience throughout the field of child development, most chapters include a box presenting the latest neuroscientific advances and their impact on our understanding of child development.

CAREERS IN CHILD DEVELOPMENT

Many chapters include an interview with a person working in a field that uses the findings of child and adolescent development. Among those interviewed are a counselor for a treatment center serving teenagers confronting substance abuse, a childcare provider, a neonatal nurse, and a preschool teacher.

FROM THE PERSPECTIVE OF ...

These questions, interspersed throughout the margins of each chapter, ask students to take the perspective of someone working in an occupation that relies on findings of child development, including the fields of health care, education, and social work.

THE CASE OF ...

Every chapter includes a case study. Case studies describe an intriguing situation related to the topics discussed in the chapter, and they end by asking students questions designed to evoke critical thinking about the case and the chapter content.

REVIEW, CHECK, AND APPLY SECTIONS

Interspersed throughout each chapter are short recaps of the chapters' main points, followed by questions designed to provoke mastery of the material and critical thinking.

RUNNING GLOSSARY

Key terms are defined in the margins of the page on which the term is presented.

END-OF-CHAPTER MATERIAL

Each chapter ends with an Epilogue that refers back to the opening Prologue, a summary, and a list of key terms and concepts. This material is designed to help students study and retain the information in the chapter.

Finally, in addition to the features described above, *Child Development: A Topical Approach* provides complete integration between the book and a huge array of digital media in *MyPsychLab*, comprising online electronic exercises, videos, assessments, and literally hundreds of activities that extend the text and make concepts come alive. The online material is referenced throughout the book in a way meant to entice students to go online and make use of the electronic materials that will help them understand the material in the book more deeply.

I am very excited about this book. I believe its topical approach, length, modular structure and other features, and media and text integration presents the material in a highly effective way and will help students learn it. Just as important, I hope the book will spark and nurture students' interest in the field of child development, drawing them into its way of looking at the world, building their understanding of developmental issues, and showing them how the field can have a significant impact on their own and others' lives.

Ancillaries

Child Development: A Topical Approach is accompanied by a superb set of teaching and learning materials.

Supplements for the Instructor

- **Instructor's Resource Manual (ISBN: 0205948197).** Each chapter of the Instructor's Resource Manual includes sample syllabi, learning objectives, key terms and concepts, chapter outlines and lecture notes, lecture suggestions and discussion topics, class activities, demonstrations, and assignments, out-of-class assignments and projects, supplemental reading lists, multimedia/video resources, and handouts.

The Instructor's Resource Manual will be available for download via the Pearson Instructor's Resource Center (www.pearsonhighered.com) or on the MyPsychLab® platform (www.mypsychlab.com).

- **Video Enhanced PowerPoint Slides.** These slides, available on the Instructor's Resource DVD (ISBN 0205947972), bring the Feldman design right into the classroom, drawing students into the lecture and providing wonderful interactive activities, visuals, and videos.

- **PowerPoint Lecture Slides (ISBN: 0205948219).** The lecture slides provide an active format for presenting concepts from each chapter and feature prominent figures and tables from the text. The PowerPoint Lecture Slides are available for download via the Pearson Instructor's Resource Center (www.pearsonhighered.com) or on the MyPsychLab® platform (www.mypsychlab.com).

- **Test Item File (ISBN: 020592350X).** The test bank contains more than 3,000 multiple-choice, true/false, and essay questions, each referenced to the relevant page in the textbook and given a rationale explaining the correct answer. Each question was accuracy checked to ensure that the correct answer was marked and the page reference was accurate. An additional feature of the test bank is the identification of each question as factual, conceptual, or applied. This allows professors to customize their tests and to ensure a balance of question types. Each chapter of the test item file begins with the Total Assessment Guide: an easy-to-reference grid that makes creating tests easier by organizing the test questions by text section, question type, and whether it is factual, conceptual, or applied.

- **MyTest (ISBN: 0205948200).** The test item file comes with the Pearson MyTest, a powerful assessment generation program that helps instructors easily create and print quizzes and exams. Questions and tests can be authored online, allowing instructors ultimate flexibility and the ability to efficiently manage assessments anytime, anywhere. For more information, go to www.PearsonMyTest.com.

- **MyVirtualChild** is an interactive simulation that allows students to raise a child from birth to age 18 and monitor the effects of their parenting decisions over time. MyVirtualChild helps students think critically as they apply their course work to the practical experiences of raising a virtual child. MyVirtualChild is available in MyPsychLab or standalone. To package the student text with MyVirtualChild use ISBN 0205941931.

- **MyPsychLab (ISBN: 0205948855).** Available at www.mypsychlab.com, this learning and assessment tool can be used to supplement a traditional lecture course or to administer a course entirely online. Instructors decide the extent of integration—from independent self-assessment for students to total course management. Students benefit from an easy-to-use site where they can test themselves on key content, track their progress, and use individually tailored study plans. MyPsychLab is an all-inclusive tool, including a Pearson eText, plus teaching and learning resources organized by chapter in the form of videos, simulations, animations, assessments, and other tools to engage students and reinforce learning. Fully customizable and easy to use, MyPsychLab meets the individual teaching and learning needs of every instructor and every student. To package MyPsychLab with the student text, use ISBN 0205959881.

  - **MyClassPrep.** Available for instructors within MyPsychLab, this exciting instructor resource makes lecture preparation easier and less time consuming. MyClassPrep collects the best class preparation resources—art and figures from our leading texts, videos, lecture activities, classroom activities, demonstrations, and much more—in one convenient online destination. You can search through MyClassPrep's extensive database of tools by content topic or by content type. You can select resources appropriate for your lecture, many of which can be downloaded directly; or you can build your own folder of resources and present from within MyClassPrep.

Video Resources for Instructors

- The **Development Video Series in MyPsychLab** engages students and brings to life a wide range of topics spanning prenatal through the end of the lifespan. New international videos shot on location allow students to observe similarities and differences in human development across various cultures.
- **Pearson Teaching Films Life Span Development Video, ISBN: 0205656021.**

Print and Media Supplements for the Student

- **MyPsychLab.** With this exciting new tool students are able to self-assess using embedded diagnostic tests and instantly view results along with a customized study plan. The customized study plan will focus on the student's strengths and weaknesses, based on the results of the diagnostic testing, and present a list of activities and resources for review and remediation, organized by chapter section. Some study resources intended for use with portable electronic devices are made available exclusively through the MyPsychLab, such as key terms flashcards and video clips. Students will be able to quickly and easily analyze their own comprehension level of the course material, and study more efficiently, leading to exceptional exam results! An access code is required and can be purchased at **www.pearsonhighered.com** or at **www.mypsychlab.com**.
- **CourseSmart eTextbook (ISBN: 0205948227).** CourseSmart offers students an online subscription to *Child Development: A Topical Approach*, Second Edition, at up to 60% savings. With the CourseSmart eTextbook, students can search the text, make notes online, print out reading assignments that incorporate lecture notes, and bookmark important passages. Ask your Pearson sales representative for details or visit **www.coursesmart.com**.

Supplementary Texts

Contact your Pearson representative to package any of these supplementary texts with *Child Development: A Topical Approach*.

- *Current Directions in Developmental Psychology* **(ISBN: 0205597505).** Readings from the American Psychological Society. This exciting reader includes more than 20 articles that have been carefully selected for the undergraduate audience, and taken from the accessible *Current Directions in Psychological Science* journal. These timely, cutting-edge articles allow instructors to bring their students a real-world perspective about today's most current and pressing issues in psychology. Discounted when packaged with this text for college adoptions.
- *Twenty Studies That Revolutionized Child Psychology* by **Wallace E. Dixon Jr.** **(ISBN: 0205948030).** The new edition of this brief text presents the seminal research studies that have shaped modern developmental psychology. It provides an overview of the environment that gave rise to each study, its experimental design, its findings, and its impact on current thinking in the discipline.
- *Human Development in Multicultural Contexts: A Book of Readings* **(ISBN: 0130195235).** Written by Michele A. Paludi, this compilation of readings highlights cultural influences in developmental psychology.
- *The Psychology Major: Careers and Strategies for Success* **(ISBN: 0205684688).** Written by Eric Landrum (Idaho State University), Stephen Davis (Emporia State University), and Terri Landrum (Idaho State University), this 160-page paperback provides valuable information on career options available to psychology majors, tips for improving academic performance, and a guide to the APA style of research reporting.

Acknowledgments

I am grateful to the following reviewers who provided a wealth of comments, constructive criticism, and encouragement:

Kristi Almeida-Bowin—Moorpark College

Bruce Anthony—Tabor College

Stephanie Babb—University of Houston–Downtown

Susan Bowers—Northern Illinois University

Heidi Burross—University of Arizona

Pamela Chibucos—Owens Community College

Marguerite Clark—California State Polytechnic University Pomona

Myra Cox—Harold Washington College

Charlene A. Drake—University of Massachusetts, Lowell

William Elmhorst—Marshfield High School

Roseanne L. Flores—Hunter College, CUNY

Karen Frye—University of Nevada, Reno

Nadine Garner—Millersville University

Jerry Green—Tarrant County College

Michael Green—University of North Carolina, Charlotte

Donnell Griffin—Davidson County Community College

Eugene Grist—Ohio University

Vivian Harper—San Joaquin Delta College

Sandra Hellyer—Ball State University

Earleen Huff—Amarillo College

Alisha Janowsky—University of Central Florida

Sara Lawrence—California State University

Mary Clare Munger—Amarillo College

Brian Parry—San Juan College

Mary Kay Reed—York College of Pennsylvania

Alesia Williams Richardson—Chicago State University

Peggy Skinner—South Plains College

Mary Hughes Stone—San Francisco State University

Patricia Weaver—Fayetteville Technical Community College

Lois Willoughby—Miami Dade College

Many others deserve a great deal of thanks. I am indebted to the numerous people who provided me with a superb education, first at Wesleyan University and later at the University of Wisconsin. Specifically, Karl Scheibe played a pivotal role in my undergraduate education, and the late Vernon Allen acted as mentor and guide through my graduate years. It was in graduate school that I learned about development, being exposed to such experts as Ross Parke, John Balling, Joel Levin, Herb Klausmeier, and many others. My education continued when I became a professor. I am especially grateful to my colleagues at the University of Massachusetts, who make the university such a wonderful place in which to teach and do research.

Several people played central roles in the development of this book. John Bickford and Christopher Poirier provided important research and editorial input, and I am thankful for their help. Most of all, John Graiff was essential in juggling and coordinating the multiple aspects of writing a book, and I am very grateful for the substantial role he played.

I am also grateful to the superb Pearson team that was instrumental in the inception and development of this book. Erin Mitchell, Executive Editor, has brought enthusiasm, creativity, and good ideas to this book. Editorial Project Manager Diane Szulecki went way beyond the call of duty to provide direction in every respect. I am grateful for their support. Finally, I'd like to thank (in advance) marketing managers Nicole Kunzmann and Jeremy Intal, on whose skills I'm counting.

I also wish to acknowledge the members of my family, who play such an essential role in my life. My brother, Michael, my sisters-in-law and brother-in-law, my nieces and nephews—all make up an important part of my life. In addition, I am indebted to the older generation of my family, who led the way in a manner I can only hope to emulate. I will always be obligated to the late Harry Brochstein, Mary Vorwerk, and Ethel Radler. Most of all, the list is headed by my father, the late Saul Feldman, and my mother, Leah Brochstein.

In the end, it is my immediate family who deserve the greatest thanks. My terrific kids, Jonathan and wife Leigh, Joshua and wife Julie, and Sarah and husband Jeffrey, not only are nice, smart, and good-looking, but my pride and joy. My grandsons Alex and Miles have brought immense happiness from the moment of their births. And my wife, Katherine Vorwerk, provides the love and grounding that makes everything worthwhile. I thank them all, with my love.

Robert S. Feldman
University of Massachusetts Amherst

About the Author

Robert S. Feldman is Professor of Psychology and Dean of the College of Social and Behavioral Sciences at the University of Massachusetts Amherst. A recipient of the College Distinguished Teacher Award, he teaches psychology classes ranging in size from 15 to nearly 500 students. During more than two decades as a college instructor, he has taught both undergraduate and graduate courses at Mount Holyoke College, Wesleyan University, and Virginia Commonwealth University in addition to the University of Massachusetts.

A Fellow of both the American Psychological Association and the Association for Psychological Science, Professor Feldman received a B.A. with High Honors from Wesleyan University (and from which he received the Distinguished Alumni Award). He has an M.S. and Ph.D. from the University of Wisconsin–Madison. He is a winner of a Fulbright Senior Research Scholar and Lecturer award, and he has written more than 100 books, book chapters, and scientific articles.

Professor Feldman has edited *Development of Nonverbal Behavior in Children* and *Applications of Nonverbal Behavioral Theory and Research*, and co-edited *Fundamentals of Nonverbal Behavior*. He is also author of *Development Across the Life Span, Understanding Psychology,* and *P.O.W.E.R. Learning: Strategies for Success in College and Life*. His books have been translated into a number of languages, including Spanish, French, Portuguese, Dutch, Chinese, Korean, Indonesian, and Japanese. His research interests include honesty and deception in everyday life, work that he described in *The Liar in Your Life,* a trade book. His research has been supported by grants from the National Institute of Mental Health and the National Institute on Disabilities and Rehabilitation Research.

Professor Feldman loves music, is an enthusiastic pianist, and enjoys cooking and traveling. He has three children, two young grandsons, and he and his wife, a psychologist, live in western Massachusetts in a home overlooking the Holyoke mountain range.

1 An Introduction to Child Development

MODULE 1.1

AN ORIENTATION TO CHILD DEVELOPMENT

- Characterizing Child Development: The Scope of the Field

DEVELOPMENTAL DIVERSITY AND YOUR LIFE:
How Culture, Ethnicity, and Race Influence Development

- Cohort Influences on Development: Developing with Others in a Social World

Review, Check, and Apply

MODULE 1.2

CHILDREN: PAST, PRESENT, AND FUTURE

- Early Views of Children
- The 20th Century: Child Development as a Discipline
- Today's Key Issues and Questions: Child Development's Underlying Themes
- The Future of Child Development

FROM RESEARCH TO PRACTICE: **Preventing Violence in Children**

ARE YOU AN INFORMED CONSUMER OF DEVELOPMENT?
Assessing Information on Child Development

Review, Check, and Apply

The Case of ... Too Many Choices

Looking Back

Key Terms and Concepts

Epilogue

PROLOGUE: Conceptions, Old and New

She was famous from the moment she was born. But it wasn't who she was that made others curious about her: It was how she was conceived.

Louise Brown, who is now in her mid-30s, has always been known as the world's first "test tube baby." She was born by *in vitro fertilization* (*IVF*), a procedure in which fertilization of a mother's egg by a father's sperm takes place outside of the mother's body.

Louise was a preschooler when her parents told her about how she was conceived, and throughout her childhood she was bombarded with questions. It became routine to explain to her classmates that she in fact was not born in a laboratory.

As a child, Louise sometimes felt isolated. "I thought it was something peculiar to me," she recalled. But as she grew older, her isolation declined as more and more children were born in the same manner.

Today, Louise is hardly isolated. More than 1.5 million babies have been born using the procedure, which has become almost routine. And at the age of 28, Louise became a mother herself, giving birth to a baby boy named Cameron—conceived, by the way, in the old-fashioned way (Moreton, 2007; Hastings, 2010).

Louise Brown and son.

>>> LOOKING AHEAD

Louise Brown's conception may have been novel, but her development, from infancy onward, has followed predictable patterns. While the specifics of our development vary—some encounter economic deprivation or live in war-torn territories; others contend with family issues such as divorce and stepparents—the broad strokes of the development set in motion in that test tube three decades ago are remarkably similar for all of us.

Louise Brown's conception in the lab is just one of the brave new worlds of the 21st century. Issues ranging from cloning to the consequences of poverty on development to the effects of culture and race raise significant developmental concerns. Underlying these are more fundamental issues: How do children develop physically? How

(continued)

does their understanding of the world grow and change over time? And how do our personalities and social world develop as we move from birth through adolescence?

These questions, and many others we'll encounter throughout this book, are central to the field of child development. Consider, for example, the range of approaches that different specialists in child development might take when considering the story of Louise Brown:

- Child development researchers who investigate behavior at the level of biological processes might determine if Louise's physical functioning before her birth was affected by her conception outside the womb.
- Specialists in child development who study genetics might examine how the biological endowment from Louise's parents affects her later behavior.
- For child development specialists who investigate the ways thinking changes during childhood, Louise's life might be examined in terms of how her understanding of the nature of her conception changed as she grew older.
- Other researchers in child development who focus on physical growth might consider whether her growth rate differed from children conceived more traditionally.
- Child development experts who specialize in the social world of children might look at the ways that Louise interacted with other children and the kinds of friendships she developed.

Although their interests take many forms, these specialists in child development share one concern: understanding the growth and change that occur during the course of childhood and adolescence. Taking many differing approaches, developmentalists study how both our biological inheritance from our parents and the environment in which we live jointly affect our behavior.

Some researchers in child development focus on explaining how our genetic background can determine not only how we look but also how we behave and how we relate to others—that is, matters of personality. These professionals explore ways to identify how much of our potential as human beings is provided—or limited—by heredity. Other child development specialists look to the environment in which we are raised, exploring ways in which our lives are shaped by the world that we encounter. They investigate the extent to which we are shaped by our early environments and how our current circumstances influence our behavior in both subtle and obvious ways.

Whether they focus on heredity or environment, all child development specialists hope that their work will ultimately inform and support the efforts of professionals whose careers are devoted to improving the lives of children. Practitioners in fields ranging from education to health care to social work draw on the findings of child development researchers, using those findings to advance children's welfare.

In this chapter, we orient ourselves to the field of child development. We begin with a discussion of the scope of the discipline, illustrating the wide array of topics it covers and the range of ages it examines, from the moment of conception through the end of adolescence. We also survey the foundations of the field and examine the key issues and questions that underlie child development. Finally, we consider where the child development field is likely to go in the future.

MODULE 1.1

AN ORIENTATION TO CHILD DEVELOPMENT

LO 1-1 What is child development?

LO 1-2 What is the scope of the field of child development?

LO 1-3 What are major societal influences that determine development?

Have you ever wondered how it is possible that an infant tightly grips your finger with tiny, perfectly formed hands? Or marveled at how a preschooler methodically draws a picture? Or pondered the way an adolescent can make involved decisions about whom to invite to a party or the ethics of downloading music files?

If you've ever wondered about such things, you are asking the kinds of questions that scientists in the field of child development pose. **Child development** is the scientific study of the patterns of growth, change, and stability that occur from conception through adolescence.

Although the definition of the field seems straightforward, the simplicity is somewhat misleading. To understand what child development is actually about, we need to look underneath the various parts of the definition.

In its study of growth, change, and stability, child development takes a scientific approach. Like members of other scientific disciplines, researchers in child development test their assumptions about the nature and course of human development by applying scientific methods. As we'll see in the next chapter, they develop theories about development, and they use methodical, scientific techniques to validate the accuracy of their assumptions systematically.

Child development focuses on *human* development. Although there are some developmentalists who study the course of development in nonhuman species, the vast majority examine growth and change in people. Some seek to understand universal principles of development, while others focus on how cultural, racial, and ethnic differences affect the course of development. Still others aim to understand the unique aspects of individuals, looking at the traits and characteristics that differentiate one person from another. Regardless of approach, however, all child developmentalists view development as a continuing process throughout childhood and adolescence.

As developmental specialists focus on the ways people change and grow during their lives, they also consider stability in children's and adolescents' lives. They ask in which areas and in what periods people show change and growth and when and how their behavior reveals consistency and continuity with prior behavior.

Finally, although child development focuses on childhood and adolescence, the process of development persists throughout *every* part of people's lives, beginning with the moment of conception and continuing until death. Developmental specialists assume that in some ways people continue to grow and change right up to the end of their lives, while in other respects their behavior remains stable. In other words, developmentalists believe that no particular, single period of life governs all development. Instead, they believe that every period of life contains the potential for both growth and decline in abilities and that individuals maintain the capacity for substantial growth and change throughout their lives.

Characterizing Child Development: The Scope of the Field

Clearly, the definition of child development is broad and the scope of the field is extensive. Consequently, professionals in child development cover several quite diverse areas, and a typical developmentalist will specialize in both a topical area and age range.

Topical Areas in Child Development.   The field of child development includes three major topics or approaches:

- Physical development
- Cognitive development
- Social and personality development

A child developmentalist might specialize in one of these topical areas. For example, some developmentalists focus on **physical development**, examining the ways in which the body's makeup—the brain, nervous system, muscles, and senses and the need for food, drink, and sleep—helps determine behavior. For example, one specialist in physical development might examine the effects of malnutrition on the pace of growth in children, while another might look at how an athlete's physical performance changes during adolescence.

Other developmental specialists examine **cognitive development**, seeking to understand how growth and change in intellectual capabilities influence a person's

child development   The field that involves the scientific study of the patterns of growth, change, and stability that occur from conception through adolescence

physical development   Development involving the body's physical makeup, including the brain, nervous system, muscles, and senses and the need for food, drink, and sleep

cognitive development   Development involving the ways that growth and change in intellectual capabilities influence a person's behavior

This wedding of two children in India is an example of how cultural factors play a significant role in determining the age when a particular event is likely to occur.

behavior. Cognitive developmentalists examine learning, memory, problem solving, and intelligence. For example, specialists in cognitive development might want to see how problem-solving changes over the course of childhood or if cultural differences exist in the ways people explain the reasons for their academic successes and failures. They would also be interested in how a person who experiences significant or traumatic events early in life remembers them later in life (Alibali, Phillips, & Fischer, 2009; Dumka et al., 2009; van Wesel et al., 2011).

Finally, some developmental specialists focus on personality and social development. **Personality development** is the study of stability and change in the enduring characteristics that differentiate one person from another. **Social development** is the way in which individuals' interactions with others and their social relationships grow, change, and remain stable over the course of life. A developmentalist interested in personality development might ask whether there are stable, enduring personality traits throughout the life span, while a specialist in social development might examine the effects of racism, poverty, or divorce on development (Lansford, 2009; Vélez et al., 2011; Carter et al., 2011). These three major topic areas—physical, cognitive, and social and personality development—are summarized in Table 1-1.

Age Ranges and Individual Differences. As they specialize in chosen topical areas, child developmentalists typically look at particular age ranges. They usually divide childhood and adolescence into broad age ranges: the prenatal period (the period from conception to birth), infancy and toddlerhood (birth to age 3), the preschool period (ages 3 to 6), middle childhood (ages 6 to 12), and adolescence (ages 12 to 20).

It's important to keep in mind that these broad periods—which are largely accepted by child developmentalists—are social constructions. A *social construction* is a shared notion of reality, one that is widely accepted but is a function of society and culture at a given time.

personality development Development involving the ways that the enduring characteristics that differentiate one person from another change over the life span

social development The way in which individuals' interactions with others and their social relationships grow, change, and remain stable over the course of life

---

TABLE 1-1 Approaches to Child Development

Orientation	Defining Characteristics	Examples of Questions Asked*
Physical Development	Examines how brain, nervous system, muscles, sensory capabilities, and needs for food, drink, and sleep affect behavior	What determines the sex of a child? (3) What are the long-term consequences of premature birth? (4) What are the benefits of breastfeeding? (4) What are the consequences of early or late sexual maturation? (5)
Cognitive Development	Emphasizes intellectual abilities, including learning, memory, language development, problem solving, and intelligence	What are the earliest memories that can be recalled from infancy? (7) What are the consequences of watching television? (15) Are there benefits to bilingualism? (8) Are there ethnic and racial differences in intelligence? (9) How does an adolescent's egocentrism affect his or her view of the world? (6)
Personality and Social Development	Examines enduring characteristics that differentiate one person from another and how interactions with others and social relationships grow and change over the life span	Do newborns respond differently to their mothers than to others? (4) What is the best procedure for disciplining children? (13) When does a sense of gender develop? (12) How can we promote cross-race friendships? (14) What are the causes of adolescent suicide? (10)

*Numbers in parenthesis indicate in which chapter the question is addressed.

Although most child developmentalists accept these broad periods, the age ranges themselves are in many ways arbitrary. Although some periods have one clear-cut boundary (infancy begins with birth, the preschool period ends with entry into public school, and adolescence starts with sexual maturity), others don't.

For instance, consider the separation between middle childhood and adolescence, which usually occurs around the age of 12. Because the boundary is based on a biological change, the onset of sexual maturation, which varies greatly from one individual to another, the specific age of entry into adolescence varies from one person to the next.

Furthermore, some developmentalists have proposed entirely new developmental periods. For instance, psychologist Jeffrey Arnett argues that adolescence extends into *emerging adulthood,* a period beginning in the late teenage years and continuing into the mid-20s. During emerging adulthood, people are no longer adolescents, but they haven't fully taken on the responsibilities of adulthood. Instead, they are still trying out different identities and engage in self-focused exploration (Schwartz, Côté, & Arnett, 2005; Lamborn & Groh, 2009; Arnett, 2010, 2011).

In short, there are substantial *individual differences* in the timing of events in people's lives. In part, this is a biological fact of life: People mature at different rates and reach developmental milestones at different points. However, environmental factors also play a significant role in determining the age at which a particular event is likely to occur. For example, the typical age at which people develop romantic attachments varies substantially from one culture to another, depending in part on the way that relationships are viewed in a given culture.

It is important to keep in mind, then, that when developmental specialists discuss age ranges, they are talking about averages—the times when people, on average, reach particular milestones. Some children will reach the milestone earlier, some later, and many—in fact, most—will reach it around the time of the average. Such variation becomes noteworthy only when children show substantial deviation from the average. For example, parents whose child begins to speak at a much later age than average might decide to have their son or daughter evaluated by a speech therapist.

Furthermore, as children grow older, they become more likely to deviate from the average and exhibit individual differences. In very young children, a good part of developmental change is genetically determined and unfolds automatically, making development fairly similar in different children. But as children age, environmental factors become more potent, leading to greater variability and individual differences as time passes.

The Links between Topics and Ages. Each of the broad topical areas of child development—physical, cognitive, and social and personality development—plays a role throughout childhood and adolescence. Consequently, some developmental experts focus on physical development during the prenatal period and others on what occurs during adolescence. Some might specialize in social development during the preschool years, while others look at social relationships in middle childhood. And still others might take a broader approach, looking at cognitive development through every period of childhood and adolescence (and beyond).

The variety of topical areas and age ranges studied within the field of child development means that specialists from many diverse backgrounds and areas of expertise consider themselves child developmentalists. Psychologists who study behavior and mental processes, educational researchers, geneticists, and physicians are only some of the people who specialize and conduct research in child development. Furthermore, developmentalists work in a variety of settings, including university departments of psychology, education, human development, and medicine, as well as nonacademic settings as varied as human service agencies and child care centers.

The diversity of specialists working under the broad umbrella of child development brings a variety of perspectives and intellectual richness to the field of child development. In addition, it permits the research findings of the field to be used by practitioners in a wide array of applied professions. Teachers, nurses, social workers, child care providers, and social policy experts all rely on the findings of child development to make decisions about how to improve children's welfare.

DEVELOPMENTAL DIVERSITY AND YOUR LIFE

How Culture, Ethnicity, and Race Influence Development

Mayan mothers in Central America are certain that almost constant contact between themselves and their infant children is necessary for good parenting, and they are physically upset if contact is not possible. They are shocked when they see a North American mother lay her infant down, and they attribute the baby's crying to the poor parenting of the North American. (Morelli et al., 1992)

What are we to make of the two views of parenting expressed above? Is one right and the other wrong? Probably not, if we take into consideration the cultural context in which the mothers are operating. In fact, different cultures and subcultures have their own views of appropriate and inappropriate child-rearing, just as they have different developmental goals for children (Tolchinsky, 2003; Feldman & Masalha, 2007; Huijbregts et al., 2009).

Specialists in child development must take into consideration broad cultural factors. For example, as we'll discuss further in Chapter 11, children growing up in Asian societies tend to have a *collectivistic orientation,* focusing on the interdependence among members of society. In contrast, children in Western societies are more likely to have an *individualistic orientation* in which they concentrate on the uniqueness of the individual.

Similarly, child developmentalists must also take into account ethnic, racial, socioeconomic, and gender differences if they are to achieve an understanding of how people change and grow throughout the life span. If these specialists succeed in doing so, not only can they achieve a better understanding of human development, but they may also be able to derive more precise applications for improving the human social condition.

Efforts to understand how diversity affects development have been hindered by difficulties in finding an appropriate vocabulary. For example, members of the research community—as well as society at large—have sometimes used terms such as *race* and *ethnic group* in inappropriate ways. *Race* is a biological concept, which should be employed to refer to classifications based on physical and structural characteristics of species. In contrast, *ethnic group* and *ethnicity* are broader terms, referring to cultural background, nationality, religion, and language.

The concept of race has proven particularly problematic. Although it formally refers to biological factors, race has taken on substantially more meanings—many of them inappropriate—that range from skin color to religion to culture. Moreover, the concept of race is exceedingly imprecise; depending on how it is defined, there are between 3 and 300 races, and no race is genetically distinct. The fact that 99.9% of humans' genetic makeup is identical in all humans makes the question of race seem insignificant (Smedley & Smedley, 2005; Coleman, 2011; Fish, 2011).

In addition, there is little agreement about which names best reflect different races and ethnic groups. Should the term *African American*—which has geographical and cultural implications—be preferred over *black*, which focuses primarily on skin color? Is *Native American* preferable to *Indian*? Is *Hispanic* more appropriate than *Latino*? And how can researchers accurately categorize people with multiethnic backgrounds? The choice of category has important implications for the validity and usefulness of research. The choice even has political implications. For example, the decision

The face of the United States is changing as the proportion of children from different backgrounds is increasing.

to permit people to identify themselves as "multiracial" on U.S. government forms and in the 2000 U.S. Census initially was highly controversial, although it is now routine (Perlmann & Waters, 2002; Saulny, 2011).

As the proportion of minorities in U.S. society continues to increase, it becomes crucial to take the complex issues associated with human diversity into account to fully understand development. In fact, it is only by looking for similarities and differences among various ethnic, cultural, and racial groups that developmental researchers can distinguish principles of development that are universal from ones that are culturally determined. In the years ahead, then, it is likely that child development will move from a discipline that primarily focuses on children with North American and European backgrounds to one that encompasses the development of children around the globe (Matsumoto & Yoo, 2006; Wardle, 2007; Kloep et al., 2009). ∎

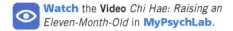

Watch the Video *Chi Hae: Raising an Eleven-Month-Old* in **MyPsychLab**.

Cohort Influences on Development: Developing with Others in a Social World

Bob, born in 1947, is a baby boomer. He was born soon after the end of World War II, when an enormous bulge in the birthrate occurred as soldiers returned to the United States from overseas. He was an adolescent at the height of the civil rights movement and the beginning of protests against the Vietnam War. His mother, Leah, was born in 1922; she is part of the generation that passed its childhood and teenage years in the shadow of the Great Depression. Bob's son, Jon, was born in 1975. Now building a career after graduating from college and starting his own family, he is a member of what has been called Generation X. Jon's younger sister, Sarah, who was born in 1982, is part of the next generation, which sociologists have called the Millennial Generation.

These people are in part products of the social times in which they live. Each belongs to a particular **cohort**, a group of people born at around the same time in the same place. Such major social events as wars, economic upturns and depressions, famines, and epidemics (such as the one due to the AIDS virus) work similar influences on members of a particular cohort (Mitchell, 2002; Dittmann, 2005).

Cohort effects provide an example of *history-graded influences,* which are biological and environmental influences associated with a particular historical moment. For instance, children who lived in New York City during the 9/11 terrorist attack on the World Trade Center experienced shared biological and environmental challenges due the attack. Their development is bound to be affected by this normative history-graded event (Bonanno, Galea, Bucciarelli, & Vlahov, 2006; Laugharne, Janca, & Widiger, 2007; Mani & Plunkett, 2011).

In contrast, *age-graded influences* are biological and environmental influences that are similar for individuals in a particular age group, regardless of when or where they are raised. For example, biological events such as puberty and menopause are universal events that occur at relatively the same time throughout all societies. Similarly, a sociocultural event such as entry into formal education can be considered a normative age-graded influence because it occurs in most cultures around age 6.

Development is also affected by *sociocultural-graded influences*, which include ethnicity, social class, subcultural membership, and other factors. For example, sociocultural-graded influences will be considerably different for immigrant children who speak English as a second language than for children born in the United States who speak English as their first language (Rose et al., 2003; Kärtner et al., 2011).

Finally, *non-normative life events* also influence development. Non-normative life events are specific, atypical events that occur in a particular person's life at a time when such events do not happen to most people. For instance, the experience of Louise Brown, who grew up with the knowledge that she was the first person to be conceived using in vitro fertilization, constitutes a non-normative life event. In addition, children can create their own non-normative life events. For instance, a high school girl who enters and wins a national science competition produces a non-normative life event for herself. In a sense, she is actively constructing her own environment, thereby participating in her own development.

FROM AN
EDUCATOR'S
PERSPECTIVE:

How would a student's cohort membership affect his or her readiness for school? For example, what would be the benefits and drawbacks of coming from a cohort in which Internet use was routine, compared with earlier cohorts prior to the appearance of the Internet?

cohort A group of people born at around the same time in the same place

Society's view of childhood and what is appropriate to ask of children has changed through the ages. These children worked full time in mines in the early 1900s.

Review, Check, and Apply

Review

1. The field of child development involves the scientific study of the ways in which children grow and develop from the time before birth to the end of adolescence.

2. Child development examines physical, cognitive, and social and personality development across broad age ranges and across individuals.

3. Development is affected by race, ethnicity, gender, and culture and is sensitive to cohort effects, age-graded influences, sociocultural influences, and non-normative life events.

Check

1. Child development takes a scientific approach to development, and it considers _____ as well as change, in the lives of children and adolescents.

2. The field of child development includes three major topics or approaches: physical development, _____ development, and social and personality development.

3. Specialists in child development must take into consideration broad _____ factors and account for ethnic, racial, socioeconomic, and gender differences if they are to understand how people change and grow throughout the life span.

4. Major social events have similar influences on members of a particular _____, a group of people born at around the same time in the same place.

Apply

1. What are some examples of the ways culture (either broad culture or aspects of culture) has affected your development?

2. How do different age-graded influences and history-graded influences contribute to making you and your parents different?

To see more review questions, log on to MyPsychLab.

ANSWERS: 1. stability 2. cognitive 3. cultural 4. cohort

MODULE 1.2

CHILDREN: PAST, PRESENT, AND FUTURE

LO 1-4 How have views of childhood changed historically?

LO 1-5 What are the key issues and questions in the field of child development?

LO 1-6 What is the future of child development likely to hold?

Children have been the target of study from the time that humans have walked the planet. Parents are endlessly fascinated by their children, and the growth displayed throughout childhood and adolescence is a source of both curiosity and wonderment. But it is relatively recent in the course of history that children have been studied from a scientific vantage point. Even a brief historical look at the field of child development shows that there has been considerable change in the way that children are viewed.

Early Views of Children

Although it is hard to imagine, some scholars believe that there was a time when childhood didn't even exist, at least in the minds of adults. According to Philippe Ariès, who studied paintings and other forms of art, children in medieval Europe were not given any special status before 1600. Instead, they were viewed as miniature, somewhat imperfect adults. They were dressed in adult clothing and not treated specially in any significant way. Childhood was not seen as a stage qualitatively different from adulthood (Ariès, 1962; Acocella, 2003; Hutton, 2004).

Although the view that children during the Middle Ages were seen simply as miniature adults may be somewhat exaggerated—Ariès's arguments were based primarily on art depicting the European aristocracy, a very limited sample of Western culture—it is clear that childhood had a considerably different meaning than it does now. Moreover, the idea that childhood could be studied systematically did not take hold until later.

Philosophers' Perspectives on Children.
During the 16th and 17th centuries, philosophers took the lead in thinking about the nature of childhood. For example, English philosopher John Locke (1632–1704) considered a child to be a *tabula rasa,* which is Latin for "blank slate." In this view, children entered the world with no specific characteristics or personalities. Instead, they were entirely shaped by their experiences as they grew up. As we'll see in the next chapter, this view was the precursor of the modern perspective known as behaviorism.

French philosopher Jean-Jacques Rousseau (1712–1778) had an entirely different view of the nature of children. He argued that children were *noble savages,* meaning that they were born with an innate sense of right and wrong and morality. Seeing humans as basically good, he argued that infants developed into admirable and worthy children and adults unless corrupted by negative circumstances in their lives. Rousseau also was one of the first observers of childhood to suggest that growth occurred in distinct, discontinuous stages that unfolded automatically—a concept that is reflected in some contemporary theories of child development that we'll discuss in the next chapter.

Baby Biographies.
Among the first instances in which children were methodically studied were *baby biographies*, which were popular in the late 1700s in Germany. Observers—typically parents—tried to trace the growth of a single child, recording the physical and linguistic milestones achieved by their child.

But it was not until Charles Darwin, who developed the theory of evolution, that observation of children took a more systematic turn. Darwin was convinced that understanding the development of individuals within a species could help identify how the species itself had developed. He made baby biographies more scientifically respectable by producing one of his own, recording his own son's development during his first year.

A wave of baby biographies was produced following publication of Darwin's book. Furthermore, other historical trends were helping to propel the development of a new scientific discipline focusing on children. Scientists were discovering the mechanisms behind conception, and geneticists were beginning to unlock the mysteries of heredity. Philosophers were arguing about the relative influences of nature (heredity) and nurture (factors in the environment).

Focus on Childhood.
As the adult labor pool increased, children were no longer needed as a source of inexpensive labor, paving the way for laws that protected children from exploitation. The advent of more universal education meant that children were separated from adults for more of the day, and educators sought to identify better ways of teaching children.

Advances in psychology led people to explore such matters as the influence of childhood events on adults' later lives. As a consequence of a growing sophistication regarding the nature and wide-ranging importance of social changes during childhood, child development became recognized as a field of its own.

The 20th Century: Child Development as a Discipline

Several figures became central to the emerging field of child development. Alfred Binet, a French psychologist, not only pioneered the study of children's intelligence but also investigated memory and mental calculation. G. Stanley Hall pioneered the use of questionnaires to

During medieval times in Europe, children were thought of as miniature, although imperfect, adults. This view of childhood was reflected in how children were dressed—identically as adults.

illuminate children's thinking and behavior. He also wrote the first book that targeted adolescence as a distinct period of development—aptly titled *Adolescence* (Hall, 1904/1916).

Contributions of Women. Even though prejudice hindered women in their pursuit of academic careers, they made significant contributions to the discipline of child development during the early 1900s. For example, Leta Stetter Hollingworth, who studied at Columbia University under Edward Thorndike, a noted pioneer in educational testing, and later became a professor of education at Columbia's Teachers College, was one of the first psychologists to focus on child development (Hollingworth, 1943/1990; Denmark & Fernandez, 1993).

During the first decades of the 1900s, one emerging trend that had enormous impact on our understanding of children's development was the rise of large-scale, systematic, and ongoing investigations of children and their development throughout the life span. For example, the Stanford Studies of Gifted Children began in the early 1920s and continue today. Similarly, the Fels Research Institute Study and the Berkeley Growth and Guidance Studies helped identify the nature of change in children's lives as they became older. Using a normative approach, these studies followed large numbers of children to determine the nature of normal growth (Dixon & Lerner, 1999).

The women and men who built the foundations of child development shared a common goal: to use scientific methods to study the nature of growth, change, and stability throughout childhood and adolescence. They helped to bring the field to where it is today.

Today's Key Issues and Questions: Child Development's Underlying Themes

Today, several key issues and questions dominate the field of child development. Among the major issues (summarized in Table 1-2) are the nature of developmental change, the importance of critical and sensitive periods, life span approaches versus more focused approaches, and the nature–nurture issue.

Continuous Change versus Discontinuous Change. One of the primary issues challenging child developmentalists is whether development proceeds in a continuous or discontinuous fashion (illustrated in Figure 1-1). In **continuous change**, development is gradual,

TABLE 1-2 Major Issues in Child Development

Continuous Change	Discontinuous Change
• Change is gradual. • Achievements at one level build on previous level. • Underlying developmental processes remain the same over the lifespan.	• Change occurs in distinct steps or stages. • Behavior and processes are qualitatively different at different stages.
Critical Periods	**Sensitive Periods**
• Certain environmental stimuli are necessary for normal development. • Emphasized by early developmentalists.	• People are susceptible to certain environmental stimuli, but consequences of absent stimuli are reversible. • Current emphasis in life span development.
Life Span Approach	**Focus on Particular Periods**
• Current theories emphasize growth and change throughout life, relatedness of different periods.	• Infancy and adolescence are emphasized by early developmentalists as most important periods.
Nature (Genetic Factors)	**Nurture (Environmental Factors)**
• Emphasis is on discovering inherited genetic traits and abilities.	• Emphasis is on environmental influences that affect a person's development.

continuous change Gradual development in which achievements at one level build on those of previous levels

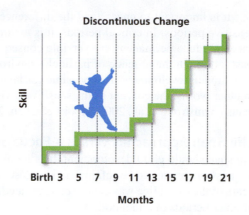

FIGURE 1-1 Two Approaches to Developmental Change

The two approaches to development are continuous change, which is gradual, with achievements at one level building on those of previous levels, and discontinuous change, which occurs in distinct steps or stages.

with achievements at one level building on those of previous levels. Continuous change is quantitative; the basic underlying developmental processes that drive change remain the same over the course of the life span. Continuous change, then, produces changes that are a matter of degree, not of kind. Changes in height prior to adulthood, for example, are continuous. Similarly, as we'll see later in the chapter, some theorists suggest that changes in people's thinking capabilities are also continuous, showing gradual quantitative improvements rather than developing entirely new cognitive processing capabilities.

In contrast, **discontinuous change** occurs in distinct steps or stages. Each stage brings about behavior that is assumed to be qualitatively different from behavior at earlier stages. Consider the example of cognitive development. We'll see in Chapter 2 that some cognitive developmentalists suggest that thinking changes in fundamental ways as children develop and that the changes are not just a matter of quantitative change, but also of qualitative change.

Most developmentalists agree that taking an either/or position on the continuous–discontinuous issue is inappropriate. While many types of developmental change are continuous, others are clearly discontinuous (Flavell, 1994; Heimann, 2003).

Critical and Sensitive Periods: Gauging the Impact of Environmental Events.
If a woman comes down with a case of rubella (German measles) in the 11th week of pregnancy, the consequences for the child she is carrying are likely to be devastating: They include the potential for blindness, deafness, and heart defects. However, if she comes down with the same strain of rubella in the 30th week of pregnancy, damage to the child is unlikely.

The differing outcomes of the disease in the two periods demonstrate the concept of critical periods. A **critical period** is a specific time during development when a particular event has its greatest consequences. Critical periods occur when the presence of certain kinds of environmental stimuli is necessary for development to proceed normally, or exposure to certain stimuli results in abnormal development. For example, mothers who take drugs at particular times while pregnant may cause permanent harm to the developing child (Uylings, 2006; Harris, 2010; Glynn & Sandman, 2011).

Although early specialists in child development placed great emphasis on the importance of critical periods, more recent thinking suggests that in many realms, individuals may be more flexible than was first thought, particularly in the domains of cognitive, personality, and social development. In these areas, there is a significant degree of **plasticity**, the degree to which a developing behavior or physical structure is modifiable. For instance, rather than suffering permanent damage from a lack of certain kinds of early social experiences, there is increasing evidence that children can use later experiences to help overcome earlier deficits.

Consequently, developmentalists are now more likely to speak of sensitive periods rather than critical periods. In a **sensitive period**, organisms are particularly susceptible to certain kinds of stimuli in their environment. A sensitive period represents the optimal period for particular capacities to emerge, and children are particularly sensitive to environmental influences. For example, a lack of exposure to language during sensitive periods may result in delayed language production in infants and toddlers.

discontinuous change Development that occurs in distinct steps or stages, with each stage bringing about behavior that is assumed to be qualitatively different from behavior at earlier stages

critical period A specific time during development when a particular event has its greatest consequences

plasticity The degree to which a developing behavior or physical structure is modifiable

sensitive period A specific time when organisms are particularly susceptible to certain kinds of stimuli in their environment

It is important to understand the difference between the concepts of critical periods and sensitive periods: In critical periods, it is assumed that certain kinds of environmental influences produce permanent, irreversible consequences for the developing individual. In contrast, although the absence of particular environmental influences during a sensitive period may hinder development, it is possible for later experiences to overcome the earlier deficits. In other words, the concept of the sensitive period recognizes the plasticity of developing humans (Armstrong et al., 2006; Hooks & Chen, 2008; Curley et al., 2011).

Life Span Approaches versus a Focus on Particular Periods.

On what part of the life span should child developmentalists focus their attention? For early developmentalists, the answers tended to be infancy and adolescence. Most research attention during the early years of the discipline was clearly concentrated on those two periods, largely to the exclusion of other periods of childhood.

Today, however, the story is different. The entire period from conception through adolescence is now regarded as important, for several reasons. One is the discovery that developmental growth and change continue during every stage of life.

Furthermore, an important part of every person's environment is the other people around him or her, the person's social environment. To understand the social influences on children of a given age, we need to understand the people who are in large measure providing those influences. For instance, to understand development in infants, we need to unravel the effects of their parents' age on their social environment. It is likely that a 15-year-old mother will provide parental influences of a different sort from those provided by a 37-year-old mother. Consequently, infant development is in part a consequence of adult development.

The Relative Influence of Nature and Nurture on Development.

One of the enduring questions of child development involves how much of people's behavior is due to their genetically determined nature and how much is due to nurture, the influences of the physical and social environment in which a child is raised. This issue, which has deep philosophical and historical roots, has dominated much work in child development (Wexler, 2006; Keating, 2011).

In this context, *nature* refers to traits, abilities, and capacities that are inherited from one's parents. It encompasses any factor that is produced by the predetermined unfolding of genetic information—a process known as **maturation**. These genetic, inherited influences are at work as we move from the one-cell organism that is created at the moment of conception to the billions of cells that make up a fully formed human.

Nature influences whether our eyes are blue or brown, whether we have thick hair throughout life or eventually go bald, and how good we are at athletics. Nature allows our brains to develop in such a way that we can read the words on this page.

In contrast, *nurture* refers to the environmental influences that shape behavior. Some of these influences may be biological, such as the impact of a pregnant mother's use of cocaine on her unborn child or the amounts and kinds of food available to children. Other environmental influences are more social, such as the ways parents discipline their children and the effects of peer pressure on an adolescent. Finally, some influences are a result of larger, societal-level factors, such as the socioeconomic circumstances in which people find themselves.

If our traits and behavior were determined solely by either nature or nurture, there would probably be little debate regarding the issue. However, for most critical behaviors, this is hardly the case. Take, for instance, one of the most controversial arenas: intelligence. As we'll consider in detail in Chapter 9, the question of whether intelligence is determined primarily by inherited, genetic factors—nature—or is shaped by environmental factors—nurture—has caused lively and often bitter arguments. Largely because of its social implications, the issue has spilled out of the scientific arena and into the realms of politics and social policy.

Implications for Child Rearing and Social Policy.

Consider the implications of the nature-versus-nurture issue: If the extent of one's intelligence is primarily determined by heredity and consequently is largely fixed at birth, then efforts to improve intellectual performance later in life may be doomed to failure. In contrast, if intelligence is primarily a result

maturation The process of the predetermined unfolding of genetic information

of environmental factors, such as the amount and quality of schooling and stimulation to which one is exposed, then we would expect that an improvement in social conditions could bring about an increase in intelligence.

The extent of social policy affected by ideas about the origins of intelligence illustrates the significance of issues that involve the nature–nurture question. As we address it in relation to several topical areas throughout this book, we should keep in mind that specialists in child development reject the notion that behavior is the result solely of either nature or nurture. Instead, the question is one of degree—and the specifics of that, too, are hotly debated.

Furthermore, the interaction of genetic and environmental factors is complex, in part because certain genetically determined traits have not only a direct influence on children's behavior but an indirect influence in shaping children's environments as well. For example, a child who is consistently cranky and who cries a great deal—a trait that may be produced by genetic factors—may influence her environment by making her parents so highly responsive to her insistent crying that they rush to comfort her whenever she cries. Their responsivity to the child's genetically determined behavior consequently becomes an environmental influence on her subsequent development (Bradley & Corwyn, 2008; Stright, Gallagher, & Kelley, 2008; Olson et al., 2011).

Similarly, although our genetic background orients us toward particular behaviors, those behaviors will not necessarily occur without an appropriate environment. People with similar genetic backgrounds (such as identical twins) may behave in very different ways; people with highly dissimilar genetic backgrounds can behave quite similarly to one another in certain areas (Gracia, Bearer, & Lerner, 2004; Kato & Pedersen, 2005; Tuvblad et al., 2011).

In sum, the question of how much of a given behavior is due to nature and how much to nurture is challenging. Ultimately, we should consider the two sides of the nature–nurture issue as opposite ends of a continuum, with particular behaviors falling somewhere between the two ends. We can say something similar about the other controversies that we have considered. For instance, continuous versus discontinuous development is not an either/or proposition; some forms of development fall toward the continuous end of the continuum, while others lie closer to the discontinuous end. In short, few statements about development involve either/or absolutes (Rutter, 2006; Deater-Deckard & Cahill, 2006).

The Future of Child Development

We've examined the foundations of the field of child development, along with the key issues and questions that underlie the discipline. But what lies ahead? Several trends appear likely to emerge:

- As research in development continues to be amassed, the field will become increasingly specialized. New areas of study and different perspectives will emerge.
- The explosion in information about genes and the genetic foundations of behavior will influence all spheres of child development. Increasingly, developmentalists will link work across biological, cognitive, and social domains, and the boundaries between different subdisciplines will be blurred.
- The increasing racial, ethnic, linguistic, and cultural variety of the population of the United States will lead the field to focus greater attention on issues of diversity.
- A growing number of professionals in a variety of fields will make use of child development's research and findings. Educators, social workers, nurses and other health-care providers, genetic counselors, toy designers, child care providers, cereal manufacturers, social ethicists, and members of dozens of other professions will all draw on the field of child development.

Work on child development will increasingly influence public interest issues. Discussion of many of the major social concerns of our time, including violence, prejudice and discrimination, poverty, changes in family life, child care, schooling, and even terrorism, can be informed by research in child development. Consequently, child developmentalists are likely to make important contributions to 21st-century society (Zigler & Finn-Stevenson, 1999; Pyszczynski, Solomon, & Greenberg, 2003; Block, Weinstein, & Seitz, 2005). (For one example of the current contributions of work in child development, see the *From Research to Practice* box.)

FROM RESEARCH TO PRACTICE
Preventing Violence in Children

"Life is hard," a probation officer had once told Jimmy Davis. Those words had made Jimmy roll his eyes. If anyone knew about life being hard, it was Jimmy. When he was five, his dad had gone to prison for gunning down a bookie. He'd never seen his father again, but he sure remembered the beatings he'd received at the hands of the old man before he got sent up.

His mom drank more after that and lost her job. Then she started bringing men home. The men either ignored Jimmy or beat him. One had threatened to set his bed on fire while he was sleeping.

Four years ago, when he was 12, he was arrested for drug possession. Last year, he got popped for stealing a car. Three days ago, he was arraigned on two counts of murder in connection with a robbery. Jimmy hadn't wanted to kill the men, but they'd been in his way. His life was too difficult to worry about anyone but himself. When his attorney asked if he was scared, Jimmy said, "No. Just sick of life."

Jimmy's descent into violence is representative of the lives of too many children and adolescents in the United States today. Many observers have called the level of violence nothing less than an epidemic. In fact, surveys find that violence and crime rank among the issues of greatest concern to people in the United States (NCADV, 2003; DocuTicker, 2010).

How can we explain the level of violence? How do people learn to be violent? How can we control and remedy aggression? And how can we discourage violence from occurring in the first place?

Child development has sought to answer such questions from several different perspectives. Consider these examples:

- *Explaining the roots of violence.* Some child developmentalists have looked at how early behavioral and physical problems may be associated with later difficulties in controlling aggression. For instance, researchers have found links between early maltreatment, physical and psychological abuse, and neglect of children and their subsequent aggressive behavior. Others have looked at hormonal influences on violent behavior (Gagné et al., 2007; Maas, Herrenkohl, & Sousa, 2008; Skårberg, Nyberg, & Engstrom, 2010).

- *Examining how exposure to aggression may lead to violence.* Other psychologists have examined how exposure to violence in the media and in video games may lead to aggression. For example, psychologist Craig Anderson has found that people who play violent video games have an altered view of the world, seeing it as more violent than those who do not play such games. In addition, those who play such violent video games are more easily triggered into aggressive behavior, and they have decreased empathy for others (Barlett, Harris, &Baldassaro, 2007; Bluemke, Friedrich, & Zumbach, 2010; Anderson et al., 2010).

- *Developing programs to reduce aggression.* According to psychologists Ervin Staub and Darren Spielman, schoolteachers and school administrators must be on the lookout for even milder forms of aggression, such as bullying. Unless such forms of aggression are checked, they are likely to endure and to escalate into more blatant forms.

To combat aggression, Staub and Spielman devised a program to help children develop constructive ways of fulfilling their basic needs. After involvement in an intervention that included role playing, videotaping, and structured discussions, participants' aggressive behavior declined (Spielman & Staub, 2003; Staub, 2011).

As these examples illustrate, developmental researchers are making progress in understanding and dealing with the violence that is increasingly part of modern society. Furthermore, violence is just one example of the areas in which experts in child development are contributing their skills for the betterment of human society. As we'll see throughout this book, the field has much to offer.

■ **Why does violence remain such a problem in the United States, and why are the levels of violence (as measured by crime statistics) worse in the United States than in other industrialized countries?**

■ **Because research shows that exposure to violent video games raises the level of aggression in players, do you think there should be legal limitations on the sale and distribution of such games? Why or why not?**

ARE YOU AN INFORMED CONSUMER OF DEVELOPMENT?

Assessing Information on Child Development

If you immediately comfort crying babies, you'll spoil them.

If you let babies cry without comforting them, they'll be untrusting and clingy as adults.

Spanking is one of the best ways to discipline your child.

Never hit your child.

If a marriage is unhappy, children are better off if their parents divorce than if they stay together.

No matter how difficult a marriage is, parents should avoid divorce for the sake of their children.

There is no lack of advice on the best way to raise a child or, more generally, to lead one's life. From best-sellers with titles such as *The No-Cry Sleep Solution* to magazine and newspaper columns that provide advice on every imaginable topic, each of us is exposed to tremendous amounts of information.

Yet not all advice is equally valid. The mere fact that something is in print, on television, or on a website does not automatically make it legitimate or accurate. Fortunately, some guidelines can help distinguish when recommendations and suggestions are reasonable and when they are not. Here are a few:

- Consider the source of the advice. Information from established, respected organizations such as the American Medical Association, the American Psychological Association, and the American Academy of Pediatrics is likely to be the result of years of study, and its accuracy is probably high.

- Evaluate the credentials of the person providing advice. Information coming from established, acknowledged researchers and experts in a field is likely to be more accurate than that coming from a person whose credentials are obscure.

- Understand the difference between anecdotal evidence and scientific evidence. Anecdotal evidence is based on one or two instances of a phenomenon, haphazardly discovered or encountered; scientific evidence is based on careful, systematic procedures.

- Keep cultural context in mind. Although an assertion may be valid in some contexts, it may not be true in all. For example, it is typically assumed that providing infants the freedom to move about and exercise their limbs facilitates their muscular development and mobility. Yet in some cultures, infants spend most of their time closely bound to their mothers with no apparent long-term damage (H. Kaplan & Dove, 1987; Tronick, Thomas, & Daltabuit, 1994).

- Don't assume that because many people believe something, it is necessarily true. Scientific evaluation has often proved that some of the most basic presumptions about the effectiveness of various techniques are invalid. For instance, consider DARE, the Drug Abuse Resistance Education anti-drug program that is used in about half the school systems in the United States. DARE is designed to prevent the spread of drugs through lectures and question-and-answer sessions run by police officers. Careful evaluation, however, finds no evidence that the program is effective in reducing drug use (Rhule, 2005; University of Akron, 2006).

In short, the key to evaluating information relating to child development is to maintain a healthy dose of skepticism. No source of information is invariably, unfailingly accurate. By keeping a critical eye on the statements you encounter, you'll be in a better position to determine the contributions made by child developmentalists in understanding how we change and grow over the course of childhood and adolescence. ■

Review, Check, and Apply

Review

1. Early philosophical views considered the child as an empty slate (*tabula rasa*) on which society had to write, or a noble savage with an innate sense of morality.

2. Advances in psychology led to a more intensive study of influences and implications of childhood events until in the 20th century the field became a formal discipline built on scientific principles.

3. Four issues have emerged as particularly significant for developmental researchers: continuity versus discontinuity in development, the importance of sensitive periods, the focus on distinct periods versus the entire life span, and the nature–nurture controversy.

4. The future of the field is tending toward increased specialization, a greater focus on genetics, the importance of diversity, and the broader use of developmental findings across fields and in public policy.

Check

1. The predetermined unfolding of genetic information is _____.

2. One key issue in child development today includes the comparison and contrast between continuous versus _____ change.

3. Another important issue involves the understanding of critical and _____ periods.

4. The relative influence of nature versus _____ on development illustrates a key question in child development.

Apply

1. What is one way in which the nature–nurture issue has been an important consideration in a modern political or societal controversy?

2. In what ways do you think food manufacturers make use of the findings of child researchers? Is such a use ever improper?

To see more review questions, log on to MyPsychLab.

ANSWERS: 1. maturation 2. discontinuous 3. sensitive 4. nurture

The CASE
of . . . *Too Many Choices*

Jenny Claymore, midway through her third year of college, is desperate to pick a career, but she hasn't a clue. The problem isn't that nothing interests her; it's that too many things do. From her reading, radio listening, and TV watching, her head is full of ideas for great-sounding careers.

Jenny loves children, having always enjoyed babysitting and her summer work as a camp counselor—so maybe she should be a teacher. She is fascinated by all she hears about DNA and genetic research—so maybe she should be a biologist or a doctor. She is concerned when she hears about school violence—from bullying to shootings—so maybe she should go into school administration or law enforcement. She is curious about how children learn language—so maybe she should go into speech pathology or, again, teaching. She is fascinated by court cases that rely on the testimony of young children, and how experts on both sides contradict each other—so maybe she should become a lawyer.

Her college counselor once said, "Begin your search for a career by thinking about the classes you've taken in high school and college." Jenny recalls a high school course in early childhood that she loved, and she knows that her favorite class in college is her Child Development course. Would considering a career in child development make sense?

1. How well might a career in the field of child development address her love of children and her interest in genetic research?

2. What sort of career might focus on the prevention of school violence?

3. How might child development relate to her interest in eyewitness testimony and memory?

4. Overall, how many careers could you think of that would fit Jenny's interests?

◀◀◀ LOOKING BACK

LO 1-1   What is child development?

- Child development is a scientific approach to questions about the growth, change, and stability that individuals experience from conception to adolescence.

LO 1-2   What is the scope of the field of child development?

- The scope of the field encompasses physical, cognitive, and social and personality development at all ages from conception through adolescence.

LO 1-3   What are major societal influences that determine development?

- Culture—both broad and narrow—is an important issue in child development. Many aspects of development are influenced not

only by broad cultural differences but also by ethnic, racial, and socioeconomic differences within a particular culture.

- Every person is subject to history-graded influences, age-graded influences, sociocultural-graded influences, and non-normative life events.

LO 1-4   How have views of childhood changed historically?

- Early views of childhood considered children as miniature adults.

- While Locke viewed a child as a *tabula rasa* (or "blank slate"), Rousseau argued that children had an inborn sense of morality.

- Later views regarded childhood as a distinct period in the life span and led to the emergence of the field of child development.

LO 1-5 What are the key issues and questions in the field of child development?

- Four key issues in child development are (1) whether developmental change is continuous or discontinuous, (2) whether development is largely governed by critical or sensitive periods during which certain influences or experiences must occur for development to be normal, (3) whether to focus on certain particularly important periods in human development or on the entire life span,

and (4) the nature–nurture question, which focuses on the relative importance of genetic versus environmental influences.

LO 1-6 What is the future of child development likely to hold?

- Future trends in the field are likely to include increasing specialization, the blurring of boundaries between different areas, increasing attention to issues involving diversity, and an increasing influence on public interest issues.

KEY TERMS AND CONCEPTS

child development (p. 5)
physical development (p. 5)
cognitive development (p. 5)
personality development (p. 6)

social development (p. 6)
cohort (p. 9)
continuous change (p. 12)
discontinuous change (p. 13)

critical period (p. 13)
plasticity (p. 13)
sensitive period (p. 13)
maturation (p. 14)

Epilogue

We have covered a lot of ground in our introduction to the growing field of child development. We have reviewed the broad scope of the field, touching on the wide range of topics that child developmentalists may address, and we have discussed the key issues and questions that have shaped the field since its inception.

Before proceeding to the next chapter, take a few minutes to reconsider the prologue of this chapter—the case of Louise Brown, the first child to be born through in vitro fertilization. Based on what you now know about child development, answer the following questions:

1. What are some of the potential benefits, and drawbacks, of the type of conception—in vitro fertilization—that was carried out for Louise's parents?

2. What are some questions that developmentalists who study either physical, cognitive, or personality and social development might ask about the effects on Louise of being conceived via in vitro fertilization?

3. The creation of complete human clones—exact genetic replicas of an individual—is still in the realm of science fiction, but the theoretical possibility does raise some important questions. For example, what would be the psychological consequences of being a clone?

4. If clones could actually be produced, how might it help scientists understand the relative impact of heredity and environment on development?

The Development Video Series in MyPsychLab

Explore the video *Sheryl: Mother of Three* by scanning this QR code with your mobile device. If you don't already have one, you may download a free QR scanner for your device wherever smartphone apps are sold. You can also view this video in MyPsychLab. For more videos related to this chapter's content, log into MyPsychLab to view the entire Development Video Series.

MyVirtualChild

- **What decisions would you make while raising a child?**
- **What would the consequences of those decisions be?**

Find out by accessing **MyVirtualChild** at
www.MyPsychLab.com
and raising your own virtual child from birth to age 18.

2 Theoretical Perspectives and Research

MODULE 2.1

PERSPECTIVES ON CHILDREN

- The Psychodynamic Perspective: Focusing on Internal Forces
- The Behavioral Perspective: Focusing on External Forces
- Classical Conditioning: Stimulus Substitution
- The Cognitive Perspective: Examining the Roots of Understanding
- The Contextual Perspective: Taking a Broad Approach to Development

CAREERS IN CHILD DEVELOPMENT: Judy Coleman Brinich

- Evolutionary Perspectives: Our Ancestors' Contributions to Behavior
- Why "Which Perspective Is Right?" Is the Wrong Question

Review, Check, and Apply

MODULE 2.2

THE SCIENTIFIC METHOD AND RESEARCH

- Theories and Hypotheses: Posing Developmental Questions
- Theories: Framing Broad Explanations
- Hypotheses: Specifying Testable Predictions
- Choosing a Research Strategy: Answering Questions
- Correlational Studies
- Experiments: Determining Cause and Effect

DEVELOPMENTAL DIVERSITY AND YOUR LIFE:
Choosing Research Participants Who Represent the Diversity of Children

Review, Check, and Apply

MODULE 2.3

RESEARCH STRATEGIES AND CHALLENGES

- Theoretical and Applied Research: Complementary Approaches
- Measuring Developmental Change

FROM RESEARCH TO PRACTICE: Using Research to Improve Public Policy

- Ethics and Research

ARE YOU AN INFORMED CONSUMER OF DEVELOPMENT? Critically Evaluating Developmental Research

Review, Check, and Apply

The Case of ... a Study in Violence

Looking Back

Key Terms and Concepts

Epilogue

PROLOGUE: The Unasked Questions

Christina-Taylor Green, 9, was excited about going to Rep. Gabrielle Giffords' informal town hall event this weekend. She started becoming interested in politics during the last presidential campaign …

Christina-Taylor was a straight-A student. The "9/11 baby" sang on the church choir and was best friends with her older brother. She had just been elected class president at Mesa Verde Elementary School and had planned to start a club at her school to help less fortunate classmates. It was that civic-mindedness that led her to a Safeway supermarket in Tucson Saturday morning.

Christina-Taylor "talked about getting all the parties to come together so we could live in a better country," her mother said Sunday. "She was going to Giffords' event to ask questions about how she could help and to learn more about politics in our country." (Clarke & Parise, 2011)

>>> LOOKING AHEAD

Christina-Taylor never got to ask her questions. She was murdered in a senseless act of violence that killed six people and wounded 12 others.

How did Christina-Taylor become as civic-minded and socially engaged as she was at the young age of 9? What accounts for her evident intelligence and her interest in politics? Where did her sweet and loving personality come from? And, conversely, what could possibly account for the rage that her killer harbored, which eventually led to Christina-Taylor's death?

More broadly, what accounts for the changes during childhood that ultimately produce a person with a given set of skills and traits? And how can children and adolescents navigate the many challenges of childhood on their way to adulthood?

The ability to answer these questions depends on the accumulated findings from literally thousands of developmental research studies. These studies have looked at questions ranging from brain development to the nature of social relationships to the way in which cognitive abilities grow throughout childhood and adolescence. The common challenge of these studies is to pose and answer questions of interest relating to development.

(continued)

Learning Objectives

MODULE 2.1

LO1 What are the basic concepts of the psychodynamic perspective?

LO2 What are the basic concepts of the behavioral perspective?

LO3 What are the basic concepts of the cognitive perspective?

LO4 What are the basic concepts of the contextual perspective?

LO5 What are the basic concepts of the evolutionary perspective?

LO6 What is the value of multiple perspectives on child development?

MODULE 2.2

LO7 What is the scientific method, and how does it help answer questions about child development?

LO8 What are the major characteristics of correlational studies and experiments, and how do they differ?

MODULE 2.3

LO9 What are the major research strategies?

LO10 What are the primary ethical principles used to guide research?

Like all of us, child developmentalists are curious about people's bodies, minds, and social interactions—and about how these aspects of human life change as people age. But to the natural curiosity that we all share, developmental scientists add one important ingredient that makes a difference in how they ask—and try to answer—questions. This ingredient is the scientific method. This structured but straightforward way of looking at phenomena elevates questioning from mere curiosity to purposeful learning. With this powerful tool, developmentalists are able not only to ask good questions but also to begin to answer them systematically.

In this chapter, we consider the way in which developmentalists ask and answer questions about the world. We begin with a discussion of the broad perspectives used in understanding children and their behavior. These perspectives provide general approaches from which to view development along multiple dimensions. We then turn to the basic building blocks of the science of child development: research tools and methods. We describe the major types of research that developmentalists perform to examine their questions and get answers to them. Finally, we focus on two important issues in developmental research: One is how to choose research participants so that results can be applied beyond the particular study setting, and the other is the central issue of ethics.

MODULE 2.1

PERSPECTIVES ON CHILDREN

LO 2-1 What are the basic concepts of the psychodynamic perspective?

LO 2-2 What are the basic concepts of the behavioral perspective?

LO 2-3 What are the basic concepts of the cognitive perspective?

LO 2-4 What are the basic concepts of the contextual perspective?

LO 2-5 What are the basic concepts of the evolutionary perspective?

LO 2-6 What is the value of multiple perspectives on child development?

When Roddy McDougall said his first word, his parents were elated—and relieved. They had anticipated the moment for what seemed a long time; most of the children of his age had already uttered their first word. In addition, his grandparents had weighed in with their concerns, his grandmother going so far as to suggest that he might be suffering from some sort of developmental delay, although that was based solely on a "feeling" she had. But the moment Roddy spoke, his parents' and grandparents' anxieties fell away, and they all simply experienced great pride in Roddy's accomplishment.

The concerns Roddy's relatives felt were based on their vague conceptions of how a normal child's development proceeds. Each of us has established ideas about the course of development, and we use them to make judgments and develop hunches about the meaning of children's behavior. Our experience orients us to certain types of behavior that we see as particularly important. For some people, it may be when a child says his or her first word; for others, it may be the way a child interacts with others.

Like laypersons, child developmentalists approach the field from a number of different perspectives. Each broad perspective encompasses one or more **theories**, broad, organized explanations and predictions concerning phenomena of interest. A theory provides a framework for understanding the relationships among a seemingly unorganized set of facts or principles.

We all develop theories about development, based on our experience, folklore, and articles in magazines and newspapers. However, theories in child development are different.

theories Explanations and predictions concerning phenomena of interest, providing a framework for understanding the relationships among an organized set of facts or principles

Whereas our own personal theories are built on unverified observations that are developed haphazardly, child developmentalists' theories are more formal, based on a systematic integration of prior findings and theorizing. These theories allow developmentalists to summarize and organize prior observations, and they allow them to move beyond existing observations to draw deductions that may not be immediately apparent. In addition, these theories are then subject to rigorous testing in the form of research. By contrast, the developmental theories of individuals are not subject to such testing and may never be questioned at all (Thomas, 2001).

We'll consider five major perspectives used in child development: the psychodynamic, behavioral, cognitive, contextual, and evolutionary perspectives. These diverse outlooks emphasize somewhat different aspects of development that steer inquiry in particular directions. Furthermore, each perspective continues to evolve and change, as befits a growing and dynamic discipline.

The Psychodynamic Perspective: Focusing on Internal Forces

When Marisol was 6 months old, she was involved in a bloody automobile accident—or so her parents tell her, since she has no conscious recollection of it. Now, however, at age 24, she is having difficulty maintaining relationships, and her therapist is seeking to determine whether her current problems are a result of the early accident.

Looking for such a link might seem a bit far-fetched, but to proponents of the **psychodynamic perspective**, it is not really improbable. Advocates of the psychodynamic perspective believe that behavior is motivated by inner forces, memories, and conflicts of which a person has little awareness or control. The inner forces, which may stem from one's childhood, continually influence behavior throughout the life span.

Freud's Psychoanalytic Theory.
The psychodynamic perspective is most closely associated with Sigmund Freud and his psychoanalytic theory. Freud, who lived from 1856 to 1939, was a Viennese physician whose revolutionary ideas ultimately had a profound effect not just on the fields of psychology and psychiatry but on Western thought in general (Masling & Bornstein, 1996; Wolitzky, 2011).

Freud's **psychoanalytic theory** suggests that unconscious forces act to determine personality and behavior. To Freud, the *unconscious* is a part of the personality about which a person is unaware. It contains infantile wishes, desires, demands, and needs that are hidden, because of their disturbing nature, from conscious awareness. Freud suggested that the unconscious is responsible for a good part of our everyday behavior.

According to Freud, everyone's personality has three aspects: id, ego, and superego. The *id* is the raw, unorganized, inborn part of personality that is present at birth. It represents primitive drives related to hunger, sex, aggression, and irrational impulses. The id operates according to the *pleasure principle*, in which the goal is to maximize satisfaction and reduce tension. The *ego* is the part of personality that is rational and reasonable. The ego acts as a buffer between the real world outside of us and the primitive id. The ego operates on the *reality principle*, in which instinctual energy is restrained to maintain the safety of the individual and help integrate the person into society.

Finally, Freud proposed that the *superego* represents a person's conscience, incorporating distinctions between right and wrong. It develops around age 5 or 6 and is learned from an individual's parents, teachers, and other significant figures.

In addition to providing an account of the various parts of the personality, Freud also suggested the ways in which personality develops during childhood. He argued that **psychosexual development** occurs as children pass through a series of stages, in which pleasure, or gratification, is focused on a particular biological function and body part. As illustrated in Table 2-1 on page 24, he suggested that pleasure shifts from the mouth (the *oral stage*) to the anus (the *anal stage*) and eventually to the genitals (the *phallic stage* and the *genital stage*).

Sigmund Freud

psychodynamic perspective   The approach to the study of development that states behavior is motivated by inner forces, memories, and conflicts of which a person has little awareness or control

psychoanalytic theory   The theory proposed by Freud that suggests that unconscious forces act to determine personality and behavior

psychosexual development   According to Freud, a series of stages that children pass through in which pleasure, or gratification, is focused on a particular biological function and body part

TABLE 2-1 Freud's and Erikson's Theories

Approximate Age	Freud's Stages of Psychosexual Development	Major Characteristics of Freud's Stages	Erikson's Stages of Psychosocial Development	Positive and Negative Outcomes of Erikson's Stages
Birth to 12–18 months	Oral	Interest in oral gratification from sucking, eating, mouthing, biting	Trust vs. mistrust	*Positive:* Feelings of trust from environmental support *Negative:* Fear and concern regarding others
12–18 months to 3 years	Anal	Gratification from expelling and withholding feces; coming to terms with society's controls relating to toilet training	Autonomy vs. shame and doubt	*Positive:* Self-sufficiency if exploration is encouraged *Negative:* Doubts about self, lack of independence
3 to 5–6 years	Phallic	Interest in the genitals; coming to terms with Oedipal conflict, leading to identification with same sex parent	Initiative vs. guilt	*Positive:* Discovery of ways to initiate actions *Negative:* Guilt from actions and thoughts
5–6 years to adolescence	Latency	Sexual concerns largely unimportant	Industry vs. inferiority	*Positive:* Development of sense of competence *Negative:* Feelings of inferiority, no sense of mastery
Adolescence to adulthood (Freud) Adolescence (Erikson)	Genital	Reemergence of sexual interests and establishment of mature sexual relationships	Identity vs. role diffusion	*Positive:* Awareness of uniqueness of self, knowledge of role to be followed *Negative:* Inability to identify appropriate roles in life
Early adulthood (Erikson)			Intimacy vs. isolation	*Positive:* Development of loving, sexual relationships and close friendships *Negative:* Fear of relationships with others
Middle adulthood (Erikson)			Generativity vs. stagnation	*Positive:* Sense of contribution to continuity of life *Negative:* Trivialization of one's activities
Late adulthood (Erikson)			Ego-integrity vs. despair	*Positive:* Sense of unity in life's accomplishments *Negative:* Regret over lost opportunities of life

According to Freud, if children are unable to gratify themselves sufficiently during a particular stage, or conversely, if they receive too much gratification, fixation may occur. *Fixation* is behavior reflecting an earlier stage of development due to an unresolved conflict. For instance, fixation at the oral stage might produce an adult unusually absorbed in oral activities—eating, talking, or chewing gum. Freud also argued that fixation is represented through symbolic sorts of oral activities, such as the use of "biting" sarcasm.

Erikson's Psychosocial Theory.

Psychoanalyst Erik Erikson, who lived from 1902 to 1994, provided an alternative psychodynamic view in his theory of psychosocial development, which emphasizes our social interaction with other people. In Erikson's view, society and culture both challenge and shape us. **Psychosocial development** encompasses changes

psychosocial development The approach to the study of development that encompasses changes in the understanding individuals have of their interactions with others, of others' behavior, and of themselves as members of society

in our interactions with and understandings of one another, as well as in our knowledge and understanding of ourselves as members of society (Erikson, 1963; Côté, 2005; Zhang & He, 2011).

Erikson's theory suggests that developmental change occurs throughout our lives in eight distinct stages (see Table 2-1 on page 24). The stages emerge in a fixed pattern and are similar for all people.

Erikson argued that each stage presents a crisis or conflict that the individual must resolve. Although no crisis is ever fully resolved, making life increasingly complicated, the individual must at least address the crisis of each stage sufficiently to deal with demands made during the next stage of development. Unlike Freud, who regarded development as relatively complete by adolescence, Erikson suggested that growth and change continue throughout the life span. For instance, he suggested that during adolescence, people pass through the identity-versus-role confusion stage, in which a growing awareness of the uniqueness of the self can produce either an understanding of the roles that one can assume in life or an inability to identify an appropriate role at all (de St. Aubin, McAdams, & Kim, 2004).

Assessing the Psychodynamic Perspective. It is hard for us to grasp the full significance of psychodynamic theories, represented by Freud's psychoanalytic theory and Erikson's theory of psychosocial development. Freud's introduction of the notion that unconscious influences affect behavior was a monumental accomplishment, and that it seems at all reasonable to us shows how extensively the idea of the unconscious has pervaded thinking in Western cultures. In fact, work by contemporary researchers studying memory and learning suggests that we carry with us memories—of which we are not consciously aware—that have a significant impact on our behavior. The example of Marisol, who was in a car accident when she was a baby, shows one application of psychodynamically based thinking and research.

Erik Erikson

Some of the most basic principles of Freud's psychoanalytic theory have been called into question, however, because they have not been validated by subsequent research. In particular, the notion that people pass through stages in childhood that determine their adult personalities has little definitive research support. In addition, because much of Freud's theory was based on a limited population of upper-middle-class Austrians living during a strict, puritanical era, its application to broad, multicultural populations is questionable. Finally, because Freud's theory focuses primarily on male development, it has been criticized as sexist and may be interpreted as devaluing women. For such reasons, many developmentalists question the validity of Freud's theory (Messer & McWilliams, 2003; Schachter, 2005; Boag, 2011).

Erikson's view that development continues throughout the life span is an important insight that influenced a good deal of thinking about how developmental change unfolds throughout life. On the other hand, the theory is vague and hard to test rigorously. Furthermore, like Freud's theory, it focuses more on men's than women's development. In sum, although the psychodynamic perspective provides reasonably good descriptions of past behavior, its predictions of future behavior are imprecise (Whitbourne et al., 1992; Zauszniewski & Martin, 1999; de St. Aubin et al., 2004).

The Behavioral Perspective: Focusing on External Forces

When Elissa Sheehan was 3, a large brown dog bit her, and she needed dozens of stitches and several operations. From the time she was bitten, she broke into a sweat whenever she saw a dog and in fact never enjoyed being around any pet.

To a child development specialist using the behavioral perspective, the explanation for Elissa's behavior is straightforward: She has a learned fear of dogs. Rather than looking inside the organism for unconscious processes, the **behavioral perspective** suggests that the keys to understanding development are observable behavior and outside stimuli in the environment. If we know the stimuli, we can predict the behavior. In this respect, the behavioral perspective reflects the view that nurture is more important to development than nature.

behavioral perspective   The approach to the study of development that suggests that the keys to understanding development are observable behavior and outside stimuli in the environment

John B. Watson

B. F. Skinner

👁 **Watch** the **Video** *The Basics: Classical Conditioning* in **MyPsychLab**.

👁 **Watch** the **Video** *The Basics: Operant Conditioning* in **MyPsychLab**.

classical conditioning   A type of learning in which an organism responds in a particular way to a neutral stimulus that normally does not bring about that type of response

operant conditioning   A form of learning in which a voluntary response is strengthened or weakened, depending on its association with positive or negative consequences

behavior modification   A formal technique for promoting the frequency of desirable behaviors and decreasing the incidence of unwanted ones

Behavioral theories reject the notion that people universally pass through a series of stages. Instead, people are assumed to be affected by the environmental stimuli to which they happen to be exposed. Developmental patterns, then, are personal, reflecting a particular set of environmental stimuli, and behavior is the result of continuing exposure to specific factors in the environment. Furthermore, developmental change is viewed in quantitative, rather than qualitative, terms. For instance, behavioral theories hold that advances in problem-solving capabilities as children age are largely a result of greater mental *capacities* rather than changes in the *kind* of thinking that children are able to bring to bear on a problem.

Classical Conditioning: Stimulus Substitution

Give me a dozen healthy infants, well-formed, and my own specified world to bring them up in and I'll guarantee to take any one at random and train him to become any type of specialist I might select—doctor, lawyer, artist, merchant-chief, and yes, even beggar-man and thief, regardless of his talents, penchants, tendencies, abilities. (J. B. Watson, 1925, p. 14)

With these words, John B. Watson, one of the first American psychologists to advocate a behavioral approach, summed up the behavioral perspective. Watson, who lived from 1878 to 1958, believed strongly that we could gain a full understanding of development by carefully studying the stimuli that make up the environment. In fact, he argued that by effectively controlling a person's environment, it was possible to produce virtually any behavior.

As we will consider further in Chapter 4, **classical conditioning** occurs when an organism learns to respond in a particular way to a neutral stimulus that normally does not evoke that type of response. For instance, if a dog is repeatedly exposed to the pairing of the sound of a bell and the presentation of meat, it may learn to react to the bell alone in the same way it reacts to the meat—by salivating and wagging its tail with excitement. Dogs don't typically respond to bells in this way; the behavior is a result of conditioning, a form of learning in which the response associated with one stimulus (food) comes to be connected to another—in this case, the bell.

The same process of classical conditioning explains how we learn emotional responses. In the case of dog-bite victim Elissa Sheehan, for instance, Watson would say that one stimulus has been substituted for another: Elissa's unpleasant experience with a particular dog (the initial stimulus) has been transferred to other dogs and to pets in general.

Operant Conditioning.   In addition to classical conditioning, other types of learning are found within the behavioral perspective. For example, **operant conditioning** is a form of learning in which a voluntary response is strengthened or weakened by its association with positive or negative consequences. It differs from classical conditioning in that the response being conditioned is voluntary and purposeful rather than automatic (such as salivating).

In operant conditioning, formulated and championed by psychologist B. F. Skinner (1904–1990), individuals learn to act deliberately on their environments to bring about desired consequences (Skinner, 1975). In a sense, then, children *operate* on their environments to bring about a desired state of affairs.

Whether children will seek to repeat a behavior depends on whether it is followed by re-inforcement. *Reinforcement* is the process by which a stimulus is provided that increases the probability that a preceding behavior will be repeated. Hence, a student is apt to work harder in school if he or she receives good grades, workers are likely to labor harder at their jobs if their efforts are tied to pay increases, and people are more apt to buy lottery tickets if they are reinforced by winning at least occasionally. In addition, *punishment*, the introduction of an unpleasant or painful stimulus or the removal of a desirable stimulus, will decrease the probability that a preceding behavior will occur in the future.

Behavior that is reinforced, then, is more likely to be repeated in the future, while behavior that receives no reinforcement or is punished is likely to be discontinued, or in the language of operant conditioning, *extinguished*. Principles of operant conditioning are used in **behavior modification**, a formal technique for promoting the frequency of desirable behaviors and decreasing the incidence of unwanted ones. Behavior modification has been used in a variety of situations, ranging from teaching severely retarded people the rudiments of language to helping people stick to diets (Hoek & Gendall, 2006; Matson & LoVullo, 2008; Holmes & Murray, 2011).

Social-Cognitive Learning Theory: Learning through Imitation.

A 5-year-old boy seriously injures his 22-month-old cousin while imitating a violent wrestling move he has seen on television. Although the infant sustained spinal cord injuries, he improved and was discharged five weeks after his hospital admission (Health eLine, 2003; Ray & Heyes, 2011).

Cause and effect? We can't know for sure, but it certainly seems possible, especially looking at the situation from the perspective of social-cognitive learning theory. According to developmental psychologist Albert Bandura and colleagues, a significant amount of learning is explained by **social-cognitive learning theory**, an approach that emphasizes learning by observing the behavior of another person, called a *model* (Bandura, 1994, 2002; MacPhee, 2011).

According to social-cognitive learning theory, observation of television programs such as *Jackass* can produce significant amounts of learning—not all of it positive.

Rather than learning being a matter of trial and error, as it is with operant conditioning, according to social-cognitive learning theory, behavior is learned through observation. We don't need to experience the consequences of a behavior ourselves to learn it. Social-cognitive learning theory holds that when we see the behavior of a model being rewarded, we are likely to imitate that behavior. For instance, in one classic experiment, children who were afraid of dogs were exposed to a model, nicknamed the "Fearless Peer," who was seen playing happily with a dog (Bandura, Grusec, & Menlove, 1967). After exposure, the children who previously had been afraid were more likely to approach a strange dog than children who had not seen the model.

Bandura suggests that social-cognitive learning proceeds in four steps (Bandura, 1986). First, an observer must pay attention and perceive the most critical features of a model's behavior. Second, the observer must successfully recall the behavior. Third, the observer must reproduce the behavior accurately. Finally, the observer must be motivated to learn and carry out the behavior.

Assessing the Behavioral Perspective.

Research based on the behavioral perspective has made significant contributions, ranging from techniques for educating children with severe mental retardation to identifying procedures for curbing aggression. At the same time, there are controversies regarding the behavioral perspective. For example, although they are part of the same general behavioral perspective, classical and operant conditioning, on the one hand, and social learning theory, on the other, disagree in some basic ways. Both classical and operant conditioning consider learning in terms of external stimuli and responses, in which the only important factors are the observable features of the environment. In such an analysis, people and other organisms are like inanimate "black boxes"; nothing that occurs inside the box is understood—nor much cared about, for that matter.

To social learning theorists, such an analysis is an oversimplification. They argue that what makes people different from rats and pigeons is mental activity, in the form of thoughts and expectations. A full understanding of people's development, they maintain, cannot occur without moving beyond external stimuli and responses.

In many ways, social learning theory has come to predominate in recent decades over classical and operant conditioning theories. In fact, another perspective that focuses explicitly on internal mental activity has become enormously influential. This is the cognitive approach, which we consider next.

The Cognitive Perspective: Examining the Roots of Understanding

When 3-year-old Jake is asked why it sometimes rains, he answers, "So the flowers can grow." When his 11-year-old sister Lila is asked the same question, she responds, "Because of evaporation from the surface of the earth." And when their cousin Ajima, who is studying

**FROM AN
EDUCATOR'S
PERSPECTIVE:**

How might the kind of social learning that comes from viewing television influence children's behavior?

social-cognitive learning theory An approach to the study of development that emphasizes learning by observing the behavior of another person, called a model

TABLE 2-2	Piaget's Stages of Cognitive Development	
Cognitive Stage	**Approximate Age Range**	**Major Characteristics**
Sensorimotor	Birth–2 years	Development of object permanence (idea that people/objects exist even when they can't be seen); development of motor skills; little or no capacity for symbolic representation
Preoperational	2–7 years	Development of language and symbolic thinking; egocentric thinking
Concrete operational	7–12 years	Development of conservation (idea that quantity is unrelated to physical appearance); mastery of concept of reversibility
Formal operational	12 years–adulthood	Development of logical and abstract thinking

meteorology in her high school science class, considers the same question, her extended answer includes a discussion of cumulonimbus clouds, the Coriolis effect, and synoptic charts.

To a developmental theorist using the cognitive perspective, the difference in the sophistication of the answers is evidence of a different degree of knowledge and understanding, or cognition. The **cognitive perspective** focuses on the processes that allow people to know, understand, and think about the world.

The cognitive perspective emphasizes how people internally represent and think about the world. By using this perspective, developmental researchers hope to understand how children and adults process information and how their ways of thinking and understanding affect their behavior. They also seek to learn how cognitive abilities change as people develop, the degree to which cognitive development represents quantitative and qualitative growth in intellectual abilities, and how different cognitive abilities are related to one another.

Piaget's Theory of Cognitive Development. No single person has had a greater impact on the study of cognitive development than Jean Piaget. A Swiss psychologist who lived from 1896 to 1980, Piaget proposed that all people pass in a fixed sequence through a series of universal stages of cognitive development (summarized in Table 2-2). He suggested that not only does the quantity of information increase in each stage, but the quality of knowledge and understanding changes as well. His focus was on the change in cognition that occurs as children move from one stage to the next (Piaget, 1952, 1962, 1983).

We'll consider Piaget's theory in detail beginning in Chapter 6, but we can get a broad sense of it now by looking at some of its main features. Piaget suggested that human thinking is arranged into *schemes*, organized mental patterns that represent behaviors and actions. In infants, such schemes represent concrete behavior—a scheme for sucking, for reaching, and for each separate behavior. In older children, the schemes become more sophisticated and abstract. Schemes are like intellectual computer software that directs and determines how data from the world are looked at and dealt with (Parker, 2005; Meltzoff, 2011).

Piaget suggests that children's *adaptation*—his term for the way in which children respond and adjust to new information—can be explained by two basic principles. *Assimilation* is the process in which people understand an experience in terms of their current stage of cognitive development and way of thinking. In contrast, *accommodation* refers to changes in existing ways of thinking in response to encounters with new stimuli or events.

Assimilation occurs when people use their current ways of thinking about and understanding the world to perceive and understand a new experience. For example, a young child

cognitive perspective The approach to the study of development that focuses on the processes that allow people to know, understand, and think about the world

who has not yet learned to count will look at two rows of buttons, each containing the same number of buttons, and say that a row in which the buttons are closely spaced together has fewer buttons in it than a row in which the buttons are more spread out. The experience of counting buttons, then, is assimilated to already existing schemes that contain the principle "bigger is more."

Later, however, when the child is older and has had sufficient exposure to new experiences, the content of the scheme will undergo change. In understanding that the quantity of buttons is identical whether they are spread out or closely spaced, the child has *accommodated* to the experience. Assimilation and accommodation work in tandem to bring about cognitive development.

Assessing Piaget's Theory.

Piaget has profoundly influenced our understanding of cognitive development and is one of the towering figures in child development. He provided masterly descriptions of how intellectual growth proceeds during childhood—descriptions that have stood the test of literally thousands of investigations. By and large, then, Piaget's broad view of the sequence of cognitive development is accurate.

However, the specifics of the theory, particularly in terms of change in cognitive capabilities over time, have been called into question. For instance, some cognitive skills clearly emerge earlier than Piaget suggested. Furthermore, the universality of Piaget's stages has been disputed. A growing amount of evidence suggests that the emergence of particular cognitive skills occurs according to a different timetable in non-Western cultures. And in every culture, some people never seem to reach Piaget's highest level of cognitive sophistication: formal, logical thought (McDonald & Stuart-Hamilton, 2003; Genovese, 2006; Richert, 2011).

Ultimately, the greatest criticism leveled at the Piagetian perspective is that cognitive development is not necessarily as discontinuous as Piaget's stage theory suggests. Remember that Piaget argued that growth proceeds in four distinct stages in which the quality of cognition differs from one stage to the next. However, many developmental researchers argue that growth is considerably more continuous. These critics have suggested an alternative perspective, known as the information processing approach, that focuses on the processes that underlie learning, memory, and thinking throughout the life span.

Information Processing Approaches.

Information processing approaches have become an important alternative to Piagetian approaches. **Information processing approaches** to cognitive development seek to identify the ways individuals take in, use, and store information.

Information processing approaches grew out of developments in the electronic processing of information, particularly as carried out by computers. They assume that even complex behavior such as learning, remembering, categorizing, and thinking can be broken down into a series of individual, specific steps.

Like computers, children are assumed by information processing approaches to have limited capacity for processing information. As they develop, though, they employ increasingly sophisticated strategies that allow them to process information more efficiently.

In stark contrast to Piaget's view that thinking undergoes qualitative advances as children age, information processing approaches assume that development is marked more by quantitative advances. Our capacity to handle information changes with age, as does our processing speed and efficiency. Furthermore, information processing approaches suggest that as people age, they are better able to control the nature of processing and can change the strategies they choose to process information.

An information-processing approach that builds on Piaget's research is known as neo-Piagetian theory. In contrast to Piaget's original work, which viewed cognition as a single system of increasingly sophisticated general cognitive abilities, *neo-Piagetian theory* considers cognition as made up of different types of individual skills. Using the terminology of information processing approaches, neo-Piagetian theory suggests that cognitive development proceeds quickly in certain areas and more slowly in others. For example, reading ability and the skills needed to recall stories may progress sooner than the sorts

information processing approaches
Approaches to the study of cognitive development that seek to identify the ways individuals take in, use, and store information

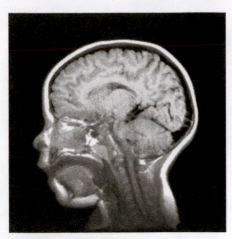

Neuroscientists have found evidence that the brains of children with autism are somewhat larger than those of children without the disorder. This finding might help identify cases of autism early, allowing for more effective intervention and treatment.

of abstract computational abilities used in algebra or trigonometry. Furthermore, in comparison with traditional Piagetian theorists, neo-Piagetian theorists believe that experience plays a greater role in advancing cognitive development (Yan & Fischer, 2002; Loewen, 2006; Miller, 2011).

Assessing Information Processing Approaches. As we'll see in future chapters, information-processing approaches have become a central part of our understanding of development. At the same time, they do not offer a complete explanation for behavior. For example, information-processing approaches have paid little attention to behavior such as creativity, in which the most profound ideas often are developed in a seemingly nonlogical, nonlinear manner. In addition, they do not take into account the social context in which development takes place. That's one of the reasons that theories that emphasize the social and cultural aspects of development have become increasingly popular—as we will see when we turn to the contextual perspective later in this chapter.

Cognitive Neuroscience Approaches. Among the most recent additions to the array of approaches taken by child developmentalists, **cognitive neuroscience approaches** look at cognitive development through the lens of brain processes. Like other cognitive perspectives, cognitive neuroscience approaches consider internal, mental processes, but they focus specifically on the neurological activity that underlies thinking, problem solving, and other cognitive behavior.

Cognitive neuroscientists seek to identify actual locations and functions within the brain that are related to different types of cognitive activity, rather than simply assuming that there are hypothetical or theoretical cognitive structures related to thinking. For example, using sophisticated brain scanning techniques, cognitive neuroscientists have demonstrated that thinking about the meaning of a word activates different areas of the brain than thinking about how the word sounds when spoken.

Work of cognitive neuroscientists is also providing clues to the cause of *autism*, a major developmental disability that can produce profound language deficits and self-injurious behavior in young children. For example, neuroscientists have found that the brains of children with the disorder show explosive, dramatic growth in the first year of life, making their heads significantly larger than those of children without the disorder. By identifying children with the disorder very early in their lives, health-care providers can provide crucial early intervention (Nadel & Poss, 2007; Lewis & Elman, 2008; Brock, 2011).

Cognitive neuroscience approaches are also on the forefront of cutting-edge research that has identified specific genes that are associated with disorders ranging from physical problems such as breast cancer to psychological disorders such as schizophrenia (Strobel et al., 2007; Ranganath, Minzenberg, & Ragland, 2008; Christoff et al., 2011). Identifying the genes that make people vulnerable to such disorders is the first step in genetic engineering, an emergent technology in which gene therapy can reduce or even prevent the disorder from occurring, as we'll discuss in Chapter 3.

Assessing Cognitive Neuroscience Approaches Cognitive neuroscience approaches represent a new frontier in child and adolescent development. Using sophisticated measurement techniques, many of them developed only in the last few years, cognitive neuroscientists are able to peer into the inner functioning of the brain. Advances in our understanding of genetics have also opened a new window into both normal and abnormal development and have suggested a variety of treatments for abnormalities.

Critics of the cognitive neuroscience approach have suggested that it sometimes provides a better *description* than *explanation* of developmental phenomena. For instance, finding that children with autism have larger brains than those without the disorder does not provide an explanation of why their brains became larger—that's a question that remains to be answered. Still, such work not only offers important clues to appropriate treatments but ultimately can lead to a fuller understanding of a range of developmental phenomena.

cognitive neuroscience approaches
Approaches to the study of cognitive development that focus on how brain processes are related to cognitive activity

The Contextual Perspective: Taking a Broad Approach to Development

Although child developmentalists often consider the course of development in terms of physical, cognitive, and personality and social factors by themselves, such a categorization has one serious drawback: In the real world, none of these broad influences occurs in isolation from any other. Instead, there is a constant, ongoing interaction between the different types of influence.

The **contextual perspective** considers the relationship between individuals and their physical, cognitive, personality, and social worlds. It suggests that a child's unique development cannot be properly viewed without seeing the child enmeshed within a complex social and cultural context. We'll consider two major theories that fall into this category, Bronfenbrenner's bioecological approach and Vygotsky's sociocultural theory.

The Bioecological Approach to Development.

In acknowledging the problem with traditional approaches to lifespan development, psychologist Urie Bronfenbrenner (1989, 2000, 2002) has proposed an alternative perspective, called the bioecological approach. The **bioecological approach** suggests there are five levels of the environment that simultaneously influence individuals. Bronfenbrenner suggests that we cannot fully understand development without considering how a person is influenced by each of these levels (illustrated in Figure 2-1).

- The *microsystem* is the everyday, immediate environment in which children lead their daily lives. Homes, caregivers, friends, and teachers all are influences that are part of the microsystem. But the child is not just a passive recipient of these influences. Instead, children actively help construct the microsystem, shaping the immediate world in which they live. The microsystem is the level at which most traditional work in child development has been directed.

- The *mesosystem* provides connections among the various aspects of the microsystem. Like links in a chain, the mesosystem binds children to parents, students to teachers, employees to bosses, friends to friends. It acknowledges the direct and indirect influences that bind us to one another, such as those that affect a mother or father who, after a bad day at the office, is short-tempered with her or his son or daughter at home.

- The *exosystem* represents broader influences, encompassing societal institutions such as local government, the community, schools, places of worship, and the local media. Each of these larger institutions of society can have an immediate, and major, impact on personal development, and each affects how the microsystem and mesosystem operate. For example, the quality of a school will affect a child's cognitive development and potentially can have long-term consequences.

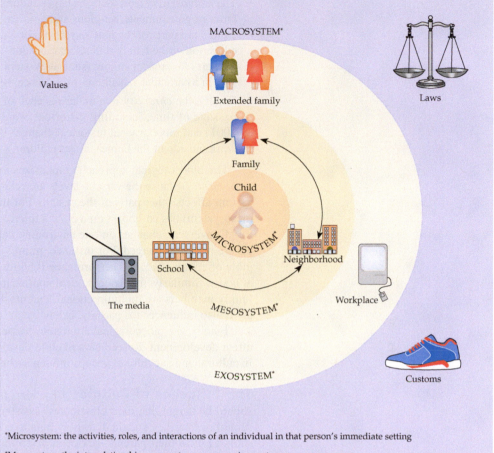

*Microsystem: the activities, roles, and interactions of an individual in that person's immediate setting

*Mesosystem: the interrelationships among two or more microsystems

*Exosystem: the social settings or organizations beyond the individual's immediate experience that affect the individual

*Macrosystem: the laws, values, and customs of the society in which the individual lives

*Chronosystem: the ways in which all of these systems interrelate to each other across time

FIGURE 2-1 Bronfenbrenner's Approach to Development

Urie Bronfenbrenner's bioecological approach to development offers five levels of the environment that simultaneously influence individuals: the macrosystem, exosystem, mesosystem, microsystem, and chronosystem.

(*Source:* Adapted from Bronfenbrenner & Morris, 1998)

contextual perspective The perspective that considers the relationship between individuals and their physical, cognitive, personality, social, and physical worlds

bioecological approach The perspective suggesting that different levels of the environment simultaneously influence every biological organism

- The *macrosystem* represents the larger cultural influences on an individual. Society in general, types of governments, religious and political value systems, and other broad, encompassing factors are parts of the macrosystem. For example, the value a culture or society places on education or the family will affect the values of the people who live in that society. Children are part of a broader culture (such as Western culture) as well as influenced by their membership in a particular subculture (for instance, being part of Mexican American subculture).

- Finally, the *chronosystem* underlies each of the previous systems. It involves the way the passage of time, including historical events (such as the terrorist attacks in September 2001) and more gradual historical changes (such as changes in the number of women who work outside of the home), affect children's development.

The bioecological approach emphasizes the *interconnectedness of the influences on development*. Because the various levels are related to one another, a change in one part of the system affects other parts of the system. For instance, a parent's loss of a job (involving the mesosystem) has an impact on a child's microsystem.

Conversely, changes on one environmental level may make little difference if other levels are not also changed. For instance, improving the school environment may have a negligible effect on academic performance if children receive little support for academic success at home. Similarly, the bioecological approach illustrates that the influences among different family members are multidirectional. Parents don't just influence their child's behavior—the child also influences the parents' behavior.

Finally, the bioecological approach stresses the importance of broad cultural factors that affect development. Researchers in child development increasingly look at how membership in cultural and subcultural groups influences behavior.

The Influence of Culture.

Consider, for instance, whether you agree that children should be taught that their classmates' assistance is indispensable to getting good grades in school or that they should definitely plan to continue their fathers' business or that children should follow their parents' advice in determining their career plans. If you have been raised in the most widespread North American culture, you would likely disagree with all three statements, because they violate the premises of *individualism*, the dominant Western philosophy that emphasizes personal identity, uniqueness, freedom, and the worth of the individual.

By contrast, if you were raised in a traditional Asian culture, it is considerably more likely that you will agree with the three statements. Why? The statements reflect the value orientation known as collectivism. *Collectivism* is the notion that the well-being of the group is more important than that of the individual. People raised in collectivistic cultures tend to emphasize the welfare of the groups to which they belong, sometimes even at the expense of their own personal well-being.

The individualism–collectivism spectrum is one of several dimensions along which cultures differ, and it illustrates differences in the cultural contexts in which people operate. Such broad cultural values play an important role in shaping the ways people view the world and behave (Garcia & Saewyc, 2007; Yu & Stiffman, 2007; Shavitt, Torelli, & Riemer, 2011).

Assessing the Bioecological Approach.

Although Bronfenbrenner considers biological influences an important component of the bioecological approach, ecological influences are central to the theory. In fact, some critics argue that the perspective pays insufficient attention to biological factors. Still, the bioecological approach is of considerable importance to child development, suggesting as it does the multiple levels at which the environment affects children's development. (Also see the *Careers in Child Development* box, which describes someone whose work involves looking at children and their parents, taking the contextual perspective into account.)

Vygotsky's Sociocultural Theory.

To Russian developmentalist Lev Semenovich Vygotsky, a full understanding of development is impossible without taking into account the culture in which children develop. Vygotsky's **sociocultural theory** emphasizes how cognitive development proceeds as a result of social interactions between members of a culture (Vygotsky, 1979, 1926/1997; Edwards, 2005; R. Miller, 2011).

sociocultural theory An approach that emphasizes how cognitive development proceeds as a result of social interactions between members of a culture

CAREERS IN CHILD DEVELOPMENT
Judy Coleman Brinich

Position: Director, Bloomsburg University Campus Child Center, Bloomsburg, Pennsylvania

Education: Bloomsburg University: B.S., Early Childhood Education, M.Ed, Elementary Education, M.S., Exceptionalities

Home: Bloomsburg, PA

Current child-care providers are far more than the babysitters they sometimes were in the past. Greater societal demands from parents needing to work full-time have required the establishment of appropriate, and often highly sophisticated, care for children and infants.

At the Bloomsburg University Campus Child Center, Judy Coleman Brinich oversees a program that serves 53 children, seven of them infants. The Center provides a safe, comfortable, stimulating yet calm and loving environment, according to Brinich.

"Our infants enjoy a relaxing environment, each with individualized schedules," says Brinich. "Conversation, music, and literature are common. We provide interactive, tactile, colorful, and interesting toys."

Parent involvement is very important, according to Brinich, and it forms the basic foundation of the care provided for the infants.

"The parent's role is extremely important because we are a community helping one another take care of our children," she notes. "We begin the process with a parent/child care staff interview and we learn from each other our expectations and determine whether or not the parent, child, facility, and child care team are the right fit."

Parents are then invited to visit the child's classroom, Brinich says. "Their input, advice and wisdom are valued components to the child's day."

As infants move into toddlerhood, the approach and care shift according to need. "At this stage they are learning to walk and talk and approach life in new and exciting ways," Brinich explains. "Everything they do is a unique experience that they will build upon to create meaning in their world."

Vygotsky, who lived a brief life from 1896 to 1934, argued that children's understanding of the world is acquired through their problem-solving interactions with adults and other children. As children play and cooperate with others, they learn what is important in their society and, at the same time, advance cognitively in their understanding of the world. Consequently, to understand the course of development, we must consider what is meaningful to members of a given culture.

More than most other theories, sociocultural theory emphasizes that development is a *reciprocal transaction* between the people in a child's environment and the child. Vygotsky believed that people and settings influence the child, who in turn influences the people and settings. This pattern continues in an endless loop, with children being both recipients of socialization influences and sources of influence. For example, a child raised with his or her extended family nearby will grow up with a different sense of family life than a child whose relatives live a considerable distance away. Those relatives, too, are affected by that situation and that child, depending upon how close and frequent their contact is with the child.

According to Vygotsky, through play and cooperation with others, children can develop cognitively in their understanding of the world and learn what is important in society.

Assessing Vygotsky's Theory. Sociocultural theory has become increasingly influential, despite Vygotsky's death almost eight decades ago. The reason is the growing acknowledgment of the central importance of cultural factors in development. Children do not develop in a cultural vacuum. Instead, their attention is directed by society to certain areas, and as a consequence, they develop particular kinds of skills that are an outcome of their cultural environment. Vygotsky was one of the first developmentalists to recognize and acknowledge the importance of culture, and—as today's society becomes increasingly multicultural—sociocultural theory is helping us to understand the rich and varied influences that shape development (Koshmanova, 2007; Rogan, 2007; Rey, 2011).

Evolutionary Perspectives: Our Ancestors' Contributions to Behavior

👁 **Watch** the **Video** *Thinking Like a Psychologist: Evolutionary Psychology* in **MyPsychLab**.

One increasingly influential approach is the evolutionary perspective, the final developmental perspective that we will consider. The **evolutionary perspective** seeks to identify behavior that is the result of our genetic inheritance from our ancestors. It focuses on how genetics and environmental factors combine to influence behavior (Bjorklund & Ellis, 2005; Goetz & Shackelford, 2006; Tomasello, 2011).

Evolutionary approaches grow out of the groundbreaking work of Charles Darwin. In 1859, Darwin argued in his book *On the Origin of Species* that a process of natural selection creates traits in a species that are adaptive to its environment. Using Darwin's arguments, evolutionary approaches contend that our genetic inheritance not only determines such physical traits as skin and eye color but also certain personality traits and social behaviors. For instance, some evolutionary developmentalists suggest that behaviors such as shyness and jealousy are produced in part by genetic causes, presumably because they were helpful in increasing the survival rates of humans' ancient relatives (Easton, Schipper, & Shackelford, 2007; Buss, 2003a, 2009).

The evolutionary perspective draws heavily on the field of *ethology*, which examines the ways in which our biological makeup influences our behavior. A primary proponent of ethology was Konrad Lorenz (1903–1989), who discovered that newborn geese are genetically preprogrammed to become attached to the first moving object they see after birth. His work, which demonstrated the importance of biological determinants in influencing behavior patterns, ultimately led developmentalists to consider the ways in which human behavior might reflect inborn genetic patterns.

As we'll consider later in the chapter, the evolutionary perspective encompasses one of the fastest growing areas within the field of life span development: behavioral genetics. *Behavioral genetics* studies the effects of heredity on behavior. Behavioral geneticists seek to understand how we might inherit certain behavioral traits and how the environment influences whether we actually display such traits. It also considers how genetic factors may produce psychological disorders such as schizophrenia (Bjorklund & Ellis, 2005; Rembis, 2009; M. Li et al., 2011).

evolutionary perspective The theory that seeks to identify behavior that is the result of our genetic inheritance from our ancestors

Assessing the Evolutionary Perspective. There is little argument among child developmentalists that Darwin's evolutionary theory provides an accurate description of basic genetic processes, and the evolutionary perspective is increasingly visible in the field of life span development. However, applications of the evolutionary perspective have been subjected to considerable criticism.

Some developmentalists are concerned that because of its focus on genetic and biological aspects of behavior, the evolutionary perspective pays insufficient attention to the environmental and social factors involved in producing children's and adults' behavior. Other critics argue that there is no good way to experimentally test theories derived from the evolutionary approach because they all happened so long ago. For example, it is one thing to say that jealousy helped individuals to survive more effectively and another thing to prove it. Still, the evolutionary approach has stimulated a significant amount of research on how our biological inheritance influences at least partially our traits and behaviors (Bjorklund, 2006; Baptista et al., 2008; Durrant & Ward, 2011).

Konrad Lorenz, seen here with geese imprinted to him, considered the ways in which behavior reflects inborn genetic patterns.

TABLE 2-3   Major Perspectives on Child Development

Perspective	Key Ideas about Human Behavior and Development	Major Proponents	Example
Psychodynamic	Behavior throughout life is motivated by inner, unconscious forces, stemming from childhood, over which we have little control.	Sigmund Freud, Erik Erikson	This view might suggest that an adolescent who is overweight has a fixation in the oral stage of development.
Behavioral	Development can be understood through studying observable behavior and environmental stimuli.	John B. Watson, B. F. Skinner, Albert Bandura	In this perspective, an adolescent who is overweight might be seen as not being rewarded for good nutritional and exercise habits.
Cognitive	Emphasis is on how changes or growth in the ways people know, understand, and think about the world affect behavior.	Jean Piaget	This view might suggest that an adolescent who is overweight hasn't learned effective ways to stay at a healthy weight and doesn't value good nutrition.
Contextual	Behavior is determined by the relationship between individuals and their physical, cognitive, personality, and social worlds.	Lev Vygotsky, Urie Bronfenbrenner	In this perspective an adolescent may become overweight because of a family environment in which food and meals are unusually important and intertwined with family rituals.
Evolutionary	Behavior is the result of genetic inheritance from our ancestors; traits and behavior that are adaptive for promoting the survival of our species have been inherited through natural selection.	Konrad Lorenz; influenced by early work of Charles Darwin	This view might suggest that an adolescent might have a genetic tendency toward obesity because extra fat helped his or her ancestors to survive in times of famine.

Why "Which Perspective Is Right?" Is the Wrong Question

We have considered five major perspectives on development: psychodynamic, behavioral, cognitive, contextual, and evolutionary (summarized in Table 2-3). It would be natural to wonder which of them provides the most accurate account of child development.

For several reasons, this is not an entirely appropriate question. For one thing, each perspective emphasizes somewhat different aspects of development. For instance, the psychodynamic approach emphasizes emotions, motivational conflicts, and unconscious determinants of behavior. In contrast, behavioral perspectives emphasize overt behavior, paying far more attention to what people *do* than to what goes on inside their heads, which is deemed largely irrelevant. The cognitive perspective looks more at what people *think* than at what they do. Finally, while the contextual perspective focuses on the interaction of environmental influences, the evolutionary perspective focuses on how inherited biological factors underlie development.

For example, a developmentalist using the psychodynamic approach might consider how the 9/11 terrorist attacks on the World Trade Center and Pentagon might affect children, unconsciously, for their entire life span. A cognitive approach might focus on how children perceived and came to interpret and understand this act of terrorism, while a contextual approach might consider what personality and social factors led the perpetrators to adopt terrorist tactics.

Clearly, each perspective is based on its own premises and focuses on different aspects of development. Furthermore, the same developmental phenomenon can be looked at from a number of perspectives simultaneously. In fact, some life span developmentalists use an *eclectic* approach, drawing on several perspectives simultaneously.

We can think of the different perspectives as analogous to a set of maps of the same general geographical area. One map may contain detailed depictions of roads; another map may show geographical features; another may show political subdivisions, such as cities, towns, and counties; and still another may highlight particular points of interest, such as scenic areas and historical landmarks. Each of the maps is accurate, but each provides a different point of view and way of thinking. No one map is "complete," but by considering them together, we can come to a fuller understanding of the area.

In the same way, the various theoretical perspectives provide different ways of looking at development. Considering them together paints a fuller portrait of the myriad ways human beings change and grow over the course of their lives. However, not all theories and claims derived from the various perspectives are accurate. How do we choose among competing explanations? The answer is *research,* which we consider in the final part of this chapter.

Review, Check, and Apply

Review

1. The psychodynamic perspective looks primarily at the influence of internal, unconscious forces on development.

2. The behavioral perspective focuses on external, observable behaviors as the key to development.

3. The cognitive perspective focuses on mental activity.

4. The contextual perspective focuses on the relationship between individuals and the context in which they lead their lives.

5. The evolutionary perspective seeks to identify behavior that is a result of our genetic inheritance.

Check

1. The major theoretical perspectives that guide the study of child development are the psychodynamic, _____, cognitive, contextual, and evolutionary perspectives.

2. The _____ perspective identifies behaviors that are the result of genetic inheritance.

3. Erikson's _____ theory was created as an alternative psychodynamic view and emphasizes social interaction with other people.

4. Vygotsky's sociocultural theory emphasizes how cognitive development proceeds as a result of _____ between members of a culture.

Apply

1. Some of the most basic principles of Freud's psychoanalytic theory have been called into question. Can you name some of these principles and explain why they have not been validated by recent research?

2. What examples of human behavior have you seen that appear to have been inherited from our ancestors because they helped individuals survive and adapt more effectively? Why do you think they are inherited?

To see more review questions, log on to MyPsychLab.

ANSWERS: 1. behavioral 2. evolutionary 3. psychosocial development 4. social interactions

MODULE 2.2

THE SCIENTIFIC METHOD AND RESEARCH

LO 2-7 What is the scientific method, and how does it help answer questions about child development?

LO 2-8 What are the major characteristics of correlational studies and experiments, and how do they differ?

The Greek historian Herodotus wrote of an experiment conducted by Psamtik, the King of Egypt in the 7th century B.C. Psamtik was eager to prove a cherished Egyptian belief, that his people were the oldest race on earth. To test this notion, he developed a hypothesis: If a child was never exposed to the language of his elders, he would instinctively adopt the primal language of humanity—the original language of the first people. Psamtik was certain this would be Egyptian.

For his experiment, Psamtik entrusted two Egyptian infants to the care of a herdsman in an isolated area. They were to be well looked after, but not allowed to leave their cottage. And they were never to hear anyone speak a single word.

When Herodotus investigated the story, he learned that Psamtik sought to learn the first word the children would say. Herodotus claims the experiment worked, but not as Psamtik had hoped. One day, when the children were two years old, they greeted the herdsman with the word "Becos!" The herdsman didn't know this word but when the children continued to use it, he contacted Psamtik. The king sent for the children who repeated the strange word to him. Psamtik did some research. Becos, it turned out, was "bread" in Phrygian. Psamtik had to conclude the Phrygians had preceded the Egyptians.

With the perspective of several thousand years, we can easily see the shortcomings—both scientific and ethical—in Psamtik's approach. Yet his procedure represents an improvement over mere speculation and as such is sometimes regarded as the first developmental experiment in recorded history (Hunt, 1993).

Theories and Hypotheses: Posing Developmental Questions

Questions such as those raised by Psamtik lie at the heart of the study of child development. The main "Psamtik question" (Is language innate?) has long been the subject of research and debate among developmentalists, and many other questions have also gained researchers' attention: What are the effects of malnutrition on later intellectual performance? How do infants form relationships with their parents, and does participation in day care disrupt such relationships? Why are adolescents susceptible to peer pressure?

To answer such questions, specialists in child development rely on the scientific method. The **scientific method** is the process of posing and answering questions using careful, controlled techniques that include systematic, orderly observation and the collection of data. As shown in Figure 2-2 on page 38, the scientific method involves three major steps: (1) identifying questions of interest, (2) formulating an explanation, and (3) carrying out research that either lends support to the explanation or refutes it.

Why use the scientific method, when our own experiences and common sense might seem to provide reasonable answers to questions? One important reason is that our own experience is limited; most of us encounter only a relatively small number of people and situations, and drawing suppositions from that restricted sample may lead us to the wrong conclusion.

Similarly, although common sense may seem helpful, it turns out that common sense often makes contradictory predictions. For example, common sense tells us that "birds of a feather flock together." But it also says that "opposites attract." You see the problem: Because common sense is often contradictory, we can't rely on it to provide objective answers to questions.

scientific method   The process of posing and answering questions using careful, controlled techniques that include systematic, orderly observation and the collection of data

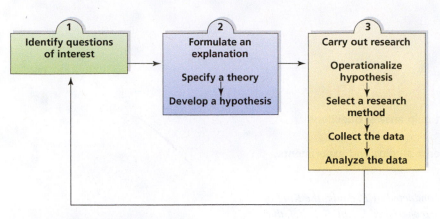

FIGURE 2-2 The Scientific Method

A cornerstone of research, the scientific method is used by psychologists as well as researchers from all other scientific disciplines.

That's why developmental psychologists insist on using the controlled procedures of the scientific method.

Theories: Framing Broad Explanations

The first step in the scientific method, the identification of questions of interest, begins when an observer puzzles over some aspect of behavior. Perhaps it is an infant who cries when she is picked up by a stranger, or a child who is doing poorly in school, or an adolescent who engages in risky behavior. Developmentalists, like all of us, start with questions about such everyday aspects of behavior, and—also like all of us—they seek to determine answers to these questions.

However, it is the way that developmental researchers try to find answers that differentiates them from more casual observers. Developmental researchers formulate *theories*, broad explanations and predictions about phenomena of interest. Using one of the major perspectives that we discussed earlier, researchers develop more specific theories.

In fact, all of us develop theories about development, based on our experience, folklore, and articles in magazines and newspapers. For instance, many people theorize that there is a crucial bonding period between parent and child immediately after birth, which is a necessary ingredient in forming a lasting parent–child relationship. Without such a bonding period, they assume, the parent–child relationship will be forever compromised.

Whenever we employ such explanations, we are developing our own theories. However, the theories in child development are different. Whereas our own personal theories are built on unverified observations that are developed haphazardly, developmentalists' theories are more formal, based on a systematic integration of prior findings and theorizing. These theories allow developmental researchers to summarize and organize prior observations and to move beyond existing observations to draw deductions that may not be immediately apparent.

Hypotheses: Specifying Testable Predictions

Although the development of theories provides a general approach to a problem, it is only the first step. To determine the validity of a theory, developmental researchers must test it scientifically. To do this, they develop hypotheses based on their theories. A **hypothesis** is a prediction stated in a way that permits it to be tested.

For instance, someone who subscribes to the general theory that bonding is a crucial ingredient in the parent–child relationship might derive the more specific hypothesis that adopted children whose adoptive parents never had the chance to bond with them immediately after birth may ultimately have less secure relationships with their adoptive parents.

Others might derive other hypotheses, such as that effective bonding occurs only if it lasts for a certain length of time or that bonding affects the mother–child relationship but not the father–child relationship. (In case you're wondering, as we'll discuss in Chapter 4, these particular hypotheses have *not* been upheld; there are no long-term reactions to the separation of parent and child immediately after birth, even if the separation lasts several days, and there is no difference in the strength of bonds with mothers and bonds with fathers.)

Choosing a Research Strategy: Answering Questions

Once researchers have formed a hypothesis, they must develop a strategy for testing its validity. The first step is to state the hypothesis in a way that will allow it to be tested. *Operationalization* is the process of translating a hypothesis into specific, testable procedures that can be measured and observed.

hypothesis   A prediction stated in a way that permits it to be tested

For example, a researcher interested in testing the hypothesis that "being evaluated leads to anxiety" might operationalize "being evaluated" as "receiving a grade from a teacher" or "listening to a friend commenting on one's athletic skills." Similarly, "anxiety" could be operationalized in terms of responses on a questionnaire or as measurements of biological reactions by an electronic instrument.

The choice of how to operationalize a variable often reflects the kind of research that is to be conducted. There are two major categories of research: correlational research and experimental research. **Correlational research** seeks to identify whether an association or relationship between two factors exists. As we'll see, correlational research cannot be used to determine whether one factor causes changes in the other. For instance, correlational research could tell us if there is an association between the number of minutes a mother and her newborn child are together immediately after birth and the quality of the mother–child relationship when the child reaches 2 years of age. Such correlational research indicates whether the two factors are *associated* or *related* to one another but not whether the initial contact caused the relationship to develop in a particular way (Schutt, 2001).

In contrast, **experimental research** is designed to discover *causal* relationships among various factors. In experimental research, researchers deliberately introduce a change in a carefully structured situation in order to see the consequences of that change. For instance, a researcher conducting an experiment might vary the number of minutes that mothers and children interact immediately following birth in an attempt to see whether the amount of bonding time measurably affects the mother–child relationship.

Because experimental research is able to answer questions of causality, it represents the heart of developmental research. However, some research questions

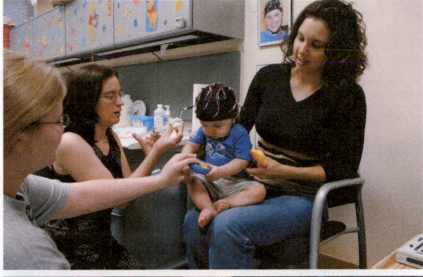

Researchers use a wide range of procedures to study human development.

cannot be answered through experiments, for either technical or ethical reasons (for example, it would be unethical to design an experiment in which a group of infants was offered no chance to bond with a caregiver). In fact, a great deal of pioneering developmental research—such as that conducted by Piaget and Vygotsky—employed correlational techniques. Consequently, correlational research remains an important tool in the developmental researcher's toolbox.

Correlational Studies

As we've noted, correlational research examines the relationship between two variables to determine whether they are associated, or *correlated*. For instance, researchers interested in the relationship between televised aggression and subsequent behavior have found that children who watch a substantial amount of aggression on television—murders, crime, shootings, and the like—tend to be more aggressive than those who watch only a little. In other words, as we'll discuss in greater detail in Chapter 13, viewing of aggression and actual aggression are strongly associated, or correlated, with each other (Brady, 2007; Feshbach & Tangney, 2008; Kirsh, 2012; Martins & Wilson, 2012).

correlational research   Research that seeks to identify whether an association or relationship between two factors exists

experimental research   Research designed to discover causal relationships between various factors

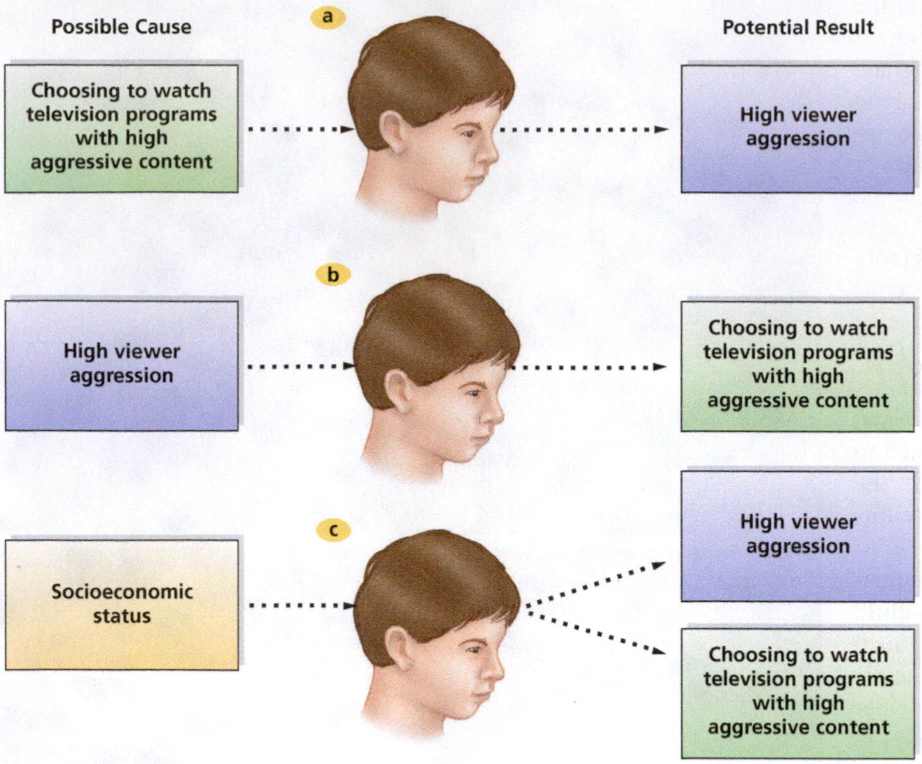

Possible Cause

Potential Result

FIGURE 2-3 Finding a Correlation

Finding a correlation between two factors does not imply that one factor causes the other factor to vary. For instance, suppose that a study found that viewing television programs with high levels of aggression is correlated with actual aggression in children. The correlation might reflect at least three possibilities: (a) watching television programs containing high levels of aggression causes aggression in viewers; (b) children who behave aggressively choose to watch television programs with high levels of aggression; or (c) some third factor, such as a child's socioeconomic status, leads to both high viewer aggression and choosing to watch television programs with high viewer aggression.

But does this mean we can conclude that the viewing of televised aggression *causes* the more aggressive behavior of the viewers? Not at all. Consider some of the other possibilities: It might be that being aggressive in the first place makes children more likely to choose to watch violent programs. In such a case, then, it is the aggressive tendency that causes the viewing behavior, not the other way around.

Or consider another possibility. Suppose that children who are raised in poverty are more likely than those raised in more affluent settings to behave aggressively *and* to watch higher levels of aggressive television. In this case, it is socioeconomic status that causes *both* the aggressive behavior and the television viewing. (The various possibilities are illustrated in Figure 2-3.)

In short, finding that two variables are correlated proves nothing about causality. Although it is possible that the variables are linked causally, this is not necessarily the case.

Nevertheless, correlational studies can provide important information. For instance, as we'll see in later chapters, we know from correlational studies that the closer the genetic link between two people, the more highly associated their intelligence. We have learned that the more parents speak to their young children, the more extensive the children's vocabularies. And we know from correlational studies that the better the nutrition that infants receive, the fewer cognitive and social problems they experience later (Hart, 2004; Colom, Lluis-Font, & Andrés-Pueyo, 2005; Robb, Richert, & Wartella, 2009).

The Correlation Coefficient. The strength and direction of a relationship between two factors is represented by a mathematical score, called a *correlation coefficient*, that ranges from +1.0 to −1.0. A positive correlation indicates that as the value of one factor increases, it can be predicted that the value of the other will also increase. For instance, if we find that the more calories children eat, the better their school performance, and the fewer calories children eat, the worse their school performance, we have found a positive correlation. (Higher values of the factor "calories" are associated with higher values of the factor "school performance," and lower values of the factor "calories" are associated with lower values of the factor "school performance.") The correlation coefficient, then, would be indicated by a positive number, and the stronger the association between calories and school performance, the closer the number would be to +1.0.

In contrast, a correlation coefficient with a negative value informs us that as the value of one factor increases, the value of the other factor declines. For example, suppose we found that the greater the number of hours adolescents spend using texting, the worse their academic performance. Such a finding would result in a negative correlation, ranging between 0 and −1.0. More instant messaging is associated with lower performance, and less texting associated with better performance. The stronger the association between texting and school performance, the closer the correlation coefficient will be to −1.0.

Finally, it is possible that two factors are unrelated to one another. For example, it is unlikely that we would find a correlation between school performance and shoe size. In this case, the lack of a relationship would be indicated by a correlation coefficient close to 0.

It is important to reiterate what we noted earlier: Even if the correlation coefficient involving two variables is very strong, there is no way we can know whether one factor causes another factor to vary. It simply means that the two factors are associated with one another in a predictable way.

Types of Correlational Studies. There are several types of correlational studies.

Naturalistic observation. **Naturalistic observation** is the observation of a naturally occurring behavior without intervention in the situation. For instance, an investigator who wishes to learn how often preschool children share toys with one another might observe a classroom over a 3-week period, recording how often the preschoolers spontaneously share with one another. The key point about naturalistic observation is that the investigator simply observes the children without interfering with the situation in any way (e.g., Prezbindowski & Lederberg, 2003; Rustin, 2006; Jankowiak, Joiner, & Khatib, 2011).

Naturalistic observation is used to examine a situation in its natural habitat without interference of any sort. What are some disadvantages of naturalistic observation?

Naturalistic observation has the advantage of identifying what children do in their "natural habitat," and it offers an excellent way for researchers to develop questions of interest. However, natural observation has a considerable drawback: Researchers are unable to exert control over factors of interest. For instance, in some cases, researchers might find so few naturally occurring instances of the behavior of interest that they are unable to draw any conclusions at all. In addition, children who know they are being watched may modify their behavior as a result of the observation. Consequently, their behavior may not be representative of how they would behave if they were not being watched.

Ethnography and qualitative research. Increasingly, naturalistic observation employs *ethnography,* a method borrowed from the field of anthropology and used to investigate cultural questions. In ethnography, a researcher's goal is to understand a culture's values and attitudes through careful, extended examination. Typically, researchers using ethnography act as participant observers, living for a period of weeks, months, or even years in another culture. By carefully observing everyday life and conducting in-depth interviews, researchers are able to obtain a deep understanding of the nature of life within another culture (Dyson, 2003).

Ethnographic studies are an example of a broader category of research known as qualitative research. In *qualitative research*, researchers choose particular settings of interest and seek to carefully describe, in narrative fashion, what is occurring, and why. Qualitative research can be used to generate hypotheses that can later be tested using more objective, quantitative methods.

Although ethnographic and qualitative studies provide a fine-grained view of behavior in particular settings, they suffer from several drawbacks. As mentioned earlier, the presence of a participant observer may influence the behavior of the individuals being studied. Furthermore, because only a small number of individuals are studied, it may be hard to generalize the findings to other settings. Finally, ethnographers carrying out cross-cultural research may misinterpret and misconceive what they are observing, particularly in cultures that are very different from their own (Polkinghorne, 2005).

Case studies. **Case studies** involve extensive, in-depth interviews with a particular individual or small group of individuals. They often are used not just to learn about the individual being interviewed but also to derive broader principles or draw tentative conclusions that might apply to others. For example, case studies have been conducted on children who display unusual genius and on children who have spent their early years in the wild without human contact. These case studies have provided important information to researchers and have suggested hypotheses for future investigation (Goldsmith, 2000; Cohen & Cashon, 2003; Wilson, 2003).

Using *diaries*, participants are asked to keep a record of their behavior on a regular basis. For example, a group of adolescents may be asked to record each time they interact with friends for more than 5 minutes, thereby providing a way to track their social behavior.

naturalistic observation Studies in which researchers observe some naturally occurring behavior without intervening or making changes in the situation

case studies Extensive, in-depth interviews with a particular individual or small group of individuals

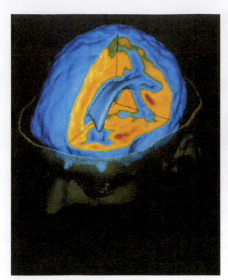

A functional magnetic resonance image (fMRI) of the brain shows brain activity at a given moment.

Survey research. You're probably familiar with an additional research strategy: survey research. In **survey research**, a group of individuals chosen to represent some larger population are asked questions about their attitudes, behavior, or thinking on a given topic. For instance, surveys have been conducted about parents' use of punishment on their children and on attitudes toward breastfeeding. From the responses, inferences are drawn regarding the larger population represented by the individuals being surveyed.

Although there's no more straightforward way of determining what people think and do than asking them directly about their behavior, survey research is not always an effective technique. For instance, adolescents asked about their sex lives may be unwilling to admit to various sexual practices for fear that confidentiality will not be complete. In addition, if the sample of people surveyed is not representative of the broader population of interest, the results of the survey have little meaning.

Psychophysiological methods. Some developmental researchers, particularly those using a cognitive neuroscience approach, make use of psychophysiological methods. **Psychophysiological methods** focus on the relationship between physiological processes and behavior. For instance, a researcher might examine the relationship between blood flow in the brain and problem-solving ability. Similarly, some studies use infants' heart rate as a measure of their interest in stimuli to which they are exposed.

Among the most frequently used psychophysiological measures:

- **Electroencephalogram (EEG).** The EEG records electrical activity within the brain recorded by electrodes placed on the outside of the skull. That brain acitivity is transformed into a pictorial representation of the brain, permitting the representation of brain wave patterns and diagnosis of disorders such as epilepsy and learning disabilities.

- **Computerized Axial Tomography (CAT) Scan.** In a CAT scan, a computer constructs an image of the brain by combining thousands of individual X-rays taken at slightly different angles. Although the CAT scan does not show brain activity, it does illuminate the structure of the brain.

- **Functional Magnetic Resonance Imaging (fMRI) Scan.** An fMRI provides a detailed, three-dimensional computer-generated image of brain activity by aiming a powerful magnetic field at the brain. It offers one of the best ways of learning about the operation of the brain, down to the level of individual nerves.

Experiments: Determining Cause and Effect

In an **experiment**, an investigator, called an *experimenter*, typically devises two different experiences for *participants*, or *subjects*. These two different experiences are called treatments. A **treatment** is a procedure applied by an investigator. One group of participants receives one of the treatments, whereas another group of participants receives either no treatment or an alternative treatment. The group receiving the treatment is known as the **treatment group** (sometimes called the *experimental group*), whereas the no-treatment or alternative-treatment group is called the **control group**.

Although the terminology may seem daunting at first, there is an underlying logic to it that helps sort it out. Think in terms of a medical experiment in which the aim is to test the effectiveness of a new drug. In testing the drug, we wish to see if the drug successfully *treats* the disease. Consequently, the group that receives the drug would be called the *treatment group*. In comparison, another group of participants would not receive the drug treatment. Instead, they would be part of the no-treatment *control group*.

Similarly, suppose we wish to explore the consequences of exposure to movie violence on viewers' subsequent aggression. We might take a group of adolescents and show them a series of movies that contain a great deal of violent imagery. We would then measure their subsequent aggression. This group would constitute the treatment group. But we would also need another group—a control group. To fulfill this need, we might take a second group of adolescents, show them movies that contain no aggressive imagery, and then measure their subsequent aggression. This would be the control group.

survey research   Research in which a group of people chosen to represent some larger population are asked questions about their attitudes, behavior, or thinking on a given topic

psychophysiological methods   A research approach that focuses on the relationship between physiological processes and behavior

experiment   A process in which an investigator, called an experimenter, devises two different experiences for subjects or participants

treatment   A procedure applied by an experimental investigator based on two different experiences devised for subjects or participants

treatment group   The group in an experiment that receives the treatment

control group   The group in an experiment that receives either no treatment or an alternative treatment

By comparing the amount of aggression displayed by members of the treatment and control groups, we would be able to determine if exposure to violent imagery produces aggression in viewers. And this is just what a group of researchers found: Running an experiment of this very sort, psychologist Jacques-Philippe Leyens and colleagues at the University of Louvain in Belgium found that the level of aggression rose significantly for the adolescents who had seen the movies containing violence (Leyens et al., 1975).

Designing an Experiment. The central feature of this experiment—and all other experiments—is the comparison of the consequences of different treatments. The use of both treatment and control groups allows researchers to rule out the possibility that something other than the experimental manipulation produced the results found in the experiment. For instance, if a control group was not used, experiments could not be certain that some other factor, such as the time of day the movies were shown, the need to sit still during the movie, or even the mere passage of time, produced the changes that were observed. By employing a control group, then, experimenters can draw accurate conclusions about causes and effects.

The formation of treatment and control groups represents the independent variable in an experiment. The **independent variable** is the variable that researchers manipulate in the experiment. In contrast, the **dependent variable** is the variable that researchers measure in an experiment and expect to change as a result of the experimental manipulation. (One way to remember the difference: A hypothesis predicts how a dependent variable *depends* on the manipulation of the independent variable.) In an experiment studying the effects of taking a drug, for instance, manipulating whether participants receive or don't receive a drug is the independent variable. Measurement of the effectiveness of the drug or no-drug treatment is the dependent variable.

To consider another example, let's take the Belgian study of the consequences of observing filmed aggression on future aggression. In this experiment, the independent variable is the *level of aggressive imagery* viewed by participants—determined by whether they viewed films containing aggressive imagery (the treatment group) or devoid of aggressive imagery (the control group). The dependent variable in the study? It was what the experimenters expected to vary as a consequence of viewing a film: the *aggressive behavior* shown by participants after they had viewed the films and measured by the experimenters. Every experiment has an independent and dependent variable.

Random Assignment. One critical step in the design of experiments is to assign participants to different treatment groups. The procedure that is used is known as random assignment. In *random assignment*, participants are assigned to different experimental groups or "conditions" on the basis of chance and chance alone. By using this technique, the laws of statistics ensure that personal characteristics that might affect the outcome of the experiment are divided proportionally among the participants in the different groups. In other words, the groups are equivalent to one another in terms of the personal characteristics of the participants. Equivalent groups achieved by random assignment allow an experimenter to draw conclusions with confidence.

Figure 2-4 on page 44 illustrates the Belgian experiment on adolescents exposed to films containing violent or nonviolent imagery and its effects on subsequent aggressive behavior. As you can see, it contains each of the elements of an experiment:

- An independent variable (the assignment to a film condition)
- A dependent variable (measurement of the adolescents' aggressive behavior)
- Random assignment to condition (viewing a film with aggressive imagery versus a film with non-aggressive imagery)
- A hypothesis that predicts the effect the independent variable will have on the dependent variable (that viewing a film with aggressive imagery will produce subsequent aggression)

Given the advantage of experimental research—that it provides a means of determining causality—why aren't experiments always used? The answer is that there are some situations that a researcher, no matter how ingenious, simply cannot control. And there are some situations that it would be unethical to control, even if it were possible. For instance, no researcher

independent variable The variable in an experiment that is manipulated by researchers

dependent variable The variable in an experiment that is measured and is expected to change as a result of the experimental manipulation

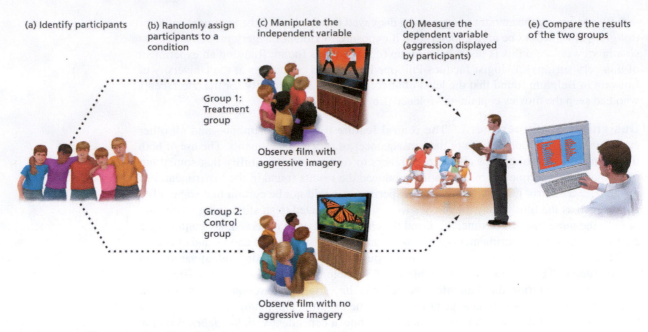

(a) Identify participants

(b) Randomly assign participants to a condition

(c) Manipulate the independent variable

Group 1: Treatment group

Observe film with aggressive imagery

Group 2: Control group

Observe film with no aggressive imagery

(d) Measure the dependent variable (aggression displayed by participants)

(e) Compare the results of the two groups

FIGURE 2-4 Elements of an Experiment

In this experiment, researchers randomly assigned a group of adolescents to one of two conditions: viewing a film that contained violent imagery, or viewing a film that lacked violent imagery (manipulation of the independent variable). Then participants were observed later to determine how much aggression they showed (the dependent variable). Analysis of the findings showed that adolescents exposed to aggressive imagery showed more aggression later. (Based on an experiment by Leyens et al., 1975.)

Leyens, J. P., Camino, L., Parke, R. D., & Berkowitz, L. (1975). Effects of movie violence on aggression in a field setting as a function of group dominance and cohesion. *Journal of Personality and Social Psychology, 32,* 346–360.

would be able to assign different groups of infants to parents of high and low socioeconomic status in order to learn the effects of such status on subsequent development. Similarly, we cannot control what a group of children watch on television throughout their childhood years to learn if childhood exposure to televised aggression leads to aggressive behavior later in life. Consequently, in situations in which experiments are logistically or ethically impossible, developmentalists employ correlational research. (See Table 2-4 for a summary of the major research strategies.)

Furthermore, keep in mind that a single experiment is insufficient to answer a research question definitively. Instead, before complete confidence can be placed in a conclusion, research must be *replicated*, or repeated, sometimes using other procedures and techniques with other participants. Sometimes developmentalists use a procedure called *meta-analysis*, which permits the combination of results of many studies into one overall conclusion (Peterson & Brown, 2005).

👁 **Watch** the **Video** *The Basics: Scientific Research Methods* in **MyPsychLab**.

Choosing a Research Setting. Deciding *where* to conduct a study may be as important as determining *what* to do. In the Belgian experiment on the influence of exposure to media aggression, the researchers used a real-world setting—a group home for boys who had been convicted of juvenile delinquency. They chose this **sample**, the group of participants chosen for the experiment, because it was useful to have adolescents whose normal level of aggression was relatively high, and because they could incorporate showing the films into the everyday life of the home with minimal disruption.

Using a real-world setting like the one in the aggression experiment is the hallmark of a field study. A **field study** is a research investigation carried out in a naturally occurring setting. Field studies may be carried out in preschool classrooms, at community playgrounds, on school buses, or on street corners. Field studies capture behavior in real-life settings, and research participants may behave more naturally than they would if they were brought into a laboratory.

sample A group of participants chosen for an experiment

field study A research investigation carried out in a naturally occurring setting

TABLE 2-4   Types of Research

Research Method	Description	Example
Naturalistic observation	An investigator systematically observes naturally occurring behavior and does not make a change in the situation.	A researcher investigating bullying carefully observes and records instances of bullying on elementary school playgrounds.
Archival research	Existing data such as census documents, college records, and newspaper clippings are examined to test a hypothesis.	College records are used to determine whether gender differences exist in math grades.
Ethnography	Careful study of a culture's values and attitudes through careful, extended examination.	A researcher lives for 6 months among families in a remote African village in order to study child-rearing practices.
Survey research	Individuals chosen to represent a larger population are asked a series of questions about their behavior, thoughts, or attitudes.	A researcher conducts a comprehensive poll asking a large group of adolescents about their attitudes toward exercise.
Case study	An in-depth, intensive investigation of an individual or small group of people.	An intensive study of a child involved in a school shooting is carried out by an investigator.
Psychophysiological research	A study of the relationship between physiological processes and behavior.	A researcher examines brain scans of children who are unusually violent to see whether there are abnormalities in brain structures and functioning.

Field studies may be used in both correlational studies and experiments. Field studies typically employ naturalistic observation, the technique we discussed previously in which researchers observe some naturally occurring behavior without intervening or making changes in the situation. For instance, a researcher might examine behavior in a child-care center, view the groupings of adolescents in high school corridors, or observe elderly adults in a senior center.

However, it often is difficult to run an experiment in real-world settings, where it is hard to exert control over the situation and environment. Consequently, field studies are more typical of correlational designs than experimental designs, and most developmental research experiments are conducted in laboratory settings. A **laboratory study** is a research investigation conducted in a controlled setting explicitly designed to hold events constant. The laboratory may be a room or building designed for research, as in a university's psychology department. Their ability to control the settings in laboratory studies enables researchers to learn more clearly how their treatments affect participants.

laboratory study   A research investigation conducted in a controlled setting explicitly designed to hold events constant

FROM AN
EDUCATOR'S
PERSPECTIVE:

Why might you criticize theories that are supported only by data collected from laboratory studies, rather than from field studies? Would such criticism be valid?

Developmentalists work in such diverse settings as in a laboratory preschool on a college campus and in human service agencies.

To understand development in all children, researchers must include participants in their studies that represent the diversity of humanity.

 DEVELOPMENTAL DIVERSITY AND YOUR LIFE

Choosing Research Participants Who Represent the Diversity of Children

For child development to represent the full range of humanity, its research must incorporate children of different races, ethnicities, cultures, genders, and other categories. However, although the field of child development is increasingly concerned with issues of human diversity, its actual progress in this domain has been slow, and in some ways, it has actually regressed.

For instance, between 1970 and 1989, only 4.6% of the articles published in *Developmental Psychology*, one of the premier journals of the discipline, focused on African American participants. Moreover, the number of published studies involving African American participants of all ages actually declined over that 20-year period (Graham, 1992; MacPhee, Kreutzer, & Fritz, 1994; Lichtenberg, 2011).

Even when minority groups are included in research, the particular participants may not represent the full range of variation that actually exists within the group. For example, African American infants used in a research study might well be disproportionally upper- and middle-class, because parents in higher socioeconomic groups may be more likely to have the time and transportation capabilities to bring their infants into a research center. In contrast, African Americans (as well as members of other groups) who are relatively poor will face more hurdles when it comes to participating in research.

Something is amiss when a science that seeks to explain children's behavior—as is the case with child development—disregards significant groups of individuals. Child developmentalists are aware of this issue, and they have become increasingly sensitive to the importance of using participants who are fully representative of the general population (Fitzgerald, 2006). ■

Review, Check, and Apply

Review

1. Theories are systematically derived explanations of facts or phenomena. Theories suggest hypotheses, which are predictions that can be tested.

2. Correlational studies examine relationships between factors without demonstrating causality, while experimental research seeks to discover cause-and-effect relationships.

3. Types of correlational studies include naturalistic observation, case studies, survey research, and, most recently, psychophysiological methods.

4. Experiments involve a randomly assigned treatment group and control group, an independent (manipulated) variable and a dependent (outcome) variable, and a testable hypothesis.

Check

1. The _____ _____ is the process of posing and answering questions using controlled techniques that include systematic, orderly observation and the collection of data.

2. A _____ is a prediction stated in a way that permits it to be tested.

3. _____ are systematically derived explanations of facts or phenomena.

4. The major research strategies associated with social science research are _____ and correlational studies.

5. In an experiment, the _____ variable is manipulated by researchers, while the effects of changes in this variable are measured through the _____ variable.

Apply

1. Formulate a theory about one aspect of human development and a hypothesis that related to it.

2. Egyptian King Psamtik's experiment of removing two children from their mothers would be unheard of today. How might a similar experiment be done today following ethical guidelines?

To see more review questions, log on to MyPsychLab.

ANSWERS: 1. scientific method 2. hypothesis 3. Theories 4. experimental 5. independent; dependent

MODULE 2.3

RESEARCH STRATEGIES AND CHALLENGES

LO 2-9 What are the major research strategies?

LO 2-10 What are the primary ethical principles used to guide research ?

Developmental researchers typically focus on one of two approaches to research: theoretical research or applied research. The two approaches are in fact complementary.

Theoretical and Applied Research: Complementary Approaches

Theoretical research is designed specifically to test some developmental explanation and expand scientific knowledge, whereas **applied research** is meant to provide practical solutions to immediate problems. For instance, if we were interested in the processes of cognitive change during childhood, we might carry out a study of how many digits children of various ages can remember after one exposure to multi-digit numbers—a theoretical approach. Alternatively, we might focus on how children learn by examining ways in which elementary school instructors can teach children to remember information more easily. Such a study would represent applied research, because the findings are applied to a particular setting and problem.

Often the distinctions between theoretical and applied research are blurred. For instance, is a study that examines the consequences of ear infections in infancy on later hearing loss theoretical or applied research? Because such a study may help illuminate the basic processes involved in hearing, it can be considered theoretical. But to the extent that the study helps us understand how to prevent hearing loss in children and how various medicines may ease the consequences of the infection, it may be considered applied research (Lerner, Fisher, & Weinberg, 2000).

In short, even the most applied research can help advance our theoretical understanding of a particular topical area, and theoretical research can provide concrete solutions to a range of practical problems. In fact, as discussed in the accompanying *From Research to Practice* box, research of both a theoretical and an applied nature has played a significant role in shaping and resolving a variety of public policy questions.

Measuring Developmental Change

For developmental researchers, the question of how people grow and change throughout the life span is central to their discipline. Consequently, one of the thorniest research issues they

theoretical research Research designed specifically to test some developmental explanation and expand scientific knowledge

applied research Research meant to provide practical solutions to immediate problems

FROM RESEARCH TO PRACTICE
Using Research to Improve Public Policy

- Is the "Race to the Top," the U.S. Department of Education program designed to improve education, effective in enhancing the lives of children?
- Does research support the legalization of marijuana?
- What are the effects of gay marriage on children in such unions?
- Should preschoolers diagnosed with attention deficit hyperactivity disorder receive drugs to treat their condition?

Each of these questions represents a national policy issue that can be answered only by considering the results of relevant research studies. By conducting controlled studies, developmental researchers have made a number of important contributions affecting education, family life, and health. Consider, for instance, the variety of ways that public policy issues have been informed by various types of research findings (Maton et al., 2004; Mervis, 2004; Aber et al., 2007; Nelson & Mann, 2011):

- **Research findings can provide policymakers a means of determining what questions to ask in the first place.** For example, studies of children's caregivers (some of which we'll consider in Chapter 15) have led policymakers to question whether the benefits of infant day care are outweighed by possible deterioration in parent–child bonds.
- **Research findings and the testimony of researchers are often part of the process by which laws are drafted.** A good deal of legislation has been passed based on findings from developmental researchers. For example, research revealed that children with developmental disabilities benefit from exposure to children without special needs, ultimately leading to passage of national legislation mandating that children with disabilities be placed in regular school classes as much as possible. Similarly, research on the benefits of foster care encouraged legislation extending eligibility for foster care to older children (Peters et al., 2008; Gustavsson & MacEachron, 2011).

- **Policymakers and other professionals use research findings to determine how best to implement programs.** Research has shaped programs designed to reduce the incidence of unsafe sex among teenagers, to reduce teenage pregnancies, and to raise class attendance rates in school-age children. The common thread among such programs is that many of the details of the programs are built upon basic research findings (Bazargan, Bazargan-Hejazi, & Hindman, 2010; J. Li, 2011).
- **Research techniques are used to evaluate the effectiveness of existing programs and policies.** Once a public policy has been implemented, it is necessary to determine whether it has been effective and successful in accomplishing its goals. To do this, researchers employ formal evaluation techniques, developed from basic research procedures. For instance, researchers have continually scrutinized the Head Start preschool program, which has received massive federal funding, to ensure that it really does what it is supposed to do—improve children's academic performance.

Developmentalists have worked hand-in-hand with policymakers, and the resulting research findings have had a substantial impact on public policies, creating potential benefits for all of us. (To learn about some of the public policies that have been most effective in the area of education, go to the the U.S. Education Department website "What Works Clearinghouse" at www.whatworks.ed.gov.)

■ **What are some policy issues affecting children that are currently being debated nationally?**

■ **Despite the existence of research data that might inform policy about development, politicians rarely discuss such data in their speeches. Why do you think that is the case?**

face concerns the measurement of change and differences over age and time. To solve this problem, researchers have developed three major strategies: longitudinal research, cross-sectional research, and sequential research.

Longitudinal Studies: Measuring Individual Change. If you were interested in learning how a child's moral development changes between 3 and 5, the most direct approach would be to take a group of 3-year-olds and follow them until they were age 5, testing them periodically.

Such a strategy illustrates longitudinal research. In **longitudinal research**, the behavior of one or more study participants is measured as they age. Longitudinal research measures change over time. By following many individuals over time, researchers can understand the general course of change across some period of life.

The granddaddy of longitudinal studies, which has become a classic, is a study of gifted children begun by Lewis Terman around 80 years ago. In the study—which has yet to be concluded—a group of 1,500 children with high IQs were tested about every 5 years. Now in their 80s, the participants—who call themselves "Termites"—have provided information

longitudinal research   Research in which the behavior of one or more individuals is measured as the subjects age

on everything from intellectual accomplishment to personality and longevity (McCullough, Tsang, & Brion, 2003; Subotnik, 2006; Campbell & Feng, 2011).

Longitudinal research has also provided great insight into language development. For instance, by tracing how children's vocabularies increase on a day-by-day basis, researchers have been able to understand the processes that underlie the human ability to become competent in using language (Oliver & Plomin, 2007; Childers, 2009; Fagan, 2009).

Longitudinal studies can provide a wealth of information about change over time. However, they have several drawbacks. For one thing, they require a tremendous investment of time, because researchers must wait for participants to become older. Furthermore, the number of active participants often decreases over the course of the research. Participants may drop out of a study, move away, or become ill or even die as the research proceeds.

Finally, participants who are observed or tested repeatedly may become "test-wise" and perform better each time they are assessed as they become more familiar with the procedure. Even if the observations of participants in a study are not terribly intrusive (such as simply recording, over a lengthy period of time, vocabulary increases in infants and preschoolers), experimental participants may be affected by the repeated presence of an experimenter or observer.

Consequently, despite the benefits of longitudinal research, particularly its ability to look at change within individuals, developmental researchers often turn to other methods in conducting research. The alternative they choose most often is the cross-sectional study.

Cross-Sectional Studies. Suppose again that you want to consider how children's moral development, their sense of right and wrong, changes from ages 3 to 5. Instead of using a longitudinal approach and following the same children over several years, we might conduct the study by simultaneously looking at three groups of children: 3-year-olds, 4-year-olds, and 5-year-olds, perhaps presenting each group with the same problem, and then seeing how they respond to it and explain their choices.

Such an approach typifies cross-sectional research. In **cross-sectional research**, people of different ages are compared at the same point in time. Cross-sectional studies provide information about differences in development among different age groups.

Cross-sectional research is considerably more economical than longitudinal research in terms of time: Participants are tested at just one point in time. For instance, Terman's study conceivably might have been completed 75 years ago if Terman had simply looked at a group of gifted 15-year-olds, 20-year-olds, 25-year-olds, and so forth, all the way through a group of 80-year-olds. Because the participants would not be periodically tested, there would be no chance that they would become test-wise, and problems of participant attrition would not occur. Why, then, would anyone choose to use a procedure other than cross-sectional research?

The answer is that cross-sectional research brings its own set of difficulties. Recall that every person belongs to a particular *cohort*, the group of people born at around the same time in the same place. If we find that people of different ages vary along some dimension, it may be due to differences in cohort membership, not age *per se.*

Consider a concrete example: If we find in a correlational study that people who are 25 perform better on a test of intelligence than those who are 75, there are several possible explanations. Although the finding may be due to decreased intelligence in older people, it may also be attributable to cohort differences. The group of 75-year-olds may have had less formal education than the 25-year-olds, because members of the older cohort were less likely to finish high school and attend college than members of the younger one. Or perhaps the older group performed less well because as infants they received less adequate nutrition than did members of the younger group. In short, we cannot fully rule out the possibility that differences we find among people of different age groups in cross-sectional studies are due to cohort differences.

Cross-sectional studies also may suffer from *selective dropout,* in which participants in some age groups are more likely than others to quit participating in a study. For example, suppose a study of cognitive development in preschoolers includes a lengthy assessment of

cross-sectional research   Research in which people of different ages are compared at the same point in time

Cross-sectional research allows researchers to compare representatives of different age groups at the same time.

 Explore *Cross-Sectional and Longitudinal Research Designs* in **MyPsychLab**.

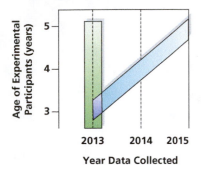

FIGURE 2-5 Research Techniques for Studying Development

In a cross-sectional study, 3-, 4-, and 5-year-olds are compared at a similar point in time (in the year 2013). In longitudinal research, a set of participants who are 3 years old in the year 2013 are studied when they are 4 years old (in 2014) and when they are 5 years old (in 2015). Finally, a sequential study combines cross-sectional and longitudinal techniques; here, a group of 3-year-olds would be compared initially in 2013 with 4- and 5-year-olds but would also be studied 1 and 2 years later, when they themselves were 4 and 5 years old. Although the graph does not illustrate this, researchers carrying out this sequential study might also choose to retest the children who were 4 and 5 in 2013 for the next 2 years. What advantages do the three kinds of studies offer?

sequential studies Studies in which researchers examine members of a number of different age groups at several points in time

cognitive abilities. It is possible that young preschoolers would find the task more difficult and demanding than older preschoolers. As a result, the younger children would be more likely than the older preschoolers to discontinue participation in the study. If the least competent young preschoolers are the ones who drop out, then the remaining sample of participants in the study will consist of the more competent young preschoolers—together with a broader and more representative sample of older preschoolers. The results of such a study would be questionable (Miller, 1998).

Finally, cross-sectional studies have an additional, and more basic, disadvantage: They are unable to inform us about changes in individuals or groups. If longitudinal studies are like videos taken of a person at various ages, cross-sectional studies are like snapshots of entirely different groups. Although we can establish differences related to age, we cannot fully determine if such differences are related to change over time.

Sequential Studies. Because both longitudinal and cross-sectional studies have drawbacks, researchers have turned to some compromise techniques. Among the most frequently employed are sequential studies, which are essentially a combination of longitudinal and cross-sectional studies.

In **sequential studies**, researchers examine a number of different age groups at several points in time. For instance, an investigator interested in children's moral behavior might begin a sequential study by examining the behavior of three groups of children, who are 3 years old, 4 years old, or 5 years old at the time the study begins. (This is no different from the way a cross-sectional study would be done.)

However, the study wouldn't stop there, but would continue for the next several years. During this period, each of the research participants would be tested annually. Thus, the 3-year-olds would be tested at ages 3, 4, and 5; the 4-year-olds at ages 4, 5, and 6; and the 5-year-olds at ages 5, 6, and 7. Such an approach combines the advantages of longitudinal and cross-sectional research, and it permits developmental researchers to tease out the consequences of age *change* versus age *difference*. (The major research techniques for studying development are summarized in Figure 2-5.)

Ethics and Research

In the "study" conducted by Egyptian King Psamtik, two children were removed from their mothers and held in isolation in an effort to learn about the roots of language. If you found yourself thinking this was extraordinarily cruel, you are in good company. Clearly, such an experiment raises blatant ethical concerns, and nothing like it would ever be done today.

But sometimes ethical issues are more subtle. For instance, in seeking to understand the roots of aggressive behavior, U.S. government researchers proposed holding a conference to examine possible genetic roots of aggression. Based on work conducted by neuroscientists and geneticists, some researchers had begun to raise the possibility that genetic markers might be found that would allow the identification of children as being particularly violence-prone. In such cases, it might be possible to track these violence-prone children and provide interventions that might reduce the likelihood of later violence.

Critics objected strenuously, however. They argued that such identification might lead to a self-fulfilling prophecy. Children labeled as violence-prone might be treated in a way that would actually *cause* them to be more aggressive than if they hadn't been so labeled. Ultimately, under intense political pressure, the conference was canceled (Wright, 1995).

To help researchers deal with such ethical problems, the major organizations of developmentalists, including the Society for Research in Child Development and the American Psychological Association, have developed comprehensive ethical guidelines for researchers. Among the basic principles that must be followed are those involving freedom from harm, informed consent, the use of deception, and maintenance of

ARE YOU AN INFORMED CONSUMER OF DEVELOPMENT?

Critically Evaluating Developmental Research

"Study Shows Adolescent Suicide Reaches New Peaks."

"Genetic Basis Found for Children's Obesity."

"New Research Points to Cure for Sudden Infant Death Syndrome."

We've all seen headlines like these, which at first glance seem to herald important, meaningful discoveries. But before we accept the findings, it is important to think critically about the research on which the headlines are based. Among the most important questions that we should consider are the following:

- Is the study grounded in theory, and what are the underlying hypotheses about the research? Research should flow from theoretical foundations, and hypotheses should be logical and based on some underlying theory. Only by considering the results in terms of theory and hypotheses can we determine how successful the research has been.

- Is this an isolated research study, or does it fit into a series of investigations addressing the same general problem? A onetime study is far less meaningful than a series of studies that build upon one another. By placing research in the context of other studies, we can be much more confident regarding the validity of the findings of a new study.

- Who took part in the study, and how far can we generalize the results beyond the participants? As we discussed earlier in the chapter, conclusions about the meaning of research can only be generalized to people who are similar to the participants in a study.

- Was the study carried out appropriately? Although it is often difficult to know the details of a study from media summaries, it is important to learn as much as possible about who did the study and how it was done. For instance, did it include appropriate control groups, and are the researchers who conducted it reputable? One clue that a study meets these criteria and is well done is whether the findings reported in the media are based on a study published in a major journal such as *Developmental Psychology, Adolescence, Child Development*, or *Science*. Each of these journals is carefully edited, and only the best, most rigorous research is reported in them.

- Were the participants studied long enough to draw reasonable developmental implications? A study that purports to study long-term development should encompass a reasonably long time frame. Furthermore, developmental implications beyond the age span studied should not be drawn. ■

participants' privacy (American Psychological Association [APA], 2002; Fisher, 2004, 2005; Nagy, 2011):

- **Researchers must protect participants from physical and psychological harm.** Their welfare, interests, and rights come before those of researchers. In research, participants' rights always come first (Sieber, 2000; Fisher, 2004; Nagy, 2011).

- **Researchers must obtain informed consent from participants before their involvement in a study.** If they are over age 7, participants must voluntarily agree to be in a study. For those under 18, their parents or guardians must also provide consent.

  The requirement for informed consent raises some difficult issues. Suppose, for instance, researchers want to study the psychological effects of abortion on adolescents. Although they may be able to obtain the consent of an adolescent who has had an abortion, the researchers may need to get her parents' permission as well, because she is a minor. But if the adolescent hasn't told her parents about the abortion, the mere request for permission from the parents would violate her privacy—leading to a breach of ethics.

- **The use of deception in research must be justified and cause no harm.** Although deception to disguise the true purpose of an experiment is permissible, any experiment that uses deception must undergo careful scrutiny by an independent panel before it is conducted. Suppose, for example, we want to know the reaction of participants to success and failure. It is ethical to tell participants that they will be playing a game when the true purpose is actually to observe how they respond to doing well or poorly on the task. However, such a procedure is ethical only if it causes no harm to participants, has been approved by a review panel, and ultimately includes a full debriefing, or explanation, for participants when the study is over (Underwood, 2005).

• **Participants' privacy must be maintained.** If participants are videotaped during the course of a study, for example, they must give their permission for the videotapes to be viewed. Furthermore, access to the tapes must be carefully restricted.

Review, Check, and Apply

Review

1. Research may be considered either applied or theoretical, but in fact the two approaches are complementary.

2. The strategies used to measure developmental change include longitudinal studies, cross-sectional studies, and sequential studies.

3. Longitudinal studies examine the same subjects over time, cross-sectional studies examine subjects of different ages at the same time, and sequential studies examine subjects from different age groups at several points in time.

4. Ethical principles that govern the conduct of developmental research include the protection of participants from physical and psychological harm, informed consent, limited use of deception, and protection of participants' privacy.

Check

1. Developmental researchers focus on _____ and applied research.

2. _____ research measures change over time.

3. The research method in which researchers examine a number of different age groups at a single point in time is called _____ research

4. In masking the true purpose of a procedure from participants, researchers must be especially careful to consider ethical principles governing _____.

Apply

1. Males born in the United States between 1910 and 1920 had a much higher incidence of early death (i.e., death before age 40) than males born between 1960 and 1970. Can you think of cohort-related influences that help to explain this difference?

2. In the age of Internet-enabled information sharing, it is common to be confronted with many "scientific" claims that appear interesting and surprising. What are some ways to check whether such claims have validity or not? Are there Internet-based strategies for doing this?

To see more review questions, log on to MyPsychLab.

The CASE
of . . . *a Study in Violence*

Don Callan loves his new job teaching fourth grade at a large public school. Lately, though, he has been concerned about the aggression he sees on the playground. He hears his students talking about movies, TV shows, and games that sound very violent.

Don decides to conduct a research study. He theorizes that "indirect" violence causes actual violence and aggression. His hypothesis is that children who encounter indirect violence at home will prefer violent images and behaviors at school.

He prepares a note for parents describing his experiment, asking them to indicate how often their children play with violent games and watch TV shows and movies that contain violence. He then plans to observe all his students for two weeks on the playground, keeping a record of any time they act aggressively. In addition, he plans to place violent and nonviolent games, comic books, and DVDs on a table and ask each child to pick one to borrow. He plans to tally their choices to see whether they choose a violent or nonviolent game.

He shows his experimental plan to his instructional supervisor and awaits her reaction.

1. Do you think Don's theory is a good example of a theory? Is his hypothesis sound?

2. Is his study an experiment or a correlational study? Why or why not?

3. Do you think Don's fourth graders would be able to understand and participate in the study and provide informed consent for their participation?

4. Do you think Don's method will yield reliable results? Why or why not?

5. What do you suppose the students' parents would think of the study? What will his instructional supervisor think? What do you think?

⫷⫷⫷ LOOKING BACK

LO 2-1 What are the basic concepts of the psychodynamic perspective?

- Five major theoretical perspectives guide the study of child development: the psychodynamic, behavioral, cognitive, contextual, and evolutionary perspectives.

- The psychodynamic perspective is exemplified by the psychoanalytic theory of Freud and the psychosocial theory of Erikson. Freud focused attention on the unconscious and on stages through which children must pass successfully to avoid harmful fixations. Erikson identified eight distinct stages of development, each characterized by a conflict, or crisis, to work out.

LO 2-2 What are the basic concepts of the behavioral perspective?

- The behavioral perspective typically concerns stimulus–response learning, exemplified by classical conditioning, the operant conditioning of Skinner, and Bandura's social-cognitive learning theory.

LO 2-3 What are the basic concepts of the cognitive perspective?

- The cognitive perspective focuses on the processes that allow people to know, understand, and think about the world. For example, Piaget identified developmental stages through which all children are assumed to pass. Each stage involves qualitative differences in thinking. In contrast, information processing approaches attribute cognitive growth to quantitative changes in mental processes and capacities. Cognitive neuroscientists seek to identify locations and functions within the brain that are related to different types of cognitive activity.

LO 2-4 What are the basic concepts of the contextual perspective?

- The contextual perspective stresses the interrelatedness of developmental areas and the importance of broad cultural factors in human development. Bronfenbrenner's ecological approach focuses on the microsystem, mesosystem, exosystem, macrosystem, and chronosystem. Vygotsky's sociocultural theory emphasizes the central influence on cognitive development exerted by social interactions between members of a culture.

LO 2-5 What are the basic concepts of the evolutionary perspective?

- The evolutionary perspective attributes behavior to genetic inheritance from our ancestors, contending that genes determine not only traits such as skin color and eye color but also certain personality traits and social behaviors.

LO 2-6 What is the value of multiple perspectives on child development?

- Each perspective is based on its own premises and focuses on different aspects of development. Combining perspectives provides a more comprehensive picture of development than relying on only one perspective in isolation.

LO 2-7 What is the scientific method, and how does it help answer questions about child development?

- The scientific method is the process of posing and answering questions using careful, controlled techniques that include systematic, orderly observation and the collection of data.

- Theories are broad explanations of facts or phenomena of interest, based on a systematic integration of prior findings and theories. Hypotheses are theory-based predictions that can be tested. Operationalization is the process of translating a hypothesis into specific, testable procedures that can be measured and observed.

- Researchers test hypotheses by correlational research (to determine if two factors are associated) and experimental research (to discover cause-and-effect relationships).

LO 2-8 What are the major characteristics of correlational studies and experiments, and how do they differ?

- Correlational studies use naturalistic observation, case studies, diaries, survey research, and psychophysiological methods to investigate whether certain characteristics of interest are associated with other characteristics. Correlational studies lead to no direct conclusions about cause and effect.

- Typically, experimental research studies are conducted on participants in a treatment group, who receive the experimental treatment, and participants in a control group, who do not. Following the treatment, differences between the two groups can help the experimenter determine the effects of the treatment. Experiments may be conducted in a laboratory or in a real-world setting.

LO 2-9 What are the major research strategies?

- Theoretical research is designed specifically to test some developmental explanation and expand scientific knowledge, whereas applied research is meant to provide practical solutions to immediate problems.

- To measure change at different ages, researchers use longitudinal studies of the same participants over time, cross-sectional studies of different-age participants conducted at one time, and sequential studies of different-age participants at several points in time.

LO 2-10 What are the primary ethical principles used to guide research ?

- Ethical guidelines for research include the protection of participants from harm, informed consent of participants, limits on the use of deception, and the maintenance of privacy.

KEY TERMS AND CONCEPTS

theories (p. 22)
psychodynamic perspective (p. 23)
psychoanalytic theory (p. 23)
psychosexual development (p. 23)
psychosocial development (p. 24)
behavioral perspective (p. 25)
classical conditioning (p. 26)
operant conditioning (p. 26)
behavior modification (p. 26)
social-cognitive learning theory (p. 27)
cognitive perspective (p. 28)
information processing approaches (p. 29)
cognitive neuroscience approaches (p. 30)

contextual perspective (p. 31)
bioecological approach (p. 31)
sociocultural theory (p. 32)
evolutionary perspective (p. 34)
scientific method (p. 37)
hypothesis (p. 38)
correlational research (p. 39)
experimental research (p. 39)
naturalistic observation (p. 41)
case studies (p. 41)
survey research (p. 42)
psychophysiological methods (p. 42)
experiment (p. 42)

treatment (p. 42)
treatment group (p. 42)
control group (p. 42)
independent variable (p. 43)
dependent variable (p. 43)
sample (p. 44)
field study (p. 44)
laboratory study (p. 45)
theoretical research (p. 47)
applied research (p. 47)
longitudinal research (p. 48)
cross-sectional research (p. 49)
sequential studies (p. 50)

Epilogue

This chapter examined the way developmentalists use theory and research to understand child development. We reviewed the broad approaches to children, examining the theories that each has produced. In addition, we looked at the ways in which research is conducted. Before proceeding to the next chapter, think about the prologue of this chapter, about the murder of Christina-Taylor Green. In light of what you now know about theories and research, consider the following questions about Christina:

1. How might child developmentalists from the psychodynamic, behavioral, cognitive, contextual, and evolutionary perspectives explain Christina's success in school?

2. What differences might there be in the questions that would interest them and the studies they might wish to conduct?

3. Formulate one hypothesis using either the behavioral or cognitive perspective to explain Christina's interest in politics.

4. Try to design a research study to test the hypothesis you generated in response to question 3.

The Development Video Series in MyPsychLab

Explore the video *The Big Picture: Genes, Evolution, and Human Behavior* by scanning this QR code with your mobile device. If you don't already have one, you may download a free QR scanner for your device wherever smartphone apps are sold. You can also view this video in MyPsychLab. For more videos related to this chapter's content, log into MyPsychLab to view the entire Development Video Series.

MyVirtualChild

- **What decisions would you make while raising a child?**
- **What would the consequences of those decisions be?**

Find out by accessing **MyVirtualChild** at
www.MyPsychLab.com
and raising your own virtual child from birth to age 18.

---

3 The Start of Life: Genetics and Prenatal Development

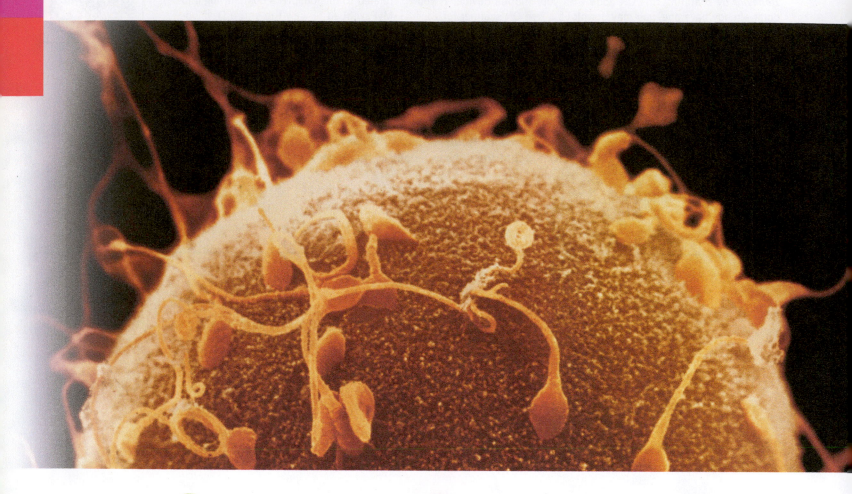

MODULE 3.1

EARLIEST DEVELOPMENT

- Genes and Chromosomes: The Code of Life
- Multiple Births: Two—or More—for the Genetic Price of One
- The Basics of Genetics: The Mixing and Matching of Traits
- Transmission of Genetic Information
- The Human Genome and Behavioral Genetics: Cracking the Genetic Code
- Inherited and Genetic Disorders: When Development Goes Awry
- Genetic Counseling: Predicting the Future from the Genes of the Present

Review, Check, and Apply

MODULE 3.2

THE INTERACTION OF HEREDITY AND ENVIRONMENT

- The Role of the Environment in Determining the Expression of Genes: From Genotypes to Phenotypes
- Studying Development: How Much Is Nature? How Much Is Nurture?
- Physical Traits: Family Resemblances
- Intelligence: More Research, More Controversy
- Genetic and Environmental Influences on Personality: Born to Be Outgoing?

DEVELOPMENTAL DIVERSITY AND YOUR LIFE:
Cultural Differences in Physical Arousal: Might a Culture's Philosophical Outlook Be Determined by Genetics?

- Psychological Disorders: The Role of Genetics and Environment
- Can Genes Influence the Environment?

Review, Check, and Apply

MODULE 3.3

PRENATAL GROWTH AND CHANGE

- Fertilization: The Moment of Conception
- The Stages of the Prenatal Period: The Onset of Development
- Pregnancy Problems
- The Prenatal Environment: Threats to Development

FROM RESEARCH TO PRACTICE: From Joy to Sorrow: When Pregnant Mothers Become Depressed

ARE YOU AN INFORMED CONSUMER OF DEVELOPMENT? Optimizing the Prenatal Environment

Review, Check, and Apply

The Case of...the Genetic Finger of Fate

Looking Back

Key Terms and Concepts

Epilogue

PROLOGUE: An Agonizing Choice

Leah and John Howard's joy at learning Leah was pregnant turned to anxiety when Leah's doctor discovered that her brother had died from Duchenne muscular dystrophy (DMD) at age 12. The disease, the doctor explained, was an X-linked inherited disorder. There was a chance Leah was a carrier. If so, there was a 50% chance that the baby would inherit the disease if it were a boy. The doctor advised them to have an ultrasound to determine the baby's sex. It turned out to be a boy.

The Howards faced new options. The doctor could take a chorion villus sampling now or wait a month and perform an amniocentesis. Both carried a very low risk for miscarriage. Leah chose amniocentesis, but the results were inconclusive. The doctor then suggested a fetal muscle biopsy to confirm the presence or lack of the muscle protein dystrophin. No dystrophin signaled DMD. The risk of miscarriage, however, was not inconsiderable.

Four months pregnant at this point and tired of the worries and tears, Leah and John decided to take their chances and look forward to their baby's birth.

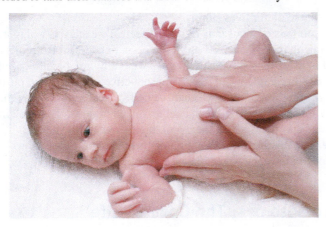

>>> LOOKING AHEAD

The Howards' decision to forego a fetal muscle biopsy does not change the outcome. They did not wish to consider a late-term abortion and DMD has no cure. But their case illustrates the difficult decisions that parents sometimes face because of advances in the identification of inherited disorders and our understanding of genetics.

In this chapter, we'll examine what developmental researchers and other scientists have learned about ways that heredity and the environment work in tandem to create and shape human beings. We begin with the basics of heredity, the genetic transmission of characteristics from biological parents to their children, by examining how we receive our genetic endowment. We consider an area of study, behavioral genetics, which specializes in the consequences of heredity on behavior. We also discuss

(continued)

Learning Objectives

MODULE 3.1

LO1 What are the basics of genetics?

LO2 How do the environment and genetics work together to determine human characteristics?

LO3 What is the purpose of genetic counseling?

MODULE 3.2

LO4 Which human characteristics are significantly influenced by heredity?

LO5 How is intelligence determined?

LO6 Can genes influence the environment?

MODULE 3.3

LO7 What happens during the prenatal stages of development?

LO8 What are the threats to the fetal environment, and what can be done about them?

LO9 How do fathers affect the prenatal environment?

what happens when genetic factors cause development to go awry, and how such problems are dealt with through genetic counseling and gene therapy.

But genes are only one part of the story of prenatal development. We also consider the ways in which a child's genetic heritage interacts with the environment in which he or she grows up—how one's family, socioeconomic status, and life events can affect a variety of characteristics, including physical traits, intelligence, and even personality.

Finally, we focus on the very first stage of development, tracing prenatal growth and change. We review some of the alternatives available to couples who find it difficult to conceive. We also talk about the stages of the prenatal period and how the prenatal environment offers both threats to—and the promise of—future growth.

MODULE 3.1

EARLIEST DEVELOPMENT

LO 3-1 What are the basics of genetics?

LO 3-2 How do the environment and genetics work together to determine human characteristics?

LO 3-3 What is the purpose of genetic counseling?

We humans begin the course of our lives simply.

Like individuals from tens of thousands of other species, we start as a single cell, a tiny speck probably weighing no more than 1/20-millionth of an ounce. But from this humble beginning, in a matter of a just several months if all goes well, a living, breathing individual infant is born. This first cell is created when a male reproductive cell, a *sperm,* pushes through the membrane of the *ovum,* the female reproductive cell. These **gametes,** as the male and female reproductive cells are also known, each contain huge amounts of genetic information. About an hour or so after the sperm enters the ovum, the two gametes suddenly fuse, becoming one cell, a **zygote.** The resulting combination of their genetic instructions—more than 2 billion chemically coded messages—is sufficient to begin creating a whole person.

Genes and Chromosomes: The Code of Life

The blueprints for creating a person are stored and communicated in our **genes,** the basic units of genetic information. The roughly 25,000 human genes are the biological equivalent of "software" that programs the future development of all parts of the body's "hardware."

All genes are composed of specific sequences of **DNA (deoxyribonucleic acid) molecules.** The genes are arranged in specific locations and in a specific order along 46 **chromosomes,** rod-shaped portions of DNA that are organized in 23 pairs. However, the sex cells—the ova and the sperm—contain half this number, so that a child's mother and father each provide one of the two chromosomes in each of the 23 pairs. The resulting 46 chromosomes (in 23 pairs) in the new zygote contain the genetic blueprint that will guide cell activity for the rest of the individual's life (Pennisi, 2000; International Human Genome Sequencing Consortium, 2001; see Figure 3-1). Through a process called *mitosis,* which accounts for the replication of most types of cells, nearly all the cells of the body will contain the same 46 chromosomes as the zygote.

Specific genes in precise locations on the chain of chromosomes determine the nature and function of every cell in the body. For instance, genes determine which cells will ultimately become part of the heart and which will become part of the muscles of the leg. Genes also establish how different parts of the body will function: how rapidly the heart will beat, or how much strength a muscle will have.

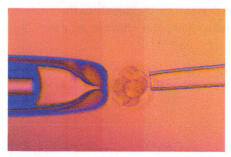

Advances in our understanding of genetics have led to major breakthroughs in genetic counseling.

Watch the **Video** *Period of the Zygote* in **MyPsychLab**.

gametes   The sex cells from the mother and father that form a new cell at conception

zygote   The new cell formed by the process of fertilization

genes   The basic unit of genetic information

DNA (deoxyribonucleic acid) molecules   The substance that genes are composed of that determines the nature of every cell in the body and how it will function

chromosomes   Rod-shaped portions of DNA that are organized in 23 pairs

If each parent provides just 23 chromosomes, where does the potential for the vast diversity of human beings come from? The answer resides primarily in the nature of the processes that underlie the cell division of the gametes. When gametes—the sex cells, sperm and ova—are formed in the adult human body in a process called *meiosis,* each gamete receives one of the two chromosomes that make up each of the 23 pairs. Because for each of the 23 pairs it is largely a matter of chance which member of the pair is contributed, there are 2^{23} or some 8 million, different combinations possible. Furthermore, other processes, such as random transformations of particular genes, add to the variability of the genetic brew. The ultimate outcome: tens of *trillions* of possible genetic combinations.

With so many possible genetic mixtures provided by heredity, there is no likelihood that someday you'll bump into a genetic duplicate of yourself—with one exception: an identical twin.

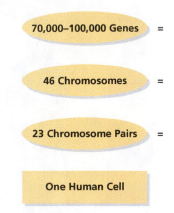

FIGURE 3-1 The Contents of a Single Human Cell

At the moment of conception, humans receive 70,000 to 100,000 genes, contained on 46 chromosomes on 23 pairs.

Multiple Births: Two—or More—for the Genetic Price of One

Although it doesn't seem surprising when dogs and cats give birth to several offspring at one time, in humans, multiple births are cause for comment. They should be: Less than 3% of all pregnancies produce twins, and the odds are even slimmer for three or more children.

Why do multiple births occur? Some occur when a cluster of cells in the ovum splits off within the first 2 weeks after fertilization. The result is two genetically identical zygotes, which, because they come from the same original zygote, are called monozygotic. **Monozygotic twins** are genetically identical. Any differences in their future development can be attributed only to environmental factors, because genetically they are exactly the same.

There is a second, and actually more common, mechanism that produces multiple births. In these cases, two separate ova are fertilized by two separate sperm at roughly the same time. Twins produced in this fashion are known as **dizygotic twins.** Because they are the result of two separate ovum–sperm combinations, they are no more genetically similar than two siblings born at different times.

Of course, not all multiple births produce only two babies. Triplets, quadruplets, and even more births are produced by either (or both) of the mechanisms that yield twins. Thus, triplets may be some combination of monozygotic, dizygotic, or trizygotic.

Although the chances of having a multiple birth are typically slim, the odds rise considerably when couples use fertility drugs to improve the probability they will conceive a child. For example, 1 in 10 couples using fertility drugs have dizygotic twins, compared to an overall figure of 1 in 86 for Caucasian couples in the United States. Older women, too, are more likely to have multiple births, and multiple births are also more common in some families than they are in others. The increased use of fertility drugs and rising average age of mothers giving birth has meant that multiple births have increased in the last 25 years (see Figure 3-2; Martin et al., 2005).

There are also racial, ethnic, and national differences in the rate of multiple births, probably due to inherited differences in the likelihood that more than one ovum will be released at a time. One out of 70 African American couples have dizygotic births, compared with 1 out of 86 for White American couples (Wood, 1997).

Mothers carrying multiple children run a higher than average risk of premature delivery and birth complications. Consequently, these mothers must be particularly concerned about their prenatal care.

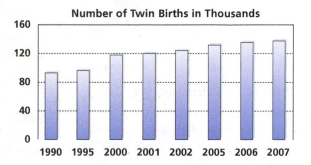

Number of Twin Births in Thousands

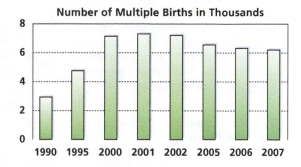

Number of Multiple Births in Thousands

FIGURE 3-2 Rising Multiples

Multiple births have increased significantly over the last 25 years. What are some of the reasons for this phenomenon?

(*Source:* Martin & Park, 2009)

Boy or Girl? Establishing the Sex of the Child.
Recall that there are 23 matched pairs of chromosomes. In 22 of these pairs, each chromosome is similar to the other member of its pair. The one exception is the 23rd pair, which is the one that determines the sex of the child. In females, the 23rd pair consists of two matching, relatively large X-shaped chromosomes, appropriately identified as XX. In males, on the other hand, the members of the pair are dissimilar. One consists of an X-shaped chromosome, but the other is a shorter, smaller Y-shaped chromosome. This pair is identified as XY.

monozygotic twins   Twins who are genetically identical

dizygotic twins   Twins who are produced when two separate ova are fertilized by two separate sperm at roughly the same time

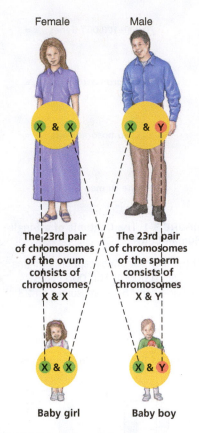

Female   Male

X & X   X & Y

The 23rd pair
of chromosomes
of the ovum
consists of
chromosomes
X & X

The 23rd pair
of chromosomes
of the sperm
consists of
chromosomes
X & Y

X & X   X & Y

Baby girl   **Baby boy**

FIGURE 3-3 Determining Sex

When an ovum and sperm meet at the moment of fertilization, the ovum is certain to provide an X chromosome, whereas the sperm will provide either an X or a Y chromosome. If the sperm contributes its X chromosome, the child will have an XX pairing on the 23rd chromosome and will be a girl. If the sperm contributes a Y chromosome, the result will be an XY pairing and will be a boy. Does this mean that girls are more likely to be conceived than are boys?

Watch the **Video** *A Preference for Sons* in **MyPsychLab**.

Monozygotic and dizygotic twins present opportunities to learn about the relative contributions of heredity and situational factors. What kinds of things can psychologists learn from studying twins?

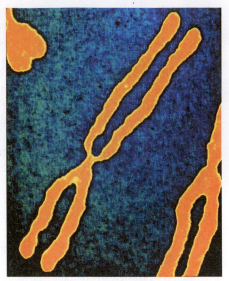

Not only is the X chromosome important in determining gender, but it is also the site of genes controlling other aspects of development.

As we discussed earlier, each gamete carries one chromosome from each of the parent's 23 pairs of chromosomes. Because a female's 23rd pair of chromosomes are both Xs, an ovum will always carry an X chromosome, no matter which chromosome of the 23rd pair it gets. A male's 23rd pair is XY, so each sperm could carry either an X or a Y chromosome.

If the sperm contributes an X chromosome when it meets an ovum (which, remember, will always contribute an X chromosome), the child will have an XX pairing on the 23rd chromosome—and will be a female. If the sperm contributes a Y chromosome, the result will be an XY pairing—a male (see Figure 3-3).

It is clear from this process that the father's sperm determines the sex of the child. This fact is the basis of emerging techniques that will allow parents to increase the chances of specifying the sex of their child. In one new technique, lasers measure the DNA in sperm. By discarding sperm that harbor the unwanted sex chromosome, the chances of having a child of the desired sex increase dramatically (Van Balen, 2005).

Of course, procedures for choosing a child's sex raise ethical and practical issues. For example, in cultures that value one sex over the other, might there be a kind of sex discrimination prior to birth? Furthermore, a shortage of children of the less preferred sex might ultimately result. Many questions must therefore be answered if sex selection is ever to become routine (Sharma, 2008; Puri et al., 2011).

The Basics of Genetics: The Mixing and Matching of Traits

What determined the color of your hair? Why are you tall or short? What made you susceptible to hay fever? And why do you have so many freckles? To answer these questions, we need to consider the basic mechanisms involved in the way that the genes we inherit from our parents transmit information.

We can start by examining the discoveries of an Austrian monk, Gregor Mendel, in the mid-1800s. In a series of simple yet convincing experiments, Mendel cross-pollinated pea plants that always produced yellow seeds with pea plants that always produced green seeds. The result was not, as one might guess, a plant with a combination of yellow and green seeds. Instead, all of the resulting plants had yellow seeds. At first it appeared that the green-seeded plants had had no influence.

However, additional research on Mendel's part proved this was not true. He bred together plants from the new, yellow-seeded generation that had resulted from his original cross-breeding of the green-seeded and yellow-seeded plants. The consistent result was a ratio of three fourths yellow seeds to one fourth green seeds.

Why did this 3-to-1 ratio of yellow to green seeds appear so consistently? It was Mendel's genius to provide an answer. Based on his experiments with pea plants, he argued that when two competing traits, such as a green or yellow coloring of seeds, were both present, only one could be expressed. The one that was expressed was called a **dominant trait.** Meanwhile, the other trait remained present in the organism, although it was not expressed (displayed). This was called a **recessive trait.** In the case of Mendel's original pea plants, the offspring plants received genetic information from both the green-seeded and the yellow-seeded parents. However, the yellow trait was dominant, and consequently the recessive green trait did not assert itself.

Keep in mind, however, that genetic material relating to both parent plants is present in the offspring, even though it cannot be seen. The genetic information is known as the organism's genotype. A **genotype** is the underlying combination of genetic material present (but outwardly invisible) in an organism. In contrast, a **phenotype** is the observable trait, the trait that actually is seen.

Although the offspring of the yellow-seeded and green-seeded pea plants all have yellow seeds (i.e., they have a yellow-seeded phenotype), the genotype consists of genetic information relating to both parents.

And what is the nature of the information in the genotype? To answer that question, let's turn from peas to people. In fact, the principles are the same not only for plants and humans but also for the majority of species.

Recall that parents transmit genetic information to their offspring via the chromosomes they contribute through the gamete they provide during fertilization. Some of the genes form pairs called *alleles,* genes governing traits that may take alternate forms, such as hair or eye color. For example, brown eye color is a dominant trait (B); blue eyes are recessive (b). A child's allele may contain similar or dissimilar genes from each parent. If the child receives similar genes, he or she is said to be **homozygous** for the trait. On the other hand, if the child receives different forms of the gene from its parents, he or she is said to be **heterozygous.** In the case of heterozygous alleles (Bb), the dominant characteristic, brown eyes is expressed. However, if the child happens to receive a recessive allele from each of its parents, and therefore lacks a dominant characteristic (bb), it will display the recessive characteristic, such as blue eyes.

Gregor Mendel's pioneering experiments on pea plants provided the foundation for the study of genetics.

Transmission of Genetic Information

We can see this process at work in humans by considering the transmission of *phenylketonuria (PKU)*, an inherited disorder in which a child is unable to make use of phenylalanine, an essential amino acid present in proteins found in milk and other foods. If left untreated, PKU allows phenylalanine to build up to toxic levels, causing brain damage and mental retardation (Moyle et al., 2007; Widaman, 2009; Cotugno et al., 2011).

PKU is produced by a single allele, or pair of genes. As shown in Figure 3-4 on page 62, we can label each gene of the pair with a *P* if it carries a dominant gene, which causes the normal production of phenylalanine, or a *p* if it carries the recessive gene that produces PKU. In cases in which neither parent is a PKU carrier, both the mother's and the father's pairs of genes are the dominant form, symbolized as *PP.* Consequently, no matter which member of the pair is contributed by the mother and father, the resulting pair of genes in the child will be *PP,* and the child will not have PKU.

However, consider what happens if one of the parents has a recessive *p* gene. In this case, which we can we symbolize as *Pp,* the parent will not have PKU, because the normal *P* gene is dominant. But the recessive gene can be passed down to the child. This is not so bad: If the child has only one recessive gene, it will not suffer from PKU. But what if both parents carry a recessive *p* gene? In this case, although neither parent has the disorder, it is possible for the child to receive a recessive gene from both parents. The child's genotype for PKU then will be *pp,* and he or she will have the disorder.

dominant trait   The one trait that is expressed when two competing traits are present

recessive trait   A trait within an organism that is present, but is not expressed

genotype   The underlying combination of genetic material present (but not outwardly visible) in an organism

phenotype   An observable trait; the trait that actually is seen

homozygous   Inheriting from parents similar genes for a given trait

heterozygous   Inheriting from parents different forms of a gene for a given trait

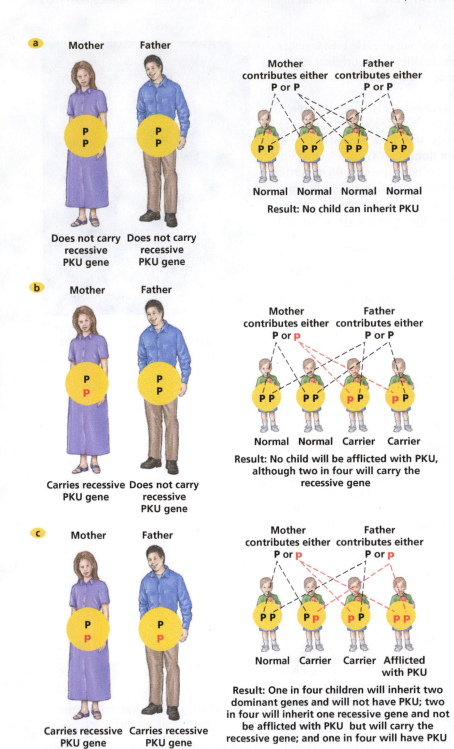

a

Mother / Father

P P / P P

Does not carry recessive PKU gene / **Does not carry recessive PKU gene**

Mother contributes either P or P / Father contributes either P or P

P P   P P   P P   P P

Normal   Normal   Normal   Normal

Result: No child can inherit PKU

b

Mother / Father

P P (p) / P P

Carries recessive PKU gene / **Does not carry recessive PKU gene**

Mother contributes either P or p / Father contributes either P or P

P P   P P   p P   p P

Normal   Normal   Carrier   Carrier

Result: No child will be afflicted with PKU, although two in four will carry the recessive gene

c

Mother / Father

P p / P p

Carries recessive PKU gene / **Carries recessive PKU gene**

Mother contributes either P or p / Father contributes either P or p

P P   P p   p P   p p

Normal   Carrier   Carrier   Afflicted with PKU

Result: One in four children will inherit two dominant genes and will not have PKU; two in four will inherit one recessive gene and not be afflicted with PKU but will carry the recessive gene; and one in four will have PKU

polygenic inheritance Inheritance in which a combination of multiple gene pairs is responsible for the production of a particular trait

X-linked genes Genes that are considered recessive and located only on the X chromosome

FIGURE 3-4 PKU Probabilities

PKU, a disease that causes brain damage and mental retardation, is produced by a single pair of genes inherited from one's mother and father. If neither parent carries a gene for the disease (a), a child cannot develop PKU. Even if one parent carries the recessive gene, but the other doesn't (b), the child cannot inherit the disease. However, if both parents carry the recessive gene (c), there is a one in four chance that the child will have PKU.

Remember, though, that even children whose parents both have the recessive gene for PKU have only a 25% chance of inheriting the disorder. Due to the laws of probability, 25% of children with *Pp* parents will receive the dominant gene from each parent (these children's genotype would be *PP*), and 50% will receive the dominant gene from one parent and the recessive gene from the other (their genotypes would be either *Pp* or *pP*). Only the unlucky 25% who receive the recessive gene from each parent and end up with the genotype *pp* will suffer from PKU.

Polygenic Traits. The transmission of PKU is a good way of illustrating the basic principles of how genetic information passes from parent to child, although the case of PKU is simpler than most cases of genetic transmission. Relatively few traits are governed by a single pair of genes. Instead, most traits are the result of polygenic inheritance. In **polygenic inheritance,** a combination of multiple gene pairs is responsible for the production of a particular trait.

Furthermore, some genes come in several alternate forms, and still others act to modify the way that particular genetic traits (produced by other alleles) are displayed. Genes also vary in terms of their *reaction range,* the potential degree of variability in the actual expression of a trait due to environmental conditions. And some traits, such as blood type, are produced by genes in which neither member of a pair of genes can be classified as purely dominant or recessive. Instead, the trait is expressed in terms of a combination of the two genes—such as type AB blood.

A number of recessive genes, called **X-linked genes,** are located only on the X chromosome. Recall that in females, the 23rd pair of chromosomes is an XX pair, whereas in males it is an XY pair. One result is that males have a higher risk for a variety of X-linked disorders—as the Howards' unborn son did in the chapter prologue—because males lack a second X chromosome that can counteract the genetic information that produces the disorder. For example, males are significantly more apt to have red-green color blindness, a disorder produced by a set of genes on the X chromosome.

Similarly, *hemophilia,* a blood disorder, is produced by X-linked genes. Hemophilia has been a recurrent problem in the royal families of Europe, as illustrated in Figure 3-5, which shows the inheritance of hemophilia in the descendants of Queen Victoria of Great Britain.

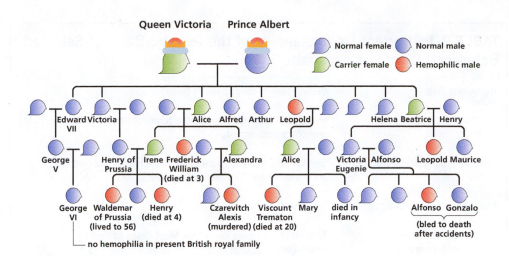

FIGURE 3-5 Inheriting Hemophilia

Hemophilia, a blood-clotting disorder, has been an inherited problem throughout the royal families of Europe, as illustrated by the descendants of Queen Victoria of Great Britain.

(*Source:* Adapted from Kimball, 1983)

The Human Genome and Behavioral Genetics: Cracking the Genetic Code

Mendel's achievements in recognizing the basics of genetic transmission of traits were trailblazing. However, they mark only the beginning of our understanding of the ways those particular sorts of characteristics are passed on from one generation to the next.

The most recent milestone in understanding genetics was reached in early 2001, when molecular geneticists succeeded in mapping the specific sequence of genes on each chromosome. This accomplishment stands as one of the most important moments in the history of genetics and, for that matter, all of biology (International Human Genome Sequencing Consortium, 2001).

Already, the mapping of the gene sequence has provided important advances in our understanding of genetics. For instance, the number of human genes, long thought to be 100,000, has been revised downward to 25,000—not many more than organisms that are far less complex (see Figure 3-6). Furthermore, scientists have discovered that 99.9% of the gene sequence is shared by all humans. What this means is that we humans are far more similar to one another than we are different. It also indicates that many of the differences that seemingly separate people—such as race—are, literally, only skin-deep. Mapping of the human genome will also help in the identification of particular disorders to which a given individual is susceptible (DeLisi & Fleischhaker, 2007; Gupta & State, 2007; Hyman, 2011).

The mapping of the human gene sequence is supporting the field of behavioral genetics. As the name implies, **behavioral genetics** studies the effects of heredity on psychological characteristics. Rather than simply examine stable, unchanging characteristics such as hair or eye color, behavioral genetics takes a broader approach, considering how our personality and behavioral habits are affected by genetic factors. Personality traits such as shyness or sociability, moodiness and assertiveness are among the areas being studied. Other behavior geneticists study psychological disorders, such as depression, attention deficit-hyperactivity disorder, and schizophrenia, looking for possible genetic links (Haeffel et al., 2008; Byerley & Badner, 2011; Curtis et al., 2011; see Table 3-1 on page 64).

The promise of behavioral genetics is substantial. For one thing, researchers working within the field have gained a better understanding of the specifics of the genetic code that underlie human behavior and development.

Even more important, researchers are seeking to identify how genetic defects may be remedied. To understand how that possibility might come about, we need to consider the ways in which genetic factors, which normally cause development to proceed so smoothly, may falter.

Inherited and Genetic Disorders: When Development Goes Awry

PKU is just one of several disorders that may be inherited. Like a bomb that is harmless until its fuse is lit, a recessive gene responsible for a disorder may be passed on unknowingly from one generation to the next, revealing itself only when, by chance, it is paired with another

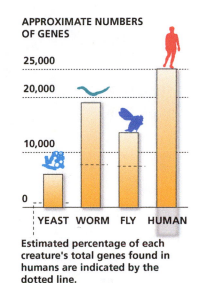

APPROXIMATE NUMBERS OF GENES

FIGURE 3-6 Uniquely Human?

Humans have about 25,000 genes, making them not much more genetically complex than some primitive species.

(*Source:* Celera Genomics: International Human Genome Sequencing Consortium, 2001)

behavioral genetics   The study of the effects of heredity on behavior

TABLE 3-1 Current Understanding of the Genetic Basis of Selected Behavioral Disorders and Traits

Behavioral Trait	Current Beliefs about Genetic Basis
Huntington's disease	Huntington gene localized to the terminal portion of the short arm of chromosome 4.
Obsessive-Compulsive Disorder (OCD)	Several potentially relevant genes have been identified but additional research is needed to verify.
Fragile X mental retardation	Two genes identified.
Early onset (familial) Alzheimer's disease	Three distinct genes identified. Most cases caused by single-gene mutation on chromosomes 21, 14, and 1.
Attention deficit hyperactivity disorder (ADHD)	Evidence in some studies has linked ADHD with the dopamine D4 and D5 genes, but the complexity of the disease makes it difficult to identify an specific gene beyond reasonable doubt.
Alcoholism	Research suggests that genes which affect the activity of neurotransmitters serotonin and GABA likely are involved in risk for alcoholism.
Schizophrenia	There is no agreement, but links to chromosomes 1, 5, 6, 10, 13, 15, and 22 have been reported.

(*Source:* Adapted from McGuffin, Riley, & Plomin, 2001)

recessive gene. It is only when two recessive genes come together like a match and a fuse that the gene will express itself and a child will inherit the genetic disorder.

But there is another way that genes are a source of concern: In some cases, genes become physically damaged. For instance, genes may break down due to wear and tear or chance events occurring during the cell division processes of meiosis and mitosis. Sometimes genes, for no known reason, spontaneously change their form, a process called *spontaneous mutation*.

Alternatively, certain environmental factors, such as exposure to X-rays or even highly polluted air, may produce a malformation of genetic material (see Figure 3-7). When such damaged genes are passed on to a child, the results can be disastrous in terms of future physical and cognitive development (Samet, MeMarini, & Malling, 2004; Olshansky, 2011).

In addition to PKU, which occurs once in 10,000 to 20,000 births, other inherited and genetic disorders include:

- *Down syndrome.* As we noted earlier, most people have 46 chromosomes, arranged in 23 pairs. One exception is individuals with **Down syndrome,** a disorder produced by the presence of an extra chromosome on the 21st pair. Once referred to as mongolism, Down syndrome is the most frequent cause of mental retardation. It occurs in about 1 in 500 births, although the risk is much greater in mothers who are unusually young or old (Sherman et al., 2007; Davis, 2008; Keck-Wherley et al., 2011).
- *Fragile X syndrome.* **Fragile X syndrome** occurs when a particular gene is injured on the X chromosome. The result is mild to moderate mental retardation (Cornish, Turk, & Hagerman, 2008; Hagerman, 2011).
- *Sickle-cell anemia.* Around one-tenth of Americans of African descent carry genes that produce sickle-cell anemia, and 1 in 400 actually has the disease. **Sickle-cell anemia** is a blood disorder that gets its name from the shape of the red blood cells in those who have it. Symptoms include poor appetite, stunted growth, swollen stomach, and yellowish eyes.

Down syndrome A disorder produced by the presence of an extra chromosome on the 21st pair; once referred to as mongolism

Fragile X syndrome A disorder produced by injury to a gene on the X chromosome, producing mild to moderate mental retardation

sickle-cell anemia A blood disorder that gets its name from the shape of the red blood cells in those who have it

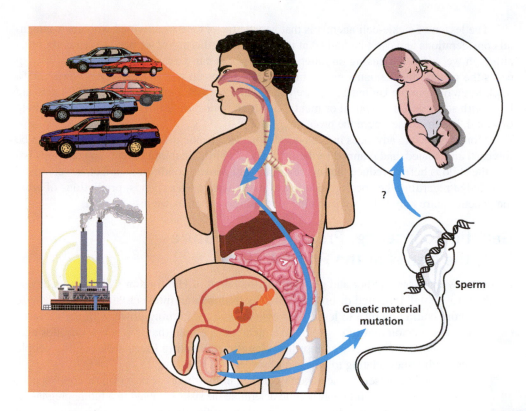

FIGURE 3-7 Inhaled Air and Genetic Mutations

Inhalation of unhealthy, polluted air may lead to mutations in genetic material in sperm. These mutations may be passed on, damaging the fetus and affecting future generations.

(*Source:* Based on Samet, MeMarini, & Malling, 2004, p. 971)

People afflicted with the most severe form of the disease rarely live beyond childhood. However, for those with less severe cases, medical advances have produced significant increases in life expectancy.

- *Tay-Sachs disease.* Occurring mainly in Jews of eastern European ancestry and in French Canadians, **Tay-Sachs disease** usually causes death before its victims reach school age. There is no treatment for the disorder, which produces blindness and muscle degeneration prior to death.

- *Klinefelter's syndrome.* One male out of every 400 is born with **Klinefelter's syndrome,** the presence of an extra X chromosome. The resulting XXY complement produces underdeveloped genitals, extreme height, and enlarged breasts. Klinefelter's syndrome is one of a number of genetic abnormalities that result from receiving the improper number of sex chromosomes. For instance, there are disorders produced by an extra Y chromosome (XYY), a missing second chromosome (called *Turner syndrome;* X0), and three X chromosomes (XXX). Such disorders are typically characterized by problems relating to sexual characteristics and by intellectual deficits (Murphy & Mazzocco, 2008; Murphy, 2009; Hazlett, Gaspar De Alba, & Hooper, 2011).

It is important to keep in mind that the mere fact a disorder has genetic roots does not mean that environmental factors do not also play a role. Consider, for instance, sickle-cell anemia, which primarily afflicts people of African descent. Because the disease can be fatal in childhood, we'd expect that those who suffer from it would be unlikely to live long enough to pass it on. And this does seem to be true, at least in the United States: Compared with parts of West Africa, the incidence in the United States is much lower.

But why shouldn't the incidence of sickle-cell anemia also be gradually reduced for people in West Africa? This question proved puzzling for many years, until scientists determined that carrying the sickle-cell gene raises immunity to malaria, which is a common disease in West Africa (Allison, 1954). This heightened immunity meant that people with the sickle-cell gene had a genetic advantage (in terms of resistance to malaria) that offset, to some degree, the disadvantage of being a carrier of the sickle-cell gene.

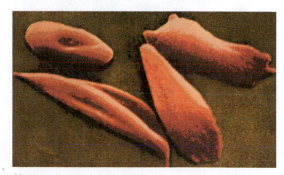

Sickle-cell anemia, named for the presence of misshapen red blood cells, is carried in the genes of 1 in 10 African Americans.

Tay-Sachs disease   A disorder that produces blindness and muscle degeneration prior to death; there is no treatment

Klinefelter's syndrome   A disorder resulting from the presence of an extra X chromosome that produces underdeveloped genitals, extreme height, and enlarged breasts

The lesson of sickle-cell anemia is that genetic factors are intertwined with environmental considerations and can't be looked at in isolation. Furthermore, we need to remember that although we've been focusing on inherited factors that can go awry, in the vast majority of cases the genetic mechanisms with which we are endowed work quite well. Overall, 95% of children born in the United States are healthy and normal. For the some 250,000 who are born with some sort of physical or mental disorder, appropriate intervention often can help treat and, in some cases, cure the problem.

Moreover, due to advances in behavioral genetics, genetic difficulties increasingly can be forecast, anticipated, and planned for before a child's birth, enabling parents to take steps before the child is born to reduce the severity of certain genetic conditions. In fact, as scientists' knowledge regarding the specific location of particular genes expands, predictions of what the genetic future may hold are becoming increasingly exact, as we discuss next.

Genetic Counseling: Predicting the Future from the Genes of the Present

Watch the **Video** *Genetic Counseling* in **MyPsychLab**.

If you knew that your mother and grandmother had died of Huntington's disease—a devastating, always fatal, inherited disorder marked by tremors and intellectual deterioration—to whom could you turn to learn your own chances of coming down with the disease? The best person to turn to would be a member of a field that, just a few decades ago, was nonexistent: genetic counseling. **Genetic counseling** focuses on helping people deal with issues relating to inherited disorders.

Genetic counselors use a variety of data in their work. For instance, couples contemplating having a child may seek to determine the risks involved in a future pregnancy. In such a case, a counselor will take a thorough family history, seeking any familial incidence of birth defects that might indicate a pattern of recessive or X-linked genes. In addition, the counselor will take into account factors such as the age of the mother and father and any previous abnormalities in other children they may have already had (Fransen, Meertens, & Schrander-Stumpel, 2006; Resta et al., 2006; Peay & Austin, 2011).

Typically, genetic counselors suggest a thorough physical examination. Such an exam may identify physical abnormalities that potential parents may have and not be aware of. In addition, samples of blood, skin, and urine may be used to isolate and examine specific chromosomes. Possible genetic defects, such as the presence of an extra sex chromosome, can be identified by assembling a *karyotype,* a chart containing enlarged photos of each of the chromosomes.

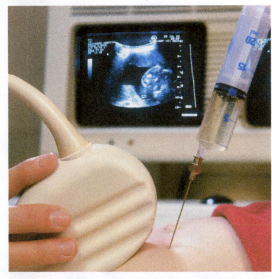
In amniocentesis, a sample of fetal cells is withdrawn from the amniotic sac and used to identify a number of genetic defects.

genetic counseling The discipline that focuses on helping people deal with issues relating to inherited disorders

ultrasound sonography A process in which high-frequency sound waves scan the mother's womb to produce an image of the unborn baby, whose size and shape can then be assessed

chorionic villus sampling (CVS) A test used to find genetic defects that involves taking samples of hairlike material that surrounds the embryo

amniocentesis The process of identifying genetic defects by examining a small sample of fetal cells drawn by a needle inserted into the amniotic fluid surrounding the unborn fetus

Prenatal Testing. A variety of techniques can be used to assess the health of an unborn child if a woman is already pregnant (see Table 3-2 for a list of currently available tests). The earliest test is a *first-trimester screen,* which combines a blood test and ultrasound sonography in the 11th to 13th week of pregnancy. In **ultrasound sonography,** high-frequency sound waves bombard the mother's womb. These waves produce a rather indistinct, but useful, image of the unborn baby, whose size and shape can then be assessed. Repeated use of ultrasound sonography can reveal developmental patterns. Although blood tests and ultrasound are not very accurate in identifying abnormalities early in pregnancy, accuracy improves later in pregnancy.

A more invasive test, **chorionic villus sampling (CVS),** can be employed in the 11th to 13th week if blood tests and ultrasound have identified a potential problem. CVS involves inserting a thin needle into the fetus and taking small samples of hairlike material that surrounds the embryo. The test can be done between the 8th and 11th week of pregnancy. However, it produces a risk of miscarriage of 1 in 100 to 1 in 200. Because of the risk, its use is relatively infrequent.

In **amniocentesis,** a small sample of fetal cells is drawn by a tiny needle inserted into the amniotic fluid surrounding the unborn fetus. Carried out 15 to 20 weeks into the pregnancy, amniocentesis allows the analysis of the fetal cells that can identify a variety of genetic defects with nearly 100% accuracy. In addition, it can determine the sex of the child. Although there is always a danger to the fetus in an invasive procedure such as amniocentesis, it is generally safe.

TABLE 3-2 Fetal Development Monitoring Techniques

Technique	Description
Amniocentesis	Done between the 15th and 20th week of pregnancy, this procedure examines a sample of the amniotic fluid, which contains fetal cells. Recommended if either parent carries Tay-Sachs, spina bifida, sickle-cell, Down syndrome, muscular dystrophy, or Rh disease.
Chorionic villus sampling (CVS)	Done at 8 to 11 weeks, either transabdominally or transcervically, depending on where the placenta is located. Involves inserting a needle (abdominally) or a catheter (cervically) into the substance of the placenta but staying outside the amniotic sac and removing 10 to 15 milligrams of tissue. This tissue is manually cleaned of maternal uterine tissue and then grown in culture, and a karyotype is made, as with amniocentesis.
Embryoscopy	Examines the embryo or fetus during the first 12 weeks of pregnancy by means of a fiberoptic endoscope inserted through the cervix. Can be performed as early as week 5. Access to the fetal circulation may be obtained through the instrument, and direct visualization of the embryo permits the diagnosis of malformations.
Fetal blood sampling (FBS)	Performed after 18 weeks of pregnancy by collecting a small amount of blood from the umbilical cord for testing. Used to detect Down syndrome and most other chromosome abnormalities in the fetuses of couples who are at increased risk of having an affected child. Many other diseases can be diagnosed using this technique.
Sonoembryology	Used to detect abnormalities in the first trimester of pregnancy. Involves high-frequency transvaginal probes and digital image processing. In combination with ultrasound, can detect more than 80% of all malformations during the second trimester.
Sonogram	Uses ultrasound to produce a visual image of the uterus, fetus, and placenta.
Ultrasound sonography	Uses very high-frequency sound waves to detect structural abnormalities or multiple pregnancies, measure fetal growth, judge gestational age, and evaluate uterine abnormalities. Also used as an adjunct to other procedures such as amniocentesis.

After the various tests are complete and all possible information is available, the couple will meet with the genetic counselor again. Typically, counselors avoid giving specific recommendations. Instead, they lay out the facts and present various options, ranging from doing nothing to taking more drastic steps, such as terminating the pregnancy through abortion. Ultimately, it is the parents who must decide what course of action to follow.

Screening for Future Problems. The newest role of genetic counselors involves testing people to identify whether they themselves, rather than their children, are susceptible to future disorders because of genetic abnormalities. For instance, Huntington's disease typically does not appear until people reach their 40s. However, genetic testing can identify much earlier whether a person carries the flawed gene that produces Huntington's disease. Presumably, knowing that they carry the gene can help people prepare themselves for the future (Cina & Fellmann, 2006; Tibben, 2007; Hinton, Grant & Grosse, 2011).

In addition to Huntington's disease, more than 1,000 disorders can be predicted on the basis of genetic testing (see Table 3-3 on page 68). Although such testing may bring welcome relief from future worries—if the results are negative—positive results may produce just the opposite effect. In fact, genetic testing raises difficult practical and ethical questions (Human Genome Project, 2006; Twomey, 2006; Wilfond & Ross, 2009).

Suppose, for instance, a woman who thought she was susceptible to Huntington's disease was tested in her 20s and found that she did not carry the defective gene. Obviously, she would experience tremendous relief. But suppose she found that she did carry the flawed gene and was therefore going to get the disease. In this case, she might well experience depression and remorse. In fact, some studies show that 10% of people who find they have the flawed gene that leads to Huntington's disease never recover fully on an emotional level (Myers, 2004; Wahlin, 2007).

TABLE 3-3 Some Currently Available DNA-Based Genetic Tests

Disease	Description
Adult polycystic kidney disease	Kidney failure and liver disease
Alpha-1-antitrypsin deficiency	Emphysema and liver disease
Alzheimer's disease	Late-onset variety of senile dementia
Amyotrophic lateral sclerosis (Lou Gehrig's disease)	Progressive motor function loss leading to paralysis and death
Ataxia telangiectasia	Progressive brain disorder resulting in loss of muscle control and cancers
Breast and ovarian cancer (inherited)	Early-onset tumors of breasts and ovaries
Charcot-Marie-Tooth	Loss of feeling in ends of limbs
Congenital adrenal hyperplasia	Hormone deficiency; ambiguous genitalia and male pseudohermaphroditism
Cystic fibrosis	Thick mucus accumulations in lungs and chronic infections in lungs and pancreas
Duchenne muscular dystrophy (Becker muscular dystrophy)	Severe to mild muscle wasting, deterioration, weakness
Dystonia	Muscle rigidity, repetitive twisting movements
Factor V-Leiden	Blood-clotting disorder
Fanconi anemia, group	Anemia, leukemia, skeletal deformities
Fragile X syndrome	Mental retardation
Gaucher disease	Enlarged liver and spleen, bone degeneration
Hemophilia A and B	Bleeding disorders
Hereditary nonpolyposis colon cancer[a]	Early-onset tumors of colon and sometimes other organs
Huntington's disease	Progressive neurological degeneration, usually beginning in midlife
Myotonic dystrophy	Progressive muscle weakness
Neurofibromatosis, type 1	Multiple benign nervous system tumors that can be disfiguring; cancers
Phenylketonuria	Progressive mental retardation due to missing enzyme; correctable by diet
Prader Willi/Angelman syndromes	Decreased motor skills, cognitive impairment, early death
Sickle-cell disease	Blood cell disorder; chronic pain and infections
Spinal muscular atrophy	Severe, usually lethal progressive muscle-wasting disorder in children
Spinocerebellar ataxia, type 1	Involuntary muscle movements, reflex disorders, explosive speech
Tay-Sachs disease	Seizures, paralysis; fatal neurological disease of early childhood
Thalassemias	Anemias

[a]These are susceptibility tests that provide only an estimated risk for developing the disorder.

(*Source:* Human Genome Project, 2006, http://www.oml.gov/scl/techresources/Human_Genome/medicine/genetest.shtml.)

Genetic testing is clearly a complicated issue. In assessing an individual's susceptibility to a disorder, it rarely provides a simple yes or no answer; instead, it typically presents a range of probabilities. In some cases, the likelihood of actually becoming ill depends on the type of environmental stressors to which a person is exposed. Personal differences also affect a given person's susceptibility to a disorder (Bonke et al., 2005; Bloss, Schork, & Topol, 2011).

As our understanding of genetics continues to grow, researchers and medical practitioners have moved beyond testing and counseling to actively working to change flawed genes. The possibilities for genetic intervention and manipulation increasingly border on what once was science fiction.

FROM A
HEALTH-CARE PROVIDER'S
PERSPECTIVE:

What are some ethical and philosophical questions that surround the issue of genetic counseling? Might it sometimes be unwise to know ahead of time about possible genetically-linked disorders that might afflict your child or yourself?

Review, Check, and Apply

Review

1. In humans, the male sex cell (the sperm) and the female sex cell (the ovum) provide the developing baby with 23 chromosomes each.

2. A genotype is the underlying but invisible combination of genetic material present in an organism; a phenotype is the visible trait, the expression of the genotype.

3. The field of behavioral genetics, a combination psychology and genetics, studies the effects of genetics on behavior.

4. Several inherited and genetic disorders are due to damaged or mutated genes.

5. Genetic counselors use a variety of data and techniques to advise future parents of possible future risks to their unborn children.

Check

1. The human genetic code, transmitted at the moment of conception and stored in our genes, is composed of specific sequences of _____.

2. _____ twins are genetically identical and come from the same zygote.

3. The _____ pair of chromosomes determines the sex of a child.

4. A _____ is the underlying combination of genetic material present (but outwardly invisible) in an organism, while a phenotype is the observable trait.

5. Mapping the gene sequence has provided support for the field of _____ genetics, which studies the effects of heredity on psychological characteristics.

Apply

1. How can the study of identical twins who were separated at birth help researchers determine the effects of genetic and environmental factors on human development?

2. If genetic testing revealed that you had what is almost always a fatal disease, what use would the information have for you? Would it change your career goals? Chosen partner? Choice of college?

To see more review questions, log on to MyPsychLab.

ANSWERS: 1. DNA 2. Monozygotic 3. 23rd 4. genotype 5. behavioral

THE INTERACTION OF HEREDITY AND ENVIRONMENT

LO 3-4 Which human characteristics are significantly influenced by heredity?

LO 3-5 How is intelligence determined?

LO 3-6 Can genes influence the environment?

Like many other parents, Jared's mother, Leesha and his father, Jamal, tried to figure out which one of them their new baby resembled the most. He seemed to have Leesha's big, wide eyes, and Jamal's generous smile. As he grew, Jared grew to resemble his mother and father even more. His hair grew in with a hairline just like Leesha's, and his teeth, when they came, made his smile resemble Jamal's even more. He also seemed to act like his parents. For example, he was a charming little baby, always ready to smile at people who visited the house—just like his friendly, jovial dad. He seemed to sleep like his mom, which was lucky because Jamal was an extremely light sleeper who could do with as little as four hours a night, whereas Leesha liked a regular 7 or 8 hours.

Were Jared's ready smile and regular sleeping habits something he just luckily inherited from his parents? Or did Jamal and Leesha provide a happy and stable home that encouraged these welcome traits? What causes our behavior? Nature or nurture? Is behavior produced by inherited, genetic influences, or is it triggered by factors in the environment?

The simple answer is: There is no simple answer.

The Role of the Environment in Determining the Expression of Genes: From Genotypes to Phenotypes

As developmental research accumulates, it is becoming increasingly clear that to view behavior as due to *either* genetic *or* environmental factors is inappropriate. A given behavior is not caused just by genetic factors; nor is it caused solely by environmental forces. Instead, as we first discussed in Chapter 1, the behavior is the product of some combination of the two.

For instance, consider **temperament,** patterns of arousal and emotionality that represent consistent and enduring characteristics in an individual. Suppose we found—as increasing evidence suggests is the case—that a small percentage of children are born with temperaments that produce an unusual degree of physiological reactivity. Having a tendency to shrink from anything unusual, such infants react to novel stimuli with a rapid increase in heartbeat and unusual excitability of the limbic system of the brain. Such heightened reactivity to stimuli at the start of life, which seems to be linked to inherited factors, is also likely to cause children, by the time they are 4 or 5 years old, to be considered shy by their parents and teachers. But not always: Some of them behave indistinguishably from their peers at the same age (Kagan & Snidman, 1991; McCrae et al., 2000; De Pauw & Mervielde, 2011).

What makes the difference? The answer seems to be the environment in which the children are raised. Children whose parents encourage them to be outgoing by arranging new opportunities for them may overcome their shyness. In contrast, children raised in a stressful environment marked by marital discord or a prolonged illness may be more likely to retain their shyness later in life. Jared, described earlier, may have been born with an easy temperament, which was easily reinforced by his caring parents (Propper & Moore, 2006; Bridgett et al., 2009; Grady, Karraker, & Metzger, 2011).

Interaction of Factors. Such findings illustrate that many traits reflect **multifactorial transmission,** meaning that they are determined by a combination of both genetic and environmental factors. In multifactorial transmission, a genotype provides a particular range

temperament Patterns of arousal and emotionality that represent consistent and enduring characteristics in an individual

multifactorial transmission The determination of traits by a combination of both genetic and environmental factors in which a genotype provides a range within which a phenotype may be expressed

Nature				Nurture
Intelligence is provided entirely by genetic factors; environment plays no role. Even a highly enriched environment and excellent education make no difference.	Although largely inherited, intelligence is affected by an extremely enriched or deprived environment.	Intelligence is affected both by a person's genetic endowment and environment. A person genetically predisposed to low intelligence may perform better if raised in an enriched environment or worse in a deprived environment. Similarly, a person genetically predisposed to higher intelligence may perform worse in a deprived environment or better in an enriched environment.	Although intelligence is largely a result of environment, genetic abnormalities may produce mental retardation.	Intelligence depends entirely on the environment. Genetics plays no role in determining intellectual success.

Possible Causes

FIGURE 3-8 Possible Causes of Intelligence

Intelligence may be explained by a range of differing possible sources, spanning the nature–nurture continuum. Which of these explanations do you find most convincing, given the evidence discussed in the chapter?

within which a phenotype may achieve expression. For instance, people with a genotype that permits them to gain weight easily may never be slim, no matter how much they diet. They may be *relatively* slim, given their genetic heritage, but they may never be able to get beyond a certain degree of thinness. In many cases, then, it is the environment that determines the way in which a particular genotype will be expressed as a phenotype (Uher, 2011).

On the other hand, certain genotypes are relatively unaffected by environmental factors. In such cases, development follows a preordained pattern, relatively independent of the specific environment in which a person is raised. For instance, research on pregnant women who were severely malnourished during famines caused by World War II found that their children were, on average, unaffected physically or intellectually as adults (Stein et al., 1975). Similarly, no matter how much health food people eat, they are not going to grow beyond certain genetically imposed limitations in height. Little Jared's hairline was probably affected very little by any actions on the part of his parents.

Ultimately, of course, it is the unique interaction of inherited and environmental factors that determines people's patterns of development.

The more appropriate question, then, is *how much* of the behavior is caused by genetic factors, and *how much* by environmental factors? (See, for example the range of possibilities for the determinants of intelligence, illustrated in Figure 3-8.) At one extreme is the idea that opportunities in the environment are solely responsible for intelligence; on the other, that intelligence is purely genetic—you either have it or you don't. Considering such extremes seems to point us toward the middle ground—that intelligence is the result of some combination of natural mental ability and environmental opportunity.

Studying Development: How Much Is Nature? How Much Is Nurture?

Developmental researchers use several strategies to try to resolve the question of the degree to which traits, characteristics, and behavior are produced by genetic or environmental factors. Their studies involve both nonhuman species and humans.

"The title of my science project is 'My Little Brother: Nature or Nurture.'"

Nonhuman Animal Studies: Controlling Both Genetics and Environment. It is relatively simple to develop breeds of animals that are genetically similar to one another in terms of specific traits. The people who raise Butterball turkeys for Thanksgiving do it all the time, producing turkeys that grow especially rapidly so that they can be brought to market inexpensively. Similarly, strains of laboratory animals can be bred to share similar genetic backgrounds.

By observing animals with similar genetic backgrounds in different environments, scientists can determine, with reasonable precision, the effects of specific kinds of environmental stimulation. For example, animals can be raised in unusually stimulating environments, with lots of items to climb over or through, or they can be raised in relatively barren environments, to determine the results of living in such different settings. Conversely, researchers can examine groups of animals that have been bred to have significantly *different* genetic backgrounds on particular traits. Then, by exposing such animals to identical environments, they can determine the role that genetic background plays.

Of course, the drawback to using nonhumans as research subjects is that we can't be sure how well the findings we obtain can be generalized to people. Still, the opportunities that animal research offers are substantial.

Contrasting Relatedness and Behavior: Adoption, Twin, and Family Studies. Obviously, researchers can't control either the genetic backgrounds or the environments of humans in the way they can with nonhumans. However, nature conveniently has provided the potential to carry out various kinds of "natural experiments"—in the form of twins.

Recall that identical, monozygotic twins are also identical genetically. Because their inherited backgrounds are precisely the same, any variations in their behavior must be due entirely to environmental factors.

It would be rather simple for researchers to make use of identical twins to draw unequivocal conclusions about the roles of nature and nurture. For instance, by separating identical twins at birth and placing them in totally different environments, researchers could assess the impact of environment unambiguously. Of course, ethical considerations make this impossible. What researchers can—and do—study, however, are cases in which identical twins have been put up for adoption at birth and are raised in substantially different environments. Such instances allow us to draw fairly confident conclusions about the relative contributions of genetics and environment (Bailey et al., 2000; Richardson & Norgate, 2007; Agrawal & Lynskey, 2008).

The data from such studies of identical twins raised in different environments are not always without bias. Adoption agencies typically take the characteristics (and wishes) of birth mothers into account when they place babies in adoptive homes. For instance, children tend to be placed with families of the same race and religion. Consequently, even when monozygotic twins are placed in different adoptive homes, there are often similarities between the two home environments. As a result, researchers can't always be certain that differences in behavior are due to differences in the environment.

Studies of nonidentical, dizygotic twins also present opportunities to learn about the relative contributions of nature and nurture. Recall that dizygotic twins are genetically no more similar than siblings in a family born at different times. By comparing behavior within pairs of dizygotic twins with that of pairs of monozygotic twins (who are genetically identical) researchers can determine whether monozygotic twins are more similar on a particular trait, on average, than dizygotic twins. If so, they can assume that genetics plays an important role in determining the expression of that trait.

Still another approach is to study people who are totally unrelated to one another and who therefore have dissimilar genetic backgrounds, but who share an environmental background. For instance, a family that adopts, at the same time, two very young unrelated children probably will provide them with quite similar environments throughout their childhood. In this case, similarities in the children's characteristics and behavior can be attributed with some confidence to environmental influences (Segal, 2000).

Finally, developmental researchers have examined groups of people in light of their degree of genetic similarity. For instance, if we find a high association on a particular trait between biological parents and their children, but a weaker association between adoptive parents and their children, we have evidence for the importance of genetics in determining the expression of that trait. On the other hand, if there is a stronger association on a trait between adoptive parents and their children than between biological parents and their children, we have evidence for the importance of the environment in determining that trait. If a particular trait tends to occur at similar levels among genetically similar individuals, but occurs at different levels among genetically more distant individuals, signs point to the fact that genetics plays an important role in the development of that trait (Buss, 2011; Ronald, 2011).

Developmental researchers have used all these approaches, and more, to study the relative impact of genetic and environmental factors. What have they found?

Before turning to specific findings, here's the general conclusion resulting from decades of research. Virtually all traits, characteristics, and behaviors are the joint result of the combination and interaction of nature and nurture. Genetic and environmental factors work in tandem, each affecting and being affected by the other, creating the unique individual that each of us is and will become (Robinson, 2004; Waterland & Jirtle, 2004).

Some traits—such as curly hair—have a clear genetic component.

Physical Traits: Family Resemblances

When patients entered the examining room of Dr. Cyril Marcus, they didn't realize that sometimes they were actually being treated by his identical twin brother, Dr. Stewart Marcus. So similar in appearance and manner were the twins that even long-time patients were fooled by this admittedly unethical behavior, which occurred in a bizarre case made famous in the film *Dead Ringers.*

Monozygotic twins are merely the most extreme example of the fact that the more genetically similar two people are, the more likely they are to share physical characteristics. Tall parents tend to have tall children, and short ones tend to have short children. Obesity, which is defined as being more than 20% above the average weight for a given height, also has a strong genetic component. For example, in one study, pairs of identical twins were put on diets that contained an extra 1,000 calories a day—and ordered not to exercise. Over a 3-month period, the twins gained almost identical amounts of weight. Moreover, different pairs of twins varied substantially in how much weight they gained, with some pairs gaining almost three times as much weight as other pairs (Bouchard et al., 1990).

Other, less obvious physical characteristics also show strong genetic influences. For instance, blood pressure, respiration rates, and even the age at which life ends are more similar in closely related individuals than in those who are less genetically alike (Melzer, Hurst, & Frayling, 2007).

Intelligence: More Research, More Controversy

No other issue involving the relative influence of heredity and environment has generated more research than the topic of intelligence. Why? The main reason is that intelligence, generally measured in terms of an IQ score, is a central human characteristic that differentiates humans from other species. In addition, intelligence is strongly related to success in scholastic endeavors and, somewhat less strongly, to other types of achievement.

Genetics plays a significant role in intelligence. In studies of both overall and general intelligence and of specific subcomponents of intelligence (such as spatial skills, verbal skills, and memory) as can be seen in Figure 3-9 on page 74, the closer the genetic link between two individuals, the greater the correspondence of their overall IQ scores.

Not only is genetics an important influence on intelligence, but also the impact increases with age. For instance, as fraternal (i.e., dizygotic) twins move from infancy to adolescence,

FIGURE 3-9 Genetics and IQ

The closer the genetic link between two individuals, the greater the correspondence between their IQ scores. Why do you think there is a sex difference in the fraternal twins' figures? Might there be other sex differences in other sets of twins or siblings, not shown on this chart?

(*Source:* Based on Bouchard & McGue, 1981)

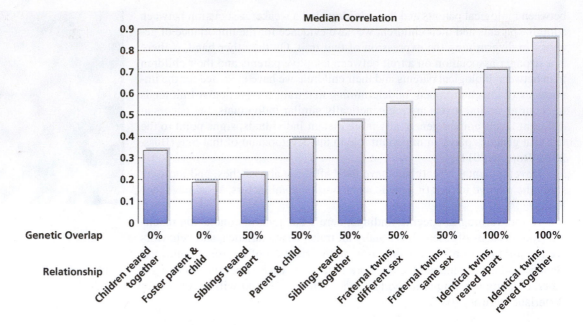

their IQ scores become less similar. In contrast, the IQ scores of identical (monozygotic) twins become increasingly similar over the course of time. These opposite patterns suggest the intensifying influence of inherited factors with increasing age (Brody, 1993; van Soelen et al., 2011).

Although it is clear that heredity plays an important role in intelligence, investigators are much more divided on the question of the degree to which it is inherited. Perhaps the most extreme view is held by psychologist Arthur Jensen (2003), who argued that as much as 80% of intelligence is a result of heredity. Others have suggested more modest figures, ranging from 50% to 70%. It is critical to keep in mind that such figures are averages across large groups of people, and any particular individual's degree of inheritance cannot be predicted from these averages (e.g., Herrnstein & Murray, 1994; Devlin, Daniels, & Roeder, 1997).

It is important to keep in mind that although heredity clearly plays an important role in intelligence, environmental factors such as exposure to books, good educational experiences, and intelligent peers are profoundly influential. Even those like Jensen who make the most extreme estimates of the role of genetics still allow for environmental factors to play a significant role. In fact, in terms of public policy, environmental influences are the focus of efforts geared toward maximizing people's intellectual success. Instead, we should be asking what can be done to maximize the intellectual development of each individual (Scarr & Carter-Saltzman, 1982; Mandelman & Grigorenko, 2011).

**FROM AN
EDUCATOR'S
PERSPECTIVE:**

Some people have used the proven genetic basis of intelligence to argue against strenuous educational efforts on behalf of individuals with below-average IQs. Does this viewpoint make sense based on what you have learned about heredity and environment? Why or why not?

Genetic and Environmental Influences on Personality: Born to Be Outgoing?

Do we inherit our personality?

At least in part. There's increasing research evidence suggesting that some of our most basic personality traits have genetic roots. For example, two of the key "Big Five" personality traits, neuroticism and extroversion, have been linked to genetic factors. *Neuroticism,* as used by personality researchers, is the degree of emotional stability an individual characteristically displays. *Extroversion* is the degree to which a person seeks to be with others, to behave in an outgoing manner, and generally to be sociable. For instance, Jared, the baby described earlier in this chapter, may have inherited a tendency to be outgoing from his extroverted father, Jamal (Zuckerman, 2003; Horwitz, Luong, & Charles, 2008; Ciani & Capiluppi, 2011).

How do we know which personality traits reflect genetics? Some evidence comes from direct examination of genes themselves. For instance, it appears that a specific gene is very influential in determining risk-taking behavior. This novelty-seeking gene affects the production of the brain chemical dopamine, making some people more prone than others to

Social potency	61%

A person high in this trait is masterful, a forceful leader.who likes to be the center of attention.

Traditionalism	60%

Follows rules and authority, endorses high moral standards and strict discipline.

Stress reaction	55%

Feels vulnerable and sensitive and is given to worries and is easily upset.

Absorption	55%

Has a vivid imagination readily captured by rich experience; relinquishes sense of reality.

Alienation	55%

Feels mistreated and used, that "the world is out to get me."

Well-being	54%

Has a cheerful disposition, feels confident and optimistic.

Harm avoidance	50%

Shuns the excitement of risk and danger, prefers the safe route even if it is tedious.

Aggression	48%

Is physically aggressive and vindictive, has taste for violence and is "out to get the world."

Achievement	46%

Works hard, strives for mastery, and puts work and accomplishment ahead of other things.

Control	43%

Is cautious and plodding, rational and sensible, likes carefully planned events.

Social closeness	33%

Prefers emotional intimacy and close ties, turns to others for comfort and help.

FIGURE 3-10 Inheriting Traits

These traits are among the personality factors that are related most closely to genetic factors. The higher the percentage, the greater the degree to which the trait reflects the influence of heredity. Do these figures mean that "leaders are born, not made"? Why or why not?

(*Source:* Adapted from Tellegen et al., 1988)

seek out novel situations and to take risks (Gillespie et al., 2003; Serretti et al., 2007; Ray et al., 2009).

Other evidence for the role of genetics in the determination of personality traits comes from studies of twins. For instance, in one major study, researchers looked at the personality traits of hundreds of pairs of twins. Because a good number of the twins were genetically identical but had been raised apart, it was possible to determine with some confidence the influence of genetic factors (Tellegen et al., 1988). The researchers found that certain traits reflected the contribution of genetics considerably more than others. As you can see in Figure 3-10, social potency (the tendency to be a masterful, forceful leader who enjoys being the center of attention) and traditionalism (strict endorsement of rules and authority) are strongly associated with genetic factors (Harris, Vernon, & Jang, 2007).

Even less basic personality traits are linked to genetics. For example, political attitudes, religious interests and values, and even attitudes toward human sexuality have genetic components (Koenig et al., 2005; Bradshaw & Ellison, 2008; Kandler et al., 2011).

Clearly, genetic factors play a role in determining personality. At the same time, the environment in which a child is raised also affects personality development. For example, some parents encourage high activity levels, seeing activity as a manifestation of independence and intelligence. Other parents may encourage lower levels of activity on the part of their children, feeling that more passive children will get along better in society. Some of these parental attitudes are culturally determined; parents in the United States may encourage higher activity levels, whereas parents in Asian cultures may encourage greater passivity. In both cases, children's personalities will be shaped in part by their parents' attitudes (Cauce, 2008; Munafò & Flint, 2011).

Because both genetic and environmental factors have consequences for a child's personality, personality development is a perfect example of a central fact of child development: the interplay between nature and nurture. Furthermore, the way in which nature and nurture interact can be reflected not only in the behavior of individuals but also in the very foundations of a culture, as we see next.

"The good news is that you will have a healthy baby girl. The bad news is that she is a congenital liar."

DEVELOPMENTAL DIVERSITY AND YOUR LIFE

Cultural Differences in Physical Arousal: Might a Culture's Philosophical Outlook Be Determined by Genetics?

The Buddhist philosophy, an inherent part of many Asian cultures, emphasizes harmony and peacefulness. In contrast, some traditional Western philosophies, such as those of Martin Luther and John Calvin, accentuate the importance of controlling the anxiety, fear, and guilt that they assume to be basic parts of the human condition.

Could such philosophical approaches reflect, in part, genetic factors? That is the controversial suggestion made by developmental psychologist Jerome Kagan and his colleagues. They speculate that the underlying temperament of a given society, determined genetically, may predispose people in that society toward a particular philosophy (Kagan, Arcus, & Snidman, 1993; Kagan, 2003a, 2011).

Kagan bases his admittedly speculative suggestion on well-confirmed findings that show clear differences in temperament between Caucasian and Asian children. For instance, one study that compared 4-month-old infants in China, Ireland, and the United States found several relevant differences. In comparison to the Caucasian American babies and the Irish babies, the Chinese babies had significantly lower motor activity, irritability, and vocalization (see Table 3-4).

Kagan suggests that the Chinese, who enter the world temperamentally calmer, may find Buddhist philosophical notions of serenity more in tune with their natural inclinations. In contrast, Westerners, who are emotionally more volatile and tense, and who report higher levels of guilt, are more likely to be attracted to philosophies that articulate the necessity of controlling the unpleasant feelings that they are more apt to encounter in their everyday experience (Kagan et al., 1994; Kagan, 2003a).

It is important to note that this does not mean that one philosophical approach is necessarily better or worse than the other. Nor does it mean that either of the temperaments from which the philosophies are thought to spring is superior or inferior to the other. Similarly, we must keep in mind that any single individual within a culture can be more or less temperamentally volatile and that the range of temperaments found even within a particular culture is vast. Finally, as we noted in our initial discussion of temperament, environmental conditions can have a significant effect on the portion of a person's temperament that is not genetically determined. But what Kagan and his colleagues' speculation does attempt to address is the back-and-forth relationship between culture and temperament. As religion may help mold temperament, so may temperament make certain religious ideals more attractive.

The notion that the very basis of culture—its philosophical traditions—may be affected by genetic factors is intriguing. More research is necessary to determine just how the unique interaction of heredity and environment within a given culture may produce a framework for viewing and understanding the world. ■

TABLE 3-4 Mean Behavioral Scores for Caucasian American, Irish, and Chinese 4-Month-Old Infants

Behavior	American	Irish	Chinese
Motor activity score	48.6	36.7	11.2
Crying (in seconds)	7.0	2.9	1.1
Fretting (% trials)	10.0	6.0	1.9
Vocalizing (% trials)	31.4	31.1	8.1
Smiling (% trials)	4.1	2.6	3.6

(*Source:* Kagan, Arcus, & Snidman, 1993.)

Psychological Disorders: The Role of Genetics and Environment

Dana Horowitz started hearing voices when she was waiting tables one summer during high school. "A customer was giving me his order and I suddenly heard him whispering, 'I'm going to kill you,'" she remembers. Coworkers recall her screaming and attacking the customer for "no reason." Several described her as "possessed."

In a sense, she was possessed: possessed with schizophrenia, one of the severest types of psychological disorder. Normal and happy through childhood, Horowitz's world took a tumble during adolescence as she increasingly lost her hold on reality. For the next 2 decades, she would be in and out of institutions, struggling to ward off the ravages of the disorder.

What was the cause of Horowitz's mental disorder? Increasing evidence suggests that schizophrenia is brought about by genetic factors. The disorder runs in families, with some families showing an unusually high incidence. Moreover, the closer the genetic links between someone with schizophrenia and another family member, the more likely it is that the other person will also develop schizophrenia. For instance, a monozygotic twin has close to a 50% risk of developing schizophrenia when the other twin develops the disorder (see Figure 3-11). On the other hand, a niece or nephew of a person with schizophrenia has less than a 5% chance of developing the disorder (Hanson & Gottesman, 2005; E Owens et al., 2011; Mitchell & Porteous, 2011).

However, these data also illustrate that genetics alone does not influence the development of the disorder. If genetics were the sole cause, the risk for an identical twin would be 100%. Consequently, other factors account for the disorder, ranging from structural abnormalities in the brain to a biochemical imbalance (e.g., Lyons, Bar, & Kremen, 2002; Hietala, Cannon, & van Erp, 2003; Howes & Kapur, 2009).

It also seems that even if individuals harbor a genetic predisposition toward schizophrenia, they are not destined to develop the disorder. Instead, they may inherit an unusual sensitivity to stress in the environment. If stress is low, schizophrenia will not occur. But if stress is sufficiently strong, it will lead to schizophrenia. On the other hand, for someone with a strong genetic predisposition toward the disorder, even relatively weak environmental stressors may lead to schizophrenia (Norman & Malla, 2001; Mittal, Ellman, & Cannon, 2008).

Several other psychological disorders have been shown to be related, at least in part, to genetic factors. For instance, major depression, alcoholism, autism, and attention-deficit hyperactivity disorder have significant inherited components (Monastra, 2008; Burbach & van der Zwaag, 2009; Hirvonen & Hietala, 2011).

The example of schizophrenia and other genetically related psychological disorders also illustrates a fundamental principle regarding the relationship between heredity and environment, one that underlies much of our previous discussion. Specifically, the role of genetics is often to produce a tendency toward a future course of development. When and whether a certain behavioral characteristic will actually be displayed depends on the nature of the environment. Thus, although a predisposition for schizophrenia may be present at birth, typically people do not show the disorder until adolescence—if at all.

Similarly, certain other kinds of traits are more likely to be displayed as the influence of parents and other socializing factors declines. For example, adopted children may, early in their lives, display traits that are relatively similar to their adoptive parents' traits, given the overwhelming influence of the environment on young children. As they get older and their parents' day-to-day influence declines, genetically influenced

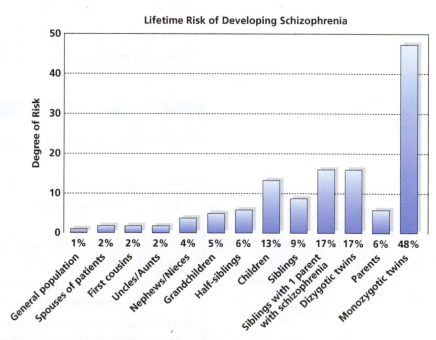

FIGURE 3-11 The Genetics of Schizophrenia

The psychological disorder of schizophrenia has clear genetic components. The closer the genetic links between someone with schizophrenia and another family member, the more likely it is that the other person will also develop schizophrenia.

(*Source:* Based on Gottesman, 1991)

Developmental psychologist Sandra Scarr argues that children's genetic characteristics actively influence and shape their environment.

traits may begin to manifest themselves as unseen genetic factors begin to play a greater role (Arseneault et al., 2003; Poulton & Caspi, 2005).

Can Genes Influence the Environment?

According to developmental psychologist Sandra Scarr (1998), the genetic endowment provided to children by their parents not only determines their genetic characteristics but also actively influences their environment. Scarr suggests three ways a child's genetic predisposition might influence his or her environment.

Children tend to actively focus on those aspects of their environment that are most connected with their genetically determined abilities. For example, an active, more aggressive child will gravitate toward sports, while a more reserved child will be more engaged by academics or solitary pursuits such as computer games or drawing. Children also pay less attention to those aspects of the environment that are less compatible with their genetic endowment. For instance, two girls may be reading the same school bulletin board. One may notice the sign advertising tryouts for Little League baseball, whereas her less coordinated but more musically endowed friend might be more apt to spot the notice recruiting students for an after-school chorus. In each case, the child is attending to those aspects of the environment in which her genetically determined abilities can flourish.

In some cases, the gene–environment influence is more passive and less direct. For example, a particularly sports-oriented parent, who has genes that promote good physical coordination, may provide many opportunities for a child to play sports.

Finally, the genetically driven temperament of a child may *evoke* certain environmental influences. For instance, an infant's demanding behavior may cause parents to be more attentive to the infant's needs than they would be if the infant were less demanding. Or, for instance, a child who is genetically inclined to be well coordinated may play ball with anything in the house so often that her parents notice. They may then decide that she should have some sports equipment.

In sum, determining whether behavior is primarily attributable to nature or nurture is a bit like shooting at a moving target. Not only are behaviors and traits a joint outcome of genetic and environmental factors, but also the relative influence of genes and environment for specific characteristics shifts over the course of people's lives. Although the pool of genes we inherit at birth sets the stage for our future development, the constantly shifting scenery and the other characters in our lives determine just how our development eventually plays out. The environment both influences our experiences and is molded by the choices we are temperamentally inclined to make.

Review, Check, and Apply

Review

1. Human characteristics and behavior are a joint outcome of genetic and environmental factors.

2. Genetic influences have been identified in physical characteristics, intelligence, and personality traits and behaviors.

3. Heredity plays a significant role in intelligence, but environmental factors such as exposure to books at home and encouragement of learning are also deeply important.

4. There is some speculation that entire cultures may be predisposed genetically toward certain types of philosophical viewpoints and attitudes, and that these predispositions affect individuals raised in those cultures.

5. Researchers are learning which psychological disorders are associated with genetic factors, and how environmental factors can strengthen or weaken genetic tendencies toward those disorders.

Check

1. If researchers find that pairs of monozygotic (identical) twins are, on average, more similar on a particular trait than dizygotic (nonidentical) twins, a probable conclusion is that _____ plays an important role in determining expression of that trait.

2. Two of the "Big Five" personality traits, neuroticism and _____, have been linked to genetic factors.

3. One _____ twin has nearly a 50% chance of developing schizophrenia when the other twin develops the disorder.

4. While many of our temperamental preferences have a genetic component, an individual's constantly shifting _____ both influences our experiences and is influenced by the choices we are genetically inclined to make.

Apply

1. How might an environment different from the one you experienced have affected the development of personality characteristics that you believe you inherited from one or both of your parents?

2. Can a person "born with" certain personality traits hope to change those traits intentionally? Can you train yourself to be less introverted? Less alienated? Less aggressive? How?

To see more review questions, log on to MyPsychLab.

ANSWERS: 1. genetics 2. extroversion 3. monozygotic (or identical) 4. environment

---

MODULE 3.3

PRENATAL GROWTH AND CHANGE

LO 3-7 What happens during the prenatal stages of development?

LO 3-8 What are the threats to the fetal environment, and what can be done about them?

LO 3-9 How do fathers affect the prenatal environment?

> *Robert accompanied Lisa to her first appointment with the midwife. The midwife checked the results of tests done to confirm the couple's own positive home pregnancy test. "Yep, you're going to have a baby," she confirmed, speaking to Lisa. "You'll need to set up monthly visits for the next 6 months, then more frequently as your due date approaches. You can get this prescription for prenatal vitamins filled at any pharmacy, and here are some guidelines about diet and exercise. You don't smoke, do you? That's good." Then she turned to Robert. "How about you? Do you smoke?" After giving lots of instructions and advice, she left the couple feeling slightly dazed, but ready to do whatever they could to have a healthy baby.*

From the moment of conception, development proceeds relentlessly. As we've seen, many aspects are guided by the complex set of genetic guidelines inherited from the parents. Of course, prenatal growth, like all development, is also influenced from the start by environmental factors. As we see later, both parents, like Lisa and Robert, can take part in providing a good prenatal environment.

FIGURE 3-12 Anatomy of the Female Reproductive Organs

The basic anatomy of the female reproductive organs is illustrated in this cutaway view.

(*Source:* Based on Moore & Persaud, 2003)

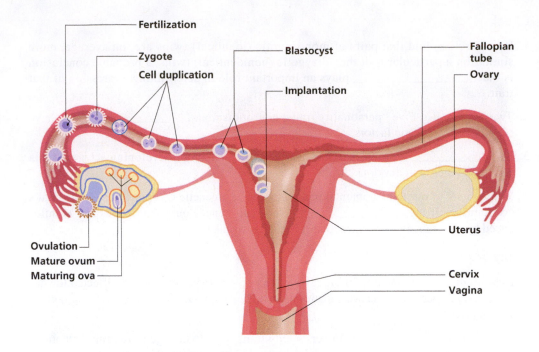

Fertilization: The Moment of Conception

When most of us think about the facts of life, we tend to focus on the events that cause a male's sperm cells to begin their journey toward a female's ovum. Yet the act of sex that brings about the potential for conception is both the consequence and the start of a long string of events that precede and follow **fertilization,** or conception: the joining of sperm and ovum to create the single-celled zygote from which each of us began our lives.

Both the male's sperm and the female's ovum come with a history of their own. Females are born with around 400,000 ova located in the two ovaries (see Figure 3-12 for the basic anatomy of the female reproductive organs). However, the ova do not mature until the female reaches puberty. From that point until she reaches menopause, the female will ovulate about every 28 days. During ovulation, an egg is released from one of the ovaries and pushed by minute hair cells through the fallopian tube toward the uterus. If the ovum meets a sperm in the fallopian tube, fertilization takes place (Aitken, 1995).

Sperm, which look a little like microscopic tadpoles, have a shorter life span. They are created by the testicles at a rapid rate: An adult male typically produces several hundred million sperm a day. Consequently, the sperm ejaculated during sexual intercourse are of considerably more recent origin than the ovum to which they are heading.

Explore *Female Reproductive Organs* in **MyPsychLab.**

When sperm enter the vagina, they begin a winding journey that takes them through the cervix, the opening into the uterus, and into the fallopian tube, where fertilization may take place. However, only a tiny fraction of the 300 million cells that are typically ejaculated during sexual intercourse ultimately survive the arduous journey. That's usually okay, though: It takes only one sperm to fertilize an ovum, and each sperm and ovum contains all the genetic data necessary to produce a new human.

The Stages of the Prenatal Period: The Onset of Development

The prenatal period consists of three phases: germinal, embryonic, and fetal. They are summarized in Table 3-5.

fertilization   The process by which a sperm and an ovum—the male and female gametes, respectively—join to form a single new cell

germinal stage   The first—and shortest—stage of the prenatal period, which takes place during the first 2 weeks following conception

The Germinal Stage: Fertilization to 2 Weeks.   In the **germinal stage,** the first—and shortest—stage of the prenatal period, the zygote begins to divide and grow in complexity during the first 2 weeks following conception. During the germinal stage, the fertilized

TABLE 3-5 Stages of the Prenatal Period

Germinal (Fertilization–2 Weeks)	Embryonic (2 Weeks–8 Weeks)	Fetal (8 Weeks–Birth)
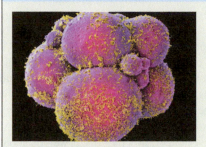	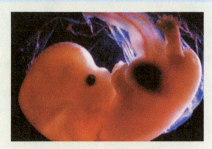	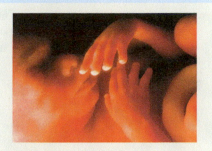
The germinal stage is the first and shortest, characterized by methodical cell division and the attachment of the organism to the wall of the uterus. Three days after fertilization, the zygote consists of 32 cells, a number that doubles by the next day. Within a week, the zygote multiplies to 100 to 150 cells. The cells become specialized, with some forming a protective layer around the zygote.	The zygote is now designated an embryo. The embryo develops three layers, which ultimately form a different set of structures as development proceeds. The layers are as follows: Ectoderm: Skin, sense organs, brain, spinal cord; Endoderm: Digestive system, liver, respiratory system; Mesoderm: Muscles, blood, circulatory system. At 8 weeks, the embryo is 1 inch long.	The fetal stage formally starts when the differentiation of the major organs has occurred. Now called a fetus, the individual grows rapidly as length increases 20 times. At 4 months, the fetus weighs an average of 4 ounces; at 7 months, 3 pounds; and at the time of birth, the average child weighs just over 7 pounds.

egg (now called a *blastocyst*) travels toward the *uterus,* where it becomes implanted in the uterus's wall, which is rich in nutrients. The germinal stage is characterized by methodical cell division, which gets off to a quick start: Three days after fertilization, the organism consists of some 32 cells, and by the next day the number doubles. Within a week, it is made up of 100 to 150 cells, and the number rises with increasing rapidity.

In addition to increasing in number, the cells of the organism become increasingly specialized. For instance, some cells form a protective layer around the mass of cells, whereas others begin to establish the rudiments of a placenta and umbilical cord. When fully developed, the **placenta** serves as a conduit between the mother and fetus, providing nourishment and oxygen via the *umbilical cord.* In addition, waste materials from the developing child are removed through the umbilical cord.

The Embryonic Stage: 2 Weeks to 8 Weeks. By the end of the germinal period—just 2 weeks after conception—the organism is firmly secured to the wall of the mother's uterus. At this point, the child is called an *embryo.* The **embryonic stage** is the period from 2 to 8 weeks following fertilization. One of the highlights of this stage is the development of the major organs and basic anatomy.

At the beginning of the embryonic stage, the developing child has three distinct layers, each of which will ultimately form a different set of structures as development proceeds. The outer layer of the embryo, the *ectoderm,* will form skin, hair, teeth, sense organs, and the brain and spinal cord. The *endoderm,* the inner layer, produces the digestive system, liver, pancreas, and respiratory system. Sandwiched between the ectoderm and endoderm is the *mesoderm,* from which the muscles, bones, blood and circulatory system are forged. Every part of the body is formed from these three layers.

If you were looking at an embryo at the end of the embryonic stage, you might be hard-pressed to identify it as human. Only an inch long, an 8-week-old embryo has what appear to be gills and a tail-like structure. On the other hand, a closer look reveals several familiar features. Rudimentary eyes, nose, lips, and even teeth can be recognized, and the embryo has stubby bulges that will form arms and legs.

The head and brain undergo rapid growth during the embryonic period. The head begins to represent a significant proportion of the embryo's size, encompassing about 50% of its total length. The growth of nerve cells, called *neurons,* is astonishing: As many as 100,000

placenta A conduit between the mother and fetus, providing nourishment and oxygen via the umbilical cord

embryonic stage The period from 2 to 8 weeks following fertilization during which significant growth occurs in the major organs and body systems

neurons are produced every minute during the second month of life! The nervous system begins to function around the 5th week, and weak brain waves begin to be produced as the nervous system starts to function (Nelson & Bosquet, 2000).

The Fetal Stage: 8 Weeks to Birth. It is not until the final period of prenatal development, the fetal stage, that the developing child becomes easily recognizable. The **fetal stage** starts at about 8 weeks after conception and continues until birth. The fetal stage formally starts when the differentiation of the major organs has occurred.

Now called a **fetus,** the developing child undergoes astoundingly rapid change during the fetal stage. For instance, it increases in length approximately 20 times, and its proportions change dramatically. At 2 months, approximately one half of the fetus is what will ultimately be its head; by 5 months, the head accounts for just over one-fourth of its total size (see Figure 3-13). The fetus also substantially increases in weight. At 4 months, the fetus weighs an average of about 4 ounces; at 7 months, it weighs about 3 pounds; and at the time of birth the average child weighs just over 7 pounds.

At the same time, the developing child is rapidly becoming more complex. Organs become more differentiated and start to work. By 3 months, for example, the fetus swallows and urinates. In addition, the interconnections between the different parts of the body become more complex and integrated. Arms develop hands; hands develop fingers; fingers develop nails.

As this is happening, the fetus makes itself known to the outside world. In the earliest stages of pregnancy, mothers may be unaware that they are, in fact, pregnant. As the fetus becomes increasingly active, however, most mothers certainly take notice. By 4 months, a mother can feel the movement of her child, and several months later others can feel the baby's kicks through the mother's skin. In addition to the kicks that alert its mother to its presence, the fetus can turn, do somersaults, cry, hiccup, clench its fist, open and close its eyes, and suck its thumb.

The brain becomes increasingly sophisticated during the fetal stage. The two symmetrical left and right halves of the brain, known as *hemispheres,* grow rapidly, and the interconnections between neurons become more complex. The neurons become coated with an insulating material called *myelin* which helps speed the transmission of messages from the brain to the rest of the body.

By the end of the fetal period, brain waves are produced that indicate the fetus passes through different stages of sleep and wakefulness. The fetus is also able to hear (and feel the vibrations of) sounds to which it is exposed. For instance, researchers Anthony DeCasper and Melanie Spence (1986) asked a group of pregnant mothers to read aloud the Dr. Seuss story *The Cat in the Hat* two times a day during the latter months of pregnancy. Three days after the babies were born, they appeared to recognize the story they had heard, responding more to it than to another story that had a different rhythm.

In weeks 8 to 24 following conception, hormones are released that lead to the increasing differentiation of male and female fetuses. For example, high levels of androgen are produced in males that affect the size of brain cells and the growth of neural connections, which, some scientists speculate, ultimately may lead to differences in male and female brain structure and even later variations in gender-related behavior (Knickmeyer & Baron-Cohen, 2006; Burton et al., 2009; Joel, 2011).

Just as no two adults are alike, no two fetuses are the same. Although development during the prenatal period follows the broad patterns outlined here, there are significant differences in the specific nature of individual fetuses' behavior. Some fetuses are exceedingly active, whereas others are more sedentary. (The more active fetuses will probably be more active after birth.) Some have relatively quick heart rates, whereas others' heart rates are slower, with the typical range varying between 120 and 160 beats per minute (DiPietro et al., 2002; Niederhofer, 2004; Tongsong et al., 2005).

Such differences in fetal behavior are due in part to genetic characteristics inherited at the moment of fertilization. Other kinds of differences, though, are brought about by the nature of the environment in which the child spends its first 9 months of life. As we will see, there are numerous ways in which the prenatal environment of infants affects their development—in good ways and bad.

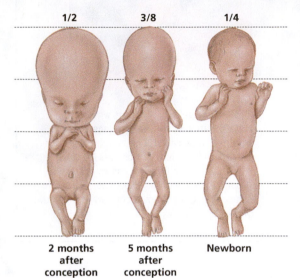

| 1/2 | 3/8 | 1/4 |

| 2 months after conception | 5 months after conception | Newborn |

FIGURE 3-13 Body Proportions

During the fetal period, the proportions of the body change dramatically. At 2 months, the head represents approximately half the fetus, but by the time of birth, it is one fourth of its total size.

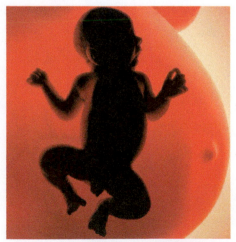

As with adults, there are broad differences in the nature of fetuses. Some are very active while others are more reserved, and these characteristics can continue after birth.

fetal stage The stage that begins at about 8 weeks after conception and continues until birth

fetus A developing child, from 8 weeks after conception until birth

Pregnancy Problems

For some couples, conception presents a major challenge. Let's consider some of the challenges—both physical and ethical—that relate to pregnancy.

Infertility. Some 15% of couples suffer from **infertility,** the inability to conceive after 12 to 18 months of trying to become pregnant. Infertility is positively correlated with age: The older the parents, the more likely infertility will occur; see Figure 3-14.

In men, infertility is typically a result of producing too few sperm. Use of illicit drugs or cigarettes and previous bouts of sexually transmitted diseases also increase infertility. For women, the most common cause of infertility is failure to release an egg through ovulation. This may occur because of a hormone imbalance, a damaged fallopian tube or uterus, stress, or abuse of alcohol or drugs (Kelly-Weeder & Cox, 2007; Wilkes et al., 2009; Peterson & Eifert, 2011).

Several treatments for infertility exist. Some difficulties can be corrected through the use of drugs or surgery. Another option may be **artificial insemination,** a procedure in which a man's sperm is placed directly into a woman's vagina by a physician. In some situations, the woman's husband provides the sperm, whereas in others the sperm come from an anonymous donor via a sperm bank.

In other cases, fertilization takes place outside of the mother's body. **In vitro fertilization (IVF)** is a procedure in which a woman's ova are removed from her ovaries, and a man's sperm are used to fertilize the ova in a laboratory. The fertilized egg is then implanted in a woman's uterus. Similarly, *gamete intrafallopian transfer (GIFT)* and *zygote intrafallopian transfer (ZIFT)* are procedures in which an egg and sperm or fertilized egg are implanted in a woman's fallopian tubes. In IVF, GIFT, and ZIFT, implantation is done either in the woman who provided the donor eggs or, in rarer instances, in a *surrogate mother,* a woman who agrees to carry the child to term. Surrogate mothers may also be used in cases in which the mother is unable to conceive; the surrogate mother is artificially inseminated by the biological father, and she agrees to give up rights to the infant (Frazier et al., 2004; Kolata, 2004).

In vitro fertilization is increasingly successful, with success rates of as high as 33% for younger women (but with lower rates for older women). It is also becoming more commonplace, with the procedure being used and publicized by women such as actresses Marcia Cross and Nicole Kidman. Worldwide, more than 3 million babies have been created through in vitro fertilization.

Furthermore, reproductive technologies are increasingly sophisticated, permitting parents to choose the sex of their baby. One technique is to separate sperm carrying the X and Y chromosome and later implanting the desired type into a woman's uterus. In another technique, eggs are removed from a woman and fertilized with sperm using in vitro fertilization. Three days after fertilization, the embryos are tested to determine their sex. If they are the desired gender, they are then implanted into the mother (Duenwald, 2003, 2004; Kalb, 2004).

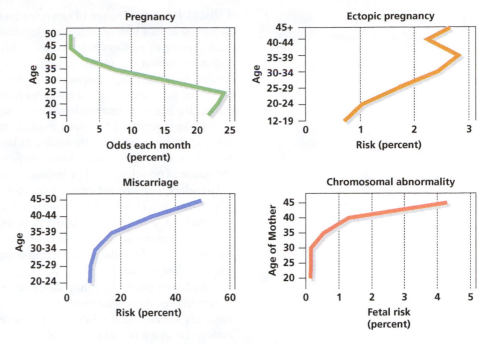

FIGURE 3-14 Older Women and Risks of Pregnancy

Not only does the rate of infertility increase as women get older, but also the risk of chromosomal abnormality.

(*Source:* Reproductive Medicine Associates of New Jersey, 2002)

"I'm their real child, and you're just a frozen embryo thingy they bought from some laboratory."

infertility   The inability to conceive after 12 to 18 months of trying to become pregnant

artificial insemination   A process of fertilization in which a man's sperm is placed directly into a woman's vagina by a physician

in vitro fertilization (IVF)   A procedure in which a woman's ova are removed from her ovaries, and a man's sperm are used to fertilize the ova in a laboratory

Ethical Issues. The use of surrogate mothers, in vitro fertilization, and sex selection techniques presents a web of ethical and legal issues, as well as many emotional concerns. In some cases, surrogate mothers have refused to give up the child after its birth, whereas in others the surrogate mother has sought to have a role in the child's life. In such cases, the rights of the mother, the father, the surrogate mother, and ultimately the baby are in conflict.

Even more troubling are concerns raised by sex selection techniques. Is it ethical to terminate the life of an embryo based on its sex? Do cultural pressures that may favor boys over girls make it permissible to seek medical intervention to produce male offspring? And—even more disturbing—if it is permissible to intervene in the reproductive process to obtain a favored sex, what about other characteristics determined by genetics that it may be possible in the future to preselect for? For instance, assuming the technology advances, would it be ethical to select for a favored eye or hair color, a certain level of intelligence, or a particular kind of personality? That's not feasible now, but it is not out the realm of possibility in the future (Bonnicksen, 2007; Mameli, 2007; Roberts, 2007).

For the moment, many of these ethical issues remain unresolved. But we can answer one question: How do children conceived using emerging reproductive technologies such as in vitro fertilization fare?

Research shows that they do quite well. In fact, some studies find that the quality of family life for those who have used such techniques may be superior to that in families with naturally conceived children. Furthermore, the later psychological adjustment of children conceived using in vitro fertilization and artificial insemination is no different from that of children conceived using natural techniques (Dipietro, Costigan, & Gurewitsch, 2005; Hjelmstedt, Widstrom, & Collins, 2006; Siegel, Dittrich, & Vollmann, 2008).

On the other hand, the increasing use of IVF techniques by older individuals (who might be quite elderly when their children reach adolescence) may change these positive findings. Because widespread use of IVF is only recent, we just don't know yet what will happen with aging parents (Colpin & Soenen, 2004).

Miscarriage and Abortion. A *miscarriage*—known as a spontaneous abortion—occurs when pregnancy ends before the developing child is able to survive outside the mother's womb. The embryo detaches from the wall of the uterus and is expelled.

Some 15% to 20% of all pregnancies end in miscarriage, usually in the first several months of pregnancy. (The term *stillbirth* is used to describe the death of a developing child 20 weeks or more after conception.) Many miscarriages occur so early that the mother is not even aware she was pregnant and may not even know she has suffered a miscarriage. Typically, miscarriages are attributable to some sort of genetic abnormality.

In *abortion*, a mother voluntarily chooses to terminate pregnancy. Involving a complex set of physical, psychological, legal, and ethical issues, abortion is a difficult choice for every woman. A task force of the American Psychological Association (APA), which looked at the aftereffects of abortion, found that, following an abortion, most women experienced a combination of relief over terminating an unwanted pregnancy and regret and guilt. However, in most cases, the negative psychological aftereffects did not last, except for a small proportion of women who already had serious emotional problems (APA Reproductive Choice Working Group, 2000).

Other research finds that abortion may be associated with an increased risk of future psychological problems. However, the findings are mixed, and there are significant individual differences in how women respond to the experience of abortion. What is clear is that in all cases, abortion is a difficult decision (Fergusson, Horwood, & Ridder, 2006).

The Prenatal Environment: Threats to Development

According to the Siriono people of South America, if a pregnant woman eats the meat of certain kinds of animals, she runs the risk of having a child who may act and look like those animals. According to opinions offered on daytime television talk, a pregnant mother should avoid getting angry in order to spare her child from entering the world with anger (Cole, 1992).

Such views are largely the stuff of folklore, although there is some evidence that a mother's anxiety during pregnancy may affect the sleeping patterns of the fetus prior to birth.

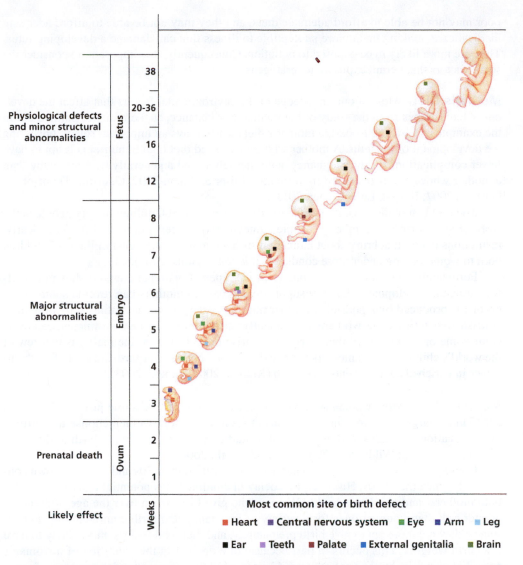

FIGURE 3-15 Teratogen Sensitivity

Depending on their state of development, some parts of the body vary in their sensitivity to teratogens.

(*Source:* Moore, 1974)

There are certain aspects of a mother's and father's behavior, both before and after conception, that can produce lifelong consequences for the child. Some consequences show up immediately, but half the possible problems aren't apparent before birth. Other problems, more insidious, may not appear until years after birth (Couzin, 2002; Glynn & Sandman, 2011).

Some of the most profound consequences are brought about by teratogenic agents. A **teratogen** is an environmental agent such as a drug, chemical, virus, or other factor that produces a birth defect. Although it is the job of the placenta to keep teratogens from reaching the fetus, the placenta is not entirely successful at this, and probably every fetus is exposed to some teratogens.

The timing and quantity of exposure to a teratogen are crucial. At some phases of prenatal development, a certain teratogen may have only a minimal impact. At other periods, however, the same teratogen may have profound consequences. Generally, teratogens have their largest effects during periods of especially rapid prenatal development. Sensitivity to specific teratogens is also related to racial and cultural background. For example, Native American fetuses are more susceptible to the effects of alcohol than those of European American descent (Kinney et al., 2003; Winger & Woods, 2004).

Furthermore, different organ systems are vulnerable to teratogens at different times during development. For example, the brain is most susceptible 15 to 25 days after conception, whereas the heart is most vulnerable 20 to 40 days following conception (see Figure 3-15; Pakjrt, 2004).

When considering the findings relating to specific teratogens, as we do next, we need to keep in mind the broader social and cultural context in which teratogen exposure occurs. For example, living in poverty increases the chances of exposure to teratogens. Mothers who are

teratogen A factor that produces a birth defect

poor may not be able to afford adequate diets, and they may not be able to afford adequate medical care, making them more susceptible to illness that can damage a developing fetus. They are more likely to be exposed to pollution. Consequently, it is important to consider the social factors that permit exposure to teratogens.

Mother's Diet. Most of our knowledge of the environmental factors that affect the developing fetus comes from the study of the mother. For instance, as the midwife pointed out in the example of Lisa and Robert, a mother's diet clearly plays an important role in bolstering the development of the fetus. A mother who eats a varied diet high in nutrients is apt to have fewer complications during pregnancy, an easier labor, and a generally healthier baby than a mother whose diet is restricted in nutrients (Kaiser & Allen, 2002; Guerrini, Thomson, & Gurling, 2007; Karp & Lutenbacher, 2011).

The problem of diet is of immense global concern, with 800 million hungry people in the world. Even worse, the number of people vulnerable to hunger is close to 1 *billion*. Clearly, restrictions in diet that bring about hunger on such a massive scale affect millions of children born to women living under those conditions (United Nations, 2004).

Fortunately, there are ways to counteract the types of maternal malnourishment that affect prenatal development. Dietary supplements given to mothers can reverse some of the problems produced by a poor diet. Furthermore, research shows that babies who were malnourished as fetuses, but who are subsequently raised in enriched environments, can overcome some of the effects of their early malnourishment. However, the reality is that few of the world's children whose mothers were malnourished *before* their birth are apt to find themselves in enriched environments after birth (Kramer, 2003; Olness, 2003).

Mother's Age. More women are giving birth later in life than was true just 2 or 3 decades ago. This is largely due to transformations in society, as more women choose to continue their education with advanced degrees and to start careers prior to giving birth to their first child (Gibbs, 2002; Wildberger, 2003; Bornstein et al., 2006).

Consequently, the number of women who give birth in their 30s and 40s has grown considerably since the 1970s. However, this delay in childbirth has potential consequences for both mothers' and children's health. Women who give birth when over the age of 30 are at greater risk than younger ones for a variety of pregnancy and birth complications. For instance, they are more apt to give birth prematurely, and their children are more likely to have low birth weights. This occurs in part because of a decline in the condition of a woman's eggs. For example, by the time they are 42 years old, 90% of a woman's eggs are no longer normal (Gibbs, 2002).

Older mothers are also considerably more likely to give birth to children with Down syndrome, a form of mental retardation. About 1 out of 100 babies born to mothers over 40 has Down syndrome; for mothers over 50, the incidence increases to 25%, or 1 in 4.

On the other hand, some research shows that older mothers are not automatically at risk for more pregnancy problems. For instance, one study found that when women in their 40s who had not experienced health difficulties were considered, they were no more likely than women in their 20s to have prenatal problems (Dildy et al., 1996).

The risks involved in pregnancy are greater not only for older mothers but also for atypically young women. Women who become pregnant during adolescence—and such pregnancies actually encompass 20% of all pregnancies—are more likely to have premature deliveries. Furthermore, the mortality rate of infants born to adolescent mothers is double that for mothers in their 20s (Kirchengast & Hartmann, 2003; Ryan et al., 2011).

Mother's Prenatal Support. Keep in mind, though, that the higher mortality rate for babies of adolescent mothers reflects more than just physiological problems related to the mothers' young age. Young mothers often face adverse social and economic factors that can affect infant health. Many teenage mothers do not have enough money or social support, a situation that prevents them from getting good prenatal care and parenting support after the baby is born. Poverty or social circumstances, such as a lack of parental involvement or supervision, may even have set the stage for the adolescent to become pregnant in the first place (Huizink, Mulder, & Buitelaar, 2004; Langille, 2007; Meade, Kershaw, & Ickovics, 2008).

◉ **Watch** the **Video** *Pregnancy and Prenatal Care Across Cultures* in **MyPsychLab**.

Mother's Health. Mothers who eat the right foods, maintain an appropriate weight, and who exercise appropriately maximize the chances of having a healthy baby. Furthermore, they can reduce the lifetime risk of obesity, high blood pressure, and heart disease in their children by maintaining a healthy lifestyle (Walker & Humphries, 2005, 2007).

In contrast, illness in a pregnant woman can have devastating consequences. For instance, the onset of *rubella* (German measles) in the mother prior to the 11th week of pregnancy is likely to cause serious consequences in the baby, including blindness, deafness, heart defects, or brain damage. In later stages of a pregnancy, however, adverse consequences of rubella become increasingly less likely.

Several other diseases may affect a developing fetus, again depending on when the illness is contracted. For instance, *chicken pox* may produce birth defects, whereas *mumps* may increase the risk of miscarriage.

Some sexually transmitted diseases such as *syphilis* can be transmitted directly to the fetus, who will be born suffering from the disease. In some cases, sexually transmitted diseases such as *gonorrhea* are communicated to the child as it passes through the birth canal to be born.

Acquired immune deficiency syndrome (AIDS) is the newest of the diseases to affect a newborn. Mothers who have the disease or who merely are carriers of the virus may pass it on to their fetuses through the blood that reaches the placenta. However, if mothers with AIDS are treated with antiviral drugs such as AZT during pregnancy, fewer than 5% of infants are born with the disease. Those infants who are born with AIDS must remain on antiviral drugs their entire lives (Nesheim et al., 2004).

Mothers' mental health status can also affect their children. For example, maternal depression while pregnant can affect children's development, as we discuss in the *From Research to Practice* box.

FROM RESEARCH TO PRACTICE
From Joy to Sorrow: When Pregnant Mothers Become Depressed

Margot Davis had invested six years and thousands of hours making her art gallery a success. And she loved every minute of it. The travel, the deal making, the splashy openings. But then she decided it was time to start a family. Her husband adored children and Margot felt one child would not cramp her high-energy style. Six months into the pregnancy she was less certain. The exhaustion typical of the first trimester had not abated. "I don't know if it's hormones or fear," she says, "but I have no interest in anything, least of all the baby." Margot talked to her doctor about antidepressants but she worries they will harm the fetus. "I don't need a guilt trip like that," she says. "I feel guilty enough already."

It's a surprising fact: As many as 10% of pregnancies are complicated by maternal depression. And not only does such depression afflict the mother, there's increasing evidence that it affects her developing fetus. For example, maternal depression is related to such harmful effects as low birth weight, premature birth, pregnancy complications, and decreased immune function (Oberlander & DiPietro, 2003; Mattes et al., 2009; Goodman et al., 2011).

Maternal depression may have even more lasting effects on a child, extending beyond birth. Some research finds that maternal depression is related to poor motor control in infancy, inadequate behavior control in childhood, and even emotional problems in adulthood. But it's difficult to know what these studies really mean because they are always correlational. Factors such as environmental stressors that might tend to coincide with depression (such as financial problems or reduced social support) can't be ruled out as the real cause of these enduring postnatal problems. Furthermore, genetic factors might be at work in both the maternal depression and in the emotional and behavioral problems in the child, independent of any specific effects of depression during pregnancy (Ji et al., 2011; Conroy et al., 2012).

Concerns over the possible harmful effects of maternal depression make it tempting for physicians to prescribe antidepressant drugs to depressed pregnant patients. But it's unclear that this solution is any less of a concern than the original problem: While most research suggests that the effects of common antidepressant drugs on a developing fetus are minimal and temporary, there's just not enough research to be certain. Research on potential long-term effects is especially lacking (Boucher, Bairm, & Beaulac-Baillargeon, 2008; Miller et al., 2008; Ramos et al., 2008; Einarson et al., 2009).

Given this reality, the best option for women who experience depression during pregnancy may be to seek out non-drug-based psychotherapeutic interventions. Forms of talk therapy offer expectant mothers an option for treatment while posing no additional risk to the developing fetus (Oberlander & DiPietro, 2003).

- **Suppose scientists found that there was a relationship between a mother's depression and her child's depression? How might both environmental factors and genetics explain such a relationship?**

- **Should mothers routinely be screened for depression during pregnancy? Why or why not?**

Mothers' Drug Use. Mothers' use of many kinds of drugs—both legal and illegal—poses serious risks to the unborn child. Even over-the-counter remedies for common ailments can have surprisingly injurious consequences. For instance, aspirin taken for a headache can lead to fetal bleeding and growth impairments (Griffith, Azuma, & Chasnoff, 1994).

Even drugs prescribed by medical professionals have sometimes had disastrous consequences. In the 1950s, many women who were told to take *thalidomide* for morning sickness during their pregnancies gave birth to children with stumps instead of arms and legs. Although the physicians who prescribed the drug did not know it, thalidomide inhibited the growth of limbs that normally would have occurred during the first 3 months of pregnancy.

Some drugs taken by mothers cause difficulties in their children literally decades after they were taken. As recently as the 1970s, the artificial hormone *diethylstilbestrol* (*DES*) was frequently prescribed to prevent miscarriage. Only later was it found that the daughters of mothers who took DES stood a much higher than normal chance of developing a rare form of vaginal or cervical cancer and had more difficulties during their pregnancies. Sons of the mothers who had taken DES had their own problems, including a higher rate than average of reproductive difficulties (Schechter, Finkelstein, & Koren, 2005).

Birth control or fertility pills taken by pregnant women before they are aware of their pregnancy can also cause fetal damage. Such medicines contain sex hormones that affect developing brain structures in the fetus. These hormones, which when produced naturally are related to sexual differentiation in the fetus and gender differences after birth, can cause significant damage (Brown, Hines, & Fane, 2002).

Illicit drugs may pose equally great, and sometimes even greater, risks for the environments of prenatal children. For one thing, the purity of drugs purchased illegally varies significantly, so drug users can never be quite sure what specifically they are ingesting. Furthermore, the effects of some commonly used illicit drugs can be particularly devastating (H. E. Jones, 2006; Mayes et al., 2007).

Consider, for instance, the use of *marijuana*. Certainly one of the most commonly used illegal drugs—millions of people in the United States have admitted trying it—marijuana used during pregnancy can restrict the oxygen that reaches the fetus. Its use can lead to infants who are irritable, nervous, and easily disturbed. Children exposed to marijuana prenatally show learning and memory deficits at the age of 10 (Smith et al., 2006; Williams & Ross, 2007; Goldschmidt et al., 2008).

During the early 1990s, *cocaine* use by pregnant women led to an epidemic of thousands of so-called crack babies. Cocaine produces an intense restriction of the arteries leading to the fetus, causing a significant reduction in the flow of blood and oxygen, increasing the risks of fetal death and a number of birth defects and disabilities (Schuetze, Eiden, & Coles, 2007).

Children whose mothers were addicted to cocaine may themselves be born addicted to the drug and may have to suffer through the pain of withdrawal. Even if not addicted, they may be born with significant problems. They are often shorter and their weight is less than average, and they may have serious respiratory problems, visible birth defects, or seizures. They behave quite differently from other infants: Their reactions to stimulation are muted, but once they start to cry, it may be hard to soothe them (Singer et al., 2000; Eiden, Foote, & Schuetze, 2007; Richardson, Goldschmidt, & Willford, 2009).

It is difficult to determine the long-term effects of mothers' cocaine use in isolation, because such drug use is often accompanied by poor prenatal care and impaired nurturing following birth. In fact, in many cases it is the poor caregiving by mothers who use cocaine that results in children's problems, and not exposure to the drug. Treatment of children exposed to cocaine consequently requires not only an end to the mother's drug use but also an improvement in the level of care the mother or other caregivers provide to the infant (Brown et al., 2004; Jones, 2006; Schempf, 2007).

Mothers' Use of Alcohol and Tobacco. A pregnant woman who reasons that having a drink every once in a while or smoking an occasional cigarette has no appreciable effect on her unborn child is, in all likelihood, kidding herself: Increasing evidence suggests that even small amounts of alcohol and nicotine can disrupt the development of the fetus.

Mothers' use of alcohol can have profound consequences for the unborn child. The children of alcoholics, who consume substantial quantities of alcohol during pregnancy, are at the greatest risk. Approximately 1 out of every 750 infants is born with **fetal alcohol syndrome (FAS),** a disorder that may include below-average intelligence and sometimes mental retardation, delayed growth, and facial deformities. FAS is now the primary preventable cause of mental retardation (Burd et al., 2003; Calhoun & Warren, 2007; May et al., 2011).

Even mothers who use smaller amounts of alcohol during pregnancy place their child at risk. **Fetal alcohol effects (FAE)** is a condition in which children display some, although not all, of the problems of FAS due to their mother's consumption of alcohol during pregnancy (Baer, Sampson, & Barr, 2003; Molina et al., 2007).

Children who do not have FAE may still be affected by their mothers' use of alcohol. Studies have found that maternal consumption of an average of just two alcoholic drinks a day during pregnancy is associated with lower intelligence in their offspring at age 7. Other research concurs, suggesting that relatively small quantities of alcohol taken during pregnancy can have future adverse effects on children's behavior and psychological functioning. Furthermore, the consequences of alcohol ingestion during pregnancy are long-lasting. For example, one study found that 14-year-olds' success on a test involving spatial and visual reasoning was related to their mothers' alcohol consumption during pregnancy. The more the mothers reported drinking, the less accurately their children responded (Lynch et al., 2003; Mattson, Calarco, & Lang, 2006; Streissguth, 2007).

Because of the risks associated with alcohol, physicians today counsel pregnant women (and even those who are trying to become pregnant) to avoid drinking any alcoholic beverages. In addition, they caution against another practice proven to have an adverse effect on an unborn child: smoking.

Smoking produces several consequences, none good. For starters, smoking reduces the oxygen content and increases the carbon monoxide of the mother's blood, which quickly reduces the oxygen available to the fetus. In addition, the nicotine and other toxins in cigarettes slow the respiration rate of the fetus and speed up its heart.

The ultimate result is an increased possibility of miscarriage and a higher likelihood of death during infancy. In fact, estimates suggest that smoking by pregnant women leads to more than 100,000 miscarriages and the deaths of 5,600 babies in the United States alone each year (Haslam & Lawrence, 2004; Triche & Hossain, 2007; Chertok et al., 2011).

Smokers are two times as likely as nonsmokers to have babies with an abnormally low birthweight, and smokers' babies are shorter, on average, than those of nonsmokers. Furthermore, women who smoke during pregnancy are 50% more likely to have mentally retarded children. Finally, mothers who smoke are more likely to have children who exhibit disruptive behavior during childhood (Wakschalg et al., 2006; McCowan et al., 2009).

The consequences of smoking are so profound that it may affect not only a mother's children but also her grandchildren. For example, children whose *grandmothers* smoked during pregnancy are more than twice as likely to develop childhood asthma than children whose grandmothers did not smoke (Li et al., 2005).

Do Fathers Affect the Prenatal Environment? It would be easy to reason that once the father has done his part in the sequence of events leading to conception, he would have no role in the *prenatal* environment of the fetus. In fact, developmental researchers have in the past generally shared this view, and there is relatively little research investigating fathers' influence on the prenatal environment.

However, it is becoming increasingly clear that fathers' behavior may well influence the prenatal environment. Consequently, as the example of Lisa and Robert's visit to the midwife, earlier in the chapter, showed, health practitioners are applying recent research findings to suggest ways fathers can support healthy prenatal development (Martin et al., 2007).

For instance, fathers-to-be should avoid smoking. Secondhand smoke from a father's cigarettes may affect the mother's health, which in turn influences her unborn child. The greater the level of a father's smoking, the lower the birthweight of his children (Tomblin, Hammer, & Zhang, 1998; Gage, Everett, & Bullock, 2011).

Similarly, a father's use of alcohol and illegal drugs can have significant effects on the fetus. Alcohol and drug use impairs sperm and may lead to chromosomal damage that may affect the fetus at conception. In addition, alcohol and drug use during pregnancy may also affect the prenatal environment by creating stress in the mother and generally producing an

fetal alcohol syndrome (FAS)   A disorder caused by the pregnant mother consuming substantial quantities of alcohol during pregnancy, potentially resulting in mental retardation and delayed growth in the child

fetal alcohol effects (FAE)   A condition in which children display some, although not all, of the problems of fetal alcohol syndrome due to the mother's consumption of alcohol during pregnancy

ARE YOU AN INFORMED CONSUMER OF DEVELOPMENT?

Optimizing the Prenatal Environment

If you are contemplating ever having a child, you may be overwhelmed, at this point in the chapter, by the number of things that can go wrong. Don't be. Although both genetics and the environment pose their share of risks, in the vast majority of cases, pregnancy and birth proceed without mishap. Moreover, there are several things that women can do—both before and during pregnancy—to optimize the probability that pregnancy will progress smoothly (Massaro, Rothbaum, & Aly, 2006). Among them:

- For women who are planning to become pregnant, several precautions are in order. First, women should have nonemergency X-rays only during the first 2 weeks after their menstrual periods. Second, women should be vaccinated against rubella (German measles) at least 3 and preferably 6 months before getting pregnant. Finally, women who are planning to become pregnant should avoid the use of birth control pills at least 3 months before trying to conceive, because of disruptions to hormonal production caused by the pills.

- Eat well, both before and during (and after, for that matter!) pregnancy. Pregnant mothers are, as the saying goes, eating for two. This means that it is more essential than ever to eat regular, well-balanced meals. In addition, physicians typically recommend taking prenatal vitamins that include folic acids, which can decrease the likelihood of birth defects (Amitai et al., 2004).

- Don't use alcohol and other drugs. The evidence is clear that many drugs pass directly to the fetus and may cause birth defects. It is also clear that the more one drinks, the greater the risk to the fetus. The best advice, whether you are already pregnant or planning to have a child: Don't use *any* drug unless directed by a physician. If you are planning to get pregnant, encourage your partner to avoid using alcohol or other drugs, too (O'Connor & Whaley, 2006).

- Monitor caffeine intake. Although it is still unclear whether caffeine produces birth defects, it is known that the caffeine found in coffee, tea, and chocolate can pass to the fetus, acting as a stimulant. Because of this, you probably shouldn't drink more than a few cups of coffee a day (Wisborg et al., 2003; Diego et al., 2007).

- Whether pregnant or not, don't smoke. This holds true for mothers, fathers, and anyone else in the vicinity of the pregnant mother, because research suggests that smoke in the fetal environment can affect birthweight.

- Exercise regularly. In most cases, women can continue to exercise, particularly exercises involving low-impact routines. On the other hand, extreme exercise should be avoided, especially on very hot or very cold days. "No pain, no gain" isn't applicable during pregnancy (Paisley, Joy, & Price, 2003; Schmidt et al., 2006; Evenson, 2011). ∎

FROM A

HEALTH-CARE PROVIDER'S

PERSPECTIVE:

In addition to avoiding smoking, what other sorts of things might fathers-to-be do to help their unborn children develop normally in the womb?

unhealthy environment. Environmental toxins in the father's workplace, such as lead or mercury, may bind to his sperm and cause birth defects (Dare et al., 2002; Choy et al., 2002).

Finally, fathers who are physically or emotionally abusive to their pregnant wives can damage their unborn children. By increasing the level of maternal stress, or actually causing physical damage, abusive fathers increase the risk of harm to their unborn children. In fact, 4% to 8% of women face physical abuse during pregnancy (Gazmarian et al., 2000; Bacchus, Mezey, & Bewley, 2006; Martin et al., 2006).

Review, Check, and Apply

Review

1. Fertilization joins the sperm and ovum to start the journey of prenatal development. Some couples, however, need medical help to conceive. Among the alternative routes to conception are artificial insemination and in vitro fertilization.

2. The prenatal period consists of three stages: germinal, embryonic, and fetal.

3. The prenatal environment significantly influences the development of the baby. The diet, age, and general health of the mother can affect the baby's health and growth.

4. Mothers' use of drugs, alcohol, tobacco, and caffeine can adversely affect the health and development of the unborn child. The behavior of fathers and others (e.g., smoking) can also affect the health of the unborn child.

Check

1. When sperm enter the vagina, they go through the cervix and into the fallopian tube, where _____ may take place.

2. Some 15% of couples suffer from _____, the inability to conceive.

3. A _____ occurs when pregnancy ends before the developing child is able to survive outside the mother's womb.

4. An environmental agent such as a drug, chemical, virus, or other factor that produces a birth defect is called a _____.

Apply

1. It is known that a mother's diet is a crucial part of the development of the fetus. What sorts of environmental and social factors affect development?

2. Studies of so-called crack babies show that when they enter school, such children have significant difficulty dealing with multiple stimuli and forming close attachments. How might a combination of genetic and environmental influences have contributed to this outcome?

To see more review questions, log on to MyPsychLab.

ANSWERS: 1. fertilization (or conception)   2. infertility   3. miscarriage   4. teratogen

The CASE
of . . . *the Genetic Finger of Fate*

Melindah and Jermain Tessel were incredibly happy last week when they learned that Melindah was pregnant with their first child, but now they're so worried they can't sleep.

When they got home from the physician's visit, they began to jokingly consider such characteristics as height (tall like Melindah or on the short side, like Jermain), tendency to obesity (like Jermain), athletic ability (like Melindah), intelligence (high, of course, like both of them), and so on. But then they turned to other traits.

Both Melindah and Jermain were overly shy and quiet, and they wished they had been more assertive. Neither was a natural leader or confident public speaker, but they wanted their children to be. Both were loners, and they agreed that their kids would have an easier time if they turned out to be more sociable and outgoing. They worried whether these personality traits were predetermined, or if their kids' fates could be changed.

Then the conversation got even more unsettling. Melindah remembered that there was some mental illness in her family and there were even rumors of violence in one of her uncles.

This prompted Jermain to recall an alcoholic cousin and a more distant relative who, he thought, had died early from sickle-cell anemia.

There seemed so many things that could go wrong—all because of the baggage they carried in their genes!

1. How would you begin to reassure Melindah and Jermain about their worries?

2. Which characteristics that they discussed are largely genetic, and which are more environmentally influenced? Are the genetic traits equivalent to fate, or can their expression be modified? Why or why not?

3. How much should Melindah worry about the mental illness and violence in her family? What would you tell her?

4. How much should Jermain worry about his children inheriting sickle-cell anemia?

5. Would you advise Melindah and Jermain to seek genetic counseling? Why or why not? What factors would you consider in advising them to visit or not to visit a counselor?

◀◀◀ LOOKING BACK

LO 3-1 What are the basics of genetics?

- A child receives 23 chromosomes from each parent. These 46 chromosomes provide the genetic blueprint that will guide cell activity for the rest of the individual's life.

- Gregor Mendel discovered an important genetic mechanism that governs the interactions of dominant and recessive genes and their expression in alleles. Traits such as hair and eye color and the presence of phenylketonuria (PKU) are alleles and follow this pattern.

- Genes may become physically damaged or may spontaneously mutate. If damaged genes are passed on to the child, the result can be a genetic disorder.

- Behavioral genetics, which studies the genetic basis of human behavior, focuses on personality characteristics and behaviors, and on psychological disorders such as schizophrenia. Researchers are now discovering how to remedy certain genetic defects through gene therapy.

LO 3-2 How do the environment and genetics work together to determine human characteristics?

- Behavioral characteristics are often determined by a combination of genetics and environment. Genetically based traits represent a potential, called the genotype, which may be affected by the environment and is ultimately expressed in the phenotype.

- To work out the different influences of heredity and environment, researchers use nonhuman studies and human studies, particularly of twins.

LO 3-3 What is the purpose of genetic counseling?

- Couples contemplating having a child may seek to determine the risks involved in a future pregnancy through genetic counseling that assesses their genetic backgrounds and predicts possible problems.

- Genetic counselors use data from tests and other sources to identify potential genetic abnormalities in women and men who plan to have children. Recently, they have begun testing individuals for genetically based disorders that may eventually appear in the individuals themselves.

LO 3-4 Which human characteristics are significantly influenced by heredity?

- Virtually all human traits, characteristics, and behaviors are the result of the combination and interaction of nature and nurture. Many physical characteristics show strong genetic influences.

- Some personality traits, including neuroticism and extroversion, have been linked to genetic factors, and even attitudes, values, and interests have a genetic component. Some personal behaviors may be genetically influenced through the mediation of inherited personality traits.

LO 3-5 How is intelligence determined?

- Although it is clear that heredity plays an important role in intelligence, investigators are much more divided on the question of the degree to which it is inherited.

- Although heredity clearly plays an important role in intelligence, environmental factors such as exposure to books, good educational experiences, and intelligent peers also are profoundly influential.

LO 3-6 Can genes influence the environment?

- The genetic endowment provided to children by their parents not only determines their genetic characteristics but also actively influences their environment.

- Behaviors and traits are a joint outcome of genetic and environmental factors, and the relative influence of genes and the environment on specific characteristics shifts over the course of people's lives.

LO 3-7 What happens during the prenatal stages of development?

- The union of a sperm and ovum at the moment of fertilization, which begins the process of prenatal development, can be difficult for some couples. Infertility, which occurs in some 15% of couples, can be treated by drugs, surgery, artificial insemination, and in vitro fertilization.

- The germinal stage (fertilization–2 weeks) is marked by rapid cell division and specialization, and the attachment of the zygote to the wall of the uterus. During the embryonic stage (2–8 weeks), the ectoderm, the mesoderm, and the endoderm begin to grow and specialize. The fetal stage (8 weeks–birth) is characterized by a rapid increase in complexity and differentiation of the organs. The fetus becomes active and most of its systems operational.

LO 3-8 What are the threats to the fetal environment, and what can be done about them?

- Factors in the mother that may affect the unborn child include diet, age, illnesses, and drug, alcohol, and tobacco use. The behaviors of fathers and others in the environment may also affect the health and development of the unborn child.

LO 3-9 How do fathers affect the prenatal environment?

- Fathers' secondhand smoke may affect the mother's health, which in turn influences her unborn child.

- A father's use of alcohol and illegal drugs can damage his sperm.

- Fathers who are physically or emotionally abusive to their pregnant wives can damage their unborn children.

KEY TERMS AND CONCEPTS

gametes (p. 58)
zygote (p. 58)
genes (p. 58)
DNA (deoxyribonucleic acid) molecules (p. 58)
chromosomes (p. 58)
monozygotic twins (p. 59)
dizygotic twins (p. 59)
dominant trait (p. 61)
recessive trait (p. 61)
genotype (p. 61)
phenotype (p. 61)
homozygous (p. 61)
heterozygous (p. 61)

polygenic inheritance (p. 62)
X-linked genes (p. 62)
behavioral genetics (p. 63)
Down syndrome (p. 64)
fragile X syndrome (p. 64)
sickle-cell anemia (p. 64)
Tay-Sachs disease (p. 65)
Klinefelter's syndrome (p. 65)
genetic counseling (p. 66)
ultrasound sonography (p. 66)
chorionic villus sampling (CVS) (p. 66)
amniocentesis (p. 66)
temperament (p. 70)

multifactorial transmission (p. 70)
fertilization (p. 80)
germinal stage (p. 80)
placenta (p. 81)
embryonic stage (p. 81)
fetal stage (p. 81)
fetus (p. 82)
infertility (p. 83)
artificial insemination (p. 83)
in vitro fertilization (IVF) (p. 83)
teratogen (p. 85)
fetal alcohol syndrome (FAS) (p. 89)
fetal alcohol effects (FAE) (p. 89)

Epilogue

In this chapter, we have discussed the basics of heredity and genetics, including the way in which the code of life is transmitted across generations through DNA. We have also seen how genetic transmission can go wrong, and we have discussed ways in which genetic disorders can be treated—and perhaps prevented—through new interventions such as genetic counseling.

One important theme in this chapter has been the interaction between hereditary and environmental factors in the determination of a number of human traits. While we have encountered a number of surprising instances in which heredity plays a part—including in the development of personality traits and even personal preferences and tastes—we have also seen that heredity is virtually never the sole factor in any complex trait. Environment nearly always plays an important role.

Finally, we reviewed the main stages of prenatal growth—germinal, embryonic, and fetal—and examined threats to the prenatal environment and ways to optimize that environment for the fetus.

Before moving on, return to the prologue of this chapter and the case of Howard's unborn daughter. Answer the following questions based on your understanding of genetics and prenatal development.

1. Do you think the Howards make a good decision to wait and see rather than having the fetal muscle biopsy? Why?

2. From the Howards' story, would you guess that Duchenne muscular distrophy is a sex-linked trait or not? Why?

3. If the Howards' pregnancy had yielded twin boys, would both boys share the same risk for developing DMD? Would it be possible for one twin to have DMD and the other not? Explain.

4. Do you think certain genetic testing (say, for predisposition to particular diseases) should become a regular part of prenatal check-ups? Why or why not?

The Development Video Series in MyPsychLab

Explore the video *The Basics: Genetic Mechanisms and Behavioral Genetics* by scanning this QR code with your mobile device. If you don't already have one, you may download a free QR scanner for your device wherever smartphone apps are sold. You can also view this video in MyPsychLab. For more videos related to this chapter's content, log into MyPsychLab to view the entire Development Video Series.

MyVirtualChild

- **What decisions would you make while raising a child?**
- **What would the consequences of those decisions be?**

Find out by accessing **MyVirtualChild** at

www.MyPsychLab.com

and raising your own virtual child from birth to age 18.

4 Birth and the Newborn Infant

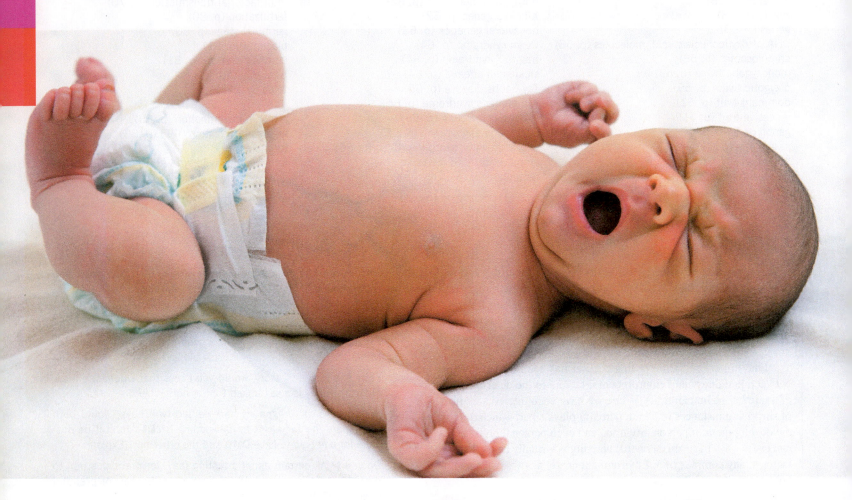

MODULE 4.1

BIRTH

- Labor: The Process of Birth Begins
- Birth: From Fetus to Neonate
- Approaches to Childbirth: Where Medicine and Attitudes Meet

FROM RESEARCH TO PRACTICE: Vaccination Wars

ARE YOU AN INFORMED CONSUMER OF DEVELOPMENT? Dealing with Labor

Review, Check, and Apply

MODULE 4.2

BIRTH COMPLICATIONS

- Preterm Infants: Too Soon, Too Small

CAREERS IN CHILD DEVELOPMENT: Clinical Nurse Specialist

- Postmature Babies: Too Late, Too Large
- Cesarean Delivery: Intervening in the Process of Birth
- Infant Mortality and Stillbirth: The Tragedy of Premature Death

DEVELOPMENTAL DIVERSITY AND YOUR LIFE: Overcoming Racial and Cultural Differences in Infant Mortality

- Postpartum Depression: Moving from the Heights of Joy to the Depths of Despair

Review, Check, and Apply

MODULE 4.3

THE COMPETENT NEWBORN

- Physical Competence: Meeting the Demands of a New Environment
- Sensory Capabilities: Experiencing the World
- Early Learning Capabilities

NEUROSCIENCE AND DEVELOPMENT: Beyond Band-Aids: How Pain in Infancy Affects Pain in Adulthood

- Social Competence: Responding to Others

Review, Check, and Apply

The Case of ... No Place Like Home?

Looking Back

Key Terms and Concepts

Epilogue

PROLOGUE: Smaller than a Soda Can

Doctors gave infant Tamera Dixon at best a 15% chance of survival. The tiny girl entered the world after only 25 weeks of gestation, months earlier than normal. When she was born, she was 10 inches long and weighed a mere 11 ounces—less than a can of soda.

Tamera was born by Cesarean section after her mother, Andrea Haws, experienced health problems during the pregnancy. "To see an 11-ounce baby, you wouldn't believe what it looked like," Andrea Haws said. "It was just skin and bones."

But Tamera beat the odds. She gained weight and began to breathe on her own. After nearly four months in the hospital, she was released to the care of her parents. At the time she went home, she weighed over four pounds. She would have been about a week old had she been carried to term.

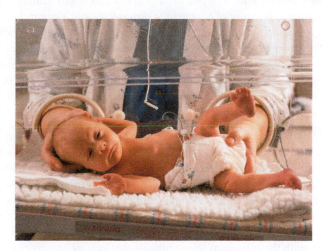

"It is a miracle," Andrea Haws said. "She is a miracle."

>>> LOOKING AHEAD

Infants were not meant to be born as early as Tamera. Yet, for a variety of reasons, more than 10% of all babies today are born prematurely, and the outlook for them to lead a normal life is improving dramatically.

All births, even those that reach full term, are tinged with a combination of excitement and some degree of anxiety. In the vast majority of cases delivery goes smoothly, and it is an amazing and joyous moment when a new being enters the world. The excitement of birth is soon replaced by wonder at the extraordinary nature of newborns themselves. Babies enter the world with a surprising array of capabilities, ready from the first moments of life outside the womb to respond to the world and the people in it.

In this chapter we examine the events that lead to the birth of a child, and take an initial look at the newborn. We first consider labor and delivery, exploring how the process usually proceeds, as well as several alternative approaches.

We next examine some of the possible complications of birth. Problems that can occur range from premature births to infant mortality.

(continued)

Learning Objectives

MODULE 4.1

LO1 What is the normal process of labor?

LO2 What are alternative birthing procedures?

MODULE 4.2

LO3 What complications can occur at birth, and what are their causes, effects, and treatments?

LO4 In what kinds of situations are Cesarean deliveries necessary?

LO5 What is postpartum depression?

MODULE 4.3

LO6 What capabilities does the newborn have?

LO7 How do newborns respond to others?

Finally, we consider the extraordinary range of capabilities of newborns. We look not only at their physical and perceptual abilities but also at the way they enter the world with the ability to learn and with skills that help form the foundations of their future relationships with others.

MODULE 4.1

BIRTH

LO 4-1 What is the normal process of labor?
LO 4-2 What are alternative birthing procedures?

I wasn't completely naïve. I mean, I knew that it was only in movies that babies come out of the womb all pink, dry, and beautiful. But still, I was initially taken aback by my son's appearance. Because of his passage through the birth canal, his head was cone-shaped, a bit like a wet, partly deflated football. The nurse must have noticed my reaction because she hastened to assure me that all this would change in a matter of days. She then moved quickly to wipe off the whitish sticky substance all over his body, informing me as she did so that the fuzzy hair on his ears was only temporary. I leaned in and put my finger into my boy's hand. He rewarded me by closing his hand around it. I interrupted the nurse's assurances. "Don't worry," I stammered, tears suddenly filling my eyes. "He's absolutely the most beautiful thing I've ever seen."

For those of us accustomed to thinking of newborns in the images of baby food commercials, this portrait of a typical newborn may be surprising. Yet most **neonates**—the term used for newborns—are born resembling this one. Make no mistake, however: Despite their temporary blemishes, babies are a welcome sight to their parents from the moment of their birth.

The neonate's outward appearance is caused by a variety of factors in its journey from the mother's uterus, down the birth canal, and out into the world. We can trace its passage, beginning with the release of the chemicals that initiate the process of labor.

Labor: The Process of Birth Begins

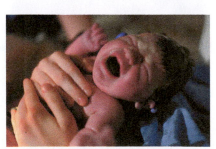

The image of newborns portrayed in commercials differs dramatically from reality.

About 266 days after conception, a protein called *corticotropin-releasing hormone* (CRH) triggers the release of various hormones, and the process that leads to birth begins. One critical hormone is *oxytocin,* which is released by the mother's pituitary gland. When the concentration of oxytocin becomes high enough, the mother's uterus begins periodic contractions (Heterelendy & Zakar, 2004; Terzidou, 2007).

During the prenatal period, the uterus, which is composed of muscle tissue, slowly expands as the fetus grows. Although for most of the pregnancy it is inactive, after the fourth month it occasionally contracts to ready itself for the eventual delivery. These contractions, called *Braxton-Hicks contractions*, are sometimes called "false labor" because, while they can fool eager and anxious expectant parents, they do not signify that the baby will be born soon.

When birth is actually imminent, the uterus begins to contract intermittently. Its increasingly intense contractions act as if it were a vise, opening and closing to force the head of the fetus against the *cervix,* the neck of the uterus that separates it from the vagina. Eventually, the force of the contractions becomes strong enough to propel the fetus slowly down the birth canal until it enters the world as a newborn. It is this exertion and the narrow birth passageway that often gives newborns the battered conehead appearance described earlier.

Labor proceeds in three stages (see Figure 4-1). In the *first stage of labor,* the uterine contractions initially occur around every 8 to 10 minutes and last about 30 seconds. As labor proceeds, the contractions occur more frequently and last longer. Toward the end of labor, the contractions may occur every two minutes and last almost two minutes. During the final

neonate   The term used for newborns

Stage 1

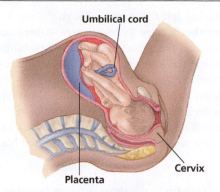

Uterine contractions initially occur every 8 to 10 minutes and last 30 seconds. Toward the end of labor, contractions may occur every 2 minutes and last as long as 2 minutes. As the contractions increase, the cervix, which separates the uterus from the vagina, becomes wider, eventually expanding to allow the baby's head to pass through.

Stage 2

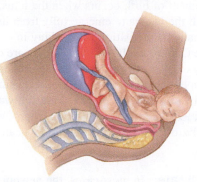

The baby's head starts to move through the cervix and birth canal. Typically lasting around 90 minutes, the second stage ends when the baby has completely left the mother's body.

Stage 3

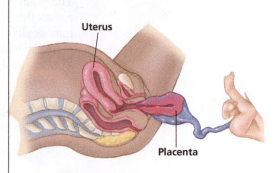

The child's umbilical cord (still attached to the neonate) and the placenta are expelled from the mother. This stage is the quickest and easiest, taking just a few minutes.

FIGURE 4-1 The Three Stages of Labor

part of the first stage of labor, the contractions increase to their greatest intensity, a period known as *transition*. The mother's cervix fully opens, eventually expanding enough (usually to around 10 cm) to allow the baby's head (the widest part of the body) to pass through.

This first stage of labor is the longest. Its duration varies significantly, depending on the mother's age, race, ethnicity, number of prior pregnancies, and a variety of other factors involving both the fetus and the mother. Typically, labor takes 16 to 24 hours for firstborn children, but there are wide variations. Births of subsequent children usually involve shorter periods of labor.

During the *second stage of labor,* which typically lasts around 90 minutes, the baby's head emerges further from the mother with each contraction, increasing the size of the vaginal opening. Because the area between the vagina and rectum must stretch a good deal, an incision called an **episiotomy** is sometimes made to increase the size of the opening of the vagina. However, this practice has been increasingly criticized in recent years as potentially causing more harm than good, and the number of episiotomies has fallen drastically in the last decades (Graham et al., 2005; Dudding, Vaizey, & Kamm, 2008; Perrier et al., 2011).

The second stage of labor ends when the baby has completely left the mother's body. Finally, the *third stage of labor* occurs when the child's umbilical cord (still attached to the neonate) and the placenta are expelled from the mother. This stage is the quickest and easiest, taking just a few minutes.

The nature of a woman's reactions to labor reflect, in part, cultural factors. Although there is no evidence that the physiological aspects of labor differ among women of different cultures, expectations about labor and interpretations of its pain do vary significantly from one culture to another (Fisher, Hauck, & Fenwick, 2006; Xirasagar et al., 2011; Redshaw & Heikkilä, 2011).

For instance, there is a kernel of truth to popular stories of pregnant women in certain societies putting down the tools with which they are tilling their fields, stepping aside and giving birth, and immediately returning to work with their neonates wrapped and bundled on their backs. Accounts of the !Kung people in Africa describe the woman in labor sitting calmly beside a tree and without much ado—or assistance—successfully giving birth to a child and quickly recovering. On the other hand, many societies regard childbirth as dangerous, and some even view it in terms befitting an illness. Such cultural perspectives color the way that people in a given society view the experience of childbirth.

Watch the **Video** *Labor* in **MyPsychLab**.

episiotomy   An incision sometimes made to increase the size of the opening of the vagina to allow the baby to pass

Birth: From Fetus to Neonate

The exact moment of birth occurs when the fetus, having left the uterus through the cervix, passes through the vagina to emerge fully from its mother's body. In most cases, babies automatically make the transition from taking in oxygen via the placenta to using their lungs to breathe air. Consequently, as soon as they are outside the mother's body, most newborns spontaneously cry. This helps them clear their lungs and breathe on their own.

What happens next varies from situation to situation and from culture to culture. In Western cultures, health-care workers are almost always on hand to assist with the birth. In the United States, 99% of births are attended by professional health-care workers, but worldwide only about 50% of births have professional health-care workers in attendance (United Nations, 1990).

The Apgar Scale. In most cases, the newborn infant first undergoes a quick visual inspection. Parents may be counting fingers and toes, but trained health-care workers look for something more. Typically, they employ the **Apgar scale**, a standard measurement system that looks for a variety of indications of good health (see Table 4-1). Developed by physician Virginia Apgar, the scale directs attention to five basic qualities, recalled most easily by using Apgar's name as a guide: *a*ppearance (color), *p*ulse (heart rate), *g*rimace (reflex irritability), *a*ctivity (muscle tone), and *r*espiration (respiratory effort).

Using the scale, health-care workers assign the newborn a score ranging from 0 to 2 on each of the five qualities, producing an overall score that can range from 0 to 10. The vast majority of children score 7 or above. The 10% of neonates who score under 7 require help to start breathing. Newborns who score under 4 need immediate, life-saving intervention.

Low Apgar scores (or low scores on other neonatal assessments, such as the *Brazelton Neonatal Behavioral Assessment Scale,* which we discuss in the next chapter) may indicate problems or birth defects that were already present in the fetus. However, the process of birth itself may sometimes cause difficulties. Among the most profound are those relating to a temporary deprivation of oxygen.

At various junctures during labor, the fetus may not get sufficient oxygen. This can happen for any of a number of reasons. For instance, the umbilical cord may get wrapped around the neck of the fetus. The cord can also be pinched during a prolonged contraction, thereby cutting off the supply of oxygen that flows through it.

Lack of oxygen for a few seconds is not harmful to the fetus, but deprivation for any longer time may cause serious harm. A restriction of oxygen, or **anoxia**, lasting a few minutes

Apgar scale A standard measurement system that looks for a variety of indications of good health in newborns

anoxia A restriction of oxygen to the baby, lasting a few minutes during the birth process, which can produce brain damage

---

TABLE 4-1   Apgar Scale

A score is given for each sign at 1 minute and 5 minutes after the birth. If there are problems with the baby, an additional score is given at 10 minutes. A score of 7–10 is considered normal, whereas 4–7 might require some resuscitative measures, and a baby with an Apgar score under 4 requires immediate resuscitation.

	Sign	0 Points	1 Point	2 Points
A	Appearance (skin color)	Blue-gray, pale all over	Normal, except for extremities	Normal over entire body
P	Pulse	Absent	Below 100 bpm	Above 100 bpm
G	Grimace (reflex irritability)	No response	Grimace	Sneezes, coughs, pulls away
A	Activity (muscle tone)	Absent	Arms and legs flexed	Active movement
R	Respiration	Absent	Slow, irregular	Good, crying

(*Source:* Apgar, 1953)

can produce cognitive deficits such as language delays and even mental retardation due to brain cell death (Hopkins-Golightly, Raz, & Sander, 2003; Lushnikova et al., 2011; Rees, Harding, & Walker, 2011).

Physical Appearance and Initial Encounters.   After assessing the newborn's health, health-care workers next deal with the remnants of the child's passage through the birth canal. You'll recall the description of the thick, greasy substance (like cottage cheese) that covers the newborn. This material, called *vernix,* smoothes the passage through the birth canal; it is no longer needed once the child is born and is quickly cleaned away. Newborns' bodies are also covered with a fine, dark fuzz known as *lanugo*; this soon disappears. The newborn's eyelids may be puffy due to an accumulation of fluids during labor, and the newborn may have blood or other fluids on parts of its body.

After being cleansed, the newborn is usually returned to the mother and the father, if he is present. The everyday and universal occurrence of childbirth makes it no less miraculous to parents, and most cherish this time to make their first acquaintance with their child.

The importance of this initial encounter between parent and child has become a matter of considerable controversy. Some psychologists and physicians argued that **bonding**, the close physical and emotional contact between parent and child during the period immediately following birth, was a crucial ingredient for forming a lasting relationship between parent and child (Lorenz, 1957). Their arguments were based in part on research conducted on nonhuman species such as ducklings. This work showed that there was a critical period just after birth when organisms showed a particular readiness to learn, or imprint, from other members of their species who happened to be present.

According to the concept of bonding applied to humans, a critical period begins just after birth and lasts only a few hours. During this period actual skin-to-skin contact between mother and child supposedly leads to deep, emotional bonding. The corollary to this assumption is that if circumstances prevent such contact, the bond between mother and child will forever be lacking in some way. Because so many babies were taken from their mothers and placed in incubators or in the hospital nursery, the fear was that medical practices prevalent at the time often left little opportunity for sustained mother and child physical contact immediately after birth.

When developmental researchers carefully reviewed the research literature, however, they found little support for the existence of a critical period for bonding at birth. Although it does appear that mothers who have early physical contact with their babies are more responsive to them than those who don't have such contact, the difference lasts only a few days. Such news is reassuring to parents whose children must receive immediate, intensive medical attention just after birth, such as in the case of Tamera Dixon, described in the chapter Prologue. It is also comforting to parents who adopt children and are not present at their births (Weinberg, 2004; Miles et al., 2006; Pearson, Lightman, & Evans, 2011).

Although mother–child bonding does not seem critical, it is important for newborns to be gently touched and massaged soon after birth by *someone*. The physical stimulation infants receive leads to the production of chemicals in the brain that instigate growth. Consequently, infant massage is related to weight gain, better sleep-waking patterns, better neuromotor development, and reduced rates of infant mortality (Field, 2001; Field, Diego, & Hernandez-Reif, 2011).

Approaches to Childbirth: Where Medicine and Attitudes Meet

In her second pregnancy, Alma Juarez knew she wanted something other than traditional obstetrics. No drugs. No lying flat on her back for the delivery (which had slowed her contractions and made an oxygen mask necessary). This time, Juarez took control. She joined an exercise class for pregnant women and read books on childbirth. She also chose a nurse-midwife instead of an obstetrician. She wanted someone to work with her, not dictate to her.

bonding   Close physical and emotional contact between parent and child during the period immediately following birth, argued by some to affect later relationship strength

In Lamaze classes, parents are taught relaxation techniques to prepare for childbirth and to reduce the need for anesthetics.

When Juarez went into labor, she called the midwife who met her at the hospital. Juarez was determined to stay on her feet, making use of gravity to hasten the birth. Her husband and the midwife took turns walking with her as the contractions got stronger. When she was fully dilated, she got on her hands and knees, a posture she knew would minimize the effort of pushing. Thirty minutes later, her daughter was born. No drugs, no extra oxygen. Juarez says, "The first birth, I was exhausted. The second birth, I was elated."

Parents in the Western world have developed a variety of strategies—and some very strong opinions—to help them deal with something as natural as giving birth, which occurs apparently without much thought throughout the nonhuman animal world. Today parents need to decide: Should the birth take place in a hospital or in the home? Should a physician, a nurse, or a midwife assist? Is the father's presence desirable? Should siblings and other family members be on hand to participate in the birth?

Most of these questions cannot be answered definitively, primarily because the choice of childbirth techniques often comes down to a matter of values and opinions. No single procedure will be effective for all mothers and fathers, and no conclusive research evidence has proven that one procedure is significantly more effective than another. As we'll see, there is a wide variety of different issues and options involved, and certainly one's culture plays a role in choices of birthing procedures.

The abundance of choices is largely due to a reaction to traditional medical practices that had been common in the United States until the early 1970s. Before that time, the typical birth went something like this: A woman in labor was placed in a room with many other women, all of whom were in various stages of childbirth, and some of whom were screaming in pain. Fathers and other family members were not allowed to be present. Just before delivery, the woman was rolled into a delivery room, where the birth took place. Often she was so drugged that she was not aware of the birth at all.

At the time, physicians argued that such procedures were necessary to ensure the health of the newborn and the mother. However, critics charged that alternatives were available that not only would maximize the medical well-being of the participants in the birth but also would represent an emotional and psychological improvement (Curl et al., 2004; Hotelling & Humenick, 2005).

Alternative Birthing Procedures. Not all mothers give birth in hospitals, and not all births follow a traditional course. Among the major alternatives to traditional birthing practices are the following:

- *Lamaze birthing techniques.* The Lamaze method has achieved widespread popularity in the United States. Based on the writings of Dr. Fernand Lamaze, the method makes use of breathing techniques and relaxation training (Lamaze, 1979). Typically, mothers-to-be participate in a series of weekly training sessions in which they learn exercises that help them relax various parts of the body on command. A "coach," most typically the father, is trained along with the future mother. The training allows women to cope with painful contractions by concentrating on their breathing and producing relaxation response, rather than by tensing up, which can make the pain more acute. Women learn to focus on a relaxing stimulus, such as a tranquil scene in a picture. The goal is to learn how to deal positively with pain and to relax at the onset of a contraction (Lothian, 2005).

  Does the procedure work? Most mothers, as well as fathers, report that a Lamaze birth is a very positive experience. They enjoy the sense of mastery that they gain over the process of labor, a feeling of being able to exert some control over what can be a formidable experience. On the other hand, we can't be sure that parents who choose the Lamaze method aren't already more highly motivated about the experience of childbirth than are parents who do not choose the technique. It is therefore possible that the accolades they express after Lamaze births are due to their initial enthusiasm, and not to the Lamaze procedures themselves (Larsen, 2001; Zwelling, 2006).

  Participation in Lamaze procedures—as well as other natural childbirth techniques in which the emphasis is on educating the parents about the process of birth and minimizing the use of drugs—is relatively rare among members of lower income groups, including many members of ethnic minorities. Parents in these groups may not have the transportation, time, or financial resources to attend childbirth preparation classes. The result is that women in lower income groups tend to be less prepared for the events of labor and consequently may suffer more pain during childbirth (Brueggeman, 1999; Lu et al., 2003).

- *Bradley Method.* The Bradley Method, which is sometimes known as "husband-coached childbirth," is based on the principle that childbirth should be as natural as possible and involve no medication or medical interventions. Women are taught to "tune into" their bodies in order to deal with the pain of childbirth.

  To prepare for childbirth, mothers-to-be are taught muscle relaxation techniques, similar to Lamaze procedures, and good nutrition and exercise during pregnancy are seen as important to prepare for delivery. Parents are urged to take responsibility for childbirth, and the use of physicians is viewed as unnecessary and sometimes even dangerous. As you might expect, the discouragement of traditional medical interventions is quite controversial (McCutcheon-Rosegg, Ingraham, & Bradley, 1996; Reed, 2005).

- *Hypnobirthing.* Hypnobirthing is a new, but increasingly popular, technique. It involves a form of self-hypnosis during delivery that produces a sense of peace and calm, thereby reducing pain. The basic concept is to produce a state of focused concentration in which a mother relaxes her body while focusing inward. Increasing research evidence shows the technique can be effective in reducing pain (Olson, 2006; White, 2007; Alexander, Turnball, & Cyna, 2009).

Childbirth attendants: Who delivers? Traditionally, *obstetricians,* physicians who specialize in delivering babies, have been the childbirth attendants of choice. In the last few decades, more mothers have chosen to use a *midwife,* a childbirth attendant who stays with the mother throughout labor and delivery. Midwives—most often nurses specializing in childbirth—are used primarily for pregnancies in which no complications are expected. The use of midwives has increased steadily in the United States—there are now 7,000 of them—and they are employed in 10% of births. Midwives help deliver some 80% of babies in other parts of the world, often at home. Home birth is common in countries at all levels of economic development. For instance, a third of all births in the Netherlands occur at home (Ayoub, 2005; MacDorman, Declercq, & Mathews, 2011).

The newest trend in childbirth assistance is also one of the oldest: the doula (pronounced doo-lah). A *doula* is trained to provide emotional, psychological, and educational support during birth. A doula does not replace an obstetrician or midwife, and does not do medical exams. Instead, doulas, who are often well-versed in birthing alternatives, provide the mother with support and makes sure parents are aware of alternatives and possibilities regarding the birth process.

Although the use of doulas is new in the United States, they represent a return to an older tradition that has existed for centuries in other cultures. Although they may not be called "doulas," supportive, experienced older women have helped mothers as they give birth in non-Western cultures for centuries.

A growing body of research indicates the presence of a doula is beneficial to the birth process, speeding deliveries and reducing reliance on drugs. Yet concerns remain about their use. Unlike certified midwives, who are nurses and receive an additional year or two of training, doulas do not need to be certified or have any particular level of education (Ballen & Fulcher, 2006; Campbell et al., 2007; Mottl-Santiago et al., 2008).

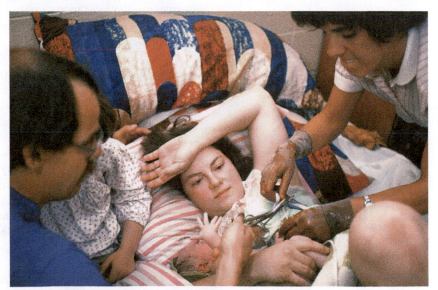

A midwife helps in this home delivery.

Pain and Childbirth. Any woman who has delivered a baby will agree that childbirth is painful. But how painful, exactly, is it?

Such a question is largely unanswerable. One reason is that pain is a subjective, psychological phenomenon, one that cannot be easily measured. No one is able to answer the question of whether their pain is "greater" or "worse" than someone else's pain, although some studies have tried to quantify it. For instance, in one survey women were asked to rate the pain they experienced during labor on a 1-to-5 scale, with 5 being the most painful (Yarrow, 1992). Nearly half (44%) said "5," and an additional one-quarter said "4."

Because pain is usually a sign that something is wrong in one's body, we have learned to react to pain with fear and concern. Yet during childbirth, pain is actually a signal that the body is working appropriately—that the contractions that are meant to propel the baby through the birth canal are doing their job. Consequently, the experience of pain during labor is difficult for women in labor to interpret, thereby potentially increasing their anxiety and making the contractions seem even more painful. Ultimately, every woman's delivery depends on such variables as how much preparation and support she has before and during delivery, her culture's view of pregnancy and delivery, and the specific nature of the delivery itself (Escott, Slade, & Spiby, 2009; Ip, Tang, & Goggins, 2009; Scotland et al., 2011).

Use of Anesthesia and Pain-Reducing Drugs. Among the greatest advances of modern medicine is the ongoing discovery of drugs that reduce pain. However, the use of medication during childbirth is a practice that holds both benefits and pitfalls.

About a third of women who receive anesthesia do so in the form of *epidural anesthesia*, which produces numbness from the waist down. Traditional epidurals produce an inability to walk and in some cases prevent women from helping to push the baby out during delivery. However, a newer form of epidural, known as a *walking epidural* or *dual spinal-epidural*, uses smaller needles and a system for administering continuous doses of anesthetic. It permits women to move about more freely during labor and has fewer side effects than traditional epidural anesthesia (Simmons et al., 2007).

It is clear that drugs hold the promise of greatly reducing, and even eliminating, pain associated with labor, which can be extreme and exhausting. However, pain reduction comes at a cost: Drugs administered during labor reach not just the mother but the fetus as well. The stronger the drug, the greater its effects on the fetus and neonate. Because of the small size of the fetus relative to the mother, drug doses that might have only a minimal effect on the mother can have a magnified effect on the fetus.

Anesthetics may temporarily depress the flow of oxygen to the fetus and slow labor. In addition, newborns whose mothers have been anesthetized are less physiologically responsive, show poorer motor control during the first days of life after birth, cry more, and may have more difficulty in initiating breastfeeding (Ransjö-Arvidson et al., 2001; Torvaldsen et al., 2006; Kraus et al., 2011).

Most research suggests that drugs, as they are currently employed during labor, produce only minimal risks to the fetus and neonate. Guidelines issued by the American College of Obstetricians and Gynecologists suggest that a woman's request for pain relief at any stage of labor should be honored, and that the proper use of minimal amounts of drugs for pain relief is reasonable and has no significant effect on a child's later well-being (ACOG, 2002; Albers et al., 2007; Wilson et al., 2011).

Postdelivery Hospital Stay: Deliver, Then Depart? When New Jersey mother Diane Mensch was sent home from the hospital just a day after the birth of her third child, she still felt exhausted. But her insurance company insisted that 24 hours was sufficient time to recover, and it refused to pay for more. Three days later, her newborn was back in the hospital, suffering from jaundice. Mensch is convinced the problem would have been discovered and treated sooner had she and her newborn been allowed to remain in the hospital longer (Begley, 1995).

Mensch's experience was not unusual. In the 1970s the average hospital stay for a normal birth was 3.9 days. By the 1990s, it was 2 days. These changes were prompted in large part by medical insurance companies, who advocated hospital stays of only 24 hours following birth to reduce costs.

Medical care providers have fought against this trend, believing that there are definite risks involved, both for mothers and for their newborns. For instance, mothers may begin to bleed if they tear tissue injured during childbirth. It is also riskier for newborns to be discharged prematurely from the intensive medical care that hospitals can provide. Furthermore, mothers are better rested and more satisfied with their medical care when they stay longer (Finkelstein, Harper, & Rosenthal, 1998).

In accordance with these views, the American Academy of Pediatrics states that except in unusual cases, women should stay in the hospital no less than 48 hours after giving birth. Furthermore, the U.S. Congress passed legislation mandating a minimum insurance coverage of 48 hours for childbirth (American Academy of Pediatrics Committee on Fetus and Newborn, 2004).

Newborn Medical Screening. Just after birth, newborns typically are tested for a variety of diseases and genetic conditions. The American College of Medical Genetics recommends that all newborns be screened for 29 disorders, ranging from hearing difficulties and sickle-cell anemia to extremely rare conditions such as isovaleric acidemia, a disorder involving metabolism. These disorders can be detected from a tiny quantity of blood drawn from an infant's heel (American College of Medical Genetics, 2006).

The advantage of newborn screening is that it permits early treatment of problems that might go undetected for years. In some cases, devastating conditions can be prevented through early treatment of the disorder, such as the implementation of a particular kind of diet (Goldfarb, 2005; Kayton, 2007; Timmermans & Buchbinder, 2011).

The exact number of tests that a newborn experiences varies drastically from state to state. In some states, only three tests are mandated, while in others more than 30 are required. In jurisdictions with only a few tests, many disorders go undiagnosed. In fact, each year around 1,000 infants in the United States suffer from disorders that could have been detected if appropriate screening had been conducted at birth (American Academy of Pediatrics, 2005; Kemper, 2011; Suida-Robinson, 2011).

Soon after birth, infants receive the first of a series of vaccinations recommended by pediatricians that extend throughout childhood to immunize children against common diseases. Vaccinations have been effective in drastically reducing the incidence of childhood diseases, and the medical community is united in recommending a series of basic ones (ACIP, 2011).

However, routine immunization has not been without controversy, as we consider in the *From Research to Practice* box.

FROM RESEARCH TO PRACTICE
Vaccination Wars

Tim Jacobs and Jeff Carlson, both 5, are best friends. "Inseparable would be more accurate," says Anne Jacobs, Tim's mom. Although Anne describes Jeff as a "great kid" and likes the Carlson family, one thing makes her nervous about the boys' friendship. "None of the three Carlson children have had any vaccinations," Anne says. "No MMR, no HepB, no polio. Nothing." The Carlsons, she explains, don't have much faith in the drug companies that make the vaccines. "They try to live outside what they call 'the money culture,'" Anne says. "They grow their own food, trade clothing with other families, and play with their kids instead of watching TV. In many ways, it's a very healthy

lifestyle, but I can't help feeling they're depending on the rest of us to have our kids immunized to protect their kids. If I was to have another baby, I would worry about what Jeff Carlson might bring into our home."

Anne Jacobs brings to light an issue that is causing some controversy for parents in our society. Although vaccinations for dangerous and deadly childhood diseases such as measles, smallpox, rubella, and polio have saved literally millions of lives, the practice has come under attack in recent years. The concern is for whether vaccinations present a danger of their own (Lantos et al., 2010; Redsell et al., 2010).

(continued)

Fear of vaccinations emerged alongside an alarming rise in the incidence of autism, a developmental disorder in which children display disturbed social functioning, lack of communication, and obsessive or repetitive behavior. Because autism often strikes children around the time they are getting their vaccinations, some observers suggested that there could be a link between the disorder and the chemicals in the vaccines (Boutot & Tincani, 2009; Mooney, 2009; Willrich, 2011).

The link between vaccinations and autism was solidified in public consciousness in 1998, when a study was published specifying what the link might be. Researchers examining the digestive systems of several children with autism and other developmental disorders found evidence of intestinal inflammation in all of them. They speculated that the common vaccine for measles, mumps, and rubella (MMR) caused this inflammation, releasing toxins that caused damage in the brain (Wakefield et al., 1998).

Although their hypothesis has since been discredited, media coverage at the time ensured that the association was firmly planted in the public consciousness. Adding to the fear was controversy surrounding the use of thimerosal, a mercury-based preservative, in prepared vaccines. Could vaccines containing mercury, a known toxin, be driving the rise in autism?

As it turns out, no. The Centers for Disease Control and Prevention and the American Academy of Pediatrics agree that the rise in autism is unconnected to the MMR vaccine. A report by the Institute of Medicine also concluded that there is no link between autism and the MMR vaccine or vaccines that contain thimerosal. Furthermore, the U.S. Court of Federal Claims handed down decisions in 2009 in three critical test cases refuting any link between autism and the MMR vaccine or vaccines with thimerosal, based on a review of the scientific literature (Centers for Disease Control and Prevention, 2008; U.S. Court of Federal Claims, 2009; Patil, 2011).

Despite these clear findings and rulings, fears persist. Urban legends such as the autism–vaccine link can be difficult to stamp out. Ironically, those who continue to advocate withholding vaccines from children out of fear of autism may be contributing to a very real social health concern. Pockets of unvaccinated children in local areas are not only themselves at risk of an outbreak of a serious disease, but they also put others at risk. As anti-vaccine sentiment builds and spreads, so too does the network of unprotected children across which a renewed disease epidemic could travel.

- **What strategies would you use to evaluate the scientific literature on the topic of vaccines and the purported link to autism?**

- **Why do some parents continue to accept the notion that vaccines are the cause of autism, despite the prevalence of scientific evidence that does not support the link?**

ARE YOU AN INFORMED CONSUMER OF DEVELOPMENT?

Dealing with Labor

Every woman who is soon to give birth has some fear of labor. Most have heard gripping tales of extended, 48-hour labors or vivid descriptions of the pain that accompanies labor. Still, few mothers would dispute the notion that the rewards of giving birth are worth the effort.

There is no single right or wrong way to deal with labor: However, several strategies can help make the process as positive as possible:

- *Be flexible.* Although you may have carefully worked out what to do during labor, don't feel an obligation to follow through exactly. If a strategy is ineffective, turn to another one.

- *Communicate with your health-care providers.* Let them know what you are experiencing. They may be able to suggest ways to deal with what you are encountering. As your labor progresses, they may also be able to give you a fairly clear idea of how much longer you will be in labor. Knowing the worst of the pain is going to last only another 20 minutes or so, you may feel you can handle it.

- *Remember that labor is ... laborious.* Expect that you may become fatigued, but realize that as the final stages of labor occur, you may well get a second wind.

- *Accept your partner's support.* If a spouse or other partner is present, allow that person to make you comfortable and provide support. Research has shown that women who are supported by a spouse or partner have a more comfortable birth experience (Bader, 1995; Kennell, 2002).

- *Be realistic and honest about your reactions to pain.* Even if you had planned an unmedicated delivery, realize that you may find the pain difficult to tolerate. At that point, consider the use of drugs. Above all, don't feel that asking for pain medication is a sign of failure. It isn't.

- *Focus on the big picture.* Keep in mind that labor is part of a process that ultimately leads to an event unmatched in the joy it can bring. ■

Review, Check, and Apply

Review

1. In the first stage of labor, contractions increase in frequency, duration, and intensity until the baby's head is able to pass through the cervix. In the second stage, the baby moves through the cervix and birth canal and leaves the mother's body. In the third stage, the umbilical cord and placenta emerge.

2. Immediately after birth, birthing attendants usually examine the neonate using a measurement system such as the Apgar scale.

3. Many birthing options are available to parents today. They may weigh the advantages and disadvantages of anesthetic drugs during birth, and they may choose alternatives to traditional hospital birthing, including the Lamaze method, the use of a birthing center, and the use of a midwife.

4. The American Academy of Pediatrics advocates hospital stays of no less than 48 hours for women who give birth to reduce risks to both mother and child. The U.S. Congress passed a law mandating insurance companies provide a minimum 48-hour coverage for childbirth.

5. Despite evidence from such sources as the Centers for Disease Control and Prevention that no link exists between childhood vaccinations and autism, some parents are still fearful and refuse to have their infants immunized. Ironically, as their numbers increase, children who have not been immunized pose a greater risk both to themselves and others for outbreak of serious disease.

Check

1. About 266 days after conception, _____ triggers the process that leads to birth.

2. The _____ is a standard measurement system designed to assess five basic qualities in a newborn: appearance (color), pulse (heart rate), grimace (reflex irritability), activity (muscle tone), and respiration (respiratory effort).

3. During delivery, a restriction of oxygen, known as _____, that lasts only a few minutes can produce long-term cognitive deficits.

4. _____ anesthesia, which produces numbness from the waist down, is used during childbirth to reduce pain in the mother.

Apply

1. How might socioeconomic factors such as level of education and income influence a woman's choice of birthing alternatives and birth attendants?

2. Are there any situations in which it may be advisable to try to talk a woman out of the birthing choices she has made?

To see more review questions, log on to MyPsychLab.

ANSWERS: 1. corticotrophin-releasing hormone (CRH)   2. Apgar scale   3. anoxia   4. Epidural

BIRTH COMPLICATIONS

LO 4-3 What complications can occur at birth, and what are their causes, effects, and treatments?

LO 4-4 In what kinds of situations are Cesarean deliveries necessary?

LO 4-5 What is postpartum depression?

When Ivy Brown's son was stillborn, a nurse told her that sad as it was, nearly 1% of births in her city, Washington, D.C., ended in death. That statistic spurred Brown to become a grief counselor, specializing in infant mortality. She formed a committee of physicians and city officials to study the capital's high infant mortality rate and find solutions to lower it. "If I can spare one mother this terrible grief, my loss will not be in vain," Brown says.

The infant mortality rate in Washington, D.C., capital of the richest country in the world, is 13.7 deaths per 1,000 births, exceeding the rate of countries such as Hungary, Cuba, Kuwait, and Costa Rica. Overall, 44 countries have better birth rates than the United States, which has 6.26 deaths for every 1,000 live births (U.S. DHHS, 2009; The World Factbook, 2009; see Figure 4-2).

Why is infant mortality higher in the United States than in other, less developed countries? To answer this question, we need to consider the nature of the problems that can occur during labor and delivery.

Preterm Infants: Too Soon, Too Small

Like Tamera Dixon, whose birth was described in the chapter prologue, 11% of infants are born earlier than normal. **Preterm infants**, or premature infants, are born prior to 38 weeks after conception. Because they have not had time to develop fully as fetuses, preterm infants are at high risk for illness and death.

The extent of danger faced by preterm babies largely depends on the child's weight at birth, which has great significance as an indicator of the extent of the baby's development. Although the average newborn weighs around 3,400 grams (about 7½ pounds), **low-birthweight infants** weigh less than 2,500 grams (around 5½ pounds). Although only 7% of all newborns in the United States fall into the low-birthweight category, they account for the majority of newborn deaths (DeVader et al., 2007).

Although most low-birthweight infants are preterm, some are small-for-gestational-age babies. **Small-for-gestational-age infants** are infants who, because of delayed fetal growth, weigh 90% (or less) of the average weight of infants of the same gestational age. Small-for-gestational-age infants are sometimes also preterm, but may not be. The syndrome may be caused by inadequate nutrition during pregnancy (Bergmann, Bergmann, & Dudenhausen, 2008; Lyndsay et al., 2011).

If the degree of prematurity is not too great and weight at birth is not extremely low, the threat to the child's well-being is relatively minor. In such cases, the main treatment may be to keep the baby in the hospital to gain weight. Additional weight is critical because fat layers help prevent chilling in neonates, who are not particularly efficient at regulating body temperature.

Newborns who are born more prematurely and who have birthweights significantly below average face a tougher road. For them, simply staying alive is a major task. For instance, low-birthweight infants are highly vulnerable to infection, and because their lungs have not had time to fully develop, they have problems taking in sufficient oxygen. As a consequence, they may experience *respiratory distress syndrome* (*RDS*), with potentially fatal consequences.

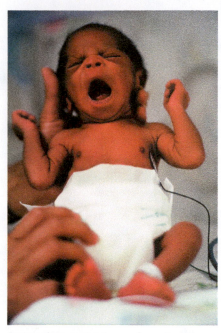

Preterm infants stand a much greater chance of survival today than they did even a decade ago.

preterm infants Infants who are born prior to 38 weeks after conception (also known as premature infants)

low-birthweight infants Infants who weigh less than 2,500 grams (around 5½ pounds) at birth

small-for-gestational-age infants Infants who, because of delayed fetal growth, weigh 90% (or less) of the average weight of infants of the same gestational age

To deal with respiratory distress syndrome, low-birthweight infants are often placed in incubators, enclosures in which temperature and oxygen content are controlled. The exact amount of oxygen is carefully monitored. Too low a concentration of oxygen will not provide relief, and too high a concentration can damage the delicate retinas of the eyes, leading to permanent blindness.

The immature development of preterm neonates makes them unusually sensitive to stimuli in their environment. They can easily be overwhelmed by the sights, sounds, and sensations they experience, and their breathing may be interrupted or their heart rates may slow. They are often unable to move smoothly; their arm and leg movements are uncoordinated, causing them to jerk about and appear startled. Such behavior is quite disconcerting to parents (Miles et al., 2006).

Despite the difficulties they experience at birth, the majority of preterm infants develop normally in the long run. However, the tempo of development often proceeds more slowly for preterm children compared to children born at full term, and more subtle problems may emerge later. For example, by the end of their first year, only 10% of prematurely born infants display significant problems, and only 5% are seriously disabled. By the age of 6, however, approximately 38% have mild problems that call for special educational interventions. For instance, some preterm children show learning disabilities, behavior disorders, or lower-than-average IQ scores. Others have difficulties with physical coordination. Still, around 60% of preterm infants are free of even minor problems (Dombrowski, Noonan, & Martin, 2007; Hall et al., 2008; Grönqvist, Brodd, & von Hofsten, 2011).

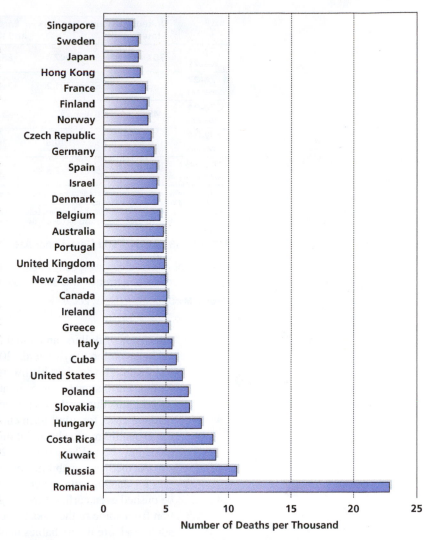

FIGURE 4-2 International Infant Mortality

Infant mortality rates in selected countries. Although the United States has greatly reduced its infant mortality rate in the past 25 years, it ranks only 26th among industrialized countries as of 1996. What are some of the reasons for this?

(*Source:* The World Factbook, 2010)

Very-Low-Birthweight Infants: The Smallest of the Small.

The story is less positive for the most extreme cases of prematurity—very-low-birthweight infants. **Very-low-birthweight infants** weigh less than 1250 grams (around 2¼ pounds) or, regardless of weight, have been in the womb less than 30 weeks.

Very-low-birthweight infants not only are tiny—some, like little Hattie Thatcher, fitting easily in the palm of the hand at birth—they hardly seem to belong to the same species as full-term newborns. Their eyes may be fused shut and their earlobes may look like flaps of skin on the sides of their heads. Their skin is a darkened red color, whatever their race.

Very-low-birthweight babies are in grave danger from the moment they are born, due to the immaturity of their organ systems. Before the mid-1980s, these babies would not have survived outside their mothers' wombs. However, medical advances have led to a higher chance of survival, pushing the *age of viability*, the point at which an infant can survive prematurely, to about 22 weeks—some four months earlier than the term of a normal delivery. Of course, the longer the period of development beyond conception, the higher are a newborn's chances of survival. A baby born earlier than 25 weeks has less than a 50-50 chance of survival (see Figure 4-3 on page 108).

The physical and cognitive problems experienced by low-birthweight and preterm babies are even more pronounced in very-low-birthweight infants, with astonishing financial consequences. A 4-month stay in an incubator in an intensive care unit can run into hundreds of

very-low-birthweight infants Infants who weigh less than 1,250 grams (around 2.25 pounds) or, regardless of weight, have been in the womb fewer than 30 weeks

	United States	Austria	Denmark	England and Wales[2]	Finland	Northern Ireland	Norway	Poland	Scotland	Sweden
22–23 weeks[1]	707.7	888.9	947.4	880.5	900.0	1,000.0	555.6	921.1	1,000.0	515.2
24–27 weeks	236.9	319.6	301.2	298.2	315.8	268.3	220.2	530.6	377.0	197.7
28–31 weeks	45.0	43.8	42.2	52.2	58.5	54.5	56.4	147.7	60.8	41.3
32–36 weeks	8.6	5.8	10.3	10.6	9.7	13.1	7.2	23.1	8.8	12.8
37 weeks or more	2.4	1.5	2.3	1.8	1.4	1.6	1.5	2.3	1.7	1.5

1 Infant mortality rates at 22–23 weeks of gestation may be unreliable due to reporting differences.
2 England and Wales provided 2005 data.
NOTE: Infant mortality rates are per 1,000 live births in specified group.
SOURCE: NCHS linked birth/infant death data set (for U.S. data), and *European Perinatal Health Report* (for European data).

FIGURE 4-3 Survival and Gestational Age

Chances of a fetus surviving greatly improve after 28 to 32 weeks. Rates shown are per 1,000 live births after specified lengths of gestation who survive the first year of life.

(*Source:* MacDorman & Mathews, 2009)

thousands of dollars, and about half of these newborns ultimately die, despite massive medical intervention (Taylor et al., 2000).

Even if a very-low-birthweight preterm infant survives, the medical costs can continue to mount. For instance, one estimate suggests that the average monthly cost of medical care for such infants during the first three years of life may be between 3 and 50 times higher than the medical costs for a full-term child. Such astronomical costs have raised ethical debates about the expenditure of substantial financial and human resources in cases in which a positive outcome may be unlikely (Prince, 2000; Doyle, 2004; Petrou, 2006).

As medical capabilities progress and developmental researchers come up with new strategies for dealing with preterm infants and improving their lives, the age of viability is likely to be pushed even earlier. Emerging evidence suggests that high-quality care can provide protection from some of the risks associated with prematurity, and that in fact by the time they reach adulthood, premature babies may be little different from other adults (Hack et al., 2002).

Research also shows that preterm infants who receive more responsive, stimulating, and organized care are apt to show more positive outcomes than those children whose care is not as good. Some of these interventions are quite simple. For example, "Kangaroo Care" in which infants are held skin-to-skin against their parents' chests appears to be effective in helping preterm infants develop. Massaging preterm infants several times a day triggers the release of hormones that promote weight gain, muscle development, and abilities to cope with stress (Erlandsson et al., 2007; Field et al., 2008; Blomqvist & Nyqvist, 2011; Feldman, 2011).

What Causes Preterm and Low-Birthweight Deliveries? About half of preterm and low-birthweight births are unexplained, but several known causes account for the remainder. In some cases, premature labor results from difficulties relating to the mother's reproductive system. For instance, mothers carrying twins have unusual stress placed on them, which can lead to early labor. In fact, most multiple births are preterm to some degree (Tan et al., 2004; Luke & Brown, 2008).

In other cases, preterm and low-birthweight babies are a result of the immaturity of the mother's reproductive system. Young mothers—under the age of 15—are more prone to deliver prematurely than older ones. In addition, a woman who becomes pregnant within six months of her previous delivery is more likely to deliver a preterm or low-birthweight infant than a woman whose reproductive system has had a chance to recover from a prior delivery. Father's age matters, too: wives of older fathers are more likely to have preterm deliveries (Smith et al., 2003; Zhu et al., 2005; Branum, 2006; Blumenshine et al., 2011).

Finally, factors that affect the general health of the mother, such as nutrition, level of medical care, amount of stress in the environment, and economic support, all are related to prematurity and low birthweight. Rates of preterm births differ between racial groups, not

---

TABLE 4-2 Factors Associated with Increased Risk of Low Birthweight

I. **Demographic Risks**

   a. Age (less than 17; over 34)
   b. Race (minority)
   c. Low socioeconomic status
   d. Unmarried
   e. Low level of education

II. **Medical Risks Predating Pregnancy**

   a. Number of previous pregnancies (0 or more than 4)
   b. Low weight for height
   c. Genitourinary anomalies/surgery
   d. Selected diseases such as diabetes, chronic hypertension
   e. Nonimmune status for selected infections such as rubella
   f. Poor obstetric history, including previous low-birthweight infant or multiple spontaneous abortions
   g. Maternal genetic factors (such as low weight at own birth)

III. **Medical Risks in Current Pregnancy**

   a. Multiple pregnancy
   b. Poor weight gain
   c. Short interpregnancy interval
   d. Low blood pressure
   e. Hypertension/preeclampsia/toxemia
   f. Selected infections such as asymptomatic bacteriuria, rubella, and cytomegalovirus
   g. First or second trimester bleeding

   h. Placental problems such as placenta previa, abruptio placentae
   i. Severe morning sickness
   j. Anemia/abnormal hemoglobin
   k. Severe anemia in a developing baby
   l. Fetal anomalies
   m. Incompetent cervix
   n. Spontaneous premature rupture of membrane

IV. **Behavioral and Environmental Risks**

   a. Smoking
   b. Poor nutritional status
   c. Alcohol and other substance abuse
   d. DES exposure and other toxic exposure, including occupational hazards
   e. High altitude

V. **Health-Care Risks**

   a. Absent or inadequate prenatal care
   b. Iatrogenic prematurity

VI. **Evolving Concepts of Risks**

   a. Stress, physical and psychosocial
   b. Uterine irritability
   c. Events triggering uterine contractions
   d. Cervical changes detected before onset of labor
   e. Selected infections such as mycoplasma and chlamydia trachomatis
   f. Inadequate plasma volume expansion
   g. Progesterone deficiency

(*Source:* Adapted from Committee to Study the Prevention of Low Birthweight, 1985.)

because of race per se, but because members of racial minorities have disproportionately lower incomes and higher stress as a result. For instance, the percentage of low-birthweight infants born to African American mothers is double that for Caucasian American mothers. (A summary of the factors associated with increased risk of low birthweight is shown in Table 4-2; Field, Diego, & Hernandex-Reif, 2006, 2008; Bergmann, Bergmann, & Dudenhausen, 2008). (Also see the *Careers in Child Development* interview with a nurse who cares for preterm and low-birthweight babies.)

Postmature Babies: Too Late, Too Large

One might imagine that a baby who spends extra time in the womb might have some advantages, given the opportunity to continue growth undisturbed by the outside world. Yet **postmature infants**—those still unborn two weeks after the mother's due date—face several risks.

For example, the blood supply from the placenta may become insufficient to nourish the still-growing fetus adequately. Consequently, the blood supply to the brain may be decreased, leading to the potential of brain damage. Similarly, labor becomes riskier (for both the child and the mother) as a fetus who may be equivalent in size to a one-month-old infant has to make its way through the birth canal (Shea, Wilcox, & Little, 1998; Fok, 2006).

Difficulties involving postmature infants are more easily prevented than those involving preterm babies, since medical practitioners can induce labor artificially if the pregnancy continues too long. Not only can certain drugs bring on labor, but physicians also have the option of performing Cesarean deliveries, a form of delivery we consider next.

postmature infants Infants still unborn 2 weeks after the mother's due date

CAREERS IN CHILD DEVELOPMENT
Clinical Nurse Specialist

Name: Patricia Clifford

Education: B.S. in Nursing, Villanova University, Villanova, PA; M.S. in Nursing, College of New Jersey

Position: Clinical Nurse Specialist at The Children's Hospital of Philadelphia

Thanks in part to modern medicine and the dedication and skill of professional medical staff such as Patricia Clifford, the survival rate of preterm infants is almost twice that of 20 years ago.

According to Clifford, a clinical nurse specialist in the neonatal intensive care unit (NICU) of The Children's Hospital of Philadelphia, preterm infants need considerable specialized attention and care.

"Preterm infants are very fragile patients who require highly technological medical care, as well as sophisticated developmental care, to ensure optimum outcomes," she noted.

"From a medical point of view, we now have multiple types and modes of ventilation that we individualize for each patient," she added. "We use double walled incubators that retain better heat as well as provide humidity."

The incubators are covered with blankets to decrease light and sound stimulation, and they are not uncovered until the infant is approximately 32 weeks, according to Clifford.

"Nurses have learned how to read the cues that these infants display to tell us what they can handle and when they are stressed," she said. "It's amazing to watch an infant display stress signs and then watch them relax and calm when the stressor is taken away."

A 75-bed unit that handles approximately 1,400 admissions a year, the Children's Hospital of Philadelphia cares for extremely low-birthweight infants born as young as 24 weeks, as well as older infants with medical problems, Clifford explains. "Approximately 30% of our infants have been born with some issue requiring surgery. Many of our infants will have surgery at the bedside with a full surgical team, rather than go to the operating room," she added.

While the infants get extensive attention and treatment, the needs of parents are tended to as well.

"At the Children's Hospital, parents have 24-hour visiting privileges and are provided with rooms in the hospital, as well as in the unit, for them to sleep if needed," Clifford said. "And nurses educate parents about stress cues and teach them how to comfort and calm their child."

The challenges are many for Clifford, but she also finds rewards in her work.

"My job provides me with the opportunity to work at the bedside helping our nurses provide the best care to our patients. It is this one-on-one interaction that gives me the greatest satisfaction," she noted.

Cesarean Delivery: Intervening in the Process of Birth

As Elena entered her 18th hour of labor, the obstetrician who was monitoring her progress began to look concerned. She told Elena and her husband, Pablo, that the fetal monitor revealed that the fetus's heart rate had begun to fall after each contraction. After trying some simple remedies, such as repositioning Elena on her side, the obstetrician came to the conclusion that the fetus was in distress. She told them that the baby should be delivered immediately, and to accomplish that, she would have to carry out a Cesarean delivery.

Elena became one of the more than one million mothers in the United States who have a Cesarean delivery each year. In a **Cesarean delivery** (sometimes known as a *C-section*), the baby is surgically removed from the uterus, rather than traveling through the birth canal.

Cesarean deliveries occur most frequently when the fetus shows distress of some sort. For instance, if the fetus appears to be in danger, as indicated by a sudden rise in its heart rate or if blood is seen coming from the mother's vagina during labor, a Cesarean may be performed. In addition, older mothers, over the age of 40, are more likely to have Cesarean deliveries than younger ones. The rate of Cesarean deliveries in the United States is now 32% of all deliveries (Tang, Wu, Liu, Lin, & Hsu, 2006; Menacker & Hamilton, 2010; Young, 2011).

Cesarean deliveries are also used in some cases of *breech position,* in which the baby is positioned feet first in the birth canal. Breech position births, which occur in about 1 out of 25 births, place the baby at risk, because the umbilical cord is more likely to be compressed, depriving the baby of oxygen. Cesarean deliveries are also more likely in *transverse position* births, in which the baby lies crosswise in the uterus, or when the baby's head is so large it has trouble moving through the birth canal.

Cesarean delivery A birth in which the baby is surgically removed from the uterus, rather than traveling through the birth canal

The routine use of **fetal monitors**, devices that measure the baby's heartbeat during labor, has contributed in part to a soaring rate of Cesarean deliveries. Because fetal monitors sometimes ambiguously indicate that the fetus is under stress, unnecessary Cesareans may result (U.S. Center for Health Statistics, 2003).

Are Cesareans an effective medical intervention? Other countries have substantially lower rates of Cesarean deliveries (see Figure 4-4), and there is no association between successful births and the rate of Cesarean deliveries. In addition, Cesarean deliveries carry dangers. Cesarean delivery represents major surgery, and the mother's recovery can be relatively lengthy, particularly when compared to a normal delivery. In addition, the risk of maternal infection is higher with Cesarean deliveries (Miesnik & Reale, 2007; Josefsson et al., 2011).

Finally, a Cesarean delivery presents some risks for the baby. Because Cesarean babies are spared the stresses of passing though the birth canal, their relatively easy passage into the world may deter the normal release of certain stress-related hormones, such as catecholamines, into the newborn's bloodstream. These hormones help prepare the neonate to deal with the stress of the world outside the womb, and their absence may be detrimental to the newborn child.

In fact, research indicates that babies born by Cesarean delivery, who have not experienced labor, are more likely to have breathing problems upon birth than those who have at least progressed through some labor prior to being born via a Cesarean delivery. Finally, mothers who deliver by Cesarean are less satisfied with the birth experience, although their dissatisfaction does not influence the quality of mother–child interactions (Porter et al., 2007; MacDorman et al., 2008; Kotaska, 2011).

Because the increase in Cesarean deliveries is, as we have said, connected to the use of fetal monitors, medical authorities now currently recommend that they not be used routinely. There is evidence that outcomes are no better for newborns who have been monitored than for those who have not been monitored. In addition, monitors tend to indicate fetal distress when there is none—false alarms—with disquieting regularity. Monitors do, however, play a critical role in high-risk pregnancies and in cases of preterm and postmature babies (Albers & Krulewitch, 1993; Freeman, 2007).

Studies examining what appear, in retrospect, to be unnecessary Cesareans have found racial and socioeconomic differences. Specifically, black mothers are more likely to have a potentially unnecessary Cesarean delivery than white mothers. In addition, Medicaid patients—who tend to be relatively poor—are more likely to have unnecessary Cesarean deliveries than non-Medicaid patients (Kabir et al., 2005).

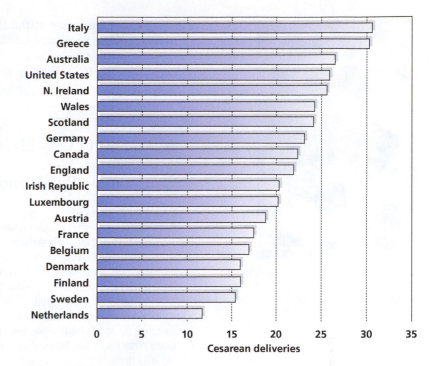

FIGURE 4-4 Cesarean Deliveries

The rate at which Cesarean deliveries are performed varies substantially from one country to another. Why do you think the United States has one of the highest rates?

(*Source:* International Cesarean Awareness Network, 2004)

Infant Mortality and Stillbirth: The Tragedy of Premature Death

The joy that accompanies the birth of a child is completely reversed when a newborn dies. The relative rarity of their occurrence makes infant deaths even harder for parents to bear.

Sometimes a child does not even live beyond its passage through the birth canal. **Stillbirth,** the delivery of a child who is not alive, occurs in fewer than 1 delivery out of 100. Sometimes the death is detected before labor begins. In this case, labor is typically induced, or physicians may carry out a Cesarean delivery to remove the body from the mother as soon as possible. In other cases of stillbirth, the baby dies during its travel through the birth canal.

Whether the death is a stillbirth or occurs after the child is born, the loss of a baby is tragic; the impact on parents, enormous. The loss and grief parents feel and their passage through it is similar to that experienced when an older loved one dies.

fetal monitor   A device that measures the baby's heartbeat during labor

stillbirth   The delivery of a child who is not alive, occurring in fewer than 1 delivery in 100

Although overall infant mortality rates have declined in the United States, there are significant differences in mortality among members of different racial and socioeconomic groups.

infant mortality   Death within the first year of life

The juxtaposition of the first dawning of life and an unnaturally early death may make the death particularly difficult to accept and handle. Depression is common, and it is often intensified owing to a lack of support. Some parents even experience post-traumatic stress disorder (Cacciatore & Bushfield, 2007; Turton, Evans, & Hughes, 2009; Robertson Blackmore et al., 2011).

🔵 DEVELOPMENTAL DIVERSITY AND YOUR LIFE

Overcoming Racial and Cultural Differences in Infant Mortality

Even though there has been a general decline in the **infant mortality** rate in the United States over the past several decades, African American babies are more than twice as likely to die before the age of 1 than white babies. This difference is largely the result of socioeconomic factors: African American women are significantly more likely to be living in poverty than Caucasian women and to receive less prenatal care. As a result, their babies are more likely to be of low birthweight—the factor most closely linked to infant mortality—than infants of mothers of other racial groups (see Figure 4-5; Stolberg, 1999; Duncan & Brooks-Gunn, 2000; Byrd et al., 2007).

But it is not just members of particular racial groups in the United States who suffer from poor mortality rates. As mentioned earlier, the rate of infant mortality in the United States is higher than the rate in many other countries. For example, the mortality rate in the United States is almost double that of Japan.

Why does the United States fare so poorly in terms of newborn survival? One answer is that the United States has a higher rate of low-birthweight and preterm deliveries than many other countries. In fact, when U.S. infants are compared to infants of the same weight who are born in other countries, the differences in mortality rates disappear (MacDorman et al., 2005).

Another reason for the higher U.S. mortality rate relates to economic diversity. The United States has a higher proportion of people living in poverty than many other countries. Because people in lower economic categories are less likely to have adequate medical care and tend to be less healthy, the relatively high proportion of economically deprived individuals in the United States has an impact on the overall mortality rate (Terry, 2000; Bremner & Fogel, 2004; MacDorman et al., 2005; Masho & Archer, 2011).

Many countries do a significantly better job than the United States in providing prenatal care to mothers-to-be. For instance, low-cost and even free care, both before and after delivery, is often available in other countries. Furthermore, paid maternity leave is frequently provided to pregnant women, lasting in some cases as long as 51 weeks (see Table 4-3).

In the United States, the *Family and Medical Leave Act* (*FMLA*) requires most employers to give new parents up to 12 weeks of unpaid leave following the birth, adoption, or foster care placement of a child. FMLA also requires employers to offer leave for the care of a child (or parent or spouse) who has a serious medical condition. However, because it is *unpaid* leave, the lack of pay is an enormous barrier for low-income workers, who rarely are able to take advantage of the opportunity to stay home with their child.

The opportunity to take an extended maternity leave can be important: Mothers who spend more time on maternity leave may have better mental health and higher quality interactions with their infants (Waldfogel, 2001).

Better health care is only part of the story. In certain European countries, in addition to a comprehensive package of services involving general practitioner, obstetrician, and midwife, pregnant women receive many privileges, such as transportation benefits for visits to health care providers. In Norway, pregnant women may be given living expenses for up to 10 days so they can be close to a hospital when it is time to give birth. And when their babies are born, new mothers receive, for just a small payment, the assistance of trained home helpers (Morice, 1998; DeVries, 2005).

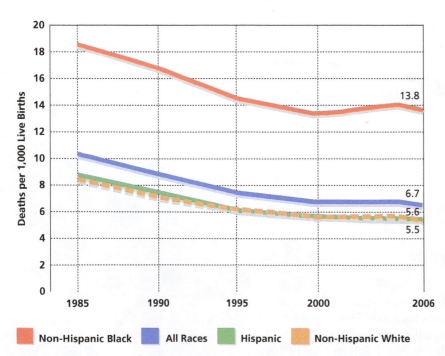

FIGURE 4-5 Race and Infant Mortality

Although infant mortality is dropping for all children in the United States, the death rate is still more than twice as high for black, non-Hispanic infants than for white, non-Hispanics. These figures show the number of deaths in the first year of life for every 1,000 live births.

(*Source:* http://childstats.gov/2009)

TABLE 4-3 Childbirth-Related Leave Policies in the United States and 10 Peer Nations

Country	Type of Leave Provided	Total Duration (in months)	Payment Rate
United States	12 weeks of family leave	2.8	Unpaid
Canada	17 weeks maternity leave 10 weeks parental leave	6.2	15 weeks at 55% of prior earnings 55% of prior earnings
Denmark	28 weeks maternity leave 1 year parental leave	18.5	60% of prior earnings 90% of unemployment benefit rate
Finland	18 weeks maternity leave 26 weeks parental leave Child rearing leave until child is 3	36.0	70% of prior earnings 70% of prior earnings Flat rate
Norway	52 weeks parental leave 2 years child rearing leave	36.0	80% of prior earnings Flat rate
Sweden	18 months parental leave	18.0	12 months at 80% of prior earnings, 3 months flat rate, 3 months unpaid
Austria	16 weeks maternity leave 2 years parental leave	27.7	100% of prior earnings 18 months of unemployment benefit rate, 6 months unpaid
France	16 weeks maternity leave Parental leave until child is 3	36.0	100% of prior earnings Unpaid for one child; paid at flat rate (income is tested) for two or more
Germany	14 weeks maternity leave 3 years parental leave	39.2	100% of prior earnings Flat rate (income-tested) for 2 years, unpaid for 3rd year
Italy	5 months maternity leave 6 months parental leave	11.0	80% of prior earnings 30% of prior earnings
United kingdom	18 weeks maternity leave 13 weeks parental leave	7.2	90% for 6 weeks and flat rate for 12 weeks, if sufficient work history; otherwise, flat rate

(*Source:* "From Maternity to Parental Leave Policies: Women's Health, Employment and Child and Family Well-Being," by S. B. Kamerman, 2000 (Spring), *The Journal of the American Women's Medical Association*, p. 55, table 1; "Parental Leave Policies: An Essential Ingredient in Early Childhood Education and Care Policies, " by S. B. Kamerman, 2000, *Social Policy Report*, p. 14. Table 1.0)

In the United States, the story is very different. The lack of national health care insurance or a national health policy means that prenatal care is often haphazardly provided to the poor. About one out of every six pregnant women has insufficient prenatal care. Some 20% of white women and close to 40% of African American women receive no prenatal care early in their pregnancies. Five percent of white mothers and 11% of African American mothers do not see a health care provider until the last three months of pregnancy; some never see a health care provider at all (Hueston, Geesey, & Diaz, 2008; Friedman, Heneghan, & Rosenthal, 2009).

Ultimately, the lack of prenatal services results in a higher mortality rate. Yet this situation can be changed if greater support is provided. A start would be to ensure that all economically disadvantaged pregnant women have access to free or inexpensive high-quality medical care from the beginning of pregnancy. Furthermore, barriers that prevent poor women from receiving such care should be reduced. For instance, programs can be developed that help pay for transportation to a health facility or for the care of older children while the mother is making a health-care visit. The cost of these programs is likely to be offset by the savings they make possible—healthy babies cost less than infants with chronic problems as a result of poor nutrition and prenatal care (Cramer et al., 2007; Edgerley et al., 2007; Barber & Gertler, 2009). ■

FROM AN EDUCATOR'S PERSPECTIVE:

Why do you think the United States lacks effective educational and health-care policies that could reduce infant mortality rates overall and among poorer people? What arguments would you make to change this situation?

Postpartum Depression: Moving from the Heights of Joy to the Depths of Despair

Renata had been overjoyed when she found out that she was pregnant and had spent the months of her pregnancy happily preparing for her baby's arrival. The birth was routine, the baby a healthy, pink-cheeked boy. But a few days after her son's birth, she sank into the depths of depression. Constantly crying, confused, feeling incapable of caring for her child, she was experiencing unshakable despair.

The diagnosis: a classic case of postpartum depression. *Postpartum depression*, a period of deep depression following the birth of a child, affects some 10% of all new mothers. Although it takes several forms, its main symptom is an enduring, deep feeling of sadness and unhappiness, lasting in some cases for months or even years. In about 1 in 500 cases, the symptoms are even worse, evolving into a total break with reality. In extremely rare instances, postpartum depression may turn deadly. For example, Andrea Yates, a mother in Texas who was charged with drowning all five of her children in a bathtub, said that postpartum depression led to her actions (Yardley, 2001; Oretti et al., 2003; Misri, 2007).

For mothers who suffer from postpartum depression, the symptoms are often bewildering. The onset of depression usually comes as a complete surprise. Certain mothers do seem more likely to become depressed, such as those who have been clinically depressed at some point in the past or who have depressed family members. Furthermore, women who are unprepared for the range of emotions that follow the birth of a child—some positive, some negative—may be more prone to depression (Kim et al., 2008; Banti et al., 2011; Iles, Slade, & Spiby, 2011).

Finally, postpartum depression may be triggered by the pronounced swings in hormone production that occur after birth. During pregnancy, the production of the female hormones estrogen and progesterone increase significantly. However, within the first 24 hours following birth, they plunge to normal levels. This rapid change may result in depression (Verkerk, Pop, & Van Son, 2003; Klier et al., 2007; Yim et al., 2009).

Whatever the cause, maternal depression leaves its marks on the infant. As we'll see later in the chapter, babies are born with impressive social capacities, and they are highly attuned to the moods of their mothers. When depressed mothers interact with their infants, they are likely to display little emotion and to act detached and withdrawn. This lack of responsiveness leads infants to display fewer positive emotions and to withdraw from contact not only with their mothers but with other adults as well. In addition, children of depressed mothers are more prone to antisocial activities such as violence (Nylen et al., 2006; Goodman et al., 2008; Garabedian et al., 2011).

Review, Check, and Apply

Review

1. Largely because of low birthweight, preterm infants may have substantial difficulties after birth and later in life.

2. Very-low-birthweight infants are in special danger because of the immaturity of their organ systems.

3. Preterm and low-birthweight deliveries can be caused by health, age, and pregnancy-related factors in the mother. Income (and, because of its relationship with income, race) is also an important factor.

4. Cesarean deliveries are performed with postmature babies or when the fetus is in distress, in the wrong position, or unable to progress through the birth canal.

5. Postpartum depression, which affects roughly 10% of new mothers, is characterized by enduring, deep feelings of sadness and unhappiness. Women who have previously suffered from clinical depression or who have family members who are depressed may be at greater risk for postpartum depression. The sharp, rapid drop of the female hormones estrogen and progesterone following delivery may also play a role.

6. Infant mortality rates can be affected by the availability of inexpensive health care and good education programs for mothers-to-be.

Check

1. Preterm infants, or premature infants, are born prior to _____ weeks after conception.

2. _____ infants weigh less than 1250 grams (around 2¼ pounds) or have been in the womb less than 30 weeks.

3. In a _____ delivery, the baby is surgically removed from the uterus, rather than traveling through the birth canal.

4. Symptoms of _____ _____ include an enduring, deep feeling of sadness and unhappiness following the birth of a child.

Apply

1. What are some ethical considerations relating to the provision of intensive medical care to very-low-birthweight babies?

2. Do you think such interventions should be routine practice? Why or why not?

To see more review questions, log on to MyPsychLab.

ANSWERS: 1. 38 2. Very-low-birthweight 3. Cesarean (or C-section) 4. postpartum depression

---

MODULE   4.3

THE COMPETENT NEWBORN

LO 4-6   What capabilities does the newborn have?

LO 4-7   How do newborns respond to others?

> *Relatives gathered around the infant car seat and its occupant, Kaita Castro. Born just two days ago, this is Kaita's first day home from the hospital with her mother. Kaita's nearest cousin, 4-year-old Tabor, seems uninterested in the new arrival. "Babies can't do anything fun. They can't even do anything at all," he says.*

Kaita's cousin Tabor is partly right. There are many things babies cannot do. Neonates arrive in the world quite incapable of successfully caring for themselves, for example. Why are human infants born so dependent, whereas members of other species seem to arrive much better equipped for their lives?

One reason is that, in one sense, humans are born too soon. The brain of the average newborn is just one fourth of what it will be at adulthood. In comparison, the brain of the macaque monkey, which is born after just 24 weeks of gestation, is 65% of its adult size. Because of the relative puniness of the infant human brain, some observers have suggested that we are propelled out of the womb some 6 to 12 months sooner than we ought to be.

In reality, evolution probably knew what it was doing: If we stayed inside our mothers' bodies an additional half-year to a year, our heads would be so large that we'd never manage to get through the birth canal (Schultz, 1969; Gould, 1977; Kotre & Hall, 1990).

The relatively underdeveloped brain of the human newborn helps explain the infant's apparent helplessness. Because of this, the earliest views of newborns focused on the things that they could not do, comparing them rather unfavorably to older members of the human species.

Today, however, such beliefs have taken a backseat to more favorable views of the neonate. As developmental researchers have begun to understand more about the nature of newborns, they have come to realize that infants enter this world with an astounding array of capabilities in all domains of development: physical, cognitive, and social.

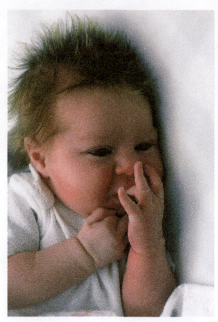

Newborns enter the world programmed to find, take in, and digest food in the form of the rooting, sucking, and swallowing reflexes.

Physical Competence: Meeting the Demands of a New Environment

The world faced by a neonate is remarkably different from the one it experienced in the womb. Consider, for instance, the significant changes in functioning that Kaita Castro encountered as she began the first moments of life in her new environment (summarized in Table 4-4).

Kaita's most immediate task was to bring sufficient air into her body. Inside her mother, air was delivered through the umbilical cord, which also provided a means for taking away carbon dioxide. The realities of the outside world are different: Once the umbilical cord was cut, Kaita's respiratory system needed to begin its lifetime's work.

For Kaita, the task was automatic. As we noted earlier, most newborn babies begin to breathe on their own as soon as they are exposed to air. The ability to breathe immediately is a good indication that the respiratory system of the normal neonate is reasonably well developed, despite its lack of rehearsal in the womb.

Neonates emerge from the uterus more practiced in other types of physical activities. For example, newborns such as Kaita show several **reflexes**—unlearned, organized, involuntary responses that occur automatically in the presence of certain stimuli. Some of these reflexes are well-rehearsed, having been present for several months before birth. The *sucking reflex* and the *swallowing reflex* permit Kaita to begin right away to ingest food. The *rooting reflex,* which involves turning in the direction of a source of stimulation (such as a light touch) near the mouth, is also related to eating. It guides the infant toward potential sources of food that are near its mouth, such as a mother's nipple.

Not all of the reflexes that are present at birth lead the newborn to seek out desired stimuli such as food. For instance, Kaita can cough, sneeze, and blink—reflexes that help her to avoid stimuli that are potentially bothersome or hazardous. (We discuss more reflexes in Chapter 5.)

Kaita's sucking and swallowing reflexes, which help her to consume her mother's milk, are coupled with the newfound ability to digest nutriments. The newborn's digestive system initially produces feces in the form of *meconium,* a greenish-black material that is a remnant of the neonate's days as a fetus.

Because the liver, a critical component of the digestive system, does not always work effectively at first, almost half of all newborns develop a distinctly yellowish tinge to their bodies and eyes. This change in color is a symptom of *neonatal jaundice.* It is most likely to occur in preterm and low-weight neonates, and it is typically not dangerous. Treatment most often consists of placing the baby under fluorescent lights or administering medicine.

TABLE 4-4   Kaita Castro's First Encounters upon Birth

1. As soon as she is through the birth canal, Kaita automatically begins to breathe on her own after no longer being attached to the umbilical cord that provided precious oxygen in the womb.

2. Reflexes—unlearned, organized involuntary responses that occur in the presence of stimuli—begin to take over. Sucking and swallowing reflexes permit Kaita immediately to ingest food.

3. The rooting reflex, which involves turning in the direction of a source of stimulation, guides Kaita toward potential sources of food that are near her mouth, such as her mother's nipple.

4. Kaita begins to cough, sneeze, and blink—reflexes that help her avoid stimuli that are potentially bothersome or hazardous.

5. Her senses of smell and taste are highly developed. Physical activities and sucking increase when she smells peppermint. Her lips pucker when a sour taste is placed on her lips.

6. Objects with colors of blue and green seem to catch Kaita's attention more than other colors, and she reacts sharply to loud, sudden noises. She will also continue to cry if she hears other newborns cry, but will stop if she hears a recording of her own voice crying.

---

reflexes   Unlearned, organized involuntary responses that occur automatically in the presence of certain stimuli

Sensory Capabilities: Experiencing the World

Just after Kaita was born, her father was certain that she looked directly at him. Did she, in fact, see him?

This is a hard question to answer for several reasons. For one thing, when sensory experts talk of "seeing," they mean both a sensory reaction due to the stimulation of the visual sensory organs and an interpretation of that stimulation (the distinction, as you might recall from an introductory psychology class, between sensation and perception). As we'll discuss further when we consider sensory capabilities during infancy in Chapter 5, it is tricky, to say the least, to pinpoint the specific sensory skills of newborns who lack the ability to explain what they are experiencing.

Still, we do have some answers to the question of what newborns are capable of seeing and, for that matter, to questions about their other sensory capabilities. For example, it is clear that neonates such as Kaita can see to some extent. Although their visual acuity is not fully developed, newborns actively pay attention to certain types of information in their environment.

Starting at birth, infants are able to distinguish colors and even show preferences for particular ones.

For instance, neonates pay closest attention to portions of scenes in their field of vision that are highest in information, such as objects that sharply contrast with the rest of their environment. Furthermore, infants can discriminate different levels of brightness. There is even evidence suggesting that newborns have a sense of size constancy. They seem aware that objects stay the same size even though the size of the image on the retina varies with distance (Chien et al., 2006; Braddick & Atkinson, 2011).

In addition, not only can newborn babies distinguish different colors, but also they seem to prefer particular ones. For example, they are able to distinguish among red, green, yellow, and blue, and they take more time staring at blue and green objects—suggesting a partiality for those colors (Dobson, 2000; Alexander & Hines, 2002; Zemach, Chang, & Teller, 2007).

Newborns are also clearly capable of hearing. They react to certain kinds of sounds, showing startle reactions to loud, sudden noises, for instance. They also exhibit familiarity with certain sounds. For example, a crying newborn will continue to cry when he or she hears other newborns crying. If the baby hears a recording of its own crying, on the other hand, he or she is more likely to stop crying, as if recognizing the familiar sound (Dondi, Simion, & Caltran, 1999; Fernald, 2001).

As with vision, however, the degree of auditory acuity is not as great as it will be later. The auditory system is not completely developed. Moreover, amniotic fluid, which is initially trapped in the middle ear, must drain out before the newborn can fully hear. In addition to sight and hearing, the other senses also function quite adequately in the newborn. It is obvious that newborns are sensitive to touch. For instance, they respond to stimuli such as the hairs of a brush, and they are aware of puffs of air so weak that adults cannot notice them (see the *Neuroscience and Development* box to learn about the long-term effects of an infant's experience of pain).

The senses of smell and taste are also well developed. Newborns suck and increase other physical activity when the odor of peppermint is placed near the nose. They also pucker their lips when a sour taste is placed on them, and respond with suitable facial expressions to other tastes as well. Such findings clearly indicate that the senses of touch, smell, and taste not only are present at birth but also are reasonably sophisticated (Cohen & Cashon, 2003; Armstrong et al., 2007).

In one sense, the sophistication of the sensory systems of newborns such as Kaita is not surprising. After all, the typical neonate has had nine months to prepare for his or her encounter with the outside world. As we discussed in Chapter 3, human sensory systems begin their development well before birth. Furthermore, the passage through the birth canal may place babies in a state of heightened sensory awareness, preparing them for the world that they are about to encounter for the first time.

Early Learning Capabilities

One-month-old Michael Samedi was on a car ride with his family when a thunderstorm suddenly began. The storm rapidly became violent, and flashes of lightning were quickly followed by loud thunderclaps. Michael was clearly disturbed and began to sob. With each new thunderclap, the pitch and fervor of his crying increased. Unfortunately, before very long it wasn't just the sound of the thunder that would raise Michael's anxiety; the sight of the

NEUROSCIENCE AND DEVELOPMENT
Beyond Band-Aids: How Pain in Infancy Affects Pain in Adulthood

More than a decade ago, researchers discovered that newborns exposed to painful stimuli early in life experience changes in their later sensory processing. For example, premature infants exposed to painful medical procedures in the neonatal intensive care unit are less sensitive to pain at 18 months of age (Grunau et al., 1994).

Is this a lasting effect? To help answer this question, neuroscientists Jamie LaPrairie and Anne Murphy administered a drug called naloxone to laboratory rats injured at birth. Naloxone blocks the actions of endogenous opioid peptides, a substance in the brain that is released following an injury and which inhibit pain. These also play an important role in motivation, emotion, and stress responses (LaPrairie & Murphy, 2009).

The birth-injured rats were again tested as adult animals, and their midbrain gray matter was examined to see if the birth trauma had altered the functioning of natural opioid. The researchers found

that the level of endogenous opioid peptides in brain-injured rats was two times higher than non-birth-injured rats. Apparently, their painful early life trauma created a brain response with fewer receptors to permit optimal sensitivity to pain medications later in life.

Of course, one critical question is whether these findings can be generalized to humans, particularly to premature infants who may experience dozens of procedures after birth. Since neonatal procedures cause such discomfort, it is conceivable that it may produce a change in the wiring of children's brain in adulthood (Simons et al., 2003; LaPrairie & Murphy, 2009).

- **What advice might you provide to a friend who has just delivered a premature infant?**

- **What questions might you suggest be asked about the infant's care?**

 Watch the **Video** *Classical Conditioning: An Involuntary Response* in **MyPsychLab**.

Developmental psychologist Tiffany Field carried out pioneering work on infants' facial expressions.

 Explore *Classical Conditioning of Little Albert* in **MyPsychLab**.

classical conditioning   A type of learning in which an organism responds in a particular way to a neutral stimulus that normally does not bring about that type of response

operant conditioning   A form of learning in which a voluntary response is strengthened or weakened, depending on its association with positive or negative consequences

lightning alone was enough to make him cry out in fear. In fact, even as an adult, Michael feels his chest tighten and his stomach churn at the mere sight of lightning.

Classical Conditioning.   The source of Michael's fear is classical conditioning, a basic type of learning first identified by Ivan Pavlov (introduced in Chapter 2). In **classical conditioning,** an organism learns to respond in a particular way to a neutral stimulus that normally does not bring about that type of response. Pavlov discovered that by repeatedly pairing two stimuli, such as the sound of a bell and the arrival of meat, he could make hungry dogs learn to respond (in this case by salivating) not only when the meat was presented but also even when the bell was sounded without the presence of meat (Pavlov, 1927).

The key feature of classical conditioning is stimulus substitution, in which a stimulus that doesn't naturally bring about a particular response is paired with a stimulus that does evoke that response. Repeatedly presenting the two stimuli together results in the second stimulus taking on the properties of the first. In effect, the second stimulus is substituted for the first.

One of the earliest examples of the power of classical conditioning in shaping human emotions was demonstrated in the case of an 11-month-old infant known by researchers as "Little Albert" (Watson & Rayner, 1920). Although he initially adored furry animals and showed no fear of rats, Little Albert learned to fear them when, during a laboratory demonstration, a loud noise was sounded every time he played with a cute and harmless white rat. In fact, the fear generalized to other furry objects, including rabbits and even a Santa Claus mask. (By the way, such a demonstration would be considered unethical today, and it would never be conducted.)

Infants are capable of learning very early through classical conditioning. For instance, one- and two-day-old newborns who are stroked on the head just before being given a drop of a sweet-tasting liquid soon learn to turn their heads and suck at the head-stroking alone. Clearly, classical conditioning is in operation from the time of birth (Dominguez, Lopez, & Molina, 1999; Kraebel, 2012; Marquis & Shi, 2012).

Operant Conditioning.   Classical conditioning is not the only mechanism through which infants learn; they also respond to **operant conditioning.** As noted in Chapter 2, operant conditioning is a form of learning in which a voluntary response is strengthened or weakened, depending on its association with positive or negative consequences. In operant conditioning, infants learn to act deliberately on their environments to bring about some desired consequence. An infant who learns that crying in a certain way is apt to bring her parents' immediate attention is displaying operant conditioning.

TABLE 4-5   Learning in Infancy: Some Basic Processes

Type	Description	Example
Classical Conditioning	A situation in which an organism learns to respond in a particular way to a neutral stimulus that normally does not bring about that type of response.	A hungry baby stops crying when her mother picks her up because she has learned to associate being picked up with subsequent feeding.
Operant Conditioning	A form of learning in which a voluntary response is strengthened or weakened, depending on its positive or negative consequences.	An infant who learns that smiling at his or her parents brings positive attention and may smile more often.
Habituation	The decrease in the response to a stimulus that occurs after repeated presentations of the same stimulus.	A baby who showed interest and surprise at first seeing a novel toy may show no interest after seeing the same toy several times.

Like classical conditioning, operant conditioning functions from the earliest days of life. For instance, researchers have found that even newborns readily learn through operant conditioning to keep sucking on a nipple when it permits them to continue hearing their mothers read a story or to listen to music.

 **Watch** the **Video** *Operant Conditioning: Learning from Consequences* in **MyPsychLab**.

Habituation. Probably the most primitive form of learning is demonstrated by the phenomenon of habituation. **Habituation** is the decrease in the response to a stimulus that occurs after repeated exposure to the same stimulus. For example, when newborns are presented with a new stimulus, they produce an *orienting response* in which they become quiet, attentive, and experience a slowed heart rate as they take in the novel stimulus. When the novelty wears off from repeated exposure, the infant no longer reacts with this orienting response. If a new and different stimulus is presented, the infant once again reacts with an orienting response. When this happens, we can say that the infant has learned to recognize the original stimulus and to distinguish it from others.

Habituation occurs in every sensory system, and researchers have studied it in several ways. One is to examine changes in sucking, which stops temporarily when a new stimulus is presented. This reaction is not unlike that of an adult who temporarily puts down her knife and fork when a dinner companion makes a statement that particularly interests her. Other measures of habituation include changes in heart rate, respiration rate, and the length of time an infant looks at a particular stimulus (Farroni et al., 2007; Colombo & Mitchell, 2009; Vaillant-Molina & Bahrick, 2012).

The development of habituation is linked to physical and cognitive maturation. It is present at birth and becomes more pronounced over the first 12 weeks of infancy. Difficulties involving habituation represent a signal of developmental problems such as mental retardation, or intellectual disability, as it is increasingly being called (Moon, 2002). (The three basic processes of learning that we've considered—classical conditioning, operant conditioning, and habituation—are summarized in Table 4-5).

 **Watch** the **Video** *Habituation* in **MyPsychLab**.

Social Competence: Responding to Others

Soon after Kaita was born, her older brother looked down at her in her crib and opened his mouth wide, pretending to be surprised. Kaita's mother, looking on, was amazed when it appeared that Kaita imitated his expression, opening her mouth as if *she* were surprised.

Was Kaita's response a happy coincidence or a true imitation of her brother's expression?

Although infants were known to have all the muscles in place to produce facial expressions related to basic emotions, the actual appearance of such expressions was assumed to be largely random. However, research beginning in the late 1970s suggested a different conclusion. For instance, developmental researchers found that when an adult modeled a behavior that the infant

habituation   The decrease in the response to a stimulus that occurs after repeated presentations of the same stimulus

TABLE 4-6 Factors that Encourage Social Interaction between Full-Term Newborns and Their Parents

Newborn	Parent
Shows a preference for particular stimuli	Offers those stimuli more than others
Begins to show a predictable cycle of arousal states	Uses the observed cycle to achieve more regulated states
Shows some consistency in time patterns	Conforms to and shapes the newborn's patterns
Shows awareness of parent's actions	Helps newborn grasp intent of actions
Reacts and adapts to actions of parent	Acts in predictable, consistent ways
Shows evidence of a desire to communicate	Works to comprehend the newborn's communicative efforts

(*Source:* Based on Eckerman & Oehler, 1992.)

already performed spontaneously, such as opening the mouth or sticking out the tongue, the newborn appeared to imitate the behavior (Meltzoff & Moore, 1977, 2002; Nagy, 2006).

Even more exciting were findings from a series of studies conducted by developmental psychologist Tiffany Field and her colleagues (Field, 1982; Field & Walden, 1982; Field et al., 1984). They initially showed that infants could discriminate among such basic facial expressions as happiness, sadness, and surprise. They then exposed newborns to an adult model with a happy, sad, or surprised facial expression. The results suggested that newborns produced a reasonably accurate imitation of the adult's expression.

However, subsequent research seemed to point to a different conclusion, as other investigators found consistent evidence only for a single imitative movement: sticking out the tongue. And even that response seemed to disappear around the age of two months. Because it seems unlikely that imitation would be limited to a single gesture and only appear for a few months, some researchers began to question the earlier findings. In fact, some researchers suggested that even sticking out the tongue was not imitation, but merely an exploratory behavior (Jones, 2006; 2007; Tissaw, 2007; Simcock, Garrity, & Barr, 2011).

The jury is still out on exactly when true imitation begins, although it seems clear that some forms of imitation begin very early in life. Such imitative skills are important, because effective social interaction with others relies in part on the ability to react to other people in an appropriate manner and to understand the meaning of others' emotional states. Consequently, newborns' ability to imitate provides them with an important foundation for social interaction later in life (Rogers & Williams, 2006; Zeedyk & Heimann, 2006; Legerstee & Markova, 2008).

Several other aspects of newborns' behavior also act as forerunners for more formal types of social interaction that they will develop as they grow. As shown in Table 4-6, certain characteristics of neonates mesh with parental behavior to help produce a social relationship between child and parent, as well as social relationships with others (Eckerman & Oehler, 1992).

For example, newborns cycle through various **states of arousal,** different degrees of sleep and wakefulness, ranging from deep sleep to great agitation. Although these cycles are disrupted immediately after birth, they quickly become more regularized. Caregivers become involved when they seek to aid the infant in transitions from one state to another. For instance, a father who rhythmically rocks his crying daughter in an effort to calm her is engaged in a joint activity that is a prelude to future social interactions of different sorts. Similarly, newborns tend to pay particular attention to their mothers' voices. In turn, parents and others modify their speech when talking to infants, using a different pitch and tempo than they use with older children and adults (De Casper & Fifer, 1980; Smith & Trainor, 2008; Barr, 2011; Morgan, Horn, & Bergman, 2011).

FROM A
CHILD CARE WORKER'S
PERSPECTIVE:
Developmental researchers no longer view the neonate as a helpless, incompetent creature, but rather as a remarkably competent, developing human being. What do you think are some implications of this change in viewpoint for methods of child rearing and child care?

states of arousal Different degrees of sleep and wakefulness through which newborns cycle

The ultimate outcome of the social interactive capabilities of the newborn infant, and the responses such behavior brings from parents, is to pave the way for future social interactions. Just as the neonate shows remarkable skills on a physical and perceptual level, its social capabilities are no less sophisticated.

Review, Check, and Apply

Review

1. Neonates, born with brains that are only a fraction of their ultimate size, are in many ways helpless. Nevertheless, studies of what newborns *can* do, rather than what they *can't* do, have revealed some surprising capabilities.

2. Newborns' respiratory and digestive systems begin to function at birth. They come equipped with an array of reflexes to help them eat, swallow, find food, and avoid unpleasant stimuli.

3. Newborns' sensory competence includes the ability to distinguish objects in the visual field and to see color differences; the ability to hear and to discern familiar sounds; and sensitivity to touch, odors, and tastes.

4. Infants are capable of learning through such simple means as classical conditioning, operant conditioning, and habituation.

5. Infants develop the foundations of social competence early. Sophisticated imitative capabilities help them react appropriately to other people's emotional states and to manage the beginnings of social interaction.

Check

1. Infants learn through both classical and _____ conditioning.

2. The decrease in the response to a stimulus that occurs after repeated presentations of the same stimulus is called _____.

3. The ability to _____ others' behavior and facial expressions provides the newborn with an important foundation for social interaction later in life.

4. Newborns cycle through various _____, different degrees of sleep and wakefulness, ranging from deep sleep to great agitation.

Apply

1. As we discussed, classical conditioning relies on stimulus substitution. Can you think of examples of the use of classical conditioning on adults in everyday life, in such areas as entertainment, advertising, or politics?

To see more review questions, log on to MyPsychLab.

ANSWERS: 1. operant 2. habituation 3. imitate 4. states of arousal

The CASE
of . . . *No Place Like Home?*

James and Roberta Calder can't quite agree on the best way for Roberta to give birth to her first child. James is enthralled by the idea of a natural, midwife-directed, at-home childbirth. His child by his first wife was born in a hospital, and he remembers the entire experience as impersonal, overmanaged, and excessively mechanical. He can still see his first wife's frightened, bewildered face as she watched dozens of people bustling about, treating her as a passive participant on what was, after all, her big day. If possible, he would like to spare Roberta that experience. After all, babies are born every day in all parts of the world, at home or out in a field—and usually without a doctor's intervention. Why should this birth be so different?

Roberta, in contrast, wants to give birth in a hospital. She approves of the idea of midwife deliveries and wants her birthing experience to be as natural as possible, but she knows too many women who tried the at-home route and ended up wishing they had the support personnel and equipment of a hospital. She knows many cases of delayed or denied anesthesia, breakneck trips to the emergency room for an unplanned Cesarean, the sudden loss of a newborn's heartbeat, and the need for heavy intervention by a team of obstetricians. These stories have made her less than entirely comfortable with a home delivery.

Both Calders want to be understanding and cooperative, but both have clear ideas about how childbirth should proceed.

1. What ideas might Roberta suggest to help James overcome his distaste for hospital deliveries? Can the hospital experience be made more personal and natural?

2. Conversely, what ideas might James propose to address Roberta's fears about at-home delivery? Are there ways to make a home birth as safe as a hospital birth?

3. If you were asked to make a recommendation for Roberta and James, what questions would you ask them?

4. Roberta and James seem stuck on the question of at-home versus in-hospital birth. Are there other options that might address both parents' concerns? What are they, and how would they address those concerns?

5. Would your recommendation change if you found out that Roberta's mother and sisters all experienced long and painful labor and ultimately had to have Cesareans? Why or why not?

◀◀◀ LOOKING BACK

LO 4-1 What is the normal process of labor?

- In the first stage of labor contractions occur about every 8 to 10 minutes, increasing in frequency, duration, and intensity until the mother's cervix expands. In the second stage of labor, which lasts about 90 minutes, the baby begins to move through the cervix and birth canal and ultimately leaves the mother's body. In the third stage of labor, which lasts only a few minutes, the umbilical cord and placenta are expelled from the mother.

- After it emerges, the newborn, or neonate, is usually given a brief visual inspection and a general health assessment. Then it is cleaned and returned to its mother and father.

- Parents-to-be have a variety of choices regarding the setting for the birth, medical attendants, and whether to use pain-reducing medication. Sometimes, medical intervention, such as Cesarean birth, becomes necessary.

LO 4-2 What are alternative birthing procedures?

- Among the major alternatives to traditional birthing practices are Lamaze, which makes use of breathing techniques and relaxation training; Bradley Method, also known as "husband-coached childbirth" and based on the principle that childbirth should be as natural as possible; and hypnobirthing, a technique that involves a form of self-hypnosis during delivery.

LO 4-3 What complications can occur at birth, and what are their causes, effects, and treatments?

- Preterm, or premature, infants, born fewer than 38 weeks following conception, generally have low birthweight, which can cause vulnerability to infection, respiratory distress syndrome, and hypersensitivity to environmental stimuli. They may even show adverse effects later in life, including slowed development, learning disabilities, behavior disorders, below-average IQ scores, and problems with physical coordination.

- Very-low-birthweight infants are in special danger because of the immaturity of their organ systems. However, medical advances have pushed the age of viability of the infant back to about 22 weeks following conception.

- Postmature babies, who spend extra time in their mothers' wombs, are also at risk. However, physicians can artificially induce labor or perform a Cesarean delivery to address this situation.

LO 4-4 In what kinds of situations are Cesarean deliveries necessary?

- In a Cesarean delivery (sometimes known as a *C-section*) the baby is surgically removed from the uterus rather than traveling through the birth canal.

- Cesarean deliveries are performed when the fetus is in distress, in the wrong position, or unable to progress through the birth canal.

LO 4-5 What is postpartum depression?

- Postpartum depression, an enduring, deep feeling of sadness, affects about 10% of new mothers. In severe cases, its effects can be harmful to the mother and the child, and aggressive treatment may be employed.

- For many mothers the onset of depression comes as a complete surprise. In some cases, depression may occur in women with a personal or family history of clinical depression, while for others depression may be triggered by the pronounced swings in hormone production.

LO 4-6 What capabilities does the newborn have?

- Human newborns quickly master breathing through the lungs, and they are equipped with reflexes to help them eat, swallow, find food, and avoid unpleasant stimuli. Their sensory capabilities are also sophisticated.

- From birth, infants learn through habituation, classical conditioning, and operant conditioning.

- Newborns can discriminate among such facial expressions as happiness, sadness, and surprise.

LO 4-7 How do newborns respond to others?

- Although there is controversy about just when the ability begins, researchers have found that newborns are capable of imitating others' behavior through facial expressions. This capability helps

them form social relationships and facilitates the development of social competence.

- Certain characteristics of neonates interact with parental behavior to help produce a social relationship between child and parent, as well as social relationships with others.

KEY TERMS AND CONCEPTS

neonate (p. 96)
episiotomy (p. 97)
Apgar scale (p. 98)
anoxia (p. 98)
bonding (p. 99)
preterm infants (p. 106)
low-birthweight infants (p. 106)

small-for-gestational-age infants (p. 106)
very-low-birthweight infants (p. 107)
postmature infants (p. 109)
Cesarean delivery (p. 110)
fetal monitor (p. 111)
stillbirth (p. 111)

infant mortality (p. 112)
reflexes (p. 116)
classical conditioning (p. 118)
operant conditioning (p. 118)
habituation (p. 119)
states of arousal (p. 120)

Epilogue

This chapter has covered the amazing and intense processes of labor and birth. There are a number of birthing options that are available to parents, and these options need to be weighed in light of possible complications that can arise during the birthing process. In addition to considering the remarkable progress that has been made regarding the various treatments and interventions available for babies that are born too early or too late, we examined the grim topics of stillbirth and infant mortality. We concluded with a discussion of the surprising capabilities of newborns and their early development of social competence.

Before we move on to a more detailed discussion of children's physical development from birth to adolescence, return for a moment to the case of the premature birth of Tamera Dixon,

discussed in the prologue. Using your understanding of the issues discussed in this chapter, answer the following questions.

1. Tamera was born more than three months early. Why was the fact that she was born alive so surprising? Can you discuss this birth in terms of "the age of viability"?

2. What procedures and activities were most likely set into motion immediately after her birth?

3. What dangers was Tamera subject to immediately after birth because of her high degree of prematurity? What dangers would be likely to continue into her childhood?

4. What ethical considerations affect the decision of whether the high costs of medical interventions for highly premature babies are justifiable? Who should pay those costs?

The Development Video Series in MyPsychLab

Explore the video **Premature Births and the Neonatal Intensive Care Unit** by scanning this QR code with your mobile device. If you don't already have one, you may download a free QR scanner for your device

wherever smartphone apps are sold. You can also view this video in MyPsychLab. For more videos related to this chapter's content, log into MyPsychLab to view the entire Development Video Series.

MyVirtualChild

- **What decisions would you make while raising a child?**
- **What would the consequences of those decisions be?**

Find out by accessing **MyVirtualChild** at
www.MyPsychLab.com

and raising your own virtual child from birth to age 18.

5 Physical Growth and Health

MODULE 5.1

PHYSICAL GROWTH AND CHANGE

- The Growing Body
- The Growing Brain

DEVELOPMENTAL DIVERSITY AND YOUR LIFE Are Gender and Culture Related to the Brain's Structure?

- Gross Motor Development
- Fine Motor Development
- Puberty: The Start of Sexual Maturation

Review, Check, and Apply

MODULE 5.2

THE DEVELOPMENT OF THE SENSES

- First Looks: Visual Perception in Infancy
- First Sounds: Auditory Perception in Infancy
- Smell and Taste in Infancy
- Infants' Sensitivity to Pain and Touch
- Multimodal Perception: Combining Individual Sensory Inputs

ARE YOU AN INFORMED CONSUMER OF DEVELOPMENT? Exercising Your Infant's Body and Senses

- Sensory Development beyond Infancy

Review, Check, and Apply

MODULE 5.3

NUTRITION AND HEALTH

- Nutrition: Links to Overall Functioning
- Malnutrition
- Childhood Obesity: Genetic and Social Factors

FROM RESEARCH TO PRACTICE: Do Media Images Affect Preadolescent Children's Body Image?

- Health and Wellness
- Sleep

Review, Check, and Apply

The Case of ... Girls Don't

Looking Back

Key Terms and Concepts

Epilogue

PROLOGUE: Waiting for Allan's First Steps

Allan's parents were starting to get anxious. After 13 months, their son had yet to take his first steps. Clearly, he was getting close. Allan was able to stand still for several moments unaided. Clutching chairs and the sides of tables, he could shuffle his way around rooms. But as for taking those first, momentous, solo steps—Allan just wasn't there yet.

Allan's older brother, Todd, had walked at 10 months. Allan's parents read stories online of children walking at 9, 8, even 6 months old! Why, then, wasn't Allan walking on his own yet?

The anticipation was building. Allan's father kept his digital camera at the ready whenever he was with his son, hoping to record Allan's milestone. Allan's mother frequently updated the family blog, keeping friends and extended family alert to Allan's progress.

Finally, the moment came. One afternoon, Allan lurched away from a chair, took a tottering step—then another, and then another. He made it all the way across the room to the opposite wall, laughing happily as he went. Allan's parents, who had been lucky enough to witness the event, were overjoyed.

⟫⟫⟫ LOOKING AHEAD

The reactions of Allan's parents in the lead-up to their son's first steps, and their elation at the steps themselves, are typical. Parents scrutinize their children's behavior, worrying over what they see as potential abnormalities (for the record, walking at 13 months is entirely consistent with healthy childhood development) and celebrating important milestones.

In this chapter, we consider the nature of physical development. We begin by considering the varied progression of physical growth during infancy, the preschool years, middle childhood, and the start of adolescence. During these years, children experience not only obvious changes in height, weight, and body shape but also less-apparent changes in the brain and nervous system. They also experience great advances in their

(continued)

Learning Objectives

MODULE 5.1

LO1 How do the body, brain, and motor skills develop during childhood?

LO2 What developmental tasks are accomplished during childhood?

LO3 What are the characteristics of puberty?

MODULE 5.2

LO4 In what ways do the senses develop as children grow?

LO5 How sensitive is an infant to pain and touch?

LO6 What sensory capabilities do people possess from the beginning of life?

MODULE 5.3

LO7 What is the role of nutrition in development, and what causes obesity?

LO8 How healthy are growing children, and what threats to wellness do they face?

motor abilities, which have important consequences not only physically but socially and emotionally as well. And during adolescence, they undergo the start of sexual maturation, with its considerable physical and social effects. As we consider many of these generally universal changes, we also try to gain some appreciation of variations due to gender and culture.

Next, we consider the development of the senses. We investigate how several individual sensory systems operate, and we examine how they are integrated with one another and how data from the sense organs are sorted out and transformed into meaningful information.

Finally, our discussion turns to nutrition and health. We examine how nutrition affects not only physical health but also emotional, social, and cognitive functioning. We end by considering health and wellness, discussing illnesses, diseases, and injuries to which developing children are likely to become exposed.

MODULE 5.1

PHYSICAL GROWTH AND CHANGE

LO 5-1 How do the body, brain, and motor skills develop during childhood?
LO 5-2 What developmental tasks are accomplished during childhood?
LO 5-3 What are the characteristics of puberty?

It is an unseasonably warm spring day at the Cushman Hill Preschool, one of the first nice days after a long winter. The children in Mary Scott's class have happily left their winter coats in the classroom for the first time this spring, and they are excitedly playing outside. Jessie plays a game of catch with Germaine, and Sarah and Molly are climbing up the slide. Craig and Marta chase one another, while Jesse and Bernstein try, with gales of giggles, to play leapfrog. Virginia and Ollie sit across from each other on the teeter-totter, successively bumping it so hard into the ground that they both are in danger of being knocked off. Erik, Jim, Scott, and Paul race around the perimeter of the playground, running for the sheer joy of it.

These same children, now so active and mobile, were unable even to crawl or walk just a few years earlier. Just how far they have developed is apparent when we look at the specific changes they have undergone in their size, shape, and physical abilities.

The Growing Body

Height and Weight The average newborn weighs just over 7 pounds, which is less than the weight of the average Thanksgiving turkey. Its length is about 20 inches, shorter than a loaf of French bread. It is helpless; if left to fend for itself, it could not survive. Yet after just a few years, the story is very different. Babies become much larger, they are mobile, and they become increasingly independent.

Growth in Infancy Infants grow at a rapid pace over the first two years of their lives. By the age of 5 months, the average infant's birthweight has doubled to around 15 pounds. By the first birthday, the baby's weight has tripled to about 22 pounds. Although the pace of weight gain slows during the second year, it continues to increase. By the end of his or her second year, the average child weighs around four times as much as he or she did at birth. Of course, there is a good deal of variation among infants. Height and weight measurements, which are taken regularly during a physician's visits during a baby's first year, provide a way to spot problems in development.

 **Watch** the **Video** *The Growing Child* in **MyPsychLab**.

The weight gains of infancy are matched by increased length. By the end of the first year, the typical baby grows almost a foot and is about 30 inches tall. By their second birthdays, children average a height of three feet.

Not all parts of an infant's body grow at the same rate. For instance, as we saw first in Chapter 4, at birth the head accounts for one-quarter of the newborn's entire body size. During the first two years of life, the rest of the body begins to catch up. By the age of 2, the baby's head is only one-fifth of its body length, and by adulthood it is only one-eighth (see Figure 5-1).

There also are gender and ethnic differences in weight and length. Girls generally are slightly shorter and weigh slightly less than boys, and these differences remain throughout childhood (and, as we will see later in this module, the disparities become considerably greater during adolescence). Furthermore, Asian infants tend to be slightly smaller than North American Caucasian infants, and African American infants tend to be slightly bigger than North American Caucasian infants.

Four Principles of Growth. The disproportionately large size of infants' heads at birth is an example of one of four major principles (summarized in Table 5-1) that govern growth.

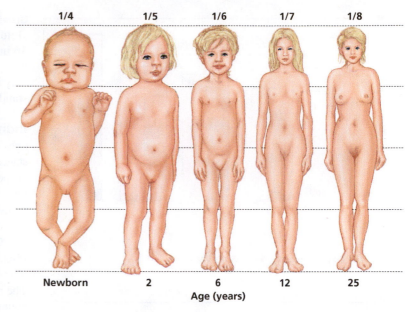

1/4   1/5   1/6   1/7   1/8

Newborn   2   6   12   25

Age (years)

FIGURE 5-1 Decreasing Proportions

At birth, the head represents one-quarter of the neonate's body. By adulthood, the head is only one-eighth the size of the body. Why is the neonate's head so large?

- The **cephalocaudal principle** states that growth follows a direction and pattern that begins with the head and upper body parts and then proceeds to the rest of the body. The cephalocaudal growth principle means that we develop visual abilities (located in the head) well before we master the ability to walk (closer to the end of the body).

- The **proximodistal principle** states that development proceeds from the center of the body outward. The proximodistal principle means that the trunk of the body grows before the extremities of the arms and legs. Furthermore, development of the ability to use various parts of the body also follows the proximodistal principle. For instance, effective use of the arms precedes the ability to use the hands.

- The **principle of hierarchical integration** states that simple skills typically develop separately and independently, but that these simple skills are integrated into more complex ones. Thus, the relatively complex skill of grasping something in the hand cannot be mastered until the developing infant learns how to control—and integrate—the movements of the individual fingers.

- Finally, the **principle of the independence of systems** suggests that different body systems grow at different rates. For instance, the patterns of growth for body size, the nervous system, and sexual maturation are quite different.

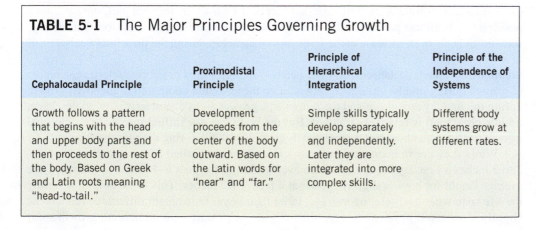

TABLE 5-1   The Major Principles Governing Growth

Cephalocaudal Principle	Proximodistal Principle	Principle of Hierarchical Integration	Principle of the Independence of Systems
Growth follows a pattern that begins with the head and upper body parts and then proceeds to the rest of the body. Based on Greek and Latin roots meaning "head-to-tail."	Development proceeds from the center of the body outward. Based on the Latin words for "near" and "far."	Simple skills typically develop separately and independently. Later they are integrated into more complex skills.	Different body systems grow at different rates.

cephalocaudal principle   The principle that growth follows a pattern that begins with the head and upper body parts and then proceeds down to the rest of the body

proximodistal principle   The principle that development proceeds from the center of the body outward

principle of hierarchical integration   The principle that simple skills typically develop separately and independently but are later integrated into more complex skills

principle of the independence of systems   The principle that different body systems grow at different rates

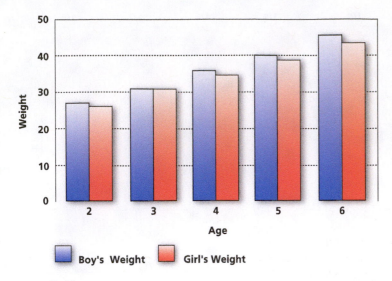

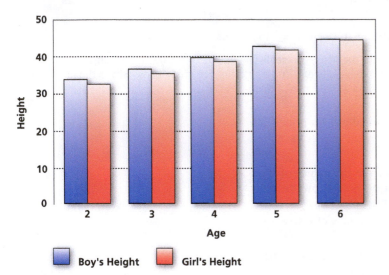

FIGURE 5-2 Gaining Height and Weight

The preschool years are marked by steady increases in height and weight. The figures show the median point for boys and girls at each age, in which 50% of children in each category are above this height or weight level and 50% are below it.

(*Source:* National Center for Health Statistics, 2000)

Growth in the Preschool Years Two years after birth, the average child in the United States weighs 25 to 30 pounds and is close to 36 inches tall—around half the height of the average adult. Children grow steadily during the preschool period, and by the time they are 6 years old, they weigh, on average, about 46 pounds and stand 46 inches tall (see Figure 5-2).

Individual Differences in Height and Weight. These averages mask great individual differences in height and weight. For instance, 10% of 6-year-olds weigh 55 pounds or more, and 10% weigh 36 pounds or less. Furthermore, average differences in height and weight between boys and girls increase during the preschool years. Although at age 2 the differences are relatively small, during the preschool years boys start becoming taller and heavier, on average, than girls.

Global economics also affect these averages. Furthermore, profound differences in height and weight exist among children in economically developed countries and those in developing countries. The better nutrition and health care received by children in developed countries translates into significant differences in growth. For instance, the average Swedish 4-year-old is as tall as the average 6-year-old in Bangladesh (Leathers & Foster, 2004; Rodriguez Martin, 2012).

Differences in height and weight reflect economic factors within the United States as well. For instance, children in families whose incomes are below the poverty level are far more likely to be unusually short than children raised in more affluent homes (Ogden et al., 2002).

Changes in Body Shape and Structure. If we compare the bodies of a 2-year-old and a 6-year-old, we find that the bodies vary not only in height and weight but also in shape. During the preschool years, boys and girls become less chubby and roundish and more slender. They begin to burn off some of the fat they have carried from their infancy, and they no longer have a pot-bellied appearance. Moreover, their arms and legs lengthen, and the size relationship between the head and the rest of the body becomes more adultlike. In fact, by the time children reach 6 years of age, their proportions are quite similar to those of adults.

The changes in size, weight, and appearance we see during the preschool years are only the tip of the iceberg. Internally, other physical changes are occurring. Children grow stronger as their muscle size increases and their bones become sturdier. The sense organs continue their development. For instance, the *eustachian tube* in the ear, which carries sounds from the external part of the ear to the internal part, moves from a position that is almost parallel to the ground at birth to a more angular position. This change sometimes leads to an increase in the frequency of earaches during the preschool years.

Growth during Middle Childhood Slow but steady—if three words could characterize the nature of growth during middle childhood, it would be these. When compared to the swift growth during the first 5 years of life and the remarkable growth spurt characteristic of adolescence, middle childhood is relatively tranquil. But the body has not shifted into neutral. Physical growth continues, although at a more stately pace than it did during the preschool years.

While they are in elementary school, children in the United States grow, on average, 2 to 3 inches a year. By the age of 11, the average height for girls is 4 feet, 10 inches, and the average height for boys is slightly shorter at 4 feet, 9 1/2 inches. This is the only time during the life span when girls are, on average, taller than boys. This height difference reflects the slightly more rapid physical development of girls, who start their adolescent growth spurt around the age of 10.

Weight gain follows a similar pattern. During middle childhood, both boys and girls gain around 5 to 7 pounds a year. Weight is also redistributed. As the rounded look of "baby fat" disappears, children's bodies become more muscular and their strength increases.

These average height and weight increases disguise significant individual differences, as anyone who has seen a line of fourth-graders walking down a school corridor has doubtless noticed. It is not unusual to see children of the same age who are six or seven inches apart in height.

Cultural Patterns of Growth. Most children in North America receive sufficient nutrients to grow to their full potential. In other parts of the world, however, inadequate nutrition and disease take their toll, producing children who are shorter and who weigh less than they would if they had sufficient nutrients.

The discrepancies can be dramatic: Children in poorer areas of cities such as Kolkata, Hong Kong, and Rio de Janeiro are smaller than their counterparts in affluent areas of the same cities.

In the United States, most variations in height and weight are the result of different people's unique genetic inheritance, including genetic factors relating to racial and ethnic background. For instance, children from Asian and Oceanic Pacific backgrounds tend to be shorter, on average, than those with northern and central European heritages. In addition, the rate of growth during childhood is generally more rapid for blacks than for whites (Deurenberg, Deurenberg-Yap, & Guricci, 2002; Deurenberg et al., 2003; Taki et al., 2012).

Even within particular racial and ethnic groups, there is significant variation between individuals. Moreover, we cannot attribute racial and ethnic differences solely to genetic factors, because dietary customs as well as possible variations in levels of affluence also may contribute to the differences. In addition, severe stress—brought on by factors such as parental conflict or alcoholism—can affect the functioning of the pituitary gland, thereby affecting growth (Koska et al., 2002).

Growth during Adolescence The growth in height and weight during **adolescence,** the development stage between childhood and adulthood, can be breathtaking. In only a few months, adolescents can grow several inches and require a virtually new wardrobe as they are transformed, at least in physical appearance, from children to young adults.

One aspect of this transformation is the **adolescent growth spurt**, a period of very rapid growth in height and weight. On average, boys grow 4.1 inches a year, and girls,

Variations of 6 inches in height between children of the same age are not unusual and are well within the normal range.

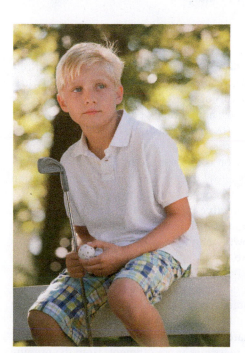

Note the changes that have occurred in just a few years in these pre- and postpuberty photos of the same boy.

adolescence   The developmental stage between childhood and adulthood

adolescent growth spurt   A period of very rapid growth in height and weight during adolescence

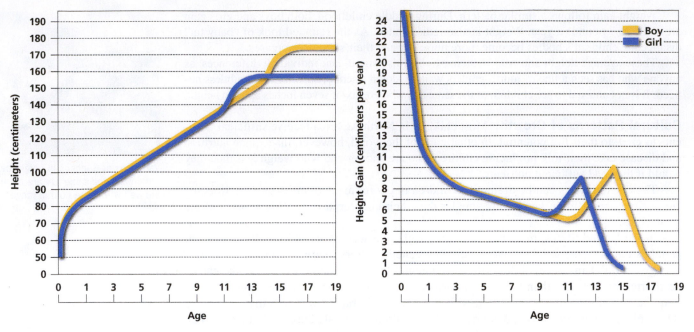

FIGURE 5-3 Growth Patterns

Patterns of growth are depicted in two ways. The figure on the left shows height at a given age, whereas the figure on the right shows the height increase that occurs from birth through the end of adolescence. Notice that girls begin their growth spurt around age 10; boys, about 2 years later. However, by the age of 13, boys tend to be taller than girls. Why is it important that educators be aware of the social consequences of being taller or shorter than average for boys and girls?

(*Source:* Adapted from Cratty, 1986)

3.5 inches a year. Some adolescents grow as much as 5 inches in a single year (Tanner, 1972; Caino et al., 2004).

Boys' and girls' adolescent growth spurts begin at different times. As you can see in Figure 5-3 girls begin their spurts around age 10, while boys start at about age 12. During the 2-year period starting at age 11, girls tend to be taller than boys. But by the age of 13, boys, on average, are taller than girls—a state of affairs that persists for the remainder of the life span.

The Growing Brain

Brain Growth during Childhood and Adolescence.
The brain grows at a faster rate than does any other part of the body. A baby's brain triples its weight during his or her first two years of life, and it reaches more than three-fourths of its adult weight and size by the age of 2. By age 5, children's brains weigh 90% of average adult brain weight. In comparison, the average 5-year-old's total body weight is just 30% of the average adult's body weight (Nihart, 1993; House, 2007).

Why does the brain grow so rapidly? One reason is an increase in the number of interconnections among cells. These interconnections allow for more complex communication between neurons, and they permit the rapid growth of cognitive skills that we discuss in later chapters. In addition, the amount of *myelin*—protective insulation that surrounds parts of neurons—increases, which speeds the transmission of electrical impulses along brain cells but also adds to brain weight. This rapid brain growth not only allows for increased cognitive abilities but also helps in the development of more sophisticated fine and gross motor skills (Dalton & Bergenn, 2007; Jolles et al., 2012).

During adolescence, the number of neurons continues to increase, and their interconnections become richer and more complex. The brain produces an oversupply of gray matter during adolescence, which is later pruned back at the rate of 1% to 2% per year. Myelination—the process in which nerve cells are insulated by a covering of fat cells—increases and continues to make the transmission of neural messages more efficient. Both the pruning process and increased myelination contribute to the growing cognitive abilities of adolescents (Sowell et al., 2003; Guevara et al., 2012).

One specific area of the brain that undergoes considerable development throughout adolescence is the prefrontal cortex, which is not fully developed until the early 20s. The *prefrontal cortex* is the part of the brain that allows people to think, evaluate, and make complex judgments in a uniquely human way. It underlies the increasingly complex intellectual achievements that are possible during adolescence.

During adolescence, the prefrontal cortex becomes increasingly efficient in communicating with other parts of the brain. This helps build a communication system within the brain that is more distributed and sophisticated, permitting the different areas of the brain to process information more effectively (Scherf, Sweeney, & Luna, 2006; Hare et al., 2008).

The prefrontal cortex also provides for impulse control. Rather than simply reacting to emotions such as anger or rage, an individual with a fully developed prefrontal cortex is able to inhibit the desire for action that stems from such emotions.

Because during adolescence the prefrontal cortex is biologically immature, the ability to inhibit impulses is not fully developed. This brain immaturity may lead to some of the risky and impulsive behaviors that are characteristic of adolescence (Eshel et al., 2007; Shad et al., 2011; Segalowitz et al., 2012).

Adolescent brain development also produces changes in regions involving dopamine sensitivity and production. As a result of these alterations, adolescents may become less susceptible to the effects of alcohol, and it requires more drinks for adolescents to experience its reinforcing qualities—leading to higher alcohol intake. In addition, alterations in dopamine sensitivity may make adolescents more sensitive to stress, leading to further alcohol use (Spear, 2002).

Lateralization. As children age, the two halves of the brain begin to become increasingly differentiated and specialized. **Lateralization,** the process in which certain functions are located more in one hemisphere than in the other, becomes more pronounced during the preschool years.

For most people, the left hemisphere is involved primarily with tasks that necessitate verbal competence, such as speaking, reading, thinking, and reasoning. The right hemisphere develops its own strengths, especially in nonverbal areas such as comprehension of spatial relationships, recognition of patterns and drawings, music, and emotional expression (Pollak, Holt, & Wismer Fries, 2004; Watling & Bourne, 2007; Szaflarski et al., 2012; see Figure 5-4).

Each of the two hemispheres also begins to process information in a slightly different manner. Whereas the left hemisphere considers information sequentially, one piece of data at a time, the right hemisphere processes information in a more global manner, reflecting on it as a whole.

Although there is some specialization of the hemispheres, in most respects the two hemispheres act in tandem. They are interdependent, and the differences between the two are minor. Even the hemispheric specialization in certain tasks is not absolute. In fact, each hemisphere can perform most of the tasks of the other. For example, the right hemisphere does some language processing and plays an important role in language comprehension (Corballis, 2003; Hall, Neal, & Dean, 2008; Rowland & Noble, 2011).

Furthermore, the brain has remarkable resiliency. In another example of human plasticity, if the hemisphere that specializes in a particular type of information is damaged, the other hemisphere can take up the slack. For instance, when young children suffer brain damage to the left side of the brain (which specializes in verbal processing) and initially lose language capabilities, the linguistic deficits are often not permanent. In such cases, the right side of the brain pitches in and may be able to compensate substantially for the damage to the left hemisphere (Kolb & Gibb, 2006; Elkana et al., 2011; Ansari, 2012).

There are also individual differences in lateralization. For example, many of the 10% of people who are left-handed or ambidextrous (able to use both hands interchangeably) have language centered in their right hemispheres or have no specific language center (Compton & Weissman, 2002; Isaacs et al., 2006). Even more intriguing are differences in lateralization related to gender and culture, as we consider next.

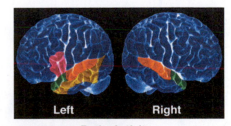

FIGURE 5-4 Brain Activity

This series of PET scans of the brain shows that activity in the right or left hemisphere of the brain differs according to the task in which a person is engaged. How might educators use this finding in their approach to teaching?

lateralization The process whereby certain functions are located more in one hemisphere of the brain than in the other

DEVELOPMENTAL DIVERSITY AND YOUR LIFE

Are Gender and Culture Related to the Brain's Structure?

Among the most controversial findings relating to the specialization of the hemispheres of the brain is evidence that lateralization is related to gender and culture. For instance, starting during the first year of life and continuing in the preschool years, boys and girls show some hemispheric differences associated with lower body reflexes and the processing of auditory information. Boys also clearly tend to show greater specialization of language in the left hemisphere; among females, language is more evenly divided between the two hemispheres. Such differences may help explain why—as we'll see later in the chapter—girls' language development proceeds at a more rapid pace during the preschool years than boys' language development (Grattan et al., 1992; Bourne & Todd, 2004; Huster, Westerhausen, & Herrmann, 2011).

Although it is clear that some kind of gender differences exist in lateralization, we still don't know the extent of the differences and why they occur. One explanation is genetic: Female brains and male brains are predisposed to function in slightly different ways. Such a view is supported by data suggesting that there are minor structural differences between males' and females' brains. For instance, a section of the corpus callosum is proportionally larger in women than in men. Furthermore, studies conducted among other species, such as primates, rats, and hamsters, have found size and structural differences in the brains of males and females (Matsumoto, 1999).

Before we accept a genetic explanation for the differences between female and male brains, we need to consider an equally plausible alternative: It may be that verbal abilities emerge earlier in girls because girls receive greater encouragement for verbal skills than boys do. For instance, even as infants, girls are spoken to more than boys (Beal, 1994). Such higher levels of verbal stimulation may produce growth in particular areas of the brain that does not occur in boys. Consequently, environmental rather than genetic factors may lead to the gender differences we find in brain lateralization.

Culture and Brain Lateralization Is the culture in which one is raised related to brain lateralization? Some research suggests it is. For instance, native speakers of Japanese process information related to vowel sounds primarily in the left hemisphere of the brain. In comparison, North and South Americans and Europeans—as well as people of Japanese ancestry who learn Japanese as a second language—process vowel sounds primarily in the brain's right hemisphere.

The explanation for this cultural difference in processing of vowels seems to rest on the nature of the Japanese language. Specifically, the Japanese language allows for the expression of complex concepts using only vowel sounds. Consequently, a specific type of brain lateralization may develop while learning and using Japanese at a relatively early age (Hiser & Kobayashi, 2003; Geuze et al., 2012).

This explanation, which is speculative, does not rule out the possibility that some type of subtle genetic difference may also be at work in determining the difference in lateralization. Once again, then, we find that teasing out the relative impact of heredity and environment is a challenging task.

Neuroscientists are just beginning to understand the ways in which brain development is related to cognitive development. For example, it appears that there are periods during childhood in which the brain shows unusual growth spurts, and these periods are linked to advances in cognitive abilities. Specifically, electrical activity in the brain shows unusual spurts at between 11/2 and 2 years, a time when language abilities increase rapidly. Other spurts occurred around other ages when cognitive advances are particularly intense (see Figure 5-5; Fischer & Rose, 1995; Mabbott et al., 2006; Westermann et al., 2007).

We do not yet know the direction of causality (does brain development produce cognitive advances, or do cognitive accomplishments fuel brain development?). However, it is clear that increases in our understanding of the physiological aspects of the brain will eventually have important implications for parents and teachers. ∎

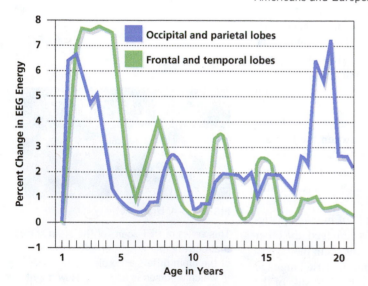

FIGURE 5-5 Brain Growth Spurt

According to one study, electrical activity in the brain has been linked to advances in cognitive abilities at various stages of life. In this graph, activity increases dramatically between 18 and 24 months, a period during which language rapidly develops.

(*Source:* Fischer & Rose, 1995)

Gross Motor Development

Suppose you were hired by a genetic engineering firm to redesign newborn humans and were charged with replacing the current version with a new, more mobile one. The first change you'd probably consider in carrying out this (luckily fictitious) job would be in the conformation and composition of the baby's body. The shape and proportions of newborn babies are simply not conducive to easy mobility. Their heads are so large and heavy that young infants lack the strength to raise them. Because their limbs are short in relation to the rest of the body, their movements are further impeded. Furthermore, their bodies are mainly fat, with a limited amount of muscle; the result is that they lack strength (Illingworth, 1973).

Fortunately, it doesn't take too long before infants begin to develop a remarkable amount of mobility. In fact, even at birth they have an extensive repertoire of behavioral possibilities brought about by innate reflexes, and their range of motor skills grows rapidly during the first 2 years of life.

Development of Gross Motor Skills.
Probably no physical changes are more obvious— and more eagerly anticipated—than the increasing array of motor skills that babies acquire during infancy. Most parents can remember their child's first steps with a sense of pride and awe at how quickly she or he changed from a helpless infant, unable even to roll over, into a person who could navigate quite effectively in the world.

Even though the motor skills of newborn infants are not terribly sophisticated, at least compared with attainments that will soon appear, young infants still are able to accomplish some kinds of movement. For instance, when placed on their stomachs they wiggle their arms and legs and may try to lift their heavy heads. As their strength increases, they are able to push hard enough against the surface on which they are resting to propel their bodies in different directions. They often end up moving backward rather than forward, but by the age of 6 months they become rather accomplished at moving themselves in particular directions. These initial efforts are the forerunners of crawling, in which babies coordinate the motions of their arms and legs and propel themselves forward. Crawling appears typically between 8 and 10 months. Figure 5-6 on page 134 provides a summary of some of the milestones of normal motor development.

Walking comes later. At around the age of 9 months, most infants are able to walk by supporting themselves on furniture, and half of all infants can walk well by the end of their first year of life.

At the same time infants are learning to move around, they are perfecting the ability to remain in a stationary sitting position. At first, babies cannot remain seated upright without support. But they quickly master this ability, and most are able to sit without support by the age of 6 months.

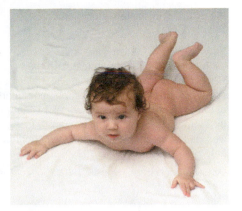
This 5-month-old girl demonstrates her gross motor skills.

Watch the **Video** *Gross Motor Skills* in **MyPsychLab**.

By 4 months of age, infants are able to reach toward an object with some degree of precision.

Watch the **Video** *Motor Development in Infants and Toddlers* in **MyPsychLab**.

During the preschool years, children grow in both gross and fine motor skills.

FIGURE 5-6 Milestones of Motor Development

Fifty percent of children are able to perform each skill at the month indicated in the figure. However, the specific timing at which each skill appears varies widely. For example, one-quarter of children are able to walk well at 11 months; by 14 months, 90% of children are walking well. Is knowledge of such average benchmarks helpful or harmful to parents?

(Adapted from Frankenburg et al., 1992)

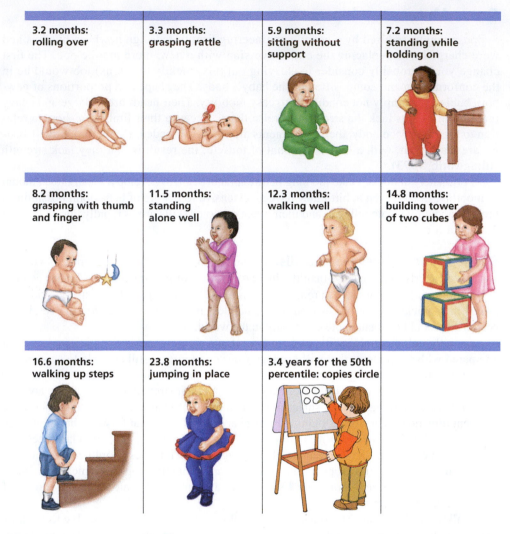

3.2 months: rolling over

3.3 months: grasping rattle

5.9 months: sitting without support

7.2 months: standing while holding on

8.2 months: grasping with thumb and finger

11.5 months: standing alone well

12.3 months: walking well

14.8 months: building tower of two cubes

16.6 months: walking up steps

23.8 months: jumping in place

3.4 years for the 50th percentile: copies circle

The Preschool Years. By the time they are 3 years old, children have mastered a variety of skills: jumping, hopping on one foot, skipping, and running. By ages 4 and 5, their skills are more refined as they gain greater control over their muscles. For instance, at age 4 they can throw a ball with enough accuracy that a friend can catch it, and by age 5 they can toss a ring and have it land on a peg five feet away. Five-year-olds can learn to ride bikes, climb ladders, and ski downhill—activities that all require considerable coordination. Figure 5-7 on page 135 summarizes major gross motor skills that emerge during the preschool years.

The advances in gross motor skills are related to brain development and myelination of neurons in areas of the brain related to balance and coordination. Another reason motor skills develop at such a rapid clip during the preschool years is that children spend a great deal of time practicing them. During this period, the general level of activity is extraordinarily high: Preschoolers seem to be perpetually in motion. In fact, the activity level is higher at age 3 than at any other point in the entire life span. In addition, as they age, preschoolers increase in general physical agility (Planinsec, 2001).

Despite generally high activity levels, there are also significant variations among children. Some differences are related to inherited temperament. Due to temperamental factors, children who were unusually active during infancy tend to continue in this way during the preschool years, whereas those who were relatively docile during infancy generally remain fairly docile during those years. Furthermore, monozygotic (identical) twins tend to show more similar activity levels than do dizygotic twins, a fact that suggests the importance of genetics in determining activity level (Wood et al., 2007).

FROM AN EDUCATOR'S PERSPECTIVE:

How might culture influence activity level in children? What might the long-term effects be on children influenced in this way?

FIGURE 5-7 Significant Gross Motor Skills in Early Childhood

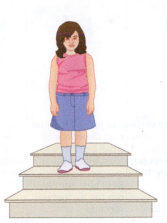

Age 3

Able to walk up
stairs, alternating
feet

Unable to stop or
turn suddenly

Able to jump a length
of 15–24 inches

Age 4

Able to walk down a
long staircase, alternating
feet, with assistance

Have some control in starting,
stopping, and turning

Length of jump
increases to 24–33 inches

Age 5

Able to walk down a
long staircase, alternating
feet

Capable of starting, stopping,
and turning in games

Able to make a running
jump of 28–36 inches

Of course, genetics is not the sole determinant of preschoolers' activity levels. Environmental factors, such as a parent's style of discipline and, more broadly, a particular culture's view of what is appropriate and inappropriate behavior, also play a role. Some cultures are fairly lenient in allowing preschoolers to play vigorously, whereas others are considerably more restrictive.

Ultimately, a combination of genetic and environmental factors determines just how active a child will be. But the preschool period generally represents the most active time of the child's entire life.

Middle Childhood. Watching a schoolyard softball player pitch a ball past a batter to the catcher or a third-grade runner reach the finish line in a race, it is hard not to be struck by the huge strides that children have made since the more awkward days of preschool. Both gross and fine motor skills improve significantly during the middle childhood years.

One important improvement in gross motor skills is in the realm of muscle coordination. For instance, most school-age children can readily learn to ride a bike, ice skate, swim, and skip rope, skills that earlier they could not perform well (see Figure 5-8 on page 136).

Do boys and girls differ in their motor skills? Years ago, developmentalists contended that gender differences in gross motor skills become increasingly pronounced during these years, with boys outperforming girls (Espenschade, 1960). However, more recent research casts some doubt on this claim. When comparisons are made between boys and girls who regularly take part in similar activities such as softball, gender variations in gross motor skills are found to be minimal (Jurimae & Saar, 2003).

What accounts for the discrepancy in earlier observations? Performance differences were probably found because of differences in motivation and expectations. Society told girls that they would do worse than boys in sports, and the girls' performance reflected that message.

Today, however, society's message has changed, at least officially. For instance, the American Academy of Pediatrics suggests that boys and girls should engage in the same sports and games and that they can do so together in mixed-gender groups. There is no reason to separate the sexes in physical exercise and sports until puberty, when the smaller size of females begins to make them more susceptible to injury in contact sports (Raudsepp & Liblik, 2002; Vilhjalmsson & Kristjansdottir, 2003; American Academy of Pediatrics, 2004).

6 Years	7 Years	8 Years	9 Years	10 Years	11 Years	12 Years
Girls superior in accuracy of movement; boys superior in more forceful, less complex acts. Can throw with the proper weight shift and step. Acquire the ability to skip.	Can balance on one foot with eyes closed. Can walk on a 2-inch-wide balance beam without falling off. Can hop and jump accurately into small squares (hopscotch). Can correctly execute a jumping-jack exercise.	Can grip objects with 12 pounds of pressure. Can engage in alternate rhythmical hopping in a 2-2, 2-3, or 3-3 pattern. Girls can throw a small ball 33 feet; boys can throw a small ball 59 feet. The number of games participated in by both sexes is the greatest at this age.	Girls can jump vertically 8.5 inches over their standing height plus reach; boys can jump vertically 10 inches. Boys can run 16.6 feet per second and throw a small ball 41 feet; girls can run 16 feet per second and throw a small ball 41 feet.	Can judge and intercept directions of small balls thrown from a distance. Both girls and boys can run 17 feet per second.	Boys can achieve standing broad jump of 5 feet; girls can achieve standing broad jump of 4.5 feet.	Can achieve high jump of 3 feet.

FIGURE 5-8 Gross Motor Skills Developed between the Ages of 6 and 12 Years

Why would it be important that a social worker be aware of this period of development?

(*Source:* Adapted from Cratty, 1979, p. 222)

Fine Motor Development

At the same time gross motor skills are developing, children are progressing in their ability to use fine motor skills, which involve smaller, more delicate body movements. Fine motor skills encompass such varied activities as using a fork and spoon, cutting with scissors, tying one's shoelaces, and playing the piano.

Infancy. As infants are perfecting their gross motor skills, such as sitting upright and walking, they are also making advances in their fine motor skills. For instance, by the age of 3 months, infants show some ability to coordinate the movements of their limbs.

Furthermore, although infants are born with a rudimentary ability to reach toward an object, this ability is neither very sophisticated nor very accurate, and it disappears around the age of 4 weeks. A different, more precise, form of reaching reappears at 4 months. It takes some time for infants to coordinate successful grasping after they reach out, but in fairly short order they are able to reach out and hold onto an object of interest (McCarty, 2003; Claxton, McCarty, & Keen, 2009; Daum, Prinz, & Aschersleben, 2011).

The sophistication of fine motor skills continues to grow. By the age of 11 months, infants are able to pick up off the ground objects as small as marbles—something caregivers need to be concerned about, because the next place such objects often go is the mouth. By the time they are 2 years old, children can carefully hold a cup, bring it to their lips, and take a drink without spilling a drop.

The Preschool Years. The skills involved in fine motor movements require a good deal of practice, as anyone who has watched a 4-year-old struggling painstakingly to copy letters of the alphabet knows. Yet fine motor skills show clear developmental patterns (see Table 5-2). At the age of 3, children can undo their clothes when they go to the bathroom, they can put a simple jigsaw puzzle together, and they can fit blocks of different shapes into matching holes.

TABLE 5-2   Fine Motor Skills in Early Childhood

3-Year-Olds	4-Year-Olds	5-Year-Olds
Cuts paper	Folds paper into triangles	Folds paper into halves and quarters
Pastes using finger	Prints name	Draws triangle, rectangle, circle
Builds bridge with three blocks	Strings beads	Uses crayons effectively
Draws O and +	Copies X	Creates clay objects
Draws doll	Builds bridge with five blocks	Copies letters
Pours liquid from pitcher without spilling	Pours from various containers	Copies two short words
Completes simple jigsaw puzzle	Opens and positions clothespins	

However, they do not show much polish in accomplishing such tasks; for instance, they may try to force puzzle pieces into place.

By the age of 4, their fine motor skills are considerably better. For example, they can fold paper into triangular designs and print their name with a crayon. And by the time they are 5, most children are able to hold and manipulate a thin pencil properly.

Middle Childhood. Typing at a computer keyboard, writing in cursive with pen or pencil, drawing detailed pictures—these are just some of the accomplishments that depend on improvements in fine motor coordination that occur during early and middle childhood. Children 6 and 7 years old are able to tie their shoes and fasten buttons; by age 8, they can use each hand independently; and by 11 and 12, they can manipulate objects with almost as much dexterity as they will have in adulthood.

One of the reasons for advances in fine motor skills is that the amount of myelin in the brain increases significantly between the ages of 6 and 8. *Myelin* provides protective insulation around parts of nerve cells. Because increased levels of myelin raise the speed at which electrical impulses travel between neurons, messages can reach muscles more rapidly and control them better.

Handedness: Separating Righties from Lefties By the end of the preschool years, most children show a clear preference for the use of one hand over the other—the development of **handedness**. Actually, some signals of future handedness are seen early in infancy, when infants may show a preference for one side of the body over the other. By the age of 7 months, some infants seem to favor one hand by grabbing more with it than the other. Many children, however, show no preference until the end of the preschool years, and a few remain ambidextrous, using both hands with equal ease (Segalowitz & Rapin, 2003; Marschik et al., 2008; Bryden, Mayer, & Roy, 2011).

By the age of 5, most children display a clear tendency to use one hand over the other, with 90% being right-handed and 10% left-handed. More boys than girls are left-handed.

Much speculation has been devoted to the meaning of handedness, fueled in part by long-standing myths about the sinister nature of left-handedness. (The word *sinister* itself is derived from a Latin word meaning "on the left.") In Islamic cultures, for instance, the left hand is generally used when going to the toilet, and it is considered uncivilized to serve food with that hand. In Christian art, portrayals of the devil often show him as left-handed.

However, there is no scientific basis for myths that suggest that there is something wrong with being left-handed. In fact, some evidence exists that left-handedness may be associated

Fine motor skills, such as typing on a keyboard, improve during early and middle childhood.

handedness   A clear preference for the use of one hand over the other with certain advantages. For example, a study of 100,000 students who took the Scholastic Assessment Test (SAT) showed that 20% in the highest-scoring category were left-handed, double the proportion of left-handed people in the general population. Such gifted individuals as Michelangelo, Leonardo da Vinci, Benjamin Franklin, and Pablo Picasso were left-handed (Bower, 1985).

Although some educators of the past tried to force left-handed children to use the right hand, particularly when learning to write, thinking has changed. Most teachers now encourage children to use whichever hand they prefer. Still, most left-handed people will agree that the design of desks, scissors, and most other everyday objects favors the right-handed. In fact, the world is so "right biased" that it may prove to be a dangerous place for lefties: Left-handed people have more accidents and are at greater risk of dying younger than right-handed people (Ellis & Engh, 2000; Bhushan & Khan, 2006; Dutta & Mandal, 2006).

When it comes to the meaning of handedness there are few conclusions. Some research finds that left-handedness is related to higher achievements, other research shows no advantage for being left-handed, and some findings suggest that children who are ambidextrous perform less well on academic tasks. Clearly, the jury is out on the consequences of handedness (Bhushan & Khan, 2006; Dutta & Mandal, 2006; Corballis, Hattie, & Fletcher, 2008).

Art: The Picture of Development.

It is a basic feature of many kitchens: the refrigerator covered with recent art created by the children of the house. Yet the art that children create is far more important than mere kitchen decoration. Developmentalists suggest that art plays an important role in honing fine motor skills, as well as in several other aspects of development.

At the most basic level, the production of art involves practice with tools such as paintbrushes, crayons, pencils, and markers. As preschoolers learn to manipulate these tools, they gain motor control skills that will help them as they learn to write.

According to developmental psychologist Howard Gardner, the rough, unformed art of preschoolers represents the equivalent of linguistic babbling in infants. He argues that the random marks that young preschoolers make contain all the building blocks of more sophisticated creations that will be produced later (Gardner & Perkins, 1989; Golomb, 2002, 2003).

Other researchers suggest that children's art proceeds through a series of stages during the preschool years (Kellogg, 1970). The first is the *scribbling* stage, in which the end product appears to be random scrawls across a paper. But this is not the case: Instead, scribbles can be categorized, consisting of 20 distinct types, such as horizontal lines and zigzags.

The *shape* stage, which is reached around the age of 3, is marked by the appearance of shapes such as squares and circles. In this stage, children draw shapes of various sorts, as well as X's and plus signs. After reaching this stage, they soon move into the *design* stage, which is characterized by the ability to combine more than one simple shape into a more complex one.

Finally, children enter the *pictorial* stage between the ages of 4 and 5. At this point, drawings begin to approximate recognizable objects (see Figure 5-9).

Watch the **Video** *Art* in **MyPsychLab**.

Puberty: The Start of Sexual Maturation

As with the physical growth spurt during adolescence, **puberty**, the period during which the sexual organs mature, begins earlier for girls than for boys. Girls start puberty at around 11 or 12 years of age, and boys begin at around 13 or 14 years of age. However, there are wide variations among individuals. For example, some girls begin puberty as early as 7 or 8 years of age or as late as 16 years of age.

Puberty begins when the pituitary gland in the brain signals other glands in children's bodies to begin producing the sex hormones, *androgens* (male hormones) or *estrogens* (female hormones), at adult levels.

It is not clear why puberty begins at a particular time. What is clear is that environmental and cultural factors play a role. For example, **menarche,** the onset of

puberty   The period of maturation during which the sexual organs mature

menarche   The onset of menstruation

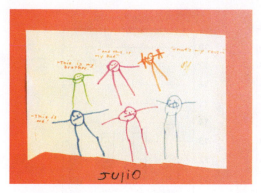 

FIGURE 5-9 Art of Development

As preschoolers enter the pictorial stage between the ages of 4 and 5, their drawings begin to approximate recognizable objects.

menstruation and probably the most obvious signal of puberty in girls, varies greatly in different parts of the world. In poorer, developing countries, menstruation begins later than it does in more economically advantaged countries. Even within wealthier countries, girls in more affluent groups begin to menstruate earlier than less affluent girls (see Figure 5-10).

Consequently, it appears that girls who are better nourished and healthier are more apt to start menstruation at an earlier age than those who suffer from malnutrition or chronic disease. In fact, some studies have suggested that weight or the proportion of fat to muscle in the body plays a critical role in the timing of menarche. For example, in the United States, athletes with a low percentage of body fat may start menstruating later than less active girls. Conversely, obesity—which results in an increase in the secretion of leptin, the hormone associated with the onset of menstruation—leads to earlier puberty (Richards, 1996; Vizmanos & Marti-Henneberg, 2000; Woelfle, Harz, & Roth, 2007).

Other factors can affect the timing of menarche. For instance, environmental stress due to such factors as parental divorce or high levels of family conflict can bring about an early onset (Kaltiala-Heino, Kosunen, & Rimpela, 2003; Ellis, 2004; Belsky et al., 2007).

Over the past 100 years or so, girls in the United States and other cultures have been experiencing puberty at earlier ages. Near the end of the 19th century, menstruation began, on average, around age 14 or 15, compared with today's age 11 or 12. Other indicators of puberty, such as the age at which adult height and sexual maturity are reached, have also appeared at earlier ages, probably due to reduced disease and improved nutrition (McDowell, Brody, & Hughes, 2007; Harris, Prior, & Koehoorn, 2008).

The earlier start of puberty is an example of a significant **secular trend,** a pattern of change occurring over several generations. Secular trends occur when a physical characteristic changes over the course of several generations, such as earlier onset of menstruation or increased height that has occurred as a result of better nutrition over the centuries.

Menstruation is just one of several changes in puberty that are related to the development of primary and secondary sex characteristics. **Primary sex characteristics** are associated with the development of the organs and structures of the body that directly relate to reproduction. In contrast, **secondary sex characteristics** are the visible signs of sexual maturity that do not involve the sex of organs directly.

In girls, the development of primary sex characteristics involves changes in the vagina and uterus. Secondary sex characteristics include the development of breasts and pubic hair.

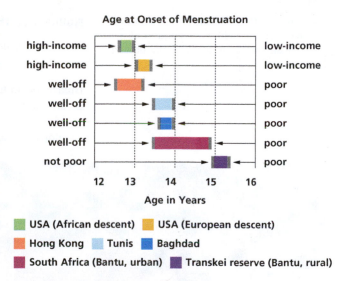

FIGURE 5-10 Onset of Menstruation

The onset of menstruation occurs earlier in more economically advantaged countries than in poorer nations. But even in wealthier countries, girls living in more affluent circumstances begin to menstruate earlier than those living in less affluent situations.

(*Source:* Adapted from Eveleth & Tanner, 1976)

secular trend A statistical tendency observed over several generations

primary sex characteristics Characteristics that are associated with the development of the organs and structures of the body that directly relate to reproduction

secondary sex characteristics The visible signs of sexual maturity that do not involve the sex organs directly

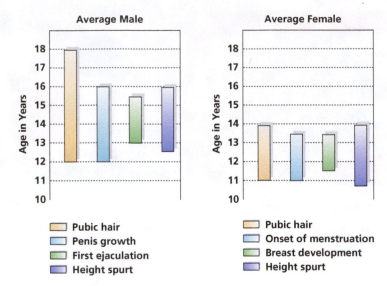

FIGURE 5-11 **The Changes of Sexual Maturation during Adolescence**

Changes in sexual maturation occur for both males and females primarily during early adolescence.

(*Source:* Adapted from Tanner, 1978)

FROM AN
EDUCATOR'S
PERSPECTIVE:

Why do you think the passage to adolescence is regarded in many cultures as a significant transition that calls for unique ceremonies?

Breasts begin to grow at about age 10, and pubic hair begins to appear at about age 11. Underarm hair appears about two years later.

For some girls, indications of puberty start unusually early. One of seven Caucasian girls develops breasts or pubic hair by age 8. Even more surprisingly, the figure is one out of two for African American girls. The reasons for this earlier onset of puberty are unclear, and the demarcation between normal and abnormal onset of puberty is a point of controversy among specialists (The Endocrine Society, 2001; Ritzen, 2003; James et al., 2012).

Boys' sexual maturation follows a somewhat different course. The penis and scrotum begin to grow at an accelerated rate at around the age of 12, and they reach adult size about 3 or 4 years later. As boys' penises enlarge, other primary sex characteristics are developing with enlargement of the prostate gland and seminal vesicles, which produce semen (the fluid that carries sperm). Secondary sex characteristics are also developing. Pubic hair begins to grow at around the age of 12, followed by the growth of underarm and facial hair. Finally, boys' voices deepen as the vocal cords become longer and the larynx becomes larger. (Figure 5-11 summarizes the changes that occur in sexual maturation during early adolescence.)

Girls begin their growth spurt several years earlier than boys, leading to significant disparities in mixed-gender settings.

Review, Check, and Apply

Review

1. Children's patterns of growth tend to be steady during the preschool and middle childhood years and accelerated during the adolescent growth spurt. The shape and structure of the body also undergo change. Regardless of general tendencies, significant individual differences and differences based on gender, culture, and environmental factors are apparent.

2. The brain grows at a faster rate than any other part of the body, largely because of a rapid increase in the number of interconnections among cells and in the amount of myelin in the brain. Lateralization, the process by which certain functions become localized more in one hemisphere than the other, becomes more pronounced.

3. Children's gross and fine motor skills also increase markedly during childhood, achieving full development during adolescence. Handedness also becomes defined, and artistic ability passes through a number of stages of increasing fluency.

4. Physical competence plays a large part in school-age children's lives and social success. Boys especially experience social benefits from physical competence that are not shared by less competent boys (or by physically competent girls).

5. Adolescence brings the onset of puberty, a period of sudden hormonal and physical changes for boys and girls that can be disturbing. Physical changes include the development of primary and secondary sex characteristics.

Check

1. The _____ _____ states that growth follows a direction and pattern that begins with the head and upper body parts and then proceeds to the rest of the body.

2. The development stage between childhood and adulthood is _____.

3. _____ sex characteristics are associated with the development of the organs and structures of the body that directly relate to reproduction. In contrast, _____ sex characteristics are the visible signs of sexual maturity that do not involve the sex of organs directly.

Apply

1. How might biology and environment combine to affect the physical growth of a child adopted as an infant from a developing country and reared in a more industrialized one?

2. What do you think Pablo Picasso meant when he said, "it has taken me a whole lifetime to learn to draw like children"? Are there other things adults can learn from children?

To see more review questions, log on to MyPsychLab.

ANSWERS: 1. cephalocaudal principle 2. adolescence 3. primary; secondary

MODULE 5.2

THE DEVELOPMENT OF THE SENSES

LO 5-4 In what ways do the senses develop as children grow?

LO 5-5 How sensitive is an infant to pain and touch?

LO 5-6 What sensory capabilities do people possess from the beginning of life?

William James, one of the founding fathers of psychology, believed the world of the infant is a "blooming, buzzing confusion" (James, 1890/1950). Was he right?

In this case, James's wisdom failed him. The newborn's sensory world does lack the clarity and stability that we can distinguish as adults, but day by day the world grows increasingly comprehensible as the infant's ability to sense and perceive the environment develops. In fact, babies appear to thrive in an environment enriched by pleasing sensations.

The processes that underlie infants' understanding of the world around them are sensation and perception. **Sensation** is the physical stimulation of the sense organs, and **perception** is the mental process of sorting out, interpretating, analyzing, and integrating stimuli from the sense organs and brain.

The study of infants' capabilities in the realm of sensation and perception challenges the ingenuity of investigators. As we'll see, researchers have developed a number of procedures for understanding sensation and perception in different realms.

sensation The stimulation of the sense organs

perception The sorting out, interpretation, analysis, and integration of stimuli involving the sense organs

A neonate's view of the world is limited to 8 to 14 inches. Objects beyond that distance are fuzzy.

A month after birth, newborns' vision has improved, but still lacks clarifying detail.

By 3 months, objects are seen with clarity.

First Looks: Visual Perception in Infancy

From the time of Lee Eng's birth, everyone who met him felt that he gazed at them intently. His eyes seemed to meet those of visitors. They seemed to bore deeply and knowingly into the faces of people who looked at him.

How good in fact was Lee's vision, and what, precisely, could he make out of his environment? Quite a bit, at least up close. According to some estimates, a newborn's distance vision ranges from 20/200 to 20/600, which means that an infant can only see with accuracy visual material up to 20 feet that an adult with normal vision is able to see with similar accuracy from a distance of between 200 and 600 feet (Haigth, 1991).

These figures indicate that infants' distance vision is one tenth to one third that of the average adult's. This isn't so bad, actually: The vision of newborns provides the same degree of distance acuity as the uncorrected vision of many adults who wear eyeglasses or contact lenses. (If you wear glasses or contact lenses, remove them to get a sense of what an infant can see of the world; see the accompanying set of photos.) Furthermore, infants' distance vision grows increasingly acute. By 6 months of age, the average infant's vision is already 20/20—in other words, identical to that of adults (Cavallini et al., 2002).

Other visual abilities grow rapidly. For instance, *binocular vision*, the ability to combine the images coming to each eye to see depth and motion, is achieved at around 14 weeks. Before then, infants do not integrate the information from each eye.

Depth perception is a particularly useful ability, helping babies acknowledge heights and avoid falls. In a classic study by developmental psychologists Eleanor Gibson and Richard Walk (1960) infants were placed on a sheet of heavy glass. A checkered pattern appeared under one-half of the glass sheet, making it seem that the infant was on a stable floor. However, in the middle of the glass sheet, the pattern dropped down several feet, forming an apparent "visual cliff." The question Gibson and Walk asked was whether infants would willingly crawl across the cliff when called by their mothers (see Figure 5-12).

The results were unambiguous. Most of the infants in the study, who ranged in age from 6 to 14 months, could not be coaxed over the apparent cliff. Clearly the ability to perceive depth had already developed in most of them by that age. On the other hand, the experiment did not pinpoint when depth perception emerged, because only infants who had already learned to crawl could be tested. But other experiments, in which infants of 2 and 3 months were placed on their stomachs above the apparent floor and above the visual cliff, revealed differences in heart rate between the two positions (Campos, Langer, & Krowitz, 1970).

Infants also show clear visual preferences, preferences that are present from birth. Given a choice, infants reliably prefer to look at stimuli that include patterns than to look at simpler

Simulate *The Visual Cliff* in **MyPsychLab**.

FIGURE 5-12 Visual Cliff

The "visual cliff" experiment examines the depth perception of infants. Most infants in the age range of 6 to 14 months cannot be coaxed to cross the cliff, apparently responding to the fact that the patterned area drops several feet.

stimuli (see Figure 5-13). How do we know? Developmental psychologist Robert Fantz (1963) created a classic test. He built a chamber in which babies could lie on their backs and see pairs of visual stimuli above them. Fantz could determine which of the stimuli the infants were looking at by observing the reflections of the stimuli in their eyes.

Fantz's work was the impetus for a great deal of research on the preferences of infants, most of which points to a critical conclusion: Infants are genetically preprogrammed to prefer particular kinds of stimuli. For instance, just minutes after birth they show preferences for certain colors, shapes, and configurations of various stimuli. They prefer curved over straight lines, three-dimensional figures to two-dimensional ones, and human faces to nonhuman faces. Such capabilities may be a reflection of the existence of highly specialized cells in the brain that react to stimuli of a particular pattern, orientation, shape, and direction of movement (Hubel & Wiesel, 2004; Kellman & Arterberry, 2006; Gliga et al., 2009).

However, genetics is not the sole determinant of infant visual preferences. Just a few hours after birth, infants have already learned to prefer their own mother's face to other faces. Similarly, between the ages of 6 and 9 months, infants become more adept at distinguishing among the faces of humans, whereas they become less able to distinguish faces of members of other species (see Figure 5-14 on page 144). They also distinguish between male and female faces. Such findings provide another clear piece of evidence of how heredity and environmental experiences are woven together to determine an infant's capabilities (Ramsey-Rennels & Langlois, 2006; Valenti, 2006; Quinn et al., 2008).

First Sounds: Auditory Perception in Infancy

What is it about a mother's lullaby that helps soothe a crying, fussy baby? Some clues emerge when we look at the capabilities of infants in the realm of auditory sensation and perception.

Infants hear from the time of birth—and even before. As we noted in Chapter 3, the ability to hear begins prenatally. Even in the womb, the fetus responds to sounds outside of its mother. Furthermore, infants are born with preferences for particular sound combinations (Trehub, 2003; Fujioka, Mourad, & Trainor, 2011).

Because they have had some practice in hearing before birth, it is not surprising that infants have reasonably good auditory perception after they are born. In fact, infants actually are more sensitive to certain very high and very low frequencies than adults—a sensitivity

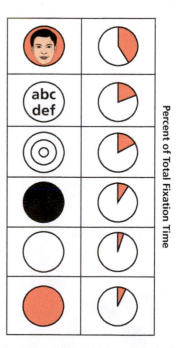

Percent of Total Fixation Time

FIGURE 5-13 Preferring Complexity

In a classic experiment, researcher Robert Fantz found that 2- and 3-month-old infants preferred to look at more complex stimuli than simple ones.

(Adapted from Fantz, 1961)

FIGURE 5-14 Distinguishing Faces

Examples of faces used in a study that found that 6-month-old infants distinguished human or monkey faces equally well, whereas 9-month-olds were less adept at distinguishing monkey faces than human faces.

(*Source:* Pascalis, de Haan, & Nelson, 2002, p. 1322)

that seems to increase during the first two years of life. On the other hand, infants are initially less sensitive than adults to middle-range frequencies. Eventually, however, their capabilities within the middle range improve (Fernald, 2001; Ertmer & Jung, 2012).

It is not fully clear what leads to the improvement during infancy in sensitivity to mid-frequency sounds, although it may be related to the maturation of the nervous system. More puzzling is why, after infancy, children's ability to hear very high and low frequencies gradually declines. One explanation may be that exposure to high levels of noise may diminish capacities at the extreme ranges (Trehub et al., 1989; Stewart, Scherer, & Lehman, 2003).

In addition to the ability to detect sound, infants need several other abilities in order to hear effectively. For instance, *sound localization* permits us to pinpoint the direction from which a sound is emanating. Compared to adults, infants have a slight handicap in this task because effective sound localization requires the use of the slight difference in the times at which a sound reaches our two ears. Sound that we hear first in the right ear tells us that the source of the sound is to our right. Because infants' heads are smaller than those of adults, the difference in timing of the arrival of sound at the two ears is less than it is in adults, so they have difficulty determining from which direction sound is coming.

Despite the potential limitation brought about by their smaller heads, infants' sound localization abilities are actually fairly good even at birth, and they reach adult levels of success by the age of 1 year. Interestingly, their improvement is not steady: Although we don't know why, studies show that the accuracy of sound localization actually declines between birth and 2 months of age, but then begins to increase (Litovsky & Ashmead, 1997; Fenwick & Morrongiello, 1998).

Infants can also discriminate groups of different sounds, in terms of their patterns and other acoustical characteristics, quite well. For instance, infants as young as 6 months old can detect the change of a single note in a six-tone melody. They also react to changes in musical key and rhythm. In sum, they listen with a keen ear to the melodies of lullabies their mothers and fathers sing to them (Masataka, 2006; Trehub & Hannon, 2009; Lewkowicz & Hansen-Tift, 2012).

Even more important to their ultimate success in the world, young infants are capable of making the fine discriminations that their future understanding of language will require. For instance, in one classic study, a group of 1- to 5-month-old infants sucked on nipples that activated a recording of a person saying "ba" every time they sucked (Eimas et al., 1971). At first, their interest in the sound made them suck vigorously. Soon, though, they became acclimated to the sound (through a process called *habituation*, discussed in Chapter 4) and sucked with less energy. On the other hand, when the experimenters changed the sound to "pa," the infants immediately showed new interest and sucked with greater vigor once again. The clear conclusion: Infants as young as 1 month old could make the distinction between the two similar sounds (Miller & Eimas, 1995; Gervain et al., 2008).

Young infants are also able to discriminate one language from another. By the age of 4 1/2 months, infants are able to discriminate their own names from other, similar-sounding words. By the age of 5 months, they can distinguish the difference between English and Spanish passages, even when the two are similar in meter, number of syllables, and speed of recitation. In fact, some evidence suggests that even 2-day-olds show preferences for the language spoken by those around them over other languages (Rivera-Gaxiola, Silva-Pereyra, & Kuhl, 2005; Kuhl, 2006).

Given their ability to discriminate a difference in speech as slight as the difference between two consonants, it is not surprising that infants can distinguish different people on the basis of voice. In fact, from an early age they show clear preferences for some voices over others. For instance, in one experiment newborns were allowed to suck a nipple that turned on a recording of a human voice reading a story. The infants sucked

By the age of 4 months, infants are able to discriminate their own names from other, similar-sounding words.

significantly longer when the voice was that of their mother than when the voice was that of a stranger (DeCasper & Fifer, 1980; Homae et al., 2012).

How do such preferences arise? One hypothesis is that prenatal exposure to the mother's voice is the key. As support for this conjecture, researchers point to the fact that newborns do not show a preference for their fathers' voices over other male voices. Furthermore, newborns prefer listening to melodies sung by their mothers before they were born to melodies that were not sung before birth. It seems, then, that the prenatal exposure to their mothers' voices—although muffled by the liquid environment of the womb—helps shape infants' listening preferences (Vouloumanous & Werker, 2007; Rosen & Iverson, 2007; Kisilevsky et al., 2009).

Smell and Taste in Infancy

What do infants do when they smell a rotten egg? Pretty much what adults do—crinkle their noses and generally look unhappy. On the other hand, the scent of bananas and butter produces a pleasant reaction on the part of infants (Steiner, 1979; Pomares, Schirrer, & Abadie, 2002).

Infants' sense of smell is so well developed that they can distinguish their mothers on the basis of smell alone.

The sense of smell is so well developed, even among very young infants, that at least some 12- to 18-day-old babies can distinguish their mothers on the basis of smell alone. For instance, in one experiment infants sniffed gauze pads worn under the arms of adults the previous evening. Infants who were being breastfed were able to distinguish their mothers' scent from that of other adults. In contrast, those who were being bottle-fed were unable to make the distinction. Moreover, both breast-fed and bottle-fed infants were unable to distinguish their fathers on the basis of odor (Mizuno & Ueda, 2004; Allam, Marlier, & Schaal, 2006).

Watch the Video *Infant Perception* in **MyPsychLab**.

Infants seem to have an innate sweet tooth (even before they have teeth!), and they show facial expressions of disgust when they taste something bitter. Very young infants smile when a sweet-tasting liquid is placed on their tongues. They also suck harder at a bottle if it is sweetened. Because breast milk has a sweet taste, it is possible that this preference may be part of our evolutionary heritage, retained because it offered a survival advantage. Infants who preferred sweet tastes may have been more likely to ingest sufficient nutrients and to survive than those who did not (Porges & Lipsitt, 1993).

Infants also develop taste preferences based on what their mothers drank while they were in the womb. For instance, one study found that women who drank carrot juice while pregnant had children who had a preference for the taste of carrots during infancy (Mennella, 2000).

Infants' Sensitivity to Pain and Touch

When Eli Rosenblatt was 8 days old, he participated in the ancient Jewish ritual of circumcision. As he lay nestled in his father's arms, the foreskin of his penis was removed. Although Eli shrieked in what seemed to his anxious parents as pain, he soon settled down and went back to sleep. Others who had watched the ceremony assured his parents that at Eli's age babies don't really experience pain, at least not in the same way that adults do.

Were Eli's relatives accurate in saying that young infants don't experience pain? In the past, many medical practitioners would have agreed. In fact, because they assumed that infants didn't experience pain in truly bothersome ways, many physicians routinely carried out medical procedures, and even some forms of surgery, without the use of painkillers or anesthesia. Their argument was that the risks from the use of anesthesia outweighed the potential pain that the young infants experienced.

Contemporary Views on Infant Pain. Today, however, it is widely acknowledged that infants are born with the capacity to experience pain. Obviously, no one can be sure whether the experience of pain in children is identical to that in adults, any more than we can tell whether an adult friend who complains of a headache is experiencing pain that is more or less severe than our own pain when we have a headache.

What we do know is that pain produces distress in infants. Their heartbeat increases, they sweat, show facial expressions of discomfort, and change the intensity and tone of crying when they are hurt (Warnock & Sandrin, 2004; Kohut & Pillai Riddell, 2009; Munsters et al., 2012).

There appears to be a developmental progression in reactions to pain. For example, a newborn infant who has her heel pricked for a blood test responds with distress, but it takes her several seconds to show the response. In contrast, only a few months later, the same procedure brings a much more immediate response. It is possible that the delayed reaction in infants is produced by the relatively slower transmission of information within the newborn's less-developed nervous system (Axia, Bonichini, & Benini, 1995; Puchalsi & Hummel, 2002).

Research with rats suggests that exposure to pain in infancy may lead to a permanent rewiring of the nervous system resulting in greater sensitivity to pain during adulthood. Such findings indicate that infants who must undergo extensive, painful medical treatments and tests may be unusually sensitive to pain when older (Ruda et al., 2000; Taddio, Shah, & Gilbert-MacLeod, 2002; Ozawa et al., 2011).

In response to increasing support for the notion that infants experience pain and that its effects may be long-lasting, medical experts now endorse the use of anesthesia and painkillers during surgery for even the youngest infants. According to the American Academy of Pediatrics, painkilling drugs are appropriate in most types of surgery—including circumcision (Sato et al., 2007; Urso, 2007; Yamada et al., 2008).

Responding to Touch. It clearly does not take the sting of pain to get an infant's attention. Even the youngest infants respond to gentle touches, such as a soothing caress, which can calm a crying, fussy infant (Hertenstein & Campos, 2001; Hertenstein, 2002).

Touch is one of the most highly developed sensory systems from the time of birth.

Touch is one of the most highly developed sensory systems in a newborn, and it is also one of the first to develop; there is evidence that by 32 weeks after conception, the entire body is sensitive to touch. Furthermore, several of the basic reflexes present at birth, such as the rooting reflex, require touch sensitivity to operate: An infant must sense a touch near the mouth in order to automatically seek a nipple to suck.

Infants' abilities in the realm of touch are particularly helpful in their efforts to explore the world. One of the ways children gain information about the world is through touching. As mentioned earlier, at the age of 6 months, infants are apt to place almost any object in their mouths, taking in data about its configuration from their sensory responses to the feel of it in their mouths (Ruff, 1989).

In addition, touch plays an important role in an organism's future development, for it triggers a complex chemical reaction that assists infants in their efforts to survive. For example, as we mentioned in Chapter 4, gentle massage stimulates the production of certain chemicals in an infant's brain that instigate growth (Field, Hernandez-Reif, & Diego, 2006; Diego, Field, & Hernandez-Reif, 2008, 2009).

Multimodal Perception: Combining Individual Sensory Inputs

When Eric Pettigrew was 7 months old, his grandparents presented him with a squeaky rubber doll. As soon as he saw it, he reached out for it, grasped it in his hand, and listened as it squeaked. He seemed delighted with the gift.

One way of considering Eric's sensory reaction to the doll is to focus on each of the senses individually: what the doll looked like to Eric, how it felt in his hand, and what it sounded like. In fact, this approach has dominated the study of sensation and perception in infancy.

Let's consider another approach: We might examine how the various sensory responses are integrated with one another. Instead of looking at each individual sensory response, we could consider how the responses work together and are combined to produce Eric's ultimate reaction. The **multimodal approach to perception** considers how information that is collected by various individual sensory systems is integrated and coordinated.

Although the multimodal approach is a relatively recent innovation in the study of how infants understand their sensory world, it raises some fundamental issues about the development of sensation and perception. For instance, some researchers argue that sensations are initially integrated with one another in the infant, while others maintain that the infant's sensory systems are initially separate and that brain development leads to increasing integration (De Gelder, 2000; Lewkowicz, 2002; Flom & Bahrick, 2007).

We do not know yet which view is correct. However, it does appear that by an early age infants are able to relate what they have learned about an object through one sensory channel to what they have learned about it through another. For instance, even one-month-old infants are able to recognize by sight objects that they have previously held in their mouths but have never seen (Steri & Spelke, 1988). Clearly, some cross-talk between various sensory channels is already possible a month after birth.

Infants' abilities at multimodal perception showcase the sophisticated perceptual abilities of infants, which continue to grow throughout the period of infancy. Such perceptual growth is aided by infants' discovery of **affordances**, the options that a given situation or stimulus provides. For example, infants learn that they might potentially fall when walking down a steep ramp—that is, the ramp *affords* the possibility of falling. Such knowledge is crucial as infants make the transition from crawling to walking. Similarly, infants learn that an object shaped in a certain way can slip out of their hands if not grasped correctly. For example, Eric is learning that his toy has several affordances: He can grab it and squeeze it, listen to it squeak, and even chew comfortably on it if he is teething (Flom & Bahrick, 2007; Wilcox et al., 2007).

FROM A HEALTH-CARE WORKER'S PERSPECTIVE: Persons who are born without the use of one sense sometimes develop unusual abilities in one or more other senses. What can health-care professionals do to help infants who are lacking in a particular sense?

ARE YOU AN INFORMED CONSUMER OF DEVELOPMENT?

Exercising Your Infant's Body and Senses

Recall how cultural expectations and environments affect the age at which various physical milestones, such as the first step, occur. Although most experts feel attempts to accelerate physical and sensory-perceptual development yield little advantage, parents should ensure that their infants receive sufficient physical and sensory stimulation. There are several specific ways to accomplish this goal:

- Carry a baby in different positions—in a backpack, in a frontpack, or in a football hold with the infant's head in the palm of your hand and its feet lying on your arm. This lets the infant view the world from several perspectives.
- Let infants explore their environment. Don't contain them too long in a barren environment. Let them crawl or wander around—after first making the environment "childproof" by removing dangerous objects.
- Engage in "rough-and-tumble" play. Wrestling, dancing, and rolling around on the floor—if not violent—are activities that are fun and that stimulate older infants' motor and sensory systems.
- Let babies touch their food and even play with it. Infancy is too early to start teaching table manners.
- Provide toys that stimulate the senses, particularly toys that can stimulate more than one sense at a time. For example, brightly colored, textured toys with movable parts are enjoyable and help sharpen infants' senses. ■

multimodal approach to perception The approach that considers how information that is collected by various individual sensory systems is integrated and coordinated

affordances The action possibilities that a given situation or stimulus provides

FIGURE 5-15 Sensory Development

Preschool-age children who view this odd vegetable-fruit-bird combination focus on the components that make it up. Not until they reach middle childhood do they begin to look at the figure as a whole in addition to its parts.

(*Source:* Elkind, 1978)

Sensory Development beyond Infancy

The increasing development of the brain permits improvements in the senses during the preschool period and beyond. For instance, brain maturation leads to better control of eye movements and focusing. Still, preschoolers' eyes are not as capable as they will be in later stages of development. Specifically, preschool-age children are unable to easily and precisely scan groupings of small letters, as is required when reading small print. Consequently, preschoolers who start to read often focus on just the initial letter of a word and guess at the rest—leading, as you might expect, to relatively frequent errors. It is not until they are approximately 6 years of age that children can effectively focus and scan. Even at this point, however, they still don't have the capabilities of adults, which gradually evolves throughout childhood (Willows, Kruk, & Corcos, 1993).

Children also begin a gradual shift in the way they view objects made up of multiple parts. For instance, consider the rather unusual vegetable-fruit-bird combination shown in Figure 5-15. Rather than identifying it as a bird, as most adults do, preschool-age children see the figure in terms of the parts that make it up ("carrots" and "cherries" and "a pear"). Not until they reach middle childhood, about the age of 7 or 8, do they begin to look at the figure in terms of both its overall organization and its parts ("a bird made of fruit").

Judgments of objects reflect the way in which their eyes move when perceiving figures (Zaporozhets, 1965). Until the age of 3 or 4, preschoolers devote most of their looking to the insides of two-dimensional objects they are scanning, concentrating on the internal details and largely ignoring the perimeter of the figure. In contrast, 4- and 5-year-olds begin to look more at the surrounding boundaries of the figure, and at 6 and 7 years of age, they look at the outside systematically, with far less scanning of the inside. The result is a greater awareness of the overall organization of the figure.

Of course, vision is not the only sense that improves during childhood. For instance, *auditory acuity*, or the sharpness of hearing, improves as well. Similarly, the other senses become more sophisticated with age.

Review, Check, and Apply

Review

1. Sensation refers to the activation of the sense organs by external stimuli. Perception is the analysis, interpretation, and integration of sensations.

2. Infants' abilities in the sensory realm are surprisingly well developed at or shortly after birth. Their perceptions through sight, hearing, smell, taste, and touch help them explore and begin to make sense of the world.

3. Very early, infants can see depth and motion, distinguish colors and patterns, localize and discriminate sounds, recognize the sound of their mothers' voices, and discern their mothers by smell alone. Moreover, infants can relate some perceptions received through one sensory channel to those received through another.

4. Infants are sensitive to pain and to touch. Most medical authorities now subscribe to procedures, including anesthesia, that minimize infants' pain.

5. The senses, especially vision and hearing, improve throughout childhood and adolescence. Control of eye movements, focusing, and the processes of visual perception all develop. Auditory acuity improves, too, although the ability to isolate individual sounds from a multitude of sounds is not yet fully developed.

Check

1. _____ is the physical stimulation of the sense organs.

2. _____ is the process of sorting out, interpretation, analysis, and integration of stimuli involving the sense organs and the brain.

3. The _____ approach to perception considers how information that is collected by various individual sensory systems is integrated and coordinated.

4. In addition to improved vision in childhood, the sharpness of hearing, or _____ _____ improves as well.

Apply

1. Given the way the brain and nervous system develop, what sort of sensory environment would probably be most conducive to healthy neural development in the infant? Why?

2. Are the processes of sensation and perception always linked? Is it possible to sense without perceiving? To perceive without sensing? How?

To see more review questions, log on to MyPsychLab.

ANSWERS: 1. sensation 2. perception 3. multimodal 4. auditory acuity

---

MODULE 5.3

NUTRITION AND HEALTH

LO 5-7 What is the role of nutrition in development, and what causes obesity?

LO 5-8 How healthy are growing children, and what threats to wellness do they face?

> *Rosa sighed as she sat down to nurse the baby—again. She had fed 5-week-old Juan about every hour today, and he still seemed hungry. Some days, it seemed like all she did was breastfeed her baby. "Well, he must be going through a growth spurt," she decided, as she settled into her favorite rocking chair and put the baby to her nipple.*

The rapid physical growth that occurs during infancy is fueled by the nutrients that infants receive. Without proper nutrition, infants cannot reach their physical potential, and they may suffer cognitive and social consequences as well (Tanner & Finn-Stevenson, 2002; Costello, Compton, & Keeler, 2003; Gregory, 2005).

Nutrition: Links to Overall Functioning

Although there are vast individual differences in what constitutes appropriate nutrition—infants differ in terms of growth rates, body composition, metabolism, and activity levels—some broad guidelines do hold. In general, infants should consume about 50 calories per day for each pound they weigh—an allotment that is twice the suggested caloric intake for adults (Dietz & Stern, 1999; Skinner et al., 2004).

Typically, though, it's not necessary to count calories for infants. Most infants regulate their caloric intake quite effectively on their own. If they are allowed consume as much as they seem to want, and not pressured to eat more, they will do fine.

Malnutrition

Malnutrition, the condition of having an improper amount and balance of nutrients, produces several results, none good. For instance, malnutrition is more common among children living in many developing countries than it is among children who live in more industrialized, affluent countries. Malnourished children in these countries begin to show a slower growth rate by the age of 6 months. By the time they reach the age of 2 years, their height and weight are only 95% the height and weight of children in more industrialized countries.

Children who have been chronically malnourished during infancy later score lower on IQ tests and tend to do less well in school. These effects may linger even after the children's diet has improved substantially (Grantham-McGregor, Ani, & Fernald, 2001; Ratanachu-Ek, 2003).

The problem of malnutrition is greatest in underdeveloped countries, where overall 10% of infants are severely malnourished. In some countries the problem is especially severe. For example, 37% of North Korean children are chronically malnourished suffering moderate to severe malnutrition (World Food Programme, 2008; also see Figure 5-16).

Problems of malnourishment are not restricted to developing countries, however. In the United States, some 13 million children—17%—live in poverty, which puts them at risk for malnutrition. In fact, the proportion of children living in low-income families has risen since 2000. Overall, some 24% of families who have children 6 years old and younger live in poverty, and 46% are classified as low income. And, as we can see in Figure 5-17, the poverty rates are even higher for Hispanic, African American, and American Indian families (Duncan & Brooks-Gunn, 2000; Douglas-Hall & Chau, 2007; National Center for Children in Poverty, 2010).

Social service programs such as these mean that children rarely become severely malnourished, but such children remain susceptible to *undernutrition,* in which there is some deficiency in diet. In fact, some surveys find that as many as a quarter of 1- to 5-year-old children in the United States have diets that fall below the minimum caloric intake recommended by nutritional experts. Although the consequences are not as severe as those of malnutrition, undernutrition also has long-term costs. For instance, cognitive development later in childhood is affected by even mild to moderate undernutrition (Pollitt et al., 1996; Tanner & Finn-Stevenson, 2002).

Severe malnutrition during infancy may lead to several disorders. Malnutrition during the first year can produce **marasmus,** a disease in which infants stop growing. Marasmus, attributable to a severe deficiency in proteins and calories, causes the body to waste away and ultimately results in death. Older children are susceptible to **kwashiorkor,** a disease in which a child's stomach, limbs, and face swell with water. To a casual observer, it appears that a child with kwashiorkor is actually chubby. However, this is an illusion: The child's body is

marasmus   A disease characterized by the cessation of growth

kwashiorkor   A disease in which a child's stomach, limbs, and face swell with water

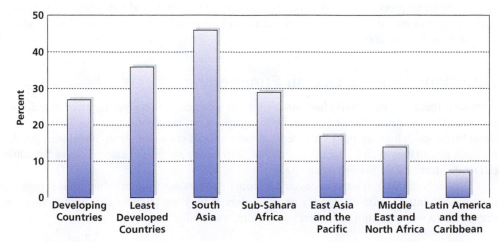

FIGURE 5-16 Underweight Children

The percentage of children under five years who are moderately or severely underweight.

(*Source:* UNICEF, *Progress for Children,* 2006)

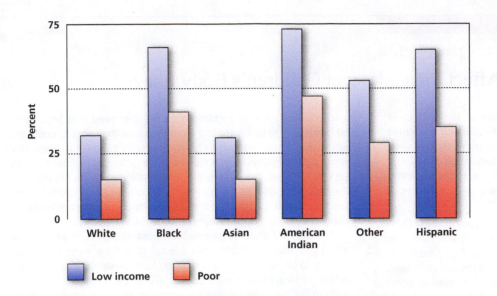

FIGURE 5-17 Children Living in Poverty

The incidence of poverty among children under the age of 6 is particularly high in minority and single-parent households.

(*Source:* National Center for Children in Poverty at the Joseph L. Mailman School of Public Health of Columbia University, 2010)

in fact struggling to make use of the few nutrients that are available (Douglass & McGadney-Douglass, 2008).

In some cases, infants who receive sufficient nutrition act as though they have been deprived of food. Looking as though they suffer from marasmus, they are underdeveloped, listless, and apathetic. The real cause, though, is emotional: They lack sufficient love and emotional support. In such cases, known as **nonorganic failure to thrive,** children stop growing not for biological reasons but due to a lack of stimulation and attention from their parents. Usually occurring by the age of 18 months, nonorganic failure to thrive can be reversed through intensive parent training or by placing children in a foster home where they can receive emotional support.

Childhood Obesity: Genetic and Social Factors

When her mother asks Ruthellen if she would like a piece of bread with her meal, Ruthellen replies that she better not—she thinks that she may be getting fat. Ruthellen, who is of normal weight and height, is 6 years old.

Although height can be of concern to both children and parents during middle childhood, maintaining the appropriate weight is an even greater worry for some. In fact, concern about weight can border on an obsession, particularly among girls. For instance, many 6-year-old girls worry about becoming "fat," and some 40% of 9- and 10-year-olds are trying to lose weight. Why? Their concern is most often the result of the U.S. preoccupation with being slim, which permeates every sector of society (see the *From Research to Practice* box; Greenwood & Pietromonaco, 2004; Armitage, 2012).

In spite of this widely held view that thinness is a virtue, increasing numbers of children are becoming obese. **Obesity** is defined as body weight that is more than 20% above the average for a person of a given age and height. By this definition, 17% of U.S. children are obese—a proportion that has more than tripled since the 1960s (see Figure 5-18 on page 152; Mann, 2005; Centers for Disease Control and Prevention, 2010; Cornwell & McAlister, 2011; Robertson et al., 2012).

Obesity is caused by a combination of genetic and environmental factors. Particular inherited genes are related to obesity and predispose certain children to be overweight. For example, adopted children tend to have weights that are more similar to those of their birth parents than to those of their adoptive parents (Whitaker et al., 1997; Bray, 2008).

But it is not just a matter of a genetic predisposition that leads to weight problems. Poor diets also contribute to obesity. Despite their knowledge that certain foods are necessary for a balanced, nutritious diet, many parents provide their children with too few fruits and

FROM AN EDUCATOR'S PERSPECTIVE:
What might be some of the reasons that malnourishment, which slows physical growth, can also lower IQ scores and school performance? How might malnourishment affect education in third world countries?

nonorganic failure to thrive A disorder in which infants stop growing due to a lack of stimulation and attention as the result of inadequate parenting

obesity A body weight more than 20% higher than the average weight for a person of a given age and height

FROM RESEARCH TO PRACTICE
Do Media Images Affect Preadolescent Children's Body Image?

Dissatisfaction with body image is on the rise. In one study of children ages 8–10, more than half of the girls and more than a third of the boys were already dissatisfied with their size, even at their young age. What's worse is that body image dissatisfaction is related to unhealthy behaviors, such as eating disorders, smoking, depression, and low self-esteem. (Wood, Becker, & Thompson, 1996; Jung & Peterson, 2007).

Why are children acquiring dissatisfaction with their bodies? One answer relates to the media. Television, magazines, and other media present models of idealized beauty and fitness as if they are the norm in the real world. Not only are certain body types overrepresented, but people with such idealized body types are portrayed as admired because of their looks. Children compare themselves to these idealized same-sex media images and often conclude that they just don't measure up (Hargreaves & Tiggemann, 2003; Morano, Colella, & Capranica, 2011).

In reality, no one can measure up to some kinds of body representations. For example, the body dimensions of male action figures marketed to young boys are so exaggerated that they are physically unattainable in real life. Furthermore, male characters in video games that are popular with young boys are also exceedingly big and muscular (Pope, Olivardia, Gruber, & Borowiecki, 1999; Scharrer, 2004; Harrison & Bond, 2007).

Research also shows that boys and girls view media differently and reach different conclusions about their own body image as a result. One study of children ages 8–11 showed that boys' ideal body image is to be bigger and more muscular than they actually are, while girls' ideal image is to be considerably thinner. Interestingly, when girls' and boys' perceptions of their actual body image are assessed, girls see themselves more accurately as being heavier than their ideal. In contrast, boys have a distorted self-perception: they see themselves as bigger and more muscular than they actually are (Jung & Peterson, 2007; Hayes & Tantleff-Dunn, 2010).

Not only are children exposed to unrealistic body image portrayals in the media, but also they are apt to admire these characters and try to be like them. Furthermore, body dissatisfaction, to some extent, is found across different racial and ethnic groups. One suggestion for how parents and teachers can try to inoculate children against media influences is to teach them that media representations are often exaggerated and unattainable. Furthermore, children should be exposed to a healthier, broader range of body types—ones with which they can identify (Jung & Peterson, 2007; George & Franko, 2010).

- **Do you think it is significant that big and strong male media characters are also often portrayed as being dominant and successful, or that slender and beautiful female media characters are also often portrayed as being popular with boys?**

- **What can parents and teachers do to reduce the influence of media images on children's body image?**

FIGURE 5-18 Obesity in Children

Obesity in children ages 6–12 has risen dramatically over the past four decades.

(*Source:* Centers for Disease Control and Prevention, 2010)

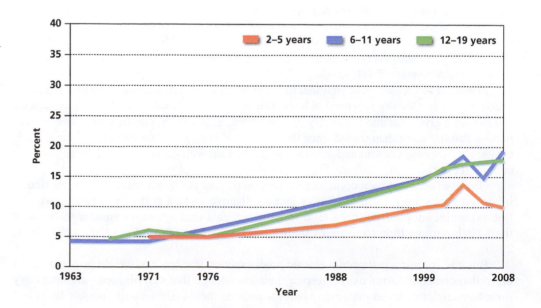

vegetables and more fats and sweets than recommended (see Figure 5-19). School lunch programs have sometimes contributed to the problem by failing to provide nutritious options (Johnston, Delva, & O'Malley, 2007; Story, Nanney, & Schwartz, 2009).

Another major factor in childhood obesity is a lack of exercise. School-age children, by and large, tend to engage in relatively little exercise and are not particularly fit. For instance, around 40% of boys 6 to 12 are unable to do more than one pull-up, and a quarter can't do any. Furthermore, school fitness surveys reveal that children in the United States have shown little or no improvement in the amount of exercise they get, despite national efforts to increase the level of fitness of school-age children. From the ages of 6 to 18, boys decrease their physical activity by 24% and girls by 36% (Moore, Gao, & Bradlee, 2003; Stork & Sanders, 2008).

Why, when our visions of childhood include children running happily on school playgrounds, playing sports, and chasing one another in games of tag, is the actual level of exercise relatively low? One answer is that many kids are inside their homes, watching television and computer screens. Such sedentary activities not only keep children from exercising, but they often snack while viewing TV, playing video games, or surfing the web (Landhuis et al., 2008; Davis et al., 2011; Goldfield, 2012).

Furthermore, many children return from school to homes without adult supervision because their parents are at work. In such situations, parents may prohibit their children from leaving the home for safety reasons, meaning that children are unable to engage in exercise even if they wanted to (Murphy & Polivka, 2007).

Dealing with Obesity. Regardless of what causes a child to become obese, treatment is tricky, because creating too strong a concern about food and dieting must be avoided. Children need to learn to control their eating themselves. Parents who are particularly controlling and directive regarding their children's eating may produce children who lack internal controls to regulate their own food intake (Wardle, Guthrie, & Sanderson, 2001; Okie, 2005).

One strategy is to control the food that is available in the home. By stuffing the cupboards and refrigerator with healthy foods—and keeping high-caloric, highly processed foods out of the house—children are essentially forced to eat a healthy diet. Furthermore, avoiding fast foods, which are high in calories and fats, is important (Campbell, Crawford, & Ball, 2006; Lindsay et al., 2006; Hoerr, Murashima, & Keast, 2008; Stotland, Larocque, & Sadikaj, 2012).

In most cases, the goal of treatment for obesity is to temporarily maintain a child's current weight through an improved diet and increased exercise, rather than actually seeking to lose weight. In time, obese children's normal growth in height will result in their weight's becoming more normal.

FIGURE 5-19 A Balanced Diet

In an effort to simplify dietary guidelines for both children and adults, the United States Department of Agriculture has released MyPlate, designed to help consumers make better food choices and build a healthy plate at meal times. MyPlate illustrates the five food groups using a familiar mealtime visual, a place setting. More information can be obtained by logging onto the USDA website at www.choosemyplate.gov.

(*Source:* U.S. Department of Agriculture, 2011)

Watch the **Video** *The Problem of Childhood Obesity* in **MyPsychLab**.

Health and Wellness

Imani was miserable. Her nose was running, her lips were chapped, and her throat was sore. Although she had been able to stay home from school and spend the day watching old reruns on TV, she still felt that she was suffering mightily.

Despite her misery, Imani's situation is not so bad. She'll get over the cold in a few days and be no worse for having experienced it. In fact, she may be a little *better* off, for she is now immune to the specific cold germs that made her ill in the first place.

Imani's cold may end up being the most serious illness that she gets during middle childhood. For most children, this is a period of robust health, and most of the ailments they do contract tend to be mild and brief. Routine immunizations during childhood have produced a considerably lower incidence of the life-threatening illnesses that 50 years ago claimed the lives of a significant number of children.

"Remember when we used to have to fatten the kids up first?"

The average preschooler has seven to ten minor colds and other minor respiratory illnesses in each of the years from ages 3 to 5. Although the sniffles and coughs that are the symptoms of such illnesses are certainly distressing to children, the unpleasantness is usually not too severe and the illnesses usually last only a few days (Kalb, 1997; Linder, 2012).

However, illness is not uncommon. For instance, more than 90% of children are likely to have at least one serious medical condition over the 6-year period of middle childhood, according to the results of one large survey. And although most children have short-term illnesses, about one in nine has a chronic, persistent condition, such as repeated migraine headaches. And some illnesses are actually becoming more prevalent (Dey & Bloom, 2005).

Actually, such minor illnesses may offer some unexpected benefits: Not only may they help children build up immunity to more severe illnesses to which they may be exposed in the future, but also may provide some emotional benefits. Specifically, some researchers argue that minor illness permits children to understand their bodies better. It also may permit them to learn coping skills that will help them deal more effectively with future, more severe diseases. Furthermore, it gives them the ability to understand better what others who are sick are going through. This ability to put oneself in another's shoes, known as empathy, may teach children to be more sympathetic and better caretakers (Notaro, Gelman, & Zimmerman, 2002; Raman & Winer, 2002; Williams & Binnie, 2002).

Serious Childhood Illnesses.

The childhood years were not always a period of relatively good health. Before the discovery of vaccines and the routine immunization of children, the preschool period was a dangerous time. Even today, this period is risky in many parts of the world, as well as in certain lower socioeconomic segments of the U.S. population (Ripple & Zigler, 2003).

asthma   A chronic condition characterized by periodic attacks of wheezing, coughing, and shortness of breath

Why does the United States, the richest nation in the world, provide less than ideal health care for its children? Culture provides a major part of the answer. The U.S. cultural tradition is that children are the complete responsibility of their parents, not of the government or of other individuals. What this means is that socioeconomic factors prevent some children from getting good health care and that members of minority groups, which tend to have less disposable income, suffer from inferior care (see Figure 5-20).

In other cultures, however, child rearing is regarded more as a shared, collective responsibility. Until the United States gives greater priority to the health of its children, the country will continue to lag behind in the effectiveness of its child care (Clinton, 1996).

Asthma.

Asthma is among the diseases that have shown a significant increase in prevalence in recent decades. **Asthma** is a chronic condition characterized by periodic attacks of wheezing, coughing, and shortness of breath. More than 7 million U.S. children suffer from the disorder, and worldwide the number is more than 150 million. Racial and ethnic minorities are particularly at risk for the disease Dey & Bloom, 2005; Centers for Disease Control, 2009; Akinbami, 2011; see Figure 5-21).

Asthma occurs when the airways leading to the lungs constrict, partially blocking the passage of air. Because the airways are obstructed, more effort is needed to push air through them, making breathing more difficult. As air is forced through the obstructed airways, it makes the whistling sound called wheezing.

Not surprisingly, children are often exceedingly frightened by asthma attacks, and the anxiety and agitation produced by their breathing difficulties may actually make the attack worse. In some cases, breathing becomes so difficult that further physical symptoms develop, including sweating, an increased heart rate, and—in the most severe cases—blueness in the face and lips due to a lack of oxygen.

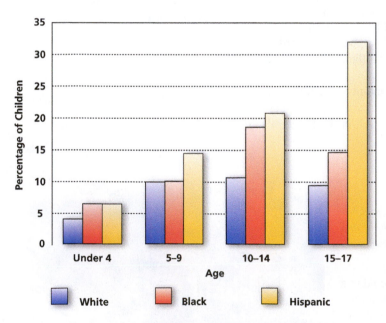

FIGURE 5-20 Children with No Physician Visits in the Past Year

In every age group, more black and Hispanic children than white children did not have a single visit to a physician during the previous year. From a social worker's perspective, what could you do to help minority children have better access to health care?

(*Source:* Health Resources and Services Administration, 2008)

Asthma attacks are triggered by a variety of factors. Among the most common are respiratory infections (such as colds or flu), allergic reactions to airborne irritants (such as pollution, cigarette smoke, dust mites, and animal dander and excretions), stress, and exercise. Sometimes even a sudden change in air temperature or humidity is enough to bring on an attack (Li et al., 2005; Noonan & Ward, 2007; Tibosch, Verhaak, & Merkus, 2011).

Although asthma can be serious, treatment is increasingly effective for those who suffer from the disorder. Some children who experience frequent asthma attacks use a small aerosol container with a special mouthpiece to spray drugs into the lungs. Other patients take tablets or receive injections (Israel, 2005).

One of the most puzzling questions about asthma is why more and more children are suffering from it. Some researchers suggest that increasing air pollution has led to the rise; others believe that cases of asthma that might have been missed in the past are being identified more accurately. Still others have suggested that exposure to "asthma triggers," such as dust, may be increasing because new buildings are more weatherproof—and therefore less drafty—than old ones, and consequently the flow of air within them is more restricted.

Finally, poverty may play an indirect role. Children living in poverty have a higher incidence of asthma than other children, probably due to poorer medical care and less sanitary living conditions. For instance, poor youngsters are more likely than more affluent ones to be exposed to triggering factors that are associated with asthma, such as dust mites, cockroach feces and body parts, and rodent feces and urine (Johnson, 2003; Caron, Gjelsvik, & Buechner, 2005; Sidora-Arcoleo et al., 2012).

Injury. The greatest risk that children face comes from neither illness nor nutritional problems but from accidents: Before the age of 10, children have twice the likelihood of dying from an injury than from an illness. In fact, children in the United States have a 1 in 3 chance every year of receiving an injury that requires medical attention (Field & Behrman, 2002; National Safety Council, 2012).

The danger of injuries during the preschool years is in part a result of the children's high levels of physical activity. A 3-year-old might think that it is perfectly reasonable to climb on an unsteady chair to get something that is out of reach, and a 4-year-old might enjoy holding on to a low tree branch and swinging her legs up and down. It is this physical activity, in combination with the curiosity and lack of judgment that also characterize this age group, that makes preschoolers so accident-prone (MacInnes & Stone, 2008).

Furthermore, some children are more apt to take risks, and such preschoolers are more likely to be injured than are their more cautious peers. Boys, who are more active than girls and tend to take more risks, have a higher rate of injuries. Ethnic differences, probably due to differences in cultural norms about how closely children need to be supervised, can also be seen in accident rates. Asian American children in the United States, who tend to be supervised particularly strictly by their parents, have one of the lowest accident rates for children. Economic factors also play a role. Children raised under conditions of poverty in urban areas, whose inner-city neighborhoods may contain more hazards than more affluent areas, are two times more likely to die of injuries than children living in affluence (Morrongiello, Midgett, & Stanton, 2000; Morrongiello & Hogg, 2004; Morrongiello, Klemencic, & Corbett, 2008).

The range of dangers that preschoolers face is wide. Injuries come from falls, burns from stoves and fires, drowning in bathtubs indoors and standing water outdoors, and suffocation in places such as abandoned refrigerators. Auto accidents also account for a large number of injuries. Finally, children face injuries from poisonous substances, such as household cleaners.

The incidence of asthma, a chronic respiratory condition, has increased dramatically over the past several decades.

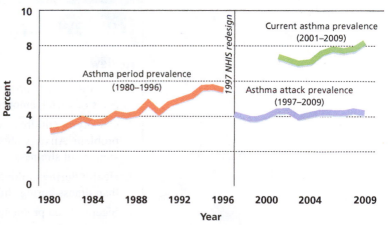

FIGURE 5-21 Rising Rates of Asthma

Since the early 1980s, the total rate of asthma has more than doubled. Of the 25 million U.S. sufferers of asthma, more than 7 million are children. A number of factors explain the rise, including increased air pollution and better means of detecting the disease.

(*Source:* Akinbami, 2011)

Preschoolers' high level of physical activity and their curiosity increase the risk of injury.

nightmares Vivid bad dreams, usually occurring toward morning

night terrors Intense psychological arousal that causes a child to wake up in a state of panic

enuresis A lack of bladder control past the age when most children are toilet trained

Sleep

No matter how tired they may be, some active children find it difficult to make the transition from the excitement of the day to settling down for a night's rest. This may lead to friction between caregivers and preschoolers over bedtime. Children may object to being told to sleep, and it may take them some time before they are able to fall asleep.

Although most children settle down fairly easily and drift off into sleep, for some sleep presents a real problem. As many as 20% to 30% of preschoolers experience difficulties lasting more than an hour in getting to sleep. Furthermore, they may wake in the night and call to their parents for comfort (Morgenthaler et al., 2006).

Once they do get to sleep, most preschoolers sleep fairly soundly through the night. However, between 10% and 50% of children ages 3 to 5 experience nightmares, with the frequency higher in boys than in girls. **Nightmares** are vivid bad dreams, usually occurring toward morning. Although an occasional nightmare is no cause for concern, when they occur repeatedly and cause a child anxiety during waking hours, they may be indicative of a problem (Pagel, 2000).

Night terrors produce intense physiological arousal and cause a child to wake up in an intense state of panic. After waking from a night terror, children are not easily comforted, and they cannot say why they are so disturbed and cannot recall having a bad dream. But the following morning, they cannot remember anything about the incident. Night terrors are much less frequent than nightmares, occurring in just 1% to 5% of children (Bootzin et al., 1993).

The most common sleep-related difficulties is **enuresis**, or a lack of bladder control past the age when most children are toilet trained. When it occurs, it usually involves bed-wetting during the night, making it a sleeping problem.

More common in boys than girls, enuresis is not, by itself, a sign of emotional difficulties. In fact, most instances spontaneously disappear as children mature and attain greater control over the muscles relating to urination. However, it can be a cause for concern if a child is upset about it or if it makes the child a target of ridicule from siblings or peers. In such cases, several types of treatments have proven effective. In particular, treatments in which children are rewarded for staying dry or are awakened by a battery device that senses when they have wet the bed are often effective (Vande et al., 2012).

Review, Check, and Apply

Review

1. Nutrition is important not only for physical growth but also because it affects many aspects of social, emotional, and cognitive functioning.

2. Obesity in children, which can be caused by genetic and social factors, can be a serious problem. Anxiety about obesity can be equally serious, especially if it leads to an obsession about slimness.

3. Health during childhood is generally good, and injury presents a far greater health risk than illness during childhood.

4. Sleep-related problems include nightmares, night terrors, and enuresis.

Check

1. _____ is body weight that is more than 20% above the average weight for a child of a given age and height.

2. A major contributor to childhood obesity is lack of _____ .

3. _____ , the condition of having an improper amount and balance of nutrients, can lead to a slower growth rate, lower IQ scores, and poorer performance in school.

4. TV, magazines, and other media present unrealistic and often unobtainable _____ _____ , which may make children anxious about their weight and general appearance.

Apply

1. What evidence can you offer that obesity is determined by both genetic and environmental factors?

2. What are some aspects of U.S. culture that may contribute to fitness and nutritional problems among school-age children?

To see more review questions, log on to MyPsychLab.

The CASE
of . . . *Girls Don't*

Jessalyn Palmer's father Dave was baffled. Jessalyn, nearly 5, had been denied admission to the Ropes & Branches course at a Native American camp she wanted to attend, and had been assigned instead to Beads and Baskets.

Jessalyn didn't want to make necklaces and baskets; she wanted to tie knots and make rope ladders and fashion slings and fly from branch to branch with the boys in Ropes & Branches. She had always been an active child, heedless of her body and happy to laugh off any hurts or bruises she earned as a result.

Dave Palmer begged the couple who ran the camp to allow Jessalyn to switch courses, but they were adamant. It would be too dangerous for her. It demanded too much brute strength and agility. Girls were better at finger skills like weaving and beading. Jessalyn would hurt herself on the ropes. They couldn't risk that.

Dave was certain they were exaggerating the risk. The camp was well staffed and had a perfect safety record. He protested that Jessalyn was as strong and agile as any boy in the course and her risk was no greater than theirs. But the owners were unmoved. When the husband remarked "Girls don't tie knots," Dave sensed that this was more than a personal judgment. The camp owners, he knew, were good and fair people, but perhaps their Native American heritage was guiding their decision.

Caught between culture and his daughter's disappointment, Dave didn't know what to do.

1. Given what you know about boys' and girls' physical characteristics at age 5, how can Dave make a case that Jessalyn's strength and agility matched those of the boys her age in the camp?

2. Could the camp owners be right about assigning Jessalyn to Beads & Baskets based on girls' superior fine motor skills? Are they justified in denying her admission to the more physical course that boys usually take?

3. What more would you need to know to decide fairly if Jessalyn would be as safe as the boys in the camp in Ropes & Branches? What policy change, if any, would you urge the owners to introduce?

4. If Jessalyn asks why she can't do Ropes & Branches, how should Dave answer? Should he tell her the truth behind the owners' decision or hide it?

5. If the owners don't change their minds, what would you advise Dave to do?

‹‹‹ LOOKING BACK

LO 5-1 How do the body, brain, and motor skills develop during childhood?

- Children's physical growth during childhood proceeds steadily until the sudden acceleration of the adolescent growth spurt. Changes in height and weight reflect genetic factors, as well as individual differences, gender, and economic status. In addition to gaining height and weight, the body changes in shape and structure.

- Brain growth is particularly rapid during the preschool years, with the number of interconnections among cells and the amount of myelin around neurons increasing greatly. Through the process of lateralization, the two halves of the brain begin to specialize in somewhat different functions. However, despite lateralization, the two hemispheres function as a unit and in fact differ only slightly. There is some evidence that the structure of the brain differs across genders and cultures.

LO 5-2   What developmental tasks are accomplished during childhood?

- Gross motor skill levels develop rapidly during childhood, and gender differences emerge, with boys displaying greater strength and activity levels, and girls showing greater coordination of arms and legs. Both genetic and social factors probably play a role in determining these differences.

- Fine motor skills also develop rapidly, with coordination achieving nearly adult levels by the beginning of adolescence. This is largely attributable to increases in the level of myelin in the brain. Handedness asserts itself during childhood, with the great majority of children showing a clear preference for the right hand by the end of the preschool years. The development of artistic expression progresses during the preschool years through the scribbling, shape, design, and pictorial stages. Artistic expression entails the development of important related skills, including planning, restraint, and self-correction.

- Physical competence is important for a number of reasons, some of which relate to self-esteem and confidence. Physical competence also brings social benefits during this period, especially for males. Because of their importance in school-age children's lives, physical skills should be encouraged. Children can be helped to place emphasis less on competition and more on achieving physical fitness, learning physical skills, and becoming comfortable with their bodies.

LO 5-3   What are the characteristics of puberty?

- The most significant event during adolescence is the onset of puberty, which begins for most girls at around age 11 and for most boys at around age 13. As puberty commences, the body begins to produce male or female hormones at adult levels, the sex organs develop and change, menstruation and ejaculation begin, and other body changes occur.

LO 5-4   In what ways do the senses develop as children grow?

- Sensation, the stimulation of the sense organs, differs from perception, the interpretation and integration of sensed stimuli. Infants' visual perception is quite good at achieving adult levels of distance acuity within 6 months. Moreover, the early achievement of binocular vision permits sophisticated perception of depth and motion by infants. Auditory perception, which begins in the womb, is also well developed in infants. They can localize sound, discriminate sound patterns and tones, and make fine sound discriminations that will be essential in the later development of language.

- The senses of smell and taste are surprisingly sophisticated in infants. Infants react as adults do to pleasant and unpleasant odors and tastes, and even very young infants can recognize their mothers' scents. The nature of infants' experiences of pain is not entirely clear, but it is clear that infants react negatively to painful stimuli. Infants use their highly developed sense of touch to explore and experience the world.

LO 5-5   How sensitive is an infant to pain and touch?

- It is widely acknowledged that infants are born with the capacity to experience pain. Touch is one of the most highly developed sensory systems in a newborn, and it is also one of the first to develop.

LO 5-6   What sensory capabilities do people posses from the beginning of life?

- Whether all sensations are initially integrated in infants and later become differentiated, or whether initially separate senses later become increasingly integrated, is an unresolved issue. However, infants are clearly able to relate perceptions from one sensory source to those from another.

LO 5-7   What is the role of nutrition in development, and what causes obesity?

- Children require balanced nutrition because of its many effects on children in the school years. In addition to enjoying purely physical benefits, well-nourished children generally show better social and emotional functioning and cognitive performance. If parents and caregivers provide a good variety of healthful foods, children will generally achieve an appropriate intake of nutrients.

- Obesity is caused by both genetic and environmental factors. Environmental influences include excessive parental interference with children's development of internal controls over eating, overindulgence in sedentary activities such as television viewing, and lack of physical exercise.

LO 5-8   How healthy are growing children, and what threats to wellness do they face?

- The health of children and adolescents is generally good, and few health hazards arise; in fact, children are more at risk from accidents than from illness.

- In the economically developed world, immunization programs have largely controlled most life-threatening diseases during childhood. However, in economically disadvantaged sectors of the world—and of the United States—immunization is not completely effective.

- Although most children sleep well at night, sleep presents real difficulties for some. Sleep-related problems include nightmares, night terrors, and enuresis.

KEY TERMS AND CONCEPTS

cephalocaudal principle (p. 127)
proximodistal principle (p. 127)
principle of hierarchical integration (p. 127)
principle of the independence of systems (p. 127)
adolescence (p. 129)
adolescent growth spurt (p. 129)
lateralization (p. 131)
handedness (p. 137)

puberty (p. 138)
menarche (p. 138)
secular trend (p. 139)
primary sex characteristics (p. 139)
secondary sex characteristics (p. 139)
sensation (p. 141)

perception (p. 141)
multimodal approach to perception (p. 147)
affordances (p. 147)
marasmus (p. 150)
kwashiorkor (p. 150)
nonorganic failure to thrive (p. 151)

obesity (p. 151)
asthma (p. 154)
nightmares (p. 156)
night terrors (p. 156)
enuresis (p. 156)

Epilogue

We saw in this chapter the enormous physical changes that accompany the move from infancy through early childhood to adolescence. Beginning with the growth of their bodies, both in weight and height, children make enormous physical strides. The brain grows rapidly, making billions of connections between neurons, and then pruning back the neurons that aren't needed, for greater efficiency. Gross motor and fine motor skills develop. Children grow more adept at sensing and perceiving their environment as the five senses of sight, hearing, smell, taste, and touch evolve. Good nutrition helps fuel all this development. Although they face threats to their health from obesity, sickness, and accidental injury, and later from the abuse of drugs and alcohol, for the most part children are healthy, energetic, inquisitive, and mastering an impressive list of physical accomplishments during the preschool years.

Before we move on to a discussion of children's cognitive development, turn back for a moment to the prologue of this chapter, about Allan's first steps, and answer these questions.

1. Which principle or principles of growth (i.e., cephalocaudal, proximodistal, hierarchical integration, independence of systems) account for the progression of physical activities that precede Allan's first steps?

2. Were Allan's parents right to worry when Allan was "behind schedule" with his first steps? What would you say to them, or to other parents in similar circumstances?

3. In walking at 10 months of age, Todd outpaced his little brother Allan by three months. Does this fact have any implications for the eventual different physical abilities of the two brothers? Why?

4. Do you think anything changed in the environment between the time Todd and Allan were born that might account for their different "first step" schedules? If you were researching this question, what environmental factors would you look for?

5. Why were Allan's parents so pleased and proud about his accomplishment, which is, after all, a routine and universal occurrence? What factors exist in U.S. culture that make the "first steps" milestone so significant?

The Development Video Series in MyPsychLab

Explore the video *Special Topics: The Plastic Brain* by scanning this QR code with your mobile device. If you don't already have one, you may download a free QR scanner for your device wherever smartphone apps are sold. You can also view this video in MyPsychLab. For more videos related to this chapter's content, log into MyPsychLab to view the entire Development Video Series.

MyVirtualChild

- **What decisions would you make while raising a child?**
- **What would the consequences of those decisions be?**

Find out by accessing **MyVirtualChild** at

www.MyPsychLab.com

and raising your own virtual child from birth to age 18.

6 Cognitive Development: Piaget and Vygotsky

MODULE 6.1

PIAGET'S APPROACH TO COGNITIVE DEVELOPMENT

- Piaget: The Master Observer of Children
- Key Elements of Piaget's Theory
- Cognitive Development in Infancy

CAREERS IN CHILD DEVELOPMENT: Stevanne Auerbach, Toy Specialist

- Cognitive Development in the Preschool Years

ARE YOU AN INFORMED CONSUMER OF DEVELOPMENT? Promoting Cognitive Development in Preschoolers: From Theory to the Classroom

- Cognitive Development in the School Years and Adolescence

Review, Check, and Apply

MODULE 6.2

APPRAISING PIAGET: SUPPORT AND CHALLENGES

- Piaget's Contributions to Developmental Science
- A Final Summation

Review, Check, and Apply

MODULE 6.3

VYGOTSKY'S VIEW OF COGNITIVE DEVELOPMENT: TAKING CULTURE INTO ACCOUNT

- The Importance of Culture
- The Zone of Proximal Development

FROM RESEARCH TO PRACTICE: Vygotsky in the Classroom

- Cultural Tools
- Evaluating Vygotsky's Contributions

DEVELOPMENTAL DIVERSITY AND YOUR LIFE: A Walk through a Cultural Landscape

Review, Check, and Apply

The Case of...the Risky Bet

Looking Back

Key Terms and Concepts

Epilogue

PROLOGUE: Jared

Jared, who is 7 months old, watches as his dad picks up his toy bell, one of his favorite playthings. Jared reaches for it, but his father slides it under the covers in his crib. Without any further sign of interest, Jared turns away, acting as if it never existed.

It is now 4 years later. Jared's parents are delighted when he comes home from kindergarten one day and explains that he has learned why the sky is blue. He talks about the Earth's atmosphere—although he doesn't pronounce the word correctly—and how tiny bits of moisture in the air reflect the sunlight. Although his explanation has rough edges (he can't quite grasp what the "atmosphere" is), he still has the general idea, and that, his parents feel, is quite an achievement for their 5-year-old.

Fast-forward 6 years. Jared, now 11, has already spent an hour laboring over his evening's homework. After completing a two-page worksheet on multiplying and dividing fractions, he begins work on his U.S. Constitution project.

Seven more years pass. Jared, now 17, is sweating as he sits on stage in the school auditorium contemplating the honors presentation he is about to make before an audience of classmates, parents, and teachers. Jared is oddly unconcerned about his actual presentation: He has worked hard on his comparison of the French and American Revolutions. No, what concerns him is that he can see Laronda Jennings in the front row and knows that she will soon be staring at him. He really, really wants not to mess up.

>>> LOOKING AHEAD

Jared is not unique in having made vast intellectual advances from early childhood through adolescence. People universally experience cognitive changes that proceed at breathtaking speed throughout these years. During this time, cognitive abilities broaden and the ability to understand and accomplish complex skills increases dramatically.

What are the advances, and the limitations, in thinking during childhood and adolescence? Several perspectives explain what goes on cognitively during this period of our lives. In this chapter, we consider cognitive development during childhood and adolescence in general, examining in detail two important theoretical perspectives. After reviewing the basics of cognitive development, we examine in

(continued)

Learning Objectives

MODULE 6.1

LO1 What are the fundamental features of Piaget's theory of cognitive development?

LO2 According to Piaget, how does cognitive development proceed during infancy?

LO3 How does Piaget explain cognitive development during the preschool years?

LO4 In what ways do children develop cognitively during middle childhood and adolescence?

MODULE 6.2

LO5 How has Piaget's theory been supported and challenged by later research?

MODULE 6.3

LO6 What is Vygotsky's approach to cognitive development?

detail the work of Swiss psychologist Jean Piaget, whose stage theory of development has served as a highly influential impetus for a considerable amount of work on cognitive development. We'll look at the foundations of Piaget's theory and trace cognitive development through the stages that Piaget identified and defined through his observations of children and adolescents.

Next we will evaluate Piaget's theory, considering both its enormous contributions to developmental research and the many criticisms of his approach that have been voiced by researchers in the field.

Finally, we will discuss the work of Lev Vygotsky, a Russian psychologist. Vygotsky's views on the importance of culture to cognitive development have become increasingly influential, particularly in his focus on the social and cultural aspects of development and learning.

MODULE 6.1

PIAGET'S APPROACH TO COGNITIVE DEVELOPMENT

LO 6-1 What are the fundamental features of Piaget's theory of cognitive development?
LO 6-2 According to Piaget, how does cognitive development proceed during infancy?
LO 6-3 How does Piaget explain cognitive development during the preschool years?
LO 6-4 In what ways do children develop cognitively during middle childhood and adolescence?

Piaget: The Master Observer of Children

Olivia's dad is wiping up the mess around the base of her high chair—for the third time today! It seems to him that 14-month-old Olivia takes great delight in dropping food from the high chair. She also drops toys, spoons—anything, it seems, just to watch how it hits the floor. She almost appears to be experimenting to see what kind of noise or what size of splatter is created by each different thing she drops.

Swiss psychologist Jean Piaget (1896–1980) probably would have said that Olivia's dad is right in theorizing that Olivia is conducting her own series of experiments to learn more about the workings of her world. Piaget's views of the ways infants learn could be summed in a simple equation: *Action = Knowledge.*

Unlike previous theorists, Piaget argued that infants do not acquire knowledge from facts communicated by others, nor through sensation and perception. Instead, Piaget suggested that knowledge is the product of direct motor behavior. Although many of his basic explanations and propositions have been challenged by subsequent research, as we discuss later, the view that in significant ways infants learn by doing remains unquestioned (Piaget, 1962, 1983; Bullinger, 1997).

Piaget's background and training influenced both the development of his theory and the methods he used to investigate it. Piaget was educated as a biologist and philosopher, and he received a Ph.D. in zoology. His initial work was aimed at producing an account of how knowledge is related to biology, which ultimately led to a theory of how children's understanding of the world develops. In doing research, Piaget relied on methods that are common among investigations of nonhuman species. For instance, his studies would often intensively focus on only a few children, including his offspring. Furthermore, he frequently would observe children in their "natural habitat," such as while they were playing games. His goal was

According to Piaget, infants learn more from doing and less from mere observation.

to understand *how* children think, rather than characterizing whether their thinking was right or wrong at a given age.

Key Elements of Piaget's Theory

As we first noted in Chapter 2, Piaget's theory is based on a stage approach to development. He assumed that all children pass through a series of four universal stages in a fixed order from birth through adolescence: sensorimotor, preoperational, concrete operational, and formal operational. He also suggested that movement from one stage to the next occurs when a child reaches an appropriate level of physical maturation *and* is exposed to relevant experiences. Without such experience, children are assumed to be incapable of reaching their cognitive potential. Some approaches to cognition focus on changes in the *content* of children's knowledge about the world, but Piaget argued that it was critical to also consider the changes in the *quality* of children's knowledge and understanding as they move from one stage to another.

For instance, as they develop cognitively, infants experience changes in their understanding about what can and cannot occur in the world. Consider a baby who participates in an experiment during which she is exposed to three identical versions of her mother all at the same time, thanks to some well-placed mirrors. A 3-month-old infant will interact happily with each of these images of mother. However, by 5 months of age, the child becomes quite agitated at the sight of multiple mothers. Apparently by this time, the child has figured out that she has but one mother, and viewing three at a time is thoroughly alarming (Bower, 1977). To Piaget, such reactions indicate that a baby is beginning to master principles regarding the way the world operates, indicating that she has begun to construct a mental sense of the world that she didn't have two months earlier.

Piaget believed that the basic building blocks of the way we understand the world are mental structures called **schemes**, organized patterns of functioning that adapt and change with mental development. At first, schemes are related to physical, or sensorimotor, activity, such as picking up or reaching for toys. As children develop, their schemes move to a mental level, reflecting thought. Schemes are similar to computer software: They direct and determine how data from the world, such as new events or objects, are considered and dealt with (Rakison & Oakes, 2003; Meltzoff, 2011).

If you give a baby a new cloth book, for example, he or she will touch it, mouth it, perhaps try to tear it or bang it on the floor. To Piaget, each of these actions may represent a scheme, and they are the infant's way of gaining knowledge and understanding of this new object. Adults, on the other hand, would use a different scheme upon encountering the book. Rather than picking it up and putting it in their mouths or banging it on the floor, they would probably be drawn to the letters on the page, seeking to understand the book through the meaning of the printed words—a very different approach.

Piaget suggested that two principles underlie the growth in children's schemes: assimilation and accommodation. **Assimilation** is the process by which people understand an experience in terms of their current stage of cognitive development and way of thinking. Assimilation occurs, then, when a stimulus or event is acted upon, perceived, and understood in accordance with existing patterns of thought. For example, an infant who tries to suck on any toy in the same way is assimilating the objects to her existing sucking scheme. Similarly, a child who encounters a flying squirrel at a zoo and calls it a "bird" is assimilating the squirrel to his existing scheme of bird.

In contrast, when we change our existing ways of thinking, understanding, or behaving in response to encounters with new stimuli or events, **accommodation** takes place. For instance, when a child sees a flying squirrel and calls it "a bird with a tail," he is beginning to *accommodate* new knowledge, modifying his scheme of bird.

Piaget believed that the earliest schemes are primarily limited to the reflexes with which we are all born, such as sucking and rooting. Infants start to modify these simple early schemes almost immediately, through the processes of assimilation and accommodation, in response to their exploration of the environment. Schemes quickly become more sophisticated as infants become more advanced in their motor capabilities—to Piaget, a signal of the potential for more advanced cognitive development.

Swiss psychologist Jean Piaget.

scheme   An organized pattern of sensorimotor functioning

assimilation   The process in which people understand an experience in terms of their current stage of cognitive development and way of thinking

accommodation   Changes in existing ways of thinking that occur in response to encounters with new stimuli or events

Cognitive Development in Infancy

Piaget's first stage of development—the sensorimotor stage—begins at birth and continues until the child is about 2 years old. Because of its fundamental importance, we consider this stage here in detail.

The Sensorimotor Period: The Earliest Stage of Cognitive Growth (Birth to 2 Years).

Piaget suggests that the **sensorimotor stage**, the initial major stage of cognitive development, can be broken down into six substages. These are summarized in Table 6-1. It is important to keep in mind that although the specific substages of the sensorimotor period may at first appear to unfold with great regularity, as though infants reach a particular age and smoothly proceed into the next substage, the reality of cognitive development is somewhat different. First, the ages at which infants actually reach a particular stage vary a good deal among different children. The exact timing of a stage reflects an interaction between the infant's level of physical maturation and the nature of the social environment in which the child is being raised. Consequently, although Piaget contended that the order of the substages does not change from one child to the next, he admitted that the timing can and does vary to some degree.

Piaget viewed development as a more gradual process than the notion of different stages might seem to imply. Infants do not go to sleep one night in one substage and wake up the next morning in the next one. Instead, there is a rather gradual and steady shifting of behavior as a child moves toward the next stage of cognitive development. Infants also pass through

sensorimotor stage (of cognitive development) Piaget's initial major stage of cognitive development, which can be broken down into six substages

---

TABLE 6-1 Piaget's Six Substages of the Sensorimotor Stage

Substage	Age	Description	Example
Substage 1: Simple reflexes	First month of life	During this period, the various reflexes that determine the infant's interactions with the world are at the center of its cognitive life.	The sucking reflex causes the infant to suck at anything placed in its lips.
Substage 2: First habits and primary circular reactions	From 1 to 4 months	At this age infants begin to coordinate what were separate actions into single, integrated activities.	An infant might combine grasping an object with sucking on it, or staring at something with touching it.
Substage 3: Secondary circular reactions	From 4 to 8 months	During this period, infants take major strides in shifting their cognitive horizons beyond themselves and begin to act on the outside world.	A child who repeatedly picks up a rattle in her crib and shakes it in different ways to see how the sound changes is demonstrating her ability to modify her cognitive scheme about shaking rattles.
Substage 4: Coordination of secondary circular reactions	From 8 to 12 months	In this stage, infants begin to use more calculated approaches to producing events, coordinating several schemes to generate a single act. They achieve object permanence during this stage.	An infant will push one toy out of the way to reach another toy that is lying, partially exposed, under it.
Substage 5: Tertiary circular reactions	From 12 to 18 months	At this age infants develop what Piaget regards as the deliberate variation of actions that bring desirable consequences. Rather than just repeat enjoyable activities, infants appear to carry out miniature experiments to observe the consequences.	A child will drop a toy repeatedly, varying the position from which he drops it, carefully observing each time to see where it falls.
Substage 6: Beginnings of thought	From 18 months to 2 years	The major achievement of Substage 6 is the capacity for mental representation or symbolic thought. Piaget argued that only at this stage can infants imagine where objects that they cannot see might be.	Children can even plot in their heads unseen trajectories of objects, so that if a ball rolls under a piece of furniture, they can figure out where it is likely to emerge on the other side.

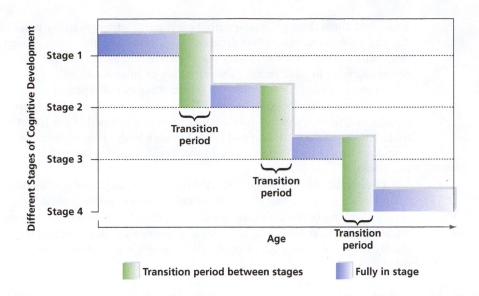

FIGURE 6-1 Transitions

Infants do not suddenly shift from one stage of cognitive development to the next. Instead, Piaget argues that there is a period of transition in which some behavior reflects one stage, while other behavior reflects the more advanced stage. Does this gradualism argue against Piaget's interpretation of stages?

periods of transition, in which some aspects of their behavior reflect the next higher stage while other aspects indicate their current stage (see Figure 6-1).

Substage 1: Simple Reflexes. The first substage of the sensorimotor period is *Substage 1: Simple reflexes*, encompassing the first month of life. During this time, the various inborn reflexes, described in Chapters 4 and 5, are at the center of a baby's physical and cognitive life, determining the nature of his or her interactions with the world. For example, the sucking reflex causes the infant to suck at anything placed in his or her lips. This sucking behavior, according to Piaget, provides the newborn with information about objects—information that paves the way to the next substage of the sensorimotor period.

At the same time, some of the reflexes begin to accommodate the infant's experience with the nature of the world. For instance, an infant who is being breastfed, but who also receives supplemental bottles, may start to change the way he or she sucks, depending on whether a nipple is on a breast or on a bottle.

Substage 2: First Habits and Primary Circular Reactions. *Substage 2: First habits and primary circular reactions*, the second substage of the sensorimotor period, occurs from 1 to 4 months of age. In this period, infants begin to coordinate what were separate actions into single, integrated activities. For instance, an infant might combine grasping an object with sucking on it, or staring at something while touching it.

If an activity engages a baby's interests, he or she may repeat it over and over, simply for the sake of continuing to experience it. Olivia's "experiments" with gravity while in her high chair (described at the beginning of the module) are an example of this. This repetition of a chance motor event helps the baby start building cognitive schemes through a process known as a *circular reaction*. *Primary circular reactions* are schemes reflecting an infant's repetition of interesting or enjoyable actions, just for the enjoyment of doing them. Piaget referred to these schemes as *primary* because the activities they involve focus on the infant's own body. Thus, when an infant first puts his thumb in his mouth and begins to suck, it is a mere chance event. However, when he repeatedly sucks his thumb in the future, it represents a primary circular reaction, which he is repeating because the sensation of sucking is pleasurable.

Substage 3: Secondary Circular Reactions. *Substage 3: Secondary circular reactions* are more purposeful. According to Piaget, this third stage of cognitive development in infancy occurs from 4 to 8 months of age. During this period, infants begin to act upon the outside world. For instance, infants now seek to repeat enjoyable events in their environments if they happen

Piaget suggests that infants increasingly seek to repeat enjoyable events by acting on their environment.

to produce them through chance activities. A child who repeatedly picks up a rattle in her crib and shakes it in different ways to see how the sound changes is demonstrating her ability to modify her cognitive scheme about shaking rattles. She is engaging in what Piaget calls secondary circular reactions.

Secondary circular reactions are schemes regarding repeated actions that bring about a desirable consequence. The major difference between primary circular reactions and secondary circular reactions is whether the infant's activity is focused on the infant and his or her own body (primary circular reactions) or involves actions relating to the world outside (secondary circular reactions).

During the third substage, babies' vocalization increases substantially as infants come to notice that if they make noises, other people around them will respond with noises of their own. Similarly, infants begin to imitate the sounds made by others. Vocalization becomes a secondary circular reaction that ultimately helps lead to the development of language and the formation of social relationships.

Substage 4: Coordination of Secondary Circular Reactions. One of the major leaps forward is in *Substage 4: Coordination of secondary circular reactions,* which lasts from around 8 months to 12 months. Before this stage, behavior involved direct action on objects. When something happened by chance that caught an infant's interest, she attempted to repeat the event using a single scheme. However, in Substage 4, infants begin to employ **goal-directed behavior**, in which several schemes are combined and coordinated to generate a single act to solve a problem. For instance, they will push one toy out of the way to reach another toy that is lying, partially exposed, under it. They also begin to anticipate upcoming events. For instance, Piaget tells of his son Laurent, who at 8 months "recognizes by a certain noise caused by air that he is nearing the end of his feeding and, instead of insisting on drinking to the last drop, he rejects his bottle" (Piaget, 1952, pp. 248–249).

Infants' newfound purposefulness, their ability to use means to attain particular ends, and their skill in anticipating future circumstances owe their appearance in part to the developmental achievement of object permanence that emerges in Substage 4. **Object permanence** is the realization that people and objects exist even when they cannot be seen. It is a simple principle, but its mastery has profound consequences.

Consider, for instance, 7-month-old Chu, who has yet to learn the idea of object permanence. Chu's father shakes a rattle in front of him, then takes the rattle and places it under a blanket. To Chu, who has not mastered the concept of object permanence, the rattle no longer exists. He will make no effort to look for it.

Several months later, when he is in Substage 4, the story is quite different (see Figure 6-2). This time, as soon as his father places the rattle under the blanket, Chu tries to toss the cover aside, eagerly searching for the rattle. Chu clearly has learned that the object continues to exist even when it cannot be seen. For the infant who achieves an understanding of object permanence, then, out of sight is decidedly not out of mind.

Watch the **Video** *Hidden Elephant (Object Permanence)* in **MyPsychLab**.

The attainment of object permanence extends not only to inanimate objects but to people, too. It gives Chu the security that his father and mother still exist even when they have left the room. This awareness is likely a key element in the development of social attachments, which we consider in Chapter 10. The recognition of object permanence also feeds infants' growing assertiveness: As they realize that an object taken away from them doesn't just cease to exist but is merely somewhere else, their only-too-human reaction may be to want it back—and quickly.

Although the understanding of object permanence emerges in Substage 4, it is only a rudimentary understanding. It takes several months for the concept to be fully comprehended, and infants continue for several months to make certain kinds of errors relating to object permanence. For instance, they often are fooled when a toy is hidden first under one blanket and then under a second blanket. In seeking out the toy, Substage 4 infants most often turn to the first hiding place, ignoring the second blanket under which the toy is currently located— even if the hiding was done in plain view. (For a more on the role of play and toys from a toy designer's perspective, see the *Careers in Child Development* interview.)

goal-directed behavior Behavior in which several schemes are combined and coordinated to generate a single act to solve a problem

object permanence The realization that people and objects exist even when they cannot be seen

Before Object Permanence

After Object Permanence

FIGURE 6-2 Object Permanence

Before an infant has understood the idea of object permanence, he will not search for an object that has been hidden right before his eyes. But several months later, he will search for it, illustrating that he has attained object permanence. Why would the concept of object permanence be important to a caregiver?

Substage 5: Tertiary Circular Reactions. *Substage 5: Tertiary circular reactions* is reached at around 12 months and extends to 18 months. As the name of the stage indicates, during this period infants develop what Piaget labeled *tertiary circular reactions*, schemes regarding the deliberate variation of actions that bring desirable consequences. Rather than just repeating

CAREERS IN CHILD DEVELOPMENT

Name: Stevanne Auerbach

Education: B.A. in education and psychology, Queens College; M.A. in special education, George Washington University; Ph.D. in child development, Union Institute

Title: Children's Toy Advocate and Author

Home: San Francisco, CA

According to play expert and researcher Stevanne Auerbach, play is a natural drive to discover and is the essence of a happy childhood.

"By absorbing, practicing, learning from mistakes, but most of all through discovery, each child will advance as individuality dictates," notes Auerbach. "As infants grow they play with innumerable things around them: their hands, toes, sunbeams coming in through the window, and soft toys, and at the same time they discover sounds, babbling and talking to themselves.

"Through play children practice the basic skills needed in the classroom—and in life. Guided play in the right environment will help a child gain the tools needed to sharpen thinking, and heighten sensitivity," she adds.

According to Auerbach, there are three types of toys that contribute to the development of children: active toys, creative toys, and educational toys.

"Active playthings, like blocks, balls, bicycles, and jump ropes, improve a child's physical activity and provide exercise, while creative toys stimulate the child's imagination at all levels, and let the child experience surprise, expand thinking, and encourage self-expression," she explains. Examples of creative toys include blocks, crafts, dollhouses, mirrors, musical instruments, puppets, stuffed animals, and art supplies.

"Educational toys have aspects that help a child learn specific skills, and sometimes several skills simultaneously. Some play items that enable these skills are board games, books, construction toys, peg-boards, puzzles, and audio and video tapes. Play objects can help with reading and writing, and can build practical skills that prepare a child for science and counting."

While a good play environment and the right types of toys are important, the participatory role of parents is crucial.

"As a 'play guide,' the parent can help the child learn more, and also informally teach the skills to be happier and get along better with others," she explains. "A playful parent encourages a child to be playful—and a more playful child is a more aware, smarter, and resilient one."

With the attainment of the cognitive skill of deferred imitation, children are able to imitate people and scenes they have witnessed in the past.

enjoyable activities, as they do with secondary circular reactions, infants appear to carry out miniature experiments to observe the consequences.

For example, Piaget observed his son Laurent dropping a toy swan repeatedly, varying the position from which he dropped it, carefully observing each time to see where it fell. Instead of just repeating the action each time (as in a secondary circular reaction), Laurent made modifications in the situation to learn about their consequences. As you may recall from our discussion of research methods in Chapter 2, this behavior represents the essence of the scientific method: An experimenter varies a situation in a laboratory to learn the effects of the variation. To infants in Substage 5, the world is their laboratory, and they spend their days leisurely carrying out one miniature experiment after another. Olivia, the baby described earlier who enjoyed dropping things from her high chair, is another little scientist in action.

What is most striking about infants' behavior during Substage 5 is their interest in the unexpected. Unanticipated events are treated not only as interesting but also as something to be explained and understood. Infants' discoveries can lead to newfound skills, some of which may cause a certain amount of chaos, as Olivia's dad realized while cleaning up around her high chair.

Substage 6: Beginnings of Thought. The final stage of the sensorimotor period is *Substage 6: Beginnings of thought*, which lasts from around 18 months to 2 years. The major achievement of Substage 6 is the capacity for mental representation, or symbolic thought. A **mental representation** is an internal image of a past event or object. Piaget argued that by this stage infants can imagine where objects might be that they cannot see. They can even plot in their heads unseen pathways of objects, so if a ball rolls under a piece of furniture, they can figure out where it is likely to emerge on the other side.

Because of children's new abilities to create internal representations of objects, their understanding of causality also becomes more sophisticated. For instance, consider Piaget's description of his son Laurent's efforts to open a garden gate:

> Laurent tries to open a garden gate but cannot push it forward because it is held back by a piece of furniture. He cannot account either visually or by any sound for the cause that prevents the gate from opening, but after having tried to force it he suddenly seems to understand; he goes around the wall, arrives at the other side of the gate, moves the armchair which holds it firm, and opens it with a triumphant expression. (Piaget, 1954, p. 296)

The attainment of mental representation also permits another important development: the ability to pretend. Using the skill of what Piaget refers to as **deferred imitation**, in which a person who is no longer present is imitated later, children are able to pretend that they are driving a car, feeding a doll, or cooking dinner long after they have witnessed such scenes played out in reality. To Piaget, deferred imitation provided clear evidence that children form internal mental representations.

Cognitive Development in the Preschool Years

Three-year-old Sam was talking to himself. As his parents listened with amusement from another room, they could hear him using two very different voices. "Find your shoes," he said in a low voice. "Not today. I'm not going. I hate the shoes," he said in a higher-pitched voice. The lower voice answered, "You are a bad boy. Find the shoes, bad boy." The higher voiced response was "No, no, no."

Sam's parents realized that he was playing a game with his imaginary friend, Gill. Gill was a bad boy who often disobeyed his mother, at least in Sam's imagination. In fact, according to Sam's musings, Gill often was guilty of the very same misdeeds for which his parents blamed Sam.

mental representation An internal image of a past event or object

deferred imitation An act in which a person who is no longer present is imitated by children who have witnessed a similar act

In some ways, the intellectual sophistication of 3-year-olds is astounding. Their creativity and imagination leap to new heights, their language is increasingly sophisticated, and they reason and think about the world in ways that would have been impossible even a few months earlier. But what underlies the dramatic advances in intellectual development that start in the preschool years and continue throughout that period? Let's take a look at Piaget's findings on the cognitive changes that occur during the preschool years.

Piaget's Stage of Preoperational Thinking (Ages 2 to 7).
Piaget saw the preschool years as a time of both stability and great change. He placed the preschool years into a single stage of cognitive development—the preoperational stage—which lasts from 2 until around 7.

During the **preoperational stage**, children's use of symbolic thinking grows, mental reasoning emerges, and the use of concepts increases. Seeing Mom's car keys may prompt a question, "Go to store?" as the child comes to see the keys as a symbol of a car ride. In this way, children become better at representing events internally, and they grow less dependent on the use of direct sensorimotor activity to understand the world around them. Yet they are still not capable of **operations**: organized, formal, logical mental processes. It is only at the end of the preoperational stage that the ability to carry out operations comes into play.

According to Piaget, a key aspect of preoperational thought is **symbolic function**, the ability to use a mental symbol, a word, or an object to stand for or represent something that is not physically present. For example, during this stage, preschoolers can use a mental symbol for a car (the word "car"), and they likewise understand that a small toy car is representative of the real thing. Because of their ability to use symbolic function, children have no need to get behind the wheel of an actual car to understand its basic purpose and use.

The Relation between Language and Thought.
Symbolic function is at the heart of one of the major advances that occurs in the preoperational period: the increasingly sophisticated use of language. As we discuss later in this book, children make substantial progress in language skills during the preschool period.

Piaget suggests that language and thinking are tightly interconnected and that the advances in language that occur during the preschool years reflect several improvements over the type of thinking that is possible during the earlier sensorimotor period. For instance, thinking embedded in sensorimotor activities is relatively slow, since it depends on actual movements of the body that are bound by human physical limitations. In contrast, the use of symbolic thought, such as the development of an imaginary friend, allows preschoolers to represent actions symbolically, permitting much greater speed.

Even more important, the use of language allows children to think beyond the present to the future. Consequently, rather than being grounded in the immediate here-and-now, preschoolers can imagine future possibilities through language in the form of sometimes elaborate fantasies and daydreams.

Do the improved language abilities of preschoolers lead to improvements in thinking, or is it the other way around, with the improvements in thinking during the preoperational period leading to enhancements in language ability? This question—whether thought determines language or language determines thought—is one of the most enduring and controversial questions within the field of psychology. Piaget's answer is that language grows out of cognitive advances, rather than the other way around. He argues that improvements during the earlier sensorimotor period are necessary for language development and that continuing growth in cognitive ability during the preoperational period provides the foundation for language ability.

Centration: What You See Is What You Think.
Place a dog mask on a cat and what do you get? According to 3- and 4-year-old preschoolers, a dog. To them, a cat with a dog mask ought to bark like a dog, wag its tail like a dog, and eat dog food. In every respect, the cat has been transformed into a dog (deVries, 1969).

To Piaget, the root of this belief is centration, a key element, and limitation, of the thinking of children in the preoperational period. **Centration** is the process of concentrating on one limited aspect of a stimulus and ignoring other aspects.

preoperational stage According to Piaget, the stage that lasts from ages 2 to 7 during which children's use of symbolic thinking grows, mental reasoning emerges, and the use of concepts increases

operations Organized, formal, logical mental processes

symbolic function According to Piaget, the ability to use a mental symbol, a word, or an object to represent something that is not physically present

centration The process of concentrating on one limited aspect of a stimulus and ignoring other aspects

FIGURE 6-3 Which Row Contains More Buttons?

When preschoolers are shown these two rows and asked the question of which row has more buttons, they usually respond that the lower row of buttons contains more, because it looks longer. They answer in this way even though they know quite well that 10 is greater than 8. Do you think an educator could teach preschoolers to answer correctly?

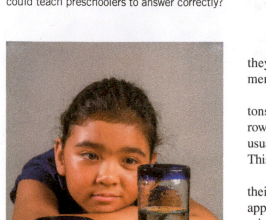

FIGURE 6-4 Which Glass Contains More?

Most 4-year-old children believe that the amount of liquid in these two glasses differs because of the differences in the containers' shapes, even though they may have seen equal amounts of liquid being poured into each.

conservation The knowledge that quantity is unrelated to the arrangement and physical appearance of objects

Preschoolers are unable to consider all available information about a stimulus. Instead, they focus on superficial, obvious elements that are within their sight. These external elements come to dominate preschoolers' thinking, leading to inaccuracy in thought.

Consider what happens when preschoolers are shown two rows of buttons, one with 10 buttons that are spaced closely together, and the other with 8 buttons spread out to form a longer row (see Figure 6-3). If asked which of the rows contains more buttons, children who are 4 or 5 usually choose the row that looks longer, rather than the one that actually contains more buttons. This occurs in spite of the fact that children this age know quite well that 10 is more than 8.

The cause of the children's mistake is that the visual image of the longer row dominates their thinking. Rather than taking into account their understanding of quantity, they focus on appearance. To a preschooler, appearance is everything. Preschoolers' focus on appearances might be related to another aspect of preoperational thought, the lack of conservation.

Conservation: Learning That Appearances Are Deceiving. Consider the following scenario:

Four-year-old Jaime is shown two drinking glasses of different shapes. One is short and broad; the other, tall and thin. A teacher half-fills the short, broad glass with apple juice. The teacher then pours the juice into the tall, thin glass. The juice fills the tall glass almost to the brim. The teacher asks Jaime a question: Is there more juice in the second glass than there was in the first?

If you view this as an easy task, so do children like Jaime. They have no trouble answering the question. However, they almost always get the answer wrong.

Most 4-year-olds respond that there is more apple juice in the tall, thin glass than there is in the short, broad one. In fact, if the juice is poured back into the shorter glass, they are quick to say that there is now less juice than there was in the taller glass (see Figure 6-4).

The reason for the error in judgment is that children of this age have not mastered conservation. **Conservation** is the knowledge that quantity is unrelated to the arrangement and physical appearance of objects. Because they are unable to conserve, preschoolers can't understand that changes in one dimension (such as a change in appearance) do not necessarily mean that other dimensions (such as quantity) change. For example, children who do not yet understand the principle of conservation feel quite comfortable in asserting that the amount of liquid changes as it is poured between glasses of different sizes. They simply are unable to realize that the transformation in appearance does not imply a transformation in quantity.

The lack of conservation also manifests itself in children's understanding of area, as illustrated by Piaget's cow-in-the-field problem (Piaget, Inhelder, & Szenubsjam, 1960). In the problem, two sheets of green paper, equal in size, are shown to a child, and a toy cow is placed in each field. Next, a toy barn is placed in each field, and children are asked which cow has more to eat. The typical—and, so far, correct—response is that the cows have the same amount.

In the next step, a second toy barn is placed in each field. But in one field, the barns are placed adjacent to one another, while in the second field, they are separated from one another. Children who have not mastered conservation usually say that the cow in the field with the adjacent barns has more grass to eat than the cow in the field with the separated barns. In contrast, children who can conserve answer, correctly, that the amount available is identical. (Some other conservation tasks are shown in Figure 6-5).

Type of Conservation	Modality	Change in Physical Appearance	Average Age Invariance Is Grasped
Number	Number of elements in a collection 	Rearranging or dislocating elements 	6–7 years
Substance (mass)	Amount of a malleable substance (e.g., clay or liquid) 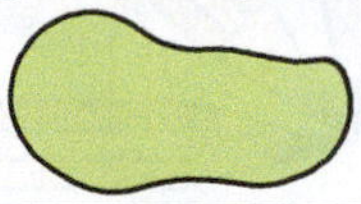	Altering shape 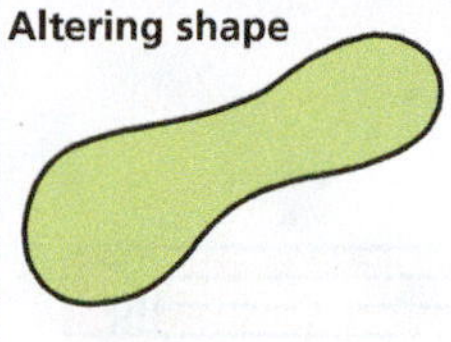	7–8 years
Length	Length of a line or object 	Altering shape or configuration 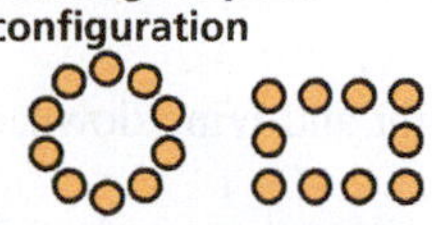	7–8 years
Area	Amount of surface covered by a set of plane figures 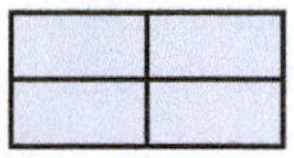	Rearranging the figures 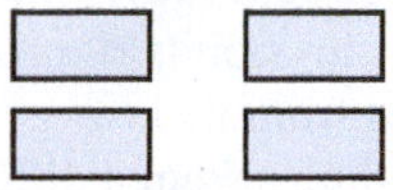	8–9 years
Weight	Weight of an object 	Altering shape 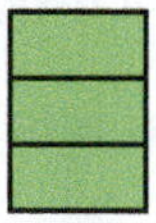	9–10 years
Volume	Volume of an object (in terms of water displacement) 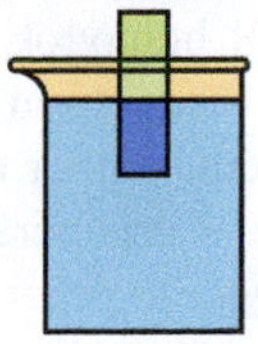	Altering shape 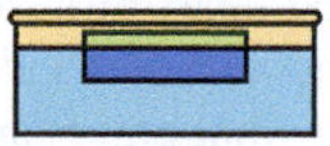	14–15 years

FIGURE 6-5 Common Tests of Children's Understanding of the Principle of Conservation

From the perspective of an educator, why would a knowledge of a child's level of conservation be important?

Why do children in the preoperational stage make errors on tasks that require conservation? Piaget suggests that the main reason is that their tendency toward centration prevents them from focusing on the relevant features of the situation. Furthermore, they cannot follow the sequence of transformations that accompanies changes in the appearance of a situation.

Watch the **Video** *Conservation Tasks* in **MyPsychLab**.

Incomplete Understanding of Transformation. A preoperational, preschool child who sees several worms during a walk in the woods may believe that they are all the same worm. The reason: She views each sighting in isolation and is unable to form an idea about the transformation it would take for the worm to move quickly from one sighting to the next. She cannot yet realize that worms can't transform themselves into creatures that can do that.

As Piaget used the term, **transformation** is the process in which one state is changed into another. For instance, adults know that if a pencil that is held upright is allowed to fall down, it passes through a series of successive stages until it reaches its final, horizontal resting spot (see Figure 6-6 on page 172). In contrast, children in the preoperational period are unable to envision or recall the successive transformations that the pencil followed in moving from the upright to the horizontal position. If asked to reproduce the sequence in a drawing,

transformation The process whereby one state is changed into another

FIGURE 6-6 The Falling Pencil

Children in Piaget's preoperational stage do not understand that as a pencil falls from the upright to the horizontal position, it moves through a series of intermediary steps. Instead, they think that there are no intermediate steps in the change from the upright to horizontal position.

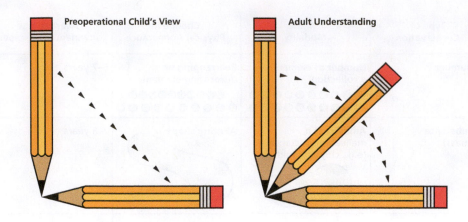

Preoperational Child's View   Adult Understanding

they draw the pencil upright and lying down, with nothing in between. Basically, they ignore the intermediate steps.

Egocentrism: The Inability to Take Others' Perspectives.

Another hallmark of the preoperational period is egocentric thinking. **Egocentric thought** is thinking that does not take into account the viewpoints of others. Preschoolers do not understand that others have different perspectives from their own. Egocentric thought takes two forms: the lack of awareness that others see things from a different physical perspective and the failure to realize that others may hold thoughts, feelings, and points of view that differ from theirs. (Note what egocentric thought does *not* imply: that preoperational children intentionally think in a selfish or inconsiderate manner.)

Egocentric thinking is what is behind children's lack of concern over their nonverbal behavior and the impact it has on others. For instance, a 4-year-old who is given an unwanted gift of socks when he was expecting something more desirable may frown and scowl as he opens the package, unaware that his face can be seen by others and may reveal his true feelings about the gift (Feldman, 1992).

Egocentrism lies at the heart of several types of behavior during the preoperational period. For instance, preschoolers may talk to themselves, even in the presence of others, and at times they simply ignore what others are telling them. Rather than being a sign of eccentricity, such behavior illustrates the egocentric nature of preoperational children's thinking: the lack of awareness that their behavior acts as a trigger to others' reactions and responses. Consequently, a considerable amount of verbal behavior on the part of preschoolers has no social motivation behind it but is meant for the preschoolers' own consumption.

Similarly, egocentrism can be seen in hiding games with children during the preoperational stage. In a game of hide-and-seek, 3-year-olds may attempt to hide by covering their faces with a pillow—even though they remain in plain view. Their reasoning: If they cannot see others, others cannot see them. They assume that others share their view.

The Emergence of Intuitive Thought.

Because Piaget labeled the preschool years as the "*pre*operational period," it is easy to assume that this is a period of marking time, waiting for the more formal emergence of operations. As if to support this view, many of the characteristics of the preoperational period highlight deficiencies, cognitive skills that the preschooler has yet to master. However, the preoperational period is far from idle. Cognitive development proceeds steadily, and in fact several new types of ability emerge. A case in point: the development of intuitive thought.

Intuitive thought refers to preschoolers' use of primitive reasoning and their avid acquisition of knowledge about the world. From about ages 4 through 7, children's curiosity blossoms. They constantly seek out the answers to a wide variety of questions, asking "Why?" about nearly everything. At the same time, children may act as if they are authorities on particular topics, feeling certain that they have the correct—and final—word on an issue. If pressed, they are unable to explain how they know what they know. In other words, their

Watch the **Video** *Egocentrism Task* in **MyPsychLab**.

egocentric thought   Thinking that does not take the viewpoints of others into account

intuitive thought   Thinking that reflects preschoolers' use of primitive reasoning and their avid acquisition of knowledge about the world

intuitive thought leads them to believe that they know answers to all kinds of questions, but there is little or no logical basis for this confidence in their understanding of the way the world operates. This may lead a preschooler to state authoritatively that airplanes can fly because they move their wings up and down like a bird, even if they have never seen an airplane's wings moving in that way.

In the late stages of the preoperational period, children's intuitive thinking does have certain qualities that prepare them for more sophisticated forms of reasoning. For instance, preschoolers come to understand that pushing harder on the pedals makes a bicycle move faster, or that pressing a button on a remote control makes the television change channels. By the end of the preoperational stage, preschoolers begin to understand the notion of *functionality*, the idea that actions, events, and outcomes are related to one another in fixed patterns. Children also begin to show an awareness of the concept of identity in the later stages of the preoperational period. *Identity* is the understanding that certain things stay the same, regardless of changes in shape, size, and appearance.

For instance, knowledge of identity allows one to understand that a lump of clay contains the same amount of clay regardless of whether it is clumped into a ball or stretched out like a snake. Comprehension of identity is necessary for children to develop an understanding of conservation, the ability to understand that quantity is not related to physical appearances, as we discussed earlier. Piaget regarded children's development of conservation as a skill that marks the transition from the preoperational period to the next stage, concrete operations, which is a hallmark of the school years.

ARE YOU AN INFORMED CONSUMER OF DEVELOPMENT?

Promoting Cognitive Development in Preschoolers: From Theory to the Classroom

Piaget's theory has had enormous influence on educational practice, particularly during the preschool years. Among the suggestions for parents and preschool teachers that arise out of the Piagetian approach are the following:

- Both parents and teachers should be aware of the general stage of cognitive development, with its capabilities and limitations, that each individual child has reached. Unless they are aware of a child's current level of development, it will be impossible to provide appropriate materials and experiences.

- Instruction should be at a level that reflects—but is just slightly higher than—each student's current level of cognitive development. For instance, Piaget suggests that cognitive growth is more likely to occur when information and material are of moderate novelty. With too little novelty, children will be bored; with too much, they will be confused.

- Instruction should be individualized as much as possible. Because children of the same age may hover around different levels of cognitive development, curriculum materials that are prepared individually stand a better chance of success.

- Children should be kept actively engaged in learning, and they should be allowed to pace themselves as they move through new material.

- Opportunities for social interaction—both with other students and with adults—should be provided. By receiving feedback from others and observing how others react in given situations, children learn new approaches and new ways of thinking about the world.

- Children should be allowed to make mistakes. Cognitive growth often flows from confronting errors.

- Because cognitive development can occur only when children have achieved the appropriate level of maturation, children should not be pushed too far ahead of their current state of cognitive development. For instance, although it may be possible through intensive training to get preoperational children to recite, in a rote manner, the correct response to a conservation problem, this does not mean that they will have true comprehension of what they are reciting. ■

Cognitive development makes substantial advances in middle childhood.

concrete operational stage The period of cognitive development between 7 and 12 years of age, characterized by the active and appropriate use of logic

decentering The ability to take multiple aspects of a situation into account

Cognitive Development in the School Years and Adolescence

As we have seen, from Piaget's perspective the preschooler thinks *preoperationally*. This type of thinking is largely egocentric, and preoperational children lack the ability to use *operations*—organized, formal, logical mental processes.

The Rise of Concrete Operational Thought (Ages 7 to 12). All this changes, according to Piaget, during the concrete operational period, which coincides with the school years. The **concrete operational stage,** which occurs between 7 and 12 years of age, is characterized by the active and appropriate use of logic.

Concrete operational thought involves applying *logical thinking* to concrete problems. For instance, when children in the concrete operational stage are confronted with a conservation problem (such as determining whether the amount of liquid poured from one container to another container of a different shape stays the same), they use cognitive and logical processes to answer, no longer being influenced solely by appearance. They are able to reason correctly that because none of the liquid has been lost, the amount stays the same. Because they are less egocentric, they can take multiple aspects of a situation into account, an ability known as **decentering.** Jared, the sixth-grader described in the chapter Prologue, was using his decentering skills to consider the views of the different factions involved in creating the U.S. Constitution.

The shift from preoperational thought to concrete operational thought does not happen overnight, of course. During the 2 years before children move firmly into the concrete operational period, they shift back and forth between preoperational and concrete operational thinking. For instance, they typically pass through a period when they can answer conservation problems correctly but can't articulate why they did so. When asked to explain the reasoning behind their answers, they may respond with an unenlightening, "Because."

Once concrete operational thinking is fully engaged, however, children show several cognitive advances representative of their logical thinking. For instance, they attain the concept of *reversibility,* which is the notion that processes transforming a stimulus can be reversed, returning it to its original form. Grasping reversibility permits children to understand that a ball of clay that has been squeezed into a long, snakelike rope can be returned to its original state. More abstractly, it allows school-age children to understand that if 3 plus 5 equals 8, then 5 plus 3 also equals 8—and later during the period, that 8 minus 3 equals 5.

Concrete operational thinking also permits children to understand such concepts as the relationship between time, speed, and distance, comprehending, for example, that an increase in speed can compensate for greater distance in a journey. For instance, consider the problem shown in Figure 6-7, in which two cars start and finish at the same points in the same amount of time but travel different routes. Children who are just entering the concrete operational period reason that the cars are traveling at the same speed. However, between the ages of 8 and 10, children begin to draw the right conclusion: that the car traveling the longer route must be moving faster if it arrives at the finish point at the same time as the car traveling the shorter route.

Despite the advances that occur during the concrete operational stage, children still experience one critical limitation in their thinking. They remain tied to concrete, physical reality. Furthermore, they are unable to understand truly abstract or hypothetical questions or ones that involve formal logic.

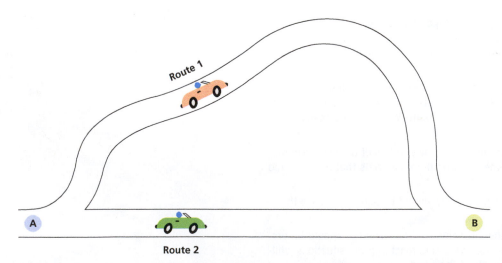

FIGURE 6-7 Sample Problem in Concrete Operational Thinking

After being told that the two cars traveling Routes 1 and 2 start and end their journeys in the same amount of time, children who are just entering the concrete operational period still reason that the cars are traveling at the same speed. Later, however, they reach the correct conclusion that the car traveling the longer route must be moving at a higher speed if it starts and ends its journey at the same time as the car traveling the shorter route.

It is this ability—to think beyond the concrete, current situation to what might or could be—that distinguishes adolescents' thinking from that of younger children. Adolescents are able to consider a variety of abstract possibilities; they can see issues in relative, as opposed to absolute, terms. When problems arise, they can perceive shadings beyond the black-and-white solutions of younger days (Keating, 1990; Lehalle, 2006).

Ms. Mejia smiled as she read a particularly creative paper. As part of her eighth-grade American Government class every year, she asked students to write about what their lives would be like if America had not won its war for independence from Britain. She had tried something similar with her sixth-graders, but many of them seemed unable to imagine anything different from what they already knew. By eighth grade, however, they were able to come up with some very interesting scenarios. One boy imagined that he would be known as Lord Lucas; a girl imagined that she would be a servant to a rich landowner; another, that she would be helping to plot an overthrow of the government.

What is it that sets adolescents' thinking apart from that of younger children? According to Piaget, with adolescence comes the formal operational stage.

Piaget's Formal Operational Stage (Ages 12 to 15). Fourteen-year-old Leigh is asked to solve a problem that anyone who has seen a grandfather's clock may have pondered: What determines the speed at which a pendulum moves back and forth? In the version of the problem that she is asked to solve, Leigh is given a weight hanging from a string. She is told that she can vary several things: the length of the string, the weight of the object at the end of the string, the amount of force used to push the string, and the height to which the weight is raised in an arc before it is released.

Leigh doesn't remember, but she was asked to solve the same problem when she was 8 years old, as part of a longitudinal research study. At that time, she was in the concrete operational period, and her efforts to solve the problem were not successful. She approached the problem haphazardly, with no systematic plan of action. For instance, she simultaneously tried to push the pendulum harder *and* shorten the length of the string *and* increase the weight on the string. Because she was varying so many factors at once, when the speed of the pendulum changed she had no way of knowing which factor or factors made a difference.

formal operational stage The stage at which people develop the ability to think abstractly

Now, however, Leigh is much more systematic. Rather than immediately beginning to push and pull at the pendulum, she stops a moment and thinks about what factors to take into account. She considers how she might test which of those factors is important, forming a hypothesis about which is most important. Then, just like a scientist conducting an experiment, she varies only one factor at a time. By examining each variable separately and systematically, she is able to come to the correct solution: The length of the string determines the speed of the pendulum.

Using Formal Operations to Solve Problems. Leigh's approach to the pendulum question, a problem devised by Piaget, illustrates that she has moved into the formal operational period of cognitive development (Piaget & Inhelder, 1958). The **formal operational stage** is the stage at which people develop the ability to think abstractly. Piaget suggested that people reach it at the start of adolescence, around the age of 12. Thus, the adolescent Leigh was able to think about the

Like scientists who form hypotheses, adolescents in the formal operational stage use hypotheticodeductive reasoning. They start with a general theory about what produces a particular outcome and then deduce explanations for specific situations in which they see that particular outcome.

various aspects of the pendulum problem in an abstract manner, and to understand how to test out the hypotheses that she had formed.

By bringing formal principles of logic to bear on problems they encounter, adolescents are able to consider problems in the abstract rather than only in concrete terms. Furthermore, they are able to test their understanding by systematically carrying out rudimentary experiments on problems and situations and observing what their experimental "interventions" bring about.

Adolescents in the formal operational stage use *hypotheticodeductive* reasoning, in which they start with a general theory about what produces a particular outcome and then deduce explanations for specific situations in which they see that particular outcome. Like scientists who form hypotheses, they can then test their theories. What distinguishes this kind of thinking from earlier cognitive stages is the ability to start with abstract possibilities and move to the concrete; in previous stages, children are tied to the concrete here-and-now. For example, at age 8, Leigh just started moving things around to see what would happen in the pendulum problem, a concrete approach. At age 12, however, she started with the abstract idea that each variable—the string, the size of the weight, and so forth—should be tested separately (Reyna et al., 2012).

Adolescents also are able to employ propositional thought during the formal operational stage. *Propositional thought* is reasoning that uses abstract logic in the absences of concrete examples. For example, propositional thinking allows adolescents to understand that if certain premises are valid, then a conclusion must also be valid. For example, consider the following:

All men are mortal.	[*premise*]
Socrates is a man.	[*premise*]
Therefore, Socrates is mortal.	[*conclusion*]

Not only can adolescents understand that if both premises are valid, then so is the conclusion, but also they are capable of using similar reasoning when premises and conclusions are stated more abstractly, as follows:

All A's are B.	[*premise*]
C is an A.	[*premise*]
Therefore, C is a B.	[*conclusion*]

Although Piaget proposed that children enter the formal operational stage at the beginning of adolescence, you may recall that he also hypothesized that—as with all the stages of cognitive development—full capabilities do not emerge suddenly, at one stroke. Instead, they gradually unfold through a combination of physical maturation and environmental experiences. According to Piaget, it is not until adolescents are around 15 years old that they are fully settled in the formal operational stage.

Some evidence suggests that a sizable proportion of people hone their formal operational skills at a later age and in some cases never fully employ formal operational thinking at all. For instance, most studies show that only 40% to 60% of college students and adults achieve formal operational thinking completely, and some estimates run as low as 25%. But many of those adults who do not show formal operational thought in every domain are fully competent in *some* aspects of formal operations (Sugarman, 1988; Keating, 1990; 2004).

Why are there inconsistencies in the use of formal operations? Why don't older adolescents consistently use formal operational thinking? One reason is that all of us often are cognitively lazy, relying on intuition and mental shortcuts rather than on formal reasoning. In addition, we are more apt to think abstractly and use formal operational thought on tasks on which we have considerable experience; in unfamiliar situations, we find it more difficult to think using formal operations. An English major finds it easy to identify the themes of a Faulkner play, while a biology major may struggle. On the other hand, the biology major may find the concepts of cell division simple, while the English major may find the concept bedeviling (Klaczynski, 2004).

Furthermore, adolescents differ in their use of formal operations because of the culture in which they were raised. People who live in isolated, scientifically unsophisticated societies and who have little formal education are less likely to perform at the formal operational level than formally educated persons living in more technologically sophisticated societies (Segall et al., 1990).

Does this mean that adolescents (and adults) from cultures in which formal operations tend not to emerge are incapable of attaining them? Not at all. A more probable conclusion is that the scientific reasoning that characterizes formal operations is not equally valued in all societies. If everyday life does not require or promote a certain type of reasoning, it is unreasonable to expect people to employ that type of reasoning when confronted with a problem (Gauvain, 1998).

The use of formal operations by this Honduran may differ from that of someone the same age raised in the United States.

The Consequences of Adolescents' Use of Formal Operations.

Adolescents' ability to reason abstractly, embodied in their use of formal operations, leads to a change in their everyday behavior. Whereas earlier they may have unquestioningly accepted rules and explanations set out for them, their increased abstract reasoning abilities may lead them to question their parents and other authority figures far more strenuously. Advances in abstract thinking also lead to greater idealism, which may make adolescents impatient with imperfections in institutions such as schools and the government.

In general, adolescents become more argumentative. They enjoy using abstract reasoning to poke holes in others' explanations, and their increased abilities to think critically make them acutely sensitive to parents' and teachers' perceived shortcomings. For instance, they may note the inconsistency in their parents' arguments against using drugs, because they know that their parents used them when they were adolescents, and nothing much came of it. At the same time, adolescents can be indecisive, as they are able to see the merits of multiple sides to issues (Alberts, Elkind, & Ginsberg, 2007; Klaczynski, 2011; Chick & Reyna, 2012; Galván, 2012).

Coping with the increased critical abilities of adolescents can be challenging for parents, teachers, and other adults. But it also makes adolescents more interesting, as they actively seek to understand the values and justifications that they encounter in their lives.

Review, Check, and Apply

Review

1. Jean Piaget argued that infants acquire knowledge directly through motor behavior, organizing their world into mental structures called *schemes* and subsequently either assimilating experiences into their current level of understanding or accommodating their ways of thinking to include the new experiences.

2. Piaget's theory is based on a stage approach to development in which children pass through a series of stages in a fixed order from birth to adolescence: sensorimotor, preoperational, concrete operational, and formal operational.

3. The key way in which Piaget differs from many theorists who preceded him is in his observation that children experience *qualitative* changes in knowledge and understanding as they move from stage to stage, not just *quantitative* changes.

4. The sensorimotor stage, from birth to about 2, involves a gradual progression through simple reflexes, single coordinated activities, manipulation of actions to produce desired outcomes, and symbolic thought. The sensorimotor stage has six substages.

5. According to Piaget, children in the preoperational stage develop symbolic function, a change in their thinking that is the foundation of further cognitive advances, but they are hampered by a tendency toward egocentric thought.

6. Children in middle childhood are in the concrete operational stage of cognitive development, characterized by the application of logical processes to concrete problems and by *decentering*, the ability to take multiple aspects of a situation into account.

7. As they enter Piaget's formal operational stage, adolescents begin to think abstractly, use logic, and perform systematic experiments to answer questions.

Check

1. Piaget's theory of cognitive development is distinctive because of its contention that cognitive development entails _____ changes in the ways individuals know and understand the world as they move from stage to stage, rather than just _____ changes.

2. According to Piaget, _____ is the process by which people understand an experience in terms of their current stage of cognitive development and way of thinking.

3. The first stage of development, according to Piaget, is the _____ stage.

4. During the _____ period children's use of symbolic thinking grows, mental reasoning emerges, and the use of concepts increases.

5. Piaget considered school-aged children to be in the _____ _____ period.

6. According to Piaget, the _____ _____ stage is the stage at which people develop the ability to think abstractly.

Apply

1. Think of a common young children's toy. How might its use be affected by the principles of assimilation and accommodation?

2. Do you think it is possible to break a preschooler's habit of egocentric thought by directly teaching him to take another person's point of view? Would showing him a picture of himself "hidden" behind a chair change his thinking? Why or why not?

To see more review questions, log on to MyPsychLab.

ANSWERS: 1. qualitative; quantitative 2. assimilation 3. sensorimotor 4. preoperational 5. concrete operational 6. formal operational

MODULE 6.2

APPRAISING PIAGET: SUPPORT AND CHALLENGES

LO 6-5 **How has Piaget's theory been supported and challenged by later research?**

Most developmental researchers would probably agree that in many significant ways, Piaget's descriptions of how cognitive development proceeds during infancy are quite accurate (Marcovitch, Zelazo, & Schmuckler, 2003). Yet, there is substantial disagreement over the validity of the theory and many of its specific predictions.

Piaget's Contributions to Developmental Science

Let's start with what is clearly correct about the Piagetian approach. Piaget was a brilliant reporter of children's behavior, and his descriptions of growth during infancy remain a monument to his powers of observation. His many books contain insightful, careful observations of children at work and play.

Furthermore, literally thousands of studies have supported Piaget's view that children learn much about the world by acting on objects in their environment. Finally, the broad outlines sketched out by Piaget of the sequence of cognitive development and the increasing cognitive accomplishments that occur during infancy are generally accurate. His theories have had powerful educational implications, and many schools use his principles to guide instruction (Brainerd, 2003; Kail, 2004).

The Critics Weigh In   Despite the powerful influence of Piaget's work, specific aspects of his theory have come under increasing scrutiny—and criticism—in the decades since he carried out his pioneering work. These criticisms are summarized below.

The Continuity of Stages.   Some researchers question the stage conception that forms the basis of Piaget's theory. Although even Piaget acknowledged that children's transitions between stages are gradual, critics contend that development proceeds in a much more continuous fashion. Rather than showing major leaps of competence at the end of one stage and the beginning of the next, improvement comes in smoother increments, growing step-by-step in a skill-by-skill manner. For instance, developmental researcher Robert Siegler suggests that cognitive development proceeds not in stages but in "waves." According to him, children don't one day drop a mode of thinking and the next take up a new form. Instead, there is an ebb and flow of cognitive approaches that children use to understand the world. One day children may use one form of cognitive strategy, while another day they may choose a less advanced strategy—moving back and forth over a period of time. Although one strategy may be used most frequently at a given age, children still may have access to alternative ways of thinking. Siegler thus sees cognitive development as in constant flux (Siegler, 2003, 2007; Aslin, 2012).

The Link between Cognitive Development and Motor Activities.   Other critics dispute Piaget's notion that cognitive development is grounded in motor activities. They charge that Piaget overlooked the importance of the sensory and perceptual systems that are present from a very early age in infancy—systems about which Piaget knew little, because so much of the research illustrating how sophisticated infants are is relatively recent. Studies of children born without arms and legs (due to their mothers' unwitting use of teratogenic drugs during pregnancy, as described in Chapter 3) show that such children display normal cognitive development, despite their lack of practice with motor activities; this is seen as further evidence that Piaget exaggerated the connection between motor development and cognitive development (Butterworth, 1994).

Timing of Mastery of Object Permanence.   Piaget's critics also point to more recent studies that cast doubt on Piaget's view that infants are incapable of mastering the concept of object permanence until they are close to a year old. For instance, some work suggests that younger infants did not appear to understand object permanence because the techniques used to test their abilities were not sensitive enough to their true capabilities (Walden et al., 2007; Baillargeon, 2004, 2008; Vallotton, 2011).

According to researcher Renée Baillargeon, infants as young as 3½ months have at least some understanding of object permanence. She argues that it may be that younger infants don't search for a rattle hidden under a blanket because they don't have the motor skills necessary to do the searching—not because they don't understand that the rattle still exists. Similarly, the apparent inability of young infants to comprehend object permanence may reflect more about infants' memory deficits than their lack of understanding of the concept: The memories of young infants may be so poor that they simply do not recall the earlier concealment of the toy (Hespos & Baillargeon, 2008).

Baillargeon has conducted ingenious experiments that demonstrate the earlier capabilities of infants in understanding object permanence. For example, in her *violation-of-expectation* studies, she repeatedly exposes infants to a physical event and then observes how they react to a variation of that event that is physically impossible. It turns out that infants as young as 3½ months show strong physiological reactions to impossible events, suggesting that they have some sense of object permanence far earlier than Piaget was able to discern (Wang, Baillargeon, & Paterson, 2005; Ruffman, Slade, & Redman, 2005; Luo, Kaufman, & Baillargeon, 2009).

Underestimation of Children's Capabilities. Other types of behavior likewise seem to emerge earlier than Piaget suggested. For instance, recall the ability of neonates to imitate basic facial expressions of adults just hours after birth, as we discussed in Chapter 4. The presence of this skill at such an early age contradicts Piaget's view that initially infants are able to imitate only behavior that they see in others, using parts of their own body that they can plainly view—such as their hands and feet. In fact, facial imitation suggests that humans may be born with a basic, innate capability for imitating others' actions, a capability that depends on certain kinds of environmental experiences, but one that Piaget believed develops later in infancy (Meltzoff & Moore, 2002; Legerstee & Markova, 2008; Vanvuchelen, Roeyers, & De Weerdt, 2011).

Many researchers contend that Piaget underestimated children's capabilities generally, in part due to the limitations of the mini-experiments he conducted. Subjected to a broader array of experimental tasks, children show less consistency within stages than Piaget predicted. Increasing evidence suggests that children's cognitive abilities emerge earlier than supposed; for example, some children demonstrate concrete operational thinking before age 7, when Piaget suggested these abilities first appear (Bjorklund, 1997b; Dawson-Tunik, Fischer, & Stein, 2004).

Children's Understanding of Numbers. Piaget may also have erred in asserting that preschoolers have little understanding of numbers, as shown by their inability to grasp conservation and reversibility (the understanding that a transformation can be reversed to return something to its original state). Recent experimental work suggests otherwise. For instance, developmental psychologist Rochel Gelman has found that children as young as 3 can easily tell the difference between rows of two and three toy animals, regardless of the animals' spacing. Older children are able to note differences in number, performing tasks such as identifying which of two numbers is larger and indicating that they understand some rudiments of addition and subtraction (Cordes & Brannon, 2009; Izard et al., 2009; McNeil, et al., 2011; Barner, Lui, & Zapf, 2012).

Based on such evidence, Gelman concludes that children have an innate ability to count, akin to the ability to use language that some theorists see as universal and genetically determined. This conclusion is clearly at odds with Piagetian notions, which suggest that children's numerical abilities do not blossom until after the preoperational period (i.e., after about age 7).

Conservation. There are further difficulties with Piaget's contention that conservation does not emerge until the end of the preoperational period. This assertion has not stood up to careful experimental scrutiny. Preoperational children can learn to answer conservation tasks correctly if they are given certain training and experiences. The fact that these children can improve their performance on these tasks argues against the Piagetian view that they have not reached a level of cognitive maturity that would permit them to understand conservation (Ping & Goldin-Meadow, 2008; Kwong See, Rasmussen, & Pertman, 2012).

Cultural Issues. Piaget's work also seems to describe children from developed, Western countries better than those in non-Western cultures. For instance, some evidence suggests cognitive skills emerge on a different timetable for children in non-Western cultures than for children living in Europe and the United States. Infants raised in the Ivory Coast of Africa, for example, reach the various substages of the sensorimotor period at an earlier age than do infants reared in France (Dasen et al., 1978; Rogoff & Chavajay, 1995; Mistry & Saraswathi, 2003).

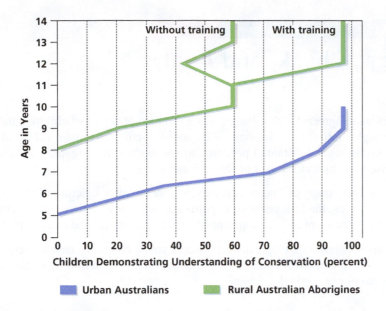

FIGURE 6-8 Understanding of Conservation among Urban and Aboriginal Australian Children

Rural Australian Aborigine children trail their urban counterparts in the development of their understanding of conservation. With training, they later catch up, but without training, around half of 14-year-old Aborigines do not understand conservation. What types of teaching programs might an educator provide to help the development of conservation?

(*Source:* Based on Dasen, Ngini, & Lavallée, 1979)

Despite these criticisms—which research has shown to be valid—we cannot dismiss Piaget. Although some early cross-cultural research seemed to imply that children in certain cultures never left the preoperational stage, failing to master conservation and to develop concrete operations, more recent research suggests otherwise. For instance, with proper training in conservation, children in non-Western cultures who do not conserve can readily learn to do so. For instance, in one study, urban Australian children—who develop concrete operations on the same timetable as Piaget suggested—were compared to rural Aborigine children, who typically do not demonstrate an understanding of conservation at the age of 14 (Dasen, Ngini, & Lavallée, 1979; Maynard & Greenfield, 2003). When the rural Aborigine children were given training, they showed conservation skills similar to their urban counterparts, although with a time lag of around 3 years (see Figure 6-8).

Furthermore, when children are interviewed by researchers from their own culture, who know the language and customs of the culture well and who use reasoning tasks that are related to domains important to the culture, the children are considerably more likely to display concrete operational thinking (Jahoda, 1983). Ultimately, such research suggests that Piaget was right when he argued that concrete operations were universally achieved during middle childhood. Although school-age children in some cultures may differ from Westerners in the demonstration of certain cognitive skills, the most probable explanation of the difference is that the non-Western children have had different sorts of experiences from those that permit children in Western societies to perform well on Piagetian measures of conservation and concrete operations. The progress of cognitive development, then, cannot be understood without considering a child's culture (Lau, Lee, & Chiu, 2004; Maynard, 2008; Crisp & Turner, 2011).

FROM A
CHILD CAREGIVER'S
PERSPECTIVE:

In general, what are some implications for child-rearing practices according to Piaget's observations about the ways children gain an understanding of the world? Would you use the same child-rearing approaches for a child growing up in a non-Western culture? Why or why not?

A Final Summation

Even Piaget's most passionate critics concede that he has provided us with an ingenious description of the broad outlines of cognitive development during infancy. His failings seem to be in underestimating the capabilities of younger infants and in his claims that sensorimotor skills develop in a consistent, fixed pattern.

Still, his influence has been enormous. Piaget's theories have inspired countless studies on the development of thinking capacities and processes, and they have spurred much classroom reform. His bold statements about the nature of cognitive development sparked opposition that brought forth new approaches, including the information processing perspective that we will discuss in the next chapter. Piaget remains a towering, pioneering figure in the field of development (Fischer & Hencke, 1996; Roth, Slone, & Dar, 2000; Kail, 2004; Maynard, 2008).

Review, Check, and Apply

Review

1. There is wide agreement that Piaget was a virtuoso observer of children and that many of his insights into the development of cognition in children remain valid and useful. His theory has brought substantial positive change to child rearing and education, and has given rise to many fruitful lines of research and study.

2. Critics question many of Piaget's conclusions, including his picture of the discontinuous nature of stages, the link between cognitive development and motor activities, and his views of the timing of the development of object permanence and conservation.

3. Critics also contend that Piaget underestimated young children's capabilities, such as their ability to grasp numerical concepts, and that his studies were limited by his narrow focus on children of one particular culture.

Check

1. The normal cognitive development of children born without arms and legs calls into question Piaget's belief that early cognitive development depends on _____ development.

2. Children's strong physiological reactions to the sudden disappearance of a toy or other object on which they were focusing suggests that they have a sense of _____ _____.

3. Children perform better on developmental assessments when they are presented with tasks that in domains that are important and relevant to their own _____.

Apply

1. Do adults ever use schemes to organize their environment? Do the principles of assimilation and accommodation apply to adult learning as well as to children's learning? How?

2. When faced with complex problems, do adults routinely use formal operations? What aspects of a culture might encourage or discourage the use application of formal operational approaches?

To see more review questions, log on to MyPsychLab.

ANSWERS: 1. motor 2. object permanence 3. culture

MODULE 6.3

VYGOTSKY'S VIEW OF COGNITIVE DEVELOPMENT: TAKING CULTURE INTO ACCOUNT

LO 6-6 What is Vygotsky's approach to cognitive development?

As her daughter watches, a member of the Chilcotin Indian tribe prepares a salmon for dinner. When the daughter asks a question about a small detail of the process, the mother takes out another salmon and repeats the entire process. According to the tribal view of learning, understanding and comprehension can come only from grasping the total procedure, and not from learning about the individual subcomponents of the task. (Tharp, 1989).

The Chilcotin view of how children learn about the world contrasts with the prevalent view of Western society, which assumes that only by mastering the separate parts of a problem can one fully comprehend it. Do differences in the ways particular cultures and societies approach problems influence cognitive development? According to Russian developmental psychologist Lev Vygotsky, who lived from 1896 to 1934, the answer is a clear Yes.

The Importance of Culture

Vygotsky viewed cognitive development as the product of social interactions in which children learn through guided participation, working with mentors to solve problems. Instead of concentrating on individual performance, as Piaget and many alternative approaches do, Vygotsky's increasingly influential view focuses on the social aspects of development and learning.

Vygotsky sees children as apprentices, learning cognitive strategies and other skills from adult and peer mentors who not only present new ways of doing things but also provide assistance, instruction, and motivation. Consequently, he focuses on the child's social and cultural world as the source of cognitive development. According to Vygotsky, children gradually grow intellectually and begin to function on their own because of the assistance that adult and peer partners provide (Vygotsky, 1926/1997; Tudge & Scrimsher, 2003; Göncü & Gauvain, 2012).

Vygotsky contends that the nature of the partnership between developing children and adults and peers is determined largely by cultural and societal factors. For instance, culture and society establish the institutions, such as preschools and play groups, that promote development by providing opportunities for cognitive growth. Furthermore, by emphasizing particular tasks, culture and society shape the nature of specific cognitive advances. Unless we look at what is important and meaningful to members of a given society, we may seriously underestimate the nature and level of cognitive abilities that ultimately will be attained (Tappan, 1997; Schaller & Crandall, 2004).

For example, children's toys reflect what is important and meaningful in a particular society. In Western societies, preschoolers commonly play with toy wagons, automobiles, and other vehicles, in part reflecting the mobile nature of the culture.

Societal expectations about gender also play a role in how children come to understand the world. For example, one study conducted at a science museum found that parents provided more detailed scientific explanations to boys than to girls at museum displays. Such differences in level of explanation may lead to more sophisticated understanding of science in boys and ultimately may produce later gender differences in science learning (Crowley et al., 2001).

Vygotsky's approach is therefore quite different from that of Piaget. Where Piaget looked at developing children and saw junior scientists, working by themselves to develop an independent understanding of the world, Vygotsky sees cognitive apprentices, learning from master teachers the skills that are important in the child's culture. Where Piaget saw preschoolers who were egocentric, looking at the world from their own, limited vantage point, Vygotsky sees preschoolers as using others to gain an understanding of the world.

In Vygotsky's view, then, children's cognitive development is dependent on interaction with others. Vygotsky argues that it is only through partnership with other people—peers, parents, teachers, and other adults—that children can fully develop their knowledge, thinking processes, beliefs, and values (Edwards, 2004; Reddy, 2012).

The Zone of Proximal Development

Vygotsky proposed that children's cognitive abilities increase through exposure to information that is new enough to be intriguing, but not too difficult for the child to contend with. He called this the **zone of proximal development, or ZPD**, the level at which a child can *almost*, but not fully, perform a task independently, but can do so with the assistance of someone more competent. When appropriate instruction is offered within the zone of proximal development, children are able to increase their understanding and master new tasks. For cognitive development to occur, new information must be presented—by parents, teachers, or more

Russian developmental psychologist Lev Vygotsky proposed that the focus of cognitive development should be on a child's social and cultural world, as opposed to the Piagetian approach, which concentrates on individual performance.

**FROM AN
EDUCATOR'S
PERSPECTIVE:**

If children's cognitive development is dependent on interactions with others, what obligations does society have regarding such social settings as preschools and neighborhoods?

zone of proximal development (ZPD)
According to Vygotsky, the level at which a child can almost, but not fully, comprehend or perform a task without assistance

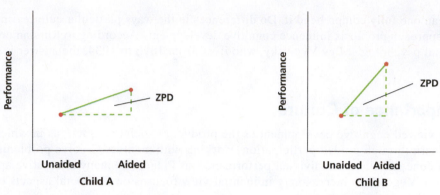

FIGURE 6-9 Sample Zones of Proximal Development (ZPDs) for Two Children

Although the two children's performance is similar when working at a task without aid, the second child benefits more from aid and therefore has a larger ZPD. Is there any way to measure a child's ZPD? Can it be enlarged?

skilled peers—within the zone of proximal development. For example, a preschooler might not be able to figure out by herself how to get a handle to stick on the clay pot she's building, but she can do it with some advice from her child-care teacher (Zuckerman & Shenfield, 2007; Norton & D'Ambrosio, 2008; Warford, 2011).

The concept of the zone of proximal development suggests that even though two children might be able to achieve the same amount without help, if one child receives aid, he or she may improve substantially more than the other. The greater the improvement that comes with help, the larger is the zone of proximal development (see Figure 6-9).

The assistance or structuring provided by others has been termed *scaffolding*. **Scaffolding** is the support for learning and problem solving that encourages independence and growth (Puntambekar & Hübscher, 2005; Blewitt et al., 2009; Jadallah et al., 2011; Hammond et al., 2012).

To Vygotsky, the process of scaffolding not only helps children solve specific problems but also aids in the development of their overall cognitive abilities. Scaffolding takes its name from the scaffolds that are put up to aid in the construction of a building and removed once the building is complete. In education, scaffolding involves, first of all, helping children think about and frame a task in an appropriate manner. In addition, a parent or teacher is likely to provide clues to task completion that are appropriate to the child's level of development and to model behavior that can lead to completion of the task. As in construction, the scaffolding that more competent people provide, which facilitates the completion of identified tasks, is removed once children are able to solve a problem on their own (Warwick & Maloch, 2003; Taumoepeau & Ruffman, 2008; Zhang & Quintana, 2012).

To illustrate how scaffolding operates, consider the following conversation between mother and son:

Mother: Do you remember how you helped me make the cookies before?

Child: No.

Mother: We made the dough and put it in the oven. Do you remember that?

Child: When Grandma came?

Mother: Yes, that's right. Would you help me shape the dough into cookies?

Child: OK.

Mother: Can you remember how big we made the cookies when Grandma was here?

Child: Big.

Mother: Right. Can you show me how big?

Child: We used the big wooden spoon.

Mother: Good boy, that's right. We used the wooden spoon, and we made big cookies. But let's try something different today by using the ice cream scoop to form the cookies.

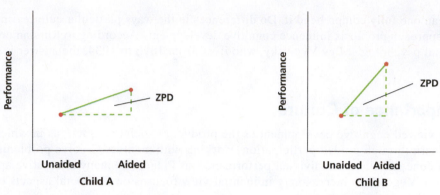

Watch the **Video** *Scaffolding* in **MyPsychLab**.

scaffolding   The support for learning and problem solving that encourages independence and growth

FROM RESEARCH TO PRACTICE
Vygotsky in the Classroom

Educators have seized on Vygotsky's notion that cognitive advances occur through exposure to information within a child's zone of proximal development, or ZPD. In the ZPD, a child can almost, but not quite, understand or perform a task.

Vygotsky's approach has particularly encouraged the development of classroom practices that promote children's active participation in their learning. Classrooms are seen as places where children should experiment and try out new activities (Vygotsky, 1926/1997; Gredler & Shields, 2008).

According to Vygotsky, education should focus on activities that involve interaction with others. Both child–adult and child–child interactions can promote cognitive growth. The interactions must be carefully structured to fall within each child's zone of proximal development.

Several current and noteworthy educational innovations have borrowed heavily from Vygotsky's work. For example, *cooperative learning, where* children work in groups to achieve a common goal, uses several aspects of Vygotsky's theory. Students working in cooperative groups benefit from the insights of others. A wrong turn by one child may be corrected by others in the group. On the other hand, not every group member is equally helpful: As Vygotsky's approach would

imply, individual children benefit most when some of the group members are more competent at the task and can act as experts (Gillies & Boyle, 2006; Law, 2008).

Reciprocal teaching, a technique to teach reading comprehension strategies, is another practice that reflects Vygotsky's approach to cognitive development. Students learn to skim the content of a passage, raise questions about its meaning, summarize, and predict what will happen next. The reciprocal nature of this technique gives students a chance to adopt the role of teacher. Teachers initially lead students through the comprehension strategies. Gradually, students progress through their zones of proximal development, taking more and more control of the strategies, until they assume the teaching role. The method has shown impressive success in raising reading comprehension levels, particularly for students with reading difficulties (Greenway, 2002; Takala, 2006; Spörer, Brunstein, & Kieschke, 2009).

- **How do Vygotsky's approaches to teaching differ from those of Piaget?**

- **Given Vygotsky's emphasis on culture, how would educational practice differ according to the culture in which education was being carried out?**

Although this conversation isn't particularly sophisticated, it illustrates the practice of scaffolding. The mother is supporting her son's efforts, and she gets him to respond conversationally. In the process, she not only expands her son's abilities by using a different tool (the scoop instead of the spoon), she models how conversations proceed.

In some societies parental support for learning differs by gender. In one study, Mexican mothers were found to provide more scaffolding than fathers. A possible explanation is that mothers may be more aware of their children's cognitive abilities than are fathers (Tenenbaum & Leaper, 1998; Tamis-LeMonda & Cabrera, 2002).

**FROM AN
EDUCATOR'S
PERSPECTIVE:**

How might a teacher use Vygotsky's approach to teach 10-year-olds about colonial America?

Cultural Tools

One key aspect of the aid that more accomplished individuals provide to learners comes in the form of cultural tools. *Cultural tools* are actual, physical items (e.g., pencils, paper, calculators, computers, and so forth), as well as an intellectual and conceptual framework for solving problems. The intellectual and conceptual framework available to learners includes the language that is used within a culture, its alphabetical and numbering schemes, its mathematical and scientific systems, and even its religious systems. These cultural tools provide a structure that can be used to help children define and solve specific problems, as well as an intellectual point of view that encourages cognitive development.

For an example of the pervasive influence of culture on thinking and action, consider the *Developmental Diversity* feature.

Evaluating Vygotsky's Contributions

Vygotsky's view has become increasingly influential, which is surprising given that he died nearly 80 years ago at the young age of 37 (Winsler, 2003; Gredler & Shields, 2008). His influence has grown because his writings are only now becoming widely disseminated in

DEVELOPMENTAL DIVERSITY AND YOUR LIFE

A Walk through a Cultural Landscape

"Dad, how far is it to school?"

"It's about three blocks past the supermarket."

"School is about a 20-minute ride downtown on the subway that stops across the street from our apartment."

"If you walk to the public well, and then walk that distance again, and then again, you will reach the school."

"You know how the boys and girls all race to that tall tree in the grove by the river? The school is maybe two of those races from our house, in the direction of the morning sun."

Our culture is all around us, as invisible and as much taken for granted as water is to fish. No matter what we do or think about, we are expressing ourselves in terms of our culture.

Consider the cultural differences in how people talk about distance. In cities, distance is usually measured in blocks ("the store is about 15 blocks away"). To a child from a rural background, more culturally meaningful terms are needed, such as yards or miles, such practical rules of thumb as "a stone's throw," or references to known distances and landmarks ("about half the distance to town"). To make matters more complicated, "how far" questions are sometimes answered in terms not of distance, but of time ("it's about 15 minutes to the store"), which will be understood variously to refer to walking or riding time, depending on context—and, if riding time, to different forms of riding—by ox cart, bicycle, bus, canoe, or automobile, again depending on cultural context.

In short, not only is the nature of the tools available to children to solve problems and perform tasks highly dependent on the culture in which they live, but also the ways they think about problems and questions, and the ways they use those tools. ■

the United States due to the increased availability of good English translations. For most of the 20th century, Vygotsky was not widely known even within his native land. His work was banned for some time, and it was not until the breakup of the Soviet Union in the 1990s that it became freely available in the formerly Soviet countries. Thus, Vygotsky, long hidden from his fellow developmentalists, didn't emerge onto the scene until long after his death (Wertsch, 2008; Aleksandrova-Howell, Abramson, & Craig, 2012).

Even more important, though, is the quality of Vygotsky's ideas. They represent a consistent theoretical system and help explain a growing body of research on the importance of social interaction in promoting cognitive development. The idea that children's comprehension of the world flows from their interactions with their parents, peers, and other members of society is both appealing and well supported by research findings. It is also consistent with a growing body of multicultural and cross-cultural research, which finds evidence that cognitive development is shaped, in part, by cultural factors (Daniels, 1996; Scrimsher & Tudge, 2003).

Of course, not every aspect of Vygotsky's theorizing has been supported, and he can be criticized for a lack of precision in his conceptualization of cognitive growth. For instance, such broad concepts as the zone of proximal development are not terribly precise, and they do not always lend themselves to experimental tests (Wertsch, 1999; Daniels, 2006).

Furthermore, Vygotsky was largely silent on how basic cognitive processes such as attention and memory develop and how children's natural cognitive capabilities unfold. Because of his emphasis on broad cultural influences, he did not focus on how individual bits of information are processed and synthesized. These processes, which must be taken into account if we are to have a complete understanding of cognitive development, are more directly addressed by information-processing theories (discussed in the next chapter).

Still, Vygotsky's melding of the cognitive and social worlds of children has been an important advance in our understanding of cognitive development. We can only imagine what his impact would have been if he had lived a longer life.

Review, Check, and Apply

Review

1. Lev Vygotsky proposed that the nature and progress of children's cognitive development are dependent on the children's social and cultural context.

2. According to Vygotsky, culture and society determine how people engage in thought and set the agenda for education and the cognitive abilities that their members are expected to attain.

3. Vygotsky's theory introduces the concepts of the zone of proximal development and scaffolding.

4. Vygotsky suggests that schoolchildren should have the opportunity to experiment and participate actively with their peers in their learning.

5. Vygotsky's ideas have influenced educational practices in the United States and other nations. In particular, the practice of cooperative learning and the technique of reciprocal teaching owe their development to his insights about how teachers can best help their students learn.

6. Despite a lack of precision about basic cognitive processes, Vygotsky has become in the years since his death an influential figure in the study of cognitive development and the practice of education.

Check

1. The _____ is the level at which a child can *almost,* but not fully, perform a task independently, but can do so with the assistance of someone more competent.

2. Providing temporary support for learning and problem solving to encourage independence and growth is a practice Vygotsky called _____.

3. When children work in groups to achieve a common learning task, they are engaged in _____ learning.

4. The reading comprehension technique by which students alternately adopt the role of student and teacher is called _____ _____.

Apply

1. If children's cognitive development is dependent on interactions with others, what obligations does society have regarding such social settings as preschools and neighborhoods?

2. In what ways have educators and others begun to apply Vygotsky's ideas in schools and communities? Should governments take an active role in this endeavor?

To see more review questions, log on to MyPsychLab.

ANSWERS: 1. zone of proximal development 2. scaffolding 3. cooperative 4. reciprocal teaching

The CASE
of . . . *the Risky Bet*

Sarah Canton, a second-grade practicum teacher, was assigned the mid-level reading group. As the group was small, she asked the reading specialist if she could add a student from the specialist's group—the children considered to be struggling.

The specialist reluctantly agreed to let Sarah put Maria Gonzales, age 8, in the mid-level group. "She will fall behind and feel worse about herself," the specialist warned. But Sarah had observed Maria, a shy girl, closely and felt she was capable of achieving more if appropriately challenged.

Sarah sat next to Maria the first week. The girl loved the attention and eagerly followed the lessons though she answered only when called upon. Sarah made sure to ask Maria questions she knew the girl could manage successfully.

The next week, Sarah moved among the children. She began asking Maria questions that required the girl to think a bit beyond the knowledge she possessed. She also asked Maria to interpret a poem the girl loved. Her interpretation was original and heartfelt, and the other children gave her positive feedback. Maria began raising her hand when Sarah asked for volunteers.

By the third week, Maria was posing questions in her reading journal and answering the other children's questions. Reading one-on-one with her, Sarah realized Maria's reading had jumped three levels. She continued to find links to Maria's interests and knowledge to advance the girl's understanding. When the marking period ended, Maria had made the most progress and was now reading above grade level. Best of all, she was writing poetry and stories of her own.

1. What Piagetian stage do you think Maria had reached by the beginning of second grade? How might Sarah have gone about deciding what "appropriate challenge" meant for Maria?

2. What considerations may have prompted Sarah's decisions to sit next to Maria for the first week and, initially, to restrict her questions to those she was certain Maria already had the knowledge to answer successfully? Can you explain these choices in terms of the theories of Piaget? Of Vygotsky?

3. Do you think Sarah was putting Maria at risk when she asked her to interpret a poem for the group? Why or why not?

4. How did the posing of questions for the group in her reading journal, and answering the other children's questions, support Maria's growth as a reader? What instructional technique is this approach an example of?

5. What is the significance of Sarah's efforts to find links in the reading lessons to Maria's interests and current knowledge? Explain your thinking in terms of Vygotsky's theories.

◀◀◀ LOOKING BACK

LO 6-1 What are the fundamental features of Piaget's theory of cognitive development?

- Piaget's stage theory asserts that children pass through stages of cognitive development in a fixed order, representing changes not only in quantity of infants' knowledge but also in the quality of that knowledge.

- According to Piaget, all children pass gradually through the four major stages of cognitive development (sensorimotor, preoperational, concrete operational, and formal operational) when they are at an appropriate level of maturation and are exposed to relevant types of experiences.

LO 6-2 According to Piaget, how does cognitive development proceed during infancy?

- During the sensorimotor period (birth to about 2 years), with its six substages, infants progress from the use of simple reflexes through the development of repeated and integrated actions that gradually increase in complexity to the ability to generate purposeful effects from their actions.

- By the end of the sixth substage of the sensorimotor period, infants are beginning to engage in symbolic thought.

LO 6-3 How does Piaget explain cognitive development during the preschool years?

- During the preoperational stage, children are not yet able to engage in organized, formal, logical thinking. However, their development

of symbolic function permits quicker and more effective thinking as they are freed from the limitations of sensorimotor learning.

- According to Piaget, children in the preoperational stage engage in intuitive thought for the first time, actively applying rudimentary reasoning skills to the acquisition of world knowledge.

LO 6-4 In what ways do children develop cognitively during middle childhood and adolescence?

- According to Piaget, school-age children enter the concrete operational period and for the first time become capable of applying logical thought processes to concrete problems.

- Cognitive growth during adolescence is rapid, with gains in abstract thinking, reasoning, and the ability to view possibilities in relative rather than in absolute terms.

- Adolescence coincides with Piaget's formal operations period of development, when people begin to engage in abstract thought and experimental reasoning.

LO 6-5 How has Piaget's theory been supported and challenged by later research?

- Piaget was a gifted reporter of children's behavior, and his descriptions of growth during infancy remain a monument to his powers of observation.

- However, subsequent research has challenged the stage conception that forms the basis of Piaget's theory, because it appears that development proceeds in a much more continuous fashion.

LO 6-6 What is Vygotsky's approach to cognitive development?

- Lev Vygotsky proposed that the nature and progress of children's cognitive development are dependent on the children's social and cultural context.

- Vygotsky proposes that children's comprehension of the world is an outcome of their interactions with their parents, peers, and other members of society. Vygotsky's theories are consistent with a growing body of multicultural and cross-cultural research, which finds evidence that cognitive development is shaped, in part, by cultural factors.

KEY TERMS AND CONCEPTS

scheme (p. 163)
assimilation (p. 163)
accommodation (p. 163)
sensorimotor stage (p. 164)
goal-directed behavior (p. 166)
object permanence (p. 166)
mental representation (p. 168)

deferred imitation (p. 168)
preoperational stage (p. 169)
operations (p. 169)
symbolic function (p. 169)
centration (p. 169)
conservation (p. 170)
transformation (p. 171)

egocentric thought (p. 172)
intuitive thought (p. 172)
concrete operational stage (p. 174)
decentering (p. 174)
formal operational stage (p. 175)
zone of proximal development (ZPD) (p. 183)
scaffolding (p. 184)

Epilogue

We have examined the work of two major cognitive development researchers, Jean Piaget and Lev Vygotsky, as well as several critics of their approaches. We have seen the weighty influence of Piaget's work on subsequent theoretical approaches and experimental work, and we have marveled at the posthumous ability of a Russian psychologist to build a structure of theory and thought that has recently gained a strong footing in American education.

Think back to Jared, the boy we looked in on at ages from 7 months to 17 years, and who began this chapter. Jared shows a pace and range of cognitive development that are on the one hand ordinary for children of all cultures, and on the other hand quite breathtaking. Consider these questions about Jared.

1. With what Piagetian stages do Jared's actions at 7 months and 5, 11, and 17 years most closely align? What are some characteristics in Jared's behavior that suggest which stage he has reached?

2. What would be Vygotsky's approach to instruction if he were a teacher in Jared's kindergarten or sixth grade? How might the U.S. Constitution project be handled differently by a teacher steeped in the zone of proximal development and scaffolding?

The Development Video Series in MyPsychLab

Explore the video **Object Permanence Across Cultures** by scanning this QR code with your mobile device. If you don't already have one, you may download a free QR scanner for your device wherever smartphone apps are sold. You can also view this video in MyPsychLab. For more videos related to this chapter's content, log into MyPsychLab to view the entire Development Video Series.

MyVirtualChild

- **What decisions would you make while raising a child?**
- **What would the consequences of those decisions be?**

Find out by accessing **MyVirtualChild** at
www.MyPsychLab.com
and raising your own virtual child from birth to age 18.

7 Cognitive Development: Information Processing

MODULE 7.1

THE BASICS OF INFORMATION PROCESSING

- Encoding, Storage, and Retrieval: The Foundations of Information Processing
- Early Abilities
- Information Processing Perspectives: Gradual Transformations in Abilities
- Egocentrism in Thinking: Adolescents' Self-Absorption

DEVELOPMENTAL DIVERSITY AND YOUR LIFE: Overcoming Gender and Racial Barriers to Achievement

Review, Check, and Apply

MODULE 7.2

MEMORY AND ATTENTION

- The Three-System Approach to Memory
- Memory During Infancy: They Must Remember This . . .
- Memory in Early Childhood
- Memory Development in the School Years
- The Cognitive Neuroscience of Memory

ARE YOU AN INFORMED CONSUMER OF DEVELOPMENT? Effective Strategies for Remembering

NEUROSCIENCE AND DEVELOPMENT: Memory and the Brain: I Am Stuck on Palmitate, and Palmitate Is Stuck in Me

- Attention

FROM RESEARCH TO PRACTICE: Attention Deficit Hyperactivity Disorder: A Failure in Attention

Review, Check, and Apply

MODULE 7.3

APPLYING INFORMATION PROCESSING APPROACHES

- Forensic Developmental Psychology: Bringing Child Development to the Courtroom
- Information Processing Contributions to the Classroom

CAREERS IN DEVELOPMENT: Mary Kriebel, Reading Resource Teacher

- Information Processing Approaches in Perspective

Review, Check, and Apply

The Case of . . . *the Frustrated Fantasy*

Looking Back

Key Terms and Concepts

Epilogue

PROLOGUE: Forgotten Memories

Arif Terzić was born during the war in Bosnia. He spent his first two years hiding in a basement with his mother. The only light he saw came from a kerosene lamp. The only sounds he heard were his mother's hushed lullabies and the explosion of shells. Someone he never saw left food for them. There was a water faucet, but sometimes the water was too filthy to drink. At one point, his mother suffered a kind of breakdown. She fed him when she remembered. But she didn't speak. Or sing.

Arif was lucky. His family emigrated to the United States when he was two. His father found work. They rented a little house. Arif went to preschool, then kindergarten. Today, he has friends, toys, a dog, and loves soccer. "He doesn't remember Bosnia," his mother says. "It's like it never happened."

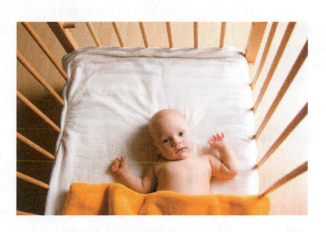

>>> LOOKING AHEAD

Did Arif really forget the first two years of his life, or do his memories still exist, hidden behind more current—and pleasant—recollections? Will he ever recall his past? Will any memories of his infancy be accurate?

We address these and related questions in this chapter as we continue our consideration of cognitive development. In this chapter we diverge from the roads that Piaget and Vygotsky laid out for us. Rather than seeking to identify universal milestones in cognitive development, as Piaget tried to do, or to recognize the contribution of the social world to thinking, as Vygotsky attempted, we now take a different approach based on *information processing*. According to the information processing approach, we can best understand cognitive development by considering the processes by which individuals acquire and use the information to which they are exposed. We focus on quantitative changes in children's mental processes and track their cognitive growth using this lens.

We first consider the notion that the foundations of information processing can be found in three elementary functions—encoding, storage, and retrieval—that are involved in any processing of information, whether by humans or computers. Using an information processing point of view, we trace some signal developmental changes in infants, children, and adolescents that are of particular importance to cognitive

(continued)

Learning Objectives

MODULE 7.1

LO1 What fundamental processes underlie information processing?

LO2 How does the information processing perspective explain cognitive development as children grow?

LO3 What are some effects of changes in information processing during adolescence?

MODULE 7.2

LO4 What is the structure of memory according to the information processing model?

LO5 How do memory processes change as children grow?

LO6 What is the role of attention in the processing of information?

MODULE 7.3

LO7 What have been some practical applications of information processing research?

LO8 Overall, what contributions has the information processing model offered to our understanding of development?

growth. We also take a close look at how a key developmental change—the emergence of metacognition—can affect adolescents' self-perceptions and behavior.

Then we turn to memory, discussing first the early development of basic memory capabilities and the surprising retention of information even at very young ages. We discuss how infants' memories become lost or corrupted, and we examine the reliability of children's memories of their own experiences. We then consider how and why memory improves as children age, and we discuss strategies that people use to control and improve cognitive processing.

We also address the topic of attention, discussing the functions and development of attention in children, the use of planning and control strategies to focus attention, and the ways that attention affects our ability to accomplish our goals and complete our tasks. As part of this discussion, we focus briefly on an increasingly prevalent attention disorder that affects learning and normal life functioning.

Finally, we conclude the chapter with a look at some practical applications of information processing theory in the courtroom and the classroom. We also offer a general appraisal of the information processing perspective and its contributions to our understanding of human cognition.

MODULE 7.1

THE BASICS OF INFORMATION PROCESSING

LO 7-1 What fundamental processes underlie information processing?

LO 7-2 How does the information processing perspective explain cognitive development as children grow?

LO 7-3 What are some effects of changes in information processing during adolescence?

Encoding, Storage, and Retrieval: The Foundations of Information Processing

Information processing approaches to cognitive development seek to identify the ways that individuals take in, use, and store information. According to this approach, the quantitative changes in our ability to organize and manipulate information are the hallmarks of cognitive development.

From this perspective, cognitive growth is characterized by increasing sophistication, speed, and capacity in information processing. Earlier, we compared Piaget's idea of schemes to computer software, which directs the computer in how to deal with data from the world. We might compare the information processing perspective on cognitive growth to the improvements that come from the use of more efficient programs that lead to increased speed and sophistication in the processing of information. Information processing approaches, then, focus on the types of "mental programs" that people use when they seek to solve problems (Cohen & Cashon, 2003; Mayer, 2012).

Information processing has three basic aspects: encoding, storage, and retrieval (see Figure 7-1). *Encoding* is the process by which information is initially recorded in a form usable to memory. People are exposed to a massive amount of information; if they tried to process it all, they would be overwhelmed. Consequently, they encode selectively, picking and choosing the information to which they will pay attention.

Even if we have been exposed to the information initially and have encoded it in an appropriate way, there is still no guarantee that we will be able to use it in the future. Information must also have been adequately stored in memory. *Storage* refers to the placement of

information-processing approaches The model that seeks to identify the way that individuals take in, use, and store information

FIGURE 7-1 Information Processing

The process by which information is encoded, stored, and retrieved.

material into memory. Finally, success in using the material in the future depends on retrieval processes. *Retrieval* is the process by which material in memory storage is located, brought into awareness, and used.

We can use our comparison to computers again here. Information processing approaches suggest that the processes of encoding, storage, and retrieval are analogous to different parts of a computer. Encoding can be thought of as a computer's keyboard, through which one inputs information; storage is the computer's hard drive, where information is stored; and retrieval is analogous to software that accesses the information for display on the screen. Only when all three processes are operating—encoding, storage, and retrieval—can information be processed.

Automatization. In some cases, encoding, storage, and retrieval are relatively automatic, while in other cases they are deliberate. *Automatization* is the degree to which an activity requires attention. Processes that require relatively little attention are automatic; processes that require relatively large amounts of attention are controlled. For example, some activities such as walking, eating with a fork, or reading may be automatic for you, but at first they required your full attention.

Automatic mental processes help children in their initial encounters with the world by enabling them to easily and "automatically" process information in particular ways. For instance, by the age of 5, children automatically encode information in terms of frequency. Without a lot of attention to counting or tallying, they become aware, for example, of how often they have encountered various people, permitting them to differentiate familiar from unfamiliar people.

Early Abilities

Without intending to and without being aware of it, infants and children develop a sense of how often different stimuli are found together simultaneously. This permits them to develop an understanding of *concepts*, categorizations of objects, events, or people that share common properties. For example, by encoding the information that four legs, a wagging tail, and barking are often found together, we learn very early in life to understand the concept of "dog." Children—as well as adults—are rarely aware of how they learn such concepts, and they are often unable to articulate the features that distinguish one concept (such as a dog) from another (such as cat). Instead, learning tends to occur automatically.

Some of the things we learn automatically are unexpectedly complex. For example, infants have the ability to learn subtle statistical patterns and relationships; these results are consistent with a growing body of research showing that the mathematical skills of infants are surprisingly good. Infants as young as 5 months are able to calculate the outcome of simple addition and subtraction problems. In a study by developmental psychologist Karen Wynn, infants first were shown an object—a 4-inch-high Mickey Mouse statuette (see Figure 7-2 on page 194). A screen was then raised, hiding the statuette. Next, the experimenter showed the infants a second, identical Mickey Mouse, and then placed it behind the same screen (Wynn, 1995, 2000).

Depending on the experimental condition, one of two outcomes occurred. In the "correct addition" condition, the screen dropped, revealing the two statuettes (analogous to $1 + 1 = 2$).

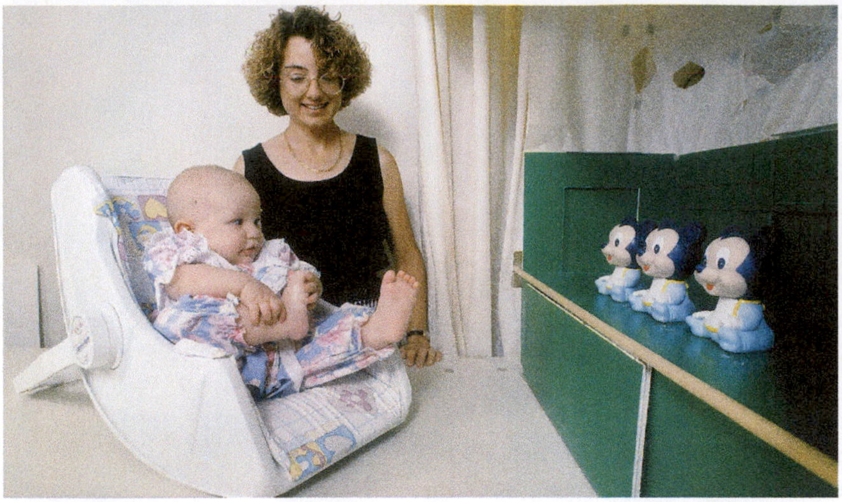

FIGURE 7-2 Mickey Mouse Math

Researcher Karen Wynn found that 5-month-olds like Michelle Follet, pictured here, reacted differently according to whether the number of Mickey Mouse statuettes they saw represented correct or incorrect addition. Do you think this ability is unique to humans? How would an educator explain the uniqueness of this ability?

But in the "incorrect addition" condition, the screen dropped to reveal just one statuette (analogous to the incorrect $1 + 1 = 1$).

Because infants look longer at unexpected occurrences than at expected ones, the researchers examined the pattern of infants' gazes under the different conditions. In support of the notion that infants can distinguish between correct and incorrect addition, the infants in the experiment gazed longer at the incorrect result than at the correct one, indicating they expected a different number of statuettes. In a similar procedure, infants also looked longer at incorrect subtraction problems than at correct ones. The conclusion: Infants have rudimentary mathematical skills that enable them to understand whether or not a quantity is accurate.

The results of this growing body of research suggest that infants have an innate grasp of certain basic mathematical functions and statistical patterns. This inborn proficiency is likely to form the basis for learning more complex mathematics and statistical relationships later in life (vanMarle & Wynn, 2006, 2009; McCrink & Wynn, 2004, 2007, 2009).

Information-Processing Perspectives: Gradual Transformations in Abilities

Cognitive Growth during the School Years.
According to *information processing approaches*, children become increasingly sophisticated in their handling of information. Like computers, they can process more data as the size of their memories increases and the "programs" they use to process information become increasingly sophisticated (Kail, 2003; Zelazo et al., 2003; Aslin, 2012).

For example, first-graders learn basic math tasks, such as addition and subtraction of single-digit numbers, as well as the spelling of simple words such as *dog* and *run*. But by the time they reach the sixth grade, children are able to work with fractions and decimals and spell such words as *exhibit* and *residence*.

Explaining the Teenage (Mental) Growth Spurt.
From the perspective of proponents of information processing approaches to cognitive development, adolescence is a particularly significant period. Clearly, adolescents' mental abilities grow gradually and continuously. Unlike Piaget's view that the increasing cognitive sophistication of the adolescent is a reflection of stagelike spurts, the *information processing perspective* sees changes in adolescents' cognitive abilities as evidence of gradual transformations in the capacity to take in, use, and store information. A number of progressive changes occur in the ways adolescents organize their thinking about the world, develop strategies for dealing with new situations, sort facts, and achieve advances in memory capacity and perceptual abilities. According to the information processing perspective, this gradual quantitative improvement is sufficient to explain the substantial changes in thinking that characterize the adolescent years (Wyer, 2004; Atkins et al., 2012).

Adolescents' general intelligence—as measured by traditional IQ tests—remains stable, but there are dramatic improvements in the specific mental abilities that underlie intelligence. Verbal, mathematical, and spatial abilities increase, making many adolescents quicker with a comeback, impressive sources of information, and accomplished athletes. Memory capacity grows, and adolescents become more adept at effectively dividing their attention across more than one stimulus at a time—such as simultaneously studying for a biology test and listening to a Lady Gaga CD.

Furthermore, as Piaget noted, adolescents grow increasingly sophisticated in their understanding of problems, their ability to grasp abstract concepts and think hypothetically, and their comprehension of the possibilities inherent in situations. This permits them, for instance, to endlessly dissect the course that their relationships might hypothetically take.

Adolescents know more about the world, too. Their store of knowledge increases as the amount of material to which they are exposed grows and their memory capacity enlarges. Taken as a whole, the mental abilities that underlie intelligence show a marked improvement during adolescence (Kail, 2003, 2004; Kail & Miller, 2006; Reyna & Dougherty, 2012).

According to information processing explanations of cognitive development during adolescence, one of the most important reasons for advances in mental abilities is the growth of metacognition. **Metacognition** is the knowledge that people have about their own thinking processes, and their ability to monitor their cognition. Although school-age children can use some metacognitive strategies, adolescents are much more adept at understanding their own mental processes.

For example, as adolescents improve their understanding of their memory capacity, they get better at gauging how long they need to study a particular kind of material to memorize it for a test. Furthermore, they can judge when they have fully memorized the material with considerably more accuracy than when they were younger. These improvements in metacognitive abilities permit adolescents to comprehend and master school material more effectively (Kuhn, 2000; Desoete, Roeyers, & De Clercq, 2003; Moshman, 2011).

These new abilities also can make adolescents particularly introspective and self-conscious—two hallmarks of the period that, as we see next, may produce a high degree of egocentrism.

Adolescents' egocentrism leads to the belief that what happens to them is unique and to feelings of invulnerability—producing risky behavior.

Egocentrism in Thinking: Adolescents' Self-Absorption

Carlos thinks of his parents as "control freaks." He cannot figure out why they insist that, when he borrows their car, he call home and let them know where he is.

Jeri is thrilled that Molly bought earrings just like hers, thinking it is the ultimate compliment, even though it's not clear that Molly even knew that Jeri had a similar pair when she bought them.

Lu is upset with his biology teacher, Ms. Sebastian, for giving a long, difficult midterm exam on which he didn't do well.

Adolescents' newly sophisticated metacognitive abilities enable them to readily imagine that others are thinking about them, and they may construct elaborate scenarios about others' thoughts. Improved metacognition is also the source of the egocentrism that sometimes dominates adolescents' thinking. **Adolescent egocentrism** is a state of self-absorption in which the world is viewed as focused on oneself. This egocentrism makes adolescents highly critical of authority figures such as parents and teachers, unwilling to accept criticism, and quick to find fault with others' behavior (Greene, Krcmar, & Rubin, 2002; Alberts, Elkind, & Ginsberg, 2007; Schwartz, Maynard, & Uzelac, 2008).

The kind of egocentrism we see in adolescence helps explain why adolescents sometimes perceive that they are the focus of everyone else's attention. In fact, adolescents may develop what has been called an **imaginary audience,** fictitious observers who pay as much attention to the adolescents' behavior as adolescents do themselves.

The imaginary audience is usually perceived as focusing on the one thing that adolescents think most about: themselves. Unfortunately, these scenarios may suffer from the same kind of egocentrism as the rest of their thinking. For instance, a student sitting in a class may be sure a teacher is focusing on her, and a teenager at a basketball game is likely to be convinced that everyone around is focusing on the pimple on his chin.

metacognition The knowledge that people have about their own thinking processes and their ability to monitor their cognition

adolescent egocentrism A state of self-absorption in which the world is viewed from one's own point of view

imaginary audience Fictitious observers who pay as much attention to adolescents' behavior as they do themselves

Watch the **Video** *Adolescent Egocentrism* in **MyPsychLab**.

Watch the **Video** *Imaginary Audience* in **MyPsychLab**.

FROM A
SOCIAL WORKER'S

PERSPECTIVE:

In what ways does adolescent egocentrism complicate adolescents' social and family relationships? Do adults entirely outgrow egocentrism and personal fables?

Egocentrism leads to a second distortion in thinking: the notion that one's experiences are unique. Adolescents develop **personal fables,** the view that what happens to them is unique, exceptional, and shared by no one else. For instance, teenagers whose romantic relationships have ended may feel that no one has ever experienced the hurt they feel, that no one has ever been treated so badly, that no one can understand what they are going through (Alberts, Elkind, & Ginsberg, 2007; Hill & Lapsley, 2011).

Personal fables also may make adolescents feel invulnerable to the risks that threaten others. Much of adolescents' risk-taking may well be traced to the personal fables they construct for themselves. They may think that there is no need to use condoms during sex because, in the personal fables they construct, pregnancy and sexually transmitted diseases such as AIDS only happen to other kinds of people, not to them. They may drive after drinking, because their personal fables paint them as careful drivers, always in control (Vartanian, 2000; Aalsma, Lapsley, & Flannery, 2006; Chick & Reyna, 2012).

 DEVELOPMENTAL DIVERSITY AND YOUR LIFE

Overcoming Gender and Racial Barriers to Achievement

In her 10th-grade math class, Frankie Teague dimmed the lights, switched on soothing music, and handed each student a whiteboard and a marker. Then, she projected an arithmetic problem onto a screen at the front of the room.

"As soon as you get the answer, hold up your board," she said, setting off a round of squeaky scribbling. The simple step of having students hold up their work, instead of raising their hands or shouting out the answer, gives a leg up to a group of pupils who have long lagged in math classes—girls. (Whalen & Begley, 2005, p. A1)

This simple innovation is part of a large-scale, and ultimately successful, effort to improve the teaching of math in British schools. Although meant to benefit all children, it has had an unintended result: erasing a gender gap that favored boys over girls in math performance.

As illustrated in Figure 7-3, the introduction of the new math curriculum in the late 1980s brought about a rise in overall math exam scores. But the rise was more pronounced for girls, and today girls outperform boys on some standardized math tests.

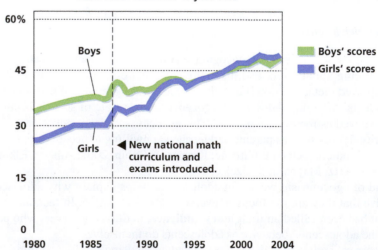

Percentage of English boys and girls earning passing grades of A through C on the state math exam for 18-year-olds

FIGURE 7-3 The New Math

After the introduction of a new math curriculum and exams in England, girls' and boys' performance began to converge.

(*Source:* Department for Education and Skills, England 2004)

personal fables   The view held by some adolescents that what happens to them is unique, exceptional, and shared by no one else

What changes in the curriculum led to the improvement in performance? Teachers were taught to be on the alert for gender stereotyping in their courses, and they were encouraged to include girls in discussions more vigorously. In addition, gender stereotypes were removed from textbooks. Classrooms were made "safer" for girls by discouraging students from shouting out answers and by encouraging girls more directly to participate. Tests were changed, too, to give partial credit when students write out their thinking—something that benefited girls, who tend to be more methodical when working on test items. ■

Academic Performance and Stereotype Threat.

Research on gender stereotypes in the United States suggests that the curricular changes adopted in England are moving in the right direction. For instance, consider this fact: When women take college classes in math, science, and engineering, they are more likely to do poorly than are men who enter college with the same level of preparation and identical SAT scores. Strangely, however, this phenomenon does not hold true for other areas of the curriculum, where men and women perform at similar levels.

According to psychologist Claude Steele, the reason behind the declining levels of performance for both women and African Americans is the same: *academic disidentification*, a lack of personal identification with an academic domain. For women, disidentification is specific to math and science; for African Americans, it is more generalized across academic domains. In both cases, negative societal stereotypes produce a state of *stereotype threat* in which members of the group fear that their behavior will indeed confirm the stereotype (Carr & Steele, 2009; Shapiro, 2012).

For instance, women seeking to achieve in nontraditional fields that rely on math and science may be hindered as they become distracted by worries about the failure that society predicts for them. In some cases, a woman may decide that failure in a male-dominated field, because it would confirm societal stereotypes, presents such great risks that, paradoxically, the struggle to succeed is not worth the effort. In that instance, the woman may not even try very hard (Inzlicht & Ben-Zeev, 2000; Logel, Peach, & Spencer, 2012).

Similarly, African Americans may work under the pressure of feeling that they must disconfirm the negative stereotype regarding their academic performance. The pressure can be anxiety-provoking and threatening, and it can reduce their performance below their true ability level. Ironically, stereotype threat may be most severe for better, more confident students, who have not internalized the negative stereotype to the extent of questioning their own abilities (Carr & Steele, 2009).

But there is a bright side to Steele's analysis: If women can be convinced that societal stereotypes regarding achievement are invalid, their performance might well improve. And in fact, this is just what Steele found in a series of experiments he conducted at the University of Michigan and Stanford University (Steele, 1997).

In one study, male and female college students were told they would be taking two math tests: one in which there were gender differences—men supposedly performed better than women—and a second in which there were no gender differences. In reality, the tests were entirely similar, drawn from the same pool of difficult items. The reasoning behind the experimental manipulation was that women would be vulnerable to societal stereotypes on a test that they thought supported those stereotypes but would not be vulnerable on a test supposedly lacking gender differences.

The results fully supported Steele's reasoning. When the women were told there were gender differences in the test, they greatly underperformed the men. But when they were told there were no gender differences, they performed virtually the same as the men.

In short, the evidence from this study and others clearly suggests that women are vulnerable to expectations regarding their future success, whether the expectations come from societal stereotypes or from information about the prior performance of women on similar tasks. More encouraging, the evidence suggests that if women can be convinced that others have been successful in given domains, they may overcome even longstanding societal stereotypes (Croizet et al., 2004; Davies, Spencer, & Steele, 2005; Good, Aronson, & Harder, 2008).

Women choosing traditionally male fields such as math and science can overcome even longstanding societal stereotypes if they are convinced that others like them.

Watch the **Video** *In the Real World: Intelligence Tests and Stereotypes* in **MyPsychLab**.

We should also keep in mind that women are not the only group susceptible to society's stereotyping. Members of minority groups, such as African Americans and Hispanic Americans, are also vulnerable to stereotypes about academic success. In fact, Steele suggests that African Americans may "disidentify" with academic success by putting forth less effort on academic tasks and generally downgrading the importance of academic achievement. Ultimately, such disidentification may act as a self-fulfilling prophecy, increasing the chances of academic failure (Perry, Steele, & Hilliard, 2003; Ryan & Ryan, 2005; Davis, Aronson, & Salinas, 2006; Kellow & Jones, 2008).

Review, Check, and Apply

Review

1. Researchers taking an information processing approach view quantitative changes in our ability to take in, use, and store information—encoding, storage, and retrieval—as the hallmarks of cognitive development. Automatization refers to the degree to which these processes require attention.

2. According to the information processing perspective, children's increasing sophistication in their handling and processing of information is a function of gradual quantitative improvements in cognition, rather than the qualitative, stagelike progressions proposed by Piaget.

3. Adolescents' increasing metacognitive abilities permit them to assess their cognitive capacities more accurately and use their mental resources more efficiently, but can also bring about adolescent egocentrism, which underlies the sense that they are being observed at all times by an imaginary audience and the creation of personal fables of invulnerability.

Check

1. The three fundamental processes involved in information processing are _____, _____, and _____.

2. The degree to which a mental activity requires attention or is performed without conscious thought is called _____.

3. Much research on infants' attention and cognition depends on the fact that infants look _____ at unexpected outcomes than at expected ones.

4. The knowledge that people have about their own thinking processes is called _____.

5. Adolescent _____ describes the tendency of adolescents to view the world as focused on themselves.

Apply

1. It has been said that poets and artists process information differently than other people. Do you agree? Why? If you agree, in which of the three basic processes—encoding, storage, or retrieval—do you think the difference mostly lies?

2. Automatization in information processing can backfire, producing an automatic response when a non-automatic response is required. Can you think of instances when this happens? Can anything be done about it?

To see more review questions, log on to MyPsychLab.

ANSWERS: 1. encoding, storage, retrieval 2. automatization 3. longer 4. metacognition 5. egocentrism

MODULE 7.2

MEMORY AND ATTENTION

LO 7-4 What is the structure of memory according to the information processing model?

LO 7-5 How do memory processes change as children grow?

LO 7-6 What is the role of attention in the processing of information?

Amber Nordstrom, 3 months old, breaks into a smile as her brother Marcus stands over her crib, picks up a doll, and makes a whistling noise through his teeth. In fact, Amber never seems to tire of Marcus's efforts at making her smile, and soon whenever Marcus appears and simply picks up the doll, her lips begin to curl into a smile.

Clearly, Amber remembers Marcus and his humorous ways. But how does she remember him? And how much else can Amber remember?

To answer questions such as these, we again need to diverge from the road that Piaget laid out for us. Rather than seeking to identify broad, universal milestones in cognitive development, as Piaget tried to do, we must consider the specific processes by which individuals acquire and use the information to which they are exposed. We need, then, to focus less on qualitative changes and more on quantitative capabilities.

The Three-System Approach to Memory

As we have seen, **memory** in the information processing model is the ability to encode, store, and retrieve information. For a child to remember a piece of information, the three processes must all function properly. Through *encoding,* the child initially records the information in a form usable to memory. Children who were never taught that 5 plus 6 equals 11 or who didn't pay attention when they were exposed to this fact will never be able to recall it. They never encoded the information in the first place.

But mere exposure to a fact is not enough; the information also has to be *stored.* In our example, the information that 5 plus 6 equals 11 must be placed and maintained in the memory system. Finally, proper functioning of memory requires that material that is stored in memory must be *retrieved.* Through retrieval, material in memory storage is located, brought into awareness, and used.

According to the *three-system approach to memory* that has come to dominate our understanding of memory, there are three different memory storage systems or stages that describe how information is processed in order for it to be recalled (Atkinson & Shiffrin, 1968, 1971). *Sensory memory* refers to the initial, momentary storage of information that lasts only an instant. Sensory memory records an exact replica of the stimulus. In the second stage, *short-term memory* (also known as *working memory*), information is stored for 15 to 25 seconds according to its meaning. Finally, the third type of storage system is *long-term memory,* in which information is stored relatively permanently, although it may be difficult to retrieve.

Watch the **Video** *Learning and Memory in Infants* in **MyPsychLab**.

Memory During Infancy: They Must Remember This . . .

Certainly, infants have memory capabilities, in that they can record, store, and retrieve information. As we've seen, infants can distinguish new stimuli from old stimuli, and this implies that some memory of the old must be present. Unless the infants had some memory of an original stimulus, it would be impossible for them to recognize that a new stimulus differed from the earlier one.

However, infants' ability to distinguish new stimuli from old tells us little about how age brings about changes in the capacities of memory and in its fundamental nature. Do infants' memory capabilities increase as they get older? The answer is clearly affirmative. In one

memory   The process by which information is initially recorded, stored, and retrieved

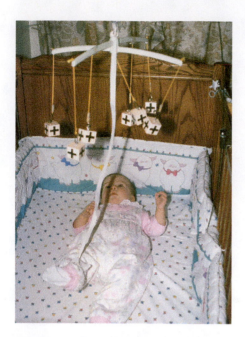

FIGURE 7-4 Early Signs of Memory

Infants who had learned the association between a moving mobile and kicking showed surprising recall ability if they were exposed to a reminder of the early memory.

study, infants were taught that they could move a mobile hanging over the crib by kicking their legs (see Figure 7-4). It took only a few days for 2-month-old infants to forget their training, but 6-month-old infants still remembered for as long as 3 weeks (Rovee-Collier, 1999; Rose et al., 2011; Cuevas, Raj, & Bell, 2012).

Furthermore, infants who were later prompted to recall the association between kicking and moving the mobile showed evidence that the memory continued to exist even longer. Infants who had received just two training sessions lasting 9 minutes each still recalled about a week later, as illustrated by the fact that they began to kick when placed in the crib with the mobile. Two weeks later, however, they made no effort to kick, suggesting that they had forgotten entirely.

But they hadn't: When the babies saw a reminder—a moving mobile—their memories were apparently reactivated. In fact, the infants could remember the association, following prompting, for as long as an additional month. Other evidence confirms these results, suggesting that hints can reactivate memories that at first seem lost, and that the older the infant, the more effective such prompting is (Sullivan, Rovee-Collier, & Tynes, 1979; Bearce & Rovee-Collier, 2006; DeFrancisco & Rovee-Collier, 2008).

Is infant memory qualitatively different from that in older children and adults? Researchers generally believe that information is processed similarly throughout the life span, even though the kind of information being processed changes and different parts of the brain may be used. According to memory expert Carolyn Rovee-Collier, people, regardless of their age, gradually lose memories, although, just like babies, they may regain them if reminders are provided. Moreover, the more times a memory is retrieved, the more enduring the memory becomes (Hsu & Rovee-Collier, 2006; Turati, 2008; Zosh, Halberda, & Feigenson, 2011).

The Duration of Memories. Although the processes that underlie memory retention and recall seem similar throughout the life span, the quantity of information stored and recalled does differ markedly as infants develop. Older infants can retrieve information more rapidly and they can remember it longer. But just how long? Can memories from infancy be recalled, for example, after babies grow up?

Researchers disagree on the age from which memories can be retrieved. Although early research supported the notion of **infantile amnesia**, the lack of memory for experiences occurring prior to 3 years of age, more recent research shows that infants do retain memories. For example, Nancy Myers and her colleagues conducted an experiment in which they showed 6-month-old children an unusual series of events, such as intermittent periods of light and dark and unusual sounds. When the children were later tested at the age of 1½ years or 2½ years, they had some memory of the earlier experience. Other research shows that infants show memory for behavior and situations that they have seen only once (Howe, Courage, & Edison, 2004; Neisser, 2004).

Such findings are consistent with evidence that the physical trace of a memory in the brain appears to be relatively permanent, suggesting that memories, even from infancy, may be enduring. However, memories may not be easily, or accurately, retrieved. For example, memories are susceptible to interference from other, newer information, which may displace or block out the older information, thereby preventing its recall.

One reason why infants appear to remember less may be because language plays a key role in determining the way in which memories from early in life can be recalled: Older children and adults may only be able to report memories using the vocabulary that they had available at the time of the initial event, when the memories were stored. Because their vocabulary at the time of initial storage may have been quite limited, they are unable to describe the event later in life, even though it is actually in their memories (Bauer et al., 2000; Simcock & Hayne, 2002; Heimann et al., 2006).

The question of how well memories formed during infancy are retained in adulthood is still not fully answered. Although infants' memories may be highly detailed and can be enduring if the infants experience repeated reminders, it is still not clear how accurate those memories remain over the course of the life span. In fact, early memories are susceptible to mis-recollection if people are exposed to related but contradictory information following the initial formation of the memory. Not only does such new information potentially impair recall

infantile amnesia The lack of memory for experiences that occurred prior to 3 years of age

of the original material, but also the new material may be inadvertently incorporated into the original memory, thereby corrupting its accuracy (DuBreuil, Garry, & Loftus, 1998; Cordon et al., 2004).

In sum, the data suggest that although it is at least theoretically possible for memories to remain intact from a very young age—if subsequent experiences do not interfere with their recollection—in most cases memories of personal experiences in infancy do not last into adulthood. Current findings suggest that memories of personal experience seem not to become accurate before age 18 to 24 months (Howe, 2003; Howe et al., 2004; Bauer, 2007).

Memory in Early Childhood

Even as an adult, Paco has clear recollections of his first trip to a farm, which he took when he was 3 years old. He was visiting his godfather, who lived in Puerto Rico, and the two of them went to a nearby farm. Paco recounts seeing what seemed like hundreds of chickens, and he clearly recalls his fear of the pigs, who seemed huge, smelly, and frightening. Most of all, he recalls the thrill of riding on a horse with his godfather.

The fact that Paco has a clear memory of his farm trip is not surprising: Most people have unambiguous, and seemingly accurate, memories dating as far back as the age of 3. But are the processes used to form memories during the preschool years similar to those that operate later in life? More broadly, what general changes in the processing of information occur during the preschool years?

Information processing approaches focus on changes in the kinds of "mental programs" that children use when approaching problems. They view the changes that occur in children's cognitive abilities during the preschool years as analogous to the way a computer program becomes more sophisticated as a programmer modifies it on the basis of experience. In fact, for many child developmentalists, information processing approaches represent the dominant, most comprehensive, and ultimately the most accurate explanation of how children develop cognitively (Lacerda, von Hofsten, & Heimann, 2001; Jack, Simcock, & Hayne, 2012).

We'll focus on two areas that highlight the approach taken by information processing theorists: understanding of numbers and memory development during the preschool years.

Preschoolers' Understanding of Numbers.
As we saw earlier, one of the flaws critics have noticed in Piaget's theory is that preschoolers have a greater understanding of numbers than Piaget thought. Researchers using information processing approaches to cognitive development have found increasing evidence for the sophistication of preschoolers' understanding of numbers. The average preschooler is able not only to count, but to do so in a fairly systematic, consistent manner.

For instance, developmental psychologist Rochel Gelman suggests that preschoolers follow a number of principles in their counting. When shown a group of several items, they know they should assign just one number to each item and that each item should be counted only once. Moreover, even when they get the *names* of numbers wrong, they are consistent in their usage. For instance, a 4-year-old who counts three items as "1, 3, 7" will say "1, 3, 7" when counting another group of different items. And she will probably say that there are 7 items in the group, if asked how many there are (Gelman, 2006; Gallistel, 2007; Le Corre & Carey, 2007).

In short, preschoolers may demonstrate a surprisingly sophisticated understanding of numbers, although their understanding is not totally precise. Still, by the age of 4, most are able to carry out simple addition and subtraction problems by counting, and they are able to compare different quantities quite successfully (Gilmore & Spelke, 2008).

Memory: Recalling the Past.
Think back to your own earliest memory. If you are like Paco, described earlier, and most other people, too, your earliest memory is probably of an event that occurred after the age of 3.

Memory requires three steps: encoding, storing, and retrieving material.

How specific and accurate will these preschoolers' memories of this event be in the future?

Autobiographical memory, memory of particular events from one's own life, achieves little accuracy until after 3 years of age. Accuracy then increases gradually and slowly throughout the preschool years (Reese & Newcombe, 2007; Wang, 2008; Bohn & Berntsen, 2011).

Preschool children's recollections of events that happened to them are sometimes, but not always, accurate. For instance, 3-year-olds can remember fairly well central features of routine occurrences, such as the sequence of events involved in eating at a restaurant. In addition, preschoolers are typically accurate in their responses to open-ended questions, such as "What rides did you like best at the amusement park?" (Price & Goodman, 1990; Wang, 2006).

The accuracy of preschoolers' memories is partly determined by how soon the memories are assessed. Unless an event is particularly vivid or meaningful, it is not likely to be remembered at all. Moreover, not all autobiographical memories last into later life. For instance, a child may remember the first day of kindergarten 6 months or a year later, but later in life might not remember that day at all.

Memories are also affected by cultural factors. For example, Chinese college students' memories of early childhood are more likely to be unemotional and reflect activities involving social roles, such as working in their family's store, whereas U.S. college students' earliest memories are more emotionally elaborate and focus on specific events such as the birth of a sibling (Wang, 2006, 2007; Peterson, Wang, & Hou, 2009).

Preschoolers' autobiographical memories not only fade, but what is remembered may not be wholly accurate. For example, if an event happens often, such as a trip to a grocery store, it may be hard to remember one specific time it happened. Preschoolers' memories of familiar events are often organized in terms of **scripts,** broad representations in memory of events and the order in which they occur.

For example, a young preschooler might represent eating in a restaurant in terms of a few steps: talking to a waitress, getting food, and eating. With age, the scripts become more elaborate: getting in the car, being seated at the restaurant, choosing food, ordering, waiting for the meal to come, eating, ordering dessert, and paying for the food. Because events that are frequently repeated tend to be melded into scripts, particular instances of a scripted event are recalled with less accuracy than those that are unscripted in memory (Sutherland, Pipe, & Schick, 2003).

There are other reasons why preschoolers may not have entirely accurate autobiographical memories. Because they have difficulty describing certain kinds of information, such as complex causal relationships, they may oversimplify recollections. For example, a child who has witnessed an argument between his grandparents may only remember that Grandma took the cake away from Grandpa, not the discussion of his weight and cholesterol that led to the action. And, as we will see later in this chapter, preschoolers' memories are susceptible to the suggestions of others. This is a special concern when children are called on to testify in legal situations, such as when abuse is suspected.

Memory Development in the School Years

During middle childhood, *short-term memory* capacity improves significantly. For instance, children are increasingly able to hear a string of digits ("1-5-6-3-4") and then repeat the string in reverse order ("4-3-6-5-1"). At the start of the preschool period, they can remember and reverse only about two digits; by the beginning of adolescence, they can perform the task with as many as six digits (Cowan, Saults, & Elliot, 2002; Towse & Cowan, 2005).

Memory capacity may shed light on another issue in cognitive development. Some developmental psychologists suggest that the difficulty children experience in solving conservation problems during the preschool period may stem from memory limitations. They argue that young children simply may not be able to recall all the necessary pieces of information that enter into the correct solution of conservation problems.

autobiographical memory Memory of particular events from one's own life

scripts Broad representations in memory of events and the order in which they occur

Metamemory, an understanding about the processes that underlie memory, also emerges and improves during middle childhood. By the time they enter first grade and their theory of mind becomes more sophisticated, children have a general notion of what memory is, and they are able to understand that some people have better memories than others (Ghetti et al., 2008; Jaswal & Dodson, 2009; Grammer et al., 2011).

School-age children's understanding of memory becomes more sophisticated as they grow older and increasingly engage in *control strategies*—conscious, intentionally used tactics to improve cognitive processing. For instance, school-age children are aware that rehearsal, the repetition of information, is a useful strategy for improving memory, and they increasingly employ it over the course of middle childhood. Similarly, they progressively make more effort to organize material into coherent patterns, a strategy that permits them to recall it better. For instance, when faced with remembering a list including cups, knives, forks, and plates, older school-age children are more likely to group the items into coherent patterns—cups and plates, forks and knives—than children just entering the school-age years (Sang, Miao, & Deng, 2002).

Similarly, children in middle childhood increasingly use *mnemonics* (pronounced "neh MON ix"), which are formal techniques for organizing information in a way that makes it more likely to be remembered. For instance, they may learn that the spaces on the music staff spell the word *FACE* or learn the rhyme "Thirty days hath September, April, June, and November" to try to recall the number of days in each month (Carney & Levin, 2003; Sprenger, 2007).

Improving Memory. Can children be trained to be more effective in the use of control strategies? Definitely. School-age children can be taught to use particular mnemonic strategies, although such teaching is not a simple matter. For instance, children need to know not only how to use a memory strategy but also when and where to use it most effectively.

Take, for example, an innovative technique called the key word strategy, which can help students learn the vocabulary of a foreign language, the capitals of the states, or other information in which two sets of words or labels are paired. In the *keyword strategy,* one word is paired with another that sounds like it (Wyra, Lawson, & Hungi, 2007).

For instance, in learning foreign language vocabulary, a foreign word is paired with a common English word that has a similar sound. The English word is the keyword. Thus, to learn the Spanish word for duck (*pato,* pronounced *pot-o*), the keyword might be "pot"; for the Spanish word for horse (*caballo,* pronounced *cob-eye-yo*), the keyword might be "eye." Once the keyword is chosen, children then form a mental image of the two words interacting with one another. For instance, a student might use an image of a duck taking a bath in a pot to remember the word *pato,* or a horse with bulging eyes to remember the word *caballo*.

Other memory strategies are discussed in the *Are You an Informed Consumer* box on page 204. Whatever memory strategies children use, they use such strategies more often and more effectively as they get older.

The Cognitive Neuroscience of Memory

Some of the most exciting research on the development of memory is coming from studies of the neurological basis of memory. Advances in brain scan technology, as well as studies of adults with brain damage, suggest that there are two separate systems involved with long-term memory. These two systems, called explicit memory and implicit memory, retain different sorts of information.

Explicit memory is memory that is conscious and that can be recalled intentionally. When we try to recall a name or phone number, we're using explicit memory. In comparison, *implicit memory* consists of memories of which we are not consciously aware but that affect performance and behavior. Implicit memory consists of motor skills, habits, and activities that can be remembered without conscious cognitive effort, such as how to ride a bike or climb a stairway.

metamemory An understanding about the processes that underlie memory that emerges and improves during middle childhood

ARE YOU AN INFORMED CONSUMER OF DEVELOPMENT?

Effective Strategies for Remembering

All of us are forgetful at one time or another. However, there are techniques that can help us remember more effectively and make it less likely that we will forget things that we wish to remember. **Mnemonics** (pronounced "nee-MON-iks") are formal strategies for organizing material in ways that make it more likely to be remembered. Among commonly used mnemonics are the following (Bloom & Lamkin, 2006; Morris & Fritz, 2006; McRae, Khalkhali, & Hare, 2012).

- *Get organized.* For people who have trouble keeping track of where they left their keys or remembering appointments, the simplest approach is for them to become more organized. Using an appointment book, hanging one's keys on a hook, or using sticky notes can help jog one's memory.

- *Pay attention.* You can improve your recall by initially paying attention when you are exposed to new information, and by purposefully thinking that you wish to recall it in the future. If you are particularly concerned about remembering something, such as where you parked your car, pay particular attention at the moment you park the car, and remind yourself that you really want to remember.

- *Use the encoding specificity phenomenon.* According to the encoding specificity phenomenon, people are most likely to recall information in environments that are similar to those in which they initially learned ("encoded") it (Tulving & Thompson, 1973). For instance, people are best able to recall information on a test if the test is held in the room in which they studied.

- *Visualize.* Making mental images of ideas can help you recall them later. For example, if you want to remember that global warming may lead to a rise in the sea level, think of yourself on a beach on a hot day, with the waves coming closer and closer to where you've set out your beach blanket.

- *Rehearse.* In the realm of memory, practice makes perfect, or if not perfect, at least better. Adults of all ages can improve their memories if they expend more effort in rehearsing what they want to remember. By practicing what they wish to recall, people can substantially improve their recall of the material. ■

Watch the **Video** *Mnemonics* in **MyPsychLab**.

Explicit and implicit memory emerge at different rates and involve different parts of the brain. Earliest memories seem to be implicit, and they involve the cerebellum and brain stem. The forerunner of explicit memory involves the hippocampus, but true explicit memory doesn't emerge until the second half of the first year. When explicit memory does emerge, it involves an increasing number of areas of the cortex of the brain (Bauer, 2007; Sauzéon et al., 2012; also see the *Neuroscience and Development* box).

Attention

Two-month-old Meredith lies in her crib. Her gaze shifts from the mobile that is slowly moving above her head, repeatedly playing "Mary Had a Little Lamb," to her father, who is singing along with the tune. At the same time, her father strokes the wisps of hair on her head, as her older brother calls out from the next room, "Dad, where are you?"

Consider the multiple sources of information in Meredith's environment: the sights of the mobile and her father, the sound of the mobile and her father's and brother's voices, and the touch of her father's hand on her head. To which of these stimuli does she pay attention?

Attention: The First Step in Information Processing.   The choices Meredith makes are determined by **attention**, information processing involving the ability to strategically choose among and sort out different stimuli in the environment. Attention is the first

mnemonics   Formal strategies for organizing material in ways that make it more likely to be remembered

attention   Information processing involving the ability to strategically choose among and sort out different stimuli in the environment

NEUROSCIENCE AND DEVELOPMENT
Memory and the Brain: I Am Stuck on Palmitate, and Palmitate Is Stuck in Me

Fats tend to have a bad reputation—after all, ingesting too much fat leads to obesity and heart attacks—but it turns out that certain kinds of fats are helpful in producing long-term memories.

Recently a team of researchers at Johns Hopkins University discovered that *palmitate*, a sticky fatty acid, is involved in activation of special brain proteins called NMDA receptors that are needed in long-term memory and learning. Palmitate helps move NMDA receptors to specific locations in the brain where cell connections are strengthened or weakened to change memory circuits (Hayashi, Thomas, & Huganir, 2009).

Why is the NMDA receptor important? Some scientists believe that the NMDA receptor is related to intelligence because it plays a significant role in the rapid, intense development of the child's brain. The discovery of the palmitate–NMDA receptor connection is thus important because it offers greater understanding of how synapses

are regulated and how memory is formed. In addition, the identification of palmitate may lead to the development of drug therapies that allow for manipulation or regulation to enhance learning and memory. Ultimately, the control of disease-induced increases or decreases in NMDA receptor activity (which in turn affects memory formation and maintenance) may occur by manipulating palmitate or palmitate-like substances in the brain.

- **What ethical questions arise if substances can be identified and produced to help enhance learning and memory beyond the levels that humans naturally achieve?**

- **If the ability to manipulate or control memory enabled scientists to erase memories completely, would there be any ethical uses of such a procedure? Would you consider undergoing such "amnesia therapy"? Why?**

step in information processing. If a child doesn't attend to a stimulus, or is unaware of it in the first place, clearly that material cannot be processed further. Furthermore, if children are constantly distracted by incoming stimuli, they will be unable to sustain focus on what they are currently involved in.

From the time of birth, infants pay more attention to some objects and less to others. What they attend to, and how long they attend to it, is largely a result of the nature of the stimuli in the environment, and the alternatives that are available. Some stimuli act as *attention-getting* stimuli due to their physical characteristics. On the other hand, some stimuli are *attention-holding*; it is their meaningfulness that sustains attention (Cohen, 1972).

The properties that make a stimulus attention-getting are fairly constant throughout the life span. For instance, a loud noise or sudden movement is apt to evoke attention in both an infant and an adult. However, attention-holding stimuli vary across the life span according to an individual's age and experience. Thus, a toy truck is more of an attention-holding stimulus to a 4-year-old than it would be to a 12-year-old, while a book is obviously of greater interest to an older reader than to a child who has not yet learned to read.

Are differences in attention due to younger children's lack of sensory capabilities? Although it seems plausible that the less well-developed sensory store of young children would render them incapable of initially taking in as much information as older individuals, in fact this does not seem to be the case. Experiments have found that initial encoding of information in the sensory store is little different between 5-year-olds and adults. On the other

FROM A
DAYCARE WORKER'S
PERSPECTIVE:
What types of stimuli would be best for the development of an infant?

Brightly colored objects act as *attention-getting* stimuli due to their physical characteristics.

Infants have the ability to plan or calculate how to produce a desired outcome.

FIGURE 7-5 Planning

When comparing whether houses such as these were different from one another, preschoolers' eye movements showed that they did not systematically compare the features of the two houses in order to make their determination. In contrast, school-age children's eye movements showed that they systematically compared the features of the houses on a window-by-window basis, and they were considerably more accurate than the younger children.

(Source: Vurpillot, 1968).

planning The ability to allocate attentional resources on the basis of goals that one wishes to achieve

hand, when 5-year-olds are asked to recall what they have been exposed to, they remember significantly less than older children and adults (Morrison, Holmes, & Haith, 1974).

In short, information appears to be initially recorded in the sensory store in the same way by children and adults. Failures of information processing, then, are more likely due to the inability to draw out information from the sensory store and to processing deficiencies in short-term memory. Several attentional factors determine whether and how effectively information is processed, including the control and planning of attention.

Control of Attention. Watching children of different ages react to their environments, it seems obvious that as they get older their attention becomes more concentrated and lasting. A 2-year-old is more apt to leap from one activity to another than a 6-year-old. Older children are better able to concentrate on a particular activity for a longer period of time, ignoring extraneous distractions. Yet even 5- and 6-year-olds don't have long attention spans, averaging only 7 minutes on a single activity during preschool play periods (Ruff & Lawson, 1990).

The increasing ability to tune into certain stimuli, while tuning out others, is an indication of increasing cognitive *control* of attention. With age, children grow more aware of their sensory and memory limitations, and they develop strategies to respond to stimuli of interest (Astheimer & Sanders, 2012).

With age, children become more effective not only at controlling what they are attending to but also at excluding irrelevant or extraneous stimuli. For instance, children who are completing a task become better at focusing on what is central to the task, and ignoring elements of the situation that will not further its completion. Thus, a preschool child might focus on the brightly colored pin worn by an individual giving directions on how to complete at task, rather than on the directions themselves, as would an older child.

Planning. With increasing age, people don't only learn to control their attention in the face of irrelevant stimuli. They also become more proficient at mapping out and devising strategies for using their attention effectively: They become better at planning. **Planning** is the ability to allocate attentional resources on the basis of goals that one wishes to achieve.

Even infants show their ability to plan. They are able to anticipate when routine child-care procedures are going to take place, beginning to shift attention according to what they expect to happen (Benson & Haith, 1995).

Despite early indication of "planfulness," young children are not highly proficient at planning, and the ability to plan effectively develops throughout the course of childhood and adolescence. For example, young children are unable to take into account all the steps that will be involved in solving complex problems. They are also less systematic than older children. For instance, in one experiment, children were asked to compare whether complex stimuli consisting of two houses were different (as in the top row of Figure 7-5) or the same (as in the bottom row of Figure 7-5).

Examination of the eye movements of preschoolers comparing the two houses showed that they did not systematically compare the features of the two houses (Vurpillot, 1968). Instead, their eyes moved back and forth in a disorderly fashion, missing key features of the houses. As a result, they frequently said two different houses were the same. In contrast, school-age children used a more systematic strategy, comparing window-to-window, and they were much more accurate in determining whether the two were the same or different.

There are several reasons why younger children are deficient in planning, even when they may know that planning will help them reach a goal (Ellis & Siegler, 1997). For one thing, planning not only requires considering what one must do, but what one must *not* do. However, the ability to refrain from acting develops relatively slowly throughout childhood.

In addition, children frequently are more optimistic about their ability to reach their goal than is warranted. Their over-optimism leaves them unmotivated to engage in planning. Furthermore, planning may require coordination with others, and young children may not have the skills to cooperate effectively with others.

Still, children's ability to determine how they will allocate their attentional resources, as well as their general ability to control attention, will grow significantly over the course of development. In fact, by the time they reach adolescence, they will be adept at effectively dividing their attention across more than one stimulus at a time—such as simultaneously studying for a biology test and listening to a CD.

The improvements that occur in the control of attention and planning related to attention are likely produced by increases in maturation of the brain, as well as by the increasing educational demands placed on children.

For some children, however, the course of attentional development is not so smooth. As we consider in the accompanying *From Research to Practice* box, attentional disorders are at the heart of a problem that strikes from 3% to 5% of the school-age population: attention deficit hyperactivity disorder.

attention deficit hyperactivity disorder (ADHD)   A learning disability marked by inattention, impulsiveness, a low tolerance for frustration, and a great deal of inappropriate activity

FROM RESEARCH TO PRACTICE
Attention Deficit Hyperactivity Disorder: A Failure in Attention

Troy Dalton, age 7, exhausted his teacher. Unable to sit still, he roamed the classroom all day, distracting the other children. In reading group, he jumped up and down in his seat, dropping his book and knocking over the whiteboard. During read aloud, he ran around the room, humming noisily and shouting, "I'm a jet plane!" Once, he flung himself through the air, landing on another boy and breaking his arm. "He's the definition of perpetual motion," the teacher told Troy's mother (who looked pretty exhausted herself). The school finally decided to split Troy's day between the three second-grade classrooms. It was not a perfect solution, but it did allow his primary teacher to do some actual teaching.

Troy suffers from attention deficit hyperactivity disorder. **Attention deficit hyperactivity disorder,** or **ADHD,** is marked by inattention, impulsiveness, a low tolerance for frustration, and generally a great deal of inappropriate activity. All children show such traits some of the time, but for those diagnosed with ADHD, such behavior is common and interferes with their home and school functioning (American Academy of Pediatrics, 2000a; Nigg, 2001; Whalen et al., 2002).

What are the most common signs of ADHD? It is often difficult to distinguish between children who simply have a high level of activity and those with ADHD. Some of the most common symptoms include the following:

- Persistent difficulty in finishing tasks, following instructions, and organizing work
- Inability to watch an entire television program
- Frequent interruption of others or excessive talking
- A tendency to jump into a task before hearing all the instructions
- Difficulty in waiting or remaining seated
- Fidgeting, squirming

Because there is no simple test to identify whether a child has ADHD, it is hard to know for sure how many children have the disorder. Most estimates put the number at between 3% to 7% of those under the age of 18. Only a trained clinician can make an accurate diagnosis, following an extensive evaluation of the child and interviews with parents and teachers (Sax & Kautz, 2003).

The treatment of children with ADHD has been a source of considerable controversy. Because it has been found that doses of Ritalin or Dexadrine (which, paradoxically, are stimulants) reduce activity levels in hyperactive children, many physicians routinely prescribe drug treatment (Kaplan et al., 2004; Schachner et al., 2008; Miller & Hinshaw, 2012).

Although in many cases such drugs are effective in increasing attention span and compliance, in some cases the side effects (such as irritability, reduced appetite, and depression) are considerable, and the long-term health consequences of this treatment are unclear. It is also true that though the drugs often help scholastic performance in the short run, the long-term evidence for continuing improvement is mixed. In fact, some studies suggest that after a few years, children treated with drugs do not perform academically any better than untreated children with ADHD. Nonetheless the drugs are being prescribed with increasing frequency (see Figure 7-6 on page 208; Mayes & Rafalovich, 2007; Rose, 2008; Vaughan, March, & Kratochvil, 2012).

In addition to the use of drugs for treating ADHD, behavior therapy is often employed. With behavior therapy, parents and teachers are trained in techniques for improving behavior, primarily involving the use of rewards (such as verbal praise) for desired behavior. In addition, teachers can increase the structure of classroom activities and use other class management techniques to help children with ADHD, who have great difficulty with unstructured tasks. (Parents and teachers can receive support from the Children and Adults with Attention-Deficit/Hyperactivity Disorder organization at www.chadd.org.)

■ **Why is ADHD sometimes over-diagnosed by educators and medical practitioners?**

■ **Why are some parents reluctant to treat the symptoms of ADHD with drugs?**

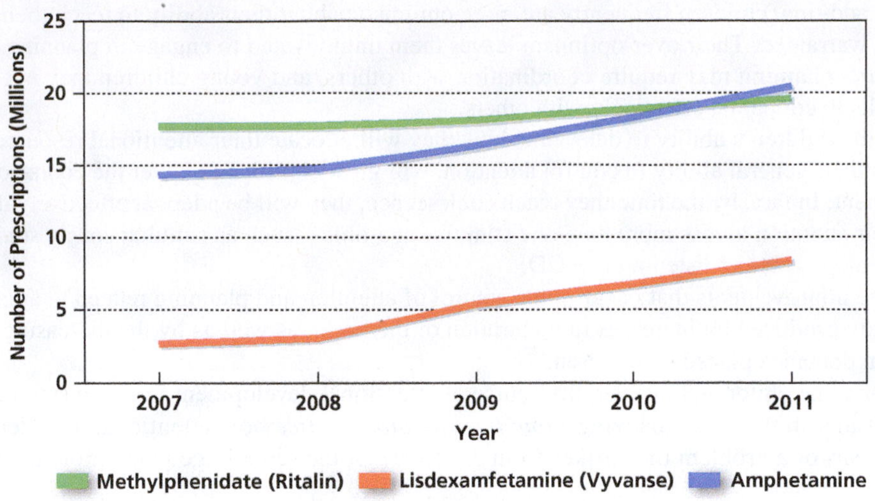

FIGURE 7-6 ADD/ADHD Stimulant Prescriptions Dispensed, 2007–2011

In spite of concerns, prescriptions for stimulants used by adults and children have steadily increased over the past six years. (Source: U.S. Drug Enforcement Administration, 2012)

Review, Check, and Apply

Review

1. According to the information processing perspective, memory comprises three systems: sensory memory, which lasts only an instant; short-term memory, which stores information for 15 to 25 seconds; and long-term memory, which holds information virtually permanently.

2. As people age, their short-term memory capacity increases and they develop metamemory, an understanding of the processes that underlie memory. This enables them to use control strategies to improve cognitive processes.

3. Infants can record, store, and retrieve information, but their ability to call upon and control these abilities is tenuous. While it is theoretically possible for memories to remain from a very young age, most memories before age 18 to 24 months lack accuracy, if they can be retrieved at all.

4. Early in life, children recall routine events in terms of scripts rather than as singular occurrences, and their recollection may be imprecise because of limitations in their inability to process complex causal relationships and interference from suggestions introduced by others.

5. As they grow older, children can learn strategies to improve their memory, including the use of mnemonic devices such as the keyword technique, rehearsal, organization, and encoding specificity.

6. Advances in brain scanning technology suggest that long-term memory consists of two systems: explicit memory, which is conscious, and implicit memory, which is not.

7. Attention is the first step in information processing, consisting of the ability to choose among and sort out different stimuli in the environment. The ability to control attention improves as children age, which leads to an improvement in planning ability.

8. Attention deficit hyperactivity disorder (ADHD) is a disorder related to attention in which the inability to complete tasks and work toward goals leads to impulsiveness and inappropriate activity.

Check

1. Working memory is also called _____-_____ memory.

2. The momentary storage of information for a second or two is called _____ memory.

3. During the school years, children develop the ability to understand the processes that underlie memory, a capability called _____.

4. _____ is the term for formal techniques for organizing information to make it more memorable.

5. A sudden loud noise is an example of an _____-_____ stimulus.

Apply

1. Are there practical applications of knowledge about attention in such areas as advertising and politics? Do these fields use attention-getting and attention-holding strategies? Do the strategies vary with intended audience?

2. Recently, there has been interest in reviving memories from early childhood and even infancy through hypnosis or other treatments. What dangers do you see in such practices? Can the accuracy of revived memories be verified?

To see more review questions, log on to MyPsychLab.

ANSWERS: 1. short-term 2. sensory 3. metamemory 4. *Mnemonics* 5. attention-getting

MODULE 7.3

APPLYING INFORMATION PROCESSING APPROACHES

LO 7-7 What have been some practical applications of information processing research?

LO 7-8 Overall, what contributions has the information processing model offered to our understanding of development?

> *A child looks at an adult and carefully explains about a mousetrap in his house. It's located in his basement, he says, next to the firewood. He was playing a game called "Operation," but then a mouse got caught in the mousetrap. And then, he explains, he caught his finger in the mousetrap, and he had to go to the hospital.*

Despite the detailed account by this 4-year-old boy of his encounter with a mousetrap and subsequent trip to the hospital, there's a problem: The incident never happened, and the memory is entirely false (Ceci & Bruck, 1993).

We turn now to two important applied areas that rely on research inspired by the information processing perspective: the courtroom and the classroom.

Forensic Developmental Psychology: Bringing Child Development to the Courtroom

The 4-year-old's explicit recounting of a mousetrap incident that had not actually occurred was the product of a study on children's memory. Each week for 11 weeks, the 4-year-old boy was told, "You went to the hospital because your finger got caught in a mousetrap. Did this ever happen to you?"

The conviction of preschool teacher Kelly Michaels for sexually molesting several preschool children may have been the result of leading questions posed to the children.

The first week, the child quite accurately said, "No. I've never been to the hospital." But by the second week, the answer changed to, "Yes, I cried." In the third week, the boy said, "Yes. My mom went to the hospital with me." By the 11th week, the answer had expanded to the quote above (Bruck & Ceci, 2004; Powell, Wright, & Hughes-Scholes, 2011).

The research study that elicited the child's false memories is part of a new and rapidly growing field within child development: forensic developmental psychology. *Forensic developmental psychology* focuses on the reliability of children's autobiographical memories in the context of the legal system. It considers children's abilities to recall events in their lives and the reliability of children's courtroom accounts where they are witnesses or victims (Bruck & Ceci, 2004; Goodman, 2006).

The embellishment of a completely false incident is characteristic of the fragility, impressionability, and inaccuracy of memory in young children. Young children may recall things quite mistakenly, but with great conviction, contending that events occurred that never really happened, and forgetting events that did occur.

Children's memories are susceptible to the suggestions of adults asking them questions. This is particularly true of preschoolers, who are considerably more vulnerable to suggestion than either adults or school-age children. Preschoolers are also more prone to make inaccurate inferences about the reasons behind others' behavior and are less able to draw appropriate conclusions based on their knowledge of a situation (e.g., "He was crying because he didn't like the sandwich.") (Loftus, 2004; Goodman & Melinder, 2007; Boseovski, 2012).

Of course, preschoolers recall many things accurately; as we discussed earlier in the chapter, children as young as 3 recall some events in their lives without distortion. However, not all recollections are accurate, and some events that are recalled with seeming accuracy never actually occurred.

The error rate for children is heightened when the same question is asked repeatedly. False memories—of the type reported by the 4-year-old who "remembered" going to the hospital after his finger was caught in a mousetrap—in fact may be more persistent than actual memories. In addition, when questions are highly suggestive (that is, when questioners attempt to lead a person to particular conclusions), children are more apt to make mistakes in recall (Loftus & Bernstein, 2005; Powell et al., 2007; Goodman & Quas, 2008).

For instance, consider the following excerpt, which presents an extreme example of a child being questioned. It comes from an actual case involving a teacher, Kelly Michaels, who was accused of sexually molesting children in a preschool:

Social worker:	Don't be so unfriendly. I thought we were buddies last time.
Child:	Nope, not any more.
Social worker:	We have gotten a lot of other kids to help us since I last saw you . . . did we tell you that Kelly is in jail?
Child:	Yes. My mother already told me.
Social worker:	Did I tell you that this is the guy (pointing to the detective) that arrested her? . . . Well, we can get out of here real quick if you just tell me what you told me the last time, when we met.
Child:	I forgot.
Social worker:	No you didn't. I know you didn't.
Child:	I did! I did!
Social worker:	I thought we were friends last time.
Child:	I'm not your friend any more!
Social worker:	How come?
Child:	Because I hate you!
Social worker:	You have no reason to hate me. We were buddies when you left.
Child:	I hate you now!

Social worker:	Oh, you do not, you secretly like me, I can tell.
Child:	I hate you.
Social worker:	Oh, come on. We talked to a few more of your buddies. And everyone told me about the nap room, and the bathroom stuff, and the music room stuff, and the choir stuff, and the peanut butter stuff, and everything . . . . All your buddies [talked] . . . . Come on, do you want to help us out? Do you want to keep her in jail? I'll let you hear your voice and play with the tape recorder; I need your help again. Come on . . . . Real quick, will you just tell me what happened with the wooden spoon? Let's go.
Child:	I forgot.
Detective:	Now listen you have to behave.
Social worker:	Do you want me to tell him to behave? Are you going to be good boy, huh? While you are here, did he [the detective] show you his badge and his handcuffs? (Ceci & Bruck, 1993, pp. 422–423)

Clearly, the interview is filled with leading questions, not to mention social pressure to conform ("all your buddies talked"), bribery ("I'll let you hear your voice and play with the tape recorder"), and even implicit threats ("did the detective show you his badge and handcuffs?").

How can children be questioned to produce the most accurate recollections? One way is to question them as soon as possible after an event has occurred. The longer the time between the actual event and questioning, the less firm are children's recollections. Furthermore, more specific questions are answered more accurately than more general ones. ("Did you go downstairs with Brian?") Asking the questions outside of a courtroom is also preferable, as the courtroom setting can be intimidating and frightening (Ceci & Bruck, 2007; Melnyk, Crossman, & Scullin, 2007; London et al., 2005).

Information Processing Contributions to the Classroom

Some of the most significant applications of information processing approaches have been made in the classroom. Not only has instruction in fundamental academic subjects been influenced by research in information processing, but efforts to teach children to think critically have also received a significant boost from researchers employing the information processing perspective.

How Should We Teach Reading?
Educators have long been engaged in an ongoing debate regarding the most effective means of teaching reading. At the heart of this debate is a disagreement about the nature of the mechanisms by which information is processed during reading. According to proponents of *code-based approaches to reading,* reading should be taught by presenting the basic skills that underlie reading. Code-based approaches emphasize the components of reading, such as the sounds of letters and their combinations—phonics—and how letters and sounds are combined to make words. They suggest that reading consists of processing the individual components of words, combining them into words, and then using the words to derive the meaning of written sentences and passages (Jimenez & Guzman, 2003; Rego, 2006; Hollingworth & Drake, 2012).

In contrast, some educators argue that reading is taught most successfully by using a whole-language approach. In *whole-language approaches to reading,* reading is viewed as a natural process, similar to the acquisition of oral language. According to this view, children should learn to read through exposure to complete writing—sentences, stories, poems, lists, charts, and other examples of actual uses of writing. Instead of being taught to sound out words, children are encouraged to make guesses about the meaning of words based on the context in which they appear. Through such a trial-and-error approach, children come to learn whole words and phrases at a time, gradually becoming proficient readers (Shaw, 2003; Sousa, 2005; Donat, 2006).

Research has found that reading instruction using code-based approaches is superior to using whole-language approaches.

CAREERS IN DEVELOPMENT
Mary Kriebel, Reading Resource Teacher

Education: Pennsylvania State University; B.S. in elementary and kindergarten education Johns Hopkins University, M.S. in communicative disorders

Position: Reading Resource Teacher

Home: Fallston, Maryland

Because so much other learning depends on it, reading is one of the fundamental tasks in the early years of school. In an effort to find the best approach for beginning readers, the teaching of reading has gone through numerous upheavals over the years, and it seems destined to continue to change.

At the Carney Elementary School in Baltimore County, Maryland, a new way to teach reading—based on a code-based approach that emphasizes the importance of phonics and grammar—was recently introduced in response to state regulations on reading instruction. At least initially, the new approach appears to be having good results.

The state regulations have shifted the direction of reading instruction to one that is very comprehensive and attentive to the needs of the children, according to Mary Kriebel, a first-grade teacher for 10 years, and now the Carney School's reading resource teacher. Kriebel feels confident that the new state guidelines will help more children learn to read better and more quickly.

"The new approach takes account of the child and his or her whole context of learning," she says. "For instance, phonics is very important for beginning readers. We work with phonics to teach word recognition in relation to basal readers and published literature. We use what's called the five-step word approach.

"First, if the student doesn't know the word, he or she is to initially skip over it. Second, the student should try to sound the word out. Third, the student should go back and look at the beginning and ending letters of the word. Fourth, the student should find the middle of the word to see if it can be blended with the two ends. The fifth and last step, if the student can't blend the word, is to ask someone.

"We also use a learning experience approach as much as possible. If children come back from a field trip, they may write about it on the board and then discuss the meaning," Kriebel notes.

"We try to integrate into our instruction the understanding that students will have to read to be informed about the subjects they are studying, such as social studies and science. We try to have them think through the whole process of reading and studying," she explains. "For example, if we are talking about the weather with first graders, we want them not only to learn about weather, types of clouds, and the effects of weather systems, but also to understand the meaning of what they are reading and learning—to think it through."

Kriebel has seen reading approaches come and go, but she feels that the new state direction is broad enough and realistic enough to be successful.

"I don't think in the past we took as close a look at the actual reading that children do and the things they need to learn. The whole language approach didn't always work because the students didn't have the fundamental skills they needed to understand what they were reading," Kriebel notes. "I feel this program is going to be successful. It allows for better grouping and gives us a way to meet the children's needs while we address their weaknesses. Phonics and other basic skills are used to make sure the students will have a good foundation to build on in the future for reading and thinking."

A growing body of data, based on careful research, suggests that code-based approaches are superior to whole-language approaches. For example, one study found that a group of children tutored in phonics for a year not only improved substantially in their reading, compared to a group of good readers, but that the neural pathways involved in reading became closer to that of good readers (see Figure 7-7; Shaywitz et al., 2004).

Based on research such as this, the National Reading Panel and National Research Council now support reading instruction using code-based approaches. Their position signals that an end may be near to the debate over which approach to teaching reading is most effective (Rayner et al., 2002).

(For more on how reading is actually taught in contemporary classrooms, see the *Careers in Development* interview.)

Teaching Critical Thinking. "There's no cereal that has more vitamins than Wheaties." "Using Crest toothpaste is the best way to fight cavities." "Be the first to buy Barbie's new playhouse."

The way that children evaluate such statements, typical of arguments made in commercials targeted to children, is dependent on their critical thinking skills. **Critical thinking** is

critical thinking Thinking that makes use of cognitive skills and strategies that increase the likelihood of solving problems, forming inferences, and making decisions appropriately and successfully

thinking that makes use of cognitive skills and strategies that increase the likelihood of solving problems, forming inferences, and making decisions appropriately and successfully. It involves not jumping to conclusions on the basis of limited facts, but considering information, weighing the alternatives, and coming to a reasoned decision. Critical thinkers scrutinize the assumptions that underlie their decisions, beliefs, and actions, and they pay attention to the contexts in which ideas are implemented.

Although all of us naturally use thinking, it is often not *critical* thinking. We jump to conclusions on the basis of limited facts and make mistakes in logic. Children, especially, are more willing to take statements, such as those made in commercials, at face value. They respond to complex questions with simple answers. Even older children and adolescents often do not take all relevant information into account, and sometimes they are unaware what significant information is missing from a problem that would be needed to come to a reasonable conclusion.

Despite the fact that educators acknowledge the importance of critical thinking, in fact the critical thinking skills of students are not terribly high. For instance, one study found that less than 40% of 17-year-olds can find, summarize, and explain information. Another study comparing Japanese and U.S. students on mathematical problem solving found that the best students from the United States scored lower than the worst Japanese students. The differences can best be attributed to a lack of critical thinking skills in the U.S. students (Izawa & Hayden, 1993; Chapman, Gamino, & Mudar, 2012).

What are the ingredients of critical thinking? There are four primary principles that must be applied if thinking is to be appropriately considered critical. First, thinkers must identify and challenge assumptions underlying a statement or contention. Second, they must check for factual accuracy and logical consistency among statements. Third, they need to take into account the context of a situation. Finally, they need to imagine and explore alternatives.

Although many children and adults could not be characterized as critical thinkers, such skills can be taught. In fact, teaching critical thinking is becoming a recommended part of the curriculum in many schools, beginning at the elementary level and running all the way up to the college level (Halpern, 1996).

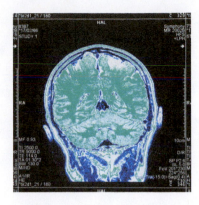

FIGURE 7-7 The Impact of Phonics Training on the Brain

Students with reading difficulties who were tutored in phonics showed improved reading proficiency and increased activity in brain areas related to skilled reading.

(Source: Darrin Jenkins/Alamy.)

Information Processing Approaches in Perspective

As we can see from this chapter, the information processing perspective on cognitive development has been a fruitful, creative area of research. This accounts for its status within the field of child development. For many child developmentalists, information processing approaches represent the dominant, most comprehensive, and ultimately most accurate explanation of how children develop cognitively.

According to information processing approaches, cognitive development consists of gradual improvements in the ways people perceive, understand, and remember information. With age and practice, children process information more efficiently and with greater sophistication, and they are able to handle increasingly complex problems. In the eyes of proponents of information processing approaches, it is these quantitative advances in information processing—and not the qualitative changes suggested by Piaget—that constitute cognitive development (Zhe & Siegler, 2000; Rose, Feldman, & Jankowski, 2009).

For supporters of information processing approaches, the reliance on well-defined processes that can be tested, with relative precision, by research is one of the perspective's most important features. Rather than relying on concepts that are somewhat vague, such as Piaget's notions of assimilation and accommodation or Vygotsky's ideas on the zone of proximal development and scaffolding, information processing approaches provide a comprehensive, logical set of concepts, focusing on the processes that underlie children's thinking.

For instance, as preschoolers grow older, they have longer attention spans, can monitor and plan what they are attending to more effectively, and become increasingly aware of their cognitive limitations. These advances may be due to brain development, and the resulting increase in attentional abilities suggests a reinterpretation of some of Piaget's findings.

For instance, increased attention allows older children to attend to both the height *and* the width of tall and short glasses into which liquid is poured. This permits them to understand that the amount of liquid in the glasses stays the same when it is poured back and forth.

Preschoolers, in contrast, are unable to attend to both dimensions simultaneously, and thus are less able to conserve (Stock, Desoete, & Roeyers, 2007).

In ways such as this, proponents of information processing theory have been successful in focusing on important cognitive processes to which alternative approaches traditionally have paid little attention, such as the contribution of mental skills such as memory and attention to children's thinking. They suggest that information processing provides a clear, logical, and full account of cognitive development.

Yet information processing approaches have their detractors, who raise significant points. For one thing, the focus on a series of single, individual cognitive processes leaves out of consideration some important factors that appear to influence cognition. For instance, information processing theorists pay relatively little attention to social and cultural factors—a deficiency that Vygotsky's approach attempts to remedy.

An even more important criticism is that information processing approaches "lose the forest for the trees." In other words, information processing approaches pay so much attention to the detailed, individual sequence of processes that compose cognitive processing and development that they never adequately paint a whole, comprehensive picture of cognitive development—which Piaget clearly did uniquely well.

Developmentalists using information processing approaches respond to such criticisms by saying that their model of cognitive development has the advantage of being precisely stated and capable of leading to testable hypotheses. They also argue that there is far more research supporting their approach than there is for alternative theories of cognitive development. In short, they suggest that their approach provides a more accurate account than any other.

What is certain is that information processing approaches have been highly influential over the past several decades. They have inspired a tremendous amount of research that has helped us gain some insights into how children develop cognitively.

Review, Check, and Apply

Review

1. Because young children's memories are highly subject to suggestion and distortion, children can be unreliable witnesses in emotionally charged law cases.

2. In the classroom, information processing approaches have supported approaches to reading instruction that are based on children's progression from low-level cognitive skills to higher-level skills. Information processing has been used to support both code-based and whole-language approaches to reading, and the best approach is probably a combination of the two.

3. Information processing approaches have also been used to develop critical thinking instruction, which focuses on the use of cognitive skills and strategies to analyze assumptions, evaluate arguments, solve problems, and make decisions.

4. The information processing perspective has proven fruitful in offering explanations of cognitive phenomena and suggesting additional research through its generation of testable hypotheses. It is less successful in accounting for social and cultural factors that affect cognitive processes and in producing a rich, comprehensive picture of cognitive development.

Check

1. When young children are led to recount untrue stories as if they were true, they are said to be creating _____ _____.

2. Investigators can elicit untrue testimony from young children by asking _____ questions that suggest the desired way to answer.

3. Essential components of _____ thinking are identification of assumptions, checking accuracy and logical consistency, considering the context of a statement, and exploring alternatives.

4. By focusing on quantitative changes rather than qualitative changes, information processing approaches have the advantage of proposing _____ that can be tested by research.

Apply

1. How do children's critical thinking limitations affect their understanding and interpretation of television commercials and written advertisements?

2. Based on your knowledge about children's critical thinking skills, do you think advertising directed to children should be closely regulated or even prohibited? Why?

To see more review questions, log on to MyPsychLab.

ANSWERS: 1. false memories 2. leading 3. critical 4. hypotheses

The CASE
of . . . *the Frustrated Fantasy*

Jared Mulford, 16, began his college search in a state of high excitement. A bright, creative student, he had already aced three AP classes and planned to take more. He was also editor of the school paper and a member of the debating team. Jared loved to lie on his bed and imagine how Harvard, Princeton, and Yale would fight over him.

To Jared's annoyance, his school college counselor did not share his vision. "It's fine to dream of Harvard, but you should pick some safety schools, Jared. You may need them."

Jared seethed at such advice. Hadn't he skipped a grade in elementary school? Wasn't he slated to be the high school valedictorian? And he was sure to get perfect SAT scores, so why bother applying to any schools but the best?

The first shock came when he received his SAT scores. Though they were quite high, they were not perfect. "Pick some safety schools," his counselor repeated. But Jared ignored her and applied only to his dream trio. His last editorial in the school paper had won a local award. He knew he was destined for special things.

Then the real shocks started hitting. First, Harvard rejected him, then Yale. Still, Jared clung to his dream until, at last, in early April, he heard from Princeton. No go.

As his friends began planning what they would take to college and arranged their freshman courses, Jared grew depressed. He had nowhere to go.

1. How do Jared's thoughts and actions reflect the egocentrism that is so typical of adolescents?

2. Why might Jared still cling to his dreams after Harvard and Yale have rejected him?

3. Is Jared's view of himself realistic? What is Jared overlooking when he fantasizes about the elite colleges fighting over him?

4. Do you think Jared's refusal to accept his college counselor's advice demonstrates growth in his cognitive abilities? Why or why not?

5. If you were Jared's college counselor, how would you have prepared him to better understand and assess the reality of his situation?

◀◀◀ LOOKING BACK

LO 7-1 What fundamental processes underlie information processing?

- Information processing approaches to the study of cognitive development seek to learn how individuals receive, organize, store, and retrieve information. These fundamental processes of information processing are called encoding, storage, and retrieval.

- Information processing approaches differ from Piaget's by attributing cognitive development to quantitative changes in children's abilities to process information rather than to the qualitative, somewhat abrupt progressions envisioned by Piaget.

LO 7-2 How does the information processing perspective explain cognitive development as children grow?

• A different approach to cognitive development is taken by proponents of information processing theories, who focus on storage and recall of information and on quantitative changes in information processing abilities (such as attention).

• According to information processing approaches, children's intellectual development in the school years can be attributed to substantial increases in memory capacity and quantitative changes in attention, permitting children to handle increasingly sophisticated mental "programs."

LO 7-3 What are some effects of changes in information processing during adolescence?

• Cognitive growth during adolescence is not abrupt, but gradual and quantitative, involving improvements in memory capacity, mental strategies, and other aspects of cognitive functioning.

• Another major area of cognitive development is the growth of metacognition, which permits adolescents to monitor their thought processes and accurately assess their cognitive capabilities.

• Hand in hand with the development of metacognition is the growth of adolescent egocentrism, a self-absorption that makes it hard for adolescents to accept criticism and tolerate authority figures.

• Adolescents may play to an imaginary audience of critical observers, and they may develop personal fables, which emphasize the uniqueness of their experiences and supposed invulnerability to risks.

LO 7-4 What is the structure of memory according to the information processing model?

• According to information processing theories, memory consists of sensory memory, the short-lived initial storage of unprocessed stimuli; short-term memory, the working area where information is processed within 15 to 25 seconds of receipt; and long-term memory, where information may be stored indefinitely.

LO 7-5 How do memory processes change as children grow?

• Infants have memory capabilities from the earliest ages, but the parts of the brain involved in memory change with age and the ability to store and retrieve memories increases.

• The accuracy of infants' and young children's memories is questionable. Autobiographical memory does not achieve much accuracy until after the age of 3.

• Short-term memory increases in capacity during childhood, largely because of increases in operating efficiency that result in greater availability of resources to store information. In addition, memory functioning improves as children use more sophisticated control strategies to improve cognitive processing. The use of scripts to store and recall information also conserves memory resources.

• Metamemory, the understanding of memory and its functioning, permits children to plan and monitor memory use to meet goals. Further, children's increasing knowledge of the world permits them to memorize and recall information more efficiently and effectively.

LO 7-6 What is the role of attention in the processing of information?

• Attention, which involves being aware of and interested in stimuli, is responsible for differences in information processing between young children and adults. Some failures of information processing appear to relate to the control and planning of attention.

• As they age, children become increasingly aware of their sensory and memory limitations and develop strategies to control their attention to stimuli of interest and exclude extraneous stimuli.

• With age, children also become more adept at planning the use of attention, allocating attentional resources to meet their goals.

• In attention deficit hyperactivity disorder (ADHD), the inability to complete tasks and work toward goals leads to impulsiveness and inappropriate activity.

LO 7-7 What have been some practical applications of information processing research?

• Information processing theories have led to practical applications in several areas of society, including the courtroom and the classroom.

• Reliance on the memories of young children in the courtroom has been shown to be risky because they are highly subject to suggestion and distortion. Recall of events is most reliable if it is obtained soon after the events. Specific questions asked in a nonthreatening setting elicit the most trustworthy results, but even so, the memories of young children must be carefully evaluated before being used.

• The information processing approach has provided insight into the way children learn to read, which has influenced the nature of reading instruction. Children progress from low-level cognitive skills to higher-level skills. The debate between code-based and whole-language approaches to reading has been informed but not definitively decided by information processing research, and the best approach is probably a combination of the two.

• Critical thinking is an important skill that information processing approaches have illuminated. As children grow, they become increasingly able to think critically, using cognitive skills and strategies to analyze assumptions, evaluate arguments, solve problems, and make decisions. However, the development of critical thinking skills is not automatic or universal; explicit instruction appears to be necessary.

LO 7-8 Overall, what contributions has the information processing model offered to our understanding of development?

• The information processing perspective has contributed significantly to our understanding of cognitive phenomena and development. It provides a coherent, logical, relatively complete account of cognitive processes in terms that permit scientific testing.

• The perspective has been criticized for failing to address social and cultural factors that affect cognitive processes and for yielding an overly mechanistic, atomistic view of cognition.

KEY TERMS AND CONCEPTS

information-processing approaches (p. 192)
metacognition (p. 195)
adolescent egocentrism (p. 195)
imaginary audience (p. 195)
personal fables (p. 196)
memory (p. 199)

infantile amnesia (p. 200)
autobiographical memory (p. 202)
scripts (p. 202)
metamemory (p. 203)
mnemonics (p. 204)
attention (p. 204)

planning (p. 206)
attention deficit hyperactivity disorder
(ADHD) (p. 207)
critical thinking (p. 212)

Epilogue

We have taken a look at information processing approaches to the study of cognitive development, discussing the basics of information processing compared with Piaget's and Vygotsky's theories. We have seen how information processing's practical, experimental methods have illuminated our understanding of memory and enlightened us as we considered some of the important issues of the day, such as the reliability of children's testimony in court and the usefulness of its insights and findings for education.

Think back to the case of Arif Terzić, the Bosnian infant who spent the first years of his life hiding in a basement with his mother. Consider these questions:

1. To what extent do you think that Arif will remember his first years when he reaches adulthood?

2. If he does recall those early years, how likely is it that his memories will be accurate?

3. Does the research on children's eyewitness testimony make you think that through appropriate questioning he could accurately recall his early years? Why?

4. Even if Arif does not remember his early years, do you think his experiences will affect his development as an adult? How?

The Development Video Series in MyPsychLab

Explore the video *Risky Behavior and Brain Development* by scanning this QR code with your mobile device. If you don't already have one, you may download a free QR scanner for your device wherever smartphone apps are sold. You can also view this video in MyPsychLab. For more videos related to this chapter's content, log into MyPsychLab to view the entire Development Video Series.

MyVirtual**Child**

- **What decisions would you make while raising a child?**
- **What would the consequences of those decisions be?**

Find out by accessing **MyVirtualChild** at
www.MyPsychLab.com
and raising your own virtual child from birth to age 18.

8 Language Development

MODULE 8.1

THE COURSE OF LANGUAGE DEVELOPMENT

- The Fundamentals of Language: From Sounds to Symbols

FROM RESEARCH TO PRACTICE: Talking with Our Hands: How Gestures Relate to Language

- Language Advances during the Preschool Years
- Language Development during Middle Childhood: Mastering Language

ARE YOU AN INFORMED CONSUMER OF DEVELOPMENT? Assessing Early Language Development

Review, Check, and Apply

MODULE 8.2

THE ORIGINS OF LANGUAGE DEVELOPMENT

- Language Acquisition
- How Are Language and Thought Related?

Review, Check, and Apply

MODULE 8.3

CHILDREN'S CONVERSATIONS: SPEAKING TO AND WITH CHILDREN

- The Language of Infant-Directed Speech

DEVELOPMENTAL DIVERSITY AND YOUR LIFE: Is Infant-Directed Speech Similar in All Cultures?

- Gender Differences in Speech Directed toward Children
- The Links between Language Development and Poverty
- Bilingualism: Speaking in Many Tongues

Review, Check, and Apply

The Case of . . . the Deedio Mystery

Looking Back

Key Terms and Concepts

Epilogue

PROLOGUE: The First Word Spoken

Vicki and Dominic were engaged in a friendly competition over whose name would be the first word their baby, Maura, said. "Say 'mama,'" Vicki would coo, before handing Maura over to Dominic for a diaper change. Grinning, he would take her and coax, "No, say 'daddy.'" Both parents ended up losing—and winning—when Maura's first word sounded more like "baba," and seemed to refer to her bottle.

Although we tend to think of language in terms of the production of words and then groups of words, infants can begin to communicate linguistically well before they say their first word.

>>> LOOKING AHEAD

Mama. No. Cookie. Dad. Jo. Most parents can remember their baby's first word, and no wonder. It's an exciting moment, this emergence of a skill that is, arguably, unique to human beings.

But those initial words are just the first and most obvious expression of language. Many months earlier, infants began to understand the language used by others to make sense of the world around them. How does this linguistic ability develop? For that matter, what is language and what are its characteristics? What is the pattern and sequence of language development? And how does the use of language transform the cognitive world of infants and their parents?

In this chapter, we address these questions as we trace the ways that language develops. We begin by considering the route of language development, examining how the use of language changes as children grow older. We consider children's first words, and how children rapidly build up a vocabulary and move from phrases to complex sentences, and ultimately, to an understanding of grammar and the pragmatic aspects of language use in social situations.

We then consider the roots of language. We present several different perspectives, and also consider the relationship between language and thought.

Finally, we conclude the chapter with a look at the ways in which adults speak to children and the influences that adult speech patterns may have on children's later

(continued)

Learning Objectives

MODULE 8.1

LO1 What is the process of language development during the childhood years?

MODULE 8.2

LO2 What are various perspectives on the origins of language development, and what evidence supports each one?

LO3 How are language and thought related?

MODULE 8.3

LO4 In what ways does the language adults use with children affect language development?

LO5 How do social issues influence language development?

development. We also examine some social issues in language development, including the relationship between poverty and language, bilingualism, and a controversy concerning the use of non-standard English in the classroom.

THE COURSE OF LANGUAGE DEVELOPMENT

LO 8-1 What is the process of language development during the childhood years?

The Fundamentals of Language: From Sounds to Symbols

Language, the systematic, meaningful arrangement of symbols, provides the basis for communication. But it does more than this: It is closely tied to the way we think and understand the world. It enables us to reflect on people and objects and to convey our thoughts to others.

Language has several formal characteristics that must be mastered as linguistic competence is developed. They include the following:

- *Phonology.* Phonology refers to the basic sounds of language, called *phonemes,* that can be combined to produce words and sentences. For instance, the "a" in "mat" and the "a" in "mate" represent two different phonemes in English. Although English employs just 40 phonemes to create every word in the language, other languages have as many as 85 phonemes—and some as few as 15 (Akmajian, Demers, & Harnish, 1984).

- *Morphemes.* A morpheme is the smallest language unit that has meaning. Some morphemes are complete words, while others add information necessary for interpreting a word, such as the endings "-s" for plural and "-ed" for past tense.

- *Semantics.* Semantics are the rules that govern the meaning of words and sentences. As their knowledge of semantics develops, children are able to understand the subtle distinction between "Ellie was hit by a ball" (an answer to the question of why Ellie doesn't want to play catch) and "A ball hit Ellie" (used to announce the current situation).

In considering the development of language, we need to distinguish between linguistic *comprehension,* the understanding of speech, and linguistic *production,* the use of language to communicate. One principle underlies the relationship between the two: Comprehension precedes production. An 18-month-old may be able to understand a complex series of directions ("pick up your coat from the floor and put it on the chair by the fireplace") but may not yet have strung more than two words together when speaking for herself. Throughout infancy comprehension also outpaces production. For instance, during infancy, comprehension of words expands at a rate of 22 new words a month, while production of words increases at a rate of about 9 new words a month, once talking begins (Rescorla, Alley, & Christine, 2001; Minagawa-Kawai et al., 2011; Lewkowicz, & Hansen-Tift, 2012; see Figure 8-1).

Early Sounds and Communication.
Spend 24 hours with even a very young infant and you will hear a variety of sounds: cooing, crying, gurgling, murmuring, and many other noises. These sounds, although not meaningful in themselves, play an important role in linguistic development, paving the way for true language (O'Grady & Aitchison, 2005).

Prelinguistic communication is communication through sounds, facial expressions, gestures, imitation, and other nonlinguistic means. When a father responds to his daughter's "ah" with an "ah" of his own, and then the daughter repeats the sound, and the father responds once again, they are engaged in prelinguistic communication. Clearly, the "ah" sound has no particular meaning. However, its repetition, which mimics the give-and-take of conversation, teaches the infant something about turn-taking and the back-and-forth of communication.

Watch the **Video** *Language Learning* in **MyPsychLab**.

language The systematic, meaningful arrangement of symbols, which provides the basis for communication

prelinguistic communication Communication through sounds, facial expressions, gestures, imitation, and other nonlinguistic means

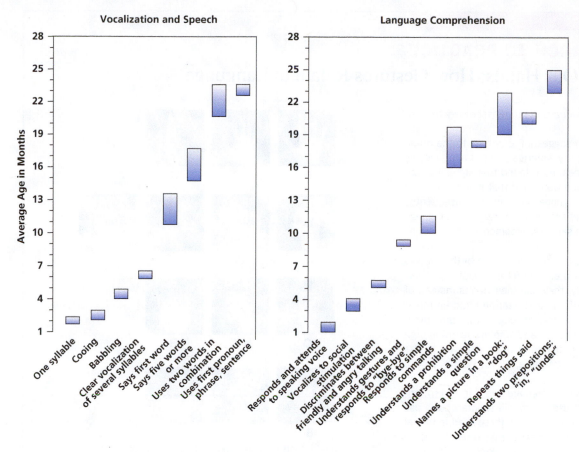

Vocalization and Speech

Average Age in Months

One syllable
Cooing
Babbling
Clear vocalization of several syllables
Says first word
Says five words or more
Uses two words in combination
Uses first pronoun, phrase, sentence

Language Comprehension

Responds and attends to speaking voice
Vocalizes to social stimulation
Discriminates between friendly and angry talking
Understands gestures and responds to "bye-bye"
Responds to simple commands
Understands a prohibition
Understands a simple question
Names a picture in a book: "dog"
Repeats things said
Understands two prepositions: "in," "under"

FIGURE 8-1 Comprehension Precedes Production

Throughout infancy, the comprehension of speech precedes the production of speech.

(*Source:* Adapted from Bornstein & Lamb, 1992a.)

The most obvious manifestation of prelinguistic communication is babbling. **Babbling,** making speechlike but meaningless sounds, starts at the age of 2 or 3 months and continues until around the age of 1 year. When they babble, infants repeat the same vowel sound over and over, changing the pitch from high to low (as in "ee-ee-ee," repeated at different pitches). After the age of 5 months, the sounds of babbling begin to expand, reflecting the addition of consonants (such as "bee-bee-bee-bee").

Babbling is a universal phenomenon, accomplished in the same way throughout all cultures. While they are babbling, infants spontaneously produce all of the sounds found in every language, not just the language they hear people around them speaking. In fact, as we discuss in the *From Research to Practice* box on page 222, even deaf children display their own form of babbling.

Babbling typically follows a progression from simple to more complex sounds. Although exposure to the sounds of a particular language does not seem to influence babbling initially, eventually experience does make a difference. By the age of 6 months, babbling reflects the sounds of the language to which infants are exposed. The difference is so noticeable that even untrained listeners can distinguish among babbling infants raised in cultures in which French, Arabic, or Cantonese languages are spoken. Furthermore, the speed at which infants begin homing in on their own language is related to the speed of later language development (Tsao, Liu, & Kuhl, 2004; Whalen, Levitt, & Goldstein, 2007).

There are other indications of prelinguistic speech. For instance, consider 5-month-old Marta, who spies her red ball just beyond her reach. After reaching for it and finding that she is unable to get to it, she makes a cry of anger that alerts her parents that something is amiss, and her mother hands it to her. Communication has occurred.

Four months later, when Marta faces the same situation, she no longer bothers to reach for the ball and doesn't respond in anger. Instead, she holds out her arm in the direction of the ball and, with great purpose, seeks to catch her mother's eye. When her mother sees the behavior, she knows just what Marta wants. Clearly, Marta's communicative skills—although still prelinguistic—have taken a leap forward.

babbling   Making speechlike but meaningless sounds

FROM RESEARCH TO PRACTICE
Talking with Our Hands: How Gestures Relate to Language

Is the ability to hear the spoken language of others necessary to learn language?

An increasing body of research suggests the answer to the question is "no." Researchers who study American Sign Language, as well as other kinds of sign languages, have found that sign language is just as complicated as the spoken word, and that it is acquired in much the same way that spoken language is acquired. Consequently, children who are unable to hear the spoken word learn sign language in much the same way, and on the same developmental schedule, as children who have hearing.

For example, infants who are profoundly deaf from birth and who are exposed to sign language show their own form of babbling. However, rather than babbling verbally, they use their hands instead of their voices. Furthermore, deaf infants and hearing children reach the same language acquisition milestones at roughly the same time. And infants who have the ability to hear and who are learning sign language babble silently using their hands when exposed to the sign language of adults (Petitto & Marentette, 1991; Petitto, 2000; Petitto et al., 2004).

There's also evidence that if deaf children are raised in an environment in which sign language is not used, they will spontaneously use gestures that are similar in form and structure to those used in formal sign languages. Even adults who are not deaf use gestures that show linguistic qualities if they are prevented from speaking. According to research by psychologist Susan Goldin-Meadow, when hearing adults typically use gestures when they are speaking, the gestures support the speech but do not show formal linguistic properties. But if hearing adults are told to use gestures only to describe an event, without speaking, the gestures they use begin to show formal linguistic properties that are similar to those found in deaf children (Goldin-Meadow, 2006, 2009; Snow & Ertmer, 2012).

In short, language acquisition appears to develop in an analogous manner in hearing and deaf individuals. Humans' sophisticated linguistic abilities

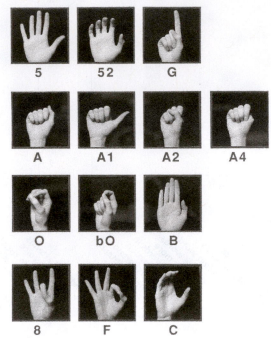

Deaf infants who are exposed to sign language do their own type of babbling, related to the use of signs.

appear in both speech and gestures, providing a highly sophisticated communication mechanism.

■ **Do you think that children who are *not* deaf also babble using gestures? Why or why not?**

■ **What does the fact that deaf children babble with their hands suggest about the origins of language development?**

Even these prelinguistic skills are supplanted in just a few months, when the gesture gives way to a new communicative skill: producing an actual word. Marta's parents clearly hear her say "ball."

First Words. When a mother and father first hear their child say "Mama" or "Dada," or even "baba," the first word spoken by Maura, the baby described earlier in this section, it is hard to be anything but delighted. But their initial enthusiasm may be dampened a bit when they find that the same sound is used to ask for a cookie, a doll, and a ratty old blanket.

First words generally are spoken somewhere around the age of 10 to 14 months but may occur as early as 9 months. Linguists differ on just how to recognize that a first word has actually been uttered. Some say it is when an infant clearly understands words and can produce a sound that is close to a word spoken by adults, such as a child who uses "mama" for any request she may have. Other linguists use a stricter criterion for the first word; they restrict "first word" to cases in which children give a clear, consistent name to a person, event, or object. In this view, "mama" counts as a first word only if it is consistently applied to the same person, seen in a variety of situations and doing a variety of things, and is not used to label other people (Hollich et al., 2000; Masataka, 2003; Watanabe, Homae, & Taga, 2012).

Although there is disagreement over when we can say a first word has been uttered, no one disputes that once an infant starts to produce words, vocabulary increases at a rapid rate. By 15 months, the average child has a vocabulary of 10 words, which methodically expands until the one-word stage of language development ends at around 18 months. At that point a sudden spurt in vocabulary occurs. In just a short period—a few weeks somewhere between 16 and 24 months of age—there is an explosion of language, in which a child's vocabulary typically increases from 50 to 400 words (Nazzi & Bertoncini, 2003; McMurray, Aslin, & Toscano, 2009; Lew-Williams & Saffran, 2012).

As you can see from the list in Figure 8-2, the first words in children's early vocabularies typically regard objects and things, both animate and inanimate. Most often they refer to people or objects that constantly appear and disappear ("Mama"), to animals ("kitty"), or to temporary states ("wet"). These first words are often **holophrases,** one-word utterances that stand for a whole phrase, whose meaning depends on the particular context in which they are used. For instance, a youngster may use the phrase "ma" to mean, depending on the context, "I want to be picked up by Mom" or "I want something to eat, Mom" or "Where's Mom?" (Dromi, 1987; O'Grady & Aitchison, 2005).

Culture has an effect on the type of first words spoken. For example, unlike North American English-speaking infants, who are more apt to use nouns initially, Chinese Mandarin-speaking infants use more verbs than nouns. On the other hand, by the age of 20 months, there are remarkable cross-cultural similarities in the types of words spoken. For example, a comparison of 20-month-olds in Argentina, Belgium, France, Israel, Italy, and the Republic of Korea found that children's vocabularies in every culture contained greater proportions of nouns than other classes of words (Tardif, 1996; Bornstein, Cote, & Maital, 2004).

First Sentences. When Aaron was 19 months old, he heard his mother coming up the back steps, as she did every day just before dinner. Aaron turned to his father and distinctly said, "Ma come." In stringing those two words together, Aaron took a giant step in his language development.

The explosive increase in vocabulary that comes at around 18 months is accompanied by another accomplishment: the linking together of individual words into sentences that convey a single thought. Although there is a good deal of variability in the time at which children first create two-word phrases, it is generally around 8 to 12 months after they say their first word.

The linguistic advance represented by two-word combinations is important because the linkage not only provides labels for things in the world but also indicates the relations between them. For instance, the combination may declare something about possession ("Mama key") or recurrent events ("Dog bark"). Interestingly, most early sentences don't represent demands or even necessarily require a response. Instead, they are often merely comments and observations about events occurring in the child's world (O'Grady & Aichison, 2005).

Two-year-olds using two-word combinations tend to employ particular sequences that are similar to the ways in which adult sentences are constructed. For instance, sentences in English typically follow a pattern in which the subject of the sentence comes first, followed by the verb, and then the object ("Josh threw the ball"). Children's speech most often uses a similar order, although not all the words are initially included. Consequently, a child might say "Josh threw" or "Josh ball" to indicate the same thought. What is significant is that the order is typically not "threw Josh" or "ball Josh," but rather the usual order of English, which makes the utterance much easier for an English speaker to comprehend (Brown, 1973; Masataka, 2003).

By the age of 2, most children use two-word phrases, such as "ball play."

holophrases One-word utterances that stand for a whole phrase, whose meaning depends on the particular context in which they are used

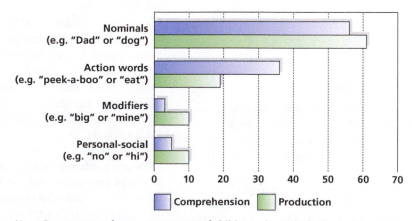

Note: Percentage refers to percentage of children who include this type of word among their first 50 words.

FIGURE 8-2 The Top 50: The First Words Children Understand and Speak

TABLE 8-1   Children's Imitation of Sentences Showing Decline in Telegraphic Speech

Sample Sentences	Speaker	26 months	29 months	32 months	35 months
I put on my shoes	Kim	Shoes	My shoes	I put on shoes	A
	Darden	Shoes on	My shoes on	Put on shoes	Put on my shoes
I will not go to bed	Kim	No bed	Not go bed	I not go bed	I not go to bed
	Darden	Not go bed	I not go bed	I not go to bed	I will not go bed
I want to ride the pony	Kim	Pony, pony	Want ride pony	I want ride pony	I want to ride pony
	Darden	Want pony	I want pony	I want the pony	A

A = accurate imitation.
(*Source:* Adapted from R. Brown & C. Fraser, 1963.)

Although the creation of two-word sentences represents an advance, the language used by children is still by no means adultlike. As we've just seen, 2-year-olds tend to leave out words that aren't critical to the message, as we might do if we were writing a telegram for which we were paying by the word. For that reason, their talk is often called **telegraphic speech.** Rather than saying, "I showed you the book," a child using telegraphic speech might say, "I show book." "I am drawing a dog" might become "Drawing dog" (see Table 8-1).

Early language has other characteristics that differentiate it from the language used by adults. For instance, consider Sarah, who refers to the blanket she sleeps with as "blankie." When her Aunt Ethel gives her a new blanket, Sarah refuses to call the new one a "blankie," restricting the word to her original blanket.

Sarah's inability to generalize the label of "blankie" to blankets in general is an example of **underextension,** using words too restrictively, which is common among children just mastering spoken language. Underextension occurs when language novices think that a word refers to a specific instance of a concept, instead of to all examples of the concept (Caplan & Barr, 1989; Masataka, 2003).

As infants like Sarah grow more adept with language, the opposite phenomenon sometimes occurs. In **overextension,** words are used too broadly, overgeneralizing their meaning. For example, when Sarah refers to buses, trucks, and tractors as "cars," she is guilty of overextension, making the assumption that any object with wheels must be a car. Although overextension reflects speech errors, it also shows that advances are occurring in the child's thought processes: The child is beginning to develop general mental categories and concepts (McDonough, 2002).

Infants also show individual differences in the style of language they use. For example, some use a **referential style,** in which language is used primarily to label objects. Others tend to use an **expressive style,** in which language is used primarily to express feelings and needs about oneself and others (Bornstein, 2000).

Language styles reflect, in part, cultural factors. For example, mothers in the United States label objects more frequently than do Japanese mothers, encouraging a more referential style of speech. In contrast, mothers in Japan are more apt to speak about social interactions, encouraging a more expressive style of speech (Fernald & Morikawa, 1993; Bornstein & Putnick, 2012).

telegraphic speech   Speech in which words not critical to the message are left out

underextension   The overly restrictive use of words, common among children just mastering spoken language

overextension   The overly broad use of words, overgeneralizing their meaning

referential style   A style of language use in which language is used primarily to label objects

expressive style   A style of language use in which language is used primarily to express feelings and needs about oneself and others

 Watch the Video *Child-Directed Speech* in MyPsychLab.

Language Advances During the Preschool Years

I tried it out and it was very great!
This is a picture of when I was running through the water with Mommy.
Where you are going when I go to the fireworks with Mommy and Daddy?
I didn't know creatures went on floats in pools.
We can always pretend we have another one.
And the teacher put it up on the counter so no one could reach it.
I really want to keep it while we're at the park.
You need to get your own ball if you want to play "hit the tree."
When I grow up and I'm a baseball player, I'll have my baseball hat, and I'll put it on, and I'll play baseball. (Shatz, 1994, p. 179)

During the preschool years, children make considerable advances in their language capabilities.

Listen to Ricky at the age of 3. In addition to recognizing most letters of the alphabet, printing the first letter of his name, and writing the word *HI*, he is readily capable of producing the complex sentences quoted above.

During the preschool years, children's language skills reach new heights of sophistication. They begin the period with reasonable linguistic capabilities, although with significant gaps in both comprehension and production. In fact, no one would mistake the language used by a 3-year-old for that of an adult. However, by the end of the preschool years, they can hold their own with adults, both comprehending and producing language that has many of the qualities of adults' language. How does this transformation occur?

Language blooms so rapidly between the late 2s and the mid-3s that researchers have yet to understand the exact pattern. What is clear is that sentence length increases at a steady pace, and the ways in which children at this age combine words and phrases to form sentences—known as **syntax**—doubles each month. By the time a preschooler is 3, the various combinations reach into the thousands (Pinker, 2005; Rowland & Noble, 2011; Kidd, 2012).

In addition to the increasing complexity of sentences, there are enormous leaps in the number of words children use. By age 6, the average child has a vocabulary of around 14,000 words. To reach this number, preschoolers acquire vocabulary at a rate of nearly one new word every 2 hours, 24 hours a day. They manage this feat through a process known as **fast mapping,** in which new words are associated with their meaning after only a brief encounter (Gershkoff-Stowe & Hahn, 2007; Krcmar, Grela, & Lin, 2007; Kan & Kohnert, 2008).

By the age of 3, preschoolers routinely use plurals and possessive forms of nouns (such as "boys" and "boy's"), employ the past tense (adding "-ed" at the end of words), and use articles ("the" and "a"). They can ask, and answer, complex questions ("Where did you say my book is?" and "Those are trucks, aren't they?").

Preschoolers' skills extend to the appropriate formation of words that they have never before encountered. For example, in one classic experiment, preschool children were shown cards with drawings of a cartoon-like bird, such as those shown in Figure 8-3 (Berko, 1958). The experimenter told the children that the figure was a "wug," and then showed them a card with two of the cartoon figures. "Now there are two of them," the children were told, and they were then asked to supply the missing word in the sentence, "There are two ____" (the answer to which, as *you* no doubt know, is "wugs").

Not only did children show that they knew rules about the plural forms of nouns, but they understood possessive forms of nouns and the third-person singular and past-tense forms of verbs—all for words that they never had previously encountered, since they were nonsense words with no real meaning (O'Grady & Aitchison, 2005).

Preschoolers also learn what *cannot* be said as they acquire the principles of grammar. **Grammar** is the system of rules that determine how our thoughts can be expressed. For instance, preschoolers come to learn that "I am sitting" is correct, while the similarly structured "I am knowing [that]" is incorrect. Although they still make frequent mistakes of one sort or another, 3-year-olds follow the principles of grammar most of the time. Some errors are very

syntax The combining of words and phrases to form sentences

fast mapping The process in which new words are associated with their meaning only after a brief encounter

grammar The system of rules that determine how our thoughts can be expressed

This is a wug.

Now there is another one.
There are two of them.
There are two _____ .

FIGURE 8-3 Appropriate Formation of Words

Even though preschoolers—like the rest of us—are unlikely to have ever before encountered a wug, they are able to produce the appropriate word to fill in the blank (which, for the record, is wugs).

(*Source:* Adapted from Berko, 1958)

noticeable—such as the use of "mens" and "catched"—but these errors are actually quite rare, occurring between one-tenth of a percent and 8% of the time. Put another way, young preschoolers are correct in their grammatical constructions more than 90% of the time (Pinker, 1994; Guasti, 2002; Witt & Vinter, 2012).

Private Speech and Social Speech. In even a short visit to a preschool, you're likely to notice some children talking to themselves during play periods. A child might be reminding a doll that the two of them are going to the grocery store later, or another child, while playing with a toy racing car, might speak of an upcoming race. In some cases, the talk is sustained, as when a child, working on a puzzle, says things like, "This piece goes here. . . . Uh-oh, this one doesn't fit. . . .Where can I put this piece? . . . This can't be right."

Some developmentalists suggest that **private speech**, speech by children that is spoken and directed to themselves, performs an important function. For instance, Vygotsky suggested that private speech is used as a guide to behavior and thought. By communicating with themselves through private speech, children are able to try out ideas, acting as their own sounding boards. In this way, private speech facilitates children's thinking and helps them control their behavior. (Have you ever said to yourself, "Take it easy" or "Calm down" when trying to control your anger over some situation?) In Vygotsky's view, then, private speech ultimately serves an important social function, allowing children to solve problems and reflect upon difficulties they encounter. He also suggested that private speech is a forerunner to the internal dialogues that we use when we reason with ourselves during thinking (Winsler, De Leon, & Wallace, 2003; Winsler et al., 2006).

In addition, private speech may be a way for children to practice the practical skills required in conversation, also known as pragmatics. **Pragmatics** is the aspect of language relating to communicating effectively and appropriately with others. The development of pragmatic abilities permits children to understand the basics of conversations—turn-taking, sticking to a topic, and what should and should not be said, according to the conventions of society. When children are taught that the appropriate response to receiving a gift is "thank you," or that they should use different language in various settings (on the playground with their friends versus in the classroom with their teacher), they are learning the pragmatics of language.

The preschool years also mark the growth of social speech. **Social speech** is speech directed toward another person and meant to be understood by that person. Before the age of 3, children may seem to be speaking only for their own entertainment, apparently uncaring whether anyone else can understand. However, during the preschool years, children begin to direct their speech to others, wanting others to listen and becoming frustrated when they cannot make themselves understood. As a result, they begin to adapt their speech to others through pragmatics, as discussed above. Recall that Piaget contended that most speech during the preoperational period was egocentric: Preschoolers were seen as taking little account of the effect their speech was having on others. However, more recent experimental evidence suggests that children are somewhat more adept in taking others into account than Piaget initially suggested.

Language Development during Middle Childhood: Mastering Language

If you listen to what school-age children say to one another, their speech, at least at first hearing, sounds not too different from that of adults. However, the apparent similarity is deceiving. The linguistic sophistication of children, particularly at the start of the school-age period, still requires refinement to reach adult levels of expertise.

Mastering the Mechanics of Language. Vocabulary continues to increase during the school years at a fairly rapid clip. For instance, the average 6-year-old has a vocabulary of from 8,000 to 14,000 words, and the vocabulary grows by another 5,000 words between the ages of 9 and 11.

School-age children's mastery of grammar also improves. For instance, the use of the passive voice is rare during the early school-age years (as in "The dog was walked by Lee,"

private speech Speech by children that is spoken and directed to themselves, performs an important function

pragmatics The aspect of language relating to communicating effectively and appropriately with others

social speech Speech directed toward another person and meant to be understood by that person

compared with the active-voice "Lee walked the dog"). Six- and 7-year-olds only infrequently use conditional sentences, such as "If Sarah will set the table, I will wash the dishes." However, over the course of middle childhood, the use of both passive voice and conditional sentences increases. In addition, children's understanding of *syntax,* the rules that indicate how words and phrases can be combined to form sentences, grows during middle childhood.

By the time they reach first grade, most children pronounce words quite accurately. However, certain *phonemes*—units of sound—remain troublesome. For instance, the ability to pronounce *j, v, th,* and *zh* sounds develops later than the ability to pronounce other phonemes.

School-age children also may have difficulty decoding sentences when the meaning depends on *intonation,* or tone of voice. For example, consider the sentence, "George gave a book to David and he gave one to Bill." If the word "he" is emphasized, the meaning is "George gave a book to David and David gave a different book to Bill." But if the intonation emphasizes the word "and," then the meaning changes to "George gave a book to David and George also gave a book to Bill." School-age children cannot easily sort out subtleties such as these (Wells, Peppé, & Goulandris, 2004).

In addition to language skills, conversational skills also develop during middle childhood. Children become more competent in their use of *pragmatics,* the rules governing the use of language to communicate in a given social setting.

For example, although children are aware of the rules of conversational turn-taking at the start of the early childhood period, their use of these rules is sometimes primitive. Consider the following conversation between 6-year-olds Yonnie and Max:

Yonnie: My dad drives a FedEx truck.

Max: My sister's name is Molly.

Yonnie: He gets up really early in the morning.

Max: She wet her bed last night.

Later, however, conversations show more give-and-take, with the second child actually responding to the comments of the first. For instance, this conversation between 11-year-olds Mia and Josh reflects a more sophisticated mastery of pragmatics:

Mia: I don't know what to get Claire for her birthday.

Josh: I'm getting her earrings.

Mia: She already has a lot of jewelry.

Josh: I don't think she has that much.

Metalinguistic Awareness. One of the most significant developments in middle childhood is children's increasing understanding of their own use of language, or **metalinguistic awareness.** By the time children are 5 or 6, they understand that language is governed by a set of rules. Whereas in the early years they learn and comprehend these rules implicitly, during middle childhood, children come to understand them more explicitly (Benelli et al., 2006; Saiegh-Haddad, 2007; D'Warte, 2012).

metalinguistic awareness Children's increasing understanding of their own use of language

Metalinguistic awareness helps children achieve comprehension when information is fuzzy or incomplete. For instance, when preschoolers are given ambiguous or unclear information, such as directions for how to play a complicated game, they rarely ask for clarification, and they tend to blame themselves if they do not understand. By the time they reach the age of 7 or 8, children realize that miscommunication may be due to factors attributable not only to themselves but also to the person communicating with them. Consequently, school-age children are more likely to ask for clarification of information that is unclear to them (Apperly & Robinson, 2002).

The increase in metalinguistic skills during middle childhood allows children to enter into the give-and-take of conversation successfully.

How Language Promotes Self-Control. The growing sophistication of their language helps school-age children control their behavior. For instance, in one experiment, children were told that they could have one marshmallow treat

ARE YOU AN INFORMED CONSUMER OF DEVELOPMENT?

Assessing Early Language Development

Given the critical role that language plays in cognitive development, parents often are concerned about whether their child's language development is proceeding on schedule. Although there are no hard-and-fast rules, given the wide variability in the timing of children's first words and the ways their vocabularies develop, there are several guidelines that indicate whether language development is normal. An infant who shows the following abilities is probably developing normally, according to psycholinguist Anne Dunlea (Fowler, 1990):

- *Understanding at least some things that are heard.* This means that, at the minimum, the child has some receptive language and can hear. For instance, most children can discriminate between friendly and angry speech by the age of 6 months.
- *Producing sounds, such as a raspberry noise, at around 6 or 7 months of age.* Children who are deaf may cease producing prelinguistic speech at this point, even if they produced it earlier, because they cannot hear themselves speaking.
- *Using gestures to communicate.* Pointing and reaching are often forerunners of language. By the age of 9 months, most children look toward an object that an adult is pointing to, and most use pointing themselves before the end of their first year.
- *Pretending to use language.* Even if the words make no sense, children may pretend to use language before they actually begin to speak, indicating that they at least know how language functions.

What if you cannot observe any of these indicators? It would be reasonable to have a pediatrician evaluate your child. Keep in mind, however, the wide range of variations in language development among different children, and the fact that the vast number of children develop quite normally. ■

if they chose to eat one immediately but two treats if they waited. Most of the children, who ranged in age from 4 to 8, chose to wait, but the strategies they used while waiting differed significantly.

The 4-year-olds often chose to look at the marshmallows while waiting, a strategy that was not terribly effective. In contrast, 6- and 8-year-olds used language to help them overcome temptation, although in different ways. The 6-year-olds spoke and sang to themselves, reminding themselves that if they waited, they would get more treats in the end. The 8-year-olds focused on aspects of the marshmallows that were not related to taste, such as their appearance, which helped them to wait.

In short, children used "self-talk" to help regulate their own behavior. Furthermore, the effectiveness of their self-control grew as their linguistic capabilities increased.

Review, Check, and Apply

Review

1. Before they *produce* their first word, infants *comprehend* many adult utterances and engage in several forms of prelinguistic communication, including the use of facial expressions, gestures, and babbling.

2. Children typically produce their first words between 10 and 14 months, and rapidly increase their vocabularies from that point on. Language development proceeds through a pattern of holophrases, two-word combinations, and telegraphic speech, and reflects a growing sense of the relations between objects in the world, and the acquisition of general mental categories and concepts.

3. In the preschool years, linguistic ability increases rapidly, including advances in sentence length, vocabulary, and syntax. Children also develop a strong sense of the grammar of their language, knowing which forms and utterances are permissible and which are not, and improve their use of pragmatics, the appropriate use of language in social situations.

4. Another linguistic development is a gradual shift from private to social speech. Piaget regards private speech as a sign of immaturity and egocentrism; Vygotsky views it as a useful cognitive mechanism that ultimately serves a social function.

5. Language development in middle childhood is characterized by improvements in vocabulary, syntax, and pragmatics; by the use of language as a self-control device; and by the growth of metalinguistic awareness.

Check

1. Language comprehension precedes language _____.

2. _____ communication begins with babbling, making speechlike but meaningless sounds around the age of 2 or 3 months.

3. The language pattern by which 2-year-olds leave out unimportant words that are not critical to the message is called _____ _____.

4. The way in which words and phrases are combined to form sentences, known as _____, increases at a steady pace during the preschool years.

5. _____ _____ is speech by children that is spoken and directed to themselves.

6. _____, the aspect of language relating to communicating effectively and appropriately with others, begins to develop in preschool and becomes more sophisticated during the school years.

7. One of the most important developments during middle childhood is the ability to understand one's own use of language, called _____ awareness.

Apply

1. We have noted that deaf children babble with their hands. What other similarities and differences do you think there might be between the development of language—spoken and signed—in hearing and non-hearing children?

2. This chapter discusses some rules of pragmatics that govern the social uses of language, such as turn-taking and addressing the same topic. Can you think of other rules of pragmatics?

To see more review questions, log on to MyPsychLab.

ANSWERS: 1. production 2. Prelinguistic 3. telegraphic speech 4. syntax 5. Private speech 6. Pragmatics 7. metalinguistic

MODULE 8.2

THE ORIGINS OF LANGUAGE DEVELOPMENT

LO 8-2 What are various perspectives on the origins of language development, and what evidence supports each one?

LO 8-3 How are language and thought related?

The immense strides in language development during childhood raise a fundamental question: How does proficiency in language come about? Linguists are deeply divided on how to answer this question. They've considered two major aspects of the question, asking how language is acquired and what relationship exists between language and thought.

Language Acquisition

Three major approaches have guided thinking on language acquisition. The first is based on learning theory, the second focuses on innate and genetically determined capabilities, and the third represents a combination of the first two approaches.

Learning Theory Approaches: Language as a Learned Skill.

One view of language development emphasizes the basic principles of learning. According to the **learning theory approach,** language acquisition follows the basic laws of reinforcement and conditioning discussed in earlier chapters (Skinner, 1957). For instance, a child who articulates the word "da" may be hugged and praised by her father, who jumps to the conclusion that she is referring to him. This reaction reinforces the child, who is more likely to repeat the word. In sum, the learning theory perspective on language acquisition suggests that children learn to speak by being rewarded for making sounds that approximate speech. Through the process of *shaping*, language becomes more and more similar to adult speech.

There's a problem, though, with the learning theory approach. It doesn't seem to adequately explain how children acquire the rules of language as readily as they do. For instance, young children are reinforced when they make errors. Parents are apt to be just as responsive if their child says, "Why the dog won't eat?" as they are if the child phrases the question more correctly ("Why won't the dog eat?"). Both forms of the question are understood correctly, and both elicit the same response; reinforcement is provided for both correct and incorrect language usage. Under such circumstances, learning theory is hard-put to explain how children learn to speak properly.

Children are also able to move beyond specific utterances they have heard and produce novel phrases, sentences, and constructions, an ability that also cannot be explained by learning theory. Furthermore, children can apply linguistic rules to nonsense words. In one study, 4-year-old children heard the nonsense verb "to pilk" in the sentence "the bear is pilking the horse." Later, when asked what was happening to the horse, they responded by placing the nonsense verb in the correct tense and voice: "He's getting pilked by the bear."

Nativist Approaches: Language as an Innate Skill.

Such conceptual difficulties with the learning theory approach have led to the development of an alternative, championed by the linguist Noam Chomsky and known as the nativist approach (1999, 2005). The **nativist approach** argues that there is a genetically determined, innate mechanism that directs the development of language. According to Chomsky, people are born with an innate capacity to use language, which emerges, more or less automatically, through maturation.

Chomsky's analysis of different languages suggests that all the world's languages share a similar underlying structure, which he calls **universal grammar.** In this view, the human brain is wired with a neural system called the **language-acquisition device (LAD)** that both permits the understanding of language structure and provides a set of strategies and techniques for learning the particular characteristics of the language to which a child is exposed. In this view, language is uniquely human, made possible by a genetic predisposition to both comprehend and produce words and sentences (Hauser, Chomsky, & Fitch, 2002; Lidz & Gleitman, 2004; Stromswold, 2006).

Support for Chomsky's nativist approach comes from identification of a specific gene related to speech production. Further support comes from research showing that language processing in infants involves brain structures similar to those in adult speech processing, suggesting an evolutionary basis to language (Wade, 2001; Dehaene-Lambertz, Hertz-Pannier, & Dubois, 2006).

According to linguist Noam Chomsky, the development of language is produced by a genetically determined process.

learning theory approach The theory that language acquisition follows the basic laws of reinforcement and conditioning

nativist approach The theory that a genetically determined, innate mechanism directs language development

universal grammar Noam Chomsky's theory that all the world's languages share a similar underlying structure

language-acquisition device (LAD) A neural system of the brain hypothesized to permit understanding of language

The view that language is an innate ability unique to humans also has its critics. For instance, some researchers argue that certain primates are able to learn at least the basics of language, an ability that calls into question the uniqueness of the human linguistic capacity. Others point out that although humans may be genetically primed to use language, language use still requires significant social experience for it to be used effectively (Goldberg, 2004).

The Interactionist Approaches.   Neither the learning theory nor the nativist perspective fully explains language acquisition. As a result, some theorists have turned to a theory that combines both schools of thought. The *interactionist perspective* suggests that language development is produced through a combination of genetically determined predispositions and environmental circumstances that help teach language.

The interactionist perspective accepts that innate factors shape the broad outlines of language development. However, interactionists also argue that the specific course of language development is determined by the language to which children are exposed and the reinforcement they receive for using language in particular ways. Social factors are considered to be key to development, because the motivation provided by one's membership in a society and culture and one's interactions with others leads to the use of language and the growth of language skills (Dixon, 2004; Yang, 2006; Arnold et al., 2012).

Just as there is support for some aspects of learning theory and nativist positions, the interactionist perspective has also received some support. We don't know, at the moment, which of these positions will ultimately provide the best explanation, if any. More likely, different factors play different roles at different times during childhood. The full explanation for language acquisition, then, remains to be determined.

How Are Language and Thought Related?

It seems reasonable that Eskimo children, whose experience with freezing precipitation is far more extensive than that of children growing up in warmer climates, would have many words in their vocabulary to describe "snow." At least that was the thinking of linguist Benjamin Lee Whorf in the early 1900s. He argued that because snow was so much a part of Eskimo lives, Eskimos had a richer snow-related vocabulary than, for example, English-speakers. Whorf's account seemed to be supported by data, and at least one expert contended that there were no fewer than 400 snow-related words in the Eskimo vocabulary—far more than in English.

Not so fast. Contemporary research has found that Whorf's claims regarding the Eskimo vocabulary were greatly exaggerated. Eskimos have no more words for "snow" than do English speakers. In fact, English contains many words of its own relating to snow: Sleet, slush, blizzard, dusting, powder, and avalanche are just a few examples (Pinker, 1994; Chiu, Leung, & Kwan, 2007).

The early contention that the Eskimo language was particularly rich in snow-related words was used to support an influential proposition called the linguistic-relativity hypothesis. The **linguistic-relativity hypothesis** states that language shapes—and, in fact, may determine the way people of a particular culture perceive and understand—the world (Whorf, 1956; Casasanto, 2008). The hypothesis suggests that language provides categories that help children construct their perceptions of people and events in their surroundings. In short, the notion is that language shapes and produces thinking.

However, the view that language shapes and produces thought is not the only plausible sequence. Consider an alternative: that instead of language being the *cause* of thought, the relationship works in the opposite direction, with language being the *result* of thinking about the world in particular ways and undergoing certain experiences. In this view, thought *produces* language.

The view that thinking shapes language is consistent with Piaget's views of the development of language. As we considered in Chapter 6, Piaget argued that the emergence of symbolic function (the ability to use mental symbols, words, and objects to represent something that is not physically present) during the preoperational period is a key aspect of the

linguistic-relativity hypothesis The theory stating language shapes—and, in fact, may determine the way people of a particular culture perceive and understand—the world

development of language skill. In short, advances in the sophistication of thinking permit language development.

Some developmentalists reject both the view that language shapes thought *and* the view that thought shapes language. Instead, they support an intermediate position: that language and thought are intertwined and influence one another. For instance, Vygotsky (1962) argues that although in the early stages of life language and thinking develop independently, by the age of 2 they become interdependent. From that point, each influences the other. More precise thought permits language to become increasingly sophisticated, and more refined language capabilities permit more advanced thought.

We now have three views about the relationship between language and thought: Language shapes thought (the linguistic-relativity hypothesis); thought shapes language; and thought and language influence one another. There is research supporting each view. Although most linguists would reject the notion that language is the *predominant* influence on thought, there is evidence that language does shape at least some kinds of thinking. For instance, the way in which information is stored and retrieved in memory is related to language, and the way that people evaluate others is influenced by the linguistic categories they have available to them (Gleitman & Papafragou, 2005; Casasanto, 2008).

On the other hand, there is also experimental support for the opposite position, that thinking shapes language. For instance, the experiences that children have shape their first words, which are usually about people, animals, and foods in their environment, regardless of the language they speak. Furthermore, cross-cultural research shows that even if there is no word for particular colors in a given language, people speaking that language can still distinguish the different colors, suggesting that language is not a prerequisite for thought (Rosch, 1974; Zhang, He, & Zhang, 2007).

The existence of evidence supporting both the language-shapes-thought and thought-shapes-language sequences suggests that the third position—that thought and language jointly influence one another—may ultimately prove to be the most accurate. In fact, such a position seems plausible and is supported by direct experimental evidence (Riley, 2008; Taylor, 2012). Most developmentalists, then, suggest that although initially language and thought may develop more or less independently, by the time children are 2, language and thinking work in tandem, as Vygotsky suggested.

Most developmentalists agree that language and thought are interdependent.

Review, Check, and Apply

Review

1. The way language develops is a complex and controversial question. Several theoretical perspectives have been adopted to explain the phenomenon, including learning theory, the nativist approach, and the interactionist approach.

2. According to the learning theory approach, language acquisition is little different from learning of any sort, with children's language reinforced and shaped by adults. The emergence of a sense of grammar is not well-explained by this approach.

3. The nativist approach, developed by Noam Chomsky, claims that humans have an innate language capacity that naturally facilitates language development. The existence of sensitive periods for learning language, the lack of language among nonhuman species, and the existence of areas of the brain associated with language support the nativist approach, while the failure to specify a truly universal grammar weakens it.

4. A compromise position is held by the interactionists, who argue that language development, while innate, is determined by social factors, such as children's linguistic environment and the reinforcement they receive from others.

5. The linguistic-relativity hypothesis, advanced by Benjamin Lee Whorf, holds that language shapes thought. However, the opposite view, that thought shapes language, as Piaget believed, is also a prevalent view, and the truth is probably that language and thought influence one another.

Check

1. The belief that children learn language by imitating their parents and shaping their sense of grammar in response to what they hear is a tenet of the _____ _____ approach.

2. In contrast, Chomsky's nativist approach holds that children are born with a _____-_____ device that enables them to draw on the universal grammar to understand and internalize the structure of their home language.

3. The _____-_____ hypothesis, originated by Whorf, claims that language shapes thought and may determine the different ways people of varied cultures perceive and understand.

Apply

1. If humans have a language-acquisition device, why do children raised in isolation not develop language naturally? Why do adults have such difficulty learning a new language?

2. Do you think language influences thought more than thought influences language? Why?

To see more review questions, log on to MyPsychLab.

ANSWERS: 1. learning theory 2. language-acquisition 3. linguistic-relativity

MODULE 8.3

CHILDREN'S CONVERSATIONS: SPEAKING TO AND WITH CHILDREN

LO 8-4 In what ways does the language adults use with children affect language development?

LO 8-5 How do social issues influence language development?

Say the following sentence aloud: *Do you like the applesauce?*

Now pretend that you are going to ask the same question of an infant, and speak it as you would for a young child's ears.

Chances are several things happened when you translated the phrase for the infant. First of all, the wording probably changed, and you may have said something like, "Does baby like the applesauce?" At the same time, the pitch of your voice probably rose, your general intonation most likely had a singsong quality, and you probably separated your words carefully.

The change in your language illustrates just one facet of the nature of conversations involving children. We turn now to several aspects of language involving children's conversations, beginning with speech directed at infants.

The Language of Infant-Directed Speech

When you talk to an infant, you naturally adjust your language; this is due to your use of **infant-directed speech,** a style of speech that characterizes much of the verbal communication directed toward infants. This type of speech pattern used to be called *motherese*, because it was assumed that it applied only to mothers. However, that assumption was wrong, and the gender-neutral term *infant-directed speech* is now used more frequently.

Infant-directed speech is characterized by short, simple sentences. Pitch becomes higher, the range of frequencies increases, and intonation is more varied. There is also repetition of words, and topics are restricted to items that are assumed to be comprehensible to infants, such as concrete objects in the baby's environment. (Infants are not the only ones who are the recipients of a specific form of speech: we change our style of speech when speaking to foreigners, as well [Soderstrom, 2007; Schachner & Hannon, 2011; Naoi et al., 2012]).

infant-directed speech A type of speech directed toward infants, characterized by short, simple sentences

Sometimes infant-directed speech includes amusing sounds that are not even words, imitating the prelinguistic speech of infants. In other cases, it has little formal structure, but is similar to the kind of telegraphic speech that infants use as they develop their own language skills.

Infant-directed speech changes as children become older. Around the end of the first year, infant-directed speech takes on more adult-like qualities. Sentences become longer and more complex, although individual words are still spoken slowly and deliberately. Pitch is also used to focus attention on particularly important words (Soderstrom et al., 2008; Kitamura & Lam, 2009).

Infant-directed speech plays an important role in infants' acquisition of language. As discussed in the *Developmental Diversity* box that follows, infant-directed speech occurs all over the world, though there are cultural variations. Newborns prefer such speech to regular language, a fact that suggests that they may be particularly receptive to it. Furthermore, some research suggests that babies who are exposed to a great deal of infant-directed speech early in life seem to begin to use words and exhibit other forms of linguistic competence earlier (Soderstrom, 2007; Werker et al., 2007; Matsuda et al., 2011).

Infant-directed speech, also known as "motherese," includes the use of short, simple sentences and is spoken using a pitch higher than that used with older children and adults.

DEVELOPMENTAL DIVERSITY AND YOUR LIFE

Is Infant-Directed Speech Similar in All Cultures?

Do mothers in the United States, Sweden, and Russia speak the same way to their infants?

In some respects, they clearly do. Although the words themselves differ across languages, the way the words are spoken to infants is quite similar. According to a growing body of research, there are basic similarities across cultures in the nature of infant-directed speech (Werker et al., 2007; Schachner & Hannon, 2011).

Consider, for instance, the comparison in Table 8-2 of the major characteristics of speech directed at infants used by native speakers of English and Spanish. Of the 10 most frequent features, 6 are common to both: exaggerated intonation, high pitch, lengthened vowels, repetition, lower volume, and instructional emphasis (i.e., heavy stress on certain key words, such as emphasizing the word "ball" in the sentence, "No, that's a *ball*") (Blount, 1982). Similarly, mothers in the United States, Sweden, and Russia all exaggerate and elongate the pronunciation of the three vowel sounds of "ee," "ah," and "oh" when speaking to infants in similar ways, despite differences in the languages in which the sounds are used (Kuhl et al., 1997).

Even deaf mothers use a form of infant-directed speech: When communicating with their infants, deaf mothers use sign language at a significantly slower tempo than when communicating with adults, and they frequently repeat the signs (Swanson, Leonard, & Gandour, 1992; Masataka, 2000).

The cross-cultural similarities in infant-directed speech are so great, in fact, that they appear in some facets of language specific to particular types of interactions. For instance, evidence comparing American English, German, and Mandarin Chinese speakers shows that in each of the languages, pitch rises when a mother is attempting to get an infant's attention or produce a response, while pitch falls when she is trying to calm an infant (Papousek & Papousek, 1991).

Why do we find such similarities across very different languages? One hypothesis is that the characteristics of infant-directed speech activate innate responses in infants. As we have noted, infants

TABLE 8-2 The Most Common Features of Infant-Directed Speech

English	Spanish
1. Stronger intonation	1. Strong intonation
2. Exaggerated breathiness	2. Repetition
3. Higher pitch	3. Higher pitch
4. More repetition	4. More instructional
5. Lower volume	5. Use of attentionals
6. Vowel sounds lengthened	6. Volume is lower
7. Creakiness in voice	7. Higher volume
8. More instruction	8. Vowel sounds lower
9. Tenseness	9. Faster speed
10. Use of falsetto	10. More substitutions of personal pronouns

(*Source:* Adapted from Blount, 1982)

seem to prefer infant-directed speech over adult-directed speech, suggesting that their perceptual systems may be more responsive to such characteristics. Another explanation is that infant-directed speech facilitates language development, providing cues as to the meaning of speech before infants have developed the capacity to understand the meaning of words (Kuhl et al., 1997; Trainor & Desjardins, 2002; Falk, 2004).

Despite the similarities in the style of infant-directed speech across diverse cultures, there are some important cultural differences in the *quantity* of speech that infants hear from their parents. For example, although the Gusii of Kenya care for their infants in an extremely close, physical way, they speak to them less than American parents do (LeVine, 1994).

There are also some stylistic differences related to cultural factors in the United States. A major factor, it seems, might be gender. ■

Gender Differences in Speech Directed toward Children

To a girl, a bird is a birdie, a blanket a blankie, and a dog a doggy. To a boy, a bird is a bird, a blanket a blanket, and a dog a dog.

At least that's what parents of boys and girls appear to think, as illustrated by the language they use toward their sons and daughters. Virtually from the time of birth, the language parents employ with their children differs depending on the child's sex, according to research conducted by developmental psychologist Jean Berko Gleason (Gleason et al., 1994; Gleason & Ely, 2002).

Gleason found that, by the age of 32 months, girls hear twice as many diminutives (words such as "kitty" or "dolly" instead of "cat" or "doll") as boys hear. Although the use of diminutives declines with increasing age, their use consistently remains higher in speech directed at girls than in that directed at boys (see Figure 8-4).

Parents also are more apt to respond differently to children's requests depending on the child's gender. For instance, when turning down a child's request, mothers are likely to respond with a firm "no" to a male child, but to soften the blow to a female child by providing a diversionary response ("Why don't you do this instead?") or by somehow making the refusal less direct. Consequently, boys tend to hear firmer, clearer language, while girls are exposed to warmer phrases, often referring to inner emotional states (Perlmann & Gleason, 1990).

Do such differences in language directed at boys and girls during infancy affect their behavior as adults? There is no direct evidence that plainly supports such an association, but men and women do use different sorts of language as adults. For instance, as adults, women tend to use more tentative, less assertive language, such as "Maybe we should try to go to a movie," than men ("I know, let's go to a movie!"). Although we don't know whether these differences are a reflection of early linguistic experiences, such findings are certainly intriguing (Tenenbaum & Leaper, 2003; Hartshorne & Ullman, 2006; Plante et al., 2006).

The Links between Language Development and Poverty

The language that preschoolers hear at home has profound implications for future cognitive success, according to results of a landmark series of studies by psychologists Betty Hart and Todd Risley (Hart & Risley, 1995; Hart, 2000, 2004). The researchers studied the language used over a 2-year period by a group of parents of varying levels of affluence as they interacted with their children. Their examination of some 1,300 hours of everyday interactions between parents and children produced several major findings:

- The greater the affluence of the parents, the more they spoke to their children. As shown in Figure 8-5, the rate at which language was addressed to children varied significantly according to the economic level of the family. The greater the affluence of the parents, the more they spoke to their children.

FROM AN
EDUCATOR'S
PERSPECTIVE:

What are some implications of differences in the ways adults speak to boys and girls? How might such speech differences contribute to later differences not only in speech but also in attitudes?

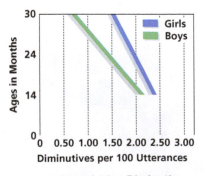

FIGURE 8-4 Diminishing Diminutives

While the use of diminutives toward both male and female infants declines with age, they are consistently used more often in speech directed at females. What do you think is the cultural significance of this?

(*Source:* Gleason et al., 1991.)

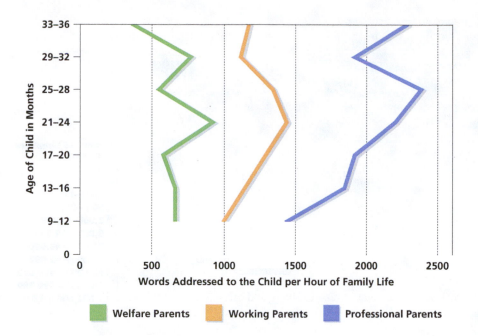

FIGURE 8-5 Different Language Exposures

Parents at differing levels of affluence provide different language experiences. Professional parents and working parents address more words to their children, on average, than parents on welfare. Why do you think this is so?

(*Source:* B. Hart & Risley, 1995, p. 239)

- In a typical hour, parents classified as professionals spent almost twice as much time interacting with their children as parents who received welfare assistance.

- By the age of 4, children in families that received welfare assistance were likely to have been exposed to some 13 million fewer words than those in families classified as professionals.

- The kind of language used in the home differed among the various types of families. Children in families that received welfare assistance were apt to hear prohibitions ("no" or "stop," for example) twice as frequently as those in families classified as professionals.

Ultimately, the study found that the type of language to which children were exposed was associated with their performance on tests of intelligence. The greater the number and variety of words children heard, for instance, the better their performance at age 3 on a variety of measures of intellectual achievement.

Although the findings are correlational, and thus cannot be interpreted in terms of cause-and-effect, they clearly suggest the importance of early exposure to language, in terms of both quantity and variety. They also suggest that intervention programs that teach parents to speak to their children more often and use more varied language may be useful in alleviating some of the potentially damaging consequences of poverty.

The research is also consistent with an increasing body of evidence that family income and poverty have powerful consequences for children's general cognitive development and behavior. By the age of 5, children raised in poverty tend to have lower IQ scores and perform less well on other measures of cognitive development than children raised in affluence. Furthermore, the longer children live in poverty, the more severe are the consequences. Poverty not only reduces the educational resources available to children, it also has such negative effects on *parents* that it limits the psychological support they can provide their families. In short, the consequences of poverty are severe, and they linger (Farah et al., 2006; Jokela et al., 2009; Barone, 2011; Maier, Vitiello, & Greenfield, 2012).

Bilingualism: Speaking in Many Tongues

John Dewey Elementary is a school known for its progressive and democratic attitudes. On the campus of a large university, it boasts a staff of classroom aides who in sum speak 15 different languages, including Hindi and Hausa. The challenge is there are more than 30 languages spoken by the students.

**FROM A
SOCIAL WORKER'S
PERSPECTIVE:**

What do you think are the underlying reasons for differences between poor and more affluent households in the use of language, and how do such language differences affect a family's social interactions?

Bilingual education, in which children are initially taught in their native language while at the same time learning English, is one approach to educating non-English speakers.

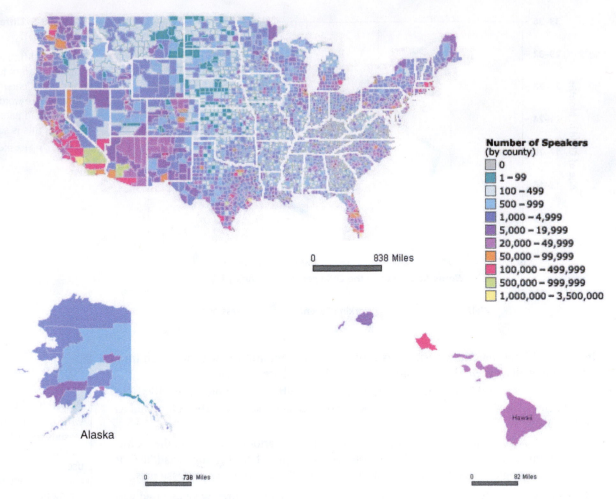

FIGURE 8-6 Languages Other Than English Spoken in the United States

These figures show the number of U.S. residents over the age of 5 who speak a language other than English at home. With increases in the number and variety of languages spoken in the United States, what types of approaches might an educator use to meet the needs of bilingual students?

(*Source:* Modern Language Association, www.mla.org/census_map, 2005. Based on data from U.S. Census Bureau, 2000)

From the smallest towns to the biggest cities, the voices with which children speak are changing. Nearly one in five people in the United States speaks a language other than English at home, a percentage that is growing. **Bilingualism**—the use of more than one language—is growing increasingly common (Graddol, 2004; Kuo & Anderson, 2012; see Figure 8-6).

Children who enter school with little or no English proficiency must learn both the standard curriculum and the language in which that curriculum is taught. One approach to educating non-English speakers is *bilingual education,* in which children are initially taught in their native language, while at the same time learning English.

With bilingual instruction, students are able to develop a strong foundation in basic subject areas using their native language. The ultimate goal of bilingual education programs is to gradually increase students' English proficiency while maintaining or improving skills in their native language.

An alternative approach is to immerse students in English as quickly as possible, teaching solely in that language, and providing only minimal instruction in a student's native language. To proponents of this approach, initially teaching students in a language other than

👁 **Watch** the **Video** *Thinking Like a Psychologist: Multilingualism* in **MyPsychLab**.

bilingualism The use of more than one language

English hinders students' efforts to learn English and slows their integration into society. Consequently, the emphasis is on English instruction.

The main drawback to the immersion approach is that it can make it more difficult for students to learn new skills if those skills are taught in a second language. For example, consider the difficulty of a student who must learn fractions in a second language to which she has been exposed for only a few months (Pearson, 2007; Jared et al., 2011; Han, 2012).

Both bilingual and immersion approaches have been highly politicized, with some politicians arguing in favor of "English-only" laws, while others urge school systems to respect the challenges faced by nonnative speakers by offering some instruction in their native language. Still, the psychological research is clear in suggesting that knowing more than one language offers several cognitive advantages. Because they have a wider range of linguistic possibilities to choose from as they assess a situation, speakers of two languages show greater cognitive flexibility. They can solve problems with greater creativity and versatility. Furthermore, learning in one's native tongue is associated with higher self-esteem in minority students (Chen & Bond, 2007; Bialystok & Viswanathan, 2009; Marinova-Todd, 2012).

Bilingual students often have greater metalinguistic awareness, understanding the rules of language more explicitly, and they often show great cognitive sophistication. They even may score higher on tests of intelligence, according to some research. Furthermore, brain scans comparing bilingual individuals with those who speak only one language find differences suggesting different types of brain activation (Swanson, Saez, & Gerber, 2004; Carlson & Meltzoff, 2008; Kovelman, Baker, & Petitto, 2008).

Finally, because many linguists contend that universal processes underlie language acquisition, as we noted earlier in this chapter, instruction in a native language may enhance instruction in a second language. In fact, many educators believe that second-language learning should be a regular part of elementary schooling for *all* children (Kecskes & Papp, 2000; McCardle & Hoff, 2006; Park, Badzakova-Trajkov, & Waldie, 2012).

Watch the **Video** *Bilingual Family* in **MyPsychLab**.

Review, Check, and Apply

Review

1. When talking to infants, adults of all cultures tend to use infant-directed speech. This type of speech seems to appeal to infants and to facilitate their linguistic development.

2. According to some research, adults tend to speak more indirectly to girls and more directly to boys, which may contribute to behavioral differences later in life.

3. Economic factors in the home have a significant influence on language development. Children raised in affluence hear a greater quantity and variety of language from their parents than children of poverty, with positive effects on later measures of intellectual achievement.

4. Bilingual students who speak more than one language show greater cognitive flexibility and metalinguistic awareness, and even seem to perform better on intelligence tests.

5. The immersion approach to school learning, with instruction delivered in the language of the dominant culture, can be problematic for children of other cultures.

Check

1. Infant directed speech is characterized by _____ sentences, _____ pitch, and more _____ intonation.

2. Economic conditions can affect the _____ of oral language that children hear at home.

3. In contrast to immersion approaches to language education, _____ education appears to offer significant benefits to language learners.

Apply

1. What are some implications of differences in the ways adults speak to boys and girls? How might such speech differences contribute to later differences not only in speech, but in attitudes?

2. If parents living in poverty are given instruction in using a greater quantity and variety of language in the home, do you think their children will thereby achieve equality with more affluent children in linguistic and cognitive areas? Why or why not?

To see more review questions, log on to MyPsychLab.

ANSWERS: 1. shorter; higher; varied 2. quantity 3. bilingual

The CASE of . . . *the Deedio Mystery*

Like most parents, Karen Muller was excited when her 10-month-old daughter, Lisa, said her first word. She was especially pleased that the word was "Mama." In the next three months, Lisa added more new words: *kitty*, *baba* (bottle), *Dada*, *hi*, *cookie*, and *bus*.

Karen waited eagerly for Lisa to begin putting words together, but the baby seemed content with her one-word utterances. Then, around 15 months, Lisa added some surprising new words: *Mammia*, *Daddio*, *Meemia*, and *Deedio*. Karen understood that *Mammia* and *Daddio* referred to her and Lisa's father, and she thought *Meemia* might be a reference to Lisa herself, but the new "fancy" labels puzzled her, and *Deedio* was a complete mystery. Also, Lisa did not use these new words in direct relation to the people they named, but in a seemingly abstract manner. For example, she said "Daddio" when her father was nowhere in sight.

Lisa's new words remained puzzling until one day, at about 18 months, as she and Karen were getting ready to go to the park, Lisa pointed to her own shoes and said, "Meemia." Then she pointed to her older brother's shoes and said, "Deedio." Karen realized two things instantly: Deedio was Lisa's brother David, and the use of "ia" and "io" endings on the familiar terms for her family and self indicated ownership.

Over the next month, Karen listened carefully to Lisa when she used these words. Daddy was still "Dada" when he was in sight, but Lisa began using two-word sentences, saying things like "Daddio coat" and "Meemia baby" (for her doll). The mystery of Deedio had been solved.

1. How would you explain to Karen the cognitive advance that was likely occurring in Lisa as she began using Mammia, Daddio, Meemia, and Deedio, even though, initially, these were one-word utterances?

2. Do you think Lisa's initial use of "Meemia" or "Daddio" could be considered telegraphic speech? Why or why not?

3. How might Karen have gone about investigating Lisa's meaning for words like "Mammia" and "Deedio" before the baby began using two-word sentences?

4. Do you think infants ever utter nonsense words, or does each word have a concrete meaning to the baby? Explain your response in terms of what we know about infant language acquisition.

5. How can a parent influence an infant's language development? In what ways is the parent's influence limited?

◀◀◀ LOOKING BACK

LO 8-1 What is the process of language development during the childhood years?

- Infants engage in prelinguistic communication, the use of sounds, gestures, facial expressions, imitation, and other nonlinguistic means to express thoughts and states. Babbling is a form of prelinguistic communication, which proceeds through regular stages and, with other forms of prelinguistic communication, prepares the infant for speech.

- Infants typically produce their first words between the ages of 10 and 14 months. Thereafter, vocabulary increases rapidly, especially during a spurt at around 18 months. At about the same time, children typically begin to link words together into primitive sentences that express single thoughts.

- Beginning speech is characterized by the use of holophrases, in which a single word conveys more complex meaning based on its context; telegraphic speech, in which only essential sentence components are used; underextension, in which an overly restrictive meaning is assigned to a word; and overextension, in which an overly generalized meaning is assigned to a word.

- Features of the child's native language begin to emerge as early as the babbling stage, when sounds other than those of the home language gradually disappear. In addition, the structure of the home language begins to be reflected even in telegraphic speech, when word order mirrors that used by mature speakers of the home language.

- The burst in language ability that occurs during the preschool years is dramatic. Children rapidly progress from two-word utterances to longer, more sophisticated expressions that reflect their growing vocabularies, sense of syntax, and emerging grasp of grammar. They also proceed along a continuum from private speech to more social speech.

- Similarly, the language development of children in the school years is substantial, with improvements in vocabulary, syntax, and pragmatics. Despite these advances, school-age children's language is still not as proficient as it will become in adulthood, and some pronunciation and comprehension difficulties are normal.

- Improvements in language help children control their behavior through linguistic strategies. Moreover, their growing metalinguistic awareness permits them to realize that language use is rule-governed and is subject to breakdowns for which they are not solely responsible, and which can be remedied by seeking clarification.

LO 8-2 What are various perspectives on the origins of language development, and what evidence supports each one?

- One theory of how humans develop language is the learning theory, which assumes that adults and children use basic behavioral processes—such as conditioning, reinforcement, and shaping—in language learning. The fact that people spontaneously develop a natural grammatical sense argues against this perspective.

- A radically different approach—the nativist approach—is proposed by Noam Chomsky, who holds that humans are genetically endowed with a language acquisition device, which permits them to detect and use the principles of universal grammar that underlie all languages. Support for this view is derived from the existence of sensitive periods for learning language, the lack of language among nonhuman species, and the existence of areas of the brain associated with language, while the failure to specify a truly universal grammar weakens it.

- An intermediate approach—the interactionist perspective—holds that children have innate linguistic capabilities that are shaped by social factors such as the language to which children are exposed and the interactions that they have with others in their environment.

LO 8-3 How are language and thought related?

- According to Benjamin Lee Whorf's linguistic-relativity hypothesis, the language that people speak influences the ways they perceive and understand the world. This view—that language shapes thought—is controversial; the opposite view—that thought shapes language—which is held by developmentalists such as Jean Piaget—is more mainstream, but also controversial. An intermediate position—that thought and language jointly influence one another—is growing in acceptance and appears to be most accurate.

LO 8-4 In what ways does the language adults use with children affect language development?

- Infant-directed speech takes on characteristics, surprisingly invariant across cultures, that make it appealing to infants and that probably facilitate language development. There is some evidence that infants are especially—and perhaps innately—attuned to the characteristics of infant-directed speech.

- Adult language also exhibits differences based on the gender of the child to whom it is directed. For example, some research indicates that adult speech addressed to boys is more direct than that addressed to girls. It is possible that gender differences in the language heard during infancy may have effects that emerge later in life.

LO 8-5 How do social issues influence language development?

- Language development and economic circumstances are significantly linked. Preschool children of poverty tend to hear a smaller quantity and variety of language from their parents and caregivers than children of affluence. This linguistic difference in turn is linked to later differential performance on a variety of measures of intellectual achievement.

- Bilingualism is an increasingly prevalent phenomenon in the school years. There is evidence that many children who are taught all subjects in the first language, with simultaneous instruction in English, experience few deficits and several linguistic and cognitive advantages.

- Immersion programs work well when majority children are immersed during the school day in a minority language, but do not work as well the other way around: when minority children are immersed in the language of the majority.

KEY TERMS AND CONCEPTS

language (p. 220)
prelinguistic communication (p. 220)
babbling (p. 221)
holophrases (p. 223)
telegraphic speech (p. 224)
underextension (p. 224)
overextension (p. 224)
referential style (p. 224)

expressive style (p. 224)
syntax (p. 225)
fast mapping (p. 225)
grammar (p. 225)
private speech (p. 226)
pragmatics (p. 226)
social speech (p. 226)
metalinguistic awareness (p. 227)

learning theory approach (p. 230)
nativist approach (p. 230)
universal grammar (p. 230)
language-acquisition device (LAD) (p. 230)
linguistic-relativity hypothesis (p. 231)
infant-directed speech (p. 234)
bilingualism (p. 238)

Epilogue

We have taken a look at the development of speech in children, observing how they progress from inaccurate users of language to accomplished speakers. The process by which they reach competence in language is complex but seems to come naturally to children. Their capabilities are so apparent that they can easily learn two or more languages if they hear them frequently and naturally—an ability envied by any school-age student or adult who has struggled with Beginning French or Mandarin Made Easy.

In the chapter prologue, we encountered Vicki and Dominic, who engaged in a friendly competition over whether their daughter Maura would first say the word "mama" or the word "daddy." The quest to encourage Maura and hear her first word was intense, keeping them occupied for months. When she at last uttered her first word, both parents were delighted—even though Maura's first word seemed to refer not to either of her parents, but to her bottle.

1. Why do you think Vicki and Dominic were so fascinated by the emergence of Maura's first word? Is it the same thrill they probably got from Maura's first steps, first solid food, first day at preschool, first sentence read, first words written? How are these experiences similar, and how are they different? Why?

2. What aspects of language are taught, and which ones develop naturally?

3. Nonhuman animals vocalize constantly. Can their oral production be called language? Why or why not? Do you think animal parents are as excited by the first meaningful sounds emitted by their offspring as Vicki and Dominic are about Maura's first word?

4. In what ways do you think nonhuman primates' language shares the formal characteristics of human speech (phonology, morphology, and semantics)? Do animal sounds display pragmatics?

The Development Video Series in MyPsychLab

Explore the video *Language Development Across Cultures* by scanning this QR code with your mobile device. If you don't already have one, you may download a free QR scanner for your device wherever smartphone apps are sold. You can also view this video in MyPsychLab. For more videos related to this chapter's content, log into MyPsychLab to view the entire Development Video Series.

MyVirtualChild

- **What decisions would you make while raising a child?**
- **What would the consequences of those decisions be?**

Find out by accessing **MyVirtualChild** at
www.MyPsychLab.com
and raising your own virtual child from birth to age 18.

9 Intelligence

MODULE 9.1

INTELLIGENCE: DETERMINING INDIVIDUAL STRENGTHS

- Intelligence Benchmarks: Differentiating the Intelligent from the Unintelligent
- Measuring IQ: Present-Day Approaches to Intelligence
- Fairness in IQ Testing

DEVELOPMENTAL DIVERSITY AND YOUR LIFE: IQ Tests: One Size Fits All?

- What IQ Tests Don't Tell: Alternative Conceptions of Intelligence
- Smart Thinking: The Triarchic Theory of Intelligence

NEUROSCIENCE AND DEVELOPMENT: When Song Is Silent: Why Amusia Sufferers Can't Hear a Tune?

- Emotional Intelligence

Review, Check, and Apply

MODULE 9.2

CONTROVERSIES INVOLVING INTELLIGENCE

- Individual Differences in Intelligence: Is One Infant Smarter Than Another?
- Information Processing Approaches to Infant Intelligence
- Group Differences in IQ
- Explaining Racial Differences in IQ

FROM RESEARCH TO PRACTICE: Take-at-Home IQ Tests: Should Parents Test Their Children's IQ?

Review, Check, and Apply

MODULE 9.3

INTELLECTUAL DEFICITS AND THE INTELLECTUALLY GIFTED

- The Least Restrictive Environment

CAREERS IN CHILD DEVELOPMENT: Christine Gonzalez, Special Education Teacher

- Below the Norm: Intellectual Disability
- Above the Norm: The Gifted and Talented

ARE YOU AN INFORMED CONSUMER OF DEVELOPMENT? How to Take an IQ Test?

Review, Check, and Apply

The Case of . . . The Worried Eighth-Grade Teacher

Looking Back

Key Terms and Concepts

Epilogue

PROLOGUE: The Exceptional Daniel Skandera

"Hey, hey, hey. Fact Track!" The 11-year-old speaker chose one of his favorite programs from the table next to the computer in his parents' dining room. He inserted the floppy disc, booted the system, and waited for the program to load.

"What is your name?" appeared on the monitor.

"Daniel Skandera," he typed. A menu scrolled up listing the program's possibilities. Daniel chose multiplication facts, Level 1.

"How many problems do you want to do?" the computer asked.

"20."

"Do you want to set a goal for yourself, Daniel?"

"Yes, 80 sec."

"Get ready!" · · ·

Randomly generated multiplication facts flashed on the screen: "4 × 6," "2 × 9," "3 × 3," "7 × 6." Daniel responded, deftly punching in his answers on the computer's numeric key-pad. Twice he recognized errors and corrected them before inputting his answers . . . .

The computer tallied the results. "You completed 20 problems in 66 seconds. You beat your goal. Problems correct = 20. Congratulations, Daniel!" And with that the 11-year-old retreated hastily to the TV room. The Lakers and 76ers were about to tip off for an NBA championship game, and Daniel wanted to see the first half before bedtime (Heward & Orlansky, 1988, p. 100)

Understanding precisely what is meant by the concept of intelligence has proven to be a major challenge for researchers.

Learning Objectives

MODULE 9.1

LO1 What is intelligence, and how has it been measured over the years?

LO2 What are newer conceptions of intelligence, and how are they measured?

MODULE 9.2

LO3 How is the intelligence of infants measured, and does infant intelligence predict adult intelligence?

LO4 Why do some groups perform better than others on IQ tests, and what do such group differences mean?

MODULE 9.3

LO5 What sorts of mental exceptionalities do people have, and what assistance do they need and receive?

>>> LOOKING AHEAD

The scene described above hardly seems out of the ordinary. But now consider an additional fact: Daniel was born with *Down syndrome*, a genetically produced disorder that causes mental retardation.

(continued)

Daniel's capabilities raise a number of issues, addressed in this chapter, about the nature of intelligence. How can we define intelligent behavior? What makes one person more, or less, intelligent than others? Ultimately, does intelligence matter?

To answer these questions, we first consider the ways that have been developed to differentiate children on the basis of intelligence. We discuss traditional measures of intelligence—IQ tests—and examine newer alternatives such as those suggested by Lev Vygotsky and information processing approaches to intelligence.

We then explore some of the controversial issues in the realm of intelligence. We consider how to measure intelligence in infancy and the meaning of racial differences in IQ scores. We also discuss the means some parents pursue to improve their children's IQ scores, considering as well the wisdom of taking this approach.

The chapter ends with an examination of the two groups that show the extremes of intelligence: people with mental retardation and gifted people. We consider the nature of the exceptionality of each of these populations and focus on the question of how exceptional children should best be integrated into society.

MODULE 9.1

INTELLIGENCE: DETERMINING INDIVIDUAL STRENGTHS

LO 9-1 What is intelligence, and how has it been measured over the years?
LO 9-2 What are newer conceptions of intelligence, and how are they measured?

"Why should you tell the truth?" "How far is Los Angeles from New York?" "A table is made of wood; a window of _____."

As 10-year-old Hyacinth sat hunched over her desk, trying to answer a long series of questions like these, she tried to guess the point of the test she was taking in her fifth-grade classroom. Clearly, the test didn't cover material that her teacher, Ms. White-Johnston, had talked about in class.

"What number comes next in this series: 1, 3, 7, 15, 31, _____?"

As she continued to work her way through the questions, she gave up trying to guess the rationale for the test. She'd leave that to her teacher, she sighed to herself. Rather than attempt to figure out what it all meant, she simply tried to do her best on the individual test items.

Hyacinth was taking an intelligence test. She might be surprised to learn that she was not alone in questioning the meaning and import of the items on the test. Intelligence test items are painstakingly prepared, and intelligence tests show a strong relationship to success in school (for reasons we soon discuss). Many developmentalists, however, would admit to harboring their own doubts as to whether questions such as those on Hyacinth's test are entirely appropriate to the task of assessing intelligence.

Understanding just what is meant by the concept of intelligence has proven to be a major challenge for researchers interested in delineating what separates intelligent from unintelligent behavior. Although nonexperts have their own conceptions of intelligence (one survey found, for instance, that laypersons believe that intelligence consists of three components: problem-solving ability, verbal ability, and social competence), it has been more difficult for experts to concur (Sternberg et al., 1981). Still, a general definition of intelligence is possible: **Intelligence** is the capacity to understand the world, think with rationality, and use resources effectively when faced with challenges.

intelligence The capacity to understand the world, think with rationality, and use resources effectively when faced with challenges

Part of the difficulty in defining intelligence stems from the many—and sometimes unsatisfactory—paths that have been followed over the years in the quest to distinguish more intelligent people from less intelligent ones. To understand how researchers have approached the task of assessing intelligence by devising intelligence tests, we need to consider some of the historical milestones in the area of intelligence.

Intelligence Benchmarks: Differentiating the Intelligent from the Unintelligent

The Paris school system was faced with a problem at the turn of the 20th century: A significant number of children were not benefiting from regular instruction. Unfortunately, these children—many of whom we would now call mentally retarded—were generally not identified early enough to shift them to special classes. The French minister of instruction approached psychologist Alfred Binet with this problem and asked him to devise a technique for the early identification of students who might benefit from instruction outside the regular classroom.

French educator Alfred Binet originated the intelligence test.

 **Watch** the **Video** *Thinking Like a Psychologist: Intelligence Tests and Success* in **MyPsychLab**.

Binet's Test. Binet tackled his task in a thoroughly practical manner. His years of observing school-age children suggested to him that previous efforts to distinguish intelligent from unintelligent students—some of which were based on reaction time or keenness of sight—were off the mark. Instead, he launched a trial-and-error process in which items and tasks were administered to students who had been previously identified by teachers as being either "bright" or "dull." Tasks that the bright students completed correctly and the dull students failed to complete correctly were retained for the test. Tasks that did not discriminate between the two groups were discarded. The result of this process was a test that reliably distinguished students who had previously been identified as fast or slow learners.

Binet's pioneering efforts in intelligence testing left several important legacies. The first was his pragmatic approach to the construction of intelligence tests. Binet did not have theoretical preconceptions about what intelligence was. Instead, he used a trial-and-error approach to psychological measurement that continues to serve as the predominant approach to test construction today. His definition of intelligence as *that which his test measured* has been adopted by many modern researchers, and it is particularly popular among test developers, who respect the widespread utility of intelligence tests but wish to avoid arguments about the underlying nature of intelligence.

Binet's legacy extends to his linking of intelligence and school success. Binet's procedure for constructing an intelligence test ensured that intelligence—defined as performance on the test—and school success would be virtually one and the same. Thus, Binet's intelligence test and today's tests that follow in Binet's footsteps have become reasonable indicators of the degree to which students possess attributes that contribute to successful school performance. On the other hand, they do not provide useful information regarding a vast number of other attributes that are largely unrelated to academic proficiency, such as social skills or personality characteristics.

Finally, Binet developed a procedure of linking each intelligence test score with a *mental age,* the age of the children taking the test who, on average, achieved that score. For example, if a 6-year-old girl received a score of 30 on the test, and this was the average score received by 10-year-olds, her mental age would be considered 10 years. Similarly, a 15-year-old boy who scored a 90 on the test—thereby matching the mean score for 15-year-olds—would be assigned a mental age of 15 years (Wasserman & Tulsky, 2005).

Although assigning a mental age to students provides an indication of whether they are performing at the same level as their peers, it does not permit adequate comparisons among students of different *chronological (physical) ages.* By using mental age alone, for instance, it would be assumed that a 15-year-old responding with a mental age of 17 years would be as

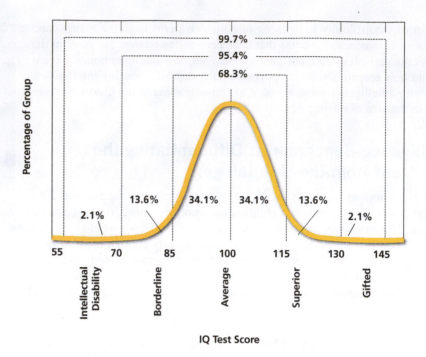

bright as a 6-year-old responding with a mental age of 8 years, when actually the 6-year-old would be showing a much greater *relative* degree of brightness.

A solution to this problem comes in the form of the **intelligence quotient (IQ),** a score that takes into account a student's mental *and* chronological age. The traditional method of calculating an IQ score uses the following formula, in which MA stands for mental age and CA stands for chronological age:

$$\text{IQ score} = \frac{\text{MA}}{\text{CA}} \times 100$$

As a bit of trial-and-error with this formula demonstrates, people whose mental age (MA) is equal to their chronological age (CA) will always have an IQ of 100. Furthermore, if the chronological age exceeds the mental age—implying below-average intelligence—the score will be below 100; and if the chronological age is lower than the mental age—suggesting above-average intelligence—the score will be above 100.

Using this formula, we can return to our earlier example of a 15-year-old who scores at a 17-year-old mental age. This student's IQ is $17/15 \times 100$, or 113. In comparison, the IQ of a 6-year-old scoring at a mental age of 8 is $8/6 \times 100$, or 133—a higher IQ score than the 15-year-old's.

IQ scores today are calculated in a more mathematically sophisticated manner and are known as *deviation IQ scores.* The average deviation IQ score remains set at 100, but tests are now devised so that the degree of deviation from this score permits the calculation of the proportion of people who have similar scores. For instance, approximately two thirds of all people fall within 15 points of the average score of 100, achieving scores between 85 and 115. As scores rise or fall beyond this range, the percentage of people in the same score category drops significantly (see Figure 9-1).

Measuring IQ: Present-Day Approaches to Intelligence

intelligence quotient (IQ) A score that takes into account a student's mental *and* chronological age

Stanford-Binet Intelligence Scales, Fifth Edition (SB5) A test that began as an American revision of Binet's original test and consists of a series of items that vary according to the age of the person being tested

Since the time of Binet, tests of intelligence have become increasingly accurate measures of IQ. Most of them can still trace their roots to his original work in one way or another. For example, one of the most widely used tests—the **Stanford-Binet Intelligence Scales, Fifth Edition (SB5)**—began as an American revision of Binet's original test. The test consists of a series of items that vary according to the age of the person being tested. For instance, young children are asked to answer questions about everyday activities or to copy complex figures. Older people are asked to explain proverbs, solve analogies, and describe similarities between groups of words. The test is administered orally, and test-takers are given progressively more difficult problems until they are unable to proceed.

The **Wechsler Intelligence Scale for Children—Fourth Edition (WISC-IV)** is another widely used intelligence test. The test (which stems from its adult counterpart, the *Wechsler Adult Intelligence Scale*) provides separate measures of verbal and performance (or nonverbal) skills, as well as a total score. As you can see from the sample items in Figure 9-2 on page 250, the verbal tasks are traditional word problems testing skills such as understanding a passage, whereas typical nonverbal tasks are copying a complex design, arranging pictures in a logical order, and assembling objects. The separate portions of the test allow for easier identification of any specific problems a test-taker may have. For example, significantly higher scores on the performance part of the test than on the verbal part may indicate difficulties in linguistic development (Zhu & Weiss, 2005).

The **Kaufman Assessment Battery for Children, Second Edition (KABC-II)** takes a different approach from that of the SB5 and WISC-IV. In it, children are tested on their ability to integrate different kinds of stimuli simultaneously and to use step-by-step thinking. A special virtue of the KABC-II is its flexibility. It allows the person giving the test to use alternative wording or gestures, or even to pose questions in a different language, in order to maximize a test-taker's performance. This capability of the KABC-II makes testing more valid and equitable for children to whom English is a second language (Kaufman et al., 2005; Kaufman et al., 2012).

Fairness in IQ Testing

A central requirement of tests that are used to make important decisions is fairness: A test with significant consequences—such as an IQ test used in assigning children to ability groups or special educational programs—has to meet stringent statistical criteria. Among the central standards of test fairness are reliability and validity.

Reliability and Validity.
Every time we weigh ourselves, we have to be able to assume that the scale will show the same number unless our weight actually changes. If the scale reports changing numbers, those numbers should reflect our fluctuating weight over time, and not inaccuracies in the scale. This property of measurement instruments—including tests—is called *reliability*. **Reliability** in testing exists when a test measures consistently what it is trying to measure. Basically, reliability equals consistency.

Consistency is particularly important—and stringently required—in an IQ test, which is assumed to measure a stable human characteristic, not a quality such as learning or achievement that is expected to change as a person grows intellectually. A reliable IQ test will produce the same score each time it is administered to a particular person. If one time IQ is reported as 105, but the next time as 130, then the test is not reliable.

But reliability is not enough. Even if a test is reliable, it is not necessarily valid. A test has **validity** when it actually measures what it is supposed to measure. For instance, just as a valid bathroom scale should measure a person's weight correctly and unambiguously, a valid IQ test should measure an individual's underlying intelligence correctly and unambiguously.

Tests can be reliable without being valid. For example, we could devise a completely reliable test for intelligence if we made the assumption that skull circumference was related to intelligence. Because measuring skull size precisely is fairly easy, and because human skulls don't change much in size over time, we would have a very reliable measure. But would such a test of intelligence be valid? Hardly, because it seems far-fetched that skull size would have much to do with anyone's intelligence. (Well, not far-fetched to everyone: There have been serious efforts in the past to match skull configuration to psychological attributes such as intelligence, although such attempts have, not surprisingly, proved unsuccessful [Gould, 1996; Deary et al., 2007].)

For intelligence to be accurately assessed, then, IQ tests must be both reliable *and* valid. Although there is wide agreement that well-established IQ tests meet the formal requirements

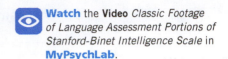
Watch the **Video** *Classic Footage of Language Assessment Portions of Stanford-Binet Intelligence Scale* in **MyPsychLab**.

Wechsler Intelligence Scale for Children—Fourth Edition (WISC-IV) A test (which stems from its adult counterpart, the *Wechsler Adult Intelligence Scale*) that provides separate measures of verbal and performance (or nonverbal) skills, as well as a total score

Kaufman Assessment Battery for Children, Second Edition (KABC-II) A scale on which children are tested on their ability to integrate different kinds of stimuli simultaneously, and to use step-by-step thinking

reliability In testing, the outcome that exists when a test consistently measures what it is trying to measure

validity The outcome when a test actually measures what it is supposed to measure

NAME	GOAL OF ITEM	EXAMPLE
VERBAL SCALE		
Information	Assess general information	How many nickels make a dime?
Comprehension	Assess understanding and evaluation of social norms and past experience	What is the advantage of keeping money in the bank?
Arithmetic	Assess math reasoning through verbal problems	If two buttons cost 15 cents, what will be the cost of a dozen buttons?
Similarities	Test understanding of how objects or concepts are alike, tapping abstract reasoning	In what way are an hour and a week alike?
PERFORMANCE SCALE		
Digit symbol	Assess speed of learning	Match symbols to numbers using key. 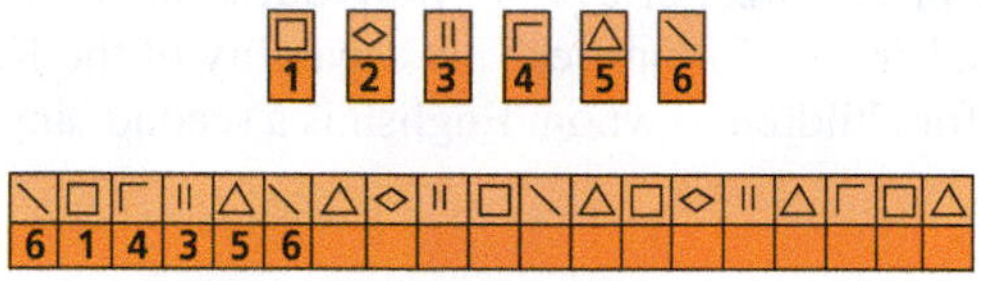
Picture completion	Visual memory and attention	Identify what is missing. 
Object assembly	Test understanding of relationship of parts to wholes	Put pieces together to form a whole. 

FIGURE 9-2 Measuring Intelligence

The Wechsler Intelligence Scales for Children (WISC-IV) includes items such as these. What do such items cover? What do they miss?

DEVELOPMENTAL DIVERSITY AND YOUR LIFE

IQ Tests: One Size Fits All?

Test critics often argue that IQ tests, however carefully constructed, are written and reviewed by people whose cultural backgrounds and assumptions may be unconsciously reflected in the test items they write. In fact, it is hard to avoid unconscious cultural assumptions when test items get beyond the $2 + 2 = 4$ variety. Think what you would do if given the task of writing items that are free of cultural traces but set, for purposes of providing real-world contexts, in airports, train stations, grocery stores, banks, living rooms, kitchens, shopping malls, classrooms, and other environments. Chances are you would imagine such settings in ways that reflect your own experiences and personal history. And that can be a problem when the test-takers are from very different cultural backgrounds.

Compounding the issue of unconscious cultural assumptions that may be built into test items is the fact that—for all the conscientious efforts of test developers—IQ tests are usually field tested among samples of people with backgrounds broadly similar to those of the test writers. The result is predictable. As we'll discuss later in the chapter, IQ tests in particular have been criticized for discriminating against members of minority racial, ethnic, and cultural groups.

To counteract possible bias, some IQ tests have been specifically designed to overcome the potential for cultural bias. *Culture-fair IQ tests* are designed to be independent of the cultural background of test-takers. For example, the *Raven Progressive Matrices Test* asks test-takers to examine abstract designs that have a missing piece and choose the missing piece from several possibilities (see Figure 9-3). Another example is the *System of Multicultural Pluralistic Assessment* (SOMPA), an IQ test designed to be culturally unbiased, which we will discuss later in this chapter.

The assumption behind culture-fair IQ tests is that no particular cultural group will be more or less acquainted with the test content, and consequently the test results will be free from cultural bias. Unfortunately, existing culture-fair tests have not been terribly successful, and disparities based on minority group membership still occur. A truly culture-fair IQ test has yet to be developed (Ostrosky-Solis & Oberg, 2006; Richards, 2012).

Another population for whom IQ tests may be unfair is the 2.6 million school-age children in the United States officially labeled as having learning disabilities. **Learning disabilities** are defined as difficulties in the acquisition and use of listening, speaking, reading, writing, reasoning, or mathematical abilities. A somewhat ill-defined category, learning disabilities are diagnosed when there is a discrepancy between children's actual academic performance and their apparent potential to learn, based on IQ scores and other ability measures (Kozey & Siegel, 2008; Geary et al., 2012).

The problem is that normal IQ tests may fail to detect abnormal learning. For instance, the most common learning disability is *attention deficit hyperactivity disorder (ADHD)*. Children with ADHD are inattentive and impulsive, with a low tolerance for frustration and generally a great deal of inappropriate activity. Yet their IQ scores are either normal or above normal. Then there is *dyslexia*, a reading disability that can result in the misperception of letters during reading and writing, unusual difficulty in sounding out letters, confusion between left and right, and difficulties in spelling. The IQ scores of dyslexic test-takers may reflect their disability more than their intelligence (Byrne, Shankweiler, & Hine, 2008; Nicolson & Fawcett, 2008; Mattison & Mayes, 2012).

The test development community is aware of these issues and is making concerted efforts to combat bias in testing. Yet for IQ testing the issue remains on the table. ■

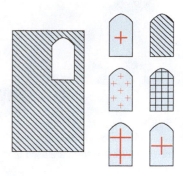

FIGURE 9-3 The Raven Progressive Matrices Test

In the Raven Progressive Matrices Test, examinees are shown an abstract figure with a missing piece. They are asked to choose from several possibilities which piece would complete the figure. The Raven is designed to be free of cultural bias because it is assumed that no group is more or less familiar with the task.

(*Source:* Based on NCS Pearson, Inc., 1998)

Watch the **Video** *Intelligence* in **MyPsychLab**.

of reliability, their validity is more problematic when they are used among some groups with characteristics or backgrounds that differ from the norm, as we see in the *Developmental Diversity* box.

The Meaning of IQ Scores.

What do the IQ scores derived from IQ tests mean? For most children, IQ scores are reasonably good predictors of their school performance. That's not surprising, given that the initial impetus for the development of intelligence tests was to identify children who were having difficulties in school (Sternberg & Grigorenko, 2002).

But when it comes to performance outside of academic spheres, the story is different. For instance, although people with higher IQ scores are apt to finish more years of schooling, once this is statistically controlled for, IQ scores are not closely related to income and later

learning disabilities Difficulties in the acquisition and use of listening, speaking, reading, writing, reasoning, or mathematical abilities

A number of different tests are used to measure intelligence.

According to Robert Sternberg's triarchic theory of intelligence, practical intelligence is as important as traditional academic intelligence in determining success.

success in life. Furthermore, IQ scores are frequently inaccurate when it comes to predicting a particular individual's future success. For example, two people with different IQ scores may both finish their bachelor's degrees at the same college, and the person with a lower IQ might end up with a higher income and a more successful career. Because of these difficulties with traditional IQ scores, researchers have turned to alternative approaches to intelligence.

What IQ Tests Don't Tell: Alternative Conceptions of Intelligence

The intelligence tests used most frequently in school settings today are based on the idea that intelligence is a single factor, a unitary mental ability. This one main attribute has commonly been called *g* (Spearman, 1927; Lubinski, 2004). The *g* factor is assumed to underlie performance on every aspect of intelligence, and it is the *g* factor that intelligence tests presumably measure.

However, many theorists dispute the notion that intelligence is one-dimensional. Some developmentalists suggest that in fact two kinds of intelligence exist: fluid intelligence and crystallized intelligence. **Fluid intelligence** reflects information-processing capabilities, reasoning, and memory. For example, a student asked to group a series of letters according to some criterion or to remember a set of numbers would be using fluid intelligence (Salthouse, Pink, & Tucker-Drob, 2008; Shangguan & Shi, 2009; Roberts & Lipnevich, 2012).

In contrast, **crystallized intelligence** is the accumulation of information, skills, and strategies that people have learned through experience and that they can apply in problem-solving situations. A student would likely be relying on crystallized intelligence to solve a puzzle or deduce the solution to a mystery, in which it was necessary to draw on past experience (Alfonso, Flanagan, & Radwan, 2005; McGrew, 2005; Buckingham, Kiernan, & Ainsworth, 2012).

Other theorists divide intelligence into an even greater number of parts. For example, psychologist Howard Gardner suggests that we have eight distinct intelligences, each relatively independent (see Figure 9-4). Gardner suggests that these separate intelligences operate not in isolation, but together, depending on the type of activity in which we are engaged (Gardner, 2003; Chen & Gardner, 2005; Gardner & Moran, 2006; also see the *Neuroscience and Development* box.).

The Russian psychologist Lev Vygotsky, whose approach to cognitive development we discussed in Chapter 6, took a very different approach to intelligence. He suggested that we should assess intelligence by looking not only at cognitive processes that are fully developed but also at processes that are currently being developed. To do this, Vygotsky contended that assessment tasks should involve cooperative interaction between the individual who is being assessed and the person who is doing the assessment—a process called *dynamic assessment*. In short, intelligence is seen as being reflected not only in how children can perform on their own but also in terms of how well they perform when helped by adults (Vygotsky, 1927/1997; Lohman, 2005; Seethaler et al., 2012).

FROM AN
EDUCATOR'S
PERSPECTIVE:

Does Howard Gardner's theory of multiple intelligences suggest that classroom instruction should be modified from an emphasis on the traditional three *R*s of reading, writing, and arithmetic?

fluid intelligence Intelligence that reflects information processing capabilities, reasoning, and memory

crystallized intelligence The accumulation of information, skills, and strategies that people have learned through experience and that they can apply in problem-solving situations

Musical intelligence (skills in tasks involving music). Case example:
When he was 3, Yehudi Menuhin was smuggled into the San Francisco Orchestra concerts by his parents. The sound of Louis Persinger's violin so entranced the youngster that he insisted on a violin for his birthday and Louis Persinger as his teacher. He got both. By the time he was 10 years old, Menuhin was an international performer.

Naturalist intelligence (ability to identify and classify patterns in nature).
Case example:
In prehistoric periods, hunter-gatherers required naturalist intelligence in order to identify what types of plants were edible.

Bodily kinesthetic intelligence (skills in using the whole body or various portions of it in the solution of problems or in the construction of products or displays, exemplified by dancers, athletes, actors, and surgeons). Case example:
Fifteen-year-old Babe Ruth played third base. During one game, his team's pitcher was doing poorly and Babe loudly criticized him from third base. Brother Mathias, the coach, called out, "Ruth, if you know so much about it, *you* pitch!" Babe was surprised and embarrassed because he had never pitched before, but Brother Mathias insisted. Ruth said later that at the very moment he took the pitcher's mound, he *knew* he was supposed to be a pitcher.

Intrapersonal intelligence (knowledge of the internal aspects of oneself; access to one's own feelings and emotions). Case example:
In her essay "A Sketch of the Past," Virginia Woolf displays deep insight into her own inner life through these lines, describing her reaction to several specific memories from her childhood that still, in adulthood, shock her: "Though I still have the peculiarity that I receive these sudden shocks, they are now always welcome; after the first surprise, I always feel instantly that they are particularly valuable. And so I go on to suppose that the shock-receiving capacity is what makes me a writer."

Gardner's Eight Intelligences

Logical mathematical intelligence (skills in problem solving and scientific thinking).
Case example:
Barbara McClintock won the Nobel Prize in medicine for her work in microbiology. She describes one of her breakthroughs, which came after thinking about a problem for half an hour...: "Suddenly I jumped and ran back to the [corn] field. At the top of the field [the others were still at the bottom] I shouted, 'Eureka, I have it!'"

Interpersonal intelligence (skills in interacting with others, such as sensitivity to the moods, temperaments, motivations, and intentions of others). Case example:
When Anne Sullivan began instructing the deaf and blind Helen Keller, her task was one that had eluded others for years. Yet, just 2 weeks after beginning her work with Keller, Sullivan achieved a great success. In her words, "My heart is singing with joy this morning. A miracle has happened! The wild little creature of 2 weeks ago has been transformed into a gentle child."

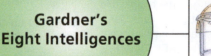

Linguistic intelligence (skills involved in the production and use of language).
Case example:
At the age of 10, T.S. Elliot created a magazine called *Fireside*, to which he was the sole contributor. In a 3-day period during his winter vacation, he created eight complete issues.

Spatial intelligence (skills involving spatial configurations, such as those used by artists and architects). Case example:
Navigation by members of the Trukese tribe is accomplished without instruments.... During the actual trip, the navigator must envision mentally a reference island as it passes under a particular star and from that he computes the number of segments completed, the proportion of the trip remaining, and any corrections in heading.

FIGURE 9-4 Gardner's Eight Intelligences

Howard Gardner has theorized that there are eight distinct intelligences, each relatively independent of one another. How do you fit into this categorization?
(*Source:* Based on Walters & Gardner, 1986)

Smart Thinking: The Triarchic Theory of Intelligence

Taking yet another approach, psychologist Robert Sternberg (2003a) suggests that intelligence is best thought of in terms of information processing. In this view, the way in which people store material in memory and later use it to solve intellectual tasks provides the most precise conception of intelligence. Rather than focus on the various subcomponents that make up the *structure* of intelligence, information-processing approaches examine the *processes* that underlie intelligent behavior (Floyd, 2005).

Studies of the nature and speed of problem-solving processes show that people with higher intelligence levels differ from others not only in the number of problems they ultimately are

NEUROSCIENCE AND DEVELOPMENT
When Song Is Silent: Why Amusia Sufferers Can't Hear a Tune

As a preschooler, Alexa put her hands over her ears when her caregiver sang or played music. In third grade her teacher reported that Alexa was disruptive in music class—often times singing the same note louder rather than following the melody of a song. It was not until she participated in a college psychology experiment that Alexa was diagnosed as one of 5% of the population with amusia, or tone deafness.

Some people cannot carry a tune, but they still process musical tones normally. In contrast, people with *amusia*, like Alexa, are unable to differentiate between pitch and often are unaware when they are singing out of tune. They also may have difficulty recognizing familiar melodies without the assistance of lyrics (Peretz et al., 2009; Marin, Gingras, & Stewart, 2012).

New brain imaging research provides insight into the brain's role in amusia. In a recent study, researchers investigated tone deafness and its association with one of the brain's neural highways and major fiber bundles called the arcuate fasciculus (AF). The AF is a white-matter, neural fiber tract that connects the right temporal lobe (where basic sound processing occurs) and frontal brain regions (where higher thinking occurs). It plays a major role in linking music and language perception with vocal production.

In the study, brain scans showed that people with amusia had less neural connectivity in the AF compared to 10 musically normal–functioning people. White matter of the people with amusia was smaller in size and possessed fewer fibers, suggesting a weaker connection. Additionally, abnormal AF branching occurred, indicating that dendrites bringing information to the AF cells and axons taking information away from AF cells were less effective in processing music-related information (Loui, Alsop, & Schlaug, 2009).

This study represents the first investigation into the structural and neural correlates of tone deafness. So the next time you hear terrible singing in a karaoke bar, forgive the singer: He or she may being suffering from amusia.

■ **Based on these findings, do you think amusia can be corrected? Why or why not?**

■ **What suggestions might you give to teachers working with children who are required to take music classes as part of their curriculum?**

---

able to solve but also in their method of solving the problems. People with high IQ scores spend more time on the initial stages of problem solving, retrieving relevant information from memory. In contrast, those who score lower on traditional IQ tests tend to spend less time on the initial stages, instead skipping ahead and making less informed guesses. The processes used in solving problems, then, may reflect important differences in intelligence (Sternberg, 2005).

Sternberg's work on information-processing approaches to intelligence has led him to develop the **triarchic theory of intelligence**. According to this model, intelligence consists of three aspects of information processing: the componential element, the experiential element, and the contextual element. The componential aspect of intelligence reflects how efficiently people can process and analyze information. Efficiency in these areas allows people to infer relationships among different parts of a problem, solve the problem, and then evaluate their solution. People who are strong on the componential element score highest on traditional tests of intelligence (Sternberg, 2005; Gardner, 2011).

The *experiential* element is the insightful component of intelligence. People who have a strong experiential element can easily compare new material with what they already know and can combine and relate facts that they already know in novel and creative ways. Finally, the *contextual* element of intelligence concerns practical intelligence, or ways of dealing with the demands of the everyday environment.

In Sternberg's view, people vary in the degree to which each of these three elements is present. Our level of success at any given task reflects the match between the task and our own specific pattern of strength on the three components of intelligence (Sternberg, 2003b, 2008).

Emotional Intelligence

In many elementary schools, the hottest topic in the curriculum has little to do with the traditional three *R*s. Instead, a significant educational trend for educators in many elementary schools throughout the United States is the use of techniques to increase students' **emotional intelligence,** the set of skills that underlie the accurate assessment, evaluation, expression, and regulation of emotions (Hastings, 2004; Fogarty, 2008; Matthews, Zeidner, & Roberts, 2012).

👁 **Watch** the **Video** *Practical Intelligence* in **MyPsychLab**.

✳ **Explore** *Sternberg's Triarchic Theory of Intelligence* in **MyPsychLab**.

triarchic theory of intelligence The belief that intelligence consists of three aspects of information processing: the componential element, the experiential element, and the contextual element

emotional intelligence The set of skills that underlie the accurate assessment, evaluation, expression, and regulation of emotions

Treating emotional intelligence as a distinct type of intelligence has gained increasing attention in recent years. People who were once dismissed as loudmouths, bullies, or hotheads are coming to be regarded as individuals with problems that affect not only their own lives but those of many others as well.

Psychologist Daniel Goleman (2005) argues that emotional literacy should be a standard part of the school curriculum. He points to several programs that succeed in teaching students to manage their emotions more effectively. For instance, in one program, children are provided with lessons in empathy, self-awareness, and social skills. In another, children are taught about caring and friendship as early as first grade through exposure to stories (Fasano & Pellitteri, 2006).

Programs meant to increase emotional intelligence have not been met with universal acceptance. Critics suggest that the nurturance of emotional intelligence is best left to students' families and that schools ought to concentrate on more traditional curriculum matters. Others suggest that adding emotional intelligence to an already crowded curriculum may reduce time spent on academics. Finally, some critics argue that there is no well-specified set of criteria for what constitutes emotional intelligence, and consequently it is difficult to develop appropriate, effective curriculum materials (Roberts, Zeidner, & Matthews, 2001).

Still, most people consider emotional intelligence worthy of nurturance. It is clear that emotional intelligence is quite different from traditional conceptions of intelligence. The goal of emotional intelligence training is to produce people who are not only cognitively sophisticated but also able to manage their emotions effectively (Brackett & Katulak, 2007; Ulutas & Ömeroglu, 2007; Davis & Humphrey, 2012).

Review, Check, and Apply

Review

1. Pinning down the meaning of intelligence and measuring it accurately have proven to be challenging tasks that have occupied psychologists for many years.

2. The measurement of intelligence began in the 20th century with the work of Alfred Binet, who took a trial-and-error approach to the question. His work is reflected in the most widely used IQ tests of today.

3. To Binet we owe three legacies: his pragmatic, non-theoretical approach to intelligence testing; his linkage of intelligence to school success; and his derivation of a mathematical means of classifying children as more or less intelligent according to IQ scores.

4. Measurements must have both reliability (defined as consistency across persons and over time) and validity (defined as measuring what they claim to measure).

5. Learning disabilities are defined as difficulties in the acquisition and use of listening, speaking, reading, writing, reasoning, or mathematical abilities.

6. While they are reasonably predictive of school success, IQ scores fall short in other realms. As a result, a number of alternative conceptions of intelligence have emerged that differentiate different kinds of intelligence.

7. One of the most successful alternative conceptions is Robert Sternberg's *triarchic theory of intelligence*, which breaks the factor down into componential, experiential, and contextual components.

Check

1. The IQ score is derived by dividing an individual's mental age by his or her _____ age and multiplying by 100.

2. If a test yields consistent results, it is said to be _____; if it measures what it is supposed to measure, it is said to be _____.

3. According to Sternberg's triarchic theory of intelligence, the three aspects of intelligence are _____, _____, and _____.

4. The set of skills that underlie the proper assessment, expression, and control of feelings is called _____ intelligence.

Apply

1. If a perfectly valid and reliable measure of intelligence were developed, how would it best be used? What uses would be inappropriate?

2. Do you think that practical and emotional intelligence are distributed equally along gender lines, or do women have more or less of one type than men do? What would be the consequences if the opposite of your answer were true?

To see more review questions, log on to MyPsychLab.

ANSWERS: 1. chronological; 2. reliable; valid 3. componential; experiential; contextual 4. emotional

M O D U L E   **9.2**

CONTROVERSIES INVOLVING INTELLIGENCE

LO 9-3 How is the intelligence of infants measured, and does infant intelligence predict adult intelligence?

LO 9-4 Why do some groups perform better than others on IQ tests, and what do such group differences mean?

> *Maddy Rodriguez is a bundle of curiosity and energy. At 6 months of age, she cries heartily if she can't reach a toy, and when she sees a reflection of herself in a mirror, she gurgles and seems, in general, to find the situation quite amusing.*
>
> *Jared Lynch, at 6 months, is a good deal more inhibited than Maddy. He doesn't seem to care much when a ball rolls out of his reach, losing interest in it rapidly. And, unlike Maddy, when he sees himself in a mirror, he pretty much ignores the reflection.*

As anyone who has spent any time at all observing more than one baby can tell you, not all infants are alike. Some are full of energy and life, apparently displaying a natural-born curiosity, while others seem, by comparison, somewhat less interested in the world around them. Does this mean that such infants differ in intelligence? Let's see what the data tell us about this and several other issues that illustrate the difficulty in classifying children on the basis of intelligence.

Determining what is meant by intelligence in infants represents a major challenge for developmentalists.

Individual Differences in Intelligence: Is One Infant Smarter Than Another?

Answering questions about how and to what degree infants vary in their underlying intelligence is not easy. Although it is clear that different infants show significant variations in their behavior, the issue of just what types of behavior may be related to cognitive ability is complicated. Interestingly, the examination of individual differences among infants was the initial approach taken by developmental specialists to understand cognitive development, and such issues still represent an important focus within the field.

TABLE 9-1 Approaches Used to Detect Differences in Intelligence during Infancy	
Developmental quotient	Formulated by Arnold Gesell, the developmental quotient is an overall developmental score that relates to performance in four domains: motor skills (balance and sitting), language use, adaptive behavior (alertness and exploration), and personal–social behavior.
Bayley Scales of Infant Development	Developed by Nancy Bayley, the Bayley Scales of Infant Development evaluate an infant's development from 2 to 42 months. The Bayley Scales focus on two areas: mental (senses, perception, memory, learning, problem solving, and language) and motor abilities (fine- and gross-motor skills).
Visual-recognition memory measurement	Measures of visual-recognition memory (the memory of and recognition of a stimulus that has been previously seen) also relate to intelligence. The more quickly an infant can retrieve a representation of a stimulus from memory, the more efficient, presumably, is that infant's information processing.

What Is Infant Intelligence? Before we can address whether and how infants may differ in intelligence, we need to consider what is meant by the term *intelligence*. Educators, psychologists, and other experts on development have yet to agree upon a general definition of intelligent behavior, even among adults. Is it the ability to do well in scholastic endeavors? Proficiency in business negotiations? Competence in navigating across treacherous seas, such as that shown by peoples of the South Pacific, who have no knowledge of Western navigational techniques?

It is even more difficult to define and measure intelligence in infants. Do we base it on the speed with which a new task is learned through classical or operant conditioning? How fast a baby becomes habituated to a new stimulus? The age at which an infant learns to crawl or walk? Even if we are able to identify particular behaviors that seem to differentiate one infant from another in terms of intelligence during infancy, we need to address a further, and probably more important, issue: How well do measures of infant intelligence relate to eventual adult intelligence?

Clearly, such questions are not simple, and no simple answers have been found. However, developmental specialists have devised several approaches (summarized in Table 9-1) to illuminate the nature of individual differences in intelligence during infancy.

Developmental Scales. Developmental psychologist Arnold Gesell formulated the earliest measure of infant development, which was designed to distinguish between normally developing babies and those with atypical development (Gesell, 1946). Gesell based his scale on examinations of hundreds of babies. He compared their performance at different ages to learn what behaviors were most common at a particular age. If an infant varied significantly from the norms of a given age, he or she was considered to be developmentally delayed or advanced.

Following the lead of researchers who sought to quantify intelligence through a specific score (known as an intelligence quotient, or IQ, score), Gesell (1946) developed a developmental quotient, or DQ. The **developmental quotient** is an overall developmental score that relates to performance in four domains: motor skills (for example, balance and sitting), language use, adaptive behavior (such as alertness and exploration), and personal–social (for example, adequately feeding and dressing oneself).

Later researchers have created other developmental scales. For instance, Nancy Bayley developed one of the most widely used measures for infants. The **Bayley Scales of Infant Development** evaluate an infant's development from 2 to 42 months. The Bayley Scales focus on two areas: mental and motor abilities. The mental scale focuses on the senses, perception, memory, learning, problem solving, and language, while the motor scale evaluates fine and gross motor skills (see Table 9-2 on page 258). Like Gesell's approach, the Bayley yields a developmental quotient (DQ). A child who scores at an average level—meaning average performance for other children at the same age—receives a score of 100 (Bayley, 1969; Gagnon & Nagle, 2000; Lynn, 2009).

developmental quotient An overall developmental score that relates to performance in four domains: motor skills, language use, adaptive behavior, and personal–social

Bayley Scales of Infant Development A set of guidelines focusing on mental and motor abilities that evaluate an infant's development from 2 to 42 months

TABLE 9-2 Sample Items from the Bayley Scales of Infant Development

Age	2 months	6 months	12 months	17–19 months	23–25 months	38–42 months
Mental Scale	Turns head to locate origin of sound; Visibly responds to disappearance of face	Picks up cup by handle; Notices illustrations in a book	Constructs tower of 2 cubes; Can turn pages in a book	Mimics crayon stroke; Labels objects in photo	Pairs up pictures; Repeats a 2-word sentence	Can identify 4 colors; Past tense evident in speech; Distinguishes gender
Motor Scale	Can hold head steady and erect for 15 seconds; Sits with assistance	Sits up without aid for 30 seconds; Grasps foot with hands	Walks when holding onto someone's hand or furniture; Holds pencil in fist	Stands on right foot without help; Remains upright climbing stairs with assistance	Strings 3 beads; Jumps length of 4 inches	Can reproduce drawing of a circle; Hops two times on one foot; Descends stairs, alternating feet

(*Source:* Based on Bayley, N. 7 1993. *Bayley scales of infant development* [*BSID-II*] 2nd ed., San Antonio, TX: The Psychological Corporation.)

FROM A
NURSE'S
PERSPECTIVE:

In what ways is the use of such developmental scales as Gesell's or Bayley's helpful? In what ways is it dangerous? How would you maximize the helpfulness and minimize the danger if you were advising a parent?

The virtue of approaches such as those taken by Gesell and Bayley is that they provide a good snapshot of an infant's current developmental level. Using these scales, we can tell in an objective manner whether a particular infant falls behind or is ahead of his or her same-age peers. The scales are particularly useful in identifying infants who are substantially behind their peers, and who therefore need immediate special attention (Aylward & Verhulst, 2000).

What such scales are not useful for is predicting a child's future course of development. An individual whose development is identified by these measures as relatively slow at the age of 1 year will not necessarily display slow development at age 5, or 12, or 25. The association between most measures of behavior during infancy and adult intelligence, then, is minimal (Murray et al., 2007).

Information-Processing Approaches to Infant Intelligence

When we speak of intelligence in everyday parlance, we often differentiate between "quick" individuals and those who are "slow." Actually, according to research on the speed of information processing, such terms hold some truth. Contemporary approaches to infant intelligence suggest that the speed with which infants process information may correlate most strongly with later intelligence, as measured by IQ tests administered during adulthood.

How can we tell whether or not a baby is processing information quickly or not? Most researchers use habituation tests. Infants who process information efficiently ought to be able to learn about stimuli more quickly. Consequently, we would expect that they would turn their attention away from a given stimulus more rapidly than those who are less efficient at information processing, leading to the phenomenon of habituation. Similarly, measures of *visual-recognition memory,* the memory and recognition of a stimulus that has been previously seen, also relate to IQ. The more quickly an infant can retrieve a representation of a stimulus from memory, the more efficient, presumably, is that infant's information processing (Rose, Jankowski, & Feldman, 2002; Robinson & Pascalis, 2005).

Research using an information processing framework clearly suggests a relationship between information processing efficiency and cognitive abilities: Measures of how quickly infants lose interest in stimuli that they have previously seen, as well as their responsiveness to new stimuli, correlate moderately well with later measures of intelligence. Infants who are more efficient information processors during the 6 months following birth tend to have higher intelligence scores between 2 and 12 years of age, as well as higher scores on other measures of cognitive competence (Fagan, Holland, & Wheeler, 2007; Domsch, Lohaus, & Thomas, 2009; Rose, Feldman, & Jankowski, 2009).

Other research suggests that abilities related to the *multimodal approach to perception,* which we considered in Chapter 5, may offer clues about later intelligence. For instance, the ability to identify a stimulus that previously has been experienced through only one sense by using another sense (called *cross-modal transference*) is associated with intelligence. A baby who is able to recognize by sight a screwdriver that she has previously only touched, but not seen, is displaying cross-modal transference. Research has found that the degree of cross-modal transference displayed by an infant at age 1—which requires a high level of abstract thinking—is associated with intelligence scores several years later (Rose, Feldman, & Jankowski, 2004; Nakato et al., 2011).

Although information processing efficiency and cross-modal transference abilities during infancy relate moderately well to later IQ scores, we need to keep in mind two qualifications. First, even though there is an association between early information processing capabilities and later measures of IQ, the correlation is only moderate in strength. Other factors, such as the degree of environmental stimulation, also play a crucial role in helping to determine adult intelligence. Consequently, we should not assume that intelligence is somehow permanently fixed in infancy.

Second, and perhaps even more important, intelligence measured by traditional IQ tests relates to a particular type of intelligence, one that emphasizes abilities that lead to academic, and certainly not artistic or professional, success. Consequently, predicting that a child may do well on IQ tests later in life is not the same as predicting that the child will be successful later in life.

Despite these qualifications, the relatively recent finding that an association exists between efficiency of information processing and later IQ scores does suggest some consistency of cognitive development across the life span. Whereas the earlier reliance on scales such as the Bayley led to the misconception that little continuity existed, the more recent information processing approaches suggest that cognitive development unfolds in a more orderly, continuous manner from infancy to the later stages of life.

Group Differences in IQ

A jontry is an example of a

   (a) rulpow
   (b) flink
   (c) spudge
   (d) bakwoe

If you were to find an item composed of nonsense words such as this on an intelligence test, your immediate—and quite legitimate—reaction would likely be to complain. How could a test that purports to measure intelligence include test items that incorporate meaningless terminology?

Yet for some people, the items actually used on traditional intelligence tests might appear equally nonsensical. To take a hypothetical example, suppose children living in rural areas were asked details about subways, while those living in urban areas were asked about the mating practices of sheep. In both cases, we would expect that the previous experiences of test-takers would have a substantial effect on their ability to answer the questions. And if questions about such matters were included on an IQ test, the test could rightly be viewed as a measure of prior experience rather than of intelligence.

Although the questions on traditional IQ tests are not so obviously dependent on test-takers' prior experiences as our examples, cultural background and experience do have the potential to affect intelligence test scores. In fact, many educators suggest that traditional measures of intelligence are subtly biased in favor of white, upper- and middle-class students, and against groups with different cultural experiences (Ortiz & Dynda, 2005).

The issue of whether racial differences in IQ exist is highly controversial and ultimately relates to questions of the genetic and environmental determinants of intelligence.

Performance on traditional IQ tests is dependent in part on test-takers' prior experiences and cultural background.

Explaining Racial Differences in IQ

The issue of how cultural background and experience influence IQ test performance has led to considerable debate among researchers. The debate has been fueled by the finding that IQ scores of certain racial groups are consistently lower, on average, than the IQ scores of other groups. For example, the mean score of African Americans tends to be about 15 IQ points lower than the mean score of whites—although the measured difference varies a great deal depending on the particular IQ test employed (Fish, 2001; Maller, 2003; Nisbett et al., 2012).

The question that emerges from such differences, of course, is whether they reflect actual differences in intelligence or, instead, are caused by bias in the intelligence tests themselves in favor of majority groups and against minorities. For example, if whites perform better on an IQ test than African Americans because of their greater familiarity with the language used in the test items, the test hardly can be said to provide a fair measure of the intelligence of African Americans. Similarly, an intelligence test that solely used African American Vernacular English could not be considered an impartial measure of intelligence for whites.

The question of how to interpret differences among intelligence scores of different cultural groups lies at the heart of one of the major controversies in child development: To what degree is an individual's intelligence determined by heredity and to what degree by environment? The issue is important because of its social implications. For instance, if intelligence is primarily determined by heredity and is therefore largely fixed at birth, attempts to alter cognitive abilities later in life, such as schooling, will meet with limited success. On the other hand, if intelligence is largely environmentally determined, modifying social and educational conditions is a more promising strategy for bringing about increases in cognitive functioning (Weiss, 2003).

***The Bell Curve* Controversy.** Although investigations into the relative contributions of heredity and environment to intelligence have been conducted for decades, the smoldering debate became a raging fire with the publication of a book by Richard J. Herrnstein and Charles Murray (1994), titled *The Bell Curve.* In the book, Herrnstein and Murray argue that the average 15-point IQ difference between whites and African Americans is due primarily to heredity rather than to environment. Furthermore, they argue that this IQ difference accounts for the higher rates of poverty, lower employment, and higher use of welfare among minority groups as compared with majority groups.

The conclusions reached by Herrnstein and Murray (1994) raised a storm of protest, and many researchers who examined the data reported in the book came to conclusions that were quite different. Most developmentalists and psychologists responded by arguing that the racial differences in measured IQ can be explained by environmental differences between the races. In fact, when a variety of indicators of economic and social factors are statistically taken into account simultaneously, mean IQ scores of black and white children turn out to be actually quite similar. For instance, children from similar middle-class backgrounds, whether African American or white, tend to have similar IQ scores (Brooks-Gunn, Klebanov, & Duncan, 1996; Alderfer, 2003).

Furthermore, critics maintained that there is little evidence to suggest that IQ is a cause of poverty and other social ills. In fact, some critics suggested, as mentioned earlier in this discussion, that IQ scores were unrelated in meaningful ways to later success in life (e.g., Reifman, 2000; Sternberg, 2005).

Finally, members of cultural and social minority groups may score lower than members of the majority group due to the nature of the intelligence tests themselves. It is clear that traditional intelligence tests may discriminate against minority groups who have not had exposure to the same environment as majority group members have experienced (Fagan, Holland & Wheeler, 2007; Razani et al., 2007).

Most traditional intelligence tests are constructed using white, English-speaking, middle-class populations as their test subjects. As a result, children from different cultural backgrounds may perform poorly on the tests—not because they are less intelligent, but because the tests use questions that are culturally biased in favor of majority group members. In fact, a classic study found that in one California school district, Mexican American students were 10 times more likely than whites to be placed in special education classes (Mercer, 1973; Hatton, 2002).

More recent findings show that nationally twice as many African American students as white students are classified as mildly retarded, a difference that experts attribute primarily to cultural bias and poverty. Although certain IQ tests (such as the *System of Multicultural Pluralistic Assessment* [SOMPA]) have been designed to be equally valid regardless of the cultural background of test-takers, no test can be completely without bias (Sandoval et al., 1998; Hatton, 2002; Ford, 2011).

In short, most experts in the area of IQ were not convinced by *The Bell Curve* contention that differences in group IQ scores are largely determined by genetic factors. Still, we cannot put the issue to rest, largely because it is impossible to design a definitive experiment that can determine the cause of differences in IQ scores among members of different groups. (Thinking about how such an experiment might be designed shows the futility of the enterprise: One cannot ethically assign children to different living conditions to find the effects of environment, nor would one wish to genetically control or alter intelligence levels in unborn children. Also see the *From Research to Practice box*.)

Today, IQ is seen as the product of *both* nature and nurture interacting with one another in a complex manner. Rather than seeing intelligence as produced by either genes or experience, genes are seen to affect experiences, and experiences are viewed as influencing the expression of genes. For instance, psychologist Eric Turkheimer has found evidence that although environmental factors play a larger role in influencing the IQ of poor children, genes are more influential in the IQ of affluent children (Turkheimer et al., 2003; Harden, Turkheimer, & Loehlin, 2007).

FROM RESEARCH TO PRACTICE
Take-at-Home IQ Tests: Should Parents Test Their Children's IQ?

One of the newest additions to the choices that parents may make in raising their children is the availability of take-at-home IQ tests. The take-at-home IQ test is designed to provide an IQ score for children as young as 6 months (Martin, 2004).

The manufacturer claims that it is responding to parents' concerns over their children's educational achievement. The reasoning goes that by learning their children's IQ scores, parents put themselves in a better position to provide either remedial help (if the IQ is low) or enrichment (if it turns out to be exceptionally high).

Although the take-at-home test seems popular—20,000 units were sold in the first few months of distribution—its availability raises several issues. First is the question of validity. Although traditional IQ tests are standardized with thousands of children before they are published, the degree of development that went into this take-at-home test is unclear. Furthermore, even if the basic material is valid, it is not obvious that parents will be able to administer the test correctly, or that the computer program that presents the test is sufficiently sophisticated to ensure correct administration. This makes the possibility of mislabeling children all too real.

But even if the IQ score a child receives is accurate, it is not apparent how knowing such information will benefit the child. Children who receive a relatively low IQ score may be seen as disappointments to their parents, and parental expectations may be lowered. It is possible that such lowered expectations may result in fewer opportunities being offered to the child, who could be seen as not worth the investment. Even holding high expectations for a child who scores well on the IQ test may not be so beneficial; such children may be seen as so "naturally" bright that they don't really need enrichment provided by extra opportunities.

It is too early to know if at-home IQ testing will become a routine part of parenting. Certainly it is unlikely that children living in families with restricted incomes will be tested, given that the IQ tests cost money and in-home computers required for the test remain comparatively rarer for families living in poverty than for affluent families. Consequently, the very real arguments against the use of take-at-home IQ tests may well impede their widespread use.

- **Why would parents choose to learn their child's IQ at an early age?**

- **What might be the drawbacks to knowing that a 6-month-old had a particularly low (or high) IQ?**

Ultimately, it may be less important to know the absolute degree to which intelligence is determined by genetic and environmental factors than it is to learn how to improve children's living conditions and educational experiences. By enriching the quality of children's environments, we will be in a better position to permit all children to reach their full potential and to maximize their contributions to society, whatever their individual levels of intelligence (Posthuma & de Geus, 2006; Nisbett, 2008; Wacker et al., 2012).

Review, Check, and Apply

Review

1. Defining infant intelligence is especially challenging, and measuring it even more so. Approaches include developmental scales, which provide good snapshots of an infant's current level of development but are unable to predict future intellectual development.

2. Information processing approaches—which have a quantitative rather than a qualitative orientation—differentiate more and less intelligent infants by observing the speed at which they process information and learn about stimuli. Visual-recognition memory and cross-modal transference are also regarded as factors in infant intelligence.

3. A major controversy in the study of intelligence is the role of cultural background in determining IQ. If intelligence levels are determined by nature, academic interventions are of little use. This is the essence of the controversy over the book *The Bell Curve*. However, most developmentalists regard cultural background as unimportant when compared with economic and social background.

Check

1. The equivalent of an IQ test for babies, a DQ test, measures a child's _____ quotient.

2. The phenomenon by which an infant processes information and then, having grown accustomed to it, turns away is called _____.

3. A baby who recognizes in the daylight a toy with which she has played only in the dark of night is demonstrating _____-_____ transference.

4. A test that reflects the experiences and social environment of one group to the exclusion of others is said to be _____ biased.

Apply

1. Why is it important to measure intelligence in infants? What can we find out? What can we do with what we find out?

2. Can you think of examples from your own experience when cultural factors may have positively influenced your performance on a test? Any examples of the opposite?

To see more review questions, log on to MyPsychLab.

ANSWERS: 1. developmental 2. habituation 3. cross-modal 4. culturally

INTELLECTUAL DEFICITS AND THE INTELLECTUALLY GIFTED

LO 9-5 What sorts of mental exceptionalities do people have, and what assistance do they need and receive?

> *Although Connie kept pace with her classmates in kindergarten, by the time she reached first grade she was academically the slowest in almost every subject. It was not that she didn't try, but rather that it took her longer than other students to catch on to new material, and she regularly required special attention to keep up with the rest of the class.*
>
> *Yet in some areas she excelled: When asked to draw or produce something with her hands, she not only matched her classmates' performance but exceeded it, producing beautiful work that was much admired by her classmates. Although the other students in the class felt that there was something different about Connie, they were hard-pressed to identify the source of the difference, and in fact they didn't spend much time pondering the issue.*

Connie's parents and teacher, though, knew what made her special. Extensive testing in kindergarten had shown that Connie's intelligence was well below normal, and she was officially classified as a special needs student.

The Least Restrictive Environment

If Connie had been attending school in earlier times, she would most likely have been placed in a special needs classroom as soon as her low IQ was identified. Such classes, consisting of students with a range of afflictions, including emotional difficulties, severe reading problems, and physical disabilities such as cerebral palsy, as well those with lower IQs, were usually kept separate from the regular educational process.

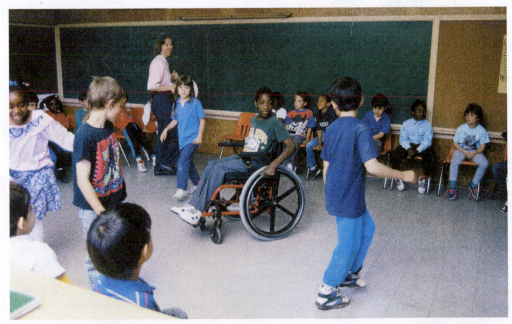

Mainstreaming of exceptional children into traditional educational systems has provided opportunities that were previously denied.

All that changed in 1975 when Congress passed Public Law 94-142, the Education for All Handicapped Children Act. The intent of the law—an intent largely realized—was to ensure that special needs children were educated in the **least restrictive environment**, that is, the setting most similar to that of children without special needs.

In practice, the law has integrated children with special needs into regular classrooms and activities to the greatest extent possible, as long as doing so is educationally beneficial. Children are to be removed from the regular classroom only for those subjects specifically affected by their exceptionality; for all other subjects, they are to be taught in regular classrooms. Of course, some children with severe handicaps still need a mostly or entirely separate education. But the law integrates exceptional children and typical children to the fullest extent possible.

This approach to special education, designed to minimize the segregation of exceptional students, is called **mainstreaming**. In mainstreaming, exceptional children are integrated as much as possible into the regular education system and provided with a broad range of alternatives (Hocutt, 1996; Belkin, 2004).

Some professionals promote an alternative model known as **full inclusion**. Full inclusion is the integration of all students, even the most severely disabled, into regular classes, thereby eliminating separate special education programs. Full inclusion is controversial, and it remains to be seen how widespread it will become (Brehm, 2003; Gersten & Dimino, 2006; Hughes-Lynch, 2012).

Regardless of whether they are educated using mainstreaming or full inclusion, children whose intelligence is significantly beyond the typical range represent a challenge for educators. We will next consider both those who are below and those who are above the norm.

FROM AN
EDUCATOR'S
PERSPECTIVE:
What are some of the challenges of teaching a class that has been mainstreamed? What are some of the advantages?

least restrictive environment   The setting most similar to that of children without special needs

mainstreaming   An approach to special education designed to minimize the segregation of exception students

full inclusion   The integration of all students, even the most severely disabled, into regular classes, thereby eliminating separate special education programs

---

CAREERS IN CHILD DEVELOPMENT

Name: Christine Gonzalez

Education: University of Florida, B.A. in Education; University of California at Los Angeles, M.Ed.

Title: Special Education Teacher, Framingham, Massachusetts, Public Schools

Teaching in a highly diverse school system that requires bilingual and English as a Second Language (ESL) services can be a challenge. Adding to the challenge is the need to teach students from a range of socioeconomic levels who also have special needs, according to Christine Gonzalez, special education teacher in the Framingham, Massachusetts, public school system.

"My caseload fluctuates through the year, but currently a paraprofessional and I support 22 students ranging from kindergarten to fifth grade," she says, "and all are classified as having a moderate disability, including learning and communications disabilities."

Gonzalez notes that modification of the curriculum is at times necessary to provide the best teaching for the special needs student.

"Our goal is to support students so that they can make effective academic progress in the least restrictive environment," she explains. "We like to offer a continuum of service, meaning that sometimes the least restrictive environment is inside the regular classroom, but sometimes it isn't.

"When the presentation of content may be disruptive within the standard class, the student may be pulled out of the regular classroom to receive specialized instruction within a small group setting," she adds.

"With accommodations, we primarily work within the regular classroom, consulting with the regular class teacher and providing direct service to the students," she notes.

"With the special education teacher in the regular class, the transition of skills and strategies becomes easier. The teacher is there to prompt students to use their strategies and skills in the regular setting, which helps to achieve academic progress in the least restrictive environment—our goal," says Gonzalez.

Gonzalez also notes that parent involvement is not only important, but encouraged.

"Parents are involved as much as possible, as we believe they can make an essential difference in a child's academic progress. During teacher conferences we encourage parents to become involved in their child's school progress in many ways, including attending meetings and other school events, and getting excited about the progress they see in their child's work.

"These parental behaviors help motivate our children," Gonzalez adds. "Students whose parents are involved often seem more excited about school and more responsible for their own learning."

Below the Norm: Intellectual Disability

Approximately 1% to 3% of the school-age population is considered to have intellectual disability. **Intellectual disability** (or, as it was formerly called, *mental retardation*) is characterized by significant limitations in intellectual functioning and in adaptive behavior involving conceptual, social, and practical skills (AAMR, 2002).

Most cases of intellectual disability are classified as *familial intellectual deficit*, in which no cause is apparent, but there is a history of retardation in the family. In other cases, there is a clear biological cause. The most common biological causes are *fetal alcohol syndrome*, which is produced by the mother's use of alcohol while pregnant, and *Down syndrome*, which results from the presence of an extra chromosome. Birth complications, such as a temporary lack of oxygen, may also produce intellectual disability (Plomin, 2005; West & Blake, 2005; Manning & Hoyme, 2007).

Degrees of Intellectual Disability.
The vast majority of individuals with intellectual disabilities—some 90%—have relatively minor levels of deficits. Classified with **mild intellectual disability**, they score in the range of 50 or 55 to 70 on IQ tests. Typically, their disability is not even identified before they reach school, although their early development is often slower than average. Once they enter elementary school, their disability and their need for special attention usually become apparent, as was the case with Connie, the first-grader profiled at the beginning of this discussion. With appropriate training, these students can ultimately reach a third- to sixth-grade educational level, and although they cannot carry out complex intellectual tasks, they are able to hold jobs and function independently and successfully.

Intellectual and adaptive limitations become more apparent, however, at more extreme levels of intellectual disability. People whose IQ scores range from around 35 or 40 to 50 or 55 are classified with **moderate intellectual disability**. Accounting for 5% to 10% of those classified as intellectually disabled, individuals with moderate intellectual disabilities display distinctive behavior early in their lives. They are slow to develop language skills, and their motor development is also affected. Regular schooling is usually not effective in training people with moderate intellectual disabilities to acquire academic skills because generally they are unable to progress beyond the second-grade level. Still, they are capable of learning occupational and social skills, and they can learn to travel independently to familiar places. Typically, they require moderate levels of supervision.

At the most significant levels of disability—in individuals with **severe intellectual disability** (IQs ranging from around 20 or 25 to 35 or 40) and **profound intellectual disability** (IQs below 20 or 25)—the ability to function is severely limited. Usually, such people produce little or no speech, have poor motor control, and may need 24-hour nursing care. At the same time, though, some people with severe intellectual disabilities are capable of learning basic self-care skills, such as dressing and eating, and they may even develop the potential to become partially independent as adults. Still, the need for relatively high levels of care continues throughout the life span, and most individuals with severe and profound intellectual disabilities are institutionalized for most of their lives.

intellectual disability (formerly known as mental retardation) A disability characterized by significant limitations in intellectual functioning and in adaptive behavior involving conceptual, social, and practical skills

mild intellectual disability Intellectual disability with IQ scores in the range of 50 or 55 to 70

moderate intellectual disability Intellectual disability with IQ scores from around 35 or 40 to 50 or 55

severe intellectual disability Intellectual disability with IQ scores that range from around 20 or 25 to 35 or 40

profound intellectual disability Intellectual disability with IQ scores below 20 or 25

Children with intellectual disability (formerly known as mental retardation) are often educated in classes with typical children and perform well.

Above the Norm: The Gifted and Talented

Amy Leibowitz picked up reading at age three. By five, she was writing her own books. First grade bored her within a week. As her school had no program for gifted children, it was suggested she skip to second grade. From there, she went to fifth grade. Her parents were proud but concerned. When they asked the fifth-grade teacher where she felt Amy really belonged, the teacher said she was ready, academically, for high school.

It sometimes strikes people as curious that the gifted and talented are considered to have a form of exceptionality. Yet, the 3% to 5% of school-age children who are gifted and talented present special challenges of their own.

Which students are considered to be **gifted and talented**? Little agreement exists among researchers on a single definition of this rather broad category of students. However, the federal government considers the term *gifted* to include "children who give evidence of high-performance capability in areas such as intellectual, creative, artistic, leadership capacity, or specific academic fields, and who require services or activities not ordinarily provided by the school in order to fully develop such capabilities" (Sec. 582, P.L. 97-35). Intellectual capabilities, then, represent only one type of exceptionality; unusual potential in areas outside the academic realm are also included in the concept. Gifted and talented children have so much potential that they, no less than students with low IQs, warrant special concern—although special school programs for them are often the first to be dropped when school systems face budgetary problems (Robinson, Zigler, & Gallagher, 2000; Schemo, 2004; Mendoza, 2006).

Despite the stereotypic description of the gifted—particularly those with exceptionally high intelligence—as "unsociable," "poorly adjusted," and "neurotic," most research suggests that highly intelligent people tend to be outgoing, well adjusted, and popular (Howe, 2004; Bracken & Brown, 2006; Shaunessy et al., 2006; Cross et al., 2008).

For instance, one landmark, long-term study of 1,500 gifted students, which began in the 1920s, found that not only were the gifted smarter than average, but also they were healthier, better coordinated, and psychologically better adjusted than their less intelligent classmates. Furthermore, their lives played out in ways that most people would envy. The subjects received more awards and distinctions, earned more money, and made many more contributions in art and literature than the average person. For instance, by the time they had reached the age of 40, they had collectively produced more than 90 books, 375 plays and short stories, and 2,000 articles, and they had registered more than 200 patents. Perhaps not surprisingly, they reported greater satisfaction with their lives than did the nongifted (Sears, 1977; Reis & Renzulli, 2004).

Yet, being gifted and talented is no guarantee of success in school, as we can see if we consider the particular components of the category. For example, the verbal abilities that allow the eloquent expression of ideas and feelings can equally permit the expression of glib and persuasive statements that happen to be inaccurate. Furthermore, teachers may sometimes misinterpret the humor, novelty, and creativity of unusually gifted children, and see their intellectual fervor to be disruptive or inappropriate. And peers are not always sympathetic: Some very bright children try to hide their intelligence in an effort to fit in better with other students (Swiatek, 2002).

gifted and talented Showing evidence of high performance capability in intellectual, creative, or artistic areas, in leadership capacity, or in specific academic fields

acceleration The provision of special programs that allow gifted students to move ahead at their own pace, even if this means skipping to higher grade levels

Educating the Gifted and Talented. Educators have devised two approaches to teaching the gifted and talented: acceleration and enrichment. **Acceleration** allows gifted students to move ahead at their own pace, even if this means skipping to higher grade levels. The materials that students receive under acceleration programs are not necessarily different from what other students receive; they simply are provided at a faster pace than the pace appropriate for the average student (Smutny, Walker, & Meckstroth, 2007; Wells, Lohman, & Marron, 2009; Steenbergen-Hu & Moon, 2011; Stambaugh & Chandler, 2012).

An alternative approach is **enrichment**, through which students are kept at grade level but are enrolled in special programs and given individual activities to allow greater depth of study on a given topic. In enrichment, the material provided to gifted students differs not only in the timing of its presentation but also in its sophistication. Thus, enrichment materials are designed to provide an intellectual challenge to the gifted student, encouraging higher order thinking (Worrell, Szarko, & Gabelko, 2001; Rotigel, 2003).

Acceleration programs can be remarkably effective. Most studies have shown that gifted students who begin school even considerably earlier than their age-mates do as well as or better than those who begin at the traditional age. One of the best illustrations of the benefits of acceleration is the "Study of Mathematically Precocious Youth," an ongoing program at Vanderbilt University. In this program, seventh- and eighth-graders who have unusual abilities in mathematics participate in a variety of special classes and workshops. The results have been nothing short of sensational, with students successfully completing college courses and sometimes even enrolling in college early. Some students have even graduated from college before the age of 18 (Lubinski & Benbow, 2001, 2006; Webb, Lubinski, & Benbow, 2002).

ARE YOU AN INFORMED CONSUMER OF DEVELOPMENT?

How to Take an IQ Test

Many of the same tips and strategies that apply to any test are applicable to IQ tests. Among the most proven test-taking strategies for multiple-choice or true/false IQ tests are:

1. Expect the unexpected. IQ tests are often very different from traditional tests in that they may use abstract designs or pictures to test logical pattern analysis skills, or they may use made-up languages to measure linguistic analysis skills.

2. Because IQ tests are different, get a practice test and get used to how they work. Unfortunately, the many IQ tests available online cost money and are often attempts to sell you something, but you should be able to find sample IQ tests in your local or school library or at low cost in a bookstore.

3. Think of an IQ test as a puzzle or a game. In fact, the test questions are similar to brain teasers, pattern puzzles, and word and math games.

4. Talk over your practice test(s) with your friends and try to understand how your reasoning compares with theirs. Try to pick up tips and strategies from them.

5. On the day of the test, before attempting the first question, relax and take a few breaths.

6. Once you begin, proceed as quickly as you comfortably can. If a question puzzles you, try to eliminate some of the obviously incorrect response choices and take an educated guess from the remaining choices.

7. If you can't answer a question after 30 seconds, mark it in the test margin (or note its number on the computer) and go back to it if you have time at the end.

8. Don't panic if time is almost up and you have a lot of questions left. Most IQ tests are designed to have more questions than the average person can answer in the time allotted. They are called *speeded* tests, because in contrast to other tests you may take, reaction time and mental processing time count on IQ tests. In fact, mental quickness is a big part of what the test is measuring.

9. Don't worry too much about your results. You may find that retaking the test at another time or after reconsidering some of your answers or your problem-solving approaches could result in better performance if you try again. Don't fall for the myth that IQ numbers are fixed, true, and permanent; they are as fallible as the results of any other test. (Murphy, 2011). ■

enrichment Approach through which students are kept at grade level but are enrolled in special programs and given individual activities to allow greater depth of study on a given topic

Review, Check, and Apply

Review

1. Students with various kinds of exceptionalities receive by federal mandate an education in the least restrictive environment.

2. Two main ways of providing special education without unduly segregating special needs students are mainstreaming and full inclusion.

3. IQ scores are also used to classify children with intellectual disabilities. This approach is more useful in measuring cognitive limitations than other limitations. Individuals with intellectual disabilities vary widely across a range of performance and independence levels.

4. A small but significant sector of students fit into the realm of the gifted and talented. To realize their potential in the school setting, they need special attention and programs, such as acceleration and enrichment programs.

Check

1. The integration of all students into regular classes, regardless of disability, and eliminating special education classes entirely is called _____ _____.

2. The older term "mental retardation" has been replaced with the term _____ _____.

3. In _____ programs for the gifted and talented, students are enrolled in special programs and provided with individual activities that allow greater depth, but they are kept a grade level.

4. In _____ programs for the gifted and talented, students are permitted to move ahead at their own pace, skipping grades as merited, but using materials similar to those of their same-level peers.

Apply

1. What are some advantages and disadvantages of mainstreaming versus full inclusion? Be sure to address multiple points of view (i.e., the student's, the teacher's, other students', the parents').

2. Should teacher time and educational resources—both of which are severely limited—be expended on gifted children? What are the ethical issues underlying your response?

To see more review questions, log on to MyPsychLab.

ANSWERS: 1. full inclusion 2. intellectual disability 3. enrichment 4. acceleration

The CASE of . . . *the Worried Eighth-Grade Teacher*

Patrice Marshall was worried about Antoine Toussaint, one of the brightest but quietest students in her class of 34 eighth-graders. The district superintendent had recently announced that eighth-graders would have to take a new IQ test. Now, with the test only two days away, Ms. Marshall considered her students. She believed that the test would work just fine for most of the class, but she knew something about Antoine that she was afraid could affect his performance: Just two days earlier Antoine's father had been rushed to the hospital following a heart attack, and he was still in critical care.

When the day of the test arrived, the class sat quietly and worked busily. Antoine seemed comfortable, apparently keeping his mind on the test. Still, Ms. Marshall worried.

When she looked at the test papers, her heart sank. Antoine's score was well below the level she expected. IQ was supposed to be accurate, unchanging, fixed—but she *knew* Antoine was more intelligent than the test showed. Could the test be wrong?

What was a responsible teacher to do?

Ms. Marshall took an extraordinary step. The district allowed teachers some discretion in re-administering tests to students who had missed school, and she intended to take advantage of this loophole to give Antoine a second chance. She "sat on" Antoine's test paper, acting as if he had somehow missed the test.

One week later, Antoine was in a different frame of mind. Over the weekend, his father had recovered completely and had come home from the hospital. On Monday, she asked Antoine to stay after school and retake the IQ test in her office. Ms. Marshall left him undisturbed while she graded papers and did her daily paperwork at her desk.

When she graded his test, she found she had been right. Antoine had improved his test score considerably. Ms. Marshall was certain that this result was the correct one. She had more faith in her instincts than in the IQ test, and in the end, her faith was justified.

1. What would account for a substantial difference in Antoine's IQ scores between the two times he took the test? Could the test have been designed to prevent such a change in score?

2. What do Antoine's scores suggest about the reliability of the test? What do they suggest about its validity? What does the score change suggest about the common view that IQ scores are accurate and unchanging?

3. Do you think Ms. Marshall was educationally right to suppress Antoine's first score? Was she morally and ethically right? Should she have acted differently?

4. Is it fair to administer important, high-consequence tests to persons who may not be at their best on a given day? Is there a practical way for test administrators to deal with this situation?

◀◀◀ LOOKING BACK

LO 9-1 What is intelligence, and how has it been measured over the years?

- It is difficult for developmental psychologists to define and measure intelligence. Alfred Binet is responsible for most 20th-century approaches to the study of intelligence.

- Binet left three major contributions to the field of intelligence measurement: using a practical, non-theoretical approach; linking intelligence to academic success; and using IQ scores to quantify intelligence.

- Measurements must be consistent (i.e., have reliability) and measure what they are expected to measure (i.e., have validity).

LO 9-2 What are newer conceptions of intelligence, and how are they measured?

- Alternative conceptions of intelligence have sprung up to explain different kinds of intelligence, including Robert Sternberg's triarchic theory of intelligence, which claims that intelligence is composed of componential, experiential, and contextual components.

- Creativity is often a young adult trait because young adults' minds are not set in habitual ways of solving problems.

LO 9-3 How is the intelligence of infants measured, and does infant intelligence predict adult intelligence?

- It is particularly difficult to define and measure infant intelligence. Approaches include developmental scales, which provide good cognitive snapshots, and information processing approaches, which focus on the speed at which infants process information and learn about stimuli.

LO 9-4 Why do some groups perform better than others on IQ tests, and what do such group differences mean?

- A major controversy in the study of intelligence is the role of nature versus nurture in IQ. Most developmentalists regard nature as less important than nurture, especially economic and social background.

LO 9-5 What sorts of mental exceptionalities do people have, and what assistance do they need and receive?

- To comply with P.L. 94-142, schools are required to provide students with exceptionalities an education in the least restrictive environment, which may mean mainstreaming or full inclusion.

- IQ scores focus primarily on academic skills and ignore other aspects of students' abilities.

- Individuals with mental retardation vary widely across a range of performance and independence levels.

- A few students may be categorized as gifted or talented, and can benefit from special programs such as acceleration and enrichment programs.

- Contrary to stereotypes, gifted and talented people are usually well adjusted and satisfied with their lives.

KEY TERMS AND CONCEPTS

intelligence (p. 246)
intelligence quotient (IQ) (p. 248)
Stanford-Binet Intelligence Scales,
  Fifth Edition (SB5) (p. 248)
Wechsler Intelligence Scale for Children—
  Fourth Edition (WISC-IV) (p. 249)
Kaufman Assessment Battery for Children,
  Second Edition (KABC-II) (p. 249)
reliability (p. 249)
validity (p. 249)

learning disabilities (p. 251)
fluid intelligence (p. 252)
crystallized intelligence (p. 252)
triarchic theory of intelligence (p. 253)
emotional intelligence (p. 254)
developmental quotient (p. 257)
Bayley Scales of Infant Development (p. 257)
least restrictive environment (p. 264)
mainstreaming (p. 264)
full inclusion (p. 264)

intellectual disability (p. 265)
mild intellectual disability (p. 265)
moderate intellectual disability (p. 265)
severe intellectual disability (p. 265)
profound intellectual disability (p. 265)
gifted and talented (p. 266)
acceleration (p. 266)
enrichment (p. 267)

Epilogue

We opened the chapter with the question of what intelligence consists of and how it can be defined. We saw some of the ways in which intelligence has been measured, and we considered controversial topics such as group performance differences on IQ tests and the need for culture-fair intelligence assessments. Our discussion of intelligence concluded with a look at two groups with intellectual exceptionalities at opposite ends of the intelligence scale: people with intellectual disabilities and people who are gifted or talented.

Think back to the case of 11-year-old Daniel Skandera, who is competent with math games on his computer and yet has Down syndrome. Daniel illustrates how persons with exceptionalities fit (and don't fit) into their worlds.

1. Does Daniel's love of and skill with computer games tell us anything about his intelligence? How do you think he would do on a traditional IQ test? Why?

2. Is there a fair way to measure Daniel's intelligence? Would Sternberg's triarchic theory work?

3. Is Daniel unique in being comparatively slow in some areas and competent in others? Based on the evidence in the prologue, does Daniel seem to be a suitable candidate for mainstreaming? For full inclusion?

The Development Video Series in MyPsychLab

Explore the video *Thinking Like a Psychologist: Intelligence Tests and Success* by scanning this QR code with your mobile device. If you don't already have one, you may download a free QR scanner for your device wherever smartphone apps are sold. You can also view this video in MyPsychLab. For more videos related to this chapter's content, log into MyPsychLab to view the entire Development Video Series.

MyVirtualChild

- What decisions would you make while raising a child?
- What would the consequences of those decisions be?

Find out by accessing **MyVirtualChild** at
www.MyPsychLab.com
and raising your own virtual child from birth to age 18.

10 Social and Emotional Development

MODULE 10.1

FORMING THE ROOTS OF SOCIABILITY

- Attachment: Forming Social Bonds
- Producing Attachment: The Roles of the Mother and Father

DEVELOPMENTAL DIVERSITY AND YOUR LIFE: Does Attachment Differ across Cultures?

- Infants' Sociability with Their Peers: Infant–Infant Interaction

Review, Check, and Apply

MODULE 10.2

EMOTIONAL DEVELOPMENT

- Emotions in Infancy: Do Infants Experience Emotional Highs and Lows?

FROM RESEARCH TO PRACTICE: Do Infants Experience Jealousy?

CAREERS IN CHILD DEVELOPMENT: Christin Poirier, Licensed Social Worker

- Social Referencing: Feeling What Others Feel
- Theory of Mind: Infants' Perspectives on the Mental Lives of Others—and Themselves
- Emotional Development in Middle Childhood
- Emotional Development in Adolescence
- Emotional Difficulties in Adolescence: Depression and Suicide

ARE YOU AN INFORMED CONSUMER OF DEVELOPMENT? Preventing Adolescent Suicide

Review, Check, and Apply

MODULE 10.3

PERSONALITY DEVELOPMENT

- Temperament: Stabilities in Behavior
- Erikson's Theory of Psychosocial Development

Review, Check, and Apply

The Case of . . . the Long Goodbye

Looking Back

Key Terms and Concepts

Epilogue

PROLOGUE: The Child-Proof Bin

Lisa Palermo, 10 months old, had Cheerios on her breath—always, especially in the late morning. At first, Mindy Crowell, Lisa's day-care teacher, thought little of it, but when she noticed that the classroom Cheerios stash was slowly dwindling, she began to wonder.

The Cheerios were stored in a plastic bin in the clothes closet. Mindy began to watch the closet out of the corner of her eye. Sure enough, she noticed Lisa crawling toward it. What she saw next astonished her. Lisa manipulated the fastener of the bin, reached in, withdrew a hand laden with Cheerios, and let the bin refasten itself, as it was designed to do.

Somehow, Lisa, barely able to hold a colored pencil, had learned how to undo the supposedly child-proof fastener—a task that Mindy herself sometimes struggled with. And what was worse, Lisa proved to be an excellent teacher.

Soon enough, Rathana, Paul, Olga, and Kelly were crawling to the bin and doing exactly the same thing. By then, though, it was too late: Because of Lisa's teaching ability, keeping the children out of the snack bin proved to be no easy task. Even more ominous was the thought that if the infants could master the fasteners on the snack bin, what would they be unfastening next?

>>> LOOKING AHEAD

As babies like Lisa show us, children are sociable from a very early age. This anecdote also demonstrates one of the side benefits of even very young children's participation in child care, and something research has begun to suggest: through their social interactions, babies acquire new skills and abilities from more "expert" peers. Children, as we will see, have an amazing capacity to learn from other children, and their interactions with others can play a central role in their developing social and emotional worlds.

In this chapter we consider social and personality development from infancy through adolescence. We begin by examining the roots of children's earliest social relationships. We look at how bonds of attachment are forged in infancy and the ways in which children increasingly interact with family members and peers.

(continued)

Learning Objectives

MODULE 10.1

LO1 What is attachment in infancy, and how does it affect an individual's future social competence?

LO2 Are there differences in attachments to fathers and mothers?

LO3 How sociable are infants with other children?

MODULE 10.2

LO4 Do infants experience emotions?

LO5 What sort of mental life does an infant lead and how does this develop in the preschool period?

LO6 What dangers do adolescents face as they deal with the stresses of adolescence?

MODULE 10.3

LO7 What individual differences distinguish one infant from another?

LO8 What is Erikson's theory of psychosocial development, and how is such development shaped by the child's environment?

We then turn to emotional development, beginning with the emotions infants feel and how well they can read others' emotions. We look at how others' responses shape children's own reactions and discuss children's growing ability to express their emotions. We consider, too, how children, even infants, view their own and others' mental lives. Next, we discuss the nature and function of emotions in adolescence and see how they learn to regulate their feelings. We include a look at the emotional difficulties adolescents may face, resulting in depression or even suicide, and discuss how suicide may be prevented.

Finally, we examine personality and the stages of children's psychosocial development. We consider the characteristics that differentiate one infant from another, and evaluate the pros and cons of day care for young children. The chapter closes with a look at a variety of theories on how personality develops in adolescence.

M O D U L E   10.1

FORMING THE ROOTS OF SOCIABILITY

LO 10-1 What is attachment in infancy, and how does it affect an individual's future social competence?

LO 10-2 Are there differences in attachments to fathers and mothers?

LO 10-3 How sociable are infants with other children?

Luis Camacho, now 38, clearly remembers the feelings that haunted him on the way to the hospital to meet his new sister Katy. Though he was only 4 at the time, that day of infamy is still vivid to him today. Luis would no longer be the only kid in the house; he would have to share his life with a baby sister. She would play with his toys, read his books, be with him in the back seat of the car.

What really bothered him, of course, was that he would have to share his parents' love and attention with a new person. And not just any new person—a girl, who would automatically have a lot of advantages. Katy would be cuter, more needy, more demanding, more interesting—more everything—than he. He would be underfoot at best, neglected at worst.

Luis also knew that he was expected to be cheerful and welcoming. So he put on a brave face at the hospital and walked without hesitation to the room where his mother and Katy were waiting.

The arrival of a newborn brings a dramatic change to a family's dynamics. No matter how welcome a baby's birth, it causes a fundamental shift in the roles that people play within the family. Mothers and fathers must start to build a relationship with their infant, and older children must adjust to the presence of a new member of the family and build their own alliance with their infant brother or sister.

Although the process of social development during infancy is neither simple nor automatic, it is crucial: The bonds that grow between infants and their parents, siblings, family, and others provide the foundation for a lifetime's worth of social relationships.

Attachment: Forming Social Bonds

The most important aspect of social development that takes place during infancy is the formation of attachment. **Attachment** is the positive emotional bond that develops between a child and a particular, special individual. When children experience attachment to a given person, they feel pleasure when they are with them and feel comforted by their presence at times of distress. The nature of our attachment

▶ Watch the **Video** *Attachment* in **MyPsychLab**.

attachment   The positive emotional bond that develops between a child and a particular individual

The bonds that children forge with others during their earliest years play a crucial role throughout their lives.

during infancy affects how we relate to others throughout the rest of our lives (Hofer, 2006; Bergman, Blom, & Polyak, 2012).

To understand attachment, the earliest researchers turned to the bonds that form between parents and children in the nonhuman animal kingdom. For instance, ethologist Konrad Lorenz (1965) observed newborn goslings, who have an innate tendency to follow their mother, the first moving object to which they typically are exposed after birth. Lorenz found that goslings whose eggs were raised in an incubator and who viewed him just after hatching would follow his every movement, as if he were their mother. He labeled this process *imprinting*: behavior that takes place during a critical period and involves attachment to the first moving object that is observed.

Lorenz's findings suggested that attachment was based on biologically determined factors, and other theorists agreed. For instance, Freud suggested that attachment grew out of a mother's ability to satisfy a child's oral needs.

It turns out, however, that the ability to provide food and other physiological needs may not be as crucial as Freud and other theorists first thought. In a classic study, psychologist Harry Harlow gave infant monkeys the choice of cuddling a wire "monkey" that provided food or a soft, terry cloth monkey that was warm but did not provide food (see Figure 10-1). Their preference was clear: Baby monkeys spent most of their time clinging to the cloth monkey, although they made occasional expeditions to the wire monkey to nurse. Harlow suggested that the preference for the warm cloth monkey provided *contact comfort* (Harlow & Zimmerman, 1959; Blum, 2002).

Harlow's work illustrates that food alone is not the basis for attachment. Given that the monkeys' preference for the soft cloth "mothers" developed some time after birth, these findings are consistent with the research we discussed in Chapter 4, showing little support for the existence of a critical period for bonding between human mothers and infants immediately following birth.

The earliest work on human attachment, which is still highly influential, was carried out by British psychiatrist John Bowlby (1951, 2007). In Bowlby's view, attachment is based primarily on infants' needs for safety and security—their genetically determined motivation to avoid predators. As they develop, infants come to learn that their safety is best provided by a particular individual. This realization ultimately leads to the development of a special relationship with that individual, who is typically the mother. Bowlby suggested that this single relationship with the primary caregiver is qualitatively different from the bonds formed with others, including the father—a suggestion that, as we'll see later, has been a source of some disagreement.

According to Bowlby, attachment provides a home base. As children become more independent, they can progressively roam further away from their secure base.

The Ainsworth Strange Situation and Patterns of Attachment.
Developmental psychologist Mary Ainsworth built on Bowlby's theorizing to develop a widely used experimental technique to measure attachment (Ainsworth, 1993). The **Ainsworth Strange Situation** consists of a sequence of staged episodes that illustrate the strength of attachment between a child and (typically) his or her mother. The "strange situation" follows this general eight-step pattern: (1) The mother and baby enter an unfamiliar room; (2) the mother sits down, leaving the baby free to explore; (3) an adult stranger enters the room and converses first with the mother and then with the baby; (4) the mother exits the room, leaving the baby alone with the stranger; (5) the mother returns, greeting and comforting the baby, and the stranger leaves; (6) the mother departs again, leaving the baby alone; (7) the stranger returns; and (8) the mother returns and the stranger leaves.

Infants' reactions to the various aspects of the Strange Situation vary considerably, depending on the nature of their attachment to their mothers. One-year-olds typically show one of four major patterns—securely attached, avoidant, ambivalent, and disorganized-disoriented (summarized in Table 10-1 on page 276). Children who have a **secure attachment pattern** use the mother as the home base that Bowlby described. These children seem at ease in the Strange Situation as long as their mothers are present. They explore independently, returning to her occasionally. Although they may or may not appear upset when she leaves, securely attached children immediately go to her when she returns and seek contact. Most North American children—about two-thirds—fall into the securely attached category.

In contrast, children with an **avoidant attachment pattern** do not seek proximity to the mother, and after she has left, they typically do not seem distressed. Furthermore, they seem

FIGURE 10-1 Monkey Mothers Matter

Harlow's research showed that monkeys preferred the warm, soft "mother" over the wire "monkey" that provided food.

Mary Ainsworth, who devised the Strange Situation to measure attachment.

Ainsworth Strange Situation A sequence of staged episodes that illustrate the strength of attachment between a child and (typically) his or her mother

secure attachment pattern A style of attachment in which children use the mother as a kind of home base and are at ease when she is present; when she leaves, they become upset and go to her as soon as she returns

avoidant attachment pattern A style of attachment in which children do not seek proximity to the mother; after the mother has left, they seem to avoid her when she returns as if they are angered by her behavior

TABLE 10-1 Classifications of Infant Attachment

	CRITERIA FOR CLASSIFICATION	
Label	Proximity with Caregiver	Contact with Caregiver
Secure	High level: Seeks proximity as base of exploration.	High level: Seeks contact, especially when distressed.
Avoidant	Low level: Avoids proximity with caregiver and others.	Low level: Avoids caregiver upon return from absence, apparently indifferent.
Ambivalent	High level: Maintains close proximity, distressed even before caregiver's absence.	High/low level: Seeks but then resists contact, sometimes appearing angry.
Disorganized-Disoriented	Inconsistent: Confused, may be near but not looking at caregiver.	Inconsistent: Contradictory behaviors, moving suddenly from calm to anger.

(*Source:* E. Walters, 1963.)

Watch the Video *Attachment in Infants* in MyPsychLab.

ambivalent attachment pattern   A style of attachment in which children display a combination of positive and negative reactions to their mothers; they show great distress when the mother leaves, but upon her return they may simultaneously seek close contact but also hit and kick her

disorganized-disoriented attachment pattern   A style of attachment in which children show inconsistent, often contradictory behavior, such as approaching the mother when she returns but not looking at her; they may be the least securely attached children of all

to avoid her when she returns. It is as if they are indifferent to her behavior. Some 20% of 1-year-old children are in the avoidant category.

Children with an **ambivalent attachment pattern** display a combination of positive and negative reactions to their mothers. Initially, ambivalent children are in such close contact with the mother that they hardly explore their environment. They appear anxious even before the mother leaves, and when she does leave, they show great distress. But upon her return, they show ambivalent reactions, seeking to be close to her but also hitting and kicking, apparently in anger. About 10% to 15% of 1-year-olds fall into the ambivalent classification (Cassidy & Berlin, 1994).

Although Ainsworth identified only three categories, a more recent expansion of her work finds that there is a fourth category: disorganized-disoriented. Children who have a **disorganized-disoriented attachment pattern** show inconsistent, contradictory, and confused behavior. They may run to the mother when she returns but not look at her, or seem initially calm and then suddenly break into angry weeping. Their confusion suggests that they may be the least securely attached children of all. About 5% to 10% of children fall into this category (Mayseless, 1996; Cole, 2005; Bernier & Meins, 2008).

A child's attachment style would be of only minor consequence were it not for the fact that the quality of attachment between infants and their mothers has significant consequences for relationships at later stages of life. For example, boys who are securely attached at the age of 1 year show fewer psychological difficulties at older ages than do avoidant or ambivalent children. Similarly, children who are securely attached as infants tend to be more socially and emotionally competent later, and others view them more positively. Adult romantic relationships are associated with the kind of attachment style developed during infancy (Simpson et al., 2007; MacDonald et al., 2008; Shaver & Mikulincer, 2012).

At the same time, we cannot say that children who do not have a secure attachment style during infancy invariably experience difficulties later in life, nor that those with a secure attachment at age 1 always have good adjustment later on. In fact, some evidence suggests that children with avoidant and ambivalent attachment—as measured

In this illustration of the Ainsworth Strange Situation, the infant first explores the playroom on his own, as long as his mother is present. But when she leaves, he begins to cry. On her return, however, he is immediately comforted and stops crying. The conclusion: he is securely attached.

by the Strange Situation—do quite well (Weinfield, Sroufe, & Egeland, 2000; Lewis, Feiring, & Rosenthal, 2000; Fraley & Spieker, 2003).

In cases in which the development of attachment has been severely disrupted, children may suffer from *reactive attachment disorder,* a psychological problem characterized by extreme problems in forming attachments to others. In young children, it can be displayed in feeding difficulties, unresponsiveness to social overtures from others, and a general failure to thrive. Reactive attachment disorder is rare and typically the result of abuse or neglect (Hornor, 2008; Schechter & Willheim, 2009; Puckering et al., 2011; Shreeve, 2012).

Producing Attachment: The Roles of the Mother and Father

As 5-month-old Annie cries passionately, her mother comes into the room and gently lifts her from her crib. After just a few moments, as her mother rocks Annie and speaks softly, Annie's cries cease, and she cuddles in her mother's arms. But the moment her mother places her back in the crib, Annie begins to wail again, leading her mother to pick her up once again.

The pattern is familiar to most parents. The infant cries, the parent reacts, and the child responds in turn. Such seemingly insignificant sequences as these, repeatedly occurring in the lives of infants and parents, help pave the way for the development of relationships between children, their parents, and the rest of the social world. We'll consider how each of the major caregivers and the infant play a role in the development of attachment.

Mothers and Attachment.
Sensitivity to their infants' needs and desires is the hallmark of mothers of securely attached infants. Such a mother tends to be aware of her child's moods, and she takes into account her child's feelings as they interact. She is also responsive during face-to-face interactions, provides feeding "on demand," and is warm and affectionate to her infant (McElwain & Booth-LaForce, 2006; Priddis & Howieson, 2009; Akhtar, 2012).

It is not only a matter of responding in *any* fashion to their infants' signals that separates mothers of securely attached and insecurely attached children. Mothers of secure infants tend to provide the appropriate level of response. In fact, research has shown that overly responsive mothers are just as likely to have insecurely attached children as under-responsive mothers. In contrast, mothers whose communication involves *interactional synchrony,* in which caregivers respond to infants appropriately and both caregiver and child match emotional states, are more likely to produce secure attachment (Hane, Feldstein, & Dernetz, 2003; Fischer, 2012).

The research showing the correspondence between mothers' sensitivity to their infants and the security of the infants' attachment is consistent with Ainsworth's arguments that attachment depends on how mothers react to their infants' emotional cues. Ainsworth suggests that mothers of securely attached infants respond rapidly and positively to their infants. For example, Annie's mother responds quickly to her cries by cuddling and comforting her. In contrast, the way for mothers to produce insecurely attached infants, according to Ainsworth, is to ignore their behavioral cues, to behave inconsistently with them, and to ignore or reject their social efforts. For example, picture a child who repeatedly and unsuccessfully tries to gain her mother's attention by calling or turning and gesturing from her stroller while her mother, engaged in conversation, ignores her. This baby is likely to be less securely attached than a child whose mother acknowledges her child more quickly and consistently (Higley & Dozier, 2009).

But how do mothers learn how to respond to their infants? One way is from their own mothers. Mothers typically respond to their infants based on their own attachment styles. As a result, there is substantial similarity in attachment patterns from one generation to the next (Peck, 2003).

It is important to realize that a mother's (and others') behavior toward infants is at least in part a reaction to the child's ability to provide effective cues. A mother may not be able to respond effectively to a child whose own behavior is unrevealing, misleading, or ambiguous. For instance, children who clearly display their anger or fear or unhappiness will be easier to read—and respond to effectively—than children whose behavior is ambiguous. Consequently, the kind of signals an infant sends may in part determine how successful the mother will be in responding.

The differences in the ways that fathers and mothers play with their children occur even in families in which the father is the primary caregiver. Based on this observation, how does culture affect attachment?

Fathers and Attachment. Up to now, we've barely touched on one of the key players involved in the upbringing of a child: the father. In fact, if you looked at the early theorizing and research on attachment, you'd find little mention of the father and his potential contributions to the life of the infant.

There are at least two reasons for this absence. First, John Bowlby, who provided the initial theory of attachment, suggested that there was something unique about the mother–child relationship. He believed the mother was uniquely equipped, biologically, to provide sustenance for the child, and he concluded that this capability led to the development of a special relationship between mothers and children. Second, the early work on attachment was influenced by the traditional social views of the time, which considered it "natural" for the mother to be the primary caregiver, while the father's role was to work outside the home to provide a living for his family.

Several factors led to the demise of this view. One was that societal norms changed, and fathers began to take a more active role in childrearing activities. More important, it became increasingly clear from research findings that—despite societal norms that relegated fathers to secondary childrearing roles—some infants formed their primary initial relationship with their fathers (Diener et al., 2008; Music, 2011; Moon, 2012).

In addition, a growing body of research has shown that fathers' expressions of nurturance, warmth, affection, support, and concern are extremely important to their children's emotional and social well-being. In fact, certain kinds of psychological disorders, such as substance abuse and depression, have been found to be related more to fathers' than mothers' behavior (Veneziano, 2003; Parke, 2004; Roelofs et al., 2006).

Infants' social bonds extend beyond their parents, especially as they grow older. For example, one study found that although most infants formed their first primary relationship with one person, around one-third had multiple relationships, and it was difficult to determine which attachment was primary. Furthermore, by the time the infants were 18 months old, most had formed multiple relationships. In sum, infants may develop attachments not only to their mothers, but to a variety of others as well (Booth, Kelly, & Spieker, 2003; Seibert & Kerns, 2009).

Are There Differences in Attachment to Mothers and Fathers? Although infants are fully capable of forming attachments to both mother and father—as well as other individuals—the nature of attachment between infants and mothers, on the one hand, and infants and fathers, on the other hand, is not identical. For example, when they are in unusually stressful circumstances, most infants prefer to be soothed by their mothers rather than by their fathers (Thompson, Easterbrooks, & Padilla-Walker, 2003; Schoppe-Sullivan et al., 2006).

One reason for qualitative differences in attachment involves the differences in what fathers and mothers do with their children. Mothers spend a greater proportion of their time feeding and directly nurturing their children. In contrast, fathers spend more time, proportionally, playing with infants. Almost all fathers do contribute to child care: Surveys show that 95% say they do some child-care chores every day. But on average they still do less than mothers. For instance, 30% of fathers with wives who work do three or more hours of daily child care. In comparison, 74% of employed married mothers spend that amount of time every day in child-care activities (Grych & Clark, 1999; Kazura, 2000; Whelan & Lally, 2002).

Furthermore, the nature of fathers' play with their babies is often quite different from that of mothers. Fathers engage in more physical, rough-and-tumble activities with their children. In contrast, mothers play traditional games such as peek-a-boo and games with more verbal elements (Paquette, Carbonneau, & Dubeau, 2003).

These differences in the ways that fathers and mothers play with their children occur even in the minority of families in the United States in which the father is the primary caregiver. Moreover, the differences occur in very diverse cultures: Fathers in Australia, Israel, India, Japan, Mexico, and even in the Aka Pygmy tribe in central Africa all engage more in play than in caregiving, although the amount of time they spend with their infants varies widely. For instance, Aka fathers spend more time caring for their infants than members of any other known culture, holding and cuddling their babies at a rate some five times higher than anywhere else in the world (Roopnarine, 1992; Hewlett & Lamb, 2002; Leavell et al., 2012).

These similarities and differences in child-rearing practices across different societies raise an important question: How does culture affect attachment?

DEVELOPMENTAL DIVERSITY AND YOUR LIFE

Does Attachment Differ across Cultures?

John Bowlby's observations of the biologically motivated efforts of the young of other species to seek safety and security were the basis for his views on attachment and his reason for suggesting that seeking attachment was a biological universal, one that we should find not only in other species but among humans of all cultures as well.

Research has shown that human attachment is not as culturally universal as Bowlby predicted. Certain attachment patterns seem more likely among infants of particular cultures. For example, one study of German infants showed that most fell into the avoidant category. Other studies, conducted in Israel and Japan, have found a smaller proportion of infants who were securely attached than in the United States. Finally, comparisons of Chinese and Canadian children show that Chinese children are more inhibited than Canadians in the Strange Situation (Takahashi, 1986; Ijzendoorn, Bakermans-Kranenburg, & Sagi-Schwartz, 2006).

Do such findings suggest that we should abandon the notion that attachment is a universal biological tendency? Not necessarily. While it is possible that Bowlby's claim that the desire for attachment is universal was too strongly stated, most of the data on attachment have been obtained by using the Ainsworth Strange Situation, which may not be the most appropriate measure in non-Western cultures. For example, Japanese parents seek to avoid separation and stress during infancy, and they don't strive to foster independence to the same degree as parents in many Western societies. Because of their relative lack of prior experience in separation, then, infants placed in the Strange Situation may experience unusual stress—producing the appearance of less secure attachment in Japanese children. If a different measure of attachment were used, one that might be administered later in infancy, more Japanese infants could likely be classified as secure (Nakagawa, Lamb, & Miyaki, 1992; Dennis, Cole, & Zahn-Waxler, 2002; Gillath, Canterberry, & Collins, 2012).

Attachment is now viewed as susceptible to cultural norms and expectations. Cross-cultural and within-cultural differences in attachment reflect the nature of the measure employed and the expectations of various cultures. Some developmental specialists suggest that attachment should be viewed as a general tendency, but one that varies in the way it is expressed according to how actively caregivers in a society seek to instill independence in their children. Secure attachment, as defined by the Western-oriented Strange Situation, may be seen earliest in cultures that promote independence, but may be delayed in societies in which independence is a less important cultural value (Rothbaum et al., 2000; Rothbaum, Rosen, & Ujiie, 2002). ■

Japanese parents seek to avoid separation and stress during infancy and do not foster independence. As a result, Japanese children often have the appearance of being less securely attached according to the Strange Situation, but using other measurement techniques they may well score higher in attachment.

Infant Interactions: Developing a Working Relationship. Research on attachment is clear in showing that infants may develop multiple attachment relationships, and that over the course of time the specific individuals with whom the infant is primarily attached may change. These variations in attachment highlight the fact that the development of relationships is an ongoing process, not only during infancy, but throughout our lifetimes.

Which processes underlie the development of relationships during infancy? One answer comes from studies that examine how parents interact with their children. For one thing, parents, and all adults, appear to be genetically preprogrammed to be sensitive to infants. For instance, brain scanning techniques have found that the facial features of infants (but not adults) activate a specialized structure in the brain called the *fusiform gyrus* within a seventh of a second. Such reactions may help elicit nurturing behavior and trigger social interaction (Zebrowitz et al., 2009; Kassuba et al., 2011; Messinger et al., 2012).

In addition, studies have found that, across almost all cultures, mothers behave in typical ways with their infants. They tend to exaggerate their facial and vocal expressions—the nonverbal equivalent of the infant-directed speech that they use when they speak to infants (as we discussed in Chapter 4). Similarly, they often imitate their infants' behavior, responding to distinctive sounds and movements by repeating them. There are even types of games, such as peek-a-boo, itsy-bitsy spider, and pat-a-cake, that are nearly universal (Harrist & Waugh, 2002; Kochanska, 2002).

Furthermore, according to the **mutual regulation model,** it is through these sorts of interactions that infants and parents learn to communicate emotional states to one another and to respond appropriately. For instance, in pat-a-cake, both infant and parent act jointly to

mutual regulation model   The model in which infants and parents learn to communicate emotional states to one another and to respond appropriately

regulate turn-taking behavior, with one individual waiting until the other completes a behavioral act before starting another. Consequently, at the age of 3 months, infants and their mothers have about the same influence on each other's behavior. Interestingly, by the age of 6 months, infants have more control over turn-taking, although by the age of 9 months both partners once again become roughly equivalent in terms of mutual influence (Tronick, 2003).

One of the ways infants and parents signal each other when they interact is through facial expressions. As we will see later in this chapter, even quite young infants are able to read, or decode, the facial expressions of their caregivers, and they react to those expressions.

For example, an infant whose mother, during an experiment, displays a stony, immobile facial expression reacts by making a variety of sounds, gestures, and facial expressions of her own in response to such a puzzling situation—and possibly to elicit some new response from her mother. Infants also show more happiness themselves when their mothers appear happy, and they look at their mothers longer. On the other hand, infants are apt to respond with sad looks and to turn away when their mothers display unhappy expressions (Crockenberg & Leerkes, 2003; Reissland & Shepherd, 2006; Yato et al., 2008).

In short, the development of attachment in infants does not merely represent a reaction to the behavior of the people around them. Instead, there is a process of **reciprocal socialization,** in which infants' behaviors invite further responses from parents and other caregivers. In turn, the caregivers' behaviors bring about a reaction from the child, continuing the cycle. Recall, for instance, Annie, the baby who kept crying to be picked up when her mother put her in her crib. Ultimately, the actions and reactions of parents and child lead to an increase in attachment, forging and strengthening bonds between infants and caregivers as babies and caregivers communicate their needs and responses to each other. Figure 10-2 summarizes the sequence of infant–caregiver interaction (Kochanska & Aksan, 2004; Spinrad & Stifter, 2006).

reciprocal socialization A process in which infants' behaviors invite further responses from parents and other caregivers, which in turn bring about further responses from the infants

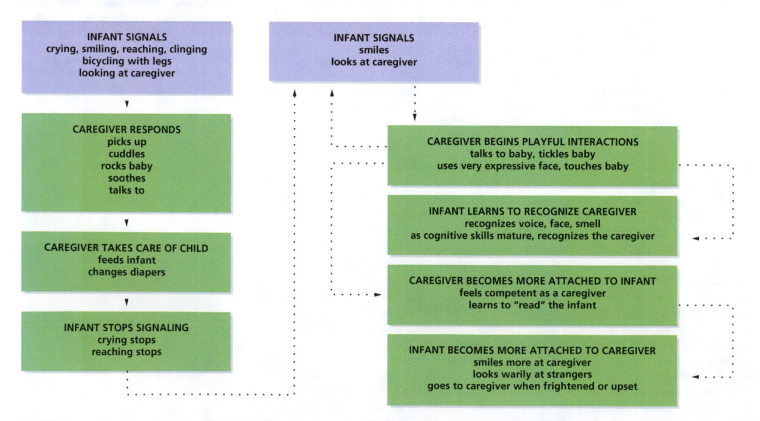

FIGURE 10-2 Sequence of Infant–Caregiver Interaction

The actions and reactions of caregivers and infants influence each other in complex ways. Do you think a similar pattern shows up in adult–adult interactions?

(Adapted from Bell & Ainsworth, 1972; Tomlinson-Keasey, 1985.)

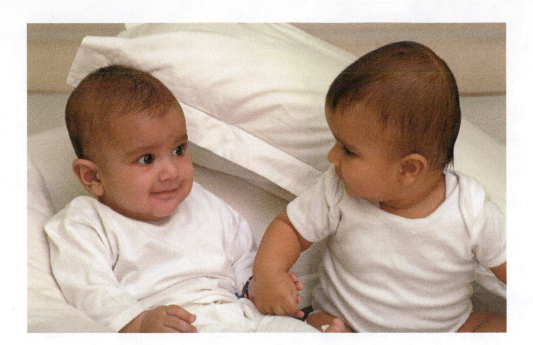

From the earliest month of life infants express sociability in several ways, showing more interest in peers than inanimate objects.

Infants' Sociability with Their Peers: Infant–Infant Interaction

How sociable are infants with other children? Although it is clear that they do not form "friendships" in the traditional sense, babies do react positively to the presence of peers from early in life, and they engage in rudimentary forms of social interaction.

Infants' sociability is expressed in several ways. From the earliest months of life, they smile, laugh, and vocalize while looking at their peers. They show more interest in peers than in inanimate objects and pay greater attention to other infants than they do to a mirror image of themselves. They also begin to show preferences for peers with whom they are familiar compared with those they do not know. For example, studies of identical twins show that twins exhibit a higher level of social behavior toward each other than toward an unfamiliar infant (Eid et al., 2003).

Infants' level of sociability generally rises with age. Nine- to 12-month-olds mutually present and accept toys, particularly if they know each other. They also play social games, such as peek-a-boo or crawl-and-chase. Such behavior is important, as it serves as a foundation for future social exchanges in which children will try to elicit responses from others and then offer reactions to those responses. These kinds of exchanges are important to learn, since they continue even into adulthood. For example, someone who says, "Hi, what's up?" may be trying to elicit a response to which he or she can then reply (Endo, 1992; Eckerman & Peterman, 2001).

Finally, as infants age, they begin to imitate each other. Such imitation serves a social function and can also be a powerful teaching tool. For example, recall the story of 10-month-old Lisa Palermo in the chapter prologue, who showed the other children in her child care center how to remove the fastener from the classroom snack bin and soon had others following her lead.

According to Andrew Meltzoff, a developmental psychologist at the University of Washington, Lisa's ability to impart this information is only one example of how so-called expert babies are able to teach skills and information to other infants. According to the research of Meltzoff and his colleagues, the abilities learned from the "experts" are retained and later utilized to a remarkable degree. Learning by exposure starts early in life. Recent evidence shows that even 7-week-old infants can perform delayed imitation of a novel stimulus to which they have earlier been exposed, such as an adult sticking the tongue out the side of the mouth (Meltzoff & Moore, 1999; Meltzoff, 2002; Meltzoff, Waismeyer, & Gopnik, 2012).

To some developmentalists, the capacity of young children to engage in imitation suggests that imitation may be inborn. In support of this view, research has identified a class of neurons in the brain that seems related to an innate ability to imitate. *Mirror neurons* are neurons that fire not only when an individual enacts a particular behavior, but also when the individual simply observes *another* organism carrying out the same behavior (Falck-Ytter, 2006; Lepage & Théret, 2007).

For example, research on brain functioning shows activation of the inferior frontal gyrus both when an individual carries out a particular task and also when observing another individual carrying out the same task. Mirror neurons may help infants to understand others' actions and to develop a theory of mind, which we discuss later in this chapter. Dysfunction of mirror neurons may be related to the development of disorders involving children's theory of mind as well as autism, a psychological disorder involving significant emotional and linguistic problems (Kilner, Friston, & Frith, 2007; Martineau et al., 2008; Welsh et al., 2009).

The idea that through exposure to other children, infants learn new behaviors, skills, and abilities has several implications. For one thing, it suggests that interactions between infants provide more than social benefits; they may have an impact on children's future cognitive development as well. Even more important, these findings illustrate that infants may benefit from participation in child-care centers (which we consider later in this chapter). Although we don't know for sure, the opportunity to learn from their peers may prove to be a lasting advantage for infants in group child-care settings.

Review, Check, and Apply

Review

1. Attachment, the positive emotional bond between an infant and a significant individual, affects a person's later social competence as an adult.

2. Qualitative differences of attachment between infants and mothers, and infants and fathers, are partly due to the different ways fathers and mothers interact with their children. Mothers spend more time feeding and directly nurturing their children, while fathers spend more time playing with them.

3. Infants and the persons with whom they interact engage in reciprocal socialization as they mutually adjust to one another's interactions.

4. Infants are sociable from the earliest months of life, smiling, laughing, and vocalizing when looking at their peers. They demonstrate more interest in peers than in inanimate objects, and they show preferences for peers with whom they are familiar compared with those they do not know.

Check

1. In British psychiatrist John Bowlby's view, attachment is based on an infant's need for _____ and _____.

2. One-year-olds show four major attachment patterns: _____, avoidant, ambivalent, and disorganized-disoriented.

3. When the development of attachment has been severely disrupted, a child may suffer from _____ _____ _____, a psychological problem characterized by extreme difficulty in forming attachments to others.

4. According to the _____ _____ model, infants and parents learn to communicate emotional states to one another and to respond appropriately.

Apply

1. In what sort of society might an avoidant attachment style be encouraged by cultural attitudes toward childrearing? In such a society, would characterizing the infant's consistent avoidance of its mother as anger be an accurate interpretation?

To see more review questions, log on to MyPsychLab.

ANSWERS: 1. safety, security 2. secure 3. reactive attachment disorder 4. mutual regulation

MODULE 10.2

EMOTIONAL DEVELOPMENT

LO 10-4 Do infants experience emotions?

LO 10-5 What sort of mental life does an infant lead and how does this develop in the preschool period?

LO 10-6 What dangers do adolescents face as they deal with the stresses of adolescence?

Germaine smiles when he catches a glimpse of his mother. Tawanda looks angry when her mother takes away the spoon that she is playing with. Sydney scowls when a loud plane flies overhead.

A smile. A look of anger. A scowl. The emotions of infancy are written all over a baby's face. Yet do infants experience emotions in the same way that adults do? When do they become capable of understanding what others are experiencing emotionally? And how do they use others' emotional states to make sense of their environment? We consider some of these questions as we seek to understand how infants develop emotionally and socially.

Emotions in Infancy: Do Infants Experience Emotional Highs and Lows?

Anyone who spends any time at all around infants knows they display facial expressions that seem indicative of their emotional states. In situations in which we expect them to be happy, they seem to smile; when we might assume they are frustrated, they show anger; and when we might expect them to be unhappy, they look sad.

These basic facial expressions are remarkably similar across the most diverse cultures. Whether we look at babies in India, the United States, or the jungles of New Guinea, the expression of basic emotions is the same (see Figure 10-3 on page 284). Furthermore, the nonverbal expression of emotion, called *nonverbal encoding*, is fairly consistent among people of all ages. These consistencies have led researchers to conclude that we are born with the capacity to display basic emotions (Scharfe, 2000; Sullivan & Lewis, 2012; Ackerman & Izard, 2004).

Infants display a fairly wide range of emotional expressions. According to research on what mothers see in their children's nonverbal behavior, almost all think that by the age of 1 month, their babies have expressed interest and joy. In addition, 84% of mothers think their infants have expressed anger, 75% surprise, 58% fear, and 34% sadness. Research using the *Maximally Discriminative Facial Movement Coding System (MAX)*, developed by psychologist Carroll Izard, also finds that interest, distress, and disgust are present at birth, and that other emotions emerge over the next few months (see Figure 10-4 on page 284; Benson, 2003; Gredebäck et al., 2012).

Although infants display similar *kinds* of emotions, the *degree* of emotional expressivity varies among infants. Children in different cultures show reliable differences in emotional

FIGURE 10-3 Universals in Facial Expressions

Across every culture, infants show similar facial expressions relating to basic emotions. Do you think such expressions are similar in nonhuman animals?

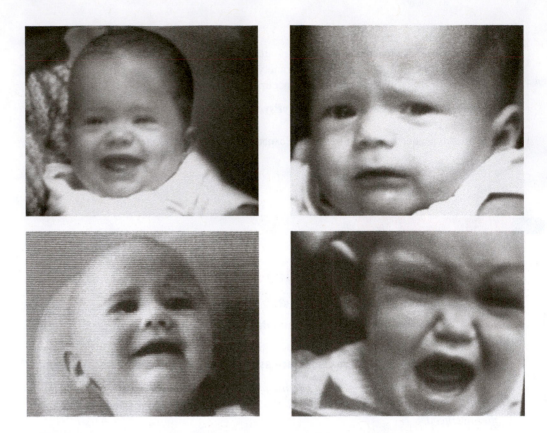

expressiveness, even during infancy. For example, by the age of 11 months, Chinese infants are generally less expressive than European, American, and Japanese infants (Camras, Meng, & Ujiie, 2002; Camras et al., 2007; Nakato et al., 2011b).

Experiencing Emotions. Does the capability of infants to express emotions nonverbally in a consistent, reliable manner mean that they actually *experience* emotions, and—if they do—is the experience similar to that of adults?

The fact that children display nonverbal expressions in a manner similar to that of adults does not necessarily mean that their actual experience is identical. In fact, if the nature of such displays is innate, or inborn, it is possible that facial expressions can occur without any accompanying awareness of our emotional experience. Nonverbal expressions, then, might be emotionless in young infants, in much the same way that your knee reflexively jerks forward when a physician taps it, without the involvement of emotions (Soussignan et al., 1997).

However, most developmental researchers do not think this is the case: They argue that the nonverbal expressions of infants represent actual emotional experiences. In fact, emotional expressions may not only reflect emotional experiences, but also help regulate the emotion itself.

It now seems clear that infants are born with an innate repertoire of emotional expressions, reflecting basic emotional states such as happiness and sadness. As infants and children grow older, they expand and modify these basic expressions and become more adept at controlling their nonverbal behavioral expressions. For example, they eventually may learn that by smiling at the right time, they can increase the chances of getting their own way. Furthermore, in addition to *expressing* a wider variety of emotions, as children develop they also *experience* a wider array of emotions (Izard et al., 2003; Buss & Kiel, 2004; Hunnius et al., 2011; also see the *From Research to Practice* box).

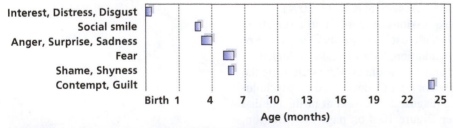

FIGURE 10-4 Emergence of Emotional Expressions

Emotional expressions emerge at roughly these times. Keep in mind that expressions in the first few weeks after birth do not necessarily reflect particular inner feelings.

FROM RESEARCH TO PRACTICE
Do Infants Experience Jealousy?

Picture tiny Consuela Marques, a sweet, lovely 6-month-old from Lubbock, Texas. Consuela is about to show her mother a new and surprising aspect of her personality.

An experimenter named Sybil Hart is having a pleasant conversation with Consuela's mother, Evita. By prearrangement, Evita ignores her daughter completely during this conversation. Consuela's reaction is unspectacular: She appears to be mildly bored, fidgeting slightly.

Next, Hart leaves the room and returns with a realistic baby doll, which she places in Evita's lap. As instructed, Evita cuddles the doll and coos to it while paying no attention to Consuela.

Consuela's reaction is immediate. First she touches her mother and smiles at her, trying to get her attention. When this fails, Consuela becomes visibly and audibly upset, wailing and kicking and ultimately turning bright red

This scenario plays out over and over in Hart's research on infant reactions to maternal unresponsiveness. If it sounds as if Consuela is jealous, that's Hart's interpretation, too. Her research shows that jealousy seems to be present in infants as young as 6 months old, and that it seems to be a functioning emotion for them—which contradicts the conventional wisdom that jealousy is a character flaw that develops later in life. Infants in Hart's research showed a wide range of distressed behaviors when their mothers held and played with the lifelike doll. Furthermore, their distress was much greater

when their mothers were distracted by the doll than when they were distracted by an interaction with another adult (Hart & Carrington, 2002; Hart, 2010).

It's the severity of the distress and the pattern of responses to the doll and to other forms of maternal unresponsiveness that led Hart to interpret the infants' behavior as jealousy. The infants did not exhibit a consistent "jealousy" behavior or expression that Hart could identify. Most commonly, the youngest infants showed sad facial expressions. Other behaviors were highly individual and included crying, wailing, rocking, and self-clinging. But other interpretations of her findings are possible. It may be, for example, that the children in her study are reacting with alternate, more basic emotions, such as sadness or anger (Hart et al., 1998; Lemerise & Dodge, 2008).

Clearly, Hart's findings need further investigation to fully understand the nature of the infants' distress responses and whether they are truly a form of jealousy. But a growing body of research suggests that, consistent with her research, infants are capable of more complex kinds of emotions than was once thought possible (Hart et al., 2004; Carver & Cornew, 2009).

- **What alternate conclusions might you draw to the conclusion that the infants are experiencing jealousy?**

- **Do you think the method used in the experiment involves ethical issues?**

The advances in infants' emotional lives are made possible by the increasing sophistication of their brain. Initially, the differentiation of emotions occurs as the cerebral cortex becomes operative in the first three months of life. By the age of 9 or 10 months, the structures that make up the limbic system (the site of emotional reactions) begin to grow. The limbic system starts to work in tandem with the frontal lobes, allowing for an increased range of emotions (Davidson, 2003; Schore, 2003; Swain et al., 2007).

Stranger Anxiety and Separation Anxiety. "She used to be such a friendly baby," thought Erika's mother. "No matter who she encountered, she had a big smile. But almost the day she turned 7 months old, she began to react to strangers as if she were seeing a ghost. Her face crinkles up with a frown, and she either turns away or stares at them with suspicion. And she doesn't want to be left with anyone she doesn't already know. It's as if she has undergone a personality transplant."

What happened to Erika is, in fact, quite typical. By the end of the first year, infants often develop both stranger anxiety and separation anxiety. **Stranger anxiety** is the caution and wariness displayed by infants when encountering an unfamiliar person. Such anxiety typically appears in the second half of the first year.

What brings on stranger anxiety? Here, too, brain development, and the increased cognitive abilities of infants, plays a role. As infants' memory develops, they are able to separate the people they know from the people they don't. The same cognitive advances that allow them to respond so positively to those people with whom they are familiar also give them the ability to recognize people who are unfamiliar. Furthermore, between 6 and 9 months, infants begin trying to make sense of their world, trying to anticipate and predict events. When something happens that they don't expect—such as with the appearance of an unknown person—they experience fear. It's as if an infant has a question but is unable to answer it (Volker, 2007).

Watch the **Video** *Stranger Anxiety* in **MyPsychLab**.

stranger anxiety The caution and wariness displayed by infants when encountering an unfamiliar person

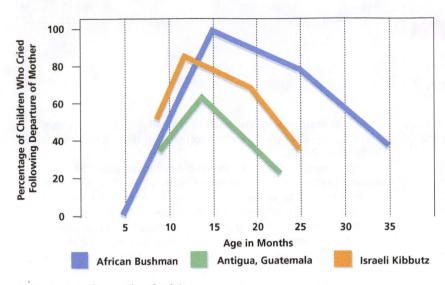

FIGURE 10-5 Separation Anxiety

Separation anxiety, the distress displayed by infants when their usual care provider leaves their presence, is a universal phenomenon beginning at around the age of 7 or 8 months. It peaks at around the age of 14 months and then begins to decline. Does separation anxiety have survival value for humans?

(*Source:* Based on Kagan, Kearsley, & Zelazo, 1978.)

Although stranger anxiety is common after the age of 6 months, significant differences exist between children. Some infants, particularly those who have a lot of experience with strangers, tend to show less anxiety than those whose experience with strangers is limited. Furthermore, not all strangers evoke the same reaction. For instance, infants tend to show less anxiety with female strangers than with male strangers. In addition, they react more positively to strangers who are children than to strangers who are adults, perhaps because their size is less intimidating (Swingler, Sweet, & Carver, 2007; Murray et al, 2007; Murray et al., 2008; Kossowsky et al., 2012).

Separation anxiety is the distress displayed by infants when a customary care provider departs. Separation anxiety, which is also universal across cultures, usually begins at about 7 or 8 months (see Figure 10-5). It peaks around 14 months and then decreases. Separation anxiety is largely attributable to the same reasons as stranger anxiety. Infants' growing cognitive skills allow them to ask reasonable questions, but they may be questions that they are too young to understand the answer to "Why is my mother leaving?" "Where is she going?" and "Will she come back?"

Stranger anxiety and separation anxiety represent important social progress. They reflect both cognitive advances and the growing emotional and social bonds between infants and their caregivers—bonds that we'll consider later in the chapter when we discuss infants' social relationships.

Watch the **Video** *Separation Anxiety* in **MyPsychLab**.

separation anxiety The distress displayed by infants when a customary care provider departs

social smile Smiling in response to other individuals

Smiling. As Luz lay sleeping in her crib, her mother and father caught a glimpse of the most beautiful smile crossing her face. Her parents were sure that Luz was having a pleasant dream. Were they right?

Probably not. The earliest smiles expressed during sleep probably have little meaning, although no one can be absolutely sure. By 6 to 9 weeks babies begin to smile reliably at the sight of stimuli that please them, including toys, mobiles, and—to the delight of parents—people. The first smiles tend to be relatively indiscriminate, as infants first begin to smile at the sight of almost anything they find amusing. However, as they get older, they become more selective in their smiles.

A baby's smile in response to another person, rather than to nonhuman stimuli, is considered a **social smile**. As babies get older, their social smiles become directed toward particular individuals, not just anyone. By the age of 18 months, social smiling, directed more toward mothers and other caregivers, becomes more frequent than smiling directed toward nonhuman objects. Moreover, if an adult is unresponsive to a child, the amount of smiling decreases. In short, by the end of the second year children are quite purposefully using smiling to communicate their positive emotions, and they are sensitive to the emotional expressions of others (Carver, Dawson, & Panagiotides, 2003; Bigelow & Rochat, 2006; Fogel et al., 2006).

Decoding Others' Facial and Vocal Expressions. In Chapter 4, we discussed the possibility that neonates can imitate adults' facial expressions minutes after birth. Although their imitative abilities certainly do not imply that they can understand the meaning of others' facial expressions, such imitation does pave the way for *nonverbal decoding* abilities, which begin to emerge fairly soon. Using these abilities, infants can interpret others' facial and vocal expressions that carry emotional meaning. For example, they can tell when a caregiver is happy to see them and pick up on worry or fear in the faces of others (Hernandez-Reif et al., 2006; Striano & Vaish, 2006; Flom & Johnson, 2011).

When infants smile at a person rather than a nonhuman stimulus, they are displaying a social smile.

CAREERS IN CHILD DEVELOPMENT

Name: Christin Poirier, LICSW

Education: B.A. in Psychology, Stonehill College; M.A. in Social Work, University of New Hampshire

Position: Licensed Social Worker

Highly trained professionals, social workers are in the front line of helping people deal with some of life's most difficult challenges, including disabilities, mental illness, discrimination, abuse, and poverty. Social workers serve individuals and families in public and private agencies, schools, hospitals, prisons, and mental health clinics.

Christin Poirier, a licensed independent clinical social worker (LICSW), incorporates child development on a daily basis as a clinician with a community mental health center.

"I provide therapy for children and adolescents who are dealing with either behavioral or emotional difficulties," said Poirier. "As a clinician, I work with individuals in a variety of settings, including school-based, community-based, and home-based settings."

She follows a number of steps to determine the proper approach with any given client.

"First, when a client enters therapy, I complete a comprehensive assessment to determine a diagnosis based on the presenting symptoms," she explains.

"Second, in order to understand what strategies are age-appropriate for a particular client, I consider their stages of development. Finally, it is necessary to consider how culture and ethnicity affect the client, so I incorporate them into the client's treatment plan," Poirier added.

Infants seem to be able to discriminate vocal expressions of emotion at a slightly earlier age than they discriminate facial expressions. Although relatively little attention has been given to infants' perception of vocal expressions, it does appear that they are able to discriminate happy and sad vocal expressions at the age of 5 months (Soken & Pick, 1999; Montague & Walker-Andrews, 2002).

Scientists know more about the *sequence* in which nonverbal facial decoding ability progresses. In the first 6 to 8 weeks, infants' visual precision is sufficiently limited that they cannot pay much attention to others' facial expressions. But they soon begin to discriminate among different facial expressions of emotion and even seem to be able to respond to differences in emotional intensity conveyed by facial expressions. They also respond to unusual facial expressions. For instance, they show distress when their mothers pose bland, unresponsive, neutral facial expressions (Adamson & Frick, 2003; Bertin & Striano, 2006; Farroni et al., 2007).

By the time they reach the age of 4 months, infants may already have begun to understand the emotions that lie behind the facial and vocal expressions of others. How do we know this? One important clue comes from a study in which 7-month-old infants were shown a pair of facial expressions relating to joy and sadness, and simultaneously heard a vocalization representing either joy (a rising tone of voice) or sadness (a falling tone of voice). When the facial expression matched the tone, infants paid more attention, suggesting that they had at least a rudimentary understanding of the emotional meaning of facial expressions and voice tones (Kahana-Kalman & Walker-Andrews, 2001; Kochanska & Aksan, 2004; Grossmann, Striano, & Friederici, 2006).

In sum, infants learn early both to produce and to decode emotions, and they begin to learn the effect of their own emotions on others. Such abilities play an important role not only in helping them experience their own emotions, but—as we see next—in using others' emotions to understand the meaning of ambiguous social situations (Buss & Kiel, 2004).

Social Referencing: Feeling What Others Feel

Twenty-three-month-old Stephania watches as her older brother Eric and his friend Chen argue loudly with each other and begin to wrestle. Uncertain of what is happening, Stephania glances at her mother. Her mother, though, wears a smile, knowing that Eric and Chen are just playing. On seeing her mother's reaction, Stephania smiles, too, mimicking her mother's facial expression.

FROM A
CHILD CARE PROVIDER'S
PERSPECTIVE:

In what situations do adults rely on social referencing to work out appropriate responses? How might social referencing be used to influence parent's behavior toward their children?

👁 **Watch** the **Video** *Social Referencing* in **MyPsychLab**.

Research suggests that this 18-month-old is exhibiting a clearly developed sense of self.

social referencing The intentional search for information about others' feelings to help explain the meaning of uncertain circumstances and events

theory of mind Knowledge and beliefs about how the mind works and how it affects behavior

Like Stephania, most of us have been in situations in which we feel uncertain. In such cases, we sometimes turn to others to see how they are reacting. This reliance on others, known as social referencing, helps us decide what an appropriate response ought to be.

Social referencing is the intentional search for information about others' feelings to help explain the meaning of uncertain circumstances and events. Like Stephania, we use social referencing to clarify the meaning of a situation and so to reduce our uncertainty about what is occurring.

Social referencing first occurs around the age of 8 or 9 months. It is a fairly sophisticated social ability: Infants need it not only to understand the significance of others' behavior, by using such cues as their facial expressions, but also understand the meaning of those behaviors within the context of a specific situation (de Rosnay et al., 2006; Carver & Vaccaro, 2007; Stenberg, 2009).

Infants make particular use of facial expressions in their social referencing, the way Stephania did when she noticed her mother's smile. For instance, in one study infants were given an unusual toy to play with. The amount of time they played with it depended on their mothers' facial expressions. When their mothers displayed disgust, they played with it significantly less than when their mothers appeared pleased. Furthermore, when given the opportunity to play with the same toy later, the infants remained reluctant to play with it, despite the mothers' now neutral-appearing facial reactions, suggesting that parental attitudes may have lasting consequences (Hertenstein & Campos, 2004; Dix et al., 2012).

Two Explanations of Social Referencing. Although it is clear that social referencing begins fairly early in life, researchers are still not certain *how* it operates. It may be that observing someone else's facial expression brings about the emotion the expression represents. That is, an infant who views someone looking sad may come to feel sad herself, and her behavior may be affected. On the other hand, it may be the case that viewing another's facial expression simply provides information. In this case, the infant does not experience the particular emotion represented by another's facial expression; she simply uses the display as data to guide her own behavior.

Both explanations for social referencing have received some support in research studies, and so we still don't know which is correct. What we do know is that social referencing is most likely to occur when a situation breeds uncertainty and ambiguity. Furthermore, infants who reach the age when they are able to use social referencing become quite upset if they receive conflicting nonverbal messages from their mothers and fathers. For example, if a mother shows with her facial expressions that she is annoyed with her son for knocking over a carton of milk, while his grandmother sees it as cute and smiles, the child receives two contradictory messages. Such mixed messages can be a real source of stress for an infant (Stenberg, 2003; Vaish & Striano, 2004).

Theory of Mind: Infants' Perspectives on the Mental Lives of Others—and Themselves

What are infants' thoughts about thinking? According to developmental psychologist John Flavell, infants begin to understand certain things about their own and others' mental processes at quite an early age. Flavell has investigated children's **theory of mind**, their knowledge and beliefs about how the mind works and how it influences behavior. Theories of mind are the explanations that children use to explain how others think.

For instance, cognitive advances during infancy that we discussed earlier permit older infants to come to see people in very different ways from other objects. They learn to see other people as *compliant agents,* beings similar to themselves who behave under their own power and who have the capacity to respond to infants' requests. For example, an infant comes to realize that she can ask her mother to get her more juice (Poulin-Dubois, 1999; Rochat, 1999, 2004; Luyten, 2011).

In addition, children's capacity to understand intentionality and causality grows during infancy. They begin to understand that others' behaviors have some meaning and that the behaviors they see people enacting are designed to accomplish particular goals, in contrast to the "behaviors" of inanimate objects. For example, a child comes to understand that his father has a specific goal when he is in the kitchen making sandwiches. In contrast, his father's car is simply parked in the driveway, having no mental life or goal (Ahn, Gelman, & Amsterlaw, 2000; Zimmer, 2003; Wellman et al., 2008).

Another piece of evidence for infants' growing sense of mental activity is that by the age of 2, infants begin to demonstrate the rudiments of empathy. **Empathy** is an emotional response that corresponds to the feelings of another person. At 24 months of age, infants sometimes comfort others or show concern for them. To do this, they need to be aware of the emotional states of others. For example, as we noted earlier, 1-year-olds are able to pick up emotional cues by observing the behavior of an actress on television (Mumme & Fernald, 2003; Liew et al., 2011; Gardner, 2012).

Further, during their second year, infants begin to use deception, both in games of "pretend" and in outright attempts to fool others. A child who plays "pretend" and who uses falsehoods must be aware that others hold beliefs about the world—beliefs that can be manipulated. In short, by the end of infancy children have developed the rudiments of their own personal theory of mind. It helps them understand the actions of others and it affects their own behavior (van der Mark et al., 2002; Caron, 2009).

Watch the **Video** *Theory of Mind* in **MyPsychLab**.

Understanding What Others Are Thinking.

As the brain matures and myelination within the frontal lobes becomes more pronounced, children develop more emotional capacity involving self-awareness. In addition, hormonal changes seem to be related to emotions that are more evaluative in nature (Davidson, 2003; Schore, 2003).

As they develop, children become more insightful regarding the motives and reasons behind people's behavior. They begin to understand that their mother is angry because she was late for an appointment, even if they themselves haven't seen her be late. Furthermore, by the age of 4, preschool-age children's understanding that people can be fooled and mistaken by physical reality (such as magic tricks involving sleight-of-hand) becomes surprisingly sophisticated. This increase in understanding helps children become more socially skilled as they gain insight into what others are thinking (Fitzgerald & White, 2003; Eisbach, 2004).

There are limits, however, to 3-year-olds' theory of mind. Although they understand the concept of "pretend" by the age of 3, their understanding of "belief" is still not complete. The difficulty experienced by 3-year-olds in comprehending "belief" is illustrated by their performance on the *false belief* task. In the false belief task, preschoolers are shown a doll named Maxi who places chocolate in a cabinet and then leaves. After Maxi is gone, though, his mother moves the chocolate somewhere else.

After viewing these events, a preschooler is asked where Maxi will look for the chocolate when he returns. Three-year-olds answer (erroneously) that Maxi will look for it in the new location. In contrast, 4-year-olds correctly realize that Maxi has the erroneous false belief that the chocolate is still in the cabinet, and that's where he will look for it (Ziv & Frye, 2003; Flynn, O'Malley, & Wood, 2004; Amsterlaw & Wellman, 2006; Brown & Bull, 2007).

By the end of the preschool years, most children easily solve false belief problems. One group has considerable difficulties throughout their lifetimes: children with autism. *Autism* is a psychological disorder that produces significant language and emotional difficulties. They find it particularly difficult to relate to others, in part because they find it difficult to understand what others are thinking. Occurring in about 4 in 10,000 people, particularly males, autism is characterized by a lack of connection to other people, even parents, and an avoidance of interpersonal situations. Individuals with autism are bewildered by false belief problems no matter how old they are (Heerey, Keltner, & Capps, 2003; Ropar, Mitchell, & Ackroyd, 2003; Ford et al., 2012).

Emotional Development in Middle Childhood

During middle childhood, children's control of their emotions grows. They begin to understand their emotions better, and they are better able to cope with their emotional highs and lows (Eisenberg, Spinrad, & Sadovsky, 2006; Rothbart, Posner, & Kieras, 2006).

In addition, children become more adept at hiding their emotions from others. Rather than showing their displeasure over a disappointing gift, they learn to hide it in a socially

empathy An emotional response that corresponds to the feelings of another person

acceptable way. Similarly, they learn to hide their anger with a teacher who is treating them unfairly (Ruihe & Guoliang, 2006; Feldman, 2009).

Children also develop empathy, in which they genuinely experience the emotions of others. Because their cognitive abilities are growing, they are able to take the perspective of other children and understand how events are affecting them. For example, a 10-year-old boy may be able to understand the sadness experienced by a classmate whose father has died, and feel that sadness himself (Eisenberg & Fabes, 2006; Oguz & Akyol, 2008).

Emotional Development in Adolescence

The range of emotions expressed by teenagers varies greatly.

Sometimes I have to stop and ask myself what kind of mood I'm in. Am I happy? Sad? Contemplative? Usually contemplative, if I'm bothering to contemplate what kind of mood I'm in. I'm kind of sad because Kyle can't come tonight . . . but kind of worried because he's sick. I'm kind of depressed feeling, too. It finally started sinking in a while ago that he's not coming back, that he has finally dropped out of my life as I feared he would.

Happy . . . sad . . . contemplative . . . worried . . . depressed . . . feared. The feelings experienced by adolescents range from the positive to the negative, as this blog comment illustrates. In fact, a traditional view of the adolescent period is that it is among the most emotionally volatile of the entire life span.

How accurate is this view? To answer the question, we first need to consider the role that emotions play during adolescence. For example, consider an adolescent girl who is experiencing sadness. As the definition suggests, sadness produces a feeling that can be differentiated from other emotions. She likely experiences physiological reactions, too, such as an increase in heart rate or sweating, that are part of her emotional reaction. In addition, the sadness has a cognitive element, in which her understanding and evaluation of the meaning of what is happening to her prompt her feelings of sadness.

It's also possible, however, to experience an emotion without the presence of cognitive elements. For example, adolescents may feel the sadness of depression without knowing why they are feeling that way. In the same way, they may react with fear to an unusual or novel situation without having an awareness or understanding of what is so frightening.

The Instability of Emotions in Adolescence.
Are adolescent emotions more volatile than at other stages of life? That's certainly the stereotype. Adolescence has traditionally been viewed as a period in which emotions run high and are easily triggered.

The stereotype does have some truth to it. Although not as extreme as the outmoded "storm and stress" view of adolescence would have us believe, emotions do tend to be more volatile during early adolescence. Younger adolescents experience emotional highs and lows, often in rapid succession. In addition, as they enter adolescence, teenagers report that they are less happy than in prior years. They are also more likely to experience mildly negative emotions as they move into adolescence (Ackerman & Izard, 2004; Reyna & Dougherty, 2012).

Not only are the emotions more negative than they were in middle childhood, adolescents' emotional responses are often more extreme than one would expect from the nature of the situation. For example, an adolescent may react with fury to a parent's suggestion that he might consider wearing a jacket to school because it is chilly. Even seemingly innocuous suggestions may be viewed as critical and reacted to with extremes of emotion.

If there is a positive side to the more explosive nature of adolescents' emotions, it is that even though they may be extreme, they don't necessary last very long. Partly because adolescents' moods change so frequently, any given emotional response is apt to be replaced by another before much time passes (Rosenbaum & Lewis, 2003; Gresham & Gullone, 2012).

Why are emotions so unstable during adolescence? One answer comes from work on the neurological underpinnings of emotion that we discuss next.

The Neurological Basis of Emotion. Emotions produce activation of specific parts of the brain. For instance, the *amygdala*, in the brain's temporal lobe, is central to the experience of emotions. It provides a link between the perception of an emotion-producing stimulus and later memory of that stimulus. For example, someone who was once frightened by a vicious dog is likely to respond with fear when he later sees the dog. Because of neural pathways connecting the amygdala, visual cortex, and the *hippocampus* (a part of the brain that is involved in the storage of memories), the emotion of fear is experienced nearly instantly. The response occurs so quickly that rational thought may not be involved at first—the fear response is literally a kind of "gut reaction" produced by the brain. It is only later that the response will be evaluated more thoroughly using rational thought processes (Adolphs, 2002; Dolan, 2002; Monk et al., 2003).

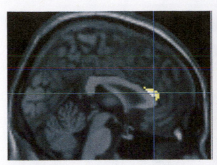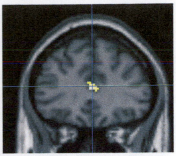

FIGURE 10-6 Brain Activity and Emotions

Although both adolescents and adults viewing pictures of faces displaying different emotions showed activation of the left ventrolateral prefrontal cortex, compared with adults, adolescents showed more activity in other areas of the brain.

(*Source*: Nelson et al., 2003. *Journal of Child Psychology and Psychiatry*, 44, 1020, bottom of Figure 2.)

Studies of brain activity help explain the greater volatility of emotions in adolescence than later in life. For example, in one study, adolescents and adults repeatedly viewed faces showing different emotions. Although both age groups showed engagement of the *left ventrolateral prefrontal cortex*, adolescents showed more activity in certain other areas of the brain when viewing familiar faces, depending on the kind of emotion being displayed (see Figure 10-6). These differences suggest emotional responses may be particularly pronounced during adolescence and affect the rationality of adolescents' evaluation of challenges they encounter and their responses to them (Nelson et al., 2003).

On the other hand, the physiological reactivity of emotions is not the full story of emotional responses during adolescence. As we'll see next, adolescents have considerable (and increasing) control over their emotions.

Emotional Self-Regulation. Throughout adolescence, both boys and girls become more adept at controlling their emotions. **Emotional self-regulation** is the ability to adjust emotions to a desired state and level of intensity. When adolescents seek to "keep cool," they are relying on emotional self-regulation.

It's not easy for any of us to regulate our emotions. For example, people asked to hide their responses to the observation of gruesome photos of accident victims show high levels of physiological reactivity as a result of their efforts to suppress their actual emotion. They also have difficulty later in recalling what they viewed. In short, emotional regulation takes both cognitive and physical effort (Richards & Gross, 2000; McRae et al., 2012).

During childhood, emotional regulation skills improve considerably, and that trend continues throughout adolescence. The demands and challenges that adolescents face lead to improvements in emotion management (Zahn-Waxler et al., 2000; Eisenberg, Spinrad & Sadovsky, 2006).

Adolescents use several strategies to regulate their emotional responses. One is to try to cognitively reappraise events that produce emotional responses. Specifically, they may try to change the way they think about something they have encountered, making it seem less bothersome. For example, an adolescent might try to convince himself that his girlfriend's decision to break up is really a good thing, because he didn't like being tied down. If he is able to convince himself of this, his initial sadness or anger might be replaced with more positive (or at least neutral) emotions.

Another emotion-regulating strategy that adolescents can use is to suppress troubling emotions. Using such a strategy involves inhibiting outward signs of inner emotional states, despite experiencing particular emotions internally. Although such a strategy may not make the individual who is suppressing the emotion feel better about negative emotions he or she might be experiencing, it can be effective in making others feel better. In fact, learning to "put on" a face

emotional self-regulation The ability to adjust emotions to a desired state and level of intensity

Between 25% to 40% of girls and 20% to 35% of boys experience occasional episodes of depression during adolescence, although the incidence of major depression is far lower.

appropriate to a particular social situation is an important advance in emotional self-regulation that occurs during adolescence.

Emotional Difficulties in Adolescence: Depression and Suicide

One day in ninth grade it struck Leanne Taunton that she was stuck without hope inside a dreadful world. "It was like the air was a big weight pressing in on me from all sides. I couldn't shake the feeling and I couldn't ignore it. There was nothing I could do."

A friend listened to her sympathetically and invited her to her basement. "We started doing drugs, using whatever was in the medicine cabinet. At first it seemed to offer some relief, but in the end we both had to go home again, if you know what I mean."

One day Leanne grabbed her father's razor, filled up the tub, and slashed her wrists. At the ripe age of 14 she had had enough.

Although by far the majority of teenagers weather the search for identity—as well as the other challenges presented by the period—without major psychological difficulties, some find adolescence particularly stressful. Some, in fact, develop severe psychological problems. Two of the most serious are adolescent depression and suicide.

Adolescent Depression. No one is immune to periods of sadness and bad moods, and adolescents are no exception. The end of a relationship, failure at an important task, the death of a loved one—all may produce profound feelings of sadness, loss, and grief. In situations such as these, depression is a fairly typical reaction.

How common are feelings of depression in adolescence? More than one fourth of adolescents report feeling so sad or hopeless for 2 or more weeks in a row that they stop doing their normal activities. Almost two thirds of teenagers say they have experienced such feelings at one time or another. On the other hand, only a small minority of adolescents—some 3%—experience *major depression,* a full-blown psychological disorder in which depression is severe and lingers for long periods (Galambos, Leadbeater, & Barker, 2004).

Gender, ethnic, and racial differences also are found in depression rates. As is the case among adults, adolescent girls, on average, experience depression more often than do boys. Some studies have found that African American adolescents have higher rates of depression than white adolescents, although not all research supports this conclusion. Native Americans, too, have higher rates of depression (Li, DiGiuseppe, & Froh, 2006; Zahn-Waxler, Shirtcliff, & Marceau, 2008; Yancey et al., 2011).

In cases of severe, long-term depression, biological factors are often involved. Although some adolescents seem to be genetically predisposed to experience depression, environmental and social factors relating to the extraordinary changes in the social lives of adolescents are also important influences. An adolescent who experiences the death of a loved one, for example, or one who grows up with an alcoholic or depressed parent, is at a higher risk of depression. In addition, being unpopular, having few close friends, and experiencing rejection are associated with adolescent depression (Eley, Liang, & Plomin, 2004; Zalsman et al., 2006; Schwartz et al., 2012).

One of the most puzzling questions about depression is why its incidence is higher among girls than boys. There is little evidence it is linked to hormone differences or a particular gene. Instead, some psychologists speculate that stress is more pronounced for girls than for boys in adolescence due to the many, sometimes conflicting demands of the traditional female gender role. For instance, an adolescent girl is worried both about doing well in school and about being popular. If she feels that academic success undermines her popularity, she is placed in a difficult bind that can leave her feeling helpless. Added to this is the fact that traditional gender roles still give higher status to men than to women (Gilbert, 2004; Hyde, Mezulis, & Abramson, 2008; Chaplin, Gillham, & Seligman, 2009).

Girls' generally higher levels of depression during adolescence may reflect gender differences in ways of coping with stress, rather than gender differences in mood. Girls may be more apt than boys are to react to stress by turning inward, thereby experiencing a sense of helplessness and hopelessness. In contrast, boys more often react by externalizing the stress and acting more impulsively or aggressively, or by turning to drugs and alcohol (Hankin & Abramson, 2001; Winstead, 2005; Wisdom et al., 2007; Wu et al., 2007).

Watch the **Video** *Sarah: Depression* in **MyPsychLab**.

Adolescent Suicide. The rate of adolescent suicide in the United States has tripled in the last 30 years. In fact, one teenage suicide occurs every 90 minutes, for an annual rate of 12.2 suicides per 100,000 adolescents. Moreover, the reported rate may actually understate the true number of suicides; parents and medical personnel are often reluctant to report a death as suicide, preferring to label it an accident. Even with underreporting, suicide is the third most common cause of death in the 15- to-24-year-old age group, after accidents and homicide. It is important to keep in mind, however, that although the rate of suicide for adolescents has risen more than for other age groups, the highest rate of suicide is found in the period of late adulthood (Grunbaum et al., 2002; Joe & Marcus, 2003; Conner & Goldston, 2007).

In adolescence, the rate of suicide is higher for boys than for girls, although girls *attempt* suicide more frequently. Suicide attempts among males are more likely to result in death because of the methods they use: Boys tend to use more violent means, such as guns, while girls are more apt to choose the more peaceful strategy of drug overdose. Some estimates suggest that there are as many as 200 attempted suicides by both sexes for every successful one (Joseph, Reznik, & Mester, 2003; Dervic et al., 2006; Pompili et al., 2009).

The reasons behind the increase in adolescent suicide over past decades are unclear. The most obvious explanation is that the stress experienced by teenagers has increased, leading those who are most vulnerable to be more likely to commit suicide. But why should stress have increased only for adolescents, given that the suicide rate for other segments of the population has remained fairly stable over the same time period?

Although we are not yet sure why adolescent suicide has increased, it is clear that certain factors heighten the risk of suicide. One factor is depression. Depressed teenagers who are experiencing a profound sense of hopelessness are at greater risk of committing suicide (although most depressed individuals do not commit suicide). In addition, social inhibition, perfectionism, and a high level of stress and anxiety are related to a greater risk of suicide. The easy availability of guns—which are more prevalent in the United States than in other industrialized nations—also contributes to the suicide rate (Zalsman, Levy, & Shoval, 2008; Wright, Wintemute, & Claire, 2008; Ougrin et al., 2012).

In addition to depression, some cases of suicide are associated with family conflicts and relationship or school difficulties. Some stem from a history of abuse and neglect. The rate of suicide among drug and alcohol abusers is also relatively high. As can be seen in Figure 10-7 on page 294, teens who called in to a hotline because they were thinking of killing themselves mentioned several other factors as well (Lyon et al., 2000; Bergen, Martin, & Richardson, 2003; Wilcox, Conner, & Caine, 2004).

Some suicides appear to be caused by exposure to the suicide of others. In *cluster suicide,* one suicide leads to attempts by others to kill themselves. For instance, some high schools have experienced a series of suicides following a well-publicized case. As a result, many schools have established crisis intervention teams to counsel students when one student commits suicide (Insel & Gould, 2008; Daniel & Goldston, 2009; Pompili et al., 2011).

FIGURE 10-7 Adolescent Difficulties

Family, peer relationships, and self-esteem problems were most often mentioned by adolescents contemplating suicide, according to a review of phone calls to a telephone help line.

(*Source:* Based on Boehm & Campbell, 1995)

ARE YOU AN INFORMED CONSUMER OF DEVELOPMENT?

Preventing Adolescent Suicide

If you suspect that an adolescent, or anyone else for that matter, is contemplating suicide, don't stand idly by. Act! Here are several suggestions:

- Talk to the person, listen without judging, and give the person an understanding forum in which to try to talk things through.
- Talk specifically about suicidal thoughts, asking such questions as: Does the person have a plan? Has he or she bought a gun? Where is it? Has he or she stockpiled pills? Where are they? The Public Health Service notes that, "contrary to popular belief, such candor will not give a person dangerous ideas or encourage a suicidal act."
- Evaluate the situation, trying to distinguish between general upset and more serious danger, as when suicide plans *have* been made. If the crisis is acute, *do not leave the person alone.*
- Be supportive, let the person know you care, and try to break down his or her feelings of isolation.
- Take charge of finding help, without concern about invading the person's privacy. Do not try to handle the problem alone; get professional help immediately.

- Make the environment safe, removing from the premises (not just hiding) weapons such as guns, razors, scissors, medication, and other potentially dangerous household items.
- Do not keep suicide talk or threats secret; these are calls for help and require immediate action.
- Do not challenge, dare, or use verbal shock treatment on the person in an effort to make them realize the errors in their thinking. These can have tragic effects.
- Make a contract with the person, getting a promise or commitment, preferably in writing, not to make any suicidal attempt until you have talked further.
- Don't be overly reassured by a sudden improvement of mood. Such seemingly quick recoveries sometimes reflect the relief of finally deciding to commit suicide or the temporary release of talking to someone, but most likely the underlying problems have not been resolved.

For immediate help with a suicide-related problem, call (800) 784-2433 or (800) 621-4000 for national hotlines staffed with trained counselors. ■

Contrary to popular belief, talking about suicide does not encourage it. In fact, it actually combats it by providing supportive feedback and breaking down the sense of isolation many suicidal people have.

Review, Check, and Apply

Review

1. Infants appear to express and to experience emotions, and their emotions broaden in range to reflect increasingly complex emotional states.
2. The ability to decode the nonverbal facial and vocal expressions of others develops early in infants.
3. During middle childhood, children gain increasing control over their emotions, as well as showing greater empathy.
4. Emotions in adolescence tend to be more changeable and more extreme than in other periods of life.
5. One of the dangers that adolescents face is depression, which affects girls more than boys.

Check

1. _____ anxiety typically appears around 6 months while separation anxiety usually begins at about 7 or 8 months.
2. _____ _____, which first occurs around the age of 8 or 9 months, is the intentional search for information about others' feelings to help explain the meaning of uncertain circumstances and events.
3. A child's _____ _____ _____ is their knowledge and beliefs about the mental world.
4. _____ _____, the ability to adjust emotions to a desired state and level of intensity, develops in adolescence.

Apply

1. Why would the sad or flat emotional expressiveness of a depressed parent be hard on an infant? How might it be counteracted?

To see more review questions, log on to MyPsychLab.

MODULE 10.3

PERSONALITY DEVELOPMENT

LO 10-7 What individual differences distinguish one infant from another?

LO 10-8 What is Erikson's theory of psychosocial development, and how is such development shaped by the child's environment?

> *Lincoln was a difficult baby, his parents both agreed. For one thing, it seemed like they could never get him to sleep at night. He cried at the slightest noise, a problem since his crib was near the windows facing a busy street. Worse yet, once he started crying, it seemed to take forever to calm him down again. One day his mother, Aisha, was telling her mother-in-law, Mary, about the challenges of being Lincoln's mom. Mary recalled that her own son, Lincoln's father Malcom, had been much the same way. "He was my first child, and I thought this was how all babies acted. So, we just kept trying different ways until we found out how he worked. I remember, we put his crib all over the apartment until we finally found out where he could sleep, and it ended up being in the hallway for a long time. Then his sister, Maleah, came along, and she was so quiet and easy, I didn't know what to do with my extra time!"*

As the story of Lincoln's family shows, babies are not all alike, and neither are their families. In fact, as we'll see, some of the differences among people seem to be present from the moment we are born. To understand how one individual differs from another, we need to consider the origins of **personality**, the sum total of enduring characteristics that differentiate one person from another. From birth onward, children begin to show unique, stable traits and behaviors that ultimately lead to their development as distinct, special individuals (Caspi, 2000; Kagan, 2000; Shiner, Masten, & Roberts, 2003).

Temperament: Stabilities in Infant Behavior

Sarah's parents thought there must be something wrong. Unlike her older brother Josh, who had been so active as an infant that he seemed never to be still, Sarah was much more placid. She took long naps and was easily soothed on those relatively rare occasions when she became agitated. What could be producing her extreme calmness?

The most likely answer: The difference between Sarah and Josh reflected differences in temperament. As we first discussed in Chapter 3, **temperament** encompasses patterns of arousal and emotionality that are consistent and enduring characteristics of an individual (Kochanska & Aksan, 2004; Rothbart, 2007; Casalin et al., 2012).

Temperament refers to *how* children behave, as opposed to *what* they do or *why* they do it. Infants show temperamental differences in general disposition from the time of birth, largely due initially to genetic factors, and temperament tends to be fairly stable well into adolescence. On the other hand, temperament is not fixed and unchangeable: Childrearing practices can modify temperament significantly. In fact, some children show little consistency in temperament from one age to another (McCrae et al., 2000; Rothbart & Derryberry, 2002; Werner et al., 2007).

personality The sum total of the enduring characteristics that differentiate one individual from another

temperament Patterns of arousal and emotionality that are consistent and enduring characteristics of an individual

Temperament is reflected in several dimensions of behavior. One central dimension is *activity level,* which reflects the degree of overall movement. Some babies (like Sarah and Maleah, in the earlier examples) are relatively placid, and their movements are slow and almost leisurely. In contrast, the activity level of other infants (like Josh) is quite high, with strong, restless movements of the arms and legs.

Another important dimension of temperament is the nature and quality of an infant's mood, and in particular a child's *irritability.* Like Lincoln, who was described in the example at the beginning of this section, some infants are easily disturbed and cry easily, while others are relatively easygoing. Irritable infants fuss a great deal, and they are easily upset. They are also difficult to soothe when they do begin to cry. Such irritability is relatively stable: Infants who are irritable at birth remain irritable at the age of 1,

Temperament is reflected in several dimensions including the nature and quality of an infant's mood.

and even at age 2 they are still more easily upset than infants who were not irritable just after birth (Worobey & Bajda, 1989). (Other aspects of temperament are listed in Table 10-2.)

Categorizing Temperament: Easy, Difficult, and Slow-to-Warm Babies. Because temperament can be viewed along so many dimensions, some researchers have asked whether there are broader categories that can be used to describe children's overall behavior. According to Alexander Thomas and Stella Chess, who carried out a large-scale study of a group of infants that has come to be known as the *New York Longitudinal Study* (Thomas & Chess, 1980), babies can be described according to one of several profiles:

- **Easy babies** have a positive disposition. Their body functions operate regularly, and they are adaptable. They are generally positive, showing curiosity about new situations, and their emotions are moderate or low in intensity. This category applies to about 40% (the largest number) of infants.

easy babies Babies who have a positive disposition; their body functions operate regularly, and they are adaptable

TABLE 10-2   Dimensions of Temperament

Dimension	Behavioral Indicators
Activity level	High: wriggles while diaper is changed Low: lies still while being dressed
Approach-withdrawal	Approach orientation: accepts novel foods and toys easily Withdrawal orientation: cries when a stranger comes near
Rhythmicity	Regular: has consistent feeding schedule Irregular: has varying sleep and waking schedule
Distractibility	Low: continues crying even when diaper is changed High: stops fussing when held and rocked
Quality of mood	Negative: cries when carriage is rocked Positive: smiles or smacks lips when tasting new food
Threshold of responsiveness	High: not startled by sudden noises or bright lights Low: pauses sucking on bottle at approach of parent or slight noise

(*Source:* Thomas, Chess, & Birch, 1968.)

- **Difficult babies** have more negative moods and are slow to adapt to new situations. When confronted with a new situation, they tend to withdraw. About 10% of infants belong in this category.
- **Slow-to-warm babies** are inactive, showing relatively calm reactions to their environment. Their moods are generally negative, and they withdraw from new situations, adapting slowly. Approximately 15% of infants are slow-to-warm.

As for the remaining 35%, they cannot be consistently categorized. These children show a variety of combinations of characteristics. For instance, one infant may have relatively sunny moods, but react negatively to new situations, or another may show little stability of any sort in terms of general temperament.

The Consequences of Temperament: Does Temperament Matter?

One obvious question to emerge from the findings of the relative stability of temperament is whether a particular kind of temperament is beneficial. The answer seems to be that no single type of temperament is invariably good or bad. Instead, children's long-term adjustment depends on the **goodness-of-fit** of their particular temperament and the nature and demands of the environment in which they find themselves. For instance, children with a low activity level and low irritability may do particularly well in an environment in which they are left to explore on their own and are allowed largely to direct their own behavior. In contrast, high-activity-level, highly irritable children may do best with greater direction, which permits them to channel their energy in particular directions (Thomas & Chess, 1980; Schoppe-Sullivan et al., 2007). Mary, the grandmother in the earlier example, found ways to adjust the environment for her son, Malcom. Malcom and Aisha may need to do the same for their own son, Lincoln.

Some research does suggest that certain temperaments are, in general, more adaptive than others. For instance, difficult children, in general, are more likely to show behavior problems by school age than those classified in infancy as easy children. But not all difficult children experience problems. The key determinant seems to be the way parents react to their infants' difficult behavior. If they react by showing anger and inconsistency—responses that their child's difficult, demanding behavior readily evokes—then the child is ultimately more likely to experience behavior problems. On the other hand, parents who display more warmth and consistency in their responses are more likely to have children who avoid later problems (Pauli-Pott, Mertesacker, & Bade, 2003; Canals, Hernández-Martínez, & Fernández-Ballart, 2011; Olafsen et al., 2012).

Furthermore, temperament seems to be at least weakly related to infants' attachment to their adult caregivers. For example, infants vary considerably in how much emotion they display nonverbally. Some are "poker-faced," showing little expressivity, while others' reactions tend to be much more easily decoded. More expressive infants may provide more easily discernible cues to others, thereby easing the way for caregivers to be more successful in responding to their needs and facilitating attachment (Meritesacker, Bade, & Haverkock, 2004; Laible, Panfile, & Makariev, 2008).

Cultural differences also have a major influence on the consequences of a particular temperament. For instance, children who would be described as "difficult" in Western cultures actually seem to have an advantage in the East African Masai culture. The reason? Mothers offer their breast to their infants only when they fuss and cry; therefore, the irritable, more difficult infants are apt to receive more nourishment than the more placid, easy infants. Particularly when environmental conditions are bad, such as during a drought, difficult babies may have an advantage (deVries, 1984; Gartstein et al., 2007).

The Biological Basis of Temperament.

Recent approaches to temperament grow out of the framework of behavioral genetics that we discussed in Chapter 3. From this perspective, temperamental characteristics are seen as inherited traits that are fairly stable during childhood and across the entire life span. These traits are viewed as making up the core of personality and playing a substantial role in future development (Sheese et al., 2009).

Consider, for example, the trait of *physiological reactivity* characterized by a high degree of motor and muscle activity in response to novel stimuli. This high reactivity, which has been termed *inhibition to the unfamiliar,* is exhibited as shyness.

---

difficult babies Babies who have negative moods and are slow to adapt to new situations; when confronted with a new situation, they tend to withdraw

slow-to-warm babies Babies who are inactive, showing relatively calm reactions to their environment; their moods are generally negative, and they withdraw from new situations, adapting slowly

goodness-of-fit The notion that development is dependent on the degree of match between children's temperament and the nature and demands of the environment in which they are being raised

A clear biological basis underlies inhibition to the unfamiliar, in which any novel stimulus produces a rapid increase in heartbeat, blood pressure, and pupil dilation, as well as high excitability of the brain's limbic system. For example, people who were categorized as inhibited at 2 years of age show high reactivity in their brain's amygdala in adulthood when viewing unfamiliar faces. The shyness associated with this physiological pattern seems to continue through childhood and even into adulthood (Schwartz et al., 2003; Propper & Moore, 2006; Kagan et al., 2007).

High reactivity to unfamiliar situations in infants has also been linked to greater susceptibility to depression and anxiety disorders in adulthood. Furthermore, when they reach adulthood, infants who are highly reactive develop an anterior prefrontal cortex that is thicker compared with those who are less reactive. Because the prefrontal cortex is closely linked to the amygdala (which controls emotional responses) and the hippocampus (which controls fear responses), the difference in prefrontal cortex may help explain the higher rates of depression and anxiety disorders (Schwartz & Rauch, 2004; Schwartz, 2008).

According to Erikson, children from 18 months to 3 years develop independence and autonomy if parents encourage exploration and freedom, within safe boundaries. What does Erikson theorize if children are restricted and overly protected at this stage?

Erikson's Theory of Psychosocial Development

As we discussed previously, some developmentalists think consistencies of behavior are present at birth, before the experiences of infancy. These consistencies are viewed as largely genetically determined and as providing the raw material of personality. However, psychologist Erik Erikson takes a different approach to personality development. **Erikson's theory of psychosocial development** considers how individuals come to understand themselves and the meaning of others'—and their own—behavior (Erikson, 1963). Building on the *psychodynamic perspective*, which suggests that unconscious influences affect behavior, Erikson's theory suggests that developmental change occurs throughout people's lives, starting in infancy.

According to Erikson, society and culture present the developing person with particular challenges, which shift as people age. Erikson believed that people pass through eight distinct stages, each characterized by a crisis or conflict that the person must resolve. Our experiences as we try to resolve these conflicts lead us to develop ideas about ourselves that can last for the rest of our lives.

According to Erikson, during the first 18 months of life, we pass through the **trust-versus-mistrust stage.** During this period, infants develop a sense of trust or mistrust, largely depending on how well their needs are met by their caregivers. Mary's attention to Malcom's needs, in the example above, probably helped him develop a basic sense of trust in the world. Erikson suggests that if infants are able to develop trust, they experience a sense of hope, which permits them to feel as if they can fulfill their needs successfully. On the other hand, feelings of mistrust lead infants to see the world as harsh and unfriendly, and they may have later difficulties in forming close bonds with others.

During the end of infancy, children enter the **autonomy-versus-shame-and-doubt stage,** which lasts from around 18 months to 3 years. During this period, children develop independence and autonomy if parents encourage exploration and freedom within safe boundaries. However, if children are restricted and overly protected, they feel shame, self-doubt, and unhappiness.

In the early part of the preschool period, children are ending the autonomy-versus-shame-and-doubt stage and entering what Erikson called the **initiative-versus-guilt stage,** which lasts from around age 3 to age 6. During this period, children's views of themselves change as preschool-age children face conflicts between the desire to act independently of their parents ("Let *me* do it" is a popular refrain among preschoolers) and the guilt that comes from the unintended consequences of their actions. They come to see themselves as persons in their own right, and they begin to make decisions on their own.

Parents who react positively to this transformation toward independence can help their children resolve the opposing forces of initiative and guilt that characterize this period. By

Erikson's theory of psychosocial development The theory that considers how individuals come to understand themselves and the meaning of others'—and their own—behavior

trust-versus-mistrust stage According to Erikson, the period during which infants develop a sense of trust or mistrust, largely depending on how well their needs are met by their caregivers

autonomy-versus-shame-and-doubt stage The period during which, according to Erikson, toddlers (ages 18 months to 3 years) develop independence and autonomy if they are allowed the freedom to explore, or shame and self-doubt if they are restricted and overprotected

initiative-versus-guilt stage Erikson's stage which lasts from around age 3 to age 6 where children's views of themselves change as they face conflicts between the desire to act independently of their parents

FROM A
CHILDCARE PROVIDER'S
PERSPECTIVE:
How would you relate Erikson's stages of trust-versus-mistrust, autonomy-versus-shame-and-doubt, and initiative-versus-guilt to the issue of secure attachment discussed in an earlier chapter?

As children become older, they begin to characterize themselves in terms of their psychological attributes (such as being a responsible and nurturing individual) as well as their physical achievements.

industry-versus-inferiority stage Erikson's stage from roughly age 6 to age 12 that is characterized by a focus on efforts to attain competence in meeting the challenges presented by parents, peers, school, clubs and groups to which they belong, and other complexities of the modern world

identity-versus-identity-confusion stage Erikson's stage during which adolescents attempt to determine what is unique and distinctive about themselves and the roles they will play in their future lives

providing their children with opportunities to act with self-reliance, while still giving them direction and guidance, parents can support and encourage their children's initiative. On the other hand, parents who discourage their children's efforts to seek independence may contribute to a sense of guilt that persists throughout their lives.

Psychosocial Development During Middle Childhood and Adolescence. Middle childhood encompasses the **industry-versus-inferiority stage**. Lasting from roughly age 6 to age 12, the industry-versus-inferiority stage is characterized by a focus on efforts to attain competence in meeting the challenges presented by parents, peers, school, clubs and groups to which they belong, and the other complexities of the modern world.

As they move through middle childhood, children direct their energies not only to mastering what they are presented in school—an enormous body of information—but also to making a place for themselves in their social worlds. Success in these efforts brings with it feelings of mastery and proficiency and a growing sense of competence.

On the other hand, difficulties in this stage lead to feelings of failure and inadequacy. Children may come to feel unskilled and incapable. As a result, they may withdraw both from academic pursuits, showing less interest and motivation to excel, and from interactions with peers.

Developing industriousness during the middle childhood years has lasting consequences. For example, one study examined how childhood industriousness and hard work were related to adult behavior by following a group of 450 men over a 35-year period, starting in early childhood. The men who were most industrious and hardworking during childhood were most successful as adults, both in occupational attainment and in their personal lives. In fact, childhood industriousness was more closely associated with adult success than was intelligence or family background (Vaillant & Vaillant, 1981).

During adolescence, teenagers enter the **identity-versus-identity-confusion stage**. In this period, adolescents attempt to determine what is unique and distinctive about themselves and the roles they will play in their future lives. As we'll consider more fully in Chapter 11, they may explore different roles, narrowing their choices and ideally finding out who they really are.

Adolescents with difficulties in resolving this stage may find it difficult to form and maintain close relationships. Alternatively, they may adopt socially inappropriate roles and fail to forge an acceptable identity.

Review, Check, and Apply

Review

1. Temperament is reflected in several dimensions of behavior. One dimension is an *activity level,* an infant's overall degree of movement. Some babies are relatively placid and their movements are slow. Other infants have a high activity level, with strong, restless movements of arms and legs. Another dimension of temperament is the nature and quality of an infant's mood, and in particular a child's *irritability.* Some infants are easily disturbed and cry easily, while others are relatively easygoing.

2. From the perspective of a behavioral geneticist, temperamental characteristics may be seen as inherited traits that are fairly stable from early childhood through the end of life. Making up the core of an individual's personality, these traits play a major role in future development.

3. Personality is the sum total of the enduring characteristics that differentiate one individual from another.

4. According to Erik Erikson, people move through the first five stages of psychosocial development between birth and adolescence, with the necessity of resolving an important conflict characteristic of each stage.

Check

1. According to Erikson, during the first 18 months of life, infants pass through the _____ stage.

2. _____ encompasses patterns of arousal and emotionality that are consistent and enduring characteristics of an individual.

3. Erikson says that adolescents are in the _____ stage, seeking to discover their individuality and identity.

Apply

1. What are the educational implications of the finding that some personality traits are inherited and remain consistent over time? Is it wiser for schools to try to change personalities or accommodate them? Why?

To see more review questions, log on to MyPsychLab.

ANSWERS: 1. trust-versus-mistrust 2. Temperament 3. identity-versus-identity-confusion

The CASE
of . . . *the Long Good-bye*

Elena Ross and her husband, Hwang Chen, were delighted to resume their pre-baby custom of going out for Sunday brunch. A friend of Elena's who had just returned to the area had proposed a childcare swap: She would look after the Ross-Chen's 8-month-old daughter, Hannah, and they would look after her son Greg, age 2, alternating Sundays.

Greg was easy. He asked a lot of delightful questions and he played nicely around Hannah, often making the baby laugh. Elena and Hwang smiled, anticipating the upcoming Sundays of newspapers and chat over omelets at their favorite restaurant. But when Elena placed Hannah in her friend's arms that first Sunday, the baby's face crumpled. Startled, Elena watched as Hannah began to cry, then howl. Her friend cuddled the baby, smiling and cooing into the tearful face, but Hannah's howls escalated. Finally, Elena took her daughter and went to a quiet room to nurse her. Hannah calmed immediately and nursed contentedly. But when Elena tried again to give Hannah to her friend, the baby resumed fussing. "Just go," her friend advised. "She'll calm down as soon as you're gone." Uncertain whether she should leave, Elena was finally convinced by Hwang to go. "I'm sure she'll stop crying," he said. But when the couple returned two hours later, Hannah was still howling, and her friend, though cheerful, was clearly exhausted.

The Hwang-Chens tried twice more to leave Hannah with Elena's friend, but each time the baby sobbed, only breaking into a wispy smile at her mother's return. They finally had to give up the arrangement. Sunday brunch just wasn't going to happen.

1. What steps might Elena have taken to make Hannah's experience more comfortable before she left her with the friend that first Sunday morning?

2. How would you explain Hannah's sudden outburst to Elena, in terms of infant social development?

3. What thoughts or questions might be going through Hannah's mind as her mother places her in the arms of her friend?

4. Not all children exhibit outbursts like Hannah's when meeting strangers or being parted from their mother. Do different parting behaviors suggest specific differences in children's environments, such as differences in parenting style? Why or why not?

‹‹‹ LOOKING BACK

LO 10-1 What is attachment in infancy, and how does it affect an individual's future social competence?

- Attachment, a strong, positive emotional bond that forms between an infant and one or more significant persons, is a crucial factor in enabling individuals to develop social relationships.

- Infants display one of four major attachment patterns: securely attached, avoidant, ambivalent, and disorganized-disoriented. Research suggests an association between an infant's attachment pattern and his or her adult social and emotional competence.

LO 10-2 Are there differences in attachments to fathers and mothers?

- Although infants are fully capable of forming attachments to both mother and father—as well as other individuals—the nature of attachment between infants and mothers, on the one hand, and infants and fathers, on the other hand, is not identical.

- For example, when they are in unusually stressful circumstances, most infants prefer to be soothed by their mothers rather than by their fathers.

LO 10-3 How sociable are infants with other children?

- From the earliest months of life, they smile, laugh, and vocalize while looking at their peers.

- Infants also show more interest in peers than in inanimate objects and pay greater attention to other infants than they do to a mirror image of themselves.

LO 10-4 Do infants experience emotions?

- Infants display a variety of facial expressions, which are similar across cultures and appear to reflect basic emotional states.

- By the end of the first year, infants often develop both stranger anxiety, wariness around an unknown person, and separation anxiety, distress displayed when a customary care provider departs.

- Early in life, infants develop the capability of nonverbal decoding: determining the emotional states of others based on their facial and vocal expressions.

- Through social referencing, infants from the age of 8 or 9 months use the expressions of others to clarify ambiguous situations and learn appropriate reactions to them.

LO 10-5 What sort of mental life does an infant lead and how does this develop in the preschool period?

- Infants begin to develop self-awareness at about the age of 12 months.

- They also begin to develop a theory of mind: knowledge and beliefs about how they and others think.

- As the brain matures, children develop more emotional capacity involving self-awareness. Their emotions become more evaluative in nature, in part because of the hormonal changes they are experiencing.

- Preschool children become more insightful about the motives and reasons behind people's behavior.

LO 10-6 What dangers do adolescents face as they deal with the stresses of adolescence?

- Many adolescents have feelings of sadness and hopelessness, and some experience major depression. Biological, environmental, and social factors contribute to depression, and there are gender, ethnic, and racial differences in its occurrence.

- The rate of adolescent suicide is rising, with suicide now the third most common cause of death in the 15- to 24-year-old bracket.

LO 10-7 What individual differences distinguish one infant from another?

- The origins of personality, the sum total of the enduring characteristics that differentiate one individual from another, arise during infancy.

- Temperament encompasses enduring levels of arousal and emotionality that are characteristic of an individual. Temperamental differences underlie the broad classification of infants into easy, difficult, and slow-to-warm categories.

- As infants age, gender differences become more pronounced, mostly due to environmental influences. Differences are accentuated by parental expectations and behavior.

LO 10-8 What is Erikson's theory of psychosocial development, and how is such development shaped by the child's environment?

- Erikson's theory of psychosocial development attempts to explain how individuals come to understand themselves and the meaning of their own—and others'—behavior.

- According to Erikson, infants' early experiences shape one of the key aspects of their personalities: whether they will be basically trusting or mistrustful.

- There are eight distinct stages of developmental change in Erikson's theory, five of which occur between birth and adolescence. In order, the first five stages are trust-versus-mistrust, autonomy-versus-shame-and-doubt, initiative-versus-guilt, industry-versus-inferiority, and identity-versus-identity-confusion.

- Parents' responses can play a key role in the psychosocial development of their children. For example, a parent who reacts in a positive manner to a toddler's growing independence is less likely to have a child who feels shame, doubt, or unhappiness than a parent who is overly protective and restrictive.

KEY TERMS AND CONCEPTS

attachment (p. 274)
Ainsworth Strange Situation (p. 275)
secure attachment pattern (p. 275)
avoidant attachment pattern (p. 275)
ambivalent attachment pattern (p. 276)

disorganized-disoriented attachment pattern (p. 276)
mutual regulation model (p. 279)
reciprocal socialization (p. 280)
stranger anxiety (p. 285)

separation anxiety (p. 286)
social smile (p. 286)
social referencing (p. 288)
theory of mind (p. 288)
empathy (p. 289)

emotional self-regulation (p. 291)
personality (p. 296)
temperament (p. 296)
easy babies (p. 297)
difficult babies (p. 298)
slow-to-warm babies (p. 298)

goodness-of-fit (p. 298)
Erikson's theory of psychosocial
   development (p. 299)
trust-versus-mistrust stage (p. 299)
autonomy-versus-shame-and-doubt
   stage (p. 299)

initiative-versus-guilt stage (p. 299)
industry-versus-inferiority stage (p. 300)
identity-versus-identity-confusion
   stage (p. 300)

Epilogue

The road children travel as they develop as social individuals is a long and winding one. We saw in this chapter how the attachment patterns that infants display can have long-term effects, influencing even what kind of parent the child eventually becomes. We also discussed how infants begin decoding and encoding emotions early, using social referencing, and eventually develop a "theory of mind" that grows more complex as they mature. In addition to examining temperament, we also explored infant child care options. We concluded with a discussion of Erik Erikson's theory of psychosocial development from infancy through adolescence.

Return to the prologue of this chapter, about Lisa Palermo's "child-proof" fastener discovery, and answer the following questions.

1. What role do you think social referencing might have played in this scenario? If Lisa's care provider had reacted negatively, would this have stopped the other children from imitating Lisa?

2. How does this story relate to the sociability of infants?

3. Can we form any opinion about Lisa's personality based on this event? Why or why not?

4. How would you evaluate the goodness of fit between the child care center provider and Lisa's temperament? How might a care provider respond to Lisa in this example to best match her actions to Lisa's personality?

5. What emotions do you think Lisa is feeling as she unfastens the snack bin and takes out a handful of Cheerios? What emotions might she feel if her care provider managed to prevent her doing so, and what impact, if any, might this have on her psychosocial development, according to Erikson's theory?

The Development Video Series in MyPsychLab

Explore the video *Social and Personality Development* by scanning this QR code with your mobile device. If you don't already have one, you may download a free QR scanner for your device wherever smartphone apps are sold. You can also view this video in MyPsychLab. For more videos related to this chapter's content, log into MyPsychLab to view the entire Development Video Series.

MyVirtualChild

• **What decisions would you make while raising a child?**
• **What would the consequences of those decisions be?**

Find out by accessing **MyVirtualChild** at
www.MyPsychLab.com
and raising your own virtual child from birth to age 18.

11 Development of the Self

MODULE 11.1

THE DEVELOPMENT OF THE SELF

- The Roots of Self-Awareness: Do Infants Know Who They Are?
- Self-Concept in the Preschool Years: Thinking about the Self

DEVELOPMENTAL DIVERSITY AND YOUR LIFE:
Developing Racial and Ethnic Awareness

- Understanding One's Self in Middle Childhood

Review, Check, and Apply

MODULE 11.2

ADOLESCENCE: THE SEARCH FOR IDENTITY

- Self-Concept: What Am I Like?
- Identity Formation: Change or Crisis?
- Marcia's Approach to Identity Development: Updating Erikson

ARE YOU AN INFORMED CONSUMER OF DEVELOPMENT? Choosing a Career

- Identity, Race, and Ethnicity

Review, Check, and Apply

MODULE 11.3

EVALUATING THE SELF

- Self-Esteem: Developing a Positive—or Negative—View of Oneself

FROM RESEARCH TO PRACTICE: The Downside of High Self-Esteem

- Self-Esteem in Adolescence: How Do I Like Myself?

DEVELOPMENTAL DIVERSITY AND YOUR LIFE: Are the Children of Immigrant Families Well Adjusted?

- Social Comparison

Review, Check, and Apply

The Case of . . . The Failed Star

Looking Back

Key Terms and Concepts

Epilogue

PROLOGUE: Who Is Karl Haglund?

Nine-year-old Karl Haglund is perched in his eagle's nest, a tree house built high in the willow that grows in his backyard. Sometimes he sits there alone among the tree's spreading branches, his face turned toward the sky, a boy clearly enjoying his solitude. Sometimes he's with his friend, engrossed in the kind of talk that boys find fascinating.

This morning Karl is busy sawing and hammering. "It's fun to build," he says. "I started the house when I was 4 years old. Then when I was about 7, my dad built me this platform. 'Cause all my places were falling apart and they were crawling with carpenter ants. So we destroyed them and then built me a deck . . ."

Sitting in his tree house, Karl thinks that someday it might be nice to have a job building things, like his dad does. "Dad's an architect and that means, like, he does buildings for the city and for other people on his own . . . . Mom's a social worker, and she talks to the parents and she goes to meetings. But I don't want to be a social worker. 'Cause I would have to be in important meetings. It's a pretty hard job. But I might be an architect, probably. Or maybe a carpenter." (Kotre & Hall, 1990, pp. 116–119)

During childhood, we develop a sense of self—who we are and what capabilities we have.

>>> LOOKING AHEAD

Karl Haglund knows who Karl Haglund is. He is someone who likes to draw, play soccer, and work with wood, and he envisions himself as perhaps an architect or a carpenter.

But is this the way Karl will see himself in a few years, or, for that matter, the way he saw himself a few years earlier? Probably not, for our view of who we are shifts considerably throughout the course of childhood.

(continued)

Learning Objectives

MODULE 11.1

LO1 How does a sense of self develop from infancy to middle childhood?

LO2 How do children develop a sense of racial and ethnic identity?

MODULE 11.2

LO3 How does the development of self-concept and identity proceed during adolescence?

LO4 What is the role of identity formation in adolescence?

MODULE 11.3

LO5 What is self-esteem, and what are some factors in and consequences of high and low self-esteem?

LO6 What is social comparison, and what role does it play in developing a self-concept and self-esteem in middle childhood and adolescence?

In this chapter, we consider the nature of the *self*, examining how we see and evaluate ourselves throughout childhood, from infancy to adolescence. We start by tracing the first evidence that we have that infants are aware of their own existence. We consider how they come to understand that they are individuals distinct from the world around them. We examine how self-concept develops in preschool and middle childhood, and how children develop racial and ethnic awareness.

We then consider how adolescents form their views of themselves in their search for identity. We discuss the roles played by society, friends, and peers in shaping an adolescent's identity, and we examine how the characteristics of crisis and commitment affect adolescents' choices and decisions as they move toward young adulthood. We also look at how race and ethnicity define identity in these years.

Next, we turn to the ways that children and adolescents develop a positive—or negative—view of themselves. We consider how adolescents' ability to differentiate various aspects of the self leads them to evaluate those aspects in different ways. We also discuss how social comparison provides a useful tool for self-evaluation by measuring one's abilities objectively within an appropriate context. We end the chapter with an evaluation of the consequences of self-esteem.

MODULE 11.1

THE DEVELOPMENT OF THE SELF

LO 11-1 How does a sense of self develop from infancy to middle childhood?
LO 11-2 How do children develop a sense of racial and ethnic identity?

Elysa, 8 months old, crawls past the full-length mirror that hangs on a door in her parents' bedroom. She barely pays any attention to her reflection as she moves by. On the other hand, her cousin Brianna, who is almost 2 years old, stares at herself in the mirror as she passes and laughs as she notices, and then rubs off, a smear of jelly on her forehead.

Perhaps you have had the experience of catching a glimpse of yourself in a mirror and noticing a hair out of place. You probably reacted by attempting to push the unruly hair back into place. Your reaction shows more than that you care about how you look. It implies that you have a sense of yourself, the awareness and knowledge that you are an independent social entity to which others react, and which you attempt to present to the world in ways that reflect favorably upon you.

The Roots of Self-Awareness: Do Infants Know Who They Are?

We are not born with the knowledge that we exist independently from others and the larger world. Very young infants do not have a sense of themselves as individuals; they do not recognize themselves in photos or mirrors. However, the roots of **self-awareness,** knowledge of oneself, begin to grow at around the age of 12 months. We know this from a simple but ingenious experimental technique. An infant's nose is secretly colored with a dab of red powder, and the infant is seated in front of a mirror. If infants touch their noses or attempt to wipe off the rouge, we have evidence that they have at least some knowledge of their physical characteristics. For them, this awareness is one step in developing an understanding of themselves as independent objects. For instance, Brianna, in the example at the beginning of this section, showed her awareness of her independence when she tried to rub the jelly off her forehead (Rochat, 2004).

Watch the **Video** *Self Awareness* in **MyPsychLab**.

self-awareness Knowledge of oneself

Although some infants as young as 12 months seem startled on seeing the rouge spot, for most a reaction does not occur until between 17 and 24 months of age. It is also around this age that children begin to show awareness of their own capabilities. For instance, infants who participate in experiments when they are between the ages of 23 and 25 months sometimes begin to cry if the experimenter asks them to imitate a complicated sequence of behaviors involving toys, although they readily accomplish simpler sequences. Their reaction suggests that they are conscious that they lack the ability to carry out difficult tasks and are unhappy about it—a reaction that provides a clear indication of self-awareness (Legerstee, 1998; Asendorpf, 2002).

Children's cultural upbringing also affects the development of self-recognition. For instance, Greek children—who experience parenting practices that emphasize autonomy and separation—show self-recognition at an earlier age than children from Cameroon in Africa. In the Cameroonian culture, parenting practices emphasize body contact and warmth, leading to more interdependence between infants and parents, and ultimately later development of self-recognition (Keller et al., 2004; Keller, Voelker, & Yovsi, 2005).

Research suggests this young child is exhibiting a sense of self.

In general, by the age of 18 to 24 months, infants in Western cultures have developed at least an awareness of their own physical characteristics and capabilities, and they understand that their appearance is stable over time. Although it is not clear how far this awareness extends, it is becoming increasingly evident, as we discussed in Chapter 10, that infants have a basic understanding of themselves as well as the beginnings of an understanding of how the mind operates—what is called a "theory of mind" (Nielsen, Dissanayake, & Kashima, 2003; Lewis & Ramsay, 2004; Lewis & Carmody, 2008).

Watch the **Video** *Self Awareness in Toddlers* in **MyPsychLab**.

self-concept   A person's identity or set of beliefs about what one is like as an individual

collectivistic orientation   A philosophy that promotes the notion of interdependence

Self-Concept in the Preschool Years: Thinking about the Self

Although the question "Who am I?" is not explicitly posed by most preschool-age children, it underlies a considerable amount of development during the preschool years. During this period, children wonder about the nature of the self, and the way they answer the "Who am I?" question may affect them for the rest of their lives.

If you ask preschool-age children to specify what makes them different from other kids, they readily respond with answers such as, "I'm a good runner" or "I like to color" or "I'm a big girl." Such answers relate to **self-concept**—their identity, or their set of beliefs about what they are like as individuals (Tessor, Felson, & Suls, 2000; Marsh, Ellis, & Craven, 2002; Bischof-Köhler, 2012).

The statements that describe children's self-concepts are not necessarily accurate. In fact, preschool children typically overestimate their skills and knowledge across all domains of expertise. Consequently, their view of the future is quite rosy: They expect to win the next game they play, to beat all opponents in an upcoming race, to write great stories when they grow up. Even when they have just experienced failure at a task, they are likely to expect to do well in the future. This optimistic view is held, in part, because they have not yet started to compare themselves and their performance against others. Their inaccuracy is also helpful, freeing them to take chances and try new activities (Dweck, 2002; Wang, 2004).

Culture and Self-Concept.   Preschool-age children's view of themselves also reflects the way their particular culture considers the self. For example, many Asian societies tend to have a **collectivistic orientation,** promoting the notion of interdependence. People in such cultures tend to regard themselves as parts of a larger social network in which they are interconnected with and responsible to

As children become older, their self-concept shifts from physical attributes to psychological traits.

DEVELOPMENTAL DIVERSITY AND YOUR LIFE

Developing Racial and Ethnic Awareness

The preschool years mark an important turning point for children. Their answer to the question of who they are begins to take into account their racial and ethnic identity.

For most preschool-age children, racial awareness comes relatively early. Certainly, even infants are able to distinguish different skin colors; their perceptual abilities allow for such color distinctions quite early in life. However, it is only later that children begin to attribute meaning to different racial characteristics.

By the time they are 3 or 4 years of age, preschool-age children notice differences among people based on skin color, and they begin to identify themselves as a member of a particular group such as "Hispanic" or "black." Although early in the preschool years they do not realize that ethnicity and race are enduring features of who they are, later they progressively begin to develop an understanding of the significance that society places on ethnic and racial membership (Quintana & McKown, 2008; McMillian, Frierson, & Campbell, 2011; Byrd, 2012).

Some preschoolers have mixed feelings about their racial and ethnic identity. Some experience **race dissonance,** the phenomenon in which minority children indicate preferences for majority values or people. For instance, some studies find that as many as 90% of African American children, when asked about their reactions to drawings of black and white children, react more negatively to the drawings of black children than to those of white children. However, these negative reactions did not translate into lower self-esteem for the African American subjects. Instead, their preferences appear to be a result of the powerful influence of the dominant white culture, rather than a disparagement of their own racial characteristics (Quintana, 2007).

Ethnic identity emerges somewhat later than racial identity, because it is usually less conspicuous than race. For instance, in one study of Mexican American ethnic awareness, preschoolers displayed only a limited knowledge of their ethnic identity. However, as they became older, they grew more aware of the significance of their ethnicity. Preschoolers who were bilingual, speaking both Spanish and English, were most apt to be aware of their ethnic identity. Ultimately, both race and ethnicity play a significant role in the development of children's overall identities (Quintana et al., 2006). ∎

The view of self that preschoolers develop depends in part on the culture in which they grow up.

Watch the **Video** *Understanding Self and Others* in **MyPsychLab**.

race dissonance The phenomenon in which minority children indicate preferences for majority values or people

individualistic orientation A philosophy that emphasizes personal identity and the uniqueness of the individual

others. In contrast, children in Western cultures are more likely to develop a view of the self reflecting an **individualistic orientation** that emphasizes personal identity and the uniqueness of the individual. They are more apt to see themselves as self-contained and autonomous, in competition with others for scarce resources. Consequently, children in Western cultures are more likely to focus on what sets them apart from others—what makes them special.

Such views pervade a culture, sometimes in subtle ways. For instance, one well-known saying in Western cultures states that "the squeaky wheel gets the grease." Preschoolers who are exposed to this perspective are encouraged to gain the attention of others by standing out and making their needs known. On the other hand, children in Asian cultures are exposed to a different perspective; they are told that "the nail that stands out gets pounded down." This perspective suggests to preschoolers that they should attempt to blend in and refrain from making themselves distinctive (Dennis et al., 2002; Lehman, Chiu, & Schaller, 2004; Wang, 2004, 2006).

Preschoolers' developing self-concepts can also be affected by their culture's attitudes toward various racial and ethnic groups, As we'll see next, preschoolers' awareness of their ethnic or racial identity develops slowly and is subtly influenced by the attitudes of the people, schools, and other cultural institutions with which they come into contact in their community.

Understanding One's Self in Middle Childhood

Eight-year-old Sonia carefully removes her muddy garden clogs and proudly plops an armload of carrots in the kitchen sink to be rinsed and scrubbed. This year, she has taken over the care for a portion of the family's vegetable garden. Having worked beside her mother since she was 6, she was able to plant and tend the carrots, zucchini, and broccoli on her own this year. Sonia smiles as she washes the vegetables, thinking about how her family depends on her, too, now.

In the opening to this chapter, we saw how Karl's growing sense of competence is reflected in his description of building a tree house with his father. Sonia, too, is coming to see herself as capable and reliable—someone her family can depend on. Conveying what psychologist Erik Erikson calls "industriousness," Karl's and Sonia's quiet pride in their accomplishments illustrates one way children's views of themselves evolve.

During middle childhood, children actively seek to answer the question "Who am I?" Although the question will assume greater urgency in adolescence, elementary-age children still try to find their place in the world.

The Shift in Self-Understanding from the Physical to the Psychological.

Children are on a quest for self-understanding during middle childhood. Helped by the cognitive advances that we discussed in Chapters 7 and 10, such as increased information processing capabilities and an increased understanding of theory of mind, they begin to view themselves less in terms of external, physical attributes and more in terms of psychological traits (Marsh & Ayotte, 2003; Lerner, Theokas, & Jelicic, 2005; Eggum et al., 2011).

For instance, 6-year-old Carey describes herself as "a fast runner and good at drawing"— both characteristics dependent on skill in external activities relying on motor skills. In contrast, 11-year-old Meiping characterizes herself as "pretty smart, friendly, and helpful to my friends." Meiping's view of herself is based on psychological characteristics, inner traits that are more abstract than the younger child's descriptions.

In addition to shifting focus from external characteristics to internal, psychological traits, children's views of who they are become more complex. In Erikson's view, as we saw in Chapter 10, children are seeking endeavors where they can be successfully industrious. As they get older, children discover that they may be good at some things and not so good at others. Ten-year-old Ginny, for instance, comes to understand that she is good at arithmetic but not very good at spelling; 11-year-old Alberto determines that he is good at softball but doesn't have the stamina to play soccer very well.

Children's self-concepts also become divided into personal and academic spheres. In fact, as can be seen in Figure 11-1, children evaluate themselves in four major areas, and each of these areas can be broken down even further. For instance, the nonacademic self-concept includes the components of physical appearance, peer relations, and physical ability. Academic self-concept is similarly divided. Research on students' self-concepts in English, mathematics, and nonacademic realms has found that the separate self-concepts are not always correlated, although there is overlap among them. For example, a child who sees herself as a star math student is not necessarily going to feel she is great at English (Burnett & Proctor, 2003; Marsh & Ayotte, 2003; Marsh & Hau, 2004).

According to Erik Erikson, middle childhood encompasses the industry-versus-inferiority stage, characterized by a focus on meeting the challenges presented by the world.

FROM AN
EDUCATOR'S
PERSPECTIVE:

As children discover their strengths and weaknesses in middle childhood, is it advisable for classroom teachers to insist on success in all academic spheres? Why or why not?

Review, Check, and Apply

Review

1. Infants develop self-awareness, the knowledge that they exist separately from the rest of the world, after about 12 months of age.

2. During the preschool years, children develop their self-concepts, beliefs about themselves that they derive from their own perceptions, their parents' behaviors, and society.

3. Racial and ethnic awareness begin to form in the preschool years.

4. In the middle childhood years, children begin to base their self-concept on psychological rather than physical characteristics.

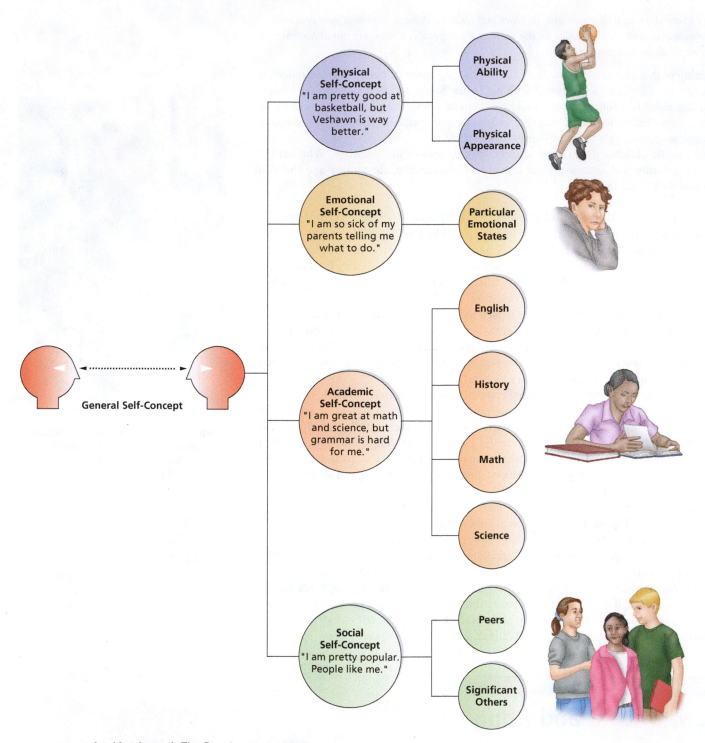

FIGURE 11-1 Looking Inward: The Development of Self

As children get older, their views of themselves become more differentiated, composed of several personal and academic spheres. What cognitive changes make this possible?

(*Source:* Adapted from Shavelson, Hubner, & Stanton, 1976)

Check

1. _____ _____ is children's identity or set of beliefs about what they are like as individuals.

2. A society that promotes interdependence and responsibility to others over the uniqueness and importance of the individual has a _____ orientation.

3. As children move through middle childhood, their view of themselves shifts from a focus on external, physical attributes to internal, _____ characteristics.

Apply

1. How might a child's developing sense of self be shaped by the culture she is born into? Think of some examples for a child born into a culture with a collectivistic orientation. What might be different for a child from a culture with an individualistic orientation?

To see more review questions, log on to MyPsychLab.

MODULE 11.2

ADOLESCENCE: THE SEARCH FOR IDENTITY

LO 11-3 How does the development of self-concept and identity proceed during adolescence?

LO 11-4 What is the role of identity formation in adolescence?

> *"You have no idea how much pressure a 13-year-old has to deal with. You've got to look cool, act cool, wear the right clothes, wear your hair a certain way—and your friends have different ideas about all these things than your parents, know what I mean? And you've got to have friends or you're nobody. And then some of your friends say you're not cool if you don't drink or do drugs, but what if you don't want that?"—Anton Merced*

The thoughts of 13-year-old Anton Merced demonstrate a clear awareness—and self-consciousness—regarding his new place in society and life. During adolescence, questions such as "Who am I?" and "Where do I belong in the world?" begin to take a front seat.

Why should issues of identity become so important during adolescence? One reason is that adolescents' intellectual capacities become more adult-like. They are able to see how they stack up to others and become aware that they are individuals, separate from everyone else. The dramatic physical changes during puberty make adolescents acutely aware of their own bodies and aware that others are reacting to them in new ways. Whatever the cause, adolescence often brings substantial changes in teenagers' self-concepts and self-esteem—in sum, their notions of their own identity.

Self-Concept: What Am I Like?

Ask Valerie to describe herself, and she says, "Others look at me as laid-back, relaxed, and not worrying too much. But really, I'm often nervous and emotional."

The fact that Valerie distinguishes others' views of her from her own perceptions represents a developmental advance of adolescence. In childhood, Valerie would have characterized herself according to a list of traits that

Adolescents' sense of who they are takes their own and others' views into account.

would not differentiate her view of herself and others' perspectives. However, adolescents are able to make the distinction, and when they try to describe who they are, they take both their own and others' views into account (Cole et al., 2001; Updegraff et al., 2004).

This broader view of themselves is one aspect of adolescents' increasing understanding of who they are. They can see various aspects of the self simultaneously, and this view of the self becomes more organized and coherent. They look at the self from a psychological perspective, viewing traits not as concrete entities but as abstractions (Adams, Montemayor, & Gullotta, 1996). For example, teenagers are more likely than younger children to describe themselves in terms of their ideology (saying something like, "I'm an environmentalist") than in terms of physical characteristics (such as, "I'm the fastest runner in my class").

In some ways, however, this broader, more multifaceted self-concept is a mixed blessing, especially during the earlier years of adolescence. At that time, adolescents may be troubled by the multiple aspects of their personalities. During the beginning of adolescence, for instance, teenagers may want to view themselves in a certain way ("I'm a sociable person and love to be with people"), and they may become concerned when their behavior is inconsistent with that view ("Even though I want to be sociable, sometimes I can't stand being around my friends and just want to be alone"). By the end of adolescence, however, teenagers find it easier to accept that different situations elicit different behaviors and feelings (Trzesniewski, Donnellan, & Robins, 2003; Hitlin, Brown, & Elder, 2006; Lucente, 2012).

Identity Formation: Change or Crisis?

According to Erik Erikson, whose theory we last discussed in Chapter 10, the search for identity inevitably leads some adolescents into substantial psychological turmoil as they encounter the adolescent identity crisis (Erikson, 1963). As we saw, Erikson's theory regarding this stage (identity-versus-identity-confusion) suggests teenagers try to figure out what is unique and distinctive about themselves—a task they manage with increasing sophistication because of the cognitive gains that occur during adolescence.

Erikson argues that adolescents strive to discover their particular strengths and weaknesses and the roles they can best play in their future lives. This discovery process often involves "trying on" different roles or choices to see if they fit an adolescent's capabilities and views about himself or herself. Through this process, adolescents seek to understand who they are by narrowing and making choices about their personal, occupational, sexual, and political commitments.

In Erikson's view, adolescents who stumble in their efforts to find a suitable identity may go off course in several ways. They may adopt socially unacceptable roles as a way of expressing what they do *not* want to be, or they may have difficulty forming and maintaining long-lasting close personal relationships. In general, their sense of self becomes "diffuse," failing to organize around a central, unified core identity.

On the other hand, those who are successful in forging an appropriate identity set a course that provides a foundation for future psychosocial development. They learn their unique capabilities and believe in them, and they develop an accurate sense of who they are. They are prepared to set out on a path that takes full advantage of what their unique strengths permit them to do (Allison & Schultz, 2001; Jones, Audley-Piotrowski, & Kiefer, 2012).

During the identity versus-identity-confusion stage, American teenagers seek to understand who they are by narrowing and making choices about their personal, occupational, sexual, and political commitments. Can this stage be applied to teenagers in other cultures? Why or why not?

Societal Pressures and Reliance on Friends and Peers.
Societal pressures are also high during the identity-versus-identity-confusion stage, as any student knows who has been repeatedly asked by parents and friends "What's your major?" and "What are you going to do when you graduate?" Adolescents feel pressure to decide whether their post–high school plans include work or college and, if they choose work, which occupational track to follow. Up to this point in their development, their educational lives have been pretty much programmed by U.S. society, which lays out a universal educational track. However, the track ends after high school and, consequently, adolescents face difficult choices about which possible future path they will follow.

During this period, adolescents increasingly rely on their friends and peers as sources of information. At the same time, their dependence on adults declines. As we discuss in Chapter14, this increasing dependence on the peer group enables adolescents to forge close relationships. Comparing themselves to others helps them clarify their own identities. This reliance on peers to help adolescents define their identities and learn how to form relationships is the link between the identity-versus-identity-confusion stage of development and the next stage Erikson proposed, known as intimacy versus isolation.

Psychological Moratorium. Because of the pressures of the identity-versus-identity-confusion period, Erikson suggested that many adolescents pursue a "psychological moratorium." The *psychological moratorium* is a period during which adolescents take time off from the upcoming responsibilities of adulthood and explore various roles and possibilities. For example, many college students take a semester or year off to travel, work, or find some other way to examine their priorities.

Teenagers who have successfully attained what James Marcia termed *identity achievement* tend to be the most psychologically healthy and *show* higher achievement motivation than adolescents of any other status.

However, for practical reasons, many adolescents cannot pursue a psychological moratorium involving a relatively leisurely exploration of various identities. Some adolescents, for economic reasons, must work part-time after school and then take jobs immediately after graduation from high school. As a result, they have little time to experiment with identities and engage in a psychological moratorium. Does this mean such adolescents will be psychologically damaged in some way? Probably not. In fact, the satisfaction that can come from successfully holding a part-time job while attending school may be a sufficient psychological reward to outweigh the inability to try out various roles.

Limitations of Erikson's Theory. One criticism that has been raised regarding Erikson's theory is that he uses male identity development as the standard against which to compare female identity. In particular, he saw males as developing intimacy only after they have achieved a stable identity, which is viewed as the normative pattern. To critics, Erikson's view is based on male-oriented concepts of individuality and competitiveness. Psychologist Carol Gilligan offers an alternative conception that suggests that women develop identity through the establishment of relationships. In her view, a key component of a woman's identity is the caring networks she builds between herself and others (Gilligan, 2004; Kroger, 2006).

Marcia's Approach to Identity Development: Updating Erikson

Using Erikson's theory as a springboard, psychologist James Marcia suggests that identity can be seen in terms of which of two characteristics—crisis or commitment—is present or absent. *Crisis* is a period of identity development in which an adolescent consciously chooses between various alternatives and makes decisions. *Commitment* is psychological investment in a course of action or an ideology. We can see the difference between an adolescent who careens from one activity to another, with nothing lasting more than a few weeks, compared with one who becomes totally absorbed in volunteer work at a homeless shelter (Peterson, Marcia, & Carpendale, 2004; Marcia, 2007).

After conducting lengthy interviews with adolescents, Marcia proposed four categories of adolescent identity (see Table 11-1 on page 314).

1. **Identity achievement.** Teenagers in this category have successfully explored and thought through who they are and what they want to do. Following a period of crisis during which they considered various alternatives, these adolescents have committed to a particular identity. Teens who have reached this identity status tend to be the most psychologically healthy, higher in achievement motivation and moral reasoning than adolescents of any other status.

2. **Identity foreclosure.** These are adolescents who have committed to an identity without passing through a period of crisis in which they explored alternatives. Instead, they

identity achievement The status of adolescents who commit to a particular identity following a period of crisis during which they consider various alternatives

identity foreclosure The status of adolescents who prematurely commit to an identity without adequately exploring alternatives

TABLE 11-1 Marcia's Four Categories of Adolescent Development

		Commitment	
		Present	**Absent**
CRISIS/EXPLORATION	**PRESENT**	**Identity achievement** "I enjoyed working at an advertising company the last two summers, so I plan to go into advertising."	**Moratorium** "I'm taking a job at my mom's bookstore until I figure out what I really want to do."
	ABSENT	**Identity foreclosure** "My dad says I'm good with kids and would be a good teacher, so I guess that's what I'll do."	**Identity diffusion** "Frankly, I have no idea what I'm going to do."

(*Source:* Based on Marcia, 1980.)

accepted others' decisions about what was best for them. Typical adolescents in this category are a son who enters the family business because it is expected of him, or a daughter who decides to become a physician simply because her mother is one. Although foreclosers are not necessarily unhappy, they tend to have what can be called "rigid strength": Happy and self-satisfied, they still have a high need for social approval and tend to be authoritarian.

3. **Moratorium.** Although adolescents in the moratorium category have explored various alternatives to some degree, they have not yet committed themselves. As a consequence, Marcia suggests, they show relatively high anxiety and experience psychological conflict, though they are often lively and appealing, seeking intimacy with others. Adolescents of this status typically settle on an identity, but only after a struggle.

4. **Identity diffusion.** Adolescents in this category neither explore nor commit to various alternatives. They tend to be flighty, shifting from one thing to the next. Although they may seem carefree, according to Marcia, their lack of commitment impairs their ability to form close relationships. In fact, they are often socially withdrawn.

It is important to note that adolescents are not necessarily stuck in one of the four categories. In fact, some move back and forth between moratorium and identity achievement in what has been called a "MAMA" cycle (**m**oratorium—identity **a**chievement—**m**oratorium—identity **a**chievement). For instance, even though a forecloser may have settled on a career path during early adolescence with little active decision making, he or she may reassess the choice later and move into another category. For some individuals, then, identity formation may take place beyond the period of adolescence. However, identity gels in the late teens and early 20s for most people (Kroger, 2007; Al-Owidha, Green, & Kroger, 2009; Dunkel, Kim, & Papini, 2012).

Identity, Race, and Ethnicity

Although the path to forming an identity is often difficult for adolescents, it presents a particular challenge for members of racial and ethnic groups that have traditionally been discriminated against. Society's contradictory values are one part of the problem. On the one hand, adolescents are told that society should be colorblind, that race and ethnic background should not matter in terms of opportunities and achievement, and that if they do achieve, society will accept them. Based on a traditional *cultural assimilation model,* this view holds that individual cultural identities should be assimilated into a unified culture in the United States—the proverbial melting pot model.

FROM A
SOCIAL WORKER'S
PERSPECTIVE:
Are there stages in Marcia's theory of development that may be more difficult to achieve for adolescents who live in poverty? Why?

moratorium The status of adolescents who may have explored various identity alternatives to some degree, but have not yet committed themselves

identity diffusion The status of adolescents who consider various identity alternatives, but never commit to one or never even consider identity options in any conscious way

ARE YOU AN INFORMED CONSUMER OF DEVELOPMENT?

Choosing a Career

One of the greatest challenges many adolescents face as they leave high school behind is making a decision that will have lifelong implications: the choice of a career. Although there is no single correct choice—most people can be happy in any of several different jobs—the options can be daunting. Here are some guidelines for at least starting to come to grips with the question of what occupational path to follow.

- Systematically evaluate a variety of choices. Libraries contain a wealth of information about potential career paths, and most colleges and universities have career centers that can provide occupational data and guidance.

- Know yourself. Evaluate your strengths and weaknesses, perhaps by completing a questionnaire at a college career center that can provide insight into your interests, skills, and values.

- Create a "balance sheet," listing the potential gains and losses that you will incur from a particular profession. First list the gains and losses that you will experience directly, and then list gains and losses for others, such as family members. Next, write down your projected self-approval or self-disapproval from the potential career. Finally, write down the projected social approval or disapproval you are likely to receive from others. By systematically evaluating a set of potential careers according to each of these criteria, you will be in a better position to compare different possibilities.

- "Try out" different careers through paid or unpaid internships. By seeing a job firsthand, interns are able to get a better sense of what an occupation is truly like.

- Remember that if you make a mistake, you can change careers. In fact, people today increasingly change careers in early adulthood and even beyond. No one should feel locked into a decision made earlier in life.

- It is reasonable to expect that shifting values, interests, abilities, and life circumstances might make a different career more appropriate later in life than the one chosen in late adolescence. ■

On the other hand, the *pluralistic society model* suggests that U.S. society is made up of diverse, coequal cultural groups that should preserve their individual cultural features. The pluralistic society model grew in part from the belief that the cultural assimilation model denigrates the cultural heritage of minorities and lowers their self-esteem.

According to this view, then, racial and ethnic factors become a central part of adolescents' identity and are not submerged in an attempt to assimilate into the majority culture. From this perspective, identity development includes development of *racial and ethnic identity*—the sense of membership in a racial or ethnic group and the feelings that are associated with that membership. It includes a sense of commitment and ties with a particular racial or ethnic group (Phinney & Alipuria, 2006; Phinney, 2008; Seaton et al., 2012).

There is a middle ground. Minority group members can form a *bicultural identity* in which they draw from their own cultural identity while integrating themselves into the dominant culture. This view suggests that an individual can live as a member of two cultures, with two cultural identities, without having to choose one over the other (Shi & Lu, 2007; Marks, Patton, & Coll, 2011; Daniel et al., 2012).

The choice of a bicultural identity is increasingly common. In fact, the number of people who identify themselves as belonging to more than one race is considerable and increased 134% from 2000 to 2010 (see Figure 11-2 on page 316; U.S. Census Bureau, 2011).

Racial and ethnic identity reflects one's sense of membership in a racial or ethnic group.

FIGURE 11-2 Increase in Bicultural Identity

The number of Americans who identified themselves as belonging to more than one race grew substantially between 2000 and 2010. Although most of those who self-identify as multi-racial report membership in two races, almost 10% report belonging to three or more races.

(U.S. Census Bureau, 2011).

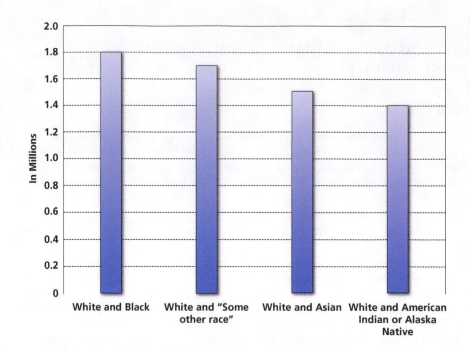

The process of identity formation is not simple for anyone and may be doubly so for minority group members. Racial and ethnic identity takes time to form, and for some individuals it may occur over a prolonged period. Still, the ultimate result can be the formation of a rich, multifaceted identity (Quintana, 2007; Jensen, 2008; Corenblum & Armstrong, 2012).

Review, Check, and Apply

Review

1. Self-concept during adolescence grows more differentiated as the view of the self becomes more organized, broader, and more abstract, and takes account of the views of others.

2. According to Erikson, adolescents try on a variety of roles as they seek to understand who they are and which choices best suit their capabilities.

3. Adolescents feel tremendous pressure from parents and friends about the choices they face regarding post–high school plans, including college or work, and which occupation to follow.

4. Marcia's four identity statuses focus on the adolescent's struggle to determine an identity and a role in society.

Check

1. According to Erikson, the search for identity leads some adolescents to experience an _____ _____, a state of substantial psychological turmoil.

2. Marcia used Erikson's theory as a springboard and suggested that identity can be seen in terms of which of two characteristics, _____ or _____, is present or absent.

3. The middle ground between the cultural assimilation model and the pluralistic society model suggests individuals can form a _____ _____, simultaneously drawing from their own culture and integrating themselves into the dominant culture.

Apply

1. Do you believe that there is an optimal length of time for the period of psychological moratorium, and at what point do you think an individual should have completed the process of identity formation? Why? Has the rapid pace of change in today's world, fueled by technological advances, had implications for the timing of identity formation?

To see more review questions, log on to MyPsychLab.

ANSWERS: 1. identity crisis 2. crisis, commitment 3. bicultural identity

MODULE 11.3

EVALUATING THE SELF

LO 11-5 What is self-esteem, and what are some factors in and consequences of high and low self-esteem?

LO 11-6 What is social comparison, and what role does it play in developing a self-concept and self-esteem in middle childhood and adolescence?

> *Kieran had been given the part of "Frog" in the second-grade class play based on the popular* Frog & Toad *stories. Somewhat shy, he was a bit nervous about this, his biggest challenge to date. His older sister helped him learn his lines, and his aunt made a frog costume. With so much support, Kieran's fear ebbed. He started to enjoy the rehearsals and when he took his bow at the close of the performance, he received more applause than anyone else. Meeting his family backstage, he beamed. "I like doing plays. Everyone thought I was great!"*

Self-Esteem: Developing a Positive—or Negative—View of Oneself

Children don't dispassionately view themselves just in terms of an itemization of physical and psychological characteristics. Instead, they make judgments about themselves as being good or bad in particular ways. **Self-esteem** is an individual's overall and specific positive and negative self-evaluation. Whereas self-concept reflects beliefs and cognitions about the self (*I am good at trumpet; I am not so good at social studies*), self-esteem is more emotionally oriented (*Everybody thinks I'm a nerd*) (Davis-Kean & Sandler, 2001; Bracken & Lamprecht, 2003; Buss, 2012).

Self-esteem develops in important ways during middle childhood. As we noted previously, children increasingly compare themselves to others, and as they do, they assess how well they measure up to society's standards. In addition, they increasingly develop their own internal standards of success, and they can see how well they compare to those. One of the advances that occurs during middle childhood is that, like self-concept, self-esteem becomes increasingly differentiated. At the age of 7, most children have self-esteem that reflects a global, fairly simple view of themselves. If their overall self-esteem is positive, they believe that they are relatively good at all things. Conversely, if their overall self-esteem is negative, they feel that they are inadequate at most things (Lerner et al., 2005; Harter, 2006a; Hoersting & Jenkins, 2011).

As children progress into the middle childhood years, however, their self-esteem is higher for some areas and lower in others. For example, a boy's overall self-esteem may be composed of positive self-esteem in some areas (such as the positive feelings he gets from his artistic ability) and more negative self-esteem in others (such as the unhappiness he feels over his athletic skills).

self-esteem An individual's overall and specific positive and negative self-evaluation

Children with high self-esteem have more positive expectations, lower anxiety and higher motivation.

Change and Stability in Self-Esteem. Generally, overall self-esteem increases during middle childhood, with a brief decline around the age of 12. Although there are probably several reasons for the decline, the main one appears to be the school transition that typically occurs around this age: Students leaving elementary school and entering either middle school or junior high school show a decline in self-esteem, which then gradually rises again (Twenge & Campbell, 2001; Robins & Trzesniewski, 2005).

On the other hand, some children have chronically low self-esteem. Children with low self-esteem face a tough road, in part because their self-esteem becomes enmeshed in a cycle of failure that grows increasingly difficult to break. Assume, for instance, that Harry, a student with chronically low self-esteem, is facing an important test. Because of his low self-esteem, he expects to do poorly. As a consequence, he is quite anxious—so anxious that he is unable to concentrate well and study effectively. Furthermore, he may decide not to study much, because he figures that if he's going to do badly anyway, why bother studying?

Ultimately, Harry's high anxiety and lack of effort bring about the result he expected: He does poorly on the test. This failure, which confirms Harry's expectation, reinforces his low self-esteem, and the cycle of failure continues (see Figure 11-3).

If a child continues to be chronically low in self-esteem in adolescence, life can be very painful. For instance, adolescents with low self-esteem respond more negatively to failure than those with high self-esteem, in part because those with low self-esteem focus on their shortcomings after experiencing failure. Like Harry, whose low expectations for his own performance led him to prepare poorly for a test—and thus fail it—adolescents with low self-esteem can become trapped in a cycle of failure. In addition, low self-esteem is related to higher levels of aggression, antisocial behavior, and delinquency in adolescence (Donnellan et al., 2005; de Jong et al., 2012).

In contrast, students with high self-esteem travel a more positive path, falling into a cycle of success. Having higher expectations leads to increased effort and lower anxiety, increasing the probability of success. In turn, this helps affirm their higher self-esteem that began the cycle.

FIGURE 11-3 Cycles of Self-Esteem

Because children with low self-esteem may expect to do poorly on a test, they may experience high anxiety and not work as hard as those with higher self-esteem. As a result, they actually do perform badly on the test, which in turn confirms their negative view of themselves. In contrast, those with high self-esteem have more positive expectations, which lead to lower anxiety and higher motivation. As a consequence, they perform better, reinforcing their positive self-image. How would a teacher help students with low self-esteem break out of their negative cycle?

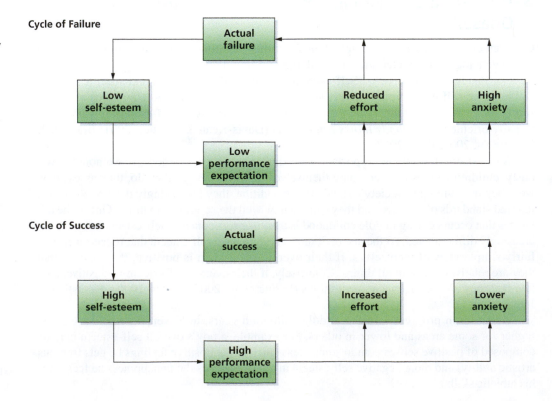

FROM RESEARCH TO PRACTICE
The Downside of High Self-Esteem

According to many, low self-esteem lies at the heart of a variety of social ills, ranging from teenage pregnancy to gang violence to drug abuse. For example, government officials in California set up a task force to encourage self-esteem, arguing that increased self-esteem might raise the general psychological health of the population and even help the state balance its budget.

But not everyone agrees with this view. According to psychologist Roy Baumeister and colleagues, if high self-esteem is unjustified by actual accomplishment, it can actually be psychologically damaging. In fact, unwarranted high self-esteem can lead to a variety of social problems, including violence (Baumeister et al., 2003; Baumeister et al., 2005).

Consider, for example, adolescents who have high, but unjustified, self-esteem—a personality type called *narcissism*. When their unwarranted positive view of themselves is disputed, they may view the challenge as so threatening that they lash out at others, behaving in a violent manner. Consequently, efforts to reduce the violence of bullies (who are typically viewed as low in self-esteem) by raising their self-esteem may backfire, unless there are actual accomplishments to accompany their raised self-esteem (Baumeister, Bushman, & Campbell, 2000; Diamantopoulou, Rydell, & Henricsson, 2008).

Similarly, efforts to boost the self-esteem of students who are facing academic difficulties to improve their performance may provoke the opposite result. For example, in one study, students who were receiving Ds and Fs in one class were divided into two groups. One group received the message that good grades were caused by a lack of confidence and low self-esteem. The other group received a different message; they were told that it was hard work that produced good grades. At the end of the semester, the group that received the self-esteem message ended up with significantly lower grades than the group that received the hard work message (Forsyth & Kerr, 1999).

Of course, such findings don't mean that high self-esteem is a bad thing. In fact, people with high self-esteem are significantly happier than those with low self-esteem, and they are less likely to be depressed. Still, the research has relevance to programs that seek to raise self-esteem in everyone. Feel-good messages ("we're all special" and "we applaud ourselves") may be off base, leading adolescents to develop unwarranted self-esteem. Instead, schools and parents should help adolescents *earn* high self-esteem through actual accomplishments (Crocker & Park, 2004; Lupien, Seery, & Almonte, 2012).

- **Under what circumstances should a school or a society seek to raise the academic self-esteem of adolescents? Is the situation different if the adolescents have high self-esteem in other areas, such as athletics or artistic accomplishments?**

- **How would you go about designing a program to address the self-esteem issues of adolescents?**

Clearly, positive self-esteem is associated with desirable consequences, and lower self-esteem is related to negative results. However, this doesn't mean we should seek to boost the self-esteem of children at any cost. For example, although higher self-esteem is associated with positive outcomes such as academic achievement, the relationship between the two factors is merely correlational. The association simply means that people with higher self-esteem are more likely to have better academic performance, and those with lower self-esteem are more likely to have poorer academic performance.

There are several possible explanations for the relationship between self-esteem and academic performance. On one hand, it may mean that higher self-esteem indeed causes better academic performance. On the other hand, it may be the reverse: that doing well academically causes higher self-esteem. Or finally, there may be some third factor (intelligence seems to be a reasonable possibility) that produces *both* higher self-esteem and better academic performance (Crocker & Knight, 2005).

In short, high self-esteem does not necessarily lead to positive outcomes. In fact, it may well be that high self-esteem can have a significant downside, as we see in the *From Research to Practice* box.

Parenting Styles and Self-Esteem. Parents can help break the cycle of failure by promoting their child's self-esteem. The best way to do this is through the use of the *authoritative* child-rearing style which we will discuss in Chapter 14. Authoritative parents are warm and emotionally supportive, while still setting clear limits for their children's behavior. In contrast, other parenting styles have less positive effects on self-esteem. Parents who are highly punitive and controlling send a message to their children that they are untrustworthy and unable to make good decisions—a message that can undermine children's sense of adequacy. Highly indulgent parents, who indiscriminately praise and reinforce their children regardless of their actual performance, can create a false sense of self-esteem in their children, which ultimately may be just as damaging to them (DeHart, Pelham, & Tennen, 2006; Rudy & Grusec, 2006; Milevsky et al., 2007).

Watch the **Video** *Parenting Styles* in **MyPsychLab**.

Self-Esteem in Adolescence: How Do I Like Myself?

Knowing who you are and *liking* who you are two different things. Although adolescents become increasingly accurate in understanding who they are (their self-concept), this knowledge does not guarantee that they like themselves (their self-esteem) any better. In fact, their increasing accuracy in understanding themselves permits them to see themselves fully—warts and all. It's what they do with these perceptions that leads them to develop a sense of their self-esteem.

The same cognitive sophistication that allows adolescents to differentiate various aspects of the self also leads them to evaluate those aspects in different ways. For instance, an adolescent may have high self-esteem in terms of academic performance, but lower self-esteem in terms of relationships with others. Or it may be just the opposite, as articulated by this adolescent:

> *How much do I like the kind of person I am? Well, I like some things about me, but I don't like others. I'm glad that I'm popular since it's really important to me to have friends. But in school I don't do as well as the really smart kids. That's OK, because if you're too smart you'll lose your friends. So being smart is just not that important. Except to my parents. I feel like I'm letting them down when I don't do as well as they want. (Harter, 1990b, p. 364)*

What determines an adolescent's self-esteem? As we'll see next, socioeconomic status and race are two factors that make a difference.

Socioeconomic Status and Race Differences in Self-Esteem.   Socioeconomic status (SES) and race also influence self-esteem. Adolescents of higher SES generally have higher self-esteem than those of lower SES, particularly during middle and later adolescence. It may be that the social status factors that especially enhance one's standing and self-esteem—such as having more expensive clothes or a car—become more conspicuous in the later periods of adolescence (Van Tassel-Baska et al., 1994).

Race and ethnicity also play a role in self-esteem, but their impact has lessened as prejudicial treatment of minorities has eased. Early studies argued that minority status would lead to lower self-esteem, and this was initially supported by research. African Americans and Hispanics, researchers explained, had lower self-esteem than did Caucasians because prejudicial attitudes in society made them feel disliked and rejected, and this feeling was incorporated into their self-concepts. More recent research paints a different picture. Most findings suggest that African American adolescents differ little from whites in their levels of self-esteem. Why should this be? One explanation is that social movements within the African American community that bolster racial pride help support African American adolescents. In fact, research finds that a stronger sense of racial identity is related to a higher level of self-esteem in African Americans and Hispanics (Phinney, 2008; Smith & Silva, 2011; Rivas-Drake, 2012).

Another reason for overall similarity in self-esteem levels between adolescents of different racial groups is that teenagers in general focus their preferences and priorities on those aspects of their lives at which they excel. Consequently, African American youths may concentrate

Research has revealed that minority status does not necessarily lead to low self-esteem. In fact, a strong sense of racial identity is tied to higher levels of self-esteem.

DEVELOPMENTAL DIVERSITY AND YOUR LIFE

Are the Children of Immigrant Families Well Adjusted?

Immigration to the United States has risen significantly in the last 30 years. Children in immigrant families account for almost 25% of children in the United States. Children of immigrant families are the fastest-growing segment of children in the country (Hernandez et al., 2008).

In many ways, children of immigrants fare quite well. On one hand, they are better off than their nonimmigrant peers. For example, they tend to have equal or better grades in school than do children whose parents were born in the United States. Psychologically, they also do quite well, showing similar levels of self-esteem to nonimmigrant children, although they do report feeling less popular and less in control of their lives (Harris, 2000; Kao, 2000; Driscoll, Russell, & Crockett, 2008).

On the other hand, many children of immigrants face challenges. Their parents often have limited education, and they work at jobs that pay poorly. Unemployment rates are often higher for immigrants than for the general population. In addition, parental English proficiency may be lower. Many children of immigrants lack good health insurance (Hernandez et al., 2008; Turney & Kao, 2009).

Even the immigrant children who are not financially well off, however, are often more highly motivated to succeed and place greater value on education than do children in nonimmigrant families. Moreover, many immigrant children come from societies that emphasize collectivism, and consequently they may feel they have a greater obligation and duty to their family to succeed. Finally, their country of origin may give some immigrant children a strong enough cultural identity to prevent them from adopting undesirable "American" behaviors—such as materialism or selfishness (Fuligni & Yoshikawa, 2003; Suárez-Orozco & Todorova Suárez-Orozco, 2008).

During the middle childhood years, it thus appears that children in immigrant families typically do quite well in the United States. The story is less clear, however, when immigrant children reach adolescence and adulthood. Research is just beginning to clarify how effectively immigrants cope over the course of the life span (Portes & Rumbaut, 2001; Fuligni & Fuligni, 2007). ■

Immigrant children tend to fare quite well in the United States, partly because many come from societies that emphasize collectivism and consequently may feel more obligation and duty to their family to succeed. What are some other cultural differences that can support the success of immigrant children?

on the things that they find most satisfying and gain self-esteem from being successful at them (Gray-Little & Hafdahl, 2000; Yang & Blodgett, 2000; Phinney, 2005).

Finally, self-esteem may be influenced not by race alone, but by a complex combination of factors. For instance, some developmentalists have considered race and gender simultaneously, coining the term *ethgender* to refer to the joint influence of race and gender. One study that simultaneously took both race and gender into account found that African American and Hispanic males had the highest levels of self-esteem, while Asian and Native American females had the lowest levels (Romero & Roberts, 2003; Saunders, Davis, & Williams, 2004; Biro et al., 2006). We will take a further look at how gender influences self-esteem in Chapter 12.

Social Identity Theory. One explanation for the complex relationship between self-esteem and minority group status comes from *social identity theory*. According to the theory, members of a minority group are likely to accept the negative views held by a majority group only if they perceive that there is little realistic possibility of changing the power and status differences between the groups. If minority group members feel that prejudice and discrimination can be reduced, and they blame society, and not themselves, for the prejudice, self-esteem should not differ between majority and minority groups (Outten et al., 2009).

In fact, as group pride and ethnic awareness on the part of minority group members has grown, differences in self-esteem among members of different ethnic groups have narrowed. This trend has further been supported by an increased sensitivity to the importance of multiculturalism (Negy, Shreve, & Jensen, 2003; Lee, 2005; Tatum, 2007).

Social Comparison

If someone asks you how good you are at math, how would you respond? Most of us would compare our performance to others who are roughly of the same age and educational level. It is unlikely that we'd answer the question by comparing ourselves either to Albert Einstein or to a kindergartner just learning about numbers.

Elementary-school-age children begin to follow the same sort of reasoning when they seek to understand how able they are. When they were younger, they tended to consider their abilities in terms of some hypothetical standard, making a judgment that they are good or bad in an absolute sense. Now they begin to use social comparison processes, comparing themselves to others, to determine their levels of accomplishment during middle childhood (Weiss, Ebbeck, & Horn, 1997).

Social comparison is the desire to evaluate one's own behavior, abilities, expertise, and opinions by comparing them to those of others. According to a theory first suggested by psychologist Leon Festinger (1954), when concrete, objective measures of ability are lacking, people turn to *social reality* to evaluate themselves. Social reality refers to understanding that is derived from how others act, think, feel, and view the world.

But who provides the most adequate comparison? When they cannot objectively evaluate their ability, children during middle childhood increasingly look to others who are similar to themselves (Summers, Schallert, & Ritter, 2003).

Downward Social Comparison.   Although children typically compare themselves to similar others, in some cases—particularly when their self-esteem is at stake—they choose to make *downward social comparisons* with others who are obviously less competent or successful (Vohs & Heatherton, 2004; Hui et al., 2006; Dunn, Ruedy, & Schweitzer, 2012).

Downward social comparison protects children's self-esteem. By comparing themselves to those who are less able, children ensure that they will come out on top and thereby preserve an image of themselves as successful.

Downward social comparison helps explain why some students in elementary schools with generally low achievement levels are found to have stronger academic self-esteem than very capable students in schools with high achievement levels. The reason seems to be that students in the low-achievement schools observe others who are not doing terribly well academically, and they feel relatively good by comparison. In contrast, students in the high-achievement schools may find themselves competing with a more academically proficient group of students, and their perception of their performance may suffer in comparison. At least in terms of self-esteem, then, it is better to be a big fish in a small pond than a small fish in a big one (Marsh & Hau, 2003; Borland & Howsen, 2003; Marsh et al., 2008).

Social Comparison in Adolescence: The Importance of Peer Groups.   Peers become more important for a number of reasons in adolescence. For one thing, they provide each other with the opportunity to compare and evaluate opinions, abilities, and even physical changes. Because physical and cognitive changes of adolescence are so unique to this age group and so pronounced, especially during the early stages of puberty, adolescents turn increasingly to others who share, and consequently can shed light on, their own experiences (Schutz, Paxton, & Wertheim, 2002; Rankin, Lane, & Gibbons, 2004; Shi & Xie, 2012).

Parents are unable to provide social comparison. Not only are they well beyond the changes that adolescents undergo, but also adolescents' questioning of adult authority and their motivation to become more autonomous make parents, other family members, and adults in general inadequate and invalid sources of knowledge. Who is left to provide such information? Peers.

Reference Groups.   As we have said, adolescence is a time of experimentation, of trying out new identities, roles, and conduct. Peers provide information about what roles and behavior are most acceptable by serving as a reference group. **Reference groups** are groups of people with whom one compares oneself. Just as a professional ballplayer is likely to compare his performance against that of other professional players, so do teenagers compare themselves to those who are similar to them.

Reference groups present a set of *norms*, or standards, against which adolescents can judge their abilities and social success. An adolescent need not even belong to a group for

Watch the **Video** *Peer Groups in Adolescence* in **MyPsychLab**.

social comparison   The collection of social skills that permit individuals to perform successfully in social settings

reference groups   Groups of people with whom one compares oneself

it to serve as a reference group. For instance, unpopular adolescents may find themselves belittled and rejected by members of a popular group, yet use that more popular group as a reference group.

Review, Check, and Apply

Review

1. During the middle childhood years, self-esteem is based on comparisons with others and internal standards of success; if self-esteem is low, the result can be a cycle of failure.

2. Self-esteem grows increasingly differentiated in adolescence as teens develop the ability to place different values on different aspects of the self.

3. Peer social groups serve as reference groups in adolescence and offer a ready means of social comparison.

4. Though they face many challenges, children of immigrant families do quite well psychologically, showing levels of self-esteem similar to nonimmigrant children.

5. Chronic low self-esteem can lead to physical illness, psychological problems, and the inability to cope with stress. Low self-esteem is also related to aggression, anti-social behavior, and delinquency in adolescence.

Check

1. _____ is an individual's overall and specific positive and negative self-evaluation.

2. Some developmentalists have considered race and gender simultaneously, coining the term _____.

3. Evaluating one's own behavior, abilities, and opinions by comparing them to those of others, generally one's peers, is known as _____ _____.

Apply

1. How would you go about designing a program for elementary students who are academic underachievers to prevent them from falling into a "cycle of failure"?

To see more review questions, log on to MyPsychLab.

ANSWERS: 1. Self-esteem 2. ethgender 3. social comparison

The CASE
of . . . *the Failed Star*

Jake Stoddard appeared to be a typical 10-year-old boy. He earned Bs in school, except in composition where he struggled to get his ideas on paper. He played trumpet in the school band and was the right fielder on his Little League team. Yes, Jake seemed an average boy to everyone—except his parents.

"You're a star, Jake. You're a winner," his parents reminded him daily. For his birthday, his dad had given him an expensive bat. "A pro deserves the best, Jake."

But Jake knew he wasn't a star, no matter how many times his parents said so. And comparing himself to the other kids, he didn't feel like a winner. Until fourth grade, Jake had tried to succeed in school, but this year he had faced facts. Writing was tough for him. He would never be as good as his friends Mark and Beth. So why try?

Though his batting was okay, his coach had already warned him about his fielding. "I like you, Jake, but if your fielding doesn't improve you may not make Little League next year," the coach said. Jake mumbled a thanks and wandered away. If he was lousy in the field, and couldn't bat like Tim or Will, maybe he should just give up the game. Then the music teacher pulled him aside. "Jake, I think maybe the trumpet isn't for you. Would you like to try another instrument?"

Jake didn't try another instrument. Instead, he continued to carry the trumpet to school. He didn't want his parents to know their "star" had failed yet again.

1. How does Jake's comparing himself to other children reflect the development of self-concept in middle childhood?

2. Why doesn't Jake believe his parents when they say he's a star and a winner? How might they change their parenting style to promote genuine self-esteem in Jake?

3. How do you see Jake's self-concept affecting the decisions he makes?

4. What specific actions would you advise Jake to take that might change his self-concept and raise his self-esteem?

◀◀◀ LOOKING BACK

LO 11-1 How does a sense of self develop from infancy to middle childhood?

- By the age of 18 to 24 months, infants have developed an awareness of their own physical characteristics and capabilities, and they understand that their appearance is stable over time.

- Preschoolers develop a self-concept, formed partly from their own perceptions and estimations of their characteristics, partly from their parents' behavior toward them, and partly from cultural influences.

- Children in the middle childhood years begin to view themselves in terms of psychological characteristics and to differentiate their self-concepts into separate areas.

LO 11-2 How do children develop a sense of racial and ethnic identity?

- Although infants are able to distinguish different skin colors, it is not until age 3 or 4 that they begin to identify themselves as a member of a particular group such as "Hispanic" or "Black."

- Some children experience race dissonance, the phenomenon in which minority children indicate preferences for majority values or people.

- Ethnic identity often emerges later than racial identity, because it is usually less conspicuous than race. Children generally display only a limited knowledge of their ethnic identity until middle childhood. However, preschoolers who are bilingual, speaking both Spanish and English, may develop an early awareness of their ethnic identity.

- Preschool-age children form racial attitudes largely in response to their environment, including parents and other influences.

LO 11-3 How does the development of self-concept and identity proceed during adolescence?

- During adolescence, self-concept differentiates to encompass others' views as well as one's own and to include multiple aspects simultaneously. Differentiation of self-concept can cause confusion as behaviors reflect a complex definition of the self.

- According to Erik Erikson, adolescents are in the identity-versus-identity-confusion stage, seeking to discover their individuality and identity. They may become confused and exhibit dysfunctional reactions, and they may rely for help and information more on friends and peers than on adults.

- James Marcia identifies four identity statuses that individuals may experience in adolescence and in later life: identity achievement, identity foreclosure, identity diffusion, and moratorium.

- The formation of an identity is challenging for members of racial and ethnic minority groups, many of whom appear to be embracing a bicultural identity approach.

LO 11-4 What is the role of identity formation in adolescence?

- Issues of identity become increasingly important during adolescence because adolescent intellectual capacities become more adult-like.

- Adolescents are better able to see how they compare to others and become aware that they are individuals, separate from their parents, peers, and others.

LO 11-5 What is self-esteem, and what are some factors in and consequences of high and low self-esteem?

- Self-esteem is the emotional side of the self-concept, involving the self-evaluative feelings that people have about various aspects of themselves.

- In middle childhood, children are developing self-esteem; those with chronically low self-esteem can become trapped in a cycle of failure in which low self-esteem feeds on itself by producing low expectations and poor performance.

- In general, adolescents with higher self-esteem hold more positive expectations about their abilities and performance, and adolescents with lower self-esteem hold more negative expectations.

- Socioeconomic status, race, and ethnicity also affect self-esteem, with African American and white adolescents generally having higher self-esteem than other groups.

- Broad, unfocused efforts at increasing self-esteem are less successful than focused efforts aimed at improving self-esteem.

LO 11-6 What is social comparison, and what role does it play in developing a self-concept and self-esteem in middle childhood and adolescence?

- School-age children and adolescents use social comparison when they seek to evaluate themselves by comparing their own behaviors, abilities, opinions, and areas of expertise with those of others, usually peers.

- Although it is typical for children to compare themselves to others they perceive as similar, they sometimes use downward social comparison to compare themselves favorably to those they perceive as less able, thus boosting or protecting their own self-esteem.

- In adolescence, peers become all-important, providing teens with reference groups from which they get information on acceptable roles and behavior, and against which they compare their own physical changes and social success, as well as opinions and abilities.

KEY TERMS AND CONCEPTS

self-awareness (p. 306)
self-concept (p. 307)
collectivistic orientation (p. 307)
race dissonance (p. 308)

individualistic orientation (p. 308)
identity achievement (p. 313)
identity foreclosure (p. 313)
moratorium (p. 314)

identity diffusion (p. 314)
self-esteem (p. 317)
social comparison (p. 322)
reference groups (p. 322)

Epilogue

"Who am I?" and "How do I feel about myself?" are two key questions in an individual's ever-evolving sense of self. In this chapter, we considered the development of the self, examining how we understand and evaluate ourselves. We began by tracing the evidence we have that infants are aware of their own existence—how they come to understand that they are individuals distinct from the world around them. We then focused on how self-concept develops in the years from preschool to adolescence, and how children develop racial and ethnic awareness. From there, we looked at self-esteem and discussed the ways that children and adolescents develop a positive—or negative—view of themselves. We then considered how adolescents are able to differentiate various aspects of the self, which leads them to evaluate those aspects in different ways. Finally, we saw how social comparison provides a useful tool for evaluating one's abilities in light of the abilities of one's peers.

Return for a moment to the opening prologue, in which we looked at Karl Haglund. In light of what you now know about the development of the self and self-evaluation in middle childhood, consider the following questions.

1. Where does Karl's description of himself place him in the shift of self-understanding that occurs in middle childhood? How would you expect his self-concept to change over the next few years?

2. How do Karl's comments demonstrate his use of social comparison to evaluate himself?

3. What educated guesses can you make about Karl's self-esteem based on the information in the Prologue?

4. In your opinion, which of psychologist James Marcia's four categories of identity will likely characterize Karl in adolescence? Why?

The Development Video Series in MyPsychLab

Explore the video *What's in it For Me?: Identity* by scanning this QR code with your mobile device. If you don't already have one, you may download a free QR scanner for your device wherever smartphone apps are sold. You can also view this video in MyPsychLab. For more videos related to this chapter's content, log into MyPsychLab to view the entire Development Video Series.

MyVirtualChild

- **What decisions would you make while raising a child?**
- **What would the consequences of those decisions be?**

Find out by accessing **MyVirtualChild** at

www.MyPsychLab.com

and raising your own virtual child from birth to age 18.

12 Gender and Sexuality

MODULE 12.1

GENDER: WHY DO BOYS WEAR BLUE AND GIRLS WEAR PINK?

- Gender Differences
- Gender Identity: Developing Femaleness and Maleness
- Explaining Gender Differences

Review, Check, and Apply

MODULE 12.2

GENDER AND SOCIAL RELATIONSHIPS

- Gender and Friendships: The Sex Segregation of Middle Childhood
- Gender Relations in Adolescence
- Dating: Close Relationships in the 21st Century

FROM RESEARCH TO PRACTICE: When Texting Turns Explicit: Sexting

Review, Check, and Apply

MODULE 12.3

SEXUAL BEHAVIOR AND TEENAGE PREGNANCY

- Becoming Sexual

CAREERS IN DEVELOPMENT: Sandra Caron, Sex Educator

- Sexual Orientation: Heterosexuality, Homosexuality, and Bisexuality

DEVELOPMENTAL DIVERSITY AND YOUR LIFE: What Determines Sexual Orientation?

- Teenage Pregnancies

ARE YOU AN INFORMED CONSUMER OF DEVELOPMENT? Preventing Unwanted Pregnancy

Review, Check, and Apply

The Case of ... The Wrong Role Models?

Looking Back

Key Terms and Concepts

Epilogue

PROLOGUE: Rules of the Game

In preschool, David was a sociable child. His ability to share toys and take turns won him many friends. He was always inventing make-believe games about pirates and knights and Star Wars. The other children liked these games, too, and were often happy to follow where David's imagination led them. Then, in first grade, soccer happened.

David liked to climb and run and jump, but he wasn't well-coordinated, and he didn't really care about scoring a goal. He joined the soccer team because his friends did, but the game bored him. His teammates began taunting him for his poor performance on the field. David didn't care about soccer, but he was sad to lose his friends.

"You don't have to be on the team if you don't want to," his dad said. "There must be something else you can do with your friends." But David knew there wasn't. His friends had discovered sports. After soccer season, they played Little League. In the fall, it was basketball, followed by Peewee hockey. Sports, David understood, were "what boys did." If he hated sports, what did that make him?

(continued)

Learning Objectives

MODULE 12.1

LO1 What differences are there between boys and girls in terms of behavior and treatment, and how does a sense of gender develop?

MODULE 12.2

LO2 How does gender affect friendships?

LO3 What are the functions and characteristics of dating during adolescence?

MODULE 12.3

LO4 How does sexuality develop in the adolescent years?

LO5 Why are there different sexual orientations, and what determines one's orientation?

LO6 What are the consequences of teen pregnancy, and how effective have abstinence programs been in preventing it?

>>> LOOKING AHEAD

David's experience appears to be a simple story about peer relationships and fitting—or not fitting—in. But underpinning the events in his story are complex expectations and norms all having to do with gender. From birth, our gender influences how we are treated and how we view ourselves. Gender definitions and expectations provide rules for what is—and what isn't—considered appropriate behavior. They define how we conduct social relationships, and—as David's story shows—with whom. However, David's story also shows one size does not fit all when it comes to what it means to be a boy, or a girl. Not every boy wants to play sports. Not every girl wants to be a ballerina.

In this chapter, we focus on gender and sexuality. We begin by looking at gender, the sense of being male or female, and how children are both treated differently and behave differently on the basis of whether they are boys or girls. We also consider the various approaches that seek to explain gender differences.

We then turn to the role gender plays in social relationships. We discuss how friendships become increasingly segregated by gender as children move through the preschool years and into middle childhood. We look at how all this changes when children reach adolescence and begin socializing in mixed gender groups, a time when self-esteem may be greatly affected by gender expectations. We then examine the role dating plays in adolescents' lives.

Finally, we look at the development of sexual relationships and consider some theories on how sexual orientation is determined. We end the chapter by examining the consequences of teen pregnancy and evaluating the success—or failure—of abstinence programs to curb it.

MODULE 12.1

GENDER: WHY DO BOYS WEAR BLUE AND GIRLS WEAR PINK?

LO 12-1 **What differences are there between boys and girls in terms of behavior and treatment, and how does a sense of gender develop?**

"It's a boy." "It's a girl."

One of these two statements, or some variant, is probably the first announcement made after the birth of a child. From the moment of birth, girls and boys are treated differently. Their parents send out different kinds of birth announcements. They are dressed in different clothes and wrapped in different-colored blankets. They are given different toys (Coltrane & Adams, 1997; Serbin et al., 2001).

Parents play with boy and girl babies differently: From birth on, fathers tend to interact more with sons than daughters, while mothers interact more with daughters. Because, as we noted in Chapter 10, mothers and fathers play in different ways (with fathers typically engaging in more physical, rough-and-tumble activities and mothers in traditional games such as peek-a-boo), male and female infants are clearly exposed to different styles of activity and interaction from their parents (Clearfield & Nelson, 2006; Parke, 2007; Biehle & Mickelson, 2012).

The behavior exhibited by girls and boys is interpreted in very different ways by adults. For instance, when researchers showed adults a video of an infant whose name was given as either "John" or "Mary," adults perceived "John" as adventurous and inquisitive, while "Mary" was fearful and anxious although it was the same baby performing a single set of behaviors (Condry & Condry, 1976). Clearly, adults view the behavior of children through the lens of gender. **Gender** refers to our sense of being male or female. The term *gender* is often used to mean the same thing as *sex*, but they are not actually the same. **Sex** typically refers to sexual anatomy and sexual behavior, while gender refers to the social perceptions of maleness or femaleness. All cultures prescribe *gender roles* for males and females, but these roles differ greatly between one culture to another.

Gender Differences

There is a considerable amount of disagreement over both the extent and causes of such gender differences, even though most agree that boys and girls do experience at least partially different worlds based on gender. Some gender differences are fairly clear from the time of birth. For example, male infants tend to be more active and fussier than female infants.

gender One's sense of being male or female

sex A reference to sexual anatomy and sexual behavior

Boys' sleep tends to be more disturbed than that of girls. Boys grimace more, although no gender difference exists in the overall amount of crying. There is also some evidence that male newborns are more irritable than female newborns, although the findings are inconsistent (Guinsburg et al., 2000; Losonczy-Marshall, 2008; Sullivan & Lewis, 2012).

Differences between male and female infants, however, are generally minor. In fact, in most ways infants seem so similar that usually adults cannot discern whether a baby is a boy or girl, as the "John" and "Mary" video research shows. Furthermore, it is important to keep in mind that there are much larger differences among individual boys and among individual girls than there are, on average, between boys and girls (Crawford & Unger, 2004).

Parents of girls who play with toys related to activities typically associated with boys are apt to be less concerned than parents of boys who play with toys typically associated with girls.

Gender Roles. Gender differences emerge more clearly as children age—and become increasingly influenced by the gender roles that society sets out for them. For instance, by the age of 1 year, infants are able to distinguish between males and females. Girls at this age prefer to play with dolls or stuffed animals, while boys seek out blocks and trucks. Often, these are the only options available to them, due to the choices their parents and other adults have made in the toys they provide (Cherney, Kelly-Vance, & Glover, 2003; Alexander, Wilcox, & Woods, 2009).

Children's preferences for certain kinds of toys are reinforced by their parents. In general, however, parents of boys are more apt to be concerned about their child's choices than are parents of girls. Boys receive more reinforcement for playing with toys that society deems appropriate for boys and this reinforcement increases with age. On the other hand, a girl playing with a truck is viewed with considerably less concern than a boy playing with a doll might be. Girls who play with toys seen by society as "masculine" are less discouraged for their behavior than boys who play with toys seen as "feminine" (Martin, Ruble, & Szkrybalo, 2002; Schmalz & Kerstetter, 2006; Hill & Flom, 2007).

Watch the **Video** *Gender Roles in the Family* in **MyPsychLab**.

By the time they reach the age of 2, boys behave more independently and less compliantly than girls. Much of this behavior can be traced to parental reactions to earlier behavior. For instance, when a child takes his or her first steps, parents tend to react differently, depending on the child's gender: Boys are encouraged more to go off and explore the world, while girls are hugged and kept close. It is hardly surprising, then, that by the age of 2, girls tend to show less independence and greater compliance (Kuczynski & Kochanska, 1990; Poulin-Dubois, Serbin, & Eichstedt, 2002).

Societal encouragement and reinforcement do not, however, completely explain differences in behavior between boys and girls. For example, as we'll discuss later in this module, one study examined girls who were exposed before birth to abnormally high levels of *androgen*, a male hormone, because their mothers unwittingly took a drug containing the hormone while pregnant. Later, these girls were more likely to play with toys stereotypically preferred by boys (such as cars) and less likely to play with toys stereotypically associated with girls (such as dolls). Although there are many alternative explanations for these results—you can probably think of several yourself—one possibility is that exposure to male hormones affected the brain development of the girls, leading them to favor toys that involve certain kinds of preferred skills (Levine et al., 1999; Mealey, 2000; Servin et al., 2003).

In sum, differences in behavior between boys and girls begin in infancy and continue throughout childhood. Although gender differences have complex causes, representing some combination of innate, biologically related factors and environmental factors, they play a profound role in the social and emotional development of infants.

Gender Identity: Developing Femaleness and Maleness

Boys' awards: Very Best Thinker, Most Eager Learner, Most Imaginative, Most Enthusiastic, Most Scientific, Best Friend, Mr. Personality, Hardest Worker, Best Sense of Humor. Girls' awards: All-Around Sweetheart, Sweetest Personality, Cutest Personality, Best Sharer, Best Artist, Biggest Heart, Best Manners, Best Helper, Most Creative.

During the preschool period, differences in play according to gender become more pronounced. In addition, boys tend to play with boys, and girls with girls.

What's wrong with this picture? To one parent, whose daughter received one of the girls' awards during a kindergarten graduation ceremony, quite a bit. While the girls were getting pats on the back for their pleasing personalities, the boys were receiving awards for their intellectual and analytic skills (Deveny, 1994).

Such a situation is not rare: Girls and boys often live in very different worlds. Differences in the ways males and females are treated begin at birth, continue during the preschool years, and as we'll see later, extend into adolescence—and beyond (Martin & Ruble, 2004; Bornstein et al., 2008; Wohlwend, 2012).

Gender, the sense of being male or female, is well established by the time children reach the preschool years. By the age of 2, children consistently label themselves and those around them as male or female (Raag, 2003; Campbell, Shirley, & Candy, 2004).

One way gender shows up is in play. Preschool boys spend more time than girls in rough-and-tumble play, while preschool girls spend more time than boys in organized games and role-playing. During this time, boys begin to play more with boys, and girls play more with girls, a trend that increases during middle childhood, as we will discuss in the next module. Girls begin to prefer same-sex playmates a little earlier than boys. They first have a clear preference for interacting with other girls at age 2, while boys don't show much preference for same-sex playmates until age 3 (Martin & Fabes, 2001; Raag, 2003).

Such same-sex preferences appear in many cultures. For instance, studies of kindergartners in mainland China show no examples of mixed-gender play. Similarly, gender "outweighs" ethnic variables when it comes to play: A Hispanic boy would rather play with a white boy than with a Hispanic girl (Whiting & Edwards, 1998; Aydt & Corsaro, 2003).

Preschool-age children often have strict ideas about how boys and girls are supposed to act. In fact, their expectations about gender-appropriate behavior are even more gender-stereotyped than those of adults and may be less flexible during the preschool years than at any other point in the life span. Beliefs in gender stereotypes become increasingly pronounced up to age 5, and although they become somewhat less rigid by age 7, they do not disappear. In fact, the gender stereotypes held by preschoolers resemble those held by traditional adults in society (Serbin, Poulin-Dubois, & Eichstedt, 2002; Lam & Leman, 2003; Ruble et al., 2007).

And what is the nature of preschoolers' gender expectations? Like adults, preschoolers expect that males are more apt to have traits involving competence, independence, forcefulness, and competitiveness. In contrast, females are viewed as more likely to have traits such as warmth, expressiveness, nurturance, and submissiveness. Although these are *expectations*, and say nothing about the way that men and women actually behave, such expectations provide the lens through which preschool-age children view the world and affect preschoolers'

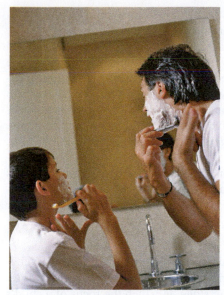

According to social learning approaches, children learn gender-related behavior and expectations from their observations of others.

behavior as well as the way they interact with peers and adults (Blakemore, 2003; Gelman, Taylor, & Nguyen, 2004).

Explaining Gender Differences

The prevalence and strength of preschoolers' gender expectations, and differences in behavior between boys and girls, have proven puzzling. Why should gender play such a powerful role during the preschool years (as well as during the rest of the life span)? Developmentalists have proposed several explanations.

Biological Perspectives on Gender.

Since gender relates to the sense of being male or female, and sex refers to the physical characteristics that differentiate males and females, it would hardly be surprising to find that the biological characteristics associated with sex might themselves lead to gender differences. This has been shown to be true.

Hormones are one sex-related biological characteristic that has been found to affect gender-based behaviors. As we mentioned earlier, girls exposed to unusually high levels of **androgens** (male hormones) prenatally are more likely to display behaviors associated with male stereotypes than are their sisters who were not exposed to androgens (Knickmeyer & Baron-Cohen, 2006; Burton et al., 2009; Mathews et al., 2009).

Androgen-exposed girls preferred boys as playmates and spent more time than other girls playing with toys associated with the male role, such as blocks and trucks. Similarly, boys exposed prenatally to atypically high levels of female hormones are apt to display more behaviors that are stereotypically female than is usual (Servin et al., 2003; Knickmeyer & Baron-Cohen, 2006; Berenbaum, Bryk & Beltz, 2012).

Moreover, biological differences exist in the structure of female and male brains. For instance, part of the **corpus callosum**, the bundle of nerves that connects the hemispheres of the brain, is proportionally larger in women than in men. To some theoreticians, evidence such as this suggests that gender differences may be produced by biological factors such as hormones (Westerhausen, 2004).

Before accepting such contentions, however, it is important to note that alternative explanations abound. For example, it may be that the *corpus callosum* is proportionally larger in women as a result of certain kinds of experiences that influence brain growth in particular ways. As we discussed earlier, girls are spoken to more than boys as infants, which might

androgens Male hormones

corpus callosum The bundle of nerves that connects the hemispheres of the brain

produce certain kinds of brain development. If this is true, environmental experience produces biological change—and not the other way around.

Other developmentalists see gender differences as serving the biological goal of survival of the species through reproduction. Basing their work on an evolutionary approach, these theorists suggest that our male ancestors who showed more stereotypically masculine qualities, such as forcefulness and competitiveness, may have been able to attract females who were able to provide them with hardy offspring. Females who excelled at stereotypically feminine tasks, such as nurturing, may have been valuable partners because they could increase the likelihood that children would survive the dangers of childhood (Browne, 2006; Ellis, 2006; McMillian, Frierson, & Campbell, 2011).

As in other domains that involve the interaction of inherited biological characteristics and environmental influences, it is difficult to attribute behavioral characteristics unambiguously to biological factors. Because of this problem, we must consider other explanations for gender differences.

Psychoanalytic Perspectives.

You may recall from Chapter 1 that Freud's psychoanalytic theory suggests that we move through a series of stages related to biological urges. To Freud, the preschool years encompass the *phallic stage,* in which the focus of a child's pleasure relates to genital sexuality. Freud argued that the end of the phallic stage is marked by an important turning point in development: the Oedipal conflict. According to Freud, the *Oedipal conflict* occurs at around the age of 5, when the anatomical differences between males and females become particularly evident. Boys begin to develop sexual interests in their mothers, viewing their fathers as rivals.

As a consequence, boys conceive a desire to kill their fathers—just as Oedipus did in the ancient Greek tragedy. However, because they view their fathers as all-powerful, boys develop a fear of retaliation, which takes the form of *castration anxiety.* To overcome this fear, boys repress their desires for their mothers and instead begin to identify with their fathers, attempting to be as similar to them as possible. **Identification** is the process in which children attempt to be similar to their same-sex parent, incorporating the parent's attitudes and values.

Girls, according to Freud, go through a different process. They begin to feel sexual attraction toward their fathers and experience *penis envy*—a view that not unexpectedly has led to accusations that Freud viewed women as inferior to men. To resolve their penis envy, girls ultimately identify with their mothers, attempting to be as similar to them as possible.

In the cases of both boys and girls, the ultimate result of identifying with the same-sex parent is that the children adopt their parents' gender attitudes and values. In this way, says Freud, society's expectations about the ways females and males "ought" to behave are perpetuated into new generations.

You may find it difficult to accept Freud's elaborate explanation of gender differences. So do most developmentalists, who believe that gender development is best explained by other mechanisms. In part, they base their criticisms of Freud on the lack of scientific support for his theories.

For example, children learn gender stereotypes much earlier than the age of 5. Furthermore, this learning occurs even in single-parent households. However, some aspects of psychoanalytic theory have been supported, such as findings indicating that preschool-age children whose same-sex parents support sex-stereotyped behavior tend to demonstrate that behavior also. Still, far simpler processes can account for this phenomenon, and many developmentalists have searched for explanations of gender differences other than Freud's (Martin & Ruble, 2004; Chen & Rao, 2011).

Social Learning Approaches.

As their name implies, social learning approaches see children as learning gender-related behavior and expectations by observing others. Children watch the behavior of their parents, teachers, siblings, and even peers. A little boy sees the glory of a major league baseball player and becomes interested in sports. A little girl watches her high school neighbor practicing cheerleading moves and begins to try them herself. The

identification The process in which children attempt to be similar to their same sex parent, incorporating the parent's attitudes and values

observation of the rewards that these others attain for acting in a gender-appropriate manner leads the child to conform to such behavior themselves (Rust et al., 2000).

Books and the media, and in particular television and video games, also play a role in perpetuating traditional views of gender-related behavior from which preschoolers may learn. Analyses of the most popular television shows, for example, find that male characters outnumber female characters by 2 to 1. Furthermore, females are more apt to appear with males, whereas female–female relationships are relatively uncommon (Calvert, Kotler, & Zehnder, 2003; Eagly & Wood, 2012).

Television also presents men and women in traditional gender roles. Television shows typically define female characters in terms of their relationships with males. Females are more likely to appear as victims than males. They are less likely to be presented as productive or as decision-makers, and more likely to be portrayed as characters interested in romance, their homes, and their families. Such models, according to social learning theory, are apt to have a powerful influence on preschoolers' definitions of appropriate behavior (Hust, Brown, & L'Engle, 2008; Nassif & Gunter, 2008; Prieler et al., 2011).

In some cases, learning of social roles does not involve models, but occurs more directly. For example, most of us have heard preschool-age children being told by their parents to act like a "little girl" or "little man." What this generally means is that girls should behave politely and courteously, or that boys should be tough and stoic—traits associated with society's traditional stereotypes of men and women. Such direct training sends a clear message about the behavior expected of a preschool-age child (Leaper, 2002).

Cognitive Approaches.   In the view of some theorists, one aspect of the desire to form a clear sense of identity is the desire to establish a **gender identity**, a perception of themselves as male or female. To do this, they develop a **gender schema**, a cognitive framework that organizes information relevant to gender (Barberá, 2003; Martin & Ruble, 2004; Signorella & Frieze, 2008).

Gender schemas are developed early in life and serve as a lens through which preschoolers view the world. For instance, preschoolers use their increasing cognitive abilities to develop "rules" about what is right and what is inappropriate for males and females. Thus, some girls decide that wearing pants is inappropriate for a female and apply the rule so rigidly that they refuse to wear anything but dresses. Or a preschool boy may reason that since makeup is typically worn by females, it is inappropriate for him to wear makeup even when he is in a preschool play and all the other boys and girls are wearing it (Frawley, 2008).

According to *cognitive-developmental theory,* proposed by Lawrence Kohlberg, this rigidity is in part a reflection of preschoolers' understanding of gender (Kohlberg, 1966). Rigid gender schemas are influenced by preschoolers' erroneous beliefs about sex differences. Specifically, young preschoolers believe that sex differences are based not on biological factors but on differences in appearance or behavior. Employing this view of the world, a girl may reason that she can be a father when she grows up, or a boy may think he could turn into a girl if he put on a dress and tied his hair in a ponytail. However, by the time they reach the age of 4 or 5, children develop an understanding of **gender constancy**, the awareness that people are permanently males or females, depending on fixed, unchangeable biological factors.

Interestingly, research on children's growing understanding of gender constancy during the preschool period indicates that it has no particular effect on gender-related behavior. In fact, the appearance of gender schemas occurs well before children understand gender constancy. Even young preschool-age children assume that certain behaviors are appropriate—and others are not—on the basis of stereotypic views of gender (Martin & Ruble, 2004; Ruble et al., 2007; Karniol, 2009).

Like the other approaches to gender development (summarized in Table 12-1 on page 334), the cognitive perspective does not imply that differences between the two sexes are in any way improper or inappropriate. Instead, it suggests that preschoolers should be taught to treat others as individuals. Furthermore, preschoolers need to learn the importance of fulfilling their own talents, acting as individuals and not as representatives of a particular gender.

gender identity   A perception of one's self as male or female

gender schema   A cognitive framework that organizes information relevant to gender

gender constancy   The awareness that people are permanently males or females, depending on fixed, unchangeable biological factors

TABLE 12-1 Four Approaches to Gender Development

Perspective	Key Concepts	Applying the Concepts to Preschool Children
Biological	Our ancestors who behaved in ways that are now stereotypically feminine or masculine may have been more successful in reproducing. Brain differences may lead to gender differences.	Girls may be genetically "programmed" by evolution to be more expressive and nurturing, whereas boys are "programmed" to be more competitive and forceful. Hormone exposure before birth has been linked to both boys' and girls' behaving in ways typically expected of the other gender.
Psychoanalytic	Gender development is the result of identification with the same-sex parent, achieved by moving through a series of stages related to biological urges.	Girls and boys whose parents of the same sex behave in stereotypically masculine or feminine ways are likely to do so, too, perhaps because they identify with those parents.
Social learning	Children learn gender-related behavior and expectations from their observation of others' behavior.	Children notice that other children and adults are rewarded for behaving in ways that conform to standard gender stereotypes, and are sometimes punished for violating those stereotypes.
Cognitive	Through the use of gender schemas, developed early in life, preschoolers form a lens through which they view the world. They use their increasing cognitive abilities to develop "rules" about what is appropriate for males and females.	Preschoolers are more rigid in their rules about proper gender behavior than are people at other ages, perhaps because they have just developed gender schemas that don't yet permit much variation from stereotypical expectations.

Review, Check, and Apply

Review

1. Mothers and fathers interact with their babies differently, with mothers interacting more with their daughters and fathers interacting more with their sons. The types of interactions they engage in also differ.

2. Some gender differences do exist in early infancy, but they are relatively minor. Gender differences become more pronounced as infants age, mostly due to environmental influences. Differences are accentuated by parental expectations and behavior.

3. Gender awareness develops in the preschool years. Explanations of this phenomenon include biological, psychoanalytical, learning, and cognitive approaches.

4. The books, television, movies, and video games young children see all play a role in perpetuating traditional stereotypes of gender-related behavior.

Check

1. _____ is one's sense of being male or female.

2. In the cognitive approach to gender identity, preschool children develop a _____ _____ from which they form rules about what is appropriate and inappropriate for each gender.

3. _____ _____ is the understanding that people are permanently males or females, based on fixed, unchangeable biological factors.

Apply

1. What sorts of activities might you encourage a preschool boy to undertake to encourage him to adopt a less stereotypical gender schema?

To see more review questions, log on to MyPsychLab.

ANSWERS: 1. Gender   2. gender schema   3. Gender constancy

MODULE 12.2

GENDER AND SOCIAL RELATIONSHIPS

LO 12-2 How does gender affect friendships?

LO 12-3 What are the functions and characteristics of dating during adolescence?

Girls rule; boys drool.

Boys are idiots. Girls have cooties.

Boys go to college to get more knowledge; girls go to Jupiter to get more stupider.

Those are the views of some boys and girls regarding members of the opposite sex during the elementary school years. As we saw earlier, these views have their roots in preschool children's preference for playmates of their own gender. It's a preference that grows stronger as children enter the school years, remaining entrenched until the onset of adolescence.

Gender and Friendships: The Sex Segregation of Middle Childhood

Avoidance of the opposite sex becomes quite pronounced during middle childhood, to the degree that the social networks of most boys and girls consist almost entirely of same-sex groupings (McHale, Dariotis, & Kauh, 2003; Mehta & Strough, 2009; MacEvoy & Asher, 2012). Technically, this sex segregation is called the **sex cleavage**.

Interestingly, the segregation of friendships according to gender occurs in almost all societies. In nonindustrialized societies, same-gender segregation may be the result of the types of activities that children engage in. For instance, in many cultures, boys are assigned one type of chore and girls another (Whiting & Edwards, 1988). Participation in different activities may not provide the whole explanation for sex segregation, however; even children in more developed countries, who attend the same schools and participate in many of the same activities, still tend to avoid members of the other gender.

When boys and girls make occasional forays into the other gender's territory, the action often has romantic overtones. For instance, girls may threaten

sex cleavage   Sex segregation in which boys interact primarily with boys and girls primarily with girls

Though same-sex groupings dominate in middle childhood, when boys and girls do make occasional forays into each others' territory, there are often romantic overtones. Such behavior has been termed "border work."

to kiss a boy, or boys might try to lure girls into chasing them. Such behavior, termed *border work,* helps emphasize the clear boundaries that exist between the two sexes. In addition, it may pave the way for future interactions that do involve romantic or sexual interests, when school-age children reach adolescence and cross-sex interactions become more socially endorsed (Beal, 1994).

The lack of cross-gender interaction in the middle childhood years means that boys' and girls' friendships are restricted to members of their own sex. Furthermore, the nature of friendships within these two groups is quite different (Rose, 2002; Lee & Troop-Gordon, 2011).

Boys typically have larger networks of friends than do girls, and they tend to play in groups, rather than pair off. Differences in status within the group are usually quite pronounced, with an acknowledged leader and members falling into particular levels of status. Because of the fairly rigid rankings that represent the relative social power of those in the group, known as the **dominance hierarchy,** members of higher status can safely question and oppose children lower in the hierarchy (Pedersen et al., 2007; Sidanius & Pratto, 2012).

Boys tend to be concerned with their place in the dominance hierarchy, and they attempt to maintain their status and improve on it. This makes for a style of play known as restrictive. In *restrictive play,* interactions are interrupted when a child feels that his status is challenged. Thus, a boy who feels that he is unjustly challenged by a peer of lower status may attempt to end the interaction by scuffling over a toy or otherwise behaving assertively. Consequently, boys' play tends to come in bursts, rather than in more extended, tranquil episodes (Estell et al., 2008).

The language of friendship used among boys reflects their concern over status and challenge. For instance, consider this conversation between two boys who were good friends:

Child 1: Give me that truck. You've had it all morning.

Child 2: I'm still using it. Go get your own truck.

Child 1: No, I want *that* truck.

Child 2: No way! And you can't make me give it to you either.

Child 1: Oh yeah?

Child 2: Yeah!

Friendship patterns among girls are quite different. Rather than having a wide network of friends, school-age girls focus on one or two "best friends" who are of relatively equal status. In contrast to boys, who seek out status differences, girls profess to avoid differences in status, preferring to maintain friendships at equal-status levels.

Conflicts among school-age girls are usually solved through compromise, by ignoring the situation, or by giving in, rather than by seeking to make one's own point of view prevail. In sum, the goal is to smooth over disagreements, making social interaction easy and nonconfrontational (Noakes & Rinaldi, 2006).

dominance hierarchy Rankings that represent the relative social power of those in a group

The motivation of girls to solve social conflict indirectly does not stem from a lack of self-confidence or from apprehension over the use of more direct approaches. In fact, when school-age girls interact with other girls who are not considered friends or with boys, they can be quite confrontational. However, among friends their goal is to maintain equal-status relationships—ones lacking a dominance hierarchy (Zahn-Waxler et al., 2008).

The language used by girls tends to reflect their view of relationships. Rather than blatant demands ("Give me the pencil"), girls are more apt to use language that is less confrontational and directive. Girls tend to use indirect forms of verbs, such as "Let's go to the movies" or "Would you want to trade books with me?" rather than "I want to go to the movies" or "Let me have these books" (Goodwin, 1990; Besag, 2006).

Gender Relations in Adolescence

As children enter adolescence from middle childhood, their groups of friends are composed almost universally of same-sex individuals. As we have seen, boys hang out with boys; girls hang out with girls.

The sex segregation of childhood continues during the early stages of adolescence. However, by the time of middle adolescence, this segregation decreases, and boys' and girls' cliques begin to converge.

However, the situation changes as members of both sexes enter puberty. Boys and girls experience the hormonal surge that marks puberty and causes the maturation of the sex organs (discussed in Chapter 5). At the same time, societal pressures suggest that the time is appropriate for romantic involvement. These developments lead to a change in the ways adolescents view the opposite sex. Where a 10-year-old is likely to see every member of the other sex as "annoying" and "a pain," heterosexual teenage boys and girls begin to regard each other with greater interest in terms of both personality and sexuality. (For gays and lesbians, pairing off holds its own complexities, as we discuss later when we consider adolescent dating.)

As they move into puberty, boys' and girls' cliques, which previously had moved along parallel but separate tracks, begin to converge. Adolescents begin to attend boy–girl dances or parties, although most of the time the boys still spend their time with boys, and the girls, with girls (Richards et al., 1998).

A little later, however, adolescents increasingly spend time with members of the other sex. New cliques emerge, composed of both males and females. Not everyone participates initially: Early on, the teenagers who are leaders of the same-sex cliques and who have the highest status lead the way. Eventually, however, most adolescents find themselves in cliques that include boys and girls.

Cliques and crowds undergo yet another transformation at the end of adolescence: They become less influential and may dissolve as a result of the increased pairing off that occurs.

Gender Expectations and Self-Esteem in Adolescence. Society's stereotypical gender expectations present challenges to adolescents' self-esteem. As we discussed in Chapter 11, many factors influence an adolescent's self-esteem: comparisons with peers, socioeconomic status, race. Gender also plays a role in how adolescents evaluate themselves.

During early adolescence, girls' self-esteem tends to be lower and more vulnerable than boys'. One reason is that, compared to boys, adolescent girls tend to be more concerned about physical appearance and social success—in addition to academic achievement. Although boys are also concerned about these things, their attitudes are often more casual. In addition, societal messages suggesting that female academic achievement is a roadblock to social success can put girls in a difficult bind: If they do well academically, they jeopardize their social

Just how well dating serves to further such functions as the development of psychological intimacy is still an open question.

success. No wonder the self-esteem of adolescent girls is more fragile than that of boys (Heaven & Ciarrochi, 2008; McLean & Breen, 2009; Armitage, 2012).

Although generally self-esteem is higher in adolescent boys than girls, boys do have vulnerabilities of their own. For example, society's stereotypical gender expectations may lead boys to feel that they should be confident, tough, and fearless all the time. Boys facing difficulties, such as not making a sports team or rejection from a girl they want to go out with, are likely to feel not only miserable about the defeat they face but also incompetent, because they don't measure up to the stereotype (Pollack, Shuster, & Trelease, 2001; Witt, Donnellan, & Trzesniewski, 2011).

Dating: Close Relationships in the 21st Century

It took him almost a month, but Sylvester Chiu finally got up the courage to ask Jackie Durbin to go to the movies. It was hardly a surprise to Jackie, though. Sylvester had first told his friend Erik about his resolve to ask Jackie out, and Erik had told Jackie's friend Cynthia about Sylvester's plans. Cynthia, in turn, had told Jackie, who was primed to say "yes" when Sylvester finally did call.

Welcome to the complex world of dating, an important and changing ritual of adolescence.

When and how adolescents begin to date is determined by cultural factors that change from one generation to another. Until fairly recently, exclusively dating a single individual was seen as something of a cultural ideal, viewed in the context of romance. In fact, society often encouraged dating in adolescence, in part as a way for adolescents to explore relationships that might eventually lead to marriage. Today, some adolescents believe that the concept of dating is outmoded and limiting, and in some places the practice of "hooking up"—a vague term that covers everything from kissing to sexual intercourse—is viewed as more appropriate. (See the *From Research to Practice* box on sexting.) Despite changing cultural norms, dating remains the dominant form of social interaction that leads to intimacy among adolescents (Manning, Giordano, & Longmore, 2006; Bogle, 2008; Sparks, Lee, & Spjeldnes, 2012).

The Functions of Dating.   Although on the surface dating is part of a pattern of courtship that can potentially lead to marriage, it actually serves other functions as well, especially early on. Dating is a way to learn how to establish intimacy with another individual. It can provide entertainment and, depending on the status of the person one is dating, prestige. It even can be used to develop a sense of one's own identity (Zimmer-Gembeck & Gallaty, 2006; Friedlander, Connolly, & Pepler, 2007; Adams & Williams, 2011).

Just how well dating serves such functions, particularly the development of psychological intimacy, is an open question. What specialists in adolescence do know, however, is surprising: Dating in early and middle adolescence is not terribly successful at facilitating intimacy. On the contrary, dating is often a superficial activity in which the participants so rarely let down their guards that they never become truly close and never expose themselves emotionally to each other. Psychological intimacy may be lacking even when sexual activity is part of the relationship (Collins, 2003; Furman & Shaffer, 2003).

True intimacy becomes more common during later adolescence. At that point, the dating relationship may be taken more seriously by both participants, and it may be seen as a way to select a mate and as a potential prelude to marriage.

For homosexual adolescents, dating presents special challenges. In some cases, blatant homophobic prejudice expressed by classmates may lead gays and lesbians to date members of the other sex in efforts to fit in. If they do seek relationships with other gays and lesbians, they may find it difficult to find partners, who may not openly express their sexual orientation. Homosexual couples who do openly date face possible harassment, making the development of a relationship all the more difficult (Savin-Williams, 2003b).

FROM RESEARCH TO PRACTICE
When Texting Turns Explicit: Sexting

One day last winter Margarite posed naked before her bathroom mirror, held up her cell phone, and took a picture. Then she sent the full-length frontal photo to Isaiah, her new boyfriend.
        Both were in eighth grade. (Hoffman, 2011, p. A1)

For an increasing number of adolescents, *sexting* (the sending of texts that contain explicit, sexually provocative photos or text) is commonplace. It is easy to do and can be used in an effort to demonstrate one's affection or loyalty to a partner in an established relationship. Sexting also may be used instead of having actual sex, or as a prelude to sex. In some cases, sexting is used to indicate interest in starting a relationship (Lenhart, Ling, & Campbell, 2010; Drouin & Landgraff, 2012).

Sexting has become commonplace: According to the results of one poll, 24% of 14- to 17-year-olds were involved in some form of naked sexting, either using cell phones or the web. Another survey found that 4% of adolescents in the same age range admitted to sending naked photos or video by cell phone, and 15% had received them (Lenhart, Ling, & Campbell, 2010; Quaid, 2011).

The consequences of sexting can be devastating. It is not uncommon for texts to be forwarded, and there are numerous incidents in which recipients of explicit photos have sent the images to friends. Ultimately, a photo may be forwarded to hundreds of others. There is also a double standard: when boys are caught sending photos of themselves, they are typically viewed more positively than girls, who may be labeled as slutty (Hoffman, 2011).

Sexting not only may produce considerable psychological harm to the person who is depicted in sexually explicit photos, but there can be legal consequences. If the image involves anyone under the age of 18 (including the subject depicted, the photographer, someone who forwards the text, or even the recipient), child pornography laws come into play. An increasing number of prosecutions have occurred as a result of sexting (Katzman, 2010; Ostrager, 2010).

■ **Why do you think there is a double standard for sexting, where boys who do it are viewed more favorably than girls?**

■ **Is it reasonable for prosecutors to use child pornography laws to deal with the problem of sexting?**

Dating, Race, and Ethnicity. Culture influences dating patterns among adolescents of different racial and ethnic groups, particularly those whose parents have immigrated to the United States from other countries. Parents may try to control their children's dating behavior in an effort to preserve their culture's traditional values or ensure that their child dates within his or her racial or ethnic group.

For example, Asian parents may be especially conservative in their attitudes and values, in part because they themselves may have had no experience of dating. (In many cases, the parents' marriage was arranged by others, and the entire concept of dating is unfamiliar.) They may insist that dating be conducted with chaperones, or not at all. As a consequence, they may find themselves involved in substantial conflict with their children (Hamon & Ingoldsby, 2003; Hoelterk, Axinn, & Ghimire, 2004; Lau et al., 2009).

Review, Check, and Apply

Review

1. Beginning in preschool, children show a marked preference for friends of their own gender, a trend that increases through middle childhood until adolescence when sex cleavage gradually diminishes and boys and girls begin to pair off.

2. In middle childhood, boys tend to play in groups, enjoying a wide network of friends, while girls typically play in pairs and prefer having one or two close friends.

3. Gender expectations play a role in self-esteem in adolescence. Girls particularly feel pressures to be attractive and socially successful, as well as smart (but not too smart!). Adolescent boys feel pressures, too, but their self-esteem is generally higher than that of girls.

4. Dating in adolescence serves a number of functions including intimacy, entertainment, and prestige.

5. Dating presents challenges for homosexual adolescents who may become the victims of classmates' homophobic prejudice. In some cases, gay and lesbian teenagers may resort to dating members of the other sex in an effort to fit in.

Check

1. _____ _____ describes the tendency in middle childhood for both boys and girls to form social networks comprised almost entirely of their own gender.

2. In a group, the relative social power of its members is known as _____ _____.

3. Dating is a way to learn how to establish _____ with another person.

Apply

1. What activities would you suggest if you were a counselor in an after-school program for elementary students, asked to plan games, crafts, and outings that would appeal to both boys and girls?

To see more review questions, log on to MyPsychLab.

ANSWERS: 1. Sex cleavage 2. dominance hierarchy 3. intimacy

MODULE 12.3

SEXUAL BEHAVIOR AND TEENAGE PREGNANCY

LO 12-4 How does sexuality develop in the adolescent years?

LO 12-5 Why are there different sexual orientations, and what determines one's orientation?

LO 12-6 What are the consequences of teen pregnancy, and how effective have abstinence programs been in preventing it?

When I started "tuning out," teachers thought I was sick—physically sick, that is. They kept sending me to the school nurse to have my temperature taken. If I'd told them I was carrying on with Beyoncé in their classes, while supposedly learning my Caesar and my Latin vocabulary, they'd have thought I was—well, delirious. I was! I'd even think of Beyoncé while jogging; I'd have to stop because it'd hurt down there! You can't run and have sex—or can you? (Based on Coles & Stokes, 1985, pp. 18–19)

Becoming Sexual

The hormonal changes of puberty bring the maturation of the sexual organs and a new range of feelings and possibilities in relations with others: sexuality. Sexual behavior and thoughts are among the central concerns of adolescents. Almost all adolescents think about sex, and many think about it a good deal of the time (Kelly, 2001; Ponton, 2001).

Masturbation. The first type of sex in which adolescents engage is often solitary sexual self-stimulation or **masturbation.** By the age of 15, some 80% of teenage boys and 20% of teenage girls report that they have masturbated. The frequency of masturbation in males occurs more in the early teens and then begins to decline, whereas in females, the frequency

masturbation Solitary sexual self-stimulation

is lower initially and increases throughout adolescence. In addition, patterns of masturbation frequency show differences according to race. For example, African American men and women masturbate less than whites do (Schwartz, 1999; Hyde & DeLamater, 2004).

Although masturbation is widespread, it still may produce feelings of shame and guilt. There are several reasons for this. One is that adolescents may believe that masturbation signifies the inability to find a sexual partner—an erroneous assumption, because statistics show that three fourths of married men and 68% of married women report masturbating between 10 and 24 times a year (Davidson, Darling, & Norton, 1995; Das, 2007; Gerressu et al., 2008).

For some, there is also a sense of shame about masturbation, the result of a lingering legacy of misguided views on the subject. For instance, 19th-century physicians and laypersons warned of the horrible effects of masturbation, including "dyspepsia, spinal disease, headache, epilepsy, various kinds of fits … impaired eyesight, palpitation of the heart, pain in the side and bleeding at the lungs, spasm of the heart, and sometimes sudden death" (Gregory, 1856). Suggested remedies included bandaging the genitals, covering them with a cage, tying the hands, male circumcision without anesthesia (so that it might better be remembered), and for girls, the administration of carbolic acid to the clitoris. One physician, J. W. Kellogg, believed that certain grains would be less likely to provoke sexual excitation—leading to his invention of corn flakes (Hunt, 1974; Michael et al., 1994).

The reality of masturbation is different. Today, experts on sexual behavior view it as a normal, healthy, and harmless activity. In fact, some suggest that it provides a useful way to learn about one's own sexuality (Levin, 2007; Hyde & DeLamater, 2010).

Sexual Intercourse. Although it may be preceded by many different types of sexual intimacy, including deep kissing, massaging, petting, and oral sex, sexual intercourse remains a major milestone in the perceptions of most adolescents. Consequently, the main focus of researchers investigating sexual behavior has been on the act of heterosexual intercourse.

The average age at which adolescents first have sexual intercourse has been steadily declining over the last 50 years, and about one in five adolescents have had sex before the age of 15. Overall, the average age of first sexual intercourse is 17, and around three-quarters of adolescents have had sex before the age of 20 (see Figure 12-1). At the same time, though, many teenagers are postponing sex, and the number of adolescents who say they have never had sexual intercourse increased by 13% from 1991 to 2007 (Dailard, 2006; MMWR, 2008; Guttmacher Institute, 2011).

There also are racial and ethnic differences in the timing of initial sexual intercourse: African Americans generally have sex for the first time earlier than do Puerto Ricans, who have sex earlier than do whites. These racial and ethnic differences likely reflect differences in socioeconomic conditions, cultural values, and family structure (Singh & Darroch, 2000; Hyde & Grabe, 2008).

It is impossible to consider sexual activities without also looking at the societal norms governing sexual conduct. The prevailing norm several decades ago was the *double standard* in which premarital sex was considered permissible for males but not for females. Women were told by society that "nice girls don't," whereas men heard that premarital sex was permissible—although they should be sure to marry virgins.

Today the double standard has begun to give way to a new norm, called *permissiveness with affection*. According to this standard, premarital intercourse is viewed as permissible for both men and women if it occurs in the context of a long-term, committed, or loving relationship (Hyde & Delamater, 2004; Earle et al., 2007).

FROM THE

PERSPECTIVE OF A

MEDICAL CARE PROVIDER:

A parent asks you how to prevent her 14-year-old son from engaging in sexual activity until he is older. What would you tell her?

Watch the **Video** *Adolescent Sexual Behavior* in **MyPsychLab**.

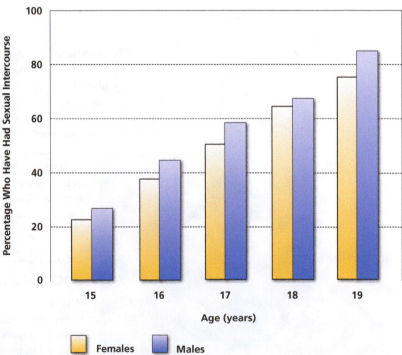

FIGURE 12-1 Adolescents and Sexual Activity

The age at which adolescents have sexual intercourse for the first time is declining, and around three-quarters have had sex before the age of 20.

(*Source:* Morbidity and Mortality Weekly Report, 2008)

CAREERS IN DEVELOPMENT
Sandra Caron, Sex Educator

Education: B.S. Health and Family Life, University of Maine; M.S., Human Development, University of Maine; Ph.D., Human Development/Family Studies, Syracuse University

Position: Professor of Family Relations/Human Sexuality, University of Maine

Dealing with the physical, emotional, and social changes related to sexuality represents some of the most important challenges faced by adolescents. However, although sexuality is a topic to which teenagers are repeatedly exposed in the media, they rarely receive accurate information.

According to Sandra Caron, professor of family relations and human sexuality and a frequent sex education lecturer, the average adolescent needs to understand more about sex.

"The fact is that many young people know very little about their own sexuality," she said. "Some are embarrassed at their ignorance and fear ridicule for not knowing more."

One of the main aspects of sex education that Caron feels is most important is teaching about relationships.

"We often emphasize the three traditional Rs, but rarely consider the fourth, relationships," Caron noted. "We seem to spend very little time explaining relationships and getting into the psychology of relationships.

"It's important to teach what it means to connect with another human being and what it means to be in a loving relationship, to have mutual respect, and understand what that means."

Being in the information age may be helpful in other areas of life, but according to Caron, when it comes to sexuality, the media only add to confusion.

"Take body image, for example. No one has a perfect body, but unfortunately the media are constantly telling us what's wrong with the way we look," she explained. "The irony with sex education is that we live in a culture where we have considerable information about many other topics. But while there is much about sex in the media, it often is not real or accurate information. The emphasis should be on trust, honesty, and committed relationships, rather than on body parts."

The demise of the double standard is far from complete, however. Attitudes toward sexual conduct are still typically more lenient for males than for females, even in relatively socially liberal cultures. And in some cultures, the standards for men and women are quite distinct. For example, in North Africa, the Middle East, and the majority of Asian countries, most women conform to societal norms suggesting that they abstain from sexual intercourse until they are married. In Mexico, where there are strict standards against premarital sex, males are also considerably more likely than females to have premarital sex. In contrast, in sub-Saharan Africa, women are more likely to have sexual intercourse prior to marriage, and intercourse is common among unmarried teenage women (Johnson et al., 1992; Peltzer & Pengpid, 2006; Wellings et al., 2006; Ghule, Balaiah, & Joshi, 2007).

Sexual Orientation: Heterosexuality, Homosexuality, and Bisexuality

When we consider adolescents' sexual development, the most frequent pattern is *heterosexuality,* sexual attraction and behavior directed to the other sex. Yet, some teenagers are *homosexual,* in which their sexual attraction and behavior is oriented to members of their own sex. (Many male homosexuals prefer the term *gay* and female homosexuals the label *lesbian,* because they refer to a broader array of attitudes and lifestyle than the term *homosexual,* which focuses on the sexual act.) Other people find they are *bisexual,* sexually attracted to people of both sexes.

The stresses of adolescence are magnified for homosexuals, who often face societal prejudice. Eventually, most adolescents come to groups with their sexual orientation, as this couple exemplifies.

Many teens experiment with homosexuality. At one time or another, around 20% to 25% of adolescent boys and 10% of adolescent girls have at least one same-sex sexual encounter. In fact, homosexuality and heterosexuality are not completely distinct sexual orientations. Alfred Kinsey, a pioneer sex researcher, argued that sexual orientation should be viewed as a continuum in which "exclusively homosexual" is at one end and "exclusively heterosexual" at the other (Kinsey, Pomeroy, & Martin, 1948). In between are people who show both homosexual and heterosexual behavior. Although accurate figures are difficult to obtain, most experts believe that between 4% and 10% of both men and women are exclusively homosexual during extended periods of their lives (Kinsey, Pomeroy, & Martin, 1948; Diamond, 2003a, 2003b; Russell & Consolacion, 2003).

The determination of sexual orientation is further complicated by distinctions between sexual orientation and gender identity. While sexual orientation relates to the object of one's sexual interests, *gender identity* is the gender a person believes he or she is psychologically. Sexual orientation and gender identity are not necessarily related to one another: A man who has a strong masculine gender identity may be attracted to other men. Consequently, the extent to which men and women enact traditional "masculine" or "feminine" behavior is not necessarily related to their sexual orientation or gender identity (Hunter & Mallon, 2000).

Some people feel they have been born the wrong physical sex, believing, for example, that they are women trapped in men's bodies. These *transgendered* individuals may pursue sexual reassignment surgery, a prolonged course of treatment in which they receive hormones and reconstructive surgery so they are able to take on the physical characteristics of the other sex.

Watch the **Video** *Adolescence: Identity and Role Development and Sexual Orientation* in **MyPsychLab**.

DEVELOPMENTAL DIVERSITY AND YOUR LIFE

What Determines Sexual Orientation?

The factors that induce people to develop as heterosexual, homosexual, or bisexual are not well understood. Evidence suggests that genetic and biological factors may play an important role. Studies of twins show that identical twins are more likely to both be homosexual than pairs of siblings who don't share their genetic makeup. Other research finds that various structures of the brain are different in homosexuals and heterosexuals, and hormone production also seems to be linked to sexual orientation (Fitzgerald, 2008; Balthazart, 2012).

Other researchers have suggested that family or peer environmental factors play a role. For example, Freud argued that homosexuality was the result of inappropriate identification with the opposite-sex parent (Freud, 1922/1959). The difficulty with Freud's theoretical perspective and other, similar perspectives that followed is that there simply is no evidence to suggest that any particular family dynamic or childrearing practice is consistently related to sexual orientation. Similarly, explanations based on learning theory, which suggest that homosexuality arises because of rewarding, pleasant homosexual experiences and unsatisfying heterosexual ones, do not appear to be the complete answer (Golombok & Tasker, 1996).

In short, there is no accepted explanation of why some adolescents develop a heterosexual orientation and others a homosexual orientation. Most experts believe that sexual orientation develops out of a complex interplay of genetic, physiological, and environmental factors (LeVay & Valente, 2003).

What is clear is that adolescents who find themselves attracted to members of the same sex may face a more difficult time than other teens. U.S. society still harbors great ignorance and prejudice regarding homosexuality, persisting in the belief that people have a choice in the matter—which they do not. Gay and lesbian teens may be rejected by their family or peers, or even harassed and assaulted if they are open about their orientation. The result is that adolescents who find themselves to be homosexual are at greater risk for depression, and suicide rates are significantly higher for homosexual adolescents than for heterosexual adolescents (Silenzio et al., 2007; Bos et al., 2008; Roberts, Schwartz, & Hart, 2011; van Gelderen et al., 2012).

Ultimately, however, most people are able to come to grips with their sexual orientation and become comfortable with it. Although lesbian, gay, and bisexuals may experience mental health difficulties as a result of the stress, prejudice, and discrimination they face, homosexuality is not considered a psychological disorder by any major psychological or medical associations. All of them endorse efforts to reduce discrimination against homosexuals (van Wormer & McKinney, 2003; Davison, 2005; Russell & McGuire, 2006). ■

This 16-year-old mother and her child are representative of a major social problem: teenage pregnancy. Why is teenage pregnancy a greater problem in the United States than in other countries?

Watch the **Video** *Teen Pregnancy* in **MyPsychLab**.

Teenage Pregnancies

Night has eased into day, but it is all the same for Tori Michel, 17. Her 5-day-old baby, Caitlin, has been fussing for hours, though she seems finally to have settled into the pink-and-purple car seat on the living-room sofa. "She wore herself out," explains Tori, who lives in a two-bedroom duplex in this St. Louis suburb with her mother, Susan, an aide to handicapped adults. "I think she just had gas."

Motherhood was not in Tori's plans for her senior year at Fort Zumwalt South High School—not until she had a "one-night thing" with James, a 21-year-old she met through friends. She had been taking birth-control pills but says she stopped after breaking up with a long-term boyfriend. "Wrong answer," she now says ruefully. (Gleick, Reed, & Schindehette, 1994)

Feedings at 3:00 a.m., diaper changes, and visits to the pediatrician are not part of most people's vision of adolescence. Yet, every year, more than 800,000 adolescents in the United States give birth. For these teenagers, life becomes increasingly challenging as they struggle with the demands of parenthood while still facing the complexities of adolescence.

The good news, though, is the number of teenage pregnancies is declining. In the last 10 years, the teenage birthrate has dropped 30%. Births to African American teenagers have shown the steepest decline, with births down by more than 40% in a decade. Overall the pregnancy rate of teenagers is 43 births per 1,000, a historic low (see Figure 12-2; Centers for Disease Control and Prevention, 2003; Colen, Geronimus, & Phipps, 2006; Hamilton et al., 2009).

Several factors explain the drop in teenage pregnancies:

* New initiatives have raised awareness among teenagers of the risks of unprotected sex. For example, about two thirds of high schools in the United States have established comprehensive sex education programs (Villarosa, 2003; Corcoran & Pillai, 2007).

* The rates of sexual intercourse among teenagers has declined, especially among younger adolescents. Only 13% of teens have ever had sex by the age of 15. (On the other hand, by their 19th birthday, 70% of teenagers of both sexes have had sexual intercourse [Guttmacher Institute, 2011].)

* The use of condoms and other forms of contraception has increased. For example, 79% of sexually experienced female teenagers use contraceptives the first time they have sex (Guttmacher Institute, 2011).

* Substitutes for sexual intercourse are more prevalent. For example, oral sex, which many teenagers do not even consider "sex," is increasingly viewed as an alternative to sexual intercourse (Bernstein, 2004).

The Challenges of Teenage Pregnancy.

Even with the decline in the birth rate for U.S. teenagers, the rate of teenage pregnancy in the United States is 2 to 10 times higher compared to that of other industrialized countries. For example, teenagers in the United States are twice as likely to become pregnant as Canadian teenagers, four times as likely as French adolescents, and six times more likely than Swedish teenagers (Singh & Darroch, 2000).

The results of an unintended pregnancy can be devastating to both mother and child. In comparison to

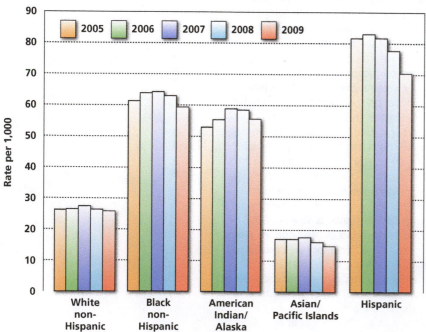

FIGURE 12-2 Teenage Pregnancy Rates

Although there has been a small increase in recent years, the rate of teenage pregnancies has dropped dramatically among all ethnic groups since 1991.

(*Source:* National Center for Chronic Disease Prevention and Health Promotion, 2011)

earlier times, teenage mothers today are much less likely to be married. In a high percentage of cases, mothers care for their children without the help of the father. Without financial or emotional support, a mother may have to abandon her own education, and consequently she may be relegated to unskilled, poorly paying jobs for the rest of her life. In other cases, she may develop long-term dependency on welfare. An adolescent mother's physical and mental health may suffer as she faces unrelenting stress due to continual demands on her time (Manlove et al., 2004; Lall, 2007; Koffman, 2012).

These difficulties affect the children of teenage mothers who also do not fare well. They are more likely to suffer from poor health and to show poorer school performance when compared to children of older mothers. Later, they are more likely to become teenage parents themselves, creating a cycle of pregnancy and poverty from which it is very difficult to extricate themselves (Carnegie Task Force, 1994; Spencer, 2001; East, Reyes, & Horn, 2007).

Virginity Pledges.   One thing that apparently *hasn't* led to a reduction in teenage pregnancies is asking adolescents to take a virginity pledge. Public pledges to refrain from premarital sex—a centerpiece of some forms of sex education—have a mixed record. Initial studies of virginity pledges were promising, showing that adolescents who took a pledge to defer sexual intercourse until marriage delayed sex about 18 months longer than those who had never taken such a pledge (Bearman & Bruckner, 2004).

But even this early research called virginity pledges into question. For example, the effectiveness of pledging depended on a student's age. For older adolescents (18 years old and above), taking a pledge had no effect. Pledges were effective only for 16- and 17-year-olds. Furthermore, the pledges worked only when a minority of people in a school took such a pledge. When more than 30% took such a pledge, the effectiveness of the pledge diminished substantially.

The reason for this surprising finding relates to why virginity pledges might work: They offer adolescents a sense of identity, similar to the way joining a club does. When a minority of students take a virginity pledge, they feel part of a special group, and they are more likely to adhere to the norms of that group—in this case, remaining a virgin. In contrast, if a majority of students take a pledge of virginity, the pledge becomes less unique and adherence is less likely.

Most recent research, however, finds that virginity pledges are ineffective. For example, in one study of 12,000 teenagers, 88% reported eventually having sexual intercourse, although taking a pledge did delay the start of sex (Bearman et al., 2004).

Because abstinence programs have not been successful, some researchers have called for more comprehensive education programs to replace ones that focus on abstinence as the only option. Most parents and teachers agree that abstinence education should be emphasized, but that information on contraception and safer sex practices should be included as well. Research supports these beliefs: While abstinence-only programs and programs that include contraception education do not clearly differ in their effects on adolescents' sexual activity, the addition of contraception education does improve adolescents' understanding and use of birth-control strategies (Giami et al., 2006; Santelli et al., 2006; Stauss, Boyas, & Murphy-Erby, 2012).

Safer Choices, a two-year program for adolescents in high school, is one such program that combines encouragement of abstinence with education on contraceptive use. Its goals are to reduce the number of students who are sexually active while in high school and to increase condom usage in students who do have sex by addressing adolescent sexual activity on multiple fronts. The program attempts to modify students' attitudes and norms about sexual behavior, abstinence, and condom use (including adolescents' perceived barriers to condom use). It also addresses students' confidence in their ability to refuse sex, to discuss safer sex with their partners, and to use a condom, and it teaches students about sexually transmitted diseases and their risks of infection. Finally, the program seeks to improve students' communication with their parents about sex (Advocates for Youth, 2003; Kirby et al., 2004).

ARE YOU AN INFORMED CONSUMER OF DEVELOPMENT?

Preventing Unwanted Pregnancy

If you're concerned about the possibility of an unwanted pregnancy and its harmful consequences, your first line of defense is to educate yourself on prevention methods. A number of birth control options are available that are appropriate for adolescents, each with its own advantages and disadvantages. A physician can help choose the method that is best for each individual. Following are some recommendations that are effective (Food and Drug Administration, 2003; Knowles, 2005).

- **Abstinence.** Abstaining from sex is the only birth control method that is guaranteed to be 100% effective. Abstinence requires no special equipment or medical supervision, costs nothing, and prevents sexually transmitted disease as well as unwanted pregnancy. The downside of abstinence is that some people find it difficult to refrain from sex, and if they have not explored alternative methods of birth control, they may not be prepared to protect themselves from unwanted pregnancy when they do become sexually active.

- **Outercourse.** *Outercourse* is sexual activity that does not involve vaginal intercourse. It may include kissing, masturbation, massage, or oral sex. Outercourse is 100% effective against pregnancy as long as no semen comes in contact with the vaginal area.

- **Condoms.** A condom, a sheath that covers the penis during intercourse, provides a barrier against the transmission of semen. Condoms are 85–98% effective against pregnancy, depending in part on how they are used (the addition of a spermicidal lubricant enhances their effectiveness). Condoms also provide protection against sexually transmitted diseases, and they are widely available and generally inexpensive. Relying on condoms to prevent unwanted pregnancy means that a condom must be used every time sexual intercourse occurs.

- **Birth control pills.** Birth control pills contain hormones that prevent pregnancy by interfering with egg fertilization. They are 92–99% effective against pregnancy, but they must be prescribed by a physician. Birth control pills have the advantage of providing continuous protection against unwanted pregnancy—you don't have to remember to do anything special at the time of intercourse. Their main disadvantage is that they must be taken daily, whether or not one is having sex.

- **Prescription barriers.** A prescription barrier, such as a diaphragm, is treated with spermicide and then inserted into the vagina before intercourse, where it blocks the transmission of semen. Prescription barriers are an alternative to daily hormone use for women who have intercourse only occasionally. They are available through a physician, and they are 84–94% effective against pregnancy. However, barriers can be difficult to use correctly, and like condoms, they must be used every time one has intercourse. ■

Review, Check, and Apply

Review

1. Masturbation, once viewed very negatively, is now generally regarded as a normal and harmless practice that continues into adulthood.

2. Sexual intercourse is a major milestone that most people reach during adolescence. The age of first intercourse reflects cultural differences and has been declining over the last 50 years.

3. Sexual orientation, which is most accurately viewed as a continuum rather than categorically, develops as the result of a complex combination of factors.

4. Teenage pregnancy is a problem in the United States, with negative consequences for adolescent mothers and their children.

Check

1. The current norm that has replaced the double standard is _____ _____ _____.

2. _____ individuals feel they have been born the wrong physical sex.

3. _____ pledges have been largely ineffective in reducing the incidence of premarital sex.

Apply

1. Do you think the double standard, which approved male sexual activity but condemned female sexual activity, has entirely disappeared? Does popular culture work to eliminate or perpetuate the double standard?

To see more review questions, log on to MyPsychLab.

ANSWERS: 1. permissiveness with affection   2. Transgendered   3. Virginity

The CASE
of . . . *the Wrong Role Models?*

Jim Martell has been watching his son Jason carefully. Because Jim runs a business 90 minutes from home, his wife Tessa, who works right in the neighborhood, has had primary responsibility for raising Jason, and Jim has been growing steadily more worried over the four years of Jason's life.

First it was Jason's quiet voice and shy, gentle mannerisms. Then it was his quiet insistence on getting a doll for Christmas at age 3, which Jim felt he had at least managed to sabotage by picking a G.I. Joe. Of course, Jim's anxiety mounted when Jason spent more time dressing Joe in different outfits than making him run around and blow things up. Then it was Jason's love of drawing and making clay models instead of playing with the neat toy guns and sports gear that Jim brought home for him.

Jim has long believed that his big mistake was letting Tessa place Jason in a local daycare where all the other kids are girls. Jim is convinced that this environment has influenced Jason's choices and made him more feminine. He is hoping that next year

Jason's kindergarten class will have more boys in it so his son can escape from the undue pressure to conform to a girl's lifestyle.

1. Given what you know about gender differences in preschoolers, are Jim's worries about Jason's mannerisms and habits justified? Why or why not?

2. Jim attributes Jason's behaviors to environmental influences. Could genetics also be a factor? Can the relative influences of nature and nurture be determined accurately?

3. If Jason attended an all-boys daycare, would his behavior and preferences necessarily be different? Why or why not?

4. Which perspective—biological, psychoanalytic, social learning, or cognitive—provides the most satisfying explanation for Jason's behavior? Why?

5. Do you think Jim is right that exposure to boys in kindergarten will change Jason's behavior? If so, how might this work?

‹‹‹ LOOKING BACK

LO 12-1 What differences are there between boys and girls in terms of behavior and treatment, and how does a sense of gender develop?

- From the moment of birth, girls and boys are treated differently and are subject to different expectations. Mothers and fathers display different interaction patterns with their children, and the toy and play preferences of boys and girls differ and are differently

encouraged by their parents. Furthermore, boys' and girls' actions are interpreted differently by parents and other adults.

- Actual biologically based behavioral differences between boy and girl infants exist, but they are minor compared to the behavioral similarities between genders. However, as children age, gender differences become more pronounced, mostly because of environmental factors.

- By the preschool years, gender is well established in terms of self-understanding and behavior. Preschoolers hold expectations about gender-appropriate behavior that are more rigid than at any other time during the life span, and they form ideas about the different careers that are appropriate for men and women.

- The strong gender expectations held by preschoolers are explained in different ways by different theorists. Some point to genetic factors as evidence for a biological explanation of gender expectations. Freud's psychoanalytic theories use a framework based on the subconscious. Social learning theorists focus on environmental influences, including parents, teachers, peers, and the media, while cognitive theorists propose that children form gender schemas, cognitive frameworks that organize information that the children gather about gender.

LO 12-2 How does gender affect friendships?

- In the preschool years, boys and girls increasingly prefer same-gender friendships, a trend that grows stronger in middle childhood with the result that most children's social networks are limited to members of their own gender.

- Male friendships in middle childhood are characterized by groups, clear dominance hierarchies, and restrictive play, while female friendships tend to involve one or two close relationships, equal status, and a reliance on cooperation.

- During adolescence, boys and girls begin to spend time together in groups and, toward the end of adolescence, to pair off.

LO 12-3 What are the functions and characteristics of dating during adolescence?

- During adolescence, dating provides intimacy, entertainment, and prestige. Achieving psychological intimacy, difficult at first, becomes easier as adolescents mature, gain confidence, and take relationships more seriously.

LO 12-4 How does sexuality develop in the adolescent years?

- For most adolescents, masturbation is often the first step into sexuality. The age of first intercourse, which is now in the teens, has declined as the double standard has faded and the norm of permissiveness with affection has gained ground. However, as more and more adolescents have become aware of the threat of STDs and AIDS, the rate of sexual intercourse has declined.

LO 12-5 Why are there different sexual orientations, and what determines one's orientation?

- The most common sexual orientation among adolescents is heterosexuality, with a smaller number of adolescents having homosexual or bisexual orientations.

- Homosexuality and heterosexuality, rather than being distinct sexual orientations, are regarded by some researchers as a continuum along which people experience their individual sexuality, which may change over time.

- The factors that cause individuals to develop as heterosexual, homosexual, or bisexual are not completely understood, but genetic and biological factors play an important role, most likely in combination with physiological and environmental factors.

- Gay and lesbian adolescents face challenges in a society that continues to be prejudiced against homosexuality, including the challenge of informing their parents of their orientation.

LO 12-6 What are the consequences of teen pregnancy, and how effective have abstinence programs been in preventing it?

- Many teenage mothers are unmarried and must care for their children without help from the father. This often means they must abandon their own education; as a result, they end up trapped in poorly paying jobs or develop a long-term dependency on welfare.

- Adolescent mothers may suffer physical and mental health problems because of the unrelenting stress they face from continual demands on their time.

- Children of teenage mothers also struggle. They are more likely to suffer from poor health and to show poorer school performance when compared to children of older mothers. They are also more likely to become teenage parents themselves, perpetuating a cycle of pregnancy and poverty.

- Virginity pledges for teenagers 18 years and older seem to have no effect. For adolescents ages 16 and 17, the pledges may be effective when only a small number of their peers pledge. The reason for this may be that having a small group involved in the pledge offers adolescents a sense of identity, similar to the way joining a club does, making them more likely to adhere to the pledge.

- Although programs focused on abstinence education have not proven successful, comprehensive sex education programs that feature abstinence as only one option, while also providing information on contraception and safer sex practices, have improved teenagers' understanding and use of birth-control strategies.

KEY TERMS AND CONCEPTS

gender (p. 328)
sex (p. 328)
androgens (p. 331)
corpus callosum (p. 331)

identification (p. 332)
gender identity (p. 333)
gender schema (p. 333)
gender constancy (p. 333)

sex cleavage (p. 335)
dominance hierarchy (p. 336)
masturbation (p. 340)

Epilogue

In this chapter we examined the development of gender awareness and how gender affects social relationships. We saw how preschoolers have a strong sense of being male or female, and of traditional gender roles and expectations. We discussed a range of theories that attempt to account for gender differences, including both biological and social theories. We also looked at how friendship, starting in the preschool years, becomes segregated by gender, a trend that continues until adolescence when teens begin socializing in mixed gender groups as a prelude to dating. We then examined the role dating plays in adolescents' lives as teens learn how to establish intimacy with another individual. Next, we discussed how adolescents become sexual and considered sexual orientation and how it is determined. In conclusion, we examined the challenges of teen pregnancy and looked at how effective abstinence programs have been in reducing it.

Turn back to the prologue to this chapter, about David's dilemma regarding sports, and answer the following questions.

1. How does this story relate to the typical gender patterns of friendship in middle childhood?

2. How do you think David's dislike of sports and the resulting drop in his popularity will affect his relationships with other boys in adolescence? With girls?

3. Based on evidence in the prologue, what might you deduce about the way David's parents treated him as an infant and preschooler in regard to gender?

4. Do you think David could find another way to be "one of the boys"? Do you think he should try? Why or why not?

The Development Video Series in MyPsychLab

Explore the video **The Basics: Sex and Gender Differences** by scanning this QR code with your mobile device. If you don't already have one, you may download a free QR scanner for your device wherever smartphone apps are sold. You can also view this video in MyPsychLab. For more videos related to this chapter's content, log into MyPsychLab to view the entire Development Video Series.

MyVirtualChild

- **What decisions would you make while raising a child?**
- **What would the consequences of those decisions be?**

Find out by accessing **MyVirtualChild** at

www.MyPsychLab.com

and raising your own virtual child from birth to age 18.

13 Moral Development and Aggression

MODULE 13.1

DEVELOPING MORALITY: FOLLOWING SOCIETY'S RIGHTS AND WRONGS

- Piaget's View of Moral Development
- Social Learning Approaches to Morality
- Empathy and Moral Behavior
- Effective Parenting: Teaching Desired Behavior

FROM RESEARCH TO PRACTICE: Parenting Coaches: Teaching Parents to Teach Their Children

Review, Check, and Apply

MODULE 13.2

MORAL REASONING AND PROSOCIAL BEHAVIOR

- Kohlberg's Approach to Moral Development
- Gilligan's Approach to Moral Development: Gender and Morality

CAREERS IN DEVELOPMENT: Jelani Quinn, Mediator

- Moral Behavior and Moral Reasoning: Why the Disconnect?

Review, Check, and Apply

MODULE 13.3

AGGRESSION AND VIOLENCE

- Aggression and Violence in Preschoolers: Sources and Consequences
- Roots of Aggression

ARE YOU AN INFORMED CONSUMER OF DEVELOPMENT? Increasing Moral Behavior and Reducing Aggression in Preschool-Age Children

DEVELOPMENTAL DIVERSITY AND YOUR LIFE: Is Aggression As American As Apple Pie?

- Schoolyard—and Cyber-Yard—Bullies
- Juvenile Delinquency: The Crimes of Adolescence

Review, Check, and Apply

The Case of . . . The Turncoat Friend

Looking Back

Key Terms and Concepts

Epilogue

PROLOGUE: Jesse's Dilemma

The most important game of the football season had ended in disappointment for Jesse and his friends. Their archrival team, the Southridge Wolverines, had trounced them 28 to 3. Now, Jesse and his friends stood before the Wolverine's empty bus, their disappointment turning to anger. Suddenly, a rock smashed one of the bus's windows. A second rock made a large dent just behind the driver's seat. "Wolverines SUCK!" the boys shouted as they lobbed every rock within their reach. Two more windows shattered. The door was bent in its frame.

Jesse stood rooted to the spot, heart pounding. He couldn't believe his friends were taking things this far. He hated the fact that his team had lost, especially to the Wolverines—rich kids from an affluent community who looked down their noses at working-class boys like Jesse—but he knew it was wrong to smash up the bus. It wouldn't solve any problems.

Glancing nervously at his friends, he confirmed his fear: He was the only one not participating in the spree of destruction. Slowly, he knelt and patted the ground in the darkness until he found a suitable rock. He stood, hefting the rock's weight, raising his arm, then lowering it.

"Cops!" one of the boys shouted. "Run!"

Jesse took careful aim and heaved his rock with his best fast ball pitch. It hit its intended target— the empty space five feet in front of the bus. Jesse turned and ran with the others into the safety of the black night.

Evaluating what is the right course of action becomes increasingly complicated as our ability to reason matures.

>>> LOOKING AHEAD

As Jesse's story illustrates, morality is a complex issue. Evaluating what is the right course of action becomes increasingly complicated as our ability to reason matures. We must take into account all the specifics of a given situation, and often weigh one imperfect course of action against another. And we must find ways to manage our more violent emotions.

In this chapter, we examine two key aspects of social behavior: moral development and aggression. We begin by considering how children develop a sense of society's

(continued)

Learning Objectives

MODULE 13.1

LO1 How do children develop a moral sense?

LO2 What sorts of disciplinary styles do parents employ, and what effects do they have?

MODULE 13.2

LO3 Through what stages does moral development progress during childhood and adolescence?

LO4 How do adolescent girls differ from boys in moral development?

LO5 As adolescents become more sophisticated morally, how does their behavior change?

MODULE 13.3

LO6 How does aggression develop in preschool-age children?

LO7 What forms does aggression take in middle childhood and adolescence, and what are some of the characteristics of its perpetrators?

rights and wrongs, and how that development can lead them to be helpful to others. We look at a variety of perspectives, ranging from Piaget's arguments about the changes in children's understanding of morality to approaches that emphasize how children learn to behave morally by imitating others' moral acts. We also consider how empathy, which begins to develop in infancy, may influence moral behavior. We then look at a range of parenting styles and discuss how parents and other authority figures use discipline to shape children's behavior.

Next, we discuss the development of moral reasoning and behavior. We see how reasoning about moral dilemmas changes in adolescence, and how the expression of moral and helping behavior develops. We also look at how gender and culture influence prosocial behavior.

We then turn to aggression and violence, considering both its sources and consequences. We ask whether aggression is an innate, genetically determined behavior and/or a response a child learns from the environment while growing up. We consider, too, ways of decreasing aggression in children and increasing their moral behaviors. We also discuss bullying, a form of aggression that has reached epidemic levels—sometimes with fatal consequences—and violence in schools. We end the chapter with a look at juvenile delinquency.

MODULE 13.1

DEVELOPING MORALITY: FOLLOWING SOCIETY'S RIGHTS AND WRONGS

LO 13-1 How do children develop a moral sense?

LO 13-2 What sorts of disciplinary styles do parents employ, and what effects do they have?

> *Lena and Carrie were part of a group of preschoolers who wanted to act out Goldilocks and the Three Bears. The teacher began assigning parts. "Carrie, you can be Baby Bear. And Lena, you be Goldilocks." Tears welled up in Carrie's eyes. "I don't want to be Baby Bear," she sobbed. Lena put her arms around Carrie. "You can be Goldilocks, too. We'll be the Goldilocks twins." Carrie cheered up at once, grateful that Lena had understood her feelings and responded with kindness.*

In this short scenario, we see many of the key elements of morality, as it is played out among preschool-age children. Changes in children's views of what is ethically right and what is the right way to behave are an important element of growth during the preschool years.

At the same time, the kind of aggression displayed by preschoolers is also changing. We can consider the development of morality and aggression as two sides of the coin of human conduct, and both involve a growing awareness of others.

Moral development refers to changes in people's sense of justice and of what is right and wrong, and in their behavior related to moral issues. Developmentalists have considered moral development in terms of children's reasoning about morality, their attitudes toward moral lapses, and their behavior when faced with moral issues. In the process of studying moral development, psychologists have evolved several approaches.

Piaget's View of Moral Development

Child psychologist Jean Piaget was one of the first to study questions of moral development. He suggested that moral development, like cognitive development, proceeds in stages (Piaget, 1932). The earliest stage is a broad form of moral thinking he called **heteronomous moral-ity,** in which rules are seen as invariant and unchangeable. During this stage, which lasts from

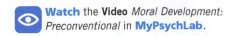

Watch the **Video** *Moral Development: Preconventional* in **MyPsychLab**.

moral development The changes in people's sense of justice and of what is right and wrong, and in their behavior related to moral issues

heteronomous morality Piaget's earliest stage of moral development lasting from about age 4 through 7 in which rules are seen as invariant and unchangeable

about age 4 through age 7, children play games rigidly, assuming that there is one, and only one, way to play and that every other way is wrong. At the same time, though, preschool-age children may not even fully grasp game rules. Consequently, a group of children may be playing together, with each child playing according to a slightly different set of rules. Nevertheless, they enjoy playing with others. Piaget suggests that every child may "win" such a game, because winning is equated with having a good time, as opposed to truly competing with others.

This rigid heteronomous morality is ultimately replaced by two later stages of morality: incipient cooperation and autonomous cooperation. As its name implies, in the **incipient cooperation stage,** which lasts from around age 7 to age 10, children's games become more clearly social. Children learn the actual formal rules of games, and they play according to this shared knowledge. Consequently, rules are still seen as largely unchangeable. There is a "right" way to play the game, and children play according to these formal rules.

It is not until the **autonomous cooperation stage,** which begins at about age 10, that children become fully aware that formal game rules can be modified if the people who play them agree. The later transition into more sophisticated forms of moral development—which we will consider further on—also is reflected in school-age children's understanding that rules of law are created by people and are subject to change according to the will of people.

Until these later stages are reached, however, children's reasoning about rules and issues of justice is bounded in the concrete. For instance, consider the following two stories:

Pedro comes home from preschool. On the table where he usually has his afternoon snack there is a plate of cookies. Thinking they are for him, he eats four cookies. His mother comes in and says she made the cookies for a bake sale to raise money for his school.

Steven's preschool class is having a party. Each child has been given two cookies and a cup of punch. Steven eats his two cookies. When he sees another child, Lizzie, leave her seat, he takes one of her cookies and eats it.

Piaget found that a preschool child in the heteronomous morality stage would judge the child who took 4 cookies as being worse than the one who took just 1 cookie. In contrast, children who have moved beyond the heteronomous morality stage would consider the child who took one cookie as being naughtier. The reason: Children in the heteronomous morality stage do not take *intention* into account.

Children in the heteronomous stage of moral development also believe in immanent justice. **Immanent justice** is the notion that rules that are broken earn immediate punishment. Preschool children believe that if they do something wrong, they will be punished instantly—even if no one sees them carrying out their misdeeds. In contrast, older children understand that punishments for misdeeds are determined and meted out by people.

Evaluating Piaget's Approach to Moral Development.
Recent research suggests that although Piaget was on the right track in his description of how moral development proceeds, his approach suffers from the same problem we encountered in his theory of cognitive development. Specifically, Piaget underestimated the age at which children's moral skills are honed.

It is now clear that preschool-age children understand the notion of intentionality by about age 3, and this allows them to make judgments based on intent at an earlier age than Piaget supposed. Specifically, when provided with moral questions that emphasize intent, preschool children judge someone who is intentionally bad as more "naughty" than someone who is unintentionally bad, but who creates more objective damage. Moreover, by the age of 4, they judge intentional lying wrong (Bussey, 1992; LoBue et al., 2011; Chee & Morachver, 2012).

Piaget believed that at the heteronomous morality stage, this child would feel that the degree to which she had done the wrong thing is directly related to the number of items broken.

incipient cooperation stage Piaget's stage of moral development lasting from around age 7 to 10 in which children's games become more clearly social

autonomous cooperation stage Piaget's stage of moral development that begins around age 10 when children become fully aware that formal game rules can be modified if the people who play them agree

immanent justice The notion that rules that are broken earn immediate punishment

Studies have shown that children who view someone behaving generously are apt to follow the model's example.

Social Learning Approaches to Morality

Social learning approaches to moral development stand in stark contrast to Piaget's approach. While Piaget emphasizes how limitations in preschoolers' cognitive development lead to particular forms of moral *reasoning,* social learning approaches focus more on how the environment in which preschoolers operate produces **prosocial behavior,** helping behavior that benefits others (Eisenberg, 2004; Spinrad, Eisenberg, & Bernt, 2007).

Social learning approaches build upon the behavioral approaches that we first discussed in Chapter 1. They acknowledge that some instances of children's prosocial behavior stem from situations in which they have received positive reinforcement for acting in a morally appropriate way. For instance, when Claire's mother tells her she has been a "good girl" for sharing a box of candy with her brother Dan, Claire's behavior has been reinforced. As a consequence, she is more likely to engage in sharing behavior in the future (Ramaswamy & Bergin, 2009; Schonert-Reichl et al., 2012).

Social learning approaches go a step further, arguing that not all prosocial behavior has to be directly performed and subsequently reinforced for learning to occur. According to social learning approaches, children also learn moral behavior more indirectly by observing the behavior of others, called *models* (Bandura, 1977). Children imitate models who receive reinforcement for their behavior, and ultimately they learn to perform the behavior themselves. For example, when Claire's friend Jake watches Claire share her candy with her brother, and Claire is praised for her behavior, Jake is more likely to engage in sharing behavior himself at some later point.

Quite a few studies illustrate the power of models and of social learning more generally in producing prosocial behavior in preschool-age children. For example, experiments have shown that children who view someone behaving generously or unselfishly are apt to follow the model's example, subsequently behaving in a generous or unselfish manner themselves when put in a similar situation. The opposite also holds true: If a model behaves selfishly, children who observe such behavior tend to behave more selfishly themselves (Hastings et al., 2007).

Not all models are equally effective in producing prosocial responses. For instance, preschoolers are more apt to model the behavior of warm, responsive adults than of adults who appear colder (Yarrow, Scott, & Waxler, 1973; Bandura, 1977). Furthermore, models viewed as highly competent or high in prestige are more effective than others.

Children do more than simply mimic unthinkingly behavior that they see rewarded in others. By observing moral conduct, they are reminded of society's norms about the importance of moral behavior as conveyed by parents, teachers, and other powerful authority figures. They notice the connections between particular situations and certain kinds of behavior. This increases the likelihood that similar situations will elicit similar behavior in the observer.

Consequently, modeling paves the way for the development of more general rules and principles in a process called **abstract modeling**. Rather than always modeling the particular behavior of others, older preschoolers begin to develop generalized principles that underlie the behavior that they observe. After observing repeated instances in which a model is rewarded for acting in a morally desirable way, children begin the process of inferring and learning the general principles of moral conduct (Bandura, 1991; Zimmerman & Schunk, 2003).

Empathy and Moral Behavior

Empathy is the understanding of what another individual feels. According to some developmentalists, empathy lies at the heart of moral behavior. The roots of empathy grow early. One-year-old infants cry when they hear other infants crying. By 2 and 3, toddlers will offer gifts and spontaneously share toys with other children and adults, even if they are strangers (Vaish, Carpenter, & Tomasello, 2009).

During the preschool years, empathy continues to grow. Some theorists believe that increasing empathy—as well as other positive emotions, such as sympathy and admiration—leads children to behave in a more moral fashion. In addition, some negative emotions—such as anger at an unfair situation or shame over previous transgressions—also may promote moral behavior (Decety & Jackson, 2006; Vinik, Almas, & Grusec, 2011; Goldstein & Winner, 2012).

prosocial behavior Helping behavior that benefits others

abstract modeling A process of modeling that paves the way for the development of more general rules and principles

empathy The understanding of what another individual feels

The notion that negative emotions may promote moral development is one that Freud first suggested in his theory of psychoanalytic personality development. Recall from our earlier discussion that Freud argued that a child's *superego,* the part of the personality that represents societal dos and don'ts, is developed through resolution of the *Oedipal conflict.* Children come to identify with their same-sex parent, incorporating that parent's standards of morality to avoid unconscious guilt raised by the Oedipal conflict.

Whether or not we accept Freud's account of the Oedipal conflict and the guilt it produces, his theory is consistent with more recent findings. These suggest that preschoolers' attempts to avoid experiencing negative emotions sometimes lead them to act in more moral, helpful ways. For instance, one reason children help others is to avoid the feelings of personal distress that they experience when they are confronted with another person's unhappiness or misfortune (Valiente, Eisenberg, & Fabes, 2004; Eisenberg, Valiente & Champion, 2005).

Children with authoritarian parents tend to be withdrawn and are not very friendly, in part because the parents are controlling and rigid. What are the consequences of parents who are too permissive? Too authoritative? Too uninvolved?

Around the start of adolescence, more sophisticated kinds of empathy begin to emerge. Adolescents experience empathy not only in specific situations but also empathy for collective groups, such as people living in poverty or victims of racism (Hoffman, 1991, 2001; Eisenberg, Fabes, & Spinread, 2006).

For example, in early adolescence, a teenager may experience empathy when she learns a friend is ill. Understanding the emotions that the friend is experiencing—concerns about missing classes, fear about falling behind, and so forth—may lead the teenager to offer help to her classmate. On the other hand, when hearing about victims of an outbreak of bird flu in China, the same girl may be emotionally unmoved.

However, later in adolescence, as her cognitive abilities increase and she can reason on more abstract levels, the same girl may feel empathy for collective groups. Not only may she feel emotionally involved over victims of specific situations (such as people who lost their homes as a consequence of Hurricane Katrina), but she may experience deep emotional responses toward abstract groups such as the homeless, whose experiences may be completely unfamiliar to her.

Effective Parenting: Teaching Desired Behavior

While she thinks no one is looking, Maria goes into her brother Alejandro's bedroom, where he has been saving the last of his Halloween candy. Just as she takes his last Reese's Peanut Butter Cup, the children's mother walks into the room and immediately takes in the situation.

If you were Maria's mother, which of the following reactions seems most reasonable?

1. Tell Maria that she must go to her room and stay there for the rest of the day, and that she is going to lose access to her favorite blanket, the one she sleeps with every night and during naps.

2. Mildly tell Maria that what she did was not such a good idea, and she shouldn't do it in the future.

3. Explain why her brother Alejandro was going to be upset, and tell her that she must go to her room for an hour as punishment.

4. Forget about it, and let the children sort it out themselves.

Each of these four alternative responses represents one of the major parenting styles identified by Diana Baumrind (1980) and updated by Eleanor Maccoby and colleagues (Maccoby & Martin, 1983).

Authoritarian parents respond as in the first alternative. They are controlling, punitive, rigid, cold. Their word is law, and they value strict, unquestioning obedience from their children. They also do not tolerate expressions of disagreement.

Permissive parents, in contrast, provide lax and inconsistent feedback, as in the second alternative. They require little of their children, and they don't see themselves as holding much responsibility for how their children turn out. They place little or no limits or control on their children's behavior.

authoritarian parents   Parents who are controlling, punitive, rigid, cold. Their word is law, and they value strict, unquestioning obedience from their children

permissive parents   Parents who require little of their children and don't see themselves as holding much responsibility for how their children turn out. They place little or no limits or control on their children's behavior

TABLE 13-1 Parenting Styles

How Demanding Parents Are of Children ▶	Demanding	Undemanding
How Responsive Parents Are to a Child ▼	**Authoritative**	**Permissive**
Highly Responsive	**Characteristics:** firm, setting clear and consistent limits. **Relationship with Children:** Although they tend to be relatively strict, like authoritarian parents, they are loving and emotionally supportive and encourage their children to be independent. They also try to reason with their children, giving explanations for why they should behave in a particular way, and communicate the rationale for any punishment they may impose.	**Characteristics:** lax and inconsistent feedback. **Relationship with Children:** They require little of their children, and they don't see themselves as holding much responsibility for how their children turn out. They place few or no limits or control on their children's behavior.
	Authoritarian	**Uninvolved**
Low Responsive	**Characteristics:** controlling, punitive, rigid, cold. **Relationship with Children:** Their word is law, and they value strict, unquestioning obedience from their children. They also do not tolerate expressions of disagreement.	**Characteristics:** displaying indifferent, rejecting behavior. **Relationship with Children:** They are detached emotionally and see their role as only providing food, clothing, and shelter. In its extreme form, this parenting style results in neglect, a form of child abuse.

(*Source:* Based on Baumrind, 1971; Maccoby & Martin, 1983.)

Authoritative parents are firm, setting clear and consistent limits. Although they tend to be relatively strict, like authoritarian parents, they are loving and emotionally supportive. They also try to reason with their children, giving explanations for why they should behave in a particular way ("Alejandro is going to be upset"), and communicating the rationale for any punishment they may impose. Authoritative parents encourage their children to be independent.

Finally, **uninvolved parents** show virtually no interest in their children, displaying indifferent, rejecting behavior. They are detached emotionally and see their role as no more than feeding, clothing, and providing shelter for their child. In its most extreme form, uninvolved parenting results in **neglect**, a form of child abuse. (The four patterns are summarized in Table 13-1.)

Does the particular style of discipline that parents use result in differences in children's behavior? The answer is very much yes—although, as you might expect, there are many exceptions (Arredondo et al., 2006; Simons & Conger, 2007; Kumar, Sharda, & Hooda, 2012):

- Children of authoritarian parents tend to be withdrawn, showing relatively little sociability. They are not very friendly, often behaving uneasily around their peers. Girls who are raised by authoritarian parents are especially dependent on their parents, whereas boys are unusually hostile.

- Permissive parents have children who, in many ways, share the undesirable characteristics of children of authoritarian parents. Children with permissive parents tend to be dependent and moody, and they are low in social skills and self-control.

- Children of authoritative parents fare best. They generally are independent, friendly with their peers, self-assertive, and cooperative. They have strong motivation to achieve, and

authoritative parents Parents who are firm, setting clear and consistent limits. Although they tend to be relatively strict, like authoritarian parents, they are loving and emotionally supportive

uninvolved parents Parents who show virtually no interest in their children, displaying indifferent, rejecting behavior. They are detached emotionally and see their role as no more than feeding, clothing, and providing shelter for their child

neglect A form of child abuse

they are typically successful and likable. They regulate their own behavior effectively, both in terms of their relationships with others and emotional self-regulation.

Some authoritative parents also display several characteristics that have come to be called *supportive parenting*, including parental warmth, proactive teaching, calm discussion during disciplinary episodes, and interest and involvement in children's peer activities. Children whose parents engage in such supportive parenting show better adjustment and are better protected from the consequences of later adversity they may encounter (Pettit, Bates, & Dodge, 1997; Belluck, 2000; Kaufmann et al., 2000).

• Children whose parents show uninvolved parenting styles are the worst off. Their parents' lack of involvement disrupts their emotional development considerably, leading them to feel unloved and emotionally detached, and impedes their physical and cognitive development as well.

The style of parenting that is most effective depends on what parents in a particular culture are taught regarding appropriate childbearing practices.

While such classification systems are useful ways of categorizing and describing parents' behavior, they are not a recipe for success. Parenting and growing up are more complicated than that! For instance, in a significant number of cases the children of authoritarian and permissive parents develop quite successfully.

Furthermore, most parents are not entirely consistent: Although the authoritarian, permissive, authoritative, and uninvolved patterns describe general styles, sometimes parents switch from their dominant mode to one of the others. For instance, when a child darts into the street, even the most laid-back and permissive parent is likely to react in a harsh, authoritarian manner, laying down strict demands about safety. In such cases, authoritarian styles may be most effective (Janssens & Dekovic, 1997; Holden & Miller, 1999; Eisenberg & Valiente, 2002; Gershoff, 2002).

Watch the **Video** *In the Real World: Parenting Styles and Socialization* in **MyPsychLab**.

Cultural Differences in Childrearing Practices.
It's important to keep in mind that the findings regarding childrearing styles we have been discussing are chiefly applicable to Western societies. The style of parenting that is most successful may depend quite heavily on the norms of a particular culture—and what parents in a particular culture are taught regarding appropriate childrearing practices (Giles-Sims & Lockhart, 2005; Dwairy et al., 2006; Hulei, Zevenbergen, & Jacobs, 2006).

For example, the Chinese concept of *chiao shun* suggests that parents should be strict, firm, and in tight control of their children's behavior. Parents are seen to have a duty to train their children to adhere to socially and culturally desirable standards of behavior, particularly those manifested in good school performance. Children's acceptance of such an approach to discipline is seen as a sign of parental respect (Wu, Robinson, & Yang, 2002; Chen, Chen, & Zhang, 2012).

Parents in China are typically highly directive with their children, pushing them to excel and controlling their behavior to a considerably higher degree than parents typically do in Western countries. And it works: Children of Asian parents tend to be quite successful, particularly academically (Steinberg, Dornbusch, & Brown, 1992; Nelson et al., 2006).

In contrast, U.S. parents are generally advised to use authoritative methods and explicitly to avoid authoritarian measures. Interestingly, it wasn't always this way. Until World War II, the point of view that dominated the advice literature was authoritarian, apparently founded on Puritan religious influences that suggested that children had "original sin" or that they needed to have their wills broken (Smuts & Hagen, 1985).

In short, the childrearing practices that parents are urged to follow reflect cultural perspectives about the nature of children as well as about the appropriate role of parents and their support system (see the *From Research to Practice* box on page 358). No single parenting pattern or style, then, is likely to be universally appropriate or likely invariably to produce successful children (Harwood et al., 1996; Hart et al., 1998; Wang & Tamis-LeMonda, 2003).

Similarly, it is important to keep in mind that childrearing practices are not the sole influence on children's development. For example, sibling and peer influences play a significant

FROM RESEARCH TO PRACTICE
Parenting Coaches: Teaching Parents to Teach Their Children

What tripped Lisa D'Annolfo Levey's maternal tolerance meter on a recent Tuesday afternoon was not just the toy fotoball her 7-year-old son, Skylar, zinged across the living room, nearly toppling her teacup. Or the karate kick sprung by her 4-year-old, Forrest, which Ms. Levey ducked, barely.

The clincher was the full-throttle duel with foam swords, her boys whooping and squealing, flailing their weapons at the blue leather couch, the yellow kidney-shaped rug, and, ultimately, their mother.

"Forrest, how about you come up and hug Skylar instead of whacking him in the head?" Ms. Levey implored. "This is stressing me out, guys." (Belluck, 2005, p. A1).

And then she called her personal parent coach to find out how to deal with the situation.

Personal parent coach? In a new and growing phenomenon, parents are turning to members of a profession that didn't exist only few years ago called *parent coaching* to help them navigate the trials of parenthood.

Less expensive than formal therapy, but more systematic than the advice one might receive from one's next-door neighbor, parent coaching provides a combination of advice and support. Some parent coaches offer specific child-rearing strategies, while others teach parents the basics of child development so that they put their child's behavior in perspective (Marchant, Young, & West, 2004).

For some parents, parent coaching is a lifeline. It provides a way for parents who might not have access to the advice of other, more experienced parents to learn how to deal with the challenges of children. It also provides a relationship with another adult who can offer social support (Smith, 2005).

Although many parents swear by the value of parent coaches, the effectiveness of parent coaching has not been established by much scientific research. In part, the lack of data is a reflection of the newness of the field. In addition, there is great heterogeneity in the qualifications of parent coaches. While some have had formal training in child development, the only qualifications of other coaches is having raised a child themselves (Leonard, 2005).

Because there is no licensing of parent coaches, parents should adopt a buyer-beware attitude. Anyone can call themselves a parent coach, and parents should examine the credentials of prospective coaches carefully. Until the field becomes more regulated—and the value of parent coaches has been formally established—parents should be cautious.

- **If you were conducting an interview with a potential parent coach, what kind of questions would you ask?**

- **Do you think parent coaches should be licensed by the government? Why or why not? What kind of qualifications would you require to get a license?**

role in children's development. Furthermore, children's behavior is in part produced by their unique genetic endowment, and their behavior can in turn shape parental behavior. In sum, parents' childrearing practices are just one of a rich array of environmental and genetic influences that influence children (Boivin et al., 2005; Loehlin, Neiderhiser, & Reiss, 2005).

Review, Check, and Apply

Review

1. Piaget believed that preschoolers are in the heteronomous morality stage of moral development, in which rules are seen as invariant and unchangeable.

2. Social learning approaches to moral development emphasize the importance of reinforcement for moral actions and the observation of models of moral conduct. Psychoanalytical and other theories focus on children's empathy with others and their wish to help others so they can avoid unpleasant feelings of guilt themselves.

3. Older preschoolers begin to use abstract modeling, a process in which they infer generalized principles and rules from observing repeated examples of a model rewarded for acting in a morally desirable way.

4. At age 1, infants cry when they hear another infant cry. By 2 or 3, children spontaneously give gifts and share toys with other children, even if they don't know them. These are examples of developing empathy.

5. There are several distinct childrearing styles including authoritarian, permissive, authoritative, and uninvolved.

6. Childrearing styles show strong cultural influences.

Check

1. Children who believe in _____ _____ think that breaking a rule earns immediate punishment.

2. _____ behavior is helping behavior that benefits others.

3. Observation of a _____ who is rewarded for prosocial behavior can lead to prosocial behavior on the part of the observer.

4. The understanding of what others feel is called _____.

5. Authoritative parents who display warmth toward their children, take an interest and involvement in their children's peer activities, use proactive teaching, and discuss issues calmly during discipline episodes are practicing _____ _____.

Apply

1. If high-prestige models of behavior are particularly effective in influencing moral attitudes and actions in children, are there implications for individuals in such industries as television, sports, and advertising?

To see more review questions, log on to MyPsychLab.

ANSWERS: 1. immanent justice 2. Prosocial 3. model 4. empathy 5. supportive parenting

MORAL REASONING AND PROSOCIAL BEHAVIOR

LO 13-3 Through what stages does moral development progress during childhood and adolescence?

LO 13-4 How do adolescent girls differ from boys in moral development?

LO 13-5 As adolescents become more sophisticated morally, how does their behavior change?

> Your wife is near death from an unusual kind of cancer. One drug exists that the physicians think might save her—a form of radium that a scientist in a nearby city has recently developed. The drug, though, is expensive to manufacture, and the scientist is charging 10 times what the drug costs him to make. He pays $1,000 for the radium and charges $10,000 for a small dose. You have gone to everyone you know to borrow money, but you can get together only $2,500—one quarter of what you need. You've told the scientist that your wife is dying and asked him to sell it more cheaply or let you pay later. But the scientist has said, "No, I discovered the drug and I'm going to make money from it." In desperation, you consider breaking into the scientist's laboratory to steal the drug for your wife. Should you do it?

Lawrence Kohlberg and Carol Gilligan present contrasting explanations for children's moral development, with Gilligan focusing on gender differences in how males and females view morality.

According to developmental psychologist Lawrence Kohlberg and his colleagues, the answer that adolescents give to this question reveals central aspects of their sense of morality and justice. He suggests that people's responses to moral dilemmas such as this one reveal the stage of moral development they have attained—as well as yield information about their general level of cognitive development (Kohlberg, 1984; Colby & Kohlberg, 1987).

Kohlberg's Approach to Moral Development

Kohlberg contends that people pass through a series of stages as their sense of justice evolves and in the kind of reasoning they use to make moral judgments. Primarily due to cognitive characteristics that we discussed earlier, younger school-age children tend to think either in terms of concrete, unvarying rules ("It is always wrong to steal" or "I'll be punished if I steal") or in terms of the rules of society ("Good people don't steal" or "What if everyone stole?").

By the time they reach adolescence, however, individuals are able to reason on a higher plane, typically having reached Piaget's stage of formal operations. They are capable of comprehending abstract, formal principles of morality, and they consider cases such as the one presented previously in terms of broader issues of morality and of right and wrong ("Stealing may be acceptable if you are following your own conscience and doing the right thing").

Kohlberg suggests that moral development emerges in a three-level sequence, which is further subdivided into six stages (see Table 13-2). At the lowest level, **preconventional morality** (Stages 1 and 2), people follow rigid rules based on punishments or rewards. For example, a student at the preconventional level might evaluate the moral dilemma posed in the story by saying that it was not worth stealing the drug because if you were caught, you would go to jail.

In the next level, that of **conventional morality** (Stages 3 and 4), people approach moral problems in terms of their own position as good, responsible members of society. Some at this level would decide *against* stealing the drug because they think they would feel guilty or dishonest for violating social norms. Others would decide *in favor* of stealing the drug because if they did nothing in this situation, they would be unable to face others. All of these people would be reasoning at the conventional level of morality.

Finally, individuals using **postconventional morality** (Stages 5 and 6) invoke universal moral principles that are considered broader than the rules of the particular society in which they live. People who feel that they would condemn themselves if they did not steal the drug because they would not be living up to their own moral principles would be reasoning at the postconventional level.

Kohlberg's theory proposes that people move through the periods of moral development in a fixed order and that they are unable to reach the highest stage until adolescence, due to deficits in cognitive development that are not overcome until then. However, not everyone is presumed to reach the highest stages: Kohlberg found that postconventional reasoning is relatively rare (Hedgepeth, 2005).

Although Kohlberg's theory provides a good account of the development of moral *judgments,* the links with moral *behavior* are less strong. Still, students at higher levels of moral reasoning are less likely to engage in antisocial behavior at school (such as breaking school rules) and in the community (engaging in juvenile delinquency; Carpendale, 2000; Paxton, Ungar, & Greene, 2012).

Furthermore, one experiment found that 15% of students who reasoned at the postconventional level of morality—the highest category—cheated when given the opportunity, although they were not as likely to cheat as those at lower levels, where more than half of the students cheated. Clearly, though, knowing what is morally right does not always mean acting that way (Hart, Burock, & London, 2003; Semerci, 2006; Krettenauer, Jia, & Mosleh, 2011).

Kohlberg's theory has also been criticized because it is based solely on observations of members of Western cultures. In fact, cross-cultural research finds that members of more industrialized, technologically advanced cultures move through the stages more rapidly than members of nonindustrialized countries. Why? One explanation is that Kohlberg's higher

preconventional morality Stages 1 and 2 of Kohlberg's theory of moral development in which people follow rigid rules based on punishments or rewards

conventional morality Stages 3 and 4 of Kohlberg's theory of moral development in which people approach moral problems in terms of their own position as good, responsible members of society

postconventional morality Stages 5 and 6 of Kohlberg's theory of moral development in which individuals invoke universal moral principles that are considered broader than the rules of the particular society in which they live

TABLE 13-2   Kohlberg's Sequence of Moral Reasoning

Level	Stage	SAMPLE MORAL REASONING	
		In Favor of Stealing	Against Stealing
Level 1 Preconventional morality The main considerations are the avoidance of punishment and the desire for rewards.	**Stage 1** Obedience and punishment orientation: People obey rules to avoid being punished. Obedience is its own reward.	"You shouldn't just let your wife die. People will blame you for not doing enough, and they'll blame the scientist for not selling you the drug for less money."	"You can't steal the drug because you'll be arrested and go to jail. Even if you aren't caught, you'll feel guilty and you'll always worry that the police may figure out what you did."
	Stage 2 Reward orientation: People obey rules in order to earn rewards for their own benefit.	"Even if you get caught, the jury will understand and give you a short sentence. Meanwhile, your wife is alive. And if you're stopped before you get the drug to your wife, you could probably just return the drug without penalty."	"You shouldn't steal the drug because you're not responsible for your wife's cancer. If you get caught, your wife will still die and you'll be in jail."
Level 2 Conventional morality Membership in society becomes important. People behave in ways that will win the approval of others.	**Stage 3** "Good boy" morality: People want to be respected by others and try to do what they're supposed to do.	"Who will blame you if you steal a life-saving drug? But if you just let your wife die, you won't be able to hold your head up in front of your family or your neighbors."	"If you steal the drug, everyone will treat you like a criminal. They will wonder why you couldn't have found some other way to save your wife."
	Stage 4 Authority and social-order-maintaining morality: People believe that only society, not individuals, can determine what is right. Obeying society's rules is right in itself.	"A husband has certain responsibilities toward his wife. If you want to live an honorable life, you can't let fear of the consequences get in the way of saving her. If you ever want to sleep again, you have to save her."	"You shouldn't let your concern for your wife cloud your judgment. Stealing the drug may feel right at the moment, but you'll live to regret breaking the law."
Level 3 Postconventional morality People accept that there are certain ideals and principles of morality that must govern our actions. These ideals are more important than any particular society's rules.	**Stage 5** Morality of contract, individual rights, and democratically accepted law: People rightly feel obligated to follow the agreed rules of society. But as societies develop over time, rules have to be updated to make societal changes reflect underlying social principles.	"If you simply follow the law, you will violate the underlying principle of saving your wife's life. If you do take the drug, society will understand your actions and respect them. You can't let an outdated law prevent you from doing the right thing."	"Rules represent society's thinking on the morality of actions. You can't let your short-term emotions interfere with the more permanent rules of society. If you do, society will judge you negatively, and in the end you will lose self-respect."
	Stage 6 Morality of individual principles and conscience: People accept that laws are attempts to write down specific applications of universal moral principles. Individuals must test these laws against their consciences, which tend to express an inborn sense of those principles.	"If you allow your wife to die, you will have obeyed the letter of the law, but you will have violated the universal principle of life preservation that resides within your conscience. You will blame yourself forever if your wife dies because you obeyed an imperfect law."	"If you become a thief, your conscience will blame you for putting your own interpretation of moral issues above the legitimate rule of law. You will have betrayed your own standards of morality."

(*Source*: Based on Kohlberg, 1969.)

stages are based on moral reasoning involving governmental and societal institutions such as the police and court system. In less industrialized areas, morality may be based more on relationships among people in a particular village. In short, the nature of morality may differ in diverse cultures, and Kohlberg's theory is more suited for Western cultures (Fu et al., 2007).

 **Watch** the **Video** *Kohlberg and the Heinz Dilemma* in **MyPsychLab**.

Carol Gilligan argues that boys and girls view morality differently, with boys seeing it primarily in terms of broad principles and girls considering it in terms of personal relationships and responsibility toward individuals.

An aspect of Kohlberg's theory that has proved even more problematic is the difficulty it has explaining *girls'* moral judgments. Because the theory initially was based largely on data from males, some researchers have argued that it does a better job describing boys' moral development than girls' moral development. This would explain the surprising finding that women typically score at a lower level than men do on tests of moral judgments using Kohlberg's stage sequence. This result has led to an alternative account of moral development for girls.

Gilligan's Approach to Moral Development: Gender and Morality

Psychologist Carol Gilligan (1996) has suggested that differences in the ways boys and girls are raised in our society lead to basic distinctions in how men and women view moral behavior. According to her, boys view morality primarily in terms of broad principles such as justice or fairness, whereas girls see it in terms of responsibility toward individuals and willingness to sacrifice themselves to help specific individuals within the context of particular relationships. Compassion for individuals, then, is a more prominent factor in moral behavior for women than it is for men (Gilligan, Lyons, & Hammer, 1990; Gump, Baker, & Roll, 2000).

Gilligan views morality as developing among females in a three-stage process (summarized in Table 13-3). In the first stage, called "orientation toward individual survival," females first concentrate on what is practical and best for them, gradually making a transition from selfishness to responsibility, in which they think about what would be best for others. In the second stage, termed "goodness as self-sacrifice," females begin to think that they must sacrifice their own wishes to what other people want.

Ideally, women make a transition from "goodness" to "truth," in which they take into account their own needs plus those of others. This transition leads to the third stage, "morality of nonviolence," in which women come to see that hurting anyone is immoral—including

---

TABLE 13-3 Gilligan's Three States of Moral Development for Women

Stage	Characteristics	Example
Stage 1 Orientation toward individual survival	Initial concentration is on what is practical and best for self. Gradual transition from selfishness to responsibility, which includes thinking about what would be best for others.	A first grader may insist on playing only games of her own choosing when playing with a friend.
Stage 2 Goodness as self-sacrifice	Initial view is that a woman must sacrifice her own wishes to what other people want. Gradual transition from "goodness" to "truth," which takes into account needs of both self and others.	Now older, the same girl may believe that to be a good friend, she must play the games her friend chooses, even if she herself doesn't like them.
Stage 3 Morality of nonviolence	A moral equivalence is established between self and others. Hurting anyone—including one's self—is seen as immoral. Most sophisticated form of reasoning, according to Gilligan.	The same girl may realize that both friends must enjoy their time together and look for activities that both she and her friend can enjoy.

CAREERS IN DEVELOPMENT
Jelani Quinn, Mediator

Education: B.A., Psychology, University of Washington, Seattle; B.A., Business Administration, University of Washington, Seattle

Position: Program Director and Lead Trainer, CRU Institute, Bellevue, Washington

Conflicts and disagreements are common among high school students, ranging from conflicts brought about stereotypes and cultural misunderstandings to teacher-student grading arguments. However, trained mediators can help defuse many situations in a fair and equitable way.

While different approaches are used depending on the conflict situation, mediators generally ask the parties involved to follow several basic ground rules, according to Jelani Quinn. Quinn was a student mediator for three years before joining the CRU Institute, a nonprofit organization whose goal is to teach young people effective, peaceful ways to resolve conflict and to develop understanding, respect, and the ability to cooperate with others.

"When students come to mediation, they are asked to sign a mediation contract and agree to abide by some basic rules," Quinn explained. "The rules are to make a commitment to solve the problem; don't interrupt; no name calling or putting down; tell the truth; no physical fighting; and everything is kept

confidential except if someone is threatening to hurt themselves or another."

Once the mediation agreement is signed, the mediator opens up a dialogue, giving each student the opportunity to offer his or her side of the story.

"One of the most important things in mediation is to get their feelings out," Quinn said. "It may be the first time they are able to express that feeling. If someone says something important, we try to get the other person to state what was said in the hope that some empathy is created between the two parties.

"If I can't keep them from arguing, I ask them what would happen if they can't settle their problem," he added. "I try to get them to look at the options they have."

Sometimes a mediation just doesn't seem to work, but according to Quinn that doesn't always produce a negative outcome.

"Sometimes there is no solution, but that can be a good thing," he explained. "The solution is not always the most important aspect of mediation. The most important part is that these two people were able to sit down and talk about the situation. A lot of the communications skills that I'm using as a mediator are reflected to these students and they can transfer that to their own actions."

hurting themselves. This realization establishes a moral equivalence between themselves and others and represents, according to Gilligan, the most sophisticated level of moral reasoning.

It is obvious that Gilligan's sequence of stages is quite different from Kohlberg's, and some developmentalists have suggested that her rejection of Kohlberg's work is too sweeping and that gender differences are not as pronounced as first thought. For instance, some researchers argue that both males and females use similar "justice" and "care" orientations in making moral judgments. Clearly, the question of how boys and girls differ in their moral orientations, as well as the nature of moral development in general, is far from settled (Weisz & Black, 2002; Jorgensen, 2006; Tappan, 2006; Donleavy, 2008).

The lingering questions about the nature of moral reasoning have not deterred people from applying what has been learned about morality to everyday life. For example, as we discuss in the *Careers in Development* box, professional mediators offer good solutions for resolving disputes.

Moral Behavior and Moral Reasoning: Why the Disconnect?

Except for social learning perspectives, most of the approaches to moral development (such as those of Kohlberg and Gilligan) focus on moral reasoning. Why has the research spotlight shone more brightly on reasoning about moral behavior, as opposed to examining actual behavior?

One reason is that the researchers have assumed that moral reasoning lies at the heart of moral behavior. If adolescents don't have a clear internal moral compass, it seems unreasonable to expect that they will behave in a moral way. Unfortunately, though, there has been a persistent disconnect between prosocial *reasoning* and prosocial *behavior*. Obviously, we'd expect moral reasoning and judgments to be closely associated, but that doesn't seem to be the case. Why?

One reason is that in the real world there are often circumstances that override our internal moral compass. Although we may know and truly believe that it is wrong to break to the law by not fully stopping at a stop sign, we may feel that because no one is around, we don't have to come to a complete stop. Or perhaps we're driving someone to a hospital emergency department, and our internal principles about aiding someone in distress are more salient at that moment than our principles about obeying traffic laws. Unlike when they are measured in experiments, moral principles in the real world occur in a particular context that brings its own situational pressures.

In addition, moral judgments are made in a variety of contexts, and it may be an over-simplification to expect that morality will be displayed in similar ways across different domains and situations. According to the **social domain approach**, moral reasoning needs to be considered in the context in which judgments are being made at a given time. Major contexts include the *moral domain* (contexts that focus on concerns about justice), the *social-conventional domain* (contexts involving the need for social groups to function well), and the *personal domain* (contexts involving matters of personal choice). The particular moral judgments are likely to vary according to the domain (Smetana & Turiel, 2003; Turiel, 2006; Richardson, Mulvey, & Killen, 2012).

Finally, adolescents sometimes look at situations through the lens of personal choices and freedom, rather than in terms of ethical dilemmas. For example, consider the decision to engage in premarital sex. For some adolescents, premarital sex is always ethically wrong, and to engage in it is, by definition, an immoral act. But to others, premarital sex is a choice to be decided upon by the individuals who are involved. Similarly, alcohol use—while illegal for adolescents younger than a certain age—may be viewed in terms of a fairly rational, cost-benefit analysis (drinking provides certain benefits, but also accrues certain costs), rather than in terms of morality. The view that such activities as taking drugs, engaging in sex, and drinking are personal, not moral, choices helps explain the lack of relationship between risk-taking and moral reasoning (Kuther, 2000; Kuther & Higgins-D'Alessandro, 2000, 2003; Eisenberg & Morris, 2004).

Prosocial Reasoning and Prosocial Behavior: The Other Side of the Coin.
We've been focusing on situations in which adolescents are faced with circumstances involving some form of wrongdoing—breaking a rule, violating a moral principle, disobeying a law. But what about the other side of the coin: doing positive, unselfish, or altruistic deeds that benefit others, sometimes at the expense of oneself?

Although there is considerably less research in this area, emerging work suggests that adolescents generally become more sophisticated in their thinking about prosocial behavior. For example, their growing cognitive abilities allow them to distinguish between prosocial behavior that is self-serving (done to gain something, such as looking better in others' eyes) or truly *altruistic* (done to help others and requiring clear self-sacrifice).

Individuals who are unusually helpful to others tend to show more sophisticated moral reasoning than adolescents who are less prosocially active. Furthermore, adolescents who show more sophisticated levels of prosocial reasoning are generally more sympathetic. There's a persistent sex difference, too: Females tend to demonstrate higher levels of prosocial reasoning than males (Eisenberg & Morris, 2004).

On the other hand, it's harder to make generalizations about prosocial *behavior*. Although some adolescents become increasingly helpful as they get older, others do not. In a way, the difficulty in finding a relationship between prosocial behavior and personal characteristics is not surprising, given the difficulty that researchers have had in finding any particular personality characteristics related to helpfulness. Most research suggests that adolescents are not invariably helpful or, for that matter, unhelpful. Instead, whether particular individuals act in a prosocial manner depends on their personality *and* the specifics of the situation. Furthermore, no single pattern of specific, individual personality traits determines prosocial behavior. Rather, the way that specific personality factors fit together, as well as the demands of the particular situation, determines whether a person will help (Eisenberg & Morris, 2004; Batson, 2012).

social domain approach An approach in which moral reasoning needs to be considered in the context in which judgments are being made at a given time

Gender and Cultural Differences in Prosocial Behavior. Both gender and culture are related to prosocial behavior. For example, quite consistently, girls are more helpful than boys. They are more caring about others, and they act in a more prosocial manner. (By the way, not only are males less likely to provide help, they are less willing to ask for help than females—something we might call the males-hating-to-ask-for-directions-even-when-they-are-lost phenomenon (Eisenberg & Morris, 2004).

On the other hand, males don't always act less helpfully than females. If the situation is one in which their behavior is public and visible to others, and the person needing help is female, males are more likely to be helpful. Having the opportunity to act like a "knight in shining armor" and come to the rescue of a damsel in distress elevates the level of male helpfulness beyond its typically more modest level (Hyde & Grabe, 2008).

The typically higher levels of prosocial behavior displayed by females reflect their tendency to hold a *communal* orientation, centering on an interest in relationships and community. In contrast, males are more likely to have an *agentic* orientation, which focuses on individuality and getting things done. Communal orientations lead to greater prosocial behavior (Mosher & Danoff-Burg, 2005; Salmivalli et al., 2005).

Parents' childrearing practices, which we discussed earlier, produce different forms of helping behavior, which emerge during childhood. For example, the level of helping behavior that children display while playing varies substantially in different cultures. Children raised in cultures in which children are taught to cooperate with other family members to do chores or to help in the upbringing of younger children (such as in Kenya, Mexico, and the Philippines) show relatively high levels of prosocial behavior. In contrast, cultures that promote competition—such as the United States—produce lower levels of prosocial behavior (Whiting & Edwards, 1988; Yablo & Field, 2007).

Furthermore, the degree to which adolescents view helping in the context of reciprocity—the view that we should help because we expect to receive help from others in the future—is related to cultural factors. For example, Hindu Indians see reciprocity as a moral obligation, whereas college students in the United States consider reciprocity as more of a personal choice (Chadha & Misra, 2004; Kärtner & Keller, 2012).

Review, Check, and Apply

Review

1. According to Kohlberg, moral development proceeds from a concern with rewards and punishments, through a focus on social conventions and rules, toward a sense of universal moral principles. Gilligan has suggested, however, that girls may follow a somewhat different progression of moral development.

2. Due to the different ways in which they are raised, Gilligan suggests boys and girls develop different views of morality. Boys see morality in terms of broad principles, while girls view it in terms of responsibility to individuals and being self-sacrificing for the good of other people in their lives.

3. Moral judgments are made in many different contexts. The social domain approach to moral reasoning cites three major contexts that influence moral judgments: the moral domain, the social-conventional domain, and the personal domain.

4. As adolescents become more cognitively sophisticated, they are better able to consider and evaluate prosocial behavior. The likelihood that a person will act prosocially depends on both the individual and the situation rather than on personality traits alone.

5. There are clear gender and cultural differences in both empathy and prosocial behavior.

Check

1. At Kohlberg's lowest level of moral development, _____ morality, people follow unvarying rules based on rewards and punishments.

2. Although Kohlberg's theory provides a good account of the development of moral judgments, it is less adequate in predicting moral _____.

3. In Gilligan's second stage of moral development, which she terms _____ _____ _____ , females begin to think that they must sacrifice their own wishes to what other people want, ultimately making the transition from "goodness" to "truth," in which they take into account their own needs plus the needs of others.

4. Using the _____ _____ approach, moral reasoning needs to be evaluated in the context in which judgments are being made at a particular moment.

Apply

1. What potential problems do adolescent girls face, in Carol Gilligan's goodness-as-self-sacrifice stage of moral development, if they decide to have serious romantic relationships with boys? What kind of program might you design to help teenage girls become more aware of their own needs and wants, and to enable them to move into Gilligan's morality-of-nonviolence stage?

To see more review questions, log on to MyPsychLab.

ANSWERS: 1. preconventional 2. behavior 3. goodness as self-sacrifice 4. social domain

---

AGGRESSION AND VIOLENCE

LO 13-6 How does aggression develop in preschool-age children?

LO 13-7 What forms does aggression take in middle childhood and adolescence, and what are some of the characteristics of its perpetrators?

> *Four-year-old Duane could not contain his anger and frustration anymore. Although he usually was mild-mannered, when Eshu began to tease him about the split in his pants and kept it up for several minutes, Duane finally snapped. Rushing over to Eshu, Duane pushed him to the ground and began to hit him with his small, closed fists. Because he was so distraught, Duane's punches were not terribly effective, but they were severe enough to hurt Eshu and bring him to tears before the preschool teachers could intervene.*

Aggression among preschoolers is quite common, though attacks such as this are not. The potential for verbal hostility, shoving matches, kicking, and other forms of aggression is present throughout the preschool period, although the degree to which aggression is acted out changes as children become older.

Aggression and Violence in Preschoolers: Sources and Consequences

Eshu's taunting was also a form of aggression. **Aggression** is intentional injury or harm to another person. Infants don't act aggressively; it is hard to contend that their behavior is *intended* to hurt others, even if they inadvertently manage to do so. In contrast, by the time they reach preschool age, children demonstrate true aggression.

aggression Intentional injury or harm to another person

During the early preschool years, some of the aggression is addressed at attaining a desired goal, such as getting a toy away from another person or using a particular space occupied by another person. Consequently, in some ways the aggression is inadvertent, and minor scuffles may be a typical part of early preschool life. It is the rare child who does not demonstrate at least an occasional act of aggression.

On the other hand, extreme and sustained aggression is a cause of concern. In most children, the amount of aggression declines as they move through the preschool years, as does the frequency and average length of episodes of aggressive behavior (Persson, 2005; Olson et al., 2011).

The child's personality and social development contribute to this decline in aggression. Throughout the preschool years, children become better at controlling the emotions that they are experiencing. **Emotional self-regulation**, as we discussed in Chapter 10, is the capability to adjust emotions to a desired state and level of intensity. Starting at age 2, children are able to talk about their feelings, and they engage in strategies to regulate them. As they get older, they develop more effective strategies, learning to better cope with negative emotions. In addition to their increasing self-control, children are also, as we've seen, developing sophisticated social skills. Most learn to use language to express their wishes, and they become increasingly able to negotiate with others (Philippot & Feldman, 2004; Cole et al., 2009; Willoughby et al., 2011; Helmsen, Koglin, & Petermann, 2012).

Aggression, both physical and verbal, is present throughout the preschool period.

Despite these typical declines in aggression, some children remain aggressive throughout the preschool period. Furthermore, aggression is a relatively stable characteristic: The most aggressive preschoolers tend to be the most aggressive children during the school-age years, and the least aggressive preschoolers tend to be the least aggressive school-age children (Tremblay, 2001; Schaeffer, Petras, & Ialongo, 2003; Davenport & Bourgeois, 2008).

Boys typically show higher levels of physical, instrumental aggression than girls. **Instrumental aggression** is aggression motivated by the desire to obtain a concrete goal, such as playing with a desirable toy that another child is playing with.

On the other hand, although girls show lower levels of instrumental aggression, they may be just as aggressive, but in different ways from boys. Girls are more likely to practice **relational aggression**, which is nonphysical aggression that is intended to hurt another person's feelings. Such aggression may be demonstrated through name-calling, withholding friendship, or simply saying mean, hurtful things that make the recipient feel bad (Murray-Close, Ostrov, & Crick, 2007; Valles & Knutson, 2008; Goldweber & Cauffman, 2012).

Watch the **Video** *Relational Aggression* in **MyPsychLab**.

Roots of Aggression

How can we explain the aggression of preschoolers? Some theoreticians suggest that to behave aggressively is an instinct, part and parcel of the human condition. For instance, Freud's psychoanalytic theory suggests that we all are motivated by sexual and aggressive instincts (Freud, 1920). According to ethologist Konrad Lorenz, an expert in animal behavior, animals—including humans—share a fighting instinct that stems from primitive urges to preserve territory, maintain a steady supply of food, and weed out weaker animals (Lorenz, 1966, 1974).

Similar arguments are made by evolutionary psychologists, scientists who consider the biological roots of social behavior. They argue that aggression leads to increased opportunities to mate, improving the likelihood that one's genes will be passed on to future generations. In addition, aggression may help to strengthen the species and its gene pool as a whole, because the strongest survive. Ultimately, then, aggressive instincts promote the survival of one's genes to pass on to future generations (Archer, 2009).

Although instinctual explanations of aggression are logical, most developmentalists believe they are not the whole story. Not only do instinctual explanations fail to take into account the increasingly sophisticated cognitive abilities that humans develop as they get older, but they also have relatively little experimental support. Moreover, they provide little guidance in determining when and how children, as well as adults, will behave aggressively, other

emotional self-regulation The capability to adjust emotions to a desired state and level of intensity

instrumental aggression Aggression motivated by the desire to obtain a concrete goal, such as playing with a desirable toy that another child is playing with

relational aggression Aggression that is nonphysical and intended to hurt another person's feelings such as name-calling, withholding friendship, or simply saying mean, hurtful things

than noting that aggression is an inevitable part of the human condition. Consequently, developmentalists have turned to other approaches to explain aggression and violence.

Social Learning Approaches to Aggression.
The day after Duane lashed out at Eshu, Lynn, who had watched the entire scene, got into an argument with Ilya. They verbally bickered for a while, and suddenly Lynn balled her hand into a fist and tried to punch Ilya. The preschool teachers were stunned: It was rare for Lynn to get upset, and she had never displayed aggression before.

Is there a connection between the two events? Most of us would answer yes, particularly if we subscribed to the view, suggested by social learning approaches, that aggression is largely a learned behavior. Social learning approaches to aggression contend that aggression is based on observation and prior learning. To understand the causes of aggressive behavior, then, we should look at the system of rewards and punishments that exists in a child's environment.

Social learning approaches to aggression emphasize how social and environmental conditions teach individuals to be aggressive. These ideas grow out of behavioral perspectives, which suggest that aggressive behavior is learned through direct reinforcement. For instance, preschool-age children may learn that they can continue to play with the most desirable toys by aggressively refusing their classmates' requests for sharing. In the parlance of traditional learning theory, they have been reinforced for acting aggressively (by continued use of the toy), and they are more likely to behave aggressively in the future.

But social learning approaches suggest that reinforcement also comes in less direct ways. A good deal of research suggests that exposure to aggressive models leads to increased aggression, particularly if the observers are themselves angered, insulted, or frustrated. For example, Albert Bandura and his colleagues illustrated the power of models in a classic study of preschool-age children (Bandura, Ross, & Ross, 1963). One group of children watched a film of an adult playing aggressively and violently with a Bobo doll (a large, inflated plastic clown designed as a punching bag for children that always returns to an upright position after being pushed down). In comparison, children in another condition watched a film of an adult playing sedately with a set of Tinkertoys (see Figure 13-1). Later the preschool-age children were allowed to play with a number of toys, which included both the Bobo doll and the Tinkertoys. But first the children were led to feel frustration by being refused the opportunity to play with a favorite toy.

As predicted by social learning approaches, the preschool-age children modeled the behavior of the adult. Those who had seen the aggressive model playing with the Bobo doll were considerably more aggressive than those who had watched the calm, unaggressive model playing with the Tinkertoys.

Later research has supported this early study, and it is clear that exposure to aggressive models increases the likelihood that aggression on the part of observers will follow. These findings have profound consequences, particularly for children who live in communities in which violence is prevalent. For instance, one survey conducted in a city public hospital found that 1 in 10 children under the age of 6 said they had witnessed a shooting or a stabbing. Other research indicates that one third of the children in some urban neighborhoods have seen a homicide and two-thirds have seen a serious assault. Such frequent exposure to violence certainly increases the probability that observers will behave aggressively themselves (Farver et al., 1997; Evans, 2004).

Viewing Violence on TV: Does It Matter?
Even the majority of preschool-age children who are not witnesses to real-life violence are typically exposed to aggression via the medium of television. Children's television programs actually contain higher levels of violence (69%) than other types of programs (57%). In an average hour, children's programs contain more than twice as many violent incidents than other types of programs (see Figure 13-2; Wilson, 2002).

This high level of televised violence, coupled with Bandura and others' research findings on modeling violence, raises a significant question: Does viewing aggression increase the likelihood that children (and later adults) will enact actual—and ultimately deadly—aggression?

FIGURE 13-1 Modeling Aggression

This series of photos is from Albert Bandura's classic Bobo doll experiment, designed to illustrate social learning of aggression. The photos clearly show how the adult model's aggressive behavior (in the first row) is imitated by children who had viewed the aggressive behavior (second and third rows).

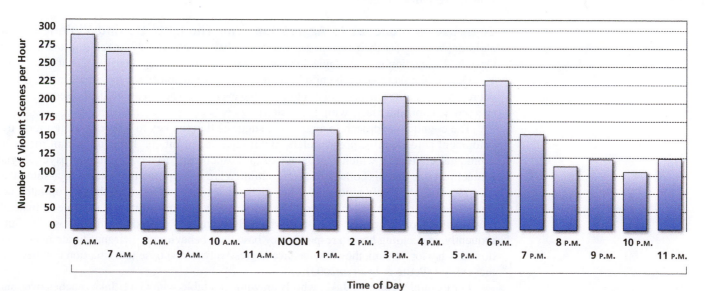

FIGURE 13-2 Televised Acts of Violence

A survey of the violence shown on the major TV networks and several cable channels in Washington, D.C., on one particular weekday found acts of violence during every time period. From the perspective of an educator, do you think depictions of violence on TV should be regulated? Why or why not?

(*Source:* Center for Media and Public Affairs, 1995.)

Social learning explanations of aggression suggest that children seeing aggression on television can prompt them to act aggressively.

FROM AN
EDUCATOR'S

PERSPECTIVE:

How might a preschool teacher or parent help children notice the violence in the programs they watch and protect them from its effects?

It is hard to answer the question definitively, primarily because scientists are unable to conduct true experiments outside laboratory settings. Although it is clear that laboratory observation of aggression on television leads to higher levels of aggression, evidence showing that real-world viewing of aggression is associated with subsequent aggressive behavior is correlational. (Think, for a moment, of what would be required to conduct a true experiment involving children's viewing habits. It would require that we control children's viewing of television in their homes for extended periods, exposing some to a steady diet of violent shows and others to nonviolent ones—something that most parents would not agree to.)

Despite the fact, then, that the results are primarily correlational, the overwhelming weight of research evidence is clear in suggesting that observation of televised aggression does lead to subsequent aggression. Longitudinal studies have found that children's preferences for violent television shows at age 8 are related to the seriousness of criminal convictions by age 30. Other evidence supports the notion that observation of media violence can lead to a greater readiness to act aggressively, bullying, and to an insensitivity to the suffering of victims of violence (Christakis & Zimmerman, 2007; Peckins et al., 2012; Miller et al., 2012).

Television is not the only source of media violence. Many video games contain a significant amount of aggressive behavior, and children are playing such games at high rates. For example, 14% of children 3 and younger and around 50% of those 4 to 6 play video games. Because research conducted with adults shows that playing violent video games is associated with behaving aggressively, children who play video games containing violence may be at higher risk for behaving aggressively (Barlett, Harris, & Baldassaro, 2007; Polman, de Castro, & van Aken, 2008; Kirsh, 2012).

Fortunately, social learning principles that lead preschoolers to learn aggression from television and video games suggest ways to reduce the negative influence of the medium. For instance, children can be explicitly taught to view violence with a more skeptical, critical eye. Being taught that violence is not representative of the real world, that the viewing of violence can affect them negatively, and that they should refrain from imitating the behavior they have seen on television can help children interpret the violent programs differently and be less influenced by them (Persson & Musher-Eizenman, 2003; Donnerstein, 2005).

Furthermore, just as exposure to aggressive models leads to aggression, observation of *non*aggressive models can *reduce* aggression. Preschoolers don't learn from others only how to be aggressive; they can also learn how to avoid confrontation and to control their aggression, as we'll discuss later.

Cognitive Approaches to Aggression: The Thoughts Behind Violence.

Two children, waiting for their turn in a game of kickball, inadvertently knock into one another. One child's reaction is to apologize; the other's is to shove, saying angrily, "Cut it out."

Despite the fact that each child bears the same responsibility for the minor event, different reactions result. The first child interprets the event as an accident, while the second sees it as a provocation and reacts with aggression.

The cognitive approach to aggression suggests that the key to understanding moral development is to examine preschoolers' interpretations of others' behavior and of the environmental context in which a behavior occurs. According to developmental psychologist Kenneth Dodge and his colleagues, some children are more prone than others to assume that actions are aggressively motivated. They are unable to pay attention to the appropriate cues in a situation and unable to interpret the behaviors in a given situation accurately. Instead, they assume—often erroneously—that what is happening is related to others' hostility. Subsequently, in deciding how to respond, they base their behavior on their inaccurate interpretation of behavior. In sum, they may behave aggressively in response to a situation that never in fact existed (Petite & Dodge, 2003).

For example, consider Jake, who is drawing at a table with Gary. Jake reaches over and takes a red crayon that Gary had just decided he was going to use next. Gary is instantly certain that Jake "knew" that he was going to use the red crayon, and that Jake is taking it just to be mean. With this interpretation in mind, Gary hits Jake for "stealing" his crayon. Although the cognitive approach to aggression provides a description of the process that leads some children to behave aggressively, it is less successful in explaining how certain children come to be inaccurate perceivers of situations in the first place. Furthermore, it fails to explain why such inaccurate perceivers so readily respond with aggression, and why they assume that aggression is an appropriate and even desirable response.

On the other hand, cognitive approaches to aggression are useful in pointing out a means to reduce aggression: By teaching preschool-age children to be more accurate interpreters of a situation, we can induce them to be less prone to view others' behavior as motivated by hostility, and consequently less likely to respond with aggression themselves. The guidelines in *Are You an Informed Consumer of Development?* are based on the various theoretical perspectives on aggression and morality that we've discussed in this chapter.

School Violence. Columbine. Jonesboro. Newtown. You may remember the names of these places where school violence occurred, and you may conclude—like many Americans—that schools are particularly dangerous places.

However, the reality of school violence is different. Despite the public perception that school violence is on the upswing, there has in fact been an overall decline in violence. Even in the year of the Columbine shooting, the number of deaths in school-related incidents dropped 40% from the previous year. School is actually one of the safest places for adolescents (Spencer, 2001; Jimerson et al., 2006; Newsome & Kelly, 2006).

In spite of high profile news reports of shootings, schools are actually one of the safest places for adolescents.

ARE YOU AN INFORMED CONSUMER OF DEVELOPMENT?

Increasing Moral Behavior and Reducing Aggression in Preschool-Age Children

The numerous points of view on what causes aggression in preschool children are useful for the various methods of encouraging children's moral conduct and reducing the incidence of aggression. Here are some of the most practical and readily accomplished strategies (Bor & Bor, 2004; Larson & Lochman, 2011):

- **Provide opportunities for preschool-age children to observe others acting in a cooperative, helpful, prosocial manner.** Encourage them to interact with peers in joint activities in which they share a common goal. Such cooperative activities can teach the importance and desirability of working with—and helping—others.
- **Do not ignore aggressive behavior.** Parents and teachers should intervene when they see aggression in preschoolers and send a clear message that aggression is an unacceptable means to resolve conflicts.
- **Help preschoolers devise alternative explanations for others' behavior.** This is particularly important for children who are prone to aggression and who may be apt to view others' conduct as more hostile than it actually is. Parents and teachers should help such children see that the behavior of their peers has several possible interpretations.
- **Monitor preschoolers' television viewing, particularly the violence that they view.** There is good evidence that observation of televised aggression results in subsequent increases in children's levels of aggression. Instead, encourage preschoolers to watch particular shows that are designed, in part, to increase the level of moral conduct, such as *Sesame Street, Dora the Explorer, Daniel Tiger's Neighborhood,* and *Barney.*
- **Help preschoolers understand their feelings.** When children become angry—and all children do—they need to learn how to deal with their feelings in a constructive manner. Tell them *specific* things they can do to improve the situation ("I see you're really angry with Jake for not giving you a turn. Don't hit him, but tell him you want a chance to play with the game.")
- **Explicitly teach reasoning and self-control.** Preschoolers can understand the rudiments of moral reasoning, and they should be reminded why certain behaviors are desirable. For instance, explicitly saying "If you take all the cookies, others will have no dessert" is preferable to saying, "Good children don't eat all the cookies." ■

The likelihood of injury from a school shooting is tiny (a child has about a one in a million chance of being killed in school). Nonetheless, parents and their children still worry about safety issues. Is it possible to identify beforehand students who pose a threat? It turns out that there are students who are prone to violence; for instance, the FBI has identified several characteristics of individuals who are at risk for carrying out violence in schools. They include a low tolerance for frustration, poor coping skills, a lack of resiliency, failed love relationships, resentment over perceived injustices, depression, self-centeredness, and alienation (O'Toole, 2000; Chisholm & Ward, 2005; Eisenbraun, 2007).

Furthermore, school shootings are rarely spontaneous. Attackers typically make plans, plotting out beforehand whom they wish to harm. Not only do they usually tell someone about their plans, they often are encouraged by others. In almost half the cases of school shootings, attackers were influenced or encouraged to act by friends or fellow students. They also have easy access to guns. In around two thirds of school shootings, the attackers used guns from their own home or that of a relative (U.S. Secret Service, 2002).

According to psychologist Elliot Aronson, students who carry out violence in schools frequently were the targets of bullying or have been rejected in some way. He notes that there are tremendous status differences in schools, and students who have been taunted and humiliated by students of higher status (or by their parents or other adults) may lash out in frustration (Aronson, 2000; 2004).

To respond to the potential of violence, many schools have instituted programs designed to prevent aggression among students. One of the most prominent is *Second Step,* which is designed to teach children to recognize and understand their feelings, experience empathy for others, make effective choices, and keep anger from escalating into violence. Carefully conducted studies have supported the program, finding improvements in students' social skills and a reduction in aggressive acts (Van Schoiack-Edstrom, Frey, & Beland, 2002; McMahon & Washburn, 2003).

Other school programs that involve cooperative learning, peer mediation, and communication skills training appear to be helpful. In addition, teaching students, parents, and educators to take threats seriously is important; many students who become violent threaten to commit violence before they actually engage in violent acts. Ultimately, schools need to be places where students feel comfortable discussing their feelings and problems, rather than sources of alienation and rejection (Aronson, 2000, 2004; Spencer, 2001; Eisenbraun, 2007).

 DEVELOPMENTAL DIVERSITY AND YOUR LIFE

Is Aggression As American As Apple Pie?

Anyone who reads a daily newspaper is exposed to a constant stream of incidents of murder, rape, mugging, and other violence, often committed by teenagers and sometimes even by younger children. Does this perception of violence match the reality, and is aggression "as American as apple pie," as one expert on aggression put it (Berkowitz, 1993)? Unfortunately, in many ways, the perception matches reality. For example, more men between the ages of 15 to 24 are murdered in the United States than in any other developed country in the world (see Figure 13-3).

On the other hand, aggression is hardly unique to the United States. In some cultures, aggression by children is substantial, while in others it is less pronounced. According to the findings of one classic study, childrearing practices help explain the substantial cross-cultural differences. In the study, researchers examined aggression in Kenya, India, Mexico, Okinawa, the Philippines, and the United States (Lambert, 1971).

In the study, researchers first examined the reactions of mothers (who were the primary caregivers in each of the cultures) to their own children's aggression. They found that Mexican parents were most strict, whereas U.S. mothers showed the greatest tolerance for aggressive behavior in their children. In contrast, for aggression against an adult, children living in Kenya, the Philippines, and Mexico received the greatest punishment, whereas children in India received the least punishment. Children living in the United States and Okinawa received a moderate degree of punishment.

As the researchers expected, mothers' reactions to aggression were related to their children's overall aggression levels, although the findings were complex. One important finding was that children with the highest activity levels learned the social values of their culture regarding aggression most effectively. Hence, active children in Mexico were less aggressive because their mothers reacted strongly to their aggression. In contrast, the more active children in the United States were more aggressive, a lesson they learned from their mother's lack of strong reactions to their aggression. In contrast, relatively inactive children, who had fewer opportunities to acquire the social values of their society, showed differing patterns of aggression from those of their more active counterparts.

Of course, we don't know from the results why, in the first place, mothers in some cultures reacted more to their children's aggression than mothers in other cultures. Still, it is clear that cultures produce a particular set of childrearing practices that are associated with different patterns of aggression in their children.

Although there are substantial cultural differences in level of aggression, in some way patterns of aggression are similar across cultures. The most significant similarity is a gender difference: In every known culture, boys are more aggressive than girls, a pattern that is mirrored in adult behavior (Knight, Fabes, & Higgins, 1996; LaFreniere et al., 2002; Verrity, 2007).

Why should boys be more aggressive than girls? Although it is tempting to look to biological or evolutionary explanations and suggest that boys are genetically preprogrammed to be aggressive, there are other possibilities. As we discussed in Chapter 12, parents and society in general hold different expectations about aggression for boys and girls, and in many cultures boys are explicitly encouraged to behave aggressively. In contrast, aggression in girls is typically discouraged (Bettencourt & Miller, 1996; Zahn-Waxler & Polanichka, 2004; Letendre, 2007).

It is also possible that boys may behave aggressively in an effort to distinguish themselves from their female caregivers, given that males in almost all societies are reared primarily by women. Behaving aggressively may make boys believe that they are adopting a behavior that is similar to that of adults (Whiting, 1965).

Although such explanations are plausible, they remain theories, and there is no definitive explanation for the higher levels of male aggression found in every culture. In any case, we should not assume that the general pervasiveness of aggressive behavior is a necessary part of children's behavior. ■

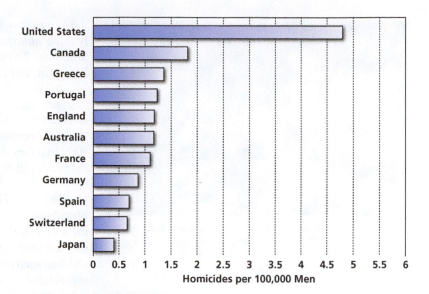

FIGURE 13-3 Tracking Murder

The murder rate (per 100,000 men) is far higher in the United States than in many other developed countries. What features of U.S. society contribute to this state of affairs?

(*Source:* United Nations Office on Drugs and Crime, 2011.)

Schoolyard—and Cyber-Yard—Bullies

Austin Rodriguez, an Ohio teen, attempted suicide after classmates bullied him for being gay. They reportedly hid his gym clothes and tried to prevent him from entering the locker room or the lunchroom. They made nasty remarks on the Internet.

Rachel Ehmke, a Minnesota seventh grader, hung herself when the bullying got too awful to live with. The 13-year-old had been hounded for months by a group of girls who called her "prostitute," scrawled "slut" all over her notebook, and harassed her online.

The sad stories of Austin and Rachel highlight a growing problem in schools and online: bullying. Almost 85% of girls and 80% of boys report experiencing some form of harassment in school at least once, and 160,000 U.S. schoolchildren stay home from school each day because they are afraid of being bullied. Others encounter bullying on

While children who are loners experience frequent bullying, some 90% of middle school students report being bullied at some point.

the Internet, which may be even more painful because often the bullying is done anonymously or may involve public postings (Mishna, Saini, & Solomon, 2009; van Goethem, Scholte, & Wiers, 2010; Juvonen, Wang, & Espinoza, 2011).

Bullying includes aggressive and hurtful acts such as name-calling, rejection, teasing, threats, and physical harm. Online, bullies may repeatedly text or email their victims with mean-spirited messages. The source of cyberbullying can remain anonymous, and the messages may be particularly abusive. Although they do not inflict physical harm, they can be psychologically damaging (Zacchilli & Valerio, 2011).

Bullies and Their Victims.

Children who experience frequent bullying are often loners who are fairly passive. They tend to cry easily, and they often lack the social skill that might otherwise defuse a bullying situation. For example, they are unable to think of humorous comebacks to bullies' taunts. But though children such as these are more likely to be bullied, even children without these characteristics occasionally are bullied during their school careers: Some 90% of middle school students report being bullied at some point in their time at school, beginning as early as the preschool years (Li, 2007; Katzer, Fetchenhauer, & Belschak, 2009; Mishna et al., 2012).

About 10% to 15% of students bully others at one time or another. About half of all bullies come from abusive homes—meaning that half don't. They tend to watch more television containing violence, and they misbehave more at home and at school than do nonbullies. When their bullying gets them into trouble, they may try to lie their way out of the situation, and they show little remorse for their victimization of others. Furthermore, bullies, compared with their peers, are more likely to break the law as adults. Although bullies are sometimes popular among their peers, some ironically become victims for bullying themselves (Haynie et al., 2001; Ireland & Archer, 2004; Barboza et al., 2009).

How can children in middle childhood deal with bullying? Among the strategies experts suggest are refusing to engage when provocations occur, speaking up against bullying (saying something such as "stop it"), and talking with parents, teachers, and other trusted adults to get their help. Ultimately, children need to recognize that one has the right *not* to be bullied. (The U.S. government website StopBullying.gov provides extensive information about bullying; NCB Now, 2011.)

The Lingering Stress of Being Bullied.

Of the many different events that occur in adolescence that are stress-provoking, one of the most stressful is being the victim of bullying. Nearly a third of all adolescents have been bullied at some point, and as many as 10% are chronically victimized.

Given that such experiences provoke negative emotions, are uncontrollable, and directly affect adolescents' lives in important ways, it's hardly surprising that being bullied is associated with anxiety, depression, and low self-worth (Hawker & Boulton, 2000; Nansel et al., 2001; Pepler et al., 2008).

Although bullying declines in frequency with age, some victims continue to be bullied throughout later adolescence and even into adulthood, where the workplace replaces the playground as a place of fear and intimidation. To understand the long-term outcomes of bullying, psychologist Matthew Newman and his colleagues explored the psychological effects during later adolescence of being bullied earlier in life. They were specifically interested in how the experience of being bullied in high school continued to affect adolescents after they made the transition to college (Newman, Holden, & Delville, 2005; Schenk & Fremouw, 2012).

University undergraduates provided data on their experiences with bullying in high school and prior to high school as well as on a variety of stress symptoms they were currently experiencing as college students. They found that the prevalence of bullying changed over time as adolescents transitioned into high school. For example, one third of the participants reported being bullied occasionally during the time before high school, and over another quarter of them reported frequent bullying during that period. But the frequency dropped off in high school, where a quarter of the participants experienced occasional bullying and fewer than 10% were bullied frequently.

Most importantly, the stress that college students currently reported was related to bullying experiences before college. Students who had been bullied more in high school reported more stress symptoms in college; interestingly, even students who had been bullied more *before* high school reported more stress symptoms in college (despite the fact that a wide majority of them reported that the bullying had decreased or stopped during high school).

Clearly, the harmful effects of being bullied during adolescence persist for years, emerging as stress symptoms after the bullied adolescents transition to college. Furthermore, the relationship between being bullied in adolescence and increased stress in college was most pronounced for students who felt the most isolated. Students who were bullied frequently in high school but nevertheless did not feel isolated from others were less likely to continue to be affected into college (Holt & Espelage, 2007; Carney, 2008).

Watch the **Video** *Bullying* in **MyPsychLab**.

Juvenile Delinquency: The Crimes of Adolescence

Adolescents, along with young adults, are more likely to commit crimes than any other age group. This is a misleading statistic in some respects: Because certain behaviors (such as drinking) are illegal for adolescents but not for older individuals, it is rather easy for adolescents to break the law by doing something that, were they a few years older, would be legal. But even when such crimes are disregarded, adolescents are disproportionately involved in violent crimes, such as murder, assaults, and rape, and in property crimes involving theft, robbery, and arson.

Although the number of violent crimes committed by U.S. adolescents over the past six years has shown a decline, delinquency among some teenagers remains a significant problem. Overall, 16% of all arrests for serious crimes involved a person under the age of 18.

Why do adolescents become involved in criminal activity? Some offenders, known as **undersocialized delinquents,** are adolescents who are raised with little discipline or with harsh, uncaring parental supervision. Although they are influenced by their peers, these children have not been socialized appropriately by their parents and were not taught standards of conduct to regulate their own behavior. Undersocialized delinquents typically begin criminal activities at an early age, well before the onset of adolescence (Hoeve et al., 2008).

Undersocialized delinquents share several characteristics. They tend to be relatively aggressive and violent fairly early in life, characteristics that lead to rejection by peers and academic failure. They also are more likely to have been diagnosed with attention deficit hyperactivity disorder as children, and they tend to be less intelligent than average (Henry et al., 1996; Silverthorn & Frick, 1999; Rutter, 2003).

Undersocialized delinquents often suffer from psychological difficulties, and as adults they fit a psychological pattern called antisocial personality disorder. They are relatively unlikely to be successfully rehabilitated, and many undersocialized delinquents live on the margins of society throughout their lives (Rönkä & Pulkkinen, 1995; Lynam, 1996; Frick et al., 2003).

A larger group of adolescent offenders are socialized delinquents. **Socialized delinquents** know and subscribe to the norms of society; they are fairly normal psychologically. For them, transgressions committed during adolescence do not lead to a life of crime. Instead, most socialized delinquents pass through a period during adolescence when they engage in some petty crimes (such as shoplifting), but they do not continue lawbreaking into adulthood.

Typically, socialized delinquents are highly influenced by their peers, and their delinquency often occurs in groups. In addition, some research suggests that parents of socialized delinquents supervise their children's behavior less closely than do other parents. But like other aspects of adolescent behavior, these minor delinquencies are often a result of giving in to group pressure or seeking to establish one's identity as an adult (Fletcher et al., 1995; Thornberry & Krohn, 1997; Goldweber et al., 2011; Henry, Knight, & Thornberry, 2012).

undersocialized delinquents Adolescents who are raised with little discipline or with harsh, uncaring parental supervision. Although they are influenced by their peers, they have not been socialized appropriately by their parents and were not taught standards of conduct to regulate their own behavior

socialized delinquents Adolescents who know and subscribe to the norms of society; they are fairly normal psychologically but pass through a period when they engage in some petty crimes (such as shoplifting), and they do not continue lawbreaking into adulthood

Watch the **Video** *Risk Taking and Delinquency* in **MyPsychLab**.

Review, Check, and Apply

Review

1. Aggression typically declines in frequency and duration as children become more able to regulate their emotions and to use language to negotiate disputes.

2. Ethologists and sociobiologists regard aggression as an innate human characteristic, while proponents of social learning and cognitive approaches focus on learned aspects of aggression.

3. Longitudinal studies have shown a relationship between children's preferences for violent television shows at age 8 and the seriousness of criminal convictions by age 30. Media violence can also lead to insensitivity toward the suffering of others and a greater readiness to act aggressively.

4. School violence receives a lot of attention from the media, but a school is in fact a safer environment for adolescents than any other.

5. The stress experienced by victims of bullies can linger into the college years and beyond.

6. Although most adolescents do not commit crimes, adolescents are disproportionately involved in criminal activities. Juvenile delinquents can be categorized as undersocialized or socialized delinquents.

Check

1. Intentional injury or harm to another person is called _____.

2. Boys tend to show higher levels of _____ aggression—aggression that is aimed at achieving a concrete goal—than girls.

3. _____ occurs in school and online, and is characterized by aggressive and hurtful acts such as name-calling, rejection, teasing, threats, and physical harm.

4. _____ delinquents are adolescents who are raised with little discipline or with harsh, uncaring parental supervision.

Apply

1. Why might being bullied be such a powerfully stressful experience for adolescents?

To see more review questions, log on to MyPsychLab.

ANSWERS: 1. aggression 2. instrumental 3. Bullying 4. Undersocialized

The CASE
of . . . *the Turncoat Friend*

Jeananne rode her bike through the autumn afternoon, thrilled and a little scared by what she was about to do. Ever since school had started—her first year in middle school—she'd wanted to be friends with Sarah Rockford and her clique. They were so cool, and Sarah attracted the kinds of boys Jeananne could only dream of. But Sarah and her friends walked by Jeananne as if she didn't exist. Until yesterday.

Yesterday, Sarah had passed her a note in math class. It said: *Some of us are going to the Beach House after school tomorrow. Want to come? P.S. Don't bring Martha. She's weird.* Jeananne couldn't believe it. The Beach House. It was *the* hangout, if you were popular. Did this mean Sarah thought Jeananne was cool enough for her crowd? Jeananne had certainly put all her energy into copying Sarah and her friends since school started. She'd changed her hair and gotten highlights, like Sarah. She'd started wearing different clothes. Ripped jeans and boots. Tiny skirts. Skinny tees. Just like Sarah and her friends. And now they were asking her to join them. But … they were also asking her to ditch Martha, her very best friend since second grade. Jeananne knew Martha wasn't weird. She was smart and funny and artistic—she even made her own clothes because she liked to be different. But … Martha wasn't cool, and Jeananne really wanted to run with Sarah's crowd.

She arrived at the Beach House, parking her bike down the block, in case none of the other kids had ridden bikes. When she entered the café/arcade, Sarah spotted her and waved her to their table. "Good," Sarah said, giving her an inclusive smile. "Glad you got my message about Martha." Jeananne looked around the table. Olivia, Danielle, and Maggie were there. And so were two

of the hottest boys in seventh grade. Jeananne greeted everyone, then turning to Sarah, she said, "I'm not really that close to Martha anymore. She's gotten sort of . . ." "Weird?" Sarah laughed, and her friends laughed, too. "Yeah," Jeananne said. "Definitely weird." She grinned. It was a relief—sort of—to have made a decision.

1. Jeananne's actions might be characterized as a disconnect between prosocial reasoning and prosocial behavior. Can her actions be defended using the social domain approach? Why or why not?

2. According to Carol Gilligan, which of the three stages of moral development characterizes Jeananne's actions? How might her actions be different in each of the other two stages?

3. Is Jeananne's betrayal of her friend Martha an act of aggression? Why or why not?

4. If Martha discovers Jeananne's betrayal, how might a mediator go about helping to create empathy between the two girls?

<<< LOOKING BACK

LO 13-1 How do children develop a moral sense?

- Piaget believed that preschool-age children are in the heteronomous morality stage of moral development, characterized by a belief in external, unchangeable rules of conduct and sure, immediate punishment for all misdeeds.

- In contrast, social learning approaches to morality emphasize interactions between environment and behavior in moral development in which models of behavior play an important role in development.

- Some developmentalists believe that moral behavior is rooted in a child's development of empathy. Other emotions, including the negative emotions of anger and shame, may also promote moral behavior.

LO 13-2 What kinds of disciplinary styles do parents employ, and what effects do they have?

- Disciplinary styles differ both individually and culturally. In the United States and other Western societies, parents' styles tend to be mostly authoritarian, permissive, uninvolved, and authoritative, the last regarded as the most effective.

- Children of authoritarian and permissive parents may develop dependency, hostility, and low self-control, while children of uninvolved parents may feel unloved and emotionally detached. Children of authoritative parents tend to be more independent, friendly, self-assertive, and cooperative.

LO 13-3 Through what stages does moral development progress during childhood and adolescence?

- According to Lawrence Kohlberg, people pass through three major levels and six stages of moral development as their sense of justice and their moral reasoning evolve. The three major levels encompass preconventional morality (motivated by rewards and punishments), conventional morality (motivated by social reference), and postconventional morality (motivated by a sense of universal moral principles)—a level that may be reached during adolescence but that many people never attain.

- Although Kohlberg's theory provides a good account of moral judgments, it is less adequate in predicting moral behavior.

- More sophisticated kinds of empathy emerge in adolescence when teens begin to experience empathy for collective groups, such as victims of racism.

LO 13-4 How do adolescent girls differ from boys in moral development?

- There appear to be gender differences in moral development not reflected in Kohlberg's work. Carol Gilligan has sketched out an alternative progression for girls, from an orientation toward individual survival through goodness as self-sacrifice to the morality of nonviolence.

LO 13-5 As adolescents become more sophisticated morally, how does their behavior change?

- Moral reasoning is not the same as moral behavior, as researchers with a social learning orientation have noted. Adolescents who understand moral issues do not invariably behave in a moral manner.

- Adolescents understand prosocial behavior and can evaluate the motivations behind it, which may be altruistic or self-serving.

- There are gender and cultural differences in empathy and prosocial behavior.

- Adolescents have a sophisticated understanding of the motivations behind lying and cheating, but their sophistication does not produce notable gains in honesty.

- Moral reasoning may vary with the context in which it occurs. Adolescents may regard some choices as personal rather than moral.

LO 13-6 How does aggression develop in preschool-age children?

- Aggression, which involves intentional harm to another person, begins to emerge in the preschool years. As children age and improve their language skills, acts of aggression typically decline in frequency and duration.

- Some ethologists, such as Konrad Lorenz, believe that aggression is simply a biological fact of human life, a belief held also by many sociobiologists, who focus on competition within species to pass genes on to the next generation.

- Social learning theorists focus on the role of the environment, including the influence of models and social reinforcement, as factors influencing aggressive behavior.

- The cognitive approach to aggression emphasizes the role of interpreting the behaviors of others in determining aggressive or non-aggressive responses.

LO 13-7 What forms does aggression take in middle childhood and adolescence, and what are some of the characteristics of its perpetrators?

- Bullying, school violence (such as the shootings at Columbine), and juvenile delinquency are all forms of aggressive behavior that may occur among school-age children or adolescents.

- Many bullies—about half—come from abusive homes. They tend to have behavior problems both at home and in school, and they may try to lie their way out of trouble when caught. They also tend to watch more television containing violence than do nonbullies, and show little remorse for their victims. They are more likely to break the law as adults than nonbullies.

- Students prone to violence are likely to be self-centered, have a low tolerance for frustration, poor coping skills, a lack of resiliency, and a resentment over perceived injustices. They may have experienced depression or a failed loved relationship and be alienated.

- Juvenile delinquents who engage in more serious criminal activities are likely to have been raised with little discipline or with harsh, uncaring parental supervision, and have not been taught how to regulate their own behavior. They tend to be relatively aggressive and violent fairly early in life, leading to rejection by peers and academic failure. They tend to have below-average intelligence and are more likely to have been diagnosed with attention deficit hyperactivity disorder as children.

KEY TERMS AND CONCEPTS

moral development (p. 352)
heteronomous morality (p. 352)
incipient cooperation stage (p. 353)
autonomous cooperation stage (p. 353)
immanent justice (p. 353)
prosocial behavior (p. 354)
abstract modeling (p. 354)
empathy (p. 354)

authoritarian parents (p. 355)
permissive parents (p. 355)
authoritative parents (p. 356)
uninvolved parents (p. 356)
neglect (p. 356)
preconventional morality (p. 360)
conventional morality (p. 360)
postconventional morality (p. 360)

social domain approach (p. 364)
aggression (p. 366)
emotional self-regulation (p. 367)
instrumental aggression (p. 367)
relational aggression (p. 367)
undersocialized delinquents (p. 375)
socialized delinquents (p. 375)

Epilogue

In this chapter, we considered both moral development and aggression. First, we looked at a variety of theories about how children develop a sense of right and wrong. We also explored a range of parenting styles and discussed their implications for shaping children's behavior, both present and future. Then, we discussed the development of moral reasoning and behavior. We saw how reasoning about moral dilemmas grows more sophisticated as children move into adolescence, and we considered how the expression of moral and helping behavior develops. We looked, too, at how prosocial behavior is influenced by gender and culture. In the final part of the chapter, we examined the sources of aggression and violence and considered the question: Is nature or nurture more responsible for aggression? We explored ways of decreasing aggression in children and increasing their moral behaviors. In conclusion, we looked at the serious consequences of bullying and examined the problem of juvenile delinquency.

Before moving on to the next chapter, take a moment to re-read the prologue to this chapter about Jesse's dilemma over the destruction of the bus, and answer the following questions:

1. Is Kohlberg's/Piaget's moral reasoning approach helpful in interpreting Jesse's actions in this instance? Why or why not?

2. Does the fact that the other boys throw rocks at the bus prove they think it's morally okay to do so? Why might there be a disconnect between their beliefs and their actions?

3. What evidence, if any, do you see in this story that Jesse has developed a set of core beliefs and values as part of his identity? What might some of those beliefs and values be?

4. Do you think Jesse's actions would have been different if a Wolverine's team member had injured one of Jesse's friends? Why or why not?

The Development Video Series in MyPsychLab

Explore the video *In the Real World: Learning Aggression* by scanning this QR code with your mobile device. If you don't already have one, you may download a free QR scanner for your device wherever smartphone apps are sold. You can also view this video in MyPsychLab. For more videos related to this chapter's content, log into MyPsychLab to view the entire Development Video Series.

My**Virtual**Child

- **What decisions would you make while raising a child?**
- **What would the consequences of those decisions be?**

Find out by accessing **MyVirtualChild** at
www.MyPsychLab.com
and raising your own virtual child from birth to age 18.

14 Friends and Family

MODULE 14.1

FRIENDSHIPS IN PRESCHOOL AND MIDDLE CHILDHOOD

- Preschoolers' Friendships
- Building Friendships in Middle Childhood
- Individual Differences in Friendship: What Makes a Child Popular?

ARE YOU AN INFORMED CONSUMER OF DEVELOPMENT? Increasing Children's Social Competence

Review, Check, and Apply

MODULE 14.2

THE ROLE OF PEERS IN ADOLESCENCE

- Peer Relationships in Adolescence: The Importance of Belonging

DEVELOPMENTAL DIVERSITY AND YOUR LIFE: Race Segregation: The Great Divide of Adolescence

- Popularity: Who's In, Who's Out?

NEUROSCIENCE AND DEVELOPMENT: A World of Faces and Facing the World

- Conformity: Peer Pressure in Adolescence

Review, Check, and Apply

MODULE 14.3

FAMILY RELATIONSHIPS

- Family Life
- Changing Family Relations and the Quest for Autonomy in Adolescence
- Family Constellations: The Array of Possibilities
- Child Abuse and Psychological Maltreatment: The Grim Side of Family Life

FROM RESEARCH TO PRACTICE: Spanking: Why the Experts Say "No"

Review, Check, and Apply

The Case of ... Too Much of a Good Thing

Looking Back

Key Terms and Concepts

Epilogue

PROLOGUE: Rewriting the Rules

Elena has been a self-care child since third grade when her parents divorced and her mom took a full-time job at a bank. The rules her mom laid down were simple: No kids in the house when she wasn't there. Call if you're going to a friend's house. Elena obeyed the rules though often she felt lonely at home on her own. Things got better in fifth grade when she began going downtown after school with her friends. Now that she's 14, Elena thinks the rules are stupid. She and her friends don't need supervision. They're not babies. She still goes downtown with her friends, which now include boys, but more and more Elena invites friends over when her mom isn't home. Sometimes things get a little out of hand. There's been some drinking, and several times Elena's bedroom has been used by the couples who are part of her clique, but no one's been hurt and nothing has been broken. "We're just normal teens,"

Elena says. "We make up our own minds about things and we don't need adults telling us every move to make." Still, Elena gets nervous when she thinks that some day her mom might come home early and discover a house full of unsupervised teens.

>>> LOOKING AHEAD

Elena's story illustrates both the quest for autonomy and the changing relationship between parents and children that characterize adolescence. Rewriting the rules is one way teens seek to establish their independence. But as Elena's concern about getting caught shows, becoming autonomous is a complex process. Along with independence comes conflict, even when parents and children truly love each other.

In this chapter, we examine family and peer relationships from the preschool years through adolescence. We begin by looking at the development of friendship and play in preschoolers. We then explore the profound changes that occur in children's notions of friendship during middle childhood. We consider, too, what makes some children more popular than others and discuss the characteristics that define social competence.

Next, we discuss the importance of peers and peer groups in adolescence. We look at the ways in which adolescents interact with their friends and the ways in which popularity is determined. We examine racial and ethnic segregation in adolescence. We also consider how peer pressure affects teens' behavior.

(continued)

Learning Objectives

MODULE 14.1

LO1 In what sorts of social relationships and play do preschool children engage?

LO2 What characterizes friendship in middle childhood, and how does social competence affect popularity?

MODULE 14.2

LO3 What role do friends and peers play in adolescence?

LO4 What are race and ethnic relationships like in adolescence?

LO5 What does it mean to be popular and unpopular in adolescence, and how do adolescents respond to peer pressure?

MODULE 14.3

LO6 How does the quality of relationships with family change as children move into adolescence?

LO7 How do today's diverse family and care arrangements affect children?

LO8 What are the forms of child abuse and psychological maltreatment, and what contributes to their occurrence?

The last part of the chapter explores the changing nature of family relationships as children grow from preschoolers to adolescents. We look at divorce and consider a variety of family constellations and their impact on children. Finally, we examine the grimmer side of family life for some children: child abuse and psychological maltreatment.

MODULE 14.1

FRIENDSHIPS IN PRESCHOOL AND MIDDLE CHILDHOOD

LO 14-1 In what sorts of social relationships and play do preschool children engage?

LO 14-2 What characterizes friendship in middle childhood, and how does social competence affect popularity?

When Juan was 3, he had his first best friend, Emilio. Juan and Emilio, who lived in the same apartment building in San Jose, were inseparable. They played incessantly with toy cars, racing them up and down the apartment hallways until some of the neighbors began to complain about the noise. They pretended to read to one another, and sometimes they slept over at each other's home—a big step for a 3-year-old. Neither boy seemed more joyful than when he was with his "best friend"—the term each used of the other.

An infant's family can provide nearly all the social contact he or she needs. Although parents and family remain very influential in the lives of preschoolers, many children, like Juan and Emilio, begin to discover the joys of friendship with their peers. Their social circles begin to expand considerably.

Preschoolers' Friendships

Before the age of 3, most social activity involves simply being in the same place at the same time, without real social interaction. However, at around the age of 3, children begin to develop real friendships like Juan and Emilio's as peers come to be seen as individuals who hold some special qualities and rewards. While preschoolers' relations with adults reflect children's needs for care, protection, and direction, their relations with peers are based more on the desire for companionship, play, and fun. Gradually, their ideas about friendship evolve. They come to view friendship as a continuing state, a stable relationship that takes place not just in the immediate moment but also offers the promise of future activity (Hay, Payne, & Chadwick, 2004; Sebanc et al., 2007; Eivers et al., 2012).

The quality and kinds of interactions children have with friends change during the preschool period. For 3-year-olds, the focus of friendship is the enjoyment of carrying out shared activities—doing things together and playing jointly, as when Juan and Emilio played with their toy cars in the hallway. Older preschoolers, however, pay more attention to abstract concepts such as trust, support, and shared interests. Throughout the preschool years, playing together remains an important part of all friendships. Like friendships, these play patterns change during the preschool years (Kawabata & Crick, 2011; Reddy, 2012).

Playing by the Rules: The Work of Play. In Rosie Graiff's class of 3-year-olds, Minnie bounces her doll's feet on the table as she sings softly to herself. Ben pushes his toy car across the floor, making motor noises. Sarah chases Abdul around and around the perimeter of the room.

As preschoolers get older, their conception of friendship evolves and the quality of their interactions changes.

Play is more than what children of preschool age do to pass the time. Instead, play helps preschoolers develop in important ways. In fact, the American Academy of Pediatrics states that play is essential for the cognitive, physical, social, and emotional well-being of children and youth. The United Nations High Commission for Human Rights maintains that play is a basic right of every child (Ginsburg et al., 2007; Whitebread et al., 2009; Fleer, 2012).

Categorizing Play.

At the beginning of the preschool years, children engage in **functional play**—simple, repetitive activities typical of 3-year-olds. Functional play may involve objects, such as dolls or cars, or repetitive muscular movements such as skipping, jumping, or rolling and unrolling a piece of clay. Functional play, then, involves doing something for the sake of being active rather than with the aim of creating some end product (Bober, Humphry, & Carswell, 2001; Kantrowitz & Evans, 2004).

As children get older, functional play declines. By the time they are 4, children become involved in a more sophisticated form of play. In **constructive play** children manipulate objects to produce or build something. A child who builds a house out of Legos or puts a puzzle together is involved in constructive play: He or she has an ultimate goal—to produce something. Such play is not necessarily aimed at creating something novel, since children may repeatedly build a house of blocks, let it fall into disarray, and then rebuild it.

Constructive play gives children a chance to test their developing physical and cognitive skills and to practice their fine muscle movements. They gain experience in solving problems about the ways and the sequences in which things fit together. They also learn to cooperate with others—a development we observe as the social nature of play shifts during the preschool period. Consequently, it's important for adults who care for preschoolers to provide a variety of toys that allow for both functional and constructive play (Edwards, 2000; Shi, 2003; Love & Burns, 2006).

The Social Aspects of Play.

If two preschoolers are sitting at a table side by side, each putting a different puzzle together, are they engaged jointly in play?

According to pioneering work done by Mildred Parten (1932), the answer is "yes." She suggests that these preschoolers are engaged in **parallel play**, in which children play with similar toys, in a similar manner, but do not interact with each other. Parallel play is typical for children during the early preschool years. Preschoolers also engage in another form of play, a highly passive one: onlooker play. In **onlooker play**, children simply watch others at play, but do not actually participate themselves. They may look on silently, or they may make comments of encouragement or advice.

As they get older, however, preschool-age children engage in more sophisticated forms of social play that involve a greater degree of interaction. In **associative play** two or more children actually interact with one another by sharing or borrowing toys or materials, although they do not do the same thing. In **cooperative play**, children genuinely play with one another, taking turns, playing games, or devising contests. (The various types of play are summarized in Table 14-1 on page 384.)

Usually associative and cooperative play do not typically become common until children reach the end of the preschool years. But children who have had substantial preschool experience are more apt to engage in more social forms of behavior, such as associative and cooperative play, fairly early in the preschool years than those with less experience (Brownell, Ramani, & Zerwas, 2006; Dyer & Moneta, 2006; Trawick-Smith & Dziurgot, 2011).

Solitary and onlooker play continue in the later stages of the preschool period. There are simply times when children prefer to play by themselves. And when newcomers join a group, one strategy for becoming part of the group—often successful—is to engage in onlooker play, waiting for an opportunity to join the play more actively (Lindsey & Colwell, 2003).

The nature of pretend, or make-believe, play also changes during the preschool period. In some ways, pretend play becomes increasingly *un*realistic—and even more imaginative—as preschoolers change from using only realistic objects to using less concrete ones. Thus, at the start of the preschool period, children may pretend to listen to a radio only if they actually have a plastic radio that looks realistic. Later, however, they are more likely to use an entirely different object, such as a large cardboard box, as a pretend radio (Bornstein et al., 1996).

In parallel play, children play with similar toys, in a similar manner, but don't necessarily interact with one another.

Watch the **Video** *Play Styles* in **MyPsychLab**.

FROM AN EDUCATOR'S PERSPECTIVE:

How might a nursery school teacher encourage a shy child to join a group of preschoolers who are playing?

functional play Play that involves simple, repetitive activities typical of 3-year-olds

constructive play Play in which children manipulate objects to produce or build something

parallel play Action in which children play with similar toys, in a similar manner, but do not interact with each other

onlooker play Action in which children simply watch others at play, but do not actually participate themselves

associative play Play in which two or more children actually interact with one another by sharing or borrowing toys or materials, although they do not do the same thing

cooperative play Play in which children genuinely interact with one another, taking turns, playing games, or devising contests

TABLE 14-1 Preschoolers' Play

Type of Play	Description	Examples
General Categories		
Functional play	Simple, repetitive activities typical of 3-year-olds. May involve objects or repetitive muscular movements.	Moving dolls or cars repetitively. Skipping, jumping, rolling or unrolling a piece of clay.
Constructive play	More sophisticated play in which children manipulate objects to produce or build something. Developed by age 4, constructive play lets children test physical and cognitive skills and practice fine muscle movements.	Building a doll house or car garage out of Legos, putting together a puzzle, making an animal out of clay.
Social Aspects of Play (Parten's Categories)		
Parallel play	Children use similar toys in a similar manner at the same time, but do not interact with each other. Typical of children during the early preschool years.	Children sitting side by side, each playing with his or her own toy car, putting together his or her own puzzle, or making an individual clay animal.
Onlooker play	Children simply watch others at play but do not actually participate. They may look on silently or make comments of encouragement or advice. Common among preschoolers and helpful when a child wishes to join a group already at play.	One child watches as a group of others play with dolls, cars, or clay; build with Legos; or work on a puzzle together.
Associative play	Two or more children interact, sharing or borrowing toys or materials, although they do not do the same thing.	Two children, each building his or her own Lego garage, may trade bricks back and forth.
Cooperative play	Children genuinely play with one another, taking turns, playing games, or devising contests.	A group of children working on a puzzle may take turns fitting in the pieces. Children playing with dolls or cars may take turns making the dolls talk or may agree on rules to race the cars.

Russian developmentalist Lev Vygotsky, whom we discussed in Chapter 6, argued that pretend play, particularly if it involves social play, is an important means for expanding preschool-age children's cognitive skills. Through make-believe play, children are able to "practice" activities (such as pretending to use a computer or read a book) that are a part of their particular culture and broaden their understanding of the way the world functions.

Furthermore, play helps the brain to develop and become more sophisticated. Based on experiments with nonhumans, neuroscientist Sergio Pellis has found not only that certain sorts of damage to the brain leads to abnormal sorts of play, but that depriving animals of the ability to play effects the course of brain development (Pellis & Pellis, 2007; Bell, Pellis, & Kolb, 2009).

For instance, in one experiment, Pellis and his colleagues observed rats under two different conditions. In the control condition, a juvenile target rat was housed with three other young females, allowing them the opportunity to engage in the equivalent of rat play. In the experimental condition, the young target rats were housed with three adult females. Although young rats caged with adults don't have the opportunity to play, they do encounter social experiences with the adults, who will groom and touch them. When Pellis examined the brains of the rats, he found that the play-deprived rats showed deficiencies in the development of their prefrontal cortex (Pellis & Pellis, 2007; Henig, 2008; Bell, Pellis, & Kolb, 2009).

Although it's a big leap from rat play to toddler play, the results of the study do suggest the significance of play in promoting brain and cognitive development. Ultimately, play may be one of the engines that fuels the intellectual development of preschoolers.

Culture also affects children's styles of play. For example, Korean American children engage in a higher proportion of parallel play than their Anglo-American counterparts, while Anglo-American preschoolers are involved in more pretend play (see Figure 14-1; Farver & Lee-Shin, 2000; Bai, 2005; Pellegrini, 2009).

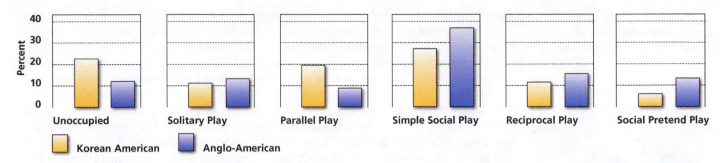

FIGURE 14-1 Comparing Play Complexity

An examination of Korean American and Anglo American preschoolers' play complexity finds clear differences in patterns of play. How would a child care provider explain this conclusion?

(*Source:* Adapted from Farver, Kim, & Lee-Shin, 1995)

How Preschoolers' Theory of Mind Affects Play. One reason behind the changes in children's play is the continuing development of preschoolers' theory of mind. As we first discussed in Chapter 7, *theory of mind* refers to knowledge and beliefs about how the mind operates. Using their theory of mind, preschool children are able to come up with explanations for how *others* think and reasons for why they behave the way they do. Increasingly they can see the world from others' perspectives. By the age of 3 or 4, preschoolers can distinguish between something in their minds and physical actuality. For instance, 3-year-olds know that they can imagine something that is not physically present, such as a zebra, and that others can do the same. They can also pretend that something has happened and react as if it really had occurred, a skill that becomes part of their imaginative play. And they know that others have the same capability (Cadinu & Kiesner, 2000; Mauritzson & Saeljoe, 2001; Andrews, Halford, & Bunch, 2003).

Building Friendships In Middle Childhood

In Lunch Room Number Two, Jamillah and her new classmates chew slowly on sandwiches and sip quietly on straws from cartons of milk. . . . Boys and girls look timidly at the strange faces across the table from them, looking for someone who might play with them in the schoolyard, someone who might become a friend.

For these children, what happens in the schoolyard will be just as important as what happens in the school. And when they're out on the playground, there will be no one to protect them. No child will hold back to keep from beating them at a game, humiliating them in a test of skill, or harming them in a fight. No one will run interference or guarantee membership in a group. Out on the playground, it's sink or swim. No one automatically becomes your friend.

(Kotre & Hall, 1990, pp. 112–113)

As Jamillah and her classmates demonstrate, friendship comes to play an increasingly important role during middle childhood. Children grow progressively more sensitive to the importance of friends, and building and maintaining friendships becomes a large part of children's social lives.

Friends influence children's development in several ways. For instance, friendships provide children with information about the world and other people as well as about themselves. Friends provide emotional support that

"We've done a lot of important playing here today."

Watch the **Video** *Friendship during Middle Childhood* in **MyPsychLab**.

Mutual trust is considered the centerpiece of friendship during middle childhood.

allows children to respond more effectively to stress. Having friends makes a child less likely to be the target of aggression, and it can teach children how to manage and control their emotions and help them interpret their own emotional experiences (Berndt, 2002).

Friendships in middle childhood also provide a training ground for communicating and interacting with others. They also can foster intellectual growth by increasing children's range of experiences (Harris, 1998; Nangle & Erdley, 2001; Gifford-Smith & Brownell, 2003).

Although friends and other peers become increasingly influential throughout middle childhood, they are not more important than parents and other family members. Most developmentalists believe that children's psychological functioning and their development in general are the product of a combination of factors, including peers and parents (Vandell, 2000; Parke, Simpkins, & McDowell, 2002; Altermatt, 2011). For that reason, we talk more about the influence of family later in this chapter.

Stages of Friendship: Changing Views of Friends.

During middle childhood, a child's conception of the nature of friendship undergoes some profound changes. According to developmental psychologist William Damon, a child's view of friendship passes through three distinct stages (Damon & Hart, 1988).

Stage 1: Basing Friendship on Others' Behaviors. In the first stage, which ranges from around 4 to 7 years of age, children see friends as others who like them and with whom they share toys and other activities. They view the children with whom they spend the most time as their friends. For instance, a kindergartner who was asked "How do you know that someone is your best friend?" responded in this way:

> I sleep over at his house sometimes. When he's playing ball with his friends he'll let me play. When I slept over, he let me get in front of him in 4-squares. He likes me. (Damon, 1983, p. 140)

What children in this first stage don't do much of, however, is take others' personal qualities into consideration. For instance, they don't see their friendship as being based on their peers' unique positive personal traits. Instead, they use a very concrete approach to deciding who is a friend, primarily dependent on others' behavior. They like those who share and with whom they can share, while they don't like those who don't share, who hit, or who don't play with them. In sum, in the first stage, friends are viewed largely in terms of presenting opportunities for pleasant interactions.

Stage 2: Basing Friendship on Trust. In the next stage, children's view of friendship becomes more complicated. Lasting from around age 8 to age 10, this stage covers a period in which children take others' personal qualities and traits as well as the rewards they provide into consideration. But the centerpiece of friendship in this second stage is mutual trust. Friends are seen as those who can be counted on to help out when they are needed. This means that violations of trust are taken very seriously, and friends cannot make amends for such violations just by engaging in positive play, as they might at earlier ages. Instead, the expectation is that formal explanations and formal apologies must be provided before a friendship can be reestablished.

Stage 3: Basing Friendship on Psychological Closeness. The third stage of friendship begins toward the end of middle childhood, from 11 to 15 years of age. During this period, children begin to develop the view of friendship that they hold during adolescence. As we will discuss in more detail later, the main criteria for friendship shift toward intimacy and loyalty. Friendship at this stage is characterized by feelings of closeness, usually brought on by sharing personal thoughts and feelings through mutual disclosure. They are also somewhat exclusive. By the time they reach the end of middle childhood, children seek out friends who will be loyal, and they come to view friendship not so much in terms of shared activities but in terms of the psychological benefits that friendship brings.

Children also develop clear ideas about which behaviors they seek in their friends—and which they dislike. As can be seen in Table 14-2, fifth- and sixth-graders most enjoy others who

TABLE 14-2 The Most-Liked and Least-Liked Behaviors That Children Note in Their Friends, in Order of Importance

Most-Liked Behaviors	Least-Liked Behaviors
Having a sense of humor	Verbal aggression
Being nice or friendly	Expressions of anger
Being helpful	Dishonesty
Being complimentary	Being critical or criticizing
Inviting one to participate in games, etc.	Being greedy or bossy
Sharing	Physical aggression
Avoiding unpleasant behavior	Being annoying or bothersome
Giving one permission or control	Teasing
Providing instructions	Interfering with achievements
Loyalty	Unfaithfulness
Performing admirably	Violating of rules
Facilitating achievements	Ignoring others

(*Source:* Based on Zarbatany, Hartmann, & Rankin, 1990.)

invite them to participate in activities and who are helpful, both physically and psychologically. In contrast, displays of physical or verbal aggression, among other behaviors, are disliked.

Individual Differences in Friendship: What Makes a Child Popular?

Children's friendships typically sort themselves out according to popularity. More popular children tend to form friendships with more popular individuals, while less popular children are more likely to have friends who are less popular. Popularity is also related to the number of friends a child has: More popular children are more apt to have a greater number of friends than those with lower popularity. In addition, more popular children are more likely to form *cliques,* groups that are viewed as exclusive and desirable, and they tend to interact with a greater number of other children.

   Why is it that some children are the schoolyard equivalent of the life of the party, while others are social isolates whose overtures toward their peers are dismissed or disdained? To answer this question, developmentalists have considered the personal characteristics of popular children.

What Makes Children Popular?
Popular children share several personality characteristics. They are usually helpful, cooperating with others on joint projects. Popular children are also funny, tending to have good senses of humor and to appreciate others' attempts at humor. Compared with children who are less popular, they are better able to read others' nonverbal behavior and understand others' emotional experiences. They also can control their nonverbal behavior more effectively, thereby presenting themselves well. In short, popular children are high in **social competence**, the collection of individual social skills that permit individuals to perform successfully in social settings (Feldman, Tomasian, & Coats, 1999).

social competence the collection of individual social skills that permit individuals to perform successfully in social setting

A variety of factors lead some children to be unpopular and socially isolated from their peers.

Although generally popular children are friendly, open, and cooperative, one subset of popular boys displays an array of negative behaviors, including being aggressive, disruptive, and causing trouble. Despite these behaviors, they may be viewed as cool and tough by their peers, and they are often remarkably popular. This popularity may occur in part because they are seen as boldly breaking rules that others feel constrained to follow (Meisinger et al., 2007; Woods, 2009; Kwon, Lease, & Hoffman, 2012).

The Social Benefits of Physical Competence.

Is Matt, a fifth-grader who is a clear standout on his Saturday morning soccer team, more popular as a result of his physical talents?

He may well be. According to a long history of research on the topic, school-age children who perform well physically are often more accepted and better liked by their peers than those who perform less well (Branta, Lerner, & Taylor, 1997).

However, the link between physical competence and popularity is considerably stronger for boys than for girls. The reason for this sex difference most likely relates to differing societal standards for appropriate male and female behavior. Despite the increasing evidence that girls and boys do not differ substantially in athletic performance, as we discussed in Chapter 5, a lingering "physical toughness" standard still exists for males but not for females. Regardless of age, males who are bigger, stronger, and more physically competent are seen as more desirable than those who are smaller, weaker, and less physically competent. In contrast, standards for females are less supportive of physical success. In fact, women receive less admiration for physical prowess than men do throughout the life span. Although these societal standards may be changing, with women's participation in sports activities becoming more frequent and valued, gender biases remain (Bowker, Gabdois, & Cornock, 2003; Hunter Smart et al., 2012).

Although the social desirability of athletically proficient boys increases throughout elementary school and continues into secondary school, at some point the positive consequences of motor ability begin to diminish.

Furthermore, it is difficult to sort out the extent that advantages from exceptional physical performance are due to actual athletic competence, as opposed to being a result of earlier maturation. Boys who physically mature at a more rapid pace than their peers or who happen to be taller, heavier, and stronger tend to perform better at athletic activities due to their relative size advantage. Consequently, it may be that early physical maturity is ultimately of greater consequence than physical skills per se.

Still, it is clear that athletic competence and motor skills in general play a notable role in school-age children's lives. However, it is important to help children avoid overemphasizing the significance of physical ability. Participation in sports should be fun, not something that separates one child from another or raises children's and parents' anxiety levels. Consequently, it is important to match the sport to a child's level of development. When the skills required by participation in a sport go beyond children's physical and mental capabilities, they may feel inadequate and frustrated (American Academy of Pediatrics, 2001).

In fact, some forms of organized sports, such as Little League baseball, are sometimes criticized for the emphasis they may place on winning at any cost. When children feel that success in sports is the sole goal, the pleasure of playing the game is diminished, particularly for children who are not naturally athletic and do not excel (Weber, 2005).

In sum, the goals of participation in sports and other physical activities should be to maintain physical fitness, to learn physical skills, and to become comfortable with one's body. And children should have fun in the process.

Social Problem-Solving Abilities.

Another factor that relates to children's popularity is their skill at social problem-solving. **Social problem-solving** refers to the use of strategies for solving social conflicts in ways that are satisfactory both to oneself and to others. Because social conflicts among school-age children are a not infrequent occurrence—even among the best of friends—successful strategies for dealing with them are an important element

social problem-solving The use of strategies for solving social conflicts in ways that are satisfactory both to oneself and to others

of social success (Rose & Asher, 1999; Murphy & Eisenberg, 2002).

According to developmental psychologist Kenneth Dodge, successful social problem-solving proceeds through a series of steps that correspond to children's information-processing strategies (see Figure 14-2). Dodge argues that the manner in which children solve social problems is a consequence of the decisions that they make at each point in the sequence (Dodge, Lansford, & Burks, 2003; Lansford et al., 2006; McLennan, 2012).

By carefully delineating each of the stages, Dodge provides a means by which interventions can be targeted toward a specific child's deficits. For instance, some children routinely misinterpret the meaning of other children's behavior (Step 2), and then respond according to their misinterpretation.

Suppose Max, a fourth-grader, is playing a game with Will. While playing the game, Will begins to get angry because he is losing and complains about the rules. If Max is not able to understand that much of Will's anger is frustration at not winning, he is likely to react in an angry way himself, defending the rules, criticizing Will, and making the situation worse. If Max interprets the source of Will's anger more accurately, Max may be able to behave in a more effective manner, perhaps by reminding Will, "Hey, you beat me at Connect Four," thereby defusing the situation.

Generally, children who are popular are better at interpreting the meaning of others' behavior accurately. Furthermore, they possess a wider inventory of techniques for dealing with social problems. In contrast, less popular children tend to be less effective at understanding the causes of others' behavior, and because of this their reactions to others may be inappropriate. In addition, their strategies for dealing with social problems are more limited; they sometimes simply don't know how to apologize or help someone who is unhappy feel better (Rose & Asher, 1999; Rinaldi, 2002).

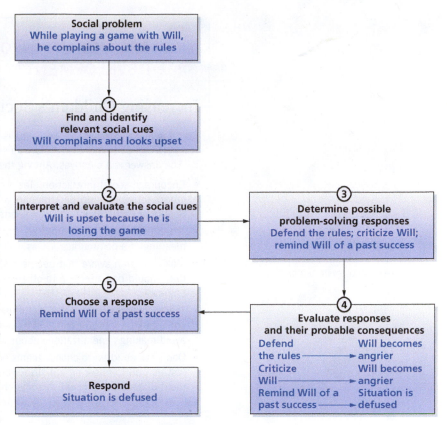

FIGURE 14-2 Problem-Solving Steps

Children's problem-solving proceeds through several steps involving different information-processing strategies. In what ways might an educator use children's problem-solving skills as a learning tool?

(*Source:* Adapted from Dodge, 1985)

Unpopular children may become victims of a phenomenon known as *learned helplessness.* Because they don't understand the root causes of their unpopularity, children may feel that they have little or no ability to improve their situation. As a result, they may simply give up and not even try to become more involved with their peers. In turn, their learned helplessness becomes a self-fulfilling prophecy, reducing the chances that they will become more popular in the future (Seligman, 2007; Aujoulat, Luminet, & Deccache, 2007).

Teaching Social Competence. Can anything be done to help unpopular children learn social competence? Happily, the answer appears to be yes. Several programs have been developed to teach children a set of social skills that seem to underlie general social competence. For example, in one experimental program, a group of unpopular fifth- and sixth-graders were taught how to hold a conversation with friends. They were taught ways to disclose material about themselves, to learn about others by asking questions, and to offer help and suggestions to others in a nonthreatening way.

Compared with a group of children who did not receive such training, the children who were in the experiment interacted more with their peers, held more conversations, developed higher self-esteem, and—most critically—were more accepted by their peers than before training (Bierman, 2004; Dollar & Stifter, 2012).

✅ ARE YOU AN INFORMED CONSUMER OF DEVELOPMENT?

Increasing Children's Social Competence

Building and maintaining friendships is critical in children's lives. Is there anything that parents and teachers can do to increase children's social competence?

The answer is a clear yes. Among the strategies that can work are the following:

- Encourage social interaction. Teachers can devise ways in which children are led to take part in group activities, and parents can encourage membership in such groups as Brownies and Cub Scouts or participation in team sports.

- Teach listening skills to children. Show them how to listen carefully and respond to the underlying meaning of a communication as well as its overt content.

- Make children aware that people display emotions and moods nonverbally and that consequently they should pay attention to others' nonverbal behavior, not only to what they are saying on a verbal level.

- Teach conversational skills, including the importance of asking questions and self-disclosure. Encourage students to use "I" statements in which they clarify their own feelings or opinions, and avoid making generalizations about others.

- Don't ask children to choose teams or groups publicly. Instead, assign children randomly: It works just as well in ensuring a distribution of abilities across groups and avoids the public embarrassment of a situation in which some children are chosen last. ■

Review, Check, and Apply

Review

1. In the preschool years, children develop friendships on the basis of personal characteristics, trust, and shared interests.

2. The character of preschoolers' play changes over time, growing more sophisticated, interactive, and cooperative, and relying increasingly on social skills.

3. Children's understanding of friendship changes from the sharing of enjoyable activities, through the consideration of personal traits that can meet their needs, to a focus on intimacy and loyalty.

4. Popular children tend to be helpful and cooperative with others. They also tend to have good senses of humor and are able to read others' nonverbal behavior and understand others' emotional experiences. Their ability to control their nonverbal behavior allows them to present themselves to good effect.

5. Children's social competence can be increased by teaching them how to communicate more effectively with others, including learning to read others' nonverbal behavior.

Check

1. Preschoolers who are playing with similar toys in a similar manner, but who are not interacting with each other, are engaging in _____ _____.

2. Functional play is the simple, repetitive activities seen among 3-year-olds. By the time children are 4, they are engaging in _____ play, manipulating objects to produce or build something.

3. _____ _____ is the collection of individual social skills that permit individuals to perform successfully in social settings.

4. The use of strategies for solving social conflicts in ways that are satisfactory both to one-self and to others is known as _____ _____.

Apply

1. How might a parent or teacher go about helping a child become more sensitive to and adept at reading others' nonverbal behaviors?

To see more review questions, log on to MyPsychLab.

ANSWERS: 1. parallel play 2. constructive 3. Social competence 4. social problem-solving

MODULE 14.2

THE ROLE OF PEERS IN ADOLESCENCE

LO 14-3 What role do friends and peers play in adolescence?

LO 14-4 What are race and ethnic relationships like in adolescence?

LO 14-5 What does it mean to be popular and unpopular in adolescence, and how do adolescents respond to peer pressure?

> *When Deborah entered middle school, she asked her parents to raise her text messaging allowance on their phone plan. "Everybody texts. That's how we communicate," Deborah explained. Her parents raised the monthly text allowance to 500 messages, surely a generous amount. But every month, Deborah exceeds the limit, once by more than 700 messages! "Why on earth do you need to text a thousand messages to people you see every day?" her mother asks, disgruntled at the third high phone bill she's received in as many months. "You don't understand!" Deborah wails. "Every one of those texts is important. Without them, I won't know what's happening."*

Peer Relationships in Adolescence: The Importance of Belonging

In the eyes of many parents, the most fitting symbols of adolescence are the computer or perhaps the cell phone, on which incessant text messaging occurs. For many of their sons and daughters, communicating with friends is experienced as an indispensable lifeline, sustaining ties to individuals with whom they may have already spent many hours earlier in the day.

The seemingly compulsive need to communicate with friends demonstrates the role that peers play in adolescence. Continuing the trend that began in middle childhood, adolescents spend increasing amounts of time with their peers, and the importance of peer relationships grows as well. In fact, there is probably no period of life in which peer relationships are as important as they are in adolescence. Even peers who are not counted as friends become extraordinarily influential in the lives of adolescents (Engels, Kerr, & Stattin, 2007; Laursen et al., 2012).

Peers grow in importance in adolescence for a variety of reasons. Peers can help adolescents satisfy personal interests and can provide them with information that they feel they need for their own purposes. For instance, an interest in conservation may cause adolescents to become part of a group dedicated to stamping out pollution. Or they may join a high school Gay, Lesbian, and Bisexual Alliance not only because of their interest in supporting people with different sexual orientations, but because they themselves are questioning their sexual identity.

Reference groups of peers provide norms for social comparison.

Watch the **Video** *Adolescent Cliques* in **MyPsychLab**.

cliques   Groups of from 2 to 12 people whose members have frequent social interactions with one another

crowds   Larger groups than cliques, composed of individuals who share particular characteristics but who may not interact with one another

In addition, some groups provide prestige. Membership on a cheerleading squad or service on the School Council may be an honor in some middle schools. (In others, membership on a cheerleading squad or School Council may be source of derision, with prestige reserved for other groups and activities.)

As we discussed earlier, peers also provide a means of social comparison, allowing teens to compare and evaluate their opinions, abilities, and even physical changes with those of others. Peers and peer groups also fill another important need for this age group: the need to *belong*.

Cliques and Crowds.   When adolescents get together, they are likely to do so in larger groups than those in which they congregated during childhood. During middle and late childhood, typical groups consisted of pairs of children, or perhaps three or four others. In contrast, adolescent groups often consist of larger collectives. As we discussed in Chapter 12, the sex segregation of childhood social groups fades in adolescence. Cliques increasingly are comprised of both boys and girls as puberty changes the way adolescents view the opposite sex.

One of the consequences of the increasing cognitive sophistication of adolescents is the ability to group others in more discriminating ways. Consequently, even if they do not belong to the group they use for reference purposes, adolescents typically are part of some identifiable group. Rather than defining people in concrete terms relating to what they do ("football players" or "musicians") as a younger school-age child might, adolescents use more abstract terms packed with greater subtleties ("jocks" or "skaters" or "stoners"; Brown, 2003).

Adolescents tend to belong to two types of groups: cliques and crowds. **Cliques** are groups of from 2 to 12 people whose members have frequent social interactions with one another. In contrast, **crowds** are larger, comprising individuals who share particular characteristics but who may not interact with one another. For instance, "jocks" and "nerds" are representative of crowds found in many high schools.

Membership in particular cliques and crowds is often determined by the degree of similarity with members of the group. One of the most important dimensions of similarity relates to substance use; adolescents tend to choose friends who use alcohol and other drugs to the same extent that they do. Their friends are also often similar in terms of their academic success, although this is not always true. For instance, during early adolescence, attraction to peers who are particularly well behaved seems to decrease, whereas, at the same time, those who behave more aggressively become more attractive (Kupersmidt & Dodge, 2004; Hutchinson & Rapee, 2007; Kiuru et al., 2009).

The emergence of distinct cliques and crowds during adolescence reflects in part the increased cognitive capabilities of adolescents. Group labels are abstractions, requiring teens to make judgments of people with whom they may interact only rarely and of whom they have little direct knowledge. It is not until mid-adolescence that teenagers are sufficiently sophisticated cognitively to make the subtle judgments that underlie distinctions between different cliques and crowds (Burgess & Rubin, 2000; Brown & Klute, 2003).

Online Social Networks: Cyberspace Peers.   Adolescents are increasingly involved in groups comprising people that they've never met in person, but with whom they are well acquainted—online. Cyberspace social networks are a growing aspect of adolescent social life, acting as virtual community centers where adolescents socialize, sometimes for hours at a time (Hempel, 2005; Rodkin & Ryan, 2012).

One of the major sites, Facebook.com, has tens of millions of members (not only adolescents, we should note). Adolescents may flirt online with total strangers or ask a person to be their friend. They are able to keep up with the latest music and films, discussing what's hot and what's out of favor.

Using virtual social networks, adolescents can also make contact with people they know in real life, as well as finding new individuals with whom to network. Several social-networking sites, such as Facebook.com, offer the opportunity to construct an elaborate webpage, post photos and favorite songs, and list the friends each member of the network has.

DEVELOPMENTAL DIVERSITY AND YOUR LIFE

Race Segregation: The Great Divide of Adolescence

When Robert Corker, a student at Tufts University, first stepped into the gym, he was immediately pulled into a pick-up basketball game. "The guys thought I'd be good at basketball just because I'm tall and black. Actually, I stink at sports and quickly changed their minds. Fortunately we all laughed about it later," Robert says.

***

When Sandra Cantú, a Puerto Rican nursing student at the University of Alabama, entered the cafeteria wearing her hospital whites, two female students assumed she was a cafeteria worker and asked her to clear off their table.

***

Race relations are no easier for white students to manage. Ted Connors, a white senior at Southern Methodist, recalls the day he asked a student in his dorm for help with his Spanish homework. "He laughed in my face," Ted recalls, "I assumed he spoke Spanish just because his name was Gonzalez. Actually, he had grown up in Michigan and spoke only English. It took quite a while to live that one down."

The pattern of racial misunderstanding experienced by these students is repeated over and over in schools and colleges throughout the United States: Even when they attend desegregated schools with significant ethnic and racial diversity, people of different ethnicities and races interact very little. Moreover, even if they have a friend of a different ethnicity within the confines of a school, most adolescents don't interact with that friend outside of school (DuBois & Hirsch, 1990).

It doesn't start out this way. During elementary school and even during early adolescence, there is a fair amount of integration among students of differing ethnicities. However, by middle and late adolescence, the amount of segregation is striking (Spencer & Dornbusch, 1990; Spencer, 1991; Ennett & Bauman, 1996).

Why should racial and ethnic segregation be the rule, even in schools that have been desegregated for some time? One reason is that minority students may actively seek support from others who share their minority status (where "minority" is used in its sociological sense to indicate a subordinate group whose members lack power, compared to members of a dominant group). By associating primarily with other members of their own group, members of minority groups are able to affirm their own identity.

Members of different racial and ethnic groups may be segregated in the classroom as well. Adolescents who are members of groups that have been historically discriminated against tend to experience less school success than members of the majority group. It may be that ethnic and racial segregation in high school is based not on ethnicity itself, but on academic achievement.

If minority group members experience less academic success, they may find themselves in classes with proportionally fewer majority group members. Similarly, majority students may be in classes with few minority students. Such class assignment practices, then, may inadvertently maintain and promote racial and ethnic segregation. This pattern would be particularly prevalent in schools where rigid academic tracking is practiced, with students assigned to "low," "medium," and "high" tracks depending on their prior achievement (Lucas & Behrends, 2002).

The lack of contact among students of different racial and ethnic backgrounds in school may also reflect prejudice, both perceived and real, toward members of other groups. Students of color may feel that the white majority is prejudiced, discriminatory, and hostile, and they may prefer to stick to same-race groups. Conversely, white students may assume that minority group members are antagonistic and unfriendly. Such mutually destructive attitudes reduce the likelihood that meaningful interaction can take place (Phinney, Ferguson, & Tate, 1997; Tropp, 2003; Hudley & Irving, 2012).

Is this sort of voluntary segregation along racial and ethnic lines found during adolescence inevitable? No. Adolescents who have interacted regularly and extensively with those of different races earlier in their lives are more likely to have friends of different races. Schools that actively promote contact among members of different ethnicities in classes help create an environment in which cross-race friendships can flourish (Hewstone, 2003).

Still, the task is daunting. Many societal pressures act to keep members of different races from interacting with one another. Peer pressure, too, may encourage this as some cliques may actively promote norms that discourage group members from crossing racial and ethnic lines to form new friendships. ■

Adolescents who have had extensive interactions with members of different races are more likely to have friends of different races.

It's too early to tell if web-based social networks will simply augment or actually replace more traditional forms of peer relationships. What is clear is that they offer adolescents a major new way both to interact with existing acquaintances and to make new friends.

Popularity: Who's In, Who's Out?

Most adolescents have well-tuned antennae when it comes to determining who is popular and who is not. In fact, for some teenagers, concerns over popularity—or lack of it—may be a central focus of their lives.

Personal Qualities and Popularity.
It's hardly surprising that adolescents' personal qualities—their personality, intelligence, and social skills—are significant factors in determining their level of popularity. Those with positive qualities are more popular than those with more disagreeable qualities.

What are the positive qualities that matter during adolescence? Popular boys and girls have high emotional intelligence, knowing how to act appropriately in a particular situation. They are

Unpopular adolescents fall into several categories. Controversial adolescents are liked by some and disliked by others, rejected adolescents are uniformly disliked, and neglected adolescents are neither liked nor disliked.

enjoyable to be around—friendly, cheerful, smart, and with a good sense of humor.

But the sheer number of qualities is not the whole story. Sometimes adolescents prefer those who have at least a few negative qualities over those who are seemingly flawless. The negative aspects of their personality make them more human and approachable (Hawley, 2003).

Furthermore, some less-than-admirable qualities are associated with popularity. For example, adolescents who lie most effectively are more popular than those who lie less well. The explanation is not that lying produces popularity. Instead, effective lying may act as a kind of social skill, allowing an adolescent to say the right thing at the right moment. In contrast, adolescents who are always truthful may hurt others' feelings with their bluntness (Feldman, Forrest, & Happ, 2002; Lansu, Cillessen, & Karremans, 2012).

Culture also plays a role in determining what qualities are associated with popularity. In Western cultures, for example, extroversion is related to popularity, while introverted adolescents are generally less popular. In contrast, in Asian cultures, shyness is viewed as a desirable trait, and introversion is more closely related to popularity (Chen et al., 2002).

Popularity and Rejection.
Actually, the social world of adolescents is divided not only into popular and unpopular individuals; the differentiations are more complex (see Figure 14-3). For instance, some adolescents are controversial; in contrast to *popular*

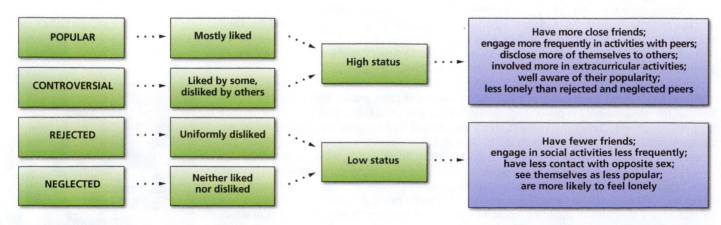

FIGURE 14-3 The Social World of Adolescence

An adolescent's popularity can fall into one of four categories, depending on the opinions of his or her peers. Popularity is related to differences in status, behavior, and adjustment.

NEUROSCIENCE AND DEVELOPMENT
A World of Faces and Facing the World

Four-year-old Duncan Mitchell looked his mother in the eye and asked, "Are you my Mommy?" When she responded, "Yes," Duncan recognized her voice and felt better—but he still didn't recognize her face.

This strange interaction led to medical examinations, revealing that Duncan suffered from prosopagnosia, a developmental condition sometime called "face blindness." Although Duncan can see perfectly, he often can't recognize others' faces—even those he knows very well.

In other ways, Duncan, now 8, is completely typical. He has a normal memory, and he can distinguish between nonhuman objects such as dogs and cars. But he is unable to distinguish human faces. (Tesoriero, 2007)

What would your life be like if you could not remember a familiar face or recognize important people in your life? For some people, diagnosed with a rare condition known as face blindness, that's an everyday experience.

Most of us, though, suffer lapses in which we are unable to remember faces due to everyday memory losses. According to new research by neuroscientist Ulrike Rimmele and colleagues (2009),

it turns out that the chemical oxytocin strengthens the neuronal systems of social memory by improving the ability to recognize familiar faces.

Rimmele's research shows that after one experimental dose of an oxytocin nasal spray, adults showed improved recognition memory for faces—but not inanimate objects. In the study, participants used the spray and were shown various images. The next day, they participated in a surprise test and were shown a collection of the same and new images. Those who used the oxytocin spray more accurately recognized the faces they had seen before than those who had not used the spray. They also improved their ability to discriminate between new and familiar faces. However, the two groups did not differ in recognizing the other, nonsocial images.

These results suggest that oxytocin specifically improves social memory and strengthens the capability to correctly discriminate faces. They also demonstrate that different mechanisms exist for social and nonsocial memory—as related to facial recognition.

■ **What types of problems might people with face blindness experience, and how might it be detrimental to their social lives?**

---

adolescents, who are mostly liked, **controversial adolescents** are liked by some and disliked by others. For example, a controversial adolescent may be highly popular within a particular group such as the string orchestra, but not popular among other classmates. Furthermore, there are **rejected adolescents**, who are uniformly disliked, and **neglected adolescents**, who are neither liked nor disliked. Neglected adolescents are the forgotten student—the ones whose status is so low that they are overlooked by almost everyone.

In most cases, popular and controversial adolescents tend to be similar in that their overall status is higher, whereas rejected and neglected adolescents share a generally lower status. Popular and controversial adolescents have more close friends, engage more frequently in activities with their peers, and disclose more about themselves to others than do less popular students. They are also more involved in extracurricular school activities. In addition, they are well aware of their popularity, and they are less lonely than their less popular classmates (Farmer et al., 2003; Zettergren, 2003; Becker & Luthar, 2007; Closson, 2009).

In contrast, the social world of rejected and neglected adolescents is considerably less pleasant. They have fewer friends, engage in social activities less frequently, and have less contact with the opposite sex. They see themselves—accurately, it turns out—as less popular, and they are more likely to feel lonely. They may find themselves in conflicts with others, some of which escalate into full-blown fights that require mediation (McElhaney, Antonishak, & Allen, 2008; to learn more about another type of difficulty in maintaining friendships, see the *Neuroscience and Development* box).

What is it that determines status in high school? As illustrated in Table 14-3 on page 396, men and women have different perceptions. For example, college men suggest that physical attractiveness is the most important factor in determining high school girls' status, whereas college women believe it is a high school girl's grades and intelligence (Suitor et al., 2001).

As they grow more confident of their own decisions, adolescents become less likely to conform to peers and parents.

controversial adolescents Children who are liked by some peers and disliked by others

rejected adolescents Children who are actively disliked, and whose peers may react to them in an obviously negative manner

neglected adolescents Children who receive relatively little attention from their peers in the form of either positive or negative interactions

TABLE 14-3 High School Status

Who Is High Status in High School?			
According to college men		**According to college women**	
High-status high school girls:	**High-status high school boys:**	**High-status high school girls:**	**High-status high school boys:**
1. are good-looking	1. take part in sports	1. have high grades and are intelligent	1. take part in sports
2. have high grades and are intelligent	2. have high grades and are intelligent	2. participate in sports	2. have high grades and are intelligent
3. take part in sports	3. are popular with girls	3. are sociable	3. are sociable
4. are sociable	4. are sociable	4. are good-looking	4. are good-looking
5. are popular with boys	5. have nice cars	5. have nice clothes	5. participate in school clubs or government

Note: Results are based on responses from students at Louisiana State University, Southeastern Louisiana University, State University of New York at Albany, State University of New York at Stony Brook, University of Georgia, and the University of New Hampshire (Suitor et al., 2001).

(*Source:* Based on Suitor et al., 2001.)

Conformity: Peer Pressure in Adolescence

Whenever Aldos Henry said he wanted to buy a particular brand of sneakers or a certain style of shirt, his parents complained that he was just giving in to peer pressure and told him to make up his own mind about things.

In arguing with Aldos, his parents were subscribing to a view of adolescence that is quite prevalent in U.S. society: that teenagers are highly susceptible to **peer pressure**, the influence of one's peers to conform to their behavior and attitudes. Were his parents correct?

The research suggests that it all depends. In some cases, adolescents *are* highly susceptible to the influence of their peers. For instance, when considering what to wear, whom to date, and what movies to see, adolescents are apt to follow the lead of their peers. Wearing the right clothes, down to the right brand of the right clothes, sometimes can be a ticket to membership in a popular group. It shows you know what's what. On the other hand, when it comes to many nonsocial matters, such as choosing a career path or trying to solve a problem, they are more likely to turn to an experienced adult (Phelan, Yu, & Davidson, 1994).

In short, particularly in middle and late adolescence, teenagers turn to those they see as experts on a given dimension. If they have social concerns, they turn to the people most likely to be experts—their peers. If the problem is one about which parents or other adults are most likely to have expertise, teenagers tend to turn to them for advice and are most susceptible to their opinions (Young & Ferguson, 1979; Perrine & Aloise-Young, 2004).

Overall, then, it does not appear that susceptibility to peer pressure suddenly soars during adolescence. Instead, adolescence brings about a change in the people to whom an individual conforms. Whereas children conform fairly consistently to their parents during childhood, in adolescence, conformity shifts to the peer group, in part because pressures to conform to peers increase as adolescents seek to establish their identity apart from their parents.

Ultimately, however, adolescents conform less to both peers *and* adults as they develop increasing autonomy over their lives. As they grow in confidence and in the ability to make their own decisions, adolescents are more apt to remain independent and to reject pressures from others, no matter who those others are. Before they learn to resist the urge to conform to their peers, however, teenagers may get into trouble, often along with their friends (Cook, Buehler, & Henson, 2009; Monahan, Steinberg, & Cauffman, 2009; Harakeh & Vollebergh, 2012).

peer pressure The influence of one's peers to conform to their behavior and attitudes

Review, Check, and Apply

Review

1. Peer groups are of great importance during adolescence, providing a way to meet personal interests, acquire information, and gain prestige.

2. Cliques and crowds serve as reference groups in adolescence and offer a ready means of social comparison. Social groups are increasingly mixed in gender.

3. Racial separation increases during adolescence, bolstered by socioeconomic status differences, different academic experiences, and mutually distrustful attitudes.

4. Degrees of popularity in adolescence include popular, controversial, neglected, and rejected adolescents.

5. Adolescents are likely to be influenced by their peers in matters of what brand clothing to wear, what movies to see, and whom to date, but when it comes to nonsocial matters, such as choosing a career path or college, they are likely to turn to a respected adult.

Check

1. Small groups of 2–12 teens whose members have frequent social interactions with one another are called _____ .

2. Popular adolescents are liked by most of their peers, whereas _____ _____ are liked by some and disliked by others.

3. The influence of one's peers to conform to their behavior and attitudes is known as _____ _____.

Apply

1. Does the popularity of online networking indicate a greater or lesser tendency to engage in social activities than face-to-face networking? Why?

To see more review questions, log on to MyPsychLab.

ANSWERS: 1. cliques 2. controversial adolescents 3. peer pressure

---

MODULE **14.3**

FAMILY RELATIONSHIPS

LO 14-6 How does the quality of relationships with family change as children move into adolescence?

LO 14-7 How do today's diverse family and care arrangements affect children?

LO 14-8 What are the forms of child abuse and psychological maltreatment, and what contributes to their occurrence?

Family Life

Four-year-old Benjamin was watching TV while his mom cleaned up after dinner. After a while, he wandered in and grabbed a towel, saying, "Mommy, let me help you do the dishes." Surprised by this unprecedented behavior, she asked him, "Where did you learn to do dishes?"

Sibling rivalry occurs when brothers and sisters compete or fight with one another.

"I saw it on Leave It to Beaver," *he replied, "Only it was the dad helping. Since we don't have a dad, I figured I'd do it."*

For an increasing number of children, life does not mirror what we see in reruns of old sit-coms. Many face the realities of an increasingly complicated world. For instance, as we will discuss in greater detail further on, children are increasingly likely to live with only one parent. In 1960, less than 10% of all children under the age of 18 lived with one parent. Now, a single parent heads a quarter of all families. There are also large racial disparities: nearly half of all African American children and a quarter of Hispanic children live with a single parent, compared with 22% of white children (Grall, 2009).

Preschoolers' Family Lives. For most children the preschool years are not a time of upheaval and turmoil. Instead, the period encompasses a growing interaction with the world at large. As we've seen, for instance, preschoolers begin to develop genuine friendships with other children, in which close ties emerge. One central factor leading preschoolers to develop friendships comes when parents provide a warm, supportive home environment. Strong, positive relationships between parents and children encourage children's relationships with others (Howes, Galinsky, & Kontos, 1998; Hill, 2012). How do parents nurture that relationship?

Family Life in Middle Childhood. During the middle years of childhood, children spend significantly less time with their parents than in earlier years. Still, parents remain the major influence in their children's lives, and they are seen as providing essential assistance, advice, and direction (Furman & Buhrmester, 1992; Parke, 2004).

Siblings also have an important influence on children during middle childhood, for good and for bad. Although brothers and sisters can provide support, companionship, and a sense of security, they can also be a source of strife.

Sibling rivalry can occur, with siblings competing or quarreling with one another. Such rivalry can be most intense when siblings are similar in age and of the same sex. Parents may intensify sibling rivalry by being perceived as favoring one child over another. Such perceptions may or may not be accurate. For example, older siblings may be permitted more freedom, which the younger sibling may interpret as favoritism. In some cases, perceived favoritism not only leads to sibling rivalry but may also damage the self-esteem of the younger sibling. On the other hand, sibling rivalry is not inevitable.

What about children who have no siblings? The only child has no opportunity to develop sibling rivalry also misses out on the benefits that siblings can bring. Generally, despite the stereotype that only children are spoiled and self-centered, the reality is that they are as well-adjusted as children with brothers and sisters. In fact, in some ways, only children are better-adjusted, often having higher self-esteem and stronger motivation to achieve. This is particularly good news for parents in China, where a strict one-child policy is in effect. Studies there show that Chinese only-children often academically outperform children with siblings (Miao & Wang, 2003).

Changing Family Relations and the Quest for Autonomy in Adolescence

When Paco Lizzagara entered junior high school, his relationship with his parents changed drastically. What had been a good relationship had become tense by the middle of seventh grade. Paco felt his parents always seemed to be "on his case." Instead of giving him more freedom, which he felt he deserved at age 13, they actually seemed to be becoming more restrictive.

Paco's parents would probably see things differently. They would likely suggest that they were not the source of the tension in the household—Paco was. From their point of view, Paco, with whom they'd established what seemed to be a close, stable, loving relationship throughout much of his childhood, suddenly seemed transformed. They felt he was shutting them out of his life, and when he did speak with them, it was merely to criticize their politics, their dress, their preferences in TV shows. To his parents, Paco's behavior was upsetting and bewildering.

Parents are sometimes angered, and even more frequently puzzled, by adolescents' conduct. Children who have previously accepted their parents' judgments, declarations, and guidelines begin to question—and sometimes rebel against—their parents' views of the world.

One reason for these clashes are the shifting roles both children and parents must deal with during adolescence. Adolescents increasingly seek **autonomy**, independence and a sense of control over their lives. Most parents intellectually realize that this shift is a normal part of adolescence, representing one of the primary developmental tasks of the period, and in many ways they welcome it as a sign of their children's growth. However, in many cases the day-to-day realities of adolescents' increasing autonomy may prove difficult for them to deal with (Smetana, 1995). But understanding this growing independence intellectually and agreeing to allow a teen to attend a party when no parents will be present are two different things. To the adolescent, her parents' refusal indicates a lack of trust or confidence. To the parent, it's simple good sense: "I trust you," they may say. "It's everyone else who will be there that I worry about."

In most families, teenagers' autonomy grows gradually over the course of adolescence. For instance, one study of changes in adolescents' views of their parents found that increasing autonomy led them to perceive parents less in idealized terms and more as persons in their own right. For example, rather than see their parents as authoritarian disciplinarians mindlessly reminding them to do their homework, they may come to see their parents' emphasis on excelling in school as evidence of parental regrets about their own lack of education and a wish to see their children have more options in life. At the same time, adolescents came to depend more on themselves and to feel more like separate individuals (see Figure 14-4).

The increase in adolescent autonomy changes the relationship between parents and teenagers. At the start of adolescence, the relationship tends to be asymmetrical: Parents hold most of the power and influence over the relationship. By the end of adolescence, however, power and influence have become more balanced, and parents and children end up in a more symmetrical, or egalitarian, relationship. Power and influence are shared, although parents typically retain the upper hand (Goede, Branje, & Meeus, 2009).

Culture and Autonomy.
The degree of autonomy that is eventually achieved varies from one family and one child to the next. Cultural factors play an important role. In Western societies, which tend to value individualism, adolescents seek autonomy at a relatively early stage of adolescence. In contrast, Asian societies are collectivistic; they promote the idea that the well-being of the group is more important than that of the individual. In such societies, adolescents' aspirations to achieve autonomy are less pronounced (Raeff, 2004; Supple et al., 2009; Schwarz et al., 2012).

Adolescents from different cultural backgrounds also vary in the degree of obligation to their family that they feel. Those in more collectivistic cultures tend to feel greater obligation to their families, in terms of fulfilling their expectations about their duty to provide assistance, show respect, and support their families in the future, than those from more individualistic societies. In such societies, the push for autonomy is less strong, and the timetable during which autonomy is expected to develop is slower (see Figure 14-5 on page 400; Chao, 2001; Fuligni & Zhang, 2004; Leung, Pe-Pua, & Karnilowicz, 2006).

For example, when asked at what age an adolescent would be expected to carry out certain behaviors (such as going to a concert with friends), adolescents and parents provide different answers depending on their cultural

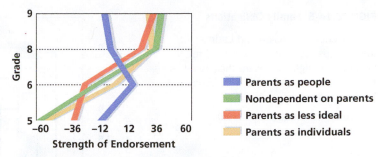

Parents as people
Nondependent on parents
Parents as less ideal
Parents as individuals

FIGURE 14-4 Changing Views of Parents

As adolescents become older, they come to perceive their parents in less idealized terms and more as individuals. What effect is this likely to have on family relations?

(*Source:* Based on Steinberg & Silverberg, 1986)

autonomy Having independence and a sense of control over one's life

In collectivistic societies, the well-being of the group is promoted as more important than individual autonomy.

FIGURE 14-5 Family Obligations

Adolescents from Asian and Latin American groups feel a greater sense of respect and obligation toward their families than do those adolescents with European backgrounds.

(*Source:* Fuligni, Tseng, & Lam, 1999)

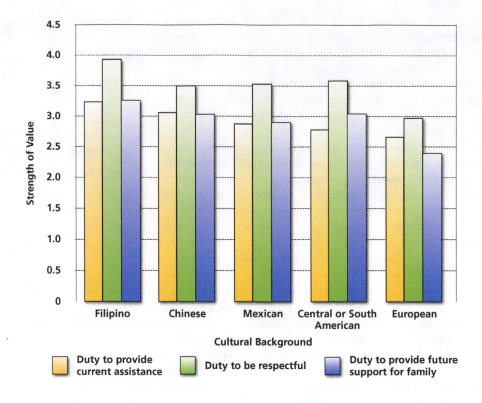

generation gap A divide between parents and adolescents in attitudes, values, aspirations, and worldviews

"*I don't blame you for everything—I blame Dad for some things, too.*"

background. In comparison to Asian adolescents and parents, Caucasian adolescents and parents indicate an earlier timetable, anticipating greater autonomy at an earlier age (Feldman & Wood, 1994).

Does the more extended timetable for the development of autonomy in more collectivistic cultures have negative consequences for adolescents in those cultures? Apparently not. The more important factor is the degree of match between cultural expectations and developmental patterns. What probably matters most is how well the development of autonomy matches societal expectations, not the specific timetable of autonomy (Zimmer-Gembeck & Collins, 2005; Updegraff et al., 2006; Perez-Brena, Updegraff, & Umaña-Taylor, 2012).

In addition to cultural factors affecting autonomy, gender also plays a role. In general, male adolescents are permitted more autonomy at an earlier age than female adolescents. The encouragement of male autonomy is consistent with more general traditional male stereotypes, in which males are perceived as more independent and females, conversely, more dependent on others. In fact, the more parents hold traditional stereotypical views of gender, the less likely they are to encourage their daughters' autonomy (Bumpus, Crouter, & McHale, 2001).

The Myth of the Generation Gap. Teen movies often depict adolescents and their parents with totally opposing points of view about the world. For example, the parent of an environmentalist teen might turn out to own a polluting factory. These exaggerations are often funny because we assume there is a kernel of truth in them, in that parents and teenagers often don't see things the same way. According to this argument, there is a **generation gap**, a deep divide between parents and children in attitudes, values, aspirations, and worldviews.

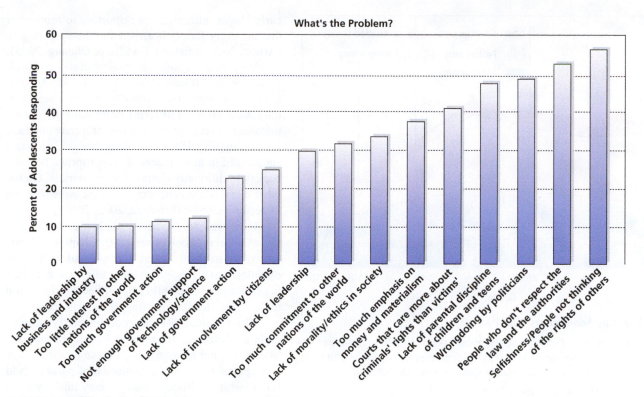

FIGURE 14-6 What's the Problem?

Adolescents' views of society's ills are ones with which their parents would likely agree.

(*Source:* PRIMEDIA/Roper National Youth Survey, 1999)

The reality, however, is quite different. The generation gap, when it exists, is really quite narrow. Adolescents and their parents tend to see eye-to-eye in a variety of domains. Republican parents generally have Republican children; members of Evangelical Christian churches have children who espouse similar views; parents who advocate for abortion rights have children who are pro-choice. On social, political, and religious issues, parents and adolescents tend to be in synch, and children's worries mirror those of their parents. Adolescents' concerns about society's problems (see Figure 14-6) are ones with which most adults would probably agree (Knafo & Schwartz, 2003; Smetana, 2005; Grønhøj & Thøgersen, 2012).

As we've said, most adolescents and their parents get along quite well. Despite their quest for autonomy and independence, most adolescents have deep love, affection, and respect for their parents—and parents feel the same way about their children. Although some parent–adolescent relationships are seriously troubled, the majority of relationships are more positive than negative and help adolescents avoid the kind of peer pressure we discuss later in the chapter (Gavin & Furman, 1996; Resnick et al., 1997; Black, 2002).

Even though adolescents spend decreasing amounts of time with their families in general, the amount of time they spend alone with each parent remains remarkably stable across adolescence (see Figure 14-7 on page 402). In short, there is no evidence suggesting that family problems are worse during adolescence than at any other stage of development (Steinberg, 1993; Larson et al., 1996; Granic, Hollenstein, & Dishion, 2003).

Conflicts with Parents. Of course, if most adolescents get along with their parents most of the time, that means some of the time they don't. No relationship is always sweetness and light. Parents and teens may hold similar attitudes about social and political issues, but they often hold different views on matters of personal taste, such as music preferences and styles of dress. Also, as we've seen, parents and children may run into disagreements when children seek to achieve autonomy and independence sooner than parents feel is right. Consequently, parent–child conflicts are more likely to occur during adolescence, particularly during the

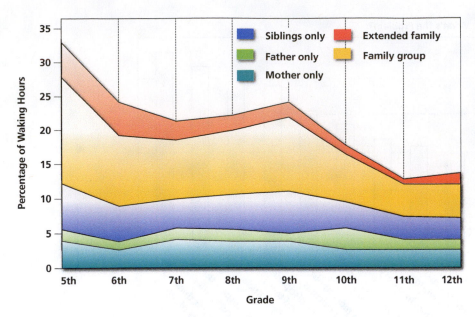

FIGURE 14-7 Time Spent by Adolescents With Parents

Despite their quest for autonomy and independence, most adolescents have deep love, affection, and respect for their parents, and the amount of time they spend alone with each parent (the lower two segments) remains remarkably stable across adolescence.

(*Source:* Larson, Richards, Moneta, Holmbeck, & Duckett, 1996)

FROM A
SOCIAL WORKER'S
PERSPECTIVE:

In what ways do you think parents with different styles—authoritarian, authoritative, permissive, and uninvolved—react to attempts to establish autonomy during adolescence? Are the styles of parenting different for a single parent? Are there cultural differences?

early stages, although it's important to remember that not every family is affected to the same degree (Arnett, 2000; Smetana, Daddis, & Chuang, 2003).

Why should conflict be greater during early adolescence than at later stages of the period? According to developmental psychologist Judith Smetana, the reason involves differing definitions of, and rationales for, appropriate and inappropriate conduct. Parents may feel, for instance, that getting one's ear pierced in three places is inappropriate because society traditionally deems it inappropriate. On the other hand, adolescents may view the issue in terms of personal choice (Smetana, 2005, 2006).

Furthermore, the newly sophisticated reasoning of adolescents (discussed in Chapter 7) leads teenagers to think about parental rules in more complex ways. Arguments that might be convincing to a school-age child ("Do it because I tell you to do it") are less compelling to an adolescent.

The argumentativeness and assertiveness of early adolescence at first may lead to an increase in conflict, but in many ways these qualities play an important role in the evolution of parent–child relationships. Although parents may initially react defensively to the challenges that their children present, and may grow inflexible and rigid, in most cases they eventually come to realize that their children *are* growing up and that they want to support them in that process.

As parents come to see that their adolescent children's arguments are often compelling and not so unreasonable, and that their daughters and sons can in fact be trusted with more freedom, they become more yielding, allowing and eventually perhaps even encouraging independence. As this process occurs during the middle stages of adolescence, the combativeness of early adolescence declines.

This pattern does not apply for all adolescents. Although the majority of teenagers maintain stable relations with their parents throughout adolescence, as many as 20% pass through a fairly rough time (Dryfoos, 1990; Dmitrieva, Chen, & Greenberger, 2004).

Cultural Differences in Parent–Child Conflicts During Adolescence. Although parent–child conflicts are found in every culture, there does seem to be less conflict between parents and their teenage children in "traditional," preindustrial cultures. Teens in such traditional cultures also experience fewer mood swings and instances of risky behavior than do teens in industrialized countries (Nelson, Badger, & Wu, 2004; Kapadia, 2008; Wu & Chao, 2011).

Why? The answer may relate to the degree of independence that adolescents expect and adults permit. In more industrialized societies, in which the value of individualism is typically high, independence is an expected component of adolescence. Consequently, adolescents and their parents must negotiate the amount and timing of the adolescent's increasing independence—a process that often leads to strife.

In contrast, in more traditional societies, individualism is not valued as highly, and therefore adolescents are less inclined to seek out independence. With diminished independence seeking on the part of adolescents, the result is less parent–child conflict (Dasen, 2000, 2002).

Family Constellations: The Array of Possibilities

Tamara's mother, Brenda, waited outside the door of her second-grade classroom for the end of the school day. Tamara came over to greet her mother as soon as she spotted her.

*"Mom, can Anna come over to play today?" Tamara demanded. Brenda had been look-
ing forward to spending some time alone with Tamara, who had spent the last 3 days
at her dad's house. But, Brenda reflected, Tamara hardly ever got to ask kids over after
school, so she agreed to the request.*

*Unfortunately, it turned out today wouldn't work for Anna's family, so they tried to
find an alternate date. "How about Thursday?" Anna's mother suggested. Before Tamara
could reply, her mother reminded her, "You'll have to ask your dad. You're at his house
that night." Tamara's expectant face fell. "OK," she mumbled.*

How will Tamara's adjustment be affected from dividing her time between the two homes
where she lives with her divorced parents? What about the adjustment of her friend, Anna,
who lives with both her parents, both of whom work outside the home? These are just a few
of the questions we need to consider as we look at the ways that children's schooling and
home life affect their lives during middle childhood.

The Changing Home Environment.
We've already noted in earlier chapters the
changes that have occurred in the structure of the family over the last few decades. With
an increase in the number of parents who both work outside of the home, a soaring divorce rate, and a rise in single-parent families, the environment faced by children passing
through middle childhood in the 21st century is very different from that faced by prior
generations.

One of the biggest challenges facing children and their parents is the increasing independence that characterizes children's behavior during middle childhood. During the period,
children move from being almost completely controlled by their parents to increasingly controlling their own destinies—or at least their everyday conduct. Middle childhood, then, is a
period of **coregulation** in which children and parents jointly control behavior. Increasingly,
parents provide broad, general guidelines for conduct, whereas children have control over
their everyday behavior. For instance, parents may urge their daughter to buy a balanced,
nutritious school lunch each day, but their daughter's decision to regularly buy pizza and two
desserts is her own.

When Both Parents Work Outside the Home: How Do Children Fare?
In most
cases, children whose parents both work full time outside the home fare quite well. Children whose parents are loving, are sensitive to their children's needs, and provide appropriate
substitute care typically develop no differently from children in families in which one of the
parents does not work (Harvey, 1999).

The good adjustment of children whose mothers and fathers both work relates to the
psychological adjustment of the parents, especially mothers. In general, women who are satisfied with their lives tend to be more nurturing with their children. When work provides a
high level of satisfaction, then, mothers who work outside of the home may be more psychologically supportive of their children. Thus, it is not so much a question of whether a mother
chooses to work full-time, to stay at home, or to arrange some combination of the two. What
matters is how satisfied she is with the choices she has made (Barnett & Rivers, 1992; Gilbert,
1994; Haddock & Rattenborg, 2003).

Although we might expect that children whose parents both work would spend comparatively less time with their parents than children with one parent at home full-time,
research suggests otherwise. Children with mothers and fathers who work full-time spend
essentially the same amount of time with family, in class, with friends, and alone as children in families where one parent stays at home (Richards & Duckett, 1994; Gottfried,
Gottfried, & Bathurst, 2002).

What are children doing during the day? The activities that take the most time are sleeping and school. The next most frequent activities are watching television and playing, followed closely by personal care and eating. This has changed little over the past 20 years
(see Figure 14-8 on page 404). What has changed is the amount of time spent in supervised,
structured settings. In 1981, 40% of a child's day was free time; by the late 1990s, only 25%
of a child's day was unscheduled (Hofferth & Sandberg, 1998).

coregulation   A period in which parents and
children jointly control children's behavior

FIGURE 14-8 How Children Spend Their Time

Whereas the amount of time children spend on certain activities has remained constant over the years, the time spent on others, such as playing and eating, has shown significant changes. What might account for these changes?

(*Source:* Hofferth & Sandberg, 1998)

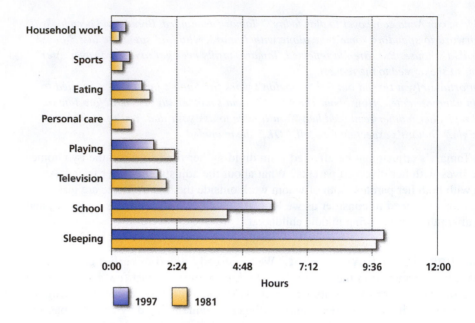

Home and Alone: What Do Children Do? When 10-year-old Johnetta Colvin comes home after finishing a day at Martin Luther King Elementary School, the first thing she does is grab a few cookies and turn on the computer. She takes a quick look at her e-mail, and then goes over to the television and typically spends the next hour watching. During commercials, she takes a look at her homework. What she doesn't do is chat with her parents, neither of whom are there. She's home alone.

Johnetta is a **self-care child,** the term for children who let themselves into their homes after school and wait alone until their parents return from work. She is far from unique. Some 12% to 14% of children in the United States between the ages of 5 and 12 spend some time alone after school, without adult supervision (Berger, 2000; Ruiz-Casares et al., 2012).

In the past, concern about self-care children centered on their lack of supervision and the emotional costs of being alone. In fact, such children were previously called *latchkey children,* raising connotations of sad, pathetic, and neglected children. However, a new view of self-care children is emerging. According to sociologist Sandra Hofferth, given the hectic schedule of many children's lives, a few hours alone may provide a helpful period of decompression. Furthermore, it may provide the opportunity for children to develop a greater sense of autonomy (Hofferth & Sandberg, 2001).

Research has identified few differences between self-care children and children who return to homes with parents. Although some children report negative experiences while at home by themselves (such as loneliness), they do not seem emotionally damaged by the experience. In addition, if they stay at home by themselves rather than "hang out" unsupervised with friends, they may avoid involvement in activities that can lead to difficulties (Belle, 1999; Goyette-Ewing, 2000).

In sum, the consequences of being a self-care child are not necessarily harmful. In fact, children may develop an enhanced sense of independence and competence. Furthermore, the time spent alone provides an opportunity to work uninterrupted on homework and school or personal projects. In fact, children with employed parents may have higher self-esteem because they feel they are contributing to the household in significant ways (Goyette-Ewing, 2000).

The Impact of Divorce on Children. Having divorced parents, like Tamara, the second-grader who was described earlier, is no longer very distinctive. Only around half the children in the United States spend their entire childhoods living in the same household with both their parents. The rest will live in single-parent homes or with stepparents, grandparents, or other nonparental relatives; and some will end up in foster care (Harvey & Fine, 2004).

self-care children Children who let themselves into their homes after school and wait alone until their caretakers return from work; previously known as *latchkey children*

How do children react to divorce? The answer depends on how soon you ask the question following a divorce as well as how old the children are at the time of the divorce. Immediately after a divorce, both children and parents may show several types of psychological maladjustment for a period that may last from 6 months to 2 years. For instance, children may be anxious, experience depression, or show sleep disturbances and phobias. Even though children most often live with their mothers following a divorce, the quality of the mother–child relationship declines in the majority of cases, often because children see themselves caught in the middle between their mothers and fathers (Juby et al., 2007; Lansford, 2009; Greenwood, 2012).

During the early stage of middle childhood, children whose parents are divorcing often blame themselves for the breakup. By the age of 10, children feel pressure to choose sides, taking the position of either the mother or the father. Because of this, they experience some degree of divided loyalty (Shaw, Winslow, & Flanagan, 1999).

Although researchers agree that the short-term consequences of divorce can be quite difficult, the longer term consequences are less clear. Some studies have found that 18 months to 2 years later, most children begin to return to their predivorce state of psychological adjustment. For many children, there are minimal long-term consequences (Hetherington & Kelly, 2002; Guttmann & Rosenberg, 2003; Harvey & Fine, 2004).

Other evidence, however, suggests that the fallout from divorce lingers. For example, twice as many children of divorced parents enter psychological counseling as children from intact families (although sometimes counseling is mandated by a judge as part of the divorce). In addition, people who have experienced parental divorce are more at risk for experiencing divorce themselves later in life (Wallerstein & Resnikoff, 2005; Huurre, Junkkari, & Aro, 2006; Ängarne-Lindberg & Wadsby, 2012).

How children react to divorce depends on several factors. One is the economic standing of the family the child is living with. In many cases, divorce brings a decline in both parents' standards of living. When this occurs, children may be thrown into poverty (Ozawa & Yoon, 2003; Fischer, 2007).

In other cases, the negative consequences of divorce are less severe because the divorce reduces the hostility and anger in the home. If the household before the divorce was overwhelmed by parental strife—as is the case in around 30% of divorces—the greater calm of a post-divorce household may be beneficial to children. This is particularly true for children who maintain a close, positive relationship with the parent with whom they do not live (Davies et al., 2002; Vélez et al., 2011).

For some children, then, divorce is an improvement over living with parents who have an intact but unhappy marriage, high in conflict. But in about 70% of divorces, the predivorce level of conflict is not high, and children in these households may have a more difficult time adjusting to divorce (Amato & Booth, 1997).

Blended Families. For many children, the aftermath of divorce includes the subsequent remarriage of one or both parents. In fact, more than 10 million households in the United States contain at least one spouse who has remarried. More than 5 million remarried couples have at least one stepchild living with them in what have come to be called **blended families**. Overall, 17% of all children in the United States live in blended families (U.S. Bureau of the Census, 2001; Bengtson et al., 2004).

Living in a blended family is challenging for the children involved. Often there is a fair amount of *role ambiguity,* in which roles and expectations are unclear. Children may be uncertain about their responsibilities, how to behave toward stepparents and stepsiblings, and how to make a host of decisions that have wide-ranging implications for their role in the family. For instance, a child in a blended family may have to choose which parent to spend each vacation and holiday with, or to decide between the conflicting advice

FROM A
HEALTH-CARE WORKER'S
PERSPECTIVE:
How might the development of self-esteem in middle childhood be affected by a divorce? Can constant hostility and tension between parents lead to a child's health problems?

blended families A remarried couple that has at least one stepchild living with them

Blended families result when previously married mothers and fathers marry.

Based on current trends, almost three-quarters of American children will spend some portion of their lives in a single-parent family. What are some possible consequences for a child raised in a single-parent household?

coming from a biological parent and a stepparent (Belcher, 2003; Sabatino & Mayer, 2011; Guadalupe & Welkley, 2012).

In many cases, however, school-age children in blended families often do surprisingly well. In comparison to adolescents, who have more difficulties, school-age children often adjust relatively smoothly to blended arrangements, for several reasons. For one thing, the family's financial situation is often improved after a parent remarries. In addition, in a blended family there are more people to share the burden of household chores. Finally, the simple fact that the family contains more individuals increases the opportunities for social interaction (Greene, Anderson, & Hetherington, 2003; Hetherington & Elmore, 2003).

On the other hand, not all children adjust well to life in a blended family. Some find the disruption of routine and of established networks of family relationships difficult. For instance, a child who is used to having her mother's complete attention may find it difficult to observe her mother showing interest and affection to a stepchild. The most successful blending of families occurs when the parents create an environment that supports children's self-esteem and creates a climate in which all family members feel a sense of togetherness. Generally, the younger the children, the easier the transition is within a blended family (Jeynes, 2006, 2007; Kirby, 2006).

Single-Parent Families. Almost three fourths of American children will spend some portion of their lives in a single-parent family before they are 18 years old. For minority children, the numbers are even higher: Almost 60% of African American children and 35% of Hispanic children under the age of 18 live in single-parent homes (U.S. Bureau of the Census, 2000; see Figure 14-9).

In rare cases, death is the reason for single parenthood. More frequently, no spouse was ever present (i.e., the mother never married), the spouses have divorced, or the spouse is absent. In the vast majority of cases, the single parent who is present is the mother.

What consequences are there for children living in homes with just one parent? This is a difficult question to answer. Much depends on whether a second parent was present earlier and the nature of the parents' relationship at that time. Furthermore, the economic status of the single-parent family plays a role in determining the consequences for children. Single-parent families are often less well-off financially than two-parent families, and living in relative poverty has a negative impact on children (Davis, 2003; Harvey & Fine, 2004; Sarsour et al., 2011).

In sum, the impact of living in a single-parent family is not, by itself, invariably negative or positive. Given the large number of single-parent households, the stigma that once existed toward such families has largely declined. The ultimate consequences for children depend on a variety of factors that accompany single parenthood, such as the economic status of the family, the amount of time that the parent is able to spend with the child, and the degree of stress in the household.

Multigenerational Families. Some households consist of several generations, in which children, parents, and grandparents live together. The presence of multiple generations in the same house can make for a rich living experience for children, who enjoy the influence of both their parents and their grandparents. On the other hand, multigenerational families also have the potential for conflict, with several adults acting as disciplinarians without coordinating what they do.

The prevalence of three-generation families who live together is greater among African Americans than among Caucasians. In addition, African American families, which are more likely than white families to be headed by single parents, often rely substantially on the help of grandparents in everyday child care, and cultural norms tend to be highly supportive of grandparents taking an active role (Oberlander, Black, & Starr, 2007; Pittman & Boswell, 2007; Kelch-Oliver, 2008).

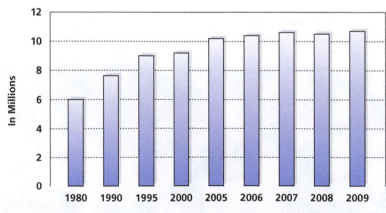

FIGURE 14-9 Increase of Single-Parent Households 1975–2003

Although the number of children living with single parents increased dramatically for several decades, it has leveled off in recent years.

(*Source:* U.S. Bureau of the Census, Statistical Abstract of the United States, 2011)

Families with Gay and Lesbian Parents. An increasing number of children have two mothers or two fathers. Estimates suggest there are between 1 and 5 million families headed by two lesbians or two gay parents in the United States, and some 6 million children have lesbian or gay parents (Patterson & Friel, 2000; Patterson, 2007).

A growing body of research on the effects of same-sex parenting on children shows that children in lesbian and gay households develop similarly to the children of heterosexual families. Their sexual orientation is unrelated to that of their parents; their behavior is no more or less gender-typed; and they seem equally well-adjusted (Patterson, 2002, 2003; Parke, 2004; Gulcher, Sutfin, & Patterson, 2008).

One recent large-scale analysis that examined 19 studies of children raised by gay and lesbian parents conducted over a 25-year period, encompassing well over a thousand gay, lesbian, and heterosexual families, confirmed these findings. The analysis found no significant differences between children raised by heterosexual parents and children raised by gay or lesbian parents on measures of children's gender role, gender identity, cognitive development, sexual orientation, and social and emotional development. The one significant difference that did emerge was the quality of the relationship between parent and child; interestingly, the gay and lesbian parents reported having *better* relationships with their children than did heterosexual parents (Crowl, Ahn, & Baker, 2008; Goldberg & Kuvalanka, 2012).

Furthermore, children of lesbian and gay parents have similar relationships with their peers as children of heterosexual parents. They also relate to adults—both those who are gay and straight—no differently from children whose parents are heterosexual. And when they reach adolescence, their romantic relationships and sexual behavior are no different from those of adolescents living with opposite-sex parents (Golombok et al., 2003; Wainright, Russell, & Patterson, 2004; Pennington & Knight, 2011).

In short, there is little developmental difference between children whose parents are gay and lesbian and those whose parents are heterosexual. What is clearly different for children with same-sex parents is the possibility of discrimination and prejudice due to their parents' homosexuality. As U.S. citizens engage in an ongoing and highly politicized debate regarding the legality of gay and lesbian marriage, children of such unions may feel singled out and victimized because of societal stereotypes and discrimination.

Race and Family Life. Although there are as many types of families as there are individuals, research does find some consistencies related to race (Parke, 2004). For example, African American families often have a particularly strong sense of family. Members of African American families are frequently willing to offer welcome and support to extended family members in their homes. Because there is a relatively high level of female-headed households among African Americans, the social and economic support of extended family often is critical. In addition, there is a relatively high proportion of families headed by older adults, such as grandparents, and some studies find that children in grandmother-headed households are particularly well adjusted (McLoyd et al., 2000; Smith & Drew, 2002; Taylor, 2002).

Hispanic families also often stress the importance of family life, as well as community and religious organizations. Children are taught to value their ties to their families, and they come to see themselves as a central part of an extended family. Ultimately, their sense of who they are becomes tied to the family. Hispanic families also tend to be relatively larger, with an average size of 3.71, compared to 2.97 for Caucasian families and 3.31 for African American families (Cauce & Domenech-Rodriguez, 2002; U.S. Census Bureau, 2003; Halgunseth, Ispa, & Rudy, 2006).

Although relatively little research has been conducted on Asian American families, emerging findings suggest that fathers are more apt to be powerful figures, maintaining discipline. In keeping with the more collectivist orientation of Asian cultures, children tend to believe that family needs have a higher priority than personal needs, and males, in particular, are expected to care for their parents throughout their lifetimes (Ishi-Kuntz, 2000).

Poverty and Family Life. Regardless of race, children living in families who are economically disadvantaged face significant hardships. Poor families have fewer basic everyday

Although the orphanages of the early 1900s were crowded and institutional (left), today the equivalent, called group homes or residential treatment centers (right), are much more pleasant.

resources, and there are more disruptions in children's lives. For example, parents may be forced to look for less expensive housing or may move the entire household in order to find work. The result frequently is family environments in which parents are less responsive to their children's needs and provide less social support (Evans, 2004).

The stress of difficult family environments, along with other stress in the lives of poor children—such as living in unsafe neighborhoods with high rates of violence and attending inferior schools—ultimately takes its toll. Economically disadvantaged children are at risk for poorer academic performance, higher rates of aggression, and conduct problems. In addition, declines in economic well-being have been linked to mental health problems (Sapolsky, 2005; Morales & Guerra, 2006; Tracy et al., 2008).

Group Care: Orphanages in the 21st Century.   The term *orphanage* evokes images of pitiful youngsters clothed in rags, eating porridge out of tin cups, and housed in huge, prison-like institutions. The reality today is different. Even the term orphanage is rarely used, having been replaced by *group home* or *residential treatment center*. Typically housing a relatively small number of children, group homes are used for children whose parents are no longer able to care for them adequately. They are typically funded by a combination of federal, state, and local aid.

Group care has grown significantly in the last decade. In fact, in the 5-year period from 1995 to 2000, the number of children in foster care increased by more than 50%. Today, more than one-half million children in the United States live in foster care (Roche, 2000; Jones-Harden, 2004; Bruskas, 2008).

About three fourths of children in group care are victims of neglect and abuse. Each year, 300,000 are removed from their homes. Most of them can be returned to their homes following intervention with their families by social service agencies. But the remaining one fourth are so psychologically damaged due to abuse or other causes that once they are placed in group care, they are likely to remain there throughout childhood. Children who have developed severe problems, such as high levels of aggression or anger, have difficulty finding adoptive families, and in fact it is often difficult to find even temporary foster families who are able to cope with their emotional and behavior problems (Bass, Shields, & Behrman, 2004; Chamberlain et al., 2006; Lee et al., 2011).

Although some politicians have suggested that an increase in group care is a solution to complex social problems associated with unwed mothers who become dependent on welfare, experts in providing social services and psychological treatment are not so sure. For one thing, group homes cannot always consistently provide the support and love potentially available in a family setting. Moreover, group care is hardly cheap: It can cost some $40,000 per

TABLE 14-4 Personal Characteristics of the Best and Worst Child- and Youth-Care Workers

Best Workers	Worst Workers
Flexible	Exhibit pathology
Mature	Selfish
Integrity	Defensive
Good judgment	Dishonest
Common sense	Abusive
Appropriate values	Abuse drugs/alcohol
Responsible	Uncooperative
Good self-image	Poor self-esteem
Self-control	Rigid
Responsive to authority	Irresponsible
Interpersonally adept	Critical
Stable	Passive-aggressive
Unpretentious	Inappropriate boundaries
Predictable/consistent	Unethical
Nondefensive	Authoritarian/coercive
Nurturant/firm	Inconsistent/unpredictable
Self-aware	Avoidant
Empowering	Don't learn from experience
Cooperative	Poor role model
Good role model	Angry/explosive

(*Source:* Adapted from Shealy, 1995.)

year to support a child in group care—about 10 times the cost of maintaining a child in foster care or on welfare (Roche, 2000; Allen & Bissell, 2004).

Other experts argue that group care is neither inherently good nor bad. Instead, the consequences of living away from one's family may be quite positive, depending on the particular characteristics of the staff of the group home and whether child- and youth-care workers are able to develop an effective, stable, and strong emotional bond with a specific child. On the other hand, if a child is unable to form a meaningful relationship with a worker in a group home, the results may well be harmful (Hawkins-Rodgers, 2007; Knorth et al., 2008; Table 14-4 shows the personal characteristics of the best—and worst—child- and youth-care workers).

FIGURE 14-10 Child Abuse

Although neglect is the most frequent form of abuse, other types of abuse are also prevalent. How can caregivers and educators, as well as health care and social workers, take the lead in identifying child abuse before it becomes serious?

(*Source:* U.S. Department of Health and Human Services, 2007)

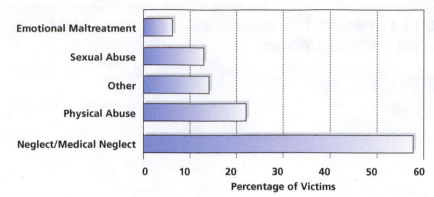

Percentage of Victims

Note: Percentage may total more that 100% because some states report more than one type of maltreatment per victim; *N* = 572,943 victims in 31 states.

Child Abuse and Psychological Maltreatment: The Grim Side of Family Life

The figures are gloomy and disheartening: In the United States, at least five children are killed by their parents or caretakers every day, and 140,000 others are physically injured every year. Around 3 million children in the United States are victims of **child abuse**, the physical and psychological maltreatment or neglect of children. The abuse takes several forms, ranging from actual physical abuse to psychological mistreatment (see Figure 14-10; U.S. Department of Health and Human Services, 2007; Maas, Herrenkohl, & Sousa, 2008).

Physical Abuse. Child abuse can occur in any household, regardless of economic well-being or the social status of the parents. It is most frequent in families living in stressful environments. Poverty, single-parenthood, and higher-than-average levels of marital conflict help create such environments. Stepfathers are more likely to commit abuse against stepchildren than genetic fathers are against their own offspring. Child abuse is also more likely when there is a history of violence between spouses (Osofsky, 2003; Evans, 2004; Herrenkohl et al., 2008). (Table 14-5 lists some of the warning signs of abuse.)

Abused children are more likely to be fussy, resistant to control, and not readily adaptable to new situations. They have more headaches and stomachaches, experience more bedwetting, are generally more anxious, and may show developmental delays (Straus & Gelles, 1990; Ammerman & Patz, 1996; Haugaard, 2000; Pandey, 2011).

Each year, more than 3 million children in the United States are victims of child abuse.

TABLE 14-5   What Are the Warning Signs of Child Abuse?

Because child abuse is typically a secret crime, identifying the victims of abuse is particularly difficult. Still, there are several signs in a child that indicate that he or she is the victim of violence (Robbins, 1990):

- Visible, serious injuries that have no reasonable explanation
- Bite or choke marks
- Burns from cigarettes or immersion in hot water
- Feelings of pain for no apparent reason
- Fear of adults or care providers
- Inappropriate attire in warm weather (long sleeves, long pants, high-necked garments)—possibly to conceal injuries to the neck, arms, and legs
- Extreme behavior—highly aggressive, extremely passive, extremely withdrawn
- Fear of physical contact

If you suspect a child is a victim of aggression, it is your responsibility to act. Call your local police or the department of social services in your city or state, or call Childhelp U.S.A at 1-800-422-4453. Talk to a teacher or a member of the clergy. Remember, by acting decisively you can literally save someone's life.

---

child abuse   The physical and psychological maltreatment or neglect of children

FROM RESEARCH TO PRACTICE
Spanking: Why the Experts Say "No"

"Spare the rod, spoil the child."

For most adults in the United States, this old proverb sums up their views: Spanking in milder forms is not only deemed acceptable to the majority of parents in the U.S., but often viewed as necessary and desirable. Almost half of mothers with children younger than 4 years of age have spanked their child in the previous week, and close to 20% of mothers believe it is appropriate to spank a child less than 1 year of age (Straus, Gelles, & Steinmetz, 2003; Gagné et al., 2007; Simons & Wurtele, 2010).

This view is at odds with the experts. There is increasing scientific evidence that spanking should be avoided. Although physical punishment may produce immediate compliance—children typically stop the behavior spanking is meant to end—there are a number of serious long-term side effects. For example, spanking is associated with lower quality of parent-child relationships, poorer mental health for both child and parent, higher levels of delinquency, and more antisocial behavior. In addition, children who experience higher levels of spanking are less able to develop their own inner sense of right and wrong than those who have been the recipients of lower amounts of spanking. Spanking also teaches children that violence is an acceptable solution to problems by serving as a model of violent, aggressive behavior (Kazdin & Benjet, 2003; Durant, 2008; MacKenzie et al., 2012).

Race, ethnicity, and culture play a key role in the nature and incidence of spanking. For instance, rates of spanking are higher among African American and Hispanic families, compared to Caucasian and Asian American families (Hawkins et al., 2010).

Austria, Germany, Israel, and Sweden outlaw any form of physical punishment directed toward a child, including spanking. In many other countries, such as China, there are strong social norms against hitting children, and spanking is rare. In the United States, where a belief in the importance of individual freedom fosters a social climate in which family life, including physical punishment

of children, is viewed as a matter of private, personal choice, high levels of spanking occur (Gershoff, 2002; Kim & Hong, 2007; Hawkins et al., 2010).

Despite the consensus view on the negative consequences of spanking, it is also clear that not all spanking is the same. Although child developmentalists, physicians, and other experts unanimously agree that severe, sustained spankings that are routinely administered produce the most negative effects, the research evidence for the negative effects of occasional, mild, and noninjurious spankings is more mixed. For instance, parents who spank their children more also hug their children less, read to them less, and play with them less than those who use spanking less frequently. They also are more physiologically volatile, reacting more quickly to stress. It's possible, then, that spanking itself is not the cause of the problems associated with spanking, but that those who spank their children more engage in a variety of behaviors that result in negative outcomes for their children (Benjet & Kazdin, 2003; Martorell & Bugental, 2006; McLoyd et al., 2007; Durant, 2008).

Even mild spanking can easily escalate into more severe spanking. Furthermore, there are a variety of techniques that are at least as effective, and often more so, than spanking for obtaining children's compliance (such as use of time-out periods). The negative consequences of spanking, and the effectiveness of nonphysical alternatives, have led the American Academy of Pediatrics to advise that spanking is not an appropriate disciplinary technique (American Academy of Pediatrics, 1998, 2002; Kazdin & Benjet, 2003; Goullatta & Blau, 2008).

- **How might you go about educating parents about the dangers of spanking?**
- **Are there any circumstances in which it is appropriate for a teacher or school administrator to spank a child? What might they be?**

As you consider this information about the characteristics of abused children, keep in mind that labeling children as being at higher risk for receiving abuse does not make them responsible for their abuse; the family members who carry out the abuse are at fault. Statistical findings simply suggest that children with such characteristics are more at risk of being the recipients of family violence.

Why does physical abuse occur? Most parents certainly do not intend to hurt their children. In fact, most parents who abuse their children later express bewilderment and regret about their own behavior.

One reason for child abuse is the vague demarcation between permissible and impermissible forms of physical punishment. The line between "spanking" and "beating" is not clear, and spankings begun in anger can escalate easily into abuse. (As we discuss in the *From Research to Practice* box, the use of physical punishment of any sort is not recommended by child care experts.)

Another factor that leads to high rates of abuse is the privacy in which child care is conducted in Western societies. In many other cultures childrearing is seen as the joint

FROM A
SOCIAL WORKER'S
PERSPECTIVE:
If a society's emphasis on family privacy contributes to the prevalence of child abuse, what sorts of social policies regarding privacy do you think are appropriate? Why?

responsibility of several people and even society as a whole. In most Western cultures—and particularly the United States—children are raised in private, isolated households. Because child care is seen as the sole responsibility of the parent, other people are typically not available to help out when a parent's patience is tested (Chaffin, 2006; Elliott & Urquiza, 2006).

Sometimes abuse is the result of an adult's unrealistically high expectations regarding children's abilities to be quiet and compliant at a particular age. Children's failure to meet these unrealistic expectations may provoke abuse (Peterson, 1994).

Many times, those who abuse children were themselves abused as children. According to the **cycle of violence hypothesis**, the abuse and neglect that children suffer predispose them as adults to abuse and neglect their own children (Miller-Perrin & Perrin, 1999; Widom, 2000; Heyman & Slep, 2002).

According to this hypothesis, victims of abuse have learned from their childhood experiences that violence is an appropriate and acceptable form of discipline. Violence may be perpetuated from one generation to another, as each generation learns to behave abusively (and fails to learn the skills needed to solve problems and instill discipline without resorting to physical violence) through its participation in an abusive, violent family (Ethier, Couture, & Lacharite, 2004; Craig & Sprang, 2007; Nickerson et al., 2012).

Being abused as a child does not inevitably lead to abuse of one's own children. In fact, statistics show that only about one third of people who were abused or neglected as children abuse their own children; the remaining two thirds of people abused as children do not turn out to be child abusers. Clearly, suffering abuse as a child is not the full explanation for child abuse in adults (Cicchetti, 1996; Straus & McCord, 1998).

Psychological Maltreatment.   Children may also be the victims of more subtle forms of mistreatment. **Psychological maltreatment** occurs when parents or other caregivers harm children's behavioral, cognitive, emotional, or physical functioning. It may occur through either overt behavior or neglect (Higgins & McCabe, 2003; Arias, 2004).

For example, abusive parents may frighten, belittle, or humiliate their children, thereby intimidating and harassing them. Children may be made to feel like disappointments or failures, or they may be constantly reminded that they are a burden to their parents. Parents may tell their children that they wish they had never had children and specifically that they wish that their children had never been born. Children may be threatened with abandonment or even death. In other instances, older children may be exploited. They may be forced to seek employment and then to give their earnings to their parents.

In other cases of psychological maltreatment, the abuse takes the form of neglect. In **child neglect**, parents ignore their children or are emotionally unresponsive to them. In such cases, children may be given unrealistic responsibilities or may be left to fend for themselves.

No one is certain how much psychological maltreatment occurs each year, because figures separating psychological maltreatment from other types of abuse are not routinely gathered. Most maltreatment occurs in the privacy of people's homes. Furthermore, psychological maltreatment typically causes no physical damage, such as bruises or broken bones, to alert physicians, teachers, and other authorities. Consequently, many cases of psychological maltreatment probably are not identified. However, it is clear that profound neglect that involves children who are unsupervised or uncared for is the most frequent form of psychological maltreatment (Hewitt, 1997).

What are the consequences of psychological maltreatment? Some children are sufficiently resilient to survive the abuse and grow into psychologically healthy adults. In many cases, however, lasting damage results. For example, psychological maltreatment has been associated with low self-esteem, lying, misbehavior, and underachievement in school. In extreme cases, it can produce criminal behavior, aggression, and murder. In other instances, children who have been psychologically maltreated become depressed and even commit suicide (Eigsti & Cicchetti, 2004; Koenig, Cicchetti, & Rogosch, 2004; Allen, 2008).

cycle of violence hypothesis   The theory that the abuse and neglect that children suffer predispose them as adults to abuse and neglect their own children

psychological maltreatment   Abuse that occurs when parents or other caregivers harm children's behavioral, cognitive, emotional, or physical functioning

child neglect   The act of parents ignoring their children or being emotionally unresponsive to them

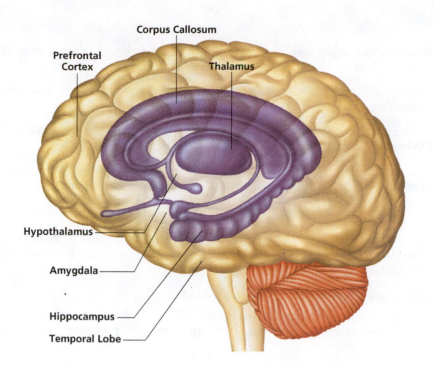

Corpus Callosum

Prefrontal
Cortex

Thalamus

Hypothalamus

Amygdala

Hippocampus

Temporal Lobe

FIGURE 14-11 Abuse Alters the Brain

The limbic system, comprising the hippocampus and amygdala, can be permanently altered as a result of childhood abuse.

(*Source: Scientific American*, March 2002, p. 71.)

One reason that psychological maltreatment—as well as physical abuse—produces so many negative consequences is that the brains of victims undergo permanent changes due to the abuse (see Figure 14-11). For example, childhood maltreatment can lead to reductions in the size of the amygdala and hippocampus in adulthood. The fear and terror produced by abuse may also lead to permanent changes in the brain due to over-excitation of the limbic system, which is involved in the regulation of memory and emotion, leading to antisocial behavior during adulthood (Watts-English et al., 2006; Rick & Douglas, 2007; Twardosz & Lutzker, 2009).

Review, Check, and Apply

Review

1. Children spend significantly less time with their parents in middle childhood, but parents are still the primary influence in their children's lives.

2. In early adolescence, teens tend to be argumentative and assertive, which may lead to increased conflict with parents. However, these qualities play an important role in the evolution of parent–child relationships, with most parents eventually realizing that their children *are* growing up and that they want to support them in that process.

3. The development of children growing up in families with same-sex parents is similar to that of children of heterosexual families.

4. How divorce affects children depends on such factors as financial circumstances and the comparative levels of tension in the family before and after the divorce.

5. The incidence of family violence is highest in families of lower socioeconomic status. A "cycle of violence" affords a partial explanation. Cultural norms may also play a role.

Check

1. Adolescents increasingly seek _____, independence and a sense of control over their lives.

2. The term for children who let themselves into their homes after school and wait alone until their parents return from work is _____.

3. _____ families encompass married couples who have at least one stepchild living with them.

4. _____ _____ occurs when parents or other caregivers harm children's behavioral, cognitive, emotional, or physical functioning.

Apply

1. Politicians often speak of "family values." How does this term relate to the diverse family situations covered in this module, including divorced parents, single parents, blended families, working parents, and gay and lesbian parents?

To see more review questions, log on to MyPsychLab

The CASE
of . . . *Too Much of a Good Thing*

Marcia Wilder was the eldest child in a close-knit family of five. Her parents took pride in the fact that the family spent all their weekends together, hiking, gardening, or going to the movies. They assumed this would always be true, and Marcia herself was happy to bask in so much familial love—until the year she turned 13. That was the year she entered middle school and her whole world changed.

Marcia discovered she had lots of interests. She joined the stage crew at her school and painted scenery for student productions. She took a photography course and began spending her afternoons in the school's darkroom, printing the photos she had taken of friends. She started babysitting two nights a week for the neighbors. On weekends, she went to the mall and the movies with friends.

"We never see you anymore," her parents complained. At first, Marcia shrugged it off, but when her parents began to criticize everything from the clothes she wore to the music she preferred, she got annoyed. When they began scrutinizing her friends and calling her cell phone every hour to see who she was with and where she was at, she became enraged. "You just won't let me have a life!" she shouted when they demanded she cancel plans with friends to spend weekend time with the family. Deep down, Marcia knew her parents loved her and she still loved them, but increasingly she felt a strong need to escape their complaints and restraints.

1. How do the changes in Marcia reflect normal social development in adolescence?

2. What specific advice would you give Marcia's parents to help ease the conflict with their daughter?

3. Do you feel Marcia is exercising an appropriate level of autonomy and independence for her age? Why or why not?

4. Given what we know about social and personality development in adolescence, what changes would you expect to occur in Marcia's relationship with her parents over the next five years?

5. Do you think Marcia and her parents are experiencing a true generation gap? Why or why not?

◀◀◀ LOOKING BACK

LO 14-1 In what sorts of social relationships and play do preschool children engage?

- Preschool social relationships begin to encompass genuine friendship, which involve trust and endure over time.
- Older preschoolers engage in more constructive play than functional play. They also engage in more associative and cooperative play than younger preschoolers, who do more parallel and onlooker playing.

LO 14-2 What characterizes friendship in middle childhood, and how does social competence affect popularity?

- Children's understanding of friendship passes through stages, from a focus on mutual liking and time spent together through the consideration of personal traits and the rewards that friendship provides to an appreciation of intimacy and loyalty.
- Popularity in children is related to traits that underlie social competence. Because of the importance of social interactions and friendships, developmental researchers have engaged in efforts to help children improve their social problem-solving skills and the processing of social information.

LO 14-3 What role do friends and peers play in adolescence?

- One of the most noticeable changes from childhood to adolescence is the greater reliance on friendships, which help adolescents define who they are.
- In addition to friends, other peers play an influential role during adolescence as parents' supervisory role begins to diminish.
- Peers influence one another in many ways during adolescence, providing support for academic achievement and prosocial behavior, and compensation for negative school or family situations.

LO 14-4 What are race and ethnic relationships like in adolescence?

- In general, segregation between people of different races and ethnicities increases in middle and late adolescence, even in schools with a diverse student body.
- Equal-status interactions among members of different racial groups can lead to improved understanding, mutual respect and acceptance, and a decreased tendency to stereotype.

LO 14-5 What does it mean to be popular and unpopular in adolescence, and how do adolescents respond to peer pressure?

- Degrees of popularity during adolescence include popular and controversial adolescents (on the high end of popularity) and neglected and rejected adolescents (on the low end).
- Peer pressure is not a simple phenomenon. Adolescents conform to their peers in areas in which they feel their peers are expert, and to adults in areas of adult expertise. As adolescents grow in confidence, their conformity to both peers and adults declines.

LO 14-6 How does the quality of relationships with family change as children move into adolescence?

- Beginning in middle childhood, children spend increasingly less time with their parents, but parents remain the most important influence in their children's lives.
- Adolescents increasingly look to peers rather than parents for guidance, especially in social matters.
- Adolescents' quest for autonomy often brings confusion and tension to their relationships with their parents, but the actual "generation gap" between parents' and teenagers' attitudes is usually small.

LO 14-7 How do today's diverse family and care arrangements affect children?

- Children in families in which both parents work outside the home generally fare well. Self-care children who fend for themselves after school may develop independence and a sense of competence and contribution.
- Immediately after a divorce, the effects on children in the middle childhood years can be serious, depending on the financial condition of the family and the hostility level between spouses before the divorce.
- The consequences of living in a single-parent family depend on the financial condition of the family and, if there had been two parents, the level of hostility that existed between them. Blended families present challenges to the child but can also offer opportunities for increased social interaction.
- Children in lesbian and gay households develop similarly to the children of heterosexual families. Their sexual orientation is unrelated to that of their parents; their behavior is no more or less gender-typed; and they seem equally well adjusted. On the other hand, children with same-sex parents may face discrimination and prejudice due to their parents' sexual orientation.

LO 14-8 **What are the forms of child abuse and psychological maltreatment, and what contributes to their occurrence?**

- Child abuse may take physical forms, but it may also be more subtle. Psychological maltreatment may involve neglect of parental responsibilities, emotional negligence, intimidation or humiliation, unrealistic demands and expectations, or exploitation of children.

- Child abuse occurs with alarming frequency in the United States and other countries, especially in stressful home environments. Firmly held notions regarding family privacy and norms that support the use of physical punishment in child rearing contribute to the high rate of abuse.

- The cycle-of-violence hypothesis points to the likelihood that persons who were abused as children may turn into abusers as adults.

KEY TERMS AND CONCEPTS

functional play (p. 383)
constructive play (p. 383)
parallel play (p. 383)
onlooker play (p. 383)
associative play (p. 383)
cooperative play (p. 383)
social competence (p. 387)
social problem-solving (p. 388)

cliques (p. 392)
crowds (p. 392)
controversial adolescents (p. 395)
rejected adolescents (p. 395)
neglected adolescents (p. 395)
peer pressure (p. 396)
autonomy (p. 399)
generation gap (p. 400)

coregulation (p. 403)
self-care child (p. 404)
blended families (p. 405)
child abuse (p. 410)
cycle of violence hypothesis (p. 412)
psychological maltreatment (p. 412)
child neglect (p. 412)

Epilogue

In this chapter, we focused on family and peer relationships from the preschool years through adolescence. We discussed how friendship and play develops in the preschool years, and the stages of friendship that occur in middle childhood. We also looked at what determines popularity and the qualities children seek in friends. We then considered the importance of peers and peer groups in adolescence, and we reflected on the different categories of popular and unpopular teens. Next, we explored the issue of race and ethnic segregation that occurs in adolescence. We also examined the issue of peer pressure and concluded that it is strongest in social matters. We looked at the changing role family plays as children mature. We discussed divorce and the many family constellations that exist today and their effects on children. In conclusion, we examined the serious problem of child abuse, both physical and psychological.

Return for a moment to the opening prologue, in which we looked at Elena's decision to disregard her mother's rules. In light of what you now know about the changing roles of family and friends in adolescence, consider the following questions.

1. In what ways does Elena's disregard for her mother's rules exemplify the changes that occur in family relationships from middle childhood to adolescence?

2. If Elena strictly followed her mother's rules, and did not allow her friends to come over when her mother is at work, how do you think it would affect her social standing with her peers? In your opinion, does peer pressure play any role in the choices Elena is making?

3. Based on the evidence in the story, how do you think Elena feels about deceiving her mother? Do you think her feelings reveal where she is in her developing autonomy? How?

4. Do you think Elena's behavior would be different if her parents had not divorced? Why or why not?

5. How would you advise Elena's mother to handle the situation if she discovers that Elena has been breaking the rules? How might Elena be expected to react?

The Development Video Series
in MyPsychLab

Explore the video *Peer Pressure* by scanning this QR code with your mobile device. If you don't already have one, you may download a free QR scanner for your device wherever smartphone apps are sold. You can also view this video in MyPsychLab. For more videos related to this chapter's content, log into MyPsychLab to view the entire Development Video Series.

MyVirtualChild

- What decisions would you make while raising a child?
- What would the consequences of those decisions be?

Find out by accessing **MyVirtualChild** at

www.MyPsychLab.com

and raising your own virtual child from birth to age 18.

15 Schooling, Culture, and Society: Living in a Multicultural World

MODULE 15.1

GETTING A START ON SCHOOLING

- Early Childhood Education: Taking the Pre-Out of Preschool

DEVELOPMENTAL DIVERSITY AND YOUR LIFE:
Preschools around the World: Why Does the United States Lag Behind?

- Does Head Start Truly Provide a Head Start?
- Learning from the Media
- Media and Technology Use by Children and Adolescents

Review, Check, and Apply

MODULE 15.2

SOCIOCULTURAL ASPECTS OF SCHOOLING

- Schooling around the World: Who Gets Educated?
- What Makes Children Ready for School?
- Educational Trends: Beyond the Three *R*s

FROM RESEARCH TO PRACTICE: **Making the Grade: Pushing Too Hard in the *Race to the Top*?**

- The Transition from Elementary to Middle School
- Homeschooling: An Alternative to Traditional Schools
- School Performance in Adolescence
- Socioeconomic Status and School Performance

Review, Check, and Apply

MODULE 15.3

LIVING IN A MULTICULTURAL WORLD

- How Culture Defines Us
- Developing an Ethnic Identity
- Multicultural Education
- Fostering a Bicultural Identity
- The Impact of Socioeconomic Status and Poverty on Children and Adolescents
- Prejudice and Discrimination

ARE YOU AN INFORMED CONSUMER OF DEVELOPMENT? **Taking a Stand against Prejudice**

Review, Check, and Apply

The Case of. . . The Secret Reader

Looking Back

Key Terms and Concepts

Epilogue

PROLOGUE: First Day

As my daughter Emily and I walked to meet the school bus for the first time, she held my hand tightly. I looked at her—this just-turned-5-year-old carrying a pink backpack that looked more like a mobile home than a schoolbag on her back—and wondered if our educators were right about this kindergarten thing. Okay, she was five and technically ready. We had read lots of books together (lately featuring stories about school) and she was good at drawing and coloring. But she was so small, so helpless. Still, when the bus arrived, off she marched like a pro, without once looking back.

>>> LOOKING AHEAD

For both preschoolers and their parents, the experience of attending school for the first time produces a combination of apprehension, exhilaration, and anticipation. It marks the start of an intellectual, as well as social, journey that will continue for many years and shape the development of children in significant ways.

In this chapter, we focus on schooling, learning, the social issues that have an impact on schooling and learning, and the choices that adolescents have to face while they are in high school and contemplating the next step, whether college or career. We conclude with a look at culture and diversity.

We begin by examining the different types of child care and preschool programs, and consider what each has to offer young children. We also examine the use of TV and the computer as teaching tools, considering the effects of television and computer media on traditional schooling.

(continued)

Learning Objectives

MODULE 15.1

LO1 What are the different kinds of preschool educational programs?

LO2 What are the consequences of enrollment in outside-the-home child care?

LO3 What effects do television and computers have on children and adolescents?

MODULE 15.2

LO4 What are some current trends that affect schooling worldwide and in the United States?

LO5 What changes have taken place in the ways U.S. schools provide instruction in the 3 Rs?

LO6 What are some of the challenges involved in educating children in the middle school years?

LO7 What are some advantages and disadvantages of homeschooling?

LO8 How do American adolescents perform in high school?

LO9 What social and cultural factors affect school performance?

MODULE 15.3

LO10 In what ways are individuals affected by culture and ethnicity?

LO11 What is multicultural education and why is it of critical importance in the United States today?

LO12 How is socioeconomic status related to race and ethnicity?

LO13 How do prejudice, stereotypes, and discrimination work together?

Next we look at the social aspects of schooling, asking what makes children ready for school and discussing current trends in education, the effectiveness of the middle school in dealing with the challenges faced by adolescents, and the rise of alternatives to traditional education such as home schooling. We then turn to a consideration of factors that affect individual student achievement, including socioeconomic factors.

In the final module, we discuss multicultural education and how a bicultural identity may be fostered in the schools. We examine the role that race, ethnicity, gender, and socioeconomic status play in determining culture. We also look at how members of different cultures relate to one another and how individuals develop an ethnic identity. Finally, we consider prejudice and discrimination.

MODULE 15.1

GETTING A START ON SCHOOLING

LO 15-1 What are the different kinds of preschool educational programs?
LO 15-2 What are the consequences of enrollment in outside-the-home child care?
LO 15-3 What effects do television and computers have on children and adolescents?

Preschoolers Steven Chen and Tracy Carroll are playing Muppets—*a game they invented based on the popular children's TV show* Sesame Street. *"C'mon Snuffy," Tracy screams. "We've got to find Alice!" Both children race to the jungle gym. Today, it's Snuffy's home— the cave where they will search for his little sister. Tomorrow, they'll play Tracy's game,* Dora the Explorer.

Ask almost any preschooler, and she or he will be able to identify Snuffleupagus as well as Big Bird, Bert, Ernie, and a host of other characters as the members of the cast of *Sesame Street*, the most successful television show in history targeted at preschoolers, with a daily audience in the millions.

However, preschoolers do more than watch TV. Many spend a good portion of their day involved in some form of child care setting outside their own homes, designed, in part, to enhance their cognitive development. What are the consequences of these activities? We turn now to a consideration of how early childhood education and television and other media are related to development.

Early Childhood Education: Taking the Pre- Out of Preschool

The term *preschool* is something of a misnomer: Almost three-quarters of children in the United States are enrolled in some form of care outside the home, much of which is designed either explicitly or implicitly to teach skills that will enhance intellectual as well as social abilities (see Figure 15-1). One important reason for this increase is the rise in the number of families in which both parents work outside the home. For instance, a very high proportion of fathers work outside the home, and 64% of women with children under 6 are employed, most of them full-time (Tamis-LeMonda & Cabrera, 2002; Bureau of Labor Statistics, 2012).

However, there is another cause, one less tied to the practical considerations of child care: Developmentalists have found increasing evidence that children can benefit substantially from involvement in some form of educational activity before they enroll in formal schooling, which typically takes place at age 5 or 6 in the United States. When compared to children who stay at home and have no formal educational involvement, those children enrolled in *good* preschools experience clear cognitive and social benefits (Friedman, 2004; National Association for the Education of Young Children, 2005; Anders et al., 2012).

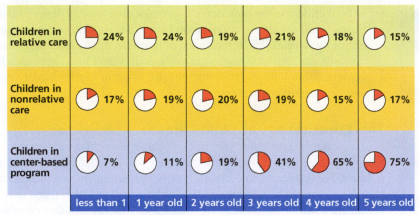

*Columns do not add up to 100 because some children participated in more than one type of day care.

FIGURE 15-1 Care Outside the Home

Approximately 75% of children in the United States are enrolled in some form of care outside the home—a trend that is the result of more parents being employed full-time. Evidence suggests that children can benefit from early childhood education. What role might a caregiver provide that can help the educational development of a child?

(*Source:* National Center for Education Statistics, 1997)

The Varieties of Early Education. The variety of early education alternatives is vast. Some outside-the-home care for children is little more than babysitting, while other options are designed to promote intellectual and social advances. Among the major choices of the latter type are the following:

- *Child-care centers* typically provide care for children all day, while their parents are at work. (Child-care centers were previously referred to as *day care centers.* However, because a significant number of parents work nonstandard schedules and therefore require care for their children at times other than the day, the preferred label has changed to child-care centers.)

  Although many child-care centers were first established as safe, warm environments where children could be cared for and could interact with other children, today their purpose tends to be broader, aimed at providing some form of intellectual stimulation. Still, their primary purpose tends to be more social and emotional than cognitive.

- Some child care is provided in *family child-care centers*, small operations run in private homes. Because centers in some areas are unlicensed, the quality of care can be uneven, and parents should consider whether a family child-care center is licensed before enrolling their children. In contrast, providers of center-based care, which is offered in institutions such as school classrooms, community centers, and churches and synagogues, are typically licensed and regulated by governmental authorities. Because teachers in such programs are more often trained professionals than those who provide family child care, the quality of care is often higher.

- *Preschools* are explicitly designed to provide intellectual and social experiences for children. They tend to be more limited in their schedules than family care centers, typically providing care for only 3 to 5 hours per day. Because of this limitation, preschools mainly serve children from middle and higher socioeconomic levels, in cases where parents don't need to work full-time.

  Like child-care centers, preschools vary enormously in the activities they provide. Some emphasize social skills, while others focus on intellectual development. Some do both.

  For instance, Montessori preschools, which use a method developed by Italian educator Maria Montessori, employ a carefully designed set of materials to create an environment that fosters sensory, motor, and language development through play. Children are provided with a variety of activities to choose from, with the option of moving from one to another (Gutek, 2003; Greenberg, 2011).

  Similarly, in the Reggio Emilia preschool approach—another Italian import—children participate in what is called a "negotiated curriculum" that emphasizes the joint participation of children and teachers. The curriculum builds on the interests of children, promoting their cognitive development through the integration of the arts and participation in week-long projects (Hong & Trepanier-Street, 2004; Rankin, 2004).

Watch the **Video** *Child Care* in **MyPsychLab**.

High-quality child care provides intellectual and social benefits while low-quality care can actually harm children.

• School child care is provided by some local school systems in the United States. Almost half the states in the United States fund prekindergarten programs for 4-year-olds, often aimed at disadvantaged children. Because they typically are staffed by better-trained teachers than less-regulated child-care centers, school child-care programs are often of higher quality than other early education alternatives.

The Effectiveness of Child Care. How effective are such programs? Most research suggests that preschoolers enrolled in child-care centers show intellectual development that at least matches that of children at home, and often is better. For instance, some studies find that preschoolers in child care are more verbally fluent, show memory and comprehension advantages, and even achieve higher IQ scores than at-home children. Other studies find that early and long-term participation in child care is particularly helpful for children from impoverished home environments or who are otherwise at risk (Clarke-Stewart & Allhusen, 2002; Vandell, 2004; Dowsett et al., 2008).

Similar advantages are found for social development. Children in high-quality programs tend to be more self-confident, independent, and knowledgeable about the social world in which they live than those who do not participate. On the other hand, not all the outcomes of outside-the-home care are positive: Children in child care have been found to be less polite, less compliant, less respectful of adults, and sometimes more competitive and aggressive than their peers. Furthermore, children who spend more than 10 hours a week in preschools have a slightly higher likelihood of being disruptive in class extending through the sixth grade (Clarke-Stewart & Allhusen, 2002; NICHHD Early Child Care Research Network, 2003; Belsky et al., 2007).

Another way to consider the effectiveness of child care is to take an economic approach. For instance, one study of prekindergarten education in Texas found that every dollar invested in high-quality preschool programs produced $3.50 in benefits. Benefits included increased graduation rates, higher earnings, savings in juvenile crime, and reductions in child welfare costs (Aguirre et al., 2006).

It is important to keep in mind that not all early childhood care programs are equally effective. One key factor is program *quality:* High-quality care provides intellectual and social benefits, while low-quality care not only is unlikely to furnish benefits, but poor programs actually may harm children (Votruba-Drzal, Coley, & Chase-Lansdale, 2004; NICHD Early Child Care Research Network, 2006; Dearing, McCartney, & Taylor, 2009; Belsky & Pluess, 2012).

The Quality of Child Care. How can we define "high quality"? The major characteristics of high-quality care include the following (Vandell, Shumow, & Posner, 2005; Lavzer & Goodson, 2006; Leach et al., 2008; Rudd, Cain, & Saxon, 2008):

• The care providers are well trained.
• The child care center has an appropriate overall size and ratio of care providers to children. Single groups should not have many more than 14 to 20 children, and there should be no more than five to ten 3-year-olds per caregiver, or seven to ten 4- or 5-year-olds per caregiver.
• The curriculum of a child-care facility is not left to chance, but is carefully planned and coordinated among the teachers.
• The language environment is rich, with a great deal of conversation.
• The caregivers are sensitive to children's emotional and social needs, and they know when and when not to intervene.
• Materials and activities are age-appropriate.
• Basic health and safety standards are followed.

"I didn't realize how much I needed to get away from that daycare grind."

No one knows how many programs in the United States can be considered "high quality," but there are many fewer than desirable. In fact, the United States lags behind almost every other industrialized country in the quality of its child care as well as in its quantity and affordability (Scarr, 1998; Muenchow & Marsland, 2007).

 ## DEVELOPMENTAL DIVERSITY AND YOUR LIFE

Preschools around the World: Why Does the United States Lag Behind?

In France and Belgium, access to preschool is a legal right. In Sweden and Finland, the governments provide child care to preschoolers whose parents work. Russia has an extensive system of state-run *yasli-sads,* nursery schools and kindergartens, attended by 75% of children age 3 to 7 in urban areas.

In contrast, the United States has no coordinated national policy on preschool education—or on the care of children in general. There are several reasons for this. For one, decisions about education have traditionally been left to the states and local school districts. For another, the United States has no tradition of teaching preschoolers, unlike other countries in which preschool-age children have been enrolled in formal programs for decades. Finally, the status of preschools in the United States has been traditionally low. Consider, for instance, that preschool and nursery school teachers are the lowest paid of all teachers. (Teacher salaries increase as the age of students rises. Thus, college and high school teachers are paid most, while preschool and elementary school teachers are paid least.)

Preschools also differ significantly from one country to another according to the views that different societies hold regarding the purpose of early childhood education. For instance, in a cross-country comparison of preschools in China, Japan, and the United States, researchers found that parents in the three countries view the purpose of preschools very differently. Whereas parents in China tend to see preschools primarily as a way of giving children a good start academically, Japanese parents view them primarily as a way of giving children the opportunity to be members of a group. In the United States, in comparison, parents regard the primary purpose of preschools as making children more independent and self-reliant, although obtaining a good academic start and having group experience are also important (see Figure 15-2; Johnson et al., 2003; Land, Lamb, & Zheng, 2011; Rao et al., 2012). ∎

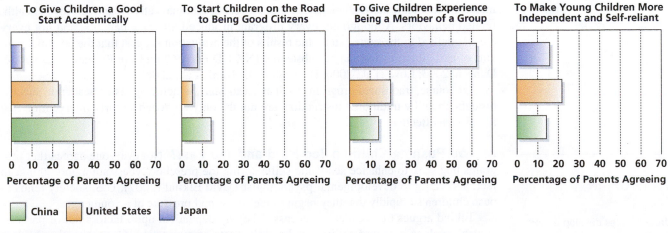

FIGURE 15-2 The Purpose of Preschool

To parents in China, Japan, and the United States, the main purpose of preschools is different. Whereas parents in China see preschools mainly as a way of giving children a good start academically, parents in Japan see them primarily as a means of giving children the experience of being a member of a group. In contrast, parents in the United States view preschools as a way of making children more independent, although obtaining a good academic start and group experience are also important. As a preschool educator, how would you interpret these findings?

(*Source:* Adapted from Tobin, Wu, & Davidson, 1989)

Does Head Start Truly Provide a Head Start?

Although many programs designed for preschoolers focus primarily on social and emotional factors, some are geared primarily toward promoting cognitive gains and preparing preschoolers for the more formal instruction they will experience when they start kindergarten. In the United States, the best-known program designed to promote future academic success is Head Start. Born in the 1960s when the United States declared a War on Poverty, the program has served more than 13 million children and their families. The program, which stresses parental involvement, was designed to serve the "whole child," including children's physical health, self-confidence, social responsibility, and social and emotional development (Zigler & Styfco, 2004; Love, Chazen-Cohen, & Raikes, 2007; Gupta et al., 2009).

Whether or not Head Start is seen as successful depends on the lens through which one is looking. If, for instance, the program is expected to provide long-term increases in IQ scores, it is a disappointment. Although graduates of Head Start programs tend to show immediate IQ gains, these increases do not last.

On the other hand, it is clear that Head Start is meeting its goal of getting preschoolers ready for school. Preschoolers who participate in Head Start are better prepared for future schooling than those who do not. Furthermore, graduates of Head Start programs have better future school adjustment than their peers, and they are less likely to be in special education classes or to be retained in grade. Finally, some research suggests that Head Start graduates even show higher academic performance at the end of high school, although the gains are modest (Brooks-Gunn, 2003; Kronholz, 2003; Bierman et al., 2009; Zhai, Raver, & Jones, 2012).

In addition to Head Start programs, other types of preschool readiness programs also provide advantages throughout the school years. Studies show that those who participate and graduate from such preschool programs are less likely to repeat grades, and they complete school more frequently than those who are not in the programs. Preschool readiness programs also appear to be cost-effective. According to a cost-benefit analysis of one readiness program, for every dollar spent on the program, taxpayers saved seven dollars by the time the graduates reached the age of 27 (Schweinhart, Barnes, & Weikart, 1993; Friedman, 2004; Gormley et al., 2005).

The most recent comprehensive evaluation of early intervention programs suggests that, taken as a group, they can provide significant benefits, and that government funds invested early in life may ultimately lead to a reduction in future costs. For instance, compared with children who did not participate in early intervention programs, participants in various programs showed gains in emotional or cognitive development, better educational outcomes, increased economic self-sufficiency, reduced levels of criminal activity, and improved health-related behaviors. Although not every program produced all these benefits, and not every child benefited to the same extent, the results of the evaluation suggest that the potential benefits of early intervention can be substantial (NICHD Early Child Care Research Network & Duncan, 2003; Love et al., 2006; Barnard, 2007; Izard et al., 2008).

Of course, traditional programs such as Head Start, which emphasize academic success brought about by traditional instruction, are not the only approach to early intervention that has proven effective.

Are We Pushing Children Too Hard and Too Fast?
Not everyone agrees that programs that seek to enhance academic skills during the preschool years are a good thing. In fact, according to developmental psychologist David Elkind (2007), U.S. society tends to push children so rapidly that they begin to feel stress and pressure at a young age.

Elkind argues that academic success is largely dependent upon factors out of parents' control, such as inherited abilities and a child's rate of maturation. Consequently, children of a particular age cannot be expected to master educational material without taking into account their current level of cognitive development. In short, children require **developmentally appropriate educational practice,** which is education that is based on both typical development and the unique characteristics of a given child (Robinson & Stark, 2005).

Rather than arbitrarily expecting children to master material at a particular age, Elkind suggests that a better strategy is to provide an environment in which learning is encouraged, but not pushed. By creating an atmosphere in which learning is facilitated—for instance,

---

FROM THE

PERSPECTIVE OF AN

EDUCATOR:
Should the United States develop a more encouraging and more supportive preschool policy? If so, what sort of policy? If not, why not?

---

developmentally appropriate educational practice Education that is based on both typical development and the unique characteristics of a given child

by reading to preschoolers—parents will allow children to proceed at their own pace rather than at one that pushes them beyond their limits (van Kleeck & Stahl, 2003).

Although Elkind's suggestions are appealing—it is certainly hard to disagree that increases in children's anxiety levels and stress should be avoided—they are not without their detractors. For instance, some educators have argued that pushing children is largely a phenomenon of the middle and higher socioeconomic levels, possible only if parents are relatively affluent. For poorer children, whose parents may not have substantial resources available to push their children nor the easy ability to create an environment that promotes learning, the benefits of formal programs that promote learning are likely to outweigh their drawbacks.

Learning from the Media

Television and digital media—including computers, iPads, cell phones, and video game players—play a central role in children's lives. Two-thirds of 0- to 8-year-olds watch television at least once every day, and almost half have a TV in their bedrooms. In almost 40% of homes, the television is on all or most of the time. Children younger than 2 years of age spend twice as much time watching TV and videos as they do reading books. Overall, children age 8 and younger spend around three hours each day involved with some form of media. Furthermore, the older they are, the greater children's media use (see Figure 15-3; Bryant & Bryant, 2001, 2003; Anand & Krosnick, 2005; Rideout, 2011).

"Say, Dad, think you could wrap it up? I have a long day tomorrow."

FIGURE 15-3 Television Time

Although 0- to 8-year-olds spend more time reading than playing video games or using a computer, they spend considerably more time watching television. As an educator, how would you instill interest in children to read more?

(*Source:* Common Sense Media, 2011)

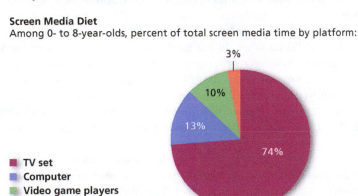

Screen Media Diet
Among 0- to 8-year-olds, percent of total screen media time by platform:

- 3%
- 10%
- 13%
- 74%

- TV set
- Computer
- Video game players
- Cell/iPod/iPad

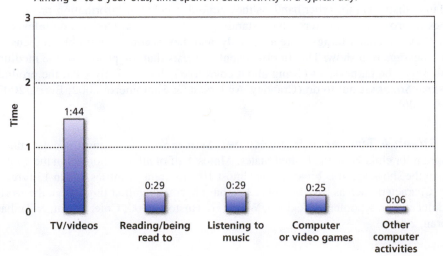

Time Spent with Media
Among 0- to 8-year-olds, time spent in each activity in a typical day:

- TV/videos: 1:44
- Reading/being read to: 0:29
- Listening to music: 0:29
- Computer or video games: 0:25
- Other computer activities: 0:06

The use of technology by preschoolers has increased dramatically, but it's still too early to know the effects of its usage.

Computers are also influential in the lives of preschoolers. Seventy percent of preschoolers between the ages of 4 and 6 have used a computer, and a quarter of them use one every day. Those who use a computer spend an average of an hour a day, and the majority use it by themselves. With help from their parents, almost one-fifth have sent an e-mail (Rideout, Vandewater, & Wartella, 2003; Glenberg, Goldberg, & Zhu, 2011; Plowman et al., 2012).

It's too early to know the effects of computer usage—and other new media such as video games—on preschoolers. However, there is a wealth of research on the consequences of viewing television, which we consider next (Pecora, Murray, & Wartella, 2007).

Television: Controlling Exposure.

Despite the introduction of a number of high-quality educational programs over the past decade, many children's programs are not of high quality or are not appropriate for a preschool audience. Accordingly, the American Academy of Pediatrics (AAP) recommends that exposure to television should be limited. They suggest that until the age of 2, children watch *no* television, and after that age, no more than 1 to 2 hours of quality programming each day. More generally, the AAP recommends that parents should limit combined screen time using television, computers, video games, and DVDs to 2 hours per day in total for preschool children (American Academy of Pediatrics, 2010).

One reason for restricting children's viewing of television relates to the inactivity it produces. Preschoolers who watch more than two hours per day of television and videos (or use computers for significant amounts of time) have a significantly higher risk of obesity than those who watch less (Danner, 2008; Jordan & Robinson, 2008; Strasburger, 2009).

What are the limits of preschoolers' "television literacy"? When they do watch television, preschool children often do not fully understand the plots of the stories they are viewing, particularly in longer programs. They are unable to recall significant story details after viewing a program, and the inferences they make about the motivations of characters are limited and often erroneous. Moreover, preschool children may have difficulty separating fantasy from reality in television programming, with some believing, for example, that there is a real Big Bird living on *Sesame Street* (Wright et al., 1994).

Preschool-age children exposed to advertising on television are not able to critically understand and evaluate the messages to which they are exposed. Consequently, they are likely to fully accept advertisers' claims about their product. The likelihood of children believing advertising messages is so high that the American Psychological Association has recommended that advertising targeting children under the age of 8 be restricted (Pine, Wilson, & Nash, 2007; Nash, Pine, & Messer, 2009; Nicklas et al., 2011).

In short, the world to which preschoolers are exposed on TV is imperfectly understood and unrealistic. On the other hand, as they get older and their information-processing capabilities improve, preschoolers' understanding of the material they see on television improves. They remember things more accurately, and they become better able to focus on the central message of a show. This improvement suggests that the powers of the medium of television may be harnessed to bring about cognitive gains—exactly what the producers of *Sesame Street* set out to do (Crawley, Anderson, & Santomero, 2002; Berry, 2003; Uchikoshi, 2006).

Sesame Street: A Teacher in Every Home?

Sesame Street is the most popular educational program for children in the United States. Almost half of all preschoolers in the United States watch the show, and it is broadcast in almost 100 different countries and in 13 foreign languages. Characters such as Big Bird and Elmo have become familiar throughout the world to both adults and preschoolers (Bickham, Wright, & Huston, 2000; Cole, Arafat, & Tidhar, 2003; Moran, 2006).

Sesame Street was devised with the express purpose of providing an educational experience for preschoolers. Its specific goals include teaching letters and numbers, increasing vocabulary, and teaching preliteracy skills. Has *Sesame Street* achieved its goals? Most evidence suggests that it has.

For example, a 2-year longitudinal study compared three groups of 3- and 5-year-olds: those who watched cartoons or other programs, those who watched the same amount of *Sesame Street,* and those who watched little or no TV. Children who watched *Sesame Street* had significantly larger vocabularies than those who watched other programs or those who watched little television. These findings held regardless of the children's gender, family size, and parent education and attitudes. Such findings are consistent with earlier evaluations of the program, which concluded that viewers showed dramatic improvements in skills that were directly taught, such as alphabet recitation, and improvements in other areas that were not directly taught, such as reading words (Rice et al., 1990; McGinn, 2002; Penuel et al., 2012).

Formal evaluations of the show find that preschoolers living in lower income households who watch the show are better prepared for school, and they perform significantly higher on several measures of verbal and mathematics ability at ages 6 and 7 than those who do not watch it. Furthermore, viewers of *Sesame Street* spend more time reading than nonviewers. And by the time they are 6 and 7, viewers of *Sesame Street* and other educational programs tend to be better readers and judged more positively by their teachers. The findings for *Sesame Street* are mirrored for other educationally oriented shows such as *Dora the Explorer* and *Blue's Clues* (Augustyn, 2003; Linebarger & Walker, 2005).

On the other hand, *Sesame Street* has not been without its critics. For instance, some educators claim the frenzied pace at which different scenes are shown makes viewers less receptive to the traditional forms of teaching that they will experience when they begin school. However, careful evaluations of the program find no evidence that viewing *Sesame Street* leads to declines in enjoyment of traditional schooling. Indeed, the most recent findings regarding *Sesame Street* and other informative programs like it show quite positive outcomes for viewers (Wright et al., 2001; Fisch, 2004; Zimmerman & Christakis, 2007).

Media and Technology Use by Children and Adolescents

According to a comprehensive survey using a sample of boys and girls 8 to 18 years old conducted by the Kaiser Family Foundation (a well-respected think tank), young people spend an average of 6.5 hours a day with media. Furthermore, because around a quarter of the time they are using more than one form of medium simultaneously, they are actually being exposed to the equivalent of 8 1/2 hours per day (Rideout, Roberts, & Foehr, 2005; see Figure 15-4).

In fact, these figures probably underestimate media use by teenagers for at least two reasons. First, the sample included preteens, many of whom likely have less opportunity and access to media than do older youth. Second, the survey was conducted in 2003 and 2004, meaning that some technologies, such as text messaging, were not as widespread as they are now, and others, such as tweeting, were not yet invented. It seems reasonable, then, that media use is even more extensive than initially found in the survey.

These varied media play a number of significant functions in adolescents' lives. Not only do media provide entertainment and information, but they also help adolescents cope with the stress of everyday life. Losing oneself in a television show or CD can be a way of escaping from one's current problems.

In addition, the media provide models and a sense of norms that operate among other adolescents. Teenagers watching reality shows not only are exposed to the lives of particular individuals, but they can also view how people look, dress, and behave (Head, 2005).

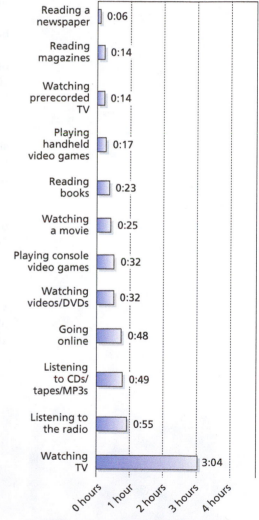

FIGURE 15-4 Time Spent with Media in a Typical Day

One comprehensive study by the Kaiser Family Foundation has show that young people spend more than 6.5 hours a day interacting with various media.

(*Source:* Rideout et al., 2005)

Clearly, the media play a number of roles in adolescents' lives. Let's look at some of the specific types of media to which teenagers are exposed and consider their consequences.

Viewing Television.

Despite the proliferation of new technologies, television viewing remains the most frequent activity. Although figures on actual exposure to television vary significantly depending on how viewing is assessed, television use is substantial, averaging around 3 hours a day. There is some change with age, though: Older adolescents watch somewhat less television than younger adolescents, in part because older adolescents begin to have more time-consuming responsibilities, such as homework and work. In addition, older adolescents have greater mobility, permitting them to leave home to participate in other activities more easily (Roberts, Henriksen, & Foehr, 2004).

It's certainly easy for adolescents to watch television, given that two-thirds of U.S. 8- to 18-year-olds have television sets in their bedrooms. But not all of that viewing is particularly attentive. Sometimes adolescents leave the television on and only monitor what is going on, rather than paying careful attention (Rideout, Roberts, & Foehr, 2005).

When they do pay attention to what they are watching, though, they are affected by their viewing in significant ways. For instance, television provides information about appropriateness of body image. In many ways, the television-based view of women's bodies is idealized in a way that barely approaches reality. Women with large breasts, small waists, and slender legs are represented as an ideal. Yet few adolescents (or anyone else) can achieve such a standard. Ultimately, the more adolescents watch television and are exposed to these idealized body images, the more negative is their own body image (Clay, Vignoles, & Dittmar, 2005; Ward & Friedman, 2006; Vandenbosch & Eggermont, 2012).

Television also may have an impact on the physical well-being of adolescents. For instance, according to the results of one survey, teenagers with the greatest number of electronic devices were twice as likely to fall asleep in school, suggesting that the availability of the equipment reduced the number of hours of sleep for the most technologically well-equipped adolescents. In addition, obesity has been linked to the level of television viewing: More hours spent viewing are associated with higher levels of adolescent obesity—largely due to the sedentary nature of television (Hancox, Milne, & Poulton, 2004; Lawlor et al., 2005; National Sleep Foundation, 2006).

Computers and the Internet: Living in a Virtual World.

Despite the fact that adolescents are spending far more time using the Internet than they did a few decades ago—when the Internet was quite new and access was limited—we still don't know a great deal about its effects on adolescent development. Surveys are only recently telling us what, at least generally, adolescents are doing when they are online.

Most of the time, adolescents are visiting websites that have to do with entertainment and sports. Older adolescents also spend more substantial amounts of time on relationship-oriented sites such as Facebook (Davis, 2012).

On the other hand, although fears that cyberspace is overrun with child molesters are exaggerated, it is true that the Internet makes available material that many parents and other adults find objectionable. In addition, there is a growing problem with Internet gambling. High school and college students can easily bet on sports events and participate in games such as poker on the web using credit cards (Dowling, Smith, & Thomas, 2005; Winters et al., 2005).

The growing use of computers also presents a challenge involving socioeconomic status, race, and ethnicity. Poorer adolescents and members of minority groups have less access to computers than more affluent adolescents and members of socially advantaged groups—a phenomenon known as the *digital divide* (Sax et al., 2004; Fetterman, 2005; Wood & Howley, 2012).

Differences in socioeconomic status also affect computer access across different countries. For example, adolescents in developing

Socioeconomic status, race and ethnicity are related to access to technology, creating a potential digital divide.

countries have less access to the Internet than those in industrialized countries. On the other hand, as computers become less expensive, their availability is becoming more common, opening up opportunities for cultural exchange among adolescents worldwide (Anderson, et al., 2003).

 **Watch** the **Video** *Media Use in Emerging Adulthood Across Cultures* **MyPsychLab**.

Review, Check, and Apply

Review

1. Nearly 75% of preschool-age children in the United States participate in some form of care outside the home, much of it intended to improve their intellectual and social skills.

2. Early education options include family or institutional child-care centers, preschools, and school child care.

3. Montessori preschools, developed in Italy, employ a carefully designed set of materials to create an environment that fosters sensory, motor, and language development through play.

4. In general, child care can be highly effective in fostering self-confidence, independence, and social skills, but children in child care tend to be less polite, compliant, and respectful of adults, and more competitive and aggressive with peers. The key element contributing to success is the quality of the child care program.

5. A focus on academic skills early in the preschool years can induce stress in young children, who should be exposed only to developmentally appropriate educational practice, which takes account of each child's level of development and unique characteristics.

6. The increasing presence of television, computers, the web, and other high-tech media in children's and adolescents' lives can have negative effects. TV watching, especially, should be limited for young children.

Check

1. _____ preschools, developed in Italy, employ a carefully designed set of materials to create an environment that fosters sensory, motor, and language development through play.

2. A key factor in the effectiveness of preschools is their level of _____.

3. David Elkind argues that children require _____ _____ educational practices, which are based on both typical development and the unique characteristics of a given child.

4. The American Academy of Pediatrics (AAP) recommends that preschool children older than 2 watch at most _____ hours of quality television per day.

Apply

1. If young children are incapable of viewing TV ads critically, should the government prohibit the airing of advertisements during children's programming? Do you think this would be advisable? Do you think it is feasible?

2. What are some advantages and disadvantages of focusing on the enhancement of academic skills during the preschool years? Is it possible to do this properly, avoiding harmful effects on children's overall development?

To see more review questions, log on to MyPsychLab.

ANSWERS: 1. Montessori 2. quality 3. developmentally appropriate 4. 1 to 2

MODULE 15.2

SOCIOCULTURAL ASPECTS OF SCHOOLING

LO 15-4 What are some current trends that affect schooling worldwide and in the United States?

LO 15-5 What changes have taken place in the ways U.S. schools provide instruction in the 3 Rs?

LO 15-6 What are some of the challenges involved in educating children in the middle school years?

LO 15-7 What are some advantages and disadvantages of homeschooling?

LO 15-8 How do American adolescents perform in high school?

LO 15-9 What social and cultural factors affect school performance?

> *As the eyes of the six other children in his reading group turned to him, Glenn shifted uneasily in his chair. Reading had never come easily to him, and he always felt anxious when it was his turn to read aloud. But as his teacher nodded in encouragement, he plunged in, hesitantly at first, then gaining momentum as he read the story about a mother's first day on a new job. He found that he could read the passage quite nicely, and he felt a surge of happiness and pride at his accomplishment. When he was done, he broke into a broad smile as his teacher said simply, "Well done, Glenn."*

Small moments such as these, repeated over and over, make—or break—a child's educational experience. Schooling marks a time when society formally attempts to transfer to new generations its accumulated body of knowledge, beliefs, values, and wisdom. The success with which this transfer is managed determines, in a very real sense, the future fortunes of the world.

Schooling around the World: Who Gets Educated?

In the United States, as in most developed countries, a primary school education is both a universal right and a legal requirement. Virtually all children are provided with a free education through the 12th grade.

Children in other parts of the world are not so fortunate. More than 160 million of the world's children do not have access to even a primary school education. An additional 100 million children do not progress beyond a level comparable to our elementary school education, and close to a billion individuals (two-thirds of them women) are illiterate throughout their lives (International Literacy Institute, 2001; see Figure 15-5).

In almost all developing countries, fewer females than males receive formal education, a discrepancy found at every level of schooling. Even in developed countries, women lag behind men in their exposure to science and technology. These differences reflect widespread and deeply held cultural and parental biases that favor males over females. Educational levels in the United States are more nearly equal between men and women, and especially in the early years of school, boys and girls share equal access to educational opportunities.

What Makes Children Ready for School?

Many parents have a hard time deciding exactly when to enroll their children in school for the first time. Do children who are younger than most of the other children in their grade suffer as a result of the age difference? According to traditional wisdom, the answer is yes. Because younger children are assumed to be slightly less advanced developmentally than their peers, it has been assumed that such children would be at a competitive disadvantage. In

In the United States and most developed countries, a primary school education is a universal right.

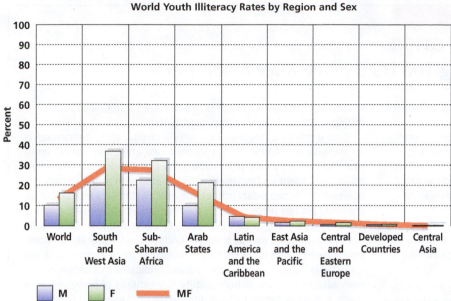

FIGURE 15-5 Plague of Illiteracy

Illiteracy remains a significant problem worldwide, particularly for women. Across the world, close to a billion people are illiterate throughout their lives.

(*Source:* UNESCO, 2006)

some cases, teachers recommended that students delay entry into kindergarten to cope better academically and emotionally (Noel & Newman, 2008).

However, a massive study conducted by developmental psychologist Frederick Morrison contradicts the traditional view. He found that children who are among the youngest in first grade progress at the same rate as the oldest. Although they were slightly behind older first-graders in reading, the difference was negligible. It was also clear that parents who chose to hold their children back in kindergarten, thereby ensuring that they would be among the oldest in first grade and after, were not doing their children a favor. These older children did no better than their younger classmates (Morrison, Bachman, & Connor, 2005; Skibbe et al., 2011).

Other research even has identified some delayed negative reaction to delayed entry. For example, one longitudinal study examined adolescents whose entrance into kindergarten was delayed by a year. Even though many seemed to show no ill effects from the delay during elementary school, during adolescence a surprising number of these children had emotional and behavioral problems (Byrd, Weitzman, & Auinger, 1997; Stipek, 2002; Winsler et al., 2012).

In short, delaying children's entry into school does not necessarily provide an advantage and in some cases may actually be harmful. Ultimately, age per se is not a critical indicator of when children should begin school. Instead, the start of formal schooling is more reasonably tied to overall developmental readiness, the product of a complex combination of several factors.

Educational Trends: Beyond the Three *R*s

Schooling in the 21st century is different from what it was as recently as a decade ago. In fact, U.S. schools are experiencing a return to the educational fundamentals embodied in the traditional three *R*s (reading, writing, and arithmetic). The focus on the fundamentals marks a departure from educational trends of prior decades when the emphasis was on students' social well-being and on allowing them to choose study topics on the basis of their interests instead of following a set curriculum (Schemo, 2003; Yinger, 2004).

Elementary school classrooms today also stress individual accountability, both for teachers and for students. Teachers are more likely to be held responsible for their students' learning, and both students and teachers are more likely to be required to take tests, developed at the state or national level, to assess their competence. As we discuss in the *From Research to Practice* box, pressures on students to succeed have grown (McDonnell, 2004).

FROM RESEARCH TO PRACTICE
Making the Grade: Pushing Too Hard in the *Race to the Top*?

Jared Reade was a happy-go-lucky boy until he started kindergarten. Now his moms Karen and Joan are concerned.

"Jared loves acting out stories," Karen says. "He remembers the plot of every book I read to him. Lately, he's been making up his own stories and dictating them to me."

"He's curious, too," Joan adds. "Last year, he asked me how they made actors small enough to fit inside the TV. Yesterday, he asked why we don't fall off the earth as it rotates."

Despite Jared's creativity and curiosity, his teacher reports he's failing. "He's not picking up reading and writing fast enough," Karen says, "but I'm more concerned that he's coming home depressed and he's not yet six years old."

The *No Child Left Behind Act,* and its successor, the *Race to the Top* program, both seek to produce educational reform, and both have a worthy goal: seeking to improve the educational success of children in the United States. For example, *No Child Left Behind* aimed to ensure that all children would be able to read by the time they reached the third grade. The law required school principals to meet this goal or risk losing their jobs and their school funding. *Race to the Top* pushes schools to adopt rigorous standards and assessments to produce "substantial" gains in student achievement through increased accountability (Paulson, 2012).

While the intentions of these initiatives are certainly good, an unforeseen outcome in some cases has been so much focus on basic topics such as reading that other topics, such as social studies and music, and activities such as recess are excluded from the school day (Abril & Gault, 2006; Paige, 2006; Sunderman, 2008).

When once kindergarten was a time for finger painting, story time, and free play, children are increasingly devoted to academic topics. Frequent testing to ensure that children are meeting short-term and long-term goals has become more commonplace. The experience of failure—and of competitive pressure to be at the top of the class—is hitting children at younger ages than before.

One trend that has many parents and educators concerned is an increase in the amount of homework assigned that has occurred over the last 20 years. But is the extra homework worth the cost? While time spent on homework is associated with greater academic achievement in secondary school, the relationship gets less strong for the lower grades; below grade 5, the relationship disappears. Experts explain this finding in terms of younger children's inability to tune out distractions as well as their yet undeveloped study skills. Moreover, research with older children shows that more homework is not necessarily better. In fact, some research indicates that unless homework assignments are of high quality, the benefits of homework may reach a plateau beyond which additional time spent on homework produces no gains (Trautwein et al., 2006; Dettmers et al., 2010; Cooper, Steenbergen-Hu, & Dent, 2012).

Some educational experts fear that the social and emotional development of children are taking a backseat to literacy education, and that the pressure, the testing, the accelerated programs, and the time spent in school—as well as in after-school programs and on homework—are robbing kids of opportunities to just be kids. Some parents, such as Jared Reade's mothers, are worried that their children are just becoming frustrated and discouraged with learning (Kohn, 2006; Bartel, 2010).

- **Why do you think students who spend a lot of time doing homework tend not to have better academic success than students who spend a moderate amount of time?**

- **Do you agree with Jared's mothers that the challenges Jared is facing are excessive? Why do you think more parents aren't expressing similar concerns?**

The Transition from Elementary to Middle School

I LOVE MIDDLE SCHOOL!!!!!!! none of my old friends are really in my classes though (ok I have some in gym and Steph in get the facs but that's only like 1 class per person) but Joe just happened to be in 4 of my classes so I spend 5 periods of every day with him, sitting by him in 3 of them. he's gotten nicer though, kinda. anyway I LOVE MIDDLE SCHOOL!!!!! it's the greatest. and plus there's Vivi who is sick right now but I have my last 3 periods with her and Morgan ... I love Latin too it's so much fun and I love my teacher Mrs. Whittaker. She's the best.

***

From 4th grade till the summer before 6th grade I was depressed. it was in 6th grade that I decided that I needed to live. I figured that since I was moving to middle school I might be able to sort of start over. however that was not the case. my brothers had by this point stopped messing with me for the most part. but school was horrible I was the kid that everyone picked on. that lasted for 2 years until I realized that if I stopped reacting to being made fun of people stopped making fun of me. so throughout middle school I was a loner. I had a lot of people who would claim to be my friends but they would still make fun of me so I became a loner.

If nothing else, middle school evokes strong feelings on the part of adolescents, as these two reactions illustrate. That's hardly surprising, given that the transition from elementary school to middle school comes at time when students are changing radically along a variety of dimensions.

The transition from elementary school to secondary education is a normative transition, meaning it is a part of the life of almost all adolescents in the United States. However, the fact that nearly everyone is doing it doesn't make it easy. The transition can be particularly difficult because of the physical, intellectual, and social changes that are occurring at about the same time.

After leaving elementary school, most students enter a *middle school,* which typically comprises grades 6 to 8. At the same time, most adolescents are beginning puberty and coming to grips with the changes taking place in their bodies. Furthermore, their thinking is becoming more sophisticated, and their relationships with their family and friends are becoming far more complicated than ever before. For most adolescents, middle schools provide a very different educational structure from the one they grew accustomed to in elementary school. Rather than spending the day in a self-contained classroom, students move from one class to another. Not only must they adapt to the demands of different teachers, but their classmates in each course may be different every class period. Those classmates may be more heterogeneous and diverse than those they encountered in their elementary schools.

Furthermore, because they are the youngest and least experienced, students in middle school enter an environment in which they suddenly find themselves at the bottom of the status hierarchy. Coming from elementary schools in which they were at the top of that status hierarchy (and at which they were physically and cognitively so different from the kindergartners and first-graders who occupied the bottom of the hierarchy), students can find the middle school experience alarming and sometimes damaging.

In addition, middle schools are typically considerably larger than elementary schools. This factor alone makes the transition to middle school more difficult. A significant amount of research demonstrates quite clearly that students do better, both academically and psychologically, in smaller, less bureaucratic educational settings (Lee & Burkam, 2003; Ready, Lee, & Welner, 2004).

In fact, from the point of view of many educators, the overall record of middle schools is subject to serious criticism. For example, consider these facts (Juvonen et al., 2004):

- Over half of eighth-graders do not achieve proficiency in reading, math, and science according to national standards.

- In comparison to their peers in other countries, eighth-graders rank in 12th place academically, which places them below average. In some cases, students from the United States who did better than their international peers in elementary school actually declined in rank when they entered middle school. For instance, in fourth grade, U.S. students are average in math and science compared to their international peers; four years later, when they enter eighth grade, they score below the international average (National Governors Association, 2008).

- The proportion of middle school students who suffer from emotional problems is higher for students in the United States than for students in all 11 of the other countries examined by the World Health Organization. U.S. middle school students exhibit higher rates of depression, a greater degree of disengagement with school, and a greater desire to drop out of school than students their age in other countries.

Although such findings suggest that middle schools have not been up to the task of educating young adolescents, it's important to keep in mind that the findings don't necessarily mean that students in middle schools fare worse than students in other school configurations. There are only a limited number of studies that compare outcomes in schools with different grade configurations. While some evidence suggests that students in some traditional configurations, such as the kindergarten-through-eighth-grade pattern, may outperform students in elementary/middle schools, the data are far from conclusive (Yecke, 2005).

Furthermore, in many cases, the philosophy behind the middle school movement—such as a focus on discovery learning—never was fully implemented. In fact, many school districts replaced large junior high schools with large middle schools and otherwise made only minimal changes, which was hardly a fair test of the middle school philosophy (Wigfield & Eccles, 2002; Wallis, 2005).

The challenges faced by students in middle schools have led adolescents and their parents to seek alternatives. We discuss one—home schooling—next.

Homeschooling, a growing educational practice, has both advantages and drawbacks.

Homeschooling: An Alternative to Traditional Schools

Teddy Pantagenes, 17, is a senior at Shoemaker High School in Kileen, Texas. But he has only one high school teacher: his mother, Delores.

Delores began homeschooling Teddy two years ago, after noticing that he never seemed happy at school. When she asked him about this situation, Teddy admitted to feeling "out of place" at Shoemaker.

"I was different from everyone else, interested in different things and never comfortable with the other kids," he says. "I really wasn't learning much."

Now Teddy is taking his remaining high school subjects at home while also attending classes at Central Texas College. "He's a different person now," Delores says. "He's cheerful, self-confident, and mature. It helps that I know what he's learning, and it doesn't hurt that he knows I care."

For students like Teddy Pantagenes, there is no distinction between their living room and classroom, because he is one of the nearly one million students who are homeschooled. Homeschooling is a major educational phenomenon in which students are taught not by teachers in schools, but by their parents in their own homes.

There are a number of reasons why parents may choose to school their adolescents at home. Some parents feel their children will thrive with the one-to-one attention that homeschooling can bring, whereas they might get lost in a larger public school. Other parents are dissatisfied with the nature of the instruction and the quality of the teachers in their public schools and feel that they can do a better job teaching their children. And some parents engage in homeschooling for religious reasons, wishing to impart particular religious beliefs and practices that would not be provided in a public school and hoping to avoid exposing their children to values and aspects of the popular culture with which they disagree (Dennis, 2004; Green & Hoover-Dempsey, 2007; Isenberg, 2007).

Homeschooling clearly works, in the sense that adolescents who have been homeschooled score generally as well on standardized tests as students who have been educated traditionally. In addition, their acceptance rate into colleges appears to be no different from that of traditionally schooled students, and they seem as well-adjusted in college as traditionally schooled students (Lines, 2001; Bolle, Wessel, & Mulvihill, 2007; Rivero, 2011).

However, the apparent academic success of adolescents schooled at home does not mean that homeschooling, per se, is effective, since parents who choose to homeschool their children may be more affluent or have the kind of well-structured family situation in which children would succeed no matter what kind of schooling they had. In contrast, parents in dysfunctional and disorganized families are unlikely to have the motivation, interest, or opportunity to homeschool their children. For adolescents from families like these, the demands and structure of a formal school are probably a good thing.

Critics of homeschooling argue that it has considerable drawbacks. For example, the social interaction with groups of adolescents that is inherent in classrooms in traditional schools is largely missing for homeschooled students. Learning in an at-home environment, while perhaps strengthening family ties, hardly provides an environment that reflects the diversity of U.S. society. Furthermore, even the best-equipped home is unlikely to have the sophisticated science materials and educational technology that are available at many schools. Finally, most parents do not have the preparation of well-trained teachers, and their teaching methods may be unsophisticated. Although parents may be successful in teaching subject areas in which their child is already interested, they may have more difficulty teaching subjects that their child seeks to avoid (Cai, Reeve, & Robinson, 2002; Apple, 2007).

Because homeschooling is relatively new, few controlled experiments have been conducted to examine its effectiveness. More research is needed to clarify how and when homeschooling is an effective way to educate adolescents.

School Performance in Adolescence

Do the advances that occur in metacognition, reasoning, and other cognitive abilities during adolescence translate into improvements in school performance? If we use students' grades as the measure, the answer is "yes." Grades awarded to high school students have shifted upward in the last decade. The mean grade point average for college-bound seniors was 3.3 (out of a scale of 4), compared with 3.1 a decade ago. More than 40% of seniors reported average grades of A+, A, or A- (College Board, 2005).

At the same time, though, independent measures of achievement, such as SAT scores, have not risen. Consequently, a more likely explanation for the higher grades is the phenomenon of grade inflation. According to this view, it is not that students have changed. Instead, instructors have become more lenient, awarding higher grades for the same performance (Cardman, 2004).

Further evidence for grade inflation comes from the relatively poor achievement of students in the United States when compared to students in other countries. For instance, students in the United States score lower on standardized math and science tests when compared to students in other industrialized countries (see Figure 15-6; OECD, 2005).

There is no single reason for this gap in the educational achievement of U.S. students, but a combination of factors, such as less time spent in classes and less intensive instruction,

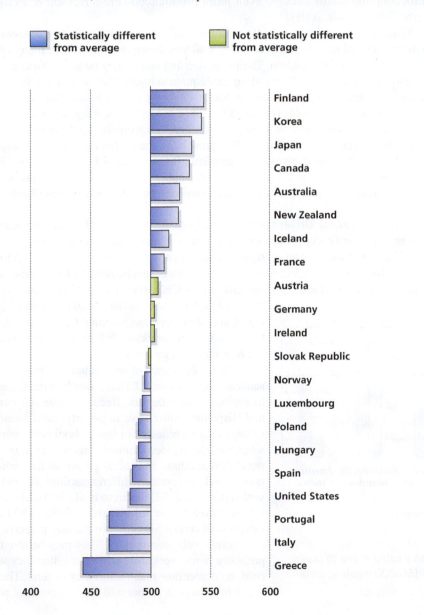

FIGURE 15-6 Not at the Top of the Class—U.S. Math Performance Lags

When compared to the academic performance of students cross the world, U.S. students perform at below-average levels.

(*Source:* Adapted from OECD, 2005)

are at work. Furthermore, the broad diversity of the U.S. school population may affect performance relative to other countries, in which the population attending school is more homogeneous and affluent (Scheme, 2001).

The poorer accomplishments of U.S. students are also reflected in high school graduation rates. Although it once stood first in the percentage of the population who graduates from high school, the United States has dropped to 22nd among industrialized countries. Only around three-quarters of U.S. high school students graduate—a rate considerably lower than other developed countries (Organization for Economic Cooperation and Development, 2009; Paulson, 2012).

Socioeconomic Status and School Performance

All students are entitled to the same opportunities in the classroom, but it is clear that certain groups have more educational advantages than others. One of the most telling indicators of this reality is the relationship between educational achievement and socioeconomic status (SES).

Middle- and high-SES students, on average, earn higher grades, score higher on standardized tests of achievement, and complete more years of schooling than do students from lower SES homes. This disparity does not start in adolescence; the same findings hold for children in lower grades. However, by the time students are in high school, the effects of socioeconomic status become even more pronounced (Frederickson & Petrides, 2008; Shernoff & Schmidt, 2008).

Why do students from middle- and high-SES homes show greater academic success? There are several reasons. For one thing, children living in poverty lack many of the advantages enjoyed by other children. Their nutrition and health may be less adequate. Often living in crowded conditions and attending inadequate schools, they may have few places to do homework. Their homes may lack the books and computers commonplace in more economically advantaged households (Prater, 2002; Chiu & McBride-Chang, 2006).

For these reasons, students from impoverished backgrounds may be at a disadvantage from the day they begin their schooling. As they grow older, their school performance may continue to lag, and in fact their disadvantage may snowball. Because later school success builds heavily on basic skills presumably learned early in school, children who experience early problems may find themselves falling increasingly behind the academic eight ball as adolescents (Biddle, 2001).

Ethnic and Racial Differences in School Achievement.
Achievement differences between ethnic and racial groups are significant, and they paint a troubling picture of American education. For instance, data on school achievement indicate that, on average, African American and Hispanic students tend to perform at lower levels, receive lower grades, and score lower on standardized tests of achievement than Caucasian students (see Figure 15-7). In contrast, Asian American students tend to receive higher grades than Caucasian students (National Center for Education Statistics, 2003; Frederickson & Petrides, 2008; Smith, Estudillo, & Kang, 2011).

What is the source of such ethnic and racial differences in academic achievement? Clearly, much of the difference is due to socioeconomic factors: Because more African American and Hispanic families live in poverty, their economic disadvantage may be reflected in their school performance. In fact, when we take socioeconomic levels into account by comparing different ethnic and racial groups at the same socioeconomic level, achievement differences diminish, but they do not vanish (Cokley, 2003; Guerrero et al., 2006; Simms, 2012).

Anthropologist John Ogbu (1988, 1992) argues that members of certain minority groups may perceive school success as relatively unimportant. They may believe that societal prejudice in the workplace will dictate that they will not succeed, no matter how much effort they expend. The conclusion is that hard work in school will have no eventual payoff.

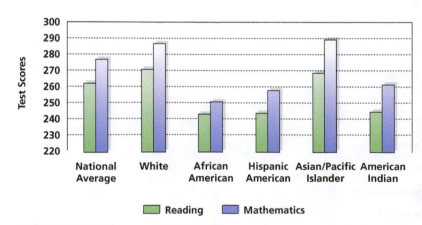

Reading **Mathematics**

FIGURE 15-7 Achievement Test Results

Racial discrepancies between groups are apparent on a national test of reading and math achievement administered to a sample of 150,000 eighth-graders.

(*Source:* NAEP, 2003)

Ogbu suggests that members of minority groups who enter a new culture voluntarily are more likely to be successful in school than those who are brought into a new culture against their will. For instance, he notes that Korean children who are the sons and daughters of voluntary immigrants to the United States tend to be, on average, quite successful in school. On the other hand, Korean children in Japan, whose parents were forced to immigrate during World War II and work as forced laborers, tend to do relatively poorly in school. The reason for the disparity? The process of involuntary immigration apparently leaves lasting scars, reducing the motivation to succeed in subsequent generations. Ogbu argues that in the United States, the involuntary immigration, as slaves, of the ancestors of many African American students might be related to their motivation to succeed.

Review, Check, and Apply

Review

1. In the United States, virtually all children receive a free education through grade 12, but in other parts of the world most children do not have access to education, and nearly one billion people are illiterate.

2. Age is not a reliable indicator of when children should start school, since delaying the start to ensure a child is on the older side of the age scale is not necessarily advantageous and may even be harmful. A better indicator is developmental readiness.

3. Handling the transition from elementary to secondary school is especially difficult for young adolescents because of the other developmental issues that they face at around the same time. These issues continue to affect school performance throughout the adolescent years.

4. In recent years, homeschooling has emerged as a way for parents to educate their children at home while meeting district and state educational requirements.

5. Performance in school depends on a number of factors, including socioeconomic status and race/ethnicity.

Check

1. In determining children's readiness for school, the most important factor is not age but _____ level.

2. The transition from elementary to secondary education is a _____ transition, in that it is a part of the life of nearly all U.S. adolescents.

3. Challenges faced by students in middle schools have led adolescents and their parents to seek alternatives, such as _____.

4. One of the most telling indicators of some students have more educational advantages is the relationship between educational achievement and _____ _____.

Apply

1. How would you advise a parent considering homeschooling to overcome the challenges of this approach with respect to their child's exposure to diversity, social interactions, and advanced school resources?

To see more review questions, log on to MyPsychLab.

ANSWERS: 1. developmental 2. normative 3. homeschooling 4. socioeconomic status

MODULE 15.3

LIVING IN A MULTICULTURAL WORLD

LO 15-10 In what ways are individuals affected by culture and ethnicity?

LO 15-11 What is multicultural education and why is it of critical importance in the United States today?

LO 15-12 How is socioeconomic status related to race and ethnicity?

LO 15-13 How do prejudice, stereotypes, and discrimination work together?

As the U.S. population has become more diverse, schools have also paid increased attention to issues involving student diversity and multiculturalism. And with good reason: Cultural, as well as language, differences affect students socially and educationally. The demographic makeup of students in the United States is undergoing an extraordinary shift. For instance, the proportion of Hispanics will in all likelihood more than double in the next 50 years. Moreover, by the year 2050, non-Hispanic Caucasians will likely become a minority of the total population of the United States (see Figure 15-8). Consequently, educators have been increasingly serious about multicultural concerns. As we will see later in this chapter, the goals for educating students from different cultures have changed significantly over the years and are still being debated today (Brock et al., 2007; U.S. Bureau of the Census, 2008).

How Culture Defines Us

An essential part of how people define themselves relates to their cultural background. Whether it involves race, ethnicity, gender, socioeconomic status, or a host of other factors, that cultural background plays a central role in determining who they are, how they view themselves, and how others treat them.

For example, because of their knowledge of their own culture, people understand what clothes are appropriate to wear, are guided in their choice of what foods to choose and what to avoid, and know which sexual practices are likely to be acceptable on a date (kissing) and which are not (forced sexual intercourse). Such knowledge reflects basic cultural beliefs and values.

We can look at culture on various levels. At the broadest level, we all belong to the human culture, sharing certain customs that are brought about by particular biological necessities (sleeping every night or eating at various times during the day rather than once every few days, for example). All humans use language, which is a defining characteristic of human culture. Furthermore, there are other cultural universals such as cooking and funeral ceremonies that, although practiced in different ways, are found in every culture.

The United States has become a more diverse culture, as we discussed earlier. Furthermore, *globalization*, the integration of cultures, social movements, and financial markets around the world, has become increasingly common across a variety of dimensions, exposing adults and children to individuals with cultural backgrounds different from their own. Ultimately, it is clear that a full understanding of human development cannot be achieved without taking culture into account.

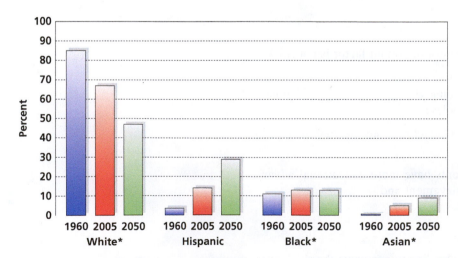

FIGURE 15-8 The Changing Face of America

Current projections of the population makeup of the United States show that by the year 2050, the proportion of non-Hispanic whites will decline as the proportion of minority group members increases. What will be some of the impacts on social workers as the result of changing demographics?

(*Source:* PEW Research Center, 2008)

Acculturation: When Cultures Collide. Let's begin our look at culture by considering the reactions of people when they encounter for sustained periods individuals from cultures other than their own, and how that may change them—a process called acculturation. **Acculturation** refers to the changes and adjustments that occur when groups of different people come into sustained firsthand contact.

The process of acculturation is particularly significant for people belonging to racial and ethnic minorities. They are faced with reconciling the demands of their own culture with those of the dominant culture. The issue of acculturation is particularly acute for adults and children who enter a new culture through immigration, an experience that typically involves leaving their native country and suddenly finding themselves in an entirely new culture. However, even members of racial and ethnic minorities who are raised their entire lives in the United States face pressures in reacting to their status as a subset of individuals living within a society in which they are a cultural minority.

The process of acculturation can produce one of four outcomes, depending on both the degree of identification with one's own culture and the strength of identification with the majority culture (illustrated in Figure 15-9):

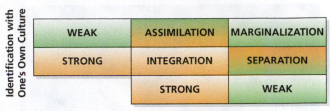

FIGURE 15-9 Four Outcomes of Acculturation

Depending on both the degree of identification with one's own culture and the strength of identification with the majority culture, the process of acculturation can produce one of the four outcomes show here.

(*Source:* Phinney et al., 1990)

- **Integration: Identifying with multiple cultures. Integration** is the process in which people maintain their own culture while simultaneously seeking to adapt and incorporate the majority culture. By embracing the dominant culture, people are able to feel more secure and assimilated. People who employ integration often have a *bicultural identity* (discussed later) in which they see themselves as part of, and comfortable with, two different cultures.

- **Assimilation: Identifying with the majority culture. Assimilation** occurs when a person begins to identify with the mainstream culture and rejects the minority culture. Assimilated people not only may adopt the values and beliefs of the majority, but, because they are only relatively weakly identified with their own culture, may reject the values and beliefs of their own culture (Unger et al., 2006).

- **Separation: Identifying with the minority culture and rejecting the majority culture. Separation** occurs when people identify with the ethnic minority culture to which they belong while rejecting or rebuffing the majority culture. Separation sometimes occurs with new immigrants, who may have difficulty with integrating into their new society because of a lack of understanding of the dominant culture. Often, they eventually take on the norms and values of the dominant culture. But the process of acculturation can be slow and painful, producing anxiety and depression (Kim et al., 2005; Sawrikar & Hunt, 2006).

  Separation may also occur voluntarily, as a political act. Some people may wish to accentuate their racial or ethnic identity by actively separating themselves, both psychologically and physically, from members of the dominant culture. This strategy of separation, which can be used to bolster group identity, can have positive psychological benefits (Phinney, 2005).

- **Marginalization: Nonidentification with minority or majority cultures. Marginalization** occurs when people identify neither with their minority culture nor with the majority culture. Marginalized people may feel isolated from both their own cultural group and from members of the majority culture, either because they have tried to connect and failed, or sometimes because they are rejected for personal reasons by others. Ultimately, they lack a clear cultural identity, and they typically feel isolated and alienated from society (Kosic, 2004; Arredondo et al., 2006).

The particular type of identification found in racial and ethnic minorities has significant implications for their well-being. Some of the outcomes—such as assimilation, integration, and occasionally even separation—can produce important psychological benefits.

On the other hand, strongly identifying with the majority culture may be seen negatively by one's minority peers. For example, although integration of majority and minority identities would seem to bring the benefits of belonging to both cultures, this may not always be true.

acculturation The changes and adjustments that occur when groups of different people come into sustained firsthand contact

integration The process in which people maintain their own culture while simultaneously seeking to adapt and incorporate the majority culture

assimilation The state that occurs when a person begins to identify with the mainstream culture and rejects the minority culture

separation The state that occurs when people identify with the ethnic minority culture to which they belong while rejecting or rebuffing the majority culture

marginalization The state that occurs when people identify neither with their minority culture nor with the majority culture

Ethnic identity, which develops in several stages, relates to the part of a person's self-concept that is derived from their awareness and knowledge that they are members of a distinct social group.

Thus, blacks who seek to integrate the majority culture into their lives may be derided for trying to "act white"—that is, trying to act like something they are not.

Similarly, it can be stressful for members of non-dominant cultures to try to integrate themselves into the majority culture if the majority culture resists their efforts. Minority members who are prevented from fully participating in the majority culture because of prejudice and discrimination may suffer psychological harm as a result (Schwartz, Montgomery, & Briones, 2006).

For some minority-culture members, the most successful approach may be to be highly adaptive, switching back and forth between the majority and minority cultures depending on the specific situation—a process called *code-switching*. For example, in some cases, minority youth are so adept at code-switching that they use different vocabulary and styles of speech depending on the group with which they are interacting (Cashman, 2005).

Developing an Ethnic Identity

Think of how you would briefly describe yourself to someone who had never met you. Would you include your ethnic background? The country from which your ancestors emigrated?

If you are a member of a minority ethnic or racial group or a recent immigrant, it is highly likely your description would prominently include that fact: "I'm a Korean American," "I'm black," or "I'm a Serb." But if you are a member of a group that is dominant in society or statistically in the majority, it might not even occur to you to say, for example, "I'm white."

The difference between the two responses reflects differences in ethnic identity and its salience in everyday life. **Ethnic identity** refers to how members of ethnic, racial, and cultural minorities view themselves, both as members of their own group and in terms of their relationships with other groups. Ethnic identity relates to the part of a person's self-concept that is derived from their awareness and knowledge that they are a member of a distinct social group (Umaña-Taylor, Bhanot, & Shin, 2006; Hudley & Irving, 2012).

According to psychologist Jean Phinney, ethnic identity develops in several stages. The first stage is *unexamined ethnic identity*, which is characterized by a lack of consideration or exploration of one's ethnicity, as well as acceptance of the norms, beliefs, and attitudes of the dominant culture. In this stage, people might not even think about ethnicity nor consider its impact on their lives. If they do think about their ethnicity, they may be embarrassed by it or reject it, believing that the dominant culture is superior (Phinney, 2003, 2006).

Although some people don't move beyond an unexamined ethnic identity, most reach the next stage, ethnic identity search. In *ethnic identity search,* people experience some sort of crisis that makes them become aware of ethnicity as a significant factor in their lives. It may be a shocking news event, such as a racially motivated killing, or they may be denied a job and suspect it's because of their race. In other cases, they may more gradually become aware that they are being treated differently by others because of their ethnicity.

Whatever the cause, people who enter the ethnic identity search phase become motivated to obtain a deeper understanding of their cultural identity. They may read books, attend ethnic celebrations and events, or—if their ethnic identity is tied to a religious group, such as Irish Catholics—may begin to attend religious services.

The ethnic identity search may produce resentment toward dominant groups in society. As they learn more about the consequences of prejudice and discrimination, people may come to believe that the majority should make amends for its discriminatory behavior.

Finally, the last stage of ethnic identity development is *achieved ethnic identity,* in which people fully embrace their ethnic identity. People in this stage develop a clear sense of themselves as members of an ethnic minority and realize that this has become part of the way that they view themselves. Their membership is viewed with pride, and they have a sense of belonging to others who share their ethnic identity.

Whereas people earlier may have experienced resentment or hostility regarding their ethnicity, directed either toward members of majority groups, others of their own ethnicity, or even themselves, they may feel more secure and optimistic after reaching the achieved ethnic identity stage. Furthermore, earlier feelings that they had two separate identities—one

ethnic identity How members of ethnic, racial, and cultural minorities view themselves, both as members of their own group and in terms of their relationships with other groups

that identified with the majority culture and one that identified with their ethnic culture—are replaced with a more unified ethnic identity that draws on both parts of who they are (Shih & Sanchez, 2005).

Achieving Ethnic Identity.   It's important to note that the stages of ethnic identity do not unfold according to any particular timetable. Some people may reach the achieved ethnic identity stage while still in adolescence, while for others it may occur later. Generally, the extent of identification with one's ethnicity increases with age.

Furthermore, some individuals may never enter the achieved ethnic identity stage or even the ethnic identity search stage at all. In such cases, ethnic identity is not perceived as part of the core of the individual. The danger is that a person will be treated (and sometimes discriminated against) by others due to his or her membership in an ethnic or racial group. Such treatment may be confusing at best and psychologically damaging at worst (Yasui, Dorham, & Dishion, 2004).

Ultimately, the nature and strength of a person's ethnic identity is determined both by parental socialization and by the particular experiences that an individual encounters. For example, ethnic minority parents teach their children, both explicitly and implicitly, about their own culture and about the dominant culture of the society in which they live. In addition, they may explicitly teach their children how to deal with the prejudice and discrimination that they are likely to encounter.

Finally, as we suggested earlier, ethnic identity is likely to be strongest for members of minority groups and weakest for members of the dominant societal group (which, in U.S. society, is whites). The reason: Members of the dominant group simply don't have to think as much about their ethnicity, given that they are not subject to the discrimination and prejudice experienced by members of ethnic minority groups. In contrast, members of minority groups expend more time and effort thinking not only about their own ethnicity but about the majority group. For ethnic minority group members, ethnicity becomes more of a part of who they are (Guinote & Fiske, 2003).

On the other hand, the fact that whites generally have less pronounced ethnic identities does not mean that ethnicity plays no role in their lives. Being a member of a particular non-racial ethnic or religious group (Italian, Jewish, or Irish, for example) may be a significant source of pride and may be perceived as a central part of identity. Furthermore, when whites find themselves in settings in which they are in the minority, their sense of racial identity may become magnified (Romero & Roberts, 2003).

Multicultural Education

It has always been the case that classrooms in the United States have been populated by individuals from a broad range of backgrounds and experiences. Yet it is only relatively recently that variations in student backgrounds have been viewed as one of the major challenges—and opportunities—that educators face.

The diversity of background and experience in the classroom relates to a fundamental objective of education, which is to provide a formal mechanism to transmit the information a society deems important. As the famous anthropologist Margaret Mead (1942, p. 633) once said, "In its broadest sense, education is the cultural process, the way in which each newborn human infant, born with a potentiality for learning greater than that of any other mammal, is transformed into a full member of a specific human society, sharing with the other members of a specific human culture."

Culture, then, can be thought of as a set of behaviors, beliefs, values, and expectations shared by members of a particular society. But although culture is often thought of in a relatively broad context (as in "Western culture" or "Asian culture"), it is also possible to focus on particular *subcultural* groups within a larger, more encompassing culture. For example, we can consider particular racial, ethnic, religious, socioeconomic, or even gender groups in the United States as manifesting characteristics of a subculture.

Pupils and teachers exposed to a diverse group can gain a better understanding of the world and greater sensitivity to the values and needs of others. What are some ways of developing greater sensitivity in the classroom?

Membership in a cultural or subcultural group might be of only passing interest to educators were it not for the fact that students' cultural backgrounds have a substantial impact on the way that they—and their peers—are educated. In fact, in recent years, a considerable amount of thought has gone into establishing **multicultural education**, a form of education in which the goal is to help minority students develop competence in the culture of the majority group while maintaining positive group identities that build on their original cultures (Nieto, 2005; Brandhorst, 2011).

Cultural Assimilation or Pluralistic Society?   Multicultural education developed in part as a reaction to a **cultural assimilation model**, in which the goal of education is to assimilate individual cultural identities into a unique, unified American culture. In practical terms, this meant, for example, that non-English-speaking students were discouraged from speaking their native tongues and were totally immersed in English.

In the early 1970s, however, educators and members of minority groups began to suggest that the cultural assimilation model ought to be replaced by a **pluralistic society model.** According to this conception, American society is made up of diverse, coequal cultural groups that should preserve their individual cultural features.

The pluralistic society model grew in part from the belief that teachers, by emphasizing the dominant culture and discouraging students who were nonnative speakers from using their native tongues, had the effect of devaluing minority subcultural heritages and lowering those students' self-esteem. Instructional materials, such as readers and history lessons, inevitably feature culture-specific events and understandings, and children who never see examples representing their own cultural heritage might never be exposed to important aspects of their backgrounds. For example, English-language texts rarely present some of the great themes that appear throughout Spanish literature and history (such as the search for the Fountain of Youth and the Don Juan legend). Hispanic students immersed in such texts might never come to understand important components of their own heritage.

Ultimately, educators began to argue that the presence of students representing diverse cultures enriched and broadened the educational experience of all students. Pupils and teachers exposed to people from different backgrounds could better understand the world and gain greater sensitivity to the values and needs of others (Gurin, Nagda, & Lopez, 2004; Zirkel & Cantor, 2004).

FROM AN
EDUCATOR'S
PERSPECTIVE:
Should one goal of instruction be to foster cultural assimilation for children from other cultures? Why or why not?

Fostering a Bicultural Identity

The pluralistic society model has an important implication for the education of minority children: that they should be encouraged to develop a bicultural identity. According to this perspective, school systems should encourage children to maintain their original cultural identities while they integrate themselves into the majority culture. This view suggests that an individual can live as a member of two cultures, with two cultural identities, without having to choose one over the other (Oyserman et al., 2003; Vyas, 2004; Marks, Patton, & Coll, 2011; Friedman et al., 2012).

The best way to achieve this goal of biculturalism is not clear. Consider, for example, children who enter a school speaking only Spanish. The traditional "melting-pot" technique would be to immerse the children in classes taught in English while providing a crash course in English-language instruction (and little else) until the children demonstrate a suitable level of proficiency. Unfortunately, the traditional approach has a considerable drawback: Until the children master English, they fall further and further behind their peers who entered school already knowing English.

More contemporary approaches emphasize a bicultural strategy in which children are encouraged to maintain simultaneous membership in more than one culture. In the case of Spanish-speaking children, for example, instruction begins in the child's native language and shifts as rapidly as possible to include English. At the same time, the school conducts a program of multicultural education for all students, in which teachers present material on the cultural backgrounds and traditions of all the students in the school. Such instruction is

multicultural education   A form of education in which the goal is to help minority students develop competence in the culture of the majority group while maintaining positive group identities that build on their original cultures

cultural assimilation model   The model in which the goal of education is to assimilate individual cultural identities into a unique, unified American culture

pluralistic society model   The model in which American society is made up of diverse, coequal cultural groups that should preserve their individual cultural features

designed to enhance the self-image of speakers from both majority and minority cultures (Bracey, Bamaca, & Umana-Taylor, 2004; Fowers & Davidov, 2006; Sánchez & Salazar, 2012).

Although most educational experts favor bicultural approaches, the general public does not always agree. For instance, the national "English-only" movement has as one of its goals the prohibition of school instruction in any language other than English. Whether such a perspective will prevail remains to be seen (Waldman, 2010).

The Impact of Socioeconomic Status and Poverty on Children and Adolescents

Although the number of youth living in low-income households began to decline in the early 1990s, it has been on the rise since 2000.

One of the greatest cultural divides between people relates to their socioeconomic status. This is a major problem that affects a significant part of the population: For example, some 15% of adolescents in the United States are living in poverty (with income levels below $19,000 per year for a family of 4), and 36% live in low-income households. Furthermore, although the number of youth living in low-income households began to decline in the early 1990s, it has been on the rise since 2000. The discrepancy between the rich and the poor also is growing (National Center for Children in Poverty, 2011).

Members of minority groups are proportionately more likely to be living in poverty than non-minority group members (see Figure 15-10). However, although Latino and black children and adolescents are disproportionately from low-income households, whites are the largest group of low-income individuals. More than half of the children of immigrant parents live in low-income families.

Poverty extends well beyond the stereotyped view of poor minority youth living in cities. Children and adolescents living in poverty are found throughout the United States in both urban and rural areas. According to Nobel winner Robert Solow, the cost of child poverty in the United States runs between $36 billion and $177 billion each year.

Poverty affects children and adolescents in a number of ways. In some households, there is not enough food, and children and adolescents go to school and to bed hungry. Because many poor households lack health insurance, children and adolescents living in poverty are unable to afford good medical care, and minor illnesses, left untreated, become major ones. The greater the degree of poverty, the higher the health risks.

As we've discussed in many of the previous chapters, the impact of poverty on human development is profound. It impedes children's and adolescents' ability to learn and can slow their cognitive development, making academic success less likely. In addition, poverty is associated with behavioral and emotional difficulties. Children and adolescents living in persistent poverty are less well adjusted and have more conduct problems, in part because their parents' emotional well-being is reduced, making them less successful caregivers (Smokowski et al., 2004; Gutman, McLoyd, & Tokoyawa, 2005).

Poverty, of course, is not an insoluble problem and solutions should be within the means of an affluent country such as the United States. However, the rate of poverty in the United

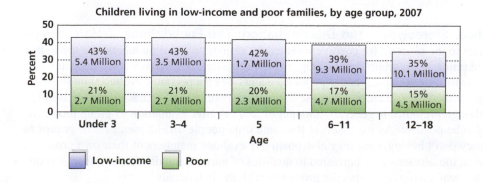

FIGURE 15-10 The Cultural Divide of Socioeconomic Status

Socioeconomic status is one of the greatest cultural divides between adolescents. According to the National Center for Children in Poverty, members of minority groups are proportionately more likely to be living in poverty than non-minority group members.

(*Source:* National Center for Children in Poverty, 2006)

States is actually higher than in many other industrialized countries. Why? The answer has a good deal to do with aggressive antipoverty measures adopted by other nations. Compared with the United States, public assistance levels for poor families are often higher, health care benefits are better, and governments have more programs to help those living in poverty (Rainwater & Smeeding, 2007).

The lower poverty rates in countries other than the United States offer a ray of hope even to poor people in this country, suggesting that the rate can be reduced. One route is clearly educational, for the higher the parental educational level, the less the chance of a child being raised in poverty. For example, only 11% of children living in poverty had at least one parent who had achieved an educational level beyond high school. In contrast, more than 80% of children whose more educated parent did not graduate from high school live in low income families (National Center for Children in Poverty, 2007).

Another route is through improvements in government programs and benefits targeted to the poor. Although current political trends and the 1996 federal welfare reform laws have been interpreted as moving the United States further from the goal of reducing poverty, some government programs on the state and local levels have been successful in breaking the bonds of poverty. Ultimately, improvements in income levels will produce substantial benefits, not just for the poor but for all children and for society in general (McLoyd, Aikens, & Burton, 2006).

Prejudice and Discrimination

When I was 17, I wanted to be "authentic" too. I was a white, suburban, middle class kid and I wanted to be tough, street-smart, and sexy. I wanted to be cool. Part of being cool was being, well—black. And since I had no hope of changing my skin color it meant listening to black music, reading black authors, and feeling, at least, a sense of solidarity with an oppressed and talented people. But in fact I had very little contact with actual black people. (http://waltersweblog.blogspot.com/2006/01/race.html, May 3, 2006)

***

Black and white kids did not play together in the schoolyard, and the black kids ate together in the cafeteria. We didn't socialize at all outside of school. This continued into high school and the only chance you might have to socialize with black people was in team sports. Even then, contact was largely limited to team activities. I did not know why this was so, and I never questioned it. It was just the way things were. (http://emergencybackupdog.blogspot.com/2005/12/my-blog-against-racism-day-post.html, May 3, 2006)

Navigating racial, ethnic, and other cultural differences is among the most difficult challenges that adolescents (and adults) face, as these blog excerpts imply. Learning how to accept and interact with individuals who are different in important ways from oneself represents an important developmental task for adolescents—a task, the success or failure of which will have consequences throughout their lives.

For some, the challenge is too great, and their prejudiced attitudes and stereotypes guide their behavior. In this final part of the final chapter, we examine the basic concepts of prejudice, stereotypes, and discrimination.

Prejudice, Stereotypes, and Discrimination: The Foundations of Hate. Preju-
dice refers to the negative (or positive) evaluations or judgments of members of a group that are based primarily on group membership, and not necessarily on the particular characteristics of individuals. For example, gender prejudice occurs when a person is evaluated on the basis of being a male or female and not because of his or her own specific characteristics or abilities.

Although prejudice is generally thought of as a negative evaluation of group members, it can also be positive: As we'll see, at the same time people dislike members of groups to which they don't belong, they may also positively evaluate members of their own group. In both cases, the assessment is unrelated to qualities of particular individuals; rather, it is due simply to membership in the specific group to which the individuals belong.

prejudice The negative (or positive) evaluations or judgments of members of a group that are based primarily on group membership, and not necessarily on the particular characteristics of individuals

The mental framework that maintains prejudice is a stereotype. A **stereotype** is a set of beliefs and expectations about members of a group that are held simply because of their membership in the group. Stereotypes are oversimplifications that people employ in an effort to make sense of the complex social environment in which they live. They determine how information is interpreted, so that even when people are exposed to evidence contrary to their stereotypes, they may interpret the information in a way that supports their prejudice (Dovidio, Glick, & Rudman, 2005; Shapiro, 2012).

Ultimately, prejudice and stereotypes can lead to **discrimination**, the negative (or sometimes positive) actions taken toward members of a particular group because of their membership in the group. Although prejudice and discrimination often go hand in hand, one may be present without the other.

In the most extreme case, people's biases lead them to engage in self-fulfilling prophecies. *Self-fulfilling prophecies* reflect the tendency of people to act in ways that are consistent with their expectations, beliefs, or cognitions about an event or behavior, thereby increasing the likelihood that the event or behavior will occur. Consequently, if a person thinks that members of a certain group are lazy, he or she may act in a way that actually elicits laziness from the members of that group.

The Roots of Prejudice.
Female. African American. Islamic fundamentalist. Gay. Quick: What images first come to mind when you read or hear each of these words? For most people, encountering a description of a person that includes such a label is enough to summon up a rich network of impressions, memories, and probably even predictions of how that person will behave in a given situation. The presence of such connections suggests that we are all susceptible to prejudice.

But where does prejudice originate? There are several sources.

Social Learning Explanations: The School of Stereotyping. Children are not born feeling prejudice and showing discrimination to members of different religions, ethnic groups, or races. It is something that is taught to them, in much the same way that they learn that $2 + 2 = 4$.

The **social learning view**, which we encountered in Chapter 13, suggests that people develop prejudice and stereotypes about members of various groups in the same way they learn other attitudes, beliefs, and values. For instance, one important source of information for children regarding stereotypes and prejudice is the behavior and teaching of parents, other adults, and peers. Through direct reinforcement, and through observation of the reinforcement given to others, people learn about members of other groups. Such learning begins at an early age: By the time they are preschoolers, children are able to distinguish between African Americans and whites, and even at that age they can possess preferential feelings for members of their own group over others (Huber, 2012).

Children are not the only ones who learn stereotypes and prejudice from others. Although significant improvements have been made in the past decade, television and other media often portray minority group members in shallow, stereotyped ways. For instance, portrayals of African Americans perpetuate some of society's most distasteful stereotypes, with many African American males being portrayed as sexually obsessed, shiftless, and speaking primarily in jive. Other groups are stereotyped in the media in equally derogatory ways, such as Godfather-like Italian mobsters, greedy Jewish bankers, and Hispanics in criminal or menial jobs (Alexander, Brewer, & Livingston, 2005; Jost, 2005).

Social Identity Theory: The Self-Esteem of Group Membership. Think about your ethnic or religious identity for a moment. Are you proud of it? Does it make you feel good to be part of the group? Would you feel threatened if your group were criticized or attacked?

Most people feel pride in the groups to which they belong. But this pride has a downside: It can lead to prejudice and discrimination. For example, according to **social identity theory**, adolescents use group membership as a source of pride and self-worth. However, to feel such pride, they must assume that their group is, in fact, superior to others. As a result, their quest for a positive social identity leads them to inflate the positive aspects of groups to which they belong and belittle groups to which they do not belong (Tajfel, 2001; Tajfel & Turner, 2004; Ellemers & Haslam, 2012).

stereotype   A set of beliefs and expectations about members of a group that are held simply because of their membership in the group

discrimination   The negative (or sometimes positive) actions taken toward members of a particular group because of their membership in the group

social learning view   The theory that suggests that people develop prejudice and stereotypes about members of various groups in the same way they learn other attitudes, beliefs, and values

social identity theory   The theory that individuals use group membership as a source of pride and self-worth

According to social identity theory, individuals use group membership as a source of pride and self-worth.

TABLE 15-1	National Pride by Countries	
Rank	**Country**	**Score**
1	Venezuela	18.4
2	United States	17.7
3	Australia	17.5
4	Austria	17.4
5	Chile	17.1
6	Canada	17.0
7	Russia	16.7
8	The Philippines	16.7
9	New Zealand	16.6
10	Spain	16.5
11	Israel	16.2
12	Slovenia	16.1
13	South Korea	16.0
14	Japan	15.9
15	Taiwan	15.6
16	Ireland	15.3
17	Poland	15.3
18	Great Britain	15.1
19	Czech Republic	15.1
20	Norway	14.9
21	Germany (Western area)	14.5
22	France	14.4
23	Switzerland	14.3
24	Germany (Eastern area)	14.2
25	Sweden	14.0

(*Source:* Data from Smith, T. W. & Seokho, K., 2006.)

Certainly, there is ample evidence that members of various cultural groups tend to see their own groups in more positive terms than others. For instance, one cross-cultural investigation that examined 17 different societies found that, universally, people rated the group to which they belonged as more peace-loving, virtuous, and obedient than other groups (Scheepers et al., 2006). Even countries in which national pride is relatively lower than that of other countries still are viewed quite positively by their citizens (see Table 15-1).

Of course, not all groups allow us to achieve the same sense of self-worth as others. It is important for groups to be small enough so that people can feel somewhat unique and special. In fact, minority group membership sometimes produces stronger feelings of social identity than majority group membership. Minority group leaders of the past who used slogans such as "Black Is Beautiful" and "Gay Pride" reflected an awareness of the importance of instilling group pride. Research has supported this strategy: Ethnic group membership can be an important source of psychological support, particularly for minority group members (Mossakowski, 2003; González & Gándara, 2005).

Overall, membership in a group provides people with a sense of personal identity and self-esteem. When a group is successful, self-esteem can rise; and, conversely, when self-esteem is threatened, people feel enhanced attraction to their own group and increased hostility toward members of other groups (Garcia et al., 2005; Martiny, Kessler, & Vignoles, 2012).

However, the use of group membership as a source of pride can lead to unfortunate consequences. For instance, in an effort to raise their own self-esteem, adolescents may come to think that their own group (known as the *ingroup*) is superior to groups to which they do not belong (the *outgroup*). Consequently, they inflate the positive aspects of the ingroup, and, at the same time, devalue outgroups and their members. Eventually they come to see members of outgroups as inferior to members of their ingroup. The ultimate result is prejudice toward members of groups of which they are not a part (Tajfel & Turner, 2004; Brown, Bradley, & Lang, 2006; Lam et al., 2006).

ARE YOU AN INFORMED CONSUMER OF DEVELOPMENT?

Taking a Stand against Prejudice

Teachers and administrators can employ a number of strategies to combat prejudice in schools and create an atmosphere of respect and tolerance. But combating prejudice is everyone's responsibility, and students can do much to get actively involved in responding to hatred in their schools and communities. The Southern Poverty Law Center (2005) has put together a list of strategies for getting started:

- **Act.** The first step to combating hatred is being willing to take responsibility for doing something about it. Standing by and doing nothing sends a message to the perpetrators, the victims, and the community that prejudice is acceptable. Apathy encourages more hatred.

- **Unite.** Get others involved in direct action, too. These could be family and friends, neighbors, church and civic group members, or teachers and administrators. Ways to get others involved range from informal discussions to writing letters to the editor of a local newspaper to organizing a community rally or event.

- **Support the victims.** Being a victim of prejudice can be a traumatic experience. Victims may feel frightened, intimidated, or alienated. Giving them your support and encouragement shows them that they are valued members of the community and that they are not alone. Even a kind word or a simple gesture can make a difference.

- **Speak up.** Prejudice has a voice; tolerance needs to have a voice as well. Condemning hateful messages is a good start, but letting others know that you actively value diversity is important, too. Create an atmosphere of tolerance by communicating your values.

- **Hold leaders accountable.** Students can do a lot to combat prejudice, but people in leadership positions enjoy special influence. The way that teachers, administrators, and other people in leadership roles respond to incidents of prejudice sends a strong message to others in the community. Quick, decisive action shows that prejudice is unacceptable; slow, uninspired action—or inaction—appears to condone it. Make sure that leaders know you expect them to respond decisively.

- **Examine your own prejudices.** Even tolerant people can harbor some prejudices. Are there any social groups you disparage or just don't know much about? Do you include people who are different from you in your circle of friends and in your group activities? Be continually on the lookout for ways to learn about different cultures and ethnicities and to build bridges across racial and ethnic divides. ■

Review, Check, and Apply

Review

1. Acculturation into a new culture can produce one of four outcomes: integration, assimilation, separation, or marginalization.

2. Developing an ethnic identity, which is especially important to members of ethnic, racial, and cultural minorities, proceeds in stages from unexamined ethnic identity, through ethnic identity search, to achieved ethnic identity.

3. The ethnic and cultural diversity in U.S. classrooms has fed the development of multicultural education, generally using the pluralistic society model as a way to help minority students gain competence in the majority culture while retaining their own cultural identities.

4. Members of minority groups are more likely to live in poverty than members of nonminority groups, with all the disadvantages and challenges that poverty brings.

5. Poverty rates in the United States are higher than in many other industrialized countries largely because policymakers have not supported aggressive antipoverty programs.

6. Children and adults must deal with prejudices (judgments of members of groups), stereotypes (beliefs and expectations about members of groups), and outright discrimination (actions taken toward members of groups).

7. The social learning view suggests that people learn prejudice the same way they learn other attitudes, beliefs, and values: from other people.

8. According to social identity theory, adolescents use group membership as a source of pride, dividing people into the ingroup and the outgroup, which is assumed to be inferior.

Check

1. The changes and adjustments that occur when people of different groups come into sustained firsthand contact are called _____.

2. When people identify with neither the minority nor the majority culture they are said to be _____.

3. According to Phinney, ethnic identity develops in several stages: unexamined ethnic identity, ethnic identity search, and _____ _____ _____.

4. The pluralistic society model of multicultural education has largely replaced the _____ _____ model, in which the goal is to immerse students in the majority culture and language, and thereby to shape individual cultures into a unified American culture.

5. Under the pluralistic society model, children from different cultures are encouraged to develop a _____ _____, maintaining their original cultural identities while integrating themselves into the majority culture.

6. _____ are beliefs and expectations about members of a group that can lead to _____, which are evaluations or judgments based on group membership. Together, they underlie _____, which refers to actions taken toward group members because of their membership in the group.

Apply

1. What advantages do you think students who are bilingual might have in today's world? How would you design a research study to demonstrate such advantages?

2. The United States has been called a "nation of immigrants," and yet feelings toward new immigrants are often negative. How might the phenomenon of cultural identity help to explain this? How might multicultural education help to change this?

To see more review questions, log on to MyPsychLab.

ANSWERS: 1. acculturation   2. marginalized   3. achieved ethnic identity   4. cultural assimilation   5. bicultural identity   6. Stereotypes; prejudices; discrimination

The CASE
of . . . *the Secret Reader*

Della Faison had handled the situation badly. As an assistant teacher in an urban preschool, she had been concerned that one of her students, Lawson Ellings, showed little interest in books and story time. She knew that Lawson's mother was a single parent who worked two jobs, and she wanted to encourage the mother to try harder to help Lawson value reading.

The next time she chatted with Mrs. Ellings, she mentioned how important it was for Lawson to take an active interest in academics, to be exposed to books in the home, and to develop an enjoyment of books and learning. When Mrs. Ellings asked what she meant, she explained that Lawson never joined reading circle and never picked a book to look through, choosing instead to play with Legos and trucks and other physical toys.

Della noticed that Mrs. Ellings paused before answering. "Thank you for your concern, Ms. Faison, but Lawson probably doesn't sit in reading circle because he is a shy boy who likes to be by himself most of the time. And he may not choose your books because he's read most of them already. I take him to the library every Wednesday evening and Saturday morning, no matter how tired I am, and I read to him and let him read to me. He's been through nearly every book in the preschool section. He may want to play with Legos because we don't have any of those at home."

Della didn't know what to say.

1. Had Della interpreted Lawson's classroom decisions accurately? Why had she made the interpretation that she had?

2. Is it plausible for a preschooler like Lawson to have a "secret reading life"? Could he really have the language skills to read books at his age?

3. Should Della still be concerned about Lawson's reading? Should she quietly test his abilities one-on-one?

4. Is it possible for an academically able student to emerge from circumstances like Lawson's? Why or why not? What factors might affect his academic achievement?

◀◀◀ LOOKING BACK

LO 15-1 What are the different kinds of preschool educational programs?

- Most preschool-age children receive some sort of care outside the home. High-quality care, whether center-based, school-based, or preschool, can lead to cognitive and social advances.

- The United States lacks a coordinated national policy on preschool education. The major federal initiative in U.S. preschool education has been the Head Start program, which has yielded mixed, although promising, results.

LO 15-2 What are the consequences of enrollment in outside-the-home child care?

- Child care has been found to be effective in increasing self-confidence, independence, and social skills, but children in child care tend to be more outspoken, less polite, less respectful of adults, and more competitive with their peers.

- An early focus on academic skills in the preschool setting can be stressful for young children. The key is to provide developmentally appropriate educational practice.

LO 15-3 What effects do television and computers have on young children?

- The effects of television watching and computer use on young children can be negative, and researchers and policymakers advise that children's use of these media be monitored and limited by adults.

LO 15-4 What are some current trends that affect schooling worldwide and in the United States?

- Virtually all children in the United States have access to free public education through high school, but this is not the case in other parts of the world.

- More than 160 million children do not receive an elementary education, and another 100 million do not progress beyond the elementary level. Nearly one billion people are illiterate throughout their lives.

- Females in many cultures are especially disadvantaged, receiving less formal education than males in developing countries, and diminished access to science and technology in developed countries.

- Concerns over the age at which children begin formal education, centering especially on holding back enrollment until the child is in the older side of the age scale, are generally unsupported by research. What matters is the developmental readiness of the child.

LO 15-5 What changes have taken place in the ways U.S. schools provide instruction in the 3 Rs?

- In recent years, schooling in the United States has largely returned to an emphasis on educational fundamentals (reading, writing, and arithmetic) instead of on students' social development.

- A key concern in U.S. educational policy has been accountability for both teachers and their students, as mandated by the federal initiatives called *No Child Left Behind* and *Race to the Top*. One result has been to place intense pressure on students to succeed academically through such means as increased homework. There is little evidence that such programs actually work.

LO 15-6 What are some of the challenges involved in educating children in the middle school years?

- The transition from elementary school to middle school can be problematic, since it typically occurs when children are entering adolescence and dealing with a host of other issues reflecting their physical, intellectual, and social development. These issues can affect school performance and effectiveness.

- The structure of the middle school environment, the large size of typical middle schools, issues of social hierarchy, and other challenges contribute to a generally unimpressive record of academic (and social-emotional) success in U.S. middle schools.

LO 15-7 What are some advantages and disadvantages of homeschooling?

- Children who are home schooled achieve comparable levels of academic success and social development as their traditionally schooled peers.

- However, home schooled students may have limited opportunities for social interaction, may not experience the diversity of the typical American classroom, and may suffer from diminished access to sophisticated learning tools such as science labs and media centers.

LO 15-8 How do American adolescents perform in high school?

- The developmental advances in metacognition, reasoning, and similar cognitive abilities during adolescence do not translate unambiguously into high academic performance. The generally high level of high school students' grades seems to reflect grade inflation rather than actual academic excellence.

- In nationally and internationally standardized comparisons, U.S. high school students perform poorly compared to students in other industrialized countries, and the U.S. high school graduation rate also compares unfavorably.

LO 15-9 What social and cultural factors affect school performance?

- There is a direct relationship between socioeconomic status and the level of a person's school achievement. Lower SES can lead to decreased nutrition, poor health, crowded living conditions, inadequate schools, a lack of books and other resources in the home, and other conditions that contribute to diminished performance.

LO 15-10 In what ways are individuals affected by culture and ethnicity?

- Culture helps individuals define themselves and make decisions ranging from what clothes to wear to what sexual practices are appropriate.

- Acculturation is the process by which an individual of a different culture adjusts to a new culture and may produce integration, assimilation, separation, or marginalization.

- It is especially important for members of minority cultures to develop an ethnic identity, a view of themselves as members of both a minority culture and a new culture.

LO 15-11 What is multicultural education and why is it of critical importance in the United States today?

- U.S. education has had to keep up with demographic changes that affect all aspects of society. The U.S. population is growing increasingly diverse, and educators have made efforts to provide multicultural education.

- The focus of U.S. multicultural education is to help students from minority cultures develop competence in the culture of the majority group while maintaining their own cultural identities.

- Present-day multicultural education seeks to supplant the old model of cultural assimilation with the pluralistic society model.

LO 15-12 How is socioeconomic status related to race and ethnicity?

- Many of the problems faced by minority adolescents are more closely linked to socioeconomic status than to ethnicity or race.

- Half of adolescents in the United States live in poverty or in low-income households, and members of minority groups are disproportionately represented in these households.

LO 15-13 How do prejudice, stereotypes, and discrimination work together?

- Evaluations of individuals on the basis of their membership in a group are reinforced by the existence of stereotypes, which are beliefs and expectations about group members.

- Prejudice and stereotypes can lead to discrimination, actions taken toward group members because of their membership in the group.

KEY TERMS AND CONCEPTS

developmentally appropriate educational practice (p. 424)
acculturation (p. 439)
integration (p. 439)
assimilation (p. 439)
separation (p. 439)

marginalization (p. 439)
ethnic identity (p. 440)
multicultural education (p. 442)
cultural assimilation model (p. 442)
pluralistic society model (p. 442)
prejudice (p. 444)

stereotype (p. 445)
discrimination (p. 445)
social learning view (p. 445)
social identity theory (p. 445)

Epilogue

In this chapter, we looked at schooling, the sociocultural aspects of attending school, and the decisions that adolescents have to make about their future, especially the choice between entering college or the world of work. We concluded with a consideration of the ramifications of living in a multicultural world. We discussed the various options that are available in preschool education and considered their benefits to young children. We examined what makes children ready for school and we considered some current trends in elementary education, including the possibility of homeschooling and the challenges of middle school education. We saw how race, ethnicity, gender, and socioeconomic status are related to academic performance. Then we discussed who goes to college and what students encounter there, and we considered the option of entering the world of work and career immediately after high school. We examined the effects of gender and ethnicity on both the college and workplace environment, and in the closing pages of the chapter, we looked at culture and diversity, examining how race, ethnicity, gender, and socioeconomic status shape culture. We concluded with a discussion of prejudice and discrimination.

Return to the prologue, which describes the start of Emily's kindergarten experience, and answer these questions.

1. What factors might Emily's parents look at in deciding if she is ready to begin formal schooling? How can they help her to succeed in school in general?

2. If Emily's teacher believes that children with summer birthdays should wait another year before starting kindergarten, how might this affect his or her expectations of Emily? How might the teacher's expectations in this case affect Emily's performance?

3. How might cultural expectations affect Emily's choice of activities, playthings, and play companions? How would you expect this to change as she grows toward adolescence?

4. If Emily's kindergarten is culturally diverse, how would you expect her to react initially to children from a culture different to her own? What factors in her upbringing might affect her reaction?

The Development Video Series in MyPsychLab

Explore the video *Are Stereotypes and Prejudice Inevitable?* by scanning this QR code with your mobile device. If you don't already have one, you may download a free QR scanner for your device wherever smartphone apps are sold. You can also view this video in MyPsychLab. For more videos related to this chapter's content, log into MyPsychLab to view the entire Development Video Series.

MyVirtualChild

- **What decisions would you make while raising a child?**
- **What would the consequences of those decisions be?**

Find out by accessing **MyVirtualChild** at
www.MyPsychLab.com
and raising your own virtual child from birth to age 18.

References

Aalsma, M., Lapsley, D., & Flannery, D. (2006, April). Personal fables, narcissism, and adolescent adjustment. *Psychology in the Schools, 43*(4), 481–491.

AAMR (American Association on Mental Retardation). (1992). *Mental retardation: Definition, classification, and systems of support.* Washington, DC: Author.

AAP/ACOG (American Academy of Pediatrics/American College of Obstetricians and Gynecologists). (1992). *Guidelines for perinatal care.* Elk Grove, IN: Author.

AARP (American Association of Retired Persons). (1990). *A profile of older Americans.* Washington, DC: Author.

AARP. (2004, May 25). *Funeral arrangements and memorial service.* Retrieved from http://www.aarp.org/griefandloss/articles/73_a.html.

AARP. (2005, October). I can see clearly now. *AARP Bulletin,* p. 34.

AAUW (American Association of University Women). (1992). *How schools shortchange women: The A.A.U.W. report.* Washington, DC: American Association of University Women Educational Foundation.

Abdo, C., Afif-Abdo, J., Otani, F., & Machado, A. (2008). Sexual satisfaction among patients with erectile dysfunction treated with counseling, sildenafil, or both. *Journal of Sexual Medicine, 5,* 1720–1726.

Abeles, R. P., Gift, H. C., & Ory, M. G. (Eds.). (1994). *Aging and quality of life.* New York: Springer.

Aber, J. L., Bishop-Josef, S. J., Jones, S. M., McLearn, K. T., & Phillips, D. A. (Eds.). (2007). *Child development a social policy: Knowledge for action.* Washington, DC: American Psychological Association.

Able, E. L., & Sokol, R. J. (1987). Incidence of fetal alcohol syndrome and economic impact of FAS-related anomalies. *Drug and Alcohol Dependence, 19,* 51–70.

Aboud, F., Mendelson, M., & Purdy, K. (2003). Cross-race peer relations and friendship quality. *International Journal of Behavioral Development, 27,* 165–173.

Aboud, F., & Sankar, J. (2007, September). Friendship and identity in a language-integrated school. *International Journal of Behavioral Development, 31*(5), 445–453.

Aboud, F. E., & Skerry, S. A. (1983). Self and ethnic concepts in relations to ethnic constancy. *Canadian Journal of Behavioral Science, 15,* 14–26.

Abrahams, N., Jewkes, R., Laubscher, R., & Hoffman, M. (2006). Intimate partner violence: Prevalence and risk factors for men in Cape Town, South Africa. *Violence and Victims, 21,* 247–264.

Abril, C., & Gault, B. (2006, March). The state of music in the elementary school: The principal's perspective. *Journal of Research in Music Education, 54,* 6–20.

Abu-Heija, A. T., Jallad, M. F., & Abukteish, F. (2000). Maternal and perinatal outcome of pregnancies after the age of 45. *Journal of Obstetrics & Gynaecology Research, 26,* 27–30.

Abushaikha, L. (2007). Methods of coping with labor pain used by Jordanian women. *Journal of Transcultural Nursing, 18,* 35–40.

Achenbach, T. A. (1992). Developmental psychopathology. In M. H. Bornstein & M. E. Lamb (Eds.), *Developmental psychology: An advanced textbook.* Hillsdale, NJ: Erlbaum.

Achter, J. A., Lubinski, D., Benbow, C. P., & Eftekhari-Sanjani, H. (1999). Assessing vocational preferences among gifted adolescents adds incremental validity to abilities: A discriminant analysis of educational out-comes over a 10-year interval. *Journal of Educational Psychology, 91,* 777–786.

ACIP Advisory Committee on Immunization Practices. (2011, January). General recommendations on immunization—recommendations of the Advisory Committee on Immunization Practices (ACIP). National Center for Immunization and Respiratory Diseases. *MMWR, Recommended Reports, 60,* 1–64.

Ackerman, B. P., & Izard, C. E. (2004). Emotion cognition in children and adolescents: Introduction [Special issue]. *Journal of Experimental Child Psychology, 89,* 271–275.

Ackerman, P., & Lohman, D. (2006). Individual differences in cognitive functions. In *Handbook of educational psychology.* Mahwah, NJ: Lawrence Erlbaum.

Acocella, J. (2003, August 18 & 25). Little people. *The New Yorker,* pp. 138–143.

ACOG (American College of Obstetricians and Gynecologists). (1994, February). *Guidelines for exercise during pregnancy and the postpartum period.* Washington, DC: Author.

ACOG (American College of Obstetricians and Gynecologists). (2002). *Guidelines for perinatal care.* Elk Grove, IN: Author.

Adair, L. (2008). Child and adolescent obesity: Epidemiology and developmental perspectives. *Physiology & Behavior, 94,* 8–16.

Adams, C., & Labouvie-Vief, G. (1986, November 20). *Modes of knowing and language processing. Symposium on developmental dimensions of adult adaptations. Perspectives in mind, self, and emotion.* Paper presented at the meeting of the Gerontological Association of America, Chicago, IL.

Adams, C. R., & Singh, K. (1998). Direct and indirect effects of school learning variables on the academic achievement of African American 10th graders. *Journal of Negro Education, 67,* 48–66.

Adams, G. R., Montemayor, R., & Gullotta, T. P. (Eds.). (1996). *Psychosocial development during adolescence.* Thousand Oaks, CA: Sage Publications.

Adams, H., & Paula, J. (2001). Gynecologic disorders and surgery. In N. L. Stotland & D. E. Stewart (Eds.), *Psychological aspects of women's health care: The interface between psychiatry and obstetrics and gynecology* (2nd ed.). Washington, DC: American Psychiatric Publishing.

Adams, H. L., & Williams, L. (2011). Advice from teens to teens about dating: Implications for healthy relationships. *Children and Youth Services Review, 33,* 254–264.

Adams, K. B. (2005). Changing investment in activities and interests in elders' lives: Theory and measurement. *International Journal of Aging and Human Development, 58,* 87–108.

Adams, R. J., Mauer, D., & Davis, M. (1986). Newborns' discrimination of chromatic from achromatic stimuli. *Journal of Experimental Child Psychology, 41,* 267–281.

Adams Hillard, P. J. (2001). Gynecologic disorders and surgery. In N. L. Stotland & D. E. Stewart (Eds.), *Psychological aspects of women's health care: The interface between psychiatry and obstetrics and gynecology* (2nd ed.). Washington, DC: American Psychiatric Publishing.

Adamson, L., & Frick, J. (2003). The still face: A history of a shared experimental paradigm. *Infancy, 4,* 451–473.

Adebayo, B. (2008). Gender gaps in college enrollment and degree attainment: An exploratory analysis. *College Student Journal, 42,* 232–237.

Adelmann, P. K., Antonucci, T. C., & Crohan, S. E. (1990). A causal analysis of employment and health in midlife women. *Women and Health, 16,* 5–20.

Ader, R., Felten, D., & Cohen, N. (2001). *Psychoneuroimmunology* (3rd ed.). San Diego: Academic Press.

Adler, P. A., & Adler, P. (1994). Observational techniques. In N. K. Denzin & Y. S. Lincoln (Eds.), *Handbook of qualitative research.* Thousand Oaks, CA: Sage Publications.

Adler, P. A., Kless, S. J., & Adler, P. (1992). Socialization to gender roles: Popularity among elementary school boys and girls. *Sociology of Education, 65,* 169–187.

Adler, S. A., Gerhardstein, P., & Rovee-Collier, C. K. (1998). Levels-of-processing effects in infant memory? *Child Development, 69,* 280–284.

Administration on Aging. (2003). *A profile of older Americans: 2003.* Washington, DC: U.S. Department of Health and Human Services.

Administration on Aging. (2006). *Profiles of older Americans 2005: Research report.* Washington, DC: U.S. Department of Health and Human Resources.

Adolph, K. E. (1997). Learning in the development of infant locomotion. With commentary by B. I. Bertenthal, S. M. Boker, E. C. Goldfield, & E. J. Gibson. *Monographs of the Society for Research in Child Development, 62,* 238–251.

Adolph, K. E., Eppler, M. A., & Gibson, E. J. (1993). Crawling versus walking infants' perception of affordances for locomotion over sloping surfaces. *Child Development, 64,* 1158–1174.

Advocates for Youth. (2003). *Science and success. Sex educations and other programs that work to prevent teen pregancy...* Washington, DC. Retrieved March 4, 2006, from http://www.advocatesforyouth.org/publications/ScienceSuccess.pdf.

Afifi, T., Brownridge, D., Cox, B., & Sareen, J. (2006, October). Physical punishment, childhood abuse and psychiatric disorders. *Child Abuse & Neglect, 30,* 1093–1103.

Agrawal, A., & Lynskey, M. (2008). Are there genetic influences on addiction: Evidence from family, adoption and twin studies. *Addiction, 103,* 1069–1081. doi:10.1111/j.1360–0443.2008.02213.x

Aguiar, A., & Baillargeon, R. (2002). Developments in young infants' reasoning about occluded objects. *Cognitive Psychology, 45,* 267–336.

Aguirre, E., Gleeson, T., McCutchen, A., Mendiola, L., Rich, K., Schroder, R., et al. (2006). *A cost-benefit analysis of universally accessible pre-kindergarten education in Texas.* Bush School of Government & Public Service: Texas A&M University.

Ah-Kion, J. (2006, June). Body image and self-esteem: A study of gender differences among mid-adolescents. *Gender & Behaviour, 4,* 534–549.

Ahmed, E., & Braithwaite, V. (2004). Bullying and victimization: Cause for concern for both families and schools. *Social Psychology of Education, 7,* 35–54.

Ahn, W., Gelman, S., & Amsterlaw, J. (2000). Causal status effect in children's categorization. *Cognition, 76,* B35–B43.

Aichhorn, T. (2008). The analytic revelation is a revolutionary force. In *Freud at 150: 21st-century essays on a man of genius.* Lanham, MD: Jason Aronson.

Aiken, L. R. (2000). *Dying, death, and bereavement.* (4th ed.). Mahwah, NJ: Erlbaum.

Ainsworth, M. D. S. (1973). The development of infant–mother attachment. In B. M. Caldwell & H. N. Ricciuti (Eds.), *Review of child development research* (Vol. 3). Chicago: University of Chicago Press.

Ainsworth, M. D. S., Blehar, M. C., Waters, E., & Wall, S. (1978). *Patterns of attachment: A psychological study of the strange situation*. Hillsdale, NJ: Erlbaum.

Ainsworth, M. D. S., & Bowlby, J. (1991). An ethological approach to personality development. *American Psychologist, 46*, 333–341.

Aitken, R. J. (1995, July 7). The complexities of conception. *Science, 269*, 39–40.

Akhtar, S. (Ed.). (2012). *The mother and her child: Clinical aspects of attachment, separation, and loss*. Lanham, MD: Jason Aronson.

Akhtar-Danesh, N., Dehghan, M., Morrison, K. M., & Fonseka, S. (2011). Parents' perceptions and attitudes on childhood obesity: A Q-methodology study. *Journal of the American Academy of Nurse Practitioners, 23*, 67–75.

Akinbami, L. J. (2011, January 12). Asthma prevalence, health care use, and mortality: United States, 2005–2009. *National Health Statistics Reports, 32*, 1–15.

Akmajian, A., Demers, R. A., & Harnish, R. M. (1984). *Linguistics*. Cambridge, MA: MIT Press.

Akshoomoff, N. (2006). Autism spectrum disorders: Introduction. *Child Neuropsychology, 12*, 245–246.

Akutsu, H. (1991). Psychophysics of reading—X. Effects of age-related changes in vision. *Journal of Gerontology: Psychological Sciences, 46*, 325–331.

Alan Guttmacher Institute. (1993a). *Report on viral sexual diseases*. Chicago: Author.

Alan Guttmacher Institute. (1993b). *Survey of male sexuality*. Chicago: Author.

Albers, L. L., & Krulewitch, C. J. (1993). Electronic fetal monitoring in the United States in the 1980s. *Obstetrics & Gynecology, 82*, 8–10.

Albers, L. L., Migliaccio, L., Bedrick, E. J., Teaf, D., & Peralta, P. (2007). Does epidural analgesia affect the rate of spontaneous obstetric lacerations in normal births? *Journal of Midwifery and Women's Health, 52*, 31–36.

Albert, R. S. (Ed.). (1992). *The social psychology of creativity and exceptional achievement* (2nd ed.). New York: Pergamon.

Alberts, A., Elkind, D., & Ginsberg, S. (2007). The personal fable and risk-taking in early adolescence. *Journal of Youth and Adolescence, 36*, 71–76.

Albrecht, G. L. (2005). *Encyclopedia of disability* (General ed.). Thousand Oaks, CA: Sage Publications.

Alderfer, C. (2003). The science and nonscience of psychologists' responses to *The Bell Curve*. *Professional Psychology: Research & Practice, 34*, 287–293.

Aldwin, C. M. (1994). *Stress, coping, and development: An integrative perspective*. New York: Guilford Press.

Aldwin, C., & Gilmer, D. (2004). *Health, illness, and optimal aging: Biological and psychosocial perspectives*. Thousand Oaks, CA: Sage Publications, Inc.

Aleksandrova-Howell, M., Abramson, C. I., & Craig, D. (2012). Coverage of Russian psychological contributions in American psychology textbooks. *International Journal of Psychology, 47*, 76–87.

Ales, K. L., Druzin, M. L., & Santini, D. L. (1990). Impact of advanced maternal age on the outcome of pregnancy. *Surgery, Gynecology & Obstetrics, 171*, 209–216.

Alessandri, S. M., Bendersky, M., & Lewis, M. (1998). Cognitive functioning in 8- to 18-month-old drug-exposed infants. *Developmental Psychology, 34*, 565–573.

Alexander, B., Turnbull, D., & Cyna, A. (2009). The effect of pregnancy on hypnotizability. *American Journal of Clinical Hypnosis, 52*, 13–22.

Alexander, G., Wilcox, T., & Woods, R. (2009). Sex differences in infants' visual interest in toys. *Archives of Sexual Behavior, 38*, 427–433.

Alexander, G. M., & Hines, M. (2002). Sex differences in response to children's toys in nonhuman primates. *Evolution and Human Behavior, 23*, 467–479.

Alexander, K. L. (2007, March 14). D.C totals for infant mortality revised. *The Washington Post*, p. BO1.

Alexandersen, P., Karsdal, M. A., & Christiansen, C. (2009). Long-term prevention with hormone-replacement therapy after the menopause: Which women should be targeted? *Womens Health (London, England), 5*, 637–647.

Alfonso, V. C., Flanagan, D. P., & Radwan, S. (2005). The impact of the Cattell-Horn-Carroll theory on test development and interpretation of cognitive and academic abilities. In D. P. Flanagan & P. L. Harrison (Eds.), *Contemporary intellectual assessment: Theories, tests, and issues*. New York: Guilford Press.

Ali, L. (2008, July 14). True or false: Having kids makes you happy. *Newsweek*, p. 62.

Alibali, M., Phillips, K., & Fischer, A. (2009). Learning new problem-solving strategies leads to changes in problem representation. *Cognitive Development, 24*, 89–101.

Alisky, J. M. (2007). The coming problem of HIV-associated Alzheimer's disease. *Medical Hypotheses, 12*, 47–55.

Allam, M., Marlier, L., & Schaal, B. (2006). Learning at the breast: Preference formation for an artificial scent and its attraction against the odor of maternal milk. *Infant Behavior & Development, 29*, 308–321.

Allan, P. (1990). Looking for work after forty: Job search experiences of older unemployed managers and professionals. *Journal of Employment Counseling, 27*, 113–121.

Allen, B. (2008). An analysis of the impact of diverse forms of childhood psychological maltreatment on emotional adjustment in early adulthood. *Child Maltreatment, 13*, 307–312.

Allen, J., Chavez, S., DeSimone, S., Howard, D., Johnson, K., LaPierre, L., et al. (2006, June). Americans' attitudes toward euthanasia and physician-assisted suicide, 1936–2002. *Journal of Sociology & Social Welfare, 33*, 5–23.

Allen, J. P., Philliber, S., Herrling, S., & Kuperminc, G. P. (1997). Preventing teen pregnancy and academic failure: Experimental evaluation of a developmentally based approach. *Child Development, 64*, 729–742.

Allen, J., Seitz, V., & Apfel, N. (2007). The sexually mature teen as a whole person: New directions in prevention and intervention for teen pregnancy and parenthood. *Child development and social policy: Knowledge for action* (pp. 185–199). Washington, DC: American Psychological Association.

Allen, M., & Bissell, M. (2004). Safety and stability for foster children: The policy context. *Future of Children, 14*, 49–74.

Allison, A. C. (1954). Protection afforded by sickle cell trait against subtertian malarial infection. *British Medical Journal, 1*, 290–294.

Allison, B., & Schultz, J. (2001). Interpersonal identity formation during early adolescence. *Adolescence, 36*, 509–523.

Alloy, L. B., Acocella, J., & Bootzin, R. R. (1996). *Abnormal psychology: Current perspectives*. New York: McGraw-Hill.

Aloise-Young, P., Slater, M., & Cruickshank, C. (2006, April). Mediators and moderators of magazine advertisement effects on adolescent cigarette smoking. *Journal of Health Communication, 11*, 281–300.

Al-Owidha, A., Green, K., & Kroger, J. (2009). On the question of an identity status category order: Rasch model step and scale statistics used to identify category order. *International Journal of Behavioral Development, 33*, 88–96.

Alper, J. (1993, April 16). The pipeline is leaking women all the way along. *Science, 260*, 409–411.

Altemus, M., Deuster, P. A., Galliven, E., Carter, C. S., & Gold, P. W. (1995). Suppression of hypothalamic pituitary adrenal axis responses to stress in lactating women. *Journal of Clinical Endocrinology and Metabolism, 80*, 2954–2959.

Altermatt, E. (2011). Capitalizing on academic success: Students' interactions with friends as predictors of school adjustment. *The Journal of Early Adolescence, 31*, 174–203.

Altholz, S., & Golensky, M. (2004). Counseling, support, and advocacy for clients who stutter. *Health & Social Work, 29*, 197–205.

Alvarez-Leon, E. E., Roman-Vinas, B., & Serra-Majem, L. (2006). Dairy products and health: A review of the epidemiological evidence. *British Journal of Nutrition, 96* (Suppl), S94–S99.

Alverdy, J., Zaborina, O., & Wu, L. (2005). The impact of stress and nutrition on bacterial–host interactions at the intestinal epithelial surface. *Current Opinion in Clinical Nutrition and Metabolic Care, 8*, 205–209.

Alzheimer's Association. (2004, May 28). Standard prescriptions for Alzheimer's. Available online at http://www.alz.org/AboutAD/Treatment/Standard.asp.

Amato, P., & Afifi, T. (2006, February). Feeling caught between parents: Adult children's relations with parents and subjective well-being. *Journal of Marriage and Family, 68*, 222–235.

Amato, P., & Booth, A. (1997). *A generation at risk*. Cambridge, MA: Harvard University Press.

Amato, P. R., & Booth, A. (2001). The legacy of parents' marital discord: Consequences for children's marital quality. *Journal of Personality and Social Psychology, 81*, 627–638.

Amato, P., & Previti, D. (2003). People's reasons for divorcing: Gender, social class, the life course, and adjustment. *Journal of Family Issues, 24*, 602–626.

Ambuel, B. (1995). Adolescents, unintended pregnancy, and abortion: The struggle for a compassionate social policy. *Current Directions in Psychological Science, 4*, 1–5.

American Academy of Family Physicians. (2002). *Position paper on neonatal circumcision*. Leawood, KS: American Academy of Family Physicians.

American Academy of Pediatrics. (1990). Bicycle helmets. *Pediatrics, 85*, 229–230.

American Academy of Pediatrics. (1995). *Policy statement on length of hospital stay following birth*. Washington, DC: Author.

American Academy of Pediatrics. (1997, April 16). Breast feeding and the use of human milk. *Pediatrics, 101*, 45–51.

American Academy of Pediatrics. (1998, April). Guidance for effective discipline. *Pediatrics, 101*, 723–728.

American Academy of Pediatrics. (1999a). *Circumcision: Information far parents*. Washington, DC: Author.

American Academy of Pediatrics. (1999b). Media education. *Pediatrics, 104*, 341–343.

American Academy of Pediatrics. (2000a). *Circumcision: Information for parents*. Washington, DC: American Academy of Pediatrics.

American Academy of Pediatrics. (2000b). Clinical practice guideline: Diagnosis and evaluation of the child with attention-deficit/hyperactivity disorder. *Pediatrics*, Retrieved from http://www.pediatrics.org/cgi/content/full/105/5/1158.

American Academy of Pediatrics. (2000c). *Recommended childhood immunization schedule, United States, January–December 2001*. Washington, DC: Author.

American Academy of Pediatrics. (2001). Organized sports for children and preadolescents. *Pediatrics, 107*, 1459–1462.

American Academy of Pediatrics. (2004, June 3). Sports programs. Retrieved from http://www.medem.com/medlb/article_detaillb_for_printer.cfm?article_ID=ZZZD2QD5M7C&sub_cat=405.

American Academy of Pediatrics. (2005a, May 12). *AAP endorses newborn screening report from the American College of Medical Genetics*. Press release.

American Academy of Pediatrics. (2005b). Breastfeeding and the use of human milk: Policy Statement. *Pediatrics, 115*, 496–506.

American Academy of Pediatrics. (2010, September 27). *Policy statement on media education*. Published online. http://pediatrics.aappublications.org/cgi/content/abstract/peds.2010–1636v1

American Academy of Pediatrics (Committee on Accident and Poison Prevention). (1990). Trampolines at home, school, and recreational centers. *Pediatrics, 103*, 1053–1056.

American Academy of Pediatrics (Committee on Fetus and Newborn). (2004). Hospital stay for healthy term newborns. *Pediatrics, 113*, 1434–2436.

American Academy of Pediatrics (Committee on Psychosocial Aspects of Child and Family Health). (1998, April). Guidance for effective discipline. *Pediatrics, 101*, 723–728.

American Academy of Pediatrics (Committee on Public Education). (1999, August). Media education (RE9911). *Pediatrics, 104*, 341–343.

American Academy of Pediatrics (Committee on Sports Medicine). (1988). Infant exercise programs. *Pediatrics, 82*, 800–825.

American Academy of Pediatrics (Committee on Sports Medicine and Committee on School Health). (1989). Organized athletics for preadolescent children. *Pediatrics, 84(3)*, 583–584.

American Academy of Pediatrics, Dietz, W. H., (Ed.), & Stern, L. (Ed.). (1999). *American Academy of Pediatrics guide to your child's nutrition: Making peace at the table and building healthy eating habits for life*. New York: Villard.

American Association of University Women. (1992). *How schools shortchange women: The AAUW report*. Washington, DC: Author.

American Association on Mental Retardation. (1992). *Mental retardation: Definition, classification, and systems of support*. Washington, DC: Author.

American Cancer Society. (1993). Cancer statistics, 1993. *Cancer Journal for Clinicians, 43*, 7–26.

American College Health Association. (1989). *Guidelines on acquaintance rape*. Washington, DC: Author.

American College of Medical Genetics. (2006). *Genetics in Medicine, 8*(5, Suppl).

American College of Obstetricians and Gynecologists. (1994, February). *Guidelines for exercise during pregnancy and the postpartum period*. Washington, DC: Author.

American College of Obstetricians and Gynecologists. (2002). *Guidelines for perinatal care*. Washington, DC: Author.

American College of Sports Medicine. (1997, November 3). *Consensus development conference statement on physical activity and cardiovascular health*. Retrieved from http://www.acsm.org/nhlbi.htm.

American College Testing Program. (2001). *National dropout rates*. Iowa City, IA: Author.

American Council on Education. (1995). *The American freshman: National norms for fall 1994*. Los Angeles: University of California Los Angeles Higher Education Research Institute.

American Council on Education. (1995–1996). *Minorities in higher education*. Washington, DC: Office of Minority Concerns.

American Heart Association. (1988). *Heart facts*. Dallas, TX: Author.

American Psychiatric Association. (1994). *Diagnostic and statistical manual of mental disorders* (4th ed.). Washington, DC: Author.

American Psychological Association. (1992). *Ethical principles of psychologists and code of conduct*. Washington, DC: Author.

American Psychological Association. (1996). *Violence and the family*. Washington, DC: Author.

American Psychological Association. (2002). *Ethical principles of psychologists and code of conduct. Updated*. Washington, DC: Author.

American Psychological Association Public Police Office. (1996). *Sex education*. Washington, DC: American Psychological Association.

American Psychological Association Reproductive Choice Working Group. (2000). *Reproductive choice and abortion: A resource packet*. Washington, DC: American Psychological Association.

American SIDS Institute. (2004). *Statistics on SIDS, based on data from the Centers for Disease Control and Prevention and the National Center for Health Statistics*. Marietta, GA: Author.

Amitai, Y., Haringman, M., Meiraz, H., Baram, N., & Leventhal, A. (2004). Increased awareness, knowledge and utilization of preconceptional folic acid in Israel following a national campaign. *Preventive Medicine: An International Journal Deveoted to Practice and Theory, 39*, 731–737.

Ammerman, R. T., & Patz, R. J. (1996). Determinants of child abuse potential: Contribution of parent and child factors. *Journal of Clinical Child Psychology, 25*, 300–307.

Amsterlaw, J., & Wellman, H. (2006). Theories of mind in transition: A microgenetic study of the development of false belief understanding. *Journal of Cognition and Development, 7*, 139–172.

An, J., & Cooney, T. (2006, September). Psychological well-being in mid to late life: The role of generativity development and parent-child relationships across the lifespan. *International Journal of Behavioral Development, 30*, 410–421.

Anand, K. J. S., & Hickey, P. R. (1992). Halothane–morphine compared with high-dose sufentanil for anesthesia and post-operative analgesia in neonatal cardiac surgery. *New England Journal of Medicine, 326*, 1–9.

Anand, S., & Krosnick, J. A. (2005). Demographic predictors of media use among infants, toddlers, and preschoolers. *American Behavioral Scientist, 48*, 539–561.

Anastasi, A. (1988). *Psychological testing* (6th ed.). New York: Macmillan.

Anders, T. F., & Taylor, T. (1994). Babies and their sleep environment. *Children's Environments, 11*, 123–134.

Anders, Y., Rossbach, H., Weinert, S., Ebert, S., Kuger, S., Lehrl, S., et al. (2012). Home and preschool learning environments and their relations to the development of early numeracy skills. *Early Childhood Research Quarterly, 27*, 231–244.

Andersen, B. L., Kiecolt-Glaser, J. K., & Glaser, R. (1994). A biobehavioral model of cancer stress and disease course. *American Psychologist, 49*, 389–404.

Andersen, S. L., & Navalta, C. P. (2004). Altering the course of neurodevelopment: A framework for understanding the enduring effects of psychotropic drugs. *Journal of Developmental Neuroscience, Special issue: Developmental aspects of addiction, 22*, 423–440.

Anderson, C., Berkowitz, L., Donnerstein, E., Huesmann, L., Johnson, J., Linz, D., et al. (2003). The influence of media violence on youth. *Psychological Science in the Public Interest, 4*, 81–110.

Anderson, C. A., Funk, Jeanne, B., & Griffiths, M. D. (2004). Contemporary issues in adolescent video game playing: Brief overview and introduction to the special issue. *Journal of Adolescence, 27*, 1–3.

Anderson C. A., Shibuya A., Ihori N., Swing E. L., Bushman B. J., et al. (2010). Violent video game effects on aggression, empathy, and prosocial behavior in eastern and western countries: A meta-analytic review. *Psychological Bulleting, 136*, 151–173.

Anderson, D., & Pempek, T. (2005). Television and very young children. *American Behavioral Scientist, 48*, 505–522.

Anderson, M. E., Johnson, D. C., & Batal, H. A. (2005). Sudden Infant Death Syndrome and prenatal maternal smoking: Rising attributed risk in the Back to Sleep era. *BMC Medical Genetics, 11*, 4.

Anderson, P., & Butcher, K. (2006, March). Childhood obesity: Trends and potential causes. *The Future of Children, 16*, 19–45.

Anderson, R. N. (2001). *United States life tables, 1998. National vital statistics reports* (Vol. 48, No. 18). Hyattsville, MD: National Center for Health Statistics.

Anderson, W. F. (1995, September.) Gene therapy. *Scientific American*, 125–128.

Anderson-Clark, T., Green, R., & Henley, T. (2008, March). The relationship between first names and teacher expectations for achievement motivation. *Journal of Language and Social Psychology, 27*(1), 94–99.

Andersson, T., & Magnusson, D. (1990). Biological maturation in adolescence and the development of drinking habits and alcohol abuse among young males: A prospective longitudinal study. *Journal of Youth and Adolescence, 19*, 33–42.

Andrew, M., McCanlies, E., Burchfiel, C., Charles, L., Hartley, T., Fekedulegn, D., et al. (2008). Hardiness and psychological distress in a cohort of police officers. *International Journal of Emergency Mental Health, 10*, 137–148.

Andrews, G., Halford, G., & Bunch, K. (2003). Theory of mind and relational complexity. *Child Development, 74*, 1476–1499.

Andrews, K., Francis, D. J., & Riese, M. L. (2000). Prenatal cocaine exposure and prematurity: Neurodevelopmental growth. *Journal of Developmental & Behavioral Pediatrics, 21*, 262–270.

Andrews, M. (1997). Life review in the context of social transition: The case of East Germany. *British Journal of Social Psychology, 36*, 273–290.

Andrikopoulou, A. (2004). Studying five-year-olds' understanding of the components of death. *Educational and Child Psychology, 21*, 41–60.

Ängarne-Lindberg, T., & Wadsby, M. (2012). Psychiatric and somatic health in relation to experience of parental divorce in childhood. *International Journal of Social Psychiatry, 58*, 16–25.

Angier, N. (2000, August 22). Do races differ? Not really, genes show. *New York Times*, pp. S1, S6.

Angus, J., & Reeve, P. (2006, April). Ageism: A threat to "aging well" in the 21st century. *Journal of Applied Gerontology, 25*, 137–152.

Anhalt, K., & Morris, T. (2003). Developmental and adjustment issues of gay, lesbian, and bisexual adolescents: A review of the empirical literature. In L. Garnets & D. Kimme (Eds.), *Psychological perspectives on lesbian, gay, and bisexual experiences* (2nd ed.). New York: Columbia University Press.

Anisfeld, M. (1996). Only tongue protrusion modeling is matched by neonates. *Developmental Review, 16*, 149–161.

Annenberg Public Policy Center. (2005). *Card playing trend in young people continues*. Philadelphia, PA: Annenberg Public Policy Center.

Annenberg Public Policy Center. (2006). *More than 1 million young people use Internet gambling sites each month*. Philadelphia, PA: Author.

Annenberg Public Policy Center. (2008). *Internet gambling stays low among youth ages 14 to 22 but access to gambling sites continues*. Philadelphia, PA: Author.

Annunziato, R., & Lowe, M. (2007, April). Taking action to lose weight: Toward an understanding of individual differences. *Eating Behaviors, 8*, 185–194.

Ansari, D. (2012). Culture and education: New frontiers in brain plasticity. *Trends in Cognitive Sciences, 16*, 93–95.

Ansberry, C. (1995, February 14). After seven decades, couple still finds romance in the 90s. *The Wall Street Journal*, pp. A1, A17.

Ansberry, C. (1997, November 14). Women of Troy: For ladies on a hill, friendships are a balm in the passages of life. *The Wall Street Journal*, pp. A1, A6.

Antonio, A., Chang, M., Hakuta, K., Kenny, D., Levin, S., & Milem, J. (2006). Effects of racial diversity on complex thinking in college students. *Psychological Science, 15*, 507–510.

Antonucci, T. C. (1990). Social supports and social relationships. In R. H. Binstock & L. K. George (Eds.), *Handbook of aging and the social sciences*. San Diego: Academic Press.

Antonucci, T. C. (2001). Social relations: An examination of social networks, social support, and sense of control. In J. E. Birren & K. W. Schaie (Eds.), *Handbook of the psychology of aging* (5th ed.). San Diego: Academic Press.

Antonucci, T. C., & Akiyama, H. (1991). Social relationships and aging well. *Generations, 15*, 39–44.

Antshel, K., & Antshel, K. (2002). Integrating culture as a means of improving treatment adherence in the Latino population. *Psychology, Health & Medicine, 7*, 435–449.

APA (American Psychological Association. (1996). *Violence and the family*. Washington, DC: Author.

American Psychological Association Reproductive Choice Working Group. (2000). *Reproductive choice and abortion: A resource packet*. Washington, DC: American Psychological Association.

Apgar, V. (1953). A proposal for a new method of evaluation in the newborn infant. *Current Research in Anesthesia and Analgesia, 32*, 260.

Apperly, I., & Robinson, E. (2002). Five-year-olds' handling of reference and description in the domains of language and mental representation. *Journal of Experimental Child Psychology, 83*, 53–75.

Apperly, I., & Robinson, E. (2003). When can children handle referential opacity? Evidence for systematic variation in 5- and 6-year-old children's reasoning about beliefs and belief reports. *Journal of Experimental Child Psychology, 85*, 297–311.

Applebome, P. (1997, March 1). Dispute over Ebonics reflects a volatile mix that roils urban education. *The New York Times*, p. 8.

Apter, A., Galatzer, A., Beth-Halachmi, N., & Laron, Z. (1981). Self-image in adolescents with delayed puberty and growth retardation. *Journal of Youth and Adolescence, 10*, 501–505.

Aquilino, W. (2006). Family relationships and support systems in emerging adulthood. *Emerging adults in America: Coming of age in the 21st century* (pp. 193–217). Washington, DC: American Psychological Association.

Arai, M. (2006, January). Elder abuse in Japan. *Educational Gerontology, 32*, 13–23.

Archer, J. (2009). The nature of human aggression. *International Journal of Law and Psychiatry, 32*, 202–208.

Archer, S. L., & Waterman, A. S. (1994). Adolescent identity development: Contextual perspectives. In C. B. Fisher & R. M. Lerner (Eds.), *Applied developmental psychology*. New York: McGraw-Hill.

Arcus, D. (2001). Inhibited and uninhibited children: Biology in the social context. In T. D. Wachs & G. A. Kohnstamm (Eds.), *Temperament in context*. Mahwah, NJ: Lawrence Erlbaum Associates.

Ardila, A., & Rosselli, M. (1994). Development of language, memory, and visuospatial ability in 5- to 12-year-old children using a neuropsychological battery. *Developmental Neuropsychology, 10*, 97–120.

Arenson, K. W. (2004, December 4). Worried colleges step up efforts over suicide. *The New York Times*, p. A1.

Arias, I. (2004). The legacy of child maltreatment: Long-term health consequences for women. *Journal of Women's Health, 13*, 468–473.

Ariès, P. (1962). *Centuries of childhood*. New York: Knopf.

Arija, V., Esparó, G., FernÁndez-Ballart, J., Murphy, M., BiarnÉs, E., & Canals, J. (2006). Nutritional status and performance in test of verbal and non-verbal intelligence in 6 year old children. *Intelligence, 34*, 141–149.

Arkoff, A., Meredith, G., & Dubanoski, J. (2004). Gains in well-being achieved through retrospective proactive life review by independent older women. *Journal of Humanistic Psychology, 44*, 204–214.

Arlotti, J. B., Cottrell, B. H., & Hughes, S. H. (1998). Breastfeeding among low-income women with and without peer support. *Journal of Community Health Nursing, 15*, 163–178.

Arluk, S., Branch, J., & Swain, D. (2003). Childhood obesity's relationship to time spent in sedentary behavior. *Military Medicine, 168*, 583–586.

Armitage, C. J. (2012). Evidence that self-affirmation reduces body dissatisfaction by basing self-esteem on domains other than body weight and shape. *Journal of Child Psychology and Psychiatry, 53*, 81–88.

Armstrong, J., Hutchinson, I., Laing, D., & Jinks, A. (2007). Facial electromyography: Responses of children to odor and taste stimuli. *Chemical Senses, 32*, 611–621.

Armstrong, P., Rounds, J., & Hubert, L. (2008). Re-conceptualizing the past: Historical data in vocational interest research. *Journal of Vocational Behavior, 72*, 284–297.

Armstrong, V., Brunet, P., He, C., Nishimura, M., Poole, H., & Spector, F. (2006). What is so critical?: A commentary on the reexamination of critical periods. *Developmental Psychobiology, 48*, 326–331.

Arnett, J. (2010). Oh, grow up! Generational grumbling and the new life stage of emerging adulthood—Commentary on Trzesniewski & Donnellan (2010). *Perspectives on Psychological Science, 5*, 89–92.

Arnett, J. (2011). Emerging adulthood(s): The cultural psychology of a new life stage. In L. Jensen (Ed.), *Bridging cultural and developmental approaches to psychology: New syntheses in theory, research, and policy*. New York: Oxford University Press.

Arnett, J. J. (2000). Emerging adulthood: A theory of development from the late teens through the twenties. *American Psychologist, 55*, 469–480.

Arnold, D. H., Kupersmidt, J. B., Voegler-Lee, M., & Marshall, N. A. (2012). The association between preschool children's social functioning and their emergent academic skills. *Early Childhood Research Quarterly*. Retrieved from http://www.sciencedirect.com/science/article/pii/S0885200612000026.

Arnold, R., & Colburn, N. (2007). Brain food. *School Library Journal, 53*, 29.

Arnold, R., & Colburn, N. (2009, September 1). Ready, set, go! Storytime can help children (and parents) become kindergarten-ready. *School Library Journal*, p. 24.

Arnon, S., Shamai, S., & Ilatov, Z. (2008). Socialization agents and activities of young adolescents. *Adolescence, 43*, 373–397.

Arnsten, A., Berridge, C., & McCracken, J. (2009). The neurobiological basis of attention-deficit/hyperactivity disorder. *Primary Psychiatry, 16*, 47–54.

Aronson, E. (1988). *The social animal* (3rd ed.). San Francisco: Freeman.

Aronson, E. (2000). *Nobody left to hate: Teaching compassion after Columbine*. New York: Freeman.

Aronson, E. (2004). Reducing hostility and building compassion: Lessons from the jigsaw classroom. *The social psychology of good and evil* (pp. 469–488). New York: Guilford Press.

Aronson, E., Stephan, W., Sikes, J., Blaney, N., & Snapp, M. (1978). *Cooperation in the classroom*. Beverly Hills, CA: Sage.

Aronson, J. D. (2007). Brain imaging, culpability and the juvenile death penalty. *Psychology, Public Policy, and Law, 13*, 115–142.

Arredondo, E., Elder, J., Ayala, G., Campbell, N., Baquero, B., & Duerksen, S. (2006, December). Is parenting style related to children's healthy eating and physical activity in Latino families? *Health Education Research, 21*, 862–871.

Arseneault, L., Moffitt, T. E., & Caspi, A. (2003). Strong genetic effects on cross-situational antisocial behavior among 5-year-old children according to mothers, teachers, examiner-observers, and twins' self-reports. *Journal of Child Psychology and Psychiatry and Allied Disciplines, 44*, 832–848.

Arseneault, L., Tremblay, R. E., Boulerice, B., & Saucier, J.-F. (2002). Obstetrical complications and violent delinquency: Testing two developmental pathways. *Child Development, 73*, 496–508.

Artal, P., Ferro, M., Miranda, I., & Navarro, R. (1993). Effects of aging in retinal image quality. *Journal of the Optical Society of America, 10*, 1656–1662.

Arts, J. A. R., Gijselaers, W. H., & Boshuizen, H. P. A. (2006). Understanding managerial problem-solving, knowledge use and information processing: Investigating stages from school to the workplace. *Contemporary Educational Psychology, 31*, 387–410.

Asch, D. A. (1996, May 23). The role of critical care nurses in euthanasia and assisted suicide. *The New England Journal of Medicine, 334*, 1374–1379.

Aseltine, R. H., Gore, S., & Colten, M. E. (1994). Depression and the social developmental context of adolescence. *Journal of Personality and Social Psychology, 67*, 252–263.

Asendorpf, J. (2002). Self-awareness, other-awareness, and secondary representation. In A. Meltzoffa & W. Prinz (Eds.), *The imitative mind: Development, evolution, and brain bases*. New York: Cambridge University Press.

Asendorpf, J. B., Warkentin, V., & Baudonniere, P. (1996). Self-awareness and other-awareness II: Mirror self-recognition, social contingency awareness, and synchronic imitation. *Developmental Psychology, 32*, 313–321.

Ash, P. (2008). Children and adolescents. In *Textbook of violence assessment and management* (pp. 359–380). Arlington, VA: American Psychiatric Publishing, Inc.

Asher, S. R., & Parker, J. G. (1991). The significance of peer relationship problems in childhood. In B. H. Schneider, G. Attili, J. Nadel, & R. P. Weisberg (Eds.), *Social competence in developmental perspective*. Amsterdam: Kluwer.

Asher, S. R., & Rose, A. J. (1997). Promoting children's social-emotional adjustment with peers. In P. Salovey & D. J. Sluyter (Eds.), *Emotional development and emotional intelligence: Educational implications* (pp. 196–230). New York: Basic Books.

Asher, S. R., Singleton, L. C., & Taylor, A. R. (1982). *Acceptance vs. friendship*. Paper presented at the meeting of the American Research Association, New York.

Ashwin, C., Baron-Cohen, S., Wheelwright, S., O'Riordan, M., & Bullmore, E. (2007). Differential activation of the amygdala and the "social brain" during fearful face-processing in Asperger syndrome. *Neuropsychologia, 45*, 2–14.

Askham, J. (1994). Marriage relationships of older people. *Reviews in Clinical Gerontology, 4*, 261–268.

Aslin, R. N. (1987). Visual and auditory development in infancy. In J. D. Osofsky (Ed.), *Handbook of infant development* (2nd ed.). New York: Wiley.

Aslin, R. N. (2012). Infant eyes: A window on cognitive development. *Infancy, 17*, 126–140.

Aspinwall, O. G., & Taylor, S. E. (1993). Effects of social comparison direction, threat, and self-esteem on affect, evaluation, and expected success. *Journal of Personality and Social Psychology, 64*, 708–722.

Astheimer, L. B., & Sanders, L. D. (2012). Temporally selective attention supports speech processing in 3- to

5-year-old children. *Developmental Cognitive Neuroscience, 2,* 120–128.

Astington, J., & Baird, J. (2005). *Why language matters for theory of mind.* New York: Oxford University Press.

Ata, R., Ludden, A., & Lally, M. (2007, November). The effects of gender and family, friend, and media influences on eating behaviors and body image during adolescence. *Journal of Youth and Adolescence, 36*(8), 1024–1037.

Atchley, R. C. (1982). Retirement: Leaving the world of work. *Annals of the American Academy of Political and Social Science, 464,* 120–131.

Atchley, R. C. (1985). *Social forces and aging: An introduction to social gerontology.* Belmont, CA: Wadsworth.

Atchley, R. C. (1989). A continuity theory of normal aging. *The Gerontologist, 29,* 183–190.

Atchley, R. C. (2000). *Social forces and aging* (9th ed.). Belmont, CA: Wadsworth Thomson Learning.

Atchley, R. (2003). Why most people cope well with retirement. In J. Ronch & J. Goldfield (Eds.), *Mental wellness in aging: Strengths-based approaches.* Baltimore, MD: Health Professions Press.

Atchley, R. C., & Barusch, A. (2005). *Social forces and aging* (10th ed.). Belmont, CA: Wadsworth.

Athanases, S., & Larrabee, T. (2003). Toward a consistent stance in teaching for equity: Learning to advocate for lesbian- and gay-identified youth. *Teaching & Teacher Education, 19,* 237–261.

Atkins, C. J., Senn, K., Rupp, J., & Kaplan, R. M. (1990). Attendance at health promotion programs: Baseline predictors and program outcomes. *Health Education Quarterly, 17,* 417–428.

Atkins, D. C., & Furrow, J. (2008, November). *Infidelity is on the rise: But for whom and why?* Paper presented at the annual meeting of the Association for Behavioral and Cognitive Therapies, Orlando, FL.

Atkins, S. M., Bunting, M. F., Bolger, D. J., & Dougherty, M. R. (2012). Training the adolescent brain: Neural plasticity and the acquisition of cognitive abilities. In V. F. Reyna, S. B. Chapman, M. R. Dougherty, J. Confrey, V. F. Reyna, S. B. Chapman, et al. (Eds.), *The adolescent brain: Learning, reasoning, and decision making.* Washington, DC: American Psychological Association.

Atkinson, R. C., & Shiffrin, R. M. (1968). Human memory: A proposed system and its control processes. In K. W. Spence & J. T. Spence (Eds.), *The psychology of learning and motivation: Advances in research and theory* (Vol. 2, pp. 80–195). New York: Academic Press.

Atkinson, R. C., & Shiffrin, R. M. (1971). The control of short-term memory. *Scientific American, 225,* 82–90.

Attie, I., & Brooks-Gunn, J. (1989). The development of eating problems in adolescent girls: A longitudinal study. *Developmental Psychology, 25,* 70–79.

Auestad, N., Scott, D. T., Janowsky, J. S., Jacobsen, C., Carroll, R. E., Montalto, M. B., et al. (2003). Visual cognitive and language assessments at 39 months: A follow-up study of children fed formulas containing long-chain polyunsaturated fatty acids to 1 year of age. *Pediatrics, 112,* e177–e183.

Augustyn, M. (2003). "G" is for growing. Thirty years of research on children and *Sesame Street. Journal of Developmental and Behavioral Pediatrics, 24,* 451.

Aunio, P., Aubrey, C., Godfrey, R., Pan, Y., & Liu, Y. (2008). Children's early numeracy in England, Finland and People's Republic of China. *International Journal of Early Years Education, 16,* 203–221.

Auyeung, B., Baron-Cohen, S., Ashwin, E., Knickmeyer, R., Taylor, K., & Hackett, G. (2009). Fetal testosterone and autistic traits. *British Journal of Psychology, 100,* 1–22.

Avalos, L., Kaskutas, L., Block, G., Abrams, B., & Li, D. (2011). Does lack of multinutrient supplementation during early pregnancy increase vulnerability to alcohol-related preterm or small-for-gestational-age births? *Maternal and Child Health Journal, 15,* 1324–1332.

Aved, B. M., Irwin, M. M., Cummings, L. S., & Findeisen, N. (1993). Barriers to prenatal care for low-income women. *Western Journal of Medicine, 158,* 493–498.

Aviezer, O., Sagi, A., & Resnick, G. (2002). School competence in young adolescence: Links to early attachment relationships beyond concurrent self-perceived competence and representations of relationships. *International Journal of Behavioral Development, 26,* 397–409.

Avis, N., Crawford, S., & Johannes, C. (2002). Menopause. In G. Wingood & R. DiClemente (Eds.), *Handbook of women's sexual and reproductive health.* New York: Kluwer Academic/Plenum Publishers.

Avis, N. E., Stellato, R., Crawford, S., Bromberger, J., Ganz, P., Cain, V., et al. (2001). Is there a menopausal syndrome? Menopausal status and symptoms across racial/ethnic groups. *Social Science & Medicine, 52,* 345–356.

Avlund, K., Lund, R., & Holstein, B. (2004). Social relations as determinant of onset of disability in aging. *Archives of Gerontology & Geriatrics, 38,* 85–99.

Axia, G., Bonichini, S., & Benini, F. (1995). Pain in infancy: Individual differences. *Perceptual and Motor Skills, 81,* 142.

Ayalon, H. (2003). Women and men go to university: Mathematical background and gender differences in choice of field in higher education. *Sex Roles, 48,* 277–282.

Aydt, H., & Corsaro, W. (2003). Differences in children's construction of gender across culture: An interpretive approach. *American Behavioral Scientist, 46,* 1306–1325.

Aylward, G. P., & Verhulst, S. J. (2000). Predictive utility of the Bayley Infant Neurodevelopmental Screener (BINS) risk status classifications: Clinical interpretation and application. *Developmental Medicine & Child Neurology, 42,* 25–31.

Ayoub, N. C. (2005, February 25). A pleasing birth: Midwives and maternity care in the Netherlands. *Chronicle of Higher Education,* p. 9.

Azar, B. (1995, January). "Gifted" label stretches, it's more than high IQ. *APA Monitor,* p. 25.

Azar, B. (1997, April). Psychologists are watching debate over 2000 census. *APA Monitor,* p. 28.

Azar, B. (2000, November). Hand-me-down skills. *Monitor on Psychology,* 64–66.

Azmitia, M. (1988). Peer interaction and problem solving: When are two heads better than one? *Child Development, 59,* 87–96.

Babad, E. (1992). Pygmalion—25 years after interpersonal expectations in the classroom. In P. D. Blanck (Ed.), *Interpersonal expectations: Theory, research and application.* Cambridge, England: Cambridge University Press.

Bacchus, L., Mezey, G., & Bewley, S. (2006). A Qualitative exploration of the nature of domestic violence in pregnancy. *Violence Against Women, 12,* 588–604.

Baddeley, A. (1993). Working memory and conscious awareness. In A. F. Collins, S. E. Gathercole, M. A. Conway, & P. E. Morris (Eds.), *Theories of memory.* Hillsdale, NJ: Lawrence Erlbaum Associates.

Baddeley, A. (1996). Exploring the central executive. *Quarterly Journal of Experimental Psychology, 49A,* 5–28.

Baddeley, A., & Wilson, B. (1985). Phonological coding and short-term memory in patients without speech. *Journal of Memory and Language, 24,* 490–502.

Badenhorst, W., Riches, S., Turton, P., & Hughes, P. (2006). The psychological effects of stillbirth and neonatal death on fathers: Systematic review. *Journal of Psychosomatic Obstetrics & Gynecology, 27,* 245–256.

Bader, A. P. (1995). Engrossment revisited: Fathers are still falling in love with their newborn babies. In J. L. Shapiro, M. J. Diamond, & M. Grenberg (Eds.), *Becoming a father.* New York: Springer.

Baer, J. (1997). *Creative teachers, creative students.* Boston, MA: Allyn & Bacon.

Baer, J. S., Sampson, P. D., & Barr, H. M. (2003). A 21-year longitudinal analysis of the effects of prenatal alcohol exposure on young adult drinking. *Archives of General Psychiatry, 60,* 377–385.

Bahrick, L. E., & Pickens, J. N. (1988). Classification of bimodal English and Spanish language passages by infants. *Infant Behavior and Development, 11,* 277–296.

Bai, L. (2005). Children at play: A childhood beyond the Confucian shadow. *Childhood: A Global Journal of Child Research, 12,* 9–32.

Bailey, J. M., Kirk, K. M., Zhu, G., Dunne, M. P., & Martin, N. G. (2000). Do individual differences in sociosexuality represent genetic or environmentally contingent strategies? Evidence from the Australian twin registry. *Journal of Personality and Social Psychology, 78,* 537–545.

Bailey, W. T. (1994). A longitudinal study of fathers' involvement with young children, infancy to age 5 years. *Journal of Genetic Psychology, 155,* 331–339.

Baillargeon, R. (1987). Object permanence in 3 1/2- and 4 1/2-month-old infants. *Developmental Psychology, 23*(5), 655–670.

Baillargeon, R. (2004). Infants' physical world. *Current Directions in Psychological Science, 13,* 89–94.

Baillargeon, R. (2008). Innate ideas revisited: For a principle of persistence in infants' physical reasoning. *Perspectives on Psychological Science, 3,* 2–13.

Baillargeon, R., & DeVos, J. (1991). Object permanence in young infants: Further evidence. *Child Development, 62,* 1227–1246.

Baines, C. J., Vidmar, M., McKeown-Eyssen, G., & Tibshirani, R. (1997, August 15). Impact of menstrual phase on false-negative mammograms in the Canadian National Breast Screening Study. *Cancer, 80,* 720–724.

Baird, A., John, R., & Hayslip, B., Jr. (2000). Custodial grandparenting among African Americans: A focus group perspective. In B. Hayslip Jr. & R. Goldberg-Glen (Eds.), *Grandparents raising grandchildren: Theoretical, empirical, and clinical perspectives.* New York: Springer.

Bajor, J., & Baltes, B. (2003). The relationship between selection optimization with compensation, conscientiousness, motivation, and performance. *Journal of Vocational Behavior, 63,* 347–367.

Baker, D. B. (1994). Parenting stress and ADHD: A comparison of mothers and fathers. *Journal of Emotional and Behavioral Disorders, 2,* 46–50.

Baker, J., Maes, H., Lissner, L., Aggen, S., Lichtenstein, P., & Kendler, K. (2009). Genetic risk factors for disordered eating in adolescent males and females. *Journal of Abnormal Psychology, 118,* 576–586.

Baker, J., Mazzeo, S., & Kendler, K. (2007). Association between broadly defined bulimia nervosa and drug use disorders: Common genetic and environmental influences. *International Journal of Eating Disorders, 40,* 673–678.

Baker, M. (2007, December). Elder mistreatment: Risk, vulnerability, and early mortality. *Journal of the American Psychiatric Nurses Association, 12,* 313–321.

Baker, S., O' Neill, B., Ginsburg, M., & Li, G. (1992). *The injury fact book* (2nd ed.). New York: Oxford University Press.

Baker, T., Brandon, T., & Chassin, L. (2004). Motivational influences on cigarette smoking. *Annual Review of Psychology, 55,* 463–491.

Baker-Sennett, J., Matusov, E., & Rogoff, B. (1992) *Sociocultural processes of creative planning in children's playcrafting.* Hillsdale, NJ: Lawrence Erlbaum Associates.

Bakker, A., & Heuven, E. (2006, November). Emotional dissonance, burnout, and in-role performance among nurses and police officers. *International Journal of Stress Management, 13,* 423–440.

Balaban, M. T., Snidman, N., & Kagan, J. (1997). Attention, emotion, and reactivity in infancy and early childhood. In P. J. Lang, R. F. Simons, & M. T. Balaban

(Eds.), *Attention and orienting: Sensory and motivational processes* (pp. 369–391). Mahwah, NJ: Erlbaum.

Ball, J. A. (1987). *Reactions to motherhood.* New York: Cambridge University Press.

Ball, K., & Rebok, G. W. (1994). Evaluating the driving ability of older adults. *Journal of Applied Gerontology, 13, Special Issue: Research translation in gerontology: A behavioral and social perspective.* 20–38.

Ball, M., & Orford, J. (2002). Meaningful patterns of activity amongst the long-term inner city unemployed: A qualitative study. *Journal of Community & Applied Social Psychology, 12,* 377–396.

Ballen, L., & Fulcher, A. (2006). Nurses and doulas: Complementary roles to provide optimal maternity care. *Journal of Obstetric, Gynecologic, & Neonatal Nursing: Clinical Scholarship for the Care of Women, Childbearing Families, & Newborns, 35,* 304–311.

Baltes, M. M. (1995). Dependency in old age: Gains and losses. *Current Directions in Psychological Science, 4,* 14–19.

Baltes, M. M. (1996). *The many faces of dependency in old age.* New York: Cambridge University Press.

Baltes, M., & Carstensen, L. (2003). The process of successful aging: Selection, optimization and compensation. In U. Staudinger & U. Lindenberger (Eds.), *Understanding human development: Dialogues with lifespan psychology.* Dordrecht, Netherlands: Kluwer Academic Publishers.

Baltes, P. B. (1987). Theoretical propositions of life-span developmental psychology: On the dynamics between growth and decline. *Developmental Psychology, 23,* 611–626.

Baltes, P. B. (1997). On the incomplete architecture of human ontogeny: Selection, optimization, and compensation as foundation of developmental theory. *American Psychologist, 52,* 366–380.

Baltes, P. B. (2003). On the incomplete architecture of human ontogeny: Selection, optimization and compensation as foundation of developmental theory. In U. M. Staudinger & U. Lindenberger (Eds.), *Understanding human development: Dialogues with lifespan psychology.* Dordrecht, Netherlands: Kluwer Academic Publishers.

Baltes, P. B., & Baltes, M. M. (1990). Psychological perspectives on successful aging: The model of selective optimization with compensation. In P. B. Baltes & M. M. Baltes (Eds.), *Successful aging: Perspectives from the behavioral sciences.* Cambridge, England: Cambridge University Press.

Baltes, P. B., & Freund, A. (2003a). Human strengths as the orchestration of wisdom and selective optimization with compensation. In L. Aspinwall & U. Staudinger (Eds.), *A psychology of human strengths: Fundamental questions and future directions for a positive psychology.* Washington, DC: American Psychological Association.

Baltes, P. B., & Freund, A. (2003b). The intermarriage of wisdom and selective optimization with compensation: Two meta-heuristics guiding the conduct of life. In C. Keyes & J. Haidt (Eds.), *Flourishing: Positive psychology and the life well-lived.* Washington, DC: American Psychological Association.

Baltes, P. B., & Schaie, K. W. (1974, March). The myth of the twilight years. *Psychology Today,* 35–38.

Baltes, P. B., & Smith, J. (2008). The fascination of wisdom: Its nature, ontogeny, and function. *Perspectives on Psychological Science, 3,* 56–64.

Baltes, P. B., & Staudinger, U. M. (2000). Wisdom: A metaheuristic (pragmatic) to orchestrate mind and virtue toward excellence. *American Psychologist, 55,* 122–136.

Baltes, P. B., Staudinger, U. M., & Lindenberger, U. (1999). Lifespan psychology: Theory and application to intellectual functioning. *Annual Review of Psychology, 50,* 471–507.

Baltes, P. B., Staudinger, U. M., Maercker, A., & Smith, J. (1995). People nominated as wise: A comparative study of wisdom-related knowledge. *Psychology and Aging, 10,* 155–166.

Balthazart, J. (2012). *The biology of homosexuality.* New York: Oxford University Press.

Baltrusch, H. J., Stangel, W., & Tirze, I. (1991). Stress, cancer and immunity: New developments in biopsychosocial and psychoneuroimmunologic research. *Acta Neurologica, 13,* 315–327.

Bamshad, M. J., & Olson, S. E. (2003, December). Does race exist? *Scientific American,* 78–85.

Bamshad, M. J., Wooding, S., Watking, W. S., Ostter, C. T., Batzer, M. H., & Jorde, L. B. (2003). Human population genetic structure and inference of group membership. *American Journal of Human Genetics, 72,* 578–589.

Bandura, A. (1977). *Social learning theory.* Englewood Cliffs, NJ: Prentice-Hall.

Bandura, A. (1978). Social learning theory of aggression. *Journal of Communication, 28,* 12–29.

Bandura, A. (1986). *Social foundations of thought and action.* Englewood Cliffs, NJ: Prentice Hall.

Bandura, A. (1991). Social cognitive theory of moral thought and action. In W. M. Kurtines & J. L. Gewirtz (Eds.), *Handbook of moral behavior and development.* Hillsdale, NJ: Erlbaum.

Bandura, A. (1994). Social cognitive theory of mass communication. In J. Bryant & D. Zillmann, (Eds.), *Media effects: Advances in theory and research. LEA's communication series.* Hillsdale, NJ: Lawrence Erlbaum.

Bandura, A. (2002). Social cognitive theory in cultural context. *Applied Psychology: An International Review, 51, Special Issue,* 269–290.

Bandura, A. (2004). Model of causality in social learning theory. *Cognition and psychotherapy* (2nd ed.). New York: Springer Publishing Co.

Bandura, A. (2007). *A history of psychology in autobiography, Vol. IX.* Washington, DC: American Psychological Association.

Bandura, A., Grusec, J. E., & Menlove, F. L. (1967). Vicarious extinction of avoidance behavior. *Journal of Personality and Social Psychology, 5,* 16–23.

Bandura, A., Pastorelli, C., Barbaranelli, C., & Caprara, G. V. (1999). Self-efficacy pathways to childhood depression. *Journal of Personality and Social Psychology, 76,* 258–269.

Bandura, A., Ross, D., & Ross, S. (1963). Vicarious extinction of avoidance behavior. *Journal of Personality and Social Psychology, 67,* 601–607.

Banich, M. T., & Nicholas, C. D. (1998). Integration of processing between the hemispheres in word recognition. In M. Beeman & C. Chiarello (Eds.), *Right hemisphere language comprehension: Perspectives from cognitive neuroscience* Mahwah, NJ: Erlbaum.

Banti, S., Mauri, M., Oppo, A., Borri, C., Rambelli, C., Ramacciotti, D., et al. (2011). From the third month of pregnancy to 1 year postpartum. Prevalence, incidence, recurrence, and new onset of depression. Results from the Perinatal Depression–Research & Screening Unit study. *Comprehensive Psychiatry, 52,* 343–351.

Baptista, T., Aldana, E., Angeles, F., & Beaulieu, S. (2008). Evolution theory: An overview of its applications in psychiatry. *Psychopathology, 41,* 17–27.

Barber, S., & Gertler, P. (2009). Empowering women to obtain high quality care: Evidence from an evaluation of Mexico's conditional cash transfer programme. *Health Policy and Planning, 24,* 18–25.

Barbera, E. (2003). Gender schemas: Configuration and activation processes. *Canadian Journal of Behavioural Science, 35,* 176–180.

Barboza, G., Schiamberg, L., Oehmke, J., Korzeniewski, S., Post, L., & Heraux, C. (2009). Individual characteristics and the multiple contexts of adolescent bullying: An ecological perspective. *Journal of Youth and Adolescence, 38,* 101–121.

Bard, D., & Rodgers, J. (2003). Sibling influence on smoking behavior: A within-family look at explanations for a birth-order effect. *Journal of Applied Social Psychology, 33,* 1773–1795.

Barer, B. M. (1994). Men and women aging differently. *International Journal of Aging and Human Development, 38,* 29–40.

Barinaga, M. (2000, June 23). A critical issue for the brain. *Science, 288,* 2116–2119.

Barker, E., & Galambos, N. (2003). Body dissatisfaction of adolescent girls and boys: Risk and resources factors. *Journal of Early Adolescence, 23,* 141–165.

Barker, V., Giles, H., & Noels, K. (2001). The English-only movement: A communication analysis of changing perceptions of language vitality. *Journal of Communication, 51,* 3–37.

Barkley, R. A. (1997a). *ADHD and the nature of self-control.* New York: Guilford Press.

Barkley, R. A. (1997b). Behavioral inhibition, sustained attention, and executive functions: Constructing a unifying theory of ADHD. *Psychological Bulletin, 121,* 65–94.

Barlett, C., Harris, R., & Baldassaro, R. (2007). Longer you play, the more hostile you feel: Examination of first person shooter video games and aggression during video game play. *Aggressive Behavior, 33,* 486–497.

Barnard, W. (2007). Publicly funded programs and their benefits for children. In *Evidence-based practices and programs for early childhood care and education* (pp. 67–87). Thousand Oaks, CA: Corwin Press.

Barner, D., Lui, T., & Zapf, J. (2012). Is two a plural marker in early child language?. *Developmental Psychology, 48,* 10–17.

Barnett, R. C., & Hyde, J. S. (2001). Women, men, work, and family. *American Psychologist, 56,* 781–796.

Barnett, R. C., Raudenbush, S. W., Brennan, R. T., Pleck, J. H., & Marshall, N. L. (1995). Change in job and marital experiences and change in psychological distress: A longitudinal study of dual-earner couples. *Journal of Personality and Social Psychology, 69,* 839–850.

Barnett, R. C., & Rivers, C. (1992). The myth of the miserable working woman. *Working Woman, 2,* 62–65, 83–85.

Barnett, R. C., & Shen, Y.-C. (1997). Gender, high- and low-schedule-control housework tasks, and psychological distress: A study of dual-earner couples. *Journal of Family Issues, 18,* 403–428.

Baron, J. B., & Sternberg, R. J. (1986). *Teaching thinking skills.* New York: Freeman.

Baron-Cohen, S. (2003). *The essential difference: Men, women and the extreme male brain.* London: Allen Lane/Penguin.

Baron-Cohen, S. (2005). Testing the extreme male brain (EMB) theory of autism: Let the data speak for themselves. *Cognitive Neuropsychiatry, 10,* 77–81.

Baron-Cohen, S., Leslie, A., & Frith, U. (1985). Does the autistic child have a "theory of mind"? *Cognition, 21,* 37–46.

Barone, D. (2011). Welcoming families: A parent literacy project in a linguistically rich, high-poverty school. *Early Childhood Education Journal, 38,* 377–384.

Barr, H. M., Streissguth, A. P., Darby, B. L., & Sampson, P. D. (1990). Prenatal exposure to alcohol, caffeine, tobacco, and aspirin: Effects on fine and gross motor performance in 4-year-old children. *Developmental Psychology, 26*(3), 339–348.

Barr, P., & Cacciatore, J. (2007). Problematic emotions and maternal grief. *Omega: Journal of Death and Dying, 56,* 331–348.

Barr, R. G. (2011). Mother and child: Preparing for a life. In D. P. Keating (Eds.), *Nature and nurture in early child development.* New York: Cambridge University Press.

Barr, R., & Hayne, H. (1999). Developmental changes in imitation from television during infancy. *Child Development, 70,* 1067–1081.

Barr, R., Lauricella, A., Zack, E., & Calvert, S. L. (2010). Infant and early childhood exposure to adult-directed and child-directed television programming: Relations with cognitive skills at age four. *Journal of Developmental Psychology, 56,* 21–48.

Barr, R., Marrott, H., & Rovee-Collier, C. (2003). The role of sensory preconditioning in memory retrieval by preverbal infants. *Learning & Behavior, 31,* 111–123.

Barr, R., Muentener, P., Garcia, A., Fujimoto, M., & Chávez, V. (2007). The effect of repetition on imitation from television during infancy. *Developmental Psychobiology, 49,* 196–207.

Barratt, M. S., Roach, M. A., Morgan, K. M., & Colbert, K. K. (1996). Adjustment to motherhood by single adolescents. *Family Relations, 45,* 209–215.

Barrett, D. E., & Frank, D. A. (1987). *The effects of undernutrition on children's behavior.* New York: Gordon & Breach.

Barrett, D. E., & Radke-Yarrow, M. R. (1985). Effects of nutritional supplementation on children's responses to novel, frustrating, and competitive situations. *American Journal of Clinical Nutrition, 42,* 102–120.

Barrett, T., & Needham, A. (2008). Developmental differences in infants' use of an object's shape to grasp it securely. *Developmental Psychobiology, 50,* 97–106.

Barringer, F. (1993, April 1). Viral sexual diseases are found in 1 of 5 in U.S. *The New York Times,* pp. A1, B9.

Barron, F. (1990). *Creativity and psychological health: Origins of personal vitality and creative freedom.* Buffalo, NY: Creative Education Foundation.

Barron, F., & Harrington, D. M. (1981). Creativity, intelligence, and personality. *Annual Review of Psychology, 32,* 439–476.

Barry, C., Padilla-Walker, L., Madsen, S., & Nelson, L. (2008). The impact of maternal relationship quality on emerging adults' prosocial tendencies: Indirect effects via regulation of prosocial values. *Journal of Youth and Adolescence, 37,* 581–591.

Barry, H., III, Josephson, L., Lauer, E., & Marshall, C. (1976). Traits inculcated in childhood: Cross-cultural codes V. *Ethnology, 15,* 83–114.

Barry, L. M., Hudley, C., Kelly, M., & Cho, S. (2009). Differences in self-reported disclosure of college experiences by first-generation college student status. *Adolescence, 44,* 55–68.

Bartecchi, C. E., MacKenzie, T. D., & Schrier, R. W. (1995, May). The global tobacco epidemic. *Scientific American,* 44–51.

Bartel, V. B. (2010). Home and school factors impacting parental involvement in a title I elementary school. *Journal of Research and Childhood Education, 24,* 209–229.

Bartholow, B., Sestir, M., & Davis, E. (2005). Correlates and consequences of exposure to video game violence: Hostile personality, empathy, and aggressive behavior. *Personality and Social Psychology Bulletin, 31,* 1573–1586.

Barton, L. J. (1997, July). A shoulder to lean on: Assisted living in the U.S. *American Demographics,* 45–51.

Barton, R. (2007). Use of medication in children with psychiatric disorders. *Journal of Community Practice, 80,* 42, 44.

Baruch, G., Vrouva, I., & Wells, C. (2011). Outcome findings from a parent training programme for young people with conduct problems. *Child and Adolescent Mental Health, 16,* 47–54.

Basak, C., Boot, W., Voss, M., & Kramer, A. (2008). Can training in a real-time strategy video game attenuate cognitive decline in older adults? *Psychology and Aging, 23,* 765–777.

Bashore, T. R., Ridderinkhof, K. R., & van der Molen, M. W. (1998). The decline of cognitive processing speed in old age. *Current Directions in Psychological Science, 6,* 163–169.

Basow, S. (2006). Gender role and gender identity development. *Handbook of girls' and women's psychological health: Gender and well-being across the lifespan* (pp. 242–251). New York: Oxford University Press.

Bass, S., Shields, M. K., & Behrman, R. E. (2004). Children, families, and foster care: Analysis and recommendations. *The Future of Children, 14,* 5–30.

Basseches, M. (1984). *Dialectical thinking and adult development.* Norwood, NJ: Ablex.

Bates, E., Bretherton, I., & Snyder, L. (1988). *From first words to grammar: Individual differences and dissociable mechanisms.* New York: Cambridge University Press.

Bates, E., Marchman, V., Thal, D., Fenson, L., Dale, P., Reznick, J. S., et al. (1994). Developmental and stylistic variation in the composition of the early vocabulary. *Journal of Child Language, 21,* 85–123.

Bates, J. E., Marvinney, D., Kelly, T., Dodge, K. A., Bennett, D. S., & Pettit, G. S. (1994). Child-care history and kindergarten adjustment. *Developmental Psychology, 30,* 690–700.

Batshaw, M. (2007). Genetics and developmental disabilities. In M. L. Batshaw, L. Pellegrino, & N. Roizen (Eds.), *Children with disabilities* (6th ed.). New York: Paul Brookes Publishing.

Batson, C. (2012). A history of prosocial behavior research. In A. W. Kruglanski & W. Stroebe (Eds.), *Handbook of the history of social psychology.* New York: Psychology Press.

Battin, M., van der Heide, A., Ganzini, L., van der Wal, G., & Onwuteaka-Philipsen, B. (2007). Legal physician-assisted dying in Oregon and the Netherlands: Evidence concerning the impact on patients in 'vulnerable' groups. *Journal of Medical Ethics, 33,* 591–597.

Bauer, P. (2006). Event memory. *Handbook of child psychology: Vol 2, Cognition, perception, and language* (6th ed.). Hoboken, NJ: John Wiley & Sons Inc.

Bauer, P. J. (1996). What do infants recall of their lives? Memory for specific events by 1- to 2-year-olds. *American Psychologist, 51,* 29–41.

Bauer, P. J. (2004). Getting explicit memory off the ground: Steps toward construction of a neuro-developmental account of changes in the first two years of life. *Developmental Review, Special Issue: Memory development in the new millennium, 24,* 347–373.

Bauer, P. J. (2007). Recall in infancy: A neurodevelopmental account. *Current Directions in Psychological Science, 16,* 142–146.

Bauer, P. J., Wenner, J. A., Dropik, P. L., & Wewerka, S. S. (2000). Parameters of remembering and forgetting in the transition from infancy to early childhood. With commentary by Mark L. Howe. *Monographs of the Society for Research in Child Development, 65,* 4.

Bauer, P. J., Wiebe, S. A., Carver, L. J., Waters, J. M., & Nelson, C. A. (2003). Developments in long-term explicit memory late in the first year of life: Behavioral and electrophysiological indices. *Psychological Science, 14,* 629–635.

Baulac, S., Lu, H., Strahle, J., Yang, T., Goldberg, M., Shen, J., et al. (2009). Increased DJ-1 expression under oxidative stress and in Alzheimer's disease brains. *Molecular Neurodegeneration, 4,* 27–37.

Bauld, R., & Brown, R. (2009). Stress, psychological distress, psychosocial factors, menopause symptoms and physical health in women. *Maturitas, 62,* 160–165.

Baum, A. (1994). Behavioral, biological, and environmental interactions in disease processes. In S. Blumenthal, K. Matthews, & S. Weiss (Eds.), *New research frontiers in behavioral medicine: Proceedings of the National Conference.* Washington, DC: NIH Publications.

Bauman, K. J. (2001, March 29–31). *Home schooling in the United States: Trends and characteristics* (Working Paper No. 53). Paper presented at the annual meeting of the Population Association of American, Washington, DC.

Baumbusch, J. (2004). Unclaimed treasures: Older women's reflections on lifelong singlehood. *Journal of Women & Aging, 16,* 105–121.

Baumeister, R. F. (Ed.). (1993). *Self-esteem: The puzzle of low self-regard.* New York: Plenum.

Baumeister, R. F., Bushman, B. J., & Campbell, W. K. (2000). Self-esteem, narcissism, and aggressions: Does violence result form low self-esteem or from threatened egotism? *Current Directions in Psychological Science, 9,* 26–29.

Baumeister, R. F., Campbell, J. D., Kreueger, J. I., & Vohs, K. D. (2003). Does high self-esteem cause better performance, interpersonal success, happiness, or healthier lifestyles? *Psychological Science in the Public Interst, 4,* 1–44.

Baumeister, R. F., Campbell, J. D., Kreueger, J. I., & Vohs, K. D. (2005, January). Exploding the self-esteem myth. *Scientific American,* 84–91.

Baumrind, D. (1971). Current patterns of parental authority. *Developmental Psychology Monographs, 4*(1, pt. 2).

Baumrind, D. (1980). New directions in socialization research. *Psychological Bulletin, 35,* 639–652.

Baumrind, D., Larzelere, R. E., & Cowan, P. A. (2002). Ordinary physical punishment: Is it harmful? Comment on Gershoff (2002). *Psychological Bulletin, 128,* 580–589.

Baydar, N., & Brooks-Gunn, J. (1998). Profiles of grandmothers who help care for their grandchildren in the United States. *Family Relations, 47,* 385–393.

Bayley, N. (1969). *Manual for the Bayley Scales of infant development.* New York: The Psychological Corporation.

Bayley, N. (1993). *Bayley Scales of Infant Development (BSID-II)* (2nd ed.). San Antonio: Psychological Corporation.

Bayley, N., & Oden, M. (1955). The maintenance of intellectual abilit y in gifted adults. *Journal of Gerontology, 10,* 91–107.

Bazargan, M., Bazargain-Hejzai, S. & Hindman, D. W. (2010). Using the information-motivation behavioral model to predict sexual behavior among underserved minority youth. *Journal of School Health, 80,* 287–295.

Beach, B. A. (2003). Rural children's play in the natural environment. In D. E. Lytle (Ed.), *Play and educational theory and practice.* Westport, CT: Praeger Publishers/ Greenwood Publishing Group.

Beal, C. R. (1994). *Boys and girls: The development of gender roles.* New York: McGraw-Hill.

Beal, C. R., & Belgrad, S. L. (1990). The development of message evaluation skills in young children. *Child Development, 61,* 705–712.

Beale, E. A., Baile, W. F., & Aaron, J. (2005). Silence is not golden: Communicating with children dying from cancer. *Journal of Clinical Oncology, 23,* 3629–3631.

Beals, K., Impett, E., & Peplau, L. (2002). Lesbians in love: Why some relationships endure and others end. *Journal of Lesbian Studies, 6,* 53–63.

Bear, G. G., & Rys, G. S. (1994). Moral reasoning, classroom behavior, and sociometric status among elementary school children. *Developmental Psychology, 30,* 633–638.

Bearce, K., & Rovee-Collier, C. (2006). Repeated priming increases memory accessibility in infants. *Journal of Experimental Child Psychology, 93,* 357–376.

Beardslee, W. R., & Goldman, S. (2003, September 22). Living beyond sadness. *Newsweek,* p. 70.

Bearman, P., & Bruckner, H. (2004). *Study on teenage virginity pledge.* Paper presented at meeting of the National STD Prevention Conference, Philadelphia, PA.

Beauchaine, T. P. (2003). Taxometrics and developmental psychopathology. *Development and Psychopathology: Special Issue, 15,* 501–527.

Beaudoin, P., & Lachance, M. (2006). Determinants of adolescents' brand sensitivity to clothing. *Family & Consumer Sciences Research Journal, 34,* 312–331.

Becahy, R. (1992, August 3). AIDS epidemic. *Newsweek,* p. 49.

Beck, M. (1991, November 11). School days for seniors. *Newsweek,* pp. 60–65.

Beck, M. (1992, May 25). Menopause. *Newsweek,* pp. 71–79.

Beck, R. W., & Beck, S. W. (1989). The incidence of extended households among middle-aged black and white women. *Journal of Family Issues, 10,* 147–168.

Becker, B., & Luthar, S. (2007, March). Peer-perceived admiration and social preference: Contextual correlates of positive peer regard among suburban and urban adolescents. *Journal of Research on Adolescence, 17,* 117–144.

Becker, G., Beyene, Y., & Newsom, E. (2003). Creating continuity through mutual assistance: Intergenerational reciprocity in four ethnic groups. *Journals of Gerontology: Series B: Psychological Sciences & Social Sciences, 58B,* S151–S159.

Beckman, M. (2004, July 30). Neuroscience: Crime, culpability, and the adolescent brain. *Science,* 305, 596–599.

Becvar, D. S. (2000). Euthanasia decisions. In F. W. Kaslow, et al. (Eds.), *Handbook of couple and family forensics: A sourcebook for mental health and legal professionals.* New York: Wiley.

Beeger, S., Rieffe, C., & Terwogt, M. M. (2003). Theory of mind-based action in children from the autism spectrum. *Journal of Autism and Developmental Disorders, 33,* 479–487.

Beehr, T. A., Glazer, S., Nielson, N. L., & Farmer, S. J. (2000). Work and nonwork predictors of employees' retirement ages. *Journal of Vocational Behavior, 57,* 206–225.

Beets, M., Flay, B., Vuchinich, S., Li, K., Acock, A., & Snyder, F. (2009). Longitudinal patterns of binge drinking among first year college students with a history of tobacco use. *Drug and Alcohol Dependence, 103,* 1–8.

Begeny, J., & Martens, B. (2007). Inclusionary education in Italy: A literature review and call for more empirical research. *Remedial and Special Education, 28,* 80–94.

Begley, S. (1991, August 26). Choosing death. *Newsweek,* pp. 43–46.

Begley, S. (1995, July 10). Deliver, then depart. *Newsweek,* p. 62.

Begley, S. (1998a). Homework. In M. L. Bote (Ed.), *How to help your child succeed in school.* (pp. 48–52) New York: Newsweek and Score.

Begley, S. (1998b, March 30). Homework doesn't help. *Newsweek, 131,* 50–51.

Begley, S. (1998c, December 28). Into the gene pool. (ethical aspects of genetic research) *Newsweek,* p. 68.

Begley, S. (1999a, March 15). Talking from hand to mouth. *Newsweek,* pp. 56–58.

Begley, S. (1999b, Spring/Summer). Understanding perimenopause. *Newsweek Special Issue,* 31–34.

Begley, S. (2000). Wired for thought. *Newsweek Special Issue: Your Child,* 25–30.

Behrend, D. A. (1988). Overextensions in early language comprehension: Evidence from a signal detection approach. *Journal of Child Language, 15,* 63–75.

Beilin, H. (1996). Mind and meaning: Piaget and Vygotsky on causal explanation. *Human Development, 39,* 277–286.

Beilin, H., & Pufall, P. (Eds.). (1992). *Piaget's theory: Prospects and possibilities.* Hillsdale, NJ: Erlbaum.

Belcher, J. R. (2003). Stepparenting: Creating and recreating families in America today. *Journal of Nervous & Mental Disease, 191,* 837–838.

Belkin, L. (1985, May 23). Parents weigh costs of children. *The New York Times,* p. A14.

Belkin, L. (1997, October 26). Pregnant with complications. *The New York Times Magazine,* pp. 54–68.

Belkin, L. (1999, July 25). Getting the girl. *The New York Times Magazine,* 26–35.

Belkin, L. (2004, September 12). The lessons of Classroom 506: What happens when a boy with cerebral palsy goes to kindergarten like all the other kids. *The New York Times Magazine,* 41–49.

Bell, A., & Weinberg, M. S. (1978). *Homosexuality: A study of diversities among men and women.* New York: Simon & Schuster.

Bell, E., Shouldice, M., & Levin, A. V. (2011). Abusive head trauma: A perpetrator confesses. *Child Abuse & Neglect, 35,* 74–77.

Bell, H., Pellis, S., & Kolb, B. (2009). Juvenile peer play experience and the development of the orbitofrontal and medial prefrontal cortices. *Behavioural Brain Research, 207,* 7–13.

Bell, I. P. (1989). The double standard: Age. In J. Freeman (Ed.), *Women: A feminist perspective* (4th ed.). Mountain View, CA: Mayfield.

Bell, J. Z. (1978). Disengagement versus engagement— A need for greater expectation. *Journal of American Geriatric Sociology, 26,* 89–95.

Bell, S. M., & Ainsworth, M. D. S. (1972). Infant crying and maternal responsiveness. *Child Development, 43,* 1171–1190.

Bella, D. (2006). *Singled out: How singles are stereotyped, stigmatized, and ignored, and still live happily every after.* New York: St. Martin's Press.

Belle, D. (1999). *The after-school lives of children: Alone and with others while parents work.* Mahwah, NJ: Erlbaum.

Bellezza, F. S., Six, L. S., & Phillips, D. S. (1992). A mnemonic for remembering long strings of digits. *Bulletin of the Psychonomic Society, 30,* 271–274.

Belluck, P. (2000, October 18). New advice for parents: Saying "That's great!" may not be. *The New York Times,* p. A14.

Belluck, P. (2005, March 13). With mayhem at home, they call a parent coach. *The New York Times,* pp. Al, A33.

Belmont, J. M. (1995). Discussion: A view from the empiricist's window. *Educational Psychologist, 30, Special Issue: Lev S. Vygotsky and contemporary educational psychology.* 99–102.

Belsky, J. (2006). Early child care and early child development: Major findings from the NICHD Study of Early Child Care. *European Journal of Developmental Psychology, 3,* 95–110.

Belsky, J. (2009). Classroom composition, childcare history and social development: Are childcare effects disappearing or spreading? *Social Development, 18,* 230–238.

Belsky, J., Fish, M., & Isabella, R. (1991). Continuity and discontinuity in infant negative and positive emotionality: Family antecedents and attachment consequences. *Developmental Psychology, 27,* 421–431.

Belsky, J., & Pluess, M. (2012). Differential susceptibility to long-term effects of quality of child care on externalizing behavior in adolescence? *International Journal of Behavioral Development, 36,* 2–10.

Belsky, J., & Rovine, M. (1988). Nonmaternal care in the first year of life and infant-parent attachment security. *Child Development, 59,* 157–167.

Belsky, J., Rovine, M., & Taylor, D. G. (1984). The Pennsylvania infant and family development project, III: The origins of individual differences in infant–mother attachment: Maternal and infant contributions. *Child Development, 55,* 718–728.

Belsky, J., Steinberg, L., & Walker, A. (1982). The ecology of day care: A critical review. *Child Development, 49,* 929–949.

Belsky, J., Vandell, D. L., Burchinal, M., Clarke-Stewart, A. K., McCartney, K., & Owen, M. T. (2007). Are there long-term effects of early child care? *Child Development, 78,* 188–193.

Bem, S. (1987). Gender schema theory and its implications for child development: Raising genderaschematic children in a gender-schematic society. In M. R. Walsh (Ed.), *The psychology of women: Ongoing debates.* New Haven, CT: Yale University Press.

Ben-Ari, A., & Livni, T. (2006). Motherhood is not a given thing: Experiences and constructed meanings of biological and nonbiological lesbian mothers. *Sex Roles, 54,* 521–531.

Benbow, C. P., Lubinski, D., & Hyde, J. S. (1997). Mathematics: Is biology the cause of gender differences in performance? In M. R. Walsh (Ed.), *Women men & gender: Ongoing debates* (pp. 271–287). New Haven, CT: Yale University Press.

Bender, D. G. (2004). Do Fourteenth Amendment considerations outweigh a potential state interest in mandating cochlear implantation for deaf children? *Journal of Deaf Studies & Deaf Education, 9,* 104–111.

Bendersky, M., & Lewis, M. (1998). Arousal modulation in cocaine-exposed infants. *Developmental Psychology, 34,* 555–564.

Benedict, H. (1979). Early lexical development: Comprehension and production. *Journal of Child Language, 6,* 183–200.

Benelli, B., Belacchi, C., Gini, G., & Lucangeli, D. (2006, February). To define means to say what you know about things: The development of definitional skills as metalinguistic acquisition. *Journal of Child Language, 33,* 71–97.

Benenson, J. F. (1994). Ages four to six years: Changes in the structures of play networks of boys and girls. *Merrill-Palmer Quarterly, 40,* 478–487.

Benenson, J. F., & Apostoleris, N. H. (1993, March). *Gender differences in group interaction in early childhood.* Paper presented at the biennial meeting of the Society for Research in Child Development, New Orleans, LA.

Bengston, V. L., Cutler, N. E., Mangen, D. J., & Marshall, V. W. (1985). Generations, cohorts, and relations between age groups. In R. H. Binstock & E. Shanas (Eds.), *Handbook of aging and the social sciences* (2nd ed.). New York: Van Nostrand Reinhold.

Bengtson, V. L., Acock, A. C., Allen, K. R., & Dilworth-Anderson, P. (Eds.). (2004) *Sourcebook of family theory and research.* Thousand Oaks, CA: Sage Publications.

Bengtson, V. L., & Schaie, K. W. (Eds.). (1999). *Handbook of theories of aging.* New York: Springer.

Benjamin, J., Ebstein, R. P., & Belmaker, R. H. (2002). Personality genetics, 2002. *Israel Journal of Psychiatry and Related Sciences, 39, Special Issue,* 271–279.

Benjet, C., & Kazdin, A. E. (2003). Spanking children: The controversies, findings and new directions. *Clinical Psychology Review, 23,* 197–224.

Benjuya, N., Melzer, I., & Kaplanski, J. (2004). Aging-induced shifts from a reliance on sensory input to muscle cocontraction during balanced standing. *Journal of Gerontology, Series A: Biological Sciences and Medical Sciences, 59,* 166–171.

Bennani, L., Allali, F., Rostom, S., Hmamouchi, I., Khazzani, H., El Mansouri, L., et al. (2009). Relationship between historical height loss and vertebral fractures in postmenopausal women. *Clinical Rheumatology, 28,* 1283–1289.

Bennett, A. (1992, October 14). Lori Schiller emerges from the torments of schizophrenia. *The Wall Street Journal,* pp. A1, A10.

Bennett, J. (2008, September 15). It's not just white girls. *Newsweek,* p. 96.

Ben-Porath, Y. (1991). Economic implications of human lifespan extension. In F. C. Ludwig (Ed.), *Lifespan extension: Consequences and open questions.* New York: Springer.

Benson, E. (2003, March). "Goo, gaa, grr?" *Monitor on Psychology,* 50–51.

Benson, H. (1993). The relaxation response. In D. Goleman & J. Guerin (Eds.), *Mind-body medicine: How to use your mind for better health.* Yonkers, NY: Consumer Reports Publications.

Benson, J. B., & Haith, M. M. (1995). Future-oriented processes: A foundation for planning behavior in infants and toddlers. *Infancia y Aprendizaje. No 69-70,* 127–140.

Bentley, E. (2007). *Adulthood: Developmental psychology*. New York: Routledge/Taylor & Francis Group.

Benton, S. A., Robertson, J. M., Tseng, W.-C., Newton, F. B., & Benton, S. L. (2003). Changes in counseling center client problems across 13 years. *Professional Psychology: Research and Practice, 34*, 66–72.

Berenbaum, S. A., & Bailey, J. M. (2003). Effects on gender identity of prenatal androgens and genital appearance: Evidence from girls with congenital adrenal hyperplasia. *Journal of Clinical Endocrinology and metabolism, 88*, 1102–1106.

Berenbaum, S. A., Bryk, K., & Beltz, A. M. (2012). Early androgen effects on spatial and mechanical abilities: Evidence from congenital adrenal hyperplasia. *Behavioral Neuroscience, 126*, 86–96.

Berenbaum, S. A., & Hines, M. (1992). Early androgens are related to sex-typed toy preferences. *Psychological Science, 3*, 202–206.

Berenbaum, S. A., & Snyder, E. (1995). Early hormonal influences on childhood sex-typed activity and playmate preferences: Implications for the development of sexual orientation. Special Issue: Sexual orientation and human development. *Developmental Psychology, 31*, 31–42.

Berenson, P. (2005). *Understand and treat alcoholism*. New York: Basic Books.

Bergeman, C., Chipuer, H., Plomin, R., Pedersen, N., McClearn, G., Nesselroade, J., et al. (1993). Genetic and environmental effects on openness to experience, agreeableness, and conscientiousness: An adoption/twin study. *Journal of Personality, 61*, 159–179.

Bergen, H., Martin, G., & Richardson, A. (2003). Sexual abuse and suicidal behavior: A model constructed from a large community sample of adolescents. *Journal of the American Academy of Child & Adolescent Psychiatry, 42*, 1301–1309.

Berger, L. (2000, April 11). What children do when home and alone. *New York Times*, p. F8.

Bergeson, T. R., Pisoni, D. B., & Davis, R. A. (2005). Development of audiovisual comprehension skills in prelingually deaf children with cochlear implants. *Ear and Hearing, 26*, 149–156.

Bergman, A., Blom, I., & Polyak, D. (2012). Attachment and separation-individuation: Two ways of looking at the mother/infant relationship. In S. Akhtar (Eds.), *The mother and her child: Clinical aspects of attachment, separation, and loss*. Lanham, MD: Jason Aronson.

Bergmann, R. L., Bergman, K. E., & Dudenhausen, J. W. (2008). Undernutrition and growth restriction in pregnancy. *Nestle Nutritional Workshop Series; Pediatrics Program, 61*, 1030–1121.

Bergstrom, M. J., & Holmes, M. E. (2000). Lay theories of successful aging after the death of a spouse: A network text analysis of bereavement advice. *Health Communication, 12*, 377–406.

Berigan, T. R., & Deagle, E. A., III. (1999). Treatment of smokeless tobacco addiction with bupropion and behavior modification. *Jama: Journal of the American Medical Association, 281*, 233.

Berk, L. E., & Spuhl, S. T. (1995). Maternal interaction, private speech, and task performance in preschool children. *Early Childhood Research Quarterly, 10*, 145–169.

Berkman, R. (Ed.). (2006). *Handbook of social work in health and aging*. New York: Oxford University Press.

Berko, J. (1958). The child's learning of English morphology. *Word, 14*, 150–177.

Berkowitz, L. (1989). Frustration-aggression hypothesis: Examination and reformulation. *Psychological Bulletin, 106*, 59–73.

Berkowitz, L. (1990). On the formation and regulation of anger and aggression: A cognitive-neoassociationistic analysis. *American Psychologist, 45*, 494–503.

Berkowitz, L. (1993). *Aggression: Its causes, consequences, and control*. New York: McGraw-Hill.

Berlin, L., Cassidy, J., & Appleyard, K. (2008). The influence of early attachments on other relationships.

Handbook of attachment: Theory, research, and clinical applications (2nd ed., pp. 333–347). New York: Guilford Press.

Berman, A. L., & Jobes, D. A. (1991). *Adolescent suicide: Assessment and intervention*. Washington, DC: American Psychological Association.

Bernal, M. E. (1994, August). *Ethnic identity of Mexican-American children*. Address at the annual meeting of the American Psychological Association, Los Angeles, CA.

Bernal, M. E., & Knight, G. P.(1997). *Ethnic identity: Formation and transmission among Hispanics and other minorities*. Albany: State University of New York Press.

Bernard, J. (1982). *The future of marriage*. New Haven, CT: Yale University Press.

Berndt, T. J. (1999). Friends' influence on students' adjustment to school. *Educational Psychologist, 34*, 15–28.

Berndt, T. J. (2002). Friendship quality and social development. *Current Directions in Psychological Science, 11*, 7–10.

Bernier, A., & Meins, E. (2008). A threshold approach to understanding the origins of attachment disorganization. *Developmental Psychology, 44*, 969–982.

Bernstein, N. (2004, March 7). Behind fall in pregnancy, a new teenage culture of restraint. *The New York Times*, pp. 1, 20.

Berrick, J. D. (1998). When children cannot remain home: Foster family care and kinship care. *Future of Children, 8*, 72–87.

Berry, G. L. (2003). Developing children and multicultural attitudes: The systemic psychosocial influences of television portrayals in a multimedia society. *Cultural Diversity and Ethnic Minority Psychology, 9*, 360–366.

Berry, J. W., Poortinga, Y. H., Segall, M. H., & Dasen, P. (1992). *Cross-cultural psychology: Research and application*. New York: Cambridge University Press.

Berscheid, E. (1985). Interpersonal attraction. In G. Lindzey & E. Aronson (Eds.), *Handbook of social psychology* (3rd ed.). New York: Random House.

Berscheid, E. (2006). Searching for the Meaning of "Love." *The new psychology of love* (pp. 171–183). New Haven, CT: Yale University Press.

Berscheid, E., & Walster, E. (1974a). Physical attractiveness. In G. Lindzey & E. Aronson (Eds.), *Handbook of social psychology* (3rd ed.). New York: Random House.

Berscheid, E., & Walster, E. (1974b). Physical attractiveness. In L. Berkowitz (Ed.), *Advances in experimental social psychology* (Vol. 7). New York: Academic Press.

Berscheid, E., Walster, E., & Bohrnstedt, G. (1973). The happy American body: A survey report. *Psychology Today, 7*(6), 119–131.

Bersoff, D. M. N., & Ogden, D. W. (1991). APA Amicus Curiae briefs: Furthering lesbian and gay male civil rights. *American Psychologist, 46*, 950–956.

Berthier, N. E. (1996). Learning to reach: A mathematical model. *Developmental Psychology, 32*, 811–823.

Bertin, E., & Striano, T. (2006, April). The still-face response in newborn, 1.5-, and 3-month-old infants. *Infant Behavior & Development, 29*, 294–297.

Bertram, L., Blacker, D., Mullin, K., Keeney, D., Jones, J., Basu, S., et al. (2000, December 23). Evidence for genetic linkage of Alzheimer's disease to chromosome 10q. *Science, 290*, 2302–2303.

Besag, Valerie E. (2006). *Understanding girls' friendships, fights and feuds: A practical approach to girls' bullying*; Maidenhead, Berkshire: Open University Press/ McGraw-Hill Education.

Besharov, D. J., & West, A. (2002). African American marriage patterns. In A. Thernstrom & S. Thernstrom (Eds.), *Beyond the color line: New perspectives on race and ethnicity in America*. Stanford, CA: Hoover Institution Press.

Besseghini, V. H. (1997). Depression and suicide in children and adolescents. In G. Creastas, G. Mastorakos, & G. P. Choursos (Eds.), *Adolescent gynecology and

endocrinology. Basic and clinical aspects* (pp. 94–98). New York: New York Academy of Sciences.

Best, C. T. (1994). The emergence of native-language phonological influences in infants: A perceptual assimilation model. In J. C. Goodman & H. C. Nusbaum (Eds.), *The development of speech perception: The transition from speech sounds to spoken words*. Cambridge, MA: MIT Press.

Best, J., Behn, C., Poe, G., & Booth, V. (2007). Neuronal models for sleep-wake regulation and synaptic reorganization in the sleeping hippocampus. *Journal of Biological Rhythms, 22*, 220–232.

Betancourt, H., & Lopez, S. R. (1993). The study of culture, ethnicity, and race in American Psychology. *American Psychologist, 48*, 1586–1596.

Bettencourt, B. A., & Miller, N. (1996). Gender differences in aggression as a function of provocation: A meta-analysis. *Psychological Bulletin, 119*, 422–447.

Bhatia, J., Greer, F., & the Committee on Nutrition. (2008). Use of soy protein-based formulas in infant feeding. *Pediatrics, 121*, 1062–1068.

Bhushan, B., & Khan, S. (2006, September). Laterality and accident proneness: A study of locomotive drivers. *Laterality: Asymmetries of Body, Brain and Cognition, 11*(5), 395–404.

Bialystok, E., & Viswanathan, M. (2009). Components of executive control with advantages for bilingual children in two cultures. *Cognition, 112*, 494–500.

Bianchi, S. M., & Casper, L. M. (2000). American Families. *Population Bulletin, 55*(4).

Bianchi, S. M., & Spain, D. (1986). *American women in transition*. New York: Russell Sage Foundation.

Bickham, D. S., Wright, J. C., & Huston, A. C. (2000). Attention, comprehension and the educational influences of television. In D. G. Singer & J. L. Singer (Eds.), *Handbook of children and the media*. Thousand Oaks, CA: Sage.

Biddle, B. J. (2001). *Social class, poverty, and education*. London: Falmer Press.

Biehle, S. N., & Mickelson, K. D. (2012). First-time parents' expectations about the division of childcare and play. *Journal of Family Psychology, 26*, 36–45.

Bierman, K. L. (2004). *Peer rejection: Developmental processes and intervention strategies*. New York: Guilford Press.

Bierman, K. L., & Furman, W. (1984). The effects of social skills training and peer involvement on the social adjustment of preadolescents. *Child Development, 55*, 151–162.

Bierman, K., Torres, M., Domitrovich, C., Welsh, J., & Gest, S. (2009). Behavioral and cognitive readiness for school: Cross-domain associations for children attending Head Start. *Social Development, 18*, 305–323.

Biernat, M., & Wortman, C. B. (1991). Sharing of home responsibilities between professionally employed women and their husbands. *Journal of Personality and Social Psychology, 60*, 844–860.

Bigelow, A., & Rochat, P. (2006). Two-month-old infants' sensitivity to social contingency in mother–infant and stranger–infant interaction. *Infancy, 9*, 313–325.

Bigler, R. S., Jones, L. C., & Lobliner, D. B. (1997). Social categorization and the formation of intergroup attitudes in children. *Child Development, 68*, 530–543.

Bijeljac-Babic, R., Bertoncini, J., & Mehler, J. (1993). How do 4-day-old infants categorize multisyllabic utterances? *Developmental Psychology, 29*, 711–721.

Bing, E. D. (1983). *Dear Elizabeth Bing: We've had our baby*. New York: Pocket Books.

Bionna, R. (2006). *Coping with stress in a changing world*. New York: McGraw-Hill.

Birch, E. E., Garfield, S., Hoffman, D. R., Uauy, R., & Birch, D. G. (2000). A randomized controlled trail of early dietary supply of long-chain polyunsaturated fatty acids and mental development in term infants. *Developmental Medicine and Child Neurology, 42*, 174–181.

Bird, G., & Melville, K. (1994). *Families and intimate relationships*. New York: McGraw-Hill.

Birlouez-Aragon, I., & Tessier, F. (2003). Antioxidant vitamins and degenerative pathologies: A review of vitamin C. *Journal of Nutrition, Health & Aging, 7*, 103–109.

Biro, F., Striegel-Moore, R., Franko, D., Padgett, J., & Bean, J. (2006, October). Self-esteem in adolescent females. *Journal of Adolescent Health, 39*, 501–507.

Birren, J. E., Woods, A. M., & Williams, M. V. (1980). Behavioral slowing with age: Causes, organization and consequences. In L. W. Poon (Ed.), *Aging in the 1980s*. Washington, DC: American Psychological Association.

Birsner, P. (1991). *Mid-career job hunting*. New York: Simon & Schuster.

Bischof-Köhler, D. (2012). Empathy and self-recognition in phylogenetic and ontogenetic perspective. *Emotion Review, 4*, 40–48.

Bishop, A. (2008). Stress and depression among older residents in religious monasteries: Do friends and God matter? *International Journal of Aging & Human Development, 67*, 1–23.

Bishop, D. V. M., & Leonard, L. B. (Eds.). (2001). *Speech and language impairments in children: Causes, characteristics, intervention and outcome*. Philadelphia, PA: Psychology Press.

Bishop, D., Meyer, B., Schmidt, T., & Gray, B. (2009). Differential investment behavior between grandparents and grandchildren: The role of paternity uncertainty. *Evolutionary Psychology, 7*, 66–77.

Bishop, J. (2006, April). Euthanasia, efficiency, and the historical distinction between killing a patient and allowing a patient to die. *Journal of Medical Ethics, 32*, 220–224.

Bivens, J. A., & Berk, L. E. (1990). A longitudinal study of the development of elementary school children's private speech. *Merrill-Palmer Quarterly, 36*, 443–463.

Bjorklund, D. (2006). Mother knows best: Epigenetic inheritance, maternal effects, and the evolution of human intelligence. *Developmental Review, 26*, 213–242.

Bjorklund, D. F. (1997a). In search of a metatheory of cognitive development (or Piaget is dead and I don't feel so good myself). *Child Development, 68*, 144–148.

Bjorklund, D. F. (1997b). The role of immaturity in human development. *Psychological Bulletin, 122*, 153–169.

Bjorklund, D. F., & Ellis, B. (2005). Evolutionary psychology and child development: An emerging synthesis. In B. J. Ellis (Ed.), *Origins of the social mind: Evolutionary psychology and child development*. New York: Guilford Press.

Bjorklund, D. F., & Pellegrini, A. D. (2000). Child development and evolutionary psychology. *Child Development, 71*, 1687–1708.

Bjorklund, D. F., & Pellegrini, A. D. (2002). *The origins of human nature: Evolutionary developmental psychology*. Washington, DC: American Psychological Association.

Bjorklund, D. F., Schneider, W., Cassel, W. S., & Ashley, E. (1994). Training and extension of a memory strategy: Evidence of utilization deficiencies in the acquisition of an organizational strategy in high- and low-IQ children. *Child Development, 65*, 951–965.

Black, J. E., & Greenough, W. T. (1986). Induction of pattern in neural structure by experience: Implication for cognitive development. In M. E. Lamb, A. L. Brown, & B. Rogoff (Eds.), *Advances in developmental psychology* (Vol. 4). Hillsdale, NJ: Erlbaum.

Black, K. (2002). Associations between adolescent–mother and adolescent–best friend interactions. *Adolescence, 37*, 235–253.

Black, M. M., & Matula, K. (1999). *Essentials of Bayley Scales of Infant Development II assessment*. New York: Wiley.

Black, P. H., & Barbutt, L. D. (2002). Stress, inflammation and cardiovascular disease. *Journal of Psychosomatic Research, 52*, 1–23.

Blaga, O., Shaddy, D., Anderson, C., Kannass, K., Little, T., & Colombo, J. (2009). Structure and continuity of intellectual development in early childhood. *Intelligence, 37*, 106–113.

Blaine, B. (2007). *Understanding the psychology of diversity*. Thousand Oaks, CA: Sage Publications, Inc.

Blaine, B. E., Rodman, J., & Newman, J. M. (2007). Weight loss treatment and psychological well-being: A review and meta-analysis. *Journal of Health Psychology, 12*, 66–82.

Blair, C., Knipe, H., Cummings, E., Baker, D., Gamson, D., Eslinger, P., et al. (2007). A developmental neuroscience approach to the study of school readiness. In *School readiness and the transition to kindergarten in the era of accountability*. Baltimore, MD: Paul H Brookes Publishing.

Blair, P., Sidebotham, P., Berry, P., Evans, M., & Fleming, P. (2006). Major epidemiological changes in sudden infant death syndrome: A 20-year population-based study in the UK. *Lancet, 367*, 314–319.

Blair, S., & Haskell, W. (2006). Objectively measured physical activity and mortality in older adults. *JAMA: Journal of the American Medical Association, 296*, 216–218.

Blair, S. N., Kohl, H. W., Paffenberger, R. S., Clark, D. G., Cooper, K. H., & Gibbons, L. W. (1989). Physical fitness and all-cause mortality: A prospective study of healthy men and women. *Journal of the American Medical Association, 262*, 2395–2401.

Blake, G., Velikonja, D., Pepper, V., Jilderda, I., & Georgiou, G. (2008). Evaluating an in-school injury prevention programme's effect on children's helmet wearing habits. *Brain Injury, 22*, 501–507.

Blake, J., & de Boysson-Bardies, B. (1992). Patterns in babbling: A cross-linguistic study. *Journal of Child Language, 19*, 51–74.

Blakemore, J. (2003). Children's beliefs about violating gender norms: Boys shouldn't look like girls, and girls shouldn't act like boys. *Sex Roles, 48*, 411–419.

Blakeslee, S. (1995, August 29). In brain's early growth, timetable may be crucial. *The New York Times*, pp. C1, C3.

Blanchard, F. A., Lilly, R., & Vaughn, L. A. (1991). Reducing the expresison of racial prejudice. *Psychological Science, 2*, 101–105.

Blank, M., & White, S. J. (1999). Activating the zone of proximal development in school: Obstacles and solutions. In P. Llyod & C. Fernyhough (Eds.), *Lev Vygotsky: Critical assessments: The zone of proximal development* (Vol. III). New York: Routledge.

Blanton, H., & Burkley, M. (2008). Deviance regulation theory: Applications to adolescent social influence. *Understanding peer influence in children and adolescents*. New York: Guilford Press.

Blascovich, J. J., & Katkin, E. S. (Eds.). (1993). *Cardiovascular reactivity to psychological stress and disease*. Washington, DC: American Psychological Association.

Blasi, H., & Bjorklund, D. F. (2003). Evolutionary developmental psychology: A new tool for better understanding human ontogeny. *Human Development, 46*, 259–281.

Blasko, D. G., Kazmerski, V. A., Corty, E. W., & Kallgren, C. A. (1998). Courseware for observational research (COR): A new approach to teaching naturalistic observation. *Behavior Research Methods, Instruments, & Computers, 30*, 217–222.

Blass, E. M., Ganchrow, J. R., & Steiner, J. E. (1984). Classical conditioning in newborn humans 2–48 hours of age. *Infant Behavior and Development, 7*, 223–235.

Blau, Z. S. (1973). *Old age in a changing society*. New York: New Viewpoints.

Blazer, D. (1991). Suicide risk factors in the elderly: An epidemiological study. *Journal of Geriatric Psychiatry, 24*, 175–190.

Blendon, R. J., Altman, D. E., Benson, J., Brodie, M., James, M., & Chervinsky, G. (1995, October). The public and the welfare reform debate. *Archives of Pediatric Adolescent Medicine, 149*, 1065–1069.

Blennow, K., & Vanmechelen, E. (2003). CSF markers for pathogenic processes in Alzheimer's disease: Diagnostic implications and use in clinical neurochemistry. *Brain Research Bulletin, 61*, 235–242.

Blewitt, P., Rump, K., Shealy, S., & Cook, S. (2009). Shared book reading: When and how questions affect young children's word learning. *Journal of Educational Psychology, 101*.

Bloch, H. (1989). On early coordinations of children and their future. In A. de Ribaupierre (Ed.), *Transition mechanisms in child development: The longitudinal perspective* (pp. 259–282). New York: Cambridge University Press.

Block, J. S., Weinstein, J., & Seitz, M. (2005). School and parent partnerships in the preschool years. In D. Zager (Ed.), *Autism spectrum disorders: Identification, education, and treatment* (3rd ed.). Mahwah, NJ: Erlbaum.

Blomqvist, Y., & Nyqvist, K. (2011). Swedish mothers' experience of continuous Kangaroo Mother Care. *Journal of Clinical Nursing, 20*, 1472–1480.

Bloom, C., & Lamkin, D. (2006). The Olympian struggle to remember the cranial nerves: Mnemonics and student success. *Teaching of Psychology, 33*, 128–129.

Bloom, L. (1993). *The transition from infancy to language: Acquiring the power of expression*. New York: Cambridge University Press.

Bloss, C. S., Schork, N.-J., & Topol E. J. (2011). Effect of direct-to-consumer genomewide profiling to assess disease risk. *The New England Journal of Medicine, 364*, 524–534.

Blount, B. G. (1982). Culture and the language of socialization: Parental speech. In D. A. Wagner & H. W. Stevenson (Eds.), *Cultural perspectives on child development*. San Francisco: Freeman.

Bluebond-Langner, M. (1977). Meanings of death to children. In H. Feifel (Ed.), *New meanings of death*. New York: McGraw-Hill.

Bluebond-Langner, M. (1980). *The private worlds of dying children*. Princeton, NJ: Princeton University Press.

Bluebond-Langner, M. (2000). *In the shadow of illness*. Princeton, NJ: Princeton University Press.

Bluemke, M., Friedrich, M., & Zumbach, J. (2010). The influence of violent and nonviolent computer games on implicit measures of aggressiveness. *Aggressive Behavior, 36*, 1–13.

Blum, D. (2002). *Love at Goon Park: Harry Harlow and the science of affection*. New York: Perseus Publishing.

Blum, N. J., Taubman, B., & Nemeth, N. (2004). Why is toilet training occurring at older ages? A study of factors associated with later training. *Journal of Pediatrics, 145*, 107–111.

Blumberg, B. D., Lewis, M. J., & Susman, E. J. (1984). Adolescence: A time of transition. In M. G. Eisenberg, L. C. Sutkin, & M. A. Jansen (Eds.), *Chronic illness and disability through the life span: Effects on self and family*. New York: Springer.

Blumenfield, M., Levy, N. B., & Kaplan, D. (1979). The wish to be informed of a fatal illness. *Omega, 9*, 323–326.

Blumenshine, P. M., Egerter, S. A., Libet, M. L., & Braveman, P. A. (2011). Father's education: An independent marker of risk for preterm birth. *Maternal and Child Health Journal, 15*, 60–67.

Blumenthal, S. (2000). Developmental aspects of violence and the institutional response. *Criminal Behaviour & Mental Health, 10*, 185–198.

Blumstein, P., & Schwartz, P. (1989). *American couples: Money, work, sex*. New York: Morrow.

Blundon, J., & Schaefer, C. (2006). The role of parent–child play in children's development. *Psychology and Education: An Interdisciplinary Journal, 43,* 1–10.

Blustein, D. L., & Palladino, D. E. (1991). Self and identity in late adolescence: A theoretical and empirical integration. *Journal of Adolescent Research, 6,* 437–453.

Boag, S. (2011). Freud and free will: Fact, fantasy, and philosophy. *Psyccritiques, 56,* 88–93.

Boatella-Costa, E., Costas-Moragas, C., Botet-Mussons, F., Fornieles-Deu, A., & De Cáceres-Zurita, M. (2007). Behavioral gender differences in the neonatal period according to the Brazelton scale. *Early Human Development, 83,* 91–97.

Boath, E. H., Pryce, A. J., & Cox, J. L. (1998). Postnatal depression: The impact on the family. *Journal of Reproductive & Infant Psychology, 16,* 199–203.

Bober, S., Humphry, R., & Carswell, H. (2001). Toddlers' persistence in the emerging occupations of functional play and self-feeding. *American Journal of Occupational Therapy, 55,* 369–376.

Bochner, S. (1996). The learning strategies of bilingual versus monolingual students. *British Journal of Educational Psychology, 66,* 83–93.

Bodell, L. P., Smith, A. R., Holm-Denoma, J. M., Gordon, K. H., & Joiner, T. E. (2011). The impact of perceived social support and negative life events on bulimic symptoms. *Eating Behaviors, 12,* 44–48.

Boden, M. A. (1994). *What is creativity?* Cambridge, MA: MIT Press.

Boden, M. A. (1996). *Creativity.* San Diego, CA: Academic Press.

Bodensteiner, J. B., & Schaefer, G. B. (1995). Evaluation of the patient with idiopathic mental retardation. *Journal of Neuropsychiatry and Clinical Neurosciences, 7,* 361–370.

Bodnar, A. G., Ouellette, M., Frolkis, M., Holt, S. E., Chiu, C. P., Morin, G. B., et al. (1998, January 16). Extension of life-span by introduction of telomerase into normal human cells. *Science, 279,* 349–352.

Boehmer, U., Linde, R., & Freund, K. M. (2005). Sexual minority women's coping and psychological adjustment after a diagnosis of breast cancer. *Journal of Women's Health, 14,* 213–224.

Boerner, K., Wortman, C. B., & Bonanno, G. A. (2005). Resilient or at risk? A 4-year study of older adults who initially showed high or low distress following conjugal loss. *Journal of Gerontology, B, Psychological Sciences and Social Sciences, 60,* P67–P73.

Bogatz, G. A., & Ball, S. (1972). *The second year of Sesame Street: A continuing evaluation.* Princeton, NJ: Educational Testing Service.

Bogenschneider, K., Wu, M.-Y., Raffaelli, M., & Tsay, J. C. (1998). Parent influences on adolescent peer orientation and substance use: The interface of parenting practices and values. *Child Development, 69,* 1672–1688.

Bogle, K. A. (2008). "Hooking Up": What educators need to know. *The Chronicle of Higher Education, 54,* p. A32.

Bohlmeijer, E., Roemer, M., Cuijpers, P., & Smit, F. (2007). The effects of reminiscence on psychological well-being in order adults: A meta-analysis. *Aging & Mental Health, 11.*

Bohlmeijer, E., Smit, F., & Cuijpers, P. (2003). Effects of reminiscence and life review on late-life depression: A meta-analysis. *International Journal of Geriatric Psychiatry, 18,* 1088–1094.

Bohlmeijer, E., Westerhof, G., & de Jong, M. (2008). The effects of integrative reminiscence on meaning in life: Results of a quasi-experimental study. *Aging & Mental Health, 12,* 639–646.

Bohn, A., & Berntsen, D. (2011). The reminiscence bump reconsidered: Children's prospective life stories show a bump in young adulthood. *Psychological Science, 22,* 197–202.

Boismier, J. D. (1977). Visual stimulation and wake-sleep behavior in human neonates. *Developmental Psychology, 10,* 219–227.

Bolger, N., Foster, M., Vinokur, A. D., & Ng, R. (1996). Close relationships and adjustments to a life crisis: The case of breast cancer. *Journal of Personality and Social Psychology, 70,* 283–294.

Bonanno, G. A. (2004). Loss, trauma, and human resilience: Have we underestimated the human capacity to thrive after extremely aversive events? *American Psychologist, 59,* 20–28.

Bonanno, G. A. (2009). *The other side of sadness.* New York: Basic Books.

Bonanno, G. A., Galea, S., Bucciarelli, A., & Vlahov, D. (2006). Psychological resilience after disaster: New York City in the aftermath of the September 11th terrorist attack. *Psychological Science, 17,* 181–186.

Bonanno, G. A., & Mancini, A. (2007, February). The human capacity to thrive in the face of potential trauma. *Pediatrics, 121*(2), 369–375.

Bonanno, G. A., Moskowitz, J. T., Papa, A., & Folkman, S. (2005). Resilience to loss in bereaved spouses, bereaved parents, and bereaved gay men. *Journal of Personality and Social Psychology, 88,* 827–843.

Bonanno, G. A., Wortman, C., & Lehman, D. (2002). Resilience to loss and chronic grief: A prospective study from preloss to 18-months postloss. *Journal of Personality & Social Psychology, 83,* 1150–1164.

Bonanno, G. A., Wortman, C. B., Lehman, D. R., Tweed, R. G., Haring, M., Sonnega, J., et al. (2002). Resilience to loss and chronic grief: a prospective study from preloss to 18-months postloss. *Journal of Personality and Social Psychology, 83,* 1150–1164.

Bonke, B., Tibben, A., Lindhout, D., Clarke, A. J., & Stijnen, T. (2005). Genetic risk estimation by healthcare professionals. *Medical Journal of Autism, 182,* 116–118.

Bonnicksen, A. (2007). Oversight of assisted reproductive technologies: The last twenty years. *Reprogenetics: Law, policy, and ethical issues.* Baltimore, MD, US: Johns Hopkins University Press.

Bookheimer, S. Y., Strojwas, M. H., Cophen, M. S., Saunders, A. M., Pericak-Vance, M. A., Mazziotta, J. C., et al. (2000, August 17). Patterns of brain activation in people at risk for Alzheimer's disease. *New England Journal of Medicine, 343,* 450–456.

Bookstein, F. L., Sampson, P. D., Streissguth, A. P., & Barr, H. M. (1996). Exploiting redundant measurement of dose and developmental outcome: New methods from the behavioral teratology of alcohol. *Developmental Psychology, 32,* 404–415.

Booth, A., & Edwards, J. N. (1989). Transmission of marital and family quality over the generations: The effect of parental divorce and unhappiness. *Journal of Divorce, 13,* 41–58.

Booth, C., Kelly, J., & Spieker, S. (2003). Toddlers' attachment security to child-care providers: The Safe and Secure Scale. *Early Education & Development, 14,* 83–100.

Booth, W. (1987, October 2). Big Brother is counting your keystrokes. *Science, 238,* 17.

Bootzin, R. R., Manber, R., Perlis, M. L., Salvio, M., & Wyatt, J. K. (1993). Sleep disorders. In P. B. Sutker & H. E. Adams (Eds.), *Comprehensive handbook of psychopathology* (2nd ed.). New York: Plenum.

Bor, W., & Bor, W. (2004). Prevention and treatment of childhood and adolescent aggression and antisocial behaviour: A selective review. *Australian & New Zealand Journal of Psychiatry, 38,* 373–380.

Borden, M. E. (1998). *Smart start: The parents' complete guide to preschool education.* New York: Facts on File.

Boren, A. N., Moum, T., Bodtker, A. S., & Ekebert, O. (2005). Reasons for induced abortion and their relation to women's emotional distress: A prospective, two-year follow-up study. *General Hospital Psychiatry, 27,* 36–43.

Borgatta, E. F. (1991). Age discrimination issues. *Research on Aging, 13,* 476–484.

Borland, M. V., & Howsen, R. M. (2003). An examination of the effect of elementary school size on student academic achievement. *International Review of Education, 49,* 463–474.

Bornstein, M. H. (1989). Sensitive periods in development: Structural characteristics and causal interpretations. *Psychological Bulletin, 105,* 179–197.

Bornstein, M. H. (2000). Infant into conversant: Language and nonlanguage processes in developing early communication. In N. Budwig & I. C. Uzgiris (Eds.), *Communication: An arena of development.* Westport, CT: Ablex Publishing.

Bornstein, M. H., & Arterberry, M. (2003). Recognition, discrimination and categorization of smiling by 5-month-old infants. *Developmental Science, 6,* 585–599.

Bornstein, M. H., & Bradley, R. H. (2003). *Socioeconomic status, parenting, and child development.* Mahwah, NJ: Lawrence Erlbaum.

Bornstein, M. H., Cote, L., & Maital, S. (2004). Cross-linguistic analysis of vocabulary in young children: Spanish, Dutch, French, Hebrew, Italian, Korean, and American English. *Child Development, 75,* 1115–1139.

Bornstein, M. H., Haynes, O. M., O'Reilly, A. W., & Painter, K. M. (1996). Solitary and collaborative pretense play in early childhood: Sources of individual variation in the development of representational competence. *Child Development, 67,* 2910–2929.

Bornstein, M. H., & Lamb, M. E. (1992a). *Development in infancy: An introduction.* New York: McGraw-Hill.

Bornstein, M. H., & Lamb, M. E. (1992b). *Developmental psychology: An advanced textbook.* Hillsdale, NJ: Erlbaum.

Bornstein, M. H., & Lamb, M. E. (Eds.). (2005). *Developmental science.* Mahwah, NJ: Lawrence Erlbaum Associates.

Bornstein, M. H., & Putnik, D. L. (2012). Stability of language in childhood: A multiage, multidomain, multimeasure, and multisource study. *Developmental Psychology, 48,* 477–491.

Bornstein, M., Putnick, D., Heslington, M., Gini, M., Suwalsky, J., Venuti, P., et al. (2008). Mother-child emotional availability in ecological perspective: Three countries, two regions, two genders. *Developmental Psychology, 44,* 666–680.

Bornstein, M. H., Putnick, D. L., Suwalsky, T. D., & Gini, M. (2006). Maternal chronological age, prenatal and perinatal history, social support, and parenting of infants. *Child Development, 77,* 875–892.

Bornstein, M. H., & Sigman, M. D. (1986). Continuity in mental development from infancy. *Child Development, 57,* 251–274.

Bornstein, M. H., & Tamis-LeMonda, C. S. (1989). Maternal responsiveness and cognitive development in children. In M. H. Bornstein (Ed.), *Maternal responsiveness: Characteristics and consequences* (pp. 49–61). San Francisco: Jossey-Bass.

Borse, N. N., Gilchrist, J., Dellinger. A. M., Rudd, R. A., Ballesteros, M. F., & Sleet, D. A. (2008). *CDC Childhood Injury Report: Patterns of unintentional injuries among 0 -19 year olds in the United States, 2000–2006.* Atlanta, GA: Centers for Disease Control and Prevention, National Center for Injury Prevention and Control.

Boruch, R. F. (1998). Randomized controlled experiments for evaluation and planning. In L. Bickman & D. J. Rog (Eds.), *Handbook of applied social research methods* (pp. 161–191). Thousand Oaks, CA: Sage.

Bos, A., Muris, P., Mulkens, S., & Schaalma, H. (2006). Changing self-esteem in children and adolescents: A roadmap for future interventions. *Netherlands Journal of Psychology, 62,* 26–32.

Bos, C. S., & Vaughn, S. S. (2005). *Strategies for teaching students with learning and behavior problems* (6th ed.). Boston: Allyn & Bacon.

Bos, H., Sandfort, T., de Bruyn, E., & Hakvoort, E. (2008). Same-sex attraction, social relationships, psychosocial functioning, and school performance in early adolescence. *Developmental Psychology, 44,* 59–68.

Bos, H., van Balen, F., & van den Boom, D. (2007, January). Child adjustment and parenting in planned lesbian-parent families. *American Journal of Orthopsychiatry, 77,* 38–48.

Boseley, S. (2008, July 24). Gates joins campaign to curb smoking in developing world: Foundation adds $125m to Bloomberg's $375m fund: Initiative to show health risks and push for bans. *The Guardian* (London), 21.

Boseovski, J. J. (2012). Trust in testimony about strangers: Young children prefer reliable informants who make positive attributions. *Journal of Experimental Child Psychology, 111,* 543–551.

Bostwick, J. (2006, February). Do SSRIs cause suicide in children? The evidence is underwhelming. *Journal of Clinical Psychology, 62*(2), 235–241.

Bosworth, K., Espelage, D. L., & Simon, T. R. (1999). Factors associated with bullying behavior in middle school students. *Journal of Early Adolescence, 19,* 341–362.

Botvin, G. J., Epstein, J. A., Schinke, S. P., & Diaz, T. (1994). Predictors of cigarette smoking among inner-city minority youth. *Journal of Developmental and Behavioral Pediatrics, 15,* 67–73.

Bouchard, C., Tremblay, A., Despres, J. P., Nadeau, A., Lupien, P. J., Theriault, G., et al. (1990). The response to long-term overfeeding in identical twins. *New England Journal of Medicine, 322,* 1477–1482.

Bouchard, T. J., Jr. (1994, June 17). Genes, environment, and personality. *Science, 264,* 1700–1701.

Bouchard, T. J., Jr. (1997, September/October). Whenever the twain shall meet. *The Sciences,* 52–57.

Bouchard, T. J., Jr. (2004). Genetic influence on human psychological traits: A survey. *Current Directions in Psychological Science, 13,* 148–153.

Bouchard, T. J., Jr., Lykken, D. T., McGue, M., Segal, N. L., & Tellegen, A. (1990, October 12). Sources of human psychological differences: The Minnesota Study of twins reared apart. *Science, 250,* 223–228.

Bouchard, T. J., Jr., & McGue, M. (1981). Familial studies of intelligence: A review. *Science, 264,* 1700–1701.

Bouchard, T. J., Jr., & Pedersen, N. (1999). Twins reared apart: Nature's double experiment. In M. C. LaBuda, E. L. Grigorenko, et al. (Eds.), *On the way to individuality: Current methodological issues in behavioral genetics.* Commack, NY: Nova.

Boucher, N., Bairam, A., & Beaulac-Baillargeon, L. (2008). A new look at the neonate's clinical presentation after in utero exposure to antidepressants in late pregnancy. *Journal of Clinical Psychopharmacology, 28,* 334–339.

Boulton, M. J. (1999). Concurrent and longitudinal relations between children's playground behavior and social preference, victimization, and bullying. *Child Development, 70,* 944–954.

Boulton, M. J., & Smith, P. K. (1990). Affective bias in children's perceptions of dominance relationships. *Child Development, 61,* 221–229.

Bourne, V., & Todd, B. (2004). When left means right: An explanation of the left cradling bias in terms of right hemisphere specializations. *Developmental Science, 7,* 19–24.

Bourque, L. M. (2005). Leave no standardized test behind. In R. P. Phelps (Ed.), *Defending standardized testing.* Mahwah, NJ: Lawrence Erlbaum Associates.

Bourque, P., Pushkar, D., Bonneville, L., & Béland, F. (2005). Contextual effects on life satisfaction of older men and women. *Canadian Journal on Aging, 24,* 31–44.

Boutot, E., & Tincani, M. (Eds.). (2009). *Autism encyclopedia: The complete guide to autism spectrum disorders.* Waco, TX: Prufrock Press.

Bove, C., & Olson, C. (2006). Obesity in low-income rural women: Qualitative insights about physical activity and eating patterns. *Women & Health, 44,* 57–78.

Bowen, D. J., Kahl, K., Mann, S. L., & Peterson, A. V. (1991). Descriptions of early triers. *Addictive Behaviors, 16,* 95–101.

Bowen, N. K., & Bowen, G. L. (1999). Effects of crime and violence in neighborhoods and schools on the school behavior and performance of adolescents. *Journal of Adolescent Research, 14,* 319–342.

Bower, B. (1985). The left hand of math and verbal talent. *Science News, 127,* 263.

Bower, T. G. R. (1977). *A primer of infant development.* San Francisco: Freeman.

Bowers, A., Gabdois, S., & Cornock, B. (2003). Sports participation and self-esteem: Variations as a function of ender and gender role orientation. *Sex Roles, 49,* 47–58.

Bowers, K. E., & Thomas, P. (1995, August). Handle with care. *Harvard Health Letter,* pp. 6–7.

Bowker, A., Gabdois, S., & Cornock, B. (2003). Sports participation and self-esteem: Variations as a function of ender and gender role orientation. *Sex Roles, 49,* 47–58.

Bowlby, J. (1951). Maternal care and mental health. *Bulletin of the World Health Organization, 3,* 355–534.

Bowlby, R. (2007). Babies and toddlers in non-parental daycare can avoid stress and anxiety if they develop a lasting secondary attachment bond with one carer who is consistently accessible to them. *Attachment & Human Development, 9, Special issue: The life and work of John Bowlby: A tribute to his centenary,* 307–319.

Boyatzis, C. J., Mallis, M., & Leon, I. (1999). Effects of game type of children's gender-based peer preferences: A naturalistic observational study. *Sex Roles, 40,* 93–105.

Boyce, P., & Parker, G. (1989). Development of a scale to measure interpersonal sensitivity. *Australian & New Zealand Journal of Psychiatry, 23,* 341–351.

Boyd, G. M., Howard, J., & Zucker, R. A. (Eds.). (1995). *Alcohol problems among adolescents: Current directions in prevention research.* Hillsdale, NJ: Erlbaum.

Boylan, P. (1990). Induction of labor, complications of labor, and postmaturity. *Current Opinion in Obstetrics & Gynecology, 2,* 31–35.

Bozett, F. W. (1981). Gay fathers: Evolution of the gay-father identity. *American Journal of Orthopsychiatry, 51,* 552–559.

Bracey, J., Bamaca, M., & Umana-Taylor, A. (2004). Examining ethnic identity and self-esteem among biracial and monoracial adolescents. *Journal of Youth & Adolescence, 33,* 123–132.

Brackbill, Y. (1979). Obstetrical medication and infant behavior. In J. D. Osofsky (Ed.), *Handbook of infant development.* New York: Wiley.

Bracken, B., & Brown, E. (2006, June). Behavioral identification and assessment of gifted and talented students. *Journal of Psychoeducational Assessment, 24,* 112–122.

Bracken, B., & Lamprecht, M. (2003). Positive self-concept: An equal opportunity construct. *School Psychology Quarterly, 18,* 103–121.

Brackett, M., & Katulak, N. (2007). Emotional intelligence in the classroom: Skill-based training for teachers and students. *Applying emotional intelligence: A practitioner's guide* (pp. 1–27). New York: Psychology Press.

Braddick, O., & Atkinson, J. (2011). Development of human visual function. *Vision Research, 51,* 1588–1609.

Braddock, O. (1993). Orientation- and motionselective mechanisms in infants. In K. Simons (Ed.), *Early visual development: Normal and abnormal* (pp. 163–177). New York: Oxford University Press.

Bradley, C. L. (1997). Generativity-stagnation: Development of a status model. *Developmental Review, 17,* 262–290.

Bradley, R. H., & Caldwell, B. M. (1995). Caregiving and the regulation of child growth and development: Describing proximal aspects of caregiving systems. *Developmental Review, 15,* 38–85.

Bradley, R. H., & Corwyn, R. (2008). Infant temperament, parenting, and externalizing behavior in first grade: A test of the differential susceptibility hypoth-

esis. *Journal of Child Psychology and Psychiatry, 49,* 124–131. Retrieved from http://search.ebscohost.com.

Bradley, R. H., Whiteside, L., Mundfrom, D. J., Casey, P. H., Kelleher, K. J., & Pope, S. K. (1994). Early indications of resilience and their relation to experiences in the home environments of low birthweight, premature children living in poverty. *Child Development, 65,* 346–360.

Bradshaw, M., & Ellison, C. (2008). Do genetic factors influence religious life? Findings from a behavior genetic analysis of twin siblings. *Journal for the Scientific Study of Religion, 47,* 529–544.

Brady, L. S. (1995, January 29). Asia Linn and Chris Applebaum. *The New York Times,* p. 47.

Brady, S. (2007). Young adults' media use and attitudes toward interpersonal and institutional forms of aggression. *Aggressive Behavior, 33,* 519–525.

Brainerd, C. (2003). Jean Piaget, learning research, and American education. In B. Zimmerman (Ed.), *Educational psychology: A century of contributions.* Mahwah, NJ: Lawrence Erlbaum Associates.

Brainerd, C. J., Reyna, V. F., & Brandse, E. (1995). Are children's false memories more persistent than their true memories? *Psychological Science, 6,* 359–364.

Brandhorst, A. R. (2011). Multicultural education reform movement. In S. Totten, J. E. Pedersen, S. Totten, & J. E. Pedersen (Eds.), *Teaching and studying social issues: Major programs and approaches.* Greenwich, CT: IAP Information Age Publishing.

Brandis, J. (2010). *$100,000 Purpose Prize winner.* Video download at http://www.purposeprize.org/video/yt_video.cfm?candidateID=3779.

Branje, S. J. T., van Lieshout, C. F. M., van Aken, M. A. G., & Haselager, G. J. T. (2004). Perceived support in sibling relationships and adolescent adjustment. *Journal of Child Psychology and Psychiatry, 45,* 1385–1396.

Branstetter, E. (1969). The young child's response to hospitalization: Separation anxiety or lack of mothering care? *American Journal of Public Health, 59,* 92–97.

Brant, M. (2003, September 8). Log on and learn. *Newsweek,* p. E14.

Branta, C. F., Lerner, J. V., & Taylor, C. S. (Eds.). (1997). *Physical activity and youth sports: Social and moral issues.* Mahwah, NJ: Erlbaum.

Branum, A. (2006). Teen maternal age and very preterm birth of twins. *Maternal & Child Health Journal, 10,* 229–233.

Braun, K. L., Pietsch, J. H., & Blanchette, P. L. (Eds.). (2000). *Cultural issues in end-of-life decision making.* Thousand Oaks, CA: Sage Publications.

Bray, G. (2008). Causes of childhood obesity. *Obesity in childhood and adolescence, Vol 1: Medical, biological, and social issues* (pp. 25–57). Westport, CT, US: Praeger Publishers/Greenwood Publishing Group.

Braza, F., Braza, P., Carreras, M. R., & Muñoz, J. M. (1997). Development of sex differences in preschool children: Social behavior during an academic year. *Psychological Reports, 80,* 179–188.

Brazelton, T. B. (1969). *Infants and mothers: Differences in development* (Rev. ed.) New York: Dell.

Brazelton, T. B. (1973). *The Neonatal Behavioral Assessment Scale.* Philadelphia: Lippincott.

Brazelton, T. B. (1983). *Infants and mothers: Differences in development* (Rev. ed.). New York: Dell.

Brazelton, T. B. (1990). Saving the bathwater. *Child Development, 61,* 1661–1671.

Brazelton, T. B. (1991). Discussion: Cultural attitudes and actions. In M. H. Bornstein (Ed.), *Cultural approaches to parenting.* Hillsdale, NJ: Erlbaum.

Brazelton, T. B. (1997). *Toilet training your child.* New York: Consumer Visions.

Brazelton, T. B., Christophersen, E. R., Frauman, A. C., Gorski, P. A., Poole, J. M., Stadtler, A. C., et al. (1999). Instruction, timeliness, and medical influences affecting toilet training. *Pediatrics, 103,* 1353–1358.

Brazelton, T. B., Nugent, J. K., & Lester, B. M. (1987). Neonatal Behavioral Assessment Scale. In J. D. Osofsky (Ed.), *Handbook of infant development* (2nd ed.). New York: Wiley.

Brazelton, T. B., & Sparrow, J. D. (2003). *Discipline: The Brazelton way.* New York: Perseus.

Brazelton, T. B., & Sparrow, J. D. (2004). *Toilet training: The Brazelton way.* Cambridge, MA: DaCapo Press.

Brazier, A., & Duff, A. J. A. (2005). Editorial: Working with childhood chronic illness: Psychosocial approaches. *Clinical Child Psychology & Psychiatry, 10,* 5–8.

Brecher, E. M., & the Editors of Consumer Reports Books. (1984). *Love, sex, and aging.* Mount Vernon, New York: Consumers Union.

Bredekamp, S. (Ed.). (1989). *Developmentally appropriate practice in early childhood programs serving children from birth through age 8.* Washington, DC: National Association for the Education of Young Children.

Bredesen, D. (2009). Neurodegeneration in Alzheimer's disease: Caspases and synaptic element interdependence. *Molecular Neurodegeneration, 4,* 52–59.

Breedlove, G. (2005). Perceptions of social support from pregnant and parenting teens using community-based doulas. *Journal of Perinatal Education, 14,* 15–22.

Breen, F., Plomin, R., & Wardle, J. (2006). Heritability of food preferences in young children. *Physiology & Behavior, 88,* 443–447.

Breheny, M., & Stephens, C. (2003). Healthy living and keeping busy: A discourse analysis of mid-aged women's attributions for menopausal experience. *Journal of Language & Social Psychology, 22,* 169–189.

Brehm, K. (2003). Lessons to be learned at the end of the day. *School Psychology Quarterly, 18,* 88–95.

Brehm, S. S. (1992). *Intimate relationships* (2nd ed.). New York: McGraw-Hill.

Bremmer, J. D. (2003). Long-term effects of childhood abuse on brain and neurobiology. *Child Adolescent Psychiatric Clinics of North America, 12,* 271–292.

Bremner, G., & Fogel, A. (Eds.). (2004). *Blackwell handbook of infant development.* Malden, MA: Blackwell Publishers.

Brennan, K. A., & Shaver, P. R. (1995). Dimensions of adult attachment, affect regulation, and romantic relationship functioning. *Personality and Social Psychology Bulletin, 21,* 267–283.

Brent, D. A., Perper, J. A., Moritz, G., & Liotus, L. (1994). Familial risk factors for adolescent suicide: A case-control study. *Acta Psychiatrica Scandinavica, 89,* 52–58.

Brescia, F. J., Sadof, M., & Barstow, J. (1984). Retrospective analysis of a home care hospice program. *Omega, 15,* 37–44.

Breslin, M. J., & Lewis, C. A. (2008). Theoretical models of the nature of prayer and health. *Mental Health, Religion & Culture, Special issue, 11,* 9–21.

Brick, J. (2008). Medical consequences of acute and chronic alcohol abuse. *Handbook of the medical consequences of alcohol and drug abuse* (2nd ed.). New York: The Haworth Press/Taylor and Francis Group.

Brick, M. (2009, February 24). At 44, a running career in ascent. *The New York Times,* p. B10.

Bridges, J. S. (1993). Pink or blue: Gender-stereotypic perceptions of infants as conveyed by birth congratulations cards. *Psychology of Women Quarterly, 17,* 193–205.

Bridgett, D., Gartstein, M., Putnam, S., McKay, T., Iddins, E., Robertson, C., et al. (2009). Maternal and contextual influences and the effect of temperament development during infancy on parenting in toddlerhood. *Infant Behavior & Development, 32,* 103–116.

Briere, J. N., Berliner, L., Bulkley, J., Jenny, C., & Reid, T. (Eds.). (1996). *The APSAC handbook on child maltreatment.* Thousand Oaks, CA: Sage.

Brislin, R. (1993). *Understanding culture's influence on behavior.* Fort Worth, TX: Harcourt Brace Jovanovich.

Brock, A. M. (1991). Economics of aging. In E. M. Baines (Ed.), *Perspectives on gerontological nursing.* Newbury Park, CA: Sage.

Brock, C., Lapp, D., Flood, J., Fisher, D., & Han, K. (2007, July). Does homework matter? An investigation of teacher perceptions about homework practices for children from nondominant backgrounds. *Urban Education, 42*(4), 349–372.

Brock, J. (2011). Commentary: Complementary approaches to the developmental cognitive neuroscience of autism—Reflections on Pelphrey et al. (2011). *Journal of Child Psychology and Psychiatry, 52,* 645–646.

Brockington, I. F. (1992). Disorders specific to the puerperium. *International Journal of Mental Health, 21,* 41–52.

Brody, J. (1994a, February 2). Fitness and the fetus: A turnabout in advice. *The New York Times,* p. C13.

Brody, J. E. (1994c, April 20). Making a strong case for antioxidants. *The New York Times,* p. B9.

Brody, J. E., & Benbow, C. P. (1987). Accelerative strategies: How effective are they for the gifted? *Gifted Child Quarterly, 3,* 105–110.

Brody, N. (1993). Intelligence and the behavioral genetics of personality. In R. Plomin & G. E. McClearn (Eds.), *Nature, nurture, and psychology.* Washington, DC: American Psychological Association.

Broen, A. N., Moum, T., Bodtker, A. S., & Ekeberg, O. (2005). Reasons for induced abortion and their relation to women's emotional distress: A prospective, two-year follow-up study. *General Hospital Psychiatry, 27,* 36–43.

Bromberger, J. T., & Matthews, K. A. (1994). Employment status and depressive symptoms in middle-aged women: A longitudinal investigation. *American Journal of Public Health, 84,* 202–206.

Bronfenbrenner, U. (1979). *The ecology of human development.* Cambridge, MA: Harvard University Press.

Bronfenbrenner, U. (1989). Ecological systems theory. In R. Vasta (Ed.), *Six theories of child development.* Greenwich, CT: JAI Press.

Bronfenbrenner, U. (2000). Ecological theory. In A. Kazdin (Ed.), *Encyclopedia of psychology.* Washington, DC, and New York: American Psychological Association/Oxford University Press.

Bronfenbrenner, U. (2002). Preparing a world for the infant in the twenty-first century: The research challenge. In J. Goes-Pedro, J. K. Nugent, J. G. Young, & T. B. Brazelton (Eds.), *The infant and family in the twenty-first century.* New York: Brunner-Routledge.

Bronfenbrenner, U., & Morris, P. (1998). The ecology of developmental processes. In W. Damon (Ed.), *Handbook of child psychology* (Vol. 1, 5th ed.). New York: Wiley.

Bronfenbrenner, U., & Morris, P. (2006). The Bioecological Model of Human Development. *Handbook of child psychology: Vol 1, Theoretical models of human development* (6th ed.). Hoboken, NJ: John Wiley & Sons Inc.

Bronson, P., & Merryman, A. (2009a). *NurtureShock: New thinking about children.* New York: Twelve.

Bronson, P., & Merryman, A. (2009b, September 14). See baby discriminate. *Newsweek,* p. 53.

Bronstein, P. (1999). Differences in mothers' and fathers' behaviors toward children: A cross-cultural comparison. In L. A. Peplau, et al. (Eds.), *Gender, culture, and ethnicity: Current research about women and men.* Mountain View, CA: Mayfield Publishing.

Bronstein, P. (2006). The family environment: Where gender role socialization begins. *Handbook of girls' and women's psychological health: Gender and well-being across the lifespan* (pp. 262–271). New York: Oxford University Press.

Brook, U., & Tepper, I. (1997). High school students' attitudes and knowledge of food consumption and body image: Implications for school-based education. *Patient Education & Counseling, 30,* 282–288.

Brooks, A. (2008). *Gross national happiness: Why happiness matters for America—and how we can get more of it.* New York: Basic Books.

Brooks, J., & Lewis, M. (1976). Infants' responses to strangers: Midget, adult, and child. *Child Development, 47,* 323–332.

Brooks-Gunn, J. (2003). Do you believe in magic?: What we can expect from early childhood intervention programs. *Social Policy Report, 17,* 3–15.

Brooks-Gunn, J., & Matthews, W. S. (1979). *He and she: How children develop their sex role identity.* Englewood Cliffs, NJ: Prentice-Hall.

Brooks-Gunn, J., Han, W. J., & Waldfogel, J. (2002). Maternal employment and child cognitive outcomes in the first three years of life: The NICHD study of early child care. *Child Development, 73,* 1052–1072.

Brooks-Gunn, J., Klebanov, P. K., & Duncan, G. J. (1996). Ethnic differences in children's intelligence test scores: Role of economic deprivation, home environment, and maternal characteristics. *Child Development, 67,* 396–408.

Brooks-Gunn, J., Petersen, A. C., & Compas, B. E. (1994). What role does biology play in childhood and adolescent depression? In I. M. Goodyear (Ed.), *Mood disorders in childhood and adolescence.* New York: Cambridge University Press.

Brooks-Gunn, J., & Reiter, E. (1990). The role of pubertal processes. In S. Feldman & G. Elliott (Eds.), *At the threshold: The developing adolescent.* Cambridge, MA: Harvard University Press.

Brotanek, J., Gosz, J., Weitzman, M., & Flores, G. (2007). Iron deficiency in early childhood in the United States: Risk factors and racial/ethnic disparities. *Pediatrics, 120,* 568–575.

Brown v. Board of Education of Topeka (1954). U.S. Supreme Court. Washington, DC.

Brown, A. L., & Ferrara, R. A. (1999). Diagnosing zones of proximal development. In P. Llyod, & C. Fernyhough (Eds.), *Lev Vygotsky: Critical assessments: The zone of proximal development* (Vol. III.) New York: Routledge.

Brown, B. (1990). Peer groups. In S. Feldman & G. Elliott (Eds.), *At the threshold: The developing adolescent.* Cambridge, MA: Harvard University Press.

Brown, B. B., & Klute, C. (2003). Friendships, cliques, and crowds. In G. R. Adams & M. D. Berzonsky (Eds.), *Blackwell handbook of adolescence.* Malden, MA: Blackwell Publishing.

Brown, B., Lohr, M., & Trujillo, C. (1983). *Adolescent peer group stereotypes, member conformity, and identity development.* Paper presented at the meeting of the Society for Research in Child Development, Detroit, MI.

Brown, C., Pikler, V., Lavish, L., Keune, K., & Hutto, C. (2008, January). Surviving childhood leukemia: Career, family, and future expectations. *Qualitative Health Research, 18*(1), 19–30.

Brown, G., McBride, B., Shin, N., & Bost, K. (2007). Parenting predictors of father-child attachment security: Interactive effects of father involvement and fathering quality. *Fathering, 5,* 197–219.

Brown, J. D. (1991). Staying fit and staying well: Physical fitness as a moderator of life stress. *Journal of Personality and Social Psychology, 60,* 368–375.

Brown, J. D. (1998). *The self.* New York: McGraw-Hill.

Brown, J. D., & McGill, K. L. (1989). The cost of good fortune: When positive life events produce negative health consequences. *Journal of Personality and Social Psychology, 57,* 1103–1110.

Brown, J. L. (1987). Hunger in the U.S. *Scientific American, 256*(2), 37–41.

Brown, J. L., & Pollitt, E. (1996, February). Malnutrition, poverty and intellectual development. *Scientific American,* 38–43.

Brown, J. V., Bakeman, R., Coles, C. D., Platzman, K. A., & Lynch, M. E. (2004). Prenatal cocaine exposure:

A comparison of 2-year-old children in prenatal and non-parental care. *Child Development, 75,* 1282–1295.

Brown, K. (1998). *Education, culture, and critical thinking.* Aldershot, England: Ashgate Publishing.

Brown, M. J. (2008). Childhood lead poisoning prevention: getting the job done by 2010. *Journal of Environmental Health,* 7056–7057.

Brown, R. (1973). *A first language.* Cambridge, MA: Harvard University Press.

Brown, R., & Fraser, C. (1963). The acquisition of syntax. In C. N. Cofer & B. Musgrave (Eds.), *Verbal behavior and learning: Problems and processes.* New York: McGraw-Hill.

Brown, S. (2003). Relationship quality dynamics of cohabitating unions. *Journal of Family Issues, 24,* 583–601.

Brown, S. (2006, March 3). A patient's story. Australian Doctor. Retrieved January 7, 2006 from LexisNexis Academic. http://www.australiandoctor.com.au/articles/93/0c03d093.asp?

Brown, W. M., Hines, M., & Fane, B. A. (2002). Masculinized finger length patterns in human males and females with congenital adrenal hyperplasia. *Hormones and Behavior, 42,* 380–386.

Browne, A. (1993). Violence against women by male partners: Prevalence, outcomes, and policy implications. *American Psychologist, 48,* 1077–1087.

Browne, B. A. (1998). Gender stereotypes in advertising on children's television in the 1990s: A cross-national analysis. *Journal of Advertising, 27,* 83–96.

Browne, K. (2006, March). Evolved sex differences and occupational segregation. *Journal of Organizational Behavior, 27,* 143–162.

Brownell, C. (1986). Convergent developments: Cognitive-developmental correlates of growth in infant/toddler peer skills. *Child Development, 57,* 275–286.

Brownell, C. A., Ramani, G. B., & Zerwas, S. (2006). Becoming a social partner with peers: Cooperation and social understanding in one- and two-year-olds. *Child Development, 77,* 803–821.

Brownell, K. D., & Rodin, J. (1994). The dieting maelstrom: Is it possible and advisable to lose weight? *American Psychologist, 49,* 781–791.

Browning, D. (2003). Pathos, paradox, and poetics: Grounded theory and the experience of bereavement. *Smith College Studies in Social Work, 73,* 325–336.

Brownlee, S. (2002, January 21). Too heavy, too young. *Time,* pp. 21–23.

Brownlee, S., Cook, G. G., & Hardigg, V. (1994, August 22). Tinkering with destiny. *U.S. News and World Report, 117,* 58–65+.

Brubaker, T. (1991). Families in later life: A burgeoning research area. In A. Booth (Ed.), *Contemporary families.* Minneapolis, MN: National Council on Family Relations.

Bruce, M. L., & Hoff, R. A. (1994). Social and physical health risk factors for first-onset major depressive disorder in a community sample. *Social Psychiatry and Psychiatric Epidemiology, 29,* 165–171.

Bruck, M., & Ceci, S. J. (1999). The suggestibility of children's memory. *Annual Review of Psychology, 50,* 419–439.

Bruck, M., & Ceci, S. J. (2004). Forensic developmental psychology: Unveiling four common misconceptions. *Current Directions in Psychological Science, 13,* 229–232.

Bruck, M., Ceci, S. J., & Francoeur, E. (2000). Children's use of anatomically detailed dolls to report genital touching in a medical examination: Developmental and gender comparisons. *Journal of Experimental Psychology: Applied, 6,* 74–83.

Bruck, M., Ceci, S. J., Francouer, E., & Renick, A. (1995). Anatomically detailed dolls do not facilitate preschoolers' reports of a pediatric examination involving genital touching. *Journal of Experimental Psychology: Applied, 1,* 95–109.

Bruck, M., Ceci, S. J., & Hembrooke, H. (1998). Reliability and credibility of young children's reports: From research to policy and practice. *American Psychologist, 53,* 136–151.

Brueggeman, I. (1999). Failure to meet ICPD goals will affect global stability, health of environment, and well-being, rights and potential of people. *Asian Forum News,* p. 8.

Brugman, G. (2006). *Wisdom and Aging.* Amsterdam, Netherlands: Elsevier.

Brune, C., & Woodward, A. (2007). Social cognition and social responsiveness in 10-month-old infants. *Journal of Cognition and Development, 8,* 133–158.

Bruner, J. S. (1981). Intention in the structure of action and interaction. In L. P. Lipsitt (Ed.), *Advances in infancy research* (Vol. 1). Norwood, NJ: Ablex.

Bruskas, D. (2008, May). Children in foster care: A vulnerable population at risk. *Journal of Child and Adolescent Psychiatric Nursing, 21*(2), 70–77.

Bryant, C. D. (Ed.). (2003). *Handbook of death and dying.* Thousand Oaks, CA: Sage Publications.

Bryant, J., & Bryant, J. A. (Eds.). (2001). *Television and the American family* (2nd ed.). Mahwah, NJ: Lawrence Erlbaum.

Bryant, J., & Bryant, J. (2003). Effects of entertainment televisual media on children. In E. Palmer & B.Young (Eds.), *The faces of televisual media: Teaching, violence, selling to children.* Mahwah, NJ: Lawrence Erlbaum Associates.

Bryden, P. J., Mayer, M. M., & Roy, E. A. (2011). Influences of task complexity, object location, and object type on hand selection in reaching in left and right-handed children and adults. *Developmental Psychobiology, 53,* 47–58.

Brzezinski, M. (2002, August 14). *CBS Evening News* [Television broadcast]. New York: WCBS.

Brzostek, T., Dekkers, W., Zalewski, Z., Januszewska, A., & Górkiewicz, M. (2008). Perception of palliative care and euthanasia among recently graduated and experienced nurses. *Nursing Ethics, 15,* 761–776.

Buchanan, A., Gentile, D. A., Nelson, D. A., Walsh, D. A., & Hensel, J. (2002, September 28). *What goes in must come out: Children's media violence consumption at home and aggressiveness at school.* Retrieved from http.www.mediafamily.org/research/reports/issbd.shtml.

Buchanan, C. M., Eccles, J. S., & Becker, J. B. (1992). Are adolescents the victims of raging hormones? Evidence for activational effects of hormones on moods and behavior at adolescence. *Psychological Bulletin, 111,* 62–107.

Buchanan, C. M., Maccoby, E. E., & Dornbusch, S. M. (1996). *Adolescents after divorce.* Cambridge, MA: Harvard University Press.

Buchmann, C., & DiPrete, T. (2006, August). The growing female advantage in college completion: The role of family background and academic achievement. *American Sociological Review, 7,* 515–541.

Buckingham, R., Kiernan, M., & Ainsworth, S. (2012). Fluid insight moderates the relationship between psychoticism and crystallized intelligence. *Personality and Individual Differences, 52,* 406–410.

Budd, K. (1999). The facts of life: Everything you wanted to know about sex (after 50). *Modern Maturity, 42,* 78.

Budris, J. (1998, April 26). Raising their children's children. *Boston Globe 55–Plus,* 8–9, 14–15.

Bugg, J., Zook, N., DeLosh, E., Davalos, D., & Davis, H. (2006, October). Age differences in fluid intelligence: Contributions of general slowing and frontal decline. *Brain and Cognition, 62,* 9–16.

Bukowski, W. M., Sippola, L. K., & Newcomb, A. F. (2000). Variations in patterns of attraction to same- and other-sex peers during early adolescence. *Developmental Psychology, 36,* 147–154.

Bull, M., & Durbin, D. (2008). Rear-facing car safety seats: Getting the message right. *Pediatrics, 121,* 619–620.

Bullinger, A. (1997). Sensorimotor function and its evolution. In J. Guimon (Ed.), *The body in psychotherapy* (pp. 25–29). Basil, Switzerland: Karger.

Bullock, J. (1988). Altering aggression in young children. *Early Childhood Education, 15,* 24–27.

Bullock, M. (1995, July/August). What's so special about a longitudinal study? *Psychological Science Agenda,* 9–10.

Bumpass, L., Sweet, J., & Martin, T. (1990). Changing patterns of remarriage. *Journal of Marriage and the Family, 52,* 747–756.

Bumpus, M. F., Crouter, A. C., & McHale, S. M. (2001). Parental autonomy granting during adolescence: Exploring gender differences in context. *Developmental Psychology, 37,* 163–173.

Burbach, J., & van der Zwaag, B. (2009). Contact in the genetics of autism and schizophrenia. *Trends in Neurosciences, 32,* 69–72.

Burbules, N. C., & Linn, M. C. (1988). Response to contradiction: Scientific reasoning during adolescence. *Journal of Educational Psychology, 80,* 67–75.

Burd, L., Cotsonas-Hassler, T. M., Martsolf, J. T., & Kerbeshian, J. (2003). Recognition and management of fetal alcohol syndrome. *Neurotoxicological Teratology, 25,* 681–688.

Burden, R. (2008). Is dyslexia necessarily associated with negative feelings of self-worth? A review and implications for future research. *Dyslexia: An International Journal of Research and Practice, 14,* 188–196.

Burdjalov, V. F., Baumgart, S., & Spitzer, A. R. (2003). Cerebral function monitoring: A new scoring system for the evaluation of brain maturation in neonates. *Pediatrics, 112,* 855–861.

Bureau of Labor Statistics. (2012). *Employment Characteristics of Families Summary—2011.* Washington, DC: United States Department of Labor.

Burgess, K. B., & Rubin, K. H. (2000). Middle childhood: Social and emotional development. In A. E. Kazdin, *Encyclopedia of psychology* (Vol. 5). Washington, DC: American Psychological Association.

Burgess, R. L., & Huston, T. L. (Eds.). (1979). *Social exchanges in developing relationships.* New York: Academic Press.

Burgio, K. L. (2004). Current perspectives on management of urgency using bladder and behavioral training. *Journal of American Academic Nurse Practitioners, 16,* 4–7.

Burgund, E., & Abernathy, A. (2008). Letter-specific processing in children and adults matched for reading level. *Acta Psychologica, 129,* 66–71.

Burkam, D. T., Ready, D. D., Lee, V., & LoGerfo, L. F., (2004). Social-class differences in summer learning between kindergarten and first grade: Model specification and estimation. *Sociology of Education, 77,* 1–31.

Burke, V., Beilin, L., Durkin, K., Stritzke, W., Houghton, S., & Cameron, C. (2006, November). Television, computer use, physical activity, diet and fatness in Australian adolescents. *International Journal of Pediatric Obesity, 1,* 248–255.

Burkhammer, M. D., Anderson, G. C., & Chiu, S.-H. (2004). Grief, anxiety, stillbirth, and perinatal problems: Healing with kangaroo care. *Journal of Obstetrics and Gynecological Neonatal Nursing, 33,* 774–782.

Burkhammer, M. D., Anderson, G. C., & Chiu, S. H. (2005). Theories of schizophrenia: A genetic-inflammatory-vascular synthesis. *BMC Medical Genetics, 11,* 7.

Burkhauser, R. V., Holden, K. C., & Feaster, D. (1988). Incidence, timing, and events associated with poverty: A dynamic view of poverty in retirement. *Journal of Gerontology, 43*(2), S46–52.

Burn, S. M. (1996). *The social psychology of gender.* New York: McGraw-Hill.

Burnett, P. C. (1996). Gender and grade differences in elementary school children's descriptive and evaluative self-statements and self-esteem. *School Psychology International, 17,* 159–170.

Burnett, P. C., & Proctor, R. (2002). Elementary school students' learner self-concept, academic self-concepts and approaches to learning. *Educational Psychology in Practice, 18,* 325–333.

Burnett-Wolle, S., & Godbey, G. (2007). Refining research on older adults' leisure: Implications of selection, optimization, and compensation and socioemotional selectivity theories. *Journal of Leisure Research, 39,* 498–513.

Burnham, M., Goodlin-Jones, B., & Gaylor, E. (2002). Nighttime sleep-wake patterns and self-soothing from birth to one year of age: A longitudinal intervention study. *Journal of Child Psychology & Psychiatry & Allied Disciplines, 43,* 713–725.

Burns, D. M. (2000). Cigarette smoking among the elderly: Disease consequences and the benefits of cessation. *American Journal of Health Promotion, 14,* 357–361.

Burns, E. (2003). *A handbook for supplementary aids and services: A best practice and IDEA guide "to enable children with disabilities to be educated with nondisabled children to the maximum extent appropriate.* Springfield, IL: Charles C Thomas Publisher.

Burrus-Bammel, L. L., & Bammel, G. (1985). Leisure and recreation. In J. E. Birren & K. W. Schaie (Eds.), *Handbook of the psychology of aging.* New York: Van Nostrand Reinhold.

Burt, V. L., & Harris, T. (1994). The third National Health and Nutrition Examination Survey: Contributing data on aging and health. *Gerontologist, 34,* 486–490.

Burtless, G. T. (1997). Welfare recipients' job skills and employment prospects. *The Future of Children, 7,* 39–51.

Burton, A., Haley, W., & Small, B. (2006, May). Bereavement after caregiving or unexpected death: Effects on elderly spouses. *Aging & Mental Health, 10,* 319–326.

Burton, L., Henninger, D., Hafetz, J., & Cofer, J. (2009). Aggression, gender-typical childhood play, and a prenatal hormonal index. *Social Behavior and Personality, 37,* 105–116.

Bushman, B. J. (1993). Human aggression while under the influence of alcohol and other drugs: An integrative research review. *Current Directions in Psychological Science, 2,* 148–152.

Bushman, B. J., & Anderson, C. A. (2001). Media violence and the American public: Scientific facts versus media misinformation. *American Psychologist, 56,* 477–489.

Bushman, B. J., & Anderson, C. A. (2002). Violent video games and hostile expectations: A test of the General Aggression Model. *Personality and Social Psychology Bulletin, 28,* 1679–1689.

Bushman, B. J., & Geen, R. G. (1990). Role of cognitive-emotional mediators and individual differences in the effects of media violence on aggression. *Journal of Personality and Social Psychology, 58,* 156–163.

Bushnell, I. W. R. (1998). The origins of face perception. In F. Simion & G. Butterworth (Eds.), *The development of sensory, motor and cognitive capacities in early infancy: From perception to cognition.* Hove, England: Psychology Press/Erlbaum (UK) Taylor & Francis.

Busick, D., Brooks, J., Pernecky, S., Dawson, R., & Petzoldt, J. (2008). Parent food purchases as a measure of exposure and preschool-aged children's willingness to identify and taste fruit and vegetables. *Appetite, 51,* 468–473.

Buss, A. H. (2011). Temperament II: Sociability and impulsiveness. In A. H. Buss (Ed.), *Pathways to individuality: Evolution and development of personality traits.* Washington, DC: American Psychological Association.

Buss, A. H. (2012). Self II: Self-esteem and identity. In A. H. Buss (Ed.), *Pathways to individuality: Evolution and development of personality traits.* Washington, DC: American Psychological Association.

Buss, A. H., & Plomin, R. (1984). *Temperament: Early developing personality traits.* Hillsdale, NJ: Erlbaum.

Buss, D. (2004). Sex differences in human mate preferences: Evolutionary hypotheses tested in 37 cultures. *Close relationships: Key readings* (pp. 135–151). Philadelphia: Taylor & Francis.

Buss, D. (2005, January 23). Sure, come back to the nest. Here are the rules. *The New York Times,* p. 8.

Buss, D. (2009). The great struggles of life: Darwin and the emergence of evolutionary psychology. *American Psychologist, 64,* 140–148.

Buss, D. M. (2003a). The dangerous passion: Why jealousy is as necessary as love and sex: Book review. *Archives of Sexual Behavior, 32,* 79–80.

Buss, D. M. (2003b). *The evolution of desire: Strategies of human mating* (Rev. ed.). New York: Basic Books.

Buss, D. M. (2004). *Evolutionary psychology: The new science of the mind* (2nd ed.). Boston: Allyn & Bacon.

Buss, D. M., & Reeve, H. K. (2003). Evolutionary psychology and developmental dynamics: Comment on Lickliter and Honeycutt. *Psychological Bulletin, 129,* 848–853.

Buss, D. M., Abbott, M., Angleitner, A., Asherian, A., Biaggio, A., Blanco-Villasenor, A., et al. (1990). International preferences in selecting mates: A study of 37 cultures. *Journal of Cross-Cultural Psychology, 21,* 5–47.

Buss, D., & Shackelford, T. (2008). Attractive women want it all: Good genes, economic investment, parenting proclivities, and emotional commitment. *Evolutionary Psychology, 6,* 134–146.

Buss, K. A., & Goldsmith, H. H. (1998). Feat and anger regulation in infancy: Effects on the temporal dynamics of affective expression. *Child Development, 69,* 359–374.

Buss, K. A., & Kiel, E. J. (2004). Comparison of sadness, anger, and fear facial expressions when toddlers look at their mothers. *Child Development, 75,* 1761–1773.

Bussey, K. (1992). Lying and truthfulness: Children's definition, standards, and evaluative reactions. *Child Development, 63,* 1236–1250.

Bussey, K., & Bandura, A. (1992). Self-regulatory mechanisms governing gender development. *Child Development, 63,* 1236–1250.

Butler, D. (2004, May 18). Science of dieting: Slim pickings. *Nature,* 252–254.

Butler, K. G., & Silliman, E. R. (Eds.). (2002). *Speaking, reading, and writing in children with language learning disabilities: New paradigms in research and practice.* Mahwah, NJ: Lawrence Erlbaum.

Butler, R. N. (1968). The life review: An interpretation of reminiscence in the aged. In B. Neugarten (Ed.), *Middle age and aging.* Chicago: University of Chicago Press.

Butler, R. N. (1990). The contributions of late-life creativity to society. *Gerontology and Geriatrics Education, 11,* 45–51.

Butler, R. N. (2002). The life review. *Journal of Geriatric Psychiatry, 35,* 7–10.

Butler, R. N., & Lewis, M. I. (1981). *Aging and mental health.* St. Louis: Mosby.

Buttelmann, D., Carpenter, M., Call, J., & Tomasello, M. (2008). Rational tool use and tool choice in human infants and great apes. *Child Development, 79,* 609–626.

Butterfield, E., & Siperstein, G. (1972). Influence of contingent auditory stimulation upon non-nutritional suckle. In J. Bosma (Ed.), *Oral sensation and perception: The mouth of the infant.* Springfield, IL: Charles C Thomas.

Butterworth, G. (1994). Infant intelligence. In J. Khalfa (Ed.), *What is intelligence? The Darwin College lecture series.* Cambridge, England: Cambridge University Press.

Button, E. (1993). *Eating disorders: Personal construct theory and change.* New York: Wiley.

Butzer, B., & Campbell, L. (2008). Adult attachment, sexual satisfaction, and relationship satisfaction: A study of married couples. *Personal Relationships, 15,* 141–154.

Buunk, B. P., & Janssen, P. P. (1992). Relative deprivation, career issues, and mental health among men in midlife. *Journal of Vocational Behavior, 40,* 338–350.

Buysse, D. J. (2005). Diagnosis and assessment of sleep and circadian rhythm disorders. *Journal of Psychiatric Practice, 11,* 102–115.

Byard, R., & Krous, H. (1999). Suffocation, shaking or sudden infant death syndrome: Can we tell the difference? *Journal of Paediatrics & Child Health, 35(5),* 432–433.

Byerley, W., & Badner, J. A. (2011). Strategies to identify genes for complex disorders: A focus on bipolar disorder and chromosome 16p. *Psychiatric Genetics, 21,* 173–182.

Byne, W., & Parsons, B. (1994, February). Biology and human sexual orientation. *Harvard Mental Health Letter, 10,* 5–7.

Byrd, C. M. (2012). The measurement of racial/ethnic identity in children: A critical review. *Journal of Black Psychology, 38,* 3–31.

Byrd, D., Katcher, M., Peppard, P., Durkin, M., & Remington, P. (2007). Infant mortality: Explaining black/white disparities in Wisconsin. *Maternal and Child Health Journal, 11,* 319–326.

Byrd, M., Nelson, E., & Manthey, L. (2006). Oral-digital habits of childhood: Thumb sucking. *Practitioner's guide to evidence-based psychotherapy.* New York: Springer Science + Business Media.

Byrd, R. S., Weitzman, M., & Auinger, P. (1997). Increased behavior problems associated with delayed school entry and delayed school progress. *Pediatrics, 100,* 654–661.

Byrne, A. (2000). Singular identities: Managing stigma, resisting voices. *Women's Studies Review, 7,* 13–24.

Byrne, B. (2000). Relationships between anxiety, fear, self-esteem, and coping strategies in adolescence. *Adolescence, 35,* 201–215.

Byrne, B., Shankweiler, D., & Hine, D. (2008). Reading development in children at risk for dyslexia. In *Brain, behavior, and learning in language and reading disorders.* New York: Guilford Press.

Cabrera, N., Shannon, J., & Tamis-LeMonda, C. (2007). Fathers' influence on their children's cognitive and emotional development: From toddlers to pre-K. *Applied Developmental Science, 11,* 208–213.

Cacciatore, J., & Bushfield, S. (2007). Stillbirth: The mother's experience and implications for improving care. *Journal of Social Work in End-of-Life & Palliative Care, 3,* 59–79.

Cadinu, M. R., & Kiesner, J. (2000). Children's development of a theory of mind. *European Journal of Psychology of Education, 15,* 93–111.

Cai, Y., Reeve., J. M., & Robinson, D. T. (2002). Home schooling and teaching style: Comparing the motivating styles of home school and public school teachers. *Journal of Educational Psychology, 94,* 372–380.

Cain, B. S. (1982, December 19). Plight of the gray divorcee. *The New York Times Magazine,* pp. 89–93.

Cain, V., Johannes, C., & Avis, N. (2003). Sexual functioning and practices in a multi-ethnic study of midlife women: Baseline results from SWAN. *Journal of Sex Research, 40,* 266–276.

Caino, S., Kelmansky, D., Lejarraga, H., & Adamo, P. (2004). Short-term growth at adolescence in healthy girls. *Annals of Human Biology, 31,* 182–195.

Caldas, S. J., & Bankston, C. (1997). Effect of school population socioeconomic status on individual academic achievement. *Journal of Educational Research, 90,* 269–277.

Caldera, Y. M., & Sciaraffa, M. A. (1998). Parent–toddler play with feminine toys: Are all dolls the same? *Sex Roles, 39,* 657–668.

Calhoun, F., & Warren, K. (2007). Fetal alcohol syndrome: Historical perspectives. *Neuroscience & Biobehavioral Reviews, 31,* 168–171.

Callen, B. (2000). Program of care for young women with iron deficiency anemia: A pilot. *Journal of Community Health Nursing, 17,* 247–262.

Callister, L. C., Khalaf, I., Semenic, S., Kartehner, R., & Vehvilainen-Julkunen, K. (2003). The pain of childbirth: Perceptions of culturally diverse women. *Pain Management Nursing, 4,* 145–154.

Calvert, S. L., Kotler, J. A., Zehnder, S., & Shockey, E. (2003). Gender stereotyping in children's reports about educational and informational television programs. *Media Psychology, 5,* 139–162.

Camarota, S. A. (2001). *Immigrants in the United States—2000: A snapshot of America's foreign-born population.* Washington, DC: Center for Immigration Studies.

Cameron, P. (2003). Domestic violence among homosexual partners. *Psychological Reports, 93,* 410–416.

Cami, J., & Farré, M. (2003). Drug addiction. *New England Journal of Medicine, 349,* 975–986.

Campbell, A., Shirley, L., & Candy, J. (2004). A longitudinal study of gender-related cognition and behaviour. *Developmental Science, 7,* 1–9.

Campbell, D., Scott, K., Klaus, M., & Falk, M. (2007). Female relatives or friends trained as labor doulas: Outcomes at 6 to 8 weeks postpartum. *Birth: Issues in Perinatal Care, 34,* 220–227.

Campbell, F. A., Pungello, E. P., Miller-Johnson, S., Ramey, C. T., & Burchinal, M. (2001). The development of cognitive and academic abilities: Growth curves from an early childhood educational experiment. *Developmental Psychology, 37,* 231–242.

Campbell, F. A., Ramey, C., & Pungello, E. (2002). Early childhood education: Young adult outcomes from the Abecedarian Project. *Applied Developmental Science, 6,* 42–57.

Campbell, J., & Feng, A. (2011). Comparing adult productivity of American mathematics, physics, and chemistry Olympians with Terman's longitudinal study. *Roeper Review: A Journal on Gifted Education, 33,* 18–25.

Campbell, J., Poland, M., Waller, J., & Ager, J. (1992). Correlates of battering during pregnancy. *Research in Nursing and Health, 15,* 219–226.

Campbell, K., Crawford, D., & Ball, K. (2006, August). Family food environment and dietary behaviors likely to promote fatness in 5-6 year-old children. *International Journal of Obesity, 30*(8), 1272–1280.

Campos, J. J., Langer, A., & Krowitz, A. (1970). Cardiac responses on the visual cliff in prelocomotor human infants. *Science, 170,* 196–197.

Camras, L. A., Malatesta, C., & Izard, C. E. (1991). The development of facial expressions in infancy. In R. S. Feldman & B. Rime (Eds.), *Fundamentals of nonverbal behavior.* Cambridge, England: Cambridge University Press.

Camras, L., Meng, Z., & Ujiie, T. (2002). Observing emotion in infants: Facial expression, body behavior, and rater judgments of responses to an expectancy-violating event. *Emotion, 2,* 179–193.

Camras, L., Oster, H., Bakeman, R., Meng, Z., Ujiie, T., & Campos, J. (2007). Do infants show distinct negative facial expressions for fear and anger? Emotional expression in 11-month-old European American, Chinese, and Japanese Infants. *Infancy, 11,* 131–155.

Camras, L. A., & Sachs, V. B. (1991). Social referencing and caretaker expressive behavior in a day care setting. *Infant Behavior and Development, 14,* 27–36.

Canals, J., Fernandez-Ballart, J., & Esparo, G. (2003). Evolution of Neonatal Behavior Assessment Scale scores in the first month life. *Infant Behavior & Development, 26,* 227–237.

Canals, J., Hernández-Martínez, C., & Fernández-Ballart, J. D. (2011). Relationships between early behavioural characteristics and temperament at 6 years. *Infant Behavior & Development, 34,* 152–160.

Canedy, D. (2001, March 3). Troubling label for Hispanics: "Girls most likely to drop out." *The New York Times,* p. A1.

Canfield, R. L., & Haith, M. M. (1991). Young infants' visual expectations for symmetric and asymmetric stimulus sequences. *Developmental Psychology, 27,* 198–208.

Canfield, R. L., Kreher, D., & Cornwell, C. (2003). Low-level lead exposure, executive functioning, and learning in early childhood. *Child Neuropsychology, 9,* 35–53.

Canfield, R. L., Smith, E. G., Breznyak, M. P., & Snow, K. L. (1997). Information processing through the first year of life: A longitudinal study using the visual expectation paradigm. With commentary by Richard N. Aslin, Marshall M. Hairth, Tara S. Wass, & Scott A. Adler. *Monographs of the Society for Research in Child Development, 62*(2 Serial No. 250).

Canning, P., Courage, M., Frizzell, L., & Seifert, T. (2007). Obesity in a provincial population of Canadian preschool children: Differences between 1984 and 1997 birth cohorts. *International Journal of Pediatric Obesity, 2,* 51–57.

Cano, A., Gillis, M., Heinz, W., Geisser, M., & Foran, H. (2004). Marital functioning, chronic pain, and psychological distress. *Pain, 107,* 99–106.

Cantin, V., Lavallière, M., Simoneau, M., & Teasdale, N. (2009). Mental workload when driving in a simulator: Effects of age and driving complexity. *Accident Analysis and Prevention, 41,* 763–771.

Caplan, L. J., & Barr, R. A. (1989). On the relationship between category intensions and extensions in children. *Journal of Experimental Child Psychology, 47,* 413–429.

Cappeliez, P., Guindon, M., & Robitaille, A. (2008). Functions of reminiscence and emotional regulation among older adults. *Journal of Aging Studies, 22,* 266–272.

Cappiello, L. A., & Troyer, R. E. (1979). A study of the role of health educators in teaching about death and dying. *Journal of School Health, 49,* 397–399.

Carbonaro, W., Ellison, B. J., & Covay, E. (2011). Gender inequalities in the college pipeline. *Social Science Research, 40,* 120–135.

Cardalda, E. B., Miranda, S. E., Perez, M., & Sierra, E. M. (2003). Attitudes toward breast-feeding working mothers. *Puerto Rican Health Science Journal, 22,* 305–310.

Cardman, M. (2004). Rising GPAs, course loads a mystery to researchers. *Education Daily, 37,* 1–3.

Cardon, L. R., & Fulker, D. (1993). Genetics of specific cognitive abilities. In R. Plomin & G. McClearn (Eds.), *Nature, nurture, and psychology* (pp. 99–120). Washington, DC: American Psychological Association.

Carey, K. (2004). *A matter of degrees: Improving graduation rates in four-year colleges and universities.* Washington, DC: Education Trust.

Carlson, E., & Hoem, J. M. (1999). Low-weight neonatal survival paradox in the Czech Republic. *American Journal of Epidemiology, 149,* 447–453.

Carlson, S. M., & Meltzoff, A. N. (2008). Bilingual experience and executive functioning in young children. *Developmental Science, 11,* 282–298.

Carmeli, A., & Josman, Z. (2006). The relationship among emotional intelligence, task performance, and organizational citizenship behaviors. *Human Performance, 19,* 403–419.

Carmichael, M. (2004, May 10). Have it your way: Redesigning birth. *Newsweek,* pp. 70–72.

Carmichael, M. (2006, May 8). Health: Does "milk" hurt kids? *Newsweek,* p. 73.

Carmody, D. (1990, March 7). College drinking: Changes in attitude and habit. *The New York Times.*

Carnegie Task Force on Meeting the Needs of Young Children. (1994). *Starting points: Meeting the needs of our youngest children.* New York: Carnegie Corporation.

Carney, J. V. (2008). Perceptions of bullying and associated trauma during adolescence. *Professional School Counseling, 11,* 179–188.

Carney, R. N., & Levin, J. R. (2003) Promoting higher order learning benefits by building lower-order mnemonic connections. *Applied Cognitive Psychology, 17,* 563–575.

Caron, A. (2009). Comprehension of the representational mind in infancy. *Developmental Review, 29,* 69–95.

Caron, C., Gjelsvik, A., & Buechner, J. S. (2005). The impact of poverty on prevention practices and health status among persons with asthma. *Medicine Health Rhode Island, 88,* 60–62.

Carpendale, J. I. M. (2000). Kohlberg and Piaget on stages and moral reasoning. *Developmental Review, 20,* 181–205.

Carpenter, D. M. H., Flowers, N., & Mertens, S. B. (2004). High expectations for every student. *Middle School Journal, 35,* 64.

Carpenter, S. (2000, October). Human genome project director says psychologists will play a critical role in the initiative's success. *Monitor on Psychology,* 14–15.

Carr, C. N., Kennedy, S. R., & Dimick, K. M. (1996). Alcohol use among high school athletes. *The Prevention Researcher, 3,* 1–3.

Carr, D. (2003). A "good death" for whom? Quality of spouse's death and psychological distress among older widowed persons. *Journal of Health and Social Behavior, 44,* 215–232.

Carr, D., & Ha, J. (2006). *Bereavement.* New York: Oxford University Press.

Carr, D., House, J. S., & Kessler, R. C. (2002). Marital quality and psychological adjustment to widowhood among older adults: A longitudinal analysis. *Journals of Gerontology: Series B: Psychological Sciences and Social Sciences, 55B*(4), S197–S207.

Carr, D., Nesse, R., & Wortman, C. (2005). *Spousal bereavement in late life.* New York: Springer.

Carr, J. (1995). *Down syndrome.* Cambridge, England: Cambridge University Press.

Carr, P., & Steele, C. (2009). Stereotype threat and inflexible perseverance in problem solving. *Journal of Experimental Social Psychology, 45,* 853–859.

Carrere, S., Buehlman, K. T., Gottman, J. M., Coan, J. A., & Ruckstuhl, L. (2000). Predicting marital stability and divorce in newlywed couples. *Journal of Family Psychology, 14,* 42–58.

Carroll, D. (1985). *Living with dying.* New York: McGraw-Hill.

Carroll, L. (2000, February 1). Is memory loss inevitable? Maybe not. *The New York Times,* pp. D1, D7.

Carson, R. G. (2005). Neural pathways mediating bilateral interactions between the upper limbs. *Brain Research Review, 49,* 641–662.

Carson, R. C., Butcher, J. N., & Coleman, J. C. (1992). *Abnormal psychology and modern life* (9th ed.). New York: HarperCollins.

Carstensen, L. L. (1995). Evidence for a life-span theory of socioemotional selectivity. *Current Directions in Psychological Science, 4,* 151–156.

Carstensen, L. L., & Charles, S. T. (1998). Emotion in the second half of life. *Current Directions in Psychological Science, 7,* 144–149.

Carstensen, L. L., Pasupathi, M., Mayr, U., Nesselroade, J. R. (2000). Emotional experience in everyday life across the adult life span. *Journal of Personality and Social Psychology, 79,* 644–655.

Carter, R. T., Mazzula, S., Victoria, R., Vazquez, R., Hall, S., Smith, S., et al. (2011). Initial development of the race-based traumatic stress symptom scale: Assessing the emotional impact of racism. *Psychological Trauma: Theory, Research, Practice, and Policy.* Retrieved from http://psycnet.apa.org/psycinfo/2011-24222-001/.

Carton, A., & Aiello, J. (2009). Control and anticipation of social interruptions: Reduced stress and improved task performance. *Journal of Applied Social Psychology, 39,* 169–185.

Carvajal, F., & Iglesias, J. (2000). Looking behavior and smiling in Down syndrome infants. *Journal of Nonverbal Behavior, 24,* 225–236.

Carver, C. S., & Scheier, M. F. (1993). On the power of positive thinking: The benefits of being optimistic. *Current Directions in Psychological Science, 2,* 26–30.

Carver, C. S., & Scheier, M. F. (2002). Coping processes and adjustment to chronic illness. In A. Christensen & M. Antoni (Eds.), *Chronic physical disorders: Behavioral medicine's perspective* (pp. 47–68). Malden: Blackwell Publishers.

Carver, L., Dawson, G., & Panagiotides, H. (2003). Age-related differences in neural correlates of face recognition during the toddler and preschool years. *Developmental Psychobiology, 42,* 148–159.

Carver, L., & Vaccaro, B. (2007, January). 12-month-old infants allocate increased neural resources to stimuli associated with negative adult emotion. *Developmental Psychology, 43,* 54–69.

Carver, L. J., & Cornew, L. (2009). The development of social information gathering in infancy: A model of neural substrates and developmental mechanisms. In M. de Haan & M. R. Gunnar (Eds.), *Handbook of developmental social neuroscience.* New York: Guilford Press.

Casalin, S., Luyten, P., Vliegen, N., & Meurs, P. (2012). The structure and stability of temperament from infancy to toddlerhood: A one-year prospective study. *Infant Behavior & Development, 35,* 94–108.

Casasanto, D. (2008). Who's afraid of the big bad whorf? Crosslinguistic differences in temporal language and thought. *Language Learning, 63*–79.

Cascalho, M., Ogle, B. M., & Platt, J. L. (2006). The future of organ transplantation. *Annals of Transplantation, 11,* 44–47.

Case, R. (1991). Stages in the development of the young child's first sense of self. *Developmental Review, 11,* 210–230.

Case, R. (1992). *Neo-Piagetian theories of intellectual development.* Hillsdale, NJ: Lawrence Erlbaum Associates.

Case, R. (1999). Conceptual development. In M. Bennett, (Ed.), *Developmental psychology: Achievements and prospects.* Philadelphia, PA: Psychology Press.

Case, R., Demetriou, A., & Platsidou, M. (2001). Integrating concepts and tests of intelligence from the differential and developmental traditions. *Intelligence, 29,* 307–336.

Case, R., & Okamoto, Y. (1996). The role of central conceptual structures in the development of children's thought. *Monographs of the Society for Research in Child Development, 61,* v–265.

Caserta, M., O'Connor, T., Wyman, P., Wang, H., Moynihan, J., Cross, W., et al. (2008). The associations between psychosocial stress and the frequency of illness, and innate and adaptive immune function in children. *Brain, Behavior, and Immunity, 22,* 933–940.

Caskey, R., Lindau, S., & Caleb Alexander, G. (2009). Knowledge and early adoption of the HPV vaccine among girls and young women: Results of a national survey. *Journal of Adolescent Health, 45,* 453–462.

Casper, M., & Carpenter, L. (2008). Sex, drugs, and politics: The HPV vaccine for cervical cancer. *Sociology of Health & Illness, 30,* 886–899.

Caspi, A. (2000). The child is father of the man: Personality continuities from childhood to adulthood. *Journal of Personality and Social Psychology, 78,* 158–172.

Caspi, A., & Moffitt, T. E. (1991). Individual differences are accentuated during periods of social change: The sample case of girls at puberty. *Journal of Personality and Social Psychology, 61,* 157–168.

Caspi, A., & Moffitt, T. E. (1993). *Continuity amidst change: A paradoxical theory of personality coherence.* Manuscript submitted for publication.

Cassel, W. S., Roebers, C. E. M., & Bjorklund, D. F. (1996). Developmental patterns of eyewitness responses to repeated and increasingly suggestive questions. *Journal of Experimental Child Psychology, 61,* 116–133.

Cassidy, J., & Berlin, L. J. (1994). The insecure/ambivalent pattern of attachment: Theory and research. *Child Development, 65,* 971–991.

Cassidy, K. W., Chu, J. Y., & Dahlsgaard, K. K. (1997). Preschoolers' ability to adopt justice and care orientations in moral dilemmas. *Early Education & Development, 8,* 419–434.

Castel, A., & Craik, F. (2003). The effects of aging and divided attention on memory for item and associative information. *Psychology & Aging, 18,* 873–885.

Catell, R. B. (1967). *The scientific analysis of personality.* Chicago: Aldine.

Catell, R. B. (1987). *Intelligence: Its structure, growth, and action.* Amsterdam: North-Holland.

Cath, S., & Shopper, M. (2001). *Stepparenting: Creating and recreating families in America today.* Hillsdale, NJ: Analytic Press, Inc.

Cattell, R. (2004). The theory of fluid and crystallized intelligence; its relationship with "culture-free" tests and its verification with children aged 9–12 years. *European Review of Applied Psychology, 54,* 47–56.

Cauce, A. (2008). Parenting, culture, and context: Reflections on excavating culture. *Applied Developmental Science, 12,* 227–229.

Cauce, A. M., Steward, A., & Domenech-Rodriguez, M. (2003). Overcoming the odds? Adolescent development in the context of urban poverty. In: S. S. Luthar (Ed.), *Resilience and vulnerability: Adaptation in the context of childhood adversities.*

Cauce, A., & Domenech-Rodriguez, M. (2002). Latino families: myths and realities. In J. M. Contreras, K. A. Kerns, & A. M. Neal-Barnett (Eds.), *Latino children and families in the United States.* Westport, CT: Praeger.

Cauffman, E., & Steinberg, L. (1996). Interactive effects of menarcheal status and dating on dieting and disordered eating among adolescent girls. *Developmental Psychology, 32,* 631–635.

Caughlin, J. (2002). The demand/withdraw pattern of communication as a predictor of marital satisfaction over time. *Human Communication Research, 28,* 49–85.

Cavallini, A., Fazzi, E., & Viviani, V. (2002). Visual acuity in the first two years of life in healthy term newborns: An experience with the Teller Acuity Cards. *Functional Neurology: New Trends in Adaptive & Behavioral Disorders, 17,* 87–92.

Cavallini, E., Pagnin, A., & Vecchi, T. (2003). Aging and everyday memory: The beneficial effect of memory training. *Archives of Gerontology & Geriatrics, 37,* 241–257.

CDC Office of Women's Health. (2008). *Leading causes of death in males in the United States, 2004.* Atlanta, GA: Centers for Disease Control and Prevention.

Ceci, S. J. (1993). Contextual trends in intellectual development. Special Issue: Setting a path for the coming decade: Some goals and challenges. *Developmental Review, 13,* 403–435.

Ceci, S. J. (2002)."I saw it with my own ears": The effects of peer conversations on preschoolers' reports of nonexperienced events. *Journal of Experimental Child Psychology, 83,* 1–25.

Ceci, S. J. (2003a). Children's memory of recurring events: Is the first event always the best remembered? *Applied Cognitive Psychology, 17,* 127–146.

Ceci, S. J. (2003b). Memory development and eyewitness testimony. In A. Slater & G. Bremmer (Eds.), *An introduction to developmental psychology.* Malden, MA: Blackwell Publishers.

Ceci, S. J., & Bruck, M. (1993). The suggestibility of the child witness: A historical review and synthesis. *Psychological Bulletin, 113,* 403–439.

Ceci, S. J., & Bruck, M. (1995). *Jeopardy in the courtroom.* Washington, DC: American Psychological Association.

Ceci, S., & Bruck, M. (2007). Loftus's lineage in developmental forensic research: Six scientific misconceptions about children's suggestibility. *Do justice and let the sky fall: Elizabeth Loftus and her contributions to science, law, and academic freedom* (pp. 65–77). Mahwah, NJ: Lawrence Erlbaum Associates.

Ceci, S. J., Fitneva, S. A., & Gilstrap, L. L. (2003). Memory development and eyewitness testimony. In A. Slater & G. Bremner (Eds.), *An introduction to developmental psychology.* Malden, MA: Blackwell Publishers.

Ceci, S. J., & Hembrooke, H. (1993). The contextual nature of earliest memories. In J. M. Puckett & H. W. Reese (Eds.), *Mechanisms of everyday cognition* (pp. 117–136). Hillsdale, NJ: Erlbaum.

Ceci, S. J., & Huffman, M. L. C. (1997). How suggestible are preschool children? Cognitive and social factors. *Journal of the American Academy of Child & Adolescent Psychiatry, 36,* 948–958.

Ceci, S. J., Loftus, E. F., Leichtman, M. D., & Bruck, M. (1994). The possible role of source misattributions in the creation of false beliefs among preschoolers. *International Journal of Clinical & Experimental Hypnosis, Special issue: Hypnosis and delayed recall: I. 42,* 304–320.

Celera Genomics: International Human Genome Sequencing Consortium. (2001). Initial sequencing and analysis of the human genome. *Nature, 409,* 860–921.

Center for Communication and Social Policy, University of California. (1998). *National television violence study, Vol. 2.* Thousand Oaks, CA: Sage.

Center for Media and Public Affairs. (1995, April 7). Adaptation analysis of violent content of broadcast and cable television stations on Thursday.

Center on Addiction and Substance Abuse. (1994). *Report on college drinking.* New York: Columbia University.

Center to Advance Palliative Care. (2004). *Technical assistance and practical resources to start and strengthen palliative care programs.* New York: Center to Advance Palliative Care.

Centers for Disease Control. (1991). *Preventing lead poisoning in young children: A statement by the Centers for Disease Control.* Atlanta, GA: U.S. Department of Health and Human Services.

Centers for Disease Control. (2003a). Incidence-surveillance, epidemiology, and end results program, 1973–2000. Atlanta, GA: Author.

Centers for Disease Control. (2003b). Rates of teenage pregnancy. *Vital and Health Statistics, Series 10, no. 219.* Washington, DC: U.S. Department of Health and Human Services.

Centers for Disease Control. (2004). Health behaviors of adults: United States, 1999–2001. *Vital and Health Statistics, Series 10, no. 219.* Washington, DC: U.S. Department of Health and Human Services.

Centers for Disease Control and Prevention. (1997). *HIV/AIDS surveillance report* (Vol. 9, No. 2). Atlanta: Author.

Centers for Disease Control and Prevention. (1998). *Youth risk behavior surveillance—United States, 1997.* Atlanta: Author.

Centers for Disease Control and Prevention. (2000). *Obesity continues to climb in 1999 among American adults.* Division of Nutrition and Physical Activity, National Center for Chronic Disease Prevention and Health Promotions. Atlanta, GA: Author.

Centers for Disease Control and Prevention. (2003). *Incidence-surveillance, epidemiology, and end results program, 1973–2000.* Atlanta, GA: Author.

Centers for Disease Control and Prevention. (2006). *HIV/AIDS surveillance report.* Atlanta: Author.

Centers for Disease Control and Prevention. (2008). *Measles, mumps and rubella (MMR) vaccine fact sheet.*

Retrieved October 9, 2009 from http://www.cdc.gov/vaccinesafety/updates/mmr_vaccine.htm.

Centers for Disease Control and Prevention. (2008). Prevalance of oversight, obesity and extreme obesity among adults: United States, trends 1960–62 through 2005–2006. *Health & Stats.*

Centers for Disease Control and Prevention. (2010). *Prevalence of obesity among children and adolescents; United States, Trends 1963–1965 Through 2007–2008.* Washington, DC: Author.

Centers for Disease Control and Prevention. (2011). *Artificial turf.* Retrieved from http://cdc.gov/nceh/lead/tips/artificialturf.htm.

Cerella, J. (1990). Aging and information-processing rate. In J. E. Birren & K. W. Schaie (Eds.), *Handbook of the psychology of aging* (3rd ed.). San Diego, CA: Academic Press.

CFCEPLA (Commonwealth Fund Commission on Elderly People Living Alone). (1986). *Problems facing elderly Americans living alone.* New York: Louis Harris & Associates.

Chaffin, M. (2006). The changing focus of child maltreatment research and practice within psychology. *Journal of Social Issues, 62,* 663–684.

Chaiklin, S. (2003). The zone of proximal development in Vygotsky's analysis of learning and instruction. In A. Kozulin & B. Gindis (Eds.), *Vygotsky's educational theory in cultural context.* New York: Cambridge University Press.

Chaker, A. M. (2003, September 23). Putting toddlers in a nursing home. *The Wall Street Journal,* p. D1.

Chall, J. (1992). The new reading debates: Evidence from science, art, and ideology. *Teachers College Record, 94,* 315–328.

Chall, J. S. (1979). The great debate: Ten years later, with a modest proposal for reading stages. In L. B. Resnick & P. A. Weaver (Eds.), *Theory and practice of early reading.* Hillsdale, NJ: Erlbaum.

Chamberlain, P., Price, J., Reid, J., Landsverk, J., Fisher, P., & Stoolmiller, M. (2006, April). Who disrupts from placement in foster and kinship care? *Child Abuse & Neglect, 30,* 409–424.

Chan, C. G., & Elder, G. H., Jr. (2000). Matrilineal advantage in grandchild-grandparent relations. *Gerontologist, 40,* 179–190.

Chan, D. W. (1997). Self-concept and global self-worth among Chinese adolescents in Hong Kong. *Personality & Individual Differences, 22,* 511–520.

Chan, W. S., Chong, K. Y., Martinovich, C., Simerly, C., & Schatten, G. (2001, January 12). Transgenic monkeys produced by retroviral gene transfer into mature oocytes. *Science, 291,* 309–312.

Chang, I., Pettit, R., & Katsurada, E. (2006, May). Where and when to spank: A comparison between U.S. and Japanese college students. *Journal of Family Violence, 21*(4), 281–286.

Chao, R. (1996). Chinese and European American mothers' beliefs about the role of parenting in children's school success. *Journal of Cross-Cultural Psychology, 27,* 403–423.

Chao, R. K. (1994). Beyond parental control and authoritarian parenting style: Understanding Chinese parenting through the cultural notion of training. *Child Development, 65,* 1111–1119.

Chao, R. K. (2001). Extending research on the consequences of parenting style for Chinese Americans and European Americans. *Child Development, 72,* 1832–1843.

Chaplin, T., Gillham, J., & Seligman, M. (2009). Gender, anxiety, and depressive symptoms: A longitudinal study of early adolescents. *The Journal of Early Adolescence, 29,* 307–327.

Chapman, S. B., Gamino, J. F., & Mudar, R. (2012). Higher order strategic gist reasoning in adolescence. In V. F. Reyna, S. B. Chapman, M. R. Dougherty, J. Confrey, V. F. Reyna, S. B. Chapman, et al. (Eds.), *The adolescent brain: Learning, reasoning, and decision making.* Washington, DC US: American Psychological Association.

Chappell, N. L. (1991). In-group differences among elders living with friends and family other than spouses. *Journal of Aging Studies, 5,* 61–76.

Chapple, A., Ziebland, S., McPherson, A., & Herxheimer, A. (2006, December). What people close to death say about euthanasia and assisted suicide: A qualitative study. *Journal of Medical Ethics, 32,* 706–710.

Charles, S., & Carstensen, L. (2010). Social and emotional aging. *Annual Review of Psychology, 61,* 383–409.

Charles, S. T., Mather, M., & Carstensen, L. L. (2003). Aging and emotional memory: The forgettable nature of negative images for older adults. *Journal of Experimental Psychology: General, 132,* 237–244.

Charles, S. T., Reynolds, C. A., & Gatz, M. (2001). Age-related differences and change in positive and negative affect over 23 years. *Journal of Personality and Social Psychology, 80,* 136–151.

Charness, N., & Boot, W. R. (2009). Aging and information technology use: Potential and barriers. *Current Directions in Psychological Science, 18,* 253–258.

Chassin, L., Macy, J., Seo, D., Presson, C., & Sherman, S. (2009). The association between membership in the sandwich generation and health behaviors: A longitudinal study. *Journal of Applied Developmental Psychology,* I31I, 38–46.

Chasteen, A. L., Bhattacharyya, S., Horhota, M., Tam, R., & Hasher, L. (2005). How feelings of stereotype threat influence older adults' memory performance. *Experimental Aging Research, 31,* 235–260.

Chatterji, M. (2004). Evidence on "what works": An argument for extended-term mixed-method (ETMM) evaluation designs. *Educational Researcher, 33,* 3–14.

Cheah, C., Leung, C., Tahseen, M., & Schultz, D. (2009). Authoritative parenting among immigrant Chinese mothers of preschoolers. *Journal of Family Psychology, 23,* 311–320.

Chee, C., & Murachver, T. (2012). Intention attribution in theory of mind and moral judgment. *Psychological Studies, 57,* 40–45.

Cheek, C., & Piercy, K. (2008). Quilting as a tool in resolving Erikson's adult stage of human development. *Journal of Adult Development, 15,* 13–24.

Chen, C., Lee, S., & Stevenson, H. W. (1996). Long-term prediction of academic achievement of American, Chinese, and Japanese adolescents. *Journal of Educational Psychology, 88,* 750–759.

Chen, C., & Stevenson, H. W. (1995). Motivation and mathematics achievement: A comparative study of Asian-American, Caucasian-American, and East Asian high school students. *Child Development, 66,* 1215–1234.

Chen, E., & Rao, N. (2011). Gender socialization in Chinese kindergartens: Teachers' contributions. *Sex Roles, 64*(1–2), 103–116.

Chen, J., Chen, T., & Zheng, X. (2012). Parenting styles and practices among Chinese immigrant mothers with young children. *Early Child Development and Care, 182,* 1–21.

Chen, J., & Gardner, H. (2005). Assessment based on multiple-intelligences theory. In D. P. Flanagan & P. L. Harrison (Eds.), *Contemporary intellectual assessment: Theories, tests, and issues.* New York: Guilford Press.

Chen, S. X., & Bond, M. H. (2007). Explaining language priming effects: Further evidence for ethnic affirmation among Chinese-English bilinguals, *Journal of Language and Social Psychology, 26,,* 398–406.

Chen, X., Hastings, P. D., Rubin, K. H., Chen, H., Cen, G., & Stewart, S. L. (1998). Child-rearing attitudes and behavioral inhibition in Chinese and Canadian toddlers: A cross-cultural study. *Developmental Psychology, 34,* 677–686.

Chen, Z., & Siegler, R. S. (2000). Across the great divide: Bridging the gap between understanding of toddlers' and older children's thinking. *Monographs of the Society for Research in Child Development, 65*(2, Serial No. 261).

Cheney, D. L., & Seyfarth, R. M. (1992). Precis of How monkeys see the world. *Behavioral & Brain Sciences, 15,* 135–182.

Cherlin, A. (1993). *Marriage, divorce, remarriage.* Cambridge, MA: Harvard University Press.

Cherlin, A., & Furstenberg, F. (1986). *The new American grandparent.* New York: Basic Books.

Cherney, I. (2003). Young children's spontaneous utterances of mental terms and the accuracy of their memory behaviors: A different methodological approach. *Infant & Child Development, 12,* 89–105.

Cherney, I., Kelly-Vance, L., & Glover, K. (2003). The effects of stereotyped toys and gender on play assessment in children aged 18 to 47 months. *Educational Psychology, 23,* 95–105.

Cherry, K. E., & Park, D. C. (1993). Individual difference and contextual variables influence spatial memory in younger and older adults. *Psychology and Aging, 8,* 517–526.

Chertok, I., Luo, J., & Anderson, R. H. (2011). Association between changes in smoking habits in subsequent pregnancy and infant birth weight in West Virginia. *Maternal and Child Health Journal, 15,* 249–254.

Cheryan, S., & Bodenhausen, G. V. (2000). When positive stereotypes threaten intellectual performance: The psychological hazards of "model minority" status. *Psychological Science, 11,* 399–402.

Cheung, A., Emslie, G., & Mayes, T. (2006, January). The use of antidepressants to treat depression in children and adolescents. *Canadian Medical Association Journal, 174*(2), 193–200.

Cheung, F. (2006). Causes and process of maturing. *PsycCRITIQUES, 51*(3).

Chicchetti, D., & Cohen, D. J. (Eds.). (2006). *Developmental psychopathology: Theory and Method, Vols. 1–3.* New York: John Wiley & Sons.

Chick, C. F., & Reyna, V. F. (2012). A fuzzy trace theory of adolescent risk taking: Beyond self-control and sensation seeking. In V. F. Reyna, S. B. Chapman, M. R. Dougherty, J. Confrey, V. F. Reyna, S. B. Chapman, et al. (Eds.), *The adolescent brain: Learning, reasoning, and decision making.* Washington, DC: American Psychological Association.

Chien, S., Bronson-Castain, K., Palmer, J., & Teller, D. (2006). Lightness constancy in 4-month-old infants. *Vision Research, 46,* 2139–2148.

Child Health USA. (1994). *Child Health.* Washington, DC: U.S. Department of Health & Human Services.

Child Health USA. (2002). *U.S. infant mortality rates by race of mother: 1980–2000.* Washington, DC: U.S. Department of Health and Human Services.

Child Health USA. (2005). U.S. Department of Health and Human Services, Health Resources and Services Administration, Maternal and Child Health Bureau. *Child health USA 2005.* Rockville, MD: U.S. Department of Health and Human Services.

Child Health USA. (2007). *Child Health USA 2007.* Rockville, MD: U.S. Department of Health and Human Services.

Child Maltreatment. (2002). *Child maltreatment.* Washington, DC: U.S. Department of Health and Human Services.

Childers, J. (2009). Early verb learners: Creative or not?. *Monographs of the Society for Research in Child Development, 74,* 133–139.

Childs, B. (2003). *Genetic medicine: A logic of disease.* Baltimore: Johns Hopkins University Press.

ChildStats.gov. (2000). *America's children 2000.* Washington, DC: National Maternal and Child Health Clearinghouse.

ChildStats.gov. (2005). *America's children 2005.* Washington, DC: National Maternal and Child Health Clearinghouse.

Chin, J. (1994). The growing impact of the HIV/AIDS pandemic on children born to HIV infected women. *Clinical Perinatalogy, 21,* 1–14.

Chira, S. (1994, July 10). Teen-agers, in a poll, report worry and distrust of adults. *The New York Times,* pp. 1, 16.

Chiriboga, D. A. (1982). Adaptation to marital separation in later and earlier life. *Journal of Gerontology, 37,* 109–114.

Chisholm, J., & Ward, A. (2005). Warning Signs. *Violence in schools: Cross-national and cross-cultural perspectives* (pp. 59–74). New York: Springer Science + Business Media.

Chisolm, T., Willott, J., & Lister, J. (2003). The aging auditory system: Anatomic and physiologic changes and implications for rehabilitation. *International Journal of Audiology, 42,* 2S3–2S10.

Chiu, C., Dweck, C. S., Yuk-yue Tong, J., & Ho-yin Fu, J. (1997). Implicit theories and conceptions of morality. *Journal of Personality and Social Psychology, 73,* 923–940.

Chiu, C., Leung, A., & Kwan, L. (2007). Language, cognition, and culture: Beyond the Whorfian hypothesis. *Handbook of cultural psychology.* New York: Guilford Press.

Chiu, M., & McBride-Chang, C. (2006). Gender, context, and reading: A comparison of students in 43 countries. *Scientific Studies of Reading, 10*(4), 331–362.

Chlebowski, R. T., Schwartz, A. G., Wakelee, H., Anderson, G. L., Stefanick, M. L., Manson, J. E., Oestrogen plus progestin and lung cancer in postmenopausal women (Women's Health Initiative trial): A post-hoc analysis of a randomised controlled trial. *Lancet, 374,* 1243–1251.

Choi, H. (2002). Understanding adolescent depression in ethnocultural context. *Advances in Nursing Science, 25,* 71–85.

Choi, H., & Marks, N. (2006, December). Transition to caregiving, marital disagreement, and psychological well-being: A prospective U.S. National Study. *Journal of Family Issues, 27,* 1701–1722.

Choi, N. G., & Mayer, J. (2000). Elder abuse, neglect, and exploitation: Risk factors and prevention strategies. *Journal of Gerontological Social Work, 33,* 5–25.

Chomsky, N. (1968). *Language and mind.* New York: Harcourt Brace Jovanovich.

Chomsky, N. (1978). On the biological basis of language capacities. In G. A. Miller & E. Lennenberg (Eds.), *Psychology and biology of language and thought* (pp. 199–220). New York: Academic Press.

Chomsky, N. (1991). Linguistics and cognitive science: Problems and mysteries. In A. Kasher (Ed.), *The Chomskyan turn.* Cambridge, MA: Blackwell.

Chomsky, N. (1999). On the nature, use, and acquisition of language. In W. C. Ritchie & T. J. Bhatia (Eds.), *Handbook of child language acquisition.* San Diego: Academic Press.

Chomsky, N. (2005). Editorial: Universals of human nature. *Psychotherapy and Psychosomatics* [serial online], *74,* 263–268.

Chong, W. (2007). The role of personal agency beliefs in academic self-regulation: An Asian perspective. *School Psychology International, 28,* 63–76.

Choy, C. M., Yeung, Q. S., Briton-Jones, C. M., Cheung, C. K., Lam, C. W., & Haines, C. J. (2002). Relationship between semen parameters and mercury concentrations in blood and in seminal fluid from subfertile males in Hong Kong. *Fertility and Sterility, 78,* 426–428.

Chrisler, J., & Smith, C. (2004). Feminism and psychology. *Praeger guide to the psychology of gender.* Westport, CT: Praeger Publishers/Greenwood Publishing Group.

Christakis, D., & Zimmerman, F. (2007). Violent television viewing during preschool is associated with antisocial behavior during school age. *Pediatrics, 120,* 993–999.

Christle, C., Jolivette, K., & Nelson, M. (2007, November). School characteristics related to high school dropout rates. *Remedial and Special Education,* 28(6), 325–339.

Christoff, K., Cosmelli, D., Legrand, D., & Thompson, E. (2011). Specifying the self for cognitive neuroscience. *Trends in Cognitive Sciences, 15,* 104–112.

Christophersen, E. R., Mortweet, S. L. (2003). Disciplining your child effectively. In E. R. Christophersen & S. L. Mortweet (Eds.), *Parenting that works: Building skills that last a lifetime.* Washington, DC, US: American Psychological Association.

Christova, P., Lewis, S., Tagaris, G., Ugurbil, K., & Georgopoulos, A. (2008). A voxel-by-voxel parametric fMRI study of motor mental rotation: hemispheric specialization and gender differences in neural processing efficiency. *Experimental Brain Research, 189,* 79–90.

Chronis, A., Jones, H., & Raggi, V. (2006, June). Evidence-based psychosocial treatments for children and adolescents with attention-deficit/hyperactivity disorder. *Clinical Psychology Review, 26,* 486–502.

Chulada, P., Corey, L., Vannappagari, V., Whitehead, N., & Blackshear, P. (2006). The feasibility of creating a population-based national twin registry in the United States. *Twin Research and Human Genetics, 9,* 919–926.

Chung, S. A., Wei, A. Q., Connor, D. E., Webb, G. C., Molloy, T., Pajic, M., & Diwan, A. D. (2007). Nucleus pulposus cellular longevity by telomerase gene therapy. *Spine, 15,* 1188–1196.

Cianciolo, A. T., Matthew, C., & Sternberg, R. J. (2006). Tacit knowledge, practical intelligence, and expertise. In K. A. Ericsson, N. Charness, P. J. Feltovich, & R. R. Hoffman, *The Cambridge handbook of expertise and expert performance.* New York: Cambridge University Press.

Ciani, A., & Capiluppi, C. (2011). Gene flow by selective emigration as a possible cause for personality differences between small islands and mainland populations. *European Journal Of Personality, 25,* 53–64.

Cicchetti, D. (1996). Child maltreatment: Implications for developmental theory and research. *Human Development, 39,* 18–39.

Cicchetti, D. (2003). Neuroendocrine functioning in maltreated children. In D. Cicchetti & E. Walker (Eds.), *Neurodevelopmental mechanisms in psychopathology.* New York: Cambridge University Press.

Cicchetti, D. (2004). An odyssey of discovery: Lessons learned through three decades of research on child maltreatment. *American Psychologist, Special issue: Awards Issue 2004, 59,* 731–741.

Cicchetti, D., & Beeghly, M. (Eds.). (1990). *Children with Down syndrome.* Cambridge: Cambridge University Press.

Cicchetti, D., & Cohen, D. J. (2006). *Developmental Psychopathology, Vol. 1: Theory and method* (2nd ed.) Hoboken, NJ: John Wiley & Sons.

Cicchetti, D., Rogosch, F. A., Maughan, A., Toth, S., & Bruce, J. (2003). False belief understanding in maltreated children. *Journal of Development and Psychopathology, Special issue, 15,* 1067–1091.

Cicchetti, D., & Toth, S. L. (1998). The development of depression in children and adolescents. *American Psychologist, 53,* 221–241.

Cicirelli, V. (2001). Personal meanings of death in older adults and young adults in relation to their fears of death. *Death Studies, 25,* 663–683.

Cillessen, A., & Borch, C. (2008). Analyzing social networks in adolescence. In *Modeling dyadic and interdependent data in the developmental and behavioral sciences* (pp. 61–85). New York: Routledge/Taylor & Francis Group.

Cillessen, A. H. N., & Mayeux, L. (2004). From censure to reinforcement: Developmental changes in the association between aggression and social status. *Child Development, 75,* 147–163.

Cimbolic, P., & Jobes, D. A. (Eds). (1990). *Youth suicide: Issues, assessment, and intervention.* Springfield, IL: Charles C Thomas.

Cina, V., & Fellmann, F. (2006). Implications of predictive testing in neurodegenerative disorders. *Schweizer Archiv für Neurologie und Psychiatrie, 157,* 359–365.

CIRE (Cooperative Institutional Research Program of the American Council on Education). (1990). *The American freshman: National norms for fall 1990.* Los Angeles: American Council on Edcuation.

Ciricelli, V. G. (1995). *Sibling relationships across the life span.* New York: Plenum.

Cirulli, F., Berry, A., & Alleva, E. (2003). Early disruption of the mother-infant relationship: Effects on brain plasticity and implications for psychopathology. *Neuroscience & Biobehavioral Reviews, 27,* 73–82.

Claes, M., Lacourse, E., & Bouchard, C. (2003). Parental practices in late adolescence, a comparison of three countries: Canada, France and Italy. *Journal of Adolescence, 26,* 387–399.

Clark, E. (1983). Meanings and concepts. In J. Flavell & E. Markham (Eds.), *Handbook of child psychology: Cognitive development* (Vol. 3). New York: Wiley.

Clark, J. E., & Humphrey, J. H. (Eds.). (1985). *Motor development: Current selected research.* Princeton, NJ: Princeton Book Company.

Clark, K. B., & Clark, M. P. (1947). Racial identification and preference in Negro children. In T. M. Newcomb & E. L. Hartley (Eds.), *Readings in social psychology.* New York: Holt, Rinehart & Winston.

Clark, L. (2010). Decision-making during gambling: an integration of cognitive and psychobiological approaches. *Philosophical Transactions of the Royal Society of London: B Biological Sciences, 365,* 319–330.

Clark, M., & Arnold, J. (2008). The nature, prevalence and correlates of generativity among men in middle career. *Journal of Vocational Behavior, 73,* 473–484.

Clark, M., & Mills, J. (1993). The difference between communal and exchange relationships: What it is and is not. *Personality and Social Psychology Bulletin, 19,* 684–691.

Clark, M. S., Mills, J. R., & Corcoran, D. M. (1989). Keeping track of needs and inputs of friends and strangers. *Personality and Social Psychology Bulletin, 15,* 533–542.

Clark, R. (1998). *Expertise.* Silver Spring, MD: International Society for Performance Improvement.

Clark, R., Hyde, J. S., Essex, M. J., & Klein, M. H. (1997). Length of maternity leave and quality of mother-infant interactions. *Child Development, 68,* 364–383.

Clarkberg, M., Stolzenberg, R. M., & Waite, L. J. (1995). Attitudes, values, and entrance into cohabitational versus marital unions. *Social Forces, 74,* 609–632.

Clarke, L. (2005). Remarriage in later life: Older women's negotiation of power, resources and domestic labor. *Journal of Women & Aging, 17,* 21–41.

Clarke, L., & Griffin, M. (2007). The body natural and the body unnatural: Beauty work and aging. *Journal of Aging Studies, 21,* 187–201.

Clarke, S., & Parise, S. (2011, January 10). Girl killed in Arizona shooting spree was born on 9/11, loved being symbol of nation's hope. *ABC Good Morning America.* Retrieved from http://abcnews.go.com/US/giffords-tucson-shooting-christina-taylor-green-born-911/story?id=12578816.

Clarke, T.-K., Treutlein, J., Zimmermann, U. S., Kiefer, F., Skowronek, M. H., Rietschel, M., et al. (2008). HPA-axis activity in alcoholism: Examples for a gene-environment interaction. *Addiction Biology, 13,* 1–14.

Clarke-Stewart, A. (1993). *Daycare.* Cambridge, MA: Harvard University Press.

Clarke-Stewart, A., & Friedman, S. (1987). *Child development: Infancy through adolescence.* New York: Wiley.

Clarke-Stewart, K., & Allhusen, V. (2002). Nonparental caregiving. In M. Bornstein (Ed.), *Handbook of parenting: Vol. 3: Being and becoming a parent* (2nd ed.). Mahwah, NJ: Lawrence Erlbaum Associates.

Clarke-Stewart, K. A., & Bailey, B. (1990). Adjusting to divorce: Why do men have it easier? *Journal of Divorce, 13,* 75–94.

Clauss-Ehlers, C. (2008). Sociocultural factors, resilience, and coping: Support for a culturally sensitive measure of resilience. *Journal of Applied Developmental Psychology, 29,* 197–212.

Claxton, L., McCarty, M., & Keen, R. (2009). Self-directed action affects planning in tool-use tasks with toddlers. *Infant Behavior & Development, 32,* 230–233.

Clearfield, M., & Nelson, N. (2006, January). Sex differences in mothers' speech and play behavior with 6-, 9-, and 14-month-old infants. *Sex Roles, 54,* 127–137.

Clements, R., & Swensen, C. (2003). Commitment to one's spouse as a predictor of marital quality among older couples. In *Love, romance, sexual interaction: Research perspectives from current psychology* (pp. 183–195). New Brunswick, NJ: Transaction Publishers.

Clemetson, L. (1998, September). Our daughters, ourselves. *Newsweek* [special issue], pp. 14–17.

Clemetson, L. (2000, September 18). Love without borders. *Newsweek,* p. 62.

Click, E. (2006). Developing a worksite lactation program. *MCN: The American Journal of Maternal/Child Nursing, 31,* 313–317.

Cliff, D. (1991). Negotiating a livable retirement: Further paid work and the quality of life in early retirement. *Aging and Society, 11,* 319–340.

Clifford, S. (2009, June 2). Online, "a reason to keep on going." *The New York Times,* P. D5.

Clifton, R. (1992). The development of spatial hearing in human infants. In L. A. Werner & E. W. Rubel (Eds.), *Developmental psychoacoustics* (pp. 135–157). Washington, DC: American Psychological Association.

Clifton, R. K., Gwiazda, Bauer, J. A., Clarkson, M. G., & Held, R. M. (1988). Growth in head size during infancy: Implications for sound localization. *Developmental Psychology, 24,* 477–483.

Clingempeel, W., Britt, S., & Henggeler, S. (2008). Beyond treatment effects: Comorbid psychopathologies and long-term outcomes among substance-abusing delinquents. *American Journal of Orthopsychiatry, 78,* 29–36.

Clinton, J. F., & Kelber, S. T. (1993). Stress and coping in fathers of newborns: Comparisons of planned versus unplanned pregnancy. *International Journal of Nursing Studies, 30,* 437–443.

Clinton, H. (1996). *It takes a village and other lessons children teach us.* New York: Touchstone.

Closson, L. (2009). Status and gender differences in early adolescents' descriptions of popularity. *Social Development, 18,* 412–426.

Cnattingius, S., Berendes, H., & Forman, M. (1993). Do delayed childbearers face increased risks of adverse pregnancy outcomes after the first birth? *Obstetrics and Gynecology, 81,* 512–516.

CNN/USA Today/Gallup Poll. (1997, February). How many children? *The Gallup Poll Monthly.*

Coats, E., & Feldman, R. S. (1995). The role of television in the socialization of nonverbal behavioral skills. *Basic and Applied Social Psychology, 17,* 327–341.

Coats, E. J., Feldman, R. S., & Schwartzberg, S. (1994). *Critical thinking: General principles and case studies.* New York: McGraw-Hill.

Cobbe, E. (2003, September 25). France ups heat toll. *CBS Evening News.*

Coelho, M., Ferreira, J., Dias, B., Sampaio, C., Martins, I., & Castro-Caldas, A. (2004). Assessment of time perception: The effect of aging. *Journal of the International Neuropsychological Society, 10,* 332–341.

Cohan, C. L., & Bradbury, T. N. (1997). Negative life events, marital interaction, and the longitudinal course of newlywed marriage. *Journal of Personality and Social Psychology, 73,* 114–128.

Cohen, J. (1999, March 19). Nurture helps mold able minds. *Science, 283,* 1832–1833.

Cohen, L. B. (1972). Attention-getting and attention-holding processes of infant visual preference. *Child Development, 43,* 869–879.

Cohen, L. B., & Cashon, C. (2003). Infant perception and cognition. In R. Lerner & M. Easterbrooks (Eds.), *Handbook of psychology: Developmental psychology* (Vol. 6, pp. 267–291). New York: Wiley.

Cohen, L. B., & Cashon, C. (2006). Infant cognition. *Handbook of child psychology: Vol 2, Cognition, perception, and language* (6th ed.). Hoboken, NJ: John Wiley & Sons Inc.

Cohen, P., Cohen, J., Kasen, S., Velez, C. N., Hartmark, C., Johnson, J., et al. (1993). An epidemiological study of disorders in late childhood and adolescence: I. Age- and gender-specfic prevalence. *Journal of Child Psychology and Psychiatry and Allied Disciplines, 34,* 851–867.

Cohen, S. E. (1995). Biosocial factors in early infancy as predictors of competence in adolescents who were born prematurely. *Journal of Developmental & Behavioral Pediatrics, 16,* 36–41.

Cohen, S., Hamrick, N., Rodriguez, M. S., Feldman, P. J., Rabin B. S., & Manuck, S. B. (2002). Reactivity and vulnerability to stress-associated risk for upper respiratory illness. *Psychosomatic Medicine, 64,* 302–310.

Cohen, S., Kamarck, T., & Mermelstein, R. (1983). A global measure of perceived stress. *Journal of Health and Social Behavior, 24,* 385–396.

Cohen, S., Tyrell, D. A., & Smith, A. P. (1993). Negative life events, perceived stress, negative affect, and susceptibility of the common cold. *Journal of Personality and Social Psychology, 64,* 131–140.

Cohen, S., Tyrell, D. A., & Smith, A. P. (1997). Psychological stress in humans and susceptibility to the common cold. In T. W. Miller (Ed.), *International Universities Press stress and health series, Monograph 7. Clinical disorders and stressful life events* (pp. 217–235). Madison, CT: International Universities Press.

Cohn, J. F., & Tronick, E. Z. (1989). Mother–infant face-to-face interaction: Influence is bidirectional and unrelated to periodic cycles in either partner's behavior. *Developmental Psychology, 24,* 386–392.

Cohn, R. M. (1982). Economic development and status change of the aged. *American Journal of Sociology, 87,* 1150–1161.

Cohrs, J., Abele, A., & Dette, D. (2006, July). Integrating situational and dispositional determinants of job satisfaction: Findings from three samples of professionals. *Journal of Psychology: Interdisciplinary and Applied, 140,* 363–395.

Cokley, K. (2003). What do we know about the motivation of African American students? Challenging the "anti-intellectual" myth. *Harvard Educational Review, 73,* 524–558.

Col, N., & Komoroff, A. L. (2004, May 10). How to think about HT. *Newsweek,* pp. 81, 83.

Colby, A., & Damon, W. (1987). Listening to a different voice: A review of Gilligan's in a different voice. In M. R. Walsh (Ed.), *The psychology of women.* New Haven, CT: Yale University Press.

Colby, A., & Kohlberg, L. (1987). *The measurement of moral adjudgment* (Vols. 1–2). New York: Cambridge University Press.

Colcombe, S. J., Erickson, K. I., Scalf, P. E., Kim, J. S., Prakash, R., McAuley, E., et al. (2006). Aerobic exercise training increases brain volume in aging humans. *Journal of Gerontology, A. Biological Sciences and Medical Sciences, 61,* 1166–1170.

Colditz, G. A., Hankinson, S. E., Hunter, D. J., Willett, W. C., Manson, J. E., Stampfer, M. J., et al. (1995, June 15). The use of estrogens and progestins and the risk of breast cancer in postmenopausal women. *The New England Journal of Medicine, 332,* 1589–1593.

Cole, C. F., Arafat, C., & Tidhar, C. (2003). The educational impact of Rechov Sumsum/Shara'a Simsim: A Sesame Street television series to promote respect and understanding among children living in Israel, the West Bank and Gaza. *International Journal of Behavioral Development, 27,* 409–422.

Cole, D. A., Maxwell, S. E., Martin, J. M., Peeke, L. G., Seroczynski, A. D., Tram, J. M., et al. (2001). The development of multiple domains of child and adolescent self-concept: A cohort sequential longitudinal design. *Child Development, 72,* 1723–1746.

Cole, M. (1992). Culture in development. In M. H. Bornstein & M. E. Lamb (Eds.), *Developmental psychology: An advanced textbook* (3rd ed.). Hillsdale, NJ: Erlbaum.

Cole, M. (1996). *Cultural psychology: A once and future discipline.* Cambridge, MA: Harvard University Press.

Cole, M. (2006). Culture and cognitive development in phylogenetic, historical, and ontogenetic perspective. In *Handbook of child psychology: Vol 2, Cognition, perception, and language* (6th ed.). Hoboken, NJ: John Wiley & Sons Inc.

Cole, M., Gay, J., Glick, J. A., & Sharp, D. W. (1971). *The cultural context of learning and thinking.* New York: Basic Books.

Cole, P., Dennis, T., Smith-Simon, K., & Cohen, L. (2009). Preschoolers' emotion regulation strategy understanding: Relations with emotion socialization and child self-regulation. *Social Development, 18,* 324–352.

Cole, S. A. (2005). Infants in foster care: Relational and environmental factors affecting attachment. *Journal of Reproductive & Infant Psychology, 23,* 43–61.

Coleman, C. A., Friedman, A. G., & Burright, R. G. (1998). The relationship of daily stress and health-related behaviors to adolescents' cholesterol levels. *Adolescence, 33,* 447–460.

Coleman, H., Chan, C., Ferris, F., & Chew, E. (2008). Age-related macular degeneration. *The Lancet, 372,* 1835–1845.

Coleman, J. (1961). *The adolescent society.* Glencoe, IL: Free Press.

Coleman, M., & Ganong, L. H. (2003). *Handbook of contemporary families: Considering the past, contemplating the future.* Thousand Oaks, CA: Sage Publications.

Coleman, M., Ganong, L., & Weaver, S. (2001). Relationship maintenance and enhancement in remarried families. In J. Harvey & A. Wenzel (Eds.), *Close romantic relationships: Maintenance and enhancement.* Mahwah, NJ: Lawrence Erlbaum Associates.

Coleman, P. (2005, July). Editorial: Uses of reminiscence: Functions and benefits. *Aging & Mental Health, 9,* 291–294.

Coleman, S. (2011). Addressing the puzzle of race. *Journal of Social Work Education, 47,* 91–108.

Colen, C., Geronimus, A., & Phipps, M. (2006, September). Getting a piece of the pie? The economic boom of the 1990s and declining teen birth rates in the United States. *Social Science & Medicine, 63,* 1531–1545.

Coles, C. D., Platzman, K. A., & Lynch, M. E. (2002). Auditory and visual sustained attention in adolescents parentally exposed to alcohol. *Clinical and Experimental Research, 26,* 263–271.

Coley, R. L., & Chase-Lansdale, P. L. (1998). Adolescent pregnancy and parenthood: Recent evidence and future directions. *American Psychologist, 53,* 152–166.

Colibazzi, T., Zhu, H., Bansal, R., Schultz, R., Wang, Z., & Peterson, B. (2008). Latent volumetric structure of the human brain: Exploratory factor analysis and structural equation modeling of gray matter volumes in healthy children and adults. *Human Brain Mapping, 29,* 1302–1312.

Colino, S. (2002, February 26). Problem kid or label? *The Washington Post,* p. HE01.

College Board. (2005). *2001 college bound seniors are the largest, most diverse group in history.* New York: College Board.

Collett, B. R., Gimpel, G. A., Greenson, J. N., & Gunderson, T. L. (2001). Assessment of discipline styles among parents of preschool through school-age children. *Journal of Psychopathology and Behavioral Assessment, 23,* 163–170.

Collins, W. (2003). More than myth: The developmental significance of romantic relationships during adolescence. *Journal of Research on Adolescence, 13,* 1–24.

Collins, W., & Andrew, L. (2004). Changing relationships, changing youth: Interpersonal contexts of adolescent development. *Journal of Early Adolescence, 24,* 55–62.

Collins, W., & Doolittle, A. (2006, December). Personal reflections of funeral rituals and spirituality in a Kentucky African American family. *Death Studies, 30,* 957–969.

Collins, W. A., Gleason, T., & Sesma, A. (1997). Internalization, autonomy, and relationships: Development during adolescence. In J. E. Grusec & L. Kuczynski (Eds.), *Parenting and children's internalization of values: A handbook of contemporary theory* (pp. 78–99). New York: Wiley.

Collins, W. A., Maccoby, E. E., Steinberg, L., Hetherington, E. M., & Bornstein, M. H. (2000). Contemporary research on parenting: The case for nature and nurture. *American Psychologist, 55,* 218–232.

Collins, W. A., & Steinberg, L. (2006). Adolescent development in interpersonal context. In *Handbook of child psychology: Vol. 3, Social, emotional, and personality development* (6th ed.). Hoboken, NJ: John Wiley & Sons Inc.

Collishaw, S., Pickles, A., Messer, J., Rutter, M., Shearer, C., & Maughan, B. (2007). Resilience to adult psychopathology following childhood maltreatment: Evidence from a community sample. *Child Abuse & Neglect, 31,* 211–229.

Colom, R., Lluis-Font, J. M., & Andrés-Pueyo, A. (2005). The generational intelligence gains are caused by decreasing variance in the lower half of the distribution: Supporting evidence for the nutrition hypothesis. *Intelligence, 33,* 83–91.

Colombo, J., & Mitchell, D. (2009). Infant visual habituation. *Neurobiology of Learning and Memory, 92,* 225–234.

Colon, J. M. (1997). Assisted reproductive technologies. In M. L. Sipski & C. J. Alexander (Eds.), *Sexual function in people with disability and chronic illness: A health professional's guide* (pp. 557–575). Gaithersburg, MD: Aspen Publishers.

Colpin, H., & Soenen, S. (2004). Bonding. Through an adoptive mother's eyes. *Midwifery Today, 70,* 30–31.

Coltrane, S., & Adams, M. (1997). Children and gender. In T. Arendell (Ed.), *Contemporary parenting: Challenges and issues. Understanding families* (Vol. 9, pp. 219–253). Thousand Oaks, CA: Sage.

Combs, D., Basso, M., Wanner, J., & Ledet, S. (2008). Schizophrenia. *Handbook of psychological assessment, case conceptualization, and treatment, Vol 1: Adults.* Hoboken, NJ: John Wiley & Sons Inc.

Committee on Children, Youth and Families. (1994). *When you need child day care.* Washington, DC: American Psychological Association.

Committee to Study the Prevention of Low Birthweight. (1985). *Preventing low birthweight.* Washington, DC: National Academy Press.

Common Sense Media. (2011). *Zero to eight: Children's media use in America.* San Francisco: Common Sense Media.

Commons, M. L., Galaz-Fontes, J. F., &Morse, S. J. (2006). Leadership, cross-cultural contact, socioeconomic status, and formal operational reasoning about moral dilemmas among Mexican non-literate adults and high school students. *Journal of Moral Education, 35,* 247–267.

Commons, M., & Richards, F. (2003). Four postformal stages. In *Handbook of adult development.* New York: Kluwer Academic/Plenum Publishers.

Compton, R., & Weissman, D. (2002). Hemispheric asymmetries in global-local perception: Effects of individual differences in neuroticism. *Laterality, 7,* 333–350.

Comstock, G., & Strasburger, V. C. (1990). Deceptive appearances: Television violence and aggressive behavior. Conference: Teens and television (1988, Los Angeles, California). *Journal of Adolescent Health Care, 11,* 31–44.

Comunian, A. L., & Gielen, U. P. (2000). Sociomoral reflection and prosocial and antisocial behavior: Two Italian studies. Psychological *Reports, 87,* 161–175.

Condit, V. (1990). Anorexia nervosa: Levels of causation. *Human Nature, 1,* 391–413.

Condly, S. (2006, May). Resilience in children: A review of literature with implications for education. *Urban Education, 41,* 211–236.

Condry, J. (1989). *The psychology of television.* Hillsdale, NJ: Erlbaum.

Condry, J., & Condry, S. (1976). Sex differences: A study of the eye of the beholder. *Child Development, 47,* 812–819.

Conel, J. L. (1930/1963). *Postnatal development of the human cortex* (Vols. 1–6). Cambridge, MA: Harvard University Press.

Conklin, H. M., & Iacono, W. G. (2002). Schizophrenia: A neurodevelopmental perspective. *Current Directions in Psychological Science, 11,* 33–37.

Conn, V. S. (2003). Integrative review of physical activity intervention research with aging adults. *Journal of the American Geriatrics Society, 51,* 1159–1168.

Connell-Carrick, K. (2006). Early child care and early child development: Major findings of the NICHD Study of Early Child Care. *Child Welfare Journal, 85,* 819–836.

Conner, K., & Goldston, D. (2007, March). Rates of suicide among males increase steadily from age 11 to 21: Developmental framework and outline for prevention. *Aggression and Violent Behavior, 12(2),* 193–207.

Connor, R. (1992). *Cracking the over-50 job market.* New York: Penguin Books.

Connor, T. (2008). Don't stress out your immune system—Just relax. *Brain, Behavior, and Immunity, 22,* 1128–1129.

Conroy, S., Pariante, C. M., Marks, M. N., Davies, H. A., Farrelly, S., Schacht, R., et al. (2012). Maternal psychopathology and infant development at 18 months: The impact of maternal personality disorder and depression. *Journal of the American Academy of Child & Adolescent Psychiatry, 51,* 51–61.

Consedine, N., Magai, C., & King, A. (2004). Deconstructing positive affect in later life: A differential functionalist analysis of joy and interest. *International Journal of Aging & Human Development, 58,* 49–68.

Conti, R., Amabile, T. M., & Pollak, S. (1995). The positive impact of creative activity: Effects of creative task engagement and motivational focus on college students' learning. *Personality and Social Psychology Bulletin, 21,* 1107–1116.

Continelli, L. (2006, December 24). From boxing to books. *Buffalo News,* p. B3.

Cook, A. S., & Oltjenbruns, K. A. (1989). *Dying and grieving: Lifespan and family perspectives.* New York: Holt, Rinehart & Winston.

Cook, E., Buehler, C., & Henson, R. (2009). Parents and peers as social influences to deter antisocial behavior. *Journal of Youth and Adolescence, 38,* 1240–1252.

Cook, L. (1994). Circumcision and sexually transmitted diseases. *American Journal of Public Health, 84,* 197–201.

Cooke, L. (2007). The importance of exposure for healthy eating in childhood: A review. *Journal of Human Nutrition and Dietetics, 20,* 294–301.

Coon, K. D., Myers, A. J., Craig, D. W., Webster, J. A., Pearson, J. V., Lince, D. H., et al. (2007). A high-density whole-genome association study reveals that APOE is the major susceptibility gene for sporadic late-onset Alzheimer's disease. *Journal of Clinical Psychiatry, 68,* 613–618.

Coons, S., & Guilleminault, C. (1982). Developments of sleep–wake patterns and non-rapid-eye-movement sleep stages during the first six months of life in normal infants. *Pediatrics, 69,* 793–798.

Cooper, B. (2001). Nature, nurture and mental disorder: Old concepts in the new millennium. *British Journal of Psychiatry, 178* (Suppl. 40), s91–s101.

Cooper, H. (1989). Synthesis of research on homework. *Educational Leadership, 47,* 85–91.

Cooper, H., Steenbergen-Hu, S., & Dent, A. L. (2012). Homework. In K. R. Harris, S. Graham, T. Urdan, A. G. Bus, S. Major, H. Swanson, et al. (Eds.), *APA educational psychology handbook, Vol 3: Application to teaching and learning.* Washington, DC: American Psychological Association.

Cooper, H., & Valentine, J. (2001). Using research to answer practical questions about homework. *Educational Psychologist, 36,* 143–153.

Cooper, N. R., Kalaria, R. N., McGeer, P. L., & Rogers, J. (2000). Key issues in Alzheimer's disease inflammation. *Neurobiology of Aging, 21,* 451–453.

Cooper, R. P., & Aslin, R. N. (1990). Preference for infant-directed speech in the first month after birth. *Child Development, 61,* 1584–1595.

Cooper, R. P., & Aslin, R. N. (1994). Developmental differences in infant attention to the spectral properties of infant-directed speech. *Child Development, 65,* 1663–1677.

Cooperative Institutional Research Program. (1990). *The American freshman: National norms for fall 1990.* Los Angeles: American Council on Education.

Cooperstock, M. S., Bakewell, J., Herman, A., & Schramm W. F. (1998). Effects of fetal sex and race on risk of very preterm birth in twins. *American Journal of Obstetrics & Gynecology, 179,* 762–765.

Copple, C., & Bredekamp, S. (1997). *Developmental appropriate practice in early childhood programs, Revised edition.* Washington, DC: National Association for the Education of Young Children.

Corballis, M. (2002). *From hand to mouth: The origins of language.* Princeton, NJ: Princeton University Press.

Corballis, M. C. (1999, March–April). The gestural origins of language. *American Scientist, 87,* 138–145.

Corballis, M. C. (2000). How laterality will survive the millennium bug. *Brain & Cognition, 42,* 160–162.

Corballis, M. C., Hattie, J., & Fletcher, R. (2008). Handedness and intellectual achievement: an even-handed look. *Neuropsychologia, 46,* 374–378.

Corballis, P. (2003). Visuospatial processing and the right-hemisphere interpreter. *Brain & Cognition, 53,* 171–176.

Corbetta, D., & Snapp-Childs, W. (2009). Seeing and touching: The role of sensory-motor experience on the development of infant reaching. *Infant Behavior & Development, 32,* 44–58.

Corbin, C. (1973). *A textbook of motor development.* Dubuque, IA: Brown.

Corbin, J. (2007). Reactive attachment disorder: A biopsychosocial disturbance of attachment. *Child & Adolescent Social Work Journal, 24,* 539–552.

Corcoran, J., & Pillai, V. (2007, January). Effectiveness of secondary pregnancy prevention programs: A meta-analysis. *Research on Social Work Practice, 17,* 5–18.

Cordes, S., & Brannon, E. (2009). Crossing the divide: Infants discriminate small from large numerosities. *Developmental Psychology, 45,* 1583–1594.

Cordón, I. M., Pipe, M., Sayfan, L., Melinder, A., & Goodman, G. S. (2004). Memory for traumatic experiences in early childhood. *Developmental Review, 24,* 101–132.

Coren, S., & Halpern, D. F. (1991). Left-handedness: A marker for decreased survival fitness. *Psychological Bulletin, 109(1),* 90–106.

Corenblum, B. B., & Armstrong, H. D. (2012). Racial-ethnic identity development in children in a racial-ethnic minority group. *Canadian Journal of Behavioural Science/Revue Canadienne Des Sciences Du Comportement.* Retrieved from http://psycnet.apa.org/psycinfo/2012-03823-001/.

Corliss, J. (1996, October 29). Alzheimer's in the news. *HealthNews*, p. 1–2.

Cormier, K., Mauk, C., & Repp, A. (1998). Manual babbling in deaf and hearing infants: A longitudinal study. In E. V. Clark (Ed.), *The proceedings of the twenty-ninth annual child language research forum.* Stanford, CA: Center for the Study of Language and Information.

Cornelius, M. D., Day, N. L., Richardson, G. A., & Taylor, P. M. (1999). Epidemiology of substance abuse during pregnancy. In P. J. Ott, R. E. Tarter, & R. T. Ammerman (Eds.), *Sourcebook on substance abuse: Etiology, epidemiology, assessment, and treatment.* Boston: Allyn & Bacon.

Cornell, T. L., Fromkin, V. A., & Mauner, G. (1993). A linguistic approach to language processing in Broca's aphasia: A paradox resolved. *Current Directions in Psychological Science, 2*, 47–52.

Cornish, K., Turk, J., & Hagerman, R. (2008). The fragile X continuum: New advances and perspectives. *Journal of Intellectual Disability Research, 52*, 469–482.

Corno, L. (1996). Homework is a complicated thing. Section 4: Grading the policymakers' solution. *Educational Researcher, 25*, 27–30.

Cornwell, T., & McAlister, A. R. (2011). Alternative thinking about starting points of obesity. Development of child taste preferences. *Appetite, 56*, 428–439.

Corr, C. (1991/1992). A task-based approach to coping with dying. *Omega, 24*, 81–94.

Corr, C. (2007). Hospice: Achievements, legacies, and challenges. *Omega: Journal of Death and Dying, 56*, 111–120.

Corr, C., & Corr, D. (2000). Anticipatory mourning and coping with dying: Similarities, differences, and suggested guidelines for helpers. In T. Rando (Ed.), *Clinical dimensions of anticipatory mourning: Theory and practice in working with the dying, their loved ones, and their caregivers.* Champaign, IL: Research Press.

Corr, C., & Corr, D. (2007). Historical and contemporary perspectives on loss, grief, and mourning. In *Handbook of thanatology: The essential body of knowledge for the study of death, dying, and bereavement* (pp. 131–142). New York; Northbrook, IL: Routledge/Taylor & Francis Group.

Corr, C., & Doka, K. (2001). Master concepts in the field of death, dying, and bereavement: Coping versus adaptive strategies. *Omega: Journal of Death & Dying, 43*, 183–199.

Corr, C., Nabe, C., & Corr, D. (2006). *Death & dying, life & living.* Belmont, CA: Thomson Wadsworth.

Coscia, J., Ris, M., & Succop, P. (2003). Cognitive development of lead exposed children from ages 6 to 15 years: An application of growth curve analysis. *Child Neuropsychology, 9*, 10–21.

Costa, P. T., Busch, C. M., Zonderman, A. B., & McCrae, R. R. (1993). Correlations of MMPI factor scales with measures of the five factor model of personality. *Journal of Personality Assessment, 50*, 640–650.

Costa, P. T., Jr., & McCrae, R. R. (1988). Personality in adulthood: A six-year longitudinal study of self-report and spouse ratings on the NEO Personality Inventory. *Journal of Personality and Social Psychology, 54*, 853–863.

Costa, P. T., Jr., & McCrae, R. R. (1989). Personality continuity and the changes of adult life. In M. Storandt & G. R. VandenBos (Eds.), *The adult years: Continuity and change.* Washington, DC: American Psychological Association.

Costa, P. T., & McCrae, R. R. (1997). Longitudinal stability of adult personality. In R. Hogan, J. A. Johnson, &

S. R. Briggs (Eds.), *Handbook of personality psychology* (pp. 269–290). San Diego, CA: Academic Press.

Costa, P., & McCrae, R. R. (2002). Looking backward: Changes in the mean levels of personality traits from 80 to 12. In D. Cervone & W. Mischel (Eds.), *Advances in personality science.* New York: Guilford Press.

Costello, E., Compton, S., & Keeler, G. (2003). Relationships between poverty and psychopathology: A natural experiment. *Journal of the American Medical Association, 290*, 2023–2029.

Costello, E., Sung, M., Worthman, C., & Angold, A. (2007, April). Pubertal maturation and the development of alcohol use and abuse. *Drug and Alcohol Dependence, 88*, S50–s59.

Costigan, A. T., Crocco, M. S., & Zumwalt, K. K. (2004). *Learning to teach in an age of accountability.* Mahwah, NJ: Lawrence Erlbaum Associates.

Côté, J. (2005). Editor's introduction. *Identity, 5*, 95–96.

Cotrufo, P., Cella, S., Cremato, F., & Labella, A. (2007, December). Eating disorder attitude and abnormal eating behaviours in a sample of 11–13 year-old school children: The role of pubertal body transformation. *Eating and Weight Disorders, 12*(4), 154–160.

Cottreaux, J. (1993). Behavioral psychotherapy applications in the medically ill. *Psychotherapy and Psychosomatics, 60*, 116–128.

Cotugno, G. G., Nicolò, R. R., Cappelletti, S. S., Goffredo, B. M., Vici, C., & Di Ciommo, V. V. (2011). Adherence to diet and quality of life in patients with phenylketonuria. *Acta Paediatrica, 100*, 1144–1149.

Coulson, N. S., Buchanan, H., & Aubeeluck, A. (2007). Social support in cyberspace: A content analysis of communication within a Huntington's disease online support group. *Patient Education and Counseling, 68*, 173–178.

Couperus, J., & Nelson, C. (2006). Early brain development and plasticity. In *Blackwell handbook of early childhood development.* Blackwell Publishing.

Courchesne, E., Carper, R., & Akshoomoff, N. (2003). Evidence of brain overgrowth in the first year of life in austism. *Journal of the American Medical Association, 290*, 337–344.

Courtney, E., Gamboz, J., & Johnson, J. (2008). Problematic eating behaviors in adolescents with low self-esteem and elevated depressive symptoms. *Eating Behaviors, 9*, 408–414.

Couzin, J. (2002, June 21). Quirks of fetal environment felt decades later. *Science, 296*, 2167–2169.

Couzin, J. (2004, July 23). Volatile chemistry: Children and antidepressants. *Science, 305*, 468–470.

Cowan, C. P., & Cowan, P. A. (1992). *When partners become parents.* New York: Wiley.

Cowan, N., Saults, J., & Elliot, E. (2002). The search for what is fundamental in the development of working memory. In R. Kail & H. Reese (Eds.), *Advances in child development and behavior* (Vol. 29). San Diego: Academic Press.

Cowgill, D. O. (1968). The social life of the aging in Thailand. *Gerontologist, 8*, 159–163.

Cowgill, D. O., & Holmes, L. D. (1972). *Aging and modernization.* New York: Appleton-Century-Crofts.

Cowley, G. (1997, June 30). How to live to 100. *Newsweek*, pp. 58–67.

Cowley, G. (2000). For the love of language. *Newsweek Special issue: Your child*, pp. 12–15.

Cowley, G. (2000, January 31). Alzheimer's: Unlocking the mystery. *Newsweek*, pp. 46–51.

Cox, C., Kotch, J., & Everson, M. (2003). A longitudinal study of modifying influences in the relationship between domestic violence and child maltreatment. *Journal of Family Violence, 18*, 5–17.

Cox, G. R. (2007). Religion, spirituality, and traumatic death. In D. Balk, C. Wogrin, G. Thornton, & D. Meagher (Eds.), *Handbook of thanatology: The essential body of knowledge for the study of death, dying, and*

bereavement. New York: Routledge/Taylor & Francis Group.

Cox, M. J., Owen, M. T., Henderson, V. K., & Margand, N. A. (1992). Prediction of infant–father and infant–mother attachment. *Developmental Psychology, 28*, 474–483.

Coyle, J. T., Oster-Granite, M. L., Reeves, R., Hohmann, C., Corsi, P., & Gearhart, J. (1991). Down syndrome and trisomy 16 mouse: Impact of gene imbalance on brain development and aging. In P. R. McHuagh & V. A. McKusick (Eds.), *Genes, brain, and behavior. Research publications: Association for Research in Nervous and Mental Disease* (Vol. 69). New York: Raven Press Publishers.

Coyne, J., Thombs, B., Stefanek, M., & Palmer, S. (2009). Time to let go of the illusion that psychotherapy extends the survival of cancer patients: Reply to Kraemer, Kuchler, and Spiegel (2009). *Psychological Bulletin, 135*, 179–182.

Craig, C., & Sprang, G. (2007, April). Trauma exposure and child abuse potential: Investigating the cycle of violence. *American Journal of Orthopsychiatry, 77*(2), 296–305.

Craik, F. I. M. (1984). Age differences in remembering. In L. R. Squire & N. Butters (Eds.), *Neuropsychology of memory.* New York: Guilford.

Craik, F. I. M. (1990). Levels of processing. In M. E. Eysenck (Ed.), *The Blackwell dictionary of cognitive psychology.* London: Blackwell.

Craik, F. I. M. (1994). Memory changes in normal aging. *Current Directions in Psychological Science, 3*, 155–158.

Craik, F. I. M., & Lockhart, R. S. (1972). Levels of processing: A framework for memory research. *Journal of Verbal Behavior, 11*, 671–684.

Craik, F. I. M., & Salthouse, T. A. (Eds.). (1999). *The handbook of aging and cognition* (2nd ed.). Mahwah, NJ: Erlbaum.

Cramer, M., Chen, L., Roberts, S., & Clute, D. (2007). Evaluating the social and economic impact of community-based prenatal care. *Public Health Nursing, 24*, 329–336.

Crane, E., & Morris, J. (2006). Changes in maternal age in England and Wales—Implications for Down syndrome. *Down Syndrome: Research & Practice, 10*, 41–43.

Cratty, B. (1979). *Perceptual and motor development in infants and children* (2nd ed.). Englewood Cliffs, NJ: Prentice-Hall.

Cratty, B. (1986). *Perceptual and motor development in infants and children* (3rd ed.). Englewood Cliffs, NJ: Prentice-Hall.

Crawford, D., Houts, R., & Huston, T. (2002). Compatiability, leisure, and satisfaction in marital relationships. *Journal of Marriage & Family, 64*, 433–449.

Crawford, M., & Unger, R. (2004). *Women and gender: A feminist psychology* (4th ed.). New York: McGraw-Hill.

Crawley, A., Anderson, D., & Santomero, A. (2002). Do children learn how to watch television? The impact of extensive experience with Blue's Clues on preschool children's television viewing behavior. *Journal of Communication, 52*, 264–280.

Crews, D. (1993). The organizational concept and vertebrates without sex chromosomes. *Brain, Behavior, and Evolution, 42*, 202–214.

Crick, N. R., Casas, J. G., & Ku, H. (1999). Relational and physical forms of peer victimization in preschool. *Developmental Psychology, 35*, 376–385.

Crisp, A., Gowers, S., Joughin, N., McClelland, L., Rooney, B., Nielsen, S., et al. (2006, May). Anorexia nervosa in males: Similarities and differences to anorexia nervosa in females. *European Eating Disorders Review, 14*, 163–167.

Crisp, R., Bache, L., & Maitner, A. (2009). Dynamics of social comparison in counter-stereotypic domains:

Stereotype boost, not stereotype threat, for women engineering majors. *Social Influence, 4,* 171–184.

Crisp, R. J., & Turner, R. N. (2011). Cognitive adaptation to the experience of social and cultural diversity. *Psychological Bulletin, 137,* 242–266.

Criss, M., & Shaw, D. (2005). Sibling relationships as contexts for delinquency training in low-income families. *Journal of Family Psychology, 19,* 592–600.

Critser, G. (2003). *Fat land: How Americans became the fattest people in the world.* Boston: Houghton Mifflin.

Crockenberg, S., & Leerkes, E. (2003). Infant negative emotionality, caregiving, and family relationships. In A. Crouter & A. Booth (Eds.), *Children's influence on family dynamics: The neglected side of family relationships* (pp. 57–78). Mahwah, NJ: Lawrence Erlbaum Associates.

Crocker, J., & Park, L. E. (2004). The costly pursuit of self-esteem. *Psychological Bulletin, 150,* 392–414.

Crockett, L. J., & Crouter, A. C. (Eds.). (1995). *Pathways through adolescence: Individual development in relation to social contexts.* Hillsdale, NJ: Erlbaum.

Croizet, J., Després, G., Gauzins, M., Huguet, P., Leyens, J., & Méot, A. (2004). Stereotype threat undermines intellectual performance by triggering a disruptive mental load. *Personality and Social Psychology Bulletin, 30,* 721–731.

Crolius, A. (1997, December 19). Living in the U.S.A. *Hampshire Life,* pp. 7, 9–11, 26.

Cromwell, E. S. (1994). *Quality child care: A comprehensive guide for administrators and teachers.* Boston: Allyn & Bacon.

Crosby, W. (1991). Studies in fetal malnutrition. *American Journal of Diseases of Children, 145,* 871–876.

Crose, R., & Drake, L. K. (1993). Older women's sexuality. *Clinical Gerontologist, 12,* 51–56.

Crosnoe, R., & Elder, G. H., Jr. (2002). Successful adaptation in the later years: A life course approach to aging. *Social Psychology Quarterly, 65,* 309–328.

Cross, T., Cassady, J., Dixon, F., & Adams, C. (2008). The psychology of gifted adolescents as measured by the MMPI-A. *Gifted Child Quarterly, 52,* 326–339.

Cross, W. W., Jr. (1991). *Shades of black: Diversity in African-American identity.* Philadelphia: Temple University Press.

Crosscope-Happel, C., Hutchins, D. E., Getz: H. G., & Hayes, G. L. (2000). Male anorexia nervosa: A new focus. *Journal of Mental Health Counseling, 22,* 365–370.

Crouter, A. (2006). Mothers and fathers at work: Implications for families and children. *Families count: Effects on child and adolescent development* (pp. 135–154). New York: Cambridge University Press.

Crowl, A., Ahn, S., & Baker, J. (2008). A meta-analysis of developmental outcomes for children of same-sex and heterosexual parents. *Journal of GLBT Family Studies, 4,* 385–407.

Crowley, B., Hayslip, B., & Hobdy, J. (2003). Psychological hardiness and adjustment to life events in adulthood. *Journal of Adult Development, 10,* 237–248.

Crowley, K., Callaman, M. A., Tenenbaum, H. R., & Allen, E. (2001). Parents explain more often to boys than to girls during shared scientific thinking. *Psychological Science, 12,* 258–261.

Crowther, M., & Rodriguez, R. (2003). A stress and coping model of custodial grandparenting among African Americans. In B. Hayslip & J. Patrick (Eds.), *Working with custodial grandparents.* New York: Springer Publishing Co.

Croyle, R. T., & Hunt, J. R. (1991). Coping with health threat: Social influence processes in reactions to medical test results. *Journal of Personality and Social Psychology, 60,* 382–389.

Crutchley, A. (2003). Bilingualism in development: language, literacy and cognition. *Child Language Teaching & Therapy, 19,* 365–367.

Cruz, N., & Bahna, S. (2006, October). Do foods or additives cause behavior disorders? *Psychiatric Annals, 36,* 724–732.

Csibra, G., Davis, G., Spratling, M. W., & Johnson, M. H. (2000, November 24). Gamma oscillations and object processing in the infant brain. *Science, 290,* 1582–1584.

Csikszentmihalyi, M., & Larson, R. (1984). *Being adolescent: Conflict and growth in the teenage years.* New York: Basic Books.

Cuddy, A. J. C., & Fiske, S. T. (2004). Doddering but dear: Process, content, and function in stereotyping of older persons. In T. Nelson (Eds.), *Ageism: Stereotyping and prejudice against older persons.* Cambridge, MA: MIT Press.

Cuervo, A. (2008). Calorie restriction and aging: The ultimate "cleansing diet." *The Journals of Gerontology: Series A: Biological Sciences and Medical Sciences, 63A,* 547–549.

Cuevas, K., Raj, V., & Bell, M. (2012). Functional connectivity and infant spatial working memory: A frequency band analysis. *Psychophysiology, 49,* 271–280.

Culbertson, J. L., & Gyurke, J. (1990). Assessment of cognitive and motor development in infancy and childhood. In J. H. Johnson & J. Goldman (Eds.), *Developmental assessment in clinical child psychology: A handbook* (pp. 100–131). New York: Pergamon Press.

Culp, A. M., Clyman, M. M., & Culp, R. E. (1995). Adolescent depressed mood, reports of suicide attempts, and asking for help. *Adolescence, 30,* 827–837.

Culver, V. (2003, August 26). Funeral expenses overwhelm survivors: $10,000-plus tab often requires aid. *The Denver Post,* p. B2.

Cumming, G. P., Currie, H. D., Moncur, R., & Lee, A. J. (2009). Web-based survey on the effect of menopause on women's libido in a computer-literate population. *Menopause International, 15,* 8–12.

Cummings, E., & Henry, W. E. (1961). *Growing old.* New York: Basic Books.

Cummings, E. M., Iannotti, R. J., & Zahn-Waxler, C. (1989). Aggression between peers in early childhood: Individual continuity and developmental change. *Child Development, 60,* 887–895.

Cunningham, J. D., & Antill, J. K. (1994). Cohabitation and marriage: Retrospective and predictive comparisons. *Journal of Social and Personal Relationships, 11,* 77–93.

Cunningham, W. R., & Hamen, K. (1992). Intellectual functioning in relation to mental health. In J. E. Birren, R. B. Sloane, & G. D. Cohen (Eds.), *Handbook of mental health and aging.* San Diego, CA: Harcourt Brace.

Curl, M., Davies, R., Lothian, S., Pascali-Bonaro, D., Scaer, R. M., & Walsh, A. (2004). Childbirth educators, doulas, nurses, and women respond to the six care practices for normal birth. *The Journal of Perinatal Education, 13*(2), 42–50.

Curl, M. N., Davies, R., Lothian, S., Pascali-Bonaro, D., Scaer, R. M., & Walsh, A. (2004). Childbirth educators, doulas, nurses, and women respond to the six care practices for normal birth. *The Journal of Perinatal Education, 13*(2), 42–50.

Curley, J. P., Jensen, C. L., Mashoodh, R. R., & Champagne, F. A. (2011). Social influences on neurobiology and behavior: Epigenetic effects during development. *Psychoneuroendocrinology, 36,* 352–371.

Currie, J., & Thomas, D. (1995). Does Head Start make a difference? *The American Economic Review, 85,* 37–49.

Curtis, D., Vine, A. E., McQuillin, A., Bass, N. J., Pereira, A., Kandaswamy, R., et al. (2011). Case–case genome-wide association analysis shows markers differentially associated with schizophrenia and bipolar disorder and implicates calcium channel genes. *Psychiatric Genetics, 21,* 1–4.

Curtis, W. J., & Cicchetti, D. (2003). Moving research on resilience into the 21st century: Theoretical and methodological considerations in examining the biological contributors to resilience. *Development and Psychopathology, 15,* 126–131.

Cutler, B. (1990). Rock-a-buy baby. *American Demographics, 12*(1), 35–39.

Cutter, J. A. (1999, June 13). Coming to terms with grief after a longtime partner dies. *The New York Times,* p. WH10.

Cwikel, J., Gramotnev, H., & Lee, C. (2006). Never-married childless women in Australia: Health and social circumstances in older age. *Social Science & Medicine, 62,* 1991–2001.

Cyna, A. M., Andrew, M. I., & McAuliffe, G. L. (2006). Antenatal self-hypnosis for labour and childbirth: A pilot study. *Anaestheology Intensive Care, 34,* 464–4699.

Cynader, M. (2000, March 17). Strengthening visual connections. *Science, 287,* 1943–1944.

Czaja, S. J., & Lee, C. C. (2007). *Information technology and older adults.* University of Miami School of Medicine., FL

D'Elia, A., Pighetti, M., & Moccia, G. (2001). Spontaneous motor activity in normal fetuses. *Early Human Development, 65,* 139–147.

da Veiga, P., & Wilder, R. (2008). Maternal smoking during pregnancy and birthweight: A propensity score matching approach. *Maternal & Child Health Journal, 12,* 194–203.

Dabelko, H., & Zimmerman, J. (2008). Outcomes of adult day services for participants: A conceptual model. *Journal of Applied Gerontology, 27,* 78–92.

Dagher, A., Tannenbaum, B., Hayashi, T., Pruessner, J., & McBride, D. (2009). An acute psychosocial stress enhances the neural response to smoking cues. *Brain Research, 129,* 340–348.

Dahl, E., & Birkelund, E. (1997). Health inequalities in later life in a social democratic welfare state. *Social Science & Medicine, 44,* 871–881.

Dahl, R. (2008). Biological, developmental, and neurobehavioral factors relevant to adolescent driving risks. *American Journal of Preventive Medicine, 35,* S278–S284.

Dailard, C. (2001). Sex education: Politicians, parents, teachers and teens. *The Guttmacher Report on Public Policy (Alan Guttmacher Institute), 4,* 1–4. Retrieved from http://www.guttmacher.org/pubs/tgr/04/1/gr040109.pdf.

Dailard, C. (2006, Summer). Legislating against arousal: The growing divide between federal policy and teenage sexual behavior. *Guttmacher Policy Review, 9,* 12–16.

Dainton, M. (1993). The myths and misconceptions of the step-mother identity. *Family Relations, 42,* 93–98.

Daley, K. C. (2004). Update on sudden infant death syndrome. *Current Opinion in Pediatrics, 16,* 227–232.

Dalton, T. C., & Bergenn, V. W. (2007). *Early experience, the brain, and consciousness: An historical and interdisciplinary synthesis.* Mahwah, NJ: Lawrence Erlbaum Associates.

Daly, M., & Wilson, M. I. (1996). Violence against stepchildren. *Current Directions in Psychological Science, 5,* 77–81.

Daly, T., & Feldman, R. S. (1994). *Benefits of social integration for typical preschoolchildren.* Unpublished manuscript.

Damon, W. (1977). *The social world of the child.* San Francisco: Jossey-Bass.

Damon, W. (1983). *Social and personality development.* New York: Norton.

Damon, W. (1988). *The moral child.* New York: Free Press.

Damon, W. (1995). *Greater expectations: Overcoming the culture of indulgence in America's homes and schools.* New York: Free Press.

Damon, W., & Hart, D. (1988). *Self-understanding in childhood and adolescence.* New York: Cambridge University Press.

Danhauer, S., McCann, J., & Gilley, D. (2004). Do behavioral disturbances in persons with Alzheimer's disease predict caregiver depression over time? *Psychology & Aging, 19,* 198–202.

Daniel, E., Schiefer, D., Möllering, A., Benish-Weisman, M., Boehnke, K., & Knafo, A. (2012). Value differentiation in adolescence: The role of age and cultural complexity. *Child Development, 83,* 322–336.

Daniel, S., & Goldston, D. (2009). Interventions for suicidal youth: A review of the literature and developmental considerations. *Suicide and Life-Threatening Behavior, 39,* 252–268.

Daniels, H. (Ed.). (1996). *An introduction to Vygotsky.* New York: Routledge.

Daniels, H. (2006, February). The "social" in post-Vygotskian theory. *Theory & Psychology, 16,* 37–49.

Danish, S. J., Taylor, T. E., & Fazio, R. J. (2006). Enhancing adolescent development through sports and leisure. In G. R. Adams & M. D. Berzonsky (Eds.), *Blackwell handbook of adolescence.* Malden, MA: Blackwell Publishing.

Danner, F. (2008). A national longitudinal study of the association between hours of TV viewing and the trajectory of BMI growth among US children. *The Journal of Pediatric Psychology, 33,* 1100–1107.

Dapretto, M., Davies, M. S., Pfeifer, J. H., Scott, A. A., Sigman, M., Bookhermer, S. Y., et al. (2006). Understanding emotions in others: Mirror neuron dysfunction in children with autism spectrum disorders. *Nature and Neuroscience, 9,* 28–30.

Dardenne, B., Dumont, M., & Bollier, T. (2007). Insidious dangers of benevolent sexism: Consequences for women's performance. *Journal of Personality and Social Psychology, 93,* 764–779.

Dare, W. N., Noronha, C. C., Kusemiju, O. T., & Okanlawon, O. A. (2002). The effect of ethanol on spermatogenesis and fertility in male Sprague-Dawley rats pretreated with acetylsalicylic acid. *Nigeria Postgraduate Medical Journal, 9,* 194–198.

Darnton, N. (1990, June 4). Mommy vs. mommy. *Newsweek,* pp. 64–67.

Darroch, J. E., & Singh, S. (1999). *Why is teenage pregnancy declining? The roles of abstinence, sexual activity and contraceptive use* (Occasional Report, No. 1). New York: The Alan Guttmacher Institute.

Das, A. (2007). Masturbation in the United States. *Journal of Sex & Marital Therapy, 33,* 301–317.

Dasen, P. (2000). Rapid social change and the turmoil of adolescence: A cross-cultural perspective. *World Psychology, 29,* 17–49.

Dasen, P. R. (1977). Are cognitive processes universal? A contribution to cross-cultural Piagetian psychology. In N. Warren (Ed.), *Studies in cross-cultural psychology* (Vol. 1). New York: Academic Press.

Dasen, P. R. (2000). Rapid social change and the turmoil of adolescence: A cross-cultural perspective. *International Journal of Group Tensions, 29,* 17–49.

Dasen, P. R., Inhelder, B., Lavallée, M., & Retschitzki, J. (1978). *Naissance de l'Intelligence chez l'enfant baoulé de Côte d'Ivoire.* Berne: Huber.

Dasen, P. R., & Mishra, R. C. (2002). Cross-cultural views on human development in the third millennium. In W. W. Hartup & R. K. Silbereisen (Eds.), *Growing points in developmental science: An introduction.* Philadelphia, PA: Psychology Press.

Dasen, P. R., Ngini, L., & Lavallee, M. (1979). Cross-cultural training studies of concrete operations. In L. H. Eckenberger, W. J. Lonner, & Y. H. Poortinga (Eds.), *Cross-cultural contributions to psychology.* Amsterdam: Swets & Zeilinger.

Daum, M. M., Prinz, W., & Aschersleben, G. (2011). Perception and production of object-related grasping in 6-month-olds. *Journal of Experimental Child Psychology, 108,* 810–818.

Davenport, B., & Bourgeois, N. (2008). Play, aggression, the preschool child, and the family: A review of literature to guide empirically informed play therapy with aggressive preschool children. *International Journal of Play Therapy, 17,* 2–23.

Davey, M. (2007, June 2). Kevorkian freed after years in prison for aiding suicide. *The New York Times,* p. A1.

Davey, M., Eaker, D. G., & Walters, L. H. (2003). Resilience processes in adolescents: Personality profiles, self-worth, and coping. *Journal of Adolescent Researech, 18,* 347–362.

Davey, S. G., Frankel S., & Yarnell, J. (1997). Sex and death: Are they related? Findings from the Caerphilly Cohort Study. *British Medical Journal, 315,* 1–4.

Davich, J. (2009, February 23). Happy kids begin with parents: What parent coaches say you need to know today. *Chicago Parent.* Retrieved from http://www.chicagoparent.com/magazines/chicago-parent/2009-march/happy-kids-begin-with-happy-parents.

Davidson, J. K., Darling, C. A., & Norton, L. (1995). Religiosity and the sexuality of women: Sexual behavior and sexual satisfaction revisited. *Journal of Sex Research, 32,* 235–243.

Davidson, R. J. (2003). Affective neuroscience: A case for interdisciplinary research. In F. Kessel & P. L. Rosenfield (Eds.), *Expanding the boundaries of health and social science: Case studies in interdisciplinary innovation.* London: Oxford University Press.

Davidson, T. (1977). Wifebeating: A recurring phenomenon throughout history. In M. Roy (Ed.), *Battered women: A psychosociological study of domestic violence.* New York: Van Nostrand Reinhold.

Davies, M., Stankov, L., & Roberts, R. D. (1998). Emotional intelligence: In search of an elusive construct. *Journal of Personality & Social Psychology, 75,* 989–1015.

Davies, P. (2005, March 29). Toddlers' implants bring upheaval to deaf education. *The Wall Street Journal,* pp. A1, A8.

Davies, P. G., Spencer, S. L., & Steele, C. M. (2005). Clearing the air: Identity safety moderates the effects of stereotype threat on women's leadership aspirations. *Journal of Personality & Social Psychology, 88,* 276–287.

Davies, P. T., & Cummings, E. M. (1994). Marital conflict and child adjustment: An emotional security hypothesis. *Psychological Bulletin, 116,* 387–411.

Davies, P. T., Harold, G. T., Goeke-Morey, M. C., & Cummings, E. M. (2002). Child emotional security and interparental conflict. *Monographs of the Society for Research in Child Development, 67.*

Davies, S., & Denton, M. (2002). The economic well-being of older women who become divorced or separated in mid- or later life. *Canadian Journal on Aging, 21,* 477–493.

Davis, A. (2003). *Your divorce, your dollars: Financial planning before, during, and after divorce.* Bellingham, WA: Self-Counsel Press.

Davis, A. (2008). Children with Down syndrome: Implications for assessment and intervention in the school. *School Psychology Quarterly, 23,* 271–281.

Davis, C., & Nolen-Hoeksema, S. (2001). Loss and meaning: How do people make sense of loss? *American Behavioral Scientist, 44,* 726–741.

Davis, C., Aronson, J., & Salinas, M. (2006, November). Shades of threat: Racial identity as a moderator of stereotype threat. *Journal of Black Psychology, 32*(4), 399–417.

Davis, C. G., Nolen-Hoeksema, S., & Larson, J. (1998). Making sense of loss and benefiting from the experience: Two construals of meaning. *Journal of Personality and Social Psychology, 75,* 561–574.

Davis, C. L., Tomporowski, P. D., McDowell, J. E., Austin, B. P., Miller, P. H., Yanasak, N. E., et al. (2011). Exercise improves executive function and achievement and alters brain activation in overweight children: A randomized, controlled trial. *Health Psychology, 30,* 91–98.

Davis, D., Shaver, P., Widaman, K., Vernon, M., Follette, W., & Beitz, K. (2006, December). "I can't get no satisfaction": Insecure attachment, inhibited sexual communication, and sexual dissatisfaction. *Personal Relationships, 13,* 465–483.

Davis, K. (2012). Friendship 2.0: Adolescents' experiences of belonging and self-disclosure online. *Journal of Adolescence.* Retrieved from http://www.sciencedirect.com/science/article/pii/S0140197112000334.

Davis, M., & Emory, E. (1995). Sex differences in neonatal stress reactivity. *Child Development, 66,* 14–27.

Davis, M., Zautra, A., Younger, J., Motivala, S., Attrep, J., & Irwin, M. (2008). Chronic stress and regulation of cellular markers of inflammation in rheumatoid arthritis: Implications for fatigue. *Brain, Behavior, and Immunity, 22,* 24–32.

Davis, S. K., & Humphrey, N. (2012). Emotional intelligence as a moderator of stressor–mental health relations in adolescence: Evidence for specificity. *Personality and Individual Differences, 52,* 100–105.

Davis, T. S., Saltzburg, S., & Locke, C. R. (2009). Supporting the emotional and psychological well being of sexual minority youth: Youth ideas for action. *Children and Youth Services Review, 31,* 1030–1041.

Davis-Floyd, R. E. (1994). The technocratic body: American childbirth as cultural expression. *Social Science & Medicine, 38,* 1125–1140.

Davis-Kean, P. E., & Sandler, H. M. (2001). A meta-analysis of measures of self-esteem for young children: A framework for future measures. *Child Development, 72,* 887–906.

Davison, G. C. (2005). Issues and nonissues in the gay-affirmative treatment of patients who are gay, lesbian, or bisexual. *Clinical Psychology: Science & Practice, 12,* 25–28.

Dawson-Tunik, T., Fischer, K., & Stein, Z. (2004). Do stages belong at the center of developmental theory? A commentary on Piaget's stages. *New Ideas in Psychology, 22,* 255–263.

de Anda, D., & Becerra, R. M. (2000). An overview of "Violence: Diverse populations and communities." *Journal of Multicultural Social Work, 8,* n1–2, p1–14.

De Angelis, T. (1994, December). What makes kids ready, set for school? *Monitor on Psychology,* 36–37.

de Bellis, M., Keshavan, M., Beers, S., Hall, J., Frustaci, K., Masalehdan, A., et al. (2001). Sex differences in brain maturation during childhood and adolescence. *Cerebral Cortex, 11,* 552–557.

de Boysson-Bardies, B., Sagart, L., & Durand, C. (1984). Discernible differences in the babbling of infants according to target language. *Journal of Child Language, 11,* 1–15.

de Boysson-Bardies, B., & Vihman, M. M. (1991). Adaptation to language: Evidence from babbling and first words in four languages. *Language, 67,* 297–307.

de Bruyn, E., & Cillessen, A. (2006, November). Popularity in early adolescence: Prosocial and antisocial subtypes. *Journal of Adolescent Research, 21,* 607–627.

De Gelder, B. (2000). Recognizing emotions by ear and by eye. In R. D. Lane, L. Nadel, et al. (Eds.), *Cognitive neuroscience of emotion. Series in affective science.* New York: Oxford University Press.

de Graaf, C., Polet, P., & van Staveren, W. A. (1994). Sensory perception and pleasantness of food flavors in elderly subjects. *Journals of Gerontology, 49,* P93–P99.

de Graaf-Peters, V., & Hadders-Algra, M. (2006). Ontogeny of the human central nervous system: What is happening when? *Early Human Development, 82,* 257–266.

de Jesus Moreno Moreno, M. (2003). Cognitive improvement in mild to moderate Alzheimer's dementia after treatment with the acetylcholine precursor choline alfoscerate: A multicenter, double-blind, randomized, placebo-controlled trial. *Clinical Therapeutics: The International Peer-Reviewed Journal of Drug Therapy, 25,* 178–193.

de Jong, P. J., Sportel, B. E., de Hullu, E. E., & Nauta, M. H. (2012). Co-occurrence of social anxiety and depression symptoms in adolescence: Differential links with implicit and explicit self-esteem? *Psychological Medicine: A Journal of Research in Psychiatry and the Allied Sciences, 42,* 475–484.

de Jong Gierveld, J. (2004). Remarriage, unmarried cohabitation, living apart together: Partner relationships following bereavement or divorce. *Journal of Marriage and Family, 66,* 236–243.

De Leo, D., Conforti, D., & Carollo, G. (1997). A century of suicide in Italy: A comparison between the old and the young. *Suicide & Life-Threatening Behavior, 27,* 239–249.

De Loache, J., & Gottlieb, A. (Eds.). (2002). *A world of babies.* Cambridge, England: Cambridge University Press.

De Meersman, R., & Stein, P. (2007, February). Vagal modulation and aging. *Biological Psychology, 74,* 165–173.

de Mooij, M. K. (1998). *Global marketing and advertising: Understanding cultural paradoxes.* Thousand Oaks, CA: Sage.

de Onis, M., Garza, C., Onyango, A. W., & Borghi, E. (2007). Comparison of the WHO child growth standards and the CDC 2000 growth charts. *Journal of Nutrition, 137,* 144–148.

De Pauw, S. W., & Mervielde, I. (2011). The role of temperament and personality in problem behaviors of children with ADHD. *Journal of Abnormal Child Psychology: An official publication of the International Society for Research in Child and Adolescent Psychopathology, 39,* 277–291.

de Rosnay, M., Cooper, P., Tsigaras, N., & Murray, L. (2006, August). Transmission of social anxiety from mother to infant: An experimental study using a social referencing paradigm. *Behaviour Research and Therapy, 44,* 1165–1175.

De Roten, Y., Favez, N., & Drapeau, M. (2003). Two studies on autobiographical narratives about an emotional event by preschoolers: Influence of the emotions experienced and the affective closeness with the interlocutor. *Early Child Development & Care, 173,* 237–248.

de Schipper, E. J., Riksen-Walraven, J. M., & Geurts, S. A. E. (2006). Effects of child-caregiver ration on the interactions between caregivers and children in child-care centers: An experimental study. *Child Development, 77,* 861–874.

de St. Aubin, E., McAdams, D. P., & Kim, T. C. (Eds.). (2004). *The generative society: Caring for future generations.* Washington, DC: American Psychological Association.

de Vries, B., Davis, C. G., Wortman, C. B., & Lehman, D. R. (1997). Long-term psychological and somatic consequences of later life parental bereavement. *Omega—Journal of Death & Dying, 35,* 97–117.

DEA (Drug Enforcement Administration). (2000, May 16). *DEA Congressional Testimony by Terrance Woodworth before the Committee on Education and the Workforce: Subcommittee on Early Childhood, Youth and Families.* Retrieved from http://www.dea.gov/pubs/cngrtest/ct051600.htm#fig2.

Deakin, M. B. (2004, May 9). The (new) parent trap. *Boston Globe Magazine,* pp. 18–21, 28–33.

Dean, A., Kolody, B., Wood, P., & Ensel, W. (1989). Measuring the communication of social support from adult children. *Journal of Marriage and the Family, 44,* 71–79.

DeAngelis, T. (1994, December). What makes kids ready, set for school? *APA Monitor,* pp. 36–37.

Dearing, E., McCartney, K., & Taylor, B. (2009). Does higher quality early child care promote low-income children's math and reading achievement in middle childhood? *Child Development, 80,* 1329–1349.

Deary, I., Ferguson, K., Bastin, M., Barrow, G., Reid, L., Seckl, J., et al. (2007). Skull size and intelligence, and King Robert Bruce's IQ. *Intelligence, 35,* 519–528.

Deater-Deckard, K., & Cahill, K. (2006). Nature and nurture in early childhood. In *Blackwell handbook of early childhood development* (pp. 3–21). New York: Blackwell Publishing.

Deaux, K. (2006). A nation of immigrants: Living our legacy. *Journal of Social Issues, 62,* 633–651.

Deaux, K., Reind, A., Mizrahi, K., & Ethier, K. A. (1995). Parameters of social identity. *Journal of Personality and Social Psychology, 68,* 280–291.

Deb, S., & Adak, M. (2006, July). Corporal punishment of children: Attitude, practice and perception of parents. *Social Science International, 22,* 3–13.

Decarrie, T. G. (1969). A study of the mental and emotional development of the thalidomide child. In B. M. Foss (Ed.), *Determinants of infant behavior* (Vol. 4). London: Methuen.

DeCasper, A. J., & Fifer, W. P. (1980). Of human bonding: Newborns prefer their mothers' voices. *Science, 208,* 1174–1176.

DeCasper, A. J., & Prescott, P. (1984). Human newborns' perception of male voices: Preference, discrimination, and reinforcing value. *Developmental Psychobiology, 17,* 481–491.

DeCasper, A. J., & Spence, M. J. (1986). Prenatal maternal speech influences newborns' perception of speech sounds. *Infant Behavior and Development, 9,* 133–150.

deCastro, J. (2002). Age-related changes in the social, psychological, and temporal influences on food intake in free-living, healthy, adult humans. *Journals of Gerontology: Series A: Biological Sciences & Medical Sciences, 57A,* M368–M377.

Decety, J., & Jackson, P. L. (2006). A social-neuroscience perspective on empathy. *Current Directions in Psychological Science, 15,* 54–61.

deChateau, P. (1980). Parent–neonate interaction and its long-term effects. In E. G. Simmel (Ed.), *Early experiences and early behavior.* New York: Academic Press.

DeClercq, E. R. (1992). The transformation of American midwifery: 1975 to 1988. *American Journal of Public Health, 82,* 680–684.

DeCristofaro, J. D., & LaGamma, E. F. (1995). Prenatal exposure to opiates. *Mental Retardation and Developmental Disabilities Research Reviews, 1,* 177–182.

Deforche, B., De Bourdeaudhuij, I., & Tanghe, A. (2006, May). Attitude toward physical activity in normal-weight, overweight and obese adolescents. *Journal of Adolescent Health, 38,* 560–568.

DeFrain, J., Martens, L., Stork, J., & Stork, W. (1991). The psychological effects of a stillbirth on surviving family members. *Omega—Journal of Death and Dying, 22,* 81–108.

DeFrancisco, B., & Rovee-Collier, C. (2008). The specificity of priming effects over the first year of life. *Developmental Psychobiology, 50,* 486–501.

DeGenova, M. K. (1993). Reflections of the past: New variables affecting life satisfaction in later life. *Educational Gerontology, 19,* 191–201.

Degnen, C. (2007). Minding the gap: The construction of old age and oldness amongst peers. *Journal of Aging Studies, 21,* 69–80.

Degroot, A., Wolff, M. C., & Nomikos, G. G. (2005). Acute exposure to a novel object during consolidation enhances cognition. *Neuroreport, 16,* 63–67.

Dehaene-Lambertz, G., Hertz-Pannier, L., & Dubois, J. (2006). Nature and nurture in language acquisition: Anatomical and functional brain-imaging studies in infants. *Neurosciences, Special issue: Nature and nurture in brain development and neurological disorders, 29,* 367–373.

DeHart, T., Pelham, B., & Tennen, H. (2006, January). What lies beneath: Parenting style and implicit self-esteem. *Journal of Experimental Social Psychology, 42,* 1–17.

Dejin-Karlsson, E., Hanson, B. S., Oestergren, P. O., Sjoeberg, N. O., & Marsal, K. (1998). Does passive smoking in early pregnancy increase the risk of small-for-gestational age infants? *American Journal of Public Health, 88,* 1523–1527.

Delaney, C. H. (1995). Rites of passage in adolescence. *Adolescence, 30,* 891–897.

DeLisi, L., & Fleischhaker, W. (2007). Schizophrenia research in the era of the genome, 2007. *Current Opinion in Psychiatry, 20,* 109–110.

Dell, D. L., & Stewart, D. E. (2000). Menopause and mood. Is depression linked with hormone changes? *Postgraduate Medicine, 108,* 34–36, 39–43.

Dellmann-Jenkins, M., & Brittain, L. (2003). Young adults' attitudes toward filial responsibility and actual assistance to elderly family members. *Journal of Applied Gerontology, 22,* 214–229.

DeLoache, J. S., & Gottlieb, A. (2000). *A world of babies: Imagined childcare guides for seven societies.* New York: Cambridge University Press.

Delpisheh, A., Attia, E., Drammond, S., & Brabin, B. (2006). Adolescent smoking in pregnancy and birth outcomes. *European Journal of Public Health, 16,* 168–172.

Delpit, L. (2006). What should teachers do? Ebonics and culturally responsive instruction. In *Dialects, Englishes, creoles, and education.* Mahwah, NJ: Lawrence Erlbaum Associates.

Delva, J., O'Malley, P., & Johnston, L. (2006, October). Racial/ethnic and socioeconomic status differences in overweight and health-related behaviors among American students: National trends 1986–2003. *Journal of Adolescent Health, 39,* 536–545.

Demaree, H. A., & Everhart, D. E. (2004). Healthy high-hostiles: Reduced parasympathetic activity and decreased sympathovagal flexibility during negative emotional processing. *Personality and Individual Differences, 36,* 457–469.

DeMaris, A., & Rao, K. V. (1992). Premarital cohabitation and subsequent marital stability in the United States: A reassessment. *Journal of Marriage and the Family, 54,* 178–190.

Dembner, A. (1995a, October 15). Marion Mealey: A determination to make it. *Boston Globe,* p. 22.

Dembner, A. (1995b, October 15). Miriam Heler: A family feeling on campus. *Boston Globe,* p. 22.

Demetriou, A., & Raftopoulos, A. (2004). *Cognitive developmental change: Theories, models and measurement.* New York: Cambridge University Press.

Demetriou, A., Shayer, M., & Efklides, A. (Eds.). (1993). *Neo-Piagetian theories of cognitive development: Implications and applications for education.* London: Routledge.

Demir, A., Ulusoy, M., & Ulusoy, M. (2003). Investigation of factors influencing burnout levels in the professional and private lives of nurses. *International Journal of Nursing Studies, 40,* 807–827.

Demo, D. H., & Acock, A. (1991). The impact of divorce on children. In A. Booth (Ed.), *Contemporary families.* Minneapolis, MN: National Council on Family Relations.

Dempster, F. N. (1981). Memory span: Sources of individual and developmental differences. *Psychological Bulletin, 89,* 63–100.

Dempster, F. N. (1993). Resistance to interference: Developmental changes in a basic processing mechanism. In R. Pasnak & M. L. Howe (Eds.), *Emerging themes in cognitive development* (Vol. 1). New York: Springer.

Deng, C., Armstrong, P., & Rounds, J. (2007). The fit of Holland's RIASEC model to US occupations. *Journal of Vocational Behavior, 71,* 1–22.

Denham, S. (1998). *Emotional development in young children.* New York: Guilford Press.

Denham, S., Mason, T., & Caverly, S. (2001). Preschoolers at play: Co-socialisers of emotional and social competence. *International Journal of Behavioral Development, 25,* 290–301.

Denizet-Lewis, B. (2004, May 30). Friends, friends with benefits and the benefits of the local mall. *The New York Times Magazine*, pp. 30–35, 54–58.

Denmark, F. L., & Fernandez, L. C. (1993). Historical development of the psychology of women. In F. L. Denmark & M. A. Paludi (Eds.), *Psychology of women: A handbook of issues and theories*. Westport, CT: Greenwood Press.

Dennis, J. G. (2004). *Homeschooling high school: Planning ahead for college admission*. Cambridge, MA: Emerald Press.

Dennis, T. A., Cole, P. M., Zahn-Wexler, C., & Mizuta, I. (2002). Self in context: Autonomy and relatedness in Japanese and U.S. mother-preschooler dyads. *Child Development, 73*, 1803–1817.

Dennis, W. (1966a). Age and creative productivity. *Journal of Gerontology, 21*, 1–8.

Dennis, W. (1966b). Creative productivity between the ages of 20 and 80 years. *Journal of Gerontology, 11*, 331–337.

Dennison, B., Edmunds, L., Stratton, H., & Pruzek, R. (2006). Rapid infant weight gain predicts childhood overweight. *Obesity, 14*, 491–499.

Denny, F. W., & Clyde, W. A. (1983). Acute respiratory tract infections: An overview. In W. A. Clyde & F. W. Denny (Eds.), Workshop on acute respiratory diseases among children of the world. *Pediatric Research, 17*, 1026–1029.

Denollet, J. (2005). DS14: Standard assessment of negative affectivity, social inhibition, and Type D personality. *Psychosomatic Medicine, 67*, 89–97.

Denollet, J., & Brutsaert, (1998). Personality, disease severity, and the risk of long-term cardiac events in patients with decreased ejection fraction after myocardial infarction. *Circulation, 97*, 167–173.

Dent, J. (1984, March). Laughter is the best medicine. *Reader's Digest, 124*, 38.

Dent-Read, C., & Zukow-Goldring, P. (Eds). (1997). *Evolving explanations of development: Ecological approaches to organism-environment systems*. Washington, DC: American Psychological Association.

Department for Education and Skills, England. (2004). *Math performance of schoolchildren*. London: Department for Education and Skills, England.

DePaulo, B. (2004). *The scientific study of people who are single: An annotated bibliography*. Glendale, CA: Unmarried America.

DePaulo, B. (2006). *Singled out: How singles are stereotyped, stigmatized, and ignored, and still live happily ever after*. New York: St Martin's Press.

DePaulo, B. M., & Morris W. L. (2006). The unrecognized stereotyping and discrimination against singles. *Current Directions in Psychological Science, 15*, 251–254.

Der, G., & Deary, I. (2006, March). Age sex differences in reaction time in adulthood: Results from the United Kingdom health and lifestyle survey. *Psychology and Aging, 21*(1), 62–73.

Deruelle, F., Nourry, C., Mucci, P., Bart, F., Grosbois, J. M., Lensel, G. H., et al. (2008). Difference in breathing strategies during exercise between trained elderly men and women. *Scandinavian Journal of Medical Science in Sports, 18*, 213–220.

Dervic, K., Friedrich, E., Oquendo, M., Voracek, M., Friedrich, M., & Sonneck, G. (2006, October). Suicide in Austrian children and young adolescents aged 14 and younger. *European Child & Adolescent Psychiatry, 15*, 427–434.

Deshields, T., Tibbs, T., Fan, M. Y., & Taylor, M. (2005, August 12). Differences in patterns of depression after treatment for breast cancer. *Psycho-Oncology*, Published Online, John Wiley & Sons.

Desmarias, S., & Curtis, J. (1997). Gender and perceived pay entitlement: Testing for effects of experience with income. *Journal of Personality and Social Psychology, 72*, 141–150.

Desoete, A., Roeyers, H., & De Clercq, A. (2003). Can offline metacognition enhance mathematical problem solving? *Journal of Educational Psychology, 95*, 188–200.

DeSpelder, L., & Strickland, A. L. (1992). *The last dance: Encountering death and dying* (3rd ed.). Palo Alto, CA: Mayfield.

DeSpelder, L., & Strickland, A. L. (2002). *The last dance: Encountering death and dying* (6th ed.). New York: McGraw-Hill.

Destounis, S., Hanson, S., Morgan, R., Murphy, P., Somerville, P., Seifert, P., et al. (2009). Computer-aided detection of breast carcinoma in standard mammographic projections with digital mammography. *International Journal of Computer Assisted Radiological Surgery, 4*, 331–336.

Dettmers, S., Trautwein, U., Lüdtke, O., Kunter, M., & Baumert, J. (2010). Homework works if homework quality is high: Using multilevel modeling to predict the development of achievement in mathematics. *Journal of Educational Psychology, 102*, 467–482.

Deurenberg, P., Deurenberg-Yap, M., Foo, L. F., Schmidt, G., & Wang, J. (2003). Differences in body composition between Singapore Chinese, Beijing Chinese and Dutch children. *European Journal of Clinical Nutrition, 57*, 405–409.

Deurenberg, P., Deurenberg-Yap, M., & Guricci, S. (2002). Asians are different from Caucasians and from each other in their body mass index/body fat percent relationship. *Obesity Review, 3*, 141–146.

Deutsch, F. M., Lussier, J. B., & Servis, L. J. (1993). Husbands at home: Predictors of paternal participation in childcare and house work. *Journal of Personality and Social Psychology, 65*, 1154–1166.

Deutsch, M. (1967). *The disadvantaged child: Selected papers of Martin Deutsch and associates*. New York: Basic Books.

Deutsch, N. (2000, September 5). *Menopause symptoms differ by race*. Retrieved from http://dailynews.yahoo.com/htx/nm/2000905/hl/monopause_1.html.

DeVader, S. R., Neeley, N. L., Myles, T. D., & Leet, T. L. (2007). Evaluation of gestational weight gain guidelines for women with normal prepregnancy body mass index. *Obstetrics and Gynecology, 110*, 745–751.

Deveny, K. (1994, December 5). Chart of kindergarten awards. *The Wall Street Journal*, p. B1.

deVilliers, P. A., & deVilliers, J. G. (1992). Language development. In M. H. Bornstein & M. E. Lamb (Eds.), *Developmental psychology: An advanced textbook*. Hillsdale, NJ: Erlbaum.

Devlin, B., Daniels, M., & Roeder, K. (1997). The heritability of IQ. *Nature, 388*, 468–471.

DeVries, H., Kerrick, S., & Oetinger, M. (2007). Satisfactions and regrets of midlife parents: A qualitative analysis. *Journal of Adult Development, 14*, 6–15.

deVries, M. W. (1984). Temperament and infant mortality among the Masai of East Africa. *American Journal of Psychiatry, 141*, 1189–1194.

deVries, R. (1969). Constancy of generic identity in the years 3 to 6. *Monographs of the Society for Research in Child Development, 34* (3, Serial No. 127).

DeVries, R. (2005). *A pleasing birth*. Philadelphia, PA: Temple University Press.

DeWitt, P. M. (1992). The second time around. *American Demographics, 14*, 60–63.

DeWolff, M. S., & van Ijzendoorn, M. H. (1997). Sensitivity and attachment: A meta-analysis on parental antecedents of infant attachment. *Child Development, 68*, 571–591.

Dey, A. N., & Bloom, B. (2005). Summary health statistics for U.S. children: National Health Interview Survey, 2003. *Vital Health Statistics, 10, 223*, 1–78.

DeYoung, C., Quilty, L., & Peterson, J. (2007). Between facets and domains: 10 aspects of the Big Five. *Journal of Personality and Social Psychology, 93*, 880–896.

Diamantopoulou, S., Rydell, A., & Henricsson, L. (2008). Can both low and high self-esteem be related to aggression in children? *Social Development, 17*, 682–698.

Diambra, L., & Menna-Barretio, L. (2004). Infradian rhythmicity in sleep/wake ratio in developing infants. *Chronobiology International, 21*, 217–227.

Diamond, L. (2003a). Love matters: Romantic relationships among sexual-minority adolescents. In P. Florsheim (Ed.), *Adolescent romantic relations and sexual behavior: Theory, research, and practical implications*. Mahwah, NJ: Lawrence Erlbaum Associates.

Diamond, L. (2003b). Was it a phase? Young women's relinquishment of lesbian/bisexual identities over a 5-year period. *Journal of Personality & Social Psychology, 84*, 352–364.

Diamond, L., & Savin-Williams, R. (2003). The intimate relationships of sexual-minority youths. In G. Adams & M. Berzonsky (Eds.), *Blackwell handbook of adolescence*. Malden, MA: Blackwell Publishers.

Dick, D., & Mustanski, B. (2006). Pubertal development and health-related behavior. *Socioemotional development and health from adolescence to adulthood* (pp. 108–125). New York: Cambridge University Press.

Dick, D. M., & Rose, R. J. (2002). Behavior genetics: What's new? What's next? *Current Directions in Psychological Science, 11*, 70–74.

Dick, D. M., Rose, R., & Kaprio, J. (2006). The next challenge for psychiatric genetics: Characterizing the risk associated with identified genes. *Annals of Clinical Psychiatry, 18*, 223–231.

Dickenson, G. (1975). Dating behavior of black and white adolescents before and after desegregation. *Journal of Marriage and the Family, 37*, 602–608.

Dickson, K. L., Walker, H., & Fogel, A. (1997). The relationship between smile type and play type during parent–infant play. *Developmental Psychology, 33*, 925–933.

Diego, M., Field, T., & Hernandez-Reif, M. (2008). Temperature increases in preterm infants during massage therapy. *Infant Behavior & Development, 31*, 149–152.

Diego, M., Field, T., & Hernandez-Reif, M. (2009). Procedural pain heart rate responses in massaged preterm infants. *Infant Behavior & Development, 32*, 226–229.

Diego, M., Field, T., Hernandez-Reif, M., Vera, Y., Gil, K., & Gonzalez-Garcia, A. (2007). Caffeine use affects pregnancy outcome. *Journal of Child & Adolescent Substance Abuse, 17*, 41–49.

Diekman, A., & Murnen, S. (2004). Learning to be little women and little men: The inequitable gender equality of nonsexist children's literature. *Sex Roles, 50*, 373–385.

Diener, E. (2000). Subjective well-being: The science of happiness and a proposal for a national index. *American Psychologist, 55*, 34–43.

Diener, E., Lucas, R. E., & Scollon, C. N. (2009). Beyond the hedonic treadmill: Revising the adaptation theory of well-being. In E. Diener (Ed.), *The science of well-being: The collected works of Ed Diener*. New York: Springer Science + Business Media.

Diener, E., Oishi, S., & Lucas, R. (2003). Personality, culture, and subjective well-being: Emotional and cognitive evaluations of life. *Annual Review of Psychology, 54*, 403–425.

Diener, E., Suh, E. M., Lucas, R. E., & Smith, H. L. (1999). Subjective well-being: Three decades of progress. *Psychological Bulletin, 125*, 276–302.

Diener, M., Isabella, R., Behunin, M., & Wong, M. (2008). Attachment to mothers and fathers during middle childhood: Associations with child gender, grade, and competence. *Social Development, 17*, 84–101.

Dieter, J., Field, T., Hernandez-Reif, M., Emory, E., & Redzepi, M. (2003). Preterm infants gain more weight and sleep less following 5 days of massage therapy. *Journal of Pediatric Psychology, 28*, 403–411.

Dietz, W. (2004). Overweight in childhood and adolescence. *New England Journal of Medicine, 350*, 855–857.

Dietz, W. H., & Stern, L. (Eds.). (1999). *American Academy of Pediatrics guide to your child's nutrition: Making peace at the table and building healthy eating habits for life*. New York: Villard.

DiFranza, J. R., & Lew, R. A. (1995, April). Effect of maternal cigarette smoking on pregnancy complications and sudden infant death syndrome. *The Journal of Family Practice, 40*, 385–394.

DiGiovanna, A. G. (1994). *Human aging: Biological perspectives*. New York: McGraw-Hill.

DiLalla, L. F., Thompson, L. A., Plomin, R., Phillips, K., Fagan, J. F., Haith, M. M., et al. (1990). Infant predictors of preschool and adult IQ: A study of infant twins and their parents. *Developmental Psychology, 26*, 433–440.

Dildy, G. A. Jackson, G. M., Fowers, G. R., Oshino, B. T., Varner, M. W., & Clark, S. C. (1996). Very advanced maternal age: Pregnancy after 45. *American Journal of Obstetrics and gynecology, 175*, 668–674.

Dillaway, H., Byrnes, M., Miller, S., & Rehan, S. (2008). Talking "among us": How women from different racial-ethnic groups define and discuss menopause. *Health Care for Women International, 29*, 766–781.

Dilworth-Bart, J., & Moore, C. (2006, March). Mercy mercy me: Social injustice and the prevention of environmental pollutant exposures among ethnic minority and poor children. *Child Development, 77*, 247–265.

DiMatteo, M. R., & Kahn, K. L. (1997). Psychosocial aspects of childbirth. In S. J. Gallant, G. P. Keita, & R. Royak-Schaler (Eds.), *Health care for women: Psychological, social, and behavioral influences*. Washington, DC: American Psychological Association.

Dinero, R., Conger, R., Shaver, P., Widaman, K., & Larsen-Rife, D. (2008). Influence of family of origin and adult romantic partners on romantic attachment security. *Journal of Family Psychology, 22*, 622–632.

Dion, K. L., & Dion, K. K. (1988). Romantic love: Individual and cultural perspectives. In R. J. Sternberg & M. L. Barnes (Eds.), *The psychology of love*. New Haven, CT: Yale University Press.

Dionigi, R., & O'Flynn, G. (2007). Performance discourses and old age: What does it mean to be an older athlete? *Sociology of Sport Journal, 24*, 359–377.

Diop, A. M. (1989). The place of the elderly in African society. *Impact of Science on Society, 153*, 93–98.

DiPietro, J. A. (2004). The role of prenatal maternal stress in child development. *Current Directions in Psychological Science, 13*, 71–73.

DiPietro, J. A., Bornstein, M. H., & Costigan, K. A. (2002). What does fetal movement predict about behavior during the first two years of life? *Developmental Psychobiology, 40*, 358–371.

Dipietro, J. A., Costigan, K. A., & Gurewitsch, E. D. (2005). Maternal psychophysiological change during the second half of gestation. *Biological Psychology, 69*, 23–39.

Dittman, M. (2005). Generational differences at work. *Monitor on Psychology, 36*, 54–55.

Dittmann, M. (2004, November). A new face to retirement. *Monitor on Psychology, 35*, 78.

Division 44/Committee on Lesbian, Gay, and Bisexual Concerns Joint Task Force on Guidelines for Psychotherapy with Lesbian, Gay, and Bisexual Clients. (2000). Guidelines for psychotherapy with lesbian, gay, and bisexual clients. *American Psychologist, 55*, 1440–1451.

Dix, T., Meunier, L. N., Lusk, K., & Perfect, M. M. (2012). Mothers' depressive symptoms and children's facial emotions: Examining the depression–inhibition hypothesis. *Development and Psychopathology, 24*, 195–210.

Dixon, L., & Browne, K. (2003). The heterogeneity of spouse abuse: A review. *Aggression & Violent Behavior, 8*, 107–130.

Dixon, R. (2003). Themes in the aging of intelligence: Robust decline with intriguing possibilities. In R. Sternberg & J. Lautrey (Eds.), *Models of intelligence:*

International perspectives. Washington, DC: American Psychological Association.

Dixon, R., & Cohen, A. (2003). Cognitive development in adulthood. In R. Lerner & M. Easterbrooks (Eds.), *Handbook of psychology: Developmental psychology* (Vol. 6). New York: John Wiley & Sons, Inc.

Dixon, R. A., & Lerner, R. M. (1999). History and systems in developmental psychology. In M. H. Bornstein & M. E. Lamb (Eds.), *Developmental psychology: An advanced textbook*. Mahwah, NJ: Erlbaum.

Dixon, W. E., Jr. (2004). There's a long, long way to go. *PsycCRITIQUES*.

Dmitrieva, J., Chen, C., & Greenberger, E. (2004). Family relationships and adolescent psychosocial outcomes: Converging findings from Eastern and Western cultures. *Journal of Research on Adolescence, 14*, 425–447.

Dobrova-Krol, N., van IJzendoorn, M., Bakermans-Kranenburg, M., Cyr, C., & Juffer, F. (2008). Physical growth delays and stress dysregulation in stunted and non-stunted Ukrainian institution-reared children. *Infant Behavior & Development, 31*, 539–553.

Dobson, V. (2000). The developing visual brain. *Perception, 29*, 1501–1503.

DocuTicker. (2010). *Lists & Rankings—City Crime Rankings 2010–2011*. Ashford, Middlesex, United Kingdom.

Dodge, K. A. (1985). A social information processing model of social competence in children. In M. Perlmutter (Ed.), *Minnesota Symposia on Child Psychology, 18*, 77–126.

Dodge, K. A., Bates, J. E., & Pettit, G. S. (1990, December 20). Mechanisms in the cycle of violence. *Science, 250*, 1678–1683.

Dodge, K. A., & Coie, J. D. (1987). Social information-processing factors in reactive and proactive aggression in children's peer groups. *Journal of Personality and Social Psychology, 53*, 1146–1158.

Dodge, K. A., & Crick, N. R. (1990). Social information-processing bases of aggressive behavior in children. *Personality and Social Psychology Bulletin, 16*, 8–22.

Dodge, K. A., Lansford, J. E., & Burks, V. S. (2003). Peer rejection and social information-processing factors in the development of aggressive behavior problems in children. *Child Development, 74*, 374–393.

Dodge, K. A., Pettit, G. S., McClasky, C. L., & Brown, M. M. (1986). Social competence in children. *Monographs of the Society for Research in Child Development, 51* (2, Serial No. 213).

Dodge, K. A., & Price, J. M. (1994). On the relation between social information processing and socially competent behavior in early school-aged children. *Child Development, 65*, 1385–1397.

Doering, M., Rhodes, S. R., & Schuster, M. (1983). *The aging worker: Research and recommendations*. Beverly Hills, CA: Sage.

Doherty, W., Carroll, J., & Waite, L. (2007). Supporting the institution of marriage: Ideological, research, and ecological perspectives. In *The family in the new millennium: World voices supporting the "natural" clan Vol 2: Marriage and human dignity* (pp. 21–51). Westport, CT: Praeger Publishers/Greenwood Publishing Group.

Doka, K. J., & Mertz, M. E. (1988). The meaning and significance of great-grandparenthood. *Gerontologist, 28*, 192–197.

Dokoupil, T. (2007, July 16). Trouble in a "black box": Did an effort to reduce teen suicides backfire? *Newsweek*, p. 48.

Dollar, J. M., & Stifter, C. A. (2012). Temperamental surgency and emotion regulation as predictors of childhood social competence. *Journal of Experimental Child Psychology*. Retrieved from http://www.ncbi.nlm.nih.gov/pubmed/22414737.

Dollard, J., Doob, L. W., Miller, N. E., Mowrer, O. H., & Sears, R. R. (1930). *Frustration and aggression*. New Haven, CT: Yale University Press.

Doman, G., & Doman, J. (2002). *How to teach your baby to read*. Glenside, PA: Gentle Revolution Press.

Dombrowski, S., Noonan, K., & Martin, R. (2007). Low birth weight and cognitive outcomes: Evidence for a gradient relationship in an urban, poor, African American birth cohort. *School Psychology Quarterly, 22*, 26–43.

Dominguez, H. D., Lopez, M. F., & Molina, J. C. (1999). Interactions between perinatal and neonatal associative learning defined by contiguous olfactory and tactile stimulation. *Neurobiology of Learning and Memory, 71*, 272–288.

Dominus, S. (2004, February 22). Life in the age of old, old age. *The New York Times Magazine*, p. 31.

Domsch, H., Lohaus, A., & Thomas, H. (2009). Prediction of childhood cognitive abilities from a set of early indicators of information processing capabilities. *Infant Behavior & Development, 32*, 91–102.

Donat, D. (2006, October). Reading their way: A balanced approach that increases achievement. *Reading & Writing Quarterly: Overcoming Learning Difficulties, 22*, 305–323.

Dondi, M., Simion, F., & Caltran, G. (1999). Can newborns discriminate between their own cry and the cry of another newborn infant? *Developmental Psychology, 35*, 418–426.

Donini, L., Savina, C., & Cannella, C. (2003). Eating habits and appetite control in the elderly: The anorexia of aging. *International Psychogeriatrics, 15*, 73–87.

Donlan, C. (1998). *The development of mathematical skills*. Philadelphia: Psychology Press.

Donleavy, G. (2008). No man's land: Exploring the space between Gilligan and Kohlberg. *Journal of Business Ethics, 80*, 807–822.

Donnerstein, E. (2005, January). *Media violence and children: What do we know, what do we do?* Paper presented at the annual National Teaching of Psychology meeting, St. Petersburg Beach, FL.

Donohue, R. (2007, April). Examining career persistence and career change intent using the career attitudes and strategies inventory. *Journal of Vocational Behavior, 70*(2), 259–276.

Dorer, H., & Mahoney, J. (2006). Self-actualization in the corporate hierarchy. *North American Journal of Psychology, 8*, 397–410.

Doress, P. B., Siegal, D. L., & The Midlife and Old Women Book Project. (1987). *Ourselves, growing older*. New York: Simon & Schuster.

Dorling, J., D'Amore, A., Salt, A., Seward, A., Kaptoge, S., Halliday, S., et al. (2006). Data collection from very low birthweight infants in a geographical region: Methods, costs, and trends in mortality, admission rates, and resource utilisation over a five-year period. *Early Human Development, 82*, 117–124.

Dorn, L., Susman, E., & Ponirakis, A. (2003). Pubertal timing and adolescent adjustment and behavior: Conclusions vary by rater. *Journal of Youth & Adolescence, 32*, 157–167.

Dornbusch, S., Carlsmith, J., Bushwall, S., Ritter, P., Leiderman, P., Hastorf, A., et al. (1985). Single parents, extended households, and the control of adolescents. *Child Development, 56*, 326–341.

Dornbusch, S. M., Ritter, P. L., & Steinberg, L. (1992). Differences between African Americans and non-Hispanic whites in the relation of family statuses to adolescent school performance. *American Journal of Education, 99*, 543–567.

Dorofaeff, T., & Denny, S. (2006, September). Sleep and adolescence. Do New Zealand teenagers get enough? *Journal of Paediatrics and Child Health, 42*, 515–520.

Dortch, S. (1997, September). Hey guys: Hit the books. *American Demographics*, pp. 4–12.

Douglas, M. J. (1991). Potential complications of spinal and epidural anesthesia for obstetrics. *Seminars in Perinatology, 15*, 368–374.

Douglass, R., & McGadney-Douglass, B. (2008). The role of grandmothers and older women in the survival of children with kwashiorkor in urban Accra, Ghana. *Research in Human Development, 5,* 26–43.

Doussard-Roosevelt, J. A., Porges, S. W., Scanlon, J. W., Alemi, B., & Scanlon, K. B. (1997). Vagal regulation of heart rate in the prediction of developmental outcome for very low birth weight preterm infants. *Child Development, 68,* 173–186.

Douvan, E., & Adelson, J. (1966). *The adolescent experience.* New York: Wiley.

Dovidio, J., Pearson, A., Gaertner, S., & Hodson, G. (2008). On the nature of contemporary prejudice: From subtle bias to severe consequences. In *Explaining the breakdown of ethnic relations: Why neighbors kill* (pp. 41–60). Malden, MA: Blackwell Publishing.

Dowling, N., Smith, D., & Thomas, T. (2005). Electronic gaming machines: Are they the "crack-cocaine" of gambling? *Addiction, 100,* 33–45.

Downe-Wamboldt, B., & Tamlyn, D. (1997). An international survey of death education trends in faculties of nursing and medicine. *Death Studies, 21,* 177–188.

Downey, G., Silver, R. C., & Wortman, C. B. (1990). Reconsidering the attribution-adjustment relation following a major negative event: Coping with the loss of a child. *Journal of Personality and Social Psychology, 59,* 227–236.

Dowsett, C., Huston, A., Imes, A., & Gennetian, L. (2008). Structural and process features in three types of child care for children from high and low income families. *Early Childhood Research Quarterly, 23,* 69–93.

Doyle, L. W., & Victorian Infant Collaborative Study Group. (2004). Neonatal intensive care at borderline viability—Is it worth it? *Early Human Development, 80,* 103–113.

Doyle, R. (1996, June). AIDS cases reported, 1994–1995 [news]. *Scientific American, 274,* 28.

Doyle, R. (2000, June). Asthma worldwide. *Scientific American, 28.*

Doyle, R. (2004a, January). Living together. *Scientific American, 28.*

Doyle, R. (2004b, April). By the numbers: A surplus of women. *Scientific American, 290,* 33.

Doyle, R. (2006, March). The honeymoon is over. *Scientific American, 34.*

Draper, T., Holman, T., Grandy, S., & Blake, W. (2008). Individual, demographic, and family correlates of romantic attachments in a group of American young adults. *Psychological Reports, 103,* 857–872.

Dreman, S. (Ed.). (1997). *The family on the threshold of the 21st century.* Mahwah, NJ: Erlbaum.

Drew, L., & Silverstein, M. (2004). Inter-generational role investments of great-grandparents: Consequences for psychological well-being. *Ageing & Society, 24,* 95–111.

Drewett, R. (2007). *The nutritional psychology of childhood.* New York: Cambridge University Press.

Drews, C. D., Murphy, C. C., Yeargin-Allsopp, M., & Decoufle, P. (1996). The relationship between idiopathic mental retardation and maternal smoking during pregnancy. *Pediatrics, 97,* 547–553.

Driedger, S. D. (1994, July 11). Cancer made me stronger. *McCleans,* p. 46.

Driscoll, A. K., Russell, S. T., & Crockett, L. J. (2008). Parenting styles and youth well-being across immigrant generations. *Journal of Family Issues, 29,* 185–209.

Driver, J., Tabares, A., & Shapiro, A. (2003). Interactional patterns in marital success and failure: Gottman laboratory studies. In F. Walsh (Ed.), *Normal family processes: Growing diversity and complexity* (3rd ed.). New York: Guilford Press.

Dromi, E. (1987). *Early lexical development.* Cambridge, England: Cambridge University Press.

Dromi, E. (1993). The development of prelinguistic communication: Implications for language evaluation. In N. J. Anastasiow & S. Harel (Eds.), *At-risk infants:*

Interventions, families, and research (pp. 19–26). Baltimore: Brookes.

Drouin, M., & Landgraff, C. (2012). Texting, sexting, and attachment in college students' romantic relationships. *Computers in Human Behavior, 28,* 444–449.

Dryfoos, J. G. (1990). *Adolescents at risk: Prevalence and prevention.* New York: Oxford University Press.

DuBois, D. L., & Hirsch, B. J. (1990). School and neighborhood friendship patterns of blacks and whites in early adolescence. *Child Development, 61,* 524–536.

DuBreuil, S. C., Garry, M., & Loftus, E. F. (1998). Tales from the crib: Age regression and the creation of unlikely memories. In S. J. Lynn & K. M. McConkey (Eds.), *Truth in memory.* New York: The Guilford Press.

Duckitt, J. (1994). Conformity to social pressure and racial prejudice among white South Africans. *Genetic, Social, and General Psychology Monographs, 120,* 121–143.

Dudding, T. C., Vaizey, C. J., & Kamm, M. A. (2008). Obstetric anal sphincter injury: Incidence, risk factors, and management. *Annals of Surgery, 247,* 224–237.

Duenwald, M. (2003, July 15). After 25 years, new ideas in the prenatal test tube. *The New York Times,* p. D5.

Duenwald, M. (2004, May 11). For couples, stress without a promise of success. *The New York Times,* p. D3.

Dufresne, A., & Kobasigawa, A. (1989). Children's spontaneous allocation of study time: Differential and sufficient aspects. *Journal of Experimental Child Psychology, 47,* 274–296.

Dugger, K. (1996). *Social location and gender-role attitudes: A comparison of black and white women.* Thousand Oaks, CA: Sage Publications.

Duke, M., & Nowicki, S., Jr. (1979). *Abnormal psychology: Perspectives on being different.* Monterey, CA: Brooks/Cole.

Dukes, R., & Martinez, R. (1994). The impact of gender on self-esteem among adolescents. *Adolescence, 29,* 105–115.

Dulin-Keita, A., Hannon, L., Fernandez, J. R., & Cockerham, W. C. (2011). The defining moment: Children's conceptualization of race and experiences with racial discrimination. *Ethnic and Racial Studies, 34,* 662–682.

Dulitzki, M., Soriano, D., Schiff, E., Chetrit, A., Mashiach, S., & Seidman, D. S. (1998). Effect of very advanced maternal age on pregnancy outcome and rate of cesarean delivery. *Obstetrics and Gynecology, 92,* 935–939.

Dumka, L., Gonzales, N., Bonds, D., & Millsap, R. (2009). Academic success of Mexican origin adolescent boys and girls: The role of mothers' and fathers' parenting and cultural orientation. *Sex Roles, 60,* 588–599. http://search.ebscohost.com, doi:10.1007/s11199-008-9518-z.

Duncan, G. J. (2003). Modeling the impacts of childcare quality on children's preschool cognitive development. *Child Development, 74,* 1454–1475.

Duncan, G. J., & Brooks-Gunn, J. (Eds.). (1997). *Consequences of growing up poor.* New York: Russell Sage Foundation.

Duncan, G. J., & Brooks-Gunn, J. (2000). Family poverty, welfare reform, and child development. *Child Development, 71,* 188–196.

Duncan, G. J., Dowsett, C., Claessens, A., Magnuson, K., Huston, A. C., Klebanov, P., et al. (2007). School readiness and later achievement. *Developmental Psychology, 43,* 1428–1446.

Duncan, G. J., & Smith, K. R. (1989). The rising affluence of the elderly: How far, how fair, and how frail. *Annual Review of Sociology.* Palo Alto, CA: Annual Reviews.

Duncan, P., Ritter, P., Dornbusch, S., Gross, R., & Carlsmith, J. (1985). The effects of pubertal timing on body image, school behavior, and deviance. *Journal of Youth and Adolescence, 14,* 227–236.

Dunham, R. M., Kidwell, J. S., & Wilson, S. M. (1986). Rites of passage at adolescence: A ritual process paradigm. *Journal of Adolescent Research, 1,* 139–153.

Dunkel, C. S., Kim, J. K., & Papini, D. R. (2012). The general factor of psychosocial development and its relation to the general factor of personality and life history strategy. *Personality and Individual Differences, 52,* 202–206.

Dunn, A. L., & Blair, S. N. (1997). Exercise prescription. In W. P. Morgan (Ed.), *Series in health psychology and behavioral medicine. Physical activity and mental health* (pp. 49–62). Washington, DC: Taylor & Francis.

Dunn, E., & Laham, S. (2006). Affective forecasting: A user's guide to emotional time travel. *Affect in social thinking and behavior.* New York: Psychology Press.

Dunn, J., Ruedy, N. E., & Schweitzer, M. E. (2012). It hurts both ways: How social comparisons harm affective and cognitive trust. *Organizational Behavior and Human Decision Processes, 117,* 2–14.

Dunn, L. M. (1968). Special education for the mildly retarded—Is much of it justifiable? *Exceptional Child, 35,* 5–22.

Dunphy, D. C. (1963). The social structure of urban adolescent peer groups. *Society, 26,* 230–246.

DuPaul, G., & Weyandt, L. (2006, June). School-based intervention for children with attention deficit hyperactivity disorder: Effects on academic, social, and behavioural functioning. *International Journal of Disability, Development and Education, 53,* 161–176.

Duplassie, D., & Daniluk, J. C. (2007). Sexuality: Young and middle adulthood. In A. Owens & M. Tupper (Eds.), *Sexual health: Volume 1, Psychological Foundations.* Westport, CT: Praeger.

DuPlessis, H. M., Bell, R., & Richards, T. (1997). Adolescent pregnancy: Understanding the impact of age and race on outcomes. *Journal of Adolescent Health, 20,* 187–197.

Dupuis, S. (2009). An ecological examination of older remarried couples. *Journal of Divorce & Remarriage, 50,* 369–387.

Durant, J. E. (1999). Evaluating the success of Sweden's corporal punishment ban. *Child Abuse & Neglect, 23,* 435–448.

Durbin, C., Hayden, E., Klein, D., & Olino, T. (2007). Stability of laboratory-assessed temperamental emotionality traits from ages 3 to 7. *Emotion, 7,* 388–399.

Durbin, J. (2003, October 6). Internet sex unzipped. *McCleans,* p. 18.

Durik, A. M., Hyde, J. S., & Clark, R. (2000). Sequelae of cesarean and vaginal deliveries: Psychosocial outcomes for mothers and infants. *Developmental Psychology, 36,* 251–260.

Durkin, K., & Nugent, B. (1998). Kindergarten children's gender-role expectations for television actors. *Sex Roles, 38,* 387–402.

Durrant, R., & Ward, T. (2011). Evolutionary explanations in the social and behavioral sciences: Introduction and overview. *Aggression and Violent Behavior, 16,* 361–370.

Dutta, T., & Mandal, M. (2006, July). Hand preference and accidents in India. *Laterality: Asymmetries of Body, Brain and Cognition, 11*(4), 368–372.

Dutton, D. G. (1988). *The domestic assault of women: Psychological and criminal justice perspectives.* Boston, MA: Allyn & Bacon.

Dutton, D. G. (1994). *The domestic assault of women: Psychological and criminal justice perspectives* (2nd ed.). Vancouver, BC, Canada: University of British Columbia Press.

Dutton, M. A. (1992). *Empowering and healing the battered woman: A model of assessment and intervention.* New York: Springer.

Dwairy, M., Achoui, M., Abouserie, R., & Farah, A. (2006, May). Parenting styles, individuation, and mental health of Arab adolescents: A third cross-regional research study. *Journal of Cross-Cultural Psychology, 37*, 262–272.

D'warte, J. (2012). Talking about texts: Middle school students' engagement in metalinguistic talk. *Linguistics and Education, 23*, 123–134.

Dweck, C. (2002). The development of ability conceptions. In A. Wigfield & J. Eccles (Eds.), *Development of achievement motivation*. San Diego: Academic Press.

Dweck, C. S. (1991). Self-theories and goals: Their role in motivation, personality and development. In R. Dienstbier (Ed.), *Nebraska symposium on motivation* (Vol. 36). Lincoln: University of Nebraska Press.

Dweck, C. S., & Bush, E. S. (1976). Sex differences in learned helplessness: I. Differential debilitation with peer and adult evaluators. *Developmental Psychology, 12*, 147–156.

Dyer, C. B., Pavlik, V. N., Murphy, K. P., & Hyman, D. J. (2000). The high prevalence of depression and dementia in elder abuse or neglect. *Journal of the American Geriatrics Society, 48*, 205–208.

Dyer, S., & Moneta, G. (2006). Frequency of parallel, associative, and co-operative play in British children of different socioeconomic status. *Social Behavior and Personality, 34*, 587–592.

Dyregrov, K., Nordanger, D., & Dyregrov, A. (2003). Predictors of psychosocial distress after suicide, SIDS and accidents. *Death Studies, 27*, 143–165.

Dyson, A. H. (2003). "Welcome to the jam": Popular culture, school literacy and making of childhoods. *Harvard Educational Review, 73*, 328–361.

Eacott, M. J. (1999). Memory of the events of early childhood. *Current Directions in Psychological Science, 8*, 46–49.

Eagly, A. H., & Steffen, V. J. (1984). Gender stereotypes stem from the distribution of women and men into social roles. *Journal of Personality and Social Psychology, 46*, 735–754.

Eagly, A. H., & Steffen, V. J. (1986). Gender and aggressive behavior: A meta-analytic review of the social psychological literature. *Psychological Bulletin, 100*, 309–330.

Eagly, A. H., & Wood, W. (2003). In C. B. Travis (Ed.), *Evolution, gender, and rape*. Cambridge, MA: MIT Press.

Eagly, A. H., & Wood, W. (2012). Social role theory. In P. M. Van Lange, A. W. Kruglanski, E. Higgins, P. M. Van Lange, A. W. Kruglanski, & E. Higgins (Eds.), *Handbook of theories of social psychology* (Vol. 2). Thousand Oaks, CA: Sage Publications Ltd.

Eaker, E. D., Sullivan, L. M., Kelly-Hayes, M., D'Agostino, R. B., Sr., & Benjamin, E. J. (2004). Anger and hostility predict the development of atrial fibrillation in men in the Framingham Offspring Study. *Circulation, 109*, 1267–1271.

Eakins, P. S. (Ed.). (1986). *The American way of birth*. Philadelphia: Temple University Press.

Eames, C., Daley, D., Hutchings, J., Whitaker, C. J., Bywater, T., Jones, K., et al. (2010). The impact of group leaders' behaviour on parents' acquisition of key parenting skills during parent training. *Behaviour Research and Therapy, 48*, 1221–1226.

Earle, J., Perricone, P., Davidson, J., Moore, N., Harris, C., & Cotten, S. (2007, March). Premarital sexual attitudes and behavior at a religiously-affiliated university: Two decades of change. *Sexuality & Culture: An Interdisciplinary Quarterly, 11*(2), 39–61.

East, P., & Khoo, S. (2005). Longitudinal pathways linking family factors and sibling relationship qualities to adolescent substance use and sexual risk behaviors. *Journal of Family Psychology, 19*, 571–580.

East, P., Reyes, B., & Horn, E. (2007, June). Association between adolescent pregnancy and a family history of teenage births. *Perspectives on Sexual and Reproductive Health, 39*(2), 108–115.

Eastman, Q. (2003, June 20). Crib death exoneration could user in new gene tests. *Science, 300*, 1858.

Easton, J., Schipper, L., & Shackelford, T. (2007). Morbid jealousy from an evolutionary psychological perspective. *Evolution and Human Behavior, 28*, 399–402.

Eaton, M. J., & Dembo, M. H. (1997). Differences in the motivational beliefs of Asian American and non-Asian students. *Journal of Educational Psychology, 89*, 433–440.

Eaton, W. O., & Enns, L. R. (1986). Sex differences in human motor activity level. *Psychological Bulletin, 100*, 19–28.

Eaton, W. O., & Yu, A. P. (1989). Are sex differences in child motor activity level a function of sex differences in maturational status? *Child Development, 60*, 1005–1011.

Eberling, J. L., Wu, C., Tong-Turnbeaugh, R., & Jagust, W. J. (2004). Estrogen- and tamoxifen-associated effects on brain structure and function. *Neuroimage, 21*, 364–371.

Ebersole, J., & Kapp, S. (2007). Stemming the tide of overrepresentation: Ensuring accurate certification of African American students in programs for the mentally retarded. *School Social Work Journal, 31*, 1–16.

Eberstadt, N. (1994). Why babies die in D.C. *The Public Interest*, 3–16.

Ebner, N., Freund, A., & Baltes, P. (2006, December). Developmental changes in personal goal orientation from young to late adulthood: From striving for gains to maintenance and prevention of losses. *Psychology and Aging, 21*, 664–678.

Ebstein, R. P., Novick, O., Umansky, R., Priel, B., Osher, Y., Blaine, D., et al. (1996). Dopamine D4 receptor (1996) exon III polymorphism associated with the human personality trait of novelty seeking. *Nature and Genetics, 12*, 78–80.

Eccles, J., Templeton, J., & Barber, B. (2003). Adolescence and emerging adulthood: The critical passage ways to adulthood. In M. Bornstein & L. Davidson (Eds.), *Well-being: Positive development across the life course*. Mahwah, NJ: Lawrence Erlbaum Associates.

Eccles, J. S., Wigfield, A., Flanagan, C., Miller, C., Reuman, D., & Yee, D. (1989). Self-concepts, domain values, and self-esteem: Relations and changes at early adolescence. *Journal of Personality and Social Psychology, 57*, 283–310.

Ecenbarger, W. (1993, April 1). America's new merchants of death. *The Reader's Digest*, 50.

Eckerd, L. (2009). Death and dying course offerings in psychology: A survey of nine Midwestern states. *Death Studies, 33*, 762–770.

Eckerman, C. O., & Oehler, J. M. (1992). Very-low-birthweight newborns and parents as early social partners. In S. L. Friedman & M. D. Sigman (Eds.), *The psychological development of low-birthweight children*. Norwood, NJ: Ablex.

Eckerman, G., & Peterman, K. (2001). Peers and infant social/communicative development. In G. Bremner & A. Fogel (Eds.), *Blackwell handbook of infant development* (pp. 326–350). Malden, MA: Blackwell Publishers.

Edelman, S., & Kidman, A. D. (1997). Mind and cancer: Is there a relationship? A review of evidence. *Australian Psychologist, 32*, 79–85.

Edelstein, B., Stoner, S., & Woodhead, E. (2008). Older adults. In *Handbook of psychological assessment, case conceptualization, and treatment, Vol 1: Adults*. Hoboken, NJ: John Wiley & Sons Inc.

Eden, D. (1990). Pygmalion without interpersonal contrast effects: Whole groups gain from raising manager expectations. *Journal of Applied Psychology, 75*, 394–398.

Edgerley, L., El-Sayed, Y., Druzin, M., Kiernan, M., & Daniels, K. (2007). Use of a community mobile health van to increase early access to prenatal care. *Maternal & Child Health Journal, 11*, 235–239.

Edmondson, B. (1997, February). Two words and a number. *American Demographics*, pp. 10–15.

Edwards, C., de Guzman, M., Brown, J., & Kumru, A. (2006). Children's social behaviors and peer interactions in diverse cultures. *Peer relationships in cultural context*. New York: Cambridge University Press.

Edwards, C. P. (2000). Children's play in cross-cultural perspective: A new look at the Six Cultures study. *Cross-Cultural Research: The Journal of Comparative Social Science, 34*, 318–338.

Edwards, S. (2004). Constructivism does not only happen in the individual: Sociocultural theory and early childhood education. *Child Development & Care, 175*, 37–47.

Edwards, S. (2005). Constructivism does not only happen in the individual: Sociocultural theory and early childhood education. *Early Child Development & Care, 17*, 37–47.

Egan, M. C. (1994). Public health nutrition: A historical perspective. *Journal of the American Dietetic Association, 94*, 298–304.

Egan, S. K., & Perry, D. G. (1998). Does low selfregard invite victimization? *Developmental Psychology, 34*, 299–309.

Egeland, B., & Farber, E. A. (1984). Infant–mother attachment: Factors related to its development and changes over time. *Child Development, 55*, 753–771.

Egeland, B., & Hiester, M. (1995). The long-term consequences of infant day-care and mother-infant attachment. *Child Development, 66*, 474–485.

Egeland, B., Pianta, R., & O'Brien, M. A. (1993). Maternal intrusiveness in infancy and child maladaptation in early school years. *Development and Psychopathology, 5*, 359–370.

Eggebeen, D. J., & Hogan, D. P. (1990). Giving between generations in American families. *Human Nature, 1*, 211–232.

Eggum, N. D., Eisenberg, N., Kao, K., Spinrad, T. L., Bolnick, R., Hofer, C., et al. (2011). Emotion understanding, theory of mind, and prosocial orientation: Relations over time in early childhood. *The Journal of Positive Psychology, 6*, 4–16.

Ehlers, C. L., Frank, E., & Kupfer, D. J. (1988). Social zeitgebers and biological rhythms: A unified approach to understanding the etiology of depression. *Archives of General Psychiatry, 45*, 948–952.

Ehrensaft, M., Cohen, P., & Brown, J. (2003). Intergenerational transmission of partner violence: A 20-year prospective study. *Journal of Consulting & Clinical Psychology, 71*, 741–753.

Eichstedt, J., Serbin, L., & Poulin-Dubois, D. (2002). Of bears and men: Infants' knowledge of conventional and metaphorical gender stereotypes. *Infant Behavior & Development, 25*, 296–310.

Eid, M., Riemann, R., Angleitner, A., & Borkenau, P. (2003). Sociability and positive emotionality: Genetic and environmental contributions to the covariation between different facets of extraversion. *Journal of Personality, 71*, 319–346.

Eiden, R., Foote, A., & Schuetze, P. (2007). Maternal cocaine use and caregiving status: Group differences in caregiver and infant risk variables. *Addictive Behaviors, 32*, 465–476.

Eigsti, I., & Cicchetti, D. (2004). The impact of child maltreatment on expressive syntax at 60 months. *Developmental Science, 7*, 88–102.

Eimas, P. D., Sigueland, E. R., Jusczyk, P., & Vigorito, J. (1971). Speech perception in infants. *Science, 171*, 303–306.

Einarson, A., Choi, J., Einarson, T., & Koren, G. (2009). Incidence of major malformations in infants following antidepressant exposure in pregnancy: Results of a large prospective cohort study. *The Canadian Journal of Psychiatry / La Revue canadienne de psychiatrie, 54*, 242–246.

Einbinder, S. D. (1992). *A statistical profile of children living in poverty: Children under three and children under six, 1990*. Unpublished document from the National Center for Children in Poverty. New York: Columbia University, School of Public Health.

Eisbach, A. O. (2004). Children's developing awareness of diversity in people's trains of thought. *Child Development, 75*, 1694–1707.

Eisenberg, M., & Resnick, M. (2006, November). Suicidality among gay, lesbian and bisexual youth: The role of protective factors. *Journal of Adolescent Health, 39*(5), 662–668.

Eisenberg, N. (2004). Another slant on moral judgment. *psycCRITQUES,* 12–15.

Eisenberg, N., & Fabes, R. (1991). Prosocial behavior and empathy: A multimethod, developmental perspective. In. M. S. Clark (Ed.), *Review of personality and social psychology* (Vol. 12). Newbury Park, CA: Sage.

Eisenberg, N., & Fabes, R. A. (2006). Emotion regulation and children's socioemotional competence. In L. Baler & C. S. Tamis-LeMonda (Eds.), *Child psychology: A handbook of contemporary issues* (2nd ed.).

Eisenberg, N., Fabes, R. A., Guthrie, I. K., & Reiser, M. (2000). Dispositional emotionality and regulation: Their role in predicting quality of social functioning. *Journal of Personality and Social Psychology, 78,* 136–157.

Eisenberg, N., Fabes, R. A, & Spinrad, T. (2006). Prosocial development. *Handbook of child psychology: Vol. 3, Social, emotional, and personality development* (6th ed.). Hoboken, NJ: John Wiley & Sons Inc.

Eisenberg, N., Futhrie, I. K., Fabes, R. A., Reiser, M., Murphy, B. C., Holgren, R., et al. (1997). The relations of regulations and emotionality to resiliency and competent social functioning in elementary school children. *Child Development, 68,* 295–311.

Eisenberg, N., Guthrie, I. K., Murphy, B. C., Shepard, S. A., Cumberland, A., & Carlo, G. (1999). Consistency and development of prosocial dispositions: A longitudinal study. *Child Development, 70,* 1360–1372.

Eisenberg, N., Spinrad, T. L., & Sadovsky, A. (2006). Empathy-related responding in children. In M. Killen & J. G., Smetana (Eds.), *Handbook of moral development.* Mahwah, NJ: Lawrence Erlbaum Associates.

Eisenberg, N., & Valiente, C. (2002). Parenting and children's prosocial and moral development. In M. Bornstein (Ed.), *Handbook of parenting: Vol. 5: Practical issues in parenting.* Mahwah, NJ: Erlbaum.

Eisenberg, N., Valiente, C., & Champion, C. (2005). Empathy-related responding: Moral, social, and socialization correlates. In A. G. Miller (Ed.), *Social psychology of good and evil.* New York: Guilford Press.

Eisenberg, N., Wolchik, S. A., Hernandez, R., & Pasternack, J. F. (1985). Parental socialization of young children's play: A short-term longitudinal study. *Child Development, 56,* 1506–1513.

Eisenberg, N., & Zhou, Q. (2000). Regulation from a developmental perspective. *Psychological Inquiry, 11,* 166–172.

Eisenbraun, K. (2007). Violence in schools: Prevalence, prediction, and prevention. *Aggression and Violent Behavior, 12,* 459–469.

Eitel, B. J. (2003). Body image satisfaction, appearance importance, and self-esteem: A comparison of Caucasian and African-American women across the adult lifespan. *Dissertation Abstracts International: Section B: The Sciences & Engineering, 63,* 5511.

Eivers, A. R., Brendgen, M., Vitaro, F., & Borge, A. H. (2012). Concurrent and longitudinal links between children's and their friends' antisocial and prosocial behavior in preschool. *Early Childhood Research Quarterly, 27,* 137–146.

Ekman, P., & O'Sullivan, M. (1991). Facial expression: Methods, means, and moues. In R. S. Feldman & B. Rime (Eds.), *Fundamentals of nonverbal behavior.* Cambridge, England: Cambridge University Press.

Elder, G. A., De Gasperi, R., & Gama Sosa, M. A. (2006). Research update: Neurogenesis in adult brain and neuropsychiatric disorders. *Mt. Sinai Journal of Medicine, 73,* 931–940.

Eley, T. C., Bolton, D., & O'Connor, T. G. (2003). A twin study of anxiety-related behaviours in pre-school children. *Journal of Child Psychology and Psychiatry and Allied Disciplines, 44,* 103–121.

Eley, T. C., Bolton, D., O'Connor, T. G., Perrin, S., Smith, P., & Plomin, R. (2003). Phenotypic and genetic differentiation of anxiety-related behaviours in young children. *Journal of Child Psychology & Psychiatry, 44,* 945–960.

Eley, T. C., Liang, H., & Plomin, R. (2004). Parental familial vulnerability, family environment, and their interactions as predictors of depressive symptoms in adolescents. *Child & Adolescent Social Work Journal, 21,* 298–306.

Eley, T. C., Lichtenstein, P., & Moffitt, T. E. (2003). A longitudinal behavioral genetic analysis of the etiology of aggressive and nonaggressive antisocial behavior. *Development and Psychopathology, 15,* 383–402.

Elkana, O., Frost, R., Kramer, U., Ben-Bashat, D., Hendler, T., Schmidt, D., et al. (2011). Cerebral reorganization as a function of linguistic recovery in children: An fMRI study. *Cortex: A Journal Devoted to the Study of the Nervous System and Behavior, 47,* 202–216.

Elkind, D. (1967). Egocentrism in adolescence. *Child Development, 38,* 1025–1034.

Elkind, D. (1978). The children's reality: Three developmental themes. In S. Coren & L. M. Ward (Eds.), *Sensation and perception.* Hillsdale, NJ: Erlbaum.

Elkind, D. (1984). *All grown up and no place to go.* Reading, MA: Addison-Wesley.

Elkind, D. (1985). Egocentrism redux. *Developmental Review, 5,* 218–226.

Elkind, D. (1988). *Miseducation.* New York: Knopf.

Elkind, D. (1994a). *A sympathetic understanding of the child: Birth to sixteen* (3rd ed). Needham Heights, MA: Allyn & Bacon.

Elkind, D. (1994b). *Ties that stress: The new family imbalance.* Cambridge, MA: Harvard University Press.

Elkind, D. (1996). Inhelder and Piaget on adolescence and adulthood: A postmodern appraisal. *Psychological Science, 7,* 216–220.

Elkind, D. (2007). *The hurried child: Growing up too fast too soon* (25th anniv.). Cambridge, MA: Da Capo Press.

Elkins, D. (2009). Why humanistic psychology lost its power and influence in American psychology: Implications for advancing humanistic psychology. *Journal of Humanistic Psychology, 49,* 267–291. http://search.ebscohost.com, doi:10.1177/0022167808323575

Ellemers, N., & Haslam, S. (2012). Social identity theory. In P. M. Van Lange, A. W. Kruglanski, E. Higgins, P. M. Van Lange, A. W. Kruglanski, & E. Higgins (Eds.), *Handbook of theories of social psychology* (Vol. 2). Thousand Oaks, CA: Sage Publications Ltd.

Elliott, K., & Urquiza, A. (2006). Ethnicity, culture, and child maltreatment. *Journal of Social Issues, 62,* 787–809.

Ellis, B. J. (2004). Timing of pubertal maturation in girls: An integrated life history approach. *Psychological Bulletin, 130,* 920–958.

Ellis, L. (2006, July). Gender differences in smiling: An evolutionary neuroandrogenic theory. *Physiology & Behavior, 88,* 303–308.

Ellis, L., & Engh, T. (2000). Handedness and age of death: New evidence on a puzzling relationship. *Journal of Health Psychology, 5,* 561–565.

Ellis, L., Ficek, C., Burke, D., & Das, S. (2008, February). Eye color, hair color, blood type, and the rhesus factor: Exploring possible genetic links to sexual orientation. *Archives of Sexual Behavior, 37*(1), 145–149.

Ellis, S., & Siegler, R. S. (1997). Planning and strategy choice, or why don't children plan when they should? In S. L. Friedman & E. K. Scholnick (Eds.), *Why, how, and when do we plan: The developmental psychology of planning.* Hillsdale, NJ: Lawrence Erlbaum Associates.

Ellis, W., & Zarbatany, L. (2007). Peer group status as a moderator of group influence on children's deviant, aggressive, and prosocial behavior. *Child Development, 78,* 1240–1254.

Elmore, J. G., Jackson, S. L., Abraham, L., Miglioretti, D. L., Carney, P. A., Geller, B. M., Yankaskas, B. C., Kerlikowske, K., Onega, T., Rosenberg, R. D., Sickles, E. A., & Buist, D. S. (2009). Variability in interpretive performance at screening mammography and radiologists' characteristics associated with accuracy. *Radiology, 253,* 641–651.

Elsayem, A., Swint, K., Fisch, M. J., Palmer, J. L., Reddy, S., Walker, P., Zhukovsky, D., Knight, P., & Bruera, E. (2004). Palliative care inpatient service in a comprehensive cancer center: Clinical and financial outcomes. *Journal of Clinical Oncology, 22,* 2008–2014.

Else-Quest, N. M., Hyde, J. S., & Clark, R. (2003). Breastfeeding, bonding, and the mother-infant relationship. *Merrill-Palmer Quarterly, 49,* 495–517.

Emack, J., Kostaki, A., Walker, C., & Matthews, S. (2008). Chronic maternal stress affects growth, behaviour and hypothalamo-pituitary-adrenal function in juvenile offspring. *Hormones and Behavior, 54,* 514–520.

Emery, R. E., & Laumann-Billings, L. (1998). An overview of the nature, causes, and consequences of abusive family relationships: Toward differentiating maltreatment and violence. *American Psychologist, 53,* 121–135.

Employment Policies Institute. (2000). *Correcting part-time misconceptions.* Washington, DC: Author.

Emslie, C., & Hunt, K. (2008). The weaker sex? Exploring lay understandings of gender differences in life expectancy: A qualitative study. *Social Science & Medicine, 67,* 808–816.

Emslie, G. J., Rush, A. J., Weinberg, W. A., Kowatch, R. A., Hughes, C. W., Carmody, T., & Rintelmann, J. A. (1997). Double-blind, randomized, placebo-controlled trial of fluoxetine in children and adolescents with depression. *Archives of General Psychiatry, 54,* 1031–1037.

Endo, S. (1992). Infant-infant play from 7 to 12 months of age: An analysis of games in infant-peer triads. *Japanese Journal of Child and Adolescent Psychiatry, 33,* 145–162.

Endocrine Society. (2001). *The Endocrine Society and Lawson Wilkins Pediatric Endocrine Society call for further research to define precocious puberty.* Bethesda, MD: Author.

Engels, R., Kerr, M., & Stattin, H. (2007). *Friends, lovers and groups: Key relationships in adolescence.* New York: John Wiley & Sons Ltd.

England, P., & Li, S. (2006, October). Desegregation stalled: The changing gender composition of college majors, 1971–2002. *Gender & Society, 20,* 657–677.

England, P., & McCreary, L. (1987). *Integrating sociology and economics to study gender and work.* Newbury Park, CA: Sage Publications.

Engle, P. L., & Breaux, C. (1998). Father's involvement with children: Perspectives from developing countries. *Social Policy Report, 12,* 1–21.

Engler, J., & Goleman, D. (1992). *The consumer's guide to psychotherapy.* New York: Simon & Schuster.

Englund, K., & Behrn, D. (2006). Changes in infant directed speech in the first six months. *Infant and Child Development, 15,* 139–160.

Englund, M. M., Levy, A. K., Hyson, D. M., & Sroufe, L. A. (2000). Adolescent social competence: Effectiveness in a group setting. *Child Development, 71,* 1049–1060.

Ennett, S. T., & Bauman, K. E. (1996). Adolescent social networks: School, demographic, and longitudinal considerations. *Journal of Adolescent Research, 11,* 194–215.

Enright, E. (2004, July & August). A house divided. *AARP Magazine,* pp. 54, 57.

Ensenauer, R. E., Michels, V. V., & Reinke, S. S. (2005). Genetic testing: Practical, ethical, and counseling considerations. *Mayo Clinic Proceedings, 80,* 63–73.

Epel, E. (2009). Telomeres in a life-span perspective: A new "psychobiomarker"? *Current Directions in Psychological Science, 18,* 6–10.

Epperson, S. E. (1988, September 16). Studies link subtle sex bias in schools with women's behavior in the workplace. *The Wall Street Journal,* p. 19.

Epstein, K. (1993). The interactions between breastfeeding mothers and their babies during the breastfeeding session. *Early Child Development and Care, 87,* 93–104.

Epstein, L., & Mardon, S. (2007, September 17). Homeroom zombies. *Newsweek,* pp. 64–65.

Erber, J. T., Rothberg, S. T., & Szuchman, L. T. (1991). Appraisal of everyday memory failures by middle-aged adults. *Educational Gerontology, 17,* 63–72.

Erber, J. T., Szuchman, L. T., & Rothberg, S. T. (1990). Everyday memory failure: Age differences in appraisal and attribution. *Psychology and Aging, 5,* 236–241.

Erel, O., Oberman, Y., & Yirmiya, N. (2000). Maternal versus nonmaternal care and seven domains of children's develoment. *Psychological Bulletin, 126,* 727–747.

Erikson, E. H. (1963). *Childhood and society.* New York: Norton.

Erlandson, D. A., Harris, E. L., Skipper, B. L., & Allen, S. D. (1993). *Doing naturalistic inquiry: A guide to methods.* Newbury Park, CA: Sage.

Erlandsson, K., Dsilna, A., Fagerberg, I., & Christensson, K. (2007). Skin-to-skin care with the father after cesarean birth and its effect on newborn crying and prefeeding behavior. *Birth: Issues in Perinatal Care, 34,* 105–114.

Eron, L. D., & Huesmann, L. R. (1985). The control of aggressive behavior by changes in attitude, values, and the conditions of learning. In R. J. Blanchard & C. Blanchard (Eds.), *Advances in the study of aggression.* New York: Academic Press.

Ertmer, D. J., & Jung, J. (2012). Prelinguistic vocal development in young cochlear implant recipients and typically developing infants: Year 1 of robust hearing experience. *Journal of Deaf Studies and Deaf Education, 17,* 116–132.

Erwin, P. (1993). *Friendship and peer relations in children.* Chichester, England: Wiley.

Escott, D., Slade, P., & Spiby, H. (2009). Preparation for pain management during childbirth: The psychological aspects of coping strategy development in antenatal education. *Clinical Psychology Review, 29,* 617–622.

Eshel, N., Nelson, E. E., Blair, R. J., Pine, D. S., & Ernst, M. (2007). Neural substrates of choice selection in adults and adolescents: Development of the ventrolateral prefrontal and anterior cingulated cortices. *Neuropsychologia, 45,* 1270–1279.

Eslea, M., Menesini, E., Morita, Y., O'Moore, M., Mora-Nerchan, J. A., Pereira, B., et al. (2004). Friendship and loneliness among bullies and victims: Data from seven countries. *Aggressive Behavior, 30,* 71–83.

Espelage, D. L., & Swearer, S. M. (2004). *Bullying in American schools.* Mahwah, NJ: Lawrence Erlbaum.

Espenschade, A. (1960). Motor development. In W. R. Johnson (Ed.), *Science and medicine of exercise and sports.* New York: Harper & Row.

Essex, M. J., & Nam, S. (1987). Marital status and loneliness among older women: The differential importance of close family and friends. *Journal of Marriage and the Family, 49,* 92–106.

Essick, K. (2009, November 23). Profiles in later life. *Wall Street Journal,* p. R8.

Estabrook, P. A., Lee, R. E., & Gyurcsik, N. C. (2003). Resources for physical activity participation: Does availability and accessibility differ by neighborhood socioeconomic status? *Annals of Behavioral Medicine, 25,* 100–104.

Estell, D. B., Jones, M. H., Pearl, R., Van Acker, R., Farmer, T. W., & Rodkin, P. C. (2008). Peer groups, popularity, and social preference: Trajectories of social functioning among students with and without learning disabilities. *Journal of Learning Disabilities, 41,* 5–14.

Ethier, L., Couture, G., & Lacharite, C. (2004). Risk factors associated with the chronicity of high potential for child abuse and neglect. *Journal of Family Violence, 19,* 13–24.

Evans, D. L. (1993, March 1). The wrong examples. *Newsweek,* p. 10.

Evans, G. W. (2004). The environment of childhood poverty. *American Psychologist, 59,* 77–92.

Evans, G. W., Boxhill, L., & Pinkava, M. (2008). Poverty and maternal responsiveness: The role of maternal stress and social resources. *International Journal of Behavioral Development, 32,* 232–237. http://search.ebscohost.com, doi:10.1177/0165025408089272

Evans, G. W., Maxwell, L. E., & Hart, B. (1999). Parental language and verbal responsiveness to children in crowded homes. *Developmental Psychology, 35,* 1020–1023.

Evans, R. (2009). A comparison of rural and urban older adults in Iowa on specific markers of successful aging. *Journal of Gerontological Social Work, 52,* 423–438.

Eveleth, P., & Tanner, J. (1976). *Worldwide variation in human growth.* New York: Cambridge University Press.

Evenson, K. R. (2011). Towards an understanding of change in physical activity from pregnancy through postpartum. *Psychology of Sport and Exercise, 12,* 36–45.

Evenson, R., & Simon, R. (2005). Clarifying the relationship between parenthood and depression. *Journal of Health and Social Behavior, 46,* 341–358.

Everett, S. A., Malarcher, A. M., Sharp, D. J., Husten, C. G., & Giovino, G. A. (2000a). Relationship between cigarette, smokeless tobacco, and cigar use, and other health risk behaviors among U.S. high school students. *Journal of School Health, 70,* 234–240.

Everett, S. A., Warren, C. W., Santelli, J. S., Kann, L., Collins, J. L., & Kolbe, L. J. (2000b). Use of birth control pills, condoms, and withdrawal among U.S. high school students. *Journal of Adolescent Health, 27,* 112–118.

Everson, M., & Boat, B. (2002). The utility of anatomical dolls and drawings in child forensic interviews. *Memory and suggestibility in the forensic interview.* Mahwah, NJ: Lawrence Erlbaum Associates.

Evinger, S. (1996, May). How to record race. *American Demographics,* 36–41.

Ewbank, J. J., Barnes, T. M., Lakowski, B., Lussier, M., Bussey, H., & Hekimi, S. (1997, February 14). Structural and functional conservation of the caenorhabditis elegans timing gene clk-1. *Science, 275,* 980.

Eyer, D. (1992). The bonding hype. In M. E. Lamb & J. B. Lancaster (Eds.), *Birth management: Biosocial perspectives.* Hawthorne, New York: Aldine de Gruyter.

Eyer, D. E. (1994). Mother–infant bonding: A scientific fiction. *Human Nature, 5,* 69–94.

Fabsitz, R. R., Carmelli, D., & Hewitt, J. K. (1992). Evidence for independent genetic influences on obesity in middle age. *International Journal of Obesity and Related Metabolic Disorders, 16,* 657–666.

Fagan, J., Holland, C., & Wheeler, K. (2007). The prediction, from infancy, of adult IQ and achievement. *Intelligence, 35,* 225–231.

Fagan, M. (2009). Mean length of utterance before words and grammar: Longitudinal trends and developmental implications of infant vocalizations. *Journal of Child Language, 36,* 495–527. Retrieved from http://search. ebscohost.com, doi:10.1017/S0305000908009070.

Fagot, B. I. (1978). The influence of sex of child on parental reactions to toddler children. *Child Development, 49,* 459–465.

Fagot, B. I. (1991). *Peer relations in boys and girls from two to seven.* Paper presented at the biennial meeting of the Society for Research in Child Development, Seattle, WA.

Fagot, B. I., & Hagan, R. (1991). Observation of parent reaction to sex-stereotyped behaviors: Age and sex effects. *Child Development, 62,* 617–628.

Fagot, B. I., & Leinbach, M. D. (1993). Gender-role development in young children: From discrimination to labeling. *Developmental Review, 13,* 205–224.

Faith, M. S., Johnson, S. L., & Allison, D. B. (1997). Putting the behavior into the behavior genetics of obesity. *Behavior Genetics, 27,* 423–439.

Falbo, T. (1992). Social norms and the one-child family: Clinical and policy implications. In F. Boer & J. Dunn (Eds.), *Children's sibling relationships.* Hillsdale, NJ: Erlbaum.

Falck-Ytter, T., Gredeback, G., & von Hofsten, C. (2006). Infants predict other people's action goals. *Nature and Neuroscience, 9,* 878–879.

Falk, D. (2004). Prelinguistic evolution in early hominins: Whence motherese? *Behavioral and Brain Sciences, 27,* 491–503.

Falk, P. J. (1989). Lesbian mothers: Psychosocial assumptions in family law. *American Psychologist, 44,* 941–947.

Families and Work Institute. (1998). *Report on men spending more time with kids.* Washington, DC: Author.

Fangman, J. J., Mark, P. M., Pratt, L., Conway, K. K., Healey, M. L., Oswald, J. W., et al. (1994). *American Journal of Obstetrical Gynecology, 170,* 744–750.

Fanshel, D., Finch, S. J., & Grundy, J. F. (1990). *Foster children in a life course perspective.* New York: Columbia University Press.

Fanshel, D., Finch, S. J., & Grundy, J. F. (1992). *Serving the urban poor.* Westport, CT: Praeger.

Fantuzzo, J. W., & Mohr, W. K. (1999). Prevalence and effects of child exposure to domestic violence. *The Future of Children, 9,* 5.

Fantz, R. (1963). Pattern vision in newborn infants. *Science, 140,* 296–297.

Fantz, R. L. (1961). The origin of form perception. *Scientific American, 72.*

Farah, M., Shera, D., Savage, J., Betancourt, L., Giannetta, J., Brodsky, N., et al. (2006, September). Childhood poverty: Specific associations with neurocognitive development. *Brain Research, 1110,* 166–174.

Farel, A. M., Hooper, S. R., Teplin, S. W., Henry, M. M., & Kraybill, E. N. (1998). Very-low-birthweight infants at seven years: An assessment of the health and neurodevelopmental risk conveyed by chronic lung disease. *Journal of Learning Disabilities, 31,* 118–126.

Farhi, P. (1995, June 21). Turning the tables on TV violence. *The Washington Post,* pp. F1, F2.

Farmer, T. W., Estell, D. B., Bishop, J. L., O'Neal, K. K., & Cairns, B. D. (2003). Rejected bullies or popular leaders? The social relations of aggressive subtypes of rural African American early adolescents. *Developmental Psychology, 39,* 992–1004.

Farrant, B., Fletcher, J., & Maybery, M. (2006, November). Specific language impairment, theory of mind, and visual perspective taking: Evidence for simulation theory and the developmental role of language. *Child Development, 77,* 1842–1853.

Farrar, M. J., & Goodman, G. S. (1992). Developmental changes in event memory. *Child Development, 63,* 173–187.

Farrar, M. J., Johnson, B., Tompkins, V., Easters, M., Zilisi-Medus, A., & Benigno, J. (2009). Language and theory of mind in preschool children with specific language impairment. *Journal of Communication Disorders, 42,* 428–441.

Farroni, T., Menon, E., Rigato, S., & Johnson, M. (2007). The perception of facial expressions in newborns. *European Journal of Developmental Psychology, 4,* 2–13.

Farver, J. M., & Branstetter, W. H. (1994). Preschoolers' prosocial responses to their peers' distress. *Developmental Psychology, 30,* 334–341.

Farver, J. M., & Frosch, D. L. (1996). L.A. stories: Aggression in preschoolers' spontaneous narratives after the riots of 1992. *Child Development, 67,* 19–32.

Farver, J. M., Kim, Y. K., & Lee-Shin, Y. (1995). Cultural differences in Korean- and Anglo-American preschoolers' social interaction and play behaviors. *Child Development, 66,* 1088–1099.

Farver, J. M., & Lee-Shin, Y. (2000). Acculturation and Korean-American children's social and play behavior. *Social Development, 9,* 316–336.

Farver, J. M., Welles-Nystrorn, B., Frosch, D. L., & Wimbarti, S. (1997). Toy stories: Aggression in children's narratives in the United States, Sweden, Germany, and Indonesia. *Journal of Cross-Cultural Psychology, 28,* 393–420.

Farzin, F., Charles, E., & Rivera, S. (2009). Development of multimodal processing in infancy. *Infancy, 14,* 563–578.

Fasano, C., & Pellitteri, J. (2006). Infusing emotional learning into the school environment. In *Emotionally intelligent school counseling* (pp. 65–79). Mahwah, NJ: Lawrence Erlbaum Associates.

Faulkner, G., & Biddle, S. (2004). Exercise and depression: Considering variability and contextuality. *Journal of Sport & Exercise Psychology, 26,* 3–18.

Fawzy, F. I. (1994). The benefits of a short-term group intervention for cancer patients. *Advances, 10,* 17–19.

Fayers, T., Crowley, T., Jenkins, J. M., & Cahill, D. J. (2003). Medical student awareness of sexual health is poor. *International Journal STD/AIDS, 14,* 386–389.

Federal Interagency Forum on Age-Related Statistics. (2000). *Older Americans 2000: Key indicators of well-being.* Hyattsville, MD: Federal Interagency Forum on Age-Related Statistics.

Federal Interagency Forum on Child and Family Statistics. (2003). *America's children: Key national indicators of well-being, 2003.* Federal Interagency Forum on Child and Family Statistics. Washington, DC: U.S. Government Printing Office.

Feeney, B., & Collins, N. (2001). Predictors of caregiving in adult intimate relationships: An attachment theoretical perspective. *Journal of Personality & Social Psychology, 80,* 972–994.

Feeney, B., & Collins, N. (2003). Motivations for caregiving in adult intimate relationships: Influences on caregiving behavior and relationship functioning. *Personality & Social Psychology Bulletin, 29,* 950–968.

Feeney, J., & Noller, P. (1996). *Adult attachment.* Thousand Oaks, CA: Sage.

Feifel, H. (1963). Relationship of physician to terminally ill patient. In N. L. Farberow (Ed.), *Taboo topics* (pp. 8–12). New York: Atherton.

Feigelman, W., Jordan, J., & Gorman, B. (2009). How they died, time since loss, and bereavement outcomes. *Omega: Journal of Death and Dying, 58,* 251–273.

Feingold, A. (1992). Matching for attractiveness in romantic partners and same-sex friends: A meta-analysis and theoretical critique. *Psychological Bulletin, 111,* 304–341.

Feinberg, A. W. (2000, October). Questions and answers. *HealthNews,* p. 10.

Feist, G., & Barron, F. (2003). Predicting creativity from early to late adulthood: Intellect, potential, and personality. *Journal of Research in Personality, 37,* 62–88.

Feldhusen, J. F. (2003a). Precocity and acceleration. *Gifted Education International, 17,* 55–58.

Feldhusen, J. F. (2003b). Lewis M. Terman: A pioneer in the development of ability tests. In B. J. Zimmerman (Ed.), *Educational psychology: A century of contributions.* Mahwah, NJ: Lawrence Erlbaum Associates.

Feldhusen, J. F., Haeger, W. W., & Pellegrino, A. S. (1989). A model training program in gifted education for school administrators. *Roeper Review, 11,* 209–214.

Feldman, D. H., & Goldsmith, L. T. (1991). *Nautre's gambit.* New York: Teachers College Press.

Feldman, R. S. (1982). *Development of nonverbal behavior in children.* New York: Springer-Verlag.

Feldman, R. S. (Ed.). (1992). *Applications of nonverbal behavioral theories and research.* Hillsdale, NJ: Erlbaum.

Feldman, R. S. (2008). Parent-infant synchrony: Biological foundations and developmental outcomes. *Current Directions in Psychological Science, 16,* 340–345.

Feldman, R. S. (2009). *The Liar in your life.* New York: Twelve.

Feldman, R. S. (2011). Maternal touch and the developing infant. In M. J. Hertenstein, S. J. Weiss, M. J. Hertenstein, & S. J. Weiss (Eds.), *The handbook of touch: Neuroscience, behavioral, and health perspectives.* New York: Springer Publishing Co.

Feldman, R. S., Coats, E. J., & Spielman, D. A. (1996). Television exposure and children's decoding of nonverbal behavior. *Journal of Applied Social Psychology, 26,* 1718–1733.

Feldman, R. S., Coats, E. J., & Philippot, P. (1998). Consequences of media exposure on the nonverbal behavior of children. In P. Philipott, R. S. Feldman, & E. J. Coats, (Eds.), *The social context of nonverbal behavior.* Cambridge, England: Cambridge University Press.

Feldman, R. S., & Eidelman, A. (2003). Direct and indirect effects of breast milk on neurobehavioral and cognitive development of premature infants. *Developmental Psychobiology, 43,* 109–119.

Feldman, R. S., Philippot, P., & Custrini, R. J. (1991). Social competence and nonverbal behavior. In R. S. Feldman & B. Rime (Eds.), *Fundamentals of nonverbal behavior.* Cambridge, England: Cambridge University Press.

Feldman, R. S., & Masalha, S. (2007). The role of culture in moderating the links between early ecological risk and young children's adaptation. *Development and Psychopathology, 19,* 1–21.

Feldman, R. S., & Prohaska, T. (1979). The student as Pygmalion: Effect of student expectation on the teacher. *Journal of Educational Psychology, 4,* 485–493.

Feldman, R. S., & Rimé, B. (Eds.). (1991). *Fundamentals of nonverbal behavior.* Cambridge, England: Cambridge University Press.

Feldman, R. S., Sussman, A., & Zigler, E. (2004). Parental leave and work adaptation at the transition to parenthood: Individual, marital, and social correlates. *Journal of Applied Developmental Psychology, 25,* 459–479.

Feldman, R. S., & Theiss, A. J. (1982). The teacher and student as Pygmalions: The joint effects of teacher and student expectation. *Journal of Educational Psychology, 74,* 217–223.

Feldman, R. S., Tomasian, J., & Coats, E. J. (1999). Adolescents' social competence and nonverbal deception abilities: Adolescents with higher social skills are better liars. *Journal of Nonverbal Behavior, 23,* 237–249.

Feldman, R. S., Weller, A., Sirota, L., & Eidelman, A. I. (2003). Testing a family intervention hypothesis: The contribution of mother–infant skin-to-skin contact (Kangaroo Care) to family interaction, proximity, and touch. *Journal of Family Psychology, 17,* 94–107.

Feldman, S. S., Biringen, Z. C., & Nash, S. C. (1981). Fluctuations of sex-related self-attributions as a function of stage of family life cycle. *Developmental Psychology, 17,* 24–35.

Feldman, S. S., & Rosenthal, D. A. (1990). The acculturation of autonomy expectations in Chinese high schoolers residing in two Western nations. *International Journal of Psychology, 25,* 259–281.

Feldman, S. S., & Wood, D. N. (1994). Parents' expectations for preadolescent sons' behavioral autonomy: A longitudinal study of correlates and outcomes. *Journal of Research on Adolescence, 4,* 45–70.

Fell, J., & Williams, A. (2008). The effect of aging on skeletal-muscle recovery from exercise: Possible implications for aging athletes. *Journal of Aging and Physical Activity, 16,* 97–115.

Feng, T. (1993). Substance abuse in pregnancy. *Current Opinion in Obstetrics & Gynecology, 5,* 16–23.

Fennell, C., Sartorius, G., Ly, L. P., Turner, L., Liu, P. Y., Conway, A. J., et al. (2009). Randomized cross-over clinical trial of injectable vs. implantable depot testosterone for maintenance of testosterone replacement therapy in androgen deficient men. *Clinical Endocrinology, 42,* 88–95.

Fenson, L., Dale, P. S., Reznick, J. S., Bates, E., Thal, D. J., & Pethick, S. J. (1994). Variability in early communicative development. *Monographs of the Society for Research in Child Development, 59*(5, Serial No. 242).

Fenwick, K., & Morrongiello, B. (1991). Development of frequency perception in infants and children. *Journal of Speech, Language Pathology, and Audiology, 15,* 7–22.

Fenwick, K. D., & Morrongiello, B. A. (1998). Spatial co-location and infants' learning of auditory-visual associations. *Behavior & Development, 21,* 745–759.

Ferber, S. G., Kuint, J., Weller, A., Feldman, R., Dollberg, S., Arbel, E., et al. (2002). Message therapy by mothers and trained professionals enhances weight gain in preterm infants. *Early Human Development, 67,* 37–45.

Ferguson, M., & Molfese, P. (2007). Breast-fed infants process speech differently from bottle-fed infants: Evidence from neuroelectrophysiology. *Developmental Neuropsychology, 31,* 337–347.

Ferguson, S. (2007). *Shifting the center: Understanding contemporary families* (3rd ed.). New York: McGraw-Hill.

Fergusson, D., Horwood, L., Boden, J., & Jenkin, G. (2007, March). Childhood social disadvantage and smoking in adulthood: Results of a 25-year longitudinal study. *Addiction, 102,* 475–482.

Fergusson, D. M., Horwood, L. J., & Ridder, E. M. (2006). Abortion in young women and subsequent mental health. *Journal of Child Psychology and Psychiatry, 47,* 16–24.

Fergusson, E., Maughan, B., & Golding, J. (2008). Which children receive grandparental care and what effect does it have? *Journal of Child Psychology and Psychiatry, 49,* 161–169.

Fernald, A. (1984). The perceptual and affective salience of mothers' speech to infants. In L. Feagans, C. Garvey, & R. Golinkoff (Eds.), *The origins and growth of communication.* Norwood, NJ: Ablex.

Fernald, A. (1989). Intonation and communicative intent in mothers' speech to infants: Is the melody the message? *Child Development, 60,* 1497–1510.

Fernald, A. (2001). Hearing, listening, and understanding: Auditory development in infancy. In G. Bremner & A. Fogel (Eds.), *Blackwell handbook of infant development.* Malden, MA: Blackwell Publishers.

Fernald, A., & Kuhl, P. (1987). Acoustic determinants of infant preference for motherese speech. *Infant Behavior and Development, 10,* 279–293.

Fernald, A., & Morikawa, H. (1993). Common themes and cultural variations in Japanese and American mothers' speech to infants. *Child Development, 64,* 637–656.

Fernald, A., Taeschner, T., Dunn, J., Papousek, M., Boysson-Bardies, B., & Fukui, I. (1989). A cross-language study of prosodic modifications in mothers' and fathers' speech to preverbal infants. *Journal of Child Language, 16,* 477–501.

Fernández, J., Casazza, K., Divers, J., & López-Alarcón, M. (2008). Disruptions in energy balance: Does nature overcome nurture? *Physiology & Behavior, 94,* 105–112.

Fernyhough, C. (1997). Vygotsky's sociocultural approach: Theoretical issues and implications for current research. In S. Hala (Ed.), *The development of social cognition* (pp. 65–92). Hove, England: Psychology Press/ Erlbaum, Taylor & Francis.

Ferrario, S., Vitaliano, P., & Zotti, A. (2003). Alzheimer's disease: Usefulness of the Family Strain Questionnaire and the Screen for Caregiver Burden in the study of caregiving-related problems. *International Journal of Geriatric Psychiatry, 18,* 1110–1114.

References

Ferri, B. A., & Connor, D. J. (2005). Tools of exclusion: Race, disability, and (re)segregated education. *Teachers College Record, 107,* 453–475.

Feshbach, S. (1980). Child abuse and the dynamics of human aggression and violence. In J. Gerbner, C. J. Ross, & E. Zigler (Eds.), *Child abuse: An agenda for action.* New York: Oxford University Press.

Feshbach, S., & Tangney, J. (2008). Television viewing and aggression: Some alternative perspectives. *Perspectives on Psychological Science, 3,* 387–389. Retrieved from http://search.ebscohost.com, doi:10.1111/j.1745–6924.2008.00086.x.

Festinger, L. (1954). A theory of social comparison processes. *Human Relations, 7,* 117–140.

Fetterman, D. M. (1998). Ethnography. In L. Bickman & D. J. Rog (Eds.), *Handbook of applied social research methods* (pp. 473–504). Thousand Oaks, CA: Sage.

Fetterman, D. M. (2005). Empowerment evaluation: From the digital divide to academic distsress. In D. Fetterman & A. Wandersman (Eds.), *Empowerment evaluation principles in practice.* New York: Guilford Press.

Fiatarone, M. S. A., & Garnett, L. R. (1997, March). Keep on keeping on. *Harvard Health Letter,* pp. 4–5.

Field, D. (2007). Death and dying. *Sociology of health and health care* (4th ed., pp. 181–203). Malden, MA: Blackwell Publishing.

Field, D., & Minkler, M. (1988). Continuity and change in social support between young-old and old-old or very-old age. *Journal of Gerontology, 43(4),* 100–106.

Field, M. J., & Behrman, R. E. (Eds.) (2002). *When children die.* Washington, DC: National Academies Press.

Field, T. (1990). *Infancy.* Cambridge, MA: Harvard University Press.

Field, T. (2001). Massage therapy facilitates weight gain in preterm infants. *Current Directions in Psychological Science, 10,* 51–54.

Field, T. M. (1979). Games parents play with normal and high-risk infants. *Child Psychiatry and Human Development, 10,* 41–48.

Field, T. M. (1981). Infant gaze aversion and heart rate during face-to-face interactions. *Infant Behavior and Development, 4,* 307–313.

Field, T. M. (1982). Individual differences in the expressivity of neonates and young infants. In R. S. Feldman (Ed.), *Development of nonverbal behavior in children.* New York: Springer-Verlag.

Field, T. M. (1987). Interaction and attachment in normal and atypical infants. *Journal of Consulting and Clinical Psychology, 14,* 183–184.

Field, T. M. (Ed.). (1988). *Stress and coping across development.* Hillsdale, NJ: Erlbaum.

Field, T. M. (1990). Alleviating stress in newborn infants in the intensive care unit. In B. M. Lester & E. Z. Tronick (Eds.), *Stimulation and the preterm infant: The limits of plasticity.* Philadelphia: Saunders.

Field, T. M. (1995a). Infant massage therapy. In T. M. Field (Ed.), *Touch in early development.* Hillsdale, NJ: Erlbaum.

Field, T. M. (1995b). Massage therapy for infants and children. *Journal of Developmental & Behavioral Pediatrics, 16,* 105–111.

Field, T. M. (1999). Sucking and massage therapy reduce stress during infancy. In M. Lewis & D. Ramsay (Eds.), *Soothing and stress.* Mahwah, NJ: Erlbaum.

Field, T. M. (2000). Infant massage therapy. In C. H. Zeanah Jr. (Ed.), *Handbook of infant mental health* (2nd ed.). New York: Guilford Press.

Field, T. M. (2001). *Touch.* Cambridge, MA: MIT Press.

Field, T., Diego, M., & Hernandez-Reif, M. (2006). Prenatal depression effects on the fetus and newborn: A review. *Infant Behavior & Development, 29,* 445–455.

Field, T., Diego, M., & Hernandez-Reif, M. (2007). Massage therapy research. *Developmental Review, 27,* 75–89.

Field, T., Diego, M., & Hernandez-Reif, M. (2008). Prematurity and potential predictors. *International Journal of Neuroscience, 118,* 277–289.

Field, T., Diego, M., & Hernandez-Reif, M. (2011). Potential underlying mechanisms for greater weight gain in massaged preterm infants. *Infant Behavior & Development, 34,* 383–389.

Field, T., Diego, M., Hernandez-Reif, M., Dieter, J., Kumar, A., Schanberg, S., et al. (2008). Insulin and insulin-like growth factor-1 increased in preterm neonates following massage therapy. *Journal of Developmental and Behavioral Pediatrics, 29,* 463–466.

Field, T. M., Greenberg, R., Woodson, R., Cohen, D., & Garcia, R. (1984). Facial expression during Brazelton neonatal assessments. *Infant Mental Health Journal, 5,* 61–71.

Field, T. M., Harding, J., Yando, R., Gonzalez, K., Lasko, D., Bendell, D., et al. (1998). Feelings and attitudes of gifted students. *Adolescence, 39,* 331–342.

Field, T. M., Hernandez-Reif, M., & Diego, M. (2006). Newborns of depressed mothers who received moderate versus light pressure massage during pregnancy. *Infant Behavior & Development, 29(1),* 54–58.

Field, T. M., & Millsap, R. E. (1991). Personality in advanced old age: Continuity or change? *Journal of Gerontology: Psychological Sciences, 46,* P299–P308.

Field, T., & Roopnarine, J. L. (1982). Infant-peer interactions. In T. Field, A. Huston, H. Quay, & G. Finley (Eds.), *Review of human development.* New York: Wiley.

Field, T., & Walden, T. (1982). Perception and production of facial expression in infancy and early childhood. In H. Reese & L. Lipsitt (Eds.), *Advances in child development and behavior* (Vol. 16). New York: Academic Press.

Fields, J., & Casper, L. M. (2001). *America's families and living arrangements: March 2000.* Current Population Reports P20–537. U.S Census Bureau Washington D.C.

Fields-Meyer, T. (1995, September 25). Having their say. *People,* pp. 50–60.

Fifer, W. (1987). Neonatal preference for mother's voice. In N. A. Kasnegor, E. M. Blass, & M. A. Hofer (Eds.), *Perinatal development: A psychobiological perspective. Behavioral biology* (pp. 111–124). Orlando, FL: Academic Press.

Figley, C. R. (1973). Child density and the marital relationship. *Journal of Marriage and the Family, 35,* 272–282.

Finch, C. E. (1990). *Longevity, senescence, and the genome.* Chicago: University of Chicago Press.

Finch, C. E., & Tanzi, R. E. (1997, October 17). Genetics of aging. *Science, 278,* 407–410.

Fincham, F. D. (1998). Child development and marital relations. *Child Development, 69,* 543–574.

Fincham, F. D. (2003). Marital conflict: Correlates, structure, and context. *Current Directions in Psychological Science, 12,* 23–27.

Fincham, F. D., Beach, S. R. H., Harold, G. T., & Osborne, L. N. (1997). Marital satisfaction and depression: Different casual relationships for men and women? *Psychological Science, 8,* 351–357.

Findlen, B. (1990). Culture: A refuge for murder. *Ms.,* pp. 1, 47.

Fingerhut, L. A., & Kleinman, J. C. (1990). International and interstate comparisons of homicide among young males. *Journal of the American Medical Association, 263,* 3292–3295.

Fingerhut, L. A., & MaKuc, D. M. (1992). Mortality among minority populations in the United States. *American Journal of Public Health, 82,* 1168–1170.

Finkbeiner, A. K. (1996). *After the death of a child: Living with loss through the years.* New York: The Free Press.

Finkel, D., Pedersen, N., Reynolds, C., Berg, S., de Faire, U., & Svartengren, M. (2003). Genetic and environmental influences on decline in biobehavioral markers of aging. *Behavior Genetics, 33,* 107–123.

Finkelhor, D. (1997). The homicides of children and youth: A developmental perspective. In G. K. Kantor & J. L. Janinski (Eds.), *Out of the darkness: Contemporary perspectives on family violence* (pp. 17–34). Thousand Oaks, CA: Sage.

Finkelstein, D. L., Harper, D. A., & Rosenthal, G. E. (1998). Does length of hospital stay during labor and delivery influence patient satisfaction? Results from a regional study. *American Journal of Managed Care, 4,* 1701–1708.

Finn, C. (2008). Neuropsychiatric aspects of genetic disorders. In *Psychiatric genetics: Applications in clinical practice.* Arlington, VA: American Psychiatric Publishing, Inc.

Finnegan, L., & Kandall, S. (2008). Perinatal substance abuse. *In The American Psychiatric Publishing textbook of substance abuse treatment* (4th ed.). Arlington, VA: American Psychiatric Publishing, Inc.

Fiore, S. M., & Schooler, J. W. (1998). Right hemisphere contributions to creative problem solving: Converging evidence for divergent thinking. In M. Beeman & C. Chiarello (Eds.), *Right hemisphere language comprehension: Perspectives from cognitive neuroscience* (pp. 349–371). Mahwah, NJ: Erlbaum.

First, J. M., & Cardenas, J. (1986). A minority view on testing. *Educational Measurement Issues and Practice, 5,* 6–11.

Fisch, S. M. (2004). *Children's learning from educational television: Sesame Street and beyond.* Mahwah, NJ: Lawrence Erlbaum.

Fischer, K. W., & Hencke, R. W. (1996). Infants' construction of actions in context: Piaget's contributions to research on early development. *Psychological Science, 7,* 204–210.

Fischer, K. W., & Rose, S. P. (1994). Dynamic development of coordination of components in brain and behavior: A framework for theory and research. In G. Dawson & K. W. Fischer (Eds.), *Human behavior and the developing brain.* New York: Guilford.

Fischer, K. W., & Rose, S. P. (1995). Concurrent cycles in the dynamic development of brain and behavior. *Newsletter of the Society for Research in Child Development,* p. 16.

Fischer, N. (2012). Mother-infant attachment: The demystification of an enigma. In S. Akhtar (Ed.), *The mother and her child: Clinical aspects of attachment, separation, and loss.* Lanham, MD: Jason Aronson.

Fischer, T. (2007). Parental divorce and children's socio-economic success: Conditional effects of parental resources prior to divorce, and gender of the child. *Sociology, 41,* 475–495.

Fish, J. M. (2011). *The concept of race and psychotherapy.* New York: Springer Science + Business Media.

Fish, J. M. (Ed.). (2001). *Race and intelligence: Separating science from myth.* Mahwah, NJ: Erlbaum.

Fishbein, H. D., & Imai, S. (1993). Preschoolers select playmates on the basis of gender and race. *Journal of Applied Developmental Psychology, 14,* 303–316.

Fishel, E. (1993, September). Starting kindergarten. *Parents,* pp. 165–169.

Fisher, C. B. (2003). *Decoding the ethics code: A practical guide for psychologists.* Thousand Oaks, CA: Sage Publications.

Fisher, C. B. (2004). Informed consent and clinical research involving children and adolescents: Implications of the revised APA ethics code and HIPAA. *Journal of Clinical Child & Adolescent Psychology, 33,* 832–839.

Fisher, C. (2005). Deception research involving children: Ethical practices and paradoxes. *Ethics & Behavior, 15,* 271–287.

Fisher, C., Hauck, Y., & Fenwick, J. (2006). How social context impacts on women's fears of childbirth: A Western Australian example. *Social Science & Medicine, 63,* 64–75.

Fisher, C., & Tokura, H. (1996). Acoustic cues to grammatical structure in infant-directed speech: Cross-linguistic evidence. *Child Development, 67,* 3192–3218.

Fisher, J., Astbury, J., & Smith, A. (1997). Adverse psychological impact of obstetric interventions: A prospective longitudinal study. *Australian & New Zealand Journal of Psychiatry, 31,* 728–738.

Fisher, J. D., & Fisher, W. A. (1992). Changing AIDS-risk behavior. *Psychological Bulletin, 111,* 455–474.

Fishman, C. (1999, May). Watching the time go by. *American Demographics,* 56–57.

Fiske, S. T., & Taylor, S. E. (1991). *Social cognition* (2nd ed.). New York: McGraw-Hill.

Fiske, S. T., & Von Hendy, H. M. (1992). Personality feedback and situational norms can control stereotyping process. *Journal of Personality and Social Psychology, 62,* 577–596.

Fiske, S. T., & Yamamoto, M. (2005). Coping with rejection: Core social motives across cultures. *The social outcast: Ostracism, social exclusion, rejection, and bullying* (pp. 185–198). New York: Psychology Press.

Fisker, T., & Strandmark, M. (2007). Experiences of surviving spouse of terminally ill spouse: A phenomenological study of an altruistic perspective. *Scandinavian Journal of Caring Sciences, 21,* 274–281.

Fitzgerald, D., & White, K. (2003). Linking children's social worlds: Perspective-taking in parent-child and peer contexts. *Social Behavior & Personality, 31,* 509–522.

Fitzgerald, H. (2006). Cross cultural research during infancy: Methodological considerations. *Infant Mental Health Journal, 27,* 612–617.

Fitzgerald, P. (2008). A neurotransmitter system theory of sexual orientation. *Journal of Sexual Medicine, 5,* 746–748.

Fivush, R. (Ed.). (1995). *Long-term retention of infant memories.* Hillsdale, NJ: Erlbaum.

Fivush, R., Kuebli, J., & Clubb, P.A. (1992). The structure of events and event representations: A developmental analysis. *Child Development, 63,* 188–201.

Flaake, K. (2005). Girls, adolescence and the impact of bodily changes: Family dynamics and social definitions of the female body. *European Journal of Women's Studies, 12,* 201–212.

Flaks, D. K., Ficher, I., Masterpasqua, F., & Joseph, G. (1995). Lesbians choosing motherhood: A comparative study of lesbian and heterosexual parents and their children. *Developmental Psychology, Special issue: Sexual orientation and human development. 31,* 105–114.

Flanigan, J. (2005, July 3). Immigrants benefit U.S. economy now as ever. *Los Angeles Times.*

Flavell, J. H. (1985). *Cognitive development* (2nd ed.). Englewood Cliffs, NJ: Prentice-Hall.

Flavell, J. H. (1994). Cognitive development: Past, present, and future. In R. D. Parke, P. A. Ornstein, J. J. Rieser, & C. Zahn-Waxler (Eds.), *A century of developmental psychology.* Washington, DC: American Psychological Association.

Flavell, J. H. (1996). Piaget's legacy. *Psychological Science, 7,* 200–203.

Flavell, J. H., Green, F. L., & Flavell, E. R. (1995). The development of children's knowledge about attentional focus. *Developmental Psychology, 31,* 706–712.

Fleer, M. (2012). The development of motives in children's play. In M. Hedegaard, A. Edwards, M. Fleer, M. Hedegaard, A. Edwards, & M. Fleer (Eds.), *Motives in children's development: Cultural-historical approaches.* New York: Cambridge University Press.

Flegal, K., Tabak, C., & Ogden, C. (2006). Overweight in children: Definitions and interpretation. *Health Education Research, 21,* 755–760.

Fleming, J. E., & Offord, D. R. (1990). Epidemiology of childhood depressive disorders: A critical review. *Journal of the American Academy of Child and Adolescent Psychiatry, 29,* 571–580.

Fleming, M., Greentree, S., Cocotti-Muller, D., Elias, K., & Morrison, S. (2006, December). Safety in cyberspace: Adolescents' safety and exposure online. *Youth & Society, 38,* 135–154.

Fleming, P., Tsogt, B., & Blair, P. (2006). Modifiable risk factors, sleep environment, developmental physiology and common polymorphisms: Understanding and preventing sudden infant deaths. *Early Human Development, 82,* 761–766.

Fletcher, A. C., Darling, N. E., Steinberg, L., & Dornbusch, S. M. (1995). The company they keep: Relation of adolescents' adjustment and behavior to their friends' perceptions of authoritative parenting in the social network. *Developmental Psychology, 31,* 300–310.

Flint, M. (1989). Cultural and subcultural meanings to the menopause. *Menopause Management, 2*(3), 11.

Flom, R., & Bahrick, L. (2007). The development of infant discrimination of affect in multimodal and unimodal stimulation: The role of intersensory redundancy. *Developmental Psychology, 43,* 238–252.

Flom, R., & Johnson, S. (2011). The effects of adults' affective expression and direction of visual gaze on 12-month-olds' visual preferences for an object following a 5-minute, 1-day, or 1-month delay. *British Journal of Developmental Psychology, 29,* 64–85.

Flor, D. L., & Knap, N. F. (2001). Transmission and transaction: Predicting adolescents' internalization of parental religious values. *Journal of Family Psychology, 15,* 627–645.

Flores, D. (2007, August 17). Tiny N.J. baby ready to return home. *Washington Post.*

Florian, V., & Kravetz, S. (1985). Children's concepts of death: A cross-cultural comparison among Muslims, Druze, Christians, and Jews in Israel. *Journal of Cross-Cultural Psychology, 16,* 174–189.

Florsheim, P. (2003). Adolescent romantic and sexual behavior: What we know and where we go from here. In P. Florsheim (Ed.), *Adolescent romantic relations and sexual behavior: Theory, research, and practical implications.* Mahwah, NJ: Lawrence Erlbaum Associates.

Flouri, E. (2005). *Fathering and child outcomes.* New York: Wiley.

Floyd, R. G. (2005). Information-processing approaches to interpretation of contemporary intellectual assessment instruments. In D. P. Flanagan & P. L. Harrison (Eds.), *Contemporary intellectual assessment: Theories, tests, and issues.* New York: Guilford Press.

Flynn, E., O'Malley, C., & Wood, D. (2004). A longitudinal, microgenetic study of the emergence of false belief understanding and inhibition skills. *Developmental Science, 7,* 103–115.

Fogarty, R. (2008). The intelligence-friendly classroom: It just makes sense. *Teaching for intelligence* (2nd ed., pp. 142–148). Thousand Oaks, CA: Corwin Press.

Fogel, A. (1980). Peer vs. mother-directed behavior in one- to three-month-old infants. *Infant Behavior and Development, 2,* 215–226.

Fogel, A., de Koeyer, I., & Bellagamba, F. (2004). The dialogical self in the first two years of life: Embarking on a journey of discovery. *Theory & Psychology, Special issue: The dialogical self, 12,* 191–205.

Fogel, A., Hsu, H., Shapiro, A., Nelson-Goens, G., & Secrist, C. (2006, May). Effects of normal and perturbed social play on the duration and amplitude of different types of infant smiles. *Developmental Psychology, 42,* 459–473.

Fogel, A., Nelson-Goens, G. C., Hsu, H., & Shapiro, A. F. (2000). Do different infant smiles reflect different positive emotions? *Social Development, 9,* 497–520.

Fok, M. S. M., & Tsang, W.Y.W. (2006). 'Development of an instrument measuring Chinese adolescent beliefs and attitudes towards substance use': Response to commentary. *Journal of Clinical Nursing, 15,* 1062–1063.

Fok, W. Y., Chan, L. Y., Tsui, M. H., Leung, T. N., Lau, T. K., & Chung, T. K. (2005). When to induce labor for post-term? A study of induction at 41 weeks versus 42 weeks. *European Journal of Obstetrics and Gynecological Reproductive Biology, 125,* 206–210.

Folkman, S., & Lazarus, R. S. (1980). An analysis of coping in a middle-aged community sample. *Journal of Health and Social Behavior, 21,* 219–239.

Folkman, S., & Lazarus, R. S. (1988). Coping as a mediator of emotion. *Journal of Personality and Social Psychology, 54,* 466–475.

Folkman, S., & Lazarus, R. S. (1990). Coping and emotion. *Psychological and biological approaches to emotion.* Hillsdale, NJ, England: Lawrence Erlbaum Associates, Inc.

Folkman, S., & Moskowitz, J. T. (2007). Positive affect and meaning-focused coping during significant psychological stress. In M. Hewstone, H. A. W. Schut, J. B. F. De Wit, K. Van Den Bos, & M. S. Stroebe (Eds.), *The scope of social psychology: Theory and applications.* New York: Psychology Press.

Ford, A. M., & Martinez-Ramirez, A. (2006). Therapeutic opportunities and targets in childhood leukemia. *Clinical and Translational Oncology, 8,* 560–565.

Ford, D. Y. (2011). *Reversing underachievement among gifted black students* (2nd ed.). Waco, TX: Prufrock Press.

Ford, J. (2007, August). Alcohol use among college students: A comparison of athletes and nonathletes. *Substance Use & Misuse, 42*(9), 1367–1377.

Ford, R. M., Driscoll, T., Shum, D., & Macaulay, C. E. (2012). Executive and theory-of-mind contributions to event-based prospective memory in children: Exploring the self-projection hypothesis. *Journal of Experimental Child Psychology, 111,* 468–489.

Forrest, R., & Forrest, M. B. (1991). *Retirement living: A guide to housing alternatives.* New York: Facts on File.

Forrester, M. (2001). The embedding of the self in early interaction. *Infant & Child Development, 10,* 189–202.

Forste, R., Weiss, J., & Lippincott, E. (2001). The decision to breastfeed in the United States: Does race matter? *Pediatrics, 108,* 291–296.

Fortunato, J., & Scheimann, A. (2008). Protein-energy malnutrition and feeding refusal secondary to food allergies. *Clinical Pediatrics, 47,* 496–499.

Fouts, G., & Burggraf, K. (1999). Television situation comedies: Female body images and verbal reinforcements. *Sex Roles, 40,* 473–482.

Fowers, B. J., & Davidov, B. J. (2006). The virtue of multiculturalism: Personal transformation, character, and openness to the other. *American Psychologist, 61,* 581–594.

Fowers, B. J., & Richardson, F. C. (1996). Why is multiculturalism good? *American Psychologist, 51,* 609–621.

Fowler, J. W., & Dell, M. L. (2006). Stages of faith from infancy through adolescence: Reflections on three decades of faith development theory. In E. C. Roehlkepartain, P. E. King, L. Wagener, & P. L. Benson (Eds.), *The handbook of spiritual development in childhood and adolescence.* Thousand Oaks, CA: Sage Publications.

Fowler, W., Ogston, K., Roberts, G., & Swenson, A. (2006). The effects of early language enrichment. *Early Child Development and Care, 176,* 777–815.

Fox, M., Pac, S., Devaney, B., & Jankowski L. (2004). Feeding infants and toddlers study: What foods are infants and toddlers eating? *Journal of the American Dietetic Association, 104,* 22–30.

Fox, N. F. (Ed.). (1994). *The development of emotion regulation: Biological and behavioral considerations* (2–3, Serial No. 240).

Fox, N., Kimmerly, N. L., & Schafer, W. D. (1991). Attachment to mother/attachment to father: A meta-analysis. *Child Development, 62,* 210–225.

Fozard, J. L., Vercruyssen, M., Reynolds, S. L., Hancock, P. A., et al. (1994). Age differences and changes in reaction time: The Baltimore Longitudinal Study of Aging. *Journal of Gerontology, 49,* 179–189.

Fraenkel, P. (2003). Contemporary two-parent families: Navigating work and family challenges. In F. Walsh (Ed.), *Normal family processes: Growing diversity and complexity* (3rd ed., pp. 61–95). New York: Guilford Press.

Fraley, R. C. (2002). Attachment stability from infancy to adulthood: Meta-analysis and dynamic modeling of developmental mechanisms. *Personality and Social Psychology Review, 6,* 123–151.

Fraley, R. C., & Spieker, S. J. (2003). Are infant attachment patterns continuously or categorically distributed? A taxometric analysis of Strange Situation behavior. *Developmental Psychology, 39,* 387–404.

Francasso, M. P., Lamb, M. E., Scholmerich, A., & Leyendecker, B. (1997). The ecology of mother–infant interaction in Euro-American and immigrant Central American families living in the United States. *International Journal of Behavioral Development, 20,* 207–217.

Franck, I., & Brownstone, D. (1991). *The parent's desk reference.* New York: Prentice-Hall.

Frankel, L. (2002). "I've never thought about it": Contradictions and taboos surrounding American males' experiences of first ejaculation (semenarche). *The Journal of Men's Studies, 11,* 37–54.

Frankel, M., & Chapman, A. (2000). *Human inheritable genetic modifications: Assessing scientific, ethical, religious, and policy issues.* Washington, DC: American Association for the Advancement of Science.

Frankenburg, W. K., Dodds, J., Archer, P., Maschka, P., Edelman, N., & Shapiro, H. (1992). *The Denver II training manual.* Denver, CO: Denver Developmental Materials.

Frankenburg, W. K., Dodds, J., Archer, P., Shapiro, H., & Bresnick, B. (1992). The Denver II: A major revision and restandardization of the Denver Developmental Screening Test. *Pediatrics, 89,* 91–97.

Franko, D., & Striegel-Moore, R. (2002). The role of body dissatisfaction as a risk factor for depression in adolescent girls: Are the differences black and white? *Journal of Psychosomatic Research, 53,* 975–983.

Fransen, M., Meertens, R., & Schrander-Stumpel, C. (2006). Communication and risk presentation in genetic counseling: Development of a checklist. *Patient Education and Counseling, 61,* 126–133.

Franzoi, S. L., Davis, M. H., & Vasquez-Suson, K. A. (1994). Two social worlds: Social correlates and stability of adolescent status groups. *Journal of Personality and Social Psychology, 67,* 462–473.

Fraser, S., Muckle, G., & Després, C. (2006, January). The relationship between lead exposure, motor function and behaviour in Inuit preschool children. *Neurotoxicology and Teratology, 28,* 18–27.

Frawley, T. (2008). Gender schema and prejudicial recall: How children misremember, fabricate, and distort gendered picture book information. *Journal of Research in Childhood Education, 22,* 291–303.

Frazier, L. M., Grainger, D. A., Schieve, L. A., & Toner, J. P. (2004). Follicle-stimulating hormone and estradiol levels independently predict the success of assisted reproductive technology treatment. *Fertility and Sterility, 82,* 834–840.

Fredrickson, B. (1998). What good are positive emotions? *Review of General Psychology, 2,* 300–319.

Frederickson, N., & Petrides, K. (2008). Ethnic, gender, and socio-economic group differences in academic performance and secondary school selection: A longitudinal analysis. *Learning and Individual Differences, 18,* 144–151.

Fredriksen, K., Rhodes, J., Reddy, R., & Way, N. (2004). Sleepless in Chicago: Tracking the effects of adolescent sleep loss during the middle school years. *Child Development, 75,* 84–95.

Freedman, A. M., & Ellison, S. (2004, May 6). Testosterone patch for women shows promise. *The Wall Street Journal,* pp. A1, B2.

Freedman, D. G. (1979, January). Ethnic differences in babies. *Human Nature,* 15–20.

Freedman, D. S., Khan, L. K., Serdula, M. K., Dietz, W. H., Sriniasan, S. R., & Berenson, G. S. (2004). Inter-relationships among childhood BMI, childhood height, and adult obesity: The Bogalusa Heart Study. *International Journal of Obesity and Related Metabolic Disorders, 28,* 10–16.

Freedman, R., Adler, L. E., & Leonard, S. (1999). Alternative phenotypes for the complex genetics of schizophrenia. *Biological Psychiatry, 45,* 551–558.

Freeman, E., Sammel, M., & Liu, L. (2004). Hormones and menopausal status as predictors of depression in women in transition to menopause. *Archives of General Psychiatry, 61,* 62–70.

Freeman, J. M. (2007). Beware: the misuse of technology and the law of unintended consequences. *Neurotherapeutics, 4,* 549–554.

Freiberg, P. (1998a, February). President's AIDS budget wins kudos. *Newsline/People with AIDS Coalition of New York,* 23–44.

Freiberg, P. (1998b, February). We know how to stop the spread of AIDS: So why can't we? *APA Monitor,* p. 32.

French, S., & Swain, J. (1997). Young disabled people. In J. Roche & S. Tucker (Eds.), *Youth in society: Contemporary theory, policy and practice* (pp. 199–206). London, England: Sage.

Frenkel, L. D., & Gaur, S. (1994). Perinatal HIV infection and AIDS. *Clinics in Perinatology, 21,* 95–107.

Frerking, B. (2006). I'm gonna keep that gray. *Slate.* Retrieved from http://www.slate.com/id/2147054/.

Freud, S. (1920). *A general introduction to psychoanalysis.* New York: Boni & Liveright.

Freud, S. (1922/1959). *Group psychology and the analysis of the ego.* London: Hogarth.

Freudenberger, H. J., & Richelson, G. (1980). *Burnout: The high cost of high achievement.* New York: Bantam.

Friborg, O., Barlaug, D., Martinussen, M., Rosenvinge, J. H., & Hjemdal, O. (2005). Resilience in relation to personality and intelligence. *International Journal of Methods in Psychiatric Research, 14,* 29–42.

Frick, P. J., Cornell, A. H., Bodin, S. D., Dane, H. A., Barry, C. T., & Loney, B. R. (2003). Callous-unemotional traits and developmental pathways to severe conduct problems. *Developmental Psychology, 39,* 246–260.

Fried, P. A., & Watkinson, B. (1990). 36- and 48-month neurobehavioral follow-up of children prenatally exposed to marijuana, cigarettes, and alcohol. *Developmental and Behavioral Pediatrics, 11,* 49–58.

Friedland, R. (2003). Fish consumption and the risk of Alzheimer disease: Is it time to make dietary recommendations? *Archives of Neurology, 60,* 923–924.

Friedlander, L. J., Connolly, J. A., & Pepler, D. J. (2007). Biological, familial, and peer influences on dating in early adolescence. *Archives of Sexual Behavior, 36,* 821–830.

Friedman, D. E. (2004). *The new economics of preschool.* Washington, DC: Early Childhood Funders' Collaborative/NAEYC.

Friedman, D., Berman, S., & Hamberger, M. (1993). Recognition memory and ERPs: Age-related changes in young, middle-aged, and elderly adults. *Journal of Psychophysiology, 7,* 181–201.

Friedman, H. S., Hawley, P. H., & Tucker, J. S. (1994). Personality, health, and longevity. *Current Directions in Psychological Science, 3,* 37–41.

Friedman, H. S., Tucker, J. S., Schwartz, J. E., Martin, L. R., Tomlinson-Keasey, C., Wingard, D. L., et al. (1995a). Childhood conscientiousness and longevity: Health behaviors and cause of death. *Journal of Personality and Social Psychology, 68,* 696–703.

Friedman, H. S., Tucker, J. S., Schwartz, J. E., Tomlinson-Keasey, C., Martin, L. R., Wingard, D. L., et al. (1995b). Psychosocial and behavioral predictors of longevity: The aging and death of the "Termites." *American Psychologist, 50,* 69–78.

Friedman, L., Kahn, J., Middleman, A., Rosenthal, S., & Zimet, G. (2006, October). Human papillomavirus (HPV) vaccine: A position statement of the society for adolescent medicine. *Journal of Adolescent Health, 39,* 620.

Friedman, R., Liu, W., Chi, S., Hong, Y., & Sung, L. (2012). Cross-cultural management and bicultural identity integration: When does experience abroad lead to appropriate cultural switching? *International Journal of Intercultural Relations, 36,* 130–139.

Friedman, S., Heneghan, A., & Rosenthal, M. (2009). Characteristics of women who do not seek prenatal care and implications for prevention. *Journal of Obstetric, Gynecologic, & Neonatal Nursing: Clinical Scholarship for the Care of Women, Childbearing Families, & Newborns, 38,* 174–181.

Friedman, W. J. (1993). Memory for the time of past events. *Psychological Bulletin, 113,* 44–66.

Friend, R. M., & Neale, J. M. (1972). Children's perceptions of success and failure: An attributional analysis of the effects of race and social class. *Developmental Psychology, 7,* 124–128.

Fries, S., Horz, H., & Haimerl, C. (2006). Pygmalion in media-based learning: Effects of quality expectancies on learning outcomes. *Learning and Instruction, 16,* 339–349.

Frisch, M., Friis, S., Kjear, S. K., & Melbye, M. (1995). Falling incidence of penis cancer in an uncircumcised population (Denmark 1943-90). *British Medical Journal, 311,* 1471.

Frishman, R. (1996, October). Hormone replacement therapy for men. *Harvard Health Letter,* pp. 6–8.

Frishman, R. G. (1997). *The aging eye.* Cambridge, MA: Harvard Medical School Health Publications Group.

Fritz, G., & Rockney, R. (2004). Summary of the practice parameter for the assessment and treatment of children and adolescents with enuresis. *Work Group on Quality Issues; Journal of the American Academy of Child & Adolescent Psychiatry, 43,* 123–125.

Frome, P., Alfeld, C., Eccles, J., & Barber, B. (2006, August). Why don't they want a male-dominated job? An investigation of young women who changed their occupational aspirations. *Educational Research and Evaluation, 12,* 359–372.

Fromholt, P., & Larsen, S. F. (1991). Autobiographical memory in normal, aging and primary degenerative dementia (dementia of the Alzheimer type). *Journal of Gerontology, 46,* 85–91.

Fry, C. L. (1985). Culture, behavior, and aging in the comparative perspective. In J. E. Birren & K. W. Schaie (Eds.), *Handbook of the psychology of aging.* New York: Van Nostrand Reinhold.

Fry, D. (2005). Rough-and-tumble social play in humans. *The nature of play: Great apes and humans.* New York: Guilford Press.

Fryer, D., & Payne, R. (1986). Being unemployed: A review of the literature on the psychological experience of unemployment. In C. L. Cooper & I. T. Robertson (Eds.), *International review of industrial and organizational psychology.* Chichester, England: Wiley.

Fu, G., Xu, F., Cameron, C., Heyman, G., & Lee, K. (2007, March). Cross-cultural differences in children's choices, categorizations, and evaluations of truths and lies. *Developmental Psychology, 43*(2), 278–293.

Fu, W., Killen, M., Culmsee, C., Dhar, S., Pandita, T. K., & Mattson, M. P. (2000). The catalytic subunit of telomerase is expressed in developing brain neurons and serves a cell survival-promoting function. *Journal of Molecular Neuroscience, 14,* 3–15.

Fu, X., & Heaton, T. (2008). Racial and educational homogamy: 1980 to 2000. *Sociological Perspectives, 51,* 735–758.

Fuchs, D., & Fuchs, L. S. (1994). Inclusive schools movement and the radicalization of special education reform. *Exceptional Children, 60,* 294–309.

Fuchs, I., Eisenberg, N., Hertz-Lazarowitz, R., & Sharabany, R. (1986). Kibbutz, Israeli city and American children's moral reasoning about prosocial moral conflicts. *Merrill-Palmer Quarterly, 32,* 37–50.

Fugate, W. N., & Mitchell, E. S. (1997). Women's images of midlife: Observations from the Seattle Midlife Women's Health Study. *Health Care for Women International, 18,* 439–453.

Fuhs, M., & Day, J. D. (2011). Verbal ability and executive functioning development in preschoolers at head start. *Developmental Psychology, 47,* 404–416.

Fujioka, T., Mourad, N., & Trainor, L. J. (2011). Development of auditory-specific brain rhythm in infants. *European Journal of Neuroscience, 33,* 521–529.

Fuligni, A. J. (1997). The academic achievement of adolescents from immigrant families: The roles of family background, attitudes, and behavior. *Child Development, 68,* 351–368.

Fuligni, A. J. (1998). The adjustment of children from immigrant families. *Current Directions in Psychological Science, 7,* 99–103.

Fuligni, A. J., & Fuligni, A. S. (2007). Immigrant families and the educational development of their children. In J. E. Lansford, K. Deater-Deckard, & M. H. Bornstein (Eds.), *Immigrant families in contemporary society.* New York: Guilford Press.

Fuligni, A. J., & Hardway, C. (2006, September). Daily variation in adolescents' sleep, activities, and psychological well-being. *Journal of Research on Adolescence, 16,* 353–378.

Fuligni, A. J., Tseng, V., & Lam, M. (1999). Attitudes toward family obligations among American adolescents with Asian, Latin American, and European backgrounds. *Child Development, 70,* 1030–1044.

Fuligni, A. J., & Yoshikawa, H. (2003). Socioeconomic resources, parenting, and child development among immigrant families. In M. Bomstein & R. Bradley (Eds.), *Socioeconomic status, parenting, and child development.* Mahwah, NJ: Erlbaum.

Fuligni, A. J., & Zhang, W. (2004). Attitudes toward family obligation among adolescents in contemporary urban and rural China. *Child Development, 75,* 180–192.

Funk, J., Buchman, D., & Jenks, J. (2003). Playing violent video games, desensitization, and moral evaluation in children. *Journal of Applied Developmental Psychology, 24,* 413–436.

Funk, L. (2010). Prioritizing parental autonomy: Adult children's accounts of feeling responsible and supporting aging parents. *Journal of Aging Studies, 24,* 57–64.

Furman, W., & Buhrmester, D. (1992). Age and sex differences in perceptions of networks of personal relationships. *Child Development, 63,* 103–115.

Furman, W., & Shaffer, L. (2003). The role of romantic relationships in adolescent development. In P. Florsheim (Ed.), *Adolescent romantic relations and sexual behavior: Theory, research, and practical implications.* Mahwah, NJ: Lawrence Erlbaum Associates.

Furnham, A., & Weir, C. (1996). Lay theories of child development. *Journal of Genetic Psychology, 157,* 211–226.

Furstenberg, F. F., Jr. (1996, June). The future of marriage. *American Demographics,* pp. 34–40.

Furstenberg, F. F., Jr., Brooks-Gunn, J., & Morgan, S. P. (1987). *Adolescent mothers in later life.* New York: Cambridge University Press.

Gabbay, S., & Wahler, J. (2002). Lesbian aging: Review of a growing literature. *Journal of Gay & Lesbian Social Services: Issues in Practice, Policy & Research, 14,* 1–21.

Gable, S., & Lutz, S. (2000). Household, parent, and child contributions to childhood obesity. *Family Relations: Interdisciplinary Journal of Applied Family Studies, 49,* 293–300.

Gabriele, A., & Schettino, F. (2008). Child malnutrition and mortality in developing countries: Evidence from a cross-country analysis. *Analyses of Social Issues and Public Policy (ASAP), 8,* 53–81.

Gadow, K. D., & Sprafkin, J. (1993). Television "violence" and children with emotional and behavioral disorders. *Journal of Emotional and Behavioral Disorders, 1,* 54–63.

Gaertner, S. L., Mann, J. A., Dovidio, J. F., Murrell, A. J., & Pomare, M. (1990). How does cooperation reduce intergroup bias? *Journal of Personality and Social Psychology, 59,* 692–704.

Gage, J. D., Everett, K. D., & Bullock, L. (2011). A theoretical explanation of male partner participation in smoking cessation during the transition to fatherhood. *Journal of Smoking Cessation, 6,* 89–96.

Gagné, M. H., Drapeau, S., Melançon, C., Saint-Jacques, M. C., & Lépine, R. (2007). Links between parental psychological violence, other family disturbances, and children's adjustment. *Family Processes, 46,* 523–542.

Gagne, M. H., Tourigny, M., Joly, J., & Pouliot-Lapointe, J. (2007). When inflicted skin injuries constitute child abuse. *Pediatrics, 110,* 644–645.

Gagnon, S. G., & Nagle, R. J. (2000). Comparison of the revised and original versions of the Bayley Scales of Infant Development. *School Psychology International, 21,* 293–305.

Galambos, N. L., & Dixon, R. A. (1984). Toward understanding and caring for latchkey children. *Child Care Quarterly, 13,* 116–125.

Galambos, N. L., Leadbeater, B., & Barker, E. (2004). Gender differences in and risk factors for depression in adolescence: A 4-year longitudinal study. *International Journal of Behavioral Development, 28,* 16–25.

Galbraith, K. M., & Dobson, K. S. (2000). The role of the psychologist in determining competence for assisted suicide/euthanasia in the terminally ill. *Canadian Psychology, 41,* 174–183.

Galic, Z. (2007). Psychological consequences of unemployment: The moderating role of education. *Review of Psychology, 14,* 25–34.

Gallagher, J. J. (1994). Teaching and learning: New models. *Annual Review of Psychology, 45,* 171–195.

Gallagher, L., Becker, K., & Kearney, G. (2003). A case of autism associated with del(2)(q32.1q32.2) or (q32.2q32.3). *Journal of Autism and Developmental Disorders, 33,* 105–108.

Gallistel, C. (2007). Commentary on Le Corre & Carey. *Cognition, 105,* 439–445.

Galluccio, L., & Rovee-Collier, C. (2006). Nonuniform effects of reinstatement within the time window. *Learning and Motivation, 37,* 1–17.

Gallup, G. G., Jr. (1977). Self-recognition in primates: A comparative approach to the bidirectional properties of consciousness. *American Psychologist, 32,* 329–337.

Gallup Poll. (1998). Ideal number of children. Appeared in March 1998. *American Demographics,* p. 35.

Gallup Poll. (2004). How many children? *The Gallup Poll Monthly.*

Galper, A., Wigfield, A., & Seefeldt, C. (1997). Head Start parents' beliefs about their children's abilities, task values, and performances on different actives. *Child Development, 68,* 897–907.

Galván, A. (2012). Risky behavior in adolescents: The role of the developing brain. In V. F. Reyna, S. B. Chapman, M. R. Dougherty, J. Confrey, V. F. Reyna, S. B. Chapman et al. (Eds.), *The adolescent brain: Learning, reasoning, and decision.* Washington, DC: American Psychological Association.

Ganger, J., & Brent, M. R. (2004). Reexamining the vocabulary spurt. *Developmental Psychology, 40,* 621–632.

Gans, J. (1990). *America's adolescents: How healthy are they?* Chicago: American Medical Association.

Ganzini, L., Beer, T., & Brouns, M. (2006, September). Views on physician-assisted suicide among family members of Oregon cancer patients. *Journal of Pain and Symptom Management, 32,* 230–236.

Garabedian, M. J., Lain, K. Y., Hansen, W. F., Garcia, L. S., Williams, C. M., & Crofford, L. J. (2011). Violence against women and postpartum depression. *Journal of Women's Health, 20,* 447–453.

Garbaciak, J. A. (1990). Labor and delivery: Anesthesia, induction of labor, malpresentation, and operative delivery. *Current Opinion in Obstetrics and Gynecology, 2,* 773–779.

Garbarino, J. (1988). Preventing childhood injury: Developmental and mental health issues. *American Journal of Orthopsychiatry, 58,* 25–45.

Garber, M. (1981). Malnutrition during pregnancy and lactation. In G. H. Bourne (Ed.), *World review of nutrition and dietetics* (Vol. 36). Basel, Switzerland: Karger.

Garcia, C., Baker, S., DeMayo, R., & Brown, G. (2005). Gestalt educational therapy. In *Gestalt therapy: History, theory, and practice.* Thousand Oaks, CA: Sage Publications, Inc.

Garcia, C., Bearer, E. L., & Lerner, R. M., (Eds.). (2004). *Nature and nurture: The complex interplay of genetic and environmental influences on human behavior and development.* Mahwah: Lawrence Erlbaum Associates.

Garcia, C., & Saewyc, E. (2007). Perceptions of mental health among recently immigrated Mexican adolescents. *Issues in Mental Health Nursing, 28,* 37–54.

Garcia, M., Shaw, D., Winslow, E., & Yaggi, K. (2000). Destructive sibling conflict and the development of conduct problems in young boys. *Developmental Psychology, 36,* 44–53.

Garcia-Moreno, C., Heise, L., Jansen, H. A. F. M., Ellsberg, M., & Watts, C. (2005, November 25). Violence against women. *Science, 310,* 1282–1283.

Garcia-Portilla, M. (2009). Depression and perimenopause: A review. *Actas españolas de psiquiatría, 37,* 231–21.

Gardner, H. (2000). *Intelligence reframed: Multiple intelligences for the 21st century.* New York: Basic Books.

Gardner, H. (2003). Three distinct meanings of intelligence. In R. Sternberg & J. Lautrey (Eds.), *Models of intelligence: International perspectives.* Washington, DC: American Psychological Association.

Gardner, H., & Moran, S. (2006). The science of multiple intelligences theory: A response to Lynn Waterhouse. *Educational Psychologist, 41,* 227–232.

Gardner, H., & Perkins, D. (1989). *Art, mind, and education: Research from Project Zero.* Champaign, IL: University of Illinois Press.

Gardner, M. K. (2011). Theories of intelligence. In M. A. Bray, T. J. Kehle, M. A. Bray, & T. J. Kehle (Eds.), *The Oxford handbook of school psychology.* New York: Oxford University Press.

Gardner, R. M., Stark, K., Friedman, B. N., & Jackson, N. A. (2000). Predictors of eating disorder scores in children ages 6 through 14: A longitudinal study. *Journal of Psychosomatic Research, 49,* 199–205.

Gargiulo, A., & Ebmeier, K. (2008, April 25). Care of the elderly: Awareness key in managing depression in later life. *The Practitioner,* p. 32.

Garland, J. E. (2004). Facing the evidence: Antidepressant treatment in children and adolescents. *Canadian Medical Association Journal, 17,* 489–491.

Garlick, D. (2003). Integrating brain science research with intelligence research. *Current Directions in Psychological Science, 12,* 185–189.

Garnefski, N., & Arends, E. (1998). Sexual abuse and adolescent maladjustment: Differences between male and female victims. *Journal of Adolescence, 21,* 99–107.

Garner, P. W. (2012). Children's emotional responsiveness and sociomoral understanding and associations with mothers' and fathers' socialization practices. *Infant Mental Health Journal, 33,* 95–106.

Garnett, L. R. (1996, May). Keeping the brain in tip-top shape. *Harvard Health Letter,* pp. 3–4.

Garrison, M., & Christakis, D. (2005). *A teacher in the living room? Educational media for babies, toddlers and preschoolers.* Menlo Park, CA: Kaiser Family Foundation.

Garrity, C., Jens, K., & Porter, W. W. (1996, August). Bully–victim problems in the school setting. Paper presented at the annual meeting of the American Psychological Association. Toronto, Canada.

Garstein, M. A., Gonzalez, C., Carranza, J. A., Ahadi, S. A., Ye, R., Rothbart, M. K., et al. (2006). Studying cross-cultural differences in the development of infant temperament: People's Republic of China, the United States of America, and Spain. *Child Psychiatry & Human Development, 37*, 145–161.

Gartstein, M. A., Slobodskaya, H., & Kinsht, I. (2003). Cross-cultural differences in temperament in the first year of life: United States of America (US) and Russia. *International Journal of Behavioral Development, 27*, 316–328.

Gathercole, S. E. (1998). The development of memory. *Journal of Child Psychology & Psychiatry & Allied Disciplines, 39*, 3–27.

Gatz, M. (1997, August). *Variations of depression in later life.* Paper presented at the Annual Convention of the American Psychological Association, Chicago.

Gaulden, M. E. (1992). Maternal age effect: The enigma of Down syndrome and other trisomic conditions. *Mutation Research, 296*, 69–88.

Gauthier, S., & Scheltens, P. (2009). Can we do better in developing new drugs for Alzheimer's disease? *Alzheimer's & Dementia, 5*, 489–491.

Gauthier, Y. (2003). Infant mental health as we enter the third millennium: Can we prevent aggression? *Infant Mental Health Journal, 24*, 101–109.

Gauvain, M. (1998). Cognitive development in social and cultural context. *Current Directions in Psychological Science, 7*, 188–194.

Gavin, L. A., & Furman, W. (1996). Adolescent girls' relationships with mothers and best friends. *Child Development, 67*, 375–386.

Gavin, T., & Myers, A. (2003). Characteristics, enrollment, attendance, and dropout patterns of older adults in beginner Tai-Chi and line-dancing programs. *Journal of Aging & Physical Activity, 11*, 123–141.

Gawande, A. (2007, April 30). The way we age now. *The New Yorker*, 49–59.

Gazmararian, J. A., Petersen, R., Spitz, A. M., Goodwin, M. M., Saltzman, L. E., & Marks, J. S. (2000). Violence and reproductive health: Current knowledge and future research directions. *Mat Child Health, 4*, 79–84.

Gazzaniga, M. S. (1983). Right-hemisphere language following brain bisection: A twenty-year perspective. *American Psychologist, 38*, 525–537.

Geary, D. (2006). Development of mathematical understanding. In *Handbook of child psychology: Vol 2, Cognition, perception, and language* (6th ed.). Hoboken, NJ: John Wiley & Sons Inc.

Geary, D. C. (1996). International differences in mathematical achievement: Their nature, causes, and consequences. *Current Directions in Psychological Science, 5*, 133–137.

Geary, D. C. (1998). *Male, female: The evolution of human sex differences.* Washington, DC: APA Books.

Geary, D. C., & Bjorklund, D. F. (2000). Evolutionary developmental psychology. *Child Development, 71*, 57–65.

Geary, D. C., Fan, L., & Bow-Thomas, C. C. (1992). Even before formal instruction, Chinese children outperform American children in mental addition. *Cognitive Development, 8*, 517–529.

Geary, D. C., Hoard, M. K., Nugent, L., & Bailey, D. H. (2012). Mathematical cognition deficits in children with learning disabilities and persistent low achievement: A five-year prospective study. *Journal of Educational Psychology, 104*, 206–223.

Geary, D. C., Liu, F., Chen, G., Saults, S., & Hoard, M. (1999). Contributions of computational fluency to cross-national differences in arithmetical reasoning abilities. *Journal of Educational Psychology, 91*, 716–719.

Geddie, L., Dawson, B., & Weunsch, K. (1998). Socioeconomic status and ethnic differences in pre-schoolers' interactions with anatomically detailed dolls. *Child Maltreatment, 3*, 43–52.

Gee, H. (2004). *Jacob's ladder: The history of the human genome.* New York: Norton.

Gelfand, D. M., & Teti, D. M. (1995). How does maternal depression affect children? *Harvard Mental Health Letter*, p. 8.

Gelfand, M. M. (2000). Sexuality among older women. *Journal of Womens Health & Gender-Based Medicine, 9*, (Suppl. 1), S-15–S-20.

Gelles, R. J. (1994). *Contemporary families.* Newbury Park, CA: Sage.

Gelman, D. (1994, April 18). The mystery of suicide. *Newsweek*, pp. 44–49.

Gelman, R. (1972). Logical capacity of very young children: Number invariance rules. *Child Development, 43*, 75–90.

Gelman, R. (2006, August). Young natural-number arithmeticians. *Current Directions in Psychological Science, 15*, 193–197.

Gelman, R., & Baillargeon, R. (1983). A review of some Piagetian concepts. In P. H. Mussen (Ed.), *Handbook of child psychology: Vol 3. Cognitive development* (4th ed., pp. 167–230). New York: Wiley.

Gelman, R., & Cordes, S. (2001). Counting in animals and humans. In E. Dupoux (Eds.), *Language, brain, and cognitive development: Essays in honor of Jacques Mehler.* Cambridge, MA: MIT Press.

Gelman, R., & Gallistel, C. R. (1978). *The child's understanding of number.* Cambridge, MA: Harvard University Press.

Gelman, R., & Gallistel, C. R. (2004, October 15). Language and the origin of numerical concepts. *Science, 306*, 441–443.

Gelman, S. A., & Kalish, C. W. (1993). Categories and causality. In R. Pasnak & M. L. Howe (Eds.), *Emerging themes in cognitive development. Vol. II: Competencies.* New York: Springer-Verlag.

Gelman, S. A., Taylor, M. G., & Nguyen, S. (2004). Mother–child conversations about gender. *Monographs of the Society for Research in Child Development, 69*.

General Social Survey. (1998). *National Opinion Research Center.* Chicago: University of Chicago.

Genesee, F. (1994). Bilingualism. In V. S. Ramachandran (Ed.), *Encyclopedia of human behavior.* San Diego: Academic Press.

Genovese, J. (2006). Piaget, pedagogy, and evolutionary psychology. *Evolutionary Psychology, 4*, 127–137.

Gentilucci, M., & Corballis, M. (2006). From manual gesture to speech: A gradual transition. *Neuroscience & Biobehavioral Reviews, 30*, 949–960.

George, J. B. E., & Franko, D. L. (2010). Cultural issues in eating pathology and body image among children and adolescents. *Journal of Pediatric Psychology, 35*, 231–242.

George-Hyslop, P. H. S. (2000, December). Piecing together Alzheimer's. *Scientific American*, 76–83.

Gerard, C. M., Harris, K. A., & Thach, B. T. (2002). Spontaneous arousals in supine infants while swaddled and unswaddled during rapid eye movement and quiet sleep. *Pediatrics, 110*, 70.

Gerber, M. S. (October 9, 2002). Eighty million strong—The singles lobby. *The Hill*, p. 45.

Gerber, P., & Coffman, K. (2007). Nonaccidental head trauma in infants. *Childs Nervous System, 23*, 499–507.

Gerend, M., Aiken, L., & West, S. (2004). Personality factors in older women's perceived susceptibility to diseases of aging. *Journal of Personality, 72*, 243–270.

Gergely, G. (2007). The social construction of the subjective self: The role of affect-mirroring, markedness, and ostensive communication in self-development. *Developmental science and psychoanalysis: Integration and innovation.* London: Karnac Books.

Gergen, M. M. (1990). Finished at 40: Women's development within the patriarchy. *Psychology of Women Quarterly, 14*, 471–493.

Gerhardt, P. (1999, August 10). Potty training: How did it get so complicated? *Daily Hampshire Gazette*, p. C1.

Gerressu, M., Mercer, C., Graham, C., Wellings, K., & Johnson, A. (2008). Prevalence of masturbation and associated factors in a British national probability survey. *Archives of Sexual Behavior, 37*, 266–278.

Gerrish, C. J., & Mennella, J. A. (2000). Short-term influence of breastfeeding on the infants' interaction with the environment. *Developmental Psychobiology, 36*, 40–48.

Gershkoff-Stowe, L., & Hahn, E. (2007). Fast mapping skills in the developing lexicon. *Journal of Speech, Language, and Hearing Research, 50*, 682–696.

Gershkoff-Stowe, L., & Thelen, E. (2004). U-shaped changes in behavior: A dynamic systems perspective. *Journal of Cognition & Development, 5*, 88–97.

Gershoff, E. (2002). Corporal punishment by parents and associated child behaviors and experiences: A meta-analytic and theoretical review. *Psychological Bulletin, 128*, 539–579.

Gersten, R., & Dimino, J. (2006, January). RTI (Response to Intervention): Rethinking special education for students with reading difficulties (yet again). *Reading Research Quarterly, 41*, 99–108.

Gerstorf, D., Ram, N., Estabrook, R., Schupp, J., Wagner, G., & Lindenberger, U. (2008). Life satisfaction shows terminal decline in old age: Longitudinal evidence from the German Socio-Economic Panel Study (SOEP). *Developmental Psychology, 44*, 1148–1159.

Gervain, J., Macagno, F., Cogoi, S., Peña, M., & Mehler, J. (2008). The neonate brain detects speech structure. *PNAS Proceedings of the National Academy of Sciences of the United States of America, 105*, 14222–14227.

Geschwind, D., & Iacoboni, M. (2007). Structural and functional asymmetries of the human frontal lobes. In B. L. Miller & J. L. Cummings (Eds), *The human frontal lobes: Functions and disorders.* New York: Guilford Press.

Gesell, A. L. (1946). The ontogenesis of infant behavior. In L. Carmichael (Ed.), *Manual of child psychology.* New York: Harper.

Gesser, G., Wong, P. T., & Reker, G. T. (1988). Death attitudes across the life span: The development and validation of the Death Attitude Profile (DAP). *Omega: Journal of Death and Dying, 18*, 113–128.

Geuze, R. H., Schaafsma, S. M., Lust, J. M., Bouma, A., Schiefenhövel, W., & Groothuis, T. G. (2012). Plasticity of lateralization: Schooling predicts hand preference but not hand skill asymmetry in a non-industrial society. *Neuropsychologia, 50*, 612–620.

Gewertz, C. (2005, April 6). Training focuses on teachers' expectations. *Education Week, 24*, 1–3.

Ghazi, A., Henis-Korenblit, S., & Kenyon, C. (2009). A transcription elongation factor that links signals from the reproductive system to lifespan extension in Caenorhabditis elegans. *PLoS Genetics, 5*, 71–77.

Ghetti, S., Lyons, K., Lazzarin, F., & Cornoldi, C. (2008, March). The development of metamemory monitoring during retrieval: The case of memory strength and memory absence. *Journal of Experimental Child Psychology, 99*(3), 157–181.

Ghule, M., Balaiah, D., & Joshi, B. (2007, September). Attitude towards premarital sex among rural college youth in Maharashtra, India. *Sexuality & Culture: An Interdisciplinary Quarterly, 11*(4), 1–17.

Giacobbi, P., Lynn, T., & Wetherington, J. (2004). Stress and coping during the transition to university for first-year female athletes. *Sport Psychologist, 18*, 1–20.

Giami, A., Ohlrichs, Y., Quilliam, S., Wellings, K., Pacey, S., & Wylie, K. (2006, November). Sex education in schools is insufficient to support adolescents in the 21st century. *Sexual and Relationship Therapy, 21*(4), 485–490.

Giammattei, J., Blix, G., Marshak, H. H., Wollitzer, A. O., & Petitt, D. J. (2003). Television watching and soft drink consumption: Associations with obesity in 11- to 13-year-old schoolchildren. *Archives of Pediatric Adolescence, 157*, 882–886.

Gibbs, N. (2002, April 15). Making time for a baby. *Time*, pp. 48–54.

Gibson, E. J., & Walk, R. D. (1960). The "visual cliff." *Scientific American, 202*, 64–71.

Gibson, F. (2004). *The past in the present: Using reminiscence in health and social care.* Baltimore, MD: Health Professions Press.

Gibson, R. C. (1986). Older black Americans. *Generations, 10*(4), 35–39.

Gidron, Y., Russ, K., Tissarchondou, H., & Warner, J. (2006, July). The relation between psychological factors and DNA-damage: A critical review. *Biological Psychology, 72*, 291–304.

Giedd, J. N. (2004). Structural magnetic resonance imaging of the adolescent brain. *Annals of the New York Academy of Sciences, 1021*, 77–85.

Gifford-Smith, M., & Brownell, C. (2003). Childhood peer relationships: Social acceptance, friendships, and peer networks. *Journal of School Psychology, 41*, 235–284.

Gilbert, K. R. (1997). Couple coping with the death of a child. In C. R. Figley, B. E. Bride, & N. Mazza (Eds.), *The series in trauma and loss. Death and trauma: The traumatology of grieving* (pp. 101–121). Washington, DC: Taylor & Francis.

Gilbert, L. A. (1994). Current perspectives on dual-career families. *Current Directions in Psychological Science, 3*, 101–105.

Gilbert, S. (2000). *Counseling for eating disorders.* Thousand Oaks, CA: Sage.

Gilbert, S. (2004, March 16). New clues to women veiled in black. *The New York Times*, pp. D1.

Gilbert, W. M., Nesbitt, T. S., & Danielsen, B. (1999). Childbearing beyond age 40: Pregnancy outcome in 24,032 cases. *Obstetrics and Gynecology, 93*, 9–14.

Giles-Sims, J., & Lockhart, C. (2005). Culturally shaped patterns of disciplining children. *Journal of Family Issues, 26*, 196–218.

Giligan, C. (2004). Recovering psyche: Reflections on life-history and history. *Annual of Psychoanalysis, 32I*, 131–147.

Gillath, O., Canterberry, M., & Collins, T. J. (2012). A multilevel, multimethod interdisciplinary approach to the understanding of attachment. In O. Gillath, G. Adams, & A. Kunkel (Eds.), *Relationship science: Integrating evolutionary, neuroscience, and sociocultural approaches.* Washington, DC: American Psychological Association.

Gillespie, N. A., Cloninger, C. R., & Heath, A. C. (2003). The genetic and environmental relationship between Cloninger's dimensions of temperament and character. *Personality and Individual Differences, 35*, 1931–1946.

Gillies, R., & Boyle, M. (2006, May). Ten Australian elementary teachers' discourse and reported pedagogical practices during cooperative learning. *The Elementary School Journal, 106*, 429–451.

Gilligan, C. (1982). *In a different voice: Psychological theory and women's development.* Cambridge, MA: Harvard University Press.

Gilligan, C. (1987). Adolescent development reconsidered. In C. E. Irwin (Ed.), *Adolescent social behavior and health.* San Francisco: Jossey-Bass.

Gilligan, C. (1996). The centrality of relationship in human development: A puzzle, some evidence, and a theory. In G. G. Noam & K.W . Fischer (Eds.), *Development and vulnerability in close relationships.* Hillsdale, NJ: Lawrence Erlbaum Associates, Inc.

Gilligan, C. (2004). Recovering psyche: Reflections on life-history and history. *Annual of Psychoanalysis, 32*, 131–147.

Gilligan, C., Brown, L. M., & Rogers, A. G. (1990). Psyche embedded: A place for body, relationships, and culture in personality theory. In A. I. Rabin & R. A. Zucker (Eds), *Studying persons and lives.* New York: Springer.

Gilligan, C., Lyons, N. P., & Hammer, T. J. (Eds.). (1990). *Making connections.* Cambridge, MA: Harvard University Press.

Gilligan, C., Ward, J. V., & Taylor, J. M. (Eds.). (1988). *Mapping the moral domain: A contribution of women's thinking to psychological theory and education.* Cambridge, MA: Harvard University Press.

Gilliland, A. L., & Verny, T. R. (1999). The effects of domestic abuse on the unborn child. *Journal of Prenatal and Perinatal Psychology and Health, Special Issue, 13*, 235–246.

Gillin, E. (2008). Visibility issues that influence older adults' line of sight during automobile driving. *Dissertation Abstracts International: Section B: The Sciences and Engineering, 69*, 980.

Gillmore, M., Gilchrist, L., Lee, J., & Oxford, M. (2006, August). Women who gave birth as unmarried adolescents: Trends in substance use from adolescence to adulthood. *Journal of Adolescent Health, 39*, 237–243.

Gilstrap, L., Laub, C., Zierten, E., & Mueller-Johnson, K. (2008). The effects of adult suggestion and child consistency on young children's reports. *Journal of Applied Social Psychology, 38*, 1905–1920.

Ginsburg, K. R., & Committee on Communications and the Committee on Psychosocial Aspects of Child and Family Health. (2007). The importance of play in promoting healthy child development and maintaining strong parent-child bonds. *Pediatrics, 119*, 182–191.

Ginzberg, E. (1972). Toward a theory of occupational choice: A restatement. *Vocational Guidance Quarterly, 12*, 10–14.

Giordana, S. (2005). *Understanding eating disorders: Conceptual and ethical issues in the treatment of anorexia (Issues in Biomedical Ethics).* New York: Oxford University Press.

Gitlin, L., Reever, K., Dennis, M., Mathieu, E., & Hauck, W. (2006, October). Enhancing quality of life of families who use adult day services: Short- and long-term effects of the Adult Day Services Plus Program. *The Gerontologist, 46*, 630–639.

Giussani, D. A., Jenkins, S. L., Mecenas, C. A., Winter, J. A., Barbera, M., Honnebier, O. M., et al. (1996). The oxytocin antagonist atosiban prevents androstenedione-induced myometrial contractions in the chronically instrumented, pregnant rhesus monkey. *Endocrinology, 137*, 3302–3307.

Gjerde, P., Block, J., & Block, J. (1988). Depressive symptoms and personality during late adolescence: Gender differences in the externalization-internalization of symptom expression. *Journal of Abnormal Psychology, 97*, 475–486.

Gladue, B. A. (1994). The biopsychology of sexual orientation. *Current Directions in Psychological Science, 3*, 150–154.

Gladue, B. A., & Bailey, J. M. (1995). Aggressiveness, competitiveness, and human sexual orientation. *Psychoneuroendocrinology, 20*, 475–485.

Glasgow, K. L., Dornbusch, S. M., Troyer, L., Steinberg, L., & Ritter, P. L. (1997). Parenting styles, adolescents' attributions, and educational outcomes in nine heterogeneous high schools. *Child Development, 68*, 507–529.

Glatt, S., Chayavichitsilp, P., Depp, C., Schork, N., & Jeste, D. (2007). Successful aging: From phenotype to genotype. *Biological Psychiatry, 62*, 282–293.

Gleason J. B. (1987). Sex differences in parent–child interaction. In S. U. Philips, S. Steele, & C. Tanz (Eds.), *Language, gender, and sex in comparative perspective.* New York: Cambridge University Press.

Gleason, J. B., & Ely, R. (2002). Gender differences in language development. In A. McGillicuddy-De Lisi & R. De Lisi (Eds.), *Biology, society, and behavior: The development of sex differences in cognition* (pp. 127–154). Westport, CT: Ablex Publishing.

Gleason, J. B., Perlmann, R. U., Ely, R., & Evans, D. W. (1994). The babytalk register: Parents' use of diminutives. In J. L. Sokolov & C. E. Snow (Eds.), *Handbook of research in language development using CHILDES.* Mahwah, NJ: Erlbaum.

Gleason, M., Iida, M., & Bolger, N. (2003). Daily supportive equity in close relationships. *Personality & Social Psychology Bulletin, 29*, 1036–1045.

Gleick, E., Reed, S., & Schindehette, S. (1994, October 24). The baby trap. *People Weekly*, 38–56.

Gleitman, L., & Landau, B. (1994). *The acquisition of the lexicon.* Cambridge, MA: Bradford.

Gleitman, L., & Papafragou, A. (2005). Language and thought. *The Cambridge handbook of thinking and reasoning.* New York: Cambridge University Press.

Glenberg, A. M., Goldberg, A. B., & Zhu, X. (2011). Improving early reading comprehension using embodied CAI. *Instructional Science, 39*, 27–39.

Glenn, N. D., & Weaver, C. N. (1977). The marital happiness of remarried divorced persons. *Journal of Marriage and the Family, 39*, 331–337.

Glenn, N. D., & Weaver, C. N. (1990). Quantitative research on marital quality in the 1980s: A critical review. *Journal of Marriage and the Family, 52*, 818–831.

Glick, P., & Fiske, S. (2003). An ambivalent alliance: Hostile and benevolent sexism as complementary justifications for gender inequality. *Understanding prejudice and discrimination* (pp. 225–236). New York: McGraw-Hill.

Glick, P., Fiske, S. T., Mladinic, A., Saiz, J. L., Abrams, D., Masser, B., et al. (2000). Beyond prejudice as simple antipathy: Hostile and benevolent sexism across cultures. *Journal of Personality and Social Psychology, 79*, 763–775.

Glick, P., Zion, C., & Nelson, C. (1988). What mediates sex discrimination in hiring decisions? *Journal of Personality and Social Psychology, 55*, 178–186.

Gliga, T., Elsabbagh, M., Andravizou, A., & Johnson, M. (2009). Faces attract infants' attention in complex displays. *Infancy, 14*, 550–562.

Gluhoski, V., Leader, J., & Wortman, C. B. (1994). Grief and bereavement. In V. S. Ramachandran (Ed.), *Encyclopedia of human behavior.* San Diego: Academic Press.

Glynn, L. M., & Sandman, C. A. (2011). Prenatal origins of neurological development: A critical period for fetus and mother. *Current Directions in Psychological Science, 20*, 384–389.

Goble, M. (2008). Medical and psychological complications of obesity. *Obesity in childhood and adolescence, Vol 1: Medical, biological, and social issues* (pp. 229–269). Westport, CT: Praeger Publishers/Greenwood Publishing Group.

Goede, I., Branje, S., & Meeus, W. (2009). Developmental changes in adolescents' perceptions of relationships with their parents. *Journal of Youth and Adolescence, 38*, 75–88.

Goetz, A., & Shackelford, T. (2006). Modern application of evolutionary theory to psychology: Key concepts and clarifications. *American Journal of Psychology, 119*, 567–584.

Goff, C., Martin, J., & Thomas, M. (2007). The burden of acting white: Implications for transition. *Career Development for Exceptional Individuals, 30*, 134–146.

Gogate, L. J., Bahrick, L. E., & Watson, J. D. (2000). A study of multimodal motherese: The role of temporal synchrony between verbal labels and gestures. *Child Development, 71*, 878–894.

Gohlke, B. C., & Stanhope, R. (2002). Final height in psychosocial short stature: Is there complete catch-up? *Acta Paediatrica, 91,* 961–965.

Goldberg, A. E. (2004). But do we need universal grammar? Comment on Lidz et al. *Cognition, 94,* 77–84.

Goldberg, A. E., & Kuvalanka, K. A. (2012). Marriage (in)equality: The perspectives of adolescents and emerging adults with lesbian, gay, and bisexual parents. *Journal of Marriage and Family, 74,* 34–52.

Goldberg, J., Holtz, D., Hyslop, T., & Tolosa, J. E. (2002). Has the use of routine episiotomy decreased? Examination of episiotomy rates from 1983 to 2000. *Obstetrics and Genecology, 99,* 395–400.

Goldberg, J., Pereira, L., & Berghella, V. (2002). Pregnancy after uterine artery emoblization. *Obstetrics and Gynecology, 100,* 869–872.

Goldberg, W., Prause, J., Lucas-Thompson, R., & Himsel, A. (2008). Maternal employment and children's achievement in context: A meta-analysis of four decades of research. *Psychological Bulletin, 134,* 77–108.

Golden, J., Conroy, R., Bruce, I., Denihan, A., Greene, E., Kirby, M., et al. (2009). Loneliness, social support networks, mood and wellbeing in community-dwelling elderly. *International Journal of Geriatric Psychiatry, 24,* 694–700.

Goldfarb, Z. (2005, July 12). Newborn medical screening expands. *Wall Street Journal,* p. D6.

Goldfield, G. S. (2012). Making access to TV contingent on physical activity: Effects on liking and relative reinforcing value of TV and physical activity in overweight and obese children. *Journal of Behavioral Medicine, 35,* 1–7.

Goldin-Meadow, S. (2006). Talking and thinking with our hands. *Current Directions in Psychological Science, 15,* 34–39.

Goldin-Meadow, S. (2009). Using the hands to study how children learn language. In J. Colombo, P. McCardle, & L. Freund, *Infant pathways to language: Methods, models, and research disorders.* New York: Psychology Press.

Goldman, R. (1964). *Religious thinking form childhood to adolescence.* London: Routledge & Kegan Paul.

Goldman, R. (2004). Circumcision policy: A psychosocial perspective. *Pediatrics and Child Health, 9,* 630–633.

Goldscheider, F. K. (1994). Divorce and remarriage: Effects on the elderly population. *Reviews in Clinical Gerontology, 4,* 253–259.

Goldschmidt, L., Richardson, G., Willford, J., & Day, N. (2008). Prenatal marijuana exposure and intelligence test performance at age 6. *Journal of the American Academy of Child & Adolescent Psychiatry, 47,* 254–263.

Goldsmith, H. H., & Gottesman, I. I. (1981). Origins of variation in behavioral style: A longitudinal study of temperament in young twins. *Child Development, 53,* 91–103.

Goldsmith, H. H., & Harman, C. (1994). Temperament and attachment: Individuals and relationships. *Current Directions in Psychological Science, 3,* 53–57.

Goldsmith, L. T. (2000). Tracking trajectories of talent: Child prodigies growing up. In R. C. Friedman & B. M. Shore (Eds.), *Talents unfolding: Cognition and development.* Washington, DC: American Psychological Association.

Goldsmith, S. K., Pellmar, T. C., Kleinman, A. M., & Bunney, W. E. (2002). *Reducing suicide: A national imperative.* Washington, DC: The National Academies Press.

Goldstein, A. P. (1999). Aggression reduction strategies: Effective and ineffective. *Psychology Quarterly, 14,* 40–58.

Goldstein, T. R., & Winner, E. (2012). Enhancing empathy and theory of mind. *Journal of Cognition and Development, 13,* 19–37.

Goldston, D. B. (2003). *Measuring suicidal behavior and risk in children and adolescents.* Washington, DC: American Psychological Association.

Goldwater, P. N. (2003). Sudden infant death syndrome: A critical review of approaches to research. *Archives of the Disabled Child, 88,* 1085–1100.

Goldweber, A., & Cauffman, E. (2012). Relational aggression and the *DSM-V:* What can clinicians tell us about female juvenile offenders? *Journal of Forensic Psychology Practice, 12,* 35–47.

Goldweber, A., Dmitrieva, J., Cauffman, E., Piquero, A. R., & Steinberg, L. (2011). The development of criminal style in adolescence and young adulthood: Separating the lemmings from the loners. *Journal of Youth and Adolescence, 40*(3), 332–346. doi:10.1007/s10964–010–9534–5

Goleman, D. (1985, February 5). Mourning: New studies affirm its benefits. *The New York Times,* pp. C1, C6.

Goleman, D. (1986, October 21). Child development theory stresses small moments. *New York Times.*

Goleman, D. (1993, July 21). Baby sees, baby does, and classmates follow. *The New York Times,* p. C10.

Goleman, D. (1995). *Emotional intelligence.* New York: Bantam.

Goleman, D. (2005). What makes a leader? In R. L. Taylor & W. E. Rosenbach (Eds.), *Military leadership: In pursuit of excellence* (5th ed.). Boulder, CO: Westview Press.

Golinkoff, R. M. (1993). When is communication a "meeting of minds"? *Journal of Child Language, 20,* 199–207.

Golmier, I., Cehbat, J. C., & Gelinas-Chebat, C. (2007). Can cigarette warnings counterbalance effects of smoking scenes in movies? *Psychological Reports, 100,* 3–18.

Golomb, C. (2002). *Child art in context.* Washington, DC: American Psychological Association.

Golomb, C. (2003). *The child's creation of a pictorial world* (2nd ed.). Mahwah, NJ: Lawrence Erlbaum.

Golombok, S., & Fivush, R. (1994). *Gender development.* Cambridge, England: Cambridge University Press.

Golombok, S., Golding, J., Perry, B., Burston, A., Murray, C., Mooney-Somers, J., et al. (2003). Children with lesbian parents: A community study. *Developmental Psychology, 39,* 20–33.

Golombok, S., Murray, C., Vasanti, J., MacCallum, F., & Lycett, E. (2004). Families created through surrogacy arrangements: Parent-child relationships in the 1st year of life. *Developmental Psychology, 40,* 400–411.

Golombok, S., & Tasker, F. (1996). Do parents influence the sexual orientation of their children? Findings from a longitudinal study of lesbian families. *Developmental Psychology, 32,* 3–11.

Golub, S., & Langer, E. (2007). Challenging assumptions about adult development: Implications for the health of older adults. *Handbook of health psychology and aging* (pp. 9–29). New York: Guilford Press.

Gomez, C. F. (1991). *Regulating death: Euthanasia and the case of the Netherlands.* New York: Free Press.

Göncü, A., & Gauvain, M. (2012). Sociocultural approaches to educational psychology: Theory, research, and application. In K. R. Harris, S. Graham, T. Urdan, C. B. McCormick, G. M. Sinatra, J. Sweller, et al. (Eds.), *APA educational psychology handbook, Vol 1: Theories, constructs, and critical issues.* Washington, DC: American Psychological Association.

Gondolf, E. W. (1985). Fighting for control: A clinical assessment of men who batter. *Social Casework, 66,* 48–54.

Gongla, P., & Thompson, E. H. (1987). Single-parent families. In M. B. Sussman & S. K. Steinmetz (Eds.), *Handbook of marriage and the family.* New York: Plenum.

Gonnerman, M. E., Jr., Lutz, G. M., Yehieli, M., & Meisinger, B. K. (2008). Religion and health connection: A study of African American, Protestant Christians.

Journal of Health Care for the Poor and Underserved, 19, 193–199.

Good, C., Aronson, J., & Harder, J. (2008, January). Problems in the pipeline: Stereotype threat and women's achievement in high-level math courses. *Journal of Applied Developmental Psychology, 29*(1), 17–28.

Good, M., & Willoughby, T. (2008). Adolescence as a sensitive period for spiritual development. *Child Development Perspectives, 2,* 32–37.

Goode, E. (1999, January 12). Clash over when, and how, to toilet-train. *The New York Times,* p. A1, A17.

Goode, E. (2004, February 3). Stronger warning is urged on antidepressants for teenagers. *The New York Times,* p. A12.

Goodglass, H. (1993). *Understanding aphasia.* San Diego, CA: Academic Press.

Goodlin-Jones, B. L., Burnham, M. M., & Anders, T. F. (2000). Sleep and sleep disturbances: Regulatory processes in infancy. In A. J. Sameroff & M. Lewis et al. (Eds.), *Handbook of developmental psychopathology* (2nd ed.). New York: Kluwer Academic/Plenum Publishers.

Goodman, G. S. (2006). Children's eyewitness memory: A modern history and contemporary commentary. *Journal of Social Issues, 62,* 811–832.

Goodman, G. S., & Reed, R. S. (1986). Age differences in eyewitness testimony. *Law and Human Behavior, 10,* 317–332.

Goodman, G., & Melinder, A. (2007, February). Child witness research and forensic interviews of young children: A review. *Legal and Criminological Psychology, 12,* 1–19.

Goodman, G., & Quas, J. (2008). Repeated interviews and children's memory: It's more than just how many. *Current Directions in Psychological Science, 17,* 386–390.

Goodman, J., Schlossberg, N. K., & Anderson, M. L. (2006). *Counseling adults in transition: Linking practice with theory.* New York: Springer.

Goodman, J. C., & Nusbaum, H. C. (Eds.). (1994). *The development of speech perception.* Cambridge, MA: Bradford.

Goodman, J. S., Fields, D. L., & Blum, T. C. (2003). Cracks in the glass ceiling: In what kinds of organizations do women make it to the top? *Group & Organization Management, 28,* 475–501.

Goodman, S., Broth, M., Hall, C., & Stowe, Z. (2008). Treatment of postpartum depression in mothers: Secondary benefits to the infants. *Infant Mental Health Journal, 29,* 492–513.

Goodman, S. H., Rouse, M. H., Connell, A. M., Broth, M., Hall, C. M., & Heyward, D. (2011). Maternal depression and child psychopathology: A meta-analytic review. *Clinical Child and Family Psychology Review, 14,* 1–27.

Goodstein, R., & Ponterotto, J. G. (1997). Racial and ethnic identity: Their relationship and their contribution to self-esteem. *Journal of Black Psychology, 23,* 275–292.

Goodwin, M. H. (1980). Directive-response speech sequences in girls' and boys' task activities. In S. McConnell-Ginet, R. Borker, & N. Furman (Eds.), *Women and language in literature and society.* New York: Praeger.

Goodwin, M. H. (1990). Tactical uses of stories: Participation frameworks within girls' and boys' disputes. *Discourse Processes, 13,* 33–71.

Googans, B., & Burden, D. (1987). Vulnerability of working parents: Balancing work and home roles. *Social Work, 32,* 295–300.

Goold, S. D., Williams, B., & Arnold, R. M. (2000). Conflicts regarding decisions to limit treatment: A differential diagnosis. *Journal of the American Medical Association, 283,* 909–914.

Goorabi, K., Hoseinabadi, R., & Share, H. (2008). Hearing aid effect on elderly depression in nursing home patients. *Asia Pacific Journal of Speech, Language, and Hearing, 11*, 119–124.

Goossens, F. A., & Van Ijzendoorn, M. H. (1990). Quality of infants' attachments to professional caregivers: Relation to infant–parent attachment and day-care characteristics. *Child Development, 61*, 832–837.

Goossens, L. (2006). The many faces of adolescent autonomy: Parent-adolescent conflict, behavioral decision-making, and emotional distancing. *Handbook of adolescent development* (pp. 135–153). New York: Psychology Press.

Gopaul-McNicol, S. A. (1995). A cross-cultural examination of racial identity and racial preference of preschool children in the West Indies. *Journal of Cross-Cultural Psychology, 26*, 141–152.

Gopnik, A., Meltzoff, A. N., & Kuhl, P. K. (2002). *The scientist in the crib: What early learning tells us about the mind.* New York: HarperCollins.

Gorchoff, S., John, O., & Helson, R. (2008). Contextualizing change in marital satisfaction during middle age: An 18-year longitudinal study. *Psychological Science, 19*, 1194–1200.

Gordon, B. N., Baker-Ward, L., & Ornstein, P. A. (2001). Children's testimony: A review of research on memory for past experiences. *Clinical Child & Family Psychology Review, 4*, 157–181.

Gordon, J. W. (1999, March 26). Genetic enhancement in humans. *Science, 283*, 2023–2024.

Gordon, N. (2007). The cerebellum and cognition. *European Journal of Paediatric Neurology, 30*, 214–220.

Goren, J. L. (2008). Antidepressants use in pediatric populations. *Expert Opinion on Drug Safety, 7*, 223–225.

Gorman, A. (2010, January 7). UCLA study says legalizing undocumented immigrants would help the economy. *Los Angeles Times.*

Gorman, K. S., & Pollitt, E. (1992). Relationship between weight and body proportionality at birth, growth during the first year of life, and cognitive development at 36, 48, and 60 months. *Infant Behavior and Development, 15*, 279–296.

Gormley, W. T., Jr., Gayer, T., Phillips, D., & Dawson, B. (2005). The effects of universal pre-K on cognitive development. *Developmental Psychology, 41*, 872–884.

Gortmaker, S. L., Dietz, W. H., & Cheung, L. W. Y. (1990). Inactivity, diet, and the fattening of America. *Journal of the American Dietetic Association, 90*, 1247–1252.

Gortmaker, S. L., Dietz, W. H., Sobol, A. M., & Welher, C. A. (1987). Increasing pediatric obesity in the United States. *American Journal of the Diseases of Children, 141*, 535–540.

Gortmaker, S. L., Must, A., Sobol, A. M., Peterson, K., Colditz, G. A., & Dietz, W. H. (1996). Television viewing as a cause of increasing obesity among children in the United States, 1896–1990. *Archives of Pediatrics & Adolescent Medicine, 150*, 356–362.

Gostin, L. (2006, April). Physician-assisted suicide: A legitimate medical practice? *JAMA: Journal of the American Medical Association, 295*, 1941–1943.

Goswami, U. (1998). *Cognition in children.* Philadelphia: Psychology Press.

Goswami, U. (2008). *Cognitive development: The learning brain.* New York: Psychology Press.

Gottesman, I. I. (1991). *Schizophrenia genesis: The origins of madness.* New York: Freeman.

Gottesman, I. I. (1993). Origins of schizophrenia: Past as prologue. In R. Plomin & G. E. McClearn (Eds.), *Nature, nurture, and psychology.* Washington, DC: American Psychological Association.

Gottfredson, G. D., & Holland, J. L. (1990). A longitudinal test of the influence of congruence: Job satisfaction, competency utilization, and counterproductive behavior. *Journal of Counseling Psychology, 37*, 389–398.

Gottfried, A. E., & Gottfried, A. W. (Eds.). (1994). *Redefining families.* New York: Plenum.

Gottfried, A., Gottfried, A., & Bathurst, K. (2002). Maternal and dual-earner employment status and parenting. In M. Bornstein (Ed.), *Handbook of parenting: Vol. 2: Biology and ecology of parenting.* Mahwah, NJ: Lawrence Erlbaum Associates.

Gottfried, A. W., Gottfried, A. E., Bathurst, K., & Guerin, D. W. (1994). *Early developmental aspects: The Fullerton Longitudinal Study.* New York: Plenum.

Gottlieb, G. (1991). Experimental canalization of behavioral development: Theory. *Developmental Psychology, 27*, 373–381.

Gottlieb, G. (2003). On making behavioral genetics truly developmental. *Human Development, 46*, 337–355.

Gottlieb, G., & Blair, C. (2004). How early experience matters in intellectual development in the case of poverty. *Preventive Science, 5*, 245–252.

Gottman, J. M. (1986). The world of coordinated play: Same- and cross-sex friendship in young children. In J. M. Gottman & J. G. Parker (Eds.), *Conversations of friends: Speculations on affective development* (pp. 139–191). Cambridge, England: Cambridge University Press.

Gottman, J. M. (1993). *What predicts divorce? The relationship between marital processes and marital outcomes.* Hillsdale, NJ: Erlbaum.

Gottman, J. M., Fainsilber-Katz, L., & Hooven, C. (1996). *Meta-emotion: How families communicate emotionally.* Mahwah, NJ: Erlbaum.

Gottman, J. M., & Katz, L. F. (1989). Effects of marital discord on young children's peer interaction and health. *Developmental Psychology, 25*, 373–381.

Gottschalk, E. C., Jr. (1983, February 21). Older Americans: The aging man gains in the 1970s, outpacing rest of the population. *The Wall Street Journal*, pp. 1, 20.

Gould, R. L. (1978). *Transformations: Growth and change in adult life.* New York: Simon Schuster.

Gould, R. L. (1980). Transformations during adult years. In R. Smelzer & E. Erickson (Eds.), *Themes of love and work in adulthood.* Cambridge, MA: Harvard University Press.

Gould, S. J. (1977). *Ontogeny and phylogeny.* Cambridge, MA: Harvard University Press.

Gow, A., Pattie, A., Whiteman, M., Whalley, L., & Deary, I. (2007). Social support and successful aging: Investigating the relationships between lifetime cognitive change and life satisfaction. *Journal of Individual Differences, 28*, 103–115.

Goyette-Ewing, M. (2000). Children's after school arrangements: A study of self-care and developmental outcomes. *Journal of Prevention & Intervention in the Community, 20*, 55–67.

Graber, J. A., Brooks-Gunn, J., & Warren, M. P. (1995). The antecedents of menarcheal age: Heredity, family environment, and stressful life events. *Child Development, 66*, 346–359.

Grabner, R. H., Neubauer, A. C., & Stern, E. (2006). Superior performance and neural efficiency: The impact of intelligence and expertise. *Brain Research Bulletin, 69*, 422–439.

Grace, D., David, B., & Ryan, M. (2008). Investigating preschoolers' categorical thinking about gender through imitation, attention, and the use of self-categories. *Child Development, 79*, 1928–1941.

Graddol, D. (2004, February 27). The future of language. *Science, 303*, 1329–1331.

Grady, C. L., McIntosh, A. R., Horwitz, B., Maison, J. M., Ungerleider, L. G., Mentis, M. J., (1995, July 14). Age-related reductions in human recognition memory due to impaired encoding. *Science, 269*, 218–221.

Grady, D. (2006, November). Management of menopausal symptoms. *New England Journal of Medicine, 355*, 2338–2347.

Grady, D., & Kolata, G. (2003, August, 29). Gene therapy used to treat patient with Parkinson's. *The New York Times*, pp. A1, A18.

Grady, J., Karraker, K., & Metzger, A. (2011). Shyness trajectories in slow-to-warm-up infants: Relations with child sex and maternal parenting. *Journal of Applied Developmental Psychology.* Retrieved from http://www.sciencedirect.com/science/article/pii/S0193397311001407.

Grady, S. (2006, December). Racial disparities in low birthweight and the contribution of residential segregation: A multilevel analysis. *Social Science & Medicine, 63*, 3013–3029.

Graf, P. (1990). Life-span changes in implicit and explicit memory. *Bulletin of the Psychonomic Society, 28*, 353–358.

Graham, E. (1995, February 9). Leah: Life is all sweetness and insecurity. *The Wall Street Journal*, p. Bl.

Graham, I., Carroli, G., Davies, C., & Medves, J. (2005). Episiotomy rates around the world: An update. *Birth: Issues in Perinatal Care, 32*, 219–223.

Graham, J., Banaschewski, T., Buitelaar, J., Gochill, D., Danckaerts, M., Dittman, R. W., et al. (2011). European guidelines on managing adverse effects of medication for ADHD. European Guidelines Group; *European Child & Adolescent Psychiatry, 20*, 17–37.

Graham, J. E., Christian, L. M., & Kiecolt-Glaser, J. K. (2006). Stress, age, and immune function: Toward a lifespan approach. *Journal of Behavioral Medicine, 29*, 389–400.

Graham, S. (1986). An attributional perspective on achievement motivation and black children. In R. S. Feldman (Ed.), *The social psychology of education: Current research and theory.* New York: Cambridge University Press.

Graham, S. (1990). Communicating low ability in the classroom: Bad things good teachers sometimes do. In S. Graham & V. S. Folkes (Eds.), *Attribution theory: Applications to achievement, mental health, and interpersonal conflict.* Hillsdale, NJ: Erlbaum.

Graham, S. (1992). "Most of the subjects were white and middle class": Trends in published research on African Americans in selected APA journals. *American Psychologist, 47*, 629–639.

Graham, S. (1994). Motivation in African Americans. *Review of Educational Research, 64*, 55–117.

Graham, S. (1997). Using attribution theory to understand social and academic motivation in African American youth. *Educational Psychologist, 32*, 21–34.

Graham, S., & Harris, K. R. (1997). Whole language and process writing: Does one approach fit all? In J. W. Lloyd, E. J. Kameenui, & D. Chard (Eds.), *Issues in educating students with disabilities* (pp. 239–258). Mahwah, NJ: Erlbaum.

Grall, T. S. (2009). Custodial mothers and fathers and their child support: 2007. Current Population Reports. Washington, DC: U.S. Bureau of the Census.

Grambs, J. D. (1989). *Women over forty: Visions and realities.* New York: Springer.

Grammer, J. K., Purtell, K. M., Coffman, J. L., & Ornstein, P. A. (2011). Relations between children's metamemory and strategic performance: Time-varying covariates in early elementary school. *Journal of Experimental Child Psychology, 108*, 139–155.

Granic, I., Hollenstein, T., & Dishion, T. (2003). Longitudinal analysis of flexibility and reorganization in early adolescence: A dynamic systems study of family interactions. *Developmental Psychology, 39*, 606–617.

Grant, C., Wall, C., Brewster, D., Nicholson, R., Whitehall, J., Super, L., et al. (2007). Policy statement on iron deficiency in pre-school-aged children. *Journal of Paediatrics and Child Health, 43*, 513–521.

Grant, J., Weaver, M., & Elliott, T. (2004). Family caregivers of stroke survivors: Characteristics of caregivers at risk for depression. *Rehabilitation Psychology, 49*, 172–179.

Grant, K. E., McMahon, S. D., Duffy, S. N., Taylor, J. J., & Compas, B. E. (2011). Stressors and mental health problems in childhood and adolescence. In R. J.

Contrada, A. Baum, R. J. Contrada, & A. Baum (Eds.), *The handbook of stress science: Biology, psychology, and health.* New York: Springer Publishing Co.

Grant, V. J. (1994). Sex of infant differences in mother–infant interaction: A reinterpretation of past findings. *Developmental Review, 14,* 1–26.

Grantham, T., & Ford, D. (2003). Beyond self-concept and self-esteem: Racial identity and gifted African American students. *High School Journal, 87,* 18–29.

Grantham-McGregor, S., Ani, C., & Fernald, L. (2001). The role of nutrition in intellectual development. In R. J. Steinberg & E. L. Grigorenko (Eds.), *Environmental effects on cognitive abilities.* Mahwah, NJ: Erlbaum.

Grantham-McGregor, S., Powell, C., Walker, S., Chang, S., & Fletcher, P. (1994). The long-term follow-up of severely malnourished children who participated in an intervention program. *Child Development, 65,* 428–439.

Gratch, G., & Schatz, J. A. (1987). Cognitive development: The relevance of Piaget's infancy books. In J. D. Osofsky (Ed.), *Handbook of infant development* (2nd ed.). New York: Wiley.

Grattan, M. P., DeVos, E. S., Levy, J., & McClintock, M. K. (1992). Asymmetric action in the human newborn: Sex differences in patterns of organization. *Child Development, 63,* 273–289.

Gray, C., Ferguson, J., Behan, S., Dunbar, C., Dunn, J., & Mitchell, D. (2007, March). Developing young readers through the linguistic phonics approach. *International Journal of Early Years Education, 15,* 15–33.

Gray, L. C., Farish, S. J., & Dorevitch, M. (1992). A population-based study of assessed applicants to long-term nursing home care. *Journal of the American Geriatric Society, 40,* 596–600.

Gray-Little, B., & Hafdahl, A. R. (2000). Factors influencing racial comparisons of self-esteem: A quantitative review. *Psychological Bulletin, 126,* 26–54.

Gredebäck, G., Eriksson, M., Schmitow, C., Laeng, B., & Stenberg, G. (2012). Individual differences in face processing: Infants' scanning patterns and pupil dilations are influenced by the distribution of parental leave. *Infancy, 17,* 79–101.

Gredler, M., & Shields, C. (2008). *Vygotsky's legacy: A foundation for research and practice.* New York: Guilford Press.

Green, C. P. (1991). Clinical considerations: Midlife daughters and their aging parents. *Journal of Gerontological Nursing, 17,* 6–12.

Green, F. (2005, September 1). The golden-touch years. *San Diego Union-Tribune,* p. C1.

Green, J., Muir, H., & Maher, M. (2011). Child pedestrian casualties and deprivation. *Accident Analysis and Prevention, 43,* 714–723.

Green, M. H. (1995). Influences of job type, job status, and gender on achievement motivation. *Current Psychology: Developmental, Learning, Personality, Social, 14,* 159–165.

Greenberg, J. (2011). The impact of maternal education on children's enrollment in early childhood education and care. *Children and Youth Services Review.*

Greenberg, J., & Becker, M. (1988). Aging parents as family resources. *Gerontologist, 28,* 786–790.

Greenberg, L. (2008). Emotion and cognition in psychotherapy: The transforming power of affect. *Canadian Psychology, 49,* 49–59.

Greenberg, J., Cwikel, J., & Mirsky, J. (2007, January). Cultural correlates of eating attitudes: A comparison between native-born and immigrant university students in Israel. *International Journal of Eating Disorders, 40,* 51–58.

Greene, K., Krcmar, M., & Rubin, D. (2002). Elaboration in processing adolescent health messages: The impact of egocentrism and sensation seeking on message processing. *Journal of Communication, 52,* 812–831.

Greene, K., Krcmar, M., Walters, L. H., Rubin, D. L., & Hale, J. L. (2000). Targeting adolescent risk-taking behaviors: The contribution of egocentrism and sensation-seeking. *Journal of Adolescence, 23,* 439–461.

Greene, R. (2008). Psychosocial theory. *Comprehensive handbook of social work and social welfare, volume 2: Human behavior in the social environment.* Hoboken, NJ: John Wiley & Sons Inc.

Greene, S., Anderson, E., & Hetherington, E. (2003). Risk and resilience after divorce. In F. Walsh (Ed.), *Normal family processes: Growing diversity and complexity.* New York: Guilford Press.

Greenfield, P. M. (1966). On culture and conservation. In J. S. Bruner, R. R. Olver, & P. M. Greenfield (Eds.), *Studies in cognitive growth.* New York: Wiley.

Greenfield, P. M. (1976). Cross-cultural research and Piagetian theory: Paradox and progress. In K. F. Riegel & J. A. Meacham (Eds.), *The developing individual in a changing world: Vol. 1.* The Hague, The Netherlands: Mouton.

Greenfield, P. M. (1995, Winter). Culture, ethnicity, race, and development: Implications for teaching theory and research. *SRCD Newsletter,* pp. 52–57.

Greenfield, P. M. (1997). You can't take it with you. Why ability assessments don't cross cultures. *American Psychologist, 52,* 1115–1124.

Greenglass, E. R., & Burke, R. J. (1991). The relationship between stress and coping among Type A's. *Journal of Social Behavior and Personality, 6,* 361–373.

Greenhill, L. L., Halperin, J. M., & Abikoff, H. (1999). Stimulant medications. *Journal of the American Academy of Child and Adolescent Psychiatry, 38,* 503–512.

Greenwald, A., Banaji, M., Rudman, L., Farnham, S., Nosek, B., & Mellott, D. (2002). A unified theory of implicit attitudes, stereotypes, self-esteem, and self-concept. *Psychological Review, 109,* 3–25.

Greenway, C. (2002). The process, pitfalls and benefits of implementing a reciprocal teaching intervention to improve the reading comprehension of a group of year 6 pupils. *Educational Psychology in Practice, 18,* 113–137.

Greenwood, D., & Isbell, L. (2002). Ambivalent sexism and the dumb blonde: Men's and women's reactions to sexist jokes. *Psychology of Women Quarterly, 26,* 341–350.

Greenwood, D. N., & Piertomonaco, P. R. (2004). The interplay among attachment orientation, idealized media images of women, and body dissatisfaction: A social psychological analysis. In L. J. Shrum (Eds.), *Psychology of entertainment media: Blurring the lines between entertainment and persuasion.* Mahwah, NJ: Lawrence Erlbaum Associates.

Greenwood, J. (2012). Parent–child relationships in the context of a mid- to late-life parental divorce. *Journal of Divorce & Remarriage, 53,* 1–17.

Greer, M. (2004, November). Retirement's road map. *Monitor on Psychology, 35,* 80.

Gregory, A. (2009, May 29). *A young at heart name for Britian's oldest mum Elizabeth Adeney.* Retrieved from http://www.mirror.co.uk/news/top-stories/2009/05/29/a-young-at-heart-name-for-britain-s-oldest-mum-115875-21397519/.

Gregory, K. (2005). Update on nutrition for preterm and full-term infants. *Journal of Obstetrics and Gynecological Neonatal Nursing, 34,* 98–108.

Gregory, S. (1856). *Facts for young women.* Boston.

Gresham, D., & Gullone, E. (2012). Emotion regulation strategy use in children and adolescents: The explanatory roles of personality and attachment. *Personality and Individual Differences, 52,* 616–621.

Greve, T. (2003). Norway: The breastfeeding top of the world. *Midwifery Today International, 67,* 57–59.

Grey, W. H., & Milken Institute, reported in Suro, R. (1999, November). Mixed doubles. *American Demographics,* 57–62.

Grieser, T., & Kuhl, P. (1988). Maternal speech to infants in atonal language: Support for universal prosodic features in motherese. *Developmental Psychology, 24,* 14–20.

Griesler, P. C., & Kandel, D. B. (1998). Ethnic differences in correlates of adolescent cigarette smoking. *Journal of Adolescent Health, 23,* 167–180.

Griffin, B. (2001). Instructor reputation and students ratings of instruction. *Contemporary Educational Psychology, 26,* 534–552.

Griffith, D. R., Azuma, S. D., & Chasnoff, I. J. (1994). Three-year outcome of children exposed prenatally to drugs. *Journal of the American Academy of Child and Adolescent Psychiatry, 33,* 20–27.

Griffith, D., & Griffith, P. (2008). Commentary on "Perspective on race and ethnicity in Alzheimer's disease research." *Alzheimer's & Dementia, 4,* 239–241.

Grigorenko, E. (2003). Intraindividual fluctuations in intellectual functioning: Selected links between nutrition and the mind. In R. Sternberg & J. Lautrey (Eds.), *Models of intelligence: International perspectives.* Washington, DC: American Psychological Association.

Grigorenko, E., Jarvin, L., Diffley, R., Goodyear, J., Shanahan, E., & Sternberg, R. (2009). Are SSATS and GPA enough? A theory-based approach to predicting academic success in secondary school. *Journal of Educational Psychology, 101,* 964–981.

Grønhøj, A., & Thøgersen, J. (2012). Action speaks louder than words: The effect of personal attitudes and family norms on adolescents' pro-environmental behaviour. *Journal of Economic Psychology, 33,* 292–302.

Grönqvist, H., Brodd, K., & von Hofsten, C. (2011). Reaching strategies of very preterm infants at 8 months corrected age. *Experimental Brain Research, 209,* 225–233.

Groome, L. J., Swiber, M. J., Atterbury, J. L., Bentz, L. S., & Holland, S. B. (1997). Similarities and differences in behavioral state organization during sleep periods in the perinatal infant before and after birth. *Child Development, 68,* 1–11.

Groome, L. J., Swiber, M. J., Bentz, L. S., Holland, S. B., & Atterbury, J. L. (1995). Maternal anxiety during pregnancy: Effect on fetal behavior at 38 to 40 weeks of gestation. *Developmental and Behavioral Pediatrics, 16,* 391–396.

Groopman, J. (1998, February 8). Decoding destiny. *New Yorker,* pp. 42–47.

Gross, J. (1991, June 16). More young single men hang on to apron strings. *The New York Times,* pp. A1, A18.

Gross, P. A. (1991). *Managing your health: Strategies for lifelong good health.* Yonkers, NY: Consumer Reports Books.

Gross, R. T., Spiker, D., & Haynes, C. W. (Eds.). (1997). *Helping low-birthweight, premature babies: The Infant Health and Development Program.* Stanford, CA: Stanford University Press.

Grossman, K. E., Grossmann, K., & Waters, E. (Eds.). (2005). *Attachment from infancy to adulthood: The major longitudinal studies.* New York: Guilford Press.

Grossmann, K. E., Grossman, K., Huber, F., & Wartner, U. (1982). German children's behavior towards their mothers at 12 months and their fathers at 18 months in Ainsworth's strange situation. *International Journal of Behavioral Development, 4,* 157–181.

Grossmann, T., Striano, T., & Friederici, A. (2006, May). Crossmodal integration of emotional information from face and voice in the infant brain. *Developmental Science, 9,* 309–315.

Groves, B., Zuckerman, B., Marans, S., & Cohen, D. (1993). Silent victims: Children who witness violence. *Journal of the American Medical Association, 269,* 262–264.

Grunbaum, J. A., Kann, L., Kinchen, S. A., Williams, B., Ross, J. G., Lowry, R., et al. (2002). *Youth risk behavior surveillance—United States, 2001.* Atlanta, GA: Centers for Disease Control.

Grunbaum, J. A., Lowry, R., & Kann, L. (2001). Prevalence of health-related behaviors among alternative high school students as compared with students attending regular high schools. *Journal of Adolescent Health, 29,* 337–343.

Grundy, E., & Henretta, J. (2006, September). Between elderly parents and adult children: A new look at the intergenerational care provided by the "sandwich generation." *Ageing & Society, 26,* 707–722.

Grusec, J. E. (1982). Socialization processes and the development of altruism. In J. P. Rushton & R. M. Sorrentino (Eds.), *Altruism and helping behavior.* Hillsdale, NJ: Erlbaum.

Grusec, J. E. (1991). The socialization of altruism. In M. S. Clark (Ed.), *Prosocial behavior.* Newbury Park, CA: Sage.

Grusec, J. E., & Goodnow, J. J. (1994). Summing up and looking to the future. *Developmental Psychology, 30,* 29–31.

Grusec, J. E., & Kuczynski, L. E. (Eds.). (1997). *Parenting and children's internalization of values: A handbook of contemporary theory.* New York: Wiley.

Grych, J. H., & Clark, R. (1999). Maternal employment and development of the father–infant relationship in the first year. *Developmental Psychology, 35,* 893–903.

Grzywacz, J., Butler, A., & Almeida, D. (2008). Work, family, and health: Work-family balance as a protective factor against stresses of daily life. *In The changing realities of work and family: A multidisciplinary approach.* Wiley-Blackwell.

Guadalupe, K. L., & Welkley, D. L. (2012). *Diversity in family constellations: Implications for practice.* Chicago: Lyceum Books.

Guan, J. (2004). Correlates of spouse relationship with sexual attitude, interest, and activity among Chinese elderly. *Sexuality & Culture: An Interdisciplinary Quarterly, 8,* 104–131.

Guarente, L. (2006, December 14). Sirtuins as potential targets for metabolic syndrome. *Nature, 14,* 868–874.

Guasti, M. T. (2002). *Language acquisition: The growth of grammar.* Cambridge, MA: MIT Press.

Gubrium, F. F. (1975). Being single in old age. *International Journal of Aging and Human Development, 6,* 29–41.

Gubrium, J. G. (1973). *The myth of the golden years: A socio-environmental theory of aging.* Springfield, IL: Thomas.

Guerrero, A., Hishinuma, E., Andrade, N., Nishimura, S., & Cunanan, V. (2006, July). Correlations among socioeconomic and family factors and academic, behavioral, and emotional difficulties in Filipino adolescents in Hawaii. *International Journal of Social Psychiatry, 52,* 343–359.

Guerrini, I., Thomson, A., & Gurling, H. (2007). The importance of alcohol misuse, malnutrition and genetic susceptibility on brain growth and plasticity. *Neuroscience & Biobehavioral Reviews, 31,* 212–220.

Guevara, M., Rizo Martínez, L., Robles Aguirre, F., & González, M. (2012). Prefrontal–parietal correlation during performance of the towers of Hanoi task in male children, adolescents and young adults. *Developmental Cognitive Neuroscience, 2,* 129–138.

Guinsburg, R., de Araújo Peres, C., Branco de Almeida, M. F., Xavier Balda, R., Bereguel, R. C., Tonelotto, J., et al. (2000). Differences in pain expression between male and female newborn infants. *Pain, 85,* 127–133.

Guisinger, S., Cowan, P., & Schuldberg, D. (1989). Changing parent and spouse relations in the first year of remarriage of divorced fathers. *Journal of Marriage and the Family, 51,* 445–456.

Gulcher, M., Sutfin, E. L., & Patterson, C. J. (2008). Individual differences in gender development: Associations with parental sexual orientation, attitudes, and division of labor. *Sex Roles, 58,* 330–341.

Gullotta, T. P., Adams, G. R., & Montemayor, R. (Eds.). (1995). *Substance misuse in adolescence.* Thousand Oaks, CA: Sage Publications.

Gullotta, T. P., & Blau, G. M. (2008). *Handbook of childhood behavioral issues: Evidence-based approaches to prevention and treatment.* New York: Routledge/Taylor & Francis Group.

Gump, L. S., Baker, R. C., & Roll, S. (2000). Cultural and gender differences in moral judgment: A study of Mexican Americans and Anglo-Americans. *Hispanic Journal of Behavioral Sciences, 22,* 78–93.

Gunnarsdottir, I., & Thorsdottir, I. (2003). Relationship between growth and feeding in infancy and body mass index at the age of 6 years. *International Journal of Obesity and Metabolic Disorders, 27,* 1523–1527.

Gupta, A., & State, M. (2007). Recent advances in the genetics of autism. *Biological Psychiatry, 61,* 429–437.

Gupta, R., Pascoe, J., Blanchard, T., Langkamp, D., Duncan, P., Gorski, P., et al. (2009). Child health in child care: A multistate survey of Head Start and non–Head Start child care directors. *Journal of Pediatric Health Care, 23,* 143–149.

Gupta, U., & Singh, P. (1982). An exploratory study of love and liking and type of marriages. *Indian Journal of Applied Psychology, 19,* 92–97.

Gur, R. C., Gur, R. E., Obrist, W. D., Hungerbuhler, J. P., Younkin, D., Rosen, A. D., et al. (1982). Sex and handedness differences in cerebral blood flow during rest and cognitive activity. *Science, 217,* 659–661.

Gur, R. C., Turetsky, B. I., Matsui, M., Yan, M., Bilker, W., Hughett, P., et al. (1999). Sex differences in brain gray and white matter in healthy young adults: Correlations with cognitive performance. *Journal of Neuroscience, 19,* 4065–4072.

Gur, R. E., & Chin, S. (1999). Laterality in functional brain imaging studies of schizophrenia. *Schizophrenia Bulletin, 25,* 141–156.

Guralnik, M. D., Ferrucci, L., Simonsick, E. M., Salive, M. E., & Wallace, R. B. (1995, March 2). Lower-extremity function in persons over the age of 70 years as a predictor of subsequent disability. *New England Journal of Medicine, 332,* 556–561.

Güre, A., Uçanok, Z., & Sayil, M. (2006). The associations among perceived pubertal timing, parental relations and self-perception in Turkish adolescents. *Journal of Youth and Adolescence, 35,* 541–550.

Gurin, P., Nagda, B. A., & Lopez, G. F. (2004). The benefits of diversity in education for democratic citizenship. *Journal of Social Issues, 60,* 17–34.

Gurin, P., Nagda, B. R. A., & Lopez, G. E. (2005). Improving the first year of college: Research and practice. *Journal of Social Issues, 60,* 17–34.

Güroglu, B., van Lieshout, C., Haselager, G., & Scholte, R. (2007). Similarity and complementary of behavioral profiles of friendship types and types of friends: Friendships and psychosocial adjustment. *Journal of Research on Adolescence, 17,* 357–386.

Gustafsson, P. A., Duchen, K., Birberg, U., & Karlsson, T. (2004). Breastfeeding, very long polyunsaturated fatty acids (PUFA) and IQ at 6 1/2 years of age. *Acta Paediatrica, 93,* 1280–1287.

Gustavsson, N. S., & MacEachron, A. E. (2011). No foster child left behind: Child welfare policy perspectives on education. *Families in Society, 92,* 276–281.

Gutek, G. L. (2003). Maria Montessori: Contributions to educational psychology. In B. J. Zimmerman (Ed.), *Educational psychology: A century of contributions.* Mahwah, NJ: Lawrence Erlbaum Associates.

Guterl, F. (2002, November 11). What Freud got right. *Newsweek,* pp. 50–51.

Guthrie, G., & Lonner, W. (1986). Assessment of personality and psychopathology. In W. Lonner & J. Berry (Eds.), *Field methods in cross-cultural research.* Newbury Park, CA: Sage.

Guttentag, R. E. (1985). Memory and aging: Implications for theories of memory development during childhood. *Developmental Review, 5,* 56–82.

Guttmacher Institute (2011, January). *Facts on American teens' sexual and reproductive health.* New York: Guttmacher Institute.

Guttman, M. (1997, May 16–18). Are you losing your mind? *USA Weekend,* pp. 4–5.

Guttmann, J., & Rosenberg, M. (2003). Emotional intimacy and children's adjustment: A comparison between single-parent divorced and intact families. *Educational Psychology, 23,* 457–472.

Guyer, B., Freedman, M. A., Strobino, D. M., & Sondik, E. J. (1995). Annual summary of vital statistics—1994. *Pediatrics, 96,* 1029–1039.

Guzzo, K. (2009). Marital intentions and the stability of first cohabitations. *Journal of Family Issues, 30,* 179–205.

Haan, N. (1985). Processes of moral development: Cognitive or social disequilibrium? *Developmental Psychology, 21,* 996–1006.

Haan, N., Millsap, R., & Hartka, E. (1986). As time goes by: Change and stability in personality over fifty years. *Psychology and Aging, 1,* 220–232.

Haas, A. P., Hendin, H., & Mann, J. J. (2003). Suicide in college students. *American Behavioral Scientist, Special issue: Suicide in Youth, 46,* 1224–1240.

Haas-Thompson, T., Alston, P., & Holbert, D. (2008). The impact of education and death-related experiences on rehabilitation counselor attitudes toward death and dying. *Journal of Applied Rehabilitation Counseling, 39,* 20–27.

Haber, D. (2006). Life review: Implementation, theory, research, and therapy. *International Journal of Aging & Human Development, 63,* 153–171.

Haberstick, B. C., Timberlake, D., Ehringer, M. A., Lessem, J. M., Hopfer, C. J., Smolen, A., et al. (2007). Can cigarette warnings counterbalance effects of smoking scenes in movies? *Addiction, 102,* 655–665.

Hack, M., Flannery, D. J., Schluchter, M., Cartar, L., Borawski, E., & Klein, N. (2002). Outcomes in young adulthood for very low birth weight infants. *New England Journal of Medicine, 346,* 149–157.

Hackel, L. S., & Ruble, D. N. (1992). Changes in the marital relationship after the first baby is born: Predicting the impact of expectancy disconfirmation. *Journal of Personality and Social Psychology, 62,* 944–957.

Haddock, S., & Rattenborg, K. (2003). Benefits and challenges of dual-earning: Perspectives of successful couples. *American Journal of Family Therapy, 31,* 325–344.

Hadley, M. (2003). Relational, indirect, adaptive, or just mean: Recent work on aggression in adolescent girls— part I. *Studies in Gender & Sexuality, 4,* 367–394.

Haederle, M. (1999, January 18). Going too far? *People Weekly,* 101–103.

Haeffel, G., Getchell, M., Koposov, R., Yrigollen, C., DeYoung, C., af Klinteberg, B., et al. (2008). Association between polymorphisms in the dopamine transporter gene and depression: Evidence for a gene-environment interaction in a sample of juvenile detainees. *Psychological Science, 19,* 62–69.

Hagerman, R. J. (2011) Fragile X syndrome and fragile X-associated disorders. In S. Goldstein & C. R. Reynolds (Eds.), *Handbook of neurodevelopmental and genetic disorders in children* (2nd ed.). New York: Guilford Press.

Hagerty, R. G., Butow, P. N., Ellis, P. A., Lobb, E. A., Pendlebury, S., Leighl, N., et al. (2004). Cancer patient preferences for communication of prognosis in the metastatic setting. *Journal of Clinical Oncology, 22,* 1721–1730.

Hagestad, G. O., & Neugarten, B. L. (1985). Age and the life course. In R. H. Binstock & E. Shanas (Eds.), *Handbook of aging and the social sciences* (2nd ed.). New York: Van Nostrand Reinhold.

Haggerty, R., Garmezy, N., Rutter, M., & Sherrod, L. (Eds.). (1994). *Stress, risk, and resilience in childhood and adolescence.* New York: Cambridge University Press.

Hahn, C.-S., & DiPietro, J. A. (2001). In vitro fertilization and the family: Quality of parenting, family functioning, and child psychosocial adjustment. *Developmental Psychology, 37,* 37–48.

Haight, B. K. (1991). Psychological illness in aging. In E. M. Baines (Ed.), *Perspectives on gerontological nursing.* Newbury Park, CA: Sage.

Haight, W. L. (2002). *African-American children at church: A sociocultural perspective.* New York: Cambridge University Press.

Haight, W. L., & Black, J. E. (2001). A comparative approach to play: Cross-species and cross-cultural perspectives of play in development. *Human Development, 44,* 228–234.

Haight, W. L., Wang, X., Fung, H. H., Williams, K., & Mintz, J. (1999). Universal developmental and variable aspects of young children's play: A cross-cultural comparison of pretending at home. *Child Development, 70,* 1477–1488.

Haines, C. (2003). Sequencing, co-ordination and rhythm ability in young children, *Child: Care, Health & Development, 29,* 395–409.

Haines, J., & Neumark-Sztainer, D. (2006, December). Prevention of obesity and eating disorders: A consideration of shared risk factors. *Health Education Research, 21,* 770–782.

Haith, M. H. (1986). Sensory and perceptual processes in early infancy. *Journal of Pediatrics, 109*(1), 158–171.

Haith, M. H. (1991, April). *Setting a path for the 90s: Some goals and challenges in infant sensory and perceptual development.* Paper presented at the biennial meeting of the Society for Research in Child Development, Seattle.

Haith, M. M. (1993). *Future-oriented processes in infancy: The case of visual expectations.* Hillsdale, NJ: Lawrence Erlbaum Associates.

Haith, M. M. (1994). *Visual expectations as the first step toward the development of future-oriented processes.* Chicago: University of Chicago Press.

Hakuta, K. U., & Garcia, E. E. (1989). Bilingualism and education. *American Psychologist, 44,* 374–379.

Halberstadt, A. G. (1991). *Toward an ecology of expressiveness: Family socialization in particular and a model in general.* New York: Cambridge University Press.

Halberstadt, A., & Eaton, K. (1998). Family factors in nonverbal behavior. In P. Philipott, R. S. Feldman, & E. J. Coats (Eds.), *The social context of nonverbal behavior.* Cambridge, England: Cambridge University Press.

Hale, M. (2009, July 15). The woman behind the boy wizard. *New York Times.*

Haleem, M., Barton, K., Borges, G., Crozier, A., & Anderson, A. (2008). Increasing antioxidant intake from fruits and vegetables: Practical strategies for the Scottish population. *Journal of Human Nutrition and Dietetics, 21,* 539–546.

Hales, D. (1992). *An invitation to health: Taking charge of your life.* Menlo Park, CA: Benjamin/Cumings.

Hales, K. A., Morgan, M. A., & Thurnau, G. R. (1993). Influence of labor and route of delivery on the frequency of respiratory morbidity in term neonates. *International Journal of Gynecology & Obstetrics, 43,* 35–40.

Haley, M., & Vasquez, J. (2008). A future in jeopardy: Sexuality issues in adolescence. In D. Capuzzi & D. R. Gross (Eds.), *Youth at risk: A prevention resource for counselors, teachers, and parents.* Alexandria, VA: American Counseling Association.

Halford, G. (2005). Development of thinking. *The Cambridge handbook of thinking and reasoning.* New York: Cambridge University Press.

Halford, G., & Andrews, G. (2006). Reasoning and problem solving. *Handbook of child psychology: Vol 2, Cognition, perception, and language* (6th ed.). Hoboken, NJ: John Wiley & Sons Inc.

Halford, G. S., Maybery, M. T., O'Hare, A. W., & Grant, P. (1994). The development of memory and processing capacity. *Child Development, 65,* 1338–1356.

Halgunseth, L. C., Ispa, J. M., & Rudy, D. (2006). Parental control in Latino families: An integrated review of the literature. *Child Development, 77,* 1282–1297.

Hall, E. G., & Lee, A. M. (1984). Sex differences in motor performance of young children: Fact or fiction? *Sex Roles, 10,* 217–230.

Hall, G. S. (1916). *Adolescence.* New York: Appleton. (Original work published 1904)

Hall, J., Neal, T., & Dean, R. (2008). Lateralization of cerebral functions. *The neuropsychology handbook* (3rd ed.). New York: Springer Publishing Co.

Hall, R. E., & Rowan, G. T. (2003). Identity development across the life span: Alternative model for biracial Americans. *Psychology and Education: An Interdisciplinary Journal, 40,* 3–12.

Hall, R., Huitt, T., Thapa, R., Williams, D., Anand, K., & Garcia-Rill, E. (2008). Long-term deficits of preterm birth: Evidence for arousal and attentional disturbances. *Clinical Neurophysiology, 119,* 1281–1291.

Hall, S. (2006). Marital meaning: Exploring young adults' belief systems about marriage. *Journal of Family Issues, 27,* 1437–1458.

Hall, S. S. (2005, October 16). The short of it. *The New York Times Magazine,* pp. 54–59.

Hallahan, D. P., Kauffman, J. M., & Lloyd, J. W. (2000). *Introduction to learning disabilities* (4th ed.). Boston: Allyn & Bacon.

Hallberg, H. (1992). Life after divorce: A five-year follow-up study of divorced middle-aged men in Sweden. *Family Practice, 9,* 49–56.

Halliday, M. A. K. (1975). *Learning how to mean— Explorations in the development of language.* London: Edward Arnold.

Hallinan, M. T., & Williams, R. A. (1989). Interracial friendship choices in secondary schools. *American Sociological Review, 54,* 67–78.

Hallpike, C. (2008). The anthropology of moral development. *Social life and social knowledge: Toward a process account of development.* New York: Taylor & Francis Group/Lawrence Erlbaum Associates.

Halpern, D. F. (1996). *Thought and knowledge: An introduction to critical thinking* (3rd ed.). Mahwah, NJ: Lawrence Erlbaum Associates.

Halpern, D. (2009). *Thought and knowledge: An introduction to critical thinking* (4th ed.). Mahwah, NJ: Erlbaum. (Kindle edition)

Halpern, D. F., Haviland, M. G., & Killian, C. D. (1998). Handedness and sex differences in intelligence: Evidence from the Medical College Admission Test. *Brain & Cognition, 38,* 87–101.

Halpern, L. F., MacLean, W. E., & Baumeister, A. A. (1995). Infant sleep-wake characteristics: Relation to neurological status and the prediction of developmental outcome. *Developmental Review, 15,* 255–291.

Halpern, S. H., Leighton, B. L., Ohlsson, A., Barrett, J. F. R., & Rice, A. (1998). Effect of epidural vs. parenteral opioid analgesia on the progress of labor. *Journal of the American Medical Association, 280,* 2105–2110.

Hamberger, L., & Holtzworth-Munroe, A. (2007). Spousal abuse. *Cognitive-behavioral strategies in crisis intervention* (3rd ed., pp. 277–299). New York: Guilford Press.

Hamilton, C. (2000). Continuity and discontinuity of attachment from infancy through adolescence. *Child Development, 71,* 690–694.

Hamilton, G. (1998). Positively testing. *Families in Society, 79,* 570–576.

Hamilton, M., & Yee, J. (1990). Rape knowledge and propensity to rape. *Journal of Research in Personality, 24,* 111–122.

Hamlin, J., Hallinan, E., & Woodward, A. (2008). Do as I do: 7-month-old infants selectively reproduce others' goals. *Developmental Science, 11,* 487–494.

Hamm, J. V. (2000). Do birds of a feather flock together? The variable bases for African American, Asian American, and European American adolescents' selection of similar friends. *Developmental Psychology, 36,* 209–219.

Hammer, J. (1992, October 26). Must blacks be buffoons? *Newsweek,* pp. 70–71.

Hammer, R. P. (1984). The sexually dimorphic region of the preoptic area in rats contains denser opiate receptor binding sites in females. *Brain Researcher, 308,* 172–176.

Hammersley, M. (1992). *What's wrong with ethnography?* New York: Routledge.

Hammersley, R. (1992). Cue exposure and learning theory. *Addictive Behaviors, 17,* 297–300.

Hammond, S. I., Müller, U., Carpendale, J. M., Bibok, M. B., & Liebermann-Finestone, D. P. (2012). The effects of parental scaffolding on preschoolers' executive function. *Developmental Psychology, 48,* 271–281.

Hammond, W. A., & Romney, D. M. (1995). Cognitive factors contributing to adolescent depression. *Journal of Youth & Adolescence, 24,* 667–683.

Hamon, R. R., & Blieszner, R. (1990). Filial responsibility expectations among adult child–older parent pairs. *Journal of Gerontology, 45,* 110–112.

Hamon, R. R., & Ingoldsby, B. B. (Eds.). (2003). *Mate selection across cultures.* Thousand Oaks, CA: Sage.

Hampson, J., & Nelson, K. (1993). The relation of maternal language to variation in rate and style of language acquisition. *Journal of Child Language, 20,* 313–342.

Han, W. (2012). Bilingualism and academic achievement. *Child Development, 83,* 300–321.

Handwerk, M. L. (2002). Least restrictive alternative: Challenging assumptions and further implications. *Children's Services: Social Policy, Research, & Practice, 5,* 99–103.

Hane, A., Feldstein, S., & Dernetz, V. (2003). The relation between coordinated interpersonal timing and maternal sensitivity in four-month-old infants. *Journal of Psycholinguistic Research, 32,* 525–539.

Haney, W. M. (2008). Evidence on education under NCLB (and how Florida boosted NAEP scores and reduced the race gap). In Gail L. Sunderman (Ed.), *Holding NCLB accountable: Achieving, accountability, equity & school reform.* Thousand Oaks, CA: Corwin Press.

Hanger, H., Fogarty, B., Wilkinson, T., & Sainsbury, R. (2000). Stroke patients' views on stroke outcomes: Death versus disability. *Clinical Rehabilitation, 14,* 417–424.

Hankin, B. L., & Abramson, L. Y. (2001). Development of gender differences in depression: An elaborated cognitive vulnerability-transactional stress theory. *Psychological Bulletin, 127,* 773–796.

Hanna, E., & Meltzoff, A. N. (1993). Peer imitation by toddlers in laboratory, home, and day-care contexts: Implications for social learning and memory. *Developmental Psychology, 29,* 701–710.

Hansen, C. H. (1989). Priming sex-role stereotypic even schemas with rock music videos: Effects on impression favorability, trait inferences, and recall of subsequent male–female interaction. *Basic and Applied Social Psychology, 10,* 371–391.

Hanson, D. R., & Gottesman, I. I. (2005). Theories of schizophrenia: A genetic-inflammatory-vascular synthesis. *BMC Medical Genetics, 6,* 7.

Hanson, R., & Hayslip, B. (2000). Widowhood in later life. In J. Harvey & E. Miller (Eds.), *Loss and trauma: General and close relationship perspectives.* New York: Brunner-Routledge.

Hanson, R. F., & Spratt, E. G. (2000). Reactive attachment disorder: What we know about the disorder and implications for treatment. *Child Maltreatment, 5*, 137–145.

Hansson, R. O., & Carpenter, B. N. (1994). *Relationship in old age: Coping with the challenge of transition.* New York: Guilford Press.

Hansson, R., Daleiden, E., & Hayslip, B. (2004). Relational competence across the life span. *Growing together: Personal relationships across the lifespan* (pp. 317–340). New York: Cambridge University Press.

Hansson, R., & Stroebe, M. (2007). *Bereavement in late life: Coping, adaptation, and developmental influences.* Washington, DC: American Psychological Association.

Happe, F. G. E., Winner, E., & Brownell, H. (1998). The getting of wisdom: Theory of mind in old age. *Developmental Psychology, 34*, 358–362.

Harakeh, Z., & Vollebergh, W. M. (2012). The impact of active and passive peer influence on young adult smoking: An experimental study. *Drug and Alcohol Dependence, 121*, 220–223.

Harden, B. (2000, January 9). Very young, smart, and restless. *New York Times Education Life,* pp. 28–31.

Harden, K., Turkheimer, E., & Loehlin, J. (2007). Genotype by environment interaction in adolescents' cognitive aptitude. *Behavior Genetics, 37*, 273–283.

Hardy, L. T. (2007). Attachment theory and reactive attachment disorder: Theoretical perspectives and treatment implications. *Journal of Child and Adolescent Psychiatric Nursing, 20*, 27–39.

Hardy, S., & Grogan, S. (2009). Preventing disability through exercise: Investigating older adults' influences and motivations to engage in physical activity. *Journal of Health Psychology, 14*, 1036–1046.

Hardy, S. A., Pratt, M. W., Pancer, S., Olsen, J. A., & Lawford, H. L. (2011). Community and religious involvement as contexts of identity change across late adolescence and emerging adulthood. *International Journal of Behavioral Development, 35*, 125–135.

Hare, T., Tottenham, N., Galvan, A., Voss, H., Glover, G., & Casey, B. (2008, May). Biological substrates of emotional reactivity and regulation in adolescence during an emotional go-nogo task. *Biological Psychiatry, 63*(10), 927–934.

Hareli, S., & Hess, U. (2008). When does feedback about success at school hurt? The role of causal attributions. *Social Psychology of Education, 11*, 259–272.

Hargreaves, D., & Tiggemann, M. (2003). The effect of "thin ideal" television commercials on body dissatisfaction and schema activation during early adolescence. *Journal of Youth and Adolescence, 32*, 367–373.

Harker, L. A., & Keltner, D. (2001). Expressions of positive emotion in women's college yearbook pictures and their relationship to personality and life outcomes across adulthood. *Journal of Personality & Social Psychology, 80*, 112–124.

Harkness, S., & Super, C. M. (1985). The cultural context of gender segregation in children's peer groups. *Child Development, 56*, 219–224.

Harlow, H. F., & Zimmerman, R. R. (1959). Affectional responses in the infant monkey. *Science, 130*, 421–432.

Harman, S., Naftolin, F., Brinton, E., & Judelson, D. (2005). Is the estrogen controversy over? Deconstructing the Women's Health Initiative study: A critical evaluation of the evidence. In M. Singh & J. Simpkins (Eds.), *The future of hormone therapy: What basic science and clinical studies teach us.* New York: New York Academy of Sciences.

Harmon, A. (1997, October 25). Internet's value in U.S. schools still in question. *The New York Times,* p. A1.

Harmon, A. (2004, August 26). Internet gives teenage bullies weapons to would from afar. *The New York Times,* A1, A21.

Harrell, J. S., Bangdiwala, S. I., Deng, S., Webb, J. P., & Bradley, C. (1998). Smoking initiation in youth: The roles of gender, race, socioeconomics, and developmental status. *Journal of Adolescent Health, 23*, 271–279.

Harrell, J. S., Gansky, S. A., Bradley, C. B., & McMurray, R. G. (1997). Leisure time activities of elementary school children. *Nursing Research, 46*, 246–253.

Harrell, S. (1981). Growing old in rural Taiwan. In P. T. Amoss & S. Harrell (Eds.), *Other ways of growing old.* Stanford, CA: Stanford University Press.

Harrell, Z., & Karim, N. (2008, February). Is gender relevant only for problem alcohol behaviors? An examination of correlates of alcohol use among college students. *Addictive Behaviors, 33*(2), 359–365.

Harrington, R., Fudge, H., Rutter, M., Pickels, A., & Hill, J. (1990). Adult outcomes of childhood and adolescent depression. *Archives of General Psychiatry, 47*, 465–473.

Harris, A. A. (2010). Practical advice for caring for women with eating disorders during the perinatal period. *Journal of Midwifery & Women's Health, 55*(6), 579–586.

Harris, A., Cronkite, R., & Moos, R. (2006, July). Physical activity, exercise coping, and depression in a 10-year cohort study of depressed patients. *Journal of Affective Disorders, 93*, 79–85.

Harris, B., Lovell, L., Smith, J., Read, G., Walker, R., & Newcombe, R. (1996). Cardiff puerperal mood and hormone study. III. Postnatal depression at 5 to 6 weeks postpartum, and its hormonal correlates across the peripartum period. *British Journal of Psychiatry, 168*, 739–744.

Harris, B., Lovell, L., Smith, J., Read, G., Walker, R., & Riad-Fahmy, D. (1994). Maternity blues and major endocrine changes: Cardiff puerperal mood and hormone study II. *British Medical Journal, 308*, 949–953.

Harris, C. M. (2004). Personality and sexual orientation. *College Student Journal, 38*, 207–211.

Harris, G. (2005, March 3). Gene therapy is facing a crucial hearing. *The New York Times,* p. A16.

Harris, J. (2004). *On cloning.* New York: Routledge.

Harris, J. (2006). *No two alike: Human nature and human individuality.* New York: W. W. Norton & Co.

Harris, J., Vernon, P., & Jang, K. (2007). Rated personality and measured intelligence in young twin children. *Personality and Individual Differences, 42*, 75–86.

Harris, J. F., Durso, F. T., Mergler, N. L., & Jones, S. K. (1990). Knowledge base influences on judgments of frequency of occurrence. *Cognitive Development, 5*, 223–233.

Harris, J. R. (1998). *The nurture assumption: Why children turn out the way they do.* New York: Free Press.

Harris, J. R. (2000). Socialization, personality development, and the child's environments: Comment on Vandell. *Developmental Psychology, 36*, 711–723.

Harris, K. M. (1999). The health status and risk behavior of adolescents in immigrant families. In D. J. Hernandez (Ed.), *Children of immigrants: Health, adjustment, and public assistance.* Washington, DC: National Academy Press.

Harris, L. K., VanZandt, C. E., & Rees, T. H. (1997). Counseling needs of students who are deaf and hard of hearing. *School Counselor, 44*, 271–279.

Harris, M., Prior, J., & Koehoorn, M. (2008). Age at menarche in the Canadian population: Secular trends and relationship to adulthood BMI. *Journal of Adolescent Health, 43*, 548–554.

Harris, M. B. (1994). Growing old gracefully: Age concealment and gender. *Journals of Gerontology, 49*, 149–158.

Harris, M. J., Milich, R., Corbitt, E. M., Hoover, D. W., & Brady, M. (1992). Self-fulfilling effects of stigmatizing information on children's social interactions. *Journal of Personality and Social Psychology, 63*, 41–50.

Harris, M. J., & Rosenthal, R. (1986). Four factors in the mediation of teacher expectancy effects. In R. S. Feldman (Ed.), *The social psychology of education.* Cambridge, MA: Cambridge University Press.

Harris, P. L. (1983). Infant cognition. In M. Haith & J. J. Campos (Eds.) & P. H. Mussen (Gen. Ed.), *Handbook of child psychology: Vol 2. Infancy and developmental psychobiology.* New York: Wiley.

Harris, P. L. (1987). The development of search. In P. Sallapatek & L. Cohen (Eds.), *Handbook of infant perception: From perception to cognition* (Vol. 2, pp. 155–207). Orlando, FL: Academic Press.

Harrison, K., & Bond, B. (2007). Gaming magazines and the drive for muscularity in preadolescent boys: A longitudinal examination. *Body Image, 4*, 269–277.

Harrison, K., & Hefner, V. (2006, April). Media exposure, current and future body ideals, and disordered eating among preadolescent girls: A longitudinal panel study. *Journal of Youth and Adolescence, 35*, 153–163.

Harrison, R. V., Gordon, K. A., & Mount, R. J. (2005). Is there a critical period for cochlear implantation in congenitally deaf children? Analyses of hearing and speech perception performance after implantation. *Developmental Psychobiology, 46*, 252–261.

Harrist, A., & Waugh, R. (2002). Dyadic synchrony: Its structure and function in children's development. *Developmental Review, 22*, 555–592.

Hart, B. (2000). A natural history of early language experience. *Topics in Early Childhood Special Education, 20*, 28–32.

Hart, B. (2004). What toddlers talk about. *First Language, 24*, 91–106.

Hart, B., & Risley, T. R. (1995). *Meaningful differences in the everyday experience of young American children.* Baltimore, MD: Paul Brookes.

Hart, C. H., Yang, C., Nelson, D. A., Jin, S., Bazarskaya, N., & Nelson, L. (1998). Peer contact patterns, parenting practices, and preschoolers' social competence in China, Russia, and the United States. In P. Slee & K. Rigby (Eds.), *Peer relations amongst children: Current issues and future directions.* London: Routledge.

Hart, D., Burock, D., & London, B. (2003). Prosocial tendencies, antisocial behavior, and moral development. In A. Slater & G. Bremner (Eds.), *An introduction to developmental psychology.* Malden, MA: Blackwell Publishers.

Hart, S., & Carrington, H. (2002). Jealousy in six-month-old infants. *Infancy, 3*, 395–402.

Hart, S., Carrington, H., Tronick, E. Z., & Carroll, S. (2004). When infants lose exclusive maternal attention: Is it jealousy? *Infancy, 6*, 57–78.

Hart, S., Field, T., del Valle, C., & Letourneau, M. (1998). Infants protest their mothers' attending to an infant-size doll. *Social Development, 7*, 54–61.

Hart, S. L. (2010). The ontogenesis of jealousy in the first year of life: A theory of jealousy as a biologically-based dimension of temperament. In S. L. Hart & M. Legerstee (Eds.), *Handbook of jealousy: Theory, research, and multidisciplinary approaches.* New York: Wiley-Blackwell.

Hart, S. N., Brassard, M. R., & Karlson, H. (1996). Psychological maltreatment. In J. N. Briere, L. Berliner, J. Bulkley, C. Jenny, & T. Reid (Eds.), *The APSAC handbook on child maltreatment.* Thousand Oaks, CA: Sage.

Harter, S. (1990a). Identity and self-development. In S. S. Feldman & G. R. Elliott (Eds.), *At the threshold: The developing adolescent.* Cambridge, MA: Harvard University Press.

Harter, S. (1990b). Issues in the assessment of self-concept of children and adolescents. In A. LaGreca (Ed.), *Through the eyes of a child.* Boston: Allyn & Bacon.

Harter, S. (2006a). The development of self-esteem. *Self-esteem issues and answers: A sourcebook of current perspectives.* New York: Psychology Press.

Harter, S. (2006b). The self. In *Handbook of child psychology: Vol. 3, Social, emotional, and personality development* (6th ed.). Hoboken, NJ: John Wiley & Sons Inc.

Hartley, A. A. (1993). Evidence for selective preservation of spatial selective attention in old age. *Psychology and Aging, 8*, 371–379.

Hartshorne, J., & Ullman, M. (2006). Why girls say "holded" more than boys. *Developmental Science, 9,* 21–32.

Hartshorne, T. S. (1994). Friendship. In V. S. Ramachandran (Ed.), *Encyclopedia of human behavior.* San Diego: Academic Press.

Hartup, W. W. (1983). Peer relations. In P. H. Mussen (Ed.), *Handbook of child psychology* (Vol. 4, 4th ed.). New York: Wiley.

Hartup, W. W., & Stevens, N. (1997). Friendships and adaptation in the life course. *Psychological Bulletin, 121,* 355–370.

Hartup, W. W., & Stevens, N. (1999). Friendships and adaptation across the life span. *Current Directions in Psychological Science, 8,* 76–79.

Harvey, A., Mullin, B., & Hinshaw, S. (2006). Sleep and circadian rhythms in children and adolescents with bipolar disorder. *Development and Psychopathology, 18,* 1147–1168.

Harvey, E. (1999). Short-term and long-term effects of early parental employment on children of the National Longitudinal Survey of Youth. *Developmental Psychology, 35,* 445–459.

Harvey, J. H., & Fine, M. A. (2004). *Children of divorce: Stories of loss and growth.* Mahwah, NJ: Lawrence Erlbaum Associates.

Harvey, J., & Weber, A. (2002). *Odyssey of the heart: Close relationships in the 21st century* (2nd ed.). Mahwah, NJ: Lawrence Erlbaum Associates.

Harvey, P. G., Hamlin, M. W., Kumar, R., & Delves, H. T. (1984). Blood lead, behavior, and intelligence test performance in preschool children. *Science of the Total Environment, 40,* 45–60.

Harway, M. (2000). Families experiencing violence. In W. C. Nichols & M. A. Pace-Nichols, et al. (Eds.), *Handbook of family development and intervention. Wiley series in couples and family dynamics and treatment.* New York: Wiley.

Harwood, R. L., Miller, J. G., & Irizarry, N. L. (1995). *Culture and attachment: Perceptions of the child in context.* New York: Guilford Press.

Harwood, R. L., Schoelmerich, A., Ventura-Cook, E., Schulze, P. A., & Wilson, S. P. (1996). Culture and class influences on Anglo and Puerto Rican mothers' beliefs regarding long-term socialization goals and child behavior. *Child Development, 67,* 2446–2461.

Hasher, L., & Zacks, R. T. (1984). Automatic processing of fundamental information: The case of frequency of occurrence. *American Psychologist, 39,* 1372–1388.

Haskett, M., Nears, K., Ward, C., & McPherson, A. (2006, October). Diversity in adjustment of maltreated children: Factors associated with resilient functioning. *Clinical Psychology Review, 26,* 796–812.

Haskins, R. (1989). Beyond metaphor: The efficacy of early childhood education. *American Psychologist, 44,* 274–282.

Haslam, C., & Lawrence, W. (2004). Health-related behavior and beliefs of pregnant smokers. *Health Psychology, 23,* 486–491.

Haslam, N. (2007). *Introduction to personality and intelligence.* Thousand Oaks, CA: Sage Publications, Inc.

Haslett, A. (2004, May 31). Love supreme. *The New Yorker,* pp. 76–80.

Hastings, D. (2010, October 4). Where is the world's first "test tube" baby now? *AOL News.* Retrieved from http://www.aolnews.com/2010/10/04/where-is-louise-brown-worlds-first-test-tube-baby/.

Hastings, P. D., McShane, K. E., Parker, R., & Ladha, F. (2007). Ready to make nice: Parental socialization of young sons' and daughters' prosocial behaviors with peers. *Journal of Genetic Psychology, 168,* 177–200.

Hastings, S. (2004, October 15). Emotional intelligence. *The Times Educational Supplement, London,* F1.

Hatfield, E. (1988). Passionate and companionate love. In R. J. Sternberg & M. L. Barnes (Eds.), *The psychology of love* (pp. 191–217). New Haven, CT: Yale University Press.

Hatfield, E., & Rapson, R. L. (1993). Historical and cross-cultural perspectives on passionate love and sexual desire. *Annual Review of Sex Research, 4,* 67–97.

Hatfield, E., & Sprecher, S. (1986). *Mirror, mirror … The importance of looks in everyday life.* Albany: State University of New York Press.

Hattery, A. (2000). *Women, work, and family: Balancing and weaving.* Thousand Oaks, CA: Sage.

Hauck, F. R. & Hunt, C. E. (2000). Sudden infant death syndrome in 2000. *Current Problems in Pediatrics, 30*(8), 237–261.

Haug, H. (1991). Aging of the brain. In F. C. Ludwig (Ed.), *Life-span extension: Consequences, intimacy, and close relationships.* New York: Springer.

Haugaard, J. J. (2000). The challenge of defining child sexual abuse. *American Psychologist, 55,* 1036–1039.

Hauser, M., Chomsky, N., & Fitch, W. (2002). The faculty of language: What is it, who has it, and how did it evolve? *Science, 298,* 1569–1579.

Hauser, S., Allen, J., & Golden, E. (2006). *Out of the woods: Tales of resilient teens.* Cambridge, MA: Harvard University Press.

Havighurst, R. J. (1973). Social roles, work, leisure, and education. In C. Eisdorfer & M. P. Lawton (Eds.), *The psychology of adult development and aging.* Washington, DC: American Psychological Association.

Havighurst, R. J., Neugarten, B. L., & Tobin, S. S. (1968). Disengagement and patterns of aging. In B. L. Neugarten (Ed.), *Middle age and aging.* Chicago: University of Chicago Press.

Haviv, S., & Leman, P. (2002). Moral decision-making in real life: Factors affecting moral orientation and behaviour justification. *Journal of Moral Education, 31,* 121–140.

Hawkins, A. O., Danielson, C. K., de Arellan, M. A., Hanson, R. F., Ruggiero, K. J., Smith, D. W., et al. (2010). Ethnic/racial differences in the prevalence of injurious spanking and other child physical abuse in a National Survey of Adolescents. *Child Maltreatment, 15,* 242–249.

Hawkins, S. A., Cockburn, M. G., Hamilton, A. S., & Mack, T. M. (2004). An estimate of physical activity prevalence in a large population-based cohort. *Medical Science and Sports Exercise, 36,* 253–260.

Hawkins-Rodgers, Y. (2007). Adolescents adjusting to a group home environment: A residential care model of reorganizing attachment behavior and building resiliency. *Children and Youth Services Review, 29,* 1131–1141.

Hawley, P. (2007). Social dominance in childhood and adolescence: Why social competence and aggression may go hand in hand. In *Aggression and adaptation: The bright side to bad behavior.* Mahwah, NJ: Lawrence Erlbaum Associates.

Hawton, K. (1986). *Suicide and attempted suicide among children and adolescents.* Newbury Park, CA: Sage.

Hay, D. F., Pawlby, S., & Angold, A. (2003). Pathways to violence in the children of mothers who were depressed postpartum. *Developmental Psychology, 39,* 1083–1094.

Hay, D., Payne, A., & Chadwick, A. (2004). Peer relations in childhood. *Journal of Child Psychology & Psychiatry & Allied Disciplines, 45,* 84–108.

Hayden, T. (1998, September 21). The brave new world of sex selection. *Newsweek,* p. 93.

Hayes, S., & Tantleff-Dunn, S. (2010). Am I too fat to be a princess? Examining the effects of popular children's media on young girls' body image. *British Journal of Developmental Psychology, 28,* 413–426.

Hayflick, L. (1974). The strategy of senescence. *The Journal of Gerontology, 14,* 37–45.

Hayflick, L. (2007). Biological aging is no longer an unsolved problem. *Annals of the New York Academy of Sciences,* pp. 1–13.

Haymes, M., Green, L., & Quinto, R. (1984). Maslow's hierarchy, moral development, and prosocial behavioral skills within a child psychiatric population. *Motivation and Emotion, 8,* 23–31.

Hayne, H., & Rovee-Collier, C. (1995). The organization of reactivated memory in infancy. *Child Development, 66,* 893–906.

Haynie, D. L., Nansel, T., Eitel, P., Crump, A. D., Saylor, K., Yu, K., et al. (2001). Bullies, victims, and bully/victims: Distinct groups of at-risk youth. *Journal of Early Adolescence, 21,* 29–49.

Hayslip, B., Servaty, H. L., Christman, T., & Mumy, E. (1997). Levels of death anxiety in terminally ill persons: A cross validation and extension. *Omega—Journal of Death & Dying, 34,* 203–217.

Hayslip, B., Jr., Shore, R. J., & Henderson, C. E. (2000). Perceptions of grandparents' influence in the lives of their grandchildren. In B. Hayslip Jr., R. Goldberg, & G. Robin (Eds.), *Grandparents raising grandchildren: Theoretical, empirical, and clinical perspectives.* New York: Springer.

Hays-Thomas, R. (2004). Why now? The contemporary focus on managing diversity. In M. S. Stockdale & F. J. Crosby, *Psychology and management of workplace diversity.* Malden, MA: Blackwell Publishers.

Hayward, M., Crimmins, E., & Saito, Y. (1997). Cause of death and active life expectancy in the older population of the United States. *Journal of Aging and Health,* 122–131.

Hazan, C., & Shaver, P. (1987). Romantic love conceptualized as an attachment process. *Journal of Personality and Social Psychology, 52,* 511–524.

Hazell, P. (1993). Adolescent suicide clusters: Evidence, mechanisms and prevention. *Australian and New Zealand Journal of Psychiatry, 27,* 653–665.

Hazell, T., Kenno, K., & Jakobi, J. (2007). Functional benefit of power training for older adults. *Journal of Aging and Physical Activity, 15,* 349–359.

Hazin, A. N., Alves, J. G., & Rodrigues Falbo, A. (2007). The myelenation process in severely malnourished children: MRI findings. *International Journal of Neuroscience, 117,* 1209–1214.

Hazlett, H., Gaspar De Alba, M., & Hooper, S. R. (2011). Klinefelter syndrome. In S. Goldstein, C. R. Reynolds, S. Goldstein, & C. R. Reynolds (Eds.), *Handbook of neurodevelopmental and genetic disorders in children* (2nd ed.). New York: Guilford Press.

Healey, J. M. (2001). *Loving lefties: How to raise your left-handed child in a right-handed world.* New York: Atria.

Health eLine. (2003, June 26). Baby's injury points to danger of kids imitating TV. *Health eLine.*

Health News. (2004). Moderate exercise, without dieting, can prevent further weight gain. *Health News, 10,* 4.

Health Resources and Services Administration. (2001). *Child Health USA, 2001.* Washington, DC: U.S. Department of Health and Human Services.

Healy, P. (2001, March 3). Data on suicides set off alarm. *Boston Globe,* p. B1.

Heath, A. C. (1994, February). Winning at sports. *Parents,* pp. 126–130.

Heath, D., & Heath, H. (2005). *Growing more mature: Insights from the lives of highly achieving men and women.* Bryn Mawr, PA: Conrow Publishing House.

Heatherton, T. F., Polivy, J., & Herman, C. P. (1991). Restraint, weight loss, and variability of body weight. *Journal of Abnormal Psychology, 100,* 78–83.

Heaven, P., & Ciarrochi, J. (2008). Parental styles, gender and the development of hope and self-esteem. *European Journal of Personality, 22,* 707–724.

Hebebrand, J., & Hinney, A. (2009). Environmental and genetic risk factors in obesity. *Child and Adolescent Psychiatric Clinics of North America, 18,* 83–94.

Hebert, T. P. (1998). Gifted black males in an urban high school: Factors that influence achievement and underachievement. *Journal for the Education of the Gifted, 21*, 385–414.

Hecht, M. L., Marston, P. J., & Larkey, L. K. (1994). Love ways and relationship quality in heterosexual relationships. *Journal of Social and Personal Relationships, 11*, 25–43.

Heckhausen, J., Dixon, R. A., & Baltes, P. B. (1989). Gains and losses in development throughout adulthood as perceived by different adult age groups. *Developmental Psychology, 25*, 109–121.

Hedge, J., Borman, W., & Lammlein, S. (2006). *Age stereotyping and age discrimination.* Washington, DC: American Psychological Association.

Hedgepeth, E. (2005). Different lenses, different vision. *School Administrator, 62*, 36–39.

Heerey, E. A., Keltner, D., & Capps, L. M. (2003). Making sense of self-conscious emotion: Linking theory of mind and emotion in children with autism. *Emotion, 3*, 394–400.

Heimann, M. (2001). Neonatal imitation—A "fuzzy" phenomenon? In F. Lacerda & C. von Hofsten (Eds.), *Emerging cognitive abilities in early infancy.* Mahwah, NJ: Lawrence Erlbaum Associates.

Heimann, M. (Ed.). (2003). *Regression periods in human infancy.* Mahwah, NJ: Lawrence Erlbaum Associates.

Heimann, M., Strid, K., Smith, L., Tjus, T., Ulvund, S., & Meltzoff, A. (2006). Exploring the relation between memory, gestural communication, and the emergence of language in infancy: A longitudinal study. *Infant and Child Development, 15*, 233–249.

Heinemann, G. D., & Evans, P. L. (1990). Widowhood: Loss, change, and adaptation. In T. H. Brubaker (Ed.), *Family relationships in later life.* Newbury Park, CA: Sage.

Heiser, S. (2007, May 23). 66-year-old woman's cross-country cycling feat tough to beat. *York Dispatch,* p. 1.

Hellman, P. (1987, November 23). *Sesame Street* smart. *New York,* pp. 49–53.

Helms, J. E., Jernigan, M., & Mascher, J. (2005). The meaning of race in psychology and how to change it: A methodological perspective. *American Psychologist, 60*, 27–36.

Helmsen, J., Koglin, U., & Petermann, F. (2012). Emotion regulation and aggressive behavior in preschoolers: The mediating role of social information processing. *Child Psychiatry and Human Development, 43*, 87–101.

Helmuth, L. (2003, February 28). The wisdom of the wizened. *Science, 299*, 1300–1302.

Helson R., & Moane, G. (1987). Personality change in women from college to midlife. *Journal of Personality and Social Psychology, 53*, 176–186.

Helson, R., & Roberts, B. W. (1994). Ego development and personality change in adulthood. *Journal of Personality and Social Psychology, 66*, 911–920.

Helson, R., & Soto, C. (2005). Up and down in middle age: Monotonic and nonmonotonic changes in roles, status, and personality. *Journal of Personality and Social Psychology, 89*, 194–204.

Helson, R., Soto, C., & Cate, R. (2006). From young adulthood through the middle ages. In *Handbook of personality development.* Mahwah, NJ: Lawrence Erlbaum Associates.

Helson, R., & Srivastava, S. (2001). Three paths of adult development: Conservers, seekers, and achievers. *Journal of Personality and Social Psychology, 80*, 995–1010.

Helson, R., Stewart, A. J., & Ostrove, J. (1995). Identity in three cohorts of midlife women. *Journal of Personality and Social Psychology, 69*, 544–557.

Helson, R., & Wink, P. (1992). Personality change in women from the early 40s to the early 50s. *Psychology and Aging, 7*, 46–55.

Hendrick, C., & Hendrick S. (1989). Research on love: Does it measure up? *Journal of Personality and Social Psychology, 56*, 784–794.

Hendrick, C., & Hendrick, S. (2003). Romantic love: Measuring cupid's arrow. In S. Lopez & C. Snyder (Eds.), *Positive psychological assessment: A handbook of models and measures.* Washington, DC: American Psychological Association.

Hendrie, H. C., Ogunniyi, A., Hall, K. S., Baiyewu, O., Unverzagt, F. W., Gureje, O., et al. (2001). Incidence of dementia and Alzheimer disease in 2 communities: Yoruba residing in Ibadan, Nigeria, and African Americans residing in Indianapolis, Indiana. *Journal of the American Medical Association, 285*, 739–747.

Henig, R. M. (2003, June). Pandora's baby. *Scientific American,* 63–67.

Henning-Stout, M. (1996). Gay and lesbian youths in schools. *Psychology Teacher Network, 6*, 2–4.

Henry, B., Caspi, A., Moffitt, T. E., & Silva, P. A. (1996). Temperamental and familial predictors of violent and nonviolent criminal convictions: Age 3 to 18. *Developmental Psychology, 32*, 614–623.

Henry, C. S., Sager, D. W., & Plunkett, S. W. (1996). Adolescents' perceptions of family system characteristics, parent-adolescent dyadic behaviors, adolescent qualities and adolescent empathy. *Family Relations: Journal of Applied Family & Child Studies, 45*, 283–292.

Henry, C. S., Stephenson, A. L., Hanson, M. F., & Hargett, W. (1993). Adolescent suicide and families: An ecological approach. *Adolescence, 28*, 291–308.

Henry, J., & McNab, W. (2003). Forever young: A health promotion focus on sexuality and aging. *Gerontology & Geriatrics Education, 23*, 57–74.

Henry, K. L., Knight, K. E., & Thornberry, T. P. (2012). School disengagement as a predictor of dropout, delinquency, and problem substance use during adolescence and early adulthood. *Journal of Youth and Adolescence, 41*, 156–166.

Henry, R., Miller, R., & Giarrusso, R. (2005). Difficulties, disagreements, and disappointments in late-life marriages. *International Journal of Aging & Human Development, 61*, 243–264.

Hensley, P. (2006, July). Treatment of bereavement-related depression and traumatic grief. *Journal of Affective Disorders, 92*, 117–124.

Hepper, P. G., Scott, D., & Shahidulla, S. (1993). Response to maternal voice. *Journal of Reproductive and Infant Psychology, 11*, 147–153.

Herbert, M. R., Ziegler, D. A., Deutsch, C. K., O'Brien, L. M., Kennedy, D. N., Filipek, P. A., et al. (2000). Brain asymmetries in autism and developmental language disorder: A nested whole-brain analysis. *Brain, 128*, 213–226.

Herbst, A. L. (1981). Diethylstilbestrol and other sex hormones during pregnancy. *Obstetrics and Gynecology, 58*, 355–405.

Herbst, A. L. (1994). The epidemiology of ovarian carcinoma and the current status of tumor markers to detect disease. *American Journal of Obstetrics and Gynecology, 170*, 1099–1105.

Herbst, J. H., McCrae, R. R., Costa, Jr., P. T., Feaganes, J. R., & Siegler, I. C. (2000). Self-perceptions of stability and change in personality at midlife: The UNC Alumni Heart Study. *Assessment, 7*, 379–388.

Herdt, G. H. (Ed.). (1998). *Rituals of manhood: Male initiation in Papua New Guinea.* Somerset, NJ: Transaction Books.

Herek, G. M. (1993). Sexual orientation and military service: A social science perspective. *American Psychologist, 48*, 538–549.

Herman, M. R. (2009). The black-white-other achievement gap: Testing theories of academic performance among multiracial and monoracial adolescents. *Sociology of Education, 82*, 20–46.

Hernandez, B. C., & Bjorklund, D. F. (2003). Evolutionary developmental psychology: A new tool for better understanding human ontogeny. *Human Development, 46*, 259–281.

Hernandez-Reif, M., Diego, M., & Field, T. (2007). Preterm infants show reduced stress behaviors and activity after 5 days of massage therapy. *Infant Behavior & Development, 30*, 557–561.

Hernandez-Reif, M., Field, T., Diego, M., Vera, Y., & Pickens, J. (2006, January). Brief report: Happy faces are habituated more slowly by infants of depressed mothers. *Infant Behavior & Development, 29*, 131–135.

Hernandez-Reif, M., Field, T. M., Krasnegor, J., Martinez, E., Schwartzmann, M., & Mavunda, K. (1999). Children with cystic fibrosis benefit from massage therapy. *Journal of Pediatric Psychology, 24*, 175–181.

Herrenkohl, T., Sousa, C., Tajima, E., Herrenkohl, R., & Moylan, C. (2008, April). Intersection of child abuse and children's exposure to domestic violence. *Trauma, Violence, & Abuse, 9*(2), 84–99.

Herrnstein, R. J., & Murray, C. (1994). *The Bell Curve: Intelligence and class structure in American life.* New York: Free Press.

Hersch, P. (1999). *A Tribe Apart.* New York: Ballantine Books.

Hersen, M., & Van Hasselt, V. B. (Eds.). (1996). *Psychological treatment of older adults: An introductory text.* New York: Plenum.

Hertel, G., & Wittchen, M. (2008). Work motivation. *An introduction to work and organizational psychology: A European perspective* (2nd ed.). Malden, MA: Blackwell Publishing.

Hertelendy, F., & Zakar, T. (2004). Prostaglandins and the mymetrium and cervix. *Prostaglandins, Leukotrienes and Essential Fatty Acids, 70*, 207–222.

Hertenstein, M. J. (2002). Touch: Its communicative functions in infancy. *Human Development, 45*, 70–94.

Hertenstein, M. J., & Campos, J. J. (2001). Emotion regulation via maternal touch. *Infancy, 2*, 549–566.

Hertenstein, M. J., & Campos, J. J. (2004). The retention effects of an adult's emotional displays on infant behavior. *Child Development, 75*, 595–613.

Hertzog, C., Kramer, A., Wilson, R., & Lindenberger, U. (2008). Enrichment effects on adult cognitive development: Can the functional capacity of older adults be preserved and enhanced? *Psychological Science in the Public Interest, 9*, 1–65.

Hespos, S. J., & Baillargeon, R. (2008). Young infants' actions reveal their developing knowledge of support variables: Converging evidence for violation-of-expectation findings. *Cognition, 107*, 304–316.

Hess, J. L. (1990). The catastrophic health care fiasco. *The Nation, 250*, 193–203.

Hess, T., Auman, C., & Colcombe, S. (2003). The impact of stereotype threat on age differences in memory performance. *Journals of Gerontology: Series B: Psychological Sciences & Social Sciences, 58B*, P3–P11.

Hess, T. M., Hinson, J. T., & Hodges, E. A. (2009). Moderators of and mechanisms underlying stereotype threat effects on older adults' memory performance. *Experimental Aging Research, 31*, 153–177.

Hess-Biber, S. (1996). *Am I thin enough yet?* New York: Oxford University Press.

Heston, C. (2002, August 9). Quoted in *Charlton Heston has Alzheimer's symptoms.* Retrieved from http://www.cnn.com/2002/US/08/09/heston.illness/.

Heterelendy, F., & Zakar, T. (2004). Prostaglandins and the mymetrium and cervix. *Prostaglandins, Leukotrienes and Essential Fatty Acids, 70*, 207–222.

Hetherington, E. M. (1989). Family relations six years after divorce. In K. Pasley & M. Ihinger-Tallman (Eds.), *Remarriage and stepparenting: Current research and theory.* New York: Guilford Press.

Hetherington, E. M. (Ed.). (1999). *Coping with divorce, single parenting, and remarriage: A risk and resiliency perspective.* Mahwah, NJ: Erlbaum.

Hetherington, E. M., & Blechman, E. A. (Eds.). (1996). *Stress, coping, and resiliency in children and families.* Hillsdale, NJ: Erlbaum.

Hetherington, E. M., Bridges, M., & Insabella, G. M. (1998). What matters? What does not? Five perspectives on the association between marital transitions and children's adjustment. *American Psychologist, 53,* 167–184.

Hetherington, E. M., & Clingempeel, W. (1992). Coping with marital transitions: A family systems perspective. *Monographs of the Society for Research in Child Development, 57,* (2–3, Serial No. 227).

Hetherington, E., & Elmore, A. (2003). Risk and resilience in children coping with their parents' divorce and remarriage. In S. Luthar (Ed.), *Resilience and vulnerability: Adaptation in the context of childhood adversities.* New York: Cambridge University Press.

Hetherington, E. M., & Kelly, J. (2002). *For better or worse: Divorce reconsidered.* New York: Norton.

Hetherington, E. M., Stanley-Hagan, M., & Anderson, E. (1989). Marital transitions: A child's perspective. *American Psychologist, 44,* 303–312.

Hetherington, T. F., & Weinberger, J. (Eds.). (1993). *Can personality change?* Washington, DC: American Psychological Association.

Heubusch, K. (1997, September). A tough job gets tougher. *American Demographics,* p. 39.

Heward, W. L., & Orlansky, M. D. (1988, October). The epidemiology of AIDS in the U.S. *Scientific American,* 72–81.

Hewett, F. M., & Forness, S. R. (1974). *Education of exceptional learners.* Boston: Allyn & Bacon.

Hewitt, B. (1997, December 15). A day in the life. *People Magazine,* pp. 49–58.

Hewlett, B., & Lamb, M. (2002). Integrating evolution, culture and developmental psychology: Explaining caregiver-infant proximity and responsiveness in central Africa and the USA. In H. Keller & Y. Poortinga (Eds.), *Between culture and biology: Perspectives on ontogenetic development* (pp. 241–269). New York: Cambridge University Press.

Hewstone, M. (2003). Intergroup contact: Panacea for prejudice? *Psychologist, 16,* 352–355.

Heyman, J. D., Breu, G., Simmons, M., & Howard, C. (2003, September 15). Drugs can make short kids grow but is it right to prescribe them? *People,* pp. 103–104.

Heyman, R., & Slep, A. M. (2002). Do child abuse and interparental violence lead to adulthood family violence? *Journal of Marriage & Family, 64,* 864–870.

HHL (Harvard Health Letter). (1997, May). *Turning up the volume,* p. 4.

HHS News. (2001, January 12). *Early Head Start shows significant results for low income children and parents.* Washington, DC: Health and Human Services.

Hietala, J., Cannon, T. D., & van Erp, T. G. M. (2003). Regional brain morphology and duration of illness in never-medicated first-episode patients with schizophrenia. *Schizophrenia, 64,* 79–81.

Higgins, D., & McCabe, M. (2003). Maltreatment and family dysfunction in childhood and the subsequent adjustment of children and adults. *Journal of Family Violence, 18,* 107–120.

Higher Education Research Institute. (2005). *The spiritual life of college students: A national study of college students' search for meaning and purpose.* Los Angeles: Higher Education Research Institute.

Highley, J. R., Esiri, M. M., McDonald, B., Cortina-Borja, M., Herron, B. M., & Crow, T. J. (1999). The size and fibre composition of the corpus callosum with respect to gender and schizophrenia: A post-mortem study. *Brian, 122,* 99–110.

Hightower, J. R. R. (2005). Women and depression. In A. Barnes (Ed.), *Handbook of women, psychology, and the law.* New York: Wiley.

Higley, E., & Dozier, M. (2009). Nighttime maternal responsiveness and infant attachment at one year. *Attachment & Human Development, 11,* 347–363.

Hildreth, K., Sweeney, B., & Rovee-Collier, C. (2003). Differential memory-preserving effects of reminders at 6 months. *Journal of Experimental Child Psychology, 84,* 41–62.

Hill, N. E. (2012). Parent–child and child–peer close relationships: Understanding parental influences on peer relations from a cultural context. In L. Campbell & T. J. Loving (Eds.), *Interdisciplinary research on close relationships: The case for integration.* Washington, DC: American Psychological Association.

Hill, P. L., & Lapsley, D. K. (2011). Adaptive and maladaptive narcissism in adolescent development. In C. T. Barry, P. K. Kerig, K. K. Stellwagen, & T. D. Barry (Eds.), *Narcissism and Machiavellianism in youth: Implications for the development of adaptive and maladaptive behavior.* Washington, DC: American Psychological Association.

Hill, R. D., Storandt, M., & Malley, M. (1993). The impact of long-term exercise training on psychological function in older adults. *Journal of Gerontology, 48,* P12–P17.

Hill, S., & Flom, R. (2007, February). 18- and 24-month-olds' discrimination of gender-consistent and inconsistent activities. *Infant Behavior & Development, 30,* 168–173.

Hillman, J. (2000). *Clinical perspectives on elderly sexuality.* Dordrecht, Netherlands: Kluwer Academic Publishers.

Hilton, J., & Anderson, T. (2009). Characteristics of women with children who divorce in midlife compared to those who remain married. *Journal of Divorce & Remarriage, 50,* 309–329.

Hinduja, S., & Patchin, J. (2008). Personal information of adolescents on the Internet: A quantitative content analysis of MySpace. *Journal of Adolescence, 31,* 125–146.

Hines, M., Golombok, S., Rust, J., Johnston, K. J., & Golding, J. (2002). Testosterone during pregnancy and gender role behavior of preschool children: A longitudinal, population study. *Child Development, 73,* 1678–1687.

Hines, M., & Kaufman, F. R. (1994). Androgen and the development of human sex-typical behavior: Rough-and-tumble play and sex of preferred playmates in children with congenital adrenal hyperplasi (CAH). *Child Development, 65,* 1042–1053.

Hinojosa, T., Sheu, C., & Michel, G. (2003). Infant hand-use preferences for grasping objects contributes to the development of a hand-use preference for manipulating objects. *Developmental Psychobiology, 43,* 328–334.

Hinshaw, S. P., Zupan, B. A., Simmel, C., Nigg, J. T., & Melnick, S. (1997). Peer status in boys with and without attention-deficit hyperactivity disorder: Predictions from overt and covert antisocial behavior, social isolation, and authoritative parenting beliefs. *Child Development, 68,* 880–896.

Hintermair, M., & Albertini, J. A. (2005). Ethics, deafness, and new medical technologies. *Journal of Deaf Studies & Deaf Education, 10,* 184–192.

Hinton, C. F., Grant, A. M., & Grosse, S. D. (2011). Ethical implications and practical considerations of ethnically targeted screening for genetic disorders: The case of hemoglobinopathy screening. *Ethnicity & Health, 16,* 377–388.

Hinton, J. M. (1967). *Dying.* Baltimore, MD: Penguin.

Hirsch, H. V., & Spinelli, D. N. (1970). Visual experience modifies distribution of horizontally and vertically oriented receptive fields in cats. *Science, 168,* 869–871.

Hirschfeld, L. (2008). Children's developing conceptions of race. In *Handbook of race, racism, and the developing child.* Hoboken, NJ: John Wiley & Sons Inc.

Hirshberg, L. (1990). When infants look to their parents: II. Twelve-month-olds' response to conflicting parental emotional signals. *Child Development, 61,* 1187–1191.

Hirshberg, L., & Svejda, M. (1990). When infants look to their parents: I. Infants' social referencing of mothers compared to fathers. *Child Development, 61,* 1175–1186.

Hirsh-Pasek, K., & Michnick-Golinkoff, R. (1995). *The origins of grammar: Evidence from early language comprehension.* Cambridge, MA: MIT Press.

Hirvonen, J., & Hietala, J. (2011). Dysfunctional brain networks and genetic risk for schizophrenia: Specific neurotransmitter systems. *CNS Neuroscience & Therapeutics, 17,* 89–96.

Hiser, E., & Kobayashi, J. (2003). Hemisphere lateralization differences: A cross-cultural study of Japanese and American students in Japan. *Journal of Asian Pacific Communication, 13,* 197–229.

Hitch, G. J., & Towse, J. N. (1995). *Working memory: What develops?* Mahwah, NJ: Lawrence Erlbaum Associates.

Hitchens, C. (2007, August 12). The boy who lived. *New York Times.* p. A4

Hitlin, S., Brown, J. S., & Elder, G. H., Jr. (2006). Racial self-categorization in adolescence: Multiracial development and social pathways. *Child Development, 77,* 1298–1308.

Hitt, J. (2000, February 20). The second sexual revolution. *The New York Times Magazine,* pp. 34–62.

Hjelmstedt, A., Widström, A., & Collins, A. (2006). Psychological correlates of prenatal attachment in women who conceived after in vitro fertilization and women who conceived naturally. *Birth: Issues in Perinatal Care, 33,* 303–310.

HMHL (Harvard Mental Health Letter). (1995, February). *Update on Alzheimer's disease—Part I.* Cambridge, MA: Harvard Medical School.

HMHL (Harvard Mental Health Letter). (2005). The treatment of attention deficit disorder: New evidence. *Harvard Mental Health Letter, 21,* 6.

Ho, B., Friedland, J., Rappolt, S., & Noh, S. (2003). Caregiving for relatives with Alzheimer's disease: Feelings of Chinese-Canadian women. *Journal of Aging Studies, 17,* 301–321.

Hobart, C., & Grigel, F. (1992). Cohabitation among Canadian students at the end of the eighties. *Journal of Comparative Family Studies, 23,* 311–337.

Hockenberry, J., & Hockenberry, A. (1996, November 22). Dance. *USA Weekend,* pp. 6–7.

Hocutt, A. M. (1996). Effectiveness of special education: Is placement the critical factor? *The Future of Children, 6,* 77–102.

Hoek, J., & Gendall, P. (2006). Advertising and obesity: A behavioral perspective. *Journal of Health Communication, 11,* 409–423.

Hoelterk L. F., Axinn, W. G., & Ghimire, D. J. (2004). Social change, premarital nonfamily experiences, and marital dynamics. *Journal of Marriage & Family, 66,* 1131–1151.

Hoerr, S., Murashima, M., & Keast, D. (2008). Nutrition and obesity. *Obesity in childhood and adolescence, Vol 1: Medical, biological, and social issues.* Westport, CT: Praeger Publishers/Greenwood Publishing Group.

Hoersting, R. C., & Jenkins, S. (2011). No place to call home: Cultural homelessness, self-esteem and cross-cultural identities. *International Journal of Intercultural Relations, 35,* 17–30.

Hoessler, C., & Chasteen, A. L. (2008). Does aging affect the use of shifting standards? *Experimental Aging Research, 34,* 1–12.

Hoeve, M., Blokland, A., Dubas, J., Loeber, R., Gerris, J., & van der Laan, P. (2008). Trajectories of delinquency and parenting styles. *Journal of Abnormal Child Psychology: An official publication of the International Society for Research in Child and Adolescent Psychopathology, 36,* 223–235.

Hofer, M. A. (2006). Psychobiological roots of early attachment. *Current Directions in Psychological Science, 15,* 84–88.

Hofferth, S. L., & Sandberg, J. (1998). *Changes in American children's time, 1981–1997.* Ann Arbor, MI: University of Michigan Institute for Social Research.

Hofferth, S., & Sandberg, J. F. (2001). How American children spend their time. *Journal of Marriage and the Family, 63,* 295–308.

Hoffman, C., Lau, I., & Johnson, D. R. (1986). The linguistic relativity of person cognition: An English-Chinese comparison. *Journal of Personality and Social Psychology, 51,* 1097–1105.

Hoffman, J. (2011, March 27). A girl's nude photo, and altered lives. *New York Times*, p. A1, A18–A19.

Hoffman, L. (2003). Why high schools don't change: What students and their yearbooks tell us. *High School Journal, 86*, 22–37.

Hoffman, L. W. (1989). Effects of maternal employment in the two-parent family. *American Psychologist, 44*, 283–292.

Hoffman, L. W., McManus, K. A., & Brackbill, Y. (1987). The value of children to young and elderly parents. *International Journal of Aging and Human Development, 25*, 309–312.

Hogg, M. A. (2003). Social identity. In M. A. Hogg (Eds.), *Handbook of self and identity*. New York: Guilford Press.

Hohm, E., Jennen-Steinmetz, C., Schmidt, M., & Laucht, M. (2007). Language development at ten months: Predictive of language outcome and school achievement ten years later? *European Child & Adolescent Psychiatry, 16*, 149–156.

Hohmann-Marriott, B. (2006, November). Shared beliefs and the union stability of married and cohabiting couples. *Journal of Marriage and Family, 68*, 1015–1028.

Holahan, C., & Chapman, J. (2002). Longitudinal predictors of proactive goals and activity participation at age 80. *Journals of Gerontology: Series B: Psychological Sciences & Social Sciences, 57B*, P418–P425.

Holahan, C. J., & Moos, R. H. (1987). Personal and contextual determinants of coping strategies. *Journal of Personality and Social Psychology, 52*, 946–955.

Holahan, C. J., & Moos, R. H. (1990). Life stressors, resistance factors, and improved psychological functioning: An extension of the stress resistance paradigm. *Journal of Personality and Social Psychology, 58*, 909–917.

Holden, C. (1987, October 9). Why do women live longer than men? *Science, 233*, 158–160.

Holden, C. (2002, February 8). The quest to reverse time's toll. *Science, 295*, 1032–1033.

Holden, G. W., & Miller, P. C. (1999). Enduring and different: A meta-analysis of the similarity in parents' child rearing. *Psychological Bulletin, 125*, 223–254.

Holland, J. (1997). *Making vocational choices: A theory of vocational personalities and work environments* (3rd ed.). Odessa, FL: Psychological Assessment Resources.

Holland, J. (2008). Reading aloud with infants: The controversy, the myth, and a case study. *Early Childhood Education Journal, 35*, 383–385.

Holland, J. C., & Lewis, S. (1993). Emotions and cancer: What do we really know? In D. Goleman & J. Gurin (Eds.), *Mind–body medicine*. Yonkers, NY: Consumer Reports Books.

Holland, J. L. (1973). *Making vocational choices: A theory of careers*. Englewood Cliffs, NJ: Prentice-Hall.

Holland, J. L. (1987). Current status of Holland's theory of careers: Another perspective. *Career Development Quarterly, 36*, 24–30.

Holland, J. L. (1997). *Making vocational choices: A theory of vocational personalities and environments* (3rd ed.). Odessa, FL: Psychological Assessment Resources.

Holland, J. M., Neimeyer, R. A., Boelen, P. A., & Prigerson, H. G. (2009). The underlying structure of grief: A taxometric investigation of prolonged and normal reactions to loss. *Journal of Psychopathology and Behavioral Assessment, 31*, 190–201.

Holland, N. (1994, August). *Race dissonance—Implications for African American children*. Paper presented at the annual meeting of the American Psychological Association, Los Angeles.

Hollenbeck, A. R., Gewirtz, J. L., Sebris, S. L., & Scanlon, J. W. (1984). Labor and delivery medication influences parent–infant interaction in the first postpartum month. *Infant Behavior and Development, 7*, 201–209.

Hollich, G. J., Hirsh-Pasek, K., Golinkoff, R. M., Brand, R. J., Brown, E. C., He, L., et al. (2000). Breaking the language barrier: An emergentist coalition model of the origins of word learning. *Monographs of the Society for Research in Child Development, 65*(3, Serial No. 262).

Hollingworth, H. L. (1943/1990). *Letta Stetter Hollingworth: A biography*. Boston: Anker.

Hollingworth, L., & Drake, H. M. (2012). *Teach reading, not testing: Best practice in an age of accountability*. Thousand Oaks, CA: Corwin Press.

Holmes, D., & Murray, S. J. (2011). Civilizing the "Barbarian": A critical analysis of behaviour modification programmes in forensic psychiatry settings. *Journal of Nursing Management, 19*, 293–301.

Holmes, E. R., & Holmes, L.D. (1995). *Other cultures, elder years*. Thousand Oaks, CA: Sage Publications.

Holmes, S. A. (1997, October 30.) Peopl can claim to be multiracial on federal forms. *The New York Times*, p. A1.

Holmes, T. H., & Rahe, R. H. (1967). The social readjustment scale. *Journal of Psychosomatic Research, 11*, 251–261.

Holowaka, S., & Petitto, L. A. (2002). Left hemisphere cerebral specialization for babies while babbling. *Science, 287*, 1515.

Holt, M. K., & Espelage, D. L. (2007). Perceived social support among bullies, victims, and bully-victims. *Journal of Youth and Adolescence, 36*, 984–994.

Holt, R. F., & Kirk, K. I. (2005). Speech and language development in cognitively delayed children with cochlear implants. *Ear and Hearing, 26*, 132–148.

Holtgraves, T. (2009). Gambling, gambling activities, and problem gambling. *Psychologically Addictive Behavior, 23*, 295–302.

Holtzman, N. A., Murphy, P. D., Watson, M. S., & Barr, P. A. (1997). Predictive genetic testing: From basic research to clinical practice. *Science, 278*, 602–604.

Holyrod, R., & Sheppard, A. (1997). Parental separation: Effects on children; implications for services. *Child: Care, Health & Development, 23*, 369–378.

Holzman, L. (1997). *Schools for growth: Radical alternatives to current educational models*. Mahwah, NJ: Erlbaum.

Homae, F., Watanabe, H., Nakano, T., & Taga, G. (2012). Functional development in the infant brain for auditory pitch processing. *Human Brain Mapping, 33*, 596–608.

Honey, J. L., Bennett, P., & Morgan, M. (2003). Predicting postnatal depression. *Journal of Affective Disorders, 76*, 201–210.

Hong, E., Milgram, R. M., & Gorsky, H. (1995). Original thinking as a predictor of creative performance in young children. *Roeper Review, 18*, 147–149.

Hong, S. B., & Trepanier-Street, M. (2004). Technology: A tool for knowledge construction in a Reggio Emilia inspired teacher education program. *Early Childhood Education Journal, 32*, 87–94.

Hood, B. M., Willen, J. D., & Driver, J. (1998). Adult's eyes trigger shifts of visual attention in human infants. *Psychological Science, 9*, 131–139.

Hooks, B., & Chen, C. (2008). Vision triggers an experience-dependent sensitive period at the retinogeniculate synapse. *The Journal of Neuroscience, 28*, 4807–4817.

Hopkins, B., & Westra, T. (1989). Maternal expectations of their infants' development: Some cultural differences. *Developmental Medicine and Child Neurology, 31*, 384–390.

Hopkins, B., & Westra, T. (1990). Motor development, maternal expectation, and the role of handling. *Infant Behavior and Development, 13*, 117–122.

Hopkins-Golightly, T., Raz, S., & Sander, C. (2003). Influence of slight to moderate risk for birth hypoxia on acquisition of cognitive and language function in the preterm infant: A cross-sectional comparison with preterm-birth controls. *Neuropsychology, 17*, 3–13.

Hoppe, M. J., Graham, L., Wilsdon, A., Wells, E. A., Nahom, D., & Morrison, D. M. (2004). Teens speak out about HIV/AIDS: Focus group discussions about risk and decision-making. *Journal of Adolescent Health, 35*, 27–35.

Hoptman, M. J., & Davidson, R. J. (1994). How and why do the two cerebral hemispheres interact? *Psychological Bulletin, 116*, 195–219.

Horiuchi, S., Finch, C., Meslé, F., & Vallin, J. (2003). Differential patterns of age-related mortality increase in middle age and old age. *Journals of Gerontology: Series A: Biological Sciences and Medical Sciences, 58A*, 495–507.

Horn, D. L., & Donaldson, G. (1980). Cognitive development II: Adulthood development of human abilities. In O. G. Brim & J. Kagan (Eds.), *Constancy and change in human development*. Cambridge, MA: Harvard University Press.

Horner, K. L. (1998). Individuality in vulnerability: Influences on physical health. *Journal of Health Psychology, 3*, 71–85.

Hornik, R., & Gunnar, M. R. (1988). A descriptive analysis of infant social referencing. *Child Development, 59*, 626–634.

Hornor, G. (2008). Reactive attachment disorder. *Journal of Pediatric Health Care, 22*, 234–239.

Horowitz, A. (1994). Vision impairment and functional disability among nursing home residents. *Gerontologist, 34*, 316–323.

Horwath, C. C. (1991). Nutrition goals for older adults: A review. *Gerontologist, 31*, 811–821.

Horwitz, B. N., Luong, G., & Charles, G. T. (2008). Neuroticism and extraversion share genetic and environmental effects with negative and positive mood spillover in a nationally representative sample. *Personality and Individual Differences, 45*, 636–642.

Hoskins, I. (1992). Social security protection of women: Prospects for the 1990s. *Aging International, 19*, 27–32.

Hossfeld, B. (2008). Developing friendships and peer relationships: Building social support with the Girls Circle program. In *Handbook of prevention and intervention programs for adolescent girls* (pp. 42–80). Hoboken, NJ: John Wiley & Sons Inc.

Hotelling, B. A., & Humenick, S. S. (2005). Advancing normal birth: Organizations, goals, and research. *Journal of Perinatal Education, 14*, 40–48.

Houle, R., & Feldman, R. S. (1991). Emotional displays in children's television programming. *Journal of Nonverbal Behavior, 15*, 261–271.

House, S. H. (2007). Nurturing the brain nutritionally and emotionally from before conception to late adolescence, *Nutritional Health, 19*, 143–161.

Houts, A. (2003). Behavioral treatment for enuresis. In A. Kazdin (Ed.), *Evidence-based psychotherapies for children and adolescents* (pp. 389–406). New York: Guilford Press.

Howard, A. (1992). Work and family crossroads spanning the career. In S. Zedeck (Ed.), *Work, families and organizations*. San Francisco: Jossey-Bass.

Howard, L., Kirkwood, G., & Latinovic, R. (2007). Sudden infant death syndrome and maternal depression. *Journal of Clinical Psychiatry, 68*, 1279–1283.

Howe, M. J. (1997). *IQ in question: The truth about intelligence*. London, England: Sage.

Howe, M. J. (2004). Some insights of geniuses into the causes of exceptional achievement. In L. V. Shavinina & M. Ferrari (Eds.), *Beyond knowledge: Extracognitive aspects of developing high ability*. Mahwah, NJ: Lawrence Erlbaum Associates.

Howe, M. L. (2003). Memories from the cradle. *Current Directions in Psychological Science, 12*, 62–65.

Howe, M. L., Courage, M. L., & Edison, S. C. (2004). When autobiographical memory begins. In S. Algarabel, A. Pitarque, T. Bajo, S. E. Gathercole, & M. A. Conway

(Eds.), *Theories of memory* (Vol. 3). New York: Psychology Press.

Howe, M. L., & O'Sullivan, J. T. (1990). The development of strategic memory: Coordinating knowledge, metamemory, and resources. In D. F. Bjorklund (Ed.), *Children's strategies: Contemporary view of cognitive development.* Hillsdale, NJ: Erlbaum.

Howe, N., & Ross, H. S. (1990). Socialization, perspective-taking, and the sibling relationship. *Developmental Psychology, 26,* 160–165.

Howes, C. (1987). Social competence with peers in young children: Developmental sequences. *Developmental Review, 7,* 252–272.

Howes, C., Galinsky, E., & Kontos, S. (1998). Childcare caregiver sensitivity and attachment. *Social Development, 7,* 25–36.

Howes, C., Unger, O., & Seidner, L. B. (1989). Social pretend play in toddlers: Parallels with social play and with solitary pretend. *Child Development, 60,* 77–84.

Howes, O., & Kapur, S. (2009). The dopamine hypothesis of schizophrenia: Version III—The final common pathway. *Schizophrenia Bulletin, 35,* 549–562.

Howie, L. (1993). Old women and widowhood: A dying status passage. *Omega, 26,* 223–233.

Howie, P. W., et al. (1990). Protective effect of breast feeding against infection. *British Journal of Medicine, 300,* 11.

Hoyer, W., & Verhaeghen, P. (2006). Memory Aging. *Handbook of the psychology of aging* (6th ed.). Amsterdam, The Netherlands: Elsevier.

Hsu, L. K. G. (1990). *Eating disorders.* New York: Guilford.

Hsu, V., & Rovee-Collier, C. (2006). Memory reactivation in the second year of life. *Infant Behavior & Development, 29,* 91–107.

Hu, G., Wilcox, H., Wissow, L., & Baker, S. (2008). Mid-life suicide: An increasing problem in U.S. whites, 1999–2005. *American Journal of Preventive Medicine, 35,* 589–593.

Huang, A., Subak, L., Thom, D., Van Den Eeden, S., Ragins, A., Kuppermann, M., et al. (2009). Sexual function and aging in racially and ethnically diverse women. *Journal of the American Geriatrics Society, 57,* 1362–1368.

Huang, J. (2004). Death: Cultural traditions. *From on our own terms: Moyers on dying.* Retrieved from www.pbs.org.

Huang, J. H., Jacobs, D. F., Derevensky, J. L., Gupta, R., & Paskus, T. S. (2007). Gambling and health risk behaviors among U.S. college student-athletes: findings from a national study. *Journal of Adolescent Health, 40,* 390–397.

Hubbs-Tait, L., Nation, J. R., Krebs, N. F., & Bellinger, D. C. (2005). Neurotoxicants, micronutrients, and social environments: Individual and combined effects on children's development. *Journal of the American Psychological Society, 6,* 57–101.

Hubel, D. H., & Wiesel, T. N. (1979). Brain mechanisms of vision. *Scientific American, 241,* 150–162.

Hubel, D. H., & Wiesel, T. N. (2004). *Brain and visual perception: The story of a 25-year collaboration.* New York: Oxford University Press.

Huber, L. (2012). What, whom, and how: Selectivity in social learning. In F. M. de Waal & P. Ferrari (Eds.), *The primate mind: Built to connect with other minds.* Cambridge, MA: Harvard University Press.

Huddleston, J., & Ge, X. (2003). Boys at puberty: Psychosocial implications. In C. Hayward (Ed.), *Gender differences at puberty.* New York: Cambridge University Press.

Hudley, C., & Irving, M. (2012). Ethnic and racial identity in childhood and adolescence. In K. R. Harris, S. Graham, T. Urdan, S. Graham, J. M. Royer, M. Zeidner et al. (Eds.), *APA educational psychology handbook, Vol 2: Individual differences and cultural and contextual factors.* Washington, DC: American Psychological Association.

Hudson, J. A., Sosa, B. B., & Shapiro, L. R. (1997). Scripts and plans: The development of preschool children's event knowledge and event planning. In S. L. Friedman & E. K. Scholnick (Eds.), *The developmental psychology of planning: Why, how and when do we plan* (pp. 77–102). Mahwah, NJ: Erlbaum.

Hudson, M. J. (1990). Hearing and vision loss in an aging population: Myths and realities. *Educational Gerontology, 16,* 87–96.

Huesmann, L. R. (1986). Psychological processes promoting the relations between exposure to media violence and aggressive behavior by the viewer. *Journal of Social Issues, 42,* 125–139.

Huesmann, L. R., Eron, L. D., Klein, R., Brice, P., & Fischer, P. (1983). Mitigating the imitation of aggressive behaviors by changing children's attitudes about media violence. *Journal of Personality and Social Psychology, 5,* 899–910.

Huesmann, L. R., Moise, J. F., & Podolski, C. (1997). The effects of media violence on the development of antisocial behavior. In D. M. Stoff, J. Breiling, & J. D. Maser (Eds.), *Handbook of antisocial behavior* (pp. 181–193). New York: Wiley.

Huesmann, L. R., Moise-Titus, J., & Podolski, C. L. (2003). Longitudinal relations between children's exposure to TV violence and their aggressive and violent behavior in young adulthood: 1977–1992. *Developmental Psychology, 39,* 201–221.

Hueston, W., Geesey, M., & Diaz, V. (2008). Prenatal care initiation among pregnant teens in the United States: An analysis over 25 years. *Journal of Adolescent Health, 42,* 243–248.

Huff, C. O. (1999). Source, recency, and degree of stress in adolescence and suicide ideation. *Adolescence, 34,* 81–89.

Hughes, F. P. (1995). *Children, play, and development* (2nd ed.). Boston: Allyn & Bacon.

Hughes-Lynch, C. E. (2012). *Teaching children with high-functioning autism: Strategies for the inclusive classroom.* Waco, TX: Prufrock Press.

Hui, A., Lau, S., Li, C., Tong, T., & Zhang, J. (2006). A cross-societal comparative study of Beijing and Hong Kong children's self-concept. *Social Behavior and Personality, 34*(5), 511–524.

Huijbregts, S., Tavecchio, L., Leseman, P., & Hoffenaar, P. (2009). Child rearing in a group setting: Beliefs of Dutch, Caribbean Dutch, and Mediterranean Dutch caregivers in center-based child care. *Journal of Cross-Cultural Psychology, 40,* 797–815.

Huizink, A., & Mulder, E. (2006). Maternal smoking, drinking or cannabis use during pregnancy and neurobehavioral and cognitive functioning in human offspring. *Neuroscience & Biobehavioral Reviews, 30,* 24–41.

Huizink, A., Mulder, E., & Buitelaar, J. (2004). Prenatal stress and risk for psychopathology: Specific effects or induction of general susceptibility? *Psychological Bulletin, 130,* 115–142.

Hulanicka, B. (1999). Acceleration of menarcheal age of girls from dysfunctional families. *Journal of Reproductive & Infant Psychology, 17,* 119–132.

Hulei, E., Zevenbergen, A., & Jacobs, S. (2006, September). Discipline behaviors of Chinese American and European American mothers. *Journal of Psychology: Interdisciplinary and Applied, 140,* 459–475.

Human Genome Program. (2003). *Genomics and its impact on science and society: A 2003 primer.* Washington, DC: U.S. Department of Energy.

Human Genome Project. (2006). Retrieved from http://www.ornl.gov/sci/techresources/Human_Genome/medicine/genetest.shtml.

Humphrey, G. M., & Zimpfer, D. G. (1996). *Counseling for grief and bereavement.* New York: Wiley.

Humphrey, N., Curran, A., Morris, E., Farrell, P., & Woods, K. (2007, April). Emotional intelligence and education: A critical review. *Educational Psychology, 27,* 235–254.

Humphreys, J. (2003). Resilience in sheltered battered women. *Issues in Mental Health Nursing, 24,* 137–152.

Humphreys, P., & Paxton, S. (2004). Impact of exposure to idealised male images on adolescent boys' body image. *Body Image, 1,* 253–266.

Hungerford, A. (2005). The use of anatomically detailed dolls in forensic investigations: Developmental considerations. *Journal of Forensic Psychology Practice, 5,* 75–87.

Hungerford, A., Brownell, C. A., & Campbell, S. B. (2000). Child care in infancy: A transactional perspective. In C. H. Zeanah Jr., et al. (Eds.), *Handbook of infant mental health* (2nd ed.). New York: Guilford Press.

Hunnius, S., de Wit, T. J., Vrins, S., & von Hofsten, C. (2011). Facing threat: Infants' and adults' visual scanning of faces with neutral, happy, sad, angry, and fearful emotional expressions. *Cognition and Emotion, 25,* 193–205.

Hunt, C., & Hauck, F. (2006, June). Sudden infant death syndrome. *Canadian Medical Association Journal, 174,* 1861–1869.

Hunt, E., & Joslyn, S. (2007). The dynamics of the relation between applied and basic research. *Expertise out of context: Proceedings of the Sixth International Conference on Naturalistic Decision Making.* Mahwah, NJ: Lawrence Erlbaum Associates.

Hunt, E., Streissguth, A. P., Kerr, B., & Olson, H. C. (1995). Mothers' alcohol consumption during pregnancy: Effects on spatial-visual reasoning in 14-year-old children. *Psychological Science, 6,* 339–342.

Hunt, J., & Hunt, L. (1975). Racial inequality and self-image: Identity maintenance as identity diffusion. *Sociology and Social Research, 61,* 539–559.

Hunt, M. (1974). *Sexual behaviors in the 1970s.* New York: Dell.

Hunt, M. (1993). *The story of psychology.* New York: Doubleday.

Hunter, G. R., McCarthy, J. P., & Bamman, M. M. (2004). Effects of resistance training on older adults. *Sports Medicine, 34,* 329–348.

Hunter, J., & Mallon, G. P. (2000). Lesbian, gay, and bisexual adolescent development: Dancing with your feet tied together. In B. Greene & G. L. Croom (Eds.), *Education, research, and practice in lesbian, gay, bisexual, and transgendered psychology: A resource manual* (Vol. 5). Thousand Oaks, CA: Sage.

Hunter, S. (2007). *Coming out and disclosures: LGBT persons across the life span.* New York: Haworth Press.

Hunter, S., & Smith, D. (2008). Predictors of children's understandings of death: Age, cognitive ability, death experience and maternal communicative competence. *Omega: Journal of Death and Dying, 57,* 143–162.

Hunter Smart, J. E., Cumming, S. P., Sherar, L. B., Standage, M., Neville, H., & Malina, R. M. (2012). Maturity associated variance in physical activity and health-related quality of life in adolescent females: A mediated effects model. *Journal of Physical Activity & Health, 9,* 86–95.

Huntsinger, C. S., Jose, P. E., Liaw, F., & Ching, W.-D. (1997). Cultural differences in early mathematics learning: A comparison of Euro-American, Chinese-American, and Taiwan-Chinese families. *International Journal of Behavioral Development, 21,* 371–388.

Huppe, M., & Cyr, M. (1997). Division of household labor and marital satisfaction of dual income couples according to family life cycle. *Canadian Journal of Counseling, 31,* 145–162.

Hust, S., & Brown, J. (2008). Gender, media use, and effects. *The handbook of children, media, and development* (pp. 98–120). Malden, MA: Blackwell Publishing.

Hust, S., Brown, J., & L'Engle, K. (2008, January). Boys will be boys and girls better be prepared: An analysis of the rare sexual health messages in young adolescents' media. *Mass Communication and Society, 11*(1), 3–23.

Huster, R. J., Westerhausen, R. R., & Herrmann, C. S. (2011). Sex differences in cognitive control are associated with midcingulate and callosal morphology. *Brain Structure & Function, 215,* 225–235.

Huston, A. (Ed.). (1991). *Children in poverty: Child development and public policy.* Cambridge, England: Cambridge University Press.

Huston, T. L., Caughlin, J. P., Houts, R. M., & Smith, S. E. (2001). The connubial crucible: Newlywed years as predictors of marital delight, distress, and divorce. *Journal of Personality and Social Psychology, 80,* 237–252.

Hutchinson, A., Whitman, R., & Abeare, C. (2003). The unification of mind: Integration of hemispheric semantic processing. *Brain & Language, 87,* 361–368.

Hutchinson, D., & Rapee, R. (2007). Do friends share similar body image and eating problems? The role of social networks and peer influences in early adolescence. *Behaviour Research and Therapy, 45,* 1557–1577.

Hutchinson, S., & Wexler, B. (2007, January). Is "raging" good for health? Older women's participation in the Raging Grannies. *Health Care for Women International, 28,* 88–118.

Hutton, P. H. (2004). *Phillippe Aries and the politics of French cultural history.* Amherst, MA: University of Massachusetts Press.

Huurre, T., Junkkari, H., & Aro, H. (2006, June). Long-term psychosocial effects of parental divorce: A follow-up study from adolescence to adulthood. *European Archives of Psychiatry and Clinical Neuroscience, 256,* 256–263.

Hwang, C. P., Lamb, M. E., & Sigel, I. E. (Eds.). (1996). *Images of childhood.* Mahwah, NJ: Erlbaum.

Hwang, S. (2004, January 19). As "doulas" enter delivery rooms, conflicts arise. *Wall Street Journal,* pp. A1, A10.

Hyde, J. S. (1994). *Understanding human sexuality* (5th ed.). New York: McGraw-Hill.

Hyde, J. S. (1995). Women and maternity leave: Empirical data and public policy. *Psychology of Women Quarterly, 19,* 299–313.

Hyde, J. S., & DeLamater, J. D. (2003). *Understanding human sexuality* (8th ed.). New York: McGraw-Hill.

Hyde, J. S., & DeLamater, J. D. (2004). *Understanding human sexuality* (9th ed.). Boston: McGraw Hill.

Hyde, J. S., Fennema, E., & Lamon, S. J. (1990). Gender differences in mathematics performance: A meta-analysis. *Psychological Bulletin, 107,* 139–155.

Hyde, J., & Grabe, S. (2008). Meta-analysis in the psychology of women. *Psychology of women: A handbook of issues and theories* (2nd ed.). Westport, CT: Praeger Publishers/Greenwood Publishing Group.

Hyde, J. S., Klein, M. H., Essex, M. J., & Clark, R. (1995). Maternity leave and women's mental health. *Psychology of Women Quarterly, 19,* 257–285.

Hyde, J., Mezulis, A., & Abramson, L. (2008, April). The ABCs of depression: Integrating affective, biological, and cognitive models to explain the emergence of the gender difference in depression. *Psychological Review, 115*(2), 291–313.

Hyde, M., & Power, D. (2006, December). Some ethical dimensions of cochlear implantation for deaf children and their families. *Journal of Deaf Studies and Deaf Education, 11*(1), 102–111.

Hyler, S. E., Gabbard, G. O., & Schneider, I. (1991). Homicidal maniacs and narcissistic parasites: Stigmatization of mentally ill persons in the movies. Annual meeting of the American Psychiatric Association (1989, San Francisco, California). *Hospital and Community Psychiatry, 42,* 1044–1048.

Hyman, S. E. (2011, February 25). The meaning of the human genome project for neuropsychiatric disorders. *Science, 331,* 1026.

Hyssaelae, L., Rautava, P., & Helenius, H. (1995). Fathers' smoking and use of alcohol: The viewpoint

of maternity health care clinics and well-baby clinics. *Family Practice, 12,* 22–27.

Iacono, W. G., & Grove, W. M. (1993). Schizophrenia reviewed: Toward an integrative genetic model. *Psychological Science, 4,* 273–276.

Ickes, W., & Turner, M. (1983). On the social advantages of having an older, opposite-sex sibling: Birth order influences in mixed-sex dyads. *Journal of Personality and Social Psychology, 45,* 210–222.

Iglesias, J., Eriksson, J., Grize, F., Tomassmi, M., & Villa, A. E. (2005). Dynamics of pruning in simulated large-scale spiking neural networks. *Biosystems, 79,* 11–20.

Ikels, C. (1989). Becoming a human being in theory and practice: Chinese views of human development. In D. I. Kertzer & K. W. Schaie (Eds.), *Age structuring in comparative perspective.* Hillsdale, NJ: Erlbaum.

Iles, J., Slade, P., & Spiby, H. (2011). Posttraumatic stress symptoms and postpartum depression in couples after childbirth: The role of partner support and attachment. *Journal of Anxiety Disorders, 25,* 101–109.

Illingworth, R. S. (1973). *Basic developmental screening: 0–2 years.* Oxford: Blackwell Scientific.

Ingersoll, E. W., & Thoman, E. B. (1999). Sleep/wake states of preterm infants: Stability, developmental change, diurnal variation, and relation with caregiving activity. *Child Development, 70,* 1–10.

Ingersoll-Dayton, B., Neal, M., & Hammer, L. (2001). Aging parents helping adult children: The experience of the sandwiched generation. *Family Relations, 50,* 263–271.

Ingram, D. K., Young, J., & Mattison, J. A. (2007). Calorie restriction in nonhuman primates: Assessing effects on brain and behavioral aging. *Neuroscience, 14,* 1359–1364.

Ingram, J., Patchin, J., Huebner, B., McCluskey, J., & Bynum, T. (2007). Parents, friends, and serious delinquency: An examination of direct and indirect effects among at-risk early adolescents. *Criminal Justice Review, 32,* 380–400.

Inoue, K., Tanii, H., Abe, S., Kaiya, H., Nata, M., & Fukunaga, T. (2006, December). The correlation between rates of unemployment and suicide rates in Japan between 1985 and 2002. *International Medical Journal, 13,* 261–263.

Insel, B., & Gould, M. (2008, June). Impact of modeling on adolescent suicidal behavior. *Psychiatric Clinics of North America, 31*(2), 293–316.

Insel, P. M., & Roth, W. T. (1991). *Core concepts in health* (6th ed.). Mountain View, CA: Mayfield.

Institute for Women's Policy Research. (2006). *The best and worst state economies for women.* (Briefing Paper No. R334). Washington, DC: Institute for Women's Policy Research.

International Cesarean Awareness Network. (2004). Retrieved from http://www.ican-online.org/.

International Human Genome Sequencing Consortium. (2001). Initial sequencing and analysis of the human genome. *Nature, 409,* 860–921.

International Literacy Institute. (2001). *Literacy overview.* Retrieved from http://www.literacyonline.org/explorer/overview.html.

Inzlicht, M., & Ben-Zeev, T. (2000). A threatening intellectual environment: Why females are susceptible to experiencing problem-solving deficits in the presence of males. *Psychological Science, 11,* 365–371.

Ip, W., Tang, C., & Goggins, W. (2009). An educational intervention to improve women's ability to cope with childbirth. *Journal of Clinical Nursing, 18,* 2125–2135.

Irani, K., Xia, Y., Zweier, J. L., Sollott, S. J., Der, C. J., Fearon, E. R., et al. (1997). Mitogenic signaling mediated by oxidants in ras-transformed fibroblasts. *Science, 275,* 1649.

Ireland, J. L., & Archer, J. (2004). Association between measures of aggression and bullying among juvenile young offenders. *Aggressive Behavior, 30,* 29–42.

Ironson, G., & Schneiderman, N. (2002). Psycholosical factors, spirituality/religiousness, and immune function in HIV/AIDS patients. In H. G. Koenig & H. J. Cohen (Eds.), *Link between religion and health: Psychoneuroimmunology and the faith factor.* London: Oxford University Press.

Irwin, E. G. (1993). A focused overview of anorexia nervosa and bulimia: I. Etiological issues. *Archives of Psychiatric Nursing, 7,* 342–346.

Isaacs, K., Barr, W., Nelson, P., & Devinsky, O. (2006, June). Degree of handedness and cerebral dominance. *Neurology, 66*(12), 1855–1858.

Isaksen, S. G., & Murdock, M. C. (1993). The emergence of a discipline: Issues and approaches to the study of creativity. In S. G. Isaksen, M. C. Murdock, R. L. Firestein, & D. J. Treffinger (Eds.), *The emergence of a discipline* (Vol. 1). Norwood, NJ: Ablex.

Isarida, T., & Isarida K. T. (2005). Effects of contextual variation during encoding on decontextualization of episodic memory. *Japanese Journal of Psychology, 76,* 105–112.

Isay, R. A. (1990). *Being homosexual: Gay men and their development.* New York: Avon.

Ishi-Kuntz, M. (2000). Diversity within Asian-American families. In D. H. Demo, K. R. Allen, & M. A. Fine (Eds.), *Handbook of family diversity.* New York: Oxford.

Ishizuka, B., Kudo, Y., & Tango, T. (2008). Cross-sectional community survey of menopause symptoms among Japanese women. *Maturitas, 61,* 260–267.

Isingrini, M., & Vazou, F. (1997). Relations between fluid intelligence and frontal lobe functioning in older adults. *International Journal of Aging & Human Development, 45,* 99–109.

Israel, E. (2005). Introduction: The rise of the age of individualism—Variability in the pathobiology, response to treatment, and treatment outcomes in asthma. *Journal of Allergy and Clinical Immunology, 115,* S525.

Iverson, T., Larsen, L., & Solem, P. (2009). A conceptual analysis of ageism. *Nordic Psychology, 61,* 4–22.

Izard, C. E., Fine, S., & Mlstow, A. (2002). Emotion processes in normal and abnormal development and preventive intervention. *Development and Psychopathology, 14,* 761–787.

Izard, C. E., Frantauzzo, C. A., Castle, J. M., Haynes, O. M., Rayias, M. F., & Putnam, P. H. (1995). The ontogeny and significance of infants' facial expressions in the first 9 months of life. *Developmental Psychology, 31,* 997–1013.

Izard, C., King, K., Trentacosta, C., Morgan, J., Laurenceau, J., Krauthamer-Ewing, E., et al. (2008, December). Accelerating the development of emotion competence in Head Start children: Effects on adaptive and maladaptive behavior. *Development and Psychopathology, 20*(1), 369–397.

Izard, C., & Malatesta, C. (1987). Perspectives on emotional development I. Differential emotions theory of early emotional development. In J. D. Osofsky (Ed.), *Handbook of infant development.* New York: Wiley.

Izard, C. E., Trentacosta, C. J., & King, K. A. (2004). An emotion-based prevention program for Head Start children. *Early Education & Development, Special issue: Prevention Interventions with Young Children, 15,* 407–422.

Izard, J., Haines, C., Crouch, R., Houston, S., & Neill, N. (2003). Assessing the impact of the teaching of modelling: Some implications. In S. Lamon, W. Parker, & K. Houston (Eds.), *Mathematical Modelling: A Way of Life: ICTMA 11.* Chichester, England: Horwood Publishing.

Izard, V., Sann, C., Spelke, E., & Streri, A. (2009). Newborn infants perceive abstract numbers. *PNAS Proceedings of the National Academy of Sciences of the United States of America, 106,* 10382–10385.

Izawa, C., & Hayden, R. G. (1993). *Race against time: Toward the principle of optimization in learning and retention.* Hillside, NJ: Lawrence Erlbaum Associates.

Jack, F., Simcock, G., & Hayne, H. (2012). Magic memories: Young children's verbal recall after a 6-year delay. *Child Development, 83,* 159–172.

Jackson, H. (2006, November 27). Boosting brain power: Computer program gives retirees a workout to keep memory sharp, thinking clear. *St. Louis Post-Dispatch,* p. H4.

Jackson, L. A., Gardner, P. D., & Sullivan, L. A. (1992). Explaining gender differences in self-pay expectations: Social comparison standards and perceptions of fair pay. *Journal of Applied Psychology, 77,* 651–663.

Jackson, T. (2006, May). Relationships between perceived close social support and health practices within community samples of American women and men. *Journal of Psychology: Interdisciplinary and Applied, 140,* 229–246.

Jacobi, C., Hayward, C., de Zwaan, M., Kraemer, H. C., & Agras, W. S. (2004). Coming to terms with risk factors for eating disorders: Application of risk terminology and suggestions for a general taxonomy. *Psychological Bulletin, 130,* 19–65.

Jacobsen, L., & Edmondson, B. (1993, August). Father figures. *American Demographics,* pp. 22–27.

Jacobson, J. W., Foxx, R. M., & Mulick, J. A. (Eds.). (2004). *Controversial therapies for developmental disabilities: Fad, fashion and science in professional practice.* Mahwah, NJ: Erlbaum.

Jacobson, N. S. (1987). Family type, visiting patterns, and children's behavior in the stepfamily: A linked family system. In K. Pasley & M. Ihinger-Tallman (Eds.), *Remarriage and stepparenting.* New York: Guilford.

Jacobson, N., & Gottman, J. (1998). *When men batter women.* New York: Simon & Schuster.

Jacobson, S. W., Fein, G. G., Jacobson, J. L., Schwartz, P. M., & Dowler, J. K. (1985). The effect of intrauterine PCB exposure on visual recognition memory. *Child Development, 56,* 853–860.

Jacoby, L. L., & Kelley, C. M. (1992). A process-dissociation framework for investigating unconscious influences: Freudian slips, projective tests, subliminal perception, and signal detection theory. *Current Directions in Psychological Science, 1,* 174–179.

Jacoby, R., & Glauberman, N. (Eds.). (1995). *The Bell Curve debate.* New York: Times Books/Random House.

Jacques, H., & Mash, E. (2004). A test of the tripartite model of anxiety and depression in elementary and high school boys and girls. *Journal of Abnormal Child Psychology, 32,* 13–25.

Jadallah, M., Anderson, R. C., Nguyen-Jahiel, K., Miller, B. W., Kim, I., Kuo, L., et al. (2011). Influence of a teacher's scaffolding moves during child-led small-group discussions. *American Educational Research Journal, 48,* 194–230.

Jager, R., Mieler, W., & Miller, J. (2008). Age-related macular degeneration. *The New England Journal of Medicine, 358,* 2606–2617.

Jahoda, G. (1980). Theoretical and systematic approaches in mass-cultural psychology. In H. C. Triandis & W. W. Lambert (Eds.), *Handbook of cross-cultural psychology* (Vol. 1). Boston: Allyn & Bacon.

Jahoda, G. (1983). European "lag" in the development of an economic concept: A study in Zimbabwe. *British Journal of Developmental Psychology, 1,* 113–120.

Jahoda, G., & Lewis, I. M. (1988). *Acquiring culture: Cross-cultural studies in child development.* London: Croom Helm.

Jahoda, M. (1982). *Employment and unemployment.* Cambridge, England: Cambridge University Press.

James, J., Ellis, B. J., Schlomer, G. L., & Garber, J. (2012). Sex-specific pathways to early puberty, sexual debut, and sexual risk taking: Tests of an integrated evolutionary–developmental model. *Developmental Psychology.* Retrieved from http://www.ncbi.nlm.nih.gov/pubmed/22268605.

James, W. (1890/1950). *The principles of psychology.* New York: Holt.

Jamieson, D. W., Lydon, J. E., Stewart, G., & Zanna, M. P. (1987). Pygmalion revisited: New evidence for student expectancy effects in the classroom. *Journal of Educational Psychology, 79,* 461–466.

Janda, L. H., & Klenke-Hamel, K. E. (1980). *Human sexuality.* New York: Van Nostrand.

Jang, K., Livesley, W., Angleitner, A., Riemann, R., & Vernon, P. (2002). Genetic and environmental influences on the covariance of facets defining the domains of the five-factor model of personality. *Personality and Individual Differences, 33,* 83–101.

Jankowiak, W., Joiner, A., & Khatib, C. (2011). What observation studies can tell us about single child play patterns, gender, and changes in Chinese society. *Cross-Cultural Research: The Journal of Comparative Social Science, 45,* 155–177.

Jansen, B. R. J., Van der Maas, W. L., & Black J. E. (2001). Evidence for the phase transition from rule I to rule II on the balance scale task. *Developmental Review, 21,* 450–494.

Janssens, J. M. A. M., & Dekovic, M. (1997). Child rearing, prosocial moral reasoning, and prosocial behaviour. *International Journal of Behavioral Development, 20,* 509–527.

Japiassu, R. (2008). Pretend play and preschoolers. In *The transformation of learning: Advances in cultural-historical activity theory.* New York: Cambridge University Press.

Jared, D., Cormier, P., Levy, B., & Wade-Woolley, L. (2011). Early predictors of biliteracy development in children in French immersion: A 4-year longitudinal study. *Journal of Educational Psychology, 103,* 119–139.

Jaswal, V., & Dodson, C. (2009). Metamemory development: Understanding the role of similarity in false memories. *Child Development, 80,* 629–635.

Javawant, S., & Parr, J. (2007). Outcome following subdural hemorrhages in infancy. *Archives of the Disabled Child, 92,* 343–347.

Jayawardena, K., & Liao, S. (2006, January). Elder abuse at end of life. *Journal of Palliative Medicine, 9,* 127–136.

Jazwinski, S. M. (1996, July 5). Longevity, genes, and aging. *Science, 273,* 54–59.

Jehlen, A., & Winans, D. (2005). No child left behind—Myth or truth? *NEA Today, 23,* 32–34.

Jeng, S., Yau, K. T., & Teng, R. (1998). Neurobehavioral development at term in very low-birthweight infants and normal term infants in Taiwan. *Early Human Development, 51,* 235–245.

Jenkins, A., Harburg, E., Weissberg, N., & Donnelly, T. (2004). The influence of minority group cultural models on persistence in college. *Journal of Negro Education, 73,* 69–80.

Jenkins, J. E. (1996). The influence of peer affiliation and student activities on adolescent drug involvement. *Adolescence, 31,* 297–306.

Jenkins, J. M., & Astington, J. W. (1996). Cognitive factors and family structure associated with theory of mind development in young children. *Developmental Psychology, 32,* 70–78.

Jensen, A. R. (2003). Regularities in Spearman's Law of Diminishing Returns. *Intelligence, 31,* 95–105.

Jensen, L. (2008). Coming of age in a multicultural world: Globalization and adolescent cultural identity formation. *Adolescent identities: A collection of readings* (pp. 3–17). New York: Analytic Press/Taylor & Francis Group.

Jeynes, W. (2007). The impact of parental remarriage on children: A meta-analysis. *Marriage & Family Review, 40,* 75–102.

Ji, S., Long, Q., Newport, D., Na, H., Knight, B., Zach, E. B., et al. (2011). Validity of depression rating scales during pregnancy and the postpartum period: Impact of trimester and parity. *Journal of Psychiatric Research, 45,* 213–219.

Jia, R., & Schoppe-Sullivan, S. J. (2011). Relations between coparenting and father involvement in families with preschool-age children. *Developmental Psychology, 47,* 106–118.

Jiang, W., Babyak, M., Krantz, D. S., Waugh, R. A., Coleman, R. E., Hanson, M. M., et al. (1996, June 5). Mental stress-induced myocardial ischemia and cardiac events. *Journal of the American Medical Association, 275,* 1651–1656.

Jiao, S., Ji, G., & Jing, Q. (1996). Cognitive development of chines urban only children and children with siblings. *Child Development, 67,* 387–395.

Ji-liang, S., Li-qing, Z., & Yan, T. (2003). The impact of intergenerational social support and filial expectation on the loneliness of elder parents. *Chinese Journal of Clinical Psychology, 11,* 167–169.

Jimenez, J., & Guzman, R. (2003). The influence of code-oriented versus meaning-oriented approaches to reading instruction on word recognition in the Spanish language. *International Journal of Psychology, 38,* 65–78.

Jimerson, S., Morrison, G., Pletcher, S., & Furlong, M. (2006). Youth engaged in antisocial and aggressive behaviors: Who are they? In *Handbook of school violence and school safety: From research to practice* (pp. 3–19). Mahwah, NJ: Lawrence Erlbaum Associates.

Joe, S., & Marcus, S (2003). Datapoints: Trends by race and gender in suicide attempts among U.S. adolescents, 1991–2001. *Psychiatric Services, 54,* 454.

Joel, D. (2011). Male or female? Brains are intersex. *Frontiers in Integrative Neuroscience.* Retrieved from http://www.ncbi.nlm.nih.gov/pmc/articles/PMC3176412/.

Johannes, L. (2003, October 9). A better test for Down syndrome. *The Wall Street Journal,* p. D1, D3.

Johannesen-Schmidt, M., & Eagly, A. (2002). Diminishing returns: The effects of income on the content stereotypes of wage earners. *Personality and Social Psychology Bulletin, 28,* 1538–1545.

Johnson, A. M., Wadsworth, J., Wellings, K., & Bradshaw, S. (1992). Sexual lifestyles and HIV risk. *Nature, 360,* 410–412.

Johnson, C. H., Vicary, J. R., Heist, C. L., & Corneal, D. A. (2001). Moderate alcohol and tobacco use during pregnancy and child behavior outcomes. *Journal of Primary Prevention, 21,* 367–379.

Johnson, C. L., & Barer, B. M. (1992). Patterns of engagement and disengagement among the oldest old. *Journal of Aging Studies, 6,* 351–364.

Johnson, D. (2003, September 22). Fighting for air. *Newsweek,* pp. 54–57.

Johnson, D., & Foster, S. (2005). The relationship between relational aggression in kindergarten children and friendship stability, mutuality, and peer liking. *Early Education and Development, 16,* 141–160.

Johnson, D., & Scelfo, J. (2003, December 15). Sex, love and nursing. *Newsweek,* 54–55.

Johnson, D. C., Kassner, C. T., & Kutner, J. S. (2004). Current use of guidelines, protocols, and care pathways for symptom management in hospice. *American Journal of Hospital Palliative Care, 21,* 51–57.

Johnson, d. J., Jaeger, E., Randolph, S. M., Cauce, A. M., Ward, J., & National Institute of Child Health and Human Development: Early Child Care Research Network. (2003). Studying the effects of early child care experiences on the development of children of color in the United States: Toward a more inclusive research agenda. *Child Development, 74,* 1227–1244.

Johnson, J. L., Primas, P. J., & Coe, M. K. (1994). Factors that prevent women of low socioeconomic status from seeking prenatal care. *Journal of the American Academy of Nurse Practitioners, 6,* 105–111.

Johnson, J., Cohen, P., Smailes, E. M., Kasen, S., & Brook, J. S. (2002, March 29). Television viewing and aggressive behavior during adolescence and adulthood. *Science, 295,* 2468–2471.

Johnson, K., & Eilers, A. (1998). Effects of knowledge and development on subordinate level categorization. *Cognitive Development, 13,* 515–545.

Johnson, M. H. (1998). The neural basis of cognitive development. In D. Kuhn & R. S. Siegler (Eds.), *Handbook of child psychology: Vol. 2: Cognition, perception, and language* (5th ed., pp. 1–49). New York: Wiley.

Johnson, M. J. (2003). Development of human brain functions. *Biological Psychiatry, 54,* 1312–1316.

Johnson, N. (2003). Psychology and health: Research, practice, and policy. *American Psychologist, 58,* 670–677.

Johnson, N. G., Roberts, M. C., & Worell, J. (Eds.). (1999). *Beyond appearance: A new look at adolescent girls.* Washington, DC: American Psychological Association.

Johnson, S. (2009). Developmental origins of object perception. *Learning and the infant mind.* New York: Oxford University Press.

Johnson, S. L., & Birch, L. L. (1994). Parents' and children's adiposity and eating style. *Pediatrics, 94,* 653–661.

Johnson, W., Emde, R. N., Pannabecker, B., Stenberg, C., & Davis, M. (1982). Maternal perception of infant emotion from birth through 18 months. *Infant Behavior and Development, 5,* 313–322.

Johnston, C. C. (1989). Pain assessment and management in infants. *Pediatrician, 16,* 16–23.

Johnston, L. D., Bachman, J. G., & O'Malley, P. M. (2010). *Monitoring the future study.* Lansing: University of Michigan.

Johnston, L., Delva, J., & O'Malley, P. (2007). Soft drink availability, contracts, and revenues in American Secondary Schools. *American Journal of Preventive Medicine, 33,* S209–SS225.

Johnston, M., & Esposito, N. (2007). Barriers and facilitators for breastfeeding among working women in the United States. *Journal of Obstetric, Gynecologic, & Neonatal Nursing: Clinical Scholarship for the Care of Women, Childbearing Families, & Newborns, 36,* 9–20.

Jokela, M., Elovainio, M., Singh-Manoux, A., & Kivimäki, M. (2009). IQ, socioeconomic status, and early death: The US National Longitudinal Study of Youth. *Psychosomatic Medicine, 71,* 322–328.

Jolles, D. D., van Buchem, M. A., Rombouts, S. B., & Crone, E. A. (2012). Practice effects in the developing brain: A pilot study. *Developmental Cognitive Neuroscience, 2*(Suppl. 1), S180–S191.

Jones, A., & Crandall, R. (Eds.). (1991). Handbook of self-actualization. *Journal of Social Behavior and Personality, 6,* 1–362.

Jones, C. (2004). *Supporting inclusion in the early years.* Maidenhead: England: Open University Press.

Jones, F., & Bright, J. (2007). Stress: Health and illness. In *The Praeger handbook on stress and coping* (Vol.1). Westport, CT: Praeger Publishers/Greenwood Publishing Group.

Jones, H. E. (2006). Drug addiction during pregnancy: Advances in maternal treatment and understanding child outcomes. *Current Directions in Psychological Science, 15,* 126–132.

Jones, M. (2003, March 16). The weaker sex. *The New York Times Magazine,* p. 56.

Jones, M. H., Audley-Piotrowski, S. R., & Kiefer, S. M. (2012). Relationships among adolescents' perceptions of friends' behaviors, academic self-concept, and math

performance. *Journal of Educational Psychology, 104,* 19–31.

Jones, S. (2006). Exploration or imitation? The effect of music on 4-week-old infants' tongue protrusions. *Infant Behavior & Development, 29,* 126–130.

Jones, S. S. (2007). Imitation in infancy: The development of mimicry. *Psychological Science, 18,* 593–599.

Jones-Harden, B. (2004). Safety and stability for foster children: A developmental perspective. *Future of Children, 14,* 31–48.

Jongudomkarn, D., & Camfield, L. (2006, September). Exploring the quality of life of people in north eastern and southern Thailand. *Social Indicators Research, 78,* 489–529.

Jordan, A., & Robinson, T. (2008, January). Children's television viewing, and weight status: Summary and recommendations from an expert panel meeting. *Annals of the American Academy of Political and Social Science, 615*(1), 119–132.

Jordan, A., Trentacoste, N., Henderson, V., Manganello, J., & Fishbein, M. (2007). Measuring the time teens spend with media: Challenges and opportunities. *Media Psychology, 9*(1), 19–41.

Jordan, J., Bardé, B., & Zeiher, A. (2007). *Contributions toward evidence-based psychocardiology: A systematic review of the literature.* Washington, DC: American Psychological Association.

Jorgensen, G. (2006, June). Kohlberg and Gilligan: duet or duel? *Journal of Moral Education, 35,* 179–196.

Jose, O., & Alfons, V. (2007). Do demographics affect marital satisfaction? *Journal of Sex and Marital Therapy, 33,* 73–85.

Josefsson, A., Gunnervik, C., Sydsjö, A., & Sydsjö, G. (2011). A comparison between Swedish midwives and obstetricians & gynecologists opinions on cesarean section. *Maternal and Child Health Journal, 15,* 555–560.

Joseph, H., Reznik, I., & Mester, R. (2003). Suicidal behavior of adolescent girls: Profile and meaning. *Israel Journal of Psychiatry & Related Sciences, 40,* 209–219.

Joseph, R. (1999). Environmental influences on neural plasticity, the limbic system, emotional development and attachment: A review. *Child Psychiatry & Human Development, 29,* 189–208.

Jost, H., & Songtag, L. (1944). The genetic factor in autonomic nervous system function. *Psychosomatic Medicine, 6,* 308–310.

Joy, M. (1997). Physician-assisted suicide: A brief historical and legal overview. *Journal of Long Term Home Health Care, 16,* 2–11.

Juby, H., Billette, J., Laplante, B., & Le Bourdais, C. (2007, September). Nonresident fathers and children: Parents' new unions and frequency of contact. *Journal of Family Issues, 28*(9), 1220–1245.

Juhn, Y. J., Sauver, J. S., Katusic, S., Vargas, D., Weaver, A., & Yunginger, J. (2005). The influence of neighborhood environment on the incidence of childhood asthma: A multilevel approach. *Social Science Medicine, 60,* 2453–2464.

Julian, T., McKenny, P. C., & McKelvey, M. W. (1992). Components of men's well-being at mid-life. *Issues in Mental Health Nursing, 13,* 285–299.

Jung, J., & Peterson, M. (2007). Body dissatisfaction and patterns of media use among preadolescent children. *Family and Consumer Sciences Research Journal, 36,* 40–54.

Juntunen, C., Wegner, K., & Matthews, L. (2002). Promoting positive career change in midlife. *Counseling across the lifespan: Prevention and treatment.* Thousand Oaks, CA: Sage Publications, Inc.

Jurimae, T., & Saar, M. (2003). Self-perceived and actual indicators of motor abilities in children and adolescents. *Perception and Motor Skills, 97,* 862–866.

Jusczyk, P. W., & Hohne, E. A. (1997, September 26). Infants' memory for spoken words. *Science, 277,* 1894–1896.

Jussim, L., Milburn, M., & Nelson, W. (1991). Emotional openness: Sex-role stereotypes and self-perceptions. *Representative Research in Social Psychology, 19,* 35–52.

Juster, F., Ono, H., & Stafford, F. (2004). *Changing times of American youth: 1981–2003.* Ann Arbor, MI: Institute for Social Research.

Juster, T., Ono, H., & Stafford, F. (2000). *Time use.* Presented at the Sloan Centers on Work and Family Conference, San Francisco.

Juvenile Justice Clearinghouse. (1995). *Current statistics on World Wide Web page.* Washington, DC.

Juvonen, J., & Graham, S. (Eds.). (2001). *Peer harassment in school: The plight of the vulnerable and victimized.* New York: Guilford Press.

Juvonen, J., Le, V.-N., Kaganoff, T., Augustine, C. H., & Constand, L. (2004). *Focus on the wonder years: Challenges facing the American middle school.* Santa Monica, CA: Rand Corporation.

Juvonen, J., Wang, Y., & Espinoza, G. (2011). Bullying experiences and compromised academic performance across middle school grades. *The Journal of Early Adolescence, 31,* 152–173.

Kabir, A. A., Pridjian, G., Steinmann, W. C., Herrera, E. A., & Khan, M. M. (2005). Racial differences in Cesareans: An analysis of U.S. 2001 national inpatient sample data. *Obstetrics & Gynecology, 105,* 710–718.

Kacapyr, E. (1997, October). Are we having fun yet? *American Demographics,* pp. 28–30.

Kagan, J. (1981). Universals in human development. In R. H. Munroe, R. L. Munroe, & B. B. Whiting (Eds.), *Handbook of crosscultural human development* (pp. 53–62). New York: Garland.

Kagan, J. (2000, October). Adult personality and early experience. *The Harvard Mental Health Letter,* pp. 4–5.

Kagan, J. (2003a). Biology, context and developmental inquiry. *Annual Review of Psychology, 54,* 1–23.

Kagan, J. (2003b). An unwilling rebel. In R. J. Sternberg (Ed.), *Psychologists defying the crowd: Stories of those who battled the establishment and won.* Washington, DC: American Psychological Association.

Kagan, J. (2008). In defense of qualitative changes in development. *Child Development, 79.*

Kagan, J. (2011). Three lessons learned. *Perspectives on Psychological Science, 6,* 107–113.

Kagan, J., Arcus, D., & Snidman, N. (1993). The idea of temperament: Where do we go from here? In R. Plomin & G. E. McClearn (Eds.), *Nature, nurture, and psychology.* Washington, DC: American Psychological Association.

Kagan, J., Arcus, D., Snidman, N., Feng, W. Y., Hendler, J., & Greene, S. (1994). Reactivity in infants: A cross-national comparison. *Developmental Psychology, 30,* 342–345.

Kagan, J., Kearsley, R., & Zelazo, P. R. (1978). *Infancy: Its place in human development.* Cambridge, MA: Harvard University Press.

Kagan, J., & Snidman, N. (1991). Infant predictors of inhibited and uninhibited profiles. *Psychological Science, 2,* 40–44.

Kagan, J., & Snidman, N. (2004). *The long shadow of temperament.* Cambridge, MA: Belknap Press/Harvard University Press.

Kagan, J., Snidman, N., Kahn, V., & Towsley, S. (2007). The preservation of two infant temperaments into adolescence. *Monographs of the Society for Research in Child Development, 72,* 1–75.

Kahana-Kalman, R., & Walker-Andrews, A. (2001). The role of person familiarity in young infants' perception of emotional expressions. *Child Development, 72,* 352–369.

Kahn, A., Groswasser, J., Franco, P., Scaillet, S., Sawaguchi, T., Kelmanson, I., & Dan, B. (2003). Sudden infant deaths: Stress, arousal and SIDS. *Early Human Development, 75* (Suppl.), 147–166.

Kahn, J. (2007, February). Maximizing the potential public health impact of HPV vaccines: A focus on parents. *Journal of Adolescent Health, 40,* 101–103.

Kahn, J. P. (2004). Hostility, coronary risk, and alpha-adrenergic to beta-adrenergic receptor density ratio. *Psychosomatic Medicine, 66,* 289–297.

Kahn, J., Hessling, R., & Russell, D. (2003). Social support, health, and well-being among the elderly: What is the role of negative affectivity? *Personality & Individual Differences, 35,* 5–17.

Kahn, P. H., Jr. (1997). Children's moral and ecological reasoning about the Prince William Sound oil spill. *Developmental Psychology, 33,* 1091–1096.

Kahn, R. L., & Rowe, J. W. (1999). *Successful aging.* New York: Dell.

Kahn, S., Zimmerman, G., Csikszentmihalyi, M., & Getzels, J. W. (1985). Relations between identity in young adulthood and intimacy at midlife. *Journal of Personality and Social Psychology, 49,* 1316–1322.

Kahneman, D., Krueger, A., Schkade, D., Schwarz, N., & Stone, A. (2006, June). Would you be happier if you were richer? A focusing illusion. *Science, 312,* 1908–1910.

Kail, R. (1991). Developmental changes in speed of processing during childhood and adolescence. *Psychological Bulletin, 109,* 490–501.

Kail, R. (2003). Information processing and memory. In M. Bornstein & L. Davidson (Eds.), *Well-being: Positive development across the life course.* Mahwah, NJ: Lawrence Erlbaum Associates.

Kail, R. V. (2004). Cognitive development includes global and domain-specific processes. *Merrill-Palmer Quarterly, 50,* 445–455.

Kail, R., & Miller, C. (2006). Developmental change in processing speed: Domain specificity and stability during childhood and adolescence. *Journal of Cognition and Development, 7(1),* 119–137.

Kaiser, L. L., Allen, L., & American Dietetic Association. (2002). Position of the American Dietetic Association: Nutrition and lifestyle for a healthy pregnancy outcome. *Journal of the American Dietetic Association, 102,* 1479–1490.

Kaitz, M., Meschulach-Sarfaty, O., Auerbach, J., & Eidelman, A. (1988). A re-examination of newborns' ability to imitate facial expressions. *Developmental Psychology, 24,* 3–7.

Kalb, C. (1997, Spring/Summer). The top 10 health worries. *Newsweek Special Issue,* 42–43.

Kalb, C. (2003, March 10). Preemies grow up. *Newsweek,* pp. 50–51.

Kalb, C. (2004, January 26). Brave new babies. *Newsweek,* pp. 45–53.

Kalb, C. (2006, December 11). Peering into the future. *Newsweek,* p. 52.

Kalichman, S. C. (1998). *Understanding AIDS, second edition: Advances in research and treatment.* Washington, DC: APA Books.

Kalish, R. A., & Reynolds, D. K. (1976). *An overview of death and ethnicity.* Farmingdale, New York: Baywood.

Kallestad, J. H., & Olweus, D. (2003). Predicting teachers' and schools' implementation of the Olweus bullying prevention program: A multilevel study. *Prevention and Treatment, 6,* 104–111.

Kalliopuska, M. (1994). Relations of retired people and their grandchildren. *Psychological Reports, 75,* 1083–1088.

Kalsi, M., Heron, G., & Charman, W. (2001). Changes in the static accommodation response with age. *Ophthalmic & Physiological Optics, 21,* 77–84.

Kaltiala-Heino, R., Kosunen, E., & Rimpela, M. (2003). Pubertal timing, sexual behaviour and self-reported depression in middle adolescence. *Journal of Adolescence, 26,* 531–545.

Kaltiala-Heino, R., Rimpelae, M., Rantanen, P., & Rimpelae, A. (2000). Bullying at school—an indicator of adolescents at risk for mental disorders. *Journal of Adolescence, 23,* 661–674.

Kamerman, S. B. (2000a). From maternity to parental leave policies: Women's health employment, and child and family well-being. *The Journal of the Women's Medical Association, 55,* Table 1.

Kamerman, S. B. (2000b). Parental leave policies: An essential ingredient in early childhood education and care policies. *Social Policy Report 14,* Table 1.0.

Kamhi, A. (1986). The elusive first word: The importance of the naming insight for the development of referential speech. *Journal of Child Language, 13,* 155–161.

Kamijo, K., Hayashi, Y., Sakai, T., Yahiro, T., Tanaka, K., & Nishihira, Y. (2009). Acute effects of aerobic exercise on cognitive function in older adults. *The Journals of Gerontology: Series B: Psychological Sciences and Social Sciences, 64B,* 356–363.

Kaminaga, M. (2007). Pubertal timing and depression in adolescents. *Japanese Journal of Educational Psychology, 55,* 370–381.

Kan, P., & Kohnert, K. (2008). Fast mapping by bilingual preschool children. *Journal of Child Language, 35,* 495–514.

Kandel, I., & Merrick, J. (2007). Delinquency and intellectual disability. *International Journal on Disability and Human Development, 6,* 273–277.

Kandler, C., Bleidorn, W., Riemann, R., Angleitner, A., & Spinath, F. M. (2011). The genetic links between the big five personality traits and general interest domains. *Personality and Social Psychology Bulletin, 37,* 1633–1643.

Kane, R. A., Caplan, A. L., Urv-Wong, E. K., & Freeman, I. C. (1997). Everyday matters in the lives of nursing home residents: Wish for and perception of choice and control. *Journal of the American Geriatrics Society, 45,* 1086–1093.

Kane, R. I., Wales, J., Bernstein, L., Leibowitz, A., & Kaplan, S. (1985, April 21). A randomized controlled trial of hospice care. *The Lancet, 302,* 890–894.

Kaneda, H., Maeshima, K., Goto, N., Kobayakawa, T., Ayabe-Kanamura, S., & Saito, S. (2000). Decline in taste and odor discrimination abilities with age, and relationship between gustation and olfaction. *Chemical Senses, 25,* 331–337.

Kanetsuna, T., Smith, P., & Morita, Y. (2006, November). Coping with bullying at school: Children's recommended strategies and attitudes to school-based interventions in England and Japan. *Aggressive Behavior, 32,* 570–580.

Kantrowitz, B., & Wingert, P. (1999, May 10). How well do you know your kid? (teenagers need adult attention). *Newsweek, 133(19),* 36.

Kantrowitz, E. J., & Evans, G. W. (2004). The relation between the ratio of children per activity area and off-task behavior and type of play in day care centers. *Environment & Behavior, 36,* 541–557.

Kao, G. (1999). Psychological well-being and educational achievement among immigrant youth. In D. J. Hernandez (Ed.), *Children of immigrants: Health, adjustment, and public assistance.* Washington, DC: National Academy Press.

Kao, G. (2000). Psychological well-being and educational achievement among immigrant youth. In D. J. Hernandez (Ed.), *Children of immigrants: Health, adjustment, and public assistance.* Washington, DC: National Academy Press.

Kao, G., & Tienda, M. (1995). Optimism and achievement: the educational performance of immigrant youth. *Social Science Quarterly, 76,* 1–19.

Kao, G., & Vaquera, E. (2006, February). The salience of racial and ethnic identification in friendship choices among Hispanic adolescents. *Hispanic Journal of Behavioral Sciences, 28,* 23–47.

Kapadia, S. (2008). Adolescent-parent relationships in Indian and Indian immigrant families in the US: Intersections and disparities. *Psychology and Developing Societies, 20,* 257–275.

Kaplan, H., & Dove, H. (1987). Infant development among the Ache of Eastern Paraguay. *Developmental Psychology, 23,* 190–198.

Kaplan, R. M., Sallis, J. F., Jr., & Patterson, T. L. (1993). Age specific breast cancer annual incidence. *Health and human behavior.* New York: McGraw-Hill.

Kaplan, S., Heiligenstein, J., West, S., Busner, J., Harder, D., Dittmann, R., et al. (2004). Efficacy and safety of atomoxetine in childhood attention-deficit/hyperactivity disorder with comorbid oppositional defiant disorder. *Journal of Attention Disorders, 8,* 45–52.

Karademas, E. C. (2007). Positive and negative aspects of well-being: Common and specific predictors. *Personality and Individual Differences, 43,* 277–287.

Karmel, B. Z., Gardner, J. M., & Magnano, C. L. (1991). Attention and arousal in early infancy. In M. J. S. Weiss & P. R. Zelazo (Eds.), *Newborn attention: Biological constraints and the influence of experience* (pp. 339–376). Norwood, NJ: Ablex.

Karney, B. R., & Bradbury, T. N. (1995). The longitudinal course of marital quality and stability: A review of theory, method, and research. *Psychological Bulletin, 118,* 3–34.

Karney, B. R., & Bradbury, T. N. (2005). Contextual influences on marriage. *Current Directions in Psychological Science, 14,* 171–174.

Karniol, R. (2009). Israeli kindergarten children's gender constancy for others' counter-stereotypic toy play and appearance: The role of sibling gender and relative age. *Infant and Child Development, 18,* 73–94.

Karoly, L. A., Greenwood, P. W., Everingham, S. S., Houbé, J., Kilburn, M. R., Rydell, C. P., et al. (1998). *Investing in our children: What we know and don't know about the costs and benefits of early childhood interventions.* Santa Monica, CA: RAND.

Karp, S. M., & Lutenbacher, M. (2011). Infant feeding practices of young mothers. *MCN: The American Journal of Maternal/Child Nursing, 36,* 98–103.

Karpov, Y. (2006). Neo-Vygotskian activity theory: Merging Vygotsky's and Piaget's theories of cognitive development. In *Frontiers in: Cognitive psychology.* Hauppauge, NY: Nova Science Publishers.

Karpov, Y. V., & Haywood, H. C. (1998). Two ways to elaborate Vygotsky's concept of mediation: Implications for instruction. *American Psychologist, 53,* 27–36.

Kart, C. S. (1990). *The realities of aging* (3rd ed.). Boston: Allyn & Bacon.

Kartman, L. L. (1991). Life review: One aspect of making meaningful music for the elderly. *Activities, Adaptations, and Aging, 15,* 42–45.

Kärtner, J., Borke, J., Maasmeier, K., Keller, H., & Kleis, A. (2011). Sociocultural influences on the development of self-recognition and self-regulation in Costa Rican and Mexican toddlers. *Journal of Cognitive Education and Psychology, 10,* 96–112.

Kärtner, J., & Keller, H. (2012). Comment: Culture-specific developmental pathways to prosocial behavior: A comment on Bischof-Köhler's universalist perspective. *Emotion Review, 4,* 49–50.

Kartrowitz, E. J., & Evans, G. W. (2004). The relation between the ratio of children per activity area and off-task behavior and type of play in day care centers. *Environment & Behavior, 36,* 541–557.

Kaslow, F. W. (2001). Families and family psychology at the millennium: Intersecting crossroads. *American Psychologist, 56,* 37–44.

Kasser, T., & Sharma, Y. S. (1999). Reproductive freedom, educational equality, and females' preference for resource-acquisition characteristics in mates. *Psychological Science, 10,* 374–377.

Kassuba, T., Klinge, C., Hölig, C., Menz, M. M., Ptito, M., Röder, B., et al. (2011). The left fusiform gyrus hosts trisensory representations of manipulable objects. *NeuroImage.* Retrieved from http://www.sciencedirect.com/science/journal/10538119.

Kastenbaum, R. (1985). Dying and death: A life-span approach. In J. E. Birren & K. W. Schaie (Eds.), *Handbook of the psychology of aging*. New York: Van Nostrand Reinhold.

Kastenbaum, R. (1999). Dying and bereavement. In J. C. Cavanaugh & S. K. Whitbourne (Eds.), *Gerontology: An interdisciplinary perspective*. New York: Oxford University Press.

Kastenbaum, R. (2000). *The psychology of death*. (3rd ed.). New York: Springer.

Kastenbaum, R. J. (1977). *Death, society and human experience*. St. Louis, MO: Mosby.

Kastenbaum, R. J. (1992). *The psychology of death*. New York: Springer-Verlag.

Katayama, A., Rodriguez, A., Brumley, K., & Warash, B. (2005). Preschoolers' judgments of object quantity under the influence of color. *Research in the Schools, 12*, 32–40.

Katchadourian, H. A. (1987). *Biological aspects of human sexuality* (3rd ed.). New York: Holt, Rinehart & Winston.

Kate, N. T. (1998, March). How many children? *American Demographics*, p. 35.

Kates, N., Grieff, B., & Hagen, D. (1990). *The psychosocial impact of job loss*. Washington, DC: American Psychiatric Press.

Kantrowitz, B., & Springen, K. (2005, May 16) A peaceful adolescence. *Newsweek International Edition*, pp. 50–52.

Kato, K., & Pedersen, N. L. (2005). Personality and coping: A study of twins reared apart and twins reared together. *Behavior Genetics, 35*, 147–158.

Katrowitz, B., & Springen, K. (2005, May 16.) A peaceful adolescence. *Newsweek International Edition*, pp. 50–52.

Katrowitz, B., & Wingert, P. (1990, Winter/Spring). Step by step. *Newsweek Special Edition*, 24–34.

Katz, D. L. (2001). Behavior modification in primary care: The Pressure System Model. *Preventive Medicine: an International Devoted to Practice & Theory, 32*, 66–72.

Katz, L. G. (1989, December). Beginners' ethics. *Parents*, p. 213.

Katz, P. (2003). Racists or tolerant multiculturalists? How do they begin? *American Psychologist, 58*, 897–909.

Katz, S., & Marshall, B. (2003). New sex for old: Lifestyle, consumerism, and the ethics of aging well. *Journal of Aging Studies, 17*, 3–16.

Katzell, R. A., & Guzzo, R. A. (1983). Psychological approaches to productivity improvement. *American Psychologist, 38*, 468–472.

Katzer, C., Fetchenhauer, D., & Belschak, F. (2009). Cyberbullying: Who are the victims?: A comparison of victimization in internet chatrooms and victimization in school. *Journal of Media Psychology: Theories, Methods, and Applications, 21*, 25–36.

Katzman, D. (2010). Sexting: Keeping teens safe and responsible in a technologically savvy world. *Paediatric Child Health, 8*, 41–45.

Kauffman, J. M. (1993). How we might achieve the radical reform of special education. *Exceptional Children, 60*, 6–16.

Kaufman, J. C., Kaufman, A. S., Kaufman-Singer, J., & Kaufman, N. L. (2005). The Kaufman Assessment Battery for Children—Second Edition and the Kaufman Adolescent and Adult Intelligence Test. In D. P. Flanagan & P. L. Harrison (Eds.), *Contemporary intellectual assessment: Theories, tests, and issues*. New York: Guilford Press.

Kaufman, J., & Sternberg, R. (2006). *The international handbook of creativity*. New York: Cambridge University Press.

Kaufman, J., & Zigler, E. (1987). Do abused children become abused parents? *American Journal of Orthopsychiatry, 57*, 186–192.

Kaufman, M. T. (1992, November 28). Teaching compassion in theater of death. *The New York Times*, p. B7.

Kaufman, S., Reynolds, M. R., Liu, X., Kaufman, A. S., & McGrew, K. S. (2012). Are cognitive g and academic achievement g one and the same g? An exploration on the Woodcock–Johnson and Kaufman tests. *Intelligence*. Retrieved from http://scottbarrykaufman.com/wp-content/uploads/2012/02/Kaufman-et-al.-2012.pdf.

Kaufmann, D., Gestert, E., Santa Lucia, R. C., Salcedo, O., Rendina-Gobioff, G., & Gadd, R. (2000). The relationship between parenting style and children's adjustment: The parents' perspective. *Journal of Child & Family Studies, 9*, 231–245.

Kavale, K. (2002). Mainstreaming to full inclusion: From orthogenesis to pathogenesis of an idea. *International Journal of Disability, Development & Education, 49*, 201—214.

Kavale, K. A., & Forness, S. R. (2000). History, rhetoric, and reality: Analysis of the inclusion debate. *Remedial and Special Education, 21*, 279–296.

Kavsek, M. (2004). Predicting later IQ from infant visual habituation and dishabituation: A meta-analysis. *Journal of Applied Developmental Psychology, 25*, 369—393.

Kawabata, Y., & Crick, N. R. (2011). The antecedents of friendships in moderately diverse classrooms: Social preference, social impact, and social behavior. *International Journal of Behavioral Development, 35*, 48–57.

Kaye, W. (2008). Neurobiology of anorexia and bulimia nervosa. *Physiology & Behavior, 94*, 121–135.

Kaye, W. H., Devlin, B., Barbarich, N., Bulik, C. M., Thornton, L., Badanu, S. A., et al. (2004). Genetic analysis of bulimia nervosa: Methods and sample description. *Journal of Eating Disorders, 35*, 556–570.

Kayton, A., (2007). Newborn screening: A literature review. *Neonatal Network, 26*, 85–95.

Kazdin, A. E. (1990). Childhood depression. *Journal of Child Psychology and Psychiatry, 31*, 121–160.

Kazdin, A. E., & Benjet, C. (2003). Spanking children: Evidence and issues. *Current Directions in Psychological Science, 12*, 99–103.

Kazura, K. (2000). Fathers' qualitative and quantitative involvement: An investigation of attachment, play, and social interactions. *Journal of Men's Studies, 9*, 41–57.

Keating, D. (1990). Adolescent thinking. In S. S. Feldman & G. R. Elliott (Eds.), *At the threshold*. Cambridge, MA: Harvard University Press.

Keating, D. (Ed.). (2011). *Nature and nurture in early child development*. New York: Cambridge University Press.

Keating, D. P. (1980). Thinking processes in adolescence. In J. Adelson (Ed.), *Handbook of adolescent psychology*. New York: Wiley.

Keating, D. P. (2004). Cognitive and brain development. In R. M. Lerner & L. Steinberg (Eds). *Handbook of adolescent psychology* (2nd ed.). Hoboken, NJ: John Wiley & Sons.

Keating, D. P., & Clark, L. V. (1980). Development of physical and social reasoning in adolescence. *Developmental Psychology, 16*, 23–30.

Keck-Wherley, J., Grover, D., Bhattacharyya, S., Xu, X., Holman, D., Lombardini, E. D., et al. (2011). Abnormal microRNA expression in Ts65Dn hippocampus and whole blood: Contributions to Down syndrome phenotypes. *Developmental Neuroscience, 33*, 451–467.

Kecskes, I., & Papp, T. (2000). *Foreign language and mother tongue*. Mahwah, NJ: Erlbaum.

Kedziora-Kornatowski, K., Szewczyk-Golec, K., Czuczejko, J., van Marke de Lumen, K., Pawluk, H., Motyl, J., Karasek, M., & Kedziora, J. (2007). Effect of melatonin on the oxidative stress in erythrocytes of healthy young and elderly subjects. *Journal of Pineal Research, 42*, 153–158.

Keefer, B. L., Kraus, R. F., Parker, B. L., Elliotst, R., et al. (1991). A state university collaboration program:

Residents' perspectives. Annual meeting of the American Psychiataric Association (1990, New York, New York). *Hospital and Community Psychiatry, 42*, 62–66.

Keel, P., & Haedt, A. (2008). Evidence-based psychosocial treatments for eating problems and eating disorders. *Journal of Clinical Child and Adolescent Psychology, 37*, 39–61.

Keel, P. K., Leon, G. R., & Fulkerson, J. A. (2001). Vulnerability to eating disorders in childhood and adolescence. In R. E. Ingram & J. M. Price (Eds.), *Vulnerability to psychopathology: Risk across the lifespan*. New York: Guilford Press.

Kelch-Oliver, K. (2008). African American grandparent caregivers: Stresses and implications for counselors. *The Family Journal, 16*, 43–50.

Keller, H., Otto, H., Lamm, B., Yovsi, R., & Kärtner, J. (2008, April). The timing of verbal/vocal communications between mothers and their infants: A longitudinal cross-cultural comparison. *Infant Behavior & Development, 31*(2), 217–226.

Keller, H., Voelker, S., & Yovsi, R. D. (2005). Conceptions of parenting in different cultural communities: The case of West African Nso and Northern German women. *Social Development, 14*, 158–180.

Keller, H., Yovsi, R., Borke, J., Kärtner, J., Henning, J., & Papaligoura, Z. (2004). Developmental consequences of early parenting experiences: Self-recognition and self-regulation in three cultural communities. *Child Development, 75*, 1745–1760.

Keller, M., & Miller, G. (2006). Resolving the paradox of common, harmful, heritable mental disorders: Which evolutionary genetic models work best? *Behavioral and Brain Sciences, 29*, 385–452.

Kellett, J. M. (1993). Sexuality in later life. *Reviews in Clinical Gerontology, 3*, 309–314.

Kellett, J. M. (2000). Older adult sexuality. In L. T. Szuchman & F. Muscarella, et al. (Eds.), *Psychological perspectives on human sexuality*. New York: Wiley.

Kelley, G., Kelley, K., Hootman, J., & Jones, D. (2009). Exercise and health-related quality of life in older community-dwelling adults: A meta-analysis of randomized controlled trials. *Journal of Applied Gerontology, 28*, 369–394.

Kelley, J. (2009, October 9). Police nab 2 alleged child predators. *Intelligencer Journal (Lancaster, PA)*, p. A1.

Kellman, P., & Arterberry, M. (2006). Infant visual perception. In W. Damon & R. M. Lerner, *Handbook of child psychology: Vol 2, Cognition, perception, and language* (6th ed.). New York: John Wiley & Sons Inc.

Kellow, J., & Jones, B. (2008, February). The effects of stereotypes on the achievement gap: Reexamining the academic performance of African American high school students. *Journal of Black Psychology, 34*(1), 94–120.

Kelly, G. (2001). *Sexuality today: A human perspective* (7th ed.) New York: McGraw-Hill.

Kelly, J. (1997, January 22). The latest in take-at-home tests: IQ. *The New York Times*, p. B7.

Kelly, J. A., Murphy, D. A., Sikkema, K.J., & Kalichman, S.C. (1993). Psychological interventions to prevent HIV infection are urgently needed. *American Psychologist, 48*, 1023–1034.

Kelly-Weeder, S., & Cox, C. (2007). The impact of lifestyle risk factors on female infertility. *Women & Health, 44*, 1–23.

Kemker, D. (2010, October 13). *Science hero: Ameen Abdulrasool*. Retrieved from http://www.myhero.com/go/hero.asp?hero=abdulrasool_06.

Kemper, A. R. (2011). Universal newborn hearing screening improves quality of life for children with permanent hearing impairment. *The Journal of Pediatrics, 158*, 88–93.

Kemper, R. L., & Vernooy, A. R. (1994). Metalinguistic awareness in first graders: A qualitative perspective. *Journal of Psycholinguistic Research, 22*, 41–57.

Kenen, R., Smith, A. C. M., Watkins, C., & Zuber-Pittore, C. (2000). To use or not to use: The prenatal genetic technology/worry conundrum. *Journal of Genetic Counseling, 9,* 203–217.

Kennedy, G. E. (1990). College students' expectations of grandparent and grandchild role behavior. *Gerontologist, 30,* 43–48.

Kennell, J. H. (2002). On becoming a family: Bonding and the changing patterns in baby and family behavior. In J. Gomes-Pedro & J. K. Nugent (Eds.), *The infant and family in the twenty-first century.* New York: Brunner-Routledge.

Kenrick, D. T., Keefe, R. C., Bryna, A., Barr, A., & Brown, S. (1995). Age preferences and mate choice among homosexuals and heterosexuals: A case for modular psychological mechanisms. *Journal of Personality and Social Psychology, 69,* 1166–1172.

Kerner, M., & Aboud, F. E. (1998). The importance of friendship qualities and reciprocity in a multi-racial school. *The Canadian Journal of Research in Early Childhood Education, 7,* 117–125.

Kerr, M., & Stattin, H. (2003). Parenting of adolescents: Action or reaction? *Children's influence on family dynamics: The neglected side of family relationships* (pp. 121–151). Mahwah, NJ: Lawrence Erlbaum Associates.

Kesler, S. (2007). Turner syndrome. *Child and Adolescent Psychiatric Clinics of North America, 16,* 709–722.

Kessels, L. E., Ruiter, R. C., Brug, J., & Jansma, B. M. (2011). The effects of tailored and threatening nutrition information on message attention. Evidence from an event-related potential study. *Appetite, 56,* 32–38.

Kessen, W. (1979). The American child and other cultural inventions. *American Psychologist, 34,* 815–820.

Kiang, L., Yip, T., & Fuligni, A. J. (2008). Multiple social identities and adjustment in young adults from ethnically diverse backgrounds. *Journal of Research on Adolescence, 18,* 643–670.

Kibria, N. (2003). *Becoming Asian American: Second-generation Chinese and Korean American identities.* Baltimore, MD: Johns Hopkins University Press.

Kidd, E. (2012). Implicit statistical learning is directly associated with the acquisition of syntax. *Developmental Psychology, 48,* 171–184.

Kidwell, J. S., Dunyam, R. M., Bacho, R. A., Pastorino, E., & Portes, P. R. (1995). Adolescent identity exploration: A test of Erikson's theory of transitional crisis. *Adolescence, 30,* 785–793.

Kiecolt, K. J., & Fossett, M. A. (1997). The effects of mate availability on marriage among black Americans: A contextual analysis. In R. J. Taylor, J. S. Jackson, & L. M. Chatters (Eds.), *Family life in black America* (pp. 63–78). Thousand Oaks, CA: Sage.

Kiecolt-Glaser, J. K. (2009). Psychoneuroimmunology: Psychology's gateway to biomedical future. *Perspectives on Psychological Science, Special issue: Next big questions in psychology, 4,* 367–369.

Kiecolt-Glaser, J. K., Bane, C., Glaser, R., & Malarkey, W. B. (2003). Love, marriage, and divorce: Newlyweds' stress hormones foreshadow relationship changes. *Journal of Consulting and Clinical Psychology, 71,* 176–188.

Kiecolt-Glaser, J. K., & Glaser, R. (1986). Behavioral influences on immune function: Evidence for the interplay between stress and health. In T. Field, P. McCabe, & N. Schneiderman (Eds.), *Stress and coping* (Vol. 2). Hillsdale, NJ: Erlbaum.

Kiecolt-Glaser, J. K., & Kiecolt-Glaser, R. (1991). Psychosocial factors, stress, disease, and immunity. In R. Ader, D. L. Felten, & N. Cohen (Eds.), *Psychoneuroimmunology.* San Diego: Academic Press.

Kiecolt-Glaser, J. K., & Newton, T. L. (2001). Marriage and health: His and hers. *Psychological Bulletin, 127,* 472–503.

Kiecolt-Glaser, R., & Kiecolt-Glaser, J. K. (1993). Mind and immunity. In D. Goleman & J. Gurin (Eds.), *Mind–body medicine.* Yonkers, NY: Consumer Reports Books.

Killen, M., & Hart, D. (Eds.). (1995). *Morality in everyday life: Developmental perspectives.* New York: Cambridge University Press.

Killeya-Jones, L., Costanzo, P., Malone, P., Quinlan, N., & Miller-Johnson, S. (2007). Norm-narrowing and self- and other-perceived aggression in early-adolescent same-sex and mixed-sex cliques. *Journal of School Psychology, 45,* 549–565.

Kilner, J. M., Friston, J. J., & Frith, C. D. (2007). Predictive coding: An account of the mirror neuron system. *Cognitive Processes, 33,* 88–997.

Kim, E., & Hong, S. (2007). First-generation Korean-American parents' perceptions of discipline, *Journal of Professional Nursing, 23,* 60–68.

Kim, E. H., & Lee, E. (2009). Effects of a death education program on life satisfaction and attitude toward death in college students. *Journal of Korean Academic Nursing, 39,* 1–9.

Kim, H., Sherman, D., & Taylor, S. (2008). Culture and social support. *American Psychologist, 63,* 518–526.

Kim, J. (1995, January). You cannot know how much freedom you have here. *Money,* 133.

Kim, J., & Cicchetti, D. (2003). Social self-efficacy and behavior problems in maltreated children. *Journal of Clinical Child & Adolescent Psychology, 32,* 106–117.

Kim, J.-S., & Lee, E.-H. (2003). Cultural and noncultural predictors of health outcomes in Korean daughter and daughter-in-law caregivers. *Public Health Nursing, 20,* 111–119.

Kim, K., & Smith, P. K. (1999). Family relations in early childhood and reproductive development. *Journal of Reproductive & Infant Psychology, 17,* 133–148.

Kim, K., Smith, P. K., & Palermiti, A. (1997). Conflict in childhood and reproductive development. *Evolution & Human Behavior, 18,* 109–142.

Kim, S., & Park, H. (2006, January). Five years after the launch of Viagra in Korea: Changes in perceptions of erectile dysfunction treatment by physicians, patients, and the patients' spouses. *Journal of Sexual Medicine, 3,* 132–137.

Kim, U., Triandis, H. C., Klggitçibais, Ç., Choi, S., & Yoon, G. (Eds.). (1994). *Individualism and collectivism: Theory, method, and applications.* Thousand Oaks, CA: Sage.

Kim, Y., Choi, J. Y., Lee, K. M., Park, S. K., Ahn, S. H., Noh, D. Y., et al. (2007). Dose-dependent protective effect of breast-feeding against breast cancer among never-lactated women in Korea. *European Journal of Cancer Prevention, 16,* 124–129.

Kim, Y., Hur, J., Kim, K., Oh, K., & Shin, Y. (2008). Prediction of postpartum depression by sociodemographic, obstetric and psychological factors: A prospective study. *Psychiatry and Clinical Neurosciences, 62,* 331–340.

Kim, Y., & Stevens, J. H. (1987). The socialization of prosocial behavior in children. *Childhood Education, 63,* 200–206.

Kim-Cohen, J. (2007). Resilience and developmental psychopathology. *Child and Adolescent Psychiatric Clinics of North America, 16,* 271–283.

Kimball, J. W. (1983). *Biology* (5th ed.). Reading, MA: Addison-Wesley.

Kimm, S. Y. (2003). Nature versus nurture in childhood obesity: A familiar old conundrum. *American Journal of Clinical Nutrition, 78,* 1051–1052.

Kimm, S. Y., Barton, B. A., Obarzanek, E., McMahon, R. P., Kronsberg, S. S., Waclawiw, M. A., et al. (2000). Obesity development during adolescence in a biracial cohort: the NHLBI Growth and Health Study. *Pediatrics, 110,* e54.

Kimm, S. Y., Glynn, N. W., Kriska, A. M., Barton, B. A., Kronsberg, S. S., Daniels, S. R., et al. (2002). Decline in physical activity in black girls and white girls during adolescence. *New England Journal of Medicine, 347,* 709–715.

Kimmel, D., & Sang, B. (2003). Lesbians and gay men in midlife. In L. Garnets & D. Kimmel (Eds.), *Psychological perspectives on lesbian, gay, and bisexual experiences.* New York: Columbia University Press.

Kincl, L., Dietrich, K., & Bhattacharya, A. (2006, October). Injury trends for adolescents with early childhood lead exposure. *Journal of Adolescent Health, 39,* 604–606.

King, K. (2003). Racism or sexism? Attributional ambiguity and simultaneous memberships in multiple oppressed groups. *Journal of Applied Social Psychology, 33,* 223–247.

Kinney, H. C., Randall, L. L., Sleeper, L. A., Willinger, M., Beliveau, R. A., Zec, N., et al. (2003). Serotonergic brainstem abnormalities in Northern Plains Indians with the sudden infant death syndrome. *Journal of Neuropathology and Experimental Neurology, 62,* 1178–1191.

Kinney, H., & Thach, B. (2009). Medical progress: The sudden infant death syndrome. *The New England Journal of Medicine, 361,* 795–805.

Kinsey, A. C., Pomeroy, W. B., & Martin, C. E. (1948). *Sexual behavior in the human male.* Philadelphia: Saunders.

Kinzie, J., Thomas, A., Palmer, M., Umbach, P., & Kuh, G. (2007, March). Women students at coeducational and women's colleges: How do their experiences compare? *Journal of College Student Development, 48*(2), 145–165.

Kirby, D., Baumler, E., Coyle, K., Basen-Engquist, K., Parcel, G., Harrist, R., et al. (2004). The "Safer Choices" intervention: Its impact on the sexual behaviors of different subgroups of high school students. *Journal of Adolescent Health, 35,* 442–452.

Kirby, J. (2006, May). From single-parent families to stepfamilies: Is the transition associated with adolescent alcohol initiation? *Journal of Family Issues, 27,* 685–711.

Kirchengast, S., & Hartmann, B. (2003). Impact of maternal age and maternal somatic characteristics on newborn size. *American Journal of Human Biology, 15,* 220–228.

Kirsh, S. J. (2012). *Children, adolescents, and media violence: A critical look at the research* (2nd ed.). Thousand Oaks, CA: Sage Publications, Inc.

Kirshner, H. S. (1995). *Classical aphasia syndromes.* New York: Marcel Dekker.

Kisilevsky, B., Hains, S., Brown, C., Lee, C., Cowperthwaite, B., Stutzman, S., et al. (2009). Fetal sensitivity to properties of maternal speech and language. *Infant Behavior & Development, 32,* 59–71.

Kisilevsky, B. S., Hains, S. M. J., Xing Xie, K. L., Huang, H., Ye, H. H., & Zhang, Z., et al. (2003). Effects of experience on fetal voice recognition. *Psychological Science, 14,* 220–224.

Kisilevsky, B., Mains, S., & Lee, K. (2003). Effects of experience on fetal voice recognition. *Psychological Science, 14,* 220–224.

Kissane, D., & Li, Y. (2008). Effects of supportive-expressive group therapy on survival of patients with metastatic breast cancer: A randomized prospective trial. *Cancer, 112,* 443–444.

Kitamura, C., & Lam, C. (2009). Age-specific preferences for infant-directed affective intent. *Infancy, 14,* 77–100.

Kitchener, R. F. (1996). The nature of the social for Piaget and Vygotsky. *Human Development, 39,* 243–249.

Kittell, L. A., & Mansfield, P. K. (2000). What perimenopausal women think about using hormones during menopause. *Women & Health, 30,* 77–91.

Kitterod, R., & Pettersen, S. (2006, September). Making up for mothers' employed working hours? Housework and childcare among Norwegian fathers. *Work, Employment and Society, 20,* 473–492.

Kitzmann, K., Gaylord, N., & Holt, A. (2003). Child witnesses to domestic violence: A meta-analytic review. *Journal of Consulting & Clinical Psychology, 71,* 339–352.

Kiuru, N., Nurmi, J., Aunola, K., & Salmela-Aro, K. (2009). Peer group homogeneity in adolescents' school adjustment varies according to peer group type and gender. *International Journal of Behavioral Development, 33*, 65–76.

Kivett, V. R. (1991). Centrality of the grandfather role among older rural black and white men. *Journal of Gerontology: Social Sciences, 46*, S250–S258.

Klaczynski, P. A. (1997). Bias in adolescents' everyday reasoning and its relationship with intellectual ability, personal theories, and self-serving motivation. *Developmental Psychology, 33*, 273–283.

Klaczynski, P. A. (2004). A dua-process model of adolescent development: Implications for decision making, reasoning, and identity. In R. V. Kail (Ed.), *Advances in child development and behavior* (Vol. 32). San Diego, CA: Elsevier Academic Press.

Klaczynski, P. A. (2011). Age differences in understanding precedent-setting decisions and authorities' responses to violations of deontic rules. *Journal of Experimental Child Psychology, 109*, 1–24.

Klaus, H. M., & Kennell, J. H. (1976). *Maternal–infant bonding.* St. Louis, MO: Mosby.

Kleespies, P. (2004). The wish to die: Assisted suicide and voluntary euthanasia. In P. Kleespies (Ed.), *Life and death decisions: Psychological and ethical considerations in end-of-life care.* Washington, DC: American Psychological Association.

Klein, M. C., Gauthier, R. J., Robbins, J. M., Kaczorowski, J., Jorgensen, S. H., Franco, E. D., et al. (1994). Relationship of episiotomy to perineal trauma and morbidity, sexual dysfunction, and pelvic floor relaxation. *American Journal of Obstetrics and Gynecology, 171*, 591–598.

Klibanoff, R., Levine, S., Huttenlocher, J., Vasilyeva, M., & Hedges, L. (2006). Preschool children's mathematical knowledge: The effect of teacher "math talk." *Developmental Psychology, 42*, 59–69.

Klier, C. M., Muzik, M., Dervic, K., Mossaheb, N., Benesch, T., Ulm, B., et al. (2007). The role of estrogen and progesterone in depression after birth. *Journal of Psychiatric Research, 41*, 273–279.

Kline, D. W., & Schieber, F. (1985). Vision and aging. In J. E. Birren & K. W. Schaie (Eds.), *Handbook of the psychology of aging* (2nd ed.). New York: Van Nostrand Reinhold.

Klinnert, M. (1984). The regulation of infant behavior by maternal facial expression. *Infant Behavior and Development, 7*, 447–465.

Klock, S. C., &Greenfeld, D. A. (2000). Psychological status of in vitro fertilization patients during pregnancy: A longitudinal study. *Fertility & Sterility, 73*, 1159–1164.

Kloep, M., Güney, N., çok, F., & Simsek, ö. (2009). Motives for risk-taking in adolescence: A cross-cultural study. *Journal of Adolescence, 32*, 135–151.

Kluger, J. (2002, January 21). Can we learn to beat the reaper? *Time Magazine*, p. 102.

Kluger, J. (2006, July 10). The new science of siblings. *Time*, pp. 47–55.

Kmiec, E. B. (1999). Gene therapy. *American Scientist, 87*, 240–247.

Knafo, A., & Plomin, R. (2006). Parental discipline and affection and children's prosocial behavior: Genetic and environmental links. *Journal of Personality and Social Psychology, 90*, 147–164.

Knafo, A., & Schwartz, S. H. (2003). Parenting and accuracy of perception of parental values by adolescents. *Child Development, 73*, 595–611.

Knaus, W. A., Conners, A. F., Dawson, N. V., Desbiens, N. A., Fulkerson, W. J., Jr., Goldman, L., et al. (1995, November 22). A controlled trial to improve care for seriously ill hospitalized patients. The study to understand prognoses and preferences for outcomes and risks of treatments (SUPPORT). *Journal of the American Medical Association, 273*, 1591–1598.

Knecht, S., Deppe, M., Draeger, B., Bobe, L., Lohmann, H., Ringelstein, E. B., et al. (2000). Language lateralization in healthy right-handers. *Brain, 123*, 74–81.

Knickmeyer, R., & Baron-Cohen, S. (2006, December). Fetal testosterone and sex differences. *Early Human Development, 82*, 755–760.

Knight, G. P., Fabes, R. A., & Higgins, D. A. (1996). Concerns about drawing casual inferences from meta-analyses: An example in the study of gender differences in aggression. *Psychological Bulletin, 119*, 410–421.

Knight, K. (1994, March). Back to basics. *Essence*, pp. 122–138.

Knittle, J. L. (1975). Early influences on development of adipose tissue. In G. A. Bray (Ed.), *Obesity in perspective.* Washington, DC: U.S. Government Printing Office.

Knorth, E., Harder, A., Zandberg, T., & Kendrick, A. (2008, February). Under one roof: A review and selective meta-analysis on the outcomes of residential child and youth care. *Children and Youth Services Review, 30*(2), 123–140.

Knutson, J. F., & Lansing, C. R. (1990). The relationship between communication problems and psychological difficulties in persons with profound acquired hearing loss. *Journal of Speech and Hearing Disorders, 55*, 656–664.

Kocarnik, R. A., & Ponzetti, J. J., Jr. (1991). The advantages and challenges of intergenerational programs in long-term care facilities. *Journal of Gerontological Social Work, 16*, 97–107.

Kochanska, G. (1997). Mutually responsive orientation between mothers and their young children: Implications for early socialization. *Child Development, 68*, 94–112.

Kochanska, G. (1998). Mother–child relationship, child fearfulness, and emerging attachment: A short-term longitudinal study. *Developmental Psychology, 34*, 480–490.

Kochanska, G., & Aksan, N. (2004). Development of mutual responsiveness between parents and their young children. *Child Development, 75*, 1657–1676.

Kochanska, G., Friesenborg, A. E., Lange, L. A., & Martel, M. M. (2004). Parents' personality and infants' temperament as contributors to their emerging relationship. *Journal of Personality and Social Psychology, 86*, 744–759.

Kodl, M., & Mermelstein, R. (2004). Beyond modeling: Parenting practices, parental smoking history, and adolescent cigarette smoking. *Addictive Behaviors, 29*, 17–32.

Koenig, A., Cicchetti, D., & Rogosch, F. (2004). Moral development: The association between maltreatment and young children's prosocial behaviors and moral transgressions. *Social Development, 13*, 97–106.

Koenig, L. B., McGue, M., Krueger, R. F., & Bouchard, T. J., Jr. (2005). Genetic and environmental influences on religiousness: Findings for retrospective and current religiousness ratings. *Journal of Personality, 73*, 471–488.

Koffman, O. (2012). Children having children? Religion, psychology and the birth of the teenage pregnancy problem. *History of the Human Sciences, 25*, 119–134.

Koh, A., & Ross, L. (2006). Mental health issues: A comparison of lesbian, bisexual and heterosexual women. *Journal of Homosexuality, 51*, 33–57.

Kohlberg, L. (1966). A cognitive-developmental anaylsis of children's sex-role concepts and attitudes. In E. E. Maccoby (Ed.), *The development of sex differences.* Stanford, CA: Stanford University Press.

Kohlberg, L. (1969). Stage and sequence: The cognitive-developmental approach to socialization. In D. Goslin (Ed.), *Handbook of socialization theory and research.* Chicago: Rand McNally.

Kohlberg, L. (1984). *The psychology of moral development: Essays on moral development* (Vol. 2). San Francisco: Harper & Row.

Kohn, A. (2006). *The homework myth: Why our kids get too much of a bad thing.* Cambridge, MA: Da Capo Press.

Kohut, S., & Riddell, R. (2009). Does the Neonatal Facial Coding System differentiate between infants experiencing pain-related and non-pain-related distress? *The Journal of Pain, 10*, 214–220.

Koivisto, M., & Revonsuo, A. (2003). Object recognition in the cerebral hemispheres as revealed by visual field experiments. *Laterality: Asymmetries of Body, Brain & Cognition, 8*, 135–153.

Kolata, G. (1994, August). Selling growth drug for children: The legal and ethical questions. *The New York Times*, pp. A1, A11.

Kolata, G. (1997, April 24). A record and big questions as woman gives birth at 63. *The New York Times*, pp. A1, A25.

Kolata, G. (1997, December 2). On cloning humans, "Never" turns swiftly into "Why not." *The New York Times*, pp. A1, A24.

Kolata, G. (1998). *Clone: The road to Dolly and the path ahead.* New York: William Morrow.

Kolata, G. (May 11, 2004). The heart's desire. *The New York Times*, p. D1.

Kolb, B. (1989). Brain development, plasticity, and behavior. *American Psychologist, 44*(9), 1203–1212.

Kolb, B. (1995). *Brain plasticity and behavior.* Mahwah, NJ: Erlbaum.

Kolb, B., & Gibb, R. (2006). Critical periods for functional recovery after cortical injury during development. *Reprogramming the cerebral cortex: Plasticity following central and peripheral lesions.* New York: Oxford University Press.

König, R. (2005). Introduction: Plasticity, learning, and cognition. In R. König, P. Heil, E. Budinger, & H. Scheich (Eds.), *Auditory cortex: A synthesis of human and animal research.* Mahwah, NJ: Lawrence Erlbaum Associates.

Konstam, V. (2007). *Emerging and young adulthood: Multiple perspectives, diverse narratives.* New York: Springer Science + Business Media.

Koopmans, S., & Kooijman, A. (2006, November). Prebyopia correction and accommodative intraocular lenses. *Gerontechnology, 5*, 222–230.

Koroukian, S. M., Trisel, B., & Rimm, A. A. (1998). Estimating the proportion of unnecessary cesarean sections in Ohio using birth certificate data. *Journal of Clinical Epidemiology, 51*, 1327–1334.

Koshmanova, T. (2007). Vygotskian scholars: Visions and implementation of cultural-historical theory. *Journal of Russian & East European Psychology, 45*, 61–95.

Koska, J., Ksinantova, L., Sebokova, E., Kvetnansky, R., Klimes, I., Chrousos, G., et al. (2002). Endocrine regulation of subcutaneous fat metabolism during cold exposure in humans. *Annals of the New York Academy of Science, 967*, 500–505.

Koski, L. R., & Shaver, P. R. (1997). Attachment and relationship satisfaction across the life span. In R. J. Sternberg & M. Hojjat (Eds.), *Satisfaction in close relationships* (pp. 26–55). New York: Guilford.

Kosmala, K., & Kloszewska, I. (2004). The burden of providing care for Alzheimer's disease patients in Poland. *International Journal of Geriatric Psychiatry, 19*, 191–193.

Koss, M. P., Dinero, T. E., Seibel, C. A., & Cox, S. L. (1988). Stranger and acquaintance rape: Are there differences in the victim's experience? *Psychology of Women Quarterly, 12*, 1–24.

Koss, M. P., Goodman, L. A., Browne, A., Fitzgerald, L. F., Keita, G. P., & Russo, N. F. (1993). *No safe haven: Violence against women, at home, at work, and in the community.* Final report of the American Psychological Association Women's Programs Office Task Force on Violence Against Women. Washington, DC: American Psychological Association.

Kossowsky, J., Wilhelm, F. H., Roth, W. T., & Schneider, S. (2012). Separation anxiety disorder in children: Disorder-specific responses to experimental separation from the mother. *Journal of Child Psychology and Psychiatry, 53*, 178–187.

Kotaska, A. (2011). Commentary: Routine cesarean section for breech: The unmeasured cost. *Birth: Issues in Perinatal Care, 38,* 162–164.

Kotre, J., & Hall, E. (1990). *Seasons of life.* Boston: Little, Brown.

Kovelman, I., Baker S. A., & Petitto, L. A. (2008). Bilingual and monolingual brains compared: A functional magnetic resonance imaging investigation of syntactic processing and a possible "neural signature" of bilingualism. *Journal of Cognitive Neuroscience, 20,* 153–169.

Kozey, M., & Siegel, L. (2008). Definitions of learning disabilities in Canadian provinces and territories. *Canadian Psychology/Psychologie Canadienne, 49,* 162–171.

Kozulin, A. (2004). Vygotsky's theory in the classroom: Introduction. *European Journal of Psychology of Education, 19,* 3–7.

Kozulin, A., & Falik, L. (1995). Dynamic cognitive assessment of the child. *Current Directions in Psychological Science, 4,* 192–196.

Kraebel, K. S. (2012). Redundant amodal properties facilitate operant learning in 3-month-old infants. *Infant Behavior & Development, 35,* 12–21.

Kraebel, K., & Gerhardstein, P. (2006). Three-month-old infants' object recognition across changes in viewpoint using an operant learning procedure. *Infant Behavior & Development, 29,* 11–23.

Kraemer, B., Noll, T., Delsignore, A., Milos, G., Schnyder, U., & Hepp, U. (2006). Finger length ratio (2D:4D) and dimensions of sexual orientation. *Neuropsychobiology, 53,* 210–214.

Kraemer, H. C., Korner, A., Anders, T., Jacklin, C. N., & Dimiceli, S. (1985). Obstetric drugs and infant behavior: A re-evaluation. *Journal of Pediatric Psychology, 10,* 345–353.

Krähenbühl, S., & Blades, M. (2006, May). The effect of question repetition within interviews on young children's eyewitness recall. *Journal of Experimental Child Psychology, 94,* 57–67.

Kramer, A. F., Erickson, K. I., & Colcombe, S. J. (2006). Exercise, cognition, and the aging brain. *Journal of Applied Physiology, 101,* 1237–1242.

Kramer, L., Perozynski, L., & Chung, T. (1999). Parental responses to sibling conflict: The effects of development and parent gender. *Child Development, 70,* 1401–1414.

Kramer, M. S. (2003a). The epidemiology of adverse pregnancy outcomes: An overview. *Journal of Nutrition, 133,* 1592S–1596S.

Kramer, M. S. (2003b). Food supplementation during pregnancy and functional outcomes. *Journal of Health, Population and Nutrition, 21,* 81–82.

Kramer, M., Aboud, F., Mironova, E., Vanilovich, I., Platt, R., Matush, L., et al. (2008). Breastfeeding and child cognitive development: New evidence from a large randomized trial. *Archives of General Psychiatry, 65,* 578–584.

Krantz, S. G. (1999). Conformal mappings. *American Scientist, 87,* 144.

Kraus, M., Segal, N., Shkolnik, M., Kochva, A., German, L., Kaplan, D., et al. (2011). The influence of epidural anesthesia on the hearing system after normal labor. *International Journal of Audiology, 50,* 519–522.

Krause, N. (2003a). Religious meaning and subjective well-being in late life. *Journals of Gerontology: Series B: Psychological Sciences and Social Sciences, 58B,* S160–S170.

Krause, N. (2003b). Praying for others, financial strain, and physical health status in late life. *Journal for the Scientific Study of Religion, 42,* 377–391.

Krause, N. (2008). The social foundation of religious meaning in life. *Research on Aging, 30,* 395–427.

Krause, N., & Borawski-Clark, E. (1994). Clarifying the functions of social support in later life. *Research on Aging, 16,* 251–279.

Kraybill, E. N. (1998). Ethical issues in the care of extremely low birth weight infants. *Seminars in Perinatology, 22,* 207–215.

Krcmar, M., Grela, B., & Lin, K. (2007). Can toddlers learn vocabulary from television? An experimental approach. *Media Psychology, 10,* 41–63.

Krebs, N. F., Himes, J. H., Jacobson, D., Nicklas, T. A., Guilday, P., & Styne, D. (2007). Assessment of child and adolescent overweight and obesity. *Pediatrics, Special issue: Assesment of childhood and adolescent overweight and obesity. 120,* S193–S228.

Kreitlow, B., & Kreitlow, D. (1997). *Creative planning for the second half of life.* Duluth, MN: Whole Person Associates.

Kremar, M., & Greene, K. (2000). Connections between violent television exposure and adolescent risk taking. *Media Psychology, 2,* 195–217.

Krettenauer, T., Jia, F., & Mosleh, M. (2011). The role of emotion expectancies in adolescents' moral decision making. *Journal of Experimental Child Psychology, 108,* 358–370.

Kringelbach M. L., Lehtonen A., Squire S., Harvey A. G., Craske M. G., et al. (2008). A specific and rapid neural signature for parental instinct. *PLoS ONE, 3*(2), e1664.

Krishnamoorthy, J. S., Hart, C., & Jelalian, E. (2006). The epidemic of childhood obesity: Review of research and implications for public policy. *Social Policy Report, 19,* 3–19.

Kroger, J. (2000). *Identity development: Adolescence through adulthood.* Thousand Oaks, CA: Sage.

Kroger, J. (2007). Why is identity achievement so elusive? *Identity, 7*(4), 331–348.

Krojgaard, P. (2005). Infants' search for hidden persons. *International Journal of Behavioral Development, 29,* 70–79.

Kronenfeld, J. J. (2002). *Health care policy: Issues and trends.* New York: Prager.

Kronholz, J. (2003, August 19). Trying to close the stubborn learning gap. *The Wall Street Journal,* pp. B1, B5.

Kronholz, J. (2003, September 2). Head Start program gets low grade. *The Wall Street Journal,* p. A4.

Krout, J. A. (1988). Rural versus urban differences in elderly parents' contact with their children. *Gerontologist, 28,* 198–203.

Krueger, G. (2006, September). Meaning-making in the aftermath of sudden infant death syndrome. *Nursing Inquiry, 13,* 163–171.

Krueger, J., & Heckhausen, J. (1993). Personality development across the adult life span: Subjective conceptions vs. cross-sectional contrasts. *Journals of Gerontology, 48,* 100–108.

Kryter, K. D. (1983). Presbycusis, sociocusis, and nosocusis. *Journal of the Acoustical Society of America, 73,* 1897–1917.

Kübler-Ross, E. (1969). *On death and dying.* New York: Macmillan.

Kübler-Ross, E. (Ed.). (1975). *Death: The final stage of growth.* Englewood Cliffs, NJ: Prentice-Hall.

Kübler-Ross, E. (1982). *Working it through.* New York: Macmillan.

Kuczaj, S. A., II, Borys, R. H., & Jones, M. (1989). On the interaction of language and thought: Some thoughts on developmental data. In A. Galletly, D. Rogers, & J. A. Sloboda (Eds.), *Cognition and the social world.* New York: Oxford University Press.

Kuczynski, L., & Kochanska, G. (1990). Development of children's noncompliance strategies from toddlerhood to age 5. *Developmental Psychology, 26,* 398–408.

Kugiumutzakis, G. (1999). Genesis and development of early infant mimesis to facial and vocal models. In. J. Nadel & G. Butterworth, *Imitation in infancy.* New York: Cambridge University Press.

Kuhl, P. (1993). Early linguistic experience and phonetic perception: Implications for theories of developmental speech perception. *Journal of Phonetics, 21,* 125–139.

Kuhl, P. (2006). *A new view of language acquisition. Language and linguistics in context: Readings and applications for teachers.* Mahwah, NJ: Lawrence Erlbaum.

Kuhl, P. K., Andruski, J. E., Chistovich, I. A., Chistovieh, L. A., Kozhevnikova, E. V., Ryskina, V. L., et al. (1977, August 1). Cross-language analysis of phonetic units in language addressed to infants. *Science, 277,* 684–686.

Kuhl, P., Tsao, F.-M., & Liu, H.-M. (2003). Foreign-language experience in infancy: Effects of short-term exposure and social interaction on phonetic learning. *Proceedings of the National Academy of Sciences, 100,* 9096–9101.

Kuhn, D. (2000). Metacognitive development. *Current Directions in Psychological Science, 9,* 178–181.

Kuhn, D. (2008). Formal operations from a twenty-first century perspective. *Human Development, 51,* 48–55.

Kuhn, D., & Franklin, S. (2006). The second decade: What develops (and how). *Handbook of child psychology: Vol 2, Cognition, perception, and language* (6th ed.). Hoboken, NJ: John Wiley & Sons Inc.

Kuhn, D., Garcia-Mila, M., Zohar, A., & Andersen, C. (1995). Strategies of knowledge acquisition. With commentary by S. H. White, D. Klahr, & S. M. Carver, and a reply by D. Kuhn. *Monographs of the Society for Research in Child Development, 60,* 122–137.

Kumar, A., Sharma, M., & Hooda, D. (2012). Perceived parenting style as a predictor of hope among adolescents. *Journal of the Indian Academy of Applied Psychology, 38,* 174–178.

Kunkel, D., Wilcox, B. L., Cantor, J., Palmer, E., Linn, S., & Dowrick, P. (2004, February 20). *Report of the APA task force on advertising and children.* Washington, DC: American Psychological Association.

Kunzmann, U., & Baltes, P. (2005). *The psychology of wisdom: Theoretical and empirical challenges.* New York: Cambridge University Press.

Kuo, L., & Anderson, R. C. (2012). Effects of early bilingualism on learning phonological regularities in a new language. *Journal of Experimental Child Psychology, 111,* 455–467.

Kupersmidt, J. B., & Dodge, K. A. (Eds.). (2004). *Children's peer relations: From development to intervention.* Washington, DC: American Psychological Association.

Kurdek, L. (2002). Predicting the timing of separation and marital satisfaction: An eight-year prospective longitudinal study. *Journal of Marriage & Family, 64,* 163–179.

Kurdek, L. (2003a). Differences between gay and lesbian cohabiting couples. *Journal of Social & Personal Relationships, 20,* 411–436.

Kurdek, L. (2003b). Negative representations of the self/spouse and marital distress. *Personal Relationships, 10,* 511–534.

Kurdek, L. (2006, May). Differences between partners from heterosexual, gay, and lesbian cohabiting couples. *Journal of Marriage and Family, 68,* 509–528.

Kurdek, L. (2007). The allocation of household labor by partners in gay and lesbian couples. *Journal of Family Issues, 28,* 132–148.

Kurdek, L. (2008). Change in relationship quality for partners from lesbian, gay male, and heterosexual couples. *Journal of Family Psychology, 22,* 701–711.

Kurdek, L. A. (1991). Correlates of relationship satisfaction in cohabiting gay and lesbian couples: Integration of contextual, investment, and problem-solving models. *Journal of Personality and Social Psychology, 61,* 910–922.

Kurdek, L. A. (1992). Relationship stability and relationship satisfaction in cohabiting gay and lesbian couples: A prospective longitudinal test of the contextual and interdependence models. *Journal of Social and Personal Relationships, 9,* 125–142.

Kurdek, L. A. (1993). The allocation of household labor in gay, lesbian, and heterosexual married children. *Journal of Social Issues, 49,* 127–139.

Kurdek, L.A. (1994). Lesbian and gay couples. In A. R. D'Augelli & C. J. Patterson (Eds.), *Lesbian and gay identities over the lifespan: psychological perspectives on personal, relational, and community processes.* New York: Oxford University Press.

Kurdek, L. A. (1995). Developmental changes in relationship quality in gay and lesbian cohabiting couples. *Developmental Psychology, 31,* 86–94.

Kurdek, L. A. (1999). The nature and predictors of the trajectory of change in marital quality for husbands and wives over the first 10 years of marriage. *Developmental Psychology, 35,* 1283–1296.

Kurdek, L. A. (2005). What do we know about gay and lesbian couples? *Current Directions in Psychological Science, 14,* 251–258.

Kurdek, L. A. (2008). A general model of relationship commitment: Evidence from same-sex partners. *Personal Relationships, 15,* 391–405.

Kurtines, W. M., & Gewirtz, J. L. (1987). *Moral development through social interaction.* New York: Wiley.

Kwant, P. B., Finocchiaro, T., Forster, F., Reul, H., Rau, G., Morshuis, M., et al. (2007). The MiniACcor: Constructive redesign of an implantable total artificial heart, initial laboratory testing and further steps. *International Journal of Artificial Organs, 30,* 345–351.

Kwon, K., Lease, A., & Hoffman, L. (2012). The impact of clique membership on children's social behavior and status nominations. *Social Development, 21,* 150–169.

Kwong See, S. T., Rasmussen, C., & Pertman, S. (2012). Measuring children's age stereotyping using a modified Piagetian conservation task. *Educational Gerontology, 38,* 149–165.

La Leche League International. (2003). *Breastfeeding around the world.* Schaumburg, IL: La Leche League International.

La Vecchia, C. (1996). Hormone replacement therapy, breasts and endometrial cancer. *European Journal of Cancer Prevention, 5,* 414–416.

Laas, I. (2006). Self-actualization and society: A new application for an old theory. *Journal of Humanistic Psychology, 46,* 77–91.

Labouvie-Vief, G. (1980). Beyond formal operations: Uses and limits of pure logic in life-span development. *Human Development, 23,* 141–161.

Labouvie-Vief, G. (1986). Modes of knowledge and the organization of development. In M. L. Commons, L. Kohlberg, F. Richards, & J. Sinnott (Eds.), *Beyond formal operations 3: Models and methods in the study of adult and adolescent thought.* New York: Praeger.

Labouvie-Vief, G. (1990). Modes of knowledge and the organization of development. In M. L. Commons, C. Armon, L. Kohlberg, F. A. Richards, T. A. Grotzer, & J. Sinnott (Eds.), *Adult development (Vol. 2). Models and methods in the study of adolescent thought.* New York: Praeger.

Labouvie-Vief, G. (2006). Emerging structures of adult thought. In J. J. Arnett & J. L. Tanner (Eds.), *Emerging adults in America: Coming of age in the 21st century.* Washington, DC: American Psychological Association.

Labouvie-Vief, G. (2009). Cognition and equilibrium regulation in development and aging. *Restorative Neurology and Neuroscience, 27,* 551–565.

Labouvie-Vief, G., & Diehl, M. (2000). Cognitive complexity and cognitive–affective integration: Related or separate domains of adult development? *Psychology & Aging, 15,* 490–504.

Lacerda, F., von Hofsten, C., & Heimann, M. (2001). *Emerging cognitive abilities in early infancy.* Mahwah, NJ: Lawrence Erlbaum Associates.

Lachmann, T., Berti, S., Kujala, T., & Schroger, E. (2005). Diagnostic subgroups of developmental dyslexia have different deficits in neural processing of tones and phonemes. *International Journal of Psychophysiology, 56,* 105–120.

Lackey, C. (2003). Violent family heritage, the transition to adulthood, and later partner violence. *Journal of Family Issues, 24,* 74–98.

Ladd, G. W. (1983). Social networks of popular, average and rejected children in social settings. *Merrill-Palmer Quarterly, 29,* 282–307.

Ladd, G., & Petry, N. (2002). Disordered gambling among university-based medical and dental patients: A focus on Internet gambling. *Psychology of Addictive Behaviors, 16,* 76–79.

Ladd, G., Herald, S., & Andrews, R. (2006). Young children's peer relations and social competence. *Handbook of research on the education of young children* (2nd ed.). Mahwah, NJ: Lawrence Erlbaum Associates.

Ladegaard, H., & Bleses, D. (2003). Gender differences in young children's speech: The acquisition of sociolinguistic competence. *International Journal of Applied Linguistics, 13,* 222–233.

Laditka, S., Laditka, J., & Probst, J. (2006). Racial and ethnic disparities in potentially avoidable delivery complications among pregnant Medicaid beneficiaries in South Carolina. *Maternal & Child Health Journal, 10,* 339–350.

Laflamme, D., Pomerleau, A., & Malcuit, G. (2002). A comparison of fathers' and mothers' involvement in childcare and stimulation behaviors during free-play with their infants at 9 and 15 months. *Sex Roles, 47,* 507–518.

LaFreniere, P., Masataka, N., Butovskaya, M., Chen, Q., Dessen, M., Atwanger, K., et al. (2002). Cross-cultural analysis of social competence and behavior problems in preschoolers. *Early Education and Development, 13,* 201–219.

LaFromboise, T., Coleman, H. L., & Gerton, J. (1993). Psychological impact of biculturalism: Evidence and theory. *Psychological Bulletin, 114,* 395–412.

Lafuente, M. J., Grifol, R., Segarra, J., & Soriano, J. (1997). Effects of the Firstart method of prenatal stimulation on psychomotor development: The first six months. *Pre- & PeriNatal Psychology, 11,* 151–162.

Lahiri, D. K., Maloney, B., Basha, M. R., Ge, Y. W., & Zawia, N. H. (2007). How and when environmental agents and dietary factors affect the course of Alzheimer's disease: The "LEARn" model (latent early-life associated regulation) may explain the triggering of AD. *Current Alzheimer Research, 4,* 219–228.

Laible, D., Panfile, T., & Makariev, D. (2008). The quality and frequency of mother-toddler conflict: Links with attachment and temperament. *Child Development, 79,* 426–443.

Lakowski, B., & Hekimi, S. (1996, May 17). Determination of life-span in caenorhabditis elegans by four clock genes. *Science, 272,* 1010.

Lall, M. (2007, August). Exclusion from school: Teenage pregnancy and the denial of education. *Sex Education, 7*(3), 219–237.

Lam, V., & Leman, P. (2003). The influence of gender and ethnicity on children's inferences about toy choice. *Social Development, 12,* 269–287.

Lamaze, F. (1970). *Painless childbirth: The Lamaze method.* Chicago: Regnery.

Lamb, D. R. (1984). *Physiology of exercise: Response and adaptation* (2nd ed.). New York: Macmillan.

Lamb, M. (1994). Infant care practices and the application of knowledge. In C. B. Fisher & R. M. Lerner (Eds.), *Applied developmental psychology.* New York: McGraw-Hill.

Lamb, M. E. (1977). The development of mother–infant and father–infant attachments in the second year of life. *Developmental Psychology, 13,* 637–648.

Lamb, M. E. (1982a). The bonding phenomenon: Misinterpretations and their implications. *Journal of Pediatrics, 101,* 555–557.

Lamb, M. E. (1982b). Paternal influences on early socio-emotional development. *Journal of Child Psychology and Psychiatry and Allied Disciplines, 23,* 185–190.

Lamb, M. E. (1987). Predictive implications of individual differences in attachment. *Journal of Consulting and Clinical Psychology, 55,* 817–824.

Lamb, M. E. (Ed.). (1986). *The father's role: Applied perspectives.* New York: Wiley.

Lamb, M. E., Morrison, D. C., & Malkin, C. M. (1987). The development of infant social expectations in face-to-face interaction. *Merrill-Palmer Quarterly, 33,* 241–254.

Lamb, M. E., Sternberg, K. J., Hwang, C. P., & Broberg, A. G. (Eds.). (1992). *Child care in context: Cross-cultural perspectives.* Hillsdale, NJ: Erlbaum.

Lambert, P., Armstrong, L., & Wagner, J. (1995, February 27). The vanishing. *People Weekly,* 32–42.

Lambert, R., Abbott-Shim, M., & McCarty, F. (2002). The relationship between classroom quality and ratings of the social functioning of Head Start children. *Early Child Development & Care, 172,* 231–245.

Lambert, W. E., & Peal, E. (1972). The relation of bilingualism to intelligence. In A. S. Dil (Ed.), *Language, psychology, and culture* (3rd ed.). New York: Wiley.

Lambert, W. W. (1971). Cross-cultural backgrounds to personality development and the socialization of aggression: Findings from the Six Culture study. In W. W. Lambert & R. Weisbrod (Eds.), *Comparative perspectives in social psychology.* Boston: Little Brown.

Lamberts, S. W. J., van den Beld, A. W., & van der Lely, A-J. (1997, October 17). The endocrinology of aging. *Science, 278,* 419–424.

Lambiase, A., Aloe, L., Centofanti, M., Parisi, V., Mantelli, F., Colafrancesco, V., et al. (2009). Experimental and clinical evidence of neuroprotection by nerve growth factor eye drops: Implications for glaucoma. *PNAS Proceedings of the National Academy of Sciences of the United States of America, 106,* 13469–13474.

Lamborn, S. D., & Groh, K. (2009). A four-part model of autonomy during emerging adulthood: Associations with adjustment. *International Journal of Behavioral Development, 33*(5), 393–401.

Lamm, B., & Keller, H. (2007). Understanding cultural models of parenting: The role of intracultural variation and response style. *Journal of Cross-Cultural Psychology, 38,* 50–57.

Lamm, H., & Wiesmann, U. (1997). Subjective attributes of attraction: How people characterize their liking, their love, and their being in love. *Personal Relationships, 4,* 271–284.

Lamont, J. A. (1997). Sexuality. In D. E. Stewart & G. E. Robinson (Eds.), *A clinician's guide to menopause. Clinical practice* (pp. 63–75). Washington, DC: Health Press International.

Lamorey, S., Robinson, B. E., & Rowland, B. H. (1998). *Latchkey kids: Unlocking doors for children and their families.* Newbury Park, CA: Sage.

Lanctot, K. L., Herrmann, N., & Mazzotta, P. (2001). Role of serotonin in the behavioral and psychological symptoms of dementia. *Journal of Neuropsychiatry & Clinical Neurosciences, 13,* 5–21.

Lancy, D. (2007). Accounting for variability in mother-child play. *American Anthropologist, Special issue: In focus: Children, childhoods, and childhood studies, 109,* 273–284.

Land, K. C., Lamb, V. L., & Zheng, H. (2011). How are the kids doing? How do we know? Recent trends in child and youth well-being in the United States and some international comparisons. *Social Indicators Research, 100,* 463–477.

Landau, R. (2008). Sex selection for social purposes in Israel: Quest for the "perfect child" of a particular gender or centuries old prejudice against women?. *Journal of Medical Ethics, 34,* Retrieved from http://search.ebscohost.com, doi:10.1136/jme.2007.023226.

Lander, E. S., & Schork, N. J. (1994, September 30). Genetic dissection of complex traits. *Science, 265,* 2037–2048.

Landhuis, C., Poulton, R., Welch, D., & Hancox, R. (2008). Programming obesity and poor fitness: The long-term impact of childhood television. *Obesity, 16,* 1457–1459.

Landrine, H., & Klonoff, E. A. (1994). Cultural diversity in causal attributions for illness: The role of the supernatural. *Journal of Behavior Medicine, 17,* 181–193.

Landström, S., Granhag, P., & Hartwig, M. (2007). Children's live and videotaped testimonies: How presentation mode affects observers' perception, assessment and memory. *Legal and Criminological Psychology, 12,* 333–347.

Landy, F. J. (1994, July/August). Mandatory retirement age: Serving the public welfare? *Psychological Science Agenda,* pp. 10–13.

Landy, F., & Conte, J. M. (2004). *Work in the 21st century.* New York: McGraw-Hill.

Lane, H. (1976). *The wild boy of Aveyron.* Cambridge, MA: Harvard University Press.

Lane, W. K. (1976, November). The relationship between personality and differential academic achievement within a group of highly gifted and high achieving children. *Dissertation Abstracts International, 37*(5-A), 2746.

Lang, A. A. (1999, June 13). Doctors are second-guessing the "miracle" of multiple births. *The New York Times,* p. WH4.

Langer, E., & Janis, I. (1979). *The psychology of control.* Beverly Hills, CA: Sage.

Langford, P. E. (1995). *Approaches to the development of moral reasoning.* Hillsdale, NJ: Erlbaum.

Langille, D. (2007). Teenage pregnancy: Trends, contributing factors and the physician's role. *Canadian Medical Association Journal, 176,* 1601–1602.

Lanphear, B. P. (1998). The paradox of lead poisoning prevention. *Science, 281,* 1617–1618.

Lansford, J. (2009). Parental divorce and children's adjustment. *Perspectives on Psychological Science, 4,* 140–152.

Lansford, J. E., Malone, P. S., Dodge, K. A., Crozier, J. C., Pettit, G. S., et al. (2006). A 12-year prospective study of patterns of social information processing, problems and externalizing behaviors. *Journal of Abnormal Child Psychology, 34,* 715–724.

Lansford, J. E., & Parker, J. G. (1999). Children's interactions in triads: Behavioral profiles and effects of gender and patterns of friendships among members. *Developmental Psychology, 35,* 80–93.

Lansu, T. M., Cillessen, A. N., & Karremans, J. C. (2012). Implicit associations with popularity in early adolescence: An approach–avoidance analysis. *Developmental Psychology, 48,* 65–75.

Lantos, J. D., Jackson, M. A., Opel, D. J., Marcuse, E. K., Myers, A. L., & Connelly, B. L. (2010). Controversies in vaccine mandates. *Current Problems in Pediatric Health Care, 40,* 38–58.

Lappi, H., Valkonen-Korhonen, M., Georgiadis, S., Tarvainen, M., Tarkka, I., Karjalainen, P., et al. (2007). Effects of nutritive and non-nutritive sucking on infant heart rate variability during the first 6 months of life. *Infant Behavior & Development, 30,* 546–556.

Lapsley, D. (2006). Moral stage theory. *Handbook of moral development.* Mahwah, NJ: Lawrence Erlbaum Associates.

Larner, M. B., Terman, D. L., & Behrman, R. E. (1997). Welfare to work: Analysis and recommendations. *The Future of Children, 7,* 4–19.

Larsen, K. E., O'Hara, M. W., & Brewer, K. K. (2001). A prospective study of self-efficacy expectancies and labor pain. *Journal of Reproductive and Infant Psychology, 19,* 203–214.

Larsen-Freeman, D., & Long, M. H. (1991). *An introduction to second language acquisition research.* London: Longman.

Larson, J., & Lochman, J. E. (2011). *Helping schoolchildren cope with anger: A cognitive-behavioral intervention* (2nd ed.). New York: Guilford Press.

Larson, M. S. (1996). Sex roles and soap operas: What adolescents learn about single motherhood. *Sex Roles, 35,* 97–110.

Larson, R. W., Clore, G. L., & Wood, G. A. (1999). The emotions of romantic relationships: Do they wreak havoc on adolescents? In W. Furman, B. B. Brown, & C. Feiring (Eds.), *The development of romantic relationships in adolescence.* New York: Cambridge University Press.

Larson, R. W., Richards, M. H., Moneta, G., Holmbeck, G., & Duckett, E. (1996). Changes in adolescents' daily interactions with their families from ages 10 to 18: Disengagement and transformation. *Developmental Psychology, 32,* 744–754.

Larsson, B., & Melin, L. (1992). Prevalence and short-term stability of depressive symptoms in school children. *Acta Psychiatrica Scandinavica, 85,* 17–22.

Larwood, L., Szwajkowski, E., & Rose, S. (1988). Sex and race discrimination resulting from manager–client relationships: Applying the rational bias theory of managerial discrimination. *Sex Roles, 18,* 9–29.

Laskas, J. (2006, December 17). Dancing with the plumber. *Washington Post Magazine,* p. W35.

Lassner, J. B., Matthews, K. A., & Stoney, C. M. (1994). Are cardiovascular reactors to asocial stress also reactors to social stress? *Journal of Personality and Social Psychology, 66,* 69–77.

Laszlo, J. (1986). Scripts for interpersonal situations. *Studia Psychologica, 28,* 125–135.

Lattibeaudiere, V. H. (2000). An exploratory study of the transition and adjustment of former home-schooled students to college life. *Dissertation Abstracts International Section A: Humanities & Social Sciences, 61,* p. 2211.

Lau, I., Lee, S., & Chiu, C. (2004). Language, cognition, and reality: Constructing shared meanings through communication. In M. Schaller & C. Crandall (Eds.), *The psychological foundations of culture.* Mahwah, NJ: Lawrence Erlbaum Associates.

Lau, M., Markham, C., Lin, H., Flores, G., & Chacko, M. (2009). Dating and sexual attitudes in Asian-American adolescents. *Journal of Adolescent Research, 24,* 91–113.

Lau, S., & Kwok, L. K. (2000). Relationship of family environment to adolescents' depression and self-concept. *Social Behavior & Personality, 28,* 41–50.

Lauer, J., & Lauer, R. (1985). Marriages made to last. *Psychology Today, 19*(6), 22–26.

Lauer, J. C., & Lauer, R. H. (1999). *How to survive and thrive in an empty nest.* Oakland, CA: New Harbinger Publications.

Laugharne, J., Janca, A., & Widiger, T. (2007). Posttraumatic stress disorder and terrorism: 5 years after 9/11. *Current Opinion in Psychiatry, 20,* 36–41.

Laumann, E. O., Paik, A., & Rosen, R. C. (1999). Sexual dysfunction in the United States: Prevalence and predictors. *Journal of the American Medical Association, 281,* 537–544.

Lauricella, T. (2001, November). The education of a home schooler. *Smart Money,* 115–121.

Laursen, B., Coy, K. C., & Collins, W. A. (1998). Reconsidering changes in parent-child conflict across adolescence: A meta-analysis. *Child Development, 69,* 817–832.

Laursen, B., Hafen, C. A., Kerr, M., & Stattin, H. (2012). Friend influence over adolescent problem behaviors as a function of relative peer acceptance: To be liked is to be emulated. *Journal of Abnormal Psychology, 121,* 88–94.

Laursen, B., Hartup, W. W., & Koplas, A. L. (1996). Towards understanding peer conflict. *Merrill-Palmer Quarterly, 42,* 76–102.

Lauter, J. L. (1998). Neuroimaging and the trimodal brain: Applications for developmental communication neuroscience. *Phoniatrica et Logopaedica, 50,* 118–145.

Lavallee, D., & Robinson, H. (2007). In pursuit of an identity: A qualitative exploration of retirement from women's artistic gymnastics. *Psychology of Sport and Exercise, 8,* 119–141.

Lavanco, G. (1997). Burnout syndrome and Type A behavior in nurses and teachers in Sicily. *Psychological Reports, 81,* 523–528.

Lavelli, M., & Fogel, A. (2005). Developmental changes in the relationship between the infant's attention and emotion during early face-to-face communication: The 2-month transition. *Developmental Psychology [serial online], 41,* 265–280.

Lavers-Preston, C., & Sonuga-Barke, E. (2003). An intergenerational perspective on parent-child relationships: The reciprocal effects of tri-generational grandparent-parent-child relationships. In R. Gupta & D. Parry-Gupta (Eds.), *Children and parents: Clinical issues for psychologists and psychiatrists.* London: Whurr Publishers, Ltd.

Lavzer, J. I., & Goodson, B. D., (2006). The "quality" of early care and education settings: Definitional and measurement issues. *Evaluation Review, 30,* 556–576.

Law, Y. (2008). Effects of cooperative learning on second graders' learning from text. *Educational Psychology, 28,* 567–582.

Lawrence, E., Rothman, A., Cobb, R., Rothman, M., & Bradbury, T. (2008). Marital satisfaction across the transition to parenthood. *Journal of Family Psychology, 22,* 41–50.

Lawton, M. P. (2001). Emotion in later life. *Current Directions in Psychological Science, 10,* 120–123.

Lawton, M. P., Kleban, M. H., Moss, M., Rovine, M., & Glicksman, A. (1989). Measuring caregiving appraisal. *Journal of Geronotology: Psychological Sciences, 44,* 61–71.

Lazarus, R. S. (1968). Emotions and adaptations: Conceptual and empirical relations. In W. Arnold (Ed.), *Nebraska symposium on motivation.* Lincoln: University of Nebraska.

Lazarus, R. S. (1991). *Emotion and adaptation.* New York: Oxford University Press.

Lazarus, R. S., & Folkman, S. (1984). *Stress, appraisal, and coping.* New York: Springer.

Le Corre, M., & Carey, S. (2007). One, two, three, four, nothing more: An investigation of the conceptual sources of the verbal counting principles. *Cognition, 105,* 395–438.

Le Vay, S., & Valente, S. M. (2003). *Human Sexuality.* Sunderland, MA: Sinauer Associates.

Leach, P., Barnes, J., Malmberg, L., Sylva, K., & Stein, A. (2008, February). The quality of different types of child care at 10 and 18 months: A comparison between types and factors related to quality. *Early Child Development and Care, 178*(2), 177–209.

Leaper, C. (2002). Parenting girls and boys. In M. Bornstein (Ed.), *Handbook of parenting: Vol. 1: Children and parenting* (2nd ed.). Mahwah, NJ: Lawrence Erlbaum Associates.

Leaper, C., Anderson, K. J., & Sanders, P. (1998). Moderators of gender effects on parents' talk to their children: A meta-analysis. *Developmental Psychology, 34,* 3–27.

Leaper, C., & Smith, T. E. (2004). A meta-analytic review of gender variations in children's language use: talkativeness, affiliative speech, and assertive speech. *Developmental Psychology, 40,* 993–1002.

Leary, W. E. (1996, November 20). U.S. rate of sexual diseases highest in developed world. *The New York Times,* p. C1.

Leathers, H. D., & Foster, P. (2004). *The world food problem: Tackling causes of undernutrition in the third world.* Boulder, CO: Lynne Rienner Publishers.

Leathers, S., & Kelley, M. (2000). Unintended pregnancy and depressive symptoms among first-time mothers and fathers. *American Journal of Orthopsychiatry, 70,* 523–531.

Leavell, A., Tamis-LeMonda, C. S., Ruble, D. N., Zosuls, K. M., & Cabrera, N. J. (2012). African American, white and Latino fathers' activities with their sons and daughters in early childhood. *Sex Roles, 66,* 53–65.

Leavitt, L. A., & Goldson, E. (1996). Introduction to special section: Biomedicine and developmental psychology: New areas of common ground. *Developmental Psychology, 32,* 387–389.

Leboyer, F. (1975). *Birth without violence.* New York: Knopf.

Lecanuet, J.-P., Fifer, W. P., Krasnegor, N. A., & Smotherman, W. P. (Eds.). (1995). *Fetal development: A psychobiological perspective.* Hillsdale, NJ: Erlbaum.

Lecanuet, J.-P., Granier-Deferre, C., & Busnel, M.-C. (1995). Human fetal auditory perception. In J.-P. Lecanuet, W. P. Fifer, N. A. Krasnegor, & W. P. Smotherman (Eds.), *Fetal development: A psychobiological perspective.* Hillsdale, NJ: Erlbaum.

Lecours, A. R. (1982). Correlates of developmental behavior in brain maturation. In T. Bever (Ed.), *Regressions in mental development.* Hillsdale, NJ: Erlbaum.

Lee, B. H., Schofer, J. L., & Koppelman, F. S. (2005). Bicycle safety helmet legislation and bicycle-related non-fatal injuries in California. *Accidental Analysis and Prevention, 37,* 93–102.

Lee, B. R., Bright, C. L., Svoboda, D. V., Fakunmoju, S., & Barth, R. P. (2011). Outcomes of group care for youth: A review of comparative studies. *Research on Social Work Practice, 21,* 177–189.

Lee, C. C., Czaja, S. J., & Sharit, J. (2009). Training older workers for technology-based employment. *Educational Gerontology, 35,* 15–31.

Lee, C.-K., Klopp, R. G., Weindruch, R., & Prolla, T. A. (1999, August 27). Gene expression profile of aging and its retardation by caloric restriction. *Science, 285,* 1390–1393.

Lee, E., & Troop-Gordon, W. (2011). Peer processes and gender role development: Changes in gender atypicality related to negative peer treatment and children's friendships. *Sex Roles, 64,* 90–102.

Lee, J. (1997). Never innocent: Breasted experiences in women's bodily narratives of puberty. *Feminism & Psychology, 7,* 453–474.

Lee, K., & Homer, B. (1999). Children as folk psychologists: The developing understanding of the mind. In A. Slater & D. Muir (Eds.), *The Blackwell reader in development psychology.* Malden, MA: Blackwell.

Lee, M. (2008). Caregiver stress and elder abuse among Korean family caregivers of older adults with disabilities. *Journal of Family Violence, 23,* 707–712.

Lee, M., Vernon-Feagans, L., & Vazquez, A. (2003). The influence of family environment and child temperament on work/family role strain for mothers and fathers. *Infant & Child Development, 12,* 421–439.

Lee, R. M. (2005). Resilience against discrimination: Ethnic identity and other-group orientation as protective factors for Korean Americans. *Journal of Counseling Psychology, 52,* 36–44.

Lee, V. E., & Burkam, D. T. (2002). *Inequality at the starting gate: Background differences in achievement as children begin school.* New York: Economic Policy Institute.

Leen-Feldner, E. W., Reardon, L .E., & Hayward, C. (2008). The relation between puberty and adolescent anxiety: Theory and evidence. In M. J. Zvolensky & J. A. J. Smits (Eds.), *Anxiety in health behaviors and physical illness.* New York: Springer Science + Business Media.

Leenaars, A. A., & Shneidman, E. S. (Eds.). (1999). *Lives and deaths; Selections from the works of Edwin S. Shneidman.* New York: Bruuner-Routledge.

Lefkowitz, E. S., Sigman, M., & Kit-fong Au, T. (2000). Helping mothers discuss sexuality and AIDS with adolescents. *Child Development, 71,* 1383–1394.

Legerstee, M. (1998). Mental and bodily awareness in infancy: Consciousness of self-existence. *Journal of Consciousness Studies, 5,* 627–644.

Legerstee, M., Anderson, D., & Schaffer, A. (1998). Five- and eight-month-old infants recognize their faces and voices as familiar and social stimuli. *Child Development, 69,* 37–50.

Legerstee, M., & Markova, G. (2008). Variations in 10-month-old infant imitation of people and things. *Infant Behavior & Development, 31,* 81–91.

Lehalle, H. (2006). Moral development in adolescence: How to integrate personal and social values? *Handbook of adolescent development.* New York: Psychology Press.

Lehman, D., Chiu, C., & Schaller, M. (2004). Psychology and culture. *Annual Review of Psychology, 55,* 689–714.

Lehr, U., Seiler, E., & Thomae, H. (2000). Aging in a cross-cultural perspective. In A. L. Comunian & U. P. Gielen (Eds.), *International perspectives on human development.* Lengerich, Germany: Pabst Science Publishers.

Lehtonen, J. (2002). Origins of dreaming. *American Journal of Psychiatry, 159,* 495–495.

Leiblum, S. R. (1990). Sexuality and the midlife woman. Special issue: Women at midlife and beyond. *Psychology of Women Quarterly, 14,* 495–508.

Leitenberg, H., Detzer, M. J., & Srebnik, D. (1993). Gender differences in masturbation and the relation of masturbation experience in preadolescence and/or early adolescence to sexual behavior and sexual adjustment in young adulthood. *Archives of Sexual Behavior, 22,* 87–98.

Leiter, J., & Johnsen, M. C. (1997). Child maltreatment and school performance declines: An event-history analysis. *American Educational Research Journal, 34,* 563–589.

Lelwica, M., & Haviland, J. (1983). *Ten-week-old infants' reactions to mothers' emotional expressions.* Paper presented at the biennial meeting of the Society for Research in Child Development.

Lemerise, E. A., & Dodge, K. A. (2008). In M. Lewis, J. Haviland-Jones, & L. F. Barrett (Eds.), *Handbook of emotions.* New York: Guilford Press.

Lemery, K., & Doelger, L. (2005). Genetic vulnerabilities to the development of psychopathology. *Development of psychopathology: A vulnerability-stress perspective.* Thousand Oaks, CA: Sage Publications, Inc.

Lemonick, M. D. (2000, October 30). Teens before their time. *Time, 67,* 68–74.

Lenhart, A., Ling, R., & Campbell, S. (2010, October 23). *Teens, adults & sexting: Data on sending and receipt of sexually suggestive nude or nearly nude images by American adolescents and adults.* Washington, DC: Pew Research Center Internet and American Life Project.

Lenssen, B. G. (1973). Infants' reactions to peer strangers. *Dissertation Abstracts International, 33,* 60–62.

Lensvelt-Mulders, G. (2003). A new approach to the multivariate genetic analysis of the consistency and variability of the big five. *Advances in psychology research* (Vol 26). Hauppauge, NY: Nova Science Publishers.

Leonard, C. M., Lombardino, L. J., Mercado, L. R., Browd, S. R., Breier, J. I., & Agee, O. F. (1996). Cerebral asymmetry and cognitive development in children: A magnetic resonance imaging study. *Psychological Science, 7,* 89–95.

Leonard, L. B. (1998). *Children with specific language impairment.* Cambridge, MA: MIT Press.

Leonard, T. (2005, March 22). Need parenting help? Call your coach. *The Daily Telegraph (London),* 15.

Lepage, J., & Théret, H. (2007). The mirror neuron system: Grasping others' actions from birth? *Developmental Science, 10,* 513–523.

Lepore, S. J., Palsane, M. N., & Evans, G. W. (1991). Daily hassles and chronic strains: A hierarchy of stressors? *Social Science and Medicine, 33,* 1029–1036.

Lerner, J. W. (2002). *Learning disabilities: Theories, diagnosis, and teaching strategies.* Boston: Houghton Mifflin.

Lerner, R. M. (2002). *Concepts and theories of human development* (3rd ed.). Mahwah, NJ: Erlbaum.

Lerner, R. M., Fisher, C. B., & Weinberg, R. A. (2000). Toward a science for and of the people: Promoting civil society through the application of developmental science. *Child Development, 71,* 11–20.

Lerner, R. M., Theokas, C., & Jelicic, H. (2005). Youth as active agents in their own positive development: A developmental systems perspective. In W. Greve, K. Rothermund, & D. Wentura (Eds.), *Adaptive self: Personal continuity and intentional self-development.* Ashland, OH: Hogrefe & Huber Publishers.

Lesaux, N. K., & Siegel, L. S. (2003). The development of reading in children who speak English as a second language. *Developmental Psychology, 39,* 1005–1019.

Lesik, S. (2006). Applying the regression-discontinuity design to infer causality with non-random assignment. *Review of Higher Education: Journal of the Association for the Study of Higher Education, 30,* 1–19.

Lesko, A., & Corpus, J. (2006, January). Discounting the difficult: How high math-identified women respond to stereotype threat. *Sex Roles, 54,* 113–125.

Leslie, A., Knobe, J., & Cohen, A. (2006). Acting intentionally and the side-effect effect: Theory of mind and moral judgment. *Psychological Science, 17,* 421–427.

Leslie, C. (1991, February 11). Classrooms of Babel. *Newsweek,* pp. 56–57.

Lesner, S. (2003). Candidacy and management of assistive listening devices: Special needs of the elderly. *International Journal of Audiology, 42,* 2S68–2S76.

Lesnoff-Caravaglia, G. (2007). Age-related changes within biological systems: Integumentary, skeletal, and muscular. *Gerontechnology: Growing old in a technological society.* Springfield, IL: Charles C. Thomas Publisher.

Lessard, A., Butler-Kisber, L., Fortin, L., Marcotte, D., Potvin, P., & Royer, É. (2008, February). Shades of disengagement: High school dropouts speak out. *Social Psychology of Education, 11*(1), 25–42.

Lester, D. (2006, December). Sexual orientation and suicidal behavior. *Psychological Reports, 99,* 923–924.

Letendre, J. (2007). "Sugar and spice but not always nice": Gender socialization and its impact on development and maintenance of aggression in adolescent girls. *Child & Adolescent Social Work Journal, 24,* 353–368.

Leung, C., Pe-Pua, R., & Karnilowicz, W. (2006, January). Psychological adaptation and autonomy among adolescents in Australia: A comparison of Anglo-Celtic and three Asian groups. *International Journal of Intercultural Relations, 30,* 99–118.

Leung, K. (2005). Special issue: Cross-cultural variations in distributive justice perception. *Journal of Cross-Cultural Psychology, 36,* 6–8.

Levano, K. J., Cunningham, F. G., Nelson, S., Roark, M., Williams, M. L., Guzick, D., et al. (1986). A prospective comparison of selective and universal electronic fetal monitoring in 34,995 pregnancies. *New England Journal of Medicine, 315,* 615–619.

LeVay, S. (1993). *The sexual brain.* Cambridge, MA: MIT Press.

LeVay, S., & Valente, S. M. (2003). *Human sexuality.* Sunderland, MA: Sinauer Associates.

Levay, S., & Valente, S. (2006). *Human sexuality* (2nd ed.). Sunderland, MA: Sinauer Associates.

Levenson, R. W., Carstensen, L. L., & Gottman, J. M. (1993). Long-term marriage: Age, gender, and satisfaction. *Psychology and Aging, 8,* 301–313.

Levick, S. E. (2004). *Clone being: Exploring the psychological and social dimensions.* Lanham, MD: Rowman & Littlefield.

Levin, R. (2007, February). Sexual activity, health and well-being—The beneficial roles of coitus and masturbation. *Sexual and Relationship Therapy, 22*(1), 135–148.

Levine, L. E., & Waite, B. M. (2000). Television viewing and attentional abilities in fourth and fifith grade children. *Journal of Applied Developmental Psychology, 21,* 667–679.

Levine, R. (1994). *Child care and culture.* Cambridge: Cambridge University Press.

Levine, R. (1997a, November). The pace of life in 31 countries. *American Demographics,* pp. 20–29.

Levine, R. (1997b). *A geography of time: The temporal misadventures of a social psychologist, or how every culture keeps time just a little bit differently.* New York: HarperCollins.

Levine, R. V. (1993, February). Is love a luxury? *American Demographics,* pp. 29–37.

LeVine, R., & Norman, K. (2008). Attachment in anthropological perspective. *Anthropology and child development: A cross-cultural reader.* Malden, MA: Blackwell Publishing.

Levine, S. C., Huttenlocher, J., Taylor, A., & Langrock, A. (1999). Early sex differences in spatial skill. *Developmental Psychology, 35,* 940–949.

Levinson, D. (1992). *The seasons of a woman's life.* New York: Knopf.

Levinson, D. J. (1986). A conception of adult development. *American Psychologist, 41,* 3–13.

Leviton, A., Bellinger, D., Allred, E. N., Rabinowitz, M., Needleman, H., & Schoenbaum, S. (1993). Pre- and postnatal low-level lead exposure and children's dysfunction in school. *Environmental Research, 60,* 30–43.

Levy, B. (2009). Stereotype embodiment: A psychosocial approach to aging. *Current Dirctions in Psychological Science, 18,* 332–336.

Levy, B. L., & Langer, E. (1994). Aging free from negative stereotypes: Successful memory in China and among the American deaf. *Journal of Personality and Social Psychology, 66,* 989–997.

Levy, B. R. (2003). Mind matters: Cognitive and physical effects of aging self-stereotypes. *Journal of Gerontology: Series B: Psychological Sciences and Social Sciences, 58B,* P203–P211.

Levy, B. R., Slade, M. D., and Kasl, S. V.(2002). Longitudinal benefit of positive self-perceptions of aging on functioning health. *Journal of Gerontology: Psychological Sciences, 57,* 166–195.

Levy, B. R., Slade, M. D., Kunkel, S. R., & Kasl, S. V. (2004). Longevity increased by positive self-perceptions of aging. *Journal of Personality and Social Psychology, 83,* 261–270.

Levy, D. A. (1997). *Tools of critical thinking: Metathoughts for psychology.* Boston: Allyn & Bacon.

Levy, D. H. (2000, August 20). Are you ready for the genome miracle? *Parade Magazine,* pp. 8–10.

Levy-Shiff, R. (1994). Individual and contextual correlates of marital change across the transition to parenthood. *Developmental Psychology, 30,* 591–601.

Lewin, T. (1995, May 11). Women are becoming equal providers: Half of working women bring home half the household income. *The New York Times,* p. A14.

Lewin, T. (2003, October 29). A growing number of video viewers watch from crib. *The New York Times,* pp. A1, A22.

Lewin, T. (2005, December 15). See baby touch a screen: But does baby get it? *New York Times,* p. A1.

Lewin, T. (2008, November 19). Teenagers' internet socializing not a bad thing. *The New York Times,* p. A20.

Lewinsohn, P. M., Roberts, R. E., Seeley, J. R., & Rohde, P. (1994). Adolescent psychopathology: II. Psychosocial risk factors for depression. *Journal of Abnormal Psychology, 103,* 302–315.

Lewinsohn, P. M., Rohde, P., & Seeley, J. R. (1994). Psychosocial risk factors for future adolescent suicide attempts. *Journal of Consulting and Clinical Psychology, 62,* 297–305.

Lewis, B., Legato, M., & Fisch, H. (2006). Medical implications of the male biological clock. *JAMA: Journal of the American Medical Association, 296,* 2369–2371.

Lewis, C. S. (1958). *The allegory of love: A study in medieval traditions.* New York: Oxford University Press.

Lewis, C. S. (1985). A grief observed. In E. S. Shneidman (Ed.), *Death: Current perspectives* (3rd ed.). Palo Alto, CA: Mayfield.

Lewis, C., & Lamb, M. (2003). Fathers' influences on children's development: The evidence from two-parent families. *European Journal of Psychology of Education, 18,* 211–228.

Lewis, C., & Mitchell, P. (Eds.). (1994). *Children's early understanding of mind: Origins and development.* Hillsdale, NJ: Erlbaum.

Lewis, D. M., & Haug, C. A. (2005). Aligning policy and methodology to achieve consistent across-grade performance standards. *Applied Measurements in Education, 18,* 11–34.

Lewis, D. O., Yeager, C. A., Loveley, R., Stein, A., & Cobham-Portorreal, C. S. (1994). A clinical follow-up of delinquent males: Ignored vulnerabilities, unmet needs, and the perpetuation of violence. *Journal of the American Academy of Child and Adolescent Psychiatry, 33,* 518–528.

Lewis, J., & Elman, J. (2008). Growth-related neural reorganization and the autism phenotype: A test of the hypothesis that altered brain growth leads to altered connectivity. *Developmental Science, 11,* 135–155.

Lewis, M., & Carmody, D. (2008). Self-representation and brain development. *Developmental Psychology, 44,* 1329–1334.

Lewis, M., Feiring, C., & Rosenthal, S. (2000). Attachment over time. *Child Development, 71,* 707–720.

Lewis, M., & Ramsay, D. (2004). Development of self-recognition, personal pronoun use, and pretend play during the 2nd year. *Child Development, 75,* 1821–1831.

Lewis, R., Freneau, P., & Roberts, C. (1979). Fathers and the postparental transition. *Family Coordinator, 28,* 514–520.

Lewis, T. E., & Phillipsen, L. C. (1998). Interactions on an elementary school playground: Variations by age, gender, race, group size, and playground area. *Child Study Journal, 28,* 309–320.

Lewis, V. (2009). Undertreatment of menopausal symptoms and novel options for comprehensive management. *Current Medical Research Opinion, 25,* 2689–2698.

Lewkowicz, D. (2002). Heterogeneity and heterochrony in the development of intersensory perception. *Cognitive Brain Research, 14,* 41–63.

Lewkowicz, D. J., & Hansen-Tift, A. M. (2012). Infants deploy selective attention to the mouth of a talking face when learning speech. *PNAS Proceedings of the National Academy of Sciences of the United States of America, 109,* 1431–1436.

Lewkowicz, D. J., & Lickliter, R. (Eds). (1994). *The development of intersensory perception: Comparative perspectives.* Hillside, NJ: Lawrence Erlbaum Associates.

Lewkowicz, D. J., & Lickliter, R. (Eds.). (2002). *Conceptions of development: Lessons from the laboratory.* New York: Psychology Press.

Lew-Williams, C., & Saffran, J. R. (2012). All words are not created equal: Expectations about word length guide infant statistical learning. *Cognition, 122,* 241–246.

Leyens, J. P., Camino, L., Parke, R. D., & Berkowitz, L. (1975). Effects of movie violence on aggression in a field setting as a function of group dominance and cohesion. *Journal of Personality and Social Psychology, 32,* 346–360.

Li, C., DiGiuseppe, R., & Froh, J. (2006, September). The roles of sex, gender, and coping in adolescent depression. *Adolescence, 41,* 409–415.

Li, G. R., & Zhu, X. D. (2007). Development of the functionally total artificial heart using an artery pump. *ASAIO Journal, 53,* 288–291.

Li, J., Laursen, T. M., Precht, D. H., Olsen, J., & Mortensen, P. B. (2005). Hospitalization for mental illness among parents after the death of a child. *New England Journal of Medicine, 352,* 1190–1196.

Li, J., Liu, H., Li, J., Luo, J., Koram, N., & Detels, R. (2011). Sexual transmissibility of HIV among opiate users with concurrent sexual partnerships: An egocentric network study in Yunnan, China. *Addiction, 106,* 1780–1787.

Li, M., Mo, Y., Luo, X., Xiao, X., Shi, L., Peng, Y., et al. (2011). Genetic association and identification of a functional SNP at GSK3β for schizophrenia susceptibility. *Schizophrenia Research, 133,* 165–171.

Li, N. P., Bailey, J. M., Kenrick, D. T., & Linsenmeier, J. A. W. (2002). The necessities and luxuries of mate preferences: Testing the tradeoffs. *Journal of Personality and Social Psychology, 82,* 947–955.

Li, Q. (2006, May). Cyberbullying in schools: A research of gender differences. *School Psychology International, 27*(2), 157–170.

Li, Q. (2007, July). New bottle but old wine: A research of cyberbullying in schools. *Computers in Human Behavior, 23*(4), 1777–1791.

Li, S. (2003). Biocultural orchestration of developmental plasticity across levels: The interplay of biology and culture in shaping the mind and behavior across the life span. *Psychological Bulletin, 129,* 171–194.

Li, Y. F., Langholz, B., Salam, M. T., & Gilliland, F. D. (2005). Maternal and grandmaternal smoking patterns are associated with early childhood asthma. *Chest, 127,* 1232–1241.

Liao, S. (2005). The ethics of using genetic engineering for sex selection. *Journal of Medical Ethics, 31,* 116–118.

Libby, A., Brent, D., Morrato, E., & Orton, H. (2007). Decline in treatment of pediatric depression after FDA advisory on risk of suicidality with SSRIs. *The American Journal of Psychiatry, 164,* 884–891.

Libby, A., Orton, H., & Valuck, R. (2009). Persisting decline in depression treatment after FDA warnings. *Archives of General Psychiatry, 66,* 633–639.

Libert, S., Zwiener, J., Chu, X., Vanvoorhies, W., Roman, G., & Pletcher, S. D. (2007, February 23). Regulation of Drosophila life span by olfaction and food-derived odors. *Science, 315,* 1133–1137.

Lichtenberg, P. A. (2011). The generalizability of a participant registry for minority health research. *The Gerontologist, 51*(Suppl. 1), S116–S124.

Lickliter, R., & Bahrick, L. E. (2000). The development of infant intersensory perception: Advantages of a comparative convergent-operations approach. *Psychological Bulletin, 126,* 260–280.

Lidz, J., & Gleitman, L. R. (2004). Yes, we still need Universal Grammar: Reply. *Cognition, 94,* 85–93.

Lieberman, A. F. (1993). *The emotional life of the toddler.* New York: The Free Press.

Liebert, R. M., & Sprafkin, J. (1988). *The early window: Effects of television on children and youth* (3rd ed.). New York: Pergamon.

Liew, J., Eisenberg, N., Spinrad, T. L., Eggum, N. D., Haugen, R. G., Kupfer, A., et al. (2011). Physiological regulation and fearfulness as predictors of young children's empathy-related reactions. *Social Development, 20,* 111–134.

Light, L. L. (1991). Memory and aging: Four hypotheses in search of data. *Annual Review of Psychology, 42,* 333–376.

Light, L. L. (2000). Memory changes in adulthood. In S. H. Qualls & N. Abeles (Eds.), *Psychology and the aging* revolution: *How we adapt to longer life* (pp. 73–97). Washington, DC: American Psychological Association.

Lightdale, J. R., & Prentice, D. A. (1994). Rethinking sex differences in aggression: Aggressive behavior in the absence of social roles. *Personality and Social Psychology Bulletin, 20,* 34–44.

Lightfoot, C. (1997). *The culture of adolescent risk-taking.* New York: Guilford Press.

Lillard, A. (1998). Ethnopsychologies: Cultural variations in theories of mind. *Psychological Bulletin, 123,* 3–32.

Lillard, A., & Else-Quest, N. (2006). Evaluating Montessori education. *Science, 313,* 1893–1894.

Lillard, L. A., & Waite, L. J. (1995). Til death do us part: Marital disruption and mortality. *American Journal of Sociology, 100,* 1131–1156.

Lillo-Martin, D. (1997). In support of the language acquisition device. In M. Marschark & P. Siple (Eds.), *Relations of language and thought: The view from sign language and deaf children. Counterpoints: Cognition, memory, and language.* New York: Oxford University Press.

Lindau, S., Schumm, L., Laumann, E., Levinson, W., O'Muircheartaigh, C., & Waite, L. (2007). A study of sexuality and health among older adults in the United States. *The New England Journal of Medicine, 357,* 762–775.

Lindemann, B. T., & Kadue, D. D. (2003). *Age discrimination in employment law.* Washington, DC: BNA Books.

Lindholm, J. A. (2006). The"interior" lives of American college students: Preliminary findings from a national study. In J. L. Heft (Ed.), *Passing on the faith: Transforming traditions for the next generation of Jews, Christians, and Muslims.* New York: Fordham University Press.

Lindholm, K. J. (1991). Two-way bilingual/immersion education: Theory, conceptual issues, and pedagogical implications. In R. V. Padilla & A. Benavides (Eds.), *Critical perspectives on bilingual education research.* Tempe, AZ: Bilingual Review Press.

Lindhout, D., Frets, P. G., & Niermeijer, M. F. (1991). Approaches to genetic counseling. *Annals of the New York Academy of Sciences, 630,* 223–229.

Lindsay, A., Sussner, K., Kim, J., & Gortmaker, S. (2006). The role of parents in preventing childhood obesity. *The Future of Children, 16,* 169–186.

Lindsay, G. (2007). Educational psychology and the effectiveness of inclusive education/mainstreaming. *British Journal of Educational Psychology, 77,* 1–24.

Lindsey, B. W., & Tropepe, V. (2006). A comparative framework for understanding the biological principles of adult neurogenesis. *Progressive Neurobiology, 80,* 281–307.

Lindsey, E., & Colwell, M. (2003). Preschoolers' emotional competence: Links to pretend and physical play. *Child Study Journal, 33,* 39–52.

Lindstrom, H., Fritsch, T., Petot, G., Smyth, K., Chen, C., Debanne, S., et al. (2005, July). The relationships between television viewing in midlife and the development of Alzheimer's disease in a case-control study. *Brain and Cognition, 58,* 157–165.

Linebarger, D. L., & Walker, D. (2005). Infants' and toddlers' television viewing and language outcomes. *American Behavioral Scientist, 48,* 624–645.

Lines, P. M. (2001). Homeschooling. *Eric Digest,* EDO-EA-10-08, 1–4.

Linn, M. C. (1997, September 19). Finding patterns in international assessments. *Science, 277,* 1743.

Lino, M. (2001). *Expenditures on Children by Families, 2000 Annual Report* (Miscellaneous Publication No. 1528-2000). Washington, DC: U.S. Department of Agriculture, Center for Nutrition Policy and Promotion.

Linz, D. G., Donnerstein, E., & Penrod, S. (1988). Effects of long-term exposure to violent and sexually degrading depictions of women. *Journal of Personality and Social Psychology, 55,* 758–768.

Lipman, J. (1992, March 10). Surgeon General says it's high time Joe Camel quit. *The Wall Street Journal,* pp. B1, B7.

Lippa, R. A. (2003). Are 2D:4D finger-length rations related to sexual orientation? Yes for men, no for women. *Journal of Personality and Social Psychology, 85,* 179–188.

Lippa, R. A., Martin, L. R., & Friedman, H. S. (2000). Gender-related individual differences and mortality in the Terman longitudinal study: Is masculinity hazardous to your health? *Personality & Social Psychology Bulletin, 26,* 1560–1570.

Lippman, J., & Lewis, P. (2008). *Divorcing with children: Expert answers to tough questions from parents and children.* Westport, CT: Praeger Publishers/Greenwood Publishing Group.

Lipsitt, L. (2003). Crib death: A biobehavioral phenomenon? *Current Directions in Psychological Science, 12,* 164–170.

Lipsitt, L. P. (1986). Toward understanding the hedonic nature of infancy. In L. P. Lipsitt & J. H. Cantor (Eds.), *Experimental child psychologist: Essays and experiments in honor of Charles C. Spiker* (pp. 97–109). Hillsdale, NJ: Erlbaum.

Liskin, L. (1985, November–December). Youth in the 1980s: Social and health concerns: 4. *Population Reports, 8*(5).

List, B. A., & Barzman, D. H. (2011). Evidence-based recommendations for the treatment of aggression in pediatric patients with attention deficit hyperactivity disorder. *Psychiatric Quarterly, 82,* 33–42.

Litovsky, R. Y., & Ashmead, D. H. (1997). Development of binaural and spatial hearing in infants and children. In R. H. Gilkey & T. R. Andersen (Eds.), *Binaural and spatial hearing in real and virtual environments* (pp. 571–592). Mahwah, NJ: Erlbaum.

Litrownik, A., Newton, R., & Hunter, W. (2003). Exposure to family violence in young at-risk children: A longitudinal look at the effects of victimization and witnessed physical and psychological aggression. *Journal of Family Violence, 18,* 59–73.

Little, T. D., & Lopez, D. F. (1997). Regularities in the development of children's causality beliefs about school performance across six sociocultural contexts. *Developmental Psychology, 33,* 165–175.

Little, T., Miyashita, T., & Karasawa, M. (2003). The links among action-control beliefs, intellective skill, and school performance in Japanese, US, and German school children. *International Journal of Behavioral Development, 27,* 41–48.

Littleton, H., & Ollendick, T. (2003). Negative body image and disordered eating behavior in children and adolescents: What places youth at risk and how can these problems be prevented? *Clinical Child & Family Psychology Review, 6,* 51–66.

Litwin, H. (2007). Does early retirement lead to longer life? *Ageing & Society, 27,* 739–754.

Litzinger, S., & Gordon, K. (2005, October). Exploring relationships among communication, sexual satisfaction, and marital satisfaction. *Journal of Sex & Marital Therapy, 31,* 409–424.

Liu, H., Kuhl, P., & Tsao, F. (2003). An association between mothers' speech clarity and infants' speech discrimination skills. *Developmental Science, 6,* F1–F10.

Liu, X., & Lesniak, K. (2006). Progression in children's understanding of the matter concept from elementary to high school. *Journal of Research in Science Teaching, 43,* 320–347.

Livingstone, S. (2008). Taking risky opportunities in youthful content creation: Teenagers' use social networking sites for intimacy, privacy and self-expression. *New Media and Society, 10,* 393–411.

Livson, N., & Peskin, H. (1980). Perspectives on adolescence from longitudinal research. In J. Adelson (Ed.), *Handbook of adolescent psychology.* New York: Wiley.

Llemery, K. S., Goldsmith, H. H., Klinnert, M. D., & Mrazek, D. A. (1999). Developmental models of infant and childhood temperament. *Developmental Psychology, 35,* 189–204.

Lloyd, B., & Duveen, G. (1991). Expressing social gender identities in the first year of school. *European Journal of Psychology of Education, 6,* 437–447.

Lloyd-Jones, D., Adams, R., Carnethon, M., De Simone, G., Ferguson, T. B., Flegal, K., et al. (2009). Heart disease and stroke statistics—2009 update: A report from the American Heart Association Statistics Committee and Stroke Statistics Subcommittee. *Circulation, 119,* e21–181.

Lobel, M., & DeLuca, R. (2007). Psychosocial sequelae of cesarean delivery: Review and analysis of their causes and implications. *Social Science & Medicine, 64,* 2272–2284.

Lobel, T. E., Bar-David, E., Gruber, R., Lau, S., & Bar-Tal, Y. (2000). Gender schema and social judgments: A developmental study of children from Hong Kong. *Sex Roles, 43,* 19–42.

Lobo, R. A. (2009). The risk of stroke in postmenopausal women receiving hormonal therapy. *Climacteric, 12* (Suppl. 1), 81–85.

Lobo, R. A., Beliske, S., Creasman, W. T., Frankel, N. R., Goodman, N. F., Hall, J. E., et al. (2006). Should symptomatic menopausal women be offered hormone therapy? *Medscape General Medicine, 8,* 40.

LoBue, V., Nishida, T., Chiong, C., DeLoache, J. S., & Haidt, J. (2011). When getting something good is bad: Even three-year-olds react to inequality. *Social Development, 20,* 154–170.

Lock, R. D. (1992). *Taking charge of your career direction* (2nd ed.). Pacific Grove, CA: Brooks/Cole.

Locke, J. L. (1983). *Phonological acquisition and change.* New York: Academic Press.

Locke, J. L. (1994). Phases in the child's development of language. *American Scientist, 82,* 436–445.

Loeb, S., Fuller, B., Kagan, S. L., & Carrol, B. (2004). Child care in poor communities: Early learning effects of type, quality and stability. *Child Development, 75,* 47–65.

Loehlin, J. C. (1992). *Genes and environment in personality development.* Newbury Park, CA: Sage.

Loehlin, J. C., Neiderhiser, J. M., Hetherington, E. M., & Plomin, R. (2000). *The relationship code: Deciphering genetic and social influences on adolescent development.* Cambridge, MA: Harvard University Press.

Loehlin, J. C., Neiderhiser, J. M., & Reiss, D. (2005). Genetic and environmental components of adolescent adjustment and parental behavior: A multivariate analysis. *Child Development, 76,* 1104–1115.

Loessl, B., Valerius, G., Kopasz, M., Hornyak, M., Riemann, D., & Voderholzer, U. (2008). Are adolescents chronically sleep-deprived? An investigation of sleep habits of adolescents in the southwest of Germany. *Child: Care, Health and Development, 34,* 549–556.

Loewen, S. (2006). Exceptional intellectual performance: A neo-Piagetian perspective. *High Ability Studies, 17,* 159–181.

Loftus, E. F. (1997, September). Creating false memories. *Scientific American,* 71–75.

Loftus, E. F. (2003, November). Make-believe memories. *American Psychologist,* 867–873.

Loftus, E. F. (2006). Memories of things unseen. *Current Directions in Psychological Science, 13,* 145–147.

Loftus, E. F., & Bernstein, D. M. (2005). Rich false memories: The royal road to success. In A. F. Healy (Ed.), *Experimental cognitive psychology and its applications.* Washington, DC: American Psychological Association.

Logan, K. J., Byrd, C. T., Mazzocchi, E. M., & Gillam, R. B. (2011). Speaking rate characteristics of elementary-school-aged children who do and do not stutter. *Journal of Communication Disorders, 44,* 130–147.

Logel, C., Peach, J., & Spencer, S. J. (2012). Threatening gender and race: Different manifestations of stereotype threat. In M. Inzlicht & T. Schmader (Eds.), *Stereotype threat: Theory, process, and application.* New York: Oxford University Press.

Logsdon, R., McCurry, S., Pike, K., & Teri, L. (2009). Making physical activity accessible to older adults with memory loss: A feasibility study. *The Gerontologist, 49* (Suppl. 1), S94–S99.

Lohman, D. F. (2005). Reasoning abilities. In R. J. Sternberg & J. E. Pretz (Eds.), *Cognition and intelligence: Identifying the mechanisms of the mind.* New York: Cambridge University Press.

Lois, J. (2006, September). Role strain, emotion management, and burnout: Homeschooling mothers' adjustment to the teacher role. *Symbolic Interaction, 29*(4), 507–530.

London, K., Bruck, M., & Ceci, S. J. (2005). Disclosure of child sexual abuse: What does the research tell us about the ways that children tell? *Psychology, Public Policy, & Law, 11,* 194–226.

Lonetto, R. (1980). *Children's conception of death.* New York: Springer.

Long, T., & Long, L. (1983). *Latchkey children.* New York: Penguin.

Lorenz, K. (1957). Companionship in bird life. In C. Scholler (Ed.), *Instinctive behavior.* New York: International Universities Press.

Lorenz, K. (1965). *Evolution and modification of behavior.* Chicago: University of Chicago Press.

Lorenz, K. (1966). *On aggression.* New York: Harcourt Brace Jovanovich.

Lorenz, K. (1974). *Civilized man's eight deadly sins.* New York: Harcourt Brace Jovanovich.

Lorion, R. P., Iscoe, I., DeLeon, P. H., & VandenBos, G. R. (Eds). (1996). *Psychology and public policy: Balancing public service and professional need.* Washington, DC: American Psychological Association.

Losonczy-Marshall, M. (2008). Gender differences in latency and duration of emotional expression in 7- through 13-month-old infants. *Social Behavior and Personality, 36,* 267–274.

Lothian, J. (2005). *The official Lamaze guide: Giving birth with confidence.* Minnetonka, MN: Meadowbrook Press.

Lourenco, O., & Machado, A. (1996). In defense of Piaget's theory: A reply to 10 common criticisms. *Psychological Review, 103,* 143–164.

Love, A., & Burns, M. (2006, December). "It's a hurricane! It's a hurricane!": Can music facilitate social constructive and sociodramatic play in a preschool classroom? *Journal of Genetic Psychology, 167*(4), 383–391.

Love, J., Chazan-Cohen, R., & Raikes, H. (2007). Forty years of research knowledge and use: From Head Start to Early Head Start and beyond. *Child development and social policy: Knowledge for action.* Washington, DC: American Psychological Association.

Love, J., Tarullo, L., Raikes, H., & Chazan-Cohen, R. (2006). Head Start: What do we know about its effectiveness? What do we need to know? In *Blackwell handbook of early childhood development.* Malden, MA: Blackwell Publishing.

Love, J. M., Harrison, L., Sagi-Schwaratz, A. (2003). Child care quality matters: How conclusions may vary with context. *Child Development, 74,* 1021–1033.

Love, J. M., Harrison, L., Sagi-Schwartz, A., van Ijzendoorn, M. H., Ross, C., Ungerer, J. A., et al. (2003). Child care quality matters: How conclusions may vary with context. *Child Development, 74,* 1021–1033.

Lovrin, M. (2009). Treatment of major depression in adolescents: Weighing the evidence of risk and benefit in light of black box warnings. *Journal of Child and Adolescent Psychiatric Nursing, 22,* 63–68.

Lowe, M. R. (1993). The effects of dieting on eating behavior: A three-factor model. *Psychological Bulletin, 114,* 100–121.

Lowe, M. R., & Timko, C. A. (2004). What a difference a diet makes: Towards an understanding of differences between restrained dieters and restrained nondieters. *Eating Behaviors, 5,* 199–208.

Lowrey, G. H. (1986). *Growth and development of children* (8th ed.). Chicago: Year Book Medical Publishers.

Lowton, K., & Higginson, I. (2003). Managing bereavement in the classroom: A conspiracy of silence? *Death Studies, 27,* 717–741.

Lozoff, B., Wolf, A. W., & Davis, N. S. (1985). Sleep problems seen in pediatric practice. *Pediatrics, 75,* 477–483.

Lu, L. (2006). The transition to parenthood: Stress, resources, and gender differences in a Chinese society. *Journal of Community Psychology, 34,* 471–488.

Lu, M. C., Prentice, J., Yu, S. M., Inkelas, M., Lange, L. O., & Halfon, N. (2003). Childbirth education classes: Sociodemographic disparities in attendance and the association of attendance with breastfeeding initiation. *Maternal Child Health, 7,* 87–93.

Lu, T., Pan, Y., Lap. S.-Y., Li, C., Kohane, I., Chang, J., et al. (2004, June 9). Gene regulation and DNA damage in the aging human brain. *Nature,* 1038.

Lu, X. (2001). Bicultural identity development and Chinese community formation: An ethnographic study of Chinese schools in Chicago. *Howard Journal of Communications, 12,* 203–220.

Lubart, T. I., & Sternberg, R. J. (1995). An investment approach to creativity: Theory and data. In S. M. Smith, T. B. Ward, & R. A. Finke (Eds.), *The creative cognition approach.* Cambridge, MA: MIT Press.

Lubinski, D. (2004). Introduction to the special section on cognitive abilities: 100 years after Spearman's (1904) "'General Intelligence,' objectively determined and measured." *Journal of Personality and Social Psychology, 86,* 96–111.

Lubinski, D., & Benbow, C. P. (2001). Choosing excellence. *American Psychologist, 56,* 76–77.

Lucas, R. E. (2005). Time does not heal all wounds: A longitudinal study of reaction and adaptation to divorce. *Psychological Science, 16,* 945–951.

Lucas, R. E. (2007). Adaptation and the set-point model of subjective well-being: Does happiness change after major life events? *Current Directions in Psychological Science, 16,* 75–79.

Lucas, S. R., & Berends, M. (2002). Sociodemographic diversity, correlated achievement, and de facto tracking. *Sociology of Education, 75,* 328–349.

Lucas-Thompson, R., Townsend, E., Gunnar, M., Georgieff, M., Guiang, S., Ciffuentes, R., et al. (2008). Developmental changes in the responses of preterm infants to a painful stressor. *Infant Behavior & Development, 31,* 614–623.

Lucente, R. L. (2012). *Character formation and identity in adolescence: Clinical and developmental issues.* Chicago: Lyceum Books.

Luchsinger, J., & Gustafson, D. (2009). Adiposity, type 2 diabetes, and Alzheimer's disease. *Journal of Alzheimer's Disease, 16,* 693–704.

Lucy, J. A. (1992). *Language diversity and thought: A reformulation of the linguistic relativity hypothesis.* Cambridge, England: Cambridge University Press.

Lundberg, U. (2006, July). Stress, subjective and objective health. *International Journal of Social Welfare, 15,* S41–S48.

Lundman, R. J. (2001). *Prevention and control of juvenile delinquency* (3rd ed.). London: Oxford University Press.

Luo, L. (2006). The transition to parenthood: Stress, resources, and gender differences in a Chinese society. *Journal of Community Psychology, 34,* 471–488.

Luo, L., & Craik, F. (2008). Aging and memory: A cognitive approach. *The Canadian Journal of Psychiatry / La Revue canadienne de psychiatrie, 53,* 346–353.

Luo, L., & Craik, F. (2009). Age differences in recollection: Specificity effects at retrieval. *Journal of Memory and Language, 60,* 421–436.

Luo, Y., Kaufman, L., & Baillargeon R. (2009). Young infants' reasoning about physical events involving inert and self-propelled objects. *Cognitive Psychology, 58,* 441–486.

Lupien, S. P., Seery, M. D., & Almonte, J. L. (2012). Unstable high self-esteem and the eliciting conditions of self-doubt. *Journal of Experimental Social Psychology.* Retrieved from http://www.sciencedirect.com/science/article/pii/S0022103112000121.

Lushnikova, I., Orlovsky, M., Dosenko, V., Maistrenko, A., & Skibo, G. (2011). Brief anoxia preconditioning and hif prolyl-hydroxylase inhibition enhances neuronal resistance in organotypic hippocampal slices on model of ischemic damage. *Brain Research, 1886,* 46–57.

Lust, B., Suner, M., & Whitman, J. (Eds.). (1995). *Syntactic theory and first language acquisition.* Hillsdale, NJ: Erlbaum.

Luster, T., & McAdoo, H. P. (1994). Factors related to the achievement and adjustment of young African American children. *Child Development, 65,* 1080–1094.

Luthar, S. S., Cicchetti, D., & Becker, B. (2000). The construct of resilience: A critical evaluation and guidelines for future work. *Child Development, 71,* 543–562.

Luyten, P. (2011). Review of "Mind to mind: Infant research, neuroscience and psychoanalysi." *Clinical Social Work Journal, 39,* 116–118.

Lyall, S. (2004, February 15). In Europe, lovers now propose: Mary me, a little. *The New York Times,* p. D2.

Lye, T. C., Piguet, O., Grayson, D. A., Creasey, H., Ridley, L. J., Bennett, H. P., et al. (2004). Hippocampal size and memory function in the ninth and tenth decades of life: The Sydney Older Persons Study. *Journal of Neurology, Neurosurgery, and Psychiatry, 75,* 548–554.

Lykken, D., Bouchard, T., McGue, M., & Tellegen, A. (1993a). Heritability of interests: A twin study. *Journal of Applied Psychology, 78,* 649–661.

Lykken, D. T., McGue, M., Tellegen, A., & Bouchard, T. J., Jr. (1993). Emergenesis: Genetic traits that may not run in families. *American Psychologist, 47,* 1565–1577.

Lyman, D. R., Milich, R., Zimmerman, R., Novak, S. P., Logan, T. K., Martin, C., et al. (1999). Project DARE: No effects at 10-year follow-up. *Journal of Consulting and Clinical Psychology, 67,* 590–593.

Lymberis, S. C., Parhar, P. K., Katsoulakis, E., & Formenti, S. C. (2004). Pharmacogenomics and breast cancer. *Pharmacogenomics, 5,* 31–55.

Lynam, D. R. (1996). Early identification of chronic offenders: Who is the fledgling psychopath? *Psychological Bulletin, 120,* 209–234.

Lynam, D., Milich, R., Zimmerman, R., Novak, S., Logan, T., Martin, C., et al. (1999). Project DARE: No effects at 10-year follow-up. *Journal of Consulting and Clinical Psychology, 67,* 590–593.

Lynch, M. E., Coles, C. D., & Corely, T. (2003). Examining delinquency in adolescents risk factors. *Journal of Studies on Alcohol, 64,* 678–686.

Lyness, S. A. (1993). Predictors of differences between Type A and B individuals in heart rate and blood pressure reactivity. *Psychological Bulletin, 114,* 266–295.

Lynn J., Teno, J. M., Phillips, R. S., Wu, A. W., Desbiens, N., Harrold J., et al. (1997). Perceptions by family members of the dying experience of older and seriously ill patients. SUPPORT Investigators. Study to Understand Prognoses and Preferences for Outcomes and Risks of Treatments [see comments]. *Annals of Internal Medicine, 126,* 164–165.

Lynn, R. (2009). What has caused the Flynn effect? Secular increases in the Development Quotients of infants. *Intelligence, 37,* 16–24.

Lynne, S., Graber, J., Nichols, T., Brooks-Gunn, J., & Botvin, G. (2007, February). Links between pubertal timing, peer influences, and externalizing behaviors among urban students followed through middle school. *Journal of Adolescent Health, 40,* 35–44.

Lynwander, L. (1995, February 5). Burying the poor. *The New York Times,* Sec. 13NJ, p. 1.

Lyon, G. R. (1996). Learning disabilities. *The Future of Children, 6,* 54–76.

Lyon, M. E., Benoit, M., O'Donnell, R. M., Getson, P. R., Silber, T., & Walsh, T. (2000). Assessing African American adolescents' risk for suicide attempts: Attachment theory. *Adolescence, 35,* 121–134.

Lyons, M. J., Bar, J. L., & Kremen, W. S. (2002). Nicotine and familial vulnerability to schizophrenia: A discordant twin study. *Journal of Abnormal Psychology, 111,* 687–693.

Lyons, T. H. (2007). Attachment theory and reactive attachment disorder: Theoretical perspectives and treatment implications. *Journal of Child and Adolescent Psychiatric Nursing, 20,* 27–40.

Lysynchuk, L. M., Pressley, M., & Vye, N. J. (1990). Reciprocal teaching improves standardized reading-comprehension performance in poor comprehenders. *Elementary School Journal, 90,* 469–484.

Ma, H., Bernstein, L., Pike, M. C., & Ursin, G. (2006). Reproductive factors and breast cancer risk according to joint estrogen and progesterone receptor status: a meta-analysis of epidemiological studies. *Breast Cancer Research, 8,* R43.

Maas, C., Herrenkohl, T. I., & Sousa, C. (2008). Review of research on child maltreatment and violence in youth. *Trauma, Violence, Abuse, 9,* 56–67.

Mabbott, D. J., Noseworthy, M., Bouffet, E., Laughlin, S., & Rockel, C. (2006). White matter growth as a mechanism of cognitive development in children. *Neuroimaging, 15,* 936–946.

MacArthur Foundation Research Network on Successful Midlife Development. (1999). *What age do you feel most of the time?* Vero Beach, FL: MIDMAC.

Maccoby, E. B. (1999). *The two sexes: Growing up apart, coming together.* New York: Belknap.

Maccoby, E. E. (1980). *Social development: Psychological growth and the parent–child relationship.* New York: Harcourt, Brace, Jovanovich.

Maccoby, E. E. (1999). *The two sexes: Growing up apart, coming together.* New York: Belknap.

Maccoby, E. E., & Lewis, C. C. (2003). Less day care or different day care? *Child Development, 74,* 1069–1075.

Maccoby, E. E., & Martin, J. A. (1983). Socialization in the context of the family: Parent–child interaction. In P. H. Mussen (Ed.) & E. M. Hetherington (Vol. Ed.), *Handbook of child psychology: Vol. 4. Socialization, personality, and social development* (4th ed., pp. 1–101). New York: Wiley.

MacDonald, G. (2007, January 25). Montessori looks back—and ahead: As name marks 100 years, movement is taking stock. *USA Today,* p. 9D.

MacDonald, H., Beeghly, M., Grant-Knight, W., Augustyn, M., Woods, R., Cabral, H., et al. (2008). Longitudinal association between infant disorganized attachment and childhood posttraumatic stress symptoms. *Development and Psychopathology, 20,* 493–508.

MacDonald, S., Hultsch, D., & Dixon, R. (2003). Performance variability is related to change in cognition: Evidence from the Victoria Longitudinal Study. *Psychology & Aging, 18,* 510–523.

MacDonald, W. (2003). The impact of job demands and workload stress and fatigue. *Australian Psychologist, 38,* 102–117.

MacDorman, M. F., Declercq, E., & Mathews, T. J. (2011). United States home births increase 20 percent from 2004 to 2008. *Birth: Issues in Perinatal Care, 38,* 185–190.

MacDorman, M., Declercq, E., Menacker, F., & Malloy, M. (2008). Neonatal mortality for primary cesarean and vaginal births to low-risk women: Application of an "intention-to-treat" model. *Birth: Issues in Perinatal Care, 35,* 3–8.

MacDorman, M. F., Martin, J. A., Mathews, T. J., Hoyert, D. L., & Ventura, S. J. (2005). Explaining the 2001–02 infant mortality increase: data from the linked birth/infant death data set. *National Vital Statistics Report, 53,* 1–22.

MacEvoy, J., & Asher, S. R. (2012). When friends disappoint: Boys' and girls' responses to transgressions of friendship expectations. *Child Development, 83,* 104–119.

Machaalani, R., & Waters, K. (2008). Neuronal cell death in the Sudden Infant Death Syndrome brainstem and associations with risk factors. *Brain: A Journal of Neurology, 131,* 218–228.

MacInnes, K., & Stone, D. H. (2008). Stages of development and injury: An epidemiological survey of young children presenting to an emergency department. *BMC Public Health, 8.*

Macionis, J. J. (2001). *Sociology.* Upper Saddle River, NJ: Prentice Hall.

Mackenzie, K., & Peters, M. (2000). Handedness, hand roles, and hand injuries at work. *Journal of Safety Research, 31,* 221–227.

MacKenzie, M. J., Nicklas, E., Waldfogel, J., & Brooks-Gunn, J. (2012). Corporal punishment and child behavioural and cognitive outcomes through 5 years of age: Evidence from a contemporary urban birth cohort study. *Infant and Child Development, 21,* 3–33.

Mackey, M. C. (1990). Women's preparation for the childbirth experience. *Maternal-Child Nursing Journal, 19,* 143–173.

Mackey, M. C., White, U., & Day, R. (1992). Reasons American men become fathers: Men's divulgences, women's perceptions. *Journal of Genetic Psychology, 153,* 435–445.

MacPhee, D., Kreutzer, J. C., & Fritz, J. J. (1994). Infusing a diversity perspective into human development courses. *Child Development, 65,* 699–715.

MacPhee, M. (2011). Learning from role models. In M. McAllister & J. B. Lowe (Eds.), *The resilient nurse: Empowering your practice.* New York: Springer Publishing Co.

MacWhinney, B. (1991). Connectionism as a framework for language acquisition. In J. Miller (Ed.), *Research on child language disorders.* Austin, TX: Pro-ed.

Madathil, J., & Benshoff, J. (2008). Importance of marital characteristics and marital satisfaction: A comparison of Asian Indians in arranged marriages and Americans in marriages of choice. *The Family Journal, 16,* 222–230.

Maddi, S. R. (2006). Hardiness: The courage to grow from stresses. *Journal of Positive Psychology, 1,* 160–168.

Maddi, S. R., Harvey, R. H., Khoshaba, D. M., Lu, J. L., Persico, M., & Brow, M. (2006). The personality construct of hardiness, III: Relationships with repression, innovativeness, authoritarianism, and performance. *Journal of Personality, 74,* 575–598.

Maddox, G. L., & Campbell, R. T. (1985). Scope, concepts, and methods in the study of aging. In R. H. Binstock & E. Shanas (Eds.), *Handbook of aging and the social sciences* (2nd ed.). New York: Van Nostrand Reinhold.

Mael, F. A. (1998). Single-sex and coeducational schooling: Relationships to socioemotional and academic development. *Review of Education Research, 68,* 101–129.

Magai, C., & McFadden, S. H. (Eds.). (1996). *Handbook of emotion, adult development, and aging.* New York: Academic Press.

Magyar, C. I. (2011). *Developing and evaluating educational programs for students with autism.* New York: Springer Science + Business Media.

Mahgoub, N., & Lantz, M. (2006, December). When older adults suffer the loss of a child. *Psychiatric Annals, 36,* 877–880.

Mahoney, E. R. (1983). *Human sexuality.* New York: McGraw-Hill.

Mahoney, J. (2009, May 3). Suicides among middle-age women are on the rise nationally. *Albuquerque (NM) Journal,* p. 6.

Mahoney, M. C., & James, D. M. (2000). Predictors of anticipated breastfeeding in an urban, lowincome setting. *Journal of Family Practice, 49,* 529–533.

Maiden, A. H. (1997). Celebrating a return to earth: Birth in indigenous aboriginal, Tibetan, Balinese, Basque and Cherokee cultures. *Pre- & Peri-Natal Psychology Journal, 11,* 251–264.

Maier, M. F., Vitiello, V. E., & Greenfield, D. B. (2012). A multilevel model of child- and classroom-level psychosocial factors that support language and literacy resilience of children in Head Start. *Early Childhood Research Quarterly, 27,* 104–114.

Maital, S., Painter, K., Park, S.-Y., Pascual, L., Pêcheux, M.-G., Ruel, J., et al. (2004). Cross-linguistic analysis of vocabulary in young children: Spanish, Dutch, French, Hebrew, Italian, Korean, and American English. *Child Development, 75,* 1115–1139.

Majdandzic, M., & van den Boom, D. (2007). Multimethod longitudinal assessment of temperament in early childhood. *Journal of Personality, 75,* 121–167.

Major, B., & Konar, E. (1984). An investigation of sex differences in pay expectations and their possible causes. *Academy of Management Journal, 27,* 777–792.

Makino, M., Hashizume, M., Tsuboi, K., Yasushi, M., & Dennerstein, L. (2006, September). Comparative study of attitudes to eating between male and female students in the People's Republic of China. *Eating and Weight Disorders, 11,* 111–117.

Makishita, H., & Matsunaga, K. (2008). Differences of drivers' reaction times according to age and mental workload. *Accident Analysis & Prevention, 40,* 567–575.

Malatesta, C. Z., & Haviland, J. M. (1986). *Measuring change in infant emotional expressivity: Two approaches applied in longitudinal investigation.* New York: Cambridge University Press.

Malchiodi, C. A. (1998). *Understanding children's drawings.* New York: Guilford Press.

Malinowski, C. I., & Smith, C. P. (1985). Moral reasoning and moral conduct: An investigation prompted by Kohlberg's theory. *Journal of Personality and Social Psychology, 49,* 1016–1027.

Maller, S. (2003). Best practices in detecting bias in nonverbal tests. In R. McCallum (Ed.), *Handbook of nonverbal assessment.* New York: Kluwer Academic/Plenum Publishers.

Malmberg, L., Wanner, B., & Little, T. (2008). Age and school-type differences in children's beliefs about school performance. *International Journal of Behavioral Development, 32,* 531–541.

Mameli, M. (2007). Reproductive cloning, genetic engineering and the autonomy of the child: The moral agent and the open future. *Journal of Medical Ethics, 33,* 87–93.

Mancini, J. A., & Blieszner, R. (1991). Aging parents and adult children. In A. Booth (Ed.), *Contemporary families.* Minneapolis, MN: National Council on Family Relations.

Mandel, D. R., Jusczyk, P. W., & Pisoni, D. B. (1995). Infants' recognition of the sound patterns of their own names. *Psychological Science, 6,* 314–317.

Mandelman, S. D., & Grigorenko, E. L. (2011). Intelligence: Genes, environments, and their interactions. In R. J. Sternberg & S. Kaufman (Eds.), *The Cambridge handbook of intelligence.* New York: Cambridge University Press.

Mandler, J. M. (1990). A new perspective on cognitive development in infancy. *American Scientist, 78,* 236–243.

Mandler, J. M., & McDonough, L. (1994). Long-term recall of event sequences in infancy. *Journal of Experimental Child Psychology, 59*, 457–474.

Manfra, L., & Winsler, A. (2006). Preschool children's awareness of private speech. *International Journal of Behavioral Development, 30*, 537–549.

Mangan, P. A. (1997, November). *Time perception*. Paper presented at the annual meeting of the Society for Neuroscience, New Orleans.

Mangelsdorf, S., Gunnar, M., Kestenbaum, R., Lang, S., & Andreas, D. (1990). Infant proneness to distress temperament, maternal personality, and mother–infant attachment: Association and goodness of fit. *Child Development, 61*, 820–831.

Mangweth, B., Hausmann, A., & Walch, T. (2004). Body fat perception in eating-disordered men. *International Journal of Eating Disorders, 35*, 102–108.

Mani, N., & Plunkett, K. (2011). Phonological priming and cohort effects in toddlers. *Cognition, 121*, 196–206

Manlove, J., Franzetta, K., McKinney, K., Romano-Papillo, A., & Terry-Humen, E. (2004). *No time to waste. Programs to reduce teen pregnancy among middle school-aged youth*. Washington, DC: National Campaign to Prevent Teen Pregnancy.

Manlove, J., Terry-Humen, E., Romano Papillo, A., Franzetta, K., Williams, S., & Ryan, S. (2002). *Preventing teenage pregnancy, childbearing, and sexually transmitted diseases: What the research shows*. Washington, DC: Child Trends. Retrieved from http://www.childtrends.org/Files/K1Brief.pdf.

Mann, C. C. (2005, March 18). Provocative study says obesity may reduce U.S. life expectancy. *Science, 307*, 1716–1717.

Mann, L. (1980). Cross-cultural studies in small groups. In H. C. Triandis & R. W. Brislin (Eds), *Handbook of cross-cultural psychology* (Vol. 5). Boston: Allyn & Bacon.

Manning, M., & Hoyme, H. (2007). Fetal alcohol spectrum disorders: A practical clinical approach to diagnosis. *Neuroscience & Biobehavioral Reviews, 31*, 230–238.

Manning, W., Giordano, P., & Longmore, M. (2006, September). Hooking up: The relationship contexts of "nonrelationship" sex. *Journal of Adolescent Research, 21*, 459–483.

Manson, A., & Shea, S. (1991). Malnutrition in elderly ambulatory medical patients. *American Journal of Public Health, 81*, 1195–1197.

Manstead, A. S. R. (1997). Situations, belongingness, attitudes, and culture: Four lessons learned from social psychology. In C. McGarty & S. A. Haslam et al. (Eds.), *The message of social psychology: Perspectives on mind in society*. Oxford, England: Blackwell Publishers, Inc.

Manstead, A. S. R., Fischer, A. H., & Jakobs, E. B. (1998). The expressive and communicative functions of facial displays. In P. Philippot, R. S. Feldman, & E. J. Coats (Eds.), *The social context of nonverbal behavior*. Cambridge, England: Cambridge University Press.

Manzoli, L., Villari, P., Pironec, G., & Boccia, A. (2007). Marital status and mortality in the elderly: A systematic review and meta-analysis. *Social Science & Medicine, 64*, 77–94.

Mao, A., Burnham, M. M., Goodlin-Jones, B. L., Gaylor, E. E., & Anders, T. F. (2004). A comparison of the sleep-wake patterns of cosleeping and solitary-sleeping infants. *Child Psychiatry and Human Development, 35*, 95–105.

Maratsos, M. P. (1983). Some current issues in the study of the acquisition of grammar. In P. H. Mussen (Ed.), *Handbook of child psychology* (Vol. 3, 4th ed.). New York: Wiley.

Marchant, M., Young, K. R., & West, R. P. (2004). The effects of parental teaching on compliance behavior of children. *Psychology in the Schools, 41*, 337–350.

Marcia, J. E. (1966). Development and validation of ego identity status. *Journal of Personality and Social Psychology, 3*(5), 551–558.

Marcia, J. E. (1980). Identity in adolescence. In J. Adelson (Ed.), *Handbook of adolescent psychology*. New York: Wiley.

Marcia, J.E. (2007). Theory and measure: The Identity Status Interview. In M. Watzlawik & A. Born (Eds.), *Capturing identity: Quantitative and qualitative methods*. Lanham, MD: University Press of America.

Marcovitch, S., Zelazo, P., & Schmuckler, M. (2003). The effect of the number of A trials on performance on the A-not-B task. *Infancy, 3*, 519–529.

Marcus, A. D. (2004, February 3). The new math on when to have kids. *The Wall Street Journal*. D1, D4.

Marczinski, C., Milliken, B., & Nelson, S. (2003). Aging and repetition effects: Separate specific and nonspecific influences. *Psychology & Aging, 18*, 780–790.

Mares, S. W., van der Vorst, H., Engels, R. E., & Lichtwarck-Aschoff, A. (2011). Parental alcohol use, alcohol-related problems, and alcohol-specific attitudes, alcohol-specific communication, and adolescent excessive alcohol use and alcohol-related problems: An indirect path model. *Addictive Behaviors, 36*, 209–216.

Margie, N., Killen, M., Sinno, S., & McGlothlin, H. (2005). Minority children's intergroup attitudes about peer relationships. *British Journal of Developmental Psychology, 23*, 251–269.

Margit, W., Vondracek, F., Capaldi, D., & Porfeli, E. (2003). Childhood and adolescent predictors of early adult career pathways. *Journal of Vocational Behavior, 63*, 305–328.

Marin, M. M., Gingras, B., & Stewart, L. (2012). Perception of musical timbre in congenital amusia: Categorization, discrimination and short-term memory. *Neuropsychologia, 50*, 367–378.

Marin, T., Chen, E., Munch, J., & Miller, G. (2009). Double-exposure to acute stress and chronic family stress is associated with immune changes in children with asthma. *Psychosomatic Medicine, 71*, 378–384.

Marinova-Todd, S. H. (2012). "Corplum is a core from a plum": The advantage of bilingual children in the analysis of word meaning from verbal context. *Bilingualism: Language and Cognition, 15*, 117–127.

Marks, A. K., Patton, F., & Coll, C. (2011). Being bicultural: A mixed-methods study of adolescents' implicitly and explicitly measured multiethnic identities. *Developmental Psychology, 47*, 270–288.

Markus, H. R., & Kitayama, S. (1991). Culture and the self: Implications for cognition, emotion, and motivation. *Psychological Review, 98*, 224–253.

Markward, N., Markward, M., & Peterson, C. (2009). Biological and genetic influences. *Obesity in youth: Causes, consequences, and cures*. Washington, DC: American Psychological Association.

Marlier, L., Schaal, B., & Soussignan, R. (1998). Neonatal responsiveness to the odor of amniotic and lacteal fluids: A test of perinatal chemosensory continuity. *Child Development, 69*, 611–623.

Marmar, C. R., Neylan, T. C., & Schoenfeld, F. B. (2002). New directions in the pharmacotherapy of post-traumatic stress disorder. *Psychiatric Quarterly, 73*, 259–270.

Marquis, A., & Shi, R. (2012). Initial morphological learning in preverbal infants. *Cognition, 122*, 61–66.

Marschark, M. (2003). Interactions of language and cognition in deaf learners: From research to practice. *International Journal of Audiology, 42*, Supplement, s41–s48.

Marschark, M., Spencer, P. E., & Newsom, C. A. (Eds.). (2003). *Oxford handbook of deaf students, language, and education*. London: Oxford University Press.

Marschik, P., Einspieler, C., Strohmeier, A., Plienegger, J., Garzarolli, B., & Prechtl, H. (2008). From the reaching behavior at 5 months of age to hand preference at preschool age. *Developmental Psychobiology, 50*, 512–518.

Marsh, H. E., Craven, R., & Debus, R. (1998). Structure, stability, and development of young children's self-concepts: A multicohort-multioccasion study. *Child Development, 69*, 1030–1053.

Marsh, H. W. (1990). Influences of internal and external frames of reference on the formation of math and English self-concepts. *Journal of Educational Psychology, 82*, 107–116.

Marsh, H., & Ayotte, V. (2003). Do multiple dimensions of self-concept become more differentiated with age? The differential distinctiveness hypothesis. *Journal of Educational Psychology, 95*, 687–706.

Marsh, H., Ellis, L., & Craven, R. (2002). How do preschool children feel about themselves? Unraveling measurement and multidimensional self-concept structure. *Developmental Psychology, 38*, 376–393.

Marsh, H. W., & Hau, K. T. (2003). Big-fish-little-pond effect on academic self-concept. *American Psychologist, 58*, 364–376.

Marsh, H., & Hau, K. (2004). Explaining paradoxical relations between academic self-concepts and achievements: Cross-cultural generalizability of the internal/external frame of reference predictions across 26 countries. *Journal of Educational Psychology, 96*, 56–67.

Marsh, H. W., & Holmes, I. W. M. (1990). Multidimensional self-concepts: Construct validation of responses by children. *American Educational Research Journal, 27*, 89–118.

Marsh, H. W., & Parker, J. W. (1984). Determinants of student self-concept: Is it better to be a relatively large fish in a small pond even if you don't learn to swim as well? *Journal of Personality and Social Psychology, 47*, 213–231.

Marsh, H., Seaton, M., Trautwein, U., Lüdtke, O., Hau, K., O'Mara, A., et al. (2008). The big-fish-little-pond-effect stands up to critical scrutiny: Implications for theory, methodology, and future research. *Educational Psychology Review, 20*, 319–350.

Marsh, H. W., & Shavelson, R. (1985). Self-concept: Its multifaceted, hierarchical structure. *Educational Psychologist, 20*, 107–123.

Marshall, E. (2000). Duke study faults overuse of stimulants for children. *Science, 289*, 721.

Marshall, E. (2000, November 17). Planned Ritalin trial for tots heads into uncharted waters. *Science, 290*, 1280–1282.

Marshall, N. L. (2004). The quality of early child care and children's development. *Current Directions in Psychological Science, 13*, 165–168.

Marshall, R., & Sutherland, P. (2008). The social relations of bereavement in the Caribbean. *Omega: Journal of Death and Dying, 57*, 21–34.

Marshall, V. W. (Ed.). (1986). *Later life: The social psychology of aging*. Beverly Hills, CA: Sage.

Martikainen, P., & Valkonen, T. (1996). Mortality after the death of a spouse: Rates and causes of death in a large Finnish cohort. *American Journal of Public Health, 86*, 1087–1093.

Martin, B. A. (1989). Gender differences in salary expectations. *Psychology of Women Quarterly, 13*, 87–96.

Martin, C. L. (1993). New directions for investigating children's gender knowledge. *Developmental Review, 13*, 184–204.

Martin, C. L. (2000). Cognitive theories of gender development. In T. Eckes & H. M. Trautner, (Eds.), *The developmental social psychology of gender*. Mahwah, NJ: Erlbaum.

Martin, C., & Fabes, R. (2001). The stability and consequences of young children's same-sex peer interactions. *Developmental Psychology, 37*, 431–446.

Martin, C. L., & Ruble, D. (2004). Children's search for gender clues: Cognitive perspectives on gender development. *Current Directions in Psychological Science, 13*, 67–70.

Martin, C. L., Ruble, D. N., & Szkrybalo, J. (2002). Cognitive theories of early gender development. *Psychological Bulletin, 128*, 903–933.

Martin, G. B., & Clark, R. D. (1982). Distress crying in neonates: Species and peer specificity. *Developmental Psychology, 18*, 3–9.

Martin, J., & D'Augelli, A. (2003). How lonely are gay and lesbian youth? *Psychological Reports, 93,* 486.

Martin, J. A., Hamilton, B. E., Sutton, P. D., Ventura, M. A., Menacker, F., & Munson, M. L. (2003, December 17). Births: Final data for 2002. *National Vital Statistics Report, 52.*

Martin, J. A., Hamilton, B. E., Sutton, P. D., Ventura, S. J., Menacker, F., & Munson, M. L. (2005). Births: Final data for 2003. *National Vital Statistics Reports, 54,* Table J, p. 21.

Martin, J. A., & Park, M. M. (1999, September 14). Trends in twin and triplet births, 1980–1997. *National Vital Statistics Reports,* pp. 1–17.

Martin, L., McNamara, M., Milot, A., Halle, T., & Hair, E. (2007). The effects of father involvement during pregnancy on receipt of prenatal care and maternal smoking. *Maternal and Child Health Journal, 11,* 595–602.

Martin, L., & Pullum, G. K. (1991). *The great Eskimo vocabulary hoax.* Chicago: University of Chicago Press.

Martin, P., Martin, D., & Martin, M. (2001). Adolescent premarital sexual activity, cohabitation, and attitudes toward marriage. *Adolescence, 36,* 601–609.

Martin, S., Li, Y., Casanueva, C., Harris-Britt, A., Kupper, L., & Cloutier, S. (2006). Intimate partner violence and women's depression before and during pregnancy. *Violence Against Women, 12,* 221–239.

Martin, W., & Freitas, M. (2002). Mean mortality among Brazilian left- and right-handers: Modification or selective elimination. *Laterality, 7,* 31–44.

Martineau, J., Cochin, S., Magne, R., & Barthelemy, C. (2008). Impaired cortical activation in autistic children: Is the mirror neuron system involved? *International Journal of Psychophysiology, 68,* 35–40.

Martinez, R., & Dukes, R. L. (1991). Ethnic and gender differences in self-esteem. *Youth and Society, 22,* 318–338.

Martinez-Torteya, C., Bogat, G., von Eye, A., & Levendosky, A. (2009). Resilience among children exposed to domestic violence: The role of risk and protective factors. *Child Development, 80,* 562–577.

Martins, N., & Wilson, B. J. (2012). Social aggression on television and its relationship to children's aggression in the classroom. *Human Communication Research, 38,* 48–71.

Martins, S. S., Storr, C. L., Ialongo, N. S., & Chilcoat, H. D. (2007). Mental health and gambling in urban female adolescents. *Journal of Adolescent Health, 40,* 463–465.

Martiny, S. E., Kessler, T., & Vignoles, V. L. (2012). Shall I leave or shall we fight? Effects of threatened group-based self-esteem on identity management strategies. *Group Processes & Intergroup Relations, 15,* 39–55.

Martorell, G.A., & Bugental, D.B. (2006). Maternal variations in stress reactivity: Implications for harsh parenting practices with very young children. *Journal of Family Psychology, 20,*641–647.

Marx, S., & Pennington, J. (2003). Pedagogies of critical race theory: Experimentations with white preservice teachers. *International Journal of Qualitative Studies in Education, 16, Special issue: Whiteness issues in teacher education,* 91–110.

Masataka, N. (1996). Perception of motherese in a signed language by 6–month-old deaf infants. *Developmental Psychology, 32,* 874–879.

Masataka, N. (1998). Perception of motherese in Japanese sign language by 6-month-old hearing infants. *Developmental Psychology, 34,* 241–246.

Masataka, N. (2000). The role of modality and input in the earliest stage of language acquisition: Studies of Japanese sign language. In C. Chamerlain & J. P. Morford, *Language acquisition by eye.* Mahwah, NJ: Lawrence Erlbaum Associates.

Masataka, N. (2003). *The onset of language.* Cambridge, England: Cambridge University Press.

Masataka, N. (2006). Preference for consonance over dissonance by hearing newborns of deaf parents and of hearing parents. *Developmental Science, 9,* 46–50.

Masataka, N., Ohnishi, T., Imabayashi, E., Hirakata, M., & Matsuda, H. (2006). Neural correlates for numerical processing in the manual mode. *Journal of Deaf Studies and Deaf Education, 11,* 144–152.

Mash, E. J., & Barkley, R. A. (1998). *Treatment of childhood disorders* (2nd ed.). New York: Guilford Press.

Mash, E. J., & Barkley, R. A. (Eds.). (2003). *Child psychopathology* (2nd ed.). New York: Guilford Press.

Masho, S. W., & Archer, P. W. (2011). Does maternal birth outcome differentially influence the occurrence of infant death among African Americans and European Americans? *Maternal and Child Health Journal, 15,* 1249–1256.

Maslach, C. (1982). *Burnout—The cost of caring.* Englewood Cliffs, NJ: Prentice-Hall.

Masling, J. M., & Bornstein, R. F. (Eds.). (1996). *Psychoanalytic perspectives on developmental psychology.* Washington, DC: American Psychological Association.

Maslow, A. H. (1970). *Motivation and personality* (2nd ed.). New York: Harper & Row.

Massaro, A., Rothbaum, R., & Aly, H. (2006). Fetal brain development: The role of maternal nutrition, exposures and behaviors. *Journal of Pediatric Neurology, 4,* 1–9.

Massimo, L. (2006). Relationship between parents and sick children: Difficulties and possibilities regarding understanding. *New developments in parent-child relations* (pp. 259–267). Hauppauge, NY: Nova Science Publishers.

Masten, A. S., & Coatsworth, J. D. (1998). The development of competence in favorable and unfavorable environments. *American Psychologist, 53,* 205–220.

Master, S., Amodio, D., Stanton, A., Yee, C., Hilmert, C., & Taylor, S. (2009). Neurobiological correlates of coping through emotional approach. *Brain, Behavior, and Immunity, 23,* 27–35.

Masters, W. H., Johnson, V., & Kolodny, R. C. (1982). *Human sexuality.* Boston: Little, Brown.

Mastropieri, M. A., & Scruggs, T. E. (1991). *Teaching students ways to remember: Strategies for learning mnemonically.* Cambridge, MA: Brookline Books.

Masunaga, H. (1998). Adult learning theory and Elderhostel. *Gerontology & Geriatrics Education, 19,* 3–16.

Maternal and Child Health Bureau. (1993). *Child Health USA '93.* Washington, DC: Health Resources and Services Administration.

Maternal and Child Health Bureau. (1994). *Child Health USA '93.* Washington, DC: U.S. Department of Health and Human Services.

Mathew, A., & Cook, M. L. (1990). The control of reaching movements by young infants. *Child Development, 61,* 1238–1257.

Mathews, G., Fane, B., Conway, G., Brook, C., & Hines, M. (2009). Personality and congenital adrenal hyperplasia: Possible effects of prenatal androgen exposure. *Hormones and Behavior, 55,* 285–291.

Mathews, J. J., & Zadak, K. (1991). The alternative birth movement in the United States: History and current status. *Women and Health, 17,* 39–56.

Mathews, J. R., Friman, P. C., Barone, V. J., Ross, L. V., & Christophersen, E. R. (1987). Decreasing dangerous infant behaviors through parent instruction. *Journal of Applied Behavior Analysis, 20,* 165–169.

Mathiesen, K., & Prior, M. (2006, December). The impact of temperament factors and family functioning on resilience processes from infancy to school age. *European Journal of Developmental Psychology, 3*(4), 357–387.

Matlin, M. (2003). From menarche to menopause: Misconceptions about women's reproductive lives. *Psychology Science, 45,* 106–122.

Matlin, M. M. (1987). *The psychology of women.* New York: Holt.

Matlock, J. R., & Green, V. P. (1990). The effects of day care on the social and emotional development of infants, toddlers and preschoolers. *Early Child Development & Care, 64,* 55–59.

Maton, K., Schellenbach, C., & Leadbeater, B. (2004). *Investing in children, youth, families, and communities: Strengths-based research and policy.* Washington, DC: American Psychological Association.

Matson, J., & LoVullo, S. (2008). A review of behavioral treatments for self-injurious behaviors of persons with autism spectrum disorders. *Behavior Modification, 32,* 61–76.

Matson, J. L., & Mulick, J. A. (Eds.). (1991). *Handbook of mental retardation* (2nd ed.). New York: Pergamon.

Matsuda, Y., Ueno, K., Waggoner, R., Erickson, D., Shimura, Y., Tanaka, K., & Mazuka, R. (2011). Processing of infant-directed speech by adults. *NeuroImage, 54,* 611–621.

Matsumoto, A. (1999). *Sexual differentiation of the brain.* Boca Raton, FL: CRC Press.

Matsumoto, D. (1993). Ethnic differences in affect intensity, emotion judgments, display rule attitudes, and self-reported emotional expression in an American sample. *Motivation & Emotion, 17,* 107–123.

Matsumoto, D., & Yoo, S. H. (2006). Toward a new generation of cross-cultural research. *Perspectives on Psychological Science, 1,* 234–250.

Mattes, E., McCarthy, S., Gong, G., van Eekelen, J., Dunstan, J., Foster, J., et al. (2009). Maternal mood scores in mid-pregnancy are related to aspects of neonatal immune function. *Brain, Behavior, and Immunity, 23,* 380–388.

Matteson, M. A. (1988). Age-related changes in the integument. In M. A. Matteson & E. S. McConnell (Eds.), *Gerontological nursing: Concepts and practice.* Philadelphia: Saunders.

Matthews, G., Zeidner, M., & Roberts, R. D. (2012). *Emotional intelligence 101.* New York: Springer Publishing Co.

Matthews, K. A. (1982). Psychological perspectives on the Type A behavior pattern. *Psychological Bulletin, 91,* 293–323.

Matthews, K. A., Wing, R. R., Kuller, L. H., Meilahn, E. N., & Owens, J. F. (2000). Menopause as a turning point in midlife. In S. B Manuck & R. Jennings (Eds.), *Behavior, health, and aging.* Mahwah, NJ: Erlbaum.

Mattison, J., Black, A., Huck, J., Moscrip, T., Handy, A., Tilmont, E., et al. (2005). Age-related decline in caloric intake and motivation for food in rhesus monkeys. *Neurobiology of Aging, 26,* 1117–1127.

Mattison, R. E., & Mayes, S. (2012). Relationships between learning disability, executive function, and psychopathology in children with ADHD. *Journal of Attention Disorders, 16,* 138–146.

Mattson, M. (2003). Will caloric restriction and folate protect against AD and PD? *Neurology, 60,* 690–695.

Mattson, S., Calarco, K., & Lang, A. (2006). Focused and shifting attention in children with heavy prenatal alcohol exposure. *Neuropsychology, 20,* 361–369.

Matusov, E., & Hayes, R. (2000). Sociocultural critique of Piaget and Vygotsky. *New Ideas in Psychology, 18,* 215–239.

Mauritzson, U., & Saeljoe, R. (2001). Adult questions and children's responses: Coordination of perspectives in studies of children's theories of other minds. *Scandinavian Journal of Educational Research, 45,* 213–231.

Maxwell, L. (2007, March). Competency in child care settings: The role of the physical environment. *Environment and Behavior, 39,* 229–245.

Maxfield, M. G., & Widom, C. S. (1996). The cycle of violence. *Archives of Pediatrics & Adolescent Medicine, 150,* 390–395.

May, P. A., Tabachnick, B. G., Gossage, J., Kalberg, W. O., Marais, A., Robinson, L. K., & … Hoyme, H. (2011). Maternal risk factors predicting child physical characteristics and dysmorphology in fetal alcohol syndrome and partial fetal alcohol syndrome. *Drug and Alcohol Dependence, 119,* 18–27.

Mayberry, R. I., & Nicoladis, E. (2001). Gesture reflects language development: Evidence from bilingual children. *Current Directions in Psychological Science, 9,* 192–195.

Mayer, J. D. (2001). Emotion, intelligence, and emotional intelligence. In J. P. Forgas (Ed), *Handbook of affect and social cognition.* Mahwah, NJ: Erlbaum.

Mayer, J. D., & Salovey, P. (1997). What is emotional intelligence? In P. Salovey & D. J. Sluyter (Eds.), *Emotional development and emotional intelligence.* New York: Basic Books.

Mayer, J. D., Salovey, P., & Caruso, D. R. (2000). Emotional intelligence as zeitgeist, as personality, and as a mental ability. In R. Bar-On, J. D. A. Parker, & D. A. James (Eds.), *The handbook of emotional intelligence: Theory, development, assessment, and application at home, school, and in the workplace.* San Francisco, CA: Jossey-Bass.

Mayer, J. D., Salovey, P., & Caruso, D. R. (2004). Emotional intelligence: Theory, findings, and implications. *Psychological Inquiry, 15,* 197–215.

Mayer, J., Salovey, P., & Caruso, D. (2008). Emotional intelligence: New ability or eclectic traits? *American Psychologist, 63,* 503–517.

Mayer, R. E. (2012). Information processing. In K. R. Harris, S. Graham, T. Urdan, C. B. McCormick, G. M. Sinatra, J. Sweller, … J. Sweller (Eds.), *APA educational psychology handbook, Vol 1: Theories, constructs, and critical issues.* Washington, DC: American Psychological Association.

Mayes, L. C., & Lombroso, P. J. (2003). Genetics of childhood disorders: L.V. prenatal drug exposure. *Journal of the American Academy of Child and Adolescent Psychiatry, 42,* 1258–1261.

Mayes, L., Snyder, P., Langlois, E., & Hunter, N. (2007). Visuospatial working memory in school-aged children exposed in Utero to cocaine. *Child Neuropsychology, 13,* 205–218.

Mayes, R., Bagwell, C., & Erkulwater, J. (2009). *Medicating children:ADHD and pediatric mental health.* Cambridge, MA: Harvard University Press.

Mayes, R., & Rafalovich, A. (2007, December). Suffer the restless children: The evolution of ADHD and paediatric stimulant use, 1900–80. *History of Psychiatry, 18*(4), 435–457.

Maynard, A. (2008). What we thought we knew and how we came to know it: Four decades of cross-cultural research from a Piagetian point of view. *Human Development, 51,* 56–65.

Maynard, A., & Greenfield, P. (2003). Implicit cognitive development in cultural tools and children: Lessons from Maya Mexico. *Cognitive Development, 18,* 489–510.

Maynard, R. A. (1995). Subsidized employment and nonlabor market alternatives for welfare recipients. In D. S. Nightingale & R. H. Haveman (Eds.), *The work alternative: Welfare reform and the realities of the job market.* Washington, DC: Urban Insittute Press.

Mayo Clinic. (2000, March). Age-related macular degeneration: Who gets it and what you can do about it. *Women's Healthsource, 4,* 1–2.

Mayseless, O. (1996). Attachment patterns and their outcomes. *Human Development, 39,* 206–223.

Mazoyer, B., Houdé, O., Joliot, M., Mellet, E., & Tzourio-Mazoyer, N. (2009). Regional cerebral blood flow increases during wakeful rest following cognitive training. *Brain Research Bulletin, 80,* 133–138. http://search.ebscohost.com, doi:10.1016/j.brainresbull.2009.06.021

McAdams, D. P., & de St. Aubin, E. (Eds.). (1998). *Generativity and adult development: How and why we care for the next generation.* Washington, DC: American Psychological Association.

McAdams, D., & Logan, R. (2004). What is generativity? In E. de St. Aubin & D. McAdams (Eds.), *Generative society: Caring for future generations* (pp. 15–31). Washington, DC: American Psychological Association.

McAdams, S., & Drake, C. (2002). Auditory perception and cognition. *Steven's handbook of experimental psychology, Vol. 1: Sensation and perception* (3rd ed.). Hoboken, NJ: John Wiley & Sons Inc.

McAdoo, H. P. (1988). *Black families.* Newbury Park, CA: Sage.

McAlister, A., & Peterson, C. (2006, November). Mental playmates: Siblings, executive functioning and theory of mind. *British Journal of Developmental Psychology, 24,* 733–751.

McArdle, E. F. (2002). New York's Do-Not-Resuscitate law: Groundbreaking protection of patient autonomy or a physician's right to make medical futility determinations? *DePaul Journal of Health Care Law, 8,* 55–82.

McAuley, E., Kramer, A. F., & Colcombe, S. J. (2004). Cardiovascular fitness and neurocognitive function in older adults: A brief review. *Brain Behavior Immunology, 18,* 214–220.

McAuliffe, S. P., & Knowlton, B. J. (2001). Hemispheric differences in object identification. *Brain & Cognition., 45,* 119–128.

McCabe, M. (1984). Toward a theory of adolescent dating. *Adolescence, 19,* 159–169.

McCabe, M., & Ricciardelli, L. (2006, June). A prospective study of extreme weight change behaviors among adolescent boys and girls. *Journal of Youth and Adolescence, 35*(3), 425–434.

McCall, R. B. (1979). *Infants.* Cambridge, MA: Harvard University Press.

McCardle, P., & Hoff, E. (Eds.). (2006). *Childhood bilingualism: Research on infancy through school age.* Clevedon, Avon: Multilingual Matters Ltd.

McCarthy, B., & Ginsberg, R. (2007). Second marriages: Challenges and risks. *The Family Journal, 15,* 119–123.

McCarthy, M. J. (1994, November 8). Hunger among elderly surges: Meal programs just can't keep up. *The Wall Street Journal,* pp. A1, A11.

McCartney, M. (2006, March 11). Mind gains: We are living longer but will we be able to keep our minds active enough to enjoy it? *Financial Times* (London, England), p. 1.

McCarty, M., & Ashmead, D. H. (1999). Visual control of reaching and grasping in infants. *Developmental Psychology, 35,* 620–631.

McCaul, K. D., Ployhart, R. E., Hinsz, V. B., & McCaul, H. S. (1995). Appraisals of a consistent versus a similar politician: Voter preferences and intuitive judgments. *Journal of Personality and Social Psychology, 68,* 292–299.

McCauley, K. M. (2007). Modifying women's risk for cardiovascular disease. *Journal of Obstetric and Gynecological Neonatal Nursing, 36,* 116–124.

McClelland, D. C. (1993). Intelligence is not the best predictor of job performance. *Current Directions in Psychological Research, 2,* 5–8.

McClement, S. E., Chochinov, H. M., Hack, T. F., Kristjanson, L. J., & Harlos, M. (2004). Dignity-conserving care: Application of research findings to practice. *International Journal of Palliative Nursing, 10,* 173–179.

McCloskey, L. A., & Bailey, J. A. (2000). The intergenerational transmission of risk for child sexual abuse. *Journal of Interpersonal Violence, 15,* 1019–1035.

McCowan, L. M. E., Dekker, G. A., Chan, E., Stewart, A., Chappell, L. C., Hunger, M., Moss-Morris, R., & North, R. A. (2009). Spontaneous preterm birth and small for gestational age infants in women who stop smoking early in pregnancy: Prospective cohort study. *BMJ: British Medical Journal, 338*(7710), Jun 27, 2009.

McCracken, A. L., & Gerdsen, L. (1991). Sharing the legacy: Hospice care principles for the terminally ill elders. *Journal of Gerontological Nursing, 17,* 4–8.

McCrae, R. R., & Costa, P. T., Jr. (1990). *Personality in adulthood.* New York: Guilford.

McCrae, R. R., & Costa, P. T., Jr. (2003). *Personality in Adulthood: A five-factor theory perspective* (2nd ed.). New York: Guilford Press.

McCrae, R. R., Costa, P. T., Jr., Ostendorf, F., Angleitner, A., Hebíková, M., Avia, M. D., Sanz, J., Sánchez-Bernardos, M. L., Kusdil, M. E., Woodfield, R., Saunders, P. R., & Smith, P. B. (2000). Nature over nurture: Temperament, personality, and life span development. *Journal of Personality and Social Psychology, 78,* 173–186.

McCrink, K., & Wynn, K. (2004). Large-number addition and subtraction by 9-month-old infants. *Psychological Science, 15,* 776–782.

McCrink, K., & Wynn, K. (2007). Ratio abstraction by 6-month- old infants. *Psychological Science, 18,* 740–745.

McCrink, K., & Wynn, K. (2009). Operational momentum in large-number addition and subtraction by 9-month-olds. *Journal of Experimental Child Psychology, 103,* 400–408.

McCullough, M. E., Tsang, J., & Brion, S. (2003). Personality traits in adolescence as predictors of religiousness in early maturity: Findings from the Terman longitudinal study. *Personality & Social Psychology Bulletin, 29,* 980–991.

McCutcheon-Rosegg, S., Ingraham, E., & Bradley, R. A. (1996). *Natural childbirth the Bradley way* (Rev. ed.) New York: Plume Books.

McDaniel, A., & Coleman, M. (2003). Women's experiences of midlife divorce following long-term marriage. *Journal of Divorce & Remarriage, 38,* 103–128.

McDaniel, K. D. (1986). Pharmacologic treatment of psychiatric and neurodevelopmental disorders in children and adolescents: III. *Clinical Pediatrics, 25,* 198–204.

McDonald, K. A. (1999, June 25). Studies of women's health produce a wealth of knowledge on the biology of gender differences. *Chronicle of Higher Education, 45,* A19, A22.

McDonald, L., & Stuart-Hamilton, I. (2003). Egocentrism in older adults: Piaget's three mountains task revisited. *Educational Gerontology, 29,* 417–425.

McDonald, M. A., Sigman, M., Espinosa, M. P., & Neumann, C. G. (1994). Impact of a temporary food shortage on children and their mothers. *Child Development, 65,* 404–415.

McDonnell, L. M. (2004). *Politics, persuasion, and educational testing.* Cambridge, MA: Harvard University Press.

McDonough, L. (2002). Basic-level nouns: First learned but misunderstood. *Journal of Child Language, 29,* 357–377.

McDougall, G. J., Blixen,C. E., & Suen, L. (1997). The process and outcome of life review psychotherapy with depressed homebound older adults. *Nursing Research, 46,* 277–283.

McDowell, M., Brody, D., & Hughes, J. (2007). Has age at menarche changed? Results from the National Health and Nutrition Examination Survey (NHANES) 1999–2004. *Journal of Adolescent Health, 40,* 227–231.

McElhaney, K., Antonishak, J., & Allen, J. (2008). "They like me, they like me not": Popularity and adolescents' perceptions of acceptance predicting social functioning over time. *Child Development, 79,* 720–731.

McElwain, N., & Booth-LaForce, C. (2006, June). Maternal sensitivity to infant distress and nondistress as predictors of infant-mother attachment security. *Journal of Family Psychology, 20,* 247–255.

McGee, G., Caplan, A., & Malhotra, R. (Eds.). (2004). *The human cloning debate.* Berkeley, CA: Hills Books.

McGinn, D. (2002, November 11). Guilt free TV. *Newsweek*, pp. 53–59.

McGlone, M., & Aronson, J. (2006, September). Stereotype threat, identity salience, and spatial reasoning. *Journal of Applied Developmental Psychology, 27,* 486–493.

McGlone, M., & Aronson, J. (2007). Forewarning and forearming stereotype-threatened students. *Communication Education, 56,* 119–133.

McGlone, M., Aronson, J., & Kobrynowicz, D. (2006, December). Stereotype threat and the gender gap in political knowledge. *Psychology of Women Quarterly, 30,* 392–398.

McGlothlin, H., Edmonds, C., & Killen, M. (2008). Children's and adolescents' decision-making about intergroup peer relationships. *Handbook of race, racism, and the developing child* (pp. 424–451). Hoboken, NJ: John Wiley & Sons Inc.

McGlothlin, H., & Killen, M. (2005). Children's perceptions of intergroup and intragroup similarity and the role of social experience. *Journal of Applied Developmental Psychology, 26,* 680–698.

McGough, R. (2003, May 20). MRIs take a look at reading minds. *The Wall Street Journal,* p. D8.

McGovern, M., & Barry, M. M. (2000). Death education: knowledge, attitudes, and perspectives of Irish parents and teachers. *Death Studies, 24,* 325–333.

McGovern, S. M. (2000). Reclaiming education: knowledge practices and indigenous communities. *Comparative Education Review, 44,* 523–529.

McGrady, A. (2007). Relaxation and meditation. *Low-cost approaches to promote physical and mental health: Theory, research, and practice.* New York: Springer Science + Business Media.

McGreal, D., Evans, B. J., & Burrows, G. D. (1997). Gender differences in coping following loss of a child through miscarriage or stillbirth: A pilot study. *Stress Medicine, 13,* 159–165.

McGrew, K. S. (2005). The Cattell-Horn-Carroll theory of cognitive abilities: Past, present, and future. In D. P. Flanagan & P. L. Harrison (Eds.), *Contemporary intellectual assessment: Theories, tests, and issues.* New York: Guilford Press.

McGue, M., Bouchard, T., Iacono, W., & Lykken, D. (1993). Behavioral genetics of cognitive ability: A life-span perspective. In R. Plomin & G. McClearn (Eds.), *Nature, nurture and psychology* (pp. 59–76). Washington, DC: American Psychological Association.

McGuffin, P., Riley, B., & Plomin, R. (2001, February 16). Toward behavioral genomics. *Science, 291,* 1232–1233.

McGuinness, D. (1972). Hearing: Individual differences in perceiving. *Perception, 1,* 465–473.

McGuire, S., McHale, S., & Updegraff, K. (1996). Children's perceptions of the sibling relationships in middle childhood: Connections within and between family relationships. *Personal Relationships, 3,* 229–239.

McHale, J. P., & Rotman, T. (2007). Is seeing believing? Expectant parents' outlooks on coparenting and later coparenting solidarity. *Infant Behavior & Development, 30,* 63–81.

McHale, S., Dariotis, J., & Kauh, T. (2003). Social development and social relationships in middle childhood. In R. Lerner & M. Easterbrooks (Eds.), *Handbook of psychology: Developmental psychology, Vol. 6.* New York: John Wiley & Sons, Inc.

McHale, S. M., Kim, J-Y., & Whiteman, S. D. (2006). Sibling relationships in childhood and adolescence. In P. Noller & J. A. Feeney (Eds.), *Close relationships: Functions, forms and processes* (pp. 127–149). Hove, England: Psychology Press/Taylor & Francis.

McHale, S. M., Shanahan, L., Updegraff, K. A., Crouter, A. C., & Booth, A. (2004). Developmental and individual differences in girls' sex-typed activities in middle childhood and adolescence. *Child Development, 75,* 1575–1593.

McKee, K., Wilson, F., Chung, M., Hinchliff, S., Goudie, F., Elford, H., et al. (2005, November). Reminiscence, regrets and activity in older people in residential care: Associations with psychological health. *British Journal of Clinical Psychology, 44,* 543–561.

McKenna, J. J. (1983). Primate aggression and evolution: An overview of sociobiological and anthropological perspectives. *Bulletin of the American Academy of Psychiatry and the Law, 11,* 105–130.

McKenna, M. C., Kear, D. J., & Ellsworth, R. A. (1995). Children's attitudes toward reading: A national survey. *Research Quarterly, 30,* 934–956.

McKenzie, R. B. (1997). Orphanage alumni: How they have done and how they evaluate their experience. *Child & Youth Care Forum, 26,* 87–111.

McKinlay, S. M., & Jefferys, M. (1974). The menopausal syndrome. *British Journal of Preventive & Social Medicine, 28,* 108–115.

McKinley, N. (2006). The developmental and cultural contexts of objectified body consciousness: A longitudinal analysis of two cohorts of women. *Developmental Psychology, 42,* 679–687.

McKown, C., & Strambler, M. (2008). Social influences on the ethnic achievement gap. *Handbook of race, racism, and the developing child* (pp. 366–396). Hoboken, NJ: John Wiley & Sons Inc.

McKown, C., & Weinstein, R. (2008). Teacher expectations, classroom context, and the achievement gap. *Journal of School Psychology, 46,* 235–261.

McLachlan, H. (2008). The ethics of killing and letting die: Active and passive euthanasia. *Journal of Medical Ethics, 34,* 636–638.

McLean, K., & Breen, A. (2009). Processes and content of narrative identity development in adolescence: Gender and well-being. *Developmental Psychology, 45,* 702–710.

McLennan, D. (2012). Using sociodrama to help young children problem solve. *Early Childhood Education Journal, 39,* 407–412.

McLoyd, V., Aikens, N., & Burton, L. (2006). Childhood Poverty, Policy, and Practice. *Handbook of child psychology, 6th ed.: Vol 4, Child psychology in practice* (pp. 700–775). Hoboken, NJ: John Wiley & Sons Inc.

McLoyd, V. C. (1998). Socioeconomic disadvantage and child development. *American Psychologist, 53,* 185–204.

McLoyd, V. C., Cauce, A. M., Takeuchi, D., & Wilson, L. (2000). Marital processes and parental socialization in families of color: A decade review of research. *Journal of Marriage and Family, 62,* 1070–1093.

McMahon, S. D., & Washburn, J. J. (2003). Violence prevention: An evaluation of program effects with urban African-American students. *Journal of Primary Prevention, 24,* 43–62.

McMillan, M. M., Frierson, H. T., & Campbell, F. A. (2011). Do gender differences exist in the academic identification of African American elementary school-aged children? *Journal of Black Psychology, 37,* 78–98.

McMillian, M. (2003-2004). Is No Child Left Behind "wise schooling" for African American male students? *High School Journal, 87,* Special Issue: From the simplicity of convention toward the complexity found in human interaction: Teaching learning and administration in high school during the 21st century, 25–33.

McMurray, B., Aslin, R. N., & Toscano, J. C. (2009). Statistical learning of phonetic categories: insights from a computational approach. *Developmental Science, 12,* 369–378.

McNeil, N. M., Fuhs, M., Keultjes, M., & Gibson, M. H. (2011). Influences of problem format and SES on preschoolers' understanding of approximate addition. *Cognitive Development, 26,* 57–71.

McNulty, J. K., & Karney, B. R. (2004). Positive expectations in the early years of marriage: Should couples expect the bests or brace for the worst? *Journal of Personality and Social Psychology, 86,* 729–743.

McRae, K., Gross, J. J., Weber, J., Robertson, E. R., Sokol-Hessner, P., Ray, R. D., & … Ochsner, K. N. (2012). The development of emotion regulation: An fMRI study of cognitive reappraisal in children, adolescents and young adults. *Social Cognitive and Affective Neuroscience, 7,* 11–22.

McRae, K., Khalkhali, S., & Hare, M. (2012). Semantic and associative relations in adolescents and young adults: Examining a tenuous dichotomy. In V. F. Reyna, S. B. Chapman, M. R. Dougherty, J. Confrey, V. F. Reyna, S. B. Chapman, … J. Confrey (Eds.), *The adolescent brain: Learning, reasoning, and decision making.* Washington, DC: American Psychological Association.

McRae, S. (1997). Cohabitation: A trial run for marriage? *Sexual & Marital Therapy, 12,* 259–273.

McVittie, C., McKinlay, A., & Widdicombe, S. (2003). Committed to (un)equal opportunities?: "New ageism" and the older worker. *British Journal of Social Psychology, 42,* 595–612.

McWhirter, D. P., Sanders, S., & Reinisch, J. M. (1990). *Homosexuality, heterosexuality: Concepts of sexual orientation.* New York: Oxford University Press.

McWhirter, L., Young, V., & Majury, Y. (1983). Belfast children's awareness of violent death. *British Journal of Psychology, 22,* 81–92.

Mead, M. (1942). *Environment and education,* a symposium held in connection with the fiftieth anniversary celebration of the University of Chicago. Chicago: University of Chicago Press.

Meade, C., Kershaw, T., & Ickovics, J. (2008). The intergenerational cycle of teenage motherhood: An ecological approach. *Health Psychology, 27,* 419–429.

Meadows, B. (2005, March 14). The Web: The bully's new playground. *People,* 152–155.

Meagher, D. (2007). How we die: Theory vs. reality. *Death Studies, 31,* 266–270.

Mealey, L. (2000). *Sex differences: Developmental and evolutionary strategies.* Orlando, FL: Academic Press.

Medeiros, R., Prediger, R. D., Passos, G. F., Pandolfo, P., Duarte, F. S., Franco, J. L., Dafre, A. L., Di Giunta, G., Figueiredo, C. P., Takahashi, R. N., Campos, M. M., & Calixto, J. B. (2007). Connecting TNF-alpha signaling pathways to iNOS expression in a mouse model of Alzheimer's disease: relevance for the behavioral and synaptic deficits induced by amyloid beta protein. *Journal of Neuroscience, 16,* 5394–5404.

Medina, A., Lederhos, C., & Lillis, T. (2009). Sleep disruption and decline in marital satisfaction across the transition to parenthood. *Families, Systems, & Health, 27,* 153–160.

Medina, J. J. (1996). *The clock of ages: Why we age—How we age—Winding back the clock.* New York: Cambridge University Press.

Mednick, S. A. (1963). Research creativity in psychology graduate students. *Journal of Consulting Psychology, 27,* 265–266.

Meece, J. L., & Kurtz-Costes, B. (2001). Introduction: The schooling of ethnic minority children and youth. *Educational Psychologist, 36,* 1–7.

Meeks, T., & Jeste, D. (2009). Neurobiology of wisdom: A literature overview. *Archives of General Psychiatry, 66,* 355–365.

Meeus, W. (1996). Studies on identity development in adolescence: An overview of research and some new data. *Journal of Youth & Adolescence, 25,* 569–598.

Meeus, W. (2003). Parental and peer support, identity development and psychological well-being in adolescence. *Psychology: The Journal of the Hellenic Psychological Society, 10,* 192–201.

Mehler, J., & DuPoux, E. (1994). *What infants know: The new cognitive science of early development.* Cambridge, MA: Blackwell.

Mehran, K. (1997). Interferences in the move from adolescence to adulthood: The development of the male. In M. Laufer (Ed.), *Adolescent breakdown and beyond* (pp. 17–25). London, England: Karnac Books.

Mehta, C. M., & Strough, J. (2009). Sex segregation in friendships and normative contexts across the life span. *Developmental Review, 29,* 201–220.

Mehta-Lissak, S. (2002). Parenting and psychosocial development of IVF children: A follow-up study. *Human Reproduction, 17,* 1116–1123.

Meier, A., Bukusi, E., & Cohen, C. (2006). Independent association of hygiene, socioeconomic status, and circumcision with reduced risk of HIV infection among Kenyan men. *Journal of Acquired Immune Deficiency Syndromes, 43,* 117–118.

Meijer, A. M., & van den Wittenboer, G. L. H. (2007). Contribution of infants' sleep and crying to marital relationship of first-time parent couples in the first year after childbirth. *Journal of Family Psychology, 21,* 49–57.

Meisels, S. J., & Plunkett, J. W. (1988). Developmental consequences of preterm birth: Are there long-term deficits? In P. B. Baltes, D. L. Featherman, & R. M. Lerner (Eds.), *Lifespan development and behavior* (Vol. 9). Hillsdale, NJ: Erlbaum.

Meiser, B., & Dunn, S. (2000). Psychological impact of genetic testing for Huntington's disease: An update of the literature. *Journal of Neurology, Neurosurgery & Psychiatry, 69,* 574–578.

Meisinger, E., Blake, J., Lease, A., Palardy, G., & Olejnik, S. (2007). Variant and invariant predictors of perceived popularity across majority-Black and majority-White classrooms. *Journal of School Psychology, 45,* 21–44.

Meister, H., & von Wedel, H. (2003). Demands on hearing aid features—special signal processing for elderly users? *International Journal of Audiology, 42,* 2S58–2S62.

Melnyk, L., Crossman, A., & Scullin, M. (2007). The suggestibility of children's memory. *The handbook of eyewitness psychology, Vol I: Memory for events.* Mahwah, NJ: Lawrence Erlbaum Associates Publishers.

Meltzoff, A. (2002). Elements of a developmental theory of imitation. In A. Meltzoff & W. Prinz (Eds.), *The imitative mind: Development, evolution, and brain bases* (pp. 19–41). New York: Cambridge University Press.

Meltzoff, A. N. (1981). Imitation, intermodal coordination and representation in early infancy. In G. Butterworth (Ed.), *Infancy and epistemology.* Brighton: Harvester Press.

Meltzoff, A. N. (2011). Social cognition and the origins of imitation, empathy, and theory of mind. In U. Goswami (Ed.), *The Wiley-Blackwell handbook of childhood cognitive development* (2nd ed.). New York: Wiley-Blackwell.

Meltzoff, A. N., & Moore, M. K. (1977). Imitation official and manual gestures by human neonates. *Science, 198,* 75–78.

Meltzoff, A. N., & Moore, M. K. (1989). Imitation in newborn infants: Exploring the range of gestures imitated and the underlying mechanisms. *Developmental Psychology, 25*(6), 954–962.

Meltzoff, A. N., & Moore, M. K. (1994). Imitation, memory, and the representation of persons. *Infant Behavior and Development, 17,* 83–99.

Meltzoff, A. N., & Moore, M. K. (1999). Persons and representation: Why infant imitation is important for theories of human development. In J. Nadel & G. Butterworth (Eds.), *Imitation in infancy. Cambridge studies in cognitive perceptual development.* New York: Cambridge University Press.

Meltzoff, A., & Moore, M. (2002). Imitation, memory, and the representation of persons. *Infant Behavior & Development, 25,* 39–61.

Meltzoff, A. N., Waismeyer, A., & Gopnik, A. (2012). Learning about causes from people: Observational causal learning in 24-month-old infants. *Developmental Psychology.* Retrieved from http://www.ncbi.nlm.nih.gov/pubmed/22369335.

Melzer, D., Hurst, A., & Frayling, T. (2007). Genetic variation and human aging: Progress and prospects. *The Journals of Gerontology: Series A: Biological Sciences and Medical Sciences, 62,* 301–307.

Menacker F., & Hamilton, B. E. (2010). Recent trends in cesarean delivery in the United States. *NCHS Data Brief, 35,* 1–8.

Mendelowitz, D. (1998). Nicotine excites cardiac vagal neurons via three sites of action. *Clinical & Experimental Pharmacology & Physiology, 25,* 453–456.

Mendelson, B. K., White, D. R., & Mendelson, M. J. (1996). Self-esteem and body esteem: Effects of gender, age, and weight. *Journal of Applied Developmental Psychology, 17,* 321–346.

Mendle, J., Turkheimer, E., & Emery, R. (2007, June). Detrimental psychological outcomes associated with early pubertal timing in adolescent girls. *Developmental Review, 27*(2), 151–171.

Mendoza, C. (2006, September). Inside today's classrooms: Teacher voices on no child left behind and the education of gifted children. *Roeper Review, 29,* 28–31.

Menella, J. (2000, June). *The psychology of eating.* Paper presented at the annual meeting of the American Psychological Society, Miami.

Meng, Z., & Jijia, Z. (2006). Effects of intonation on 6 to 10-year-old children's cognition of different types of irony. *Acta Psychologica Sinica, 38,* 197–206.

Menkens, K. (2005). Stereotyping older workers and retirement: The managers point of view. *Canadian Journal on Aging, 24,* 353–366.

Mennella, J., Kennedy, J., & Beauchamp, G. (2006). Vegetable acceptance by infants: Effect of formula flavors. *Early Human Development, 82,* 463–468.

Menzel, J. (2008). Depression in the elderly after traumatic brain injury: A systematic review. *Brain Injury, 22,* 375–380.

Mercado, E. (2009). Cognitive plasticity and cortical modules. *Current Directions in Psychological Science, 18,* 153–158.

Mercer, C. (1992). *Students with learning disabilities* (4th ed.). Columbus, OH: Merrill.

Mercer, J. R. (1973). *Labeling the mentally retarded.* Berkeley: University of California Press.

Meredith, H.V. (1971). Growth in body size: A compendium of findings on contemporary children living in different parts of the world. *Child Development & Behavior, 6,* 153–238.

Merewood, A. (2006). Race, ethnicity, and breastfeeding. *Pediatrics, 118,* 1742–1743.

Merill, D. M. (1997). *Caring for elderly parents: Juggling work, family, and caregiving in middle and working class families.* Wesport, CT: Auburn House/Greenwood Publishing Group.

Meritesacker, B., Bade, U., & Haverkock, A. (2004). Predicting maternal reactivity/sensitivity: The role of infant emotionality, maternal depressiveness/anxiety, and social support. *Infant Mental Health Journal, 25,* 47–61.

Merlo, L., Bowman, M., & Barnett, D. (2007). Parental nurturance promotes reading acquisition in low socioeconomic status children. *Early Education and Development, 18,* 51–69.

Merrell, K. (2008). *Behavioral, social, and emotional assessment of children and adolescents* (3rd ed.). Mahwah, NJ: Lawrence Erlbaum Associates Publishers.

Merriman, W., & Lipko, A. (2008). A dual criterion account of the development of linguistic judgment in early childhood. *Journal of Memory and Language, 58,* 1012–1031.

Merry, T. (2008). The actualization conundrum. *Reflections on human potential: Bridging the person-centered approach and positive psychology.* Ross-on-Wye England: PCCS Books.

Mervis, J. (2004, June 11). Meager evaluations make it hard to find out what works. *Science, 304,* 1583.

Messer, S. B., & McWilliams, N. (2003). The impact of Sigmund Freud and *The Interpretation of Dreams.* In R. J. Sternberg (Ed.), *The anatomy of impact: What makes the great works of psychology great* (pp. 71–88). Washington, DC: American Psychological Association.

Messinger, D. (2002). Positive and negative infant facial expressions and emotions. *Current Directions in Psychological Science, 11,* 1–6.

Messinger, D. S., Ekas, N. V., Ruvolo, P., & Fogel, A. D. (2012). "Are you interested, baby?" Young infants exhibit stable patterns of attention during interaction. *Infancy, 17,* 233–244.

MetLife Mature Market Institute. (2003). *The MetLife Market Survey of Nursing Home & Home Care Costs 2003.* Westport, CT: MetLife Mature Market Institute.

MetLife Mature Market Institute. (2007). *The MetLife Market Survey of Nursing Home & Home Care Costs 2006.* Westport, CT: Author.

Meyer, I. H. (2003). Prejudice, social stress, and mental health in lesbian, gay, and bisexual populations: Conceptual issues and research evidence. *Psychological Bulletin, 129,* 574–697.

Meyer, M., Wolf, D., & Himes, C. (2006, March). Declining eligibility for social security spouse and widow benefits in the United States? *Research on Aging, 28,* 240–260.

Meyer-Bahlburg, H. F. L., Ehrhardt, A. A., Rosen, L. R., Gruen, R. S., Veridiano, N. P., Vann, F. H., & Neuwalder, H. F. (1995). Prenatal estrogens and the development of homosexual orientation. *Developmental Psychology, 31,* 12–21.

Meyerhoff, M. K., & White, B. L. (1986, September). Making the grade as parents. *Psychology Today,* pp. 38–45.

Meyers, R. H. (2004). Huntington's Disease genetics. *NeuroRx, 2,* 255–262.

Mezuk, B., Prescott, M., Tardiff, K., Vlahov, D., & Galea, S. (2008). Suicide in older adults in long-term care: 1990 to 2005. *Journal of the American Geriatrics Society, 56,* 2107–2111.

Miao, X., & Wang, W. (2003). A century of Chinese developmental psychology. *International Journal of Psychology, 38,* 258–273.

Michael, R. T., Gagnon, J. H., Laumann, E. O., & Kolata, G. (1994). *Sex in America: A definitive survey.* Boston: Little, Brown.

Michaels, M. (2006). Factors that contribute to stepfamily success: A qualitative analysis. *Journal of Divorce & Remarriage, 44,* 53–66.

Michel, G. L. (1981). Right-handedness: A consequence of infant supine head-orientation preference? *Science, 212,* 685–687.

Midaeva, E., & Lyubimova, Z. (2008). Formation of language-specific characteristics of speech sounds in early ontogeny. *Human Physiology, 34,* 649–652.

Midlarsky, E., & Bryan, J. H. (1972). Affect expressions and children's imitative altruism. *Journal of Experimental Research in Personality, 6,* 195–203.

Miehl, N. J. (2005). Shaken baby syndrome. *Journal of Forensic Nursing, 1,* 111–117.

Miesnik, S., & Reale, B. (2007). A review of issues surrounding medically elective cesarean delivery. *Journal of Obstetric, Gynecologic, & Neonatal Nursing: Clinical Scholarship for the Care of Women, Childbearing Families, & Newborns, 36,* 605–615.

Mikami, A. Y., Lerner, M. D., Griggs, M. S., McGRath, A., & Calhoun, C. D. (2010). Parental influence on children with attention-deficit/hyperactivity disorder: II. Results of a pilot intervention training parents as friendship coaches for children. *Journal of Abnormal Child Psychology: An official publication of the International Society for Research in Child and Adolescent Psychopathology, 38,* 737–749.

Mikhail, B. (2000). Prenatal care utilization among low-income African American women. *Journal of Community Health Nursing, 17,* 235–246.

Mikulincer, M., & Shaver, P. R., (2007). *Attachment in adulthood: Structure, dynamics, and change.* New York: Guilford Press.

Mikulincer, M., & Shaver, P. (2009). An attachment and behavioral systems perspective on social support. *Journal of Social and Personal Relationships, 26*, 7–19.

Mikulovic, J., Marcellini, A., Compte, R., Duchateau, G., Vanhelst, J., Fardy, P. S., & Bui-Xuan, G. (2011). Prevalence of overweight in adolescents with intellectual deficiency. Differences in socio-educative context, physical activity and dietary habits. *Appetite, 56*, 403–407.

Miles, M., Holditch-Davis, D., Schwartz, T., & Scher, M. (2007). Depressive symptoms in mothers of prematurely born infants. *Journal of Developmental & Behavioral Pediatrics, 28*, 36–44.

Miles, R., Cowan, F., Glover, V., Stevenson, J., & Modi, N. (2006). A controlled trial of skin-to-skin contact in extremely preterm infants. *Early Human Development, 2(7)*, 447–455.

Milevsky, A., Schlechter, M., Netter, S., & Keehn, D. (2007). Maternal and paternal parenting styles in adolescents: Associations with self-esteem, depression and life-satisfaction. *Journal of Child and Family Studies, 16*, 39–47.

Miller, A. B. (1991). Is routine mammography screening appropriate for women 40–49 years of age? *American Journal of Preventive Medicine, 7*, 55–62.

Miller, B. (1997a, April). Population update for April. *American Demographics*, p. 18.

Miller, B. (1997b, March). The quest for lifelong learning. *American Demographics*, pp. 20–22.

Miller, C. A. (1987). A review of maternity care programs in western Europe. *Family Planning Perspectives, 19(5)*, 207–211.

Miller, D. A., McCluskey-Fawcett, K., & Irving, L. (1993). Correlates of bulimia nervosa: Early family mealtime experiences. *Adolescence, 28*, 621–635.

Miller, E. M. (1998). Evidence from opposite-sex twins for the effects of prenatal sex hormones. In L. Ellis & L. Ebertz (Eds.), *Males, females, and behavior: Toward biological understanding.* Westport, CT: Praeger Publishers/Greenwood Publishing Group.

Miller, G., & Cohen, S. (2001). Psychological interventions and the immune system: A meta-analytic review and critique. *Health Psychology, 20*, 47–63.

Miller, G. A. (1956). The magical number seven, plus or minus two: Some limits on our capacity for processing information. *Psychology Review, 63*, 81–97.

Miller, J. L., & Eimas, P. D. (1995). Speech perception: From signal to word. *Annual Review of Psychology, 46*, 467–492.

Miller, K. J., & Mizes, J. S. (Eds.). (2000). *Comparative treatments for eating disorders.* New York: Springer.

Miller, L., Bishop, J., Fischer, J., Geller, S., & Macmillan, C. (2008). Balancing risks: Dosing strategies for antidepressants near the end of pregnancy. *Journal of Clinical Psychiatry, 69*, 323–324.

Miller, L. E., Grabell, A., Thomas, A., Bermann, E., & Graham-Bermann, S. A. (2012). The associations between community violence, television violence, intimate partner violence, parent-child aggression, and aggression in sibling relationships of a sample of preschoolers. *Psychology of Violence, 2*, 165–178.

Miller, M., & Hinshaw, S. P. (2012). Attention-deficit/hyperactivity disorder. In P. C. Kendall (Ed.), *Child and adolescent therapy: Cognitive-behavioral procedures* (4th ed.). New York: Guilford Press.

Miller, N., & Brewer, M. (1984). *Groups in contact: The psychology of desegregation.* New York: Academic Press.

Miller, P. A., & Jansen op de Haar, M. A. (1997). Emotional, cognitive, behavioral, and temperament characteristics of high-empathy children. *Motivation and Emotion, 21*, 109–125.

Miller, P. H. (2011). Piaget's theory: Past, present, and future. In U. Goswami (Ed.), *The Wiley-Blackwell handbook of childhood cognitive development* (2nd ed.). New York: Wiley-Blackwell.

Miller, P. H., & Seier, W. L. (1994). *Strategy utilization deficiencies in children: When, where, and why.* San Diego: Academic Press.

Miller, P. H., Woody-Ramsey, J., & Aloise, P. A. (1991). The role of strategy effortfulness in strategy effectiveness. *Developmental Psychology, 27*, 738–745.

Miller, R. (2011). *Vygotsky in perspective.* New York: Cambridge University Press.

Miller, R. B., Hemesath, K., & Nelson, B. (1997). Marriage in middle and later life. In T. D. Hargrave & S. M. Hanna (Eds.), *The aging family: New visions in theory, practice, and reality* (pp. 178–198). New York: Brunner/Mazel.

Miller, S. A. (1998). *Developmental research methods.* (2nd ed.). Upper Saddle River, NJ: Prentice-Hall.

Miller, S. M., & Mangan, C. E. (1983). Interacting effects of information and coping style in adapting to gynecologic stress: Should the doctor tell all? *Journal of Personality and Social Psychology, 45*, 223–236.

Miller, T., Smith, R., Kordasiewicz, H., & Kaspar, B. (2008). Gene-targeted therapies for the central nervous system. *Archives of Neurology, 65*, 447–451.

Miller, T. Q., Smith, T. W., Turner, C. W., Guijarro, M. L., & Hallet, A. J. (1996). A meta-analytic review of research on hostility and physical health. *Psychological Bulletin, 119*, 322–348.

Miller-Perrin, C. L., & Perrin, R. D. (1999). *Child maltreatment: An introduction.* Thousand Oaks, CA: Sage.

Mills, E., & Siegfried, N. (2006). Cautious optimism for new HIV/AIDS prevention strategies. *Lancet, 368*, 1236–1236.

Mills, J. L. (1999). Cocaine, smoking, and spontaneous abortion. *New England Journal of Medicine, 340*, 380–381.

Milner, J. (1995, January). Paper presented at a conference, "Violence against children in the family and the community: a conference on causes, developmental consequences, interventions and prevention." Los Angeles: University of Southern California.

Mimura, K., Kimoto, T., & Okada, M. (2003). Synapse efficiency diverges due to synaptic pruning following overgrowth. *Phys Rev E Stat Nonlinear Soft Matter Physics, 68*, 124–131.

Minagawa-Kawai, Y., van der Lely, H., Ramus, F., Sato, Y., Mazuka, R., & Dupoux, E. (2011). Optical brain imaging reveals general auditory and language-specific processing in early infant development. *Cerebral Cortex, 21*, 254–261.

Minaker, K. L., & Frishman, R. (1995, October). Love gone wrong. *Harvard Health Letter*, pp. 9–12.

Mindell, J. A., & Cashman, L. (1995). Sleep disorders. In A. R. Eisen, C. A. Kearney, & C. E. Schaefer (Eds.), *Clinical handbook of anxiety disorders in children and adolescents.* Northvale, NJ: Aronson.

Minkowski, A. (1967). *Regional development of the brain in early life.* Oxford: Blackwell.

Mino, X., & Wang, W. (2003). A century of Chinese developmental psychology. *International Journal of Psychology, 38*, 258–273.

Minorities in Higher Education. (1990). *Report on minorities in higher education.* Washington, DC: Minorities in Higher Education.

Minorities in Higher Education. (1995). *Annual status report on minorities in higher education.* Washington, DC: Author.

Mirowsky, J., & Ross, C. (2003). *Education, social status, and health.* Hawthorne, NY: Aldine de Gruyter.

Mirsky, S., & Rennie, J. (1997, June). What cloning means for gene therapy. *Scientific American*, 122–123.

Mishna, F., Khoury-Kassabri, M., Gadalla, T., & Daciuk, J. (2012). Risk factors for involvement in cyber bullying: Victims, bullies and bully–victims. *Children And Youth Services Review, 34*, 63–70.

Mishna, F., Saini, M., & Solomon, S. (2009). Ongoing and online: Children and youth's perceptions of cyber bullying. *Children and Youth Services Review, 31*, 1222–1228.

Mishra, R. (2001). Cognition across cultures. *The handbook of culture and psychology.* New York: Oxford University Press.

Mishra, R. C. (1997). Cognition and cognitive development. In J. W. Berry, P. R. Dasen, & T. S. Saraswathi (Eds.), *Handbook of cross-cultural psychology, Vol. 2: Basic processes and human development* (2nd ed., pp. 143–175). Boston, MA: Allyn & Bacon.

Mishra, R., & Stainthorp, R. (2007). The relationship between phonological awareness and word reading accuracy in Oriya and English: A study of Oriya-speaking fifth-graders. *Journal of Research in Reading, 30*, 23–37.

Misra, D. P., Astone, N., & Lynch, C. D. (2005). Maternal smoking and birth weight: Interaction with parity and mother's own in utero exposure to smoking. *Epidemiology, 16*, 288–293.

Misri, S. (2007). Suffering in silence: The burden of perinatal depression. *The Canadian Journal of Psychiatry / La Revue canadienne de psychiatrie, 52*, 477–478.

Mistretta, C. M. (1990). Taste development. In J. R. Coleman (Ed.), *Development of sensory systems in mammals* (pp. 567–613). New York: Wiley.

Mistry, J., & Saraswathi, T. (2003). The cultural context of child development. In R. Lerner & M. Easterbrooks (Eds.), *Handbook of psychology: Developmental psychology* (Vol. 6, pp. 267–291). New York: John Wiley & Sons, Inc.

Mitchell, B. A. (2006). *The boomerang age: Transitions to adulthood in families.* New Brunswick, NJ: AldineTransaction.

Mitchell, B., Carleton, B., Smith, A., Prosser, R., Brownell, M., & Kozyrskyj, A. (2008). Trends in psychostimulant and antidepressant use by children in 2 Canadian provinces. *The Canadian Journal of Psychiatry / La Revue canadienne de psychiatrie, 53*, 152–159.

Mitchell, D., Haan, M., & Steinberg, F. (2003). Body composition in the elderly: The influence of nutritional factors and physical activity. *Journal of Nutrition, Health & Aging, 7*, 130–139.

Mitchell, E. (2009). What is the mechanism of SIDS? Clues from epidemiology. *Developmental Psychobiology, 51*, 215–222.

Mitchell, K. J., Finkelhor, D., Wolak, J., Ybarra, M. L., & Turner, H. (2011). Youth Internet victimization in a broader victimization context. *Journal of Adolescent Health, 48*, 128–134.

Mitchell, K. J., & Porteous, D. J. (2011). Rethinking the genetic architecture of schizophrenia. *Psychological Medicine: A Journal of Research in Psychiatry and the Allied Sciences, 41*, 19–32.

Mitchell, K., Wolak, J., & Finkelhor, D. (2007, February). Trends in youth reports of sexual solicitations, harassment and unwanted exposure to pornography on the Internet. *Journal of Adolescent Health, 40*, 116–126.

Mitchell, S. (2002). *American generations: Who they are, how they live, what they think.* Ithaca, NY: New Strategists Publications.

Mittal, V., Ellman, L., & Cannon, T. (2008). Gene-environment interaction and covariation in schizophrenia: The role of obstetric complications. *Schizophrenia Bulletin, 34*, 1083–1094.

Mittendorf, R., Williams, M. A., Berkey, C. S., & Cotter, R. F. (1990). The length of uncomplicated human gestation. *Obstetrics and Gynecology, 75*, 73–78.

Mix, K. S., Huttenlocher, J., & Levine, S. C. (Eds.). (2001). *Quantitative development in infancy and early childhood.* New York: Oxford University Press.

Mix, K. S., Huttenlocher, J., & Levine, S. C. (2002). Multiple cues for quantification in infancy: Is number one of them? *Psychological Bulletin, 128* 278–294.

Mix, K. S., Huttenlocher, J., & Levine, S. C. (2003). Quantitative development in infancy and early childhood. *Infant & Child Development, 12*, 110–112.

Miyamoto, R. H., Hishinuma, E. S., Nishimura, S. T., Nahulu, L. B., Andrade, N. N., & Goebert, D. A. (2000). Variation in self-esteem among adolescents in an Asian/Pacific-Islander sample. *Personality & Individual Differences, 29*, 13–25.

Mizuno, K., & Ueda, A. (2004). Antenatal olfactory learning influences infant feeding. *Early Human Development, 76*, 83–90.

Mizuta, I., Zahn-Waxler, C., Colre, P. M., & Hiruma, N. (1996). A cross-cultural study of preschoolers' attachment: Security and sensitivity in Japanese and U.S. dads. *International Journal of Behavioral Development, 19*, 141–159.

MMWR. (2008, August 1). Trens in HIV- and STD-Related risk behaviors among high school students—United States, 1991-2007. *Morbidity and Mortality Weekly Report, 57*, 817–822.

Modern Language Association. (2005). www.mla.org/census_map. Based on data from the U.S. Census Bureau, 2000.

Mogelonsky, M. (1996, May). The rocky road to adulthood. *American Demographics*, pp. 26–35, 56.

Mohajeri, M., & Leuba, G. (2009). Prevention of age-associated dementia. *Brain Research Bulletin, 80*, 315–325.

Mohammed, A., Attalla, B., Bashir, F., Ahmed, F., Hassan, A., et al. (2006). Relationship of the sickle cell gene to the ethnic and geographic groups populating the Sudan. *Community Genetics, 9*, 113–120.

Mohler, M. (2009). So much homework, so little time. *Parents Website*. Retrieved from http://www.parents.com/teens-tweens/school-college/school-college/so-much-homework-so-little-time/.

Moldin, S. O., & Gottesman, I. I. (1997). Genes, experience, and chance in schizophrenia—Positioning for the 21st century. *Schizophrenia Bulletin, 23*, 547–561.

Molfese, V. J., & Acheson, S. (1997). Infant and preschool mental and verbal abilities: How are infant scores related to preschool scores? *International Journal of Behavioral Development, 20*, 595–607.

Molina, J. C., Spear, N. E., Spear, L. P., Mennella, J. A., & Lewis, M. J. (2007). The International society for developmental psychobiology 39th annual meeting symposium: Alcohol and development: Beyond fetal alcohol syndrome. *Developmental Psychobiology, 49*, 227–242.

Monahan, K., Steinberg, L., & Cauffman, E. (2009). Affiliation with antisocial peers, susceptibility to peer influence, and antisocial behavior during the transition to adulthood. *Developmental Psychology, 45*, 1520–1530.

Monastra, V. (2008). The etiology of ADHD: A neurological perspective. *Unlocking the potential of patients with ADHD: A model for clinical practice*. Washington, DC, US: American Psychological Association.

Mondloch, C. J., Lewis, T. L., Budreau, D. R., Maurer, D., Dannemiller, J. L., Stephens, B. R., & Kleiner-Gathercoal, K. A. (1999). Face perception during early infancy. *Psychological Science, 10*, 419–422.

Mones, P. (1995, July 28). Life and death and Susan Smith. *The New York Times*, p. A27.

Money, J., & Ehrhardt, A. A. (1972). *Man and woman, boy and girl: The differentiation and dimorphism of gender identity from conception to maturity*. Baltimore: Johns Hopkins University Press.

Mongan, M. F. (2005). *HypnoBirthing: The Mongan method: A natural approach to a safe, easier, more comfortable birthing* (3rd ed.). Deerfield Beach, FL: Health Communications, Inc.

Montague, D., & Walker-Andrews, A. (2001). Peekaboo: A new look at infants' perception of emotion expressions. *Developmental Psychology, 37*, 826–838.

Montague, D., & Walker-Andrews, A. (2002). Mothers, fathers, and infants: The role of person familiarity and parental involvement in infants' perception of emotion expressions. *Child Development, 73*, 1339–1352.

Montemayor, R., Adams, G. R., & Gulotta, T. P. (Eds.). (1994). *Personal relationships during adolescence*. Newbury Park, CA: Sage.

Montessori, M. (1964). *The Montessori method*. New York: Schocken.

Montgomery, C., Reilly, J. J., Jackson, D. M., Kelly, L. A., Slater, C., Paton, J. Y., & Grant, S. (2004). Relation between physical activity and energy expenditure in a representative sample of young children. *American Journal of Clinical Nutrition, 80*, 591–596.

Montgomery-Downs, H., & Thomas, E. B. (1998). Biological and behavioral correlates of quiet sleep respiration rates infants. *Physiology and Behavior, 64*, 637–643.

Montpetit, M., & Bergeman, C. (2007). Dimensions of control: Mediational analyses of the stress-health relationship. *Personality and Individual Differences, 43*, 2237–2248.

Moon, C. (2002). Learning in early infancy. *Advances in Neonatal Care, 2*, 81–83.

Moon, C., Cooper, R. P., & Fifer, W. (1993). Two-day-olds prefer their native language. *Infant Behavior and Development, 16*, 495–500.

Moon, M. (2012). Self and vested interests: Predictors of fathers' views of child care. *Journal of Applied Social Psychology, 42*, 308–319.

Mooney, C. (2009, June). Vaccination nation. *Discover*, p. 58.

Moore, B. N., & Parker, R. (2008). *Critical thinking*. New York: McGraw-Hill.

Moore, C. (1996). Theories of mind in infancy. *British Journal of Developmental Psychology, 14*, 19–40.

Moore, C., Pure, K., & Furrow, D. (1990). Children's understanding of the modal expression of certainty and uncertainty and its relation to the development of a representational theory of mind. *Child Development, 61*, 722–730.

Moore, D. S. (2002, December 31). Americans' view of influence of religion settling back to pre-September 11 levels. *Gallup Poll Tuesday Briefing*.

Moore, K. L. (1974). *Before we are born: Basic embryology and birth defects*. Philadelphia: Saunders.

Moore, K. L., & Persaud, T. V. N. (2003). *Before we were born* (6th ed.). Philadelphia, PA: Saunders.

Moore, L., Gao, D., & Bradlee, M. (2003). Does early physical activity predict body fat change throughout childhood? *Preventive Medicine: An International Journal Devoted to Practice & Theory, 37*, 10–17.

Moore, S., & Rosenthal, D. (2006). *Sexuality in adolescence: Current trends*. New York: Routledge/Taylor & Francis Group.

Moores, D. F. (2004). No child left behind: The good, the bad, and the ugly. *American Annals of the Deaf, 148*, 347–348.

Moores, D., & Meadow-Orlans, K. (1990). *Educational and developmental aspects of deafness*. Washington, DC: Gallaudet University Press.

Moos, R. H., & Lemke, S. (1985). Specialized living environments for older people. In J. E. Birren & K. W. Schaie (Eds.), *Handbook of the psychology of aging*. New York: Van Nostrand Reinhold.

Morales, J. R., & Guerra, N. F. (2006). Effects of multiple context and cumulative stress on urban children's adjustment in elementary school. *Child Development, 77*, 907–923.

Moran, K. C. (2006). The global expansion of children's television: A case study of the adaptation of Sesame Street in Spain. *Learning, Media & Technology, 31*, 287–300.

Morange, M. (2002). *The misunderstood gene*. Cambridge, MA: Harvard University Press.

Morano, M., Colella, D., & Capranica, L. (2011). Body image, perceived and actual physical abilities in normal-weight and overweight boys involved in individual and team sports. *Journal of Sports Sciences, 29*, 355–362.

Morelli, G. A., Rogoff, B., Oppenheim, D., & Goldsmith, D. (1992). Cultural variation in infants' sleeping arrangements: Questions of independence. Special section: Cross-cultural studies of development. *Developmental Psychology, 28*, 604–613.

Moreton, C. (2007, January 14). World's first test-tube baby Louise Brown has child of her own. *The Independent*.

Morfei, M. Z., Hooker, K., Carpenter, J., Blakeley, E., & Mix, C. (2004). Agentic and communal generative behavior in four areas of adult life: Implications for psychological well-being. *Journal of Adult Development, 11*, 55–58.

Morgan, B. E., Horn, A. R., & Bergman, N. J. (2011). Should neonates sleep alone? *Biological Psychiatry, 70*, 817–825.

Morgan, L. (1991). *After marriage ends*. Newbury Park, CA: Sage.

Morgan, R., Garavan, H., & Smith, E. (2001). Early lead exposure produces lasting changes in sustained attention, response initiation, and reactivity to errors. *Neurotoxicology & Teratology, 23*, 519–531.

Morgane, P., Austin-LaFrance, R., Bronzino, J., Tonkiss, J., Diaz-Cintra, S., Cintra, L., Kemper, T., & Galler, J. (1993). Prenatal malnutrition and development of the brain. *Neuroscience and Biobehavioral Reviews, 17*, 91–128.

Morice, A. (1998, February 27–28). Future moms, please note: Benefits vary. *The Wall Street Journal*, p. 15.

Morita, J., Miwa, K., Kitasaka, T., Mori, K., Suenaga, Y., Iwano, S., et al. (2008). Interactions of perceptual and conceptual processing: Expertise in medical image diagnosis. *International Journal of Human-Computer Studies, 66*, 370–390.

Morita, Y., & Tilly, J. L. (2000). Sphingolipid regulation of female gonadal cell apoptosis. *Annals of the New York Academy of Sciences, 905*, 209–220.

Morra, S. (2008). Memory components and control processes in children's drawing. *Children's understanding and production of pictures, drawings, and art: Theoretical and empirical approaches* (pp. 53–85). Ashland, OH: Hogrefe & Huber Publishers.

Morra, S., Gobbo, C., Marini, Z., & Sheese, R. (2008). *Cognitive development: Neo-Piagetian perspectives*. New York: Taylor & Francis Group/Lawrence Erlbaum Associates.

Morris, A., Yelin, E., Wong, B., & Katz, P. (2008). Patterns of psychosocial risk and long-term outcomes in rheumatoid arthritis. *Psychology, Health & Medicine, 13*, 529–544.

Morris, L. B. (March 21, 2001). For elderly, relief for emotional ills can be elusive. *The New York Times*, A6.

Morris, P., & Fritz, C. (2006, October). How to improve your memory. *The Psychologist, 19*, 608–611.

Morrison, F. J. (1993). Phonological processes in reading acquisition: Toward a unified conceptualization. Special Issue: Phonological processes and learning disability. *Developmental Review, 13*, 279–285.

Morrison, F. J., Bachman, H. J., & Connor, C. M. (2005) *Improving literacy in America: Guidelines from research*. New Haven, CT: Yale University Press.

Morrison, F. J., Holmes, D. L., & Hairth, M. M. (1974). A developmental study of the effects of familiarity on short-term visual memory. *Journal of Experimental Child Psychology, 18*, 412–425.

Morrison, F. J., Smith, L., & Dow-Ehrensberger, M. (1995). Education and cognitive development: A natural experiment. *Developmental Psychology, 31*, 789–799.

Morrison, J. H., & Hof, P. R. (1997, October 17). Life and death of neurons in the aging brain. *Science, 278*, 412–417.

Morrison, M. F., & Tweedy, K. (2000). Effects of estrogen on mood and cognition in aging women. *Psychiatric Annals, 30*, 113–119.

Morrison, S., & Meier, D. E. (Eds.). (2003). *Geriatric palliative care.* New York: Oxford University Press.

Morrongiello, B. A. (1997). Children's perspectives on injury and close call experiences: Sex differences in injury-outcome process. *Journal of Pediatric Psychology, 22*, 499–512.

Morrongiello, B., Corbett, M., & Bellissimo, A. (2008). "Do as I say, not as I do": Family influences on children's safety and risk behaviors. *Health Psychology, 27*, 498–503.

Morrongiello, B., Corbett, M., McCourt, M., & Johnston, N. (2006, July). Understanding unintentional injury-risk in young children I. The nature and scope of caregiver supervision of children at home. *Journal of Pediatric Psychology, 31*, 529–539.

Morrongiello, B., & Hogg, K. (2004). Mothers' reactions to children misbehaving in ways that can lead to injury: Implications for gender differences in children's risk taking and injuries. *Sex Roles, 50*, 103–118.

Morrongiello, B., Klemencic, N., & Corbett, M. (2008). Interactions between child behavior patterns and parent supervision: Implications for children's risk of unintentional injury. *Child Development, 79*, 627–638.

Morrongiello, B., Midgett, C., & Stanton, K. (2000). Gender biases in children's appraisals of injury risk and other children's risk-taking behaviors. *Journal of Experimental Child Psychology, 77*, 317–336.

Morrongiello, B., Zdzieborski, D., Sandomierski, M., & Lasenby-Lessard, J. (2009). Video messaging: What works to persuade mothers to supervise young children more closely in order to reduce injury risk? *Social Science & Medicine, 68*, 1030–1037.

Morry, M. (2007, February). The attraction-similarity hypothesis among cross-sex friends: Relationship satisfaction, perceived similarities, and self-serving perceptions. *Journal of Social and Personal Relationships, 24*, 117–138.

Morse, R. M., & Flavin, D. K. (1992). The definition of alcoholism. *Journal of the American Medical Association, 268*, 1012–1014.

Mortensen, E. L., Michaelsen, K. F., Sanders, S. A., & Reinisch, J. M. (2002). The association between duration of breast feeding and adult intelligence. *Journal of the American Medical Association, 287*, 2365.

Moses, L. J., & Chandler, M. J. (1992). Traveler's guide to children's theories of mind. *Psychological Inquiry, 3*, 286–301.

Mosher, D. L., & Anderson, R. D. (1986). Macho personality, sexual aggression, and reactions to guided imagery of realistic rape. *Journal of Research in Personality, 20*, 77–94.

Moshman, D. (2011). *Adolescent rationality and development: Cognition, morality, and identity* (3rd ed.). New York: Psychology Press.

Moshman, D., Glover, J. A., & Bruning, R. H. (1987). *Developmental psychology.* Boston: Little, Brown.

Moss, M. (1997, March 31). Golden years? For one 73-year-old, punching time clock isn't a labor of love. *The Wall Street Journal*, pp. A1, A8.

Motschnig, R., & Nykl, L. (2003). Toward a cognitive-emotional model of Rogers's person-centered approach. *Journal of Humanistic Psychology, 43*, 8–45.

Mottl-Santiago, J., Walker, C., Ewan, J., Vragovic, O., Winder, S., & Stubblefield, P. (2008). A hospital-based doula program and childbirth outcomes in an urban, multicultural setting. *Maternal and Child Health Journal, 12*, 372–377.

Mouw, T., & Entwisle, B. (2006). Residential segregation and interracial friendship in schools. *American Journal of Sociology, 112*, 394–441.

Mowry, B. J., Nancarrow, D. J., & Levinson, D. F. (1997). The molecular genetics of schizophrenia: An update. *Australian & New Zealand Journal of Psychiatry, 31*, 704–713.

Moyad, M. A. (2004). Preventing male osteoporosis: Prevalence, risks, diagnosis and imaging tests. *Urological Clinics of North America, 31*, 321–330.

Moyer, M. S. (1992). Sibling relationships among older adults. *Generations, 16*, 55–58.

Moyle, J., Fox, A., Arthur, M., Bynevelt, M., & Burnett, J. (2007). Meta-analysis of neuropsychological symptoms of adolescents and adults with PKU. *Neuropsychology Review, 17*, 91–101. http://search.ebscohost.com, doi:10.1007/s11065–007-9021–2

Mroczek, D. K., & Kolarz, C. M. (1998). The effect of age on positive and negative affect: A developmental perspective on happiness. *Journal of Personality and Social Psychology, 75*, 1333–1349.

Muehlenhard, C. L., & Hollabaugh, L. C. (1988). Do women sometimes say no when they mean yes? The prevalence and correlates of women's token resistance to sex. *Journal of Personality and Social Psychology, 54*, 872–879.

Mueller, E., & Vandell, D. (1979). Infant-infant interactions. In J. Osofsky (Ed.), *Handbook of infant development.* New York: Wiley.

Mueller, M., Wilhelm, B., & Elder, G. (2002). Variations in grandparenting. *Research on Aging, 24*, 360–388.

Mueller, N., & Knight, R. (2002). Age-related changes in fronto-parietal networks during spatial memory: An ERP study. *Cognitive Brain Research, 13*, 221–234.

Muenchow, S., & Marsland, K. (2007). Beyond baby steps: Promoting the growth and development of U.S. child-care policy. *Child development and social policy: Knowledge for action.* Washington, DC: American Psychological Association.

Muhuri, P. K., MacDorman, M. F., & Ezzati-Rice, T. M. (2004). Racial differences in leading causes of infant death in the United States. *Paediatric and Perinatal Epidemiology, 18*, 51–60.

Muldoon, K., Lewis, C., & Francis, B. (2007). Using cardinality to compare quantities: The role of social-cognitive conflict in early numeracy. *Developmental Science, 10*, 694–711.

Mulvaney, M., & Mebert, C. (2007, September). Parental corporal punishment predicts behavior problems in early childhood. *Journal of Family Psychology, 21*(3), 389–397.

Mumme, D., & Fernald, A. (2003). The infant as onlooker: Learning from emotional reactions observed in a television scenario. *Child Development, 74*, 221–237.

Munafò, M. R., & Flint, J. (2011). Dissecting the genetic architecture of human personality. *Trends in Cognitive Sciences, 15*, 395–400.

Munakata, Y., McClelland, J. L., Johnson, M. H., & Siegler, R. S. (1997). Rethinking infant knowledge: Toward an adaptive process account of the successes and failures in object permanence tasks. *Psychological Review, 104*, 686–713.

Munsters, J., Wallström, L., Ågren, J., Norsted, T., & Sindelar, R. (2012). Skin conductance measurements as pain assessment in newborn infants born at 22–27 weeks gestational age at different postnatal age. *Early Human Development, 88*, 21–26.

Munzar, P., Cami, J., & Farré, M. (2003). Mechanisms of drug addiction. *New England Journal of Medicine, 349*, 2365–2365.

Murdock, T. B., & Bolch, M. B. (2005). Risk and protective factors for poor school adjustment in lesbian, gay, and bisexual (LGB) high school youth: Variable and person-centered analyses. *Psychology in the Schools, 42*, 159–172.

Murguia, A., Peterson, R. A., & Zea, M. C. (1997, August). *Cultural health beliefs.* Paper presented at the annual meeting of the American Psychological Association, Toronto, Canada.

Murphy, B., & Eisenberg, N. (2002). An integrative examination of peer conflict: Children's reported goals, emotions, and behaviors. *Social Development, 11*, 534–557.

Murphy, C. (2008). The chemical senses and nutrition in older adults. *Journal of Nutrition for the Elderly, 27*, 247–265.

Murphy, M. (2009). Language and literacy in individuals with Turner syndrome. *Topics in Language Disorders, 29*, 187–194.

Murphy, M., & Mazzocco, M. (2008). Mathematics learning disabilities in girls with fragile X or Turner syndrome during late elementary school. *Journal of Learning Disabilities, 41*, 29–46.

Murphy, M., & Polivka, B. (2007). Parental perceptions of the schools' role in addressing childhood obesity. *The Journal of School Nursing, 23*, 40–46.

Murphy, S. (2008). The loss of a child: Sudden death and extended illness perspectives. *Handbook of bereavement research and practice: Advances in theory and intervention* (pp. 375–395). Washington, DC: American Psychological Association.

Murphy, S., Johnson, L., & Wu, L. (2003). Bereaved parents' outcomes 4 to 60 months after their children's death by accident, suicide, or homicide: A comparative study demonstrating differences. *Death Studies, 27*, 39–61.

Murray, B. (1996, July). Getting children off the couch and onto the field. *Monitor on Psychology*, pp. 42–43.

Murray, G., Jones, P., Kuh, D., & Richards, M. (2007). Infant developmental milestones and subsequent cognitive function. *Annals of Neurology, 62*, 128–136.

Murray, J. (2008). Media violence: The effects are both real and strong. *American Behavioral Scientist, 51*, 1212–1230.

Murray, J. A., Terry, D. J., Vance, J. C., Battistutta, D., & Connolly, Y. (2000). Effects of a program of intervention on parental distress following infant death. *Death Studies, 4*, 275–305.

Murray, K. E. (2011). Sleep in infants—Sleeping through the night. *Journal of Developmental and Behavioral Pediatrics, 32*, 175–176.

Murray, L., & Cooper, P. J. (Eds.). (1997). *Postpartum depression and child development.* New York: Guilford Press.

Murray, L, Cooper, P., Creswell, C., Schofield, E., & Sack, C. (2007). The effects of maternal social phobia on mother-infant interactions and infant social responsiveness. *Journal of Child Psychology and Psychiatry, 48*, 45–52.

Murray, L., de Rosnay, M., Pearson, J., Bergeron, C., Schofield, E., Royal-Lawson, M., et al. (2008). Intergenerational transmission of social anxiety: The role of social referencing processes in infancy. *Child Development, 79*, 1049–1064.

Murray, S., Bellavia, G., & Rose, P. (2003). Once hurt, twice hurtful: How perceived regard regulates daily marital interactions. *Journal of Personality & Social Psychology, 84*, 126–147.

Murray, S., Griffin, D., Rose, P., & Bellavia, G. (2006). For better or worse? Self-esteem and the contingencies of acceptance in marriage. *Personality and Social Psychology Bulletin, 32*, 866–880.

Murray-Close, D., Ostrov, J., & Crick, N. (2007, December). A short-term longitudinal study of growth of relational aggression during middle childhood: Associations with gender, friendship intimacy, and internalizing problems. *Development and Psychopathology, 19*, 187–203.

Murstein, B. I. (1976). *Who will marry whom? Theories and research in marital choice.* New York: Springer.

Murstein, B. I. (1986). *Paths to marriage.* Beverly Hills, CA: Sage.

Murstein, B. I. (1987). A clarification and extension of the SVR theory of dyadic pairing. *Journal of Marriage and the Family, 49*, 929–933.

Music, G. (2011). *Nurturing natures: Attachment and children's emotional, sociocultural and brain development*. New York: Psychology Press.

Musick, J. (1993). *Young, poor, and pregnant: The psychology of teenage motherhood*. New Haven: Yale University Press.

Musolino, J., & Lidz, J. (2006). Why children aren't universally successful with quantification. *Linguistics, 44*, 817–852.

Mussen, P. H. (1969). Early sex-role development. In D. A. Goslin (Eds.), *Handbook of socialization theory and research* (pp. 707–732). Chicago: Rand McNally.

Mussen, P. H., & Jones, M. C. (1957). Self-conceptions, motivations, and interpersonal attitudes of late- and early-maturing boys. *Child Development, 28*, 243–256.

Mutran, E. J., Reitzes, D. C., & Fernandez, M. E. (1997). Factors influencing attitudes toward retirement. *Research on Aging, 19*, 251–273.

Mutrie, N. (1997). The therapeutic effects of exercise on the self. In K. R. Fox (Ed.), *The physical self: From motivation to well being* (pp. 287–314). Champaign, IL: Human Kinetics.

Myers, B.J., Dawson, K. S., Britt, G. C., Lodder, D. E., Meloy, L. D., Saunders, M. K., Meadows, S. L., & Elswick, R. K. (2003). Prenatal cocaine exposure and infant performance on the Brazelton Neonatal Behavioral Assessment Scale. *Substance Use and Misuse, 38*, 2065–2096.

Myers, D. (2000). *A quiet world: Living with hearing loss*. New Haven: Yale University Press.

Myers, K. (2003). Mood management leader's manual: A cognitive- behavioral skills-building program for adolescents: Mood Management: A cognitive-behavioral Skills-building program for adolescents, skills workbook. *Journal of the American Academy of Child & Adolescent Psychiatry, 42*, 1533–1534.

Myers, M. G., Martin, R. A., Rohsenow, D. J., & Monti, P. M. (1996). The relapse situation appraisal questionnaire: Initial psychometric characteristics and validation. *Psychology of Addictive Behaviors, 10*, 237–247.

Myers, N. A., Clifton, R. K., & Clarkson, M. G. (1987). When they were very young: Almost-threes remember two years ago. *Infant Behavior and Development, 10*, 123–132.

Myers, R. H. (2004). Huntington's disease genetics. *NeuroRx, 1*, 255–262.

Myklebust, B. M., & Gottlieb, G. L. (1993). Development of the stretch reflex in the newborn: Reciprocal excitation and reflex irradation. *Child Development, 64*, 1036–1045.

Myrtek, M. (2007). *Type A behavior and hostility as independent risk factors for coronary heart disease*. Washington, DC: American Psychological Association.

Myslinski, N. R. (1990). The effects of aging on the sensory systems of the nose and mouth. *Topics in Geriatric Rehabilitation, 5*, 21–30.

NAACP Education Department. (2003). *NAACP call for action in education*. Baltimore, MD: NAACP.

Nachtigall, L., & Heilman, J. R. (1995). *Estrogen* (2nd ed.). New York: Harperperennial Library.

Nadal, K. (2004). Filipino American identity development model. *Journal of Multicultural Counseling & Development, 32*, 45–62.

Nadeau, L., Boivin, M., Tessier, R., Lefebvre, F., & Robaey, P. (2001). Mediators of behavioral problems in 7-year-old children born after 24 to 28 weeks of gestation. *Journal of Developmental & Behavioral Pediatrics, 22*, 1–10.

Nadel, S., & Poss, J. (2007). Early detection of autism spectrum disorders: Screening between 12 and 24 months of age. *Journal of the American Academy of Nurse Practitioners, 19*, 408–417.

Nagabhushan, P. (2011). Review of "Asian American parenting and parent-adolescent relationships." *Journal of Youth and Adolescence, 40*, 245–247.

Nagda, B. R. A., Gurin, P., & Johnson, S. M. (2005). Living, doing and thinking diversity: How does pre-college diversity experience affect first-year students' engagement with college diversity? In R. S. Feldman, *Improving the first year of college: Research and practice*. Mahwah, NJ: Lawrence Erlbaum.

Nagy, E. (2006). From imitation to conversation: The first dialogues with human neonates. *Infant and Child Development, 15*, 223–232.

Nagy, M. (1948). The child's theories concerning death. *Journal of Genetic Psychology, 73*, 3–27.

Nagy, T. F. (2011). *Essential ethics for psychologists: A primer for understanding and mastering core issues*. Washington, DC: American Psychological Association.

Nahmiash, D. (2006). *Abuse and neglect of older adults: What do we know about it and how can we identify it?* Westport, CT: Praeger Publishers/Greenwood Publishing Group.

Naik, G. (2002, November 22). The grim mission of a Swiss group: Visitor's suicides. *The Wall Street Journal*, A1, A6.

Naik, G. (2004, March 10). Unlikely way to cut hospital costs: Comfort the dying. *The Wall Street Journal*, A1, A12.

Naik, G. (2009, February 3). Parents agonize over treatment in the womb. *Wall Street Journal*, p. D1.

Nair, K. (2008). A plea for a holistic approach to aging. *Discourses on aging and dying*. New Delhi: Sage Publications India.

Nakagawa, M., Lamb, M. E., & Miyaki, K. (1992). Antecedents and correlates of the Strange Situation behavior of Japanese infants. *Journal of Cross-Cultural Psychology, 23*, 300–310.

Nakamura, M., Kyo, S., Kanaya, T., Yatabe, N., Maida, Y., Tanaka, M., Ishida, Y., Fujii, C., Kondo, T., Inoue, M., & Mukaida, N. (2004). hTERT-promoter-based tumor-specific expression of MCP-1 effectively sensitizes cervical cancer cells to a low dose of cisplatin. *Cancer Gene Therapy, 2*, 1–7.

Nakato, E., Otsuka, Y., Kanazawa, S., Yamaguchi, M. K., Honda, Y., & Kakigi, R. (2011). I know this face: Neural activity during mother' face perception in 7- to 8-month-old infants as investigated by near-infrared spectroscopy. *Early Human Development, 87*, 1–7.

Nakato, E., Otsuka, Y., Kanazawa, S., Yamaguchi, M. K., & Kakigi, R. (2011). Distinct differences in the pattern of hemodynamic response to happy and angry facial expressions in infants—A near-infrared spectroscopic study. *NeuroImage, 54*, 1600–1606.

Nam, C. B., & Boyd, M. (2004). Occupational status in 2000: Over a century of census-based measurement. *Population Research and Policy Review, 23*, 327–358.

Nanda, S., & Konnur, N. (2006, October). Adolescent drug & alcohol use in the 21st century. *Psychiatric Annals, 36*, 706–712.

Nangle, D. W., & Erdley, C. A. (Eds.). (2001). *The role of friendship in psychological adjustment*. San Francisco: Jossey-Bass.

Naoi, N., Minagawa-Kawai, Y., Kobayashi, A., Takeuchi, K., Nakamura, K., Yamamoto, J., & Kojima, S. (2012). Cerebral responses to infant-directed speech and the effect of talker familiarity. *Neuroimage, 59*, 1735–1744.

Nappi, R., & Polatti, F. (2009). The use of estrogen therapy in women's sexual functioning. *Journal of Sexual Medicine, 6*, 603–616.

Nash, A., Pine, K., & Messer, D. (2009). Television alcohol advertising: Do children really mean what they say? *British Journal of Developmental Psychology, 27*, 85–104.

Nassif, A., & Gunter, B. (2008). Gender representation in television advertisements in Britain and Saudi Arabia. *Sex Roles, 58*, 752–760.

Nathanielsz, P. W. (1996). The timing of birth. *American Scientist, 84*, 562–569.

Nathanson, A., Wilson, B., & McGee, J. (2002). Counteracting the effects of female stereotypes on television via active mediation. *Journal of Communication, 52*, 922–937.

Nation, M., & Heflinger, C. (2006). Risk factors for serious alcohol and drug use: The role of psychosocial variables in predicting the frequency of substance use among adolescents. *American Journal of Drug and Alcohol Abuse, 32*, 415–433.

National Association for the Education of Young Children. (2005). *Position statements of the NAEYC*. Retrieved from http://www.naeyc.org/about/positions.asp#where.

National Campaign to Prevent Youth Pregnancy (NCPYP). (2003). *14 and younger: The sexual behavior of young adolescents*. Washington, DC.

National Center for Children in Poverty. (2005). *Basic facts about low-income children in the United States*. New York: National Center for Children in Poverty.

National Center for Children in Poverty. (2010). *Basic facts about low-income children, 2009*. New York: National Center for Children in Poverty.

National Center for Chronic Disease Prevention and Health Promotion. (2011). *Teen pregnancy: Improving the lives of oung people and strengthening communities by reducing teen pregnancy*. Washington, DC: Centers for Disease Control.

National Center for Education Statistics. (1997). *Digest of education statistics, 1997*. Washington, DC: U.S. Government Printing Office.

National Center for Education Statistics. (2000). *Dropout rates in the United States: 1999*. Washington, DC: National Center for Education Statistics.

National Center for Education Statistics. (2001). *Time spent on homework and on the job (Indicator No. 21)*. Retrieved from http/nces.ed.gov/programs/coe/2001/section3/indicator21.asp.

National Center for Education Statistics. (2002). *Dropout rates in the United States: 2000*. Washington, DC: NCES.

National Center for Education Statistics. (2003). *Public high school dropouts and completers from the common core of data: School year 2000–01 statistical analysis report*. Washington, DC: NCES.

National Center for Education Statistics. (2004). *The condition of education, 2004*. Washington, DC: National Center for Education Statistics.

National Center for Health Statistics. (1993a). Advance report of final natality statistics, 1991. *Monthly Vital Statistics Report*. Washington, DC: Public Health Service.

National Center for Health Statistics. (1993b). *Health United States, 1992*. Washington, DC: Public Health Service.

National Center for Health Statistics. (1994). *Division of vital statistics*. Washington, DC: Public Health Service.

National Center for Health Statistics. (1996). *Percentage of births to single mothers*. Washington, DC: National Center for Health Statistics.

National Center for Health Statistics. (1997). *Asthma conditions of children under 18*. Washington, DC: Public Health Service.

National Center for Health Statistics. (2000). *Health United States, 2000 with adolescent health chartbook*. Hyattsville, MD.

National Center for Health Statistics. (2001a). *Division of vital statistics*. Washington, DC: Public Health Service.

National Center for Health Statistics. (2001b). *Obesity in children*. Washington, DC: National Center for Health Statistics.

National Center for Health Statistics. (2003). *Division of vital statistics*. Washington, DC: Public Health Service.

National Center for Health Statistics. (2004). *SIDS death rate: 1980–2000*. Washington, DC: National Center for Health Statistics.

National Center for Health Statistics. (2006). National Hospital Discharge Survey: 2004 annual summary with detailed diagnosis and procedure data. *Vital and Health Statistics, 13*(162).

National Center for Health Statistics (Infant and Child Health Studies Branch). (1997). *Survival rates of infants.* Washington, DC: National Center for Health Statistics.

National Center for Health Statistics (Infant and Child Health Studies Branch). (2003). *Rates of cesarean births.* Washington, DC: National Center for Health Statistics.

National Center for Missing and Exploited Children. (1994). *Safety guidelines for children.* Alexandria, VA: Author. Retrieved from http://www.missingkids.com./html/ncmec_default_ec_internetsafty.html.

National Center for Missing and Exploited Children. (2002). *Internet rules.* Alexandria, VA: Author. Retrieved from http://www.missingkids.com.

National Clearinghouse on Child Abuse and Neglect Information. (2004). *Child maltreatment 2002: Summary of key findings/National Clearinghouse on Child Abuse and Neglect Information.* Washington, DC: Author.

National Coalition Against Domestic Violence (NCADC). (2003). *Poll finds domestic violence is women's main concern.* Denver, CO: NCADC.

National Committee to Prevent Child Abuse. (1995). *Current trends in child abuse reporting and fatalities: The results of the 1995 Annual Fifty State Survey, Working Paper Number 808.* Chicago, IL: NCPCA.

National Highway Traffic Safety Administration. (1994). *Age-related incidence of traffic accidents.* Washington, DC: National Highway Traffic Safety Administration.

National Institute of Aging. (2004, May 31). Sexuality in later life. Available online at http://www.niapublications.org/engagepages/sexuality.asp.

National Institute of Child Health and Human Development (NICHD). (1999). Child care and mother-child interaction in the first 3 years of life. *Developmental Psychology, 35,* 1399–1413.

National Institute of Child Health and Human Development Early Child Care Research Network. (2003). Does amount of time spent in child care predict socioemotional adjustment during the transition to kindergarten? *Child Development, 74,* 976–1005.

National Institute of Child Health and Human Development Early Child Care Research Network & Duncan, G. J. (2003). Modeling the impacts of child care quality on child care quality on children's preschool cognitive development. *Child Development, 74,* 1454–1475.

National Institutes of Health. (2006, December 13) Adult male circumcision significantly reduces risk of acquiring HIV. NIH News release. Retrieved from http://www.nih.gov/news/pr/dec2006/niaid-13.htm.

National Longitudinal Study on Adolescent Health. (2000). *Teenage stress.* Chapel Hill, NC: Carolina Population Center.

National Research Council. (1991). *Caring for America's children.* Washington, DC: National Academy Press.

National Research Council. (1997). *Racial and ethnic differences in the health of older Americans.* New York: Author.

National Safety Council. (1989). *Accident facts: 1989 edition.* Chicago: National Safety Council.

National Science Foundation (NSF), Division of Science Resources Statistics. (2002). *Women, minorities, and persons with disabilities in science and engineering: 2002.* Arlington, VA: National Science Foundation.

National Sleep Foundation. (2002a). *Adolescents and sleep.* Washington, DC: National Sleep Foundation.

National Sleep Foundation. (2002b). *Americans favor later high school start times, according to National Sleep Foundation Poll.* Washington, DC: National Sleep Foundation.

Navarro, M. (2006, May 25). Families add 3rd generation to households. *The New York Times,* A1, A22.

Nawaz, S., Griffiths, P., & Tappin, D. (2002). Parent-administered modified dry-bed training for childhood nocturnal enuresis: Evidence for superiority over urine-alarm conditioning when delivery factors are controlled. *Behavioral Interventions, 17,* 247–260.

Nazzi, T., & Bertoncini, J. (2003). Before and after the vocabulary spurt: Two modes of word acquisition? *Developmental Science, 6,* 136–142.

NCADC (National Coalition Against Domestic Violence). (2003). *Poll finds domestic violence is women's main concern.* Denver, CO: Author.

NCB (National Children's Bureau) Now. (2011, February 8.) *ABA's anti-bullying tools for schools.* London: England.

NCES (National Center of Educational Statistics). (2000). *Digest of educational statistics.* Washington, DC: U.S. Department of Education, Office of Educational Research and Improvement.

NCPYP (National Campaign to Prevent Youth Pregnancy). (2003). *14 and younger: The sexual behavior of young adolescents.* Washington, D.C.

Needleman, H. L., & Bellinger, D. (Eds.). (1994). *Prenatal exposure to toxicants: Developmental consequences.* Baltimore: Johns Hopkins University Press.

Needleman, H. L., Riess, J. A., Tobin, M. J., Biesecker, G. E., & Greenhouse, J. B. (1996, February 7). Bone lead levels and delinquent behavior. *Journal of the American Medical Association, 2755,* 363–369.

Negy, C., Shreve, T., & Jensen, B. (2003). Ethnic identity, self-esteem, and ethnocentrism: A study of social identity versus multicultural theory of development. *Cultural Diversity & Ethnic Minority Psychology, 9,* 333–344.

Neher, A. (1991). Maslow's theory of motivation: A critique. *Journal of Humanistic Psychology, 31,* 89–112.

Neisser, U. (2004). Memory development: New questions and old. *Developmental Review, 24,* 154–158.

Nelis, D., Quoidbach, J., Mikolajczak, M., & Hansenne, M. (2009). Increasing emotional intelligence: (How) is it possible? *Personality and Individual Differences, 47,* 36–41.

Nelson, C. A. (1987). The recognition of facial expressions in the first two years of life: Mechanisms of development. *Child Development, 58,* 889–909.

Nelson, C. A. (1995). The ontogeny of human memory: A cognitive neuroscience perspective. *Developmental Psychology, 31,* 723–738.

Nelson, C. A., & Bosquet, M. (2000). Neurobiology of fetal and infant development: Implications for infant mental health. In C. H. Zeanah Jr. (Ed.), *Handbook of infant mental health* (2nd ed.). New York: Guilford Press.

Nelson, D. A., Hart, C. H., Yang, C., Olsen, J. A., & Jin, S. (2006). Aversive parenting in China: Associations with child physical and relational aggression. *Child Development, 77,* 554–572.

Nelson, D. G. K., Jusczyk, P. W., Mandel, D. R., Myers, J., et al. (1995). *Infant Behavior & Development, 18,* 111–116.

Nelson, F., & Mann, T. (2011). Opportunities in public policy to support infant and early childhood mental health: The role of psychologists and policymakers. *American Psychologist, 66,* 129–139.

Nelson, H. D., Tyne, K., Naik, A., Bougatsos, C., Chan, B. K., & Humphrey, L. (2009). Screening for breast cancer: An update for the U.S. Preventive Services Task Force. *Annals of Internal Medicine, 151,* 727–737.

Nelson, K. (1981). Individual differences in language development: Implications for development and language. *Developmental Psychology, 17*(2), 170–187.

Nelson, K. (1986). *Event knowledge: Structure and function in development.* Hillsdale, NJ: Erlbaum.

Nelson, K. (1989). Remembering: A functional developmental perspective. In P. R. Solomon, G. R. Goethels, C. M. Kelley, & B. R. Stephens (Eds.), *Memory: An interdisciplinary approach.* New York: Springer-Verlag.

Nelson, K. (1992). Emergence of autobiographical memory at age 4. *Human Development, 35,* 172–177.

Nelson, K. (1996). *Language in cognitive development: Emergence of the mediated mind.* New York: Cambridge University Press.

Nelson, K., & Arkenberg, M. (2008). Language and reading development reflect dynamic mixes of learning conditions. *Brain, behavior, and learning in language and reading disorders.* New York: Guilford Press.

Nelson, K., & Fivush, R. (2004). The emergence of autobiographical memory: A social cultural developmental theory. *Psychological Review, 111,* 486–511.

Nelson, L., Badger, S., & Wu, B. (2004). The influence of culture in emerging adulthood: Perspectives of Chinese college students. *International Journal of Behavioral Development, 28,* 26–36.

Nelson, L. D., Scheibel, K. E., & Ringman, J. M. (2007). An experimental approach to detecting dementia in Down syndrome: A paradigm for Alzheimer's disease. *Brain and Cognition, 64,* 92–103.

Nelson, L. J., & Cooper, J. (1997). Gender differences in children's reactions to success and failure with computers. *Computers in Human Behavior, 13,* 247–267.

Nelson, P., Adamson, L., & Bakeman, R. (2008). Toddlers' joint engagement experience facilitates preschoolers' acquisition of theory of mind. *Developmental Science, 11,* 847–859.

Nelson, T. (2002). *The psychology of prejudice.* Needham Heights, MA: Allyn & Bacon.

Nelson, T. (2004). *Ageism: Stereotyping and prejudice against older persons.* Cambridge, MA: MIT Press.

Nelson, T. O. (1994). Metacognition. In V. S. Ramachandran (Ed.), *Encyclopedia of human behavior* (Vol. 3). San Diego: Academic Press.

Nelson, T., & Wechsler, H. (2003). School spirits: Alcohol and collegiate sports fans. *Addictive Behaviors, 28,* 1–11.

Nemeth, C. (1992). Minority dissent as a stimulant to group performance. In S. Worchel, W. Wood, & J. Simpson (Eds.), *Group processes and productivity.* Newbury Park, CA: Sage Publications.

Nesheim, S., Henderson, S., Lindsay, M., Zuberi, J., Grimes, V., Buehler, J., Lindegren, M. L., & Bulterys, M. (2004). *Prenatal HIV testing and antiretroviral prophylasix at an urban hospital—Atlanta, Georgia, 1997–2000.* Atlanta, GA: Centers for Disease Control.

Ness, J., Aronow, W., & Beck, G. (2006). Menopausal symptoms after cessation of hormone replacement therapy. *Maturitas, 53,* 356–361.

Ness, R. B., Grisso, J. A., Hirschinger, N., Markovic, N., Shaw, L. M., Day, N. L., & Kline, J. (1999). Cocaine and tobacco use and the risk of spontaneous abortion. *New England Journal of Medicine, 340,* 333–339.

Nettelbeck, T., & Rabbitt, P. M. (1992). Aging, cognitive performance, and mental speed. *Intelligence, 16,* 189–205.

Nettles, S. M., & Pleck, J. H. (1990). Risk, resilience, and development: The multiple ecologies of black adolescents. In R. J. Haggerty, N. Garmezy, M. Rutter, & L. Sherrod (Eds.), *Risk and resilience in children: Developmental approaches.* New York: Cambridge University Press.

Neugarten, B. (1967). The awareness of middle age. In R. Owen (Ed.), *Middle age.* London: BBC.

Neugarten, B. L. (1972). Personality and the aging process. *The Gerontologist, 12,* 9–15.

Neugarten, B. L. (1977). Personality and aging. In J. E. Birren & K. W. Schaie (Eds.), *Handbook for the psychology of aging.* New York: Van Nostrand Reinhold.

Neugarten, B. L. (1979). Time, age, and the life cycle. *American Journal of Psychiatry, 136,* 887–893.

Neugarten, B. L., & Neugarten, D. A. (1987). The changing meanings of age. *Psychology Today, 21,* 29–33.

Newbart, D. (2006, October 8). Record freshman diversity at U. of C.: 1 in 4 students black, Hispanic or from abroad. *Chicago Sun Times,* p. A09.

Newbart, D. (2009, October 11). "Silent addiction" on campus: Gambling. *Chicago Sun Times*, p. A12.

Newcomb, A. F., & Bagwell, C. L. (1995). Children's friendship relations: A meta-analytic review. *Psychological Bulletin, 117*, 306–347.

Newcombe, N., Drummey, A. B., & Lie, E. (1995). Children's memory for early experience. *Journal of Experimental Child Psychology, 59*, 337–342.

Newman, R., & Hussain, I. (2006). Changes in preference for infant-directed speech in low and moderate noise by 4.5- to 13-month-olds. *Infancy, 10*, 61–76.

Newport, F. (2008, April 4). Wives still do laundry, men do yard work. Gallup Poll: Princeton, NJ.

Newsome, W., & Kelly, M. (2006). Bullying behavior and school violence. *Fostering child & adolescent mental health in the classroom* (pp. 183–201). Thousand Oaks, CA: Sage Publications, Inc.

Newston, R. L., & Keith, P. M. (1997). Single women later in life. In J. M. Coyle (Ed.), *Handbook on women and aging* (pp. 385–399). Westport, CT: Greenwood Press.

Newton, K., Reed, S., LaCroix, A., Grothaus, L., Ehrlich, K., & Guiltinan, J. (2006). Treatment of vasomotor symptoms of menopause with black cohosh, multibotanicals, soy, hormone therapy, or placebo. *Annals of Internal Medicine, 145*, 869–879.

Ney, P. G., Fung, T., & Wickett, A. R. (1993). Child neglect: The precursor to child abuse. *Pre- and Peri-Natal Psychology Journal, 8*, 95–112.

Ng, F., Pomerantz, E., & Lam, S. (2007, September). European American and Chinese parents' responses to children's success and failure: Implications for children's responses. *Developmental Psychology, 43*(5), 1239–1255.

Ng, S. (2002). Will families support their elders? Answers from across cultures. In T. Nelson (Ed.), *Ageism: Stereotyping and prejudice against older persons*. Cambridge, MA: The MIT Press.

Ng, T., & Feldman, D. (2008). The relationship of age to ten dimensions of job performance. *Journal of Applied Psychology, 93*, 392–423.

Nguyen, L., & Frye, D. (1999). Children's theory of mind: Understanding of desire, belief and emotion with social referents. *Social Development, 8*, 70–92.

Ní Bhrolcháin, M. (2006). The age difference between partners: A matter of female choice? *Human clocks: The bio-cultural meanings of age* (pp. 289–312). New York: Peter Lang Publishing.

NIAAA (National Institute on Alcohol Abuse and Alcoholism). (1990). *Alcohol and health*. Washington, DC: U.S. Government Printing Office.

NICHD Early Child Care Research Network. (1997). The effects of infant child care on infant–mother attachment security: Results of the NICHD study of early child care. *Child Development, 68*, 860–879.

NICHD Early Child Care Research Network. (2000). The relation of child care to cognitive and language development. *Child Development, 71*, 960–980.

NICHD Early Child Care Research Network. (2001a). Child care and children's peer interaction at 24 and 36 months: The NICHD study of early child care. *Child Development, 72*, 1478–1500.

NICHD Early Child Care Research Network. (2001b). Child-care and family predictors of preschool attachment and stability from infancy. *Developmental Psychology, 37*, 847–862.

NICHD Early Child Care Research Network. (2002). Child-care structure process outcome. Dicert and indirect effect of child-care quality on young children's development. *Psychological Science, 13*, 199–306.

NICHD Early Child Care Research Network. (2003a). Does quality of child care affect child outcomes at age 41/2? *Developmental Psychology, 39*, 451–469.

NICHD Early Child Care Research Network. (2003b). Families matter—even for kids in child care. *Journal of Developmental and Behavioral Pediatrics, 24*, 58–62.

NICHD Early Child Care Research Network. (2005). *Child care and child development: Results from the NICHD study of early child care and youth development*. New York: Guilford Press.

NICHD Early Child Care Research Network. (2006a). *Child care and child development: Results from the NICHD study of early child care and youth development*. New York: Guilford Press.

NICHD Early Child Care Research Network. (2006b). *The NICHD Study of Early Child Care and Youth Development (SECCYD): Findings for children up to age 4 1/2 years*. (Figure 5, p. 20). Washington, DC: National Institute of Child Health and Human Development.

NICHD Early Child Care Research Network. (2008). Social competence with peers in third grade: Associations with earlier peer experiences in childcare. *Social Development, 17*, 419–453.

Nickerson, A., Aderka, I. M., Bryant, R. A., & Hofmann, S. G. (2012). The relationship between childhood exposure to trauma and intermittent explosive disorder. *Psychiatry Research*. Retrieved from http://www.ncbi.nlm.nih.gov/pubmed/22464047.

Nicklas, T. A., Goh, E., Goodell, L., Acuff, D. S., Reiher, R., Buday, R., & Ottenbacher, A. (2011). Impact of commercials on food preferences of low-income, minority preschoolers. *Journal of Nutrition Education and Behavior, 43*, 35–41.

Nickman, S. L. (1996, January). Challenges of adoption. *The Harvard Mental Health Letter*, pp. 5–7.

Nicolson, R., & Fawcett, A. (2008). *Dyslexia, learning, and the brain*. Cambridge, MA: MIT Press.

Niederhofer, H. (2004). A longitudinal study: Some preliminary results of association of prenatal maternal stress and fetal movements, temperament factors in early childhood and behavior at age 2 years. *Psychological Reports, 95*, 767–770.

Nielsen, M. (2006). Copying actions and copying outcomes: Social learning through the second year. *Developmental Psychology, 42*, 555–565.

Nielsen, M., Dissanayake, C., & Kashima, Y. (2003). A longitudinal investigation of self–other discrimination and the emergence of minor self-recognition. *Infant Behavior & Development, 26*, 213–226.

Nieto, S. (2005). Public Education in the twentieth century and beyond: High hopes, broken promises, and an uncertain future. *Harvard Educational Review, 75*, 43–65.

Nigg, J. T. (2001). Is ADHD a disinhibatory disorder? *Psychological Bulletin, 127*, 571–598.

Nigg, J., Knottnerus, G., Martel, M., Nikolas, M., Cavanagh, K., Karmaus, W., et al. (2008). Low blood lead levels associated with clinically diagnosed attention-deficit/hyperactivity disorder and mediated by weak cognitive control. *Biological Psychiatry, 63*, 325–331.

Nihart, M. A. (1993). Growth and development of the brain. *Journal of Child and Adolescent Psychiatric and Mental Health Nursing, 6*, 39–40.

Nilsen, E., & Graham, S. (2009). The relations between children's communicative perspective-taking and executive functioning. *Cognitive Psychology, 58*, 220–249.

Nilsson, L. (1990). *A child is born*. New York: Dell.

Nilsson, L. (2003). Memory function in normal aging. *Acta Neurologica Scandinavica, 107*, 7–13.

Nilsson, L. G., Bäckman, L., Erngrund, K., Nyberg, L., et al. (1997). The Betula prospective cohort study: Memory, health, and aging. *Aging Neuropsychology & Cognition, 4*, 1–32.

Nimrod, G., & Adoni, H. (2006, July). Leisure-styles and life satisfaction among recent retirees in Israel. *Ageing & Society, 26*, 607–630.

Niparko, J. K. (2004). Speech, language, and reading skills after early cochlear implantation. *JAMA: Journal of the American Medical Association, 291*, 2378–2380.

Nisbett, R. (1994, October 31). Blue genes. *New Republic, 211*, 15.

Nisbett, R. E., Aronson, J., Blair, C., Dickens, W., Flynn, J., Halpern, D. F., & Turkheimer, E. (2012). Intelligence: New findings and theoretical developments. *American Psychologist, 67*, 130–159.

Nishi, D. (2008, December 23). Segueing from a life of rock 'n' roll into therapy. *Wall Street Journal*, p. D6.

Nixon-Cave, K. (2001). *Influence of cultural/ethnic beliefs and behaviors and family environment on the motor development of infants 12–18 months of age in three ethnic groups: African-American, Hispanic/Latino and Anglo-European*. Unpublished doctoral dissertation, Temple University, PA.

Noakes, M. A., & Rinaldi, C. M. (2006). Age and gender differences in peer conflict, *Journal of Youth and Adolescence, 35*, 881–891.

Nobuyuki, I. (1997). Simple reaction times and timing of serial reactions of middle-aged and old men. *Perceptual & Motor Skills, 84*, 219–225.

Nockels, R., & Oakeshott, P. (1999). Awareness among young women of sexually transmitted chlamydia infection. *Family Practice, 16*, 94.

Noel, A., & Newman, J. (2008). Mothers' plans for children during the kindergarten hold-out year. *Early Child Development and Care, 178*(3), 289–303.

Nolen-Hoeksema, S. (2001). Ruminative coping and adjustment to bereavement. In M. Stroebe & R. Hansson (Eds.), *Handbook of bereavement research: Consequences, coping, and care*. Washington, DC: American Psychological Association.

Nolen-Hoeksema, S. (2003). *Women who think too much: How to break free of overthinking and reclaim your life*. New York: Henry Holt.

Nolen-Hoeksema, S., & Davis, C. (2002). Positive responses to loss: Perceiving benefits and growth. In C. Snyder & S. Lopez (Eds.), *Handbook of positive psychology*. London: Oxford University Press.

Nolen-Hoeksema, S., & Girgus, J. S. (1994). The emergence of gender differences in depression during adolescence. *Psychological Bulletin, 115*, 424–443.

Nolen-Hoeksema, S., & Larson, J. (1999). *Coping with loss*. Mahwah, NJ: Erlbaum.

Nolen-Hoeksema, S., McBraide, A., & Larson, J. (1997). Rumination and psychological distress among bereaved partners. *Journal of Personality and Social Psychology, 72*, 855–862.

Noller, P., Feeney, J. A., & Ward, C. M. (1997). Determinants of marital quality: A partial test of Lewis and Spanier's model. *Journal of Family Studies, 3*, 226–251.

Noonan, C., & Ward, T. (2007, November). Environmental tobacco smoke, woodstove heating and risk of asthma symptoms. *Journal of Asthma, 44*(9), 735–738.

Noonan, D. (2003a, September 29). High on testosterone. *Newsweek*, pp. 50–52.

Noonan, D. (2003b, September 22). When safety is the name of the game. *Newsweek*, pp. 64–66.

Noone, J., Stephens, C., & Alpass, F. (2009). Preretirement planning and well-being in later life: A prospective study. *Research on Aging, 31*, 295–317.

Nordenmark, M., & Stattin, M. (2009). Psychosocial wellbeing and reasons for retirement in Sweden. *Ageing & Society, 29*, 413–430.

Nordin, S., Razani, L., & Markison, S. (2003). Age-associated increases in intensity discrimination for taste. *Experimental Aging Research, 29*, 371–381.

Norlander, T., Von Schedvin, H., & Archer, T. (2005). Thriving as a function of affective personality: Relation to personality factors, coping strategies and stress. *Anxiety, Stress & Coping: An International Journal, 18*, 105–116.

Norman, R. (2008). Reproductive changes in the female lifespan. *The active female: Health issues throughout the lifespan* (pp. 17–24). Totowa, NJ: Humana Press.

Norman, R. M. G., & Malla, A. K. (2001). Family history of schizophrenia and the relationship of stress to symptoms: Preliminary findings. *Australian & New Zealand Journal of Psychiatry, 35,* 217–223.

Northcote, J. (2006). Nightclubbing and the search for identity: Making the transition from childhood to adulthood in an urban milieu. *Journal of Youth Studies, 9,* 1–16.

Norton, A., & D'Ambrosio, B. (2008). ZPC and ZPD: Zones of teaching and learning. *Journal for Research in Mathematics Education, 39,* 220–246.

Norton, M., Skoog, I., Toone, L., Corcoran, C., Tschanz, J., Lisota, R., et al. (2006). Three-year incidence of first-onset depressive syndrome in a population sample of older adults: The Cache County Study. *American Journal of Geriatric Psychiatry, 14,* 237–245.

Nossiter, A. (1995, September 5). Asthma common and on rise in the crowded South Bronx. *The New York Times,* pp. A1, B2.

Notaro, P., Gelman, S., & Zimmerman, M. (2002). Biases in reasoning about the consequences of psychogenic bodily reactions: Domain boundaries in cognitive development. *Merrill-Palmer Quarterly, 48,* 427–449.

Notzon, F. C. (1990). International differences in the use of obstetric interventions. *Journal of the American Medical Association, 263,* 3286–3291.

Nowak, C. A. (1977). Does youthfulness equal attractiveness? In L. E. Troll, J. Israel, & K. Israel (Eds.), *Looking ahead.* Englewood, Cliffs, NJ: Prentice Hall.

Nowak, M. A., Komarova, N. L., & Niyogi, P. (2001, January 5). Evolution of universal grammar. *Science, 291,* 114–116.

Nowak, M., Komarova, N., & Niyogi, P. (2002). Computational and evolutionary aspects of language. *Nature, 417,* 611–617.

Nowak, R. (1994a, July 22). Genetic testing set for take-off. *Science, 265,* 464–467.

Nowak, R. (1994b, March 18). Nicotine scrutinized as FDA seeks to regulate cigarettes. *Science, 263,* 1555–1556.

Nowicki, S., & Oxenford, C. (1989). The relation of hostile nonverbal communication styles to popularity in preadolescent children. *Journal of Genetic Psychology, 150,* 39–44.

NPD Group. (1998). The reality of children's diet. Port Washington, NY: NPD Group.

NPD Group. (2004). The reality of children's diet. Port Washington, NY: NPD Group.

Nucci, L. P., Saxe, G., & Turiel, E. (Eds.). (2000). *Culture, thought, and development.* Mahwah, NJ: Lawrence Erlbaum Associates.

Nugent, J. K., Lester, B. M., & Brazelton, T. B. (Eds.). (1989). *The cultural context of infancy, Vol. 1: Biology, culture, and infant development.* Norwood, NJ: Ablex.

Nuttman-Shwartz, O. (2007). Is there life without work? *International Journal of Aging & Human Development, 64,* 129–147.

Nwoye, J., & Tung, P. (2002). Federal educational policies and innovations: Impacts on educating all students. In F. E. Obiakor & P. A. Grant (Eds.), *Educating all learners: Refocusing the comprehensive support model.* Springfield, IL: Charles C Thomas.

Nyiti, R. M. (1982). The validity of "culture differences explanations" for cross-cultural variation in the rate of Piagetian cognitive development. In D. Wagner & H. Stevenson (Eds.), *Cultural perspectives on child development.* New York: Freeman.

Nylen, K., Moran, T., Franklin, C., & O'Hara, M. (2006). Maternal depression: A review of relevant treatment approaches for mothers and infants. *Infant Mental Health Journal, 27,* 327–343.

O'Bryant, S. L., & Morgan, L. A. (1989). Financial experience and well-being among mature widowed women. *Gerontologist, 29,* 245–251.

O'Connor, M. J., Sigman, M., & Brill, N. (1987). Disorganization of attachment in relation to maternal alcohol consumption. *Journal of Consulting and Clinical Psychology, 55*(6), 831–836.

O'Connor, M., & Whaley, S. (2006). Health care provider advice and risk factors associated with alcohol consumption following pregnancy recognition. *Journal of Studies on Alcohol, 67,* 22–31.

O'Connor, P. (1994). Very close parent/child relationships: The perspective of the elderly person. *Journal of Cross-Cultural Gerontology, 9,* 53–76.

O'Connor, T., Heron, J., Glover, V., & The ALSPAC Study Team. (2002). Antenatal anxiety predicts child behavioral/emotional problems independently of postnatal depression. *Academy of Child and Adolescent Psychology, 41,* 1470–1477.

O'Dea, J., & Wilson, R. (2006). Socio-cognitive and nutritional factors associated with body mass index in children and adolescents: Possibilities for childhood obesity prevention. *Health Education Research, 21,* 796–805.

O'Grady, W., & Aitchison, J. (2005). *How children learn language.* New York: Cambridge University Press.

O'Hara, R., Schroder, C., Bloss, C., Bailey, A., Alyeshmerni, A., Mumenthaler, M., Friedman, L., & Yesavage, J. (2005). Hormone replacement therapy and longitudinal cognitive performance in postmenopausal women. *American Journal of Geriatric Psychiatry, 13,* 1107–1110.

O'Hare, W. (1997, September). *American Demographics,* pp. 50–56.

O'Leary, S. G. (1995). Parental discipline mistakes. *Current Directions in Psychological Science, 4,* 11–13.

O'Neill, C. (1994, May 17). Exercise just for the fun of it. *The Washington Post,* p. WH18.

O'Sullivan, J. T. (1993). Applying cognitive developmental principles in classrooms. In R. Pasnak & M. L. Howe (Eds.), *Emerging themes in cognitive development* (Vol. 2). New York: Springer-Verlag.

O'Toole, M. E. (2000). *The school shooter: A threat assessment perspective.* Washington, DC: Federal Bureau of Investigation.

O'Toole, M. L., Sawicki, M. A., & Artal, R. (2003). Structured diet and physical activity prevent postpartum weight retention. *Journal of Women's Health, 12,* 991–998.

Oashi, O. (2003). A review on the psychological interventions for the modification of Type A behavior pattern. *Japanese Journal of Counseling Science, 36,* 175–186.

Oberlander, S., Black, M., & Starr, R. (2007, March). African American adolescent mothers and grandmothers: A multigenerational approach to parenting. *American Journal of Community Psychology, 39*(1), 37–46.

Oblinger, D. G., & Rush, S. C. (1997). *The learning revolution: The challenge of information technology in the academy.* Bolton, MA: Anker Publishing Co.

Ochsner Clinic Foundation. (2003). *Adult preventive health care screening recommendations.* New Orleans, LA: Ochsner Clinic Foundation.

O'Connor, M., & Whaley, S. (2006). Health care provider advice and risk factors associated with alcohol consumption following pregnancy recognition. *Journal of Studies on Alcohol, 67,* 22–31.

Ocorr, K., Reeves, N. L., Wessells, R. J., Fink, M., Chen, H. S., Akasaka, T., Yasuda, S., Metzger, J. M., Giles, W., Posakony, J. W., & Bodmer, R. (2007). KCNQ potassium channel mutations cause cardiac arrhythmias in Drosophila that mimic the effects of aging. *Proceedings of the National Academy of Sciences, 104,* 3943–3948.

OECD (Organization for Economic Cooperation and Development). (1998). *Education at a glance: OECD indicators, 1998.* Paris: Author.

OECD. (2005). *Math performance of students around the world.* Paris: Author.

Oesterdiekhoff, G. (2007). The reciprocal causation of intelligence and culture: A commentary based on a Piagetian perspective. *European Journal of Personality, 21,* 742–743.

Ogbu, J. (1992). Understanding cultural diversity and learning. *Educational Researcher, 21,* 5–14.

Ogbu, J. (2002). Cultural amplifiers of intelligence: IQ and minority status in cross-cultural perspective. *Race and intelligence: Separating science from myth* (pp. 241–278). Mahwah, NJ: Lawrence Erlbaum Associates.

Ogbu, J. U. (1988). Black education: A cultural-ecological perspective. In H. P. McAdoo (Ed.), *Black families.* Beverly Hills, CA: Sage.

Ogden, C. L., Kuczmarski, R. J., Flegal, K. M., Mei, Z., Guo, S., Wei, R., Grummer-Strawn, L. M., Curtin, L. R., Roche, A. F., & Johnson, C. L. (2002). Centers for Disease Control and Prevention 2000 growth charts for the United States: Improvements to the 1977 National Center for Health Statistics Version. *Pediatrics, 109,* 45–60.

Ogilvy-Stuart, A. L., & Gleeson, H. (2004). Cancer risk following growth hormone use in childhood: Implications for current practice. *Drug Safety, 27,* 369–382.

Oğuz, V., & Akyol, A. K. (2008). Perspective-taking skills of 6-year-old children: Preschool attendance and mothers' and fathers' education and empathetic skills. *Perceptual and Motor Skills, 107,* 481–493.

Okie, S. (2005). *Winning the war against childhood obesity.* Washington, DC: Joseph Henry Publications.

Olafsen, K. S., Rønning, J. A., Handegård, B., Ulvund, S., Dahl, L., & Kaaresen, P. (2012). Regulatory competence and social communication in term and preterm infants at 12 months corrected age. Results from a randomized controlled trial. *Infant Behavior & Development, 35,* 140–149.

Olds, T., Wake, M., Patton, G., Ridley, K., Waters, E., Williams, J., et al. (2009). How do school-day activity patterns differ with age and gender across adolescence? *Journal of Adolescent Health, 44,* 64–72.

Olivardia, R., & Pope, H. (2002). Body image disturbance in childhood and adolescence. In D. Castle & K. Phillips (Eds.), *Disorders of body image.* Petersfield, UK: Wrightson Biomedical Publishing.

Oliver, B., & Plomin, R. (2007). Twins' Early Development Study (TEDS): A multivariate, longitudinal genetic investigation of language, cognition and behavior problems from childhood through adolescence. *Twin Research and Human Genetics, 10,* 96–105.

Oliver, M. B., & Hyde, J. S. (1993). Gender differences in sexuality: A meta-analysis. *Psychological Bulletin, 114,* 29–51.

Ollendick, T. H., Yang, B., King, N. J., Dong, Q., & Akande, A. (1996). Fears in American, Australian, Chinese, and Nigerian children and adolescents: A cross-cultural study. *Journal of Child Psychology and Psychiatry and Allied Disciplines, 37,* 213–220.

Oller, D. K., Eilers, R. E., Urbano, R., & Cobo-Lewis, A. B. (1997). Development of precursors to speech in infants exposed to two languages. *Journal of Child Language, 24,* 407–425.

Olness, K. (2003). Effects on brain development leading to cognitive impairment: A worldwide epidemic. *Journal of Developmental & Behavioral Pediatrics, 24,* 120–130.

Olsen, S. (2009, October 30). Will the digital divide close by itself? *The New York Times.* Retrieved from http://bits.blogs.nytimes.com/2009/10/30/will-the-digital-divide-close-by-itself/.

Olshansky, S. (2011). Trends in longevity and prospects for the future. In R. H. Binstock & L. K. George (Eds.), *Handbook of aging and the social sciences* (7th ed.). San Diego, CA: Elsevier Academic Press.

Olshansky, S. J., Passaro, D. J., Hershow, R. C., Layden, J., Carnes, B. A., Brody, J., Hayflick, L., Butler,

R. N., Allison, D. B., & Ludwig, D. S. (2005, March 17). Special report: A potential decline in life expectancy in the United States in the 21st century. *The New England Journal of Medicine, 352,* 1138–1145.

Olsho, L. W., Harkins, S. W., & Lenhardt, M. L. (1985). Aging and the auditory system. In J. E. Birren & K. W. Schaie (Eds.), *Handbook of the psychology of aging* (2nd ed.). New York: Van Nostrand Reinhold.

Olson, E. (2006, April 27). You're in labor, and getting sleeeepy. *New York Times,* p. C2.

Olson, J. M., Vernon, P. A., & Harris, J. A. (2001). The heritability of attitudes: A study of twins. *Journal of Personality & Social Psychology, 80,* 845–860.

Olson, R. K., Keenan, J. M., Byrne, B., Samuelsson, S., Coventry, W. L., Corley, R., & . . . Hulslander, J. (2011). Genetic and environmental influences on vocabulary and reading development. *Scientific Studies of Reading, 15,* 26–46.

Olson, S. (2003). *Mapping human history: Genes, race, and our common origins.* New York: Mariner Books.

Olson, S. L., Lopez-Duran, N., Lunkenheimer, E. S., Chang, H., & Sameroff, A. J. (2011). Individual differences in the development of early peer aggression: Integrating contributions of self-regulation, theory of mind, and parenting. *Development and Psychopathology, 23,* 253–266.

Oltjenbruns, K., & Balk, D. (2007). Life span issues and loss, grief, and mourning: Part 1: The importance of a developmental context: Childhood and adolescence as an example; Part 2: Adulthood. *Handbook of thanatology: The essential body of knowledge for the study of death, dying, and bereavement* (pp. 143–163). Northbrook, IL: Routledge/Taylor & Francis Group.

O'Luanaigh, C., & Lawlor, B. (2008). Loneliness and the health of older people. *International Journal of Geriatric Psychiatry, 23,* 1213–1221.

Olweus, D. (1995). Bullying or peer abuse at school: Facts and intervention. *Current Directions in Psychological Science, 4,* 196–200.

O'Neal, E. (1997). As American as apple pie. *PsycCRITIQUES, 42,* 998–999.

Onishi, K., & Baillargeon, R. (2005). Do 15-month-old infants understand false beliefs? *Science, 308,* 255–258.

Ono, Y. (1995, October 15). Ads do push kids to smoke, study suggests. *The Wall Street Journal,* pp. B1–B2.

Onslow, M. (1992). Choosing a treatment program for early stuttering: Issues and future directions. *Journal of Speech and Hearing Research, 35,* 983–993.

Opfer, V. D., Henry, G. T., & Mashburn, A. J. (2008). The district effect: Systemic responses to high stakes accountability policies in six southern states. *American Journal of Education, 114,* 299–332.

Orbuch, T. L., House, J. S., Mero, R. P., & Webster, P. S. (1996). Marital quality over the life course. *Social Psychology Quarterly, 58,* 162–171.

Orenstein, P. (1994). *Schoolgirls: Young women, self-esteem, and the confidence gap.* New York: Doubleday.

Oretti, R. G., Harris, B., & Lazarus, J. H. (2003). Is there an association between life events, postnatal depression and thyroid dysfunction in thyroid antibody positive women? *International Journal of Social Psychiatry, 49,* 70–76.

Organization for Economic Cooperation and Development. (1998). *Education at a glance: OECD indicators, 1998.* Paris: Author.

Organization for Economic Cooperation and Development. (2001). *Education at a glance: OECD indicators, 2001.* Paris: Author.

Organization for Economic Cooperation and Development. (2009). *International high school graduation rates.* Montreal: UNESCO Institute for Statistics. World Education Indicators Programme.

Ormont, L. R. (2001). Developing emotional insulation. In L. B. Fugeri (Ed.), *The technique of group treatment:*

The collected papers of Louis R. Ormont. Madison, CT: Psychosocial Press.

Ornstein, P. A., & Elischberger, H. B. (2004). Studies of suggestibility: Some observations and suggestions. [Special issue: Individual and developmental differences in suggestibility]. *Applied Cognitive Psychology, 18,* 1129–1141.

Orr, A. L. (1991). The psychosocial aspects of aging and vision loss. *Journal of Gerontological Social Work, 17,* 1–14.

Ortega, S., Beauchemin, A., & Kaniskan, R. (2008, December). Building resiliency in families with young children exposed to violence: The safe start initiative pilot study. *Best Practices in Mental Health: An International Journal, 4*(1), 48–64.

Ortiz, S. O., & Dynda, A. M. (2005). Use of intelligence tests with culturally and linguistically diverse populations. In D. P. Flanagan & P. L. Harrison (Eds.), *Contemporary intellectual assessment: Theories, tests, and issues.* New York: Guilford Press.

Osofsky, J. (2003). Prevalence of children's exposure to domestic violence and child maltreatment: Implications for prevention and intervention. *Clinical Child & Family Psychology Review, 6,* 161–170.

Osofsky, J. D. (1995a). Children who witness domestic violence: The invisible victims. *Social Policy Report, 9,* 1–16.

Osofsky, J. D. (1995b). The effects of exposure to violence on young children. *American Psychologist, 50,* 782–788.

Ostrager, B. (2010). SMS. OMG! LOL! TTYL: Translating the law to accommodate today's teens and the evolution from texting to sexting. *Family Court Review, 48,* 712–726.

Ostrosky-Solís, F., & Oberg, G. (2006). Neuropsychological functions across the world— Common and different features: From digit span to moral judgment. *International Journal of Psychology, 41,* 321–323.

Ostrov, J., Gentile, D., & Crick, N. (2006, November). Media exposure, aggression and prosocial behavior during early childhood: A longitudinal study. *Social Development, 15,* 612–627.

O'Sullivan, L., Mantsun, M., Harris, K., & Brooks-Gunn, J. (2007). I wanna hold your hand: The progression of social, romantic and sexual events in adolescent relationships. *Perspectives on Sexual and Reproductive Health, 39,* 100–107.

Oswalt, W. (2001). *Eskimos and explorers.* Minneapolis: Sagebrush Educational Resources.

O'Toole, M. L., Sawicki, M. A., & Artal, R. (2003). Structured diet and physical activity prevent postpartum weight retention. *Journal of Women's Health, 12,* 991–998.

Ott, C., Sanders, S., & Kelber, S. (2007). Grief and personal growth experience of spouses and adult-child caregivers of individuals with Alzheimer's disease and related dementias. *The Gerontologist, 47,* 798–809.

Ougrin, D., Zundel, T., Kyriakopoulos, M., Banarsee, R., Stahl, D., & Taylor, E. (2012). Adolescents with suicidal and nonsuicidal self-harm: Clinical characteristics and response to therapeutic assessment. *Psychological Assessment, 24,* 11–20.

Outten, H., Schmitt, M., Garcia, D., & Branscombe, N. (2009). Coping options: Missing links between minority group identification and psychological well-being. *Applied Psychology: An International Review, 58,* 146–170.

Ouwehand, C., de Ridder, D. T., & Bensing, J. M. (2007). A review of successful aging models: Proposing proactive coping as an important additional strategy. *Clinical Psycholgoy Review, 43,* 101–116.

Owen, J. E., Klapow, J. C., Roth, D. L., Nabell, L., & Tucker, D. C. (2004). Improving the effectiveness of adjuvant psychological treatment for women with breast cancer. The feasibility of providing online support. *Psycho-Oncology, 13,* 281–292.

Owens, J. (2008). Socio-cultural considerations and sleep practices in the pediatric population. *Sleep Medicine Clinics, 3,* 97–107.

Owens, S. F., Picchioni, M. M., Rijsdijk, F. V., Stahl, D. D., Vassos, E. E., Rodger, A. K., & . . . Toulopoulou, T. T. (2011). Genetic overlap between episodic memory deficits and schizophrenia: Results from the Maudsley Twin Study. *Psychological Medicine: A Journal of Research in Psychiatry and the Allied Sciences, 41,* 521–532.

Ownby, R. L., Czaja, S. J., Loewenstein, D., & Rubert, M. (2008). Cognitive abilities that predict success in a computer-based training program. *The Gerontologist, 48,* 170–180.

Owsley, C., Stalvey, B., & Phillips, J. (2003). The efficacy of an educational intervention in promoting self-regulation among high-risk older drivers. *Accident Analysis & Prevention, 35,* 393–400.

Oxford, M., Gilchrist, L., Gillmore, M., & Lohr, M. (2006, July). Predicting variation in the life course of adolescent mothers as they enter adulthood. *Journal of Adolescent Health, 39,* 20–26.

Oyebode, J. (2008). Death, dying and bereavement. *Handbook of the clinical psychology of ageing* (2nd ed., pp. 75–94). New York: John Wiley & Sons Ltd.

Oyserman, D., Kemmelmeier, M., Fryberg, S., Brosh, H., & Hart-Johnson, T. (2003). Racial ethnic self-schemas. *Social Psychology Quarterly, 66,* 333–347.

Ozawa, M., Kanda, K., Hirata, M., Kusakawa, I., & Suzuki, C. (2011). Influence of repeated painful procedures on prefrontal cortical pain responses in newborns. *Acta Paediatrica, 100,* 198–203.

Ozawa, M., & Yoon, H. (2003). Economic impact of marital disruption on children. *Children & Youth Services Review, 25,* 611–632.

Pachter, L. M., & Weller, S. C. (1993). Acculturation and compliance with medical therapy. *Journal of Development and Behavior Pediatrics, 14,* 163–168.

Paffenbarger, R. S., Kampert, J. B., Lee, I. M., Hyde, R. T., et al. (1994). Changes in physical activity and other lifeway patterns influencing longevity. *Medicine and Science in Sports and Exercise, 26,* 857–865.

Pagani, L. S., Remblay, R. E., Nagain, D., Zoccolillo, M., Vitaro, F., & McDuff, P. (2004). Risk factor models for adolescent verbal and physical aggression toward mothers. *International Journal of Behavioral Development, 28,* 528–537.

Pagel, J. F. (2000). Nightmares and disorders of dreaming. *American Family Physician, 61,* 2037–2042, 2044.

Paige, R. (2006, December). No Child Left Behind: The ongoing movement for public education reform. *Harvard Educational Review, 76,* 461–473.

Paikoff, R. L., & Brooks-Gunn, J. (1990). Physiological processes: What role do they play during the transition to adolescence? In R. Montemayor, G. R. Adams, & T. P. Gulotta (Eds.), *From childhood to adolescence: A transitional period?* Newbury Park, CA: Sage.

Painter, K. (1997, August 15–17). Doctors have prenatal tests for 450 genetic diseases. *USA Today,* pp. 1–2.

Paisley, T. S., Joy, E. A., & Price, R. J., Jr. (2003). Exercise during pregnancy: A practical approach. *Current Sports Medicine Reports, 2,* 325–330.

Pajkrt, E., Weisz, B., Firth, H. V., & Chitty, L. S. (2004). Fetal cardiac anomalies and genetic syndromes. *Prenatal Diagnosis, 24,* 1104–1115.

Pajulo, M., Helenius, H., & MaYes, L. (2006, May). Prenatal views of baby and parenthood: Association with sociodemographic and pregnancy factors. *Infant Mental Health Journal, 27,* 229–250.

Palan, P. R., Connell, K., Ramirez, E., Inegbenijie, C., Gavara, R. Y., Ouseph, J. A., & Mikhail, M. S. (2005). Effects of menopause and hormone replacement therapy on serum levels of coenzyme Q10 and other lipid-soluble antioxidants. *Biofactors, 25,* 61–66.

Palfai, T., Halperin, S., & Hoyer, W. (2003). Age inequalities in recognition memory: Effects of stimulus presentation time and list repetitions. *Aging, Neuropsychology, & Cognition, 10,* 134–140.

Palincsar, A. S., Brown, A. L., & Campione, J. C. (1993). First-grade dialogues for knowledge acquisition and use. In E. Forman, N. Minick, & C. A. Stone (Eds.), *Contexts for Learning: Sociocultural Dynamics in Children's Development.* New York: Oxford University Press.

Palincsar, A. S., & Klenk, L. (1992). Fostering literacy learning in supportive contexts. *Journal of Learning Disabilities, 25,* 211–225, 229.

Palmore, E. (1975). *The honorable elders: A cross-cultural analysis of aging in Japan.* Durham, NC: Duke University Press.

Palmore, E. (1979). Predictors of successful aging. *Gerontologist, 19,* 427–431.

Palmore, E. B. (1988). *The facts on aging quiz.* New York: Springer.

Palmore, E. B. (1992). Knowledge about aging: What we know and need to know. *Gerontologist, 32,* 149–150.

Palmore, E. B. (1999). *Ageism: Negative and positive.* New York: Springer Publishing Co.

Pandey, S. (2011). Cognitive functioning in children: The role of child abuse, setting and gender. *Journal of the Indian Academy of Applied Psychology, 37,* 98–105.

Paneth, N. S. (1995). The problem of low birthweight. *Future of Children, 5,* 19–34.

Panneton, R. K. (1985). *Prenatal auditory experience with melodies: Effects on postnatal auditory preferences in human newborns.* Unpublished doctoral dissertation, University of North Carolina, Greensboro.

Papaharitou, S., Nakopoulou, E., Kirana, P., Giaglis, G., Moraitou, M., & Hatzichristou, D. (2008). Factors associated with sexuality in later life: An exploratory study in a group of Greek married older adults. *Archives of Gerontology and Geriatrics, 46,* 191–201.

Papousek, H., & Bernstein, P. (1969). The functions of conditioning stimulation in human neonates and infants. In A. Ambrose (Ed.), *Stimulation in early infancy.* New York: Academic Press.

Pappano, L. (1994, November 27). The new old generation. *The Boston Globe Magazine,* pp. 18–38.

Papps, F., Walker, M., Trimboli, A., & Trimboli, C. (1995). Parental discipline in Anglo, Greek, Lebanese, and Vietnamese cultures. *Journal of Cross-Cultural Psychology, 26,* 49–64.

Paquette, D., Carbonneau, R., & Dubeau, D. (2003). Prevalence of father-child rough-and-tumble play and physical aggression in preschool children. *European Journal of Psychology of Education, 18,* 171–189.

Parcel, T. L., & Menaghan, E. G. (1997). Effects of low-wage employment on family well-being. *The Future of Children, 7,* 116–121.

Pardee, P., Norman, G., Lustig, R., Preud'homme, D., & Schwimmer, J. (2007, December). Television viewing and hypertension in obese children. *American Journal of Preventive Medicine, 33*(6), 439–443.

Paris, J. (1999). *Nature and nurture in psychiatry: A predisposition-stress model of mental disorders.* Washington, DC: American Psychiatric Press.

Park, A. (2008, June 23). Living Large. *Time,* pp. 90–92.

Park, H. P., Badzakova-Trajkov, G., & Waldie, K. E. (2012, March 7). Language lateralisation in late proficient bilinguals: A lexical decision fmri study. *Neuropsychologia.* Retrieved from http://www.ncbi.nlm.nih.gov/pubmed/22245007.

Park, K. A., Lay, K., & Ramsay, L. (1993). Individual differences and developmental changes in preschoolers' friendships. *Developmental Psychology, 29,* 264–270.

Park, L., & Maner, J. (2009, January). Does self-threat promote social connection? The role of self-esteem and contingencies of self-worth. *Journal of Personality and Social Psychology, 96,* 203–217.

Park, R. D., & Buriel, R. (1998). Socialization in the family: Ethnic and ecological perspectives. In N. W. Damon & N. Eisnberg (Eds.), *Social, emotional and personality development. Vol, 3. Handbook of child psychology.* New York: Wiley.

Parke, R. D. (1989). Social development in infancy: A twenty-five year perspective. In D. Palermo (Ed.), *Advances in child development and behaviors.* New York: Academic Press.

Parke, R. D. (1990). In search of fathers: A narrative of an empirical journey. In I. Sigel & G. Brody (Eds.), *Methods of family research* (Vol. 1). Hillsdale, NJ: Erlbaum.

Parke, R. D. (1996). *New fatherhood.* Cambridge, MA: Harvard University Press.

Parke, R. D. (2004). Development in the family. *Annual Review of Psychology, 55,* 365–399.

Parke, R. D. (2007). Fathers, families, and the future: A plethora of plausible predictions. In G. W. Ladd (Ed.), *Appraising the human developmental sciences: Essays in honor of Merrill-Palmer Quarterly.* Detroit, MI: Wayne State University Press.

Parke, R., Ornstein, P. A., Rieser, J. J., & Zahn-Waxler, C. (1994). The past as prologue: An overview of a century of developmental psychology. In R. D. Parke, P. A. Ornstein, J. J. Rieser, & C. Zahn-Waxler (Eds.), *A century of developmental psychology.* Washington, DC: American Psychological Association.

Parke, R., Simpkins, S., & McDowell, D. (2002). Relative contributions of families and peers to children's social development. In P. Smith & C. Hart (Eds.), *Blackwell handbook of childhood social development.* Malden, MA: Blackwell Publishers.

Parker, J., Summerfeldt, L., & Hogan, M. (2004). Emotional intelligence and academic success: Examining the transition from high school to university. *Personality & Individual Differences, 36,* 163–172.

Parker, S. T. (2005). Piaget's legacy in cognitive constructivism, niche construction, and phenotype development and evolution. In S. T. Parker & J. Langer (Eds.), *Biology and knowledge revisited: From neurogenesis to psychogenesis.* Mahwah, NJ: Lawrence Erlbaum Associates.

Parker, S., & Langer, J. (Eds.). (2005). *Biology and knowledge revisited: From neurogenesis to psychogenesis.* Mahwah, NJ: Lawrence Erlbaum Associates.

Parker-Pope, T. (2003, December 9). How to give your child a longer life. *The Wall Street Journal,* p. R1.

Parker-Pope, T. (2003, October 21). The case for hormone therapy. *The Wall Street Journal,* pp. R1, R3.

Parker-Pope, T. (2004, May 4). When your spouse makes you sick: Research probes toll of marital stress. *The Wall Street Journal,* p. D1.

Parkes, C. M. (1997). Normal and abnormal responses to stress—A developmental approach. In D. Black, M. Newman, J. Harris-Hendricks, & G. Mezey (Eds.), *Psychological trauma: A developmental approach* (pp. 10–18). London, UK: Gaskell/Royal College of Psychiatrists.

Parks, C. A. (1998). Lesbian parenthood: A review of the literature. *American Journal of Orthopsychiatry, 68,* 376–389.

Parks, C., Sanna, L., & Posey, D. (2003). Retrospection in social dilemmas: How thinking about the past affects future cooperation. *Journal of Personality & Social Psychology, 84,* 988–996.

Parlee, M. B. (1979, October). The friendship bond. *Psychology Today, 13,* 43–45.

Parmalee, A. H., Jr., & Sigman, M. D. (1983). Prenatal brain development and behavior. In P. H. Mussen (Ed.), *Handbook of child psychology* (Vol. 2, 4th ed.). New York: Wiley.

Parmalee, A. H., Wenner, W., & Schulz, H. (1964). Infant sleep patterns from birth to 16 weeks of age. *Journal of Pediatrics, 65,* 572–576.

Parnell, T. F., & Day, D. O. (Eds.). (1998). *Munchausen by proxy syndrome: Misunderstood child abuse.* Thousand Oaks, CA: Sage.

Parritz, R. H., Mangelsdorf, S., & Gunnar, M. R. (1992). Control, social referencing, and the infants' appraisal of threat. In S. Feinman (Ed.), *Social referencing and the social construction of reality in infancy.* New York: Plenum.

Parten, M. B. (1932). Social participation among preschool children. *Journal of Abnormal and Social Psychology, 27,* 243–269.

Pascalis, O., de Haan, M., & Nelson, C. A. (2002). Is face processing species-specific during the first year of life? *Science, 296,* 1321–1323.

Pascoe, J. M. (1993). Social support during labor and duration of labor: A community-based study. *Public Health Nursing, 10,* 97–99.

Pascual-Leone, J., & Johnson, J. (2005). A dialectical constructivist view of developmental intelligence. *Handbook of understanding and measuring intelligence.* Thousand Oaks, CA: Sage Publications, Inc.

Pashos, A., & McBurney, D. (2008). Kin relationships and the caregiving biases of grandparents, aunts, and uncles: A two-generational questionnaire study. *Human Nature, 19,* 311–330.

Pasqualotto, F. F., Lucon, A. M., Sobreiro, B. P., Pasqualotto, E. B., & Arap, S. (2005). Effects of medical therapy, alcohol, smoking, and endocrine disrupters on male infertility. *Revista do Hospital das Clinicas, 59,* 375–382.

Patchin, J., & Hinduja, S. (2006, April). Bullies move beyond the schoolyard: A preliminary look at cyberbullying. *Youth Violence and Juvenile Justice, 4,* 148–169.

Patenaude, A. F., Guttmacher, A. E., & Collins, F. S. (2002). Genetic testing and psychology: New roles, new responsibilities. *American Psychologist, 57,* 271–282.

Paterson, D. S., Trachtenberg, F. L., Thompson, E. G., Belliveau, R. A., Beggs, A. H., Darnall, R., Chadwick, A. E., Krous, H. F., & Kinney, H. C. (2006). Multiple serotonergic brainstem abnormalities in sudden infant death syndrome. *JAMA: Journal of the American Medical Association, 296,* 2124–2132.

Patil, R. R. (2011). MMR vaccination and autism: Learnings and implications. *Human Vaccinations, 7,* 12–21.

Patterson, C. (1994). Children of the lesbian baby boom: Behavioral adjustment, self-concepts, and sex-role identity. In B. Greene & G. Herek (Eds.), *Contemporary perspectives of gay and lesbian psychology: Theory, research, and applications.* Beverly Hills, CA: Sage.

Patterson, C. (1995). Lesbian mothers, gay fathers and their children. In A. R. D'Augelli & C. Patterson (Eds.), *Lesbian, gay and bisexual identities across the lifespan: Psychological perspectives.* New York: Oxford University Press.

Patterson, C. (2003). Children of lesbian and gay parents. In L. Garnets & D. Kimmel (Eds.), *Psychological perspectives on lesbian, gay, and bisexual experiences* (2nd ed.). New York: Columbia University Press.

Patterson, C. (2006, October). Children of lesbian and gay parents. *Current Directions in Psychological Science, 15,* 241–244.

Patterson, C. (2009). Children of lesbian and gay parents: Psychology, law, and policy. *American Psychologist, 64,* 727–736.

Patterson, C. J. (1992). Children of lesbian and gay parents. *Child Development, 63,* 1025–1042.

Patterson, C. J. (1994). Lesbians and gay families. *Current Directions in Psychological Science, 3,* 62–64.

Patterson, C. J. (1995). Families of the baby boom: Parents' division of labor and children's adjustment [Special issue: Sexual orientation and human development]. *Developmental Psychology, 31,* 115–123.

Patterson, C. J. (2002). Lesbian and gay parenthood. In M. Bornstein (Ed.), *Handbook of parenting.* Mahwah, NJ: Erlbaum.

Patterson, C. J. (2007). *Handbook of counseling and psychotherapy with lesbian, gay, bisexual, and transgender clients* (2nd ed.). K. J. Bieschke, R. M. Perez, & K. A. DeBord (Eds.). Washington, DC: American Psychological Association.

Patterson, C., & Friel, L. V. (2000). Sexual orientation and fertility. In G. R. Bentley & N. Mascie-Taylor (Eds.), *Infertility in the modern world: Biosocial perspectives.* Cambridge, UK: Cambridge University Press.

Patterson, C. J., & Redding, R. E. (1996). Lesbian and gay families with children: Implications of social science research for policy. *Journal of Social Issues, 52,* 29–50.

Patterson, K., Dancer, J., & Clark, D. (1990). Myth perceptions of hearing loss, hearing aids, and aging. *Educational Gerontology, 16,* 289–296.

Patterson, M., & Bigler, R. (2006). Preschool children's attention to environmental messages about groups: Social categorization and the origins of intergroup bias. *Child Development, 77,* 847–860.

Pattison, E. M. (1977). *The experience of dying.* Englewood Cliffs, NJ: Prentice Hall.

Patton, G. C., Coffey, C., Carlin, J. B., Sawyer, S. M., Williams, J., Olsson, C. A., & Wake, M. (2011). Overweight and obesity between adolescence and young adulthood: A 10-year prospective cohort study. *Journal of Adolescent Health, 48,* 275–280.

Pauker, S., & Arond, M. (1989). *The first year of marriage: What to expect, what to accept and what you can change.* New York: Warner Books.

Paul, J. P., Catania, J., Pollack, L., Moskowitz, J., Canchola, J., Mills, T., Binson, D., & Stall, R. (2002). Suicide attempts among gay and bisexual men: Lifetime prevalence and antecedents. *American Journal of Public Health, 92,* 1338–1345.

Paul, K., & Moser, K. (2009). Unemployment impairs mental health: Meta-analyses. *Journal of Vocational Behavior, 74,* 264–282.

Paul, P. (2006, January 16). Want a brainier baby? *Time, 167*(3), 104.

Paul, P. (2007, November 21). Tutors for toddlers. *Time,* pp. 91–92.

Paulesu, E., Démonet, J. F., Fazio, F., McCrory, E., Chanoine, V., Brunswick, N., Cappa, S. F., Cossu, G., Habib, M., Frith, C. D., & Frith, U. (2001, March 16). Dyslexia: Cultural diversity and biological unity. *Science, 291,* 2165–2167.

Pauli-Pott, U., Mertesacker, B., & Bade, U. (2003). Parental perceptions and infant temperament development. *Infant Behavior & Development, 26,* 27–48.

Paulson, A. (2012, March 13). US high school graduation rate inches past 75 percent. *Christian Science Monitor.* Retrieved from http://www.csmonitor.com/USA/Education/2012/0319/US-high-school-graduation-rate-inches-past-75-percent.

Pavis, S., Cunningham-Burley, S., & Amos, A. (1997). Alcohol consumption and young people: Exploring meaning and social context. *Health Education Research, 12,* 311–322.

Pavlov, I. P. (1927). *Conditioned reflexes.* London: Oxford University Press.

Paxton, J. M., Ungar, L., & Greene, J. D. (2012). Reflection and reasoning in moral judgment. *Cognitive Science: A Multidisciplinary Journal, 36,* 163–177.

Paxton, S. J., Schutz, H. K., Wertheim, E. H., & Muir, S. L. (1999). Friendship clique and peer influences on body image concerns, dietary restraint, extreme weight-loss behaviors, and binge eating in adolescent girls. *Journal of Abnormal Psychology, 108,* 255–266.

Payne, J. S., Kauffman, J. M., Brown, G. B., & DeMott, R. M. (1974). *Exceptional children in focus.* Columbus, OH: Merrill.

Payne, K., Thaler, L., Kukkonen, T., Carrier, S., & Binik, Y. (2007). Sensation and sexual arousal in circumcised and uncircumcised men. *Journal of Sexual Medicine, 4,* 667–674.

Pear, R. (2000, March 19). Proposal to curb the use of drugs to calm the young. *The New York Times,* p. 1.

Pearlman, D., Zierler, S., Meersman, S., Kim, H., Viner-Brown, S., & Caron, C. (2006, February). Race disparities in childhood asthma: Does where you live matter? *Journal of the National Medical Association, 98,* 239–247.

Pearson, B. Z. (2007). Social factors in childhood bilingualism in the United States. *Applied Psycholinguistics, 28,* 399–410.

Pearson, R. M., Lightman, S. L., & Evans, J. J. (2011). The impact of breastfeeding on mothers' attentional sensitivity towards infant distress. *Infant Behavior & Development, 34,* 200–205.

Peay, H., & Austin, J. (2011) *How to talk with families about: Genetics and psychiatric illness.* New York: W. W. Norton & Co.

Peck, R. C. (1968). Psychological developments in the second half of life. In B. L. Neugarten (Ed.), *Middle age and aging.* Chicago: University of Chicago Press.

Peck, S. (2003). Measuring sensitivity moment-by-moment: A microanalytic look at the transmission of attachment. *Attachment & Human Development, 5,* 38–63.

Peckins, M. K., Dockray, S., Eckenrode, J. L., Heaton, J., & Susman, E. J. (2012). The longitudinal impact of exposure to violence on cortisol reactivity in adolescents. *Journal Of Adolescent Health.* Retrieved from http://www.jahonline.org/article/S1054-139X%2812%2900016-X/abstract.

Pecora, N., Murray, J., & Wartella, E. (2007). *Children and television: Fifty years of research.* Mahwah, NJ: Lawrence Erlbaum Associates.

Pedersen, N. L., Plomin, R., Nesselroade, J. R., & McClearn, G. E. (1992). A quantitative genetic analysis of cognitive abilities during the second half of the life span. *Psychological Science, 3,* 346–353.

Pedersen, S., Vitaro, F., Barker, E. D., & Borge, A. I. H. (2007). The timing of middle-childhood peer rejection and friendship: Linking early behavior to early-adolescent adjustment. *Child Development, 78,* 1037–1051.

Pedersen, S., Yagensky, A., Smith, O., Yagenska, O., Shpak, V., & Denollet, J. (2009). Preliminary evidence for the cross-cultural utility of the type D personality construct in the Ukraine. *International Journal of Behavioral Medicine, 16,* 108–115.

Pedlow, R., Sanson, A., Prior, M., & Oberklaid, F. (1993). Stability of maternally reported temperament from infancy to 8 years. *Developmental Psychology, 29,* 998–1007.

Peirano, P., Algarin, C., & Uauy, R. (2003). Sleep–wake states and their regulatory mechanisms throughout early human development. *Journal of Pediatrics, 143*(Suppl.), S70–S79.

Peisah, C., Latif, E., Wilhelm, K., & Williams, B. (2009). Secrets to psychological success: Why older doctors might have lower psychological distress and burnout than younger doctors. *Aging & Mental Health, 13,* 300–307.

Peisner-Feinberg, E. S., Burchinal, M. R., Clifford, R. M., Culkin, M. L., Howes, C., Kagan, S. L., & Yazejian, N. (2001). The relation of preschool child-care quality to children's cognitive and social developmental trajectories through second grade. *Child Development, 72,* 1534–1553.

Pelham, B., & Hetts, J. (2001). Underworked and overpaid: Elevated entitlement in men's self-pay. *Journal of Experimental Social Psychology, 37,* 93–103.

Pellegrini, A. (2007). Is aggression adaptative? Yes: Some kinds are and in some ways. *Aggression and adaptation: The bright side to bad behavior.* Mahwah, NJ: Lawrence Erlbaum Associates.

Pellegrini, A. D. (2009). *The role of play in human development.* New York: Oxford University Press.

Pellicano, E. (2007). Links between theory of mind and executive function in young children with autism: Clues to developmental primacy. *Developmental Psychology, 43,* 974–990.

Pelligrini, A. D., & Smith, P. K. (1998). Physical activity play: The nature and function of a neglected aspect of play. *Child Development, 69,* 577–598.

Pellis, S. M., & Pellis, V. C. (2007). Rough-and-tumble play and the development of the social brain. *Current Directions in Psychological Science, 16,* 95–98.

Peltonen, L., & McKusick, V. A. (2001, February 16). Dissecting the human disease in the postgenomic era. *Science, 291,* 1224–1229.

Peltzer, K., & Pengpid, S. (2006). Sexuality of 16- to 17- year-old South Africans in the context of HIV/AIDS. *Social Behavior and Personality, 34,* 239–256.

Pempek, T. A., Demers, L. B., Hanson, K. G., Kirkorian, H. L., & Anderson, D. R. (2011). The impact of infant-directed videos on parent–child. *Journal of Applied Developmental Psychology, 32,* 10–19.

Pence, E., & Shepard, M. (1988). Integrating feminist theory and practice: The challenge of the battered women's movement. In K. Yllo & M. Bograd (Eds.), *Feminist perspectives on wife abuse.* Berkeley, CA: Sage.

Pennington, S. B. (1987). Children of lesbian mothers. In F. W. Bozett (Ed.), *Gay and lesbian parents.* New York: Praeger.

Penninx, B., Guralnik, J. M., Ferrucci, L., Simonsick, E. M., Deeg, D., & Wallace, R. B. (1998). Depressive symptoms and physical decline in community-dwelling older persons. *Journal of the American Medical Association, 279,* 1720–1726.

Pennisi, E. (1997, August 1). Transgenic lambs from cloning lab. *Science, 277,* 631.

Pennisi, E. (2000, May 19). And the gene number is...? *Science, 288,* 1146–1147.

Pennisi, E., & Vogel, G. (2000, June 9). Clones: A hard act to follow. *Science, 288,* 1722–1727.

Penuel, W. R., Bates, L., Gallagher, L. P., Pasnik, S., Llorente, C., Townsend, E., & . . . VanderBorght, M. (2012). Supplementing literacy instruction with a media-rich intervention: Results of a randomized controlled trial. *Early Childhood Research Quarterly, 27,* 115–127.

People Weekly. (1995, December 25). Oklahoma journey: Children of J. Denny recover from injuries. *People Weekly, 44,* 136–141.

People Weekly. (2000, May 8). Giant steps. p. 117.

Peplau, L. A., Padesky, C., & Hamilton, M. (1982). Satisfaction in lesbian relationships. *Journal of Homosexuality, 8,* 23–25.

Pepler, D., Jiang, D., Craig, W., & Connolly, J. (2008). Developmental trajectories of bullying and associated factors. *Child Development, 79,* 325–338.

Pereira, A. C., Huddleston, D. E., Brickman, A. M., Sosunov, A. A., Hen, R., McKhann, G. M., Sloan, R., Gage, F. H., Brown, T. R., & Small, S. A. (2007). An in vivo correlate of exercise-induced neurogenesis in the adult dentate gyrus. *Proceedings of the National Academy of Sciences, 104,* 5638–5643.

Pereira-Smith, O., Smith, J., et al. (1988, August). Paper presented at the annual meeting of the International Genetics Congress, Toronto.

Perez, C. M., & Widom, C. S. (1994). Childhood victimization and long-term intellectual and academic outcomes. *Child Abuse & Neglect, 18,* 617–633.

Perez, E. M., Dempers, G., van Heerden, A. E., & Hendricks, M. K. (1997). A comparative study of well nourished and malnourished under-five clinic attenders: Risk factors and caregiver psychosocial functioning. *Southern African Journal of Child and Adolescent Mental Health, 9,* 87–94.

Perez-Brena, N. J., Updegraff, K. A., & Umaña-Taylor, A. J. (2012). Father- and mother-adolescent decision-making in Mexican-origin families. *Journal of Youth and Adolescence, 41,* 460–473.

Peritto, L. A., Holowka, S., & Sergio, L. E. (2004). Baby hands that move to the rhythm of language: Hearing babies acquiring sign languages babble silently on the hands. *Cognition, 93,* 43–73.

Perlmann, J., & Waters, M. (Eds.). (2002). *The new race question: How the census counts multiracial individuals.* New York: Russell Sage Foundation.

Perlmann, R. Y., & Gleason, J. B. (1990, July). *Patterns of prohibition in mothers' speech to children.* Paper presented at the Fifth International Congress for the Study of Child Language, Budapest, Hungary.

Perlmutter, M., & Hall, E. (1992). *Adult development and aging* (2nd ed.). New York: Wiley.

Perlmutter, M., Kaplan, M., & Nyquist, L. (1990). Development of adaptive competence in adulthood. *Human Development, 33,* 185–197.

Perner, J., & Ruffman, T. (2005). Infants' insight into the mind: How deep? *Science, 308,* 214–216.

Perozzi, J. A., & Sanehez, M. C. (1992). The effect of instruction in L1 on receptive acquisition of L2 for bilingual children with language delay. *Language, Speech, and Hearing Services in Schools, 23,* 348–352.

Perreault, A., Fothergill-Bourbonnais, F., & Fiset, V. (2004). The experience of family members caring for a dying loved one. *International Journal of Palliative Nursing, 10,* 133–143.

Perreira, K., Harris, K., & Lee, D. (2007). Immigrant youth in the labor market. *Work and Occupations, 34,* 5–34.

Perrier, L., Mrklas, K., Shepperd, S., Dobbins, M., McKibbon, K., & Straus, S. E. (2011). Interventions encouraging the use of systematic reviews in clinical decision-making: A systematic review. *Journal of General Internal Medicine, 26,* 419–426.

Perrine, N. E., & Aloise-Young, P. A. (2004). The role of self-monitoring in adolescents' susceptibility to passive peer pressure. *Personality & Individual Differences, 37,* 1701–1716.

Perry, T., Steele, C., & Hilliar, A., III. (2003). *Promoting high achievement among African-American students.* Boston: Beacon Press.

Perry, W. G. (1970). *Forms of intellectual and ethical development in the college years.* New York: Holt.

Persson, A., & Musher-Eizenman, D. R. (2003). The impact of a prejudice-prevention television program on young children's ideas about race. *Early Childhood Research Quarterly, 18,* 530–546.

Persson, G. E. B. (2005). Developmental perspectives on prosocial and aggressive motives in preschoolers' peer interactions. *International Journal of Behavioral Development, 29,* 80–91.

Pérusse, D., Dionne, G., Saysset, V., Zoccolillo, M., Tarabulsy, G. M., Tremblay, N., & Tremblay, R. E. (2005). The genetic-environmental etiology of parents' perceptions and self-assessed behaviours toward their 5-month-old infants in a large twin and singleton sample. *Journal of Child Psychology and Psychiatry, 46,* 612–630.

Peters, A. (2003). Isolation or inclusion: Creating safe spaces for lesbian and gay youth. *Families in Society, 84,* 331–337.

Peters, C., Claussen Bell, K. S., Zinn, A., Goerge, R. M., & Courtney, M. E. (2008). *Continuing in foster care beyond age 18: How courts can help.* Chicago: Chapin Hall at the University of Chicago.

Petersen, A. (2000). A longitudinal investigation of adolescents' changing perceptions of pubertal timing. *Developmental Psychology, 36,* 37–43.

Petersen, A. C., & Crockett, L. (1985). Pubertal timing and grade effects on adjustment. *Journal of Youth and Adolescence, 14,* 191–206.

Petersen, A. C., Sarigiani, P. A., & Kennedy, R. E. (1991). Adolescent depression: Why more girls? *Journal of Youth and Adolescence, 20,* 247–271.

Peterson, A. C. (1988, September). Those gangly years. *Psychology Today,* pp. 28–34.

Peterson, B. (2006, June). Generativity and successful parenting: An analysis of young adult outcomes. *Journal of Personality, 74,* 847–869.

Peterson, B. D., & Eifert, G. H. (2011). Using Acceptance and Commitment Therapy to treat infertility stress. *Cognitive And Behavioral Practice, 18,* 577–587.

Peterson, C., & Park, N. (2007). Explanatory style and emotion regulation. In J. J. Gross (Ed.), *Handbook of emotion regulation.* New York: Guilford Press.

Peterson, C., & Roberts, C. (2003). Like mother, like daughter: Similarities in narrative style. *Developmental Psychology, 39,* 551–562.

Peterson, C., Wang, Q., & Hou, Y. (2009). "When I was little": Childhood recollections in Chinese and European Canadian grade school children. *Child Development, 80,* 506–518.

Peterson, D. M., Marcia, J. E., & Carpendale, J. I. M. (2004). Identity: Does thinking make it so? In C. Lightfoot, C. Lalonde, & M. Chandler (Eds.), *Changing conceptions of psychological life.* Mahwah, NJ: Erlbaum.

Peterson, L. (1994). Child injury and abuse-neglect: Common etiologies, challenges, and courses toward prevention. *Current Directions in Psychological Science, 3,* 116–120.

Peterson, M., & Wilson, J. (2004). Work stress in America. *International Journal of Stress Management, 11,* 91–113.

Peterson, R. A., & Brown, S. P. (2005). On the use of beta coefficients in meta-analysis. *Journal of Applied Psychology, 90,* 175–181.

Petit, G., & Dodge, K. A. (2003). Violent children: Bridging development, intervention, and public policy. *Developmental Psychology, Special Issues: Violent Children, 39,* 187–188.

Petitto, L. A. (2002). The acquisition of natural signed languages: Lessons in the nature of human language and its biological foundations. In C. Chamerlain, J. P. Morford, & R. I. Mayberry (Eds.), *Language acquisition by eye.* Mahwah, NJ: Lawrence Erlbaum Associates.

Petitto, L. A., Holowka, S., Sergio, L., Bronna, L., & Ostry, D. L. (2004). Baby hands that move to the rhythm of language: Hearing babies acquiring sign languages babble silently on the hands. *Cognition, 93,* 43–73.

Petitto, L. A., & Marentette, P. F. (1991, March 22). Babbling in the manual mode: Evidence for the ontogeny of language. *Science, 251,* 1493–1496.

Petkoska, J., & Earl, J. (2009). Understanding the influence of demographic and psychological variables on retirement planning. *Psychology and Aging, 24,* 245–251.

Petraitis, J., Flay, B. R., & Miller, T. Q. (1995). Reviewing theories of adolescent substance use: Organizing pieces in the puzzle. *Psychological Bulletin, 117,* 67–86.

Petrashek, A. R., & Friedman, O. (2011). The signature of inhibition in theory of mind: Children's predictions of behavior based on avoidance desire. *Psychonomic Bulletin & Review, 18,* 199–203.

Petrou, S. (2006). Preterm birth—What are the relevant economic issues? *Early Human Development, 82*(2), 75–76.

Pettingale, K. W., Morris, T., Greer, S., & Haybittle, J. L. (1985). Mental attitudes to cancer: An additional prognostic factor. *Lancet, 310,* 750.

Pettit, G. S., Bates, J. E., & Dodge, K. A. (1997). Supportive parenting, ecological context, and children's adjustment: A seven-year longitudinal study. *Child Development, 68,* 908–923.

Pettle, S. A., & Britten, C. M. (1995). Talking with children about death and dying. *Child: Care, Health & Development, 21,* 395–404.

Pew Forum on Religion & Public Life. (2008). *U.S. Religious Landscape Survey.* Washington, DC: Pew Forum on Religion & Public Life.

Pfeiffer, S. I. (2001). Emotional intelligence: Popular but elusive construct. *Roeper Review, 23,* 138–142.

Pfeiffer, S. I., & Stocking, V. B. (2000). Vulnerabilities of academically gifted students. *Special Services in the Schools, 16,* 83–93.

Phelan, P., Yu, H. C., & Davidson, A. L. (1994). Navigating the psychosocial pressures of adolescence: The voices and experiences of high school youth. *American Educational Research Journal, 31,* 415–447.

Philippot, P., & Feldman, R. S. (Eds.). (2004). *The regulation of emotion.* Mahwah, NJ: Lawrence Erlbaum Associates.

Phillips, D. (1992, September). Death postponement and birthday celebrations. *Psychosomatic Medicine, 26,* 12–18.

Phillips, D., Mekos, D., & Scarr, S. (2000). Within and beyond the classroom door: Assessing quality in child care centers. *Early Childhood Research Quarterly, 15,* 475–496.

Phillips, D., & Smith, D. (1990, April 11). Postponement of death until symbolically meaningful occasions. *Journal of the American Medical Association, 269,* 27–38.

Phillips, D. A., & Zimmerman, M. (1990). The developmental course of perceived competence and incompetence among competent children. In R. Sternberg & J. Kolligian (Eds.), *Competence considered.* New Haven, CT: Yale University Press.

Phillips, D. A., Voran, M., Kisker, E., Howes, C., & Whitebook, M. (1994). Child care for children in poverty: Opportunity or inequity? *Child Development, 65,* 472–492.

Phillips, L., & Henry, J. (2008). Adult aging and executive functioning. *Executive functions and the frontal lobes: A lifespan perspective.* Philadelphia: Taylor & Francis.

Phillips, R. D., Wagner, S. H., Fells, C. A., & Lynch, M. (1990). Do infants recognize emotion in facial expressions?: Categorical and "metaphorical" evidence. *Infant Behavior and Development, 13,* 71–84.

Phillips, S., King, S., & DuBois, L. (1978). Spontaneous activities of female versus male newborns. *Child Development, 49,* 590–597.

Phillips-Silver, J., & Trainor, L. J. (2005, June 3). Feeling the beat: Movement influences infant rhythm perception. *Science, 308,* 1430.

Phillipson, S. (2006, October). Cultural variability in parent and child achievement attributions: A study from Hong Kong. *Educational Psychology, 26,* 625–642.

Phinney, J. (2006). Ethnic identity exploration in emerging adulthood. *Emerging adults in America: Coming of age in the 21st century.* Washington, DC: American Psychological Association.

Phinney, J. S. (2005). Ethnic identity in late modern times: A response to Rattansi and Phoenix. *Identity, 5,* 187–194.

Phinney, J. S. (2008). Ethnic identity exploration in emerging adulthood. In D. L. Browning (Ed), *Adolescent identities: A collection of readings.* New York: The Analytic Press/Taylor & Francis Group.

Phinney, J. S., & Alipuria, L. L. (1990). Ethnic identity in college students from four ethnic groups. *Journal of Adolescence, 13,* 171–183.

Phinney, J. S., & Alipuria, L. L. (1996). At the interface of cultures: Multiethnic/multiracial high school and college students. *Journal of Social Psychology, 136,* 139–158.

Phinney, J. S., & Alipuria, L. L. (2006). Multiple social categorization and identity among multiracial, multiethnic, and multicultural individuals: Processes and implications. In R. J. Crips & M. Hewstone (Eds), *Multiple social categorization: Processes, models and applications.* New York: Psychology Press.

Phinney, J. S., Ferguson, D. L., & Tate, J. D. (1997). Intergroup attitudes among ethnic minority adolescents: A causal model. *Child Development, 68,* 955–969.

Phinney, J., Lochner, B., & Murphy, R. (1990). Ethnic identity development and psychological adjustment in adolescence. In A. Stiffman & L. Davis (Eds.), *Advances in adolescent mental health, Vol. 5: Ethnic issues.* Greenwich, CT: JAI Press.

Phipps, M. G., Blume, J. D., & DeMonner, S. M. (2002). *Obstetrics and Gynecology, 100*, 481–486.

Piaget, J. (1932). *The moral judgment of the child.* New York: Harcourt, Brace & World.

Piaget, J. (1952). *The origins of intelligence in children.* New York: International Universities Press.

Piaget, J. (1954). *The construction of reality in the child* (Margaret Cook, Trans.). New York: Basic Books.

Piaget, J. (1962). *Play, dreams and imitation in childhood.* New York: Norton.

Piaget, J. (1983). Piaget's theory. In W. Kessen (Ed.), P. H. Mussen (Series Ed.), *Handbook of child psychology: Vol 1. History, theory, and methods* (pp. 103–128). New York: Wiley.

Piaget, J., & Inhelder, B. (1958). *The growth of logical thinking from childhood to adolescence* (A. Parsons & S. Seagrin, Trans.). New York: Basic Books.

Piaget, J., Inhelder, B., & Szeminska, A. (1960). *The child's conception of geometry.* New York: Basic Books. (Original work published 1948)

Picard, A. (2008, February 14). Health study: Tobacco will soon claim one million lives a year. *The Globe and Mail*, A15.

Picard, E. M., Del Dotto, J. E., & Breslau, N. (2000). Prematurity and low birthweight. In K. O. Yeates & M. D. Ris (Eds.), *Pediatric neuropsychology: Research, theory, and practice. The science and practice of neuropsychology: A Guilford series.* New York: Guilford Press.

Picavet, H. S., & Hoeymans, N. (2004). Health related quality of life in multiple musculoskeletal diseases: SF-36 and EQ-5D in the DMC3 study. *Annals of the Rheumatic Diseases, 63*, 723–729.

Pietrobelli, A., Espinoza, M. C., & De Cristofaro, P. (2008). Childhood obesity: Looking into the future. *Angiology, 11*, 29–34.

Pillay, A. L., & Wassenaar, D. R. (1997). Recent stressors and family satisfaction in suicidal adolescents in South Africa. *Journal of Adolescence, 20*, 155–162.

Pine, K., Wilson, P., & Nash, A. (2007, December). The relationship between television advertising, children's viewing and their requests to Father Christmas. *Journal of Developmental & Behavioral Pediatrics, 28*(6), 456–461.

Ping, R., & Goldin-Meadow, S. (2008). Hands in the air: Using ungrounded iconic gestures to teach children conservation of quantity. *Developmental Psychology, 44*, 1277–1287.

Pingree, A. (2008). Teaching, learning, and spirituality in the college classroom. *Teaching Excellence, 19*, 1–2.

Pinker, S. (1994). *The language instinct.* New York: William Morrow.

Pinker, S. (2005). So how does the mind work? *Mind & Language, 20*, 1–24.

Pintney, R., Forlands, F., & Freedman, H. (1937). Personality and attitudinal similarity among classmates. *Journal of Applied Psychology, 21*, 48–55.

Pipe, M., Lamb, M., Orbach, Y., & Esplin, P. (2004). Recent research on children's testimony about experienced and witnessed events. *Developmental Review, 24*, 440–468.

Piper, W. E., Ogrodniczuk, J. S., Joyce, A. S., & Weidman, R. (2009). Follow-up outcome in short-term group therapy for complicated grief. *Group Dynamics: Theory, Research, and Practice, 13*, 46–58.

Plomin, R. (1994a). Nature, nurture, and social development. *Social Development, 3*, 37–53.

Pipp, S., Easterbrooks, M., & Brown, S. R. (1993). Attachment status and complexity of infants' self- and other-knowledge when tested with mother and father. *Social Development, 2*, 1–14.

Pipp-Siegel, S., & Foltz, C. (1997). Toddlers' acquisition of self/other knowledge: Ecological and interpersonal aspects of self and other. *Child Development, 68*, 69–79.

Pittman, L., & Boswell, M. (2007). The role of grandmothers in the lives of preschoolers growing up in urban poverty. *Applied Developmental Science, 11*(1), 20–42.

Pitts, D. G. (1982). The effects of aging upon selected visual functions. In R. Sekuler, D. Kline, & K. Dismukes (Eds.), *Aging and human visual function.* New York: Alan R. Liss.

Planinsec, J. (2001). A comparative analysis of the relations between the motor dimensions and cognitive ability of pre-school girls and boys. *Kinesiology, 33*, 56–68.

Plante, E., Schmithorst, V., Holland, S., & Byars, A. (2006). Sex differences in the activation of language cortex during childhood. *Neuropsychologia, 44*, 1210–1221.

Plomin, R. (1994a). The genetic basis of complex human behaviors. *Science, 264*, 1733–1739.

Plomin, R. (1994b). *Genetics and experience: The interplay between nature and nurture.* Newbury Park, CA: Sage.

Plomin, R. (1994c). Nature, nurture, and social development. *Social Development, 3*, 37–53.

Plomin, R. (2005). Finding genes in child psychology and psychiatry: When are we going to be there? *Journal of Child Psychology and Psychiatry, 46*, 1030–1038.

Plomin, R. (2007). *Genetics and developmental psychology.* Detroit, MI: Wayne State University Press.

Plomin, R., & Caspi, A. (1998). DNA and personality. *European Journal of Personality, 12*, 387–407.

Plomin, R., & McClearn, G. E. (Eds.). (1993). *Nature, nurture, and psychology.* Washington, DC: American Psychological Association.

Plomin, R., & McGuffin, P. (2003). Psychopathology in the postgenomic era. *Review of Psychology, 54*, 205–228.

Plomin, R., & Rutter, M. (1998). Child development, molecular genetics, and what to do with genes once they are found. *Child Development, 69*, 1223–1242.

Plonczynski, D. J., & Plonczynski, K. J. (2007). Hormone therapy in perimenopausal and postmenopausal women: Examining the evidence on cardiovascular disease risks. *Journal of Gerontological Nursing, 33*, 48–55.

Plosker, G., & Keam, S. (2006). Bimatoprost: A pharmacoeconomic review of its use in open-angle glaucoma and ocular hypertension. *PharmacoEconomics, 24*, 297–314.

Plowfield, L.A. (2007). HIV disease in children 25 years later. *Pediatric Nursing, 33*, 274–278, 273.

Plowman, L., Stevenson, O., Stephen, C., & McPake, J. (2012). Preschool children's learning with technology at home. *Computers & Education, 59*, 30–37.

Poest, C. A., Williams, J. R., Witt, D. D., & Atwood, M. E. (1990). Challenge me to move: Large muscle development in young children. *Young Children, 45*, 4–10.

Polansky, E. (1976). Take him home, Mrs. Smith. *Healthright, 2*(2).

Poling, D., & Evans, E. (2004). Are dinosaurs the rule or the exception? Developing concepts of death and extinction. *Cognitive Development, 19*, 363–383.

Polivka, B. (2006, January). Needs assessment and intervention strategies to reduce lead-poisoning risk among low-income Ohio toddlers. *Public Health Nursing, 23*, 52–58.

Polivy, J., & Herman, C. P. (1991). Good and bad dieters: Self-perception and reaction to a dietary challenge. *International Journal of Eating Disorders, 10*, 91–99.

Polivy, J., & Herman, C. (1999). The effects of resolving to diet on restrained and unrestrained eaters: The "false hope syndrome." *International Journal of Eating Disorders, 26*, 434–447.

Polivy, J., & Herman, C. (2002). If at first you don't succeed: False hopes of self-change. *American Psychologist, 57*, 677–689.

Polkinghorne, D. E. (2005). Language and meaning: Data collection in qualitative research [Special Issue:

Knowledge in context: Qualitative methods in counseling psychology research]. *Journal of Counseling Psychology, 52*, 137–145.

Pollack, W. (1999). *Real boys: Rescuing our sons from the myths of boyhood.* New York: Owl Books.

Pollack, W. (2006). The "war" for boys: Hearing "real boys" voices, healing their pain. *Professional Psychology: Research and Practice, 37*, 190–195.

Pollack, W., Shuster, T., & Trelease, J. (2001). *Real boys voices.* New York: Penguin.

Pollak, S., Holt, L., & Wismer Fries, A. (2004). Hemispheric asymmetries in children's perception of nonlinguistic human affective sounds. *Developmental Science, 7*, 10–18.

Pollatou, E., Karadimou, K., & Gerodimos, V. (2005). Gender differences in musical aptitude, rhythmic ability and motor performance in preschool children. *Early Child Development and Care, 175*, 361–369.

Pollitt, E. (1994). Poverty and child development: Relevance of research in developing countries to the United States. *Child Development, 65*, 283–295.

Pollitt, E., Golub, M., Gorman, K., GranthamMcGregor, S., Levitsky, D., Schürch, B., Strupp, B., & Wachs, T. (1996). A reconceptualization of the effects of undernutrition on children's biological, psychosocial, and behavioral development. *Social Policy Report, 10*, 1–22.

Pollitt, E., Gorman, K. S., Engle, P. L., Martorell, R., & Rivera, J. (1993). Early supplementary feeding and cognition: Effects over two decades. *Monographs of the Society for Research in Child Development, 58*, v–99.

Polman, H., de Castro, B., & van Aken, M. (2008). Experimental study of the differential effects of playing versus watching violent video games on children's aggressive behavior. *Aggressive Behavior, 34*, 256–264.

Pomares, C. G., Schirrer, J., & Abadie, V. (2002). Analysis of the olfactory capacity of healthy children before language acquisition. *Journal of Developmental Behavior and Pediatrics, 23*, 203–207.

Pomerleau, O. F., & Pomerleau, C. S. (1989). A biobehavioral perspective on smoking. In T. Ney & A. Gale (Eds.), *Smoking and human behavior.* New York: Wiley.

Pompili, M., Innamorati, M., Girardi, P., Tatarelli, R., & Lester, D. (2011). Evidence-based interventions for preventing suicide in youths. In M. Pompili & R. Tatarelli (Eds.), *Evidence-based practice in suicidology: A source book.* Cambridge, MA: Hogrefe Publishing.

Pompili, M., Masocco, M., Vichi, M., Lester, D., Innamorati, M., Tatarelli, R., et al. (2009). Suicide among Italian adolescents: 1970–2002. *European Child & Adolescent Psychiatry, 18*, 525–533.

Ponton, L. E. (1999, May 10). Their dark romance with risk. *Newsweek*, pp. 55–58.

Ponton, L. E. (2001). *The sex lives of teenagers: Revealing the secret world of adolescent boys and girls.* New York: Penguin Putnam.

Ponza, M., & Wray, L. (1990). *Evaluation of the food assistance needs of the low-income elderly and their participation in USDA programs: Final results of the elderly programs study.* Princeton, NJ: Mathematical Policy Research.

Poole, D., & Lamb, M. (1998). *Investigative interviews of children: A guide for helping professionals.* Washington, DC: American Psychological Association.

Poon, H. F., Calabrese, V., Scapagnini, G., & Butterfield, D. A. (2004). Free radicals and brain aging. *Clinical Geriatric Medicine, 20*, 329–359.

Poon, L. W. (1985). Differences in human memory with aging: Nature, causes, and clinical implications. In J. E. Birren & K. W. Schaie (Eds.), *Handbook of the psychology of aging* (2nd ed.). New York: Van Nostrand Reinhold.

Pope, A. W., & Bierman, K. L. (1999). Predicting adolescent peer problems and antisocial activities: The relative roles of aggression and dysregulation. *Developmental Psychology, 35*, 335–346.

Pope, H., Olivardia, R., Gruber, A., & Borowiecki, J. (1999). Evolving ideals of male body image as seen through action toys. *International Journal of Eating Disorders, 26,* 65–72.

Popenoe, D. (1987). Beyond the nuclear family: A statistical portrait of the changing family in Sweden. *Journal of Marriage and the Family, 49,* 173–183.

Population Council Report. (1995, May 30). The decay of families is global, studies says. *The New York Times,* p. A5.

Porath, A. J., & Fried, P. A. (2005). Effects of prenatal cigarette and marijuana exposure on drug use among offspring. *Neurotoxicological Teratology, 27,* 267–277.

Porges, S. W., & Lipsitt, L. P. (1993). Neonatal responsivity to gustatory stimulation; The gustatory-vagal hypothesis. *Infant Behavior & Development, 16,* 487–494.

Porter, E. J. (1997). Parental actions to reduce children's exposure to lead: Some implications for primary and secondary prevention. *Family & Community Health, 20,* 24–37.

Porter, E., & Walsh, M. (2005, February 9). Retirement becomes a rest stop as pensions and benefits shrink. *The New York Times,* p. A1.

Porter, F. L., Porges, S. W., & Marshall, R. E. (1988). Newborn pain cries and vagal tone: Parallel changes in response to circumcision. *Child Development, 59,* 495–515.

Porter, M., van Teijlingen, E., Yip, L., & Bhattacharya, S. (2007). Satisfaction with cesarean section: Qualitative analysis of open-ended questions in a large postal survey. *Birth: Issues in Perinatal Care, 34,* 148–154.

Porter, R. H., Balogh, R. D., & Malkin, J. W. (1988). Olfactory influences on mother–infant interactions. In C. Rovee-Collier & L. Lipsitt (Eds.), *Advances in infancy research* (Vol. 5). Norwood, NJ: Ablex.

Portes, A. (2005). English-only triumphs, but the costs are high. *Critical social issues in American education: Democracy and meaning in a globalizing world* (3rd ed.). Mahwah, NJ: Lawrence Erlbaum Associates.

Portes, A., & Rumbaut, R. (2001). *Legacies: The story of the immigrant second generation.* Los Angeles: University of California Press.

Porzelius, L. K., Dinsmore, B. D., & Staffelbach, D. (2001). Eating disorders. In M. Hersen & V. B. Van Hasselt (Eds.), *Advanced abnormal psychology* (2nd ed.). New York: Kluwer Academic/Plenum Publishers.

Posthuma, D., & de Geus, E. (2006, August). Progress in the molecular-genetic study of intelligence. *Current Directions in Psychological Science, 15,* 151–155.

Poulain, M., Doucet, M., Major, G., Drapeau, V., Sériès, F., Boulet, L., et al. (2006, April). The effect of obesity on chronic respiratory diseases: Pathophysiology and therapeutic strategies. *Canadian Medical Association Journal, 174,* 1293–1299.

Poulin-Dubois, D. (1999). Infants' distinction between animate and inanimate objects: The origins of naive psychology. In P. Rochat, *Early social cognition.* Hillsdale, NJ: Lawrence Erlbaum Associates.

Poulin-Dubois, D., Frank, I., & Graham, S. A. (1999). The role of shape similarity in toddlers' lexical extensions. *British Journal of Developmental Psychology, 17,* 21–36.

Poulin-Dubois, D., Serbin, L., & Eichstedt, J. (2002). Men don't put on make-up: Toddlers' knowledge of the gender stereotyping of household activities. *Social Development, 11,* 166–181.

Poulin-Dubois, D., Serbin, L. A., Kenyon, B., & Derbyshire, A. (1994). Infants' intermodal knowledge about gender. *Developmental Psychology, 30,* 436–442.

Poulton, R., & Caspi, A. (2005). Commentary: How does socioeconomic disadvantage during childhood damage health in adulthood? Testing psychosocial pathways. *International Journal of Epidemiology, 23,* 51–55.

Powdthavee, N. (2008). Putting a price tag on friends, relatives, and neighbours: Using surveys of life satisfaction to value social relationships. *Journal of Socio-Economics, 37,* 1459–1480.

Powdthavee, N. (2009). Think having children will make you happy. *The Psychologist, 22,* 308–310.

Powell, G. F., Brasel, J. A., & Blizzard, R. M. (1967). Emotional deprivation and growth retardation simulating idiopathic hypopituitarism: I. Clinical evaluation of the syndrome. *New England Journal of Medicine, 276,* 1272–1278.

Powell, M. B., Thomson, D. M., & Ceci, S. J. (2003). Children's memory of recurring events: Is the first event always the best remembered? *Applied Cognitive Psychology, 17,* 127–146.

Powell, M. B., Wright, R., & Hughes-Scholes, C. H. (2011). Contrasting the perceptions of child testimony experts, prosecutors and police officers regarding individual child abuse interviews. *Psychiatry, Psychology and Law, 18,* 33–43.

Powell, M., Roberts, K., Thomson, D., & Ceci, S. (2007). The impact of experienced versus non-experienced suggestions on children's recall of repeated events. *Applied Cognitive Psychology, 21,* 649–667.

Powell, R. (2004, June 19). Colleges construct housing for elderly: Retiree students move to campus. *The Washington Post,* F13.

Power, T. G. (1999). *Play and exploration in children and animals.* Mahwah, NJ: Erlbaum.

Power, T. G., & Parke, R. D. (1982). Play as a context for early learning: Lab and home analyses. In L. M. Laosa & I. E. Sigal (Eds.), *The family as a learning environment.* New York: Plenum.

Prater, L. (2002). African American families: Equal partners in general and special education. In F. Obiakor & A. Ford (Eds.), *Creating successful learning environments for African American learners with exceptionalities.* Thousand Oaks, CA: Corwin Press, Inc.

Pratt, H., Phillips, E., & Greydanus, D. (2003). Eating disorders in the adolescent population: Future directions. *Journal of Adolescent Research, 18,* 297–317.

Pratt, M. W., Danso, H. A., Arnold, M. L., Norris, J. E., & Filyer, R. (2001). Adult generativity and the socialization of adolescents: Relations to mothers' and fathers' parenting beliefs, styles, and practices. *Journal of Personality, 69,* 89–120.

Pratt, W. F., Mosher, W. D., Bachrach, C., & Horn, M. (1984). *Understanding U.S. fertility: Findings from the National Survey of Family Growth.* Washington, DC: Population Reference Bureau.

Pratto, F., Stallworth, L. M., Sidanius, J., & Siers, B. (1997). The gender gap in occupational role attainment: A social dominance approach. *Journal of Personality and Social Psychology, 72,* 37–53.

Prechtl, H. F. R. (1982). Regressions and transformations during neurological development. In T. G. Bever (Ed.), *Regressions in mental development.* Hillsdale, NJ: Erlbaum.

Prentice, A. (1991). Can maternal dietary supplements help in preventing infant malnutrition? *Acta Paediatrica Scandinaica* (Supp. 374), 67–77.

Prentice, A., Schoenmakers, I., Laskey, M. A., de Bono, S., Ginty, F., & Goldberg, G. R. (2006). Nutrition and bone growth and development. *Proceedings of the Nutritional Society, 65,* 348–360.

Prescott, C. A., Caldwell, C. B., Carey, G., Vogler, G. P., Trumbetta, S. L., & Gottesman, I. I. (2005). The Washington University Twin Study of alcoholism. *American Journal of Medical Genetics, B, Neuropsychiatric Genetics, 31.*

Prescott, C., & Gottesman, I. (1993). Genetically mediated vulnerability to schizophrenia. *Psychiatric Clinics of North America, 16,* 245–267.

Press, I., & McKool, M., Jr. (1972). Social structure and status of the aged: Toward some valid crosscultural generalizations. *Aging and Human Development, 3,* 297–306.

Pressley, M. (1987). Are keyword method effects limited to slow presentation rates? An empirically based reply to Hall and Fuson (1986). *Journal of Educational Psychology, 79,* 333–335.

Pressley, M. (1994). State-of-the-science primary-grades reading instruction or whole language? *Educational Psychologist, 29,* 211–215.

Pressley, M. (1995). *What is intellectual development about in the 1990s? Good information processing.* Mahwah, NJ: Lawrence Erlbaum Associates.

Pressley, M., & Levin, J. R. (1983). *Cognitive strategy research: Psychological foundations.* New York: Springer-Verlag.

Pressley, M., & Schneider, W. (1997). *Introduction to memory development during childhood and adolescence.* Mahwah, NJ: Erlbaum.

Pressley, M., & VanMeter, P. (1993). Memory strategies: Natural development and use following instruction. In R. Pasnak & M. L. Howe (Eds.), *Emerging themes in cognitive development* (Vol. II). New York: Springer-Verlag.

Prezbindowski, A. K., & Lederberg, A. R. (2003). Vocabulary assessment of deaf and hard-of-hearing children from infancy through the preschool years. *Journal of Deaf Studies and Deaf Education, 8,* 383–400.

Price, D. W., & Goodman, G. S. (1990). Visiting the wizard: Children's memory for a recurring event. *Child Development, 61,* 664–680.

Price, R., & Gottesman, I. (1991). Body fat in identical twins reared apart: Roles for genes and environment. *Behavior Genetics, 21,* 1–7.

Priddis, L., & Howieson, N. (2009). The vicissitudes of mother-infant relationships between birth and six years. *Early Child Development and Care, 179,* 43–53.

Prieler, M., Kohlbacher, F., Hagiwara, S., & Arima, A. (2011). Gender representation of older people in Japanese television advertisements. *Sex Roles, 64,* 405–415.

Prigerson, H. (2003). Costs to society of family caregiving for patients with end-stage Alzheimer's disease. *New England Journal of Medicine, 349,* 1891–1892.

Prigerson, H. G., Frank, E., Kasl, S. V., et al. (1995). Complicated grief and bereavement-related depression as distinct disorders: Preliminary empirical validation in elderly bereaved spouses. *American Journal of Psychiatry, 152,* 22–30.

Primedia/Roper. (1998). *Adolescents' view of society's ills.* Storrs, CT: Roper Center for Public Opinion Research.

Primedia/Roper National Youth Survey. (1999). *Adolescents' view of society's ills.* Storrs, CT: Roper Center for Public Opinion Research.

Prince, M. (2000, November 13). How technology has changed the way we have babies. *The Wall Street Journal,* pp. R4, R13.

Prince, R. L., Smith, M., Dick, I. M., Price, R. I., Webb, P. G., Henderson, N. K., & Harris, M. M. (1991). Prevention of postmenopausal osteoporosis. A comparative study of exercise, calcium supplementation, and hormone replacement therapy. *New England Journal of Medicine, 325,* 1189–1195.

Principe, G. F., & Ceci, S. J. (2002). "I saw it with my own ears": The effects of peer conversations on preschoolers' reports of nonexperienced events. *Journal of Experimental Child Psychology, 83,* 1–25.

Probert, B. (2004). "I just couldn't fit in": Gender and unequal outcomes in academic careers. *Gender, Work & Organization, 12,* 50–72.

Pronin, E., Steele, C., & Ross, L. (2004). Identity bifurcation in response to stereotype threat: Women and mathematics. *Journal of Experimental Social Psychology, 40,* 152–168.

Proper, K., Cerin, E., & Owen, N. (2006, April). Neighborhood and individual socio-economic variations in the contribution of occupational physical activity to total physical activity. *Journal of Physical Activity & Health, 3,* 179–190.

Propper, C., & Moore, G. (2006, December). The influence of parenting on infant emotionality: A multi-level psychobiological perspective. *Developmental Review, 26,* 427–460.

Pruchno, R., & Rosenbaum, J. (2003). Social relationships in adulthood and old age. In R. Lerner & M. Easterbrooks (Eds.), *Handbook of psychology: Developmental psychology, Vol. 6.* New York: John Wiley & Sons, Inc.

Pryor, J. B., & Reeder, G. D. (Eds.). (1993). *The social psychology of HIV infection.* Hillsdale, NJ: Erlbaum.

Pryor, J. H., Hurtado, S., Saenz, V. B., Korn, J. S., Santos, J. S., & Korn, W. S. (2006). *The American freshman: National norms for fall 2006.* Los Angeles: Higher Education Research Institute, UCLA.

Pryor, J. H., Hurtado, S., Saenz, V. B., Santos, J. L., & Korn, W. S. (2007). *The American freshman: National norms for fall 2007.* Los Angeles: Higher Education Research Institute, UCLA.

Puchalski, M., & Hummel, P. (2002). The reality of neonatal pain. *Advances in Neonatal Care, 2,* 245–247.

Puckering, C., Connolly, B., Werner, C., Toms-Whittle, L., Thompson, L., Lennox, J., & Minnis, H. (2011). Rebuilding relationships: A pilot study of the effectiveness of the Mellow Parenting Programme for children with Reactive Attachment Disorder. *Clinical Child Psychology and Psychiatry, 16,* 73–87.

Pudrovska, T., Schieman, S., & Carr, D. (2006). Strains of singlehood in later life: Do race and gender matter? *Journals of Gerontology: Series B: Psychological Sciences and Social Sciences, 61B,* S315–S322.

Pugh, K. R., Mencl, W. E., Jenner, A. R., Katz, L., Frost, S. J., Lee, J. R., Shaywitz, S. E., & Shaywitz, B. A. (2000). Functional neuroimaging studies of reading and reading disability (developmental dyslexia). *Mental Retardation & Developmental Disabilities Research Reviews, 6,* 207–213.

Puntambekar, S., & Hubscher, R. (2005). Tools for scaffolding students in a complex learning environment: What have we gained and what have we missed? *Educational Psychologist, 40,* 1–12.

Purdy, M. (1995, November 6). A kind of sexual revolution. *The New York Times,* pp. B1, B6.

Puri, S., Adams, V., Ivey, S., & Nachtigall, R. D. (2011). "There is such a thing as too many daughters, but not too many sons": A qualitative study of son preference and fetal sex selection among Indian immigrants in the United States. *Social Science & Medicine, 72,* 1169–1176.

Putney, N. M., & Bengtson, V. L. (2001). Families, intergenerational relationships, and kinkeeping in midlife. In M. E. Lachman (Ed.), *Handbook of midlife development.* Hoboken, NJ: John Wiley & Sons.

Putterman, E., & Linden, W. (2004). Appearance versus health: Does the reason for dieting affect dieting behavior? *Journal of Behavioral Medicine, 27,* 185–204.

Pyryt, M. C., & Mendaglio, S. (1994). The multidimensional self-concept: A comparison of figted and average-ability adolescents. *Journal for the Education of the Gifted, 17,* 299–305.

Pyszczynski, T., Greenberg, J., & LaPrelle, J. (1985). Social comparison after success and failure: Biased search for information consistent with a self-servicing conclusion. *Journal of Experimental Social Psychology, 21,* 195–211.

Pyszczynski, T., Solomon, S., & Greenberg, J. (2003). *In the wake of 9/11: The psychology of terror.* Washington, DC: American Psychological Association.

Qian, Z-C., & Lichter, D. T. (2007). Social boundary and marital assimilation: Evaluating trends in racial and ethnic intermarriage. *American Sociological Review, 72,* 68–94.

Quade, R. (1994, July 10). Day care brightens young and old. *The New York Times,* p. B8.

Quaid, L. (2011). "Sexting" is more common than you might think. Retrieved from http://www.newsvine.com/_news/2009/12/03/3581416-sexting-is-more-common-than-you-might-think.

Qualter, P., & Munn, P. (2005). The friendships and play partners of lonely children. *Journal of Social and Personal Relationships, 22,* 379–397.

Quartz, S. R. (2003). Toward a developmental evolutionary psychology: Genes, development, and the evolution of human cognitive architecture. In S. J. Scher & F. Rauscher (Eds.), *Evolutionary psychology: Alternative approaches.* Dordrecht, Netherlands: Kluwer Academic Publishers.

Quatromoni, P., Pencina, M., Cobain, M., Jacques, P., & D'Agostino, R. (2006, August). Dietary quality predicts adult weight gain: Findings from the Framingham Offspring Study. *Obesity, 14,* 1383–1391.

Quinn, J. B. (1993, April 5). What's for dinner, Mom? *Newsweek,* p. 68.

Quinn, M. (1990, January 29). Don't aim that pack at us. *Time,* p. 60.

Quinn, P. (2008). In defense of core competencies, quantitative change, and continuity. *Child Development, 79,* 1633–1638.

Quinn, P. C., & Eimas, P. D. (1996). *Perceptual organization and categorization in young infants.* Norwood, NJ: Ablex.

Quinn, P., Uttley, L., Lee, K., Gibson, A., Smith, M., Slater, A., et al. (2008). Infant preference for female faces occurs for same- but not other-race faces. *Journal of Neuropsychology, 2,* 15–26.

Quinnan, E. J. (1997). Connection and autonomy in the lives of elderly male celibates: Degrees of disengagement. *Journal of Aging Studies, 11,* 115–130.

Quintana, C. (1998, May 17). Riding the rails. *The New York Times Magazine,* pp. 22–24, 66.

Quintana, S. (2004). Race, ethnicity, and culture in child development. *Child Development, 75,* v–vi.

Quintana, S. (2007, July). Racial and ethnic identity: Developmental perspectives and research. *Journal of Counseling Psychology, 54*(3), 259–270.

Quintana, S. M., Aboud, F. E., Chao, R. K., Contreras-Grau, J., Cross Jr, W. E., Hudley, C., Hughes, D., Liben, L. S., Nelson-Le Gall, S., & Vietze, D. L. (2006). Race, ethnicity, and culture in child development: Contemporary research and future directions. *Child Development, 77,* 1129–1141.

Quintana, S. M., & McKown, C. (Eds.). (2008). *Handbook of race, racism, and the developing child.* Hoboken, NJ: John Wiley & Sons Inc.

Quintana, S. M., McKown, C., Cross, W. E., & Cross, T. B. (2008). *Handbook of race, racism, and the developing child.* Hoboken, NJ: John Wiley & Sons Inc.

Raag, T. (2003). Racism, gender identities and young children: Social relations in a multi-ethnic, inner-city primary school. *Archives of Sexual Behavior, 32,* 392–393.

Rabain-Jamin, J., & Sabeau-Jouannet, E. (1997). Maternal speech to 4-month-old infants in two cultures: Wolof and French. *International Journal of Behavioral Development, 20,* 425–451.

Rabin, R. (2006, June 13). Breast-feed or else. *The New York Times,* D1.

Rabkin, J., Remien, R., & Wilson, C. (1994). *Good doctors, good patients: Partners in HIV treatment.* New York: NCM Publishers.

Radetsky, P. (1994, December 2). Stopping premature births before it's too late. *Science, 266,* 1486–1488.

Radke-Yarrow, M., Zahn-Waxler, C., & Chapman, M. (1983). Children's prosdcial dispositions and behavior. In E. M. Hetherington (Ed.), *Handbook of child psychology: Vol. 4. Socialization, personality, and social development* (pp. 469–545). New York: Wiley.

Radziszewska, B., & Rogoff, B. (1988). Influence of adult and peer collaborators on children's planning skills. *Developmental Psychology, 24,* 840–848.

Raeburn, P. (2004, October 1). Too immature for the death penalty? *The New York Times Magazine,* 26–29.

Raeff, C. (2004). Within-culture complexities: multifaceted and interrelated autonomy and connectedness characteristics in late adolescent selves. In M. E. Mascolo & J. Li (Eds.), *Culture and developing selves: Beyond dichotomization.* San Francisco, CA: Jossey-Bass.

Raffaelli, M., & Crockett, L. J. (2003). Sexual risk taking in adolescence: The role of self-regulation and attraction to risk. *Developmental Psychology, 39,* 1036–1046.

Rahman, Q., & Wilson, G. (2003). Born gay? The psychobiology of human sexual orientation. *Personality & Individual Differences, 34,* 1337–1382.

Raikes, H., Pan, B. A., Luze, G., Tamis-Le Monda, C. S., Brooks-Gunn, J., Constantine, J., Tarullo, L. B., Raikes, H. A., & Rodriguez, E. (2006). Mother-child book reading in low-income families: Correlations and outcomes during the first three years of life. *Child Development,* 954–953.

Raikkonen, K., Keskivaara, P., Keltikangas, J. L., & Butzow, E. (1995). Psychophysiological arousal related to Type A components in adolescent boys. *Scandinavian Journal of Psychology, 36,* 142–152.

Rainwater, L., & Smeeding, T. (2007). Is there hope for America's low-income children? *Shifting the center: Understanding contemporary families* (3rd ed., pp. 770–779). New York: McGraw-Hill.

Raji, C., Ho, A., Parikshak, N., Becker, J., Lopez, O., Kuller, L., Hua, X., Leow, A., Toga, A., & Thompson, P. (in press). Brain structure and obesity. *Human Brain Mapping.*

Rakison, D., & Oakes, L. (2003). *Early category and concept development: Making sense of the blooming, buzzing confusion.* London: Oxford University Press.

Raman, L., & Winer, G. (2002). Children's and adults' understanding of illness: Evidence in support of a coexistence model. *Genetic, Social, & General Psychology Monographs, 128,* 325–355.

Ramaswamy, V., & Bergin, C. (2009). Do reinforcement and induction increase prosocial behavior? Results of a teacher-based intervention in preschools. *Journal of Research in Childhood Education, 23,* 527–538.

Ramey, C. T., & Ramey, S. L. (1998). Early intervention and early experience. *American Psychologist, 53,* 109–120.

Ramey, S. L. (1999). Head Start and preschool education. *American Psychologist, 54,* 344–346.

Ramos, é., St-André, M., Rey, é., Oraichi, D., & Bérard, A. (2008). Duration of antidepressant use during pregnancy and risk of major congenital malformations. *British Journal of Psychiatry, 192,* 344–350.

Ramsay, D. S. (1980). Onset of unimanual handedness in infants. *Infant Behavior and Development, 3,* 377–385.

Ramsey, P. G. (1995). Changing social dynamics in early childhood classrooms. *Child Development, 66,* 764–773.

Ramsey-Rennels, J. L., & Langlois, J. H. (2006). Infants' differential processing of female and male faces. *Current Directions in Psychological Science, 15,* 59–62.

Ranade, V. (1993). Nutritional recommendations for children and adolescents. *International Journal of Clinical Pharmacology, Therapy, and Toxicology, 31,* 285–290.

Randahl, G. J. (1991). A typological analysis of the relations between measured vocational interests and abilities. *Journal of Vocational Behavior, 38,* 333–350.

Rando, T. A. (1993). *Treatment of complicated mourning.* Champaign, IL: Research Press.

Ranganath, C., Minzenberg, M., & Ragland, J. (2008). The cognitive neuroscience of memory function and dysfunction in schizophrenia. *Biological Psychiatry, 64,* 18–25.

Rank, M. R., & Hirschl, T. A. (1999). Estimating the proportion of Americans ever experiencing poverty during their elderly years. *Journals of Gerontology Series B-Psychological Science and Social Sciences, 54,* S184–S193.

Rankin, B. (2004). The importance of intentional socialization among children in small groups: A conversation with

Loris Malaguzzi. *Early Childhood Education Journal, 32*, 81–85.

Rankin, J., Lane, D., & Gibbons, F. (2004). Adolescent self-consciousness: Longitudinal age changes and gender differences in two cohorts. *Journal of Research on Adolescence, 14*, 1–21.

Ransjö-Arvidson, A. B., Matthiesen, A. S., Lilja, G., Nissen, E., Widströ, A. M., & Unväs-Moberg. (2001). Maternal analgesia during labor disturbs newborn behavior: Effects on breastfeeding, temperature, and crying. *Birth, 28*, 5–12.

Ransom, R. L., Sutch, R., & Williamson, S. H. (1991). Retirement: Past and present. In A. H. Munnell (Ed.), *Retirement and public policy: Proceedings of the Second Conference of the National Academy of Social Insurance,* Dubuque, IA: Kendall/Hunt.

Rao, N., Sun, J., Zhou, J., & Zhang, L. (2012). Early achievement in rural China: The role of preschool experience. *Early Childhood Research Quarterly, 27*, 66–76.

Rao, V. (1997). Wife-beating in rural South India: A qualitative and econometric analysis. *Social Science & Medicine, 44*, 1169–1180.

Rapkin, B. D., & Fischer, K. (1992). Personal goals of older adults: Issues in assessment and prediction. *Psychology and Aging, 7*, 127–137.

Rapp, M., Krampe, R., & Balles, P. (2006, January). Adaptive task prioritization in aging: Selective resource allocation to postural control is preserved in Alzheimer Disease. *American Journal of Geriatric Psychiatry, 14*, 52–61.

Raskauskas, J., & Stoltz, A. D. (2007). Involvement in traditional and electronic bullying among adolescents. *Developmental Psychology, 43*, 564–575.

Ratanachu-Ek, S. (2003). Effects of multivitamin and folic acid supplementation in malnourished children. *Journal of the Medical Association of Thailand, 4*, 86–91.

Rattan, S. I. S., Kristensen, P., & Clark, B. F. C. (Eds.). (2006). *Understanding and modulating aging.* Malden, MA: Blackwell Publishing on behalf of the New York Academy of Sciences, 2006.

Rattner, A., & Nathans, J. (2006, November). Macular degeneration: Recent advances and therapeutic opportunities. *Nature Reviews Neuroscience, 7*, 860–872.

Rauch-Elnekave, H. (1994). Teenage motherhood: Its relationship to undetected learning problems. *Adolescence, 29*, 91–103.

Raudsepp, L., & Liblik, R. (2002). Relationship of perceived and actual motor competence in children. *Perception and Motor Skills, 94*, 1059–1070.

Raup, J., & Myers, J. (1989). The empty nest syndrome: Myth or reality? *Journal of Counseling and Development, 68*, 180–183.

Ravitch, D. (1985). *The troubled crusade: American education 1945–1980.* New York: Basic Books.

Ray, E., & Heyes, C. (2011). Imitation in infancy: The wealth of the stimulus. *Developmental Science, 14*, 92–105.

Ray, L., Bryan, A., MacKillop, J., McGeary, J., Hesterberg, K., & Hutchison, K. (2009). The dopamine D receptor (4) gene exon III polymorphism, problematic alcohol use and novelty seeking: Direct and mediated genetic effects. *Addiction Biology, 14*, 238–244.

Ray, O. (2004). How the mind hurts and heals the body. *American Psychologist, 59*, 29–40.

Raymond, J. (2000). The world of the senses. *Newsweek Special Issue: Your Child*, pp. 16–18.

Rayner, E., Joyce, A., Rose, J., Twyman, M., & Clulow, C. (2005). *Human development: An introduction to the psychodynamics of growth, maturity and ageing* (4th ed.). New York: Routledge.

Rayner, K., Foorman, B. R., Perfetti, C. A., Pesetsky, D., & Seidenberg, M. S. (2002, March). How should reading be taught? *Scientific American*, 85–91.

Raynor, K., & Pollatsek, A. (Eds.). (1989). *The psychology of reading.* Englewood Cliffs, NJ: Prentice-Hall.

Raz, N., Rodrigue, K., Kennedy, K., & Acker, J. (2007, March). Vascular health and longitudinal changes in brain and cognition in middle-aged and older adults. *Neuropsychology, 21*, 149–157.

Razani, J., Murcia, G., Tabares, J., & Wong, J. (2007). The effects of culture on WASI test performance in ethnically diverse individuals. *The Clinical Neuropsychologist, 21*, 776–788.

Rebekah, A., Richert, M. B., Robb, M. A., Fender, J. G., & Wartella, E. (2010). Word learning from BabVideos. *Archives of Pediatric Adolescent Medicine, 164*, 432–437.

Reblin, M., & Uchino, B. (2008). Social and emotional support and its implication for health. *Current Opinions in Psychiatry, 21*, 201–205.

Redcay, E., & Courchesne, E. (2005). When is the brain enlarged in Autism? A meta-analysis of all brain size reports. *Biological Psychiatry, 58*, 1–9.

Reddy, L. A. (2012). III. Group play interventions. In L. A. Reddy (Ed.), *Group play interventions for children: Strategies for teaching prosocial skills.* Washington, DC: American Psychological Association.

Reddy, L. A., & Pfeiffer, S. I. (1997). Effectiveness of treatment of foster care with children and adolescents: A review of outcome studies. *Journal of the American Academy of Child & Adolescent Psychiatry, 36*, 381–588.

Reddy, V. (1999). Prelinguistic communication. In M. Barrett (Ed.), *The development of language* (pp. 25–50). Philadelphia: Psychology Press.

Redsell, S. A., Bedford, H., Siriwardena, A. N., Collier, J., & Atkinson, P. (2010). Exploring communication strategies to use with parents on childhood immunisation. *Nursing Times, 106*, 19–22.

Redshaw, M. E. (1997). Mothers of babies requiring special care: Attitudes and experiences. *Journal of Reproductive & Infant Psychology, 15*, 109–120.

Redshaw, M., & Heikkilä, K. (2011). Ethnic differences in women's worries about labour and birth. *Ethnicity & Health, 16*, 213–223.

Ree, M., & Carretta, T. (2002). g2K. *Human Performance, 15*, 3–24.

Reed, R. K. (2005). *Birthing fathers: The transformation of men in American rites of birth.* New Brunswick, NJ: Rutgers University Press.

Rees, A. (2003). How homophobia hurts children: Nurturing diversity at home, at school, and in the community. *Sex Roles, 49*, 555–556.

Rees, S., Harding, R., & Walker, D. (2011). The biological basis of injury and neuroprotection in the fetal and neonatal brain. *International Journal of Developmental Neuroscience, 29*, 551–563.

Reese, E., & Cox, A. (1999). Quality of adult book reading affects children's emergent literacy. *Developmental Psychology, 35*, 20–28.

Reese, E., & Newcombe, R. (2007). Training mothers in elaborative reminiscing enhances children's autobiographical memory and narrative. *Child Development, 78*, 1153–1170.

Rego, A. (2006). The alphabetic principle, phonics, and spelling: Teaching students the code. *Reading assessment and instruction for all learners* (pp. 118–162). New York: Guilford Press.

Reichert, F., Menezes, A., Wells, J., Dumith, C., & Hallal, P. (2009). Physical activity as a predictor of adolescent body fatness: A systematic review. *Sports Medicine, 39*, 279–294.

Reid, K. J., Zeldow, M., Teplin, L. A., McClelland, G. M., Atom, K. A., & Zee, P. C. (2002). *Steep habits of juvenile detainees in the Chicago area.* Paper presented at the annual meeting of the American Academy of Neurology, Denver.

Reid, M., Miller, W., & Kerr, E. (2004). Sex-based glass ceilings in U.S. state-level bureaucracies, 1987–1997. *Administration & Society, 36*, 377–405.

Reifman, A. (2000). Revisiting the bell curve. *Psycoloquy, 11*.

Reifsteck, J. (2005). Failure and success in foster care programs. *North American Journal of Psychology, 7*, 313–326.

Reiner, W. G., & Gearhart, J. P. (2004). Discordant sexual identity in some genetic males with cloacal exstrophy assigned to female sex at birth. *The New England Journal of Medicine, 350*, 333–341.

Reinis, S., & Goldman, J. M. (1980). *The development of the brain: Biological and functional perspectives.* Springfield, IL: Charles C Thomas.

Reis, H. T., Collins, W. A., & Berscheid, E. (2000). The relationship context of human behavior and development. *Psychological Bulletin, 126*, 844–872.

Reis, S., & Renzulli, J. (2004). Current research on the social and emotional development of gifted and talented students: good news and future possibilities. *Psychology in the Schools, 41*, 119–130.

Reiss, I. L. (1960). *Premarital sexual standards in America.* New York: Free Press.

Reiss, M. J. (1984). Human sociobiology. *Zygon Journal of Religion and Science, 19*, 117–140.

Reissland, N. (1988). Neonatal imitation in the first hour of life: Observations in rural Nepal. *Developmental Psychology, 24*, 450–469.

Reissland, N., & Shepherd, J. (2006, March). The effect of maternal depressed mood on infant emotional reaction in a surprise-eliciting situation. *Infant Mental Health Journal, 27*, 173–187.

Reitman, V. (1994, February 15). Tots do swimmingly in language-immersion programs. *The Wall Street Journal*, p. B1.

Rembis, M. (2009). (Re)defining disability in the "genetic age": Behavioral genetics, "new" eugenics and the future of impairment. *Disability & Society, 24*, 585–597.

Remien, R., & Rabkin, J. (2002). Managing chronic disease: Individual counseling with medically ill patients. *Innovative approaches to health psychology: Prevention and treatment lessons from AIDS* (pp. 117–139). Washington, DC: American Psychological Association.

Remondet, J. H., & Hansson, R. O. (1991). Jobrelated threats to control among older employees. *Journal of Social Issues, 47*, 129–141.

Renkl, M. (2009). Renkl, M. Five facts about kids' social lives. Retrieved from http://www.parenting.com/article/Child/Development/5-Facts-About-Kids-Social-Lives/1.

Renner, L., & Slack, K. (2006, June). Intimate partner violence and child maltreatment: Understanding intra- and intergenerational connections. *Child Abuse & Neglect, 30*, 599–617.

Rennie, S., Muula, A., & Westreich, D. (2007). Male circumcision and HIV prevention: Ethical, medical and public health tradeoffs in low-income countries. *Journal of Medical Ethics, 33*, 357–361.

Reproductive Medicine Associates of New Jersey. (2002). *Older women and risks of pregnancy.* Princeton, NJ: American Society for Reproductive Medicine.

Reschly, D. J. (1996). Identification and assessment of students with disabilities. *The Future of Children, 6*, 40–53.

Rescorla, L., Alley, A., & Christine, J. (2001). Word frequencies in toddlers' lexicons. *Journal of Speech, Language, & Hearing Research, 44*, 598–609.

Resnick, B. (2000). A seven step approach to starting an exercise program for older adults. *Patient Education & Counseling, 39*, 243–252.

Resnick, M. D., Bearman, P. S., Blum, R. W., Bauman, K. E., Harris, M. R., Jones, L., Tabor, J., Beuhring, T., Sieving, R., Shew, M., Ireland, M., Bearinger, L. H., & Udry, J. R. (1997). Protecting adolescents from harm: Findings from the National Longitudinal Study on Adolescent Health. *Journal of the American Medical Association, 278*, 823–832.

Ressner, J. (2001, March 6). When a coma isn't one. *Time Magazine*, p. 62.

Resta, R., Biesecker, B. B., Bennett, R. L., Blum, S., Estabrooks. H. S., Strecker, M. N., & Williams J. L. (2006). A new definition of genetic counseling: National Society of Genetic Counselors' Task Force Report. *Journal of Genetic Counseling, 15*, 77–83.

Rethorst, C., Wipfli, B., & Landers, D. (2009). The antidepressive effects of exercise: A meta-analysis of randomized trials. *Sports Medicine, 39*, 491–511.

Rettew, D. (2008). In this issue/abstract thinking: Prenatal environment and mental health outcomes. *Journal of the American Academy of Child & Adolescent Psychiatry, 47*, 1101–1102.

Reuters Health eLine. (2002, June 26). Baby's injuring points to danger of kids imitating television. *Reuters Health eLine.*

Reutzel, D., Fawson, P., & Smith J. (2006). Words to go!: Evaluating a first-grade parent involvement program for "making" words at home. *Reading Research and Instruction, 45*, 119–159.

Rey, F. (2011). A re-examination of defining moments in Vygotsky's work and their implications for his continuing legacy. *Mind, Culture, and Activity, 18*, 257–275.

Reyna, V., Chapman, S., Dougherty, M., & Confrey, J. (Eds.). (2012). *The adolescent brain: Learning, reasoning, and decision making.* Washington, DC: American Psychological Association.

Reyna, V. F. (1997). Conceptions of memory development with implications for reasoning and decision making. In R. Vasta (Ed.), *Annals of child development: A research annual* (Vol. 12, pp. 87–118). London, UK: Jessica Kingsley Publishers.

Reyna, V. F., & Dougherty, M. R. (2012). Paradoxes of the adolescent brain in cognition, emotion, and rationality. In V. F. Reyna, S. B. Chapman, M. R. Dougherty, J. Confrey, V. F. Reyna, S. B. Chapman, … J. Confrey (Eds.), *The adolescent brain: Learning, reasoning, and decision making.* Washington, DC: American Psychological Association.

Reyna, V. F., & Farley, F. (2006). Risk and rationality in adolescent decision making. *Psychological Science in the Public Interest, 7*, 1–44.

Rhoades, G., Stanley, S., & Markman, H. (2006, December). Pre-engagement cohabitation and gender asymmetry in marital commitment. *Journal of Family Psychology, 20*, 553–560.

Rhoades, G., Stanley, S., & Markman, H. (2009). The pre-engagement cohabitation effect: A replication and extension of previous findings. *Journal of Family Psychology, 23*, 107–111.

Rhodes, G. (2006). The evolutionary psychology of facial beauty. *Annual Review of Psychology, 57*, 199–226.

Rhodes, R., Mitchell, S., Miller, S., Connor, S., & Teno, J. (2008). Bereaved family members' evaluation of hospice care: What factors influence overall satisfaction with services? *Journal of Pain and Symptom Management, 35*, 365–371.

Rholes, W., Simpson, J., Tran, S., Martin, A., & Friedman, M. (2007, March). Attachment and information seeking in romantic relationships. *Personality and Social Psychology Bulletin, 33*, 422–438.

Rhule, D. (2005). Take care to do no harm: Harmful interventions for youth problem behavior. *Professional Psychology: Research and Practice, 36*, 618–625.

Ribeiro, O., & Paul, C. (2008). Older male carers and the positive aspects of care. *Ageing & Society, 28*, 165–183.

Ricciardelli, L. A. (1992). Bilingualism and cognitive development in relation to threshold theory. *Journal of Psycholinguistic Research, 21*, 301–316.

Ricciardelli, L., & McCabe, M. (2003). Sociocultural and individual influences on muscle gain and weight loss strategies among adolescent boys and girls. *Psychology in the Schools, 40*, 209–224.

Ricciardelli, L. A., & McCabe, M. P. (2004). A biopsychosocial model of disordered eating and the pursuit of muscularity in adolescent boys. *Psychological Bulletin, 130*, 179–205.

Ricciuti, H. N. (1993). Nutrition and mental development. *Current Directions in Psychological Science, 2*, 43–46.

Rice, F. P. (1999). *Intimate relationships, marriages, & families* (4th ed.). Mountain View, CA: Mayfield.

Rice, M. L., Huston, A. C., Truglio, R., & Wright, J. (1990). Words from "Sesame Street": Learning vocabulary while viewing. *Developmental Psychology, 26*(3), 421–428.

Richards, G. (2012). *"Race," racism and psychology: Towards a reflexive history* (2nd ed.). New York: Routledge/Taylor & Francis Group.

Richards, H. D., Bear, G. G., Stewart, A. L., & Norman, A. D. (1992). Moral reasoning and classroom conduct: Evidence of a curvilinear relationship. *Merrill-Palmer Quarterly, 38*, 176–190.

Richards, M. H., Casper, R. C., Larson, R. W. (1990). Weight and eating concerns among pre- and young adolescent boys and girls. *Journal of Adolescent Health Care, 11*, 203–209.

Richards, M. H., Crowe, P. A., Larson, R., & Swarr, A. (1998). Developmental patterns and gender differences in the experience of peer companionship during adolescence. *Child Development, 69*, 154–163.

Richards, M. H., & Duckett, E. (1991). Maternal employment and adolescents. In J. V. Lerner & N. Galambos (Eds.), *Employed mothers and their children.* New York: Garland.

Richards, M. H., & Duckett, E. (1994). The relationship of maternal employment to early adolescent daily experience with and without parents. *Child Development, 65*, 225–236.

Richards, M. H., Crowe, P. A., Larson, R., & Swarr, A. (1998). Developmental patterns and gender differences in the experience of peer companionship during adolescence. *Child Development, 69*, 154–163.

Richards, M. P. M. (1996). The childhood environment and the development of sexuality. In C. J. K. Henry & S. J. Ulijaszek (Eds.), *Long-term consequences of early environment: Growth, development and the lifespan developmental perspective.* Cambridge, UK: Cambridge University Press.

Richards, R., Kinney, D. K., Benet, M., & Merzel, A. P. C. (1990). Assessing everyday creativity: Characteristics of the lifetime creativity scales and validation with three large samples. *Journal of Personality and Social Psychology, 54*, 476–485.

Richardson, C. B., Mulvey, K., & Killen, M. (2012). Extending social domain theory with a process-based account of moral judgments. *Human Development, 55*, 4–25.

Richardson, G. A., & Day, N. L. (1994). Detrimental effects of prenatal cocaine exposure: Illusion or reality? *Journal of the American Academy of Child & Adolescent Psychiatry, 33*, 28–34.

Richardson, G. A., Ryan, C., & Willford, J. (2002). Prenatal alcohol and marijuana exposure: Effects on neuropsychological outcomes at 10 years. *Neurotoxicology and Teratology, 24* [Special Issue], 311–320.

Richardson, G., Goldschmidt, L., & Willford, J. (2009). Continued effects of prenatal cocaine use: Preschool development. *Neurotoxicology and Teratology, 31*, 325–333.

Richardson, H., Walker, A., & Horne, R. (2009). Maternal smoking impairs arousal patterns in sleeping infants. *Sleep: Journal of Sleep and Sleep Disorders Research, 32*, 515–521.

Richardson, K., & Norgate, S. (2007). A critical analysis of IQ studies of adopted children. *Human Development, 49*, 319–335.

Richardson, V., & Champion, V. (1992). The relationship of attitudes, knowledge, and social support to breastfeeding. *Issues in Comprehensive Pediatric Nursing, 15*, 183–197.

Richert, A. J. (2011). Johnson's philosophy of personal meaning and theoretical integration. *Journal of Psychotherapy Integration, 21*, 400–411.

Richeson, N., & Thorson, J. (2002). The effect of autobiographical writing on the subjective well-being of older adults. *North American Journal of Psychology, 4*, 395–404.

Rick, S., & Douglas, D. (2007). Neurobiologlcal effects of childhood abuse. *Journal of Psychosocial Nursing & Mental Health Services, 45*, 47–54.

Rickel, A. U., & Becker, E. (1997). *Keeping children from harm's way: How national policy affects psychological development.* Washington, DC: American Psychological Association.

Rickford, J. R. (2006). Linguistics, education and the Ebonics firestorm. In S. J. Nero (Ed.), *Dialects, Englishes, Creoles, and education.* Mahwah, NJ: Lawrence Erlbaum Associates.

Rideout, V. (2011). *Zero to eight: Children's media use in America.* San Francisco: Common Sense Media.

Rideout, V. J., Vandewater, E. A., & Wartella, E. A. (2003). *Zero to six: Electronic media in the lives of infants, toddlers and preschoolers.* Menlo Park, CA: Henry J. Kaiser Foundation.

Riebe, D., Burbank, P., & Garber, C. (2002). Setting the stage for active older adults. In P. Burbank & D. Riebe (Eds.), *Promoting exercise and behavior change in older adults: Interventions with the transtheoretical mode.* New York: Springer Publishing Co.

Rigby, K., & Bagshaw, D. (2003). Prospects of adolescent students collaborating with teachers in addressing issues of bullying and conflict in schools. *Educational Psychology, 23*, 535–546.

Riley, K. (2008). Language socialization. *The handbook of educational linguistics.* Malden, MA: Blackwell Publishing.

Riley, L., & Bowen, C. (2005, January). The sandwich generation: Challenges and coping strategies of multigenerational families. *The Family Journal, 13*, 52–58.

Rimer, B. K., Meissner, H., Breen, N., Legler, J., & Coyne, C. A. (2001). Social and behavioral interventions to increase breast cancer screening. In N. Schneiderman & M. A. Speers (Eds.), *Integrating behavioral and social sciences with public health.* Washington, DC: American Psychological Association.

Rimm, S. B., & Lovance, K. J. (1992). The use of subject and grade skipping for the prevention and reversal of underachievement. Special Issue: Challenging the gifted: Grouping and acceleration. *Gifted Child Quarterly, 36*, 100–105.

Rinaldi, C. (2002). Social conflict abilities of children identified as sociable, aggressive, and isolated: Developmental implications for children at-risk for impaired peer relations. *Developmental Disabilities Bulletin, 30*, 77–94.

Ripple, C. H., Gilliam, W. S., Chanana, N., & Zigler, E. (1999). Will fifty cooks spoil the broth? The debate over entrusting Head Start to the states. *American Psychologist, 54*, 327–343.

Ripple, C., & Zigler, E. (2003). Research, policy, and the federal role in prevention initiatives for children. *American Psychologist, 58*, 482–490.

Riso, L., & McBride, C. (2007). Introduction: A return to a focus on cognitive schemas. *Cognitive schemas and core beliefs in psychological problems: A scientist-practitioner guide.* Washington, DC: American Psychological Association.

Ritchie, L. (2003). Adult day care: Northern perspectives. *Public Health Nursing, 20*, 120–131.

Ritzen, E. M. (2003). Early puberty: What is normal and when is treatment indicated? *Hormone Research, 60*(Suppl.), 31–34.

Rivas-Drake, D. (2012). Ethnic identity and adjustment: The mediating role of sense of community. *Cultural Diversity and Ethnic Minority Psychology.* Retrieved from http://www.ncbi.nlm.nih.gov/pubmed/22309502.

Rivera-Gaziola, M., Silva-Pereyra, J., & Kuhl, P. K. (2005). Brain potentials to native and non-native speech contrasts in 7- and 11-month-old American infants. *Developmental Science, 8,* 162–172.

Rizza, M. G., & Morrison, W. F. (2003). Uncovering stereotypes and identifying characteristics of gifted students and students with emotional/behavioral disabilities. *Roeper Review, 25,* 73–77.

Rizzo, T. A., Metzger, B. E., Dooley, S. L., & Cho, N. H. (1997). Early malnutrition and child neurobehavioral development: Insights from the study of children of diabetic mothers. *Child Development, 68,* 26–38.

Robb, A., & Dadson, M. (2002). Eating disorders in males. *Child & Adolescent Psychiatric Clinics of North America, 11,* 399–418.

Robb, M., Richert, R., & Wartella, E. (2009). Just a talking book? Word learning from watching baby videos. *British Journal of Developmental Psychology, 27,* 27–45.

Robbins, M. W. (1990, December 10). Sparing the child: How to intervene when you suspect abuse. *The New York Times Magazine,* pp. 42–53.

Robbins, M., Francis, L. J., & Edwards, B. (2008). Prayer, personality and happiness: A study among undergraduate students in Wales. *Mental Health, Religion & Culture, 11,* Special Issue, 93–99.

Robergeau, K., Joseph, J., & Silber, T. (2006, December). Hospitalization of children and adolescents for eating disorders in the state of New York. *Journal of Adolescent Health, 39,* 806–810.

Roberto, K. A. (1987). Exchange and equity in friendships. In R. G. Admas & R. Blieszner (Eds.), *Older adult friendships: Structure and process.* Newbury Park, CA: Sage.

Roberto, K., & Jarrott, S. (2008). Family caregivers of older adults: A life span perspective. *Family Relations, 57,* 100–111.

Roberts, B., Helson, R., & Klohnen, E. (2002). Personality development and growth in women across 30 years: Three perspectives. *Journal of Personality, 70,* 79–102.

Roberts, B. W., Walton, K. E., & Viechtbauer, W. (2006). Patterns of mean-level change in personality traits across the life course: A meta-analysis of longitudinal studies. *Psychological Bulletin, 132,* 1–25.

Roberts, E. (2007). Extra embryos: The ethics of cryopreservation in Ecuador and elsewhere. *American Ethnologist, 34,* 181–199.

Roberts, K. E., Schwartz, D., & Hart, T. A. (2011). Social anxiety among lesbian, gay, bisexual, and transgender adolescents and young adults. In C. A. Alfano & D. C. Beidel (Eds.), *Social anxiety in adolescents and young adults: Translating developmental science into practice.* Washington, DC: American Psychological Association.

Roberts, R. D., & Lipnevich, A. A. (2012). From general intelligence to multiple intelligences: Meanings, models, and measures. In K. R. Harris, S. Graham, T. Urdan, S. Graham, J. M. Royer, M. Zeidner, … M. Zeidner (Eds.), *APA educational psychology handbook, Vol 2: Individual differences and cultural and contextual factors.* Washington, DC: American Psychological Association.

Roberts, R. D., Zeidner, M., & Matthews, G. (2001). Does emotional intelligence meet traditional standards for an intelligence? Some new data and conclusions. *Emotion, 1,* 196–231.

Roberts, R. E., Phinney, J. S., Masse, L. C., Chen, Y. R., Roberts, C. R., & Romero, A. (1999). The structure of ethnic identity of young adolescents from diverse ethnocultural groups. *Journal of Early Adolescence, 19,* 301–322.

Roberts, R., Roberts, C., & Duong, H. (2009). Sleepless in adolescence: Prospective data on sleep deprivation, health and functioning. *Journal of Adolescence, 32,* 1045–1057.

Roberts, R. E., Roberts, C., & Xing, Y. (2011). Restricted sleep among adolescents: Prevalence, incidence, persistence, and associated factors. *Behavioral Sleep Medicine, 9,* 18–30.

Roberts, S. (2006, Ocotber 15). It's official: To be married means to be outnumbered. *The New York Times,* 22.

Roberts, S. (2007, January 16). 51% of women are now living without spouse. *The New York Times,* p. A1.

Roberts, S. (2009, November 24). Economy is forcing young adults back home in big numbers, survey finds. *New York Times,* p. A16.

Robertson, S. S. (1982). Intrinsic temporal patterning in the spontaneous movement of awake neonates. *Child Development, 53,* 1016–1021.

Robertson, W., Thorogood, M., Inglis, N., Grainger, C., & Stewart-Brown, S. (2012). Two-year follow-up of the "Families for Health" programme for the treatment of childhood obesity. *Child: Care, Health and Development, 38,* 229–236.

Robertson Blackmore, E., Côté-Arsenault, D., Tang, W., Glover, V., Evans, J., Golding, J., & O'Connor, T. G. (2011). Previous prenatal loss as a predictor of perinatal depression and anxiety. *British Journal of Psychiatry, 198,* 373–378.

Robins, R. W., & Trzesniewski, K. H. (2005). Self-esteem development across the lifespan. *Current Directions in Psychological Science, 14,* 158–162.

Robinson, A. J., & Pascalis, O. (2004). Development of flexible visual recognition memory in human infants. *Developmental Science, 7,* 527–533.

Robinson, A., & Stark, D. R. (2005). *Advocates in action.* Washington, DC: National Association for the Education of Young Children.

Robinson, D. L. (1997). Age differences, cerebral arousability, and human intelligence. *Personality and Individual Differences, 23,* 601–618.

Robinson, G. (2002). Cross-cultural perspectives on menopause. In A. Hunter & C. Forden (Eds.), *Readings in the psychology of gender: Exploring our differences and commonalities.* Needham Heights, MA: Allyn & Bacon.

Robinson, G. E. (2004, April 16). Beyond nature and nurture. *Science, 304,* 397–399.

Robinson, J. P., & Bianchi, S. (1997, December). The children's hours. *American Demographics,* pp. 20–23.

Robinson, J. P., & Godbey, G. (1997). *Time for life: The surprising ways Americans use their time.* College Park: Pennsylvania State University Press.

Robinson, N. M., Zigler, E., & Gallagher, J. J. (2000). Two tails of the normal curve: Similarities and differences in the study of mental retardation and giftedness. *American Psychologist, 55,* 1413–1421.

Robinson, W. P., & Gillibrand, E. (2004, May 14). Single-sex teaching and achievement in science. *International Journal of Science Education, 26,* 659.

Rochat, P. (Ed.). (1999). *Early social cognition: Understanding others in the first months of life.* Mahwah, NJ: Erlbaum.

Rochat, P. (2004). Emerging co-awareness. In G. Bremnery & A. Slater (Eds.), *Theories of infant development.* Maiden, MA: Blackwell Publishers.

Rochat, P., & Goubet, N. (1995). Development of sitting and reaching in 5- and 6-month-old infants. *Infant Behavior and Development, 18,* 53–68.

Roche, T. (2000, November 13). The crisis of foster care. *Time,* pp. 74–82.

Rodgers, K. A., & Summers, J. J. (2008). African American students at predominantly white institutions: A motivational and self-systems approach to understanding retention. *Educational Psychology Review, 20,* 171–190.

Rodkin, P. C., Farmer, T. W., Pearl, R., & Van Acker, R. (2000). Heterogeneity of popular boys: Antisocial and prosocial configurations. *Developmental Psychology, 36,* 14–24.

Rodkin, P. C., & Ryan, A. M. (2012). Child and adolescent peer relations in educational context. In K. R. Harris, S. Graham, T. Urdan, S. Graham, J. M. Royer, M. Zeidner, … M. Zeidner (Eds.), *APA educational psychology handbook, Vol 2: Individual differences and cultural and contextual factors.* Washington, DC: American Psychological Association.

Rodrigues, T., & Barros, H. (2007). Comparison of risk factors for small-for-gestational-age and preterm in a Portuguese cohort of newborns. *Maternal & Child Health Journal, 11,* 417–424.

Rodríguez Martín, J. (2012). An index of child health in the least developed countries (LDCs) of Africa. *Social Indicators Research, 105,* 309–322.

Roecke, C., & Cherry, K. (2002). Death at the end of the 20th century: Individual processes and developmental tasks in old age. *International Journal of Aging & Human Development, 54,* 315–333.

Roehrig, M., Masheb, R., White, M., & Grilo, C. (2009). Dieting frequency in obese patients with binge eating disorder: Behavioral and metabolic correlates. *Obesity, 17,* 689–697.

Roelofs, J., Meesters, C., Ter Huurne, M., Bamelis, L., & Muris, P. (2006, June). On the links between attachment style, parental rearing behaviors, and internalizing and externalizing problems in non-clinical children. *Journal of Child and Family Studies, 15,* 331–344.

Roffwarg, H. P., Muzio, J. N., & Dement, W. C. (1966). Ontogenetic development of the human sleep–dream cycle. *Science, 152,* 604–619.

Rogan, J. (2007). How much curriculum change is appropriate? Defining a zone of feasible innovation. *Science Education, 91,* 439–460.

Rogan, W. J., & Gladen, B. C. (1993). Breast-feeding and cognitive development. *Early Human Development, 31,* 181–193.

Rogers, A., & Hayden, T. (1997, June 30). Miracles that may keep you going. *Newsweek,* p. 59.

Rogers, C., Floyd, F., Seltzer, M., Greenberg, J., & Hong, J. (2008). Long-term effects of the death of a child on parents' adjustment in midlife. *Journal of Family Psychology, 22,* 203–211.

Rogers, C. R. (1971). A theory of personality. In S. Maddi (Ed.), *Perspectives on personality.* Boston: Little Brown.

Rogers, S., & Willams, J. (2006). *Imitation and the social mind: Autism and typical development.* Guilford Press.

Roggeveen, A. B., Prime, D. J., & Ward, L. M. (2007). Lateralized readiness potentials reveal motor slowing in the aging brain. *Journal of Gerontology, B, Psychological Science and Social Science, 62,* P78–P84.

Rogler, L. H. (1999). Methodological sources of cultural insensitivity in mental health research. *American Psychologist, 54,* 424–433.

Rogoff, B. (1990). *Apprenticeship in thinking: Cognitive development in social context.* New York: Oxford University Press.

Rogoff, B. (1995). *Observing sociocultural activity on three planes: Participatory appropriation, guided participation, and apprenticeship.* New York: Cambridge University Press.

Rogoff, B., & Chavajay, P. (1995). What's become of research on the cultural basis of cognitive development? *American Psychologist, 50,* 859–877.

Rohm, W. G. (2003, October). The test-tube family reunion. *Wired,* pp. 156–157.

Rokeach, M. (1971). Long-range experimental modification of values, attitudes, and behavior. *American Psychologist, 26,* 453–459.

Rolland, J., & Williams, J. (2006). Toward a psychosocial model for the new era of genetics. In S. M. Miller, S. H. McDaniel, J. S. Rolland & S. L. Feetham (Eds.), *Individuals, families, and the new era of genetics: Biopsychosocial perspectives.* New York: W. W. Norton & Co.

Rolls, E. (2000). Memory systems in the brain. *Annual Review of Psychology, 51,* 599–630.

Rom, S. A., Miller, L., & Peluso, J. (2009). Playing the game: psychological factors in surviving cancer. *International Journal of Emergency Mental Health, 11,* 25–35.

Romaine, S. (1994). *Bilingualism* (2nd ed.). London: Blackwell.

Romero, A., & Roberts, R. (2003). The impact of multiple dimensions of ethnic identity on discrimination and adolescents' self-esteem. *Journal of Applied Social Psychology, 33,* 2288–2305.

Ron, P. (2006). Care giving offspring to aging parents: How it affects their marital relations, parenthood, and mental health. *Illness, Crisis, & Loss, 14,* 1–21.

Ronald, A. (2011). Is the child "father of the man"? Evaluating the stability of genetic influences across development. *Developmental Science, 14,* 1471–1478.

Rönkä, A., & Pulkkinen, L. (1995). Accumulation of problems in social functioning in young adulthood: A developmental approach. *Journal of Personality and Social Psychology, 69,* 381–391.

Roodenrys, S., Hulme, C., & Brown, G. (1993). The development of short-term memory span: Separable effects of speech rate and long-term memory. *Journal of Experimental Child Psychology, 56,* 431–442.

Roopnarine, J. (1992). Father–child play in India. In K. MacDonald (Ed.), *Parent–child play.* Albany: State University of New York Press.

Roopnarine, J. (2002). *Conceptual, social-cognitive, and contextual issues in the fields of play.* Westport, CT: Ablex Publishing.

Roopnarine, J. L., Johnson, J. E., & Hooper, F. H. (Eds.). (1994). *Children's play in diverse cultures.* Albany: State University of New York Press.

Roopnarine, J., & Metindogan, A. (2006). Early childhood education research in cross-national perspective. *Handbook of research on the education of young children* (2nd ed., pp. 555–571). Mahwah, NJ: Lawrence Erlbaum Associates Publishers.

Ropar, D., Mitchell, P., & Ackroyd, K. (2003). Do children with autism find it difficult to offer alternative interpretations to ambiguous figures? *British Journal of Developmental Psychology, 21,* 387–395.

Roper Starch Worldwide. (1997, August). Romantic resurgence. *American Demographics,* p. 35.

Rosch, E. (1974). Linguistic relativity. In A. Silverstein (Ed.), *Human communication: Theoretical explorations.* (pp. 95–121). New York: Halstead Press.

Rose, A. J. (2002). Co-rumination in the friendships of girls and boys. *Child Development, 73,* 1830–1843.

Rose, A. J., & Asher, S. R. (1999). Children's goals and strategies in response to conflicts within a friendship. *Developmental Psychology, 35,* 69–79.

Rose, H. (2004, October 29). Ceausescu's orphans 20 years on. *The Daily Telegraph (London).* Pg 7.

Rose, M. R. (1999, December). Can human aging be postponed? *Scientific American,* 106–110.

Rose, R. J., Viken, R. J., Dick, D.M., Bates, J. E., Pulkkinen, L., & Kaprio, J. (2003). It *does* take a village: Nonfamilial environments and children's behavior. *Psychological Science, 14,* 273–278.

Rose, S. (2008, January). Drugging unruly children is a method of social control. *Nature, 451*(7178), 521–528.

Rose, S. A., & Feldman, J. F. (1995). Prediction of IQ and specific cognitive abilities at 11 years from infancy measures. *Developmental Psychology, 31,* 685–696.

Rose, S. A., & Feldman, J. F. (1997). Memory and speed: Their role in the relation of infant information processing to later IQ. *Child Development, 68,* 630–641.

Rose, S., Feldman, J., & Jankowski, J. (1999). Visual and auditory temporal processing, cross-modal transfer, and reading. *Journal of Learning Disabilities, 32,* 256–266.

Rose, S. A., Feldman, J. F., & Jankowski, J. J. (2004a). Dimensions of cognition in infancy. *Intelligence, 32,* 245–262.

Rose, S., Feldman, J., & Jankowski, J. (2004b). Infant visual recognition memory. *Developmental Review, 24,* 74–100.

Rose, S., Feldman, J., & Jankowski, J. (1999). Visual and auditory temporal processing, cross-modal transfer, and reading. *Journal of Learning Disabilities, 32,* 256–266.

Rose, S., Feldman, J., & Jankowski, J. (2009). Information processing in toddlers: Continuity from infancy and persistence of preterm deficits. *Intelligence, 37,* 311–320.

Rose, S. A., Feldman, J. F., Jankowski, J. J., & Van Rossem, R. (2011). The structure of memory in infants and toddlers: An SEM study with full-terms and preterms. *Developmental Science, 14,* 83–91.

Rose, S. A., Feldman, J. F., Wallace, I. F., & McCarton, C. (1991). Information processing at 1 year: Relation to birth status and developmental outcome during the first 5 years. *Developmental Psychology, 27,* 723–737.

Rose, S., Jankowski, J., & Feldman, J. (2002). Speed of processing and face recognition at 7 and 12 months. *Infancy, 3,* 435–455.

Rose, S. A., & Ruff, H. A. (1987). Cross-modal abilities in human infants. In J. D. Osofsky (Ed.), *Handbook of infant development* (2nd ed.). New York: Wiley.

Roseberry, S., Hirsh-Pasek, K., Parish-Morris, J., & Golinkoff, R. (2009). Live action: Can young children learn verbs from video? *Child Development, 80,* 1360–1375.

Rosen, D. (1997, March 25). The physician's perspective. *HealthNews,* 3.

Rosen, D. (1997, October 28). Making sense of SIDS. *HealthNews,* p. 4.

Rosen, E., Ackerman, L., & Zosky, D. (2002). The sibling empty nest syndrome: The experience of sadness as siblings leave the family home. *Journal of Human Behavior in the Social Environment, 6,* 65–80.

Rosen, K. H. (1998). The family roots of aggression and violence: A life span perspective. In L. L'Abate (Ed.), *Family psychopathology: The relational roots of dysfunctional behavior.* New York: Guilford Press.

Rosen, K. S., & Burke, P. B. (1999). Multiple attachment relationships within families: Mothers and fathers with two young children. *Developmental Psychology, 35,* 436–444.

Rosen, S., & Iverson, P. (2007). Constructing adequate non-speech analogues: What is special about speech anyway? *Developmental Science, 10,* 165–168.

Rosen, W. D., Adamson, L. B., & Bakeman, R. (1992). An experimental investigation of infant social referencing: Mothers' messages and gender differences. *Developmental Psychology, 28,* 1172–1178.

Rosenblatt, P. C. (1988). Grief: The social context of private feelings. *Journal of Social Issues, 44,* 67–78.

Rosenblatt, P. C. (2001). A social constructionist perspective on cultural differences in grief. In M. S. Stroebe, R. O. Hansson, W. Stroebe, & H. Schut (Eds.), *Handbook of bereavement research: Consequences, coping, and care.* Washington, DC: American Psychological Association Press.

Rosenblatt, P. C., & Wallace, B. R. (2005). *African American grief.* New York: Brunner-Routledge.

Rosenfeld, A. A., Pilowsky, D. J., & Fine, P. (1997). Foster care: An update. *Journal of the American Academy of Child & Adolescent Psychiatry, 36,* 448–457.

Rosenfeld, B., Krivo, S., Breitbart, W., & Chochinov, H. M. (2000). Suicide, assisted suicide, and euthanasia in the terminally ill. In H. M. Chochinov & W. Breitbart (Eds.), *Handbook of psychiatry in palliative medicine.* New York: Oxford University Press.

Rosenfeld, M. E., & Curiel, D. T. (1996). Gene therapy strategies for novel cancer therapeutics. *Current Opinion in Oncology, 8,* 72–77.

Rosenfeld, M., & Owens, W. A., Jr. (1965, April). *The intrinsic–extrinsic aspects of work and their demographic correlates.* Paper presented at the Midwestern Psychological Association, Chicago.

Rosenman, R. H. (1990). Type A behavior pattern: A personal overview. *Journal of Social Behavior and Personality, 5,* 1–24.

Rosenman, R. H., Brand, R. J., Sholtz, R. I., & Friedman, M. (1976). Multivariate prediction of coronary heart disease during 8.5 year follow-up in the Western Collaborative Group Study. *American Journal of Cardiology, 37,* 903–910.

Rosenstein, D., & Oster, H. (1988). Differential facial responses to four basic tastes in newborns. *Child Development, 59,* 1555–1568.

Rosenthal, A. M. (1993, July 27). The torture continues. *New York Times,* p. A13.

Rosenthal, H., & Crisp, R. (2006, April). Reducing stereotype threat by blurring intergroup boundaries. *Personality and Social Psychology Bulletin, 32,* 501–511.

Rosenthal, M. (1998). Women and infertility. *Psychopharmacology Bulletin, 34,* 307–308.

Rosenthal, R. (1987). Pygmalion effects: Existence, magnitude, and social importance. *Educational Researcher,* 37–40.

Rosenthal, R. (1994). Interpersonal expectancy effects: A 30-year perspective. *Current Directions in Psychological Science, 3,* 176–179.

Rosenthal, R. (2002). The Pygmalion effect and its mediating mechanisms. In J. Aronson (Ed.), *Improving academic achievement: Impact of psychological factors on education.* San Diego: Academic Press.

Rosenthal, R., & Jacobson, L. (1968). *Pygmalion in the classroom: Teacher expectation and pupils' intellectual development.* New York: Holt, Rinehart & Winston.

Rosenzweig, M. R., & Bennett, E. L. (1976). Enriched environments: Facts, factors, and fantasies. In L. Petrinovich & J. L. McGaugh (Eds.), *Knowing, thinking, and believing.* New York: Plenum.

Ross Laboratories. (1993). *Ross Laboratories mothers' survey, 1992.* Division of Abbott Laboratories, USA, Columbus, OH. Unpublished data.

Ross, C. E., Microwsky, J., & Goldsteen, K. (1991). The impact of the family on health. In A. Booth (Ed.), *Contemporary families.* Minneapolis, MN: National Council on Family Relations.

Ross, J., Stefanatos, G., & Roeltgen, D. (2007). Klinefelter syndrome. *Neurogenetic developmental disorders: Variation of manifestation in childhood.* Cambridge, MA: The MIT Press.

Ross, M., & Wilson, A. E. (2003). Autobiographical memory and conceptions of self: Getting better all the time. *Current Directions in Psychological Science, 12,* 66–69.

Ross, R. K., & Yu, M. C. (1994, June 9). Breast feeding and breast cancer. *New England Journal of Medicine, 330,* 1683–1684.

Rosser, P. L., & Randolph, S. M. (1989). Black American infants: The Howard University normative study. In J. K. Neugent, B. M. Lester, & T. B. Brazelton (Eds.), *The cultural context of infancy: Vol. I. Biology, culture, and infant development.* Norwood, NJ: Ablex.

Rossman, I. (1977). Anatomic and body composition changes with aging. In C. E. Finch & L. Hayflick (Eds.), *Handbook of the biology of aging.* New York: Van Nostrand Reinhold.

Rossouw, J. E. (2006). Implications of recent clinical trials of postmenopausal hormone therapy for management of cardiovascular disease. *Annals of the New York Academy of Sciences, 1089,* 444–453.

Rossouw, J. E., Prentice, R. L., Manson, J. E., Wu, L., Barad, D., Barnabei, V. M., Ko, M., LaCroix, A. Z., Margolis, K. L., & Stefanick, M. L. (2007). Postmenopausal hormone therapy and risk of cardiovascular disease by age and years since menopause. *Journal of the American Medical Association, 297,* 1465–1477.

Rotenberg, K., Boulton, M., & Fox, C. (2005). Cross-sectional and longitudinal relations among children's trust beliefs, psychological maladjustment and social relationships: Are very high as well as very low trusting children at risk? *Journal of Abnormal Child Psychology, 33*, 595–610.

Rotenberg, K. J., & Morrison, J. (1993). Loneliness and college achievement: Do loneliness scale scores predict college drop-out? *Psychological Reports, 73*, 1283–1288.

Roth, D., Slone, M., & Dar, R. (2000). Which way cognitive development? An evaluation of the Piagetian and the domain-specific research programs. *Theory & Psychology, 10*, 353–373.

Rothbart, M. (2007). Temperament, development, and personality. *Current Directions in Psychological Science, 16*, 207–212.

Rothbart, M. K., Ahadi, S. A., & Evans, D. E. (2000). Temperament and personality: Origins and outcomes. *Journal of Personality and Social Psychology, 78*, 122–135.

Rothbart, M. K., & Bates, J. E. (1998). Temperament. In N. Eisenberg (Ed.), *Handbook of child psychology: Vol. 3. Social, emotional, and personality development* (5th ed.) New York: Wiley.

Rothbart, M., & Derryberry, D. (2002). Temperament in children. In C. von Hofsten & L. Backman (Eds.), *Psychology at the turn of the millennium, vol. 2: Social, developmental, and clinical perspectives.* Florence, KY: Taylor & Frances/Routledge.

Rothbart, M. K., Derryberry, D., & Hershey, K. (2000). Stability of temperament in childhood: Laboratory infant assessment to parent report at seven years. In V. J. Molfese & D. L. Molfese (Eds.), *Temperament and personality development across the life span.* Mahwah, NJ: Erlbaum.

Rothbart, M. K., Posner, M. I., Kieras, J. (2006). Temperament, Attention, and the Development of Self-Regulation. In K. McCartney & D. Phillips, *Blackwell handbook of early childhood development.* Malden, MA: Blackwell Publishing.

Rothbaum, F., Rosen, K., & Ujiie, T. (2002). Family systems theory, attachment theory and culture. *Family Process, 41*, 328–350.

Rothbaum, F., Weisz, J., Pott, M., Miyake, K., & Morelli, G. (2000). Attachment and culture: Security in the United States and Japan. *American Psychologist, 55*, 1093–1104.

Rothrauff, T., Middlemiss, W., & Jacobson, L. (2004). Comparison of American and Austrian infants' and toddlers' sleep habits: A retrospective, exploratory study. *North American Journal of Psychology, 6*, 125–144.

Rotigel, J. V. (2003). Understanding the young gifted child: Guidelines for parents, families, and educators. *Early Childhood Education Journal, 30*, 209–214.

Roush, W. (1995, March 31). Arguing over why Johnny can't read. *Science, 267*, 1896–1998.

Rovee-Collier, C. K. (1987). Learning and memory in infancy. In J. D. Osofsky (Ed.), *Handbook of infant development* (2nd ed.). New York: Wiley.

Rovee-Collier, C. (1993). The capacity for long-term memory in infancy. *Current Directions in Psychological Science, 2*, 130–135.

Rovee-Collier, C. (1999). The development of infant memory. *Current Directions in Psychological Science, 8*, 80–85.

Rovee-Collier, C., & Barr, R. (2002). Infant cognition. *Stevens' handbook of experimental psychology (3rd ed.), Vol. 4: Methodology in experimental psychology.* Hoboken, NJ: John Wiley & Sons Inc.

Rovee-Collier, C., & Gerhardstein, P. (1997). The development of infant memory. In N. Cowan (Ed.), *The development of memory in childhood* (pp. 5–39). Hove, UK: Psychology Press/Erlbaum, Taylor, & Francis.

Rovee-Collier, C. K., & Hayne, H. (1987). Reactivation and infant long-term memory. In H. W. Reese (Ed.), *Advances in child development and behavior* (Vol. 20). New York: Academic.

Rovee-Collier, C., Hayne, H., & Colombo, M. (2001). *The development of implicit and explicit memory.* Philadelphia, PA: John Benjamins.

Rovner, B. W., & Katz, I. R. (1993). Psychiatric disorders in the nursing home: A selective review of studies related to clinical care. *International Journal of Geriatric Psychiatry, 8, Special Issue*, 75–87.

Row, J. W., & Kahn, R. L. (2000). *Breaking down the myths of aging. Successful aging.* New York: Dell Publications.

Rowe, D. C. (1994). *The effects of nurture on individual natures.* New York: Guilford Press.

Rowe, D. C. (1999). Heredity. In V. J. Derlega & B. A. Winstead (Eds.), *Personality: Contemporary theory and research* (2nd ed.). Chicago: Nelson-Hall Publishers.

Rowe, J. W., & Kahn, R. L. (1997). Successful aging. *Gerontologist, 37*, 433–440.

Rowe, J. W., & Kahn, R. L. (1998). *Successful aging.* New York: Pantheon.

Rowland, C. F., & Noble, C. L. (2011). The role of syntactic structure in children's sentence comprehension: Evidence from the dative. *Language Learning and Development, 7*, 55–75.

Rowley, S., Burchinal, M., Roberts, J., & Zeisel, S. (2008). Racial identity, social context, and race-related social cognition in African Americans during middle childhood. *Developmental Psychology, 44*, 1537–1546.

Roy, A., Nielsen, D., Rylander, G., Sarchiapone, M., & Segal, N. L. (1999). Genetics of suicide in depression. *Journal of Clinical Psychology, 60*, 12–17.

Rubenstein, A. J., Kalakanis, L., & Langlois, J. H. (1999). Infant preferences for attractive faces: A cognitive explanation. *Developmental Psychology, 35*, 848–855.

Rubin, D. C. (1985, September). The subtle deceiver: Recalling our past. *Psychology Today*, pp. 39–46.

Rubin, D. C. (1986). *Autobiographical memory.* Cambridge, England: Cambridge University Press.

Rubin, D. C. (Ed.). (1996). *Remembering our past: Studies in autobiographical memory.* New York: Cambridge University Press.

Rubin, D. C. (2000). Autobiographical memory and aging. In C. D. Park & N. Schwarz et al. (Eds.), *Cognitive aging: A primer.* Philadelphia: Psychology Press/Taylor & Francis.

Rubin, D., & Greenberg, D. (2003). The role of narrative in recollection: A view from cognitive psychology and neuropsychology. In G. Fireman & T. McVay (Eds.), *Narrative and consciousness: Literature, psychology, and the brain.* London: Oxford University Press.

Rubin, D. H., Krasilnikoff, P. A., Leventhal, J. M., Weile, B., & Berget, A. (1986, August 23). Effects of passive smoking on birthweight. *Lancet, 315*, 415–417.

Rubin, K. H. (1998). Social and emotional development from a cultural perspective. *Developmental Psychology, 34*, 611–615.

Rubin, K. H., & Chung, O. B. (Eds.). (2006). *Parenting beliefs, behaviors, and parent-child relations: A cross-cultural perspective.* New York: Psychology Press.

Rubin, K. H., Fein, G., & Vandenberg, B. (1983). In E. M. Hetherington (Ed.), *Handbook of child psychology. Vol. 4. Socialization, personality and social development* (pp. 693–774). New York: Wiley.

Ruble, D. (1983). The development of social comparison processes and their role in achievementrelated self-actualization. In E. T. Higgins, D. N. Ruble, & W. W. Hartup (Eds.), *Social cognition and social development.* New York: Cambridge University Press.

Ruble, D. N., Boggiano, A. K., Feldman, N. S., & Loebl, J. H. (1989). Developmental analysis of the role of social comparison in self-evaluation. *Developmental Psychology, 16*, 105–115.

Ruble, D., & Brooks-Gunn, J. (1982). The experience of menarche. *Child Development, 53*, 1557–1566.

Ruble, D., Taylor, L., Cyphers, L., Greulich, F., Lurye, L., & Shrout, P. (2007, July). The role of gender constancy in early gender development. *Child Development, 78*(4), 1121–1136.

Ruda, M. A., Ling, Q.-D., Hohmann, A. G., Peng, Y. B., & Tachibana, T. (2000, July 28). Altered nociceptive neuronal circuits after neonatal peripheral inflammation. *Science, 289*, 628–630.

Ruda, M. A., Ling, Q-D., Hohmann, A. G., Peng, Y. B., & Tachibana, T. (2000, July 28). Altered nociceptive neuronal circuits after neonatal peripheral inflammation. *Science, 289*, 628–630.

Rudd, L., Cain, D., & Saxon, T. (2008). Does improving joint attention in low-quality child-care enhance language development? *Early Child Development and Care, 178*(3), 315–338.

Rudy, D., & Grusec, J. (2006, March). Authoritarian parenting in individualist and collectivist groups: Associations with maternal emotion and cognition and children's self-esteem. *Journal of Family Psychology, 20*, 68–78.

Ruff, H. A. (1989). The infant's use of visual and haptic information in the perception and recognition of objects. *Canadian Journal of Psychology, 43*, 302–319.

Ruff, H. A., & Lawson, K. R. (1990). Development of sustained, focused attention in young children during free play. *Developmental Psychology, 26*, 85–93.

Ruffman, T., Perner, J., Naito, M., Parkin, L., & Clements, W.A. (1998). Older (but not younger) siblings facilitate false belief understanding. *Developmental Psychology, 34*, 161–174.

Ruffman, T., Slade, L., & Redman, J. (2005). Young infants' expectations about hidden objects. *Cognition [serial online], 97*, B35–B43.

Ruihe, H., & Guoliang, Y. (2006). Children's understanding of emotional display rules and use of strategies. *Psychological Science (China), 29*, 18–21.

Ruiz-Casares, M., Rousseau, C., Currie, J. L., & Heymann, J. (2012). "I hold on to my teddy bear really tight": Children's experiences when they are home alone. *American Journal of Orthopsychiatry, 82*, 97–103.

Rule, B. G., & Ferguson, T. J. (1986). The effects of media violence on attitudes, emotions and cognitions. *Journal of Social Issues, 42*, 29–50.

Rumelhart, D. E. (1984). Schemata and the cognitive system. In R. S. Wyer Jr. & T. K. Siull (Eds.), *Handbook of social cognition.* Hillsdale, NJ: Erlbaum.

Runco, M. A. (1992). On creativity and human capital. *Creativity Research Journal, 5*, 373–378.

Runeson, I., Martenson, E., & Enskar, K. (2007). Children's knowledge and degree of participation in decision making when undergoing a clinical diagnostic procedure. *Pediatric Nursing, 33*, 505–511.

Runyan, D. (2008). The challenges of assessing the incidence of inflicted traumatic brain injury: A world perspective. *American Journal of Preventive Medicine, 34*, S112–SS115.

Rupp, D., Vodanovich, S., & Credé, M. (2006, June). Age bias in the workplace: The impact of ageism and causal attributions. *Journal of Applied Social Psychology, 36*, 1337–1364.

Russell, G., & Radojevic, M. (1992). The changing role of fathers? Current understandings and future directions for research and practice. Special Section: Australian Regional Meeting: Attachment and the relationship the infant and caregivers. *Infant Mental Health Journal, 13*, 296–311.

Russell, S., & Consolacion, T. (2003). Adolescent romance and emotional health in the United States: Beyond binaries. *Journal of Clinical Child & Adolescent Psychology, 32*, 499–508.

Russell, S., & McGuire, J. (2006). Critical mental health issues for sexual minority adolescents. *The crisis in youth mental health: Critical issues and effective programs, Vol. 2: Disorders in adolescence.* Westport, CT: Praeger Publishers/Greenwood Publishing Group.

Russo, R., & Parkin, A. J. (1993). Age differences in implicit memory: More apparent than real. *Memory and Cognition, 21*, 73–80.

Russon, A. E., & Waite, B. E. (1991). Patterns of dominance and imitation in an infant peer group. *Ethology & Sociobiology, 12,* 55–73.

Rust, J., Golombok, S., Hines, M., Johnston, K., & Golding, J.; ALSPAC Study Team. (2000). The role of brothers and sisters in the gender development of preschool children. *Journal of Experimental Child Psychology, 77,* 292–303.

Rustin, M. (2006). Infant observation research: What have we learned so far? *Infant Observation, 9,* 35–52.

Rusting, R. (1990, March). Safe passage? *Scientific American, 262,* 36.

Rutter, M. (1987). Continuities and discontinuities from infancy. In J. D. Osofsky (Ed.), *Handbook of infant development* (2nd ed.). New York: Wiley.

Rutter, M. (2003). Commentary: Causal processes leading to antisocial behavior. *Developmental Psychology, 39,* 372–378.

Rutter, M. (2006). *Genes and behavior: Nature-nurture interplay explained.* New York: Blackwell Publishing.

Rutter, M., Bailey, A., Bolton, P., & LeCouteur, A. (1993). Autism: Syndrome definition and possible genetic mechanisms. In R. Plomin & G. E. McClearn (Eds.), *Nature, nurture, and psychology.* Washington, DC: American Psychological Association.

Rutter, M., Dunn, J., Plomin, R., & Simonoff, E. (1997). Integrating nature and nurture: Implications of person-environment correlations and interactions for developmental psychopathology. *Development and Psychopathology, 9,* 335–364.

Rutter M., & Garmezy, N. (1983). Developmental psychopathology. In E. M. Hetherington (Ed.), *Handbook of child psychology. Vol. IV. Socialization, personality, and social development.* New York: Wiley.

Ryan, A. S. (1997). The resurgence of breastfeeding in the United States. *Pediatrics, 99,* e12.

Ryan, B. P. (2001). *Programmed therapy for stuttering in children and adults* (2nd ed.). Springfield, IL: Charles C. Thomas.

Ryan, C., & Rivers, I. (2003). Lesbian, gay, bisexual and transgender youth: Victimization and its correlates in the USA and UK. *Culture, Health & Sexuality, 5,* 103–119.

Ryan, D., & Martin, A. (2000). Lesbian, gay, bisexual, and transgender parents in the school systems. *The School Psychology Review, 29,* 207–216.

Ryan, J. A., Casapía, M., Aguilar, E., Silva, H., Rahme, E., Gagnon, A. J., & … Gyorkos, T. W. (2011). A comparison of low birth weight among newborns of early adolescents, late adolescents, and adult mothers in the Peruvian Amazon. *Maternal and Child Health Journal, 15,* 587–596.

Ryan, J. J., Sattler, J. M., & Lopez, S. J. (2000). Age effects on Wechsler Adult Intelligence Scale-III subtests. *Archives of Clinical Neuropsychology, 15,* 311–317.

Ryan, K. E., & Ryan, A. M. (2005). Psychological process underlying stereotype threat and standardized math test performance. *Educational Psychologist, 40,* 53–63.

Rycek, R. F., Stuhr, S. L., McDermott, J., Benker, J., & Swartz, M. D. (1998). Adolescent egocentrism and cognitive functioning during late adolescence. *Adolescence, 33,* 745–749.

Ryff, C. D., & Singer, B. (2003). Flourishing under fire: Resilience as a prototype of challenged thriving. In C. L. Keyes & J. Haidt (Eds.), *Flourishing: Positive psychology and the life well-lived* (pp. 15–36). Washington, DC: American Psychological Association.

Saad, L. (2002, May 16). "Cloning" humans is a turnoff to most Americans. *Gallup News Service.* Retrieved from http:/www.gallup.com.

Saarni, C. & Weber, H. (1998). Emotional displays and dissemblance in childhood: Implication and self-presentation. In P. Philipott, R. S. Feldman, & E. J. Coats (Eds.), *The social context of nonverbal behavior.* Cambridge, UK: Cambridge University Press.

Sabatino, C., & Mayer, L. (2011). Supporting today's blended family. In C. Franklin & R. Fong (Eds.), *The church leader's counseling resource book: A guide to mental health and social problems.* New York: Oxford University Press.

Sabbagh, M. (2009). Drug development for Alzheimer's disease: Where are we now and where are we headed? *American Journal of Geriatric Pharmacotherapy (AJGP), 7,* 167–185.

Sabbagh, M., Bowman, L., Evraire, L., & Ito, J. (2009). Neurodevelopmental correlates of theory of mind in preschool children. *Child Development, 80,* 1147–1162.

Sachs, J. (2006, April 1). Will your child be fat? *Parenting, 20,* 112.

Sack, K. (1999, March 21). Older students bring new life to campuses. *The New York Times,* p. WH8.

Sacks, M. H. (1993). Exercise for stress control. In D. Goleman & J. Gurin (Eds.), *Mind–body medicine.* Yonkers, NY: Consumer Reports Books.

Saczynski, J., Willis, S., & Schaie, K. (2002). Strategy use in reasoning training with older adults. *Aging, Neuropsychology, & Cognition, 9,* 48–60.

Sadeh, A., Flint-Ofir, E., Tirosh, T., & Tikotzky, L. (2007, March). Infant sleep and parental sleep-related cognitions. *Journal of Family Psychology, 21,* 74–87.

Sadker, M., & Sadker, D. (1994). *Failing at fairness: How America's schools cheat girls.* New York: Scribner's.

Sadker, D., & Sadker, M. (2005). *Teachers, schools, and society.* New York: McGraw-Hill.

Saffran, J., Werker, J., & Werner, L. (2006). The infant's auditory world: Hearing, speech, and the beginnings of language. In W. Damon & R. M. Lerner (Eds.), *Handbook of child psychology: Vol 2, Cognition, perception, and language* (6th ed.). New York: John Wiley & Sons Inc.

Saffran, J. R., Aslin, R. N., & Newport, E. L. (1996, December 13). Statistical learning by 8-mont-old infants. *Science, 274,* 1926–1928.

Sagi, A. (1990). Attachment theory and research from a cross-cultural perspective. *Human Development, 33,* 10–22.

Sagi, A., Donnell, F., van Ijzendoorn, M. H., Mayseless, O., & Aviezer, O. (1994). Sleeping out of home in a kibbutz communal arrangement: It makes a difference for infant– mother attachment. *Child Development, 65,* 992–1004.

Sagi, A., van Ijzendoorn, M. H., Aviezer, O., Donnell, F., Koren-Karie, N., Joels, T., & Harel, Y. (1995). Attachments in multiple-caregiver and multiple-infant environment: The case of the Israeli kibbutzim. *Monographs of the Society for Research in Child Development, 44,* 121-129..

Sagi, A., van Ijzendoorn, M. H., & Koren-Karie, N. (1991). Primary appraisal of the Strange Situation: A cross-cultural analysis of preseparation episodes. *Developmental Psychology, 27,* 587–596.

Sagrestano, L. M., McCormick, S. H., Paikoff, R. L., & Holmbeck, G. N. (1999). Pubertal development and parent–child conflict in low-income, urban, African American adolescents. *Journal of Research on Adolescence, 9,* 85–107.

Saiegh-Haddad, E. (2007). Epilinguistic and metalinguistic phonological awareness may be subject to different constraints: Evidence from Hebrew. *First Language, 27,* 385–405.

Salber, E. J., Freeman, H. E., & Abelin, T. (1968). Needed research on smoking: Lessons from the Newton study. In E. F. Borgatta & R. R. Evans (Eds.), *Smoking, health, and behavior.* Chicago: Aldine.

Sales, B. D., & Folkman, S. (Eds.). (2000). *Ethics in research with human participants.* Washington, DC: American Psychological Association.

Sallis, J., & Glanz, K. (2006, March). The role of built environments in physical activity, eating, and obesity in childhood. *The Future of Children, 16,* 89–108.

Salmon, D. K. (1993, September). Getting through labor. *Parents,* pp. 62–66.

Salovey, P., & Pizarro, D. (2003). The value of emotional intelligence. In R. Sternberg & J. Lautrey (Eds.), *Models of intelligence: International perspectives.* Washington, DC: American Psychological Association.

Salovey, P., & Sluyter, D. J. (Eds.). (1997). *Emotional development and emotional intelligence.* New York: Basic Books.

Salthouse, T. A. (1984). Effects of age and skill in typing. *Journal of Experimental Psychology: General, 113,* 345–371.

Salthouse, T. A. (1989). Age-related changes in basic cognitive processes. In APA Master Lectures, *The adult years: Continuity and change.* Washington, DC: American Psychological Association.

Salthouse, T. A. (1990). Cognitive competence and expertise in aging. In J. E. Birren, W. K. Schaie, (Eds.), *Handbook of the psychology of aging* (3rd ed.). San Diego, CA: Academic Press.

Salthouse, T. A. (1991). Mediation of adult age differences in cognition by reductions in working memory and speed of processing. *Psychological Science, 2,* 179–183.

Salthouse, T. A. (1993). Speed mediation of adult age differences in cognition. *Developmental Psychology, 29,* 722–738.

Salthouse, T. A. (1994a). Aging associations: Influence of speed on adult age differences in associative learning. *Journal of Experimental Psychology: Learning, Memory, and Cognition, 20,* 1486–1503.

Salthouse, T. A. (1994b). The aging of working memory. *Neuropsychology, 8,* 535–543.

Salthouse, T. (2006a). Aging of thought. *Lifespan cognition: Mechanisms of change.* New York: Oxford University Press.

Salthouse, T. A. (2006b). Mental exercise and mental aging: Evaluating the validity of the "Use it or lose it" hypothesis. *Perspectives on Psychological Science, 1,* 68–87.

Salthouse, T. (2009). When does age-related cognitive decline begin? *Neurobiology of Aging, 30,* 507–514.

Salthouse, T. A., Atkinson, T. M., & Berish, D. E. (2003). Executive functioning as a potential mediator of age-related cognitive decline in normal adults. *Journal of Experimental Psychology, General, 132,* 566–594.

Salthouse, T., Pink, J., & Tucker-Drob, E. (2008). Contextual analysis of fluid intelligence. *Intelligence, 36,* 464–486.

Samet, J. H., Memarini, D. M., & Malling, H. V. (2004, May 14). Do airborne particles induce heritable mutations? *Science, 304,* 971.

Sammons, M. (2009). Writing a wrong: Factors influencing the overprescription of antidepressants to youth. *Professional Psychology: Research and Practice, 40,* 327–329.

Sampson, J., & Chason, A. (2008). Helping gifted and talented adolescents and young adults: Make informed and careful career choices. *Handbook of giftedness in children: Psychoeducational theory, research, and best practices.* New York: Springer Science + Business Media.

Samuels, C. A. (2005). Special educators discuss NCLB effect at national meeting. *Education Week, 24,* 12.

Samuelsson, I., & Johansson, E. (2006, January). Play and learning—inseparable dimensions in preschool practice. *Early Child Development and Care, 176,* 47–65.

Sánchez, P., & Salazar, M. (2012). Transnational computer use in urban Latino immigrant communities: Implications for schooling. *Urban Education, 47,* 90–116.

Sandberg, D. E., & Voss, L. D. (2002). The psychosocial consequences of short stature: A review of the evidence. *Best Practice and Research Clinical Endocrinology and Metabolism, 16,* 449–463.

Sanders, C. M. (1988). Risk factors in bereavement outcome. *Journal of Social Issues, 44,* 97–111.

Sanders, N. (2010). *The quick guide to parenting solutions: Parenting 101 success.* CreateSpace.

Sanders, S., Ott, C., Kelber, S., & Noonan, P. (2008). The experience of high levels of grief in caregivers of persons with Alzheimer's disease and related dementia. *Death Studies, 32,* 495–523.

Sanderson, C. A., & Cantor, N. (1995). Social dating goals in late adolescence: Implications for safer sexual activity. *Journal of Personality and Social Psychology, 68,* 1121–1134.

Sandis, E. (2000). The aging and their families: A cross-national review. In A. L. Comunian & U. P. Gielen (Eds.), *International perspectives on human development.* Lengerich, Germany: Pabst Science Publishers.

Sandler, B. (1994, January 31). First denial, then a near-suicidal plea: "Mom, I need your help." *People Weekly,* 56–58.

Sandoval, J., Frisby, C. L., Geisinger, K. F., Scheuneman, J. D., & Grenier, J. R. (Eds.). (1998). *Test interpretation and diversity: Achieving equity in assessment.* Washington, DC: APA Books.

Sandoval, J., Scott, A., & Padilla, I. (2009). Crisis counseling: An overview. *Psychology in the Schools, 46,* 246–256.

Sanefuji, W., Ohgami, H., & Hashiya, K. (2006). Preference for peers in infancy. *Infant Behavior & Development, 29,* 584–593.

Sang, B., Miao, X., & Deng, C. (2002). The development of gifted and nongifted young children in metamemory knowledge. *Psychological Science (China), 25,* 406–409, 424.

Sangree, W. H. (1989). Age and power: Life-course trajectories and age structuring of power relations in East and West Africa. In D. I. Kertzer & K. W. Schaie (Eds.), *Age structuring in comparative perspective.* Hillsdale, NJ: Erlbaum.

Sankar, A. (1981). The conquest of solitude: Singlehood and old age in traditional Chinese society. In C. L. Fry (Ed.), *Dimensions: Aging, culture and health.* New York: Praeger.

Sankupellay, M., Wilson, S. S., Heussler, H. S., Parsley, C. C., Yuill, M. M., & Dakin, C. C. (2011). Characteristics of sleep EEG power spectra in healthy infants in the first two years of life. *Clinical Neurophysiology, 122,* 236–243.

Sanoff, A. P., & Minerbrook, S. (1993, April 19). Race on campus. *U.S. News and World Report,* pp. 52–64.

Sanson, A., & diMuccio, C. (1993). The influence of aggressive and neutral cartoons and toys on the behavior of preschool children. *Australian Psychologist, 28,* 93–99.

Santelli, J., Ott, M., Lyon, M., Rogers, J., Summers, D., & Schleifer, R. (2006). Abstinence and abstinence-only education: A review of U.S. policies and programs. *Journal of Adolescent Health, 38,* 72–81.

Santesso, D., Schmidt, L., & Trainor, L. (2007). Frontal brain electrical activity (EEG) and heart rate in response to affective infant-directed (ID) speech in 9-month-old infants. *Brain and Cognition, 65,* 14–21. http://search.ebscohost.com, doi:10.1016/j.bandc.2007.02.008

Santos, M., Richards, C., & Bleckley, M. (2007). Comorbidity between depression and disordered eating in adolescents. *Eating Behaviors, 8,* 440–449.

Santtila, P., Sandnabba, N., Harlaar, N., Varjonen, M., Alanko, K., & von der Pahlen, B. (2008, January). Potential for homosexual response is prevalent and genetic. *Biological Psychology, 77*(1), 102–105.

Sapolsky, R. (2005, December). Sick of poverty. *Scientific American,* 93–99.

Sarantakos, S. (1991). Cohabitation revisited: Paths of change among cohabiting and non-cohabiting couples. *Australian Journal of Marriage and the Family, 12,* 144–155.

Sarason, S., Johnson, J. H., & Siegel, J. M. (1978). Assessing the impact of life changes: Development of the Life Experiences Survey. *Journal of Consulting and Clinical Psychology, 46,* 932–946.

Saravi, F. (2007). The elusive search for a "gay gene." *Tall tales about the mind & brain: Separating fact from fiction* (pp. 461–477). New York: Oxford University Press.

Sargent, J. D., Tanski, S. E., & Gibson, J. (2007). Exposure to movie smoking among U.S. adolescents aged 10 to 14 years: A population estimate. *Pediatrics, 119,* 1167–1176.

Sarrel, P. M. (2000). Effects of hormone replacement therapy on sexual psychophysiology and behavior in postmenopause. *Journal of Womens Health & Gender-Based Medicine, 9,* (Suppl. 1), S-25–S-32.

Sarsour, K., Sheridan, M., Jutte, D., Nuru-Jeter, A., Hinshaw, S., & Boyce, W. (2011). Family socioeconomic status and child executive functions: The roles of language, home environment, and single parenthood. *Journal of the International Neuropsychological Society, 17,* 120–132.

Sasser-Coen, J. R. (1993). Qualitative changes in creativity in the second half of life: A life-span developmental perspective. *Journal of Creative Behavior, 27,* 18–27.

Satel, S. (2004, May 25). Antidepressants: Two countries, two views. *The New York Times,* p. H2.

Sato, Y., Fukasawa, T., Hayakawa, M., Yatsuya, H., Hatakeyama, M., Ogawa, A., et al. (2007). A new method of blood sampling reduces pain for newborn infants: A prospective, randomized controlled clinical trial. *Early Human Development, 83,* 389–394.

Sattler, J. M. (1992). *Assessment of children: WISC—III and WPPSI—R supplement.* San Diego, CA: Jerome M. Sattler.

Saudino, K., & McManus, I. C. (1998). Handedness, footedness, eyedness, and earedness in the Colorado Adoption Project. *British Journal of Developmental Psychology, 16,* 167–174.

Saulny, S. (2006, March 3.). In baby boomlet, preschool derby is the fiercest yet. *New York Times.* C4.

Saulny, S. (2011, January 30). Black? While? Asian? More young Americans choose all of the above. *The New York Times,* p. 1.

Saunders, J., Davis, L., & Williams, T. (2004). Gender differences in self-perceptions and academic outcomes: A study of African American high school students. *Journal of Youth & Adolescence, 33,* 81–90.

Sauzéon, H., Déjos, M., Lestage, P., Pala, P., & N'Kaoua, B. (2012). Developmental differences in explicit and implicit conceptual memory tests: A processing view account. *Child Neuropsychology, 18,* 23–49.

Savage, J. (2008). The role of exposure to media violence in the etiology of violent behavior: A criminalist weighs in. *American Behavioral Scientist, 51,* 1123–1136.

Savage-Rumbaugh, E. S., Murphy, J., Sevcik, R. A., Brakke, K. E., Williams, S. L., & Rumbaugh, D. M. (1993). Language and comprehension in ape and child. *Monographs of the Society for Research in Child Development, 58,* (3–4, Serial No. 233).

Savin-Williams, R. C. (2003a). Are adolescent same-sex romantic relationships on our radar screen? In P. Florsheim (Ed.), *Adolescent romantic relations and sexual behavior: Theory, research, and practical implications.* Mahwah, NJ: Erlbaum.

Savin-Williams, R. C. (2003b). Lesbian, gay, and bisexual youths' relationships with their parents. In L. Garnets & D. Kimme (Eds.), *Psychological perspectives on lesbian, gay, and bisexual experience* (2nd ed.). New York: Columbia University Press.

Savin-Williams, R. C., & Berndt, T. J. (1990). Friendship and peer relations. In S. Feldman & G. Elliott (Eds.), *At the threshold: The developing adolescent.* Cambridge, MA: Harvard University Press.

Savin-Williams, R., & Demo, D. (1983). Situational and transituational determinants of adolescent self-feelings. *Journal of Personality and Social Psychology, 44,* 824–833.

Savin-Williams, R., & Ream, G. (2003). Suicide attempts among sexual-minority male youth. *Journal of Clinical Child & Adolescent Psychology, 32,* 509–522.

Savina, C., Donini, L., & Canniella, C. (2006). Anorexia of aging. *New developments in eating disorders research.* Hauppauge, NY: Nova Science Publishers.

Sawatzky, J., & Naimark, B. (2002). Physical activity and cardiovascular health in aging women: A health-promotion perspective. *Journal of Aging & Physical Activity, 10,* 396–412.

Sax, L. (2005, March 2). The promise and peril of single-sex public education. *Education Week, 24,* 48–51.

Sax, L., et al. (2004). *The American freshman: National norms for fall 2004.* Los Angeles: Higher Education Research Institute, UCLA.

Sax, L. J., Astin, A. W., Korn, W. S., & Mahoney, K. M. (2000). *The American freshman: National norms for fall 2000.* Los Angeles: University of California, Higher Education Research Institute.

Sax, L., Kautz, K. J. (2003). Who first suggests the diagnosis of attention-deficit/hyperactivity disorder? *Annals of Family Medicine, 1,* 171–174.

Saywitz, K. J., & Nathanson, R. (1993). Children's testimony and their perceptions of stress in and out of the courtroom. *Child Abuse & Neglect, 17,* 613–622.

Scafidi, F., & Field, T. (1996). Massage therapy improves behavior in neonates born to HIV-positive mothers. *Journal of Pediatric Psychology, 21,* 889–897.

Scanlon, J. W., & Hollenbeck, A. R. (1983). Neonatal behavioral effects of anesthetic exposure during pregnancy. In A. E. Friedman, A. Milusky, & A. Gluck (Eds.), *Advances in perinatal medicine.* New York: Plenum.

Scarr, S. (1992). Developmental theories for the 1990s: Development and individual differences. *Child Development, 63,* 1–19.

Scarr, S. (1993). Biological and cultural diversity: The legacy of Darwin for development. *Child Development, 64,* 1333–1353.

Scarr, S. (1996). Child care research, social values, and public policy. *The American Academy of Arts and Sciences Bulletin, 1,* 28–45.

Scarr, S. (1997). Why child care has little impact on most children's development. *Current Directions in Psychological Science, 6,* 143–147.

Scarr, S. (1998). American child care today. *American Psychologist, 53,* 95–108.

Scarr, S., & Carter-Saltzman, L. (1982). Genetics and intelligence. In R. J. Sternberg (Ed.), *Handbook of human intelligence* (pp. 792–896). Cambridge, UK: Cambridge University Press.

Scarr, S., Phillips, D., & McCartney, K. (1989). Working mothers and their families. *American Psychologist, 44,* 1402–1409.

Schachner, A., & Hannon, E. E. (2011). Infant-directed speech drives social preferences in 5-month-old infants. *Developmental Psychology, 47,* 19–25.

Schachner, D., Shaver, P., & Gillath, O. (2008). Attachment style and long-term singlehood. *Personal Relationships, 15,* 479–491.

Schachter, E. P. (2005). Erikson meets the postmodern: Can classic identity theory rise to the challenge? *Identity, 5,* 137–160.

Schaefer, R. T., & Lamm, R. P. (1992). *Sociology* (4th ed.). New York: McGraw-Hill.

Schaeffer, C., Petras, H., & Ialongo, N. (2003). Modeling growth in boys' aggressive behavior across elementary school: Links to later criminal involvement, conduct disorder, and antisocial personality disorder. *Developmental Psychology, 39,* 1020–1035.

Schaie, K. W. (1977–1978). Toward a stage of adult theory of adult cognitive development. *Journal of Aging and Human Development, 8,* 129–138.

Schaie, K. W. (1991). Developmental designs revisited. In S. H. Cohen & H. W. Reese (Eds.), *Life-span developmental psychology: Methodological innovations*. Hillsdale, NJ: Erlbaum.

Schaie, K. W. (1993). The Seattle longitudinal studies of adult intelligence. *Current Directions in Psychological Science, 2*, 171–175.

Schaie, K. W. (1994). The course of adult intellectual development. *American Psychologist, 49*, 304–313.

Schaie, K. W., & Willis, S. L. (1986). Can decline in adult intellectual functioning be reversed? *Developmental Psychology, 22*, 223–232.

Schaie, K. W., & Willis, S. L. (1993). Age difference patterns of psychometric intelligence in adulthood: Generalizability within and across ability domains. *Psychology and Aging, 8*, 44–55.

Schaie, K. W., Willis, S. L., Jay, G., & Chipuer, H. (1989). Structural invariance of cognitive abilities across the adult life span: A cross-sectional study. *Developmental Psychology, 25*, 652–662.

Schaie, K. W., & Zanjani, F. A. K. (2006). Intellectual development across adulthood. In C. Hoare (Ed.), *Handbook of adult development and learning*. New York: Oxford University Press.

Schaller, M., & Crandall, C. S. (Eds.). (2004). *The psychological foundations of culture*. Mahwah, NJ: Lawrence Erlbaum Associates.

Schanberg, S., Field, T., Kuhn, C., & Bartolome, J. (1993). Touch: A biological regulator of growth and development in the neonate. *Verhaltenstherapie, 3*(Suppl. 1), 15.

Scharfe, E. (2000). Development of emotional expression, understanding, and regulation in infants and young children. In R. Bar-On & J. Parker (Eds.), *The handbook of emotional intelligence: Theory, development, assessment, and application at home, school, and in the workplace*. San Francisco, CA: Jossey-Bass/Pfeiffer.

Scharrer, E. (2004). Virtual violence: Gender and aggression in video game advertisements. *Mass Communication & Society, 7*, 393–412.

Scharrer, E., Kim, D., Lin, K., & Liu, Z. (2006). Working hard or hardly working? Gender, humor, and the performance of domestic chores in television commercials. *Mass Communication and Society, 9*, 215–238.

Schatz, M. (1994). *A toddler's life*. New York: Oxford University Press.

Schaufeli, W., & Salanova, M. (2007). Efficacy or inefficacy, that's the question: Burnout and work engagement, and their relationships with efficacy beliefs. *Anxiety, Stress & Coping: An International Journal, 20*, 177–196.

Schechter, D., & Willheim, E. (2009). Disturbances of attachment and parental psychopathology in early childhood. *Child and Adolescent Psychiatric Clinics of North America, 18*, 665–686.

Schechter, T., Finkelstein, Y., & Koren, G. (2005). Pregnant "DES daughters" and their offspring. *Canadian Family Physician, 51*, 493–494.

Scheepers, D., Spears, R., Doosje, B., & Manstead, A. (2006). The social functions of ingroup bias: Creating, confirming, or changing social reality. *European Review of Social Psychology, 17*, 359–396.

Scheibel, A. B. (1992). Structural changes in the aging brain. In J. E. Birren, R. B. Sloane, & G. D. Cohen (Eds.), *Handbook of mental health and aging* (2nd ed.). San Diego: Harcourt Brace.

Scheiber, F., et al. (1992). Aging and the senses. In J. E. Birren, R. B. Sloane, & G. D. Cohen (Eds.), *Handbook of mental health and aging* (2nd ed.). San Diego: Harcourt Brace.

Schellenberg, E. G., & Trehub, S. E. (1996). Natural musical intervals: Evidence from infant listeners. *Psychological Science, 7*, 272–277.

Scheme, D. J. (2001, December 5). U.S. students prove middling on 32-nation test. *The New York Times*, p. A21.

Schemo, D. J. (2003, November 13). Students' scores rise in math, not in reading. *The New York Times*, p. A2.

Schemo, D. J. (2004, March 2). Schools, facing tight budgets, leave gifted programs behind. *The New York Times*, pp. A1, A18.

Schempf, A. H. (2007). Illicit drug use and neonatal outcomes: a critical review. *Obstetrics and Gynecological Surveys, 62*, 745–757.

Schenk, A. M., & Fremouw, W. J. (2012). Prevalence, psychological impact, and coping of cyberbully victims among college students. *Journal of School Violence, 11*, 21–37.

Scher, S. J., & Rauscher, F. (Eds.). (2003). *Evolutionary psychology: Alternative approaches*. Dordrecht, The Netherlands: Kluwer Academic Publishers.

Scherer, M. (2004). Contrasting inclusive with exclusive education. In M. Scherer, *Connecting to learn: Educational and assistive technology for people with disabilities*. Washington, DC: American Psychological Association.

Scherf, K. S., Sweeney, J. A., & Luna, B. (2006). Brain basis of developmental change in visuospatial working memory. *Journal of Cognitive Neuroscience, 18*, 1045–1058.

Schiavi, R. C. (1990). Sexuality and aging in men. *Annual Review of Sex Research, 1*, 227–249.

Schieber, F., Sugar, J. A., & McDowd, J. M. (1992). Behavioral sciences and aging. In J. E. Birren, B. R. Sloan, G. D. Cohen, N. R. Hooyman, & B. D. Lebowitz (Eds.), *Handbook of mental health and aging* (2nd ed.). San Diego, CA: Academic Press, 1992.

Schieman, S., McBrier, D. B., & van Gundy, K. (2003). Home-to-work conflict, work qualities, and emotional distress. *Sociological Forum, 18*, 137–164.

Schiffer, A., Pavan, A., Pedersen, S., Gremigni, P., Sommaruga, M., & Denollet, J. (2006, March). Type D personality and cardiovascular disease: Evidence and clinical implications. *Minerva Psichiatrica, 47*(1), 79–87.

Schiffer, A., Pedersen, S., Broers, H., Widdershoven, J., & Denollet, J. (2008). Type-D personality but not depression predicts severity of anxiety in heart failure patients at 1-year follow-up. *Journal of Affective Disorders, 106*, 73–81.

Schiffer, A. A., Pedersen, S. S., Widdershoven, J. W., Hendriks, E. H., Winter, J. B., & Denollet, J. (2005). The distressed (type D) personality is independently associated with impaired health status and increased depressive symptoms in chronic heart failure. *European Journal of Cardiovascular Prevention and Rehabilitation, 12*, 341–346.

Schiller, J. S., & Bemadel, L. (2004). Summary health statistics for the U.S. population: National Health Interview Survey, 2002. *Vital Health Statistics, 10*, 1–110.

Schindehette, S. (1997, December 8). Coming up roses. *People Weekly, 48*, 54–60.

Schindehette, S., Fowler, J., Grisby, L., & Breu, G. (1997, December 12). Coming up roses. *People*, pp. 54–60.

Schkade, D. A., & Kahneman, D. (1998). Does living in California make people happy? A focusing illusion on judgments of life satisfaction. *Psychological Science, 9*, 340–346.

Schlegel, A., & Barry, H., III. (1991). *Adolescence: An anthropological inquiry*. New York: The Free Press.

Schlossberg, N. (2004). *Retire smart, retire happy: Finding your true path in life*. Washington, DC: American Psychological Association.

Schmalz, D., & Kerstetter, D. (2006). Girlie girls and manly men: Chidren's stigma consciousness of gender in sports and physical activities. *Journal of Leisure Research, 38*, 536–557.

Schmidley, D. A. (2001). *Profile of the foreign-born population in the United States: 2000. Current Population Reports, Special Studies*: Washington, DC: U.S. Census Bureau.

Schmidt, M., Pekow, P., Freedson, P., Markenson, G., & Chasan-Taber, L. (2006). Physical activity patterns during pregnancy in a diverse population of women. *Journal of Women's Health, 15*, 909–918.

Schmidt, P. J., & Rubinow, D. R. (1991). Menopause-related affective disorders: A justification for further study. *American Journal of Psychiatry, 148*, 844–852.

Schmitt, D. (2004). Patterns and universals of mate poaching across 53 nations: The effects of sex, culture, and personality on romantically attracting another person's partner. *Journal of Personality and Social Psychology, 86*, 560–584.

Schmitt, E. (2001, March 13). For 7 million people in census, one race category isn't enough. *The New York Times*, p. A1, A14.

Schmitt, M., Kliegel, M., & Shapiro, A. (2007). Marital interaction in middle and old age: A predictor of marital satisfaction? *International Journal of Aging & Human Development, 65*, 283–300.

Schneider, B. (1997). Psychoacoustics and aging: Implications for everyday listening. *Journal of Speech-Language Pathology & Audiology, 21*, 111–124.

Schneider, B. A., Atkinson, L., & Tardif, C. (2001). Child–parent attachment and children's peer relations: A quantitative review. *Developmental Psychology, 37*, 86–100.

Schneider, B. A., Bull, D., & Trehub, S. E. (1988). Binaural unmasking in infants. *Journals of the Acoustical Society of America, 83*, 1124–1132.

Schneider, B. A., Trehub, S. E., & Bull, D. (1980). High-frequency sensitivity in infants. *Science, 207*, 1003–1004.

Schneider, E. L. (1999, February 5). Aging in the third millennium. *Science, 283*, 796–797.

Schneider, W., & Pressley, M. (1989). *Memory between two and twenty*. New York: Springer-Verlag.

Schneider, W., & Pressley, M. (1997). *Memory development between two and twenty* (2nd ed.). Mahwah, NJ: Lawrence Erlbaum Associates.

Schneiderman, N. (1983). Animal behavior models of coronary hearty disease. In D. S. Kranz, A. Baum, & J. E. Singer (Eds.), *Handbook of psychology and health* (Vol. 3). Hillsdale, NJ: Erlbaum.

Schnitzer, P. G. (2006). Prevention of unintentional childhood injuries. *American Family Physician, 74*, 1864–1869.

Schnur, E., & Belanger, S. (2000). What works in Head Start. In M. P. Kluger & G. Alexander et al. (Eds.), *What works in child welfare*. Washington, DC: Child Welfare League of America.

Schofield, J. W., & Francis, W. D. (1982). An observational study of peer interaction in racially mixed "accelerated" classrooms. *Journal of Educational Psychology, 74*, 722–732.

Schöner, G., & Thelen, E. (2006). Using dynamic field theory to rethink infant habituation. *Psychological Review, 113*, 273–299.

Schonert-Reichl, K. A., Smith, V., Zaidman-Zait, A., & Hertzman, C. (2012). Promoting children's prosocial behaviors in school: Impact of the "Roots of Empathy" program on the social and emotional competence of school-aged children. *School Mental Health, 4*, 1–21.

Schönpflug, U., & Bilz, L. (2009). The transmission process: Mechanisms and contexts. *Cultural transmission: Psychological, developmental, social, and methodological aspects*. New York: Cambridge University Press.

Schoppe-Sullivan, S., Diener, M., Mangelsdorf, S., Brown, G., McHale, J., & Frosch, C. (2006, July). Attachment and sensitivity in family context: The roles of parent and infant gender. *Infant and Child Development, 15*, 367–385.

Schoppe-Sullivan, S., Mangelsdorf, S., Brown, G., & Sokolowski, M. (2007, February). Goodness-of-fit in family context: Infant temperament, marital quality, and early coparenting behavior. *Infant Behavior & Development, 30*, 82–96.

Schor, E. L. (1987). Unintentional injuries: Patterns within families. *American Journal of the Diseases of Children, 141,* 1280.

Schore, A. (2003). *Affect regulation and the repair of the self.* New York: W. W. Norton.

Schreiber, G. B., Robins, M., Striegel-Moore, R., Obarzanek, M., Morrison, J. A., & Wright, D. J. (1996). Weight modification efforts reported by black and white preadolescent girls: National Heart, Lung, and Blood Institute Growth and Health Study. *Pediatrics, 98,* 63–70.

Schuetze, P., Eiden, R., & Coles, C. (2007). Prenatal cocaine and other substance exposure: Effects on infant autonomic regulation at 7 months of age. *Developmental Psychobiology, 49,* 276–289.

Schulenberg, J. E., Asp, C. E., & Peterson, A. C. (1984). School from the young adolescent's perspective. *Journal of Early Adolescence, 4,* 107–130.

Schulman, M. (1991). *The passionate mind: Bringing up an intelligent and creative child.* New York: Free Press.

Schulman, M., & Mekler, E. (1994). *Bringing up a moral child: A new approach for teaching your child to be kind, just, and responsible.* Reading, MA: Addison-Wesley.

Schulman, P., Keith, D., & Seligman, M. (1993). Is optimism heritable? A study of twins. *Behavior Research and Therapy, 31,* 569–574.

Schultz, A. H. (1969). *The life of primates.* New York: Universe.

Schultz, N. (2009, August 22). Do expanding waistlines cause shrinking brains? *New Scientist,* p. 9.

Schultz, R., & Curnow, C. (1988). Peak performance and age among superathletes: Track and field, swimming, baseball, tennis, and golf. *Journal of Gerontology, 43,* P113–P120.

Schultz, R., & Heckhausen, J. (1996). A life span model of successful aging. *American Psychologist, 51,* 702–714.

Schulz, R. (Ed.). (2000). *Handbook on dementia caregiving: Evidence-based interventions for family caregivers.* New York: Springer Publishing.

Schulz, R., & Aderman, D. (1976). How medical staff copes with dying patients. *Omega, 7,* 11–21.

Schulz, R., & Ewen, R. B. (1988). *Adult development and aging: Myths and emerging realities.* New York: Macmillan.

Schumer, F. (2009, September 29). After a death, the pain that doesn't go away. *The New York Times,* p. D1.

Schumm, W. R. (2004). What was really learned from Tasker and Golombok's (1995) study of lesbian and single parent mothers? *Psychological Reports, 94,* 422–424.

Schuster, C. S., & Ashburn, S. S. (1986). *The process of human development* (2nd ed.). Boston, MA: Little, Brown.

Schutt, R. K. (2001). *Investigating the social world: The process and practice of research.* Thousand Oaks, CA: Sage.

Schutz, H., Paxton, S., & Wertheim, E. (2002). Investigation of body comparison among adolescent girls. *Journal of Applied Social Psychology, 32,* 1906–1937.

Schwartz, B. S., & Stewart, W. F. (2007). Lead and cognitive function in adults: a questions and answers approach to a review of the evidence for cause, treatment, and prevention. *International Review of Psychiatry, 19,* 671–692.

Schwartz, C. E., & Rauch, S. L. (2004). Temperament and its implications for neuroimaging of anxiety disorders. *CNS Spectrums, 9,* 284–291.

Schwartz, C. E., Wright, C. L., Shin, L. M., Kagan, J., & Rauch, S. L. (2003, June 20). Inhibited and uninhibited infants "grown up": Adult amygdalar response to novelty. *Science, 300,* 1952–1953.

Schwartz, D., Dodge, K. A., Pettit, G. S., & Bates, J. E. (1997). The early socialization of aggressive victims of bullying. *Child Development, 68,* 665–675.

Schwartz, I. M. (1999). Sexual activity prior to coital interaction: A comparison between males and females. *Archives of Sexual Behavior, 28,* 63–69.

Schwartz, J. E., Friedman, H. S., Tucker, J. S., Tomlinson-Keasey, C., Wingard, D. L., & Criqui, M. H. (1995). Childhood sociodemographic and psychosocial factors as predictors of longevity across the life-span. *American Journal of Public Health, 85,* 1237–1245.

Schwartz, M. (2006, June 11). The hold-'em holdup. *The New York Times Magazine,* 52–58.

Schwartz, O. S., Dudgeon, P., Sheeber, L. B., Yap, M. H., Simmons, J. G., & Allen, N. B. (2012). Parental behaviors during family interactions predict changes in depression and anxiety symptoms during adolescence. *Journal of Abnormal Child Psychology, 40,* 59–71.

Schwartz, P., Maynard, A., & Uzelac, S. (2008). Adolescent egocentrism: A contemporary view. *Adolescence, 43,* 441–448.

Schwartz, S. J., Côté, J. E., & Arnett, J. (2005). Identity and agency in emerging adulthood: Two developmental routes in the individualization process. *Youth & Society, 37*(2), 201–229.

Schwarz, B., Mayer, B., Trommsdorff, G., Ben-Arieh, A., Friedlmeier, M., Lubiewska, K., & … Peltzer, K. (2012). Does the importance of parent and peer relationships for adolescents' life satisfaction vary across cultures? *The Journal of Early Adolescence, 32,* 55–80.

Schwarzer, R., & Knoll, N. (2007). Functional roles of social support within the stress and coping process: A theoretical and empirical overview. *International Journal of Psychology, 42,* 243–252.

Schwebel, D.C., & Gaines, J. (2007). Pediatric unintentional injury: Behavioral risk factors and implications for prevention. *Journal of Developmental and Behavioral Pediatrics. 28,* 245–254.

Schwebel, M., Maher, C. A., & Fagley, N. S. (Eds.). (1990). *Promoting cognitive growth over the life span.* Hillsdale, NJ: Erlbaum.

Schweinhart, L. J., Barnes, H. V., & Weikart, D. P. (1993). *Significant benefits: The High/Scope Perry Preschool Study through age 27 (Monographs of the High/Scope Educational Research Foundation, No. 10).* Ypsilanti, MI: High/Scope Press.

Schwenkhagen, A. (2007). Hormonal changes in menopause and implications on sexual health. *The Journal of Sexual Medicine, 4* (Suppl.), 220–226.

Sciarra, D. T., & Ambrosino, K. E. (2011). Post-secondary expectations and educational attainment. *Professional School Counseling, 14,* 231–241.

Scopesi, A., Zanobini, M., & Carossino, P. (1997). Childbirth in different cultures: Psychophysical reactions of women delivering in U.S., German, French, and Italian hospitals. *Journal of Reproductive & Infant Psychology, 15,* 9–30.

Scotland, G. S., McNamee, P., Cheyne, H., Hundley, V., & Barnett, C. (2011). Women's preferences for aspects of labor management: Results from a discrete choice experiment. *Birth: Issues in Perinatal Care, 38,* 36–46.

Scrimsher, S., & Tudge, J. (2003). The teaching/learning relationship in the first years of school: Some revolutionary implications of Vygotsky's theory. *Early Education and Development, 14* [Special issue], 293–312.

Scruggs, T. E., & Mastropieri, M. A. (1994). Successful mainstreaming in elementary science classes: A qualitative study of three reputational cases. *American Educational Research Journal, 31,* 785–811.

Sears, R. R. (1977). Sources of life satisfaction of the Terman gifted men. *American Psychologist, 32,* 119–129.

Seaton, E. K., Yip, T., Morgan-Lopez, A., & Sellers, R. M. (2012). Racial discrimination and racial socialization as predictors of African American adolescents' racial identity development using latent transition analysis. *Developmental Psychology, 48,* 448–458.

Sebanc, A., Kearns, K., Hernandez, M., & Galvin, K. (2007). Predicting having a best friend in young children: Individual characteristics and friendship features. *Journal of Genetic Psychology, 168,* 81–95.

Secouler, L. M. (1992). Our elders: At high risk for humiliation. Special Issue: The humiliation dynamic: Viewing the task of prevention from a new perspective: II. *Journal of Primary Prevention, 12,* 195–208.

Sedikides, C., Gaertner, L., & Toguchi, Y. (2003). Pancultural self-enhancement. *Journal of Personality and Social Psychology, 84,* 60–79.

SEER. (2005). Surveillance, Epidemiology, and End Results Program (SEER) Program. (www.seer.cancer. gov) SEER*Stat Database: Incidence—SEER 9 Regs Public-Use, Nov 2004 Sub (1973–2002), National Cancer Institute, DCCPS, Surveillance Research Program, Cancer Statistics Branch, released April 2005, based on the November 2004 submission.

Seethaler, P. M., Fuchs, L. S., Fuchs, D., & Compton, D. L. (2012). Predicting first graders' development of calculation versus word-problem performance: The role of dynamic assessment. *Journal of Educational Psychology, 104,* 224–234.

Segal, B. M., & Stewart, J. C. (1996). Substance use and abuse in adolescence: An overview. *Child Psychiatry & Human Development, 26,* 193–210.

Segal, J., & Segal, Z. (1992, September). No more couch potatoes. *Parents,* p. 235.

Segal, N. L. (1993). Twin, sibling, and adoption methods: Tests of evolutionary hypotheses. *American Psychologist, 48,* 943–956.

Segal, N. L. (2000). Virtual twins: New findings on within-family environmental influences on intelligence. *Journal of Educational Psychology, 92,* 188–194.

Segal, N., McGuire, S., Havlena, J., Gill, P., & Hershberger, S. (2007). Intellectual similarity of virtual twin pairs: Developmental trends. *Personality and Individual Differences, 42,* 1209–1219.

Segall, M. H. (1988). Cultural roots of aggressive behavior. In M. Bond (Ed.), *The cross-cultural challenge to social psychology.* New York: Sage Publications

Segall, M. H., Dasen, P. R., Berry, J. W., & Poortinga, Y. H. (1990). *Human behavior in global perspective.* Boston: Allyn & Bacon.

Segalowitz, S. J., & Rapin I. (Eds.). (2003). *Child neuropsychology, Part I.* Amsterdam, The Netherlands: Elsevier Science.

Segalowitz, S. J., Santesso, D. L., Willoughby, T., Reker, D. L., Campbell, K., Chalmers, H., & Rose-Krasnor, L. (2012). Adolescent peer interaction and trait surgency weaken medial prefrontal cortex responses to failure. *Social Cognitive and Affective Neuroscience, 7,* 115–124.

Segrè, F. (2009, August 16). Anne Miller and Michael Davoli. *The New York Times,* p. ST13.

Seibert, A., & Kerns, K. (2009). Attachment figures in middle childhood. *International Journal of Behavioral Development, 33,* 347–355.

Seidman, S. (2003). The aging male: Androgens, erectile dysfunction, and depression. *Journal of Clinical Psychiatry, 64,* 31–37.

Seidman, S. N., & Rieder, R. O. (1994). A review of sexual behavior in the United States. *American Journal of Psychiatry, 151,* 330–341.

Seifer, R., Schiller, M., & Sameroff, A. J. (1996). Attachment, maternal sensitivity, and infant temperament during the first year of life. *Developmental Psychology, 32,* 12–25.

Selfhout, M., Denissen, J., Branje, S., & Meeus, W. (2009). In the eye of the beholder: Perceived, actual, and peer-rated similarity in personality, communication, and friendship intensity during the acquaintanceship process. *Journal of Personality and Social Psychology, 96,* 1152–1165.

Selig, S., Tomlinson, T., & Hickey, T. (1991). Ethical dimensions of intergenerational reciprocity: Implications for practice. *Gerontologist, 31,* 624–630.

Seligman, L. (1995). *Promoting a fighting spirit: Psychotherapy for cancer patients, survivors, and their families.* San Francisco: Jossey-Bass.

Seligman, M. E. P. (2007). Coaching and positive psychology. *Australian Psychologist, 42,* 266–267.

Semerci, Ç. (2006). The opinions of medicine faculty students regarding cheating in relation to Kohlberg's moral development concept. *Social Behavior and Personality, 34,* 41–50.

Sener, A., Terzioglu, R., & Karabulut, E. (2007, January). Life satisfaction and leisure activities during men's retirement: A Turkish sample. *Aging & Mental Health, 11,* 30–36.

Senghas, A., Kita, S., & özyürek, A. (2004, September, 17). Children creating core properties of language: Evidence from an emerging sign language in Nicaragua. *Science, 305,* 1779–1782.

Senter, L., Sackoff, J., Landi, K., & Boyd, L. (2011). Studying sudden and unexpected infant deaths in a time of changing death certification and investigation practices: Evaluating sleep-related risk factors for infant death in New York City. *Maternal and Child Health Journal, 15,* 242–248.

Seppa, N. (1996, December). Keeping schoolyards safe from bullies. *APA Monitor,* p. 41.

Seppa, N. (1997, February). Wisdom: A quality that may defy age. *APA Monitor,* pp. 1, 9.

Serbin, L., & Karp, J. (2004). The intergenerational transfer of psychosocial risk: Mediators of vulnerability and resilience. *Annual Review of Psychology, 55,* 333–363.

Serbin, L., Poulin-Dubois, D., & Colburne, K. (2001). Gender stereotyping in infancy: Visual preferences for and knowledge of gender-stereotyped toys in the second year. *International Journal of Behavioral Development, 25,* 7–15.

Serbin, L. A., Poulin-Dubois, D., Colburne, K. A., Sen, M. G., & Eichstedt, J. A. (2001). Gender stereotyping in infancy: Visual preferences for and knowledge of gender-stereotyped toys in the second year. *International Journal of Behavioral Development, 25,* 7–15.

Serbin, L., Poulin-Dubois, D., & Eichstedt, J. (2002). Infants' response to gender-inconsistent events. *Infancy, 3,* 531–542.

Serovich, J. M., & Greene, K. (1997). Predictors of adolescent risk taking behaviors which put them at risk for contracting HIV. *Journal of Youth & Adolescence, 26,* 429–444.

Serretti, A., Calati, R., Ferrari, B., & De Ronchi, D. (2007). Personality and genetics. *Current Psychiatry Reviews, 3,* 147–159.

Servin, A., Nordenström, A., Larsson, A., & Bohlin, G. (2003). Prenatal androgens and gender-typed behavior: A study of girls with mild and severe forms of congenital adrenal hyperplasia. *Developmental Psychology, 39,* 440–450.

Serwint, J. R., Dias, M., & White, J. (2000). Effects of lead counseling for children with lead levels >=20 mug/dL: Impact on parental knowledge, attitudes, and behavior. *Clinical Pediatrics, 39,* 643–650.

Sesser, S. (1993, September 13). Opium war redux. *The New Yorker,* pp. 78–89.

Settersten, R. (2002). Social sources of meaning in later life. In R. Weiss & S. Bass (Eds.), *Challenges of the third age: Meaning and purpose in later life.* London: Oxford University Press.

Seva, N., Kempe, V., Brooks, P., Mironova, N., Pershukova, A., & Fedorova, O. (2007). Crosslinguistic evidence for the diminutive advantage: Gender agreement in Russian and Serbian children. *Journal of Child Language, 34,* 111–131.

Seven, R. (2006, November 26). The road taken. *The Seattle Times Pacific Northwest Sunday Magazine,* p. 6.

Seyfarth, R., & Cheney, D. (1996). *Inside the mind of a monkey.* Cambridge, MA: MIT Press.

Seymour, H. N., Abdulkarim, L., & Johnson, V. (1999). The Ebonics controversy: An educational and clinical dilemma. *Topics in Language Disorders, 19,* 66–77.

Seymour, J., Payne, S., Chapman, A., & Holloway, M. (2007). Hospice or home? Expectations of end-of-life care among white and Chinese older people in the UK. *Sociology of Health & Illness, 29,* 872–890.

Shad, M. U., Bidesi, A. S., Chen, L., Thomas, B. P., Ernst, M., & Rao, U. (2011). Neurobiology of decision-making in adolescents. *Behavioural Brain Research, 217,* 67–76.

Shafer, R. G. (1990, March 12). An anguished father recounts the battle he lost—Trying to rescue a teenage son from drugs. *People Weekly,* 81–83.

Shaffer, D., Bautista, C., Sateren, W., Sawe, F., Kiplangat, S., Miruka, A., et al. (2007). The protective effect of circumcision on HIV incidence in rural low-risk men circumcised predominantly by traditional circumcisers in Kenya: Two-year follow-up of the Kericho HIV Cohort Study. *JAIDS Journal of Acquired Immune Deficiency Syndromes, 45,* 371–379.

Shala, M., & Bahtiri, A. (2011). Differences in gross motor achievements among children of four to five years of age in private and public institutions in Prishtinë, Kosovo. *Early Child Development and Care, 181,* 55–61.

Shangguan, F., & Shi, J. (2009). Puberty timing and fluid intelligence: A study of correlations between testosterone and intelligence in 8- to 12-year-old Chinese boys. *Psychoneuroendocrinology, 34,* 983–988.

Shantz, C. U., & Hartup, W. W. (Eds.). (1995). *Conflict in child and adolescent development.* New York: Cambridge University Press.

Shapiro, A. F., Gottman, J. M., & Carrère, S. (2000). The baby and the marriage: Identifying factors that buffer against decline in marital satisfaction after the first baby arrives. *Journal of Family Psychology, 14,* 124–130.

Shapiro, J. R. (2012). Types of threats: From stereotype threat to stereotype threats. In M. Inzlicht & T. Schmader (Eds.), *Stereotype threat: Theory, process, and application.* New York: Oxford University Press.

Shapiro, L. (1997, Spring/Summer). Beyond an apple a day. *Newsweek Special Issue,* 52–56.

Shapiro, L., & Solity, J. (2008). Delivering phonological and phonics training within whole-class teaching. *British Journal of Educational Psychology, 78,* 597–620.

Sharf, R. S. (1992). *Applying career development theory to counseling.* Pacific Grove, CA: Brooks/Cole.

Sharma, M. (2008). Twenty-first century pink or blue: How sex selection technology facilitates gendercide and what we can do about it. *Family Court Review, 46,* 198–215.

Sharp, D. (1997, March 14–16). Your kids' education is at stake. *USA Weekend,* 4–6.

Sharpe, R. (1994, July 18). Better babies: School gets kids to do feats at a tender age, but it's controversial. *The Wall Street Journal,* pp. A1, A6.

Shaunessy, E., Suldo, S., Hardesty, R., & Shaffer, E. (2006, December). School functioning and psychological well-being of International Baccalaureate and general education students: A preliminary examination. *Journal of Secondary Gifted Education, 17,* 76–89.

Shavelson, R., Hubner, J. J., & Stanton, J. C. (1976). Self-concept: Validation of construct interpretations. *Review of Educational Research, 46,* 407–441.

Shaver, P. (1994, August). *Attachment and care giving in adult romantic relationships.* Invited address presented at the annual meeting of the American Psychological Association, Los Angeles.

Shaver, P. R., Hazan, C., & Bradshaw, D. (1988). Love as attachment: The integration of three behavioral systems. In R. J. Sternberg & M. L. Barnes (Eds.), *The psychology of love* (pp. 68–99). New Haven, CT: Yale University Press.

Shaver, P. R., & Mikulincer, M. (2012). Attachment theory. In P. M. Van Lange, A. W. Kruglanski, E. Higgins, P. M. Van Lange, A. W. Kruglanski, & E. Higgins (Eds.), *Handbook of theories of social psychology* (Vol. 2). Thousand Oaks, CA: Sage Publications Ltd.

Shavitt, S., Torelli, C. J., & Riemer, H. (2011). Horizontal and vertical individualism and collectivism: Implications for understanding psychological processes. In M. J. Gelfand, C. Chiu, & Y. Hong (Eds.), *Advances in culture and psychology* (Vol. 1). New York: Oxford University Press.

Shaw, D. S., Winslow, E. B., & Flanagan, C. (1999). A prospective study of the effects of marital status and family relations on young children's adjustment among African American and European American families. *Child Development, 70,* 742–755.

Shaw, J. (1994). Aging and sexual potential. *Journal of Sex Education and Therapy, 20,* 134–139.

Shaw, L. R., Chan, F., & McMahon, B. T. (2012). Intersectionality and disability harassment: The interactive effects of disability, race, age, and gender. *Rehabilitation Counseling Bulletin, 55,* 82–91.

Shaw, M. L. (2003). Creativity and whole language. In J. Houtz (Ed.), *The educational psychology of creativity.* Cresskill, NJ: Hampton Press.

Shaw, P., Eckstrand, K., Sharp, W., Blumenthal, J., Lerch, J. P., Greenstein, D., Classen, L., Evans, A., Giedd, J., & Rapoport, J. L. (2007). Attention-deficit/hyperactivity disorder is characterized by a delay in cortical maturation. *Proceedings of the National Academy of Sciences, 104,* 19649–19654.

Shaywitz, B. A., Shaywitz, S. E., Blachman, B. A., Pugh, K. R., Fulbright, R. K., Skudlarski, P., Mencl, W. E., Constable, R. T., Holahan, J. M., Marchione, K. E., Fletcher, J. M., Lyon, G. R., & Gore, J. C. (2004). Development of left occipitotemporal systems for skilled reading in children after a phonologically-based intervention. *Biological Psychiatry, 55,* 926–933.

Shaywitz, S. (2004). *Overcoming dyslexia: A new and complete science-based program for reading problems at any level.* New York: Vintage.

Shaywitz, S. E. (1996, November). Dyslexia. *Scientific American,* 98–104.

Shaywitz, S. E., Shaywitz, B. A., Pugh, K. R., Fulbright, R. K., Skudlarski, P., Mencl, W. E., Constable, R. T., Naftolin, F., Palter, S. F., Marchione, K. E., Katz, L., Shankweiler, D. P., Fletcher, J. M., Lacadie, C., Keltz, M., & Gore, J. C. (1999). Effect of estrogen on brain activation patterns in postmenopausal women during working memory tasks. *Journal of the American Medical Association, 281,* 1197–1202.

Shea, J. (2006, September). Cross-cultural comparison of women's midlife symptom-reporting: A China study. *Culture, Medicine and Psychiatry, 30,* 331–362.

Shea, J. D. (1985). Studies of cognitive development in Papua, New Guinea. *International Journal of Psychology, 20,* 33–61.

Shea, K. M., Wilcox, A. J., & Little, R. E. (1998). Postterm delivery: A challenge for epidemiologic research. *Epidemiology, 9,* 199–204.

Shealy, C. N. (1995). From Boys Town to Oliver Twist: Separating fact from fiction in welfare reform and out-of-home placement of children and youth. *American Psychologist, 50,* 565–580.

Sheehan, N., & Petrovic, K. (2008). Grandparents and their adult grandchildren: Recurring themes from the literature. *Marriage & Family Review, 44,* 99–124.

Sheehy, G. (1976). *Passages.* New York: Dutton.

Sheese, B., Voelker, P., Posner, M., & Rothbart, M. (2009). Genetic variation influences on the early development of reactive emotions and their regulation by attention. *Cognitive Neuropsychiatry, 14,* 332–355.

Sheets, R. H., & Hollins, E. R. (1999). *Racial and ethnic identity in school practices.* Mahwah, NJ: Lawrence Erlbaum.

Sheffield, J. V. (1997). General medicine update: NIDDM, prevention of CAD, & risks & benefits of hormone replacement therapy. *Comprehensive Therapy, 23,* 303–309.

Sheingold, K., & Tenney, Y. J. (1982). Memory for a salient childhood event. In U. Neisser (Ed.), *Memory observed.* New York: Freeman.

Shelby, R., Crespin, T., Wells-Di Gregorio, S., Lamdan, R., Siegel, J., & Taylor, K. (2008). Optimism, social support, and adjustment in African American women with breast cancer. *Journal of Behavioral Medicine, 31,* 433–444.

Sheldon, K. M., Elliot, A. J., Kim, Y., & Kasser, T. (2001). What is satisfying about satisfying events? Testing 10 candidate psychological needs. *Journal of Personality and Social Psychology, 80,* 325–339.

Sheldon, K. M., Joiner, T. E., Jr., & Pettit, J. W. (2003). Reconciling humanistic ideals and scientific clinical practice. *Clinical Psychology, 10,* 302–315.

Sheldon, S., & Wilkinson, S. (2004). Should selecting saviour siblings be banned? *Journal of Medical Ethics, 30,* 533–537.

Shellenbarger, S. (2003, January 9). Yes, that weird day-care center could scar your child, researchers say. *The Wall Street Journal,* p. D1.

Shenkin, S. D., Starr, J. M., & Deary, I. J. (2004). Birth weight and cognitive ability in childhood: A systematic review. *Psychological Bulletin, 130,* 989–1013.

Shepard, G. B. (1991). A glimpse of kindergarten—Chinese style. *Young Children, 47,* 11–15.

Sheridan, C., & Radmacher, S. (2003). Significance of psychosocial factors to health and disease. In L. Schein & H. Bernard (Eds.), *Psychosocial treatment for medical conditions: Principles and techniques.* New York: Brunner-Routledge.

Sherman, E. (1991). *Reminiscence and the self in old age.* New York: Springer.

Sherman, S., Allen, E., Bean, L., & Freeman, S. (2007). Epidemiology of Down syndrome. *Mental Retardation and Developmental Disabilities Research Reviews, 13,* 221–227.

Shernoff, D., & Schmidt, J. (2008). Further evidence of an engagement-achievement paradox among U.S. high school students. *Journal of Youth and Adolescence, 37,* 564–580.

Sherry, B., Springer, D. A., Connell, F. A., & Garrett, S. M. (1992). Short, thin, or obese? Comparing growth indexes of children from high- and low-poverty areas. *Journal of the American Dietetic Association, 92,* 1092–1095.

Sherwin, B. B. (1991). The psychoendocrinology of aging and female sexuality. *Annual Review of Sex Research, 2,* 181–198.

Shevron, R. H., & Lumsden, D. B. (1985). *Introduction to educational gerontology* (2nd ed.). New York: Hemisphere.

Shi, B., & Xie, H. (2012). Socialization of physical and social aggression in early adolescents' peer groups: High-status peers, individual status, and gender. *Social Development, 21,* 170–194.

Shi, L. (2003). Facilitating constructive parent–child play: Family therapy with young children. *Journal of Family Psychotherapy, 14,* 19–31.

Shi, X., & Lu, X. (2007, October). Bilingual and bicultural development of Chinese American adolescents and young adults: A comparative study. *Howard Journal of Communications, 18*(4), 313–333.

Shimizu, M., & Pelham, B. (2004). The unconscious cost of good fortune: Implicit and explicit self-esteem, positive life events, and health. *Health Psychology, 23,* 101–105.

Shin, H. B., & Bruno. R. (2003). *Language use and English speaking ability: 2000.* Washington, DC: U.S. Census Bureau.

Shiner, R., Masten, A., & Roberts, J. (2003). Childhood personality foreshadows adult personality and life outcomes two decades later. *Journal of Personality, 71,* 1145–1170.

Shiono, P. H., & Behrman, R. E. (1995). Low birth weight: Analysis and recommendations. *The Future of Children, 5,* 4–18.

Shneidman, E. S. (1983). *Deaths of man.* New York: Jason Aronson.

Shock, N. W. (1962). *The physiology of aging.* San Francisco, CA: Freeman.

Shonk, S. M., & Cicchetti, D. (2001). Maltreatment, competency deficits, and risk for academic and behavioral maladjustment. *Developmental Psychology, 37,* 3–17.

Shook, J., Vaughn, M., Litschge, C., Kolivoski, K., & Schelbe, L. (2009). The importance of friends among foster youth aging out of care: Cluster profiles of deviant peer affiliations. *Children and Youth Services Review, 31,* 284–291.

Shor, R. (2006, May). Physical punishment as perceived by parents in Russia: Implications for professionals involved in the care of children. *Early Child Development and Care, 176,* 429–439.

Short, L. (2007, February). Lesbian mothers living well in the context of heterosexism and discrimination: Resources, strategies and legislative change. *Feminism & Psychology, 17,* 57–74.

Short, R. J., & Talley, R. C. (1997). Rethinking psychology and the schools: Implications of recent national policy. *American Psychologist, 52,* 234–240.

Shreeve, D. F. (2012). *Reactive attachment disorder: A case-based approach.* New York: Springer Science + Business Media.

Shriver, M. D., & Piersel, W. (1994). The long-term effects of intrauterine drug exposure: Review of recent research and implications for early childhood special education. *Topics in Early Childhood Special Education, 14,* 161–183.

Shrum, W., Cheek, N., Jr., & Hunter, S. M. (1988). Friendship in school: Gender and racial homophily. *Sociology of Education, 61,* 227–239.

Shucard, J., Shucard, D., Cummins, K., & Campso, J. (1981). Auditory evoked potentials and sexrelated differences in brain development. *Brain and Language, 13,* 91–102.

Shulman, S., & Ben-Artzi, E. (2003). Age-related differences in the transition from adolescence to adulthood and links with family relationships. *Journal of Adult Development, 10,* 217–226.

Shumaker, S. A., & Smith, T. R. (1994). The politics of women's health. *Journal of Social Issues, 50,* 189–202.

Shurkin, J. N. (1992). *Terman's kids: The groundbreaking study of how the gifted grow up.* Boston: Little, Brown.

Shute, N. (1997, November 10). No more hard labor. *U.S. News & World Report,* pp. 92–95.

Shute, R., & Charlton, K. (2006). Anger or compromise? Adolescents' conflict resolution strategies in relation to gender and type of peer relationship. *International Journal of Adolescence and Youth, 13,* 55–69.

Shweder, R. A. (Ed.). (1998). *Welcome to middle age (and other cultural fictions).* Chicago, IL: University of Chicago Press.

Sidanius, J., & Pratto, F. (2012). Social dominance theory. In P. M. Van Lange, A. W. Kruglanski, & E. Higgins, (Eds.), *Handbook of theories of social psychology* (Vol. 2). Thousand Oaks, CA: Sage Publications Ltd.

Sidora-Arcoleo, K., Feldman, J. M., Serebrisky, D., & Spray, A. (2012). A multi-factorial model for examining racial and ethnic disparities in acute asthma visits by children. *Annals of Behavioral Medicine, 43,* 15–28.

Sieber, J. E. (1998). Planning ethically responsible research. In L. Bickman & D. J. Rog (Eds.), *Handbook of applied social research methods* (pp. 127–156). Thousand Oaks, CA: Sage.

Sieber, J. E. (2000). Planning research: Basic ethical decision-making. In B. D. Sales & S. Folkman (Eds.), *Ethics in research with human participants.* Washington, DC: American Psychological Association.

Siegal, M. (1997). *Knowing children: Experiments in conversation and cognition* (2nd ed.). Hove, England: Psychology Press/Erlbaum, Taylor & Francis.

Siegal, M. (2003). Cognitive development. *An introduction to developmental psychology.* Malden, MA: Blackwell Publishing.

Siegel, B. (1996). Is the emperor wearing clothes? Social policy and the empirical support for full inclusion of children with disabilities in the preschool and early elementary grades. *Social Policy Report, 10,* 2–17.

Siegel, L. J., & Davis, L. (2008). Somatic disorders. In R. J. Morris & T. R. Kratochwill (Eds.), *The practice of child therapy* (4th ed.). Mahwah, NJ: Lawrence Erlbaum Associates.

Siegel, L. S. (1989). A reconceptualization of prediction from infant test scores. In M. H. Bornstein & N. A. Krasnegor (Eds.), *Stability and continuity in mental development: Behavioral and biological perspectives.* Hillsdale, NJ: Erlbaum.

Siegel, S., Dittrich, R., & Vollmann, J. (2008). Ethical opinions and personal attitudes of young adults conceived by in vitro fertilisation. *Journal of Medical Ethics, 34,* 236–240.

Siegler, I. C., & Costa, P. T. (1985). Health behavior relationships. In J. E. Birren & K. W. Schaie (Eds.), *Handbook of the psychology of aging* (2nd ed.). New York: Van Nostrand Reinhold.

Siegler, R. (2003). Thinking and intelligence. In M. Bornstein & L. Davidson (Eds.), *Well-being: Positive development across the life course* (pp. 311–320). Mahwah, NJ: Lawrence Erlbaum Associates.

Siegler, R. (2007). Cognitive variability. *Developmental Science, 10,* 104–109.

Siegler, R. S. (1994). Cognitive variability: A key to understanding cognitive development. *Current Directions in Psychological Science, 3,* 1–5.

Siegler, R. S. (1995). How does change occur? A microgentic study of number conservation. *Cognitive Psychology, 28,* 225–273.

Siegler, R. S. (1998). *Children's thinking* (3rd ed.). Upper Saddle River, NJ: Prentice-Hall.

Siegler, R. S., & Ellis, S. (1996). Piaget on childhood. *Psychological Science, 7,* 211–215.

Siegler, R. S., & Richards, D. (1982). The development of intelligence. In R. Sternberg (Ed.), *Handbook of human intelligence.* London: Cambridge University Press.

Siegman, A. W., & Smith, T. W. (Eds.). (1994). *Anger, hostility and the heart.* Mahwah, NJ: Erlbaum.

Sierra, F. (2006, June). Is (your cellular response to) stress killing you? *Journals of Gerontology: Series A: Biological Sciences and Medical Sciences, 61,* 557–561.

Sigman, M. (1995). Nutrition and child development: More food for thought. *Current Directions in Psychological Science, 4,* 52–55.

Sigman, M., Cohen, S. E., & Beckwith, L. (1997). Why does infant attention predict adolescent intelligence? *Infant Behavior & Development, 20,* 133–140.

Sigman, M., Cohen, S., & Beckwith, L. (2000). Why does infant attention predict adolescent intelligence? In D. Muir & A. Slater (Eds.), *Infant development: The essential readings* (pp. 239–253). Malden, MA: Blackwell Publishers.

Sigman, M., Cohen, S. E., Beckwith, L., Asarnow, R., & Parmelee, A. H. (1991). Continuity in cognitive abilities from infancy to 12 years of age. *Cognitive Development* 6, 47-57.

Sigman, M. D., Cohen, S. E., Beckwith, L., Asarnow, R., & Parmelee, A. H. (1992). The prediction of cognitive abilities at 8 and 12 years of age from neonatal assessments of preterm infants. In S. L. Friedman & M. D. Sigman (Eds.), *The psychological development of low birthweight children.* Norwood, NJ: Ablex.

Sigman, M., Neumann, C., Jansen, A. A. J., & Bwibo, N. (1989). Cognitive abilities of Kenyan children in relation to nutrition, family characteristics, and education. *Child Development, 60,* 1463–1474.

Sigmund, E., De Ste Croix, M., Miklánková, L., & Frömel, K. (2007, December). Physical activity patterns of kindergarten children in comparison to teenagers and young adults. *European Journal of Public Health, 17*(6), 646–651.

Signorella, M. L., Bigler, R. S., & Liben, L. (1993). Development differences in children's gender schemata about others: A meta-analytic review. *Developmental Review, 13,* 106–126.

Signorella, M., & Frieze, I. (2008). Interrelations of gender schemas in children and adolescents: Attitudes, preferences, and self-perceptions. *Social Behavior and Personality, 36,* 941–954.

Silbereisen, R., Peterson, A., Albrecht, H., & Krache, B. (1989). Maturational timing and the development of problem behavior: Longitudinal studies in adolescence. *Journal of Early Adolescence, 9,* 247.

Silenzio, V., Pena, J., Duberstein, P., Cerel, J., & Knox, K. (2007, November). Sexual orientation and risk factors for suicidal ideation and suicide attempts among adolescents and young adults. *American Journal of Public Health, 97*(11), 2017–2019.

Silva, M., Groeger, J., & Bradshaw, M. (2006). Attention-memory interactions in scene perception. *Spatial Vision, 19,* 9–19.

Silverstein, L. B., & Auerbach, C. F. (1999). Deconstructing the essential father. *American Psychologist, 54,* 397–407.

Silverthorn, P., & Frick, P. J. (1999). Developmental pathways to antisocial behavior: The delayed-onset pathway in girls. *Developmental & Psychopathology, 11,* 101–126.

Simcock, G., Garrity, K., & Barr, R. (2011). The effect of narrative cues on infants' imitation from television and picture books. *Child Development, 82,* 1607–1619.

Simcock, G., & Hayne, H. (2002). Breaking the barrier? Children fail to translate their preverbal memories into language. *Psychological Science, 13,* 225–231.

Simmons, R. (2002). *Odd girl out: The hidden culture of aggression in girls.* Orlando, FL: Harcourt.

Simmons, R., & Blyth, D. (1987). *Moving into adolescence.* New York: Aldine de Gruyter.

Simmons, S. W., Cyna, A. M., Dennis, A. T., & Hughes, D. (2007). Combined spinal-epidural versus epidural analgesia in labour. *Cochrane Database and Systematic Review, 18,* CD003401.

Simms, K. (2012). A hierarchical examination of the immigrant achievement gap: The additional explanatory power of nationality and educational selectivity over traditional explorations of race and socioeconomic status. *Journal of Advanced Academics, 23,* 72–98.

Simon, R. W. (2008). The joys of parenthood, reconsidered. *Contexts, 7,* 40–45.

Simonoff, E., Bolton, P., & Rutter, M. (1996). Mental retardation: Genetic findings, clinical implications and research agenda. *Journal of Child Psychology and Psychiatry and Allied Disciplines, 37,* 259–280.

Simons, D. A., & Wurtele, S. K. (2010). Relationships between parents' use of corporal punishment and their children's endorsement of spanking and hitting other children. *Child Abuse & Neglect, 34,* 639–646.

Simons, K. (Ed.). (1993). *Early visual development: normal and abnormal.* New York: Oxford University Press.

Simons, L., & Conger, R. (2007, February). Linking mother–father differences in parenting to a typology of family parenting styles and adolescent outcomes. *Journal of Family Issues, 28,* 212–241.

Simons, M. (1995, September 11). Dutch doctors to tighten rules on mercy killings. *The New York Times,* p. A7.

Simons, S. H., van Dijk, M., Anand, K. S., Roofthooft, D., van Lingen, R. A., & Tibboel. D., (2003). Do we still hurt newborn babies? A prospective study of procedural pain and analgesia in neonates. *Archives of Pediatrics and Adolescence, 157,* 1058–1064.

Simonton, D. K. (1989). The swan-song phenomenon: Last-works effects for 172 classical composers. *Psychology and Aging, 4,* 42–47.

Simonton, D. K. (1994). *Greatness: Who makes history and why.* New York: Guilford.

Simonton, D. K. (1997). Creative productivity: A predictive and explanatory model of career trajectories and landmarks. *Psychological Review, 104,* 66–89.

Simonton, D. K. (2009). Varieties of (scientific) creativity: A hierarchical model of domain-specific disposition, development, and achievement. *Perspectives on Psychological Science, 4,* 441–452.

Simpkins, S., Parke, R., Flyr, M., & Wild, M. (2006, November). Similarities in children's and early adolescents? Perceptions of friendship qualities across development, gender, and friendship qualities. *Journal of Early Adolescence, 26,* 491–508.

Simpson, J. A. (1990). Influence of attachment styles on romantic relationships. *Journal of Personality & Social Psychology, 59,* 971–980.

Simpson, J. M., Thompson, J. F., & Ellwood, D. A. (2006). Intrapartum epidural analgesia and breastfeeding: A prospective cohort study. *International Breastfeeding Journal, 11,* 1–24.

Simpson, J., Collins, W., Tran, S., & Haydon, K. (2007, February). Attachment and the experience and expression of emotions in romantic relationships: A developmental perspective. *Journal of Personality and Social Psychology, 92,* 355–367.

Simpson, R., & Otten, K. (2005). Structuring behavior management strategies and building social competence. In D. Zager, *Autism spectrum disorders: Identification, education, and treatment* (3rd ed.). Mahwah, NJ: Lawrence Erlbaum Associates.

Simson, S., Thompson, E., & Wilson, L. B. (2001). Who is teaching lifelong learners? A study of peer educators in institutes for learning in retirement. *Gerontology & Geriatrics Education, 22,* 31–43.

Simson, S., Wilson, L., & Harlow-Rosentraub, K. (2006). *Civic engagement and lifelong learning institutes: Current status and future directions.* New York: Haworth Press.

Sinclair, D. A., & Guarente, L. (2006). Unlocking the secrets of longevity genes. *Scientific American, 294,* 48–51, 54–57.

Singer, D. G., & Singer, J. L. (Eds.). (2000). *Handbook of children and the media.* Thousand Oaks, CA: Sage.

Singer, L. T., Arendt, R., Minnes, S., Farkas, K., & Salvator, A. (2000). Neurobehavioral outcomes of cocaine-exposed infants. *Neurotoxicology & Teratology, 22,* 653–666.

Singer, M. S., Stacey, B. G., & Lange, C. (1993). The relative utility of expectancy-value theory and social cognitive theory in predicting psychology student course goals and career aspirations. *Journal of Social Behavior and Personality, 8,* 703–714.

Singh, B. R. (1991). Teaching methods for reducing prejudice and enhancing academic achievement for all children. *Educational Studies, 17,* 157–171.

Singh, G. K., & Yu, S. M. (1995). Infant mortality in the United States: Trends, differentials, and projections 1950 through 2010. *The American Journal of Public Health, 85,* 957–964.

Singh, S., & Darroch, J. E. (2000). Adolescent pregnancy and childbearing: Levels and trends in developed countries. *The Canadian Journal of Human Sexuality, 9,* 67.

Singleton, L. C., & Asher, S. R. (1979). Racial integration and children's peer preferences. *Child Development, 50,* 936–941.

Sinnott, J. (2003). Postformal thought and adult development: Living in balance. *Handbook of adult development.* New York: Kluwer Academic/Plenum Publishers.

Sinnott, J. D. (1998a). Career paths and creative lives: A theoretical perspective on late-life potential. In C. Adams-Price (Ed.), *Creativity and successful aging: Theoretical and empirical approaches.* New York: Springer.

Sinnott, J. D. (1998b). *The development of logic in adulthood: Postformal thought and its applications.* New York: Plenum.

Sinnott, J. D. (2008). Cognitive and representational development in adults. In B. Kelly (Ed.), *Literacy processes: Cognitive flexibility in learning and teaching.* New York: Guilford Press.

Sinnott-Armstrong, W. (2008). *Moral psychology, Vol 3: The neuroscience of morality: Emotion, brain disorders, and development.* Cambridge, MA: MIT Press.

Sirois, B., & Burg, M. (2003). Negative emotion and coronary heart disease: A review. *Behavior Modification, 27,* 83–102.

Skårberg, K., Nyberg, F., & Engström, I. (2010). Is there an association between the use of anabolic-androgenic steroids and criminality? *European Addiction Research, 16*(4), 213–219.

Skibbe, L. E., Connor, C., Morrison, F. J., & Jewkes, A. M. (2011). Schooling effects on preschoolers' self-regulation, early literacy, and language growth. *Early Childhood Research Quarterly, 26,* 42–49.

Skinner, B. F. (1957). *Verbal behavior.* New York: Appleton-Century-Crofts.

Skinner, B. F. (1975). The steep and thorny road to a science of behavior. *American Psychologist, 30,* 42–49.

Skinner, J., Carruth, B., Wendy, B., & Ziegler, P. (2002). Children's food preferences: A longitudinal analysis. *Journal of the American Dietetic Association, 102,* 1638–1647.

Skinner, J. D., Ziegler, P., Pac, S., & Devaney, B. (2004). Meal and snack patterns of infants and toddlers. *Journal of the American Dietary Association, 104,* s65–s70.

Skipper, J. K., & Nass, G. (1966). Dating behavior: A framework of analysis and an illustration. *Journal of Marriage and the Family, 28,* 412–420.

Skowronski, J., Walker, W., & Betz, A. (2003). Ordering our world: An examination of time in autobiographical memory. *Memory, 11,* 247–260.

Slater, A. (1995). Individual differences in infancy and later IQ. *Journal of Child Psychology and Psychiatry and Allied Disciplines, 36,* 69–112.

Slater, A., & Butterworth, G. (1997). Perception of social stimuli: Face perception and imitation. In G. Bremmer, A. Slater, & G. Butterworth (Eds.), *Infant development: Recent advances* (pp. 223–245). Hove, UK: Psychology Press/Erlbaum, Taylor & Francis.

Slater, A., & Johnson, S. P. (1998). Visual sensory and perceptual abilities of the newborn: Beyond the blooming, buzzing confusion. In F. Simion, G. Butterworth, et al. (Eds.), *The development of sensory, motor and cognitive capacities in early infancy: From perception to cognition.* Hove, UK: Psychology Press/Erlbaum (Uk) Taylor & Francis.

Slater, A., Mattock, A., & Brown, E. (1990). Size constancy at birth: Newborn infants' responses to retinal and real size. *Journal of Experimental Child Psychology, 49,* 314–322.

Slater, M., Henry, K., & Swaim, R. (2003). Violent media content and aggressiveness in adolescents: A downward spiral model. *Communication Research, 30,* 713–736.

Slavin, R. E. (1995). Enhancing intergroup relations in schools: Cooperative learning and other strategies. In W. D. Hawley & A. W. Jackson (Eds.), *Toward a common destiny: Improving race and ethnic relations in America.* San Francisco: Jossey-Bass.

Sleek, S. (1997, June). Can "emotional intelligence" be taught in today's schools? *APA Monitor,* p. 25.

Slep, A. M., Smith, R., & O'Leary, S. G. (2001). Examining partner and child abuse: Are we ready for a more integrated approach to family violence? *Clinical Child & Family Psychology Review, 4,* 87–107.

Sliwinski, M., Buschke, H., Kuslansky, G., & Senior, G. (1994). Proportional slowing and addition speed in old and young adults. *Psychology and Aging, 9,* 72–80.

Sliwinski, M., Stawski, R., Hall, C., Katz, M., Verghese, J., & Lipton, R. (2006). Distinguishing preterminal and terminal cognitive decline. *European Psychologist, 11,* 172–181.

Sloan, S., Gildea, A., Stewart, M., Sneddon, H., & Iwaniec, D. (2008). Early weaning is related to weight and rate of weight gain in infancy. *Child: Care, Health and Development, 34,* 59–64.

Slobin, D. (1970). Universals of grammatical development in children. In G. Flores D'Arcais & W. Levelt (Eds.), *Advances in psycholinguistics.* New York: American Elsevier.

Small, B. J., & Bäckman, L. (1999). Time to death and cognitive performance. *Current Directions in Psychological Science, 8,* 168–172.

Small, G. W. (1991). Recognition and treatment of depression in the elderly. The clinician's challenge: Strategies for treatment of depression in the 1990s, Phoenix, Arizona. *Journal of Clinical Psychiatry, 52* (Suppl.), 11–22.

Small, G. W., Mazziotta, J. C., Collins, M. T., et al. (1995). Apolipoprotein E. type 4 allele and cerebral glucose metabolism in relatives at risk for familial Alzheimer's disease. *Journal of the American Medical Association, 273,* 942–947.

Smalls, C., White, R., Chavous, T., & Sellers, R. (2007). Racial ideological beliefs and racial discrimination experiences as predictors of academic engagement among African American adolescents. *Journal of Black Psychology, 33,* 299–330.

Smedley, A., & Smedley, B. D. (2005). Race as biology is fiction, racism as a social problem is real: Anthropological and historical perspectives on the social construction of race. *American Psychologist, 60,* 16–26.

Smedley, B. D., & Syme, S. L. (Eds.). (2000). *Promoting health: Intervention strategies from social and behavioral research.* Washington, DC: National Academy of Sciences.

Smetana, J. (1988). Concepts of self and social convention: Adolescents' and parents' reasoning about hypothetical and actual family conflicts. In M. Gunnar (Ed.), *21st Minnesota Symposium on Child Psychology.* Hillsdale, NJ: Erlbaum.

Smetana, J. (1989). Adolescents' and parents' reasoning about actual family conflict. *Child Development, 60,* 1052–1067.

Smetana, J. (2006). Social-cognitive domain theory: Consistencies and variations in children's moral and social judgments. *Handbook of moral development.* Mahwah, NJ: Lawrence Erlbaum Associates.

Smetana, J. G. (1995). Parenting styles and conceptions of parental authority during adolescence. *Child Development, 66,* 299–316.

Smetana, J. G. (2005). Adolescent-parent conflict: Resistance and subversion as developmental process. In L. Nucci, *Conflict, contradiction, and contrarian elements in moral development and education.* Mahwah, NJ: Lawrence Erlbaum Associates.

Smetana, J., Daddis, C., & Chuang, S. (2003)."Clean your room!" A longitudinal investigation of adolescent-parent conflict and conflict resolution in middle-class African American families. *Journal of Adolescent Research, 18,* 631–650.

Smetana, J., Yau, J., & Hanson, S. (1991). Conflict resolution in families with adolescents. *Journal of Research on Adolescence, 1,* 189–206.

Smith, A., Fried, P., Hogan, M., & Cameron, I. (2006). Effects of prenatal marijuana on visuospatial working memory: An fMRI study in young adults. *Neurotoxicology and Teratology, 28,* 286–295.

Smith, G. C., Pell, S. P., & Dobbie, R. (2003). Interpregnancy interval and risk of preterm birth and neonatal death. *British Medical Journal, 327,* 313–316.

Smith, J. (2005, April 7). Coaches help mom, dad see "big picture" in parenting. *The Oregonian,* 8.

Smith, J. S., Estudillo, A. G., & Kang, H. (2011). Racial differences in eighth grade students' identification with academics. *Education and Urban Society, 43,* 73–90.

Smith, J., & Baltes, P. B. (1997). Profiles of psychological functioning in the old and oldest old. *Psychology and Aging, 12,* 458–472.

Smith, M. (1990). Alternative techniques. *Nursing Times, 86,* 43–45.

Smith, N., & Trainor, L. (2008). Infant-directed speech is modulated by infant feedback. *Infancy, 13,* 410–420.

Smith, P. K. (1978). A longitudinal study of social participation in preschool children: Solitary and parallel play re-examined. *Developmental Psychology, 12,* 517–523.

Smith, P. K. (1995). Grandparenthood. In M. H. Bornstein, *Handbook of parenting.* Hillsdale, NJ: Erlbaum.

Smith, P., & Drew, L. (2002). Grandparenthood. In M. Bornstein (Ed.), *Handbook of parenting: Vol. 3: Being and becoming a parent* (2nd ed., pp. 141–172). Mahwah, NJ: Lawrence Erlbaum Associates.

Smith, P. K., Pepler, D., & Rigby, K. (Eds.). (2004). *Bullying in schools: How successful can interventions be?* New York: Cambridge University Press.

Smith, R. (1999, March). The timing of birth. *Scientific American,* 68–75.

Smith, R. J., Bale, J. F., Jr., & White, K. R. (2005, March 2). Sensorineural hearing loss in children. *Lancet, 365,* 879–890.

Smith, S., Quandt, S., Arcury, T., Wetmore, L., Bell, R., & Vitolins, M. (2006, January). Aging and eating in the rural, southern United States: Beliefs about salt and its effect on health. *Social Science & Medicine, 62,* 189–198.

Smith, T. B., & Silva, L. (2011). Ethnic identity and personal well-being of people of color: A meta-analysis. *Journal of Counseling Psychology, 58,* 42–60.

Smith, T. W. (1992). Hostility and health: Current status of a psychosomatic hypothesis. *Health Psychology, 11,* 139–150.

Smith, W., Mitchell, P., Webb, K., & Leeder, S. R. (1999). Dietary antioxidants and age-related maculopathy: The Blue Mountains Eye Study. *Opthalmology, 106,* 761–767.

Smorti, A. (2008). Everyday life reasoning, possible worlds and cultural processes. *Integrative Psychological & Behavioral Science, 42,* 224–232.

Smotherman, W. P., & Robinson, S. R. (1996). The development of behavior before birth. *Developmental Psychology, 32,* 425–434.

Smutny, J., Walker, S., & Meckstroth, E. (2007). *Acceleration for gifted learners, K–5.* Thousand Oaks, CA: Corwin Press.

Smuts, A. B., & Hagen, J. W. (1985). History of the family and of child development: Introduction to Part 1. *Monographs of the Society for Research in Child Development, 50* (4–5, Serial No. 211).

Snarey, J. R. (1985). Cross-cultural universality of social-moral development. A critical review of Kohlbergian research. *Psychological Bulletin, 97,* 202–232.

Snarey, J. R. (1995). In a communitarian voice: The sociological expansion of Kohlbergian theory, research, and practice. In W. M. Kurtines & J. L. Gerwirtz (Eds.), *Moral development: An introduction.* Boston: Allyn and Bacon.

Snow, D., & Ertmer, D. (2012). Children's development of intonation during the first year of cochlear implant experience. *Clinical Linguistics & Phonetics, 26,* 51–70.

Snow, R. (1969). Unfinished Pygmalion. *Contemporary Psychology, 14,* 197–199.

Snowdon, D. A., Kemper, S. J., Mortimer, J. A., Greiner, L. H., Wekstein, D. R., & Markesbery, W. R. (1996, February 21). Linguistic ability in early life and cognitive function and Alzheimer's disease in late life: Findings from the nun study. *Journal of the American Medical Association, 275,* 528–532.

Snowling, M. (2000). *Dyslexia: A cognitive developmental perspective* (2nd ed.). New York: Blackwell Publishers.

Snyder, H. M. (2002). *Juvenile arrests 2000.* Washington, DC: National Center for Juvenile Justice.

Snyder, J., Cramer, A., & Afrank, J. (2005). The contributions of ineffective discipline and parental hostile attributions of child misbehavior to the development of conduct problems at home and school. *Developmental Psychology, 41,* 30–41.

Snyder, J., Horsch, E., & Childs, J. (1997). Peer relationships of young children: Affiliative choices and the shaping of behavior. *Journal of Clinical Child Psychology, 26,* 145–156.

Snyder, M. (1974). The self-monitoring of expressive behavior. *Journal of Personality and Social Psychology, 30,* 526–537.

Snyder, R. A., Verderber, K. S., Langmeyer, L., & Myers, M. (1992). A reconsideration of self- and organization-referent attitudes as "causes" of the glass ceiling effect. *Group and Organization Management, 17,* 260–278.

Socolar, R. R. S., & Stein, R. E. K. (1995). Spanking infants and toddlers: Maternal belief and practice. *Pediatrics, 95,* 105–111.

Socolar, R. R. S., & Stein, R. E. K. (1996). Maternal discipline of young children: Context, belief, and practice. *Developmental and Behavioral Pediatrics, 17,* 1–8.

Soderstrom, M. (2007). Beyond babytalk: Re-evaluating the nature and content of speech input to preverbal infants. *Developmental Review, 27,* 501–532.

Soderstrom, M., Blossom, M., Foygel, R., & Morgan, J. (2008). Acoustical cues and grammatical units in speech to two preverbal infants. *Journal of Child Language, 35,* 869–902.

Sohal, R. S., & Weindruch, R. (1996, July 5). Oxidative stress, caloric restriction, and aging. *Science, 273,* 59–63.

Soken, N. H., & Pick, A.D. (1999). Infants' perception of dynamic affective expressions: Do infants distinguish specific expressions? *Child Development. 70,* 1275–1282.

Solantaus, T., Leinonen, J., & Punamäki, R-L. (2004). Children's mental health in times of economic recession: Replication and extension of the family economic stress model in Finland. *Developmental Psychology, 40,* 412–429.

Soldo, B.J. (1996). Cross-pressures on middle-aged adults: A broader view. *Journal of Gerontology: Psychological Sciences and Social Sciences, 51B,* 271–273.

Solomon, A. (1995, May 22). A death of one's own. *New Yorker,* pp. 54–69.

Solomon, G. E. A., & Cassimatis, N. L. (1999). On facts and conceptual systems: Young children's integration of their understandings of germs and contagion. *Developmental Psychology, 35,* 113–126.

Somerset, W., Newport, D., Ragan, K., & Stowe, Z. (2006). Depressive disorders in women: From menarche to beyond the menopause. In L. M. Keyes & S. H. Goodman (Eds.), *Women and depression: A handbook for the social, behavioral, and biomedical sciences.* New York: Cambridge University Press.

Son Hing, L., Chung-Yan, G., Hamilton, L., & Zanna, M. (2008). A two-dimensional model that employs explicit and implicit attitudes to characterize prejudice. *Journal of Personality and Social Psychology, 94,* 971–987.

Sondik, E. J. (1988). Progress in cancer prevention and control. *Transactions & Studies of the College of Physicians of Philadelphia, 10,* 111–131.

Song, K., & Porath, M. (2005). Common and domain-specific cognitive characteristics of gifted students: An integrated model of human abilities. *High Ability Studies, 16,* 229–246.

Sonnen, J., Larson, E., Gray, S., Wilson, A., Kohama, S., Crane, P., et al. (2009). Free radical damage to cerebral cortex in Alzheimer's disease, microvascular brain injury, and smoking. *Annals of Neurology, 65,* 226–229.

Sontag, S. (1979). The double standard of aging. In J. H. Williams (Ed.), *Psychology of women: Selected readings.* New York: Norton.

Sophian, C., Garyantes, D., & Chang, C. (1997). When three is less than two: Early developments in children's understanding of fractional quantities. *Developmental Psychology, 33,* 731–744.

Sorensen, K. (1992). Physical and mental development of adolescent males with Klinefelter syndrome. *Hormone Research, 37* (Suppl. 3), 55–61.

Sorensen, T., Nielsen, G., Andersen, P., & Teasdale, T. (1988). Genetic and environmental influences on premature death in adult adoptees. *New England Journal of Medicine, 318,* 727–732.

Sotiriou, A., & Zafiropoulou, M. (2003). Changes of children's self-concept during transition from kindergarten to primary school. *Psychology: The Journal of the Hellenic Psychological Society, 10,* 96–118.

Sotos, J. F. (1997). Overgrowth: Section IV: Genetic disorders associated with overgrowth. *Clinical Pediatrics, 36,* 37–49.

Sousa, D. L. (2005). *How the brain learns to read.* Thousand Oaks, CA: Corwin Press.

Soussignan, R., Schaal, B., Marlier, L., & Jiang, T. (1997). Facial and autonomic responses to biological and artificial olfactory stimuli in human neonates: Re-examining early hedonic discrimination of odors. *Physiology and Behavior, 62,* 745–758.

Southern, W. T., Jones, E. D., & Stanley, J. C. (1993). Acceleration and enrichment: The context and development of program options. In K. A. Heller, F. J. Monks, & A. H. Passow (Eds.), *International handbook of research and development of giftedness and talent.* Oxford, England: Pergamon.

Sowell, E. R., Peterson, B. S., Thompson, P. M., Welcome, S. E., Henkenius, A. L., & Toga, A. W. (2003). Mapping cortical change across the human life span. *Nature Neuroscience, 6,* 309–315.

Sowell, E. R., Thompson, P. M., Holmes, C. J., Jerrigan, T. L., & Toga, A. W. (1999). In vivo evidence for post-adolescent brain maturation in frontal and striatal regions. *Nature Neuroscience, 10,* 859–861.

Sowell, E. R., Thompson, P. M., Tessner, K. D., & Toga, A. W. (2001). Mapping continued brain growth and gray matter density reduction in dorsal frontal cortex: Inverse relationships during postadolescent brain maturation. *Journal of Neuroscience, 15,* 1119–1129.

Sparks, A., Lee, M., & Spjeldnes, S. (2012). Evaluation of the high school relationship curriculum connections: Dating and emotions. *Child & Adolescent Social Work Journal, 29,* 21–40.

Spear, L. P. (2002). The adolescent brain and the college drinker: Biological basis of propensity to use and misuse alcohol. *Journal of Studies on Alcohol, Special Issue: College drinking, what it is, and what to do about it: Review of the state of the science,* Suppl. 14, 71–81.

Spear, P. D. (1993). Neural bases of visual deficits during aging. *Vision Research, 33,* 2589–2609.

Spearman, C. (1927). *The abilities of man.* London: Macmillan.

Spector, H. (2005, February 6). Awaiting a cancer cure; Mother's last hope is experimental gene therapy for her son. *Cleveland Plain Dealer,* A1.

Spelke, E. (1987). The development of intermodal perception. In P. Salapatek & L. Cohen (Eds.), *Handbook of infant perception* (Vol. 2). Orlando, FL: Academic Press.

Spelke, E. S. (1991). Physical knowledge in infancy: Reflections on Piaget's theory. In S. Carey & R. Gelman (Eds.), *The epigenesis of mind.* Hillsdale, NJ: Erlbaum.

Spence, S. H. (1997). Sex and relationships. In W. K. Halford & H. J. Markman (Eds.), *Clinical handbook of marriage and couples interventions* (pp. 73–105). Chichester, England: Wiley.

Spence-Cochran, K., & Pearl, C. (2006). Moving toward full inclusion. *Life beyond the classroom: Transition strategies for young people with disabilities* (4th ed.). Baltimore, MD: Paul H Brookes Publishing.

Spencer, J. (2001). How to battle school violence. *MSNBC News.* Retrieved from http://www.msnbc.com/news/.

Spencer, M. B. (1991). Identity, minority development of. In R. M. Lerner, A. C. Petersen, & J. Brooks-Gunn (Eds.), *Encyclopedia of adolescence* (Vol. 1). New York: Garland.

Spencer, M. B., & Dornbusch, S. M. (1990). Challenges in studying minority youth. In S. Feldman & G. Elliott (Eds.), *At the threshold: The developing adolescent.* Cambridge, MA: Harvard University Press.

Spencer, N. (2001). The social patterning of teenage pregnancy. *Journal of Epidemiology & Community Health, 55,* 5.

Spencer, S. J., Fein, S., Zanna, M. P., & Olson, J. M. (Eds.) (2003). *Motivated social perception: The Ontario Symposium,* Vol. 9. Mahwah, NJ: Erlbaum.

Spencer, S., Steele, C. M., & Quinn, D. (1997). *Under suspicion of inability: Stereotype thrat and women's math performance.* Manuscript submitted for publication. Cited in Steele, 1997.

Spencer, S., Steele, C. M.,& Quinn, D. (1999). Under suspicion of inability: Stereotype threat and women's math performance. *Journal of Experimental Social Psychology, 35,* 4–28.

Spiegel, D. (1993). Social support: How friends, family, and groups can help. In D. Goleman & J. Gurin (Eds.), *Mind-body medicine.* Yonkers, NY: Consumer Reports Books.

Spiegel, D. (1996). Dissociative disorders. In R. E. Hales & S. C. Yudofsky (Eds.), *The American Psychiatric Press synopsis of psychiatry.* Washington, DC: American Psychiatric Press.

Spiegel, D. (1996, July). Cancer and depression. *British Journal of Psychiatry, 168,* 109–116.

Spiegel, D., Bloom, J. R., Kraemer, H. C., & Gottheil, E. (1989, October 14). Effect of psychosocial treatment on survival of patients with metastatic breast cancer. *Lancet, 2,* 888–891.

Spiegel, D., & Giese-Davis, J. (2003). Depression and cancer: Mechanisms and disease progression. *Biological Psychiatry, 54,* 269–282.

Spielman, D. A., & Staub, E. (2003). Reducing Boy's aggression: Learning to fulfill basic needs constructively. In E. Staub (Ed.), *The psychology of good and evil.* Cambridge, England: Cambridge University Press.

Spinrad, T., Eisenberg, N., & Bernt, F. (2007, June). Introduction to the special issues on moral development: Part I. *Journal of Genetic Psychology, 168*(2), 101–104.

Spinrad, T. L., & Stifler, C. A. (2006). Toddlers' empathy-related responding to distress: predictions from negative emotionality and maternal behavior in infancy. *Infancy, 10,* 97–121.

Spira, A., Bajos, N., Bejin, A., & Beltzer, N. (1992). AIDS and sexual behavior in France. *Nature, 360,* 407–409.

Spitze, G., & Logan, J. (1990). More evidence on women (and men) in the middle. *Research on Aging, 12,* 182–198.

Spörer, N., Brunstein, J., & Kieschke, U. (2009). Improving students' reading comprehension skills: Effects of strategy instruction and reciprocal teaching. *Learning and Instruction, 19,* 272–286.

Spraggins, R. E. (2003). *Women and men in the United States: March 2002.* Washington, DC: U.S. Department of Commerce.

Sprecher, S., Sullivan, Q., & Hatfield, E. (1994). Mate selection preferences: Gender differences examined in a national sample. *Journal of Personality and Social Psychology, 66,* 1074–1080.

Sprenger, M. (2007). *Memory 101 for educators.* Thousand Oaks, CA: Corwin Press.

Springen, K. (2000). The circumcision decision. *Newsweek Special Issue: Your Child,* 50.

Springen, K. (2000, October 16). On spanking. *Newsweek,* pp. 64.

Springer, S. P., & Deutsch, G. (1989). *Left brain, right brain* (3rd ed.). New York: Freeman.

Squatriglia, C. (2007, February 16). Ted Soulis—charitable painter, businessman. *San Francisco Chronicle,* p. B7.

Squire, L. R., & Knowlton, B. J. (1995). Memory, hippocampus, and brain systems. In M. S. Gazzaniga, *Cognitive neurosciences.* Cambridge, MA: The MIT Press.

Squires, S. (1991, September 17). Lifelong fitness depends on teaching children to love exercise. *The Washington Post,* p. WH16.

Srivastava, S., John, O., & Gosling, S. (2003). Development of personality in early and middle adulthood: Set like plaster or persistent change? *Journal of Personality & Social Psychology, 84,* 1041–1053.

Sroufe, L. A. (1994). Pathways to adaptation and maladaptation: Psychopathology as developmental deviation. In D. Cicchetti (Ed.), *Developmental psychopathology: Past, present, and future.* Hillsdale, NJ: Erlbaum.

Sroufe, L. A. (1996). *Emotional development: The organization of emotional life in the early years.* New York: Cambridge University Press.

Stack, D., & Muir, D. (1992). Adult tactile stimulation during face-to-face interactions modulates five-month-olds' affect and attention. *Child Development, 63,* 1509–1525.

Stacy, A. W., Sussman, S., Dent, C. W., Burton, D., et al. (1992). Moderators of peer social influence in adolescent smoking. *Personality & Social Psychology Bulletin, 18,* 163–172.

Stadtler, A. C., Gorski, P. A., & Brazelton, T. B. (1999). Toilet training methods, clinical interventions, and recommendations. *Pediatrics, 103,* 1359–1361.

Staff, J., Mortimer, J. T., & Uggen, C. (2004). Work and leisure in adolescence. In R. M. Lerner & L. Steinberg (Eds.) *Handbook of adolescent psychology* (2nd ed.) New York: Wiley.

Stahl, S. M. (1997). Estrogen makes the brain a sex organ. *Journal of Clinical Psychiatry, 58,* 421–422.

Stahl, S., & Nagy, W. (2006). *Teaching word meanings.* Mahwah, NJ: Lawrence Erlbaum Associates.

Stahl, S. A., McKenna, M. C., & Pagnucco, J. R. (1994). The effects of whole-language instruction: An update and a reappraisal. *Educational Psychologist, 29,* 175–185.

Stambaugh, T., & Chandler, K. L. (2012). *Effective curriculum for underserved gifted students: A CEC-TAG educational resource.* Waco, TX: Prufrock Press.

Stangor, C., Lynch, L., Duan, C. & Glas, B. (1992). Categorization of individuals on the basis of multiple social features. *Journal of Personality & Social Psychology, 62,* 207–218.

Stanjek, K. (1978). Das Uberreichen von Gaben: Funktion und Entwicklung in den ersten Lebensjahren. *Zeitschrift fur Entwicklungpsychologie und Pedagogische Psychologie, 10,* 103–113.

Stanley, J. C., & Benbow, C. P. (1983). SMPY's first decade: Ten years of posing problems and solving them. *Journal of Special Education, 17,* 11–25.

Starfield, B. (1991). Childhood morbidity: Comparisons, clusters, and trends. *Pediatrics, 88,* 519–526.

Staub, E. (1977). A child in distress: The influence of nurturance and modeling on children's attempts to help. *Developmental Psychology, 5,* 124–133.

Staub, E. (2011). *Overcoming evil: Genocide, violent conflict, and terrorism.* New York: Oxford University Press.

Staudenmeier, J. J., Jr. (1999). Children and computers. *Journal of the American Academy of Child and Adolescent Psychiatry, 38,* 5.

Stauder, J. A., Cornet, L. M., & Ponds, R. M. (2011). The extreme male brain theory and gender role behaviour in persons with an autism spectrum condition. *Research in Autism Spectrum Disorders, 5,* 1209–1214.

Staudinger, U. (2008). A psychology of wisdom: History and recent developments. *Research in Human Development, 5,* 107–120.

Staudinger, U. M., & Baltes, P. B. (1996). Interactive minds: A facilitative setting for wisdom-related performance? *Journal of Personality and Social Psychology, 71,* 746–762.

Staudinger, U. M., Fleeson, W., & Baltes, P. B. (1999). Predictors of subjective physical health and global well-being: Similarities and differences between the United States and German. *Journal of Personality and Social Psychology, 76,* 305–319.

Staudinger, U. M., & Leipold, B. (2003). The assessment of wisdom-related performance. In C. R. Snyder (Ed.), *Positive psychological assessment: A handbook of models and measures.* Washington, DC: American Psychological Association.

Staudinger, U. M., Marsiske, M., & Baltes, P. B. (1993). Resilience and levels of reserve capacity in later adulthood: Perspectives from life-span theory. *Development and Psychopathology, 5,* 541–566.

Staunton, H. (2005). Mammalian sleep. *Naturwissenschaften, 35,* 15.

Staus, M. A., Gelles, R. J., & Steinmetz, S. K. (2003). Spare the rod? In M. Silberman (Ed.), *Violence and society: A reader.* Upper Saddle River, NJ: Prentice Hall.

Stauss, K., Boyas, J., & Murphy-Erby, Y. (2012). Implementing and evaluating a rural community-based sexual abstinence program: Challenges and solutions. *Sex Education, 12,* 47–63.

Stearns, E., & Glennie, E. (2006, September). When and why dropouts leave high school. *Youth & Society, 38,* 29–57.

Stedman, L. C. (1997). International achievement differences: An assessment of a new perspective. *Educational Reseaqrcher, 26,* 4–15.

Steele, C. (2003). Through the back door to theory. *Psychological Inquiry, 14,* 314–317.

Steele, C. M. (1997). A threat in the air: How stereotypes shape intellectual identity and performance. *American Psychologist, 52,* 613–629.

Steele, C. M., & Aronson, J. (1995). Stereotype threat and the intellectual test performance of African Americans. *Journal of Personality and Social Psychoilogy, 69,* 797–811.

Steenbergen-Hu, S., & Moon, S. M. (2011). The effects of acceleration on high-ability learners: A meta-analysis. *Gifted Child Quarterly, 55,* 39–53.

Steers, R. M., & Porter, L. W. (1991). *Motivation and work behavior* (5th ed.). New York: McGraw-Hill.

Stein, D., Latzer, Y., & Merick, J. (2009). Eating disorders: From etiology to treatment. *International Journal of Child and Adolescent Health, 2,* 139–151.

Stein, J. (2009, September 28). The vaccination war. *Time,* p. 72.

Stein, J. A., Lu, M. C., & Gelberg, L. (2000). Severity of homelessness and adverse birth outcomes. *Health Psychology, 19,* 524–534.

Stein, J. H., & Reiser, L. W. (1994). A study of white middle-class adolescent boys' responses to "semenarche" (the first ejaculation). *Journal of Youth and Adolescence, 23,* 373–384.

Stein, M. T., Kennell, J. H., & Fulcher, A. (2003). Benefits of a doula present at the birth of a child. *Journal of Developmental and Behavioral Pediatrics, 24,* 195–198.

Stein, Z., Susser, M., Saenger, G., & Marolla, F. (1975). *Famine and human development: The Dutch hunger winter of 1944–1945.* New York: Oxford University Press.

Steinberg, J. (1997, January 2). Turning words into meaning. *The New York Times,* pp. B1–B2.

Steinberg, J. (1998, March 19). Experts call for mix of two methods to teach reading. *The New York Times,* p. A1, A17.

Steinberg, K. K., Thacker, S. B., Smith, S. J., Stroup, D. F., Zack, M. M., Flanders, W. D., & Berkelman, R. L. (1991). A meta-analysis of the effect of estrogen replacement therapy on the risk of breast cancer. *Journal of the American Medical Association, 265,* 1985–1990.

Steinberg, L. (1990). Autonomy, conflict, and harmony in the family relationship. In S. Feldman & G. Elliott (Eds.), *At the threshold: The developing adolescent.* Cambridge, MA: Harvard University Press.

Steinberg, L. (1993). *Adolescence.* New York: McGraw-Hill.

Steinberg, L. (1997, January 2). Turning words into meaning. *The New York Times,* pp. B1–B2.

Steinberg, L., Dornbusch, S., & Brown, B. B. (1992). Ethnic differences in adolescent achievement: An ecological perspective. *American Psychologist, 47,* 723–729.

Steinberg, L., Lamborn, S. D., Darling, N., Mounts, N. S., & Dornbusch, S. M. (1994). Over-time changes in adjustment and competence among adolescents from authoritative, authoritarian, indulgent, and neglectful families. *Child Development, 65,* 754–770.

Steinberg, L., & Monahan, K. (2007, November). Age differences in resistance to peer influence. *Developmental Psychology, 43*(6), 1531–1543.

Steinberg, L. D., & Scott, S. S. (2003). Less guilty by reason of adolescence: Developmental immaturity, diminished responsibility, and the juvenile death penalty. *American Psychologist, 58,* 1009–1018.

Steinberg, L., & Silverberg, S. (1986). The vicissitudes of autonomy in early adolescence. *Child Development, 57,* 841–851.

Steiner, J. E. (1979). Human facial expressions in response to taste and smell stimulation. *Advances in Child Development and Behavior, 13,* 257.

Steinert, S., Shay, J. W., & Wright, W. E. (2000). Transient expression of human telomerase extends the life span of normal human fibroblasts. *Biochemical & Biophysical Research Communications, 273,* 1095–1098.

Steinhausen, H. C., & Spohr, H. L. (1998). Long-term outcome of children with fetal alcohol syndrome: Psychopathology, behavior, and intelligence. *Alcoholism, Clinical & Experimental Research, 22,* 334–338.

Stella, L., Verreschi, L., & Lipay, M. (2008). Chimeric hermaphroditism: An overview. *International Journal of Child and Adolescent Health, 1,* 5–9.

Stenberg, G. (2003). Effects of maternal inattentiveness on infant social referencing. *Infant & Child Development, 12,* 399–419.

Stenberg, G. (2009). Selectivity in infant social referencing. *Infancy, 14,* 457–473.

Stephens, C., Pachana, N., & Bristow, V. (2006). The effect of hormone replacement therapy on mood and everyday memory in younger and mid-life women. *Psychology, Health & Medicine, 11,* 461–469.

Steri, A. O., & Spelke, E. S. (1988). Haptic perception of objects in infancy. *Cognitive Psychology, 20,* 1–23.

Stern, G. (1994, November, 30). Going back to college has special meaning for Mrs. McAlpin. *The Wall Street Journal,* p. A1.

Sternberg, J. (2005). The triarchic theory of successful intelligence. In D. P. Flanagan & P. L. Harrison (Eds.), *Contemporary intellectual assessment: Theories, tests, and issues.* New York: Guilford Press.

Sternberg, R. J. (1997). *Educating intelligence: Infusing the Triarchic Theory into school instruction.* New York: Cambridge University Press.

Sternberg, R. (2003a). A broad view of intelligence: The theory of successful intelligence. *Consulting Psychology Journal: Practice & Research, 55,* 139–154.

Sternberg, R. (2003b). Our research program validating the triarchic theory of successful intelligence: Reply to Gottfredson. *Intelligence, 31,* 399–413.

Sternberg, R. (2006). A duplex theory of love. *The new psychology of love* (pp. 184–199). New Haven, CT: Yale University Press.

Sternberg, R. (2007, January). A systems model of leadership: WICS. *American Psychologist, 62,* 34–42.

Sternberg, R. (2008, March). Applying psychological theories to educational practice. *American Educational Research Journal, 45*(1), 150–165.

Sternberg, R. J. (1982). Reasoning, problems solving, and intelligence. In R. J. Sternberg (Ed.), *Handbook of human intelligence* (pp. 225–307). Cambridge, England: Cambridge University Press.

Sternberg, R. J. (1985). *Beyond IQ: A triarchic theory of human intelligence.* New York: Cambridge University Press.

Sternberg, R. J. (1986). Triangular theory of love. *Psychological Review, 93,* 119–135.

Sternberg, R. J. (1987). Liking versus loving: A comparative evaluation of theories. *Psychological Bulletin, 102,* 331–345.

Sternberg, R. J. (1988). *The nature of creativity.* Cambridge, England: Cambridge University Press.

Sternberg, R. J. (1988). Triangulating love. In R. J. Sternberg & M. J. Barnes (Eds.), *The psychology of love.* New Haven, CT: Yale University Press.

Sternberg, R. J. (1990). *Metaphors of mind: Conceptions of the nature of intelligence.* Cambridge, England: Cambridge University Press.

Sternberg, R. J. (1991). Theory-based testing of intellectual abilities: Rationale for the Sternberg triarchic abilities test. In H. A. H. Rowe (Ed.), *Intelligence: Reconceptualization and measurement.* Hillsdale, NJ: Erlbaum.

Sternberg, R. J. (1995). For whom the bell curve tolls: A review of *The Bell Curve. Psychological Science, 6,* 257–261.

Sternberg, R. J. (1996). Educating intelligence: Infusing the triarchic theory into school instruction. In R. J. Sternberg & E. Grigorenko (Eds.), *Intelligence, heredity, and environment.* New York: Cambridge University Press.

Sternberg, R. J. (1997). Intelligence and lifelong learning: What's new and how can we use it? *American Psychologist, 52,* 1134–1139.

Sternberg, R. J. (2005). The triarchic theory of successful intelligence. In D. P. Flanagan & P. L. Harrison (Eds.), *Contemporary intellectual assessment: Theories, tests, and issues.* New York, Guilford Press.

Sternberg, R. J. (2006). Intelligence. In K. Pawlik & G. d'Ydewalle (Eds.), *Psychological concepts: An international historical perspective.* Hove, England: Psychology Press/Taylor & Francis.

Sternberg, R. J. (2009). The nature of creativity. In R. J. Sternberg, J. C. Kaufman, & E. L. Grigorenko, (Eds.), *The essential Sternberg: Essays on intelligence, psychology, and education.* New York: Springer Publishing Co.

Sternberg, R. J., Conway, B. E., Ketron, J. L., & Bernstein, M. (1981). Peoples' conceptions of intelligence. *Journal of Personality and Social Psychology, 41,* 37–55.

Sternberg, R. J., & Grigorenko, E. L. (Eds.). (1996). *Intelligence, heredity, and environment.* New York: Cambridge University Press.

Sternberg, R. J., & Grigorenko, E. L. (Eds.). (2002). *The generalfactor of intelligence: How general is it?* Mahwah, NJ: Lawrence Erlbaum.

Sternberg, R., Kaufman, J., & Grigorenko, E. (2008). *Applied intelligence.* New York: Cambridge University Press.

Sternberg, R. J., Kaufman, J. C., & Pretz, J. E. (2002). *The creativity conundrum: A propulsion model of creative contributions.* Philadelphia, PA: Psychology Press.

Sternberg, R. J., & Lubart, T. I. (1992). Buy low and sell high: An investment approach to creativity. *Current Directions in Psychological Science, 1,* 1–5.

Sternberg, R. J., & Lubart, T. I. (1995). An investment perspective on creative insight. In R. J. Sternberg & J. E. Davidson, (Eds.). *The nature of insight.* Cambridge, MA: MIT Press.

Sternberg, R. J., & Lubart, T. I. (1996). Investing in creativity. *American Psychologist, 51,* 677–688.

Sternberg, R. J., & The Rainbow Project Collaborators. (2006). The Rainbow Project: Enhancing the SAT through assessments of analytical, practical, and creative skills. *Intelligence, 34.*

Sternberg, R. J., & Wagner, R. K. (1993). The g-ocentric view of intelligence and job performance is wrong. *Current Directions in Psychological Science, 2,* 1–5.

Sternberg, R. J., & Wagner, R. K. (Eds.). (1986). *Practical intelligence: Nature and origins of competence in the everyday world.* New York: Cambridge University Press.

Sternberg, R. J., Wagner, R. K., Williams, W. M., & Horvath, J. A. (1997). Testing common sense. In D. Russ-Eft, H. Preskill, & C. Sleezer (Eds.), *Human resource development review: Research and implications* (pp. 102–132). Thousand Oaks, CA: Sage.

Sterns, H. L., Barrett, G. V., & Alexander, R. A. (1985). Accidents and the aging individual. In J. E. Birren & K. W. Schaie (Eds.), *Handbook of the psychology of aging* (2nd ed.). New York: Van Nostrand Reinhold.

Stettler, N. (2007). Nature and strength of epidemiological evidence for origins of   childhood and adulthood obesity in the first year of life. *International Journal of Obesity, 31,* 1035–1043.

Stevens, J., Cai, J., Evenson, K. R., & Thomas, R. (2002). Fitness and fatness as predictors of mortality from all causes and from cardiovascular disease in men and women in the lipid research clinics study. *American Journal of Epidemiology, 156,* 832–841.

Stevens, J. C., Cain, W. S., Demarque, A., & Ruthruff, A. (1991). On the discrimination of missing ingredients: Aging and salt flavor. *Appetite, 16,* 129–140.

Stevens, N., Martina, C., & Westerhof, G. (2006, August). Meeting the need to belong: Predicting effects of a friendship enrichment program for older women. *The Gerontologist, 46,* 495–502.

Stevens, W., Hasher, L., Chiew, K., & Grady, C. (2008). A neural mechanism underlying memory failure in older adults. *The Journal of Neuroscience, 28,* 12820–12824.

Stevens-Ratchford, R. G. (1993). The effect of life review reminiscence activities on depression and self-esteem in older adults. *American Journal of Occupational Therapy, 47,* 413–420.

Stevens-Simon, C., & White, M. M. (1991). Adolescent pregnancy. *Pediatric Annals, 20,* 322–331.

Stevenson, C., & White, M. (2000). Outside in: The tension between curatorial practice and research. *Teacher Education Quarterly, 27,* 25–33.

Stevenson, H. W., Chen, C., & Lee, S. Y. (1992). A comparison of the parent–child relationship in Japan and the United States. In L. L. Roopnarine & D. B. Carter (Eds.), *Parent-child socialization in diverse cultures.* Norwood, NJ: Ablex.

Stevenson, H. W., & Lee, S. Y. (1990). Contexts of achievement: A study of American, Chinese, and Japanese children. *Monographs of the Society for Research in Child Development, 55,* 1–123.

Stevenson, H. W., & Lee, S. (1996). The academic achievement of Chinese students. In M. H. Bond (Ed.), *Handbook of Chinese psychology.* London: Oxford University Press.

Stevenson, H. W., Lee, S., & Mu, X. (2000). Successful achievement in mathematics: China and the United States. In C. F. M. van Lieshout & P. G. Heymans, *Developing talent across the life span.* Philadelphia, PA: Psychology Press.

Stevenson, J. (2005). Alcohol use, misuse, abuse, and dependence in later adulthood. *Annual Review of Nursing Research, 23,* 245–280.

Stevenson, M., Henderson, T., & Baugh, E. (2007, February). Vital defenses: Social support appraisals of Black grandmothers parenting grandchildren. *Journal of Family Issues, 28,* 182–211.

Steward, E. P. (1995). *Beginning writers in the zone of proximal development.* Hillsdale, NJ: Erlbaum.

Stewart, A. J., Copeland, A. P., Chester, N. L., Mallery, J. E., & Barenbaum, N. B. (1997). *Separating together: How divorce transforms families.* New York: Guilford Press.

Stewart, A. J., & Ostrove, J. M. (1998). Women's personality in middle age: Gender, history, and midcourse corrections. *American Psychologist, 53,* 1185–1194.

Stewart, A. J., & Vandewater, E. A. (1999). "If I had it to do over again …": Midlife review, midcourse corrections, and women's well-being in midlife. *Journal of Personality and Social Psychology, 76,* 270–283.

Stewart, D., Rolfe, D., & Robertson, E. (2004). Depression, estrogen, and the women's health initiative. *Psychosomatics 45,* 445–447.

Stewart, M., Scherer, J., & Lehman, M. (2003). Perceived effects of high frequency hearing loss in a farming population. *Journal of the American Academy of Audiology, 14,* 100–108.

Stice, E. (2003). Puberty and body image. In C. Hayward (Ed.), *Gender differences at puberty.* New York: Cambridge University Press.

Stice, E., Presnell, K., & Bearman, K. (2001). Relation of early menarche to depression, eating disorders, substance abuse, and comorbid psychopathology among adolescent girls. *Developmental Psychology, 37,* 608–619.

Stice, E., & Shaw, H. (2004). Eating disorder prevention programs: A meta-analytic review. *Psychological Bulletin, 130,* 206–227.

Stiles, J., Moses, P., & Paul, B. M. (2006). The longitudinal study of spatial cognitive development in children with pre- or perinatal focal brain injury: Evidence for cognitive compensation and for the emergence of alternative profiles of brain organization. In S. G. Lomber & J. J. Eggermont (Eds.), *Reprogramming the cerebral cortex: Plasticity following central and peripheral lesions.* New York: Oxford University Press, 2006.

Stipek, D. (2002). At what age should children enter kindergarten? A question for policy makers and parents. *Social Policy Report, 16,* 3–16.

Stipek, D. J. (1984). Sex differences in children's attributions for success and failure on math and spelling tests. *Sex Roles, 11,* 969–981.

Stipek, D. J., & Hoffman, J. (1980). Development of children's performance-related judgments. *Child Development, 51,* 912–914.

Stitch, S. (2006, December 4). Going it alone. *Time,* p. F3.

Stock, G., & Campbell, J. (2000). *Engineering the human germline: An exploration of the science and ethics of altering the genes we pass to our children.* New York: Oxford University Press.

Stock, P., Desoete, A., & Roeyers, H. (2007). Early markers for arithmetic difficulties. *Educational and Child Psychology, 24,* 28–39.

Stockdale, M. S., & Crosby, F. J. (2004). *Psychology and management of workplace diversity.* Malden, MA: Blackwell Publishers.

Stohs, J. H. (1992). Intrinsic motivation and sustained art activity among male fine and applied artists. *Creativity Research Journal, 5,* 245–252.

Stolberg, S. G. (1998, April 3). Rise in smoking by young Blacks erodes a success story in health. *The New York Times,* p. A1.

Stolberg, S. G. (1999, August 8). Black mothers' mortality rate under scrutiny. *The New York Times,* pp. 1, 18.

Stolberg, S. G. (2001, August 15). Researchers discount a caution in debate over cloned humans. *The New York Times,* p. A18.

Stone, C. (2003). Counselors as advocates for gay, lesbian, and bisexual youth: A call for equity and action. *Journal of Multicultural Counseling & Development, 31,* 143–155.

Stone, R., Cafferata, G. L., & Sangl, J. (1987). Caregivers of the frail elderly: A national profile. *Gerontologist, 27,* 616–626.

Stone, S. (2003). Disability, dependence, and old age: Problematic constructions. *Canadian Journal on Aging, 22,* 59–67.

Storfer, M. (1990). *Intelligence and giftedness: The contributions of heredity and early environment.* San Francisco: Jossey-Bass.

Stork, S., & Sanders, S. (2008, January). Physical education in early childhood. *The Elementary School Journal, 108*(3), 197–206.

Story, M., Nanney, M., & Schwartz, M. (2009). Schools and obesity prevention: Creating school environments and policies to promote healthy eating and physical activity. *Milbank Quarterly, 87,* 71–100.

Stotland, S., Larocque, M., & Sadikaj, G. (2012). Positive and negative dimensions of weight control motivation. *Eating Behaviors, 13,* 20–26.

Strasburger, V. (2009). Media and children: What needs to happen now? *JAMA: Journal of the American Medical Association, 301,* 2265–2266.

Strauch, B. (1997, August 10). Use of antidepression medicine for young patients has soared. *The New York Times,* p. A1, A24.

Straus, M. A., & Gelles, R. J. (Eds.). (1990). *Physical violence in American families.* New Brunswick, NJ: Transaction.

Straus, M., Gelles, R., & Steinmetz, S. K. (1980). *Behind closed doors: Violence in the American family.* Garden City, NY: Anchor Press.

Straus, M. A., Gelles, R. J., & Steinmetz, S. K. (2003). The marriage license as a hitting license. In M. Silberman, *Violence and society: A reader.* Upper Saddle River, NJ: Prentice Hall.

Straus, M. A., & McCord, J. (1998). Do physically punished children become violent adults? In S. Nolen-Hoeksema (Ed.), *Clashing views on abnormal psychology: A Taking Sides custom reader* (pp. 130–155). Guilford, CT: Dushkin/McGraw-Hill.

Straus, M. A., Sugarman, D. B., & Giles-Sims, J. (1997). Spanking by parents and subsequent antisocial behavior of children. *Archives of Pediatrics and Adolescent Medicine, 151,* 761–767.

Straus, M. A., & Yodanis, C. L. (1996). Corporal punishment in adolescence and physical assaults on spouses in later life: What accounts for the link? *Journal of Marriage and the Family, 58,* 825–841.

Streissguth, A. (1997). *Fetal alcohol syndrome: A guide for families and communities.* Baltimore, MD: Paul H. Brookes.

Streissguth, A. (2007). Offspring effects of prenatal alcohol exposure from birth to 25 years: The Seattle Prospective Longitudinal Study. *Journal of Clinical Psychology in Medical Settings, 14,* 81–101.

Streissguth, A. P., Randels, S. P., & Smith, D. F. (1991). A test-retest study of intelligence in patients with fetal alcohol syndrome: Implications for care. *Journal of the American Academy of Child & Adolescent Psychiatry, 30,* 584–587.

Strelau, J. (1998). *Temperament: A psychological perspective.* New York: Plenum Publishers.

Strength, J. (1999). Grieving the loss of a child. *Journal of Psychology & Christianity, 18,* 338–353.

Streri, A. (2003). Intermodal relations in infancy. *Touching for knowing: Cognitive psychology of haptic manual perception.* Amsterdam, Netherlands: John Benjamins Publishing Company.

Streri, A. O., & Spelke, E. S. (1988). Haptic perception of objects in infancy. *Cognitive Psychology, 20,* 1–23.

Striano, T., & Vaish, A. (2006, November). Seven- to 9-month-old infants use facial expressions to interpret others' actions. *British Journal of Developmental Psychology, 24,* 753–760.

Striegel-Moore, R. H. (1997). Risk factors for eating disorders. In M. S. Jacobson, J. M. Rees, N. H. Golden, & C. E. Irwin (Eds.), *Annals of the New York Academy of Sciences: Vol. 817. Adolescent nutritional disorders: Prevention and treatment* (pp. 98–109). New York: New York Academy of Sciences.

Stright, A., Gallagher, K., & Kelley, K. (2008). Infant temperament moderates relations between maternal parenting in early childhood and children's adjustment in first grade. *Child Development, 79*(1), 186–200.

Strobel, A., Dreisbach, G., Müller, J., Goschke, T., Brocke, B., & Lesch, K. (2007, December). Genetic variation of serotonin function and cognitive control. *Journal of Cognitive Neuroscience, 19,* 1923–1931.

Stroebe, M. S., Stroebe, W., & Hansson, R. O. (Eds.). (1993). *Handbook of bereavement: Theory, research, and intervention.* Cambridge, England: Cambridge University Press.

Stroebe, W. (2008). Energy balance and the genetics of body weight. *Dieting, overweight, and obesity: Self-regulation in a food-rich environment.* Washington, DC: American Psychological Association.

Stroebe, W., Stroebe, M., Abakoumkin, G., & Schut, H. (1996). The role of loneliness and social support in adjustment to loss: A test of attachment versus stress theory. *Journal of Personality and Social Psychology, 70,* 1241–1249.

Stroh, L., K., Langlands, C. L., & Simpson, P. A. (2004). Shattering the glass ceiling in the new millennium. In M. S. Stockdale & F. J. Crosby (Eds.), *Psychology and management of workplace diversity.* Malden, MA: Blackwell Publishers.

Stromswold, K. (2006). Why aren't identical twins linguistically identical? Genetic, prenatal and postnatal factors. *Cognition, 101,* 333–384.

Strube, M. (Ed.). (1990). Type A behavior. *Journal of Social Behavior and Personality, 5* [Special issue].

Stuen, C., & Fischer, M. (2007). Gerontechnology and vision. *Gerontechnology: Growing old in a technological society.* Springfield, IL: Charles C. Thomas Publisher.

Stutts, M., Zank, G. M., Smith, K. H., & Williams, S. A. (2011). Nutrition information and children's fast food menu choices. *Journal of Consumer Affairs, 45,* 52–86.

Stutzer, A., & Frey, B. (2006, April). Does marriage make people happy, or do happy people get married? *The Journal of Socio-Economics, 35,* 326–347.

Suarez, E. C., & Williams, R.B., Jr. (1992). Interactive models of reactivity: The relationship between hostility and potentially pathogenic physiological responses to social stressors. In N. Schneiderman, P. McCabe, & A. Baum (Eds.), *Stress and disease processes.* Hillsdale, NJ: Erlbaum.

Suarez-Orozco, C., Suarez-Orozco., & Todorova, I. (2008). *Learning a new land: Immigrant students in American society.* Cambridge, MA: Belknap Press/Harvard University Press.

Subotnik, R. (2006). Longitudinal studies: Answering our most important questions of prediction and effectiveness. *Journal for the Education of the Gifted, 29,* 379–383.

Subrahmanyam, K., & Smahel, D. (2011). *Digital youth: The role of media in development.* New York: Springer Science + Business Media.

Sudia-Robinson, T. (2011, March 14). Ethical implications of newborn screening, life-limiting conditions, and palliative care. *MCN, American Journal of Maternal Child Nursing.* Retrieved from http://journals.lww.com/mcnjournal/Abstract/publishahead/Ethical_Implications_of_New

born_Screening,.99982.aspx.

Sugarman, S. (1988). *Piaget's construction of the child's reality.* Cambridge, England: Cambridge University Press.

Sugden, J. (1995, January 23). Sanctuaries for broken children. *People Weekly,* 39.

Suinn, R. M. (2001). The terrible twos—Anger and anxiety: Hazardous to your health. *American Psychologist, 56,* 27–36.

Suitor, J. J., Minyard, S. A., & Carter, R. S. (2001). "Did you see what I saw?" Gender differences in perceptions of avenues to prestige among adolescents. *Sociological Inquiry, 71,* 437–454.

Sullivan, K. (2000). *The anti-bullying handbook.* New York: Oxford University Press.

Sullivan, M. W., & Lewis, M. (2012). Relations of early goal-blockage response and gender to subsequent tantrum behavior. *Infancy, 17,* 159–178.

Sullivan, M. W., Rovee-Collier, C. K., & Tynes, D. M. (1979). A conditioning analysis of infant long-term memory. *Child Development, 50,* 152–162.

Suls, J., & Wallston, K. (2003). *Social psychological foundations of health and illness.* Malden, MA: Blackwell Publishers.

Suls, J., & Wills, T. A. (Eds.). (1991). *Social comparison: Contemporary theory and research.* Hillsdale, NJ: Erlbaum.

Sulzer-Azaroff, B., & Mayer, R. (1991). *Behavior analysis and lasting change.* New York: Holt.

Summers, J., Schallert, D., & Ritter, P. (2003). The role of social comparison in students' perceptions of ability: An enriched view of academic motivation in middle school students. *Contemporary Educational Psychology, 28,* 510–523.

Sun, J., & Nathans, J. (2001, October). The challenge of macular degeneration. *Scientific American,* 69–75.

Sunderman, G. (2008). *Holding NCLB accountable: Achieving, accountability, equity, & school reform.* Thousand Oaks, CA: Corwin Press.

Sundin, O., Ohman, A., Palm, T., & Strom, G. (1995). Cardiovascular reactivity, Type A behavior, and coronary heart disease: Comparisons between myocardial infarction patients and controls during laboratory-induced stress. *Psychophysiology, 32,* 28–35.

Sung, B. L. (1985). Bicultural conflicts in Chinese immigrant children. *Journal of Comparative Family Studies, 16,* 255–270.

Super, C. M. (1976). Environmental effects on motor development: A case of African infant precocity. *Developmental Medicine and Child Neurology, 18,* 561–576.

Super, C. M., & Harkness, S. (1982). The infant's niche in rural Kenya and metropolitan America. In L. Adler (Ed.), *Issues in cross-cultural research.* New York: Academic Press.

Super, C., & Harkness, S. (1999). The environment as culture in developmental research. *Measuring environment across the life span: Emerging methods and concepts.* Washington, DC: American Psychological Association.

Supple, A., Ghazarian, S., Peterson, G., & Bush, K. (2009). Assessing the cross-cultural validity of a parental autonomy granting measure: Comparing adolescents in the United States, China, Mexico, and India. *Journal of Cross-Cultural Psychology, 40,* 816–833.

Suresh, I. S., Rattan, P. K., & Clark, B.F.C. (Eds.). (2006). *Understanding and modulating aging.* Malden, MA: Blackwell Publishing on behalf of the New York Academy of Sciences.

Suro, R. (1999, November). Mixed doubles. *American Demographics,* pp. 57–62.

Suskind, R. (1994, September 24). Class struggle: Poor, black, and smart. *The New York Times,* p. A1.

Suskind, R. (1999). *A hope in the unseen: An American odyssey from the inner city to the Ivy League.* New York: Broadway Books.

Susman-Stillman, A., Kalkose, M., Egeland, B., & Waldman, I. (1996). Infant temperament and maternal sensitivity as predictors of attachment security. *Infant Behavior & Development, 19,* 33–47.

Sussman, S. K., & Sussman, M. B. (Eds.). (1991). *Families: Intergenerational and generational connections.* Binghamton, NY: Haworth.

Sutherland, R., Pipe, M., & Schick, K. (2003). Knowing in advance: The impact of prior event information on memory and event knowledge. *Journal of Experimental Child Psychology, 84,* 244–263.

Sutton, J. (2002). Cognitive conceptions of language and the development of autobiographical memory. *Language & Communication, 22,* 375–390.

Suzuki, L., & Aronson, J. (2005). The cultural malleability of intelligence and its impact on the racial/ethnic hierarchy. *Psychology, Public Policy, and Law, 11,* 320–327.

Suzuki, L. A., & Valencia, R. R. (1997). Race-ethnicity and measured intelligence. *American Psychologist, 52,* 1103–1114.

Swaim, R., Barner, J., & Brown, C. (2008). The relationship of calcium intake and exercise to osteoporosis health beliefs in postmenopausal women. *Research in Social & Administrative Pharmacy, 4,* 153–163.

Swain, J. (2004). Is placement in the least restrictive environment a restricted debate? *PsycCRITIQUES,* pp. 23–30.

Swain, J. E., Lorberbaum, J. P., Kose, S., & Strathearn, L. (2007). Brain basis of early parent-*infant* interactions: Psychology, physiology, and in vivo functional neuroimaging studies. *Journal of Child Psychology and Psychiatry, 48,* 262–287.

Swan, S. H. (1997). Hormone replacement therapy and the risk of reproductive cancers. *Journal of Psychosomatic Obstetrics and Gynaecology, 18,* 165–174.

Swanson, H., Saez, L., & Gerber, M. (2004). Literacy and cognitive functioning in bilingual and nonbilingual children at or not at risk for reading disabilities. *Journal of Educational Psychology, 96,* 3–18.

Swanson, L. A., Leonard, L. B., & Gandour, J. (1992). Vowel duration in mothers' speech to young children. *Journal of Speech and Hearing Research, 35,* 617–625.

Sweet, E. (1985, October). Date rape: The story of an epidemic and those who deny it. *Ms/Campus Times,* pp. 56–59.

Swendsen, J. D., & Mazure, C. M. (2000). Life stress as a risk factor for postpartum depression: Current research and methodological issues. *Clinical Psychology-Science & Practice, 7,* 17–31.

Swiatek, M. (2002). Social coping among gifted elementary school students. *Journal for the Education of the Gifted, 26,* 65–86.

Swingler, M. M., Sweet, M. A., & Carver, L. J. (2007). Relations between mother-child interaction and the neural correlates of face processing in 6-month-olds. *Infancy, 11,* 63–86.

Swingley, D. (2008). The roots of the early vocabulary in infants' learning from speech. *Current Directions in Psychological Science, 17,* 308–312.

Sy, T., Tram, S., & O'Hara, L. (2006, June). Relation of employee and manager emotional intelligence to job satisfaction and performance. *Journal of Vocational Behavior, 68,* 461–473.

Szaflarski, J., Holland, S., Schmithorst, V., & Byars, A. (2006, March). fMRI study of language lateralization in children and adults. *Human Brain Mapping, 27,* 202–212.

Szaflarski, J. P., Rajagopal, A., Altaye, M., Byars, A. W., Jacola, L., Schmithorst, V. J., & ... Holland, S. K. (2012). Left-handedness and language lateralization in children. *Brain Research, 143,* 85–97.

Taddio, A., Shah, V., & Gilbert-MacLeod, C. (2002). Conditioning and hyperalgesia in newborns exposed to repeated heel lances. *Journal of the American Medical Association, 288,* 857–861.

Tadinac, M., & Hromatko, I. (2007). Own mate value and relative importance of a potential mate's qualities. *Studia Psychologica, 49,* 251–264.

Taga, K., Markey, C., & Friedman, H. (2006, June). A longitudinal investigation of associations between boys' pubertal timing and adult behavioral health and well-being. *Journal of Youth and Adolescence, 35,* 401–411.

Tajfel, H. (1982). *Social identity and intergroup relations.* London: Cambridge University Press.

Takahashi, K. (1986). Examining the Strange Situation procedure with Japanese mothers and 12-month-old infants. *Developmental Psychology, 22,* 265–270.

Takala, M. (2006, November). The effects of reciprocal teaching on reading comprehension in mainstream and special (SLI) education. *Scandinavian Journal of Educational Research, 50,* 559–576.

Takanishi, R., Hamburg, D. A., & Jacobs, K. (Eds.). (1997). *Preparing adolescents for the twenty-first century: Challenges facing Europe and the United States.* New York: Cambridge University Press.

Taki, Y., Hashizume, H., Sassa, Y., Takeuchi, H., Asano, M., Asano, K., & … Kawashima, R. (2012). Correlation among body height, intelligence, and brain gray matter volume in healthy children. *Neuroimage, 59,* 1023–1027.

Talkington-Boyer, S., & Snyder, D. K. (1994). Assessing impact on family caregivers to Alzheimer's disease patients. *American Journal of Family Therapy, 22,* 57–66.

Tallandini, M., & Scalembra, C. (2006). Kangaroo mother care and mother-premature infant dyadic interaction. *Infant Mental Health Journal, 27,* 251–275.

Tamis-LeMonda, C. (2004). Conceptualizing fathers' roles: Playmates and more. *Human Development, 47,* 220–227.

Tamis-LeMonda, C. S., & Bornstein, M. H. (1993). Antecedents of exploratory competence at one year. *Infant Behavior and Development, 16,* 423–439.

Tamis-LeMonda, C. S., & Cabrera, N. (1999). Perspectives on father involvement: Research and policy. *Social Policy Report, 13,* 1–31.

Tamis-LeMonda, C., & Cabrera, N. (2002). *Handbook of father involvement: Multidisciplinary perspectives.* Mahwah, NJ: Lawrence Erlbaum Associates.

Tan, H., Wen, S. W., Mark, W., Fung, K. F., Demissie, K., & Rhoads, G. G. (2004). The association between fetal sex and preterm birth in twin pregnancies. *Obstetrics and Gynecology, 103,* 327–332.

Tanaka, K., Kon, N., Ohkawa, N., Yoshikawa, N., & Shimizu, T. (2009). Does breastfeeding in the neonatal period influence the cognitive function of very-low-birth-weight infants at 5 years of age?. *Brain & Development, 31,* 288–293.

Tang, C., Wu, M., Liu, J., Lin, H., & Hsu, C. (2006). Delayed parenthood and the risk of cesarean delivery—Is paternal age an independent risk factor?. *Birth: Issues in Perinatal Care, 33,* 18—26.

Tang, W. R., Aaronson, L. S., & Forbes, S. A. (2004). Quality of life in hospice patients with terminal illness. *Western Journal of Nursing Research, 26,* 113–128.

Tang, Z., & Orwin, R. (2009). Marijuana initiation among American youth and its risks as dynamic processes: Prospective findings from a national longitudinal study. *Substance Use & Misuse, 44,* 195–211.

Tangney, J., & Dearing, R. (2002). Gender differences in morality. In R. Bornstein & J. Masling (Eds.), *The psychodynamics of gender and gender role.* Washington, DC: American Psychological Association.

Tangri, S., Thomas, V., & Mednick, M. (2003). Predictors of satisfaction among college-educated African American women in midlife. *Journal of Adult Development, 10,* 113–125.

Tannen, D. (1991). *You just don't understand.* New York: Ballantine.

Tanner, E., & Finn-Stevenson, M. (2002). Nutrition and brain development: Social policy implications. *American Journal of Orthopsychiatry, 72,* 182–193.

Tanner, J. M. (1972). Sequence, tempo, and individual variation in growth and development of boys and girls aged twelve to sixteen. In J. Kagan & R. Coles (Eds.), *Twelve to sixteen: Early adolescence.* New York: Norton.

Tanner, J. M. (1978). *Education and physical growth* (2nd ed.). New York: International Universities Press.

Tappan, M. (2006, March). Moral functioning as mediated action. *Journal of Moral Education, 35,* 1–18.

Tappan, M. B. (1997). Language, culture, and moral development: A Vygotskian perspective. *Developmental Review, 17,* 199–212.

Tardif, T. (1996). Nouns are not always learned before verbs: Evidence from Mandarin speakers' early vocabularies. *Developmental Psychology, 32,* 492–504.

Tardif, T., Wellman, H. M., & Cheung, K. M. (2004). False belief understanding in Cantonese-speaking children. *Journal of Child Language, 31,* 779–800.

Taris, T., van Horn, J., & Schaufeli, W. (2004). Inequity, burnout and psychological withdrawal among teachers: A dynamic exchange model. *Anxiety, Stress & Coping: An International Journal, 17,* 103–122.

Tartamella, L., Herscher, E., & Woolston, C. (2005). *Generation extra large: Rescuing our children fro the epidemic of obesity.* New York: Basic.

Task Force on College Gambling Policies. (2009). *A call to action addressing college gambling: Recommendations for science-based policies and programs.* Cambridge, MA: Division on Addictions at the Cambridge Health Alliance.

Task Force on Sudden Infant Death Syndrome. (2005). The changing concept of sudden infant death syndrome: Diagnostic coding shifts, controversies regarding the sleeping environment, and new variables to consider in reducing risk. *Pediatrics, 105,* 650–656.

Tasker, F. L., & Golombok, S. (1997). *Growing up in a lesbian family: Effects on child development.* New York: Guilford Press.

Tate, D. C., Reppucci, N. D., & Mulvey, E. P. (1995). Violent juvenile delinquents: Treatment effectiveness and implications for future action. *American Psychologist, 50,* 777–781.

Tatum, B. (1997). *"Why are all the black kids sitting together in the cafeteria?": And other conversations about race.* New York: Basic Books.

Tatum, B. (2007). *Can we talk about race?: And other conversations in an era of school resegregation.* Boston: Beacon Press.

Taubes, G. (1997, February 21). The breast-screening brawl. *Science, 275,* 1056–1059.

Taumoepeau, M., & Ruffman, T. (2008, March). Stepping stones to others' minds: Maternal talk relates to child mental state language and emotion understanding at 15, 24, and 33 months. *Child Development, 79(2),* 284–302.

Tauriac, J., & Scruggs, N. (2006, January). Elder abuse among African Americans. *Educational Gerontology, 32,* 37–48.

Taveras, E., Sandora, T., Shih, M., Ross-Degnan, D., Goldmann, D., & Gillman, M. (2006, November). The association of television and video viewing with fast food intake by preschool-age children. *Obesity, 14,* 2034–2041.

Tavris, C., & Sadd, S. (1977). The *Redbook* report on female sexuality. New York: Delacorte.

Taylor, C., Ahn, D., & Winkleby, M. (2006). Neighborhood and Individual Socioeconomic Determinants of Hospitalization. *American Journal of Preventive Medicine, 31,* 127–134.

Taylor, D. M. (2002). *The quest for identity: From minority groups to Generation Xers.* Westport, CT: Praeger Publishers/Greenwood Publishing.

Taylor, H. G., Klein, N., Minich, N. M., & Hack, M. (2000). Middle-school-age outcomes in children with very low birthweight. *Child Development, 71,* 1495–1511.

Taylor, R. J., Chatters, L. M., Tucker, M. B., & Lewis, E. (1991). Developments in research on black families. In A. Booth (Ed.), *Contemporary families.* Minneapolis, MN: National Council on Family Relations.

Taylor, R. L. (2000). A diversity within African American Families. In D. H. Demo, K. R. Allen, & M. A. Fine (Eds.), *Handbook of family diversity.* New York: Oxford University Press.

Taylor, R. L., & Rosenbach, W. E. (2005). (Eds.), *Military leadership: In pursuit of excellence* (5th ed.). Boulder, CO: Westview Press

Taylor, S. E. (1991). *Health psychology* (2nd ed.). New York: McGraw-Hill.

Taylor, S., & Stanton, A. (2007). Coping resources, coping processes, and mental health. *Annual Review of Clinical Psychology, 3,* 377–401.

Taylor, T. J. (2012). Understanding others and understanding language: How do children do it? *Language Sciences, 34,* 1–12.

Teerikangas, O. M., Aronen, E. T., Martin, R. P., & Huttunen, M. O. (1998). Effects of infant temperament and early intervention on the psychiatric symptoms of adolescents. *Journal of the American Academy of Child & Adolescent Psychiatry, 37,* 1070–1076.

Tegano, D. W., Lookabaugh, S., May, G. E., & Burdette, M. P. (1991). Constructive play and problem solving: The role of structure and time in the classroom. *Early Child Development and Care, 68,* 27–35.

Teicher, M. H., Anderson, S. L., Polcari, A., Anderson, C. M., & Navalta, C. P. (2002). Developmental neurobiology of childhood stress and trauma. *Psychiatric Clinics of North America, 25,* 397–426.

Teicher, M. H., Anderson, S. L., Polcari, A., Anderson, C. M., Navalta, C. P., & Kim, D. M. (2003). The neurobiological consequences of early stress and childhood maltreatment. *Neuroscience and Biobehavioral Review, 27,* 33–44.

Tellegen, A., Lykken, D. T., Bouchard, T. J., Jr., Wilcox, K. J., Segal, N. L., & Rich, S. (1988). Personality similarity in twins reared apart and together. *Journal of Personality and Social Psychology, 54,* 1031–1039.

Tenenbaum, H. R., & Leaper, C. (1998). Gender effects on Mexican-descent parents' questions and scaffolding during toy play: A sequential analysis. *First Language, 18,* 129–147.

Tenenbaum, H., & Leaper, C. (2003). Parent-child conversations about science: The socialization of gender inequities? *Developmental Psychology, 39,* 34–47.

Terman, D. L., Larner, M. B., Stevenson, C. S., & Behrman, R. E. (1996). Special education for students with disabilities: Analysis and recommendations. *The future of children, 6,* 4–24.

Terman, L. M., & Oden, M. H. (1959). *The gifted group at mid-life: Thirty-five years follow-up of the superior child.* Standord, CA: Standord University Press.

Termin, N. T., & Izard, C. E. (1988). Infants' responses to their mothers' expressions of joy and sadness. *Developmental Psychology, 24,* 223–229.

Terracciano, A., McCrae, R., & Costa, P. (2009). Intra-individual change in personality stability and age. *Journal of Research in Personality, 27,* 88–97.

Terry, D. (1994, December 12). When the family heirloom is homicide. *New York Times,* pp. A1, B7.

Terry, D. (2000, August, 11). U.S. child poverty rate fell as economy grew, but is above 1979 level. *The New York Times,* p. A10.

Terzidou, V. (2007). Preterm labour. Biochemical and endocrinological preparation for parturition. *Best Practices of Research in Clinical Obstetrics and Gynecology, 21,* 729–756.

Tesman, J. R., & Hills, A. (1994). Developmental effects of lead exposure in children. *Social Policy Report, 8,* 1–17.

Tessor, A., Felson, R. B., & Suls, J. M. (Eds.). (2000). *Psychological perspectives on self and identity.* Washington, DC: American Psychological Association.

Teutsch, C. (2003). Patient–doctor communication. *Medical Clinics of North America, 87,* 1115–1147.

Tharp, R. G. (1989). Psychocultural variables and constants: Effects on teaching and learning in schools: Special issue: Children and their development: Knowledge base, research agenda, and social policy application. *American Psychologist, 44,* 349–359.

Thatcher, S., & Greer, L. (2008). Does it really matter if you recognize who I am? The implications of identity comprehension for individuals in work teams. *Journal of Management, 34,* 5–24.

The Albert Shanker Institute. (2009). *Preschool curriculum: What's in it for children and teachers.* Retrieved from http://www.shankerinstitute.org/Downloads/Early%20Childhood%2012-11-08.pdf.

The Boston Globe. (2004, April 26). Oregon's vital experiment. *The Boston Globe,* A12.

The Endocrine Society. (2001, March 1). *The Endocrine Society and Lawson Wilkins Pediatric Endocrine Society call for further research to define precocious puberty.* Bethesda, MD: The Endocrine Society.

The Future of Children. (1991). Recommendations in "Executive Summary, Welfare to Work." *The Future of Children,* pp. 1–8.

The Future of Children. (2001). *Caring for infants and toddlers* (Vol. 11). Los Altos, CA: David and Lucile Packard Foundation.

Thelen, E. (1979). Rhythmical stereotypes in normal human infants. *Animal Behavior, 27,* 699–715.

Thelen, E. (1994). Three-month-old infants can learn task-specific patterns of interlimb coordination. *Psychological Science, 5,* 280–285.

Thelen, E. (2002). Motor development as foundation and future of developmental psychology. In W. W. Hartup, W. Willard, & R. K. Silbereisen (Eds.), *Growing points in developmental science: An introduction.* Philadelphia, PA: Psychology Press.

Thelen, E., & Bates, E. (2003). Connectionism and dynamic systems: Are they really different? *Developmental Science, 6,* 378–391.

Thelen, E., & Smith, L. (2006). Dynamic systems theories. *Handbook of child psychology* (6th ed.): *Volume 1, Theoretical models of human development* New York: John Wiley & Sons Inc.

Thiel de Bocanegra, H. (1998). Breast-feeding in immigrant women: The role of social support and acculturation. *Hispanic Journal of Behavioral Sciences, 20,* 448–467.

Thiessen, E., Hill, E., & Saffran, J. (2005). Infant-directed speech facilitates word segmentation. *Infancy* [serial online], *7,* 53–71.

Thivel, D., Isacco, L., Rousset, S., Boirie, Y., Morio, B., & Duché, P. (2011). Intensive exercise: A remedy for childhood obesity? *Physiology & Behavior, 102,* 132–136.

Thoma, S. J., & Rest, J. R. (1999). The relationship between moral decision making and patterns of consolidation and transition in moral judgment development. *Developmental Psychology, 35,* 323–334.

Thoman, E. B. (1990). Sleeping and waking states in infants: A functional perspective. *Neuroscience and Biobehavioral Review, 14,* 93–107.

Thoman, E. B., & Whitney, M. P. (1989). Sleep states of infants monitored in the home: Individual differences, developmental trends, and origins of diurnal cyclicity. *Infant Behavior and Development, 12,* 59–75.

Thoman, E. B., & Whitney, M. P. (1990). Behavioral states in infants: Individual differences and individual analyses. In J. Colombo & J. Fagen (Eds.), *Individual differences in infancy: Reliability, stability, prediction* (pp. 113–136). Hillsdale, NJ: Erlbaum.

Thomas, A., & Chess, S. (1977). *Temperament and development.* New York: Brunner-Mazel.

Thomas, A., & Chess, S. (1980). *The dynamics of psychological development.* New York: Brunner-Mazel.

Thomas, A., Chess, S., & Birch, H. G. (1968). *Temperament and behavior disorders in children.* New York: New York University Press.

Thomas, A., & Sawhill, I. (2005). For love and money? The impact of family structure on family income. *The Future of Children, 15,* 57–74.

Thomas, C. B., Duszynski, K. R., & Schaffer, J. W. (1979). Family attitudes reported in youth as potential predictors of cancer. *Psychosomatic Medicine, 4,* 287–302.

Thomas, J. (1986). Gender differences in satisfaction with grandparenting. *Psychology and Aging, 1,* 215–219.

Thomas, P. (1994, September 6). Washington's infant mortality rate, more than twice the U.S. average, reflects urban woes. *The Wall Street Journal,* p. A14.

Thomas, P., & Fenech, M. (2007). A review of genome mutation and Alzheimer's disease. *Mutagenesis, 22,* 15–33.

Thomas, P., Lalloué, F., Preux, P., Hazif-Thomas, C., Pariel, S., Inscale, R., et al. (2006, January). Dementia patients caregivers quality of life: The PIXEL study. *International Journal of Geriatric Psychiatry, 21,* 50–56.

Thomas, R. M. (2001). *Recent human development theories.* Thousand Oaks, CA: Sage.

Thomas, S. (2006, December). From the editor—the phenomenon of cyberbullying. *Issues in Mental Health Nursing, 27,* 1015–1016.

Thompson, C., & Prottas, D. (2006, January). Relationships among organizational family support, job autonomy, perceived control, and employee well-being. *Journal of Occupational Health Psychology, 11,* 100–118.

Thompson, P. (1993). "I don't feel old": The significance of the search for meaning in later life. *International Journal of Geriatric Psychiatry, 8,* 685–692.

Thompson, R., Easterbrooks, M., & Padilla-Walker, L. (2003). Social and emotional development in infancy. In R. Lerner and M. Easterbrooks (Eds.), *Handbook of psychology: Developmental psychology, Vol. 6* (pp. 91–112). New York: John Wiley & Sons, Inc.

Thompson, R. A., & Limber, S. P. (1990). Social anxiety in infancy: Stranger and separation reactions. In H. Leitenberg (Ed.), *Handbook of social and evaluation anxiety.* New York: Plenum.

Thompson, R. A., & Nelson, C. A. (2001, January). Developmental science and the media: Early Brain Development. *American Psychologist, 5,* 5–15.

Thompson, W. C., Clarke-Stewart, K. A., & Lepore, S. J. (1997). What did the janitor do? Suggestive interviewing and the accuracy of children's accounts. *Law & Human Behavior, 21,* 405–426.

Thoms, K. M., Kuschal, C., & Emmert, S., (2007). Lessons learned from DNA repair defective syndromes. *Experimental Dermatology, 16,* 532–544.

Thomson, J. A., Ampofo-Boateng, K., Lee, D. N., Grieve, R., Pitcairn, T. K., & Demetre, J. D. (1998). The effectiveness of parents in promoting the development of road crossing skills in young children. *British Journal of Educational Psychology, 68,* 475–491.

Thordstein, M., Löfgren, N., Flisberg, A., Lindecrantz, K., & Kjellmer, I. (2006). Sex differences in electrocortical activity in human neonates. *Neuroreport: For Rapid Communication of Neuroscience Research, 17,* 1165–1168.

Thoresen, C. E., & Bracke, P. (1997). Reducing coronary recurrences and coronary-prone behavior: A structures group treatment approach. In J. L. Sira (Ed.), *Group therapy for medically ill patients* (pp. 92–129). New York: Guilford Press.

Thornberry, T. P., & Krohn, M. D. (1997). Peers, drug use, and delinquency. In D. M. Stoff, J. Breiling, & J. D. Maser (Eds.), *Handbook of antisocial behavior* (pp. 218–233). New York: Wiley.

Thornburg, K. R., Pearl, P., Crompton, D., & Ispa, J. M. (1990). Development of kindergarten children based on child care arrangements. *Early Childhood Research Quarterly, 5,* 27–42.

Thorne, B. (1986). Girls and boys together, but mostly apart. In W. W. Hartup & Z. Rubin (Eds.), *Relationships and development* (pp. 167–184). Hillsdale, NJ: Erlbaum.

Thorne, B., & Luria, Z. (2003). Putting boundaries around the sexes: Sexuality and gender in children's daily worlds. *Down to earth sociology: Introductory readings* (12th ed.). New York, NY: Free Press.

Thornton, J. (2002). Myths of aging or ageist stereotypes. *Educational Gerontology, 28,* 301–312.

Thornton, J. (2004). Lifespan learning: A developmental perspective. *International Journal of Aging & Human Development, 57,* 55–76.

Thorpe, J. A., Hu, D. H., Albin, R. M., McNitt, J., Meyer, B. A., Cohen, J. R., & Yeast, J. D. (1993). The effect of intrapartum epidural analgesia on nulliparous labor: A randomized, controlled prospective trial. *American Journal of Obstetrics and Gynecology, 169,* 851–858.

Thorsheim, H. I., & Roberts, B. B. (1990). *Reminiscing together: Ways to help us keep mentally fit as we grow older.* Minneapolis: CompCare Publishers.

Thorson, J. A., Powell, F., Abdel-Khalek, A. M., & Beshai, J. A. (1997). Constructions of religiosity and death anxiety in two cultures: The United States and Kuwait. *Journal of Psychology and Theology, 25,* 374–383.

Thorvaldsson, V., Hofer, S., Berg, S., Skoog, I., Sacuiu, S., & Johansson, B. (2008). Onset of terminal decline in cognitive abilities in individuals without dementia. *Neurology, 71,* 882–887.

Thurlow, M. L., Lazarus, S. S., & Thompson, S. J. (2005). State policies on assessment participation and accommodations for students with disabilities. *Journal of Special Education, 38,* 232–240.

Tibben, A. (2007). Predictive testing for Huntington's disease. *Brain Research Bulletin, 72,* 165–171.

Tibosch, M. M., Verhaak, C. M., & Merkus, P. M. (2011). Psychological characteristics associated with the onset and course of asthma in children and adolescents: A systematic review of longitudinal effects. *Patient Education and Counseling, 82,* 11–19.

Tikotzky, L., & Sadeh, A. (2009). Maternal sleep-related cognitions and infant sleep: A longitudinal study from pregnancy through the 1st year. *Child Development, 80,* 860–874.

Time. (1980, September 8). People section.

Timmermans, S., & Buchbinder, M. (2011). Improving expanded newborn screening: A reply to Watson, Howell, and Rinaldo. *Journal of Health and Social Behavior, 52,* 279–281.

Tincoff, R., & Jusczyk, P. W. (1999). Some beginnings of word comprehension in 6-month-olds. *Psychological Science, 10,* 172–175.

Ting, Y. (1997). Determinants of job satisfaction of federal government employees. *Public Personnel Management, 26,* 313–334.

Tinsley, B., Lees, N., & Sumartojo, E. (2004). Child and adolescent HIV risk: Familial and cultural perspectives. *Journal of Family Psychology, 18,* 208–224.

Tissaw, M. (2007). Making sense of neonatal imitation. *Theory & Psychology, 17,* 217–242.

Tisserand, D., & Jolles, J. (2003). On the involvement of prefrontal networks in cognitive ageing. *Cortex, 39,* 1107–1128.

Tobin, J. J., Wu, D. Y. H., & Davidson, D. H. (1989). *Preschool in three cultures: Japan, China, and the United States.* New Haven, CT: Yale University Press.

Tobin-Richards, M. H., Boxer, A. M., & Petersen, A. C. (1983). The psychological significance of pubertal change: Sex differences in perceptions of self during early adolescence. In J. Brooks-Gunn & A. C. Petersen (Eds.), *Girls at puberty*. New York: Plenum.

Toch, T. (1995, January 2). Kids and marijuana: The glamour is back. *U.S. News and World Report*, p. 12.

Toda, S., & Fogel, A. (1993). Infant response to the still-face situation at 3 and 6 months. *Developmental Psychology, 29,* 532–538.

Toga, A. W., & Thompson, P. M. (2003). Temporal dynamics of brain anatomy. *Annual Review of Biomedical Engineering, 5,* 119–145.

Toga, A. W., Thompson, P. M., & Sowell, E. R. (2006). Mapping brain maturation. *Trends in Neuroscience, 29,* 148–159.

Tolan, P. H., & Dodge, K. A. (2005). Children's mental health as a primary care and concern: A system for comprehensive support and service. *American Psychologist, 60,* 601–614.

Tolchinsky, L. (2003). *The cradle of culture and what children know about writing and numbers before being taught*. Mahwah, NJ: Lawrence Erlbaum Associates.

Tomasello, M. (1995)."Thinking in niches: Sociocultural influences on cognitive development": Comment. *Human Development, 38,* 46–52.

Tomasello, M. (2011). Human culture in evolutionary perspective. In M. J. Gelfand, C. Chiu, Y. Hong, M. J. Gelfand, C. Chiu, & Y. Hong (Eds.), *Advances in culture and psychology* (Vol. 1). New York: Oxford University Press.

Tomasello, M., Carpenter, M., Call, J., Behne, T., & Moll, H. (2005). Understanding and sharing intentions: The origins of cultural cognition. *Behavioral and Brain Sciences, 28,* 675–735.

Tomasello, M., Carpenter, M., & Liszkowski, U. (2007). A new look at infant pointing. *Child Development, 78,* 705–722.

Tomblin, J. B., Hammer, C. S., & Zhang, X. (1998). The association of prenatal tobacco use and SLI. *International Journal of Language and Communication Disorders, 33,* 357–368.

Tomlinson-Keasey, C. (1985). *Child development: Psychological, sociological, and biological factors*. Homewood, IL: Dorsey.

Tongsong, T., Iamthongin, A., Wanapirak, C., Piyamongkol, W., Sirichotiyakul, S., Boonyanurak, P., Tatiyapornkul, T., & Neelasri, C. (2005). Accuracy of fetal heart-rate variability interpretation by obstetricians using the criteria of the National Institute of Child Health and Human Development compared with computer-aided interpretation. *Journal of Obstetric and Gynaecological Research, 31,* 68–71.

Topolnicki, D. M. (1995, January). The real immigrant story: Making it big in America. *Money*, pp. 129–138.

Torges, C., Stewart, A., & Nolen-Hoeksema, S. (2008). Regret resolution, aging, and adapting to loss. *Psychology and Aging, 23,* 169–180.

Torvaldsen, S., Roberts, C. L, Simpson, J. M., Thompson, J. F., & Ellwood, D. A. (2006). Intrapartum epidural analgesia and breastfeeding: A prospective cohort study. *International Breastfeeding Journal, 24,* 1–24.

Toschke, A. M., Grote, V., Koletzko, B., & von Kries, R. (2004). Identifying children at high risk for overweight at school entry by weight gain during the first 2 years. *Archives of Pediatric Adolescence, 158,* 449–452.

Touwen, B. C. L. (1984). Primitive reflexes: Conceptual or semantic problem? In H. F. R. Prechtl (Ed.), *Continuity of neural functions from prenatal to postnatal life*. Philadelphia: Lippincott.

Townsend, A., Noelker, L., Deimling, G., & Bass, D. (1989). Longitudinal impact of interhousehold caregiving on adult children's mental health. *Psychology and Aging, 4,* 393–401.

Towse, J., & Cowan, N. (2005). Working memory and its relevance for cognitive development. In W. Schneider, R. Schumann-Hengsteler, & B. Sodian, *Young children's cognitive development: Interrelationships among executive functioning, working memory, verbal ability, and theory of mind*. Mahwah, NJ: Lawrence Erlbaum Associates.

Tracy, J., Shaver, P., & Albino, A. (2003). Attachment styles and adolescent sexuality. In P. Florsheim (Ed.), *Adolescent romantic relations and sexual behavior: Theory, research, and practical implications*. Mahwah, NJ: Lawrence Erlbaum Associates.

Tracy, M., Zimmerman, F., Galea, S., McCauley, E., & Vander Stoep, A. (2008). What explains the relation between family poverty and childhood depressive symptoms? *Journal of Psychiatric Research, 42,* 1163–1175.

Trainor, L. J., Austin, C. M., & Desjardins, R. N. (2000). Is infant-directed speech prosody a result of the vocal expression of emotion? *Psychological Science, 11,* 188–195.

Trainor, L., & Desjardins, R. (2002). Pitch characteristics of infant-directed speech affect infants' ability to discriminate vowels. *Psychonomic Bulletin & Review, 9,* 335–340.

Trautwein, U., Lüdtke, O., Kastens, C., & Köller, O. (2006). Effort on homework in grades 5–9: Development, motivational antecedents, and the association with effort on classwork. *Child Development, 77,* 1094–1111.

Trawick-Smith, J., & Dziurgot, T. (2011). "Good-fit" teacher–child play interactions and the subsequent autonomous play of preschool children. *Early Childhood Research Quarterly, 26,* 110–123.

Traywick, L., & Schoenberg, N. (2008). Determinants of exercise among older female heart attack survivors. *Journal of Applied Gerontology, 27,* 52–77.

Treas, J., & Bengston, V. L. (1987). The family in later years. In M. B. Sussman & S. K. Steinmetz (Eds.), *Handbook of marriage and the family*. New York: Plenum.

Treasure, J., & Tiller, J. (1993). The aetiology of eating disorders: Its biological basis. *International Review of Psychiatry, 5,* 23–31.

Treffers, P. E., Eskes, M., Kleiverda, G., & van Alten, D. (1990). Home births and minimal medical interventions. *Journal of the American Medical Association, 2624*(7), 2203, 2207–2208.

Trehub, S. E. (2003). The developmental origins of musicality. *Nature Neuroscience, 6,* 669–673.

Trehub, S., & Hannon, E. (2009). Conventional rhythms enhance infants' and adults' perception of musical patterns. *Cortex, 45,* 110–118.

Trehub, S. E., Schneider, B. A., Morrongiello, B. A., & Thorpe, L. A. (1988). Auditory sensitivity in school-age children. *Journal of Experimental Child Psychology, 46,* 272–285.

Trehub, S. E., Schneider, B. A., Morrongiello, B. A., & Thorpe, L. A. (1989). Developmental changes in high-frequency sensitivity. *Audiology, 28,* 241–249.

Trehub, S. E., Thorpe, L. A., & Morrongiello, B. A. (1985). Infants' perception of melodies: Changes in a single tone. *Infant Behavior and Development, 8,* 213–223.

Tremblay, R. E. (2001). The development of physical aggression during childhood and the prediction of later dangerousness. In G. F. Pinard & L. Pagani (Eds.). *Clinical assessment of dangerousness: Empirical contributions*. New York: Cambridge University Press.

Triandis, H. C. (1994). *Culture and social behavior*. New York: McGraw-Hill.

Triandis, H. C. (1995). *Individualism and collectivism*. Boulder, CO: Westview Press.Triche, E. W., & Hossain, N. (2007). Environmental factors implicated in the causation of adverse pregnancy outcome. *Seminars in Perinatology, 31,* 240–242.

Trickett, P. K., Kurtz, D. A., & Pizzigati, K. (2004). Resilient outcomes in abused and neglected children: Bases for strengths-based intervention and prevention policies. In K. I. Maton & C. J. Schellenbach (Eds.), *Investing in children, youth, families and communities: Strength-based research and policy*. Washington, DC: American Psychological Association.

Trippet, S. E. (1991). Being aware: The relationship between health and social support among older women. *Journal of Women and Aging, 3,* 69–80.

Troiano, R. P., Flegal, K. M., Kuczmarski, R. J., Campbell, S. M., & Johnson, C. L. (1995). Overweight prevalence and trends for children and adolescents. The National Health and Nutrition Examination Surveys, 1963–1992. *Archives of Pediatric and Adolescent Medicine, 10,* 1085–1091.

Troll, L. E. (1985). *Early and middle adulthood* (2nd ed.). Monterey, CA: Brooks/Cole.

Troll, L. E. (1986). Parents and children in later life. *Generations, 10,* 23–25.

Troll, L. E. (1989). Myths of midlife intergenerational relationships. In S. Hunter & M. Sundel (Eds.), *Midlife myths*. Newbury Park, CA: Sage.

Tronick, E. (2003). Emotions and emotional communication in infants. In J. Raphael-Leff (Ed.), *Parent-infant psychodynamics: Wild things, mirrors and ghosts* (pp. 35–53). London: Whurr Publishers, Ltd.

Tronick, E. Z. (1995). Touch in mother–infant interactions. In T. M. Field (Ed.), *Touch in early development*. Hillsdale, NJ: Erlbaum.

Tronick, E. Z. (1998). Dyadically expanded states of consciousness and the process of therapeutic change. *Infant Mental Health Journal, 19,* 290–299.

Tronick, E. Z., Thomas, R. B., & Daltabuit, M. (1994). The Quechua manta pouch: A caretaking practice for buffering the Peruvian infant against the multiple stressors of high altitude. *Child Development, 65,* 1005–1013.

Tropp, L. (2003). The psychological impact of prejudice: Implications for intergroup contact. *Group Processes & Intergroup Relations, 6,* 131–149.

Tropp, L., & Wright, S. (2003). Evaluations and perceptions of self, ingroup, and outgroup: Comparisons between Mexican-American and European-American children. *Self & Identity, 2,* 203–221.

Trotter, A. (2004, December 1). Web searches often overwhelm young researchers. *Education Week, 24,* 8.

Trouilloud, D., Sarrazin, P., Bressoux, P., & Bois, J. (2006, February). Relation between teachers' early expectations and students' later perceived competence in physical education classes: autonomy-supportive climate as a moderator. *Journal of Educational Psychology, 98*(1), 75–86.

Tryon, W. (2008). Historical and theoretical foundations. In M. Hersen & A. M. Gross (Eds), *Handbook of clinical psychology, Vol 1: Adults*. Hoboken, NJ: John Wiley & Sons Inc.

Trzesniewski, K. H., Donnellan, M. B., & Robins, R. W. (2003). Stability of self-esteem across the life span. *Journal of Personality and Social Psychology, 84,* 205–220.

Tsao, F-M., Liu, H-M., & Kuhl, P. K. (2004). Speech perception in infancy predicts language development in the second year of life: A longitudinal study. *Child Development, 75,* 1067–1084.

Tsapelas, I., Aron, A., & Orbuch, T. (2000). Marital boredom now predicts less satisfaction 9 years later. *Psychological Science, 20,* 543–545.

Tse, T., & Howie, L. (2005, September). Adult day groups: Addressing older people's needs for activity and companionship. *Australasian Journal on Ageing, 24,* 134–140.

Tsunoda, T. (1985). *The Japanese brain: Uniqueness and universality*. Tokyo: Taishukan.

Tucker, J. S., Friedman, H. S., Schwartz, J. E., Criqui, M. H., Tomlinson-Keasey, C., Wingard, D. L., & Martin, L. R. (1997). Parental divorce: Effects on individual behavior and longevity. *Journal of Personality and Social Psychology, 73,* 381–391.

Tucker, J., Martínez, J., Ellickson, P., & Edelen, M. (2008, March). Temporal associations of cigarette smoking with social influences, academic performance, and delinquency: A four-wave longitudinal study from ages 13-23. *Psychology of Addictive Behaviors, 22*(1), 1–11.

Tucker, M. B., & Mitchell-Kernan, C. (Eds.). (1995). *The decline in marriage among African Americans: Causes, consequences, and policy implications.* New York: Russell Sage.

Tucker, P., & Aron, A. (1993). Passionate love and marital satisfaction at key transition points in the family life cycle. *Journal of Social and Clinical Psychology, 12,* 135–147.

Tudge, J., & Scrimsher, S. (2003). Lev S. Vygotsky on education: A cultural-historical, interpersonal, and individual approach to development. In B. Zimmerman (Ed.), *Educational psychology: A century of contributions.* Mahwah, NJ: Lawrence Erlbaum Associates.

Tulving, E., & Thompson, D. M. (1973). Encoding specificity and retrieval processes in episodic memory. *Psychological Review, 80,* 352–373.

Turati, C. (2008). Newborns' memory processes: A study on the effects of retroactive interference and repetition priming. *Infancy, 13,* 557–569.

Turati, C., Cassia, V. M., Simion, F., & Leo, I. (2006). Newborns' face recognition: Role of inner and outer facial features. *Child Development, 77,* 297–311.

Turkheimer, E., Haley, A., Waldreon, M., D'Onofrio, B., & Gottesman, I. I. (2003). Socioeconomic status modifies heritability of IQ in young children. *Psychological Science, 14,* 623–628.

Turner, J. C. (1987). *Rediscovering the social group: A self-categorization theory.* New York: Basil Blackwell.

Turner, J. C., & Onorato, R. S. (1999). Social identity, personality, and the self-concept: A self-categorizing perspective. In T. R. Tyler & R. M. Kramer (Eds.), *The psychology of the social self: Applied social research.* Mahwah, NJ: Erlbaum.

Turner, J. S., & Helms, D. B. (1994). *Contemporary adulthood* (5th ed.). Forth Worth, TX: Harcourt Brace.

Turner, M. E., Pratkanis, A. R., Probasco, P., & Leve, C. (1992). Threat, cohesion, and group effectiveness: Testing a social identity maintenance perspective on groupthink. *Journal of Personality and Social Psychology, 63,* 781–796.

Turner, P. H., Scadden, L., & Harris, M. B. (1990). Parenting in gay and lesbian families. *Journal of Gay and Lesbian Psychotherapy, 1,* 55–66.

Turner, P. J., Gervai, J., & Hinde, R. A. (1993). Gendertyping in young children: Preferences, behavior and cultural differences. *British Journal of Developmental Psychology, 11,* 323–342.

Turner-Bowker, D. M. (1996). Gender stereotyped descriptors in children's picture books: Does "Curious Jane" exist in the literature? *Sex Roles, 35,* 461–488.

Turney, K., & Kao, G. (2009). Barriers to school involvement: Are immigrant parents disadvantaged? *Journal of Educational Research, 102,* 257–271.

Turton, P., Evans, C., & Hughes, P. (2009). Long-term psychosocial sequelae of stillbirth: Phase II of a nested case-control cohort study. *Archives of Women's Mental Health, 12,* 35–41.

Tuvblad, C., Narusyte, J., Grann, M., Sarnecki, J., & Lichtenstein, P. (2011). The genetic and environmental etiology of antisocial behavior from childhood to emerging adulthood. *Behavior Genetics, 41,* 629–640.

Twardosz, S., & Lutzker, J. (2009). Child maltreatment and the developing brain: A review of neuroscience perspectives. *Aggression and Violent Behavior, 15,* 59–68.

Twenge, J. M., & Campbell, W. K. (2001). Age and birth cohort differences in self-esteem: A cross-temporal meta-analysis. *Personality and Social Psychology Review, 5,* 321–344.

Twenge, J. M., & Crocker, J. (2002). Race and self-esteem: Meta-analyses comparing whites, blacks, Hispanics, Asians, and American Indians and comment on Gray-Little and Hafdahl (2000). *Psychological Bulletin, 128,* 371–408.

Twomey, J. (2006). Issues in genetic testing of children. *MCN: The American Journal of Maternal/Child Nursing, 31,* 156–163.

Tyler, K., Dillihunt, M., Boykin, A., Coleman, S., Scott, D., Tyler, C., et al. (2008). Examining cultural socialization within African American and European American households. *Cultural Diversity and Ethnic Minority Psychology, 14,* 201–204.

Tyre, P. (2004, January 19). In a race against time. *Newsweek,* pp. 62–66.

Tyre, P. (2006, September 11). The new first grade: Too much too soon? *Newsweek,* pp. 34–44.

Tyre, P., & McGinn, D. (2003, May 12). She works, he doesn't. *Newsweek,* pp. 45–52.

Tyre, P., Philips, M., Scelfo, J., Skipp, C., Joseph, N., Tolme, P., & Shenfeld, H. (2006, September 11). The new first grade: Too much too soon. *Newsweek,* p. 34.

Tyre, P., & Scelfo, J. (2003, September 22). Helping kids get fit. *Newsweek,* pp. 60–62.

U.S. Advisory Board on Child Abuse and Neglect. (1995). *A nation's shame: Fatal child abuse and neglect in the United States.* Washington, DC: Superintendent of Documents.

U.S. Bureau of Labor Statistics. (1995). *Workforce demographics and makeup.* Washington, DC: U.S. Department of Labor.

U.S. Bureau of Labor Statistics. (2003). *Wages earned by women.* Washington, DC: U.S Bureau of Labor Statistics.

U.S. Bureau of Labor, Women's Bureau. (1998). *The median wages of women as a proportion of the wages that men receive.* Washington, DC: U.S. Bureau of Labor.

U.S. Bureau of the Census. (1990a). *Statistical abstract of the United States: 1990* (110th ed.). Washington, DC: U.S. Government Printing Office.

U.S. Bureau of the Census. (1990b). *Studies in marriage and the family: Single parents and their children.* (Current Population Reports, Series P-23, No. 167). Washington, DC: U.S. Government Printing Office.

U.S. Bureau of the Census. (1990c). *Current population reports* (pp. 25–917, 25–1095). Washington, DC: U.S. Government Printing Office.

U.S. Bureau of the Census. (1992). *Poverty in the United States: 1991.* (Current Population Reports, Series P-60, No. 181). Washington, D.C: U.S. Government Printing Office.

U.S. Bureau of the Census. (1993). *Child health USA.* Washington, DC: U.S. Government Printing Office.

U.S. Bureau of the Census. (1994). Household statistics, 1993. *Current population reports.* Washington, DC: U.S. Govrnment Printing Office.

U.S. Bureau of the Census. (1995). *Higher education statistics.* (Current Population Reports). Washington, DC: U.S. Government Printing Office.

U.S. Bureau of the Census. (1997). *Who's minding our preschoolers?* Washington, DC: U.S. Government Printing Office.

U.S. Bureau of the Census. (1998). *Statistical abstract of the United States* (118th ed.). Washington, DC: U.S. Government Printing Office.

U.S. Bureau of the Census. (2000). *Current population reports.* Washington, DC: U.S. Government Printing Office.

U.S. Bureau of the Census. (2001a). *Living arrangements of children.* Washington, DC: U.S. Government Printing Office.

U.S. Bureau of the Census. (2001b). *Statistical abstract of the United States, 2001.* Washington, DC: U.S. Government Printing Office.

U.S. Bureau of the Census. (2002). *Statistical abstract of the United States* (122nd ed.). Washington, DC: U.S. Government Printing Office.

U.S. Bureau of the Census. (2004). *Current Population Survey, 2004 Annual Social and Economic Supplement.* Washington, DC: U.S. Bureau of the Census.

U.S. Bureau of the Census. (2005). *Current population survey.* Washington, DC: US. Bureau of the Census.

U.S. Bureau of the Census. (2008). *Statistical abstract of the United States, 2008.* Washington, DC: U.S. Government Printing Office.

U.S. Bureau of the Census. (2009). *Statistical abstract of the United States.* Washington, DC: U.S. Government Printing Office.

U.S. Census Bureau. (1996). *Population statistics.* Washington, D.C.

U.S. Census Bureau. (1997). *Poverty by educational attainment.* Washington, DC: U.S. Census Bureau.

U.S. Census Bureau. (2000). The condition of education. *Current Population Surveys, October 2000.* Washington, DC: U.S. Census Bureau.

U.S. Census Bureau. (2003). *Population reports.* Washington, DC: GPO.

U.S. Census Bureau. (2011). *Overview of race and Hispanic origin: 2010–2010 Census briefs* Washington, DC: U.S. Department of Commerce.

U.S. Department of Agriculture. (1999). *Dietary guidelines.* Washington, DC: U.S. Government Printing Office.

U.S. Department of Education (2005). 2003–04 National Postsecondary Student Aid Study (NPSAS:04), unpublished tabulations. Washington, DC: U.S. Department of Education

U.S. Department of Education. (2005). 2003–04 National Postsecondary Student Aid Study (NPSAS:04), unpublished tabulations. Washington, DC: U.S. Department of Education.

U.S. Department of Education. (2008). *Helping your child become a reader.* Retrieved from http://www.aft.org/pubs-reports/downloads/teachers/Help-English.pdf.

U.S. Department of Education, Office of Special Education and Rehabilitative Services. (1987). *Eighth Annual Report to Congress on the implementation of the education of the Handicapped Act, 1986.* Washington, DC: U.S. Government Printing Office.

U.S. Department of Health and Human Services, Administration on Children Youth and Families. (2007). *Child Maltreatment 2005. Washington, DC: U.S. Government Printing Office.*

U.S. Drug Enforcement Administration, Office of Diversion Control. (2012). National Forensic Laboratory Information System Special Report: ADD/ADHD Stimulants in NFLIS, 2007-2011. Springfield, VA: U.S. Drug Enforcement Administration.

U.S. National Center for Education Statistics. (1997). *Digest of education statistics 1997.* Washington, DC: U.S. Government Printing Office.

U.S.D.A. (1992). *Dietary guidelines.* Washington, DC: Author.

Ubell, E. (1996, September 15). Are you at risk? *Parade Magazine,* pp. 20–21.

Uchikoshi, Y. (2006). Early reading in bilingual kindergartners: Can educational television help? *Scientific Studies of Reading, 10,* 89–120.

Uchitelle, L. (1994, November 28). A generation transformed—A special report: Women in their 50's follow many paths into workplace. *The New York Times,* B8.

Uher, R. (2011). Genes, environment, and personalized treatment for depression. In K. A. Dodge & M. Rutter, (Eds.), *Gene–environment interactions in developmental psychopathology.* New York: Guilford Press.

Uhlenberg, P., Cooney, T., & Boyd, R. (1990). Divorce for women after midlife. *Journal of Gerontology, 45(1),* S3–S11.

Ulutas, I., & Ömeroglu, E. (2007). The effects of an emotional intelligence education program on the emotional intelligence of children. *Social Behavior and Personality, 35*(10), 1365–1372.

Umana-Taylor, A. J., Diversi, M., & Fine, M. A. (2002). Ethnic identity and self-esteem of Latino adolescents: Distinctions among the Latino populations. *Journal of Adolescent Research, 17,* 303–327.

Umana-Taylor, A., & Fine, M. (2004). Examining ethnic identity among Mexican-origin adolescents living in the United States. *Hispanic Journal of Behavioral Sciences, 26,* 36–59.

Umberson, D., Williams, K., Powers, D., Chen, M., & Campbell, A. (2005). As good as it gets? A life course perspective on marital quality. *Social Forces, 81,* 493–511.

UNAIDS & World Health Organization. (2001). *Cases of AIDS around the world.* New York: United Nations.

UNAIDS & World Health Organization. (2006). *AIDS epidemic update.* Paris: World Health Organization. ·

UNC Center for Civil Rights. (2005, January 7). *The socioeconomic compositions of the public schools: A crucial consideration in student assignment policy.* Chapel Hill: The University of North Carolina at Chapel Hill.

Underwood, M. (2003). *Social aggression among girls.* New York: Guilford Press.

Underwood, M. (2005). Introduction to the special section: Deception and observation. *Ethics & Behavior, 15,* 233–234.

UNESCO. (2006). *Compendium of statistics on illiteracy.* Paris: UNESCO.

Unger, R. K. (Ed.). (2001). *Handbook of the psychology of women and gender.* New York: John Wiley & Sons.

Unger, R., & Crawford, M. (1992). *Women and gender: A feminist psychology* (2nd ed.). New York: McGraw-Hill.

Unger, R., & Crawford, M. (1996). *Women and gender: A feminist psychology* (3rd ed.). New York: McGraw-Hill.

Unger, R., & Crawford, M. (1999). *Women and gender: A feminist psychology* (4th ed.). New York: McGraw-Hill.

Unger, R., & Crawford, M. (2004). *Women and gender: A feminist psychology* (4th ed.). New York: McGraw-Hill.

Ungrady, D. (1992, October 19). Getting physical: Fitness experts are helping shape up young America. *The Washington Post,* p. B5.

UNICEF. (2005). *The state of the world's children.* New York: The United Nations Children's Fund U.S. Bureau of the Census. (2006). Women's earnings as a percentage of men's earnings: 1960–2005. Historical Income Tables-People. Table P-40. Washington, DC: U.S. Bureau of the Census.

United Nations. (1990). *Declaration of the world summit for children.* New York: Author.

United Nations. (1991). *Declaration of the world summit for children.* New York: Author.

United Nations. (2002). *Building a Society for all ages.* New York: United Nations.

United Nations. (2004). *Hunger and the world's children.* New York: United Nations.

United Nations Children's Fund. (2006). *Childhood under threat.* New York: United Nations.

United Nations Office on Drugs and Crime. (2011). *Homicide statistics.* Vienna: United Nations Office on Drugs and Crime.

United Nations Population Division. (2002). *World population ageing: 1950–2050.* New York: United Nations.

United Nations World Food Programme. (2004). Retrieved from http://www.wfp.org.

University of Akron. (2006). *A longitudinal evaluation of the new curricula for the D.A.R.E. middle (7th grade) and high school (9th grade) programs: Take Charge of Your Life.* Akron, OH: University of Akron.

Unruh, D. (1989). Toward a social psychology of reminiscence. In D. Unruh & G. S. Livings (Eds.), *Personal history through the life course.* Greenwich, CT: JAI Press.

Updegraff, K. A., Helms, H. M., McHale, S. M., Crouter, A. C., Thayer, S. M., & Sales, L. H. (2004). Who's the boss? Patterns of perceived control in adolescents' friendships. *Journal of Youth & Adolescence, 33,* 403–420.

Updegraff, K., McHale, S., & Crouter, A. (2000). Adolescents' sex-typed friendship experiences: Does having a sister versus a brother matter? *Child Development, 71,* 1597–1610.

Updegraff, K. A., McHale, S. M., Whiteman, S. D., Thayer, S. M., & Crouter, A. C. (2006). The nature and correlates of Mexican-American adolescents' time with parents and peers. *Child Development, 77,* 1470–1486.

Urberg, K. A. (1982). The development of the concepts of masculinity and femininity in young children. *Sex Roles, 8,* 659–668.

Urberg, K. A., Degirmencioglu, S. M., & Pilgrim, C. (1997). Close friend and group influence on adolescent cigarette smoking and alcohol use. *Developmental Psychology, 33,* 834–844.

Urberg, K., Luo, Q., & Pilgrim, C. (2003). A two-stage model of peer influence in adolescent substance use: Individual and relationship-specific differences in susceptibility to influence. *Addictive Behaviors, 28,* 1243–1256.

Urquidi, V., Tarin, D., & Goodison, S. (2000). Role of telomerase in cell senescence and oncogenesis. *Annual Review of Medicine, 51,* 65–79.

Urso, A. (2007). The reality of neonatal pain and the resulting effects. *Journal of Neonatal Nursing, 13,* 236–238.

Usdansky, M. L. (1992, July 17). Wedded to the single life: Attitudes, economy delaying marriages. *USA Today,* p. A8.

USDHHS (U.S. Department of Health and Human Services). (1990). *Health United States 1989* (DHHS Publication No. PHS 90–1232). Washington, DC: U.S. Government Printing Office.

Uther, M., Knoll, M. A., & Burnham, D. (2007). Do you speak E-NG-L-I-SH? A comparison of foreigner- and infant-directed speech. Speech Communication, 49, 2–7.

Uylings, H. (2006). Development of the human cortex and the concept of "critical" or "sensitive" periods. *Language Learning, 56,* 59–90.

Vaillancourt, T., & Hymel, S. (2006, July). Aggression and social status: The moderating roles of sex and peer-valued characteristics. *Aggressive Behavior, 32,* 396–408.

Vaillant, G. (2003). Mental health. *American Journal of Psychiatry, 160,* 1373–1384.

Vaillant, G. E. (1977). *Adaptation to life.* Boston: Little, Brown.

Vaillant, G. E., & Vaillant, C. O. (1981). Natural history of male psychological health, X: Work as a predictor of positive mental health. *The American Journal of Psychiatry, 138,* 1433–1440.

Vaillant, G. E., & Vaillant, C. O. (1990). Natural history of male psychological health, XII: A 45-year study of predictors of successful aging. *American Journal of Psychiatry, 147*(1), 31–37.

Vaillant-Molina, M., & Bahrick, L. E. (2012). The role of intersensory redundancy in the emergence of social referencing in 51/2-month-old infants. *Developmental Psychology, 48,* 1–9.

Vaish, A., Carpenter, M., & Tomasello, M. (2009). Sympathy through affective perspective taking and its relation to prosocial behavior in toddlers. *Developmental Psychology, 45,* 534–543.

Vaish, A., & Striano, T. (2004). Is visual reference necessary? Contributions of facial versus vocal cues in 12-month-olds' social referencing behavior. *Developmental Science, 7,* 261–269.

Vajragupta, O., Monthakantirat, O., Wongkrajang, Y., Watanabe, H., & Peungvicha, P. (2000). Chroman amide 12P inhibition of lipid peroxidation and protection against learning and memory impairment. *Life Sciences, 67,* 1725–1734.

Valenti, C. (2006). Infant vision guidance: Fundamental vision development in infancy. *Optometry and Vision Development, 37,* 147–155.

Valiente, C., Eisenberg, N., & Fabes, R. A. (2004). Prediction of children's empathy-related responding from their effortful control and parents' expressivity. *Developmental Psychology, 40,* 911–926.

Valles, N., & Knutson, J. (2008). Contingent responses of mothers and peers to indirect and direct aggression in preschool and school-aged children. *Aggressive Behavior, 34,* 497–510.

Vallotton, C. (2011). Babies open our minds to their minds: How "listening" to infant signs complements and extends our knowledge of infants and their development. *Infant Mental Health Journal, 32,* 115–133.

Van Balen, F. (1998). Development of IVF children. *Developmental Review, 18,* 30–46.

Van Balen, F. (2005). The choice for sons or daughters. *Journal of Psychosomatic Obstetrics & Gynecology, 26,* 229–320.

Van Biema, D. (1995, December 11). Abandoned to her fate. *Time,* pp. 32–36.

Van de Graaf, K. (2000). *Human anatomy* (5th ed.). p. 339. Boston: McGraw-Hill.

Van den Bergh, B., Van Calster, B., Puissant, S., & Van Huffel, S. (2008). Self-reported symptoms of depressed mood, trait anxiety and aggressive behavior in post-pubertal adolescents: Associations with diurnal cortisol profiles. *Hormones and Behavior, 54,* 253–257.

van den Hoonaard, D. K. (1994). Paradise lost: Widowhood in a Florida retirement community. *Journal of Aging Studies, 8,* 121–132.

van der Mark, I., van IJzendoorn, M., & Bakermans-Kranenburg, M. (2002). Development of empathy in girls during the second year of life: Associations with parenting, attachment, and temperament. *Social Development, 11,* 451–468.

van Der Veer, R., & Valsiner, J. (1991). *Understanding Vygotsky: A quest for synthesis.* Cambridge, MA: Blackwell.

Van Der Veer, R., & Valsiner, J. (1993). *Understanding Vygotsky.* Oxford, England: Blackwell.

Van Der Veer, R., & Valsiner, J. (Eds.). (1994). *The Vygotsky reader.* Oxford, England: Blackwell.

van Geert, P. (1998). A dynamic systems model of basic developmental mechanisms: Piaget, Vygotsky, and beyond. *Psychological Review, 105,* 634–677.

van Gelderen, L., Gartrell, N., Bos, H. W., van Rooij, F. B., & Hermanns, J. A. (2012). Stigmatization associated with growing up in a lesbian-parented family: What do adolescents experience and how do they deal with it?. *Children and Youth Services Review.* Retrieved from http://williamsinstitute.law.ucla.edu/research/parenting/stigmatization-associated-with-growing-up-in-a-lesbian-parented-family/.

van Goethem, A. A. J., Scholte, R. H. J., & Wiers, R. W. (2010). Explicit- and implicit attitudes in relation to bullying behavior. *Journal of Abnormal Child Psychology: An official publication of the International Society for Research in Child and Adolescent Psychopathology, 38,* 829–842.

van Honk, J., Schutter, D. L., Hermans, E. J., & Putman, P. (2004). Testosterone, cortisol, dominance, and submission: Biologically prepared motivation, no psychological mechanisms involved. *Behavioral & Brain Sciences, 27,* 160–161.

van Jaarsveld, C., Fidler, J., Simon, A., & Wardle, J. (2007, October). Persistent impact of pubertal timing on trends in smoking, food choice, activity, and stress in adolescence. *Psychosomatic Medicine, 69*(8), 798–806.

van Kleeck, A., & Stahl, S. (2003). *On reading books to children: Parents and teachers.* Mahwah, NJ: Lawrence Erlbaum Associates.

van Leeuwen, M., van den Berg, S., & Boomsma, D. (2008). A twin-family study of general IQ. *Learning and Individual Differences, 18,* 76–88.

Van Manen, S., & Pietromonaco, P. (1993). *Acquaintance and consistency influence memory from interpersonal information.* Unpublished manuscript, University of Massachusetts, Amherst.

Van Mark, K., & Wynn, K. (2006). Six-month-old infants use analog magnitudes to represent duration. *Developmental Science, 9,* F41–F49.

van Marle, K., & Wynn, K. (2009). Infants' auditory enumeration: Evidence for analog magnitudes in the small number range. *Cognition, 111,* 302–316.

Van Riper, C. (1972). *Speech correction: Principles and methods.* Englewood Cliffs, NJ: Prentice-Hall.

Van Schoiack-Edstrom, L., Frey, K. S., & Beland, K. (2002). Changing adolescents' attitudes about relational and physical aggression. *School Psychology Review, 31,* 201–216.

van Soelen, I. C., Brouwer, R. M., van Leeuwen, M., Kahn, R. S., Pol, H., & Boomsma, D. I. (2011). Heritability of verbal and performance intelligence in a pediatric longitudinal sample. *Twin Research And Human Genetics, 14,* 119–128.

van Strien, T., & Bazelier, F. (2007). Perceived parental control of food intake is related to external, restrained and emotional eating in 7-12-year-old boys and girls. *Appetite, 49,* 618–625.

Van Tassel-Baska, J. (1986). Effective curriculum and instructional models for talented students. *Gifted Child Quarterly, 30,* 164–169.

Van Tassel-Baska, J., Olszewski-Kubilius, P., & Kulieke, M. (1994). A study of self-concept and social support in advantaged and disadvantaged seventh and eighth grade gifted students. *Roeper Review, 16,* 186–191.

van Wesel, F., Boeije, H., Alisic, E., & Drost, S. (2011). I'll be working my way back: A qualitative synthesis on the trauma experience of children. *Psychological Trauma: Theory, Research, Practice, and Policy.* Retrieved from http://psycnet.apa.org/psycinfo/2011-24222-001/.

van Wormer, K., & McKinney, R. (2003). What schools can do to help gay/lesbian/bisexual youth: A harm reduction approach. *Adolescence, 38,* 409–420.

van't Spijker, A., & ten Kroode, H. F. (1997). Psychological aspects of genetic counseling: A review of the experience with Huntington's disease. *Patient Education and Counseling, 32,* 33–40.

Vance, B., Hankins, N., & Brown, W. (1988). Ethnic and sex differences on the Test of Nonverbal Intelligence, Quick Test of intelligence, and Wechsler Intelligence Scale for Children–Revised. *Journal of Clinical Psychology, 44,* 261–265.

VandeBerg, L. R., & Streckfuss, D. (1992). Prime-time television's portrayal of women and the world of work: A demographic profile. *Journal of Broadcasting and Electronic Media, 36,* 195–208.

Vandell, D. L. (2000). Parents, peer groups, and other socializing influences. *Developmental Psychology, 36,* 699–710.

Vandell, D. L. (2004). Early child care: The known and the unknown. *Merrill-Palmer Quarterly, 50,* Special issue: The maturing of human developmental sciences: Appraising past, present, and prospective agendas, 387–414.

Vandell, D. L., & Pierce, K. M. (2003). Child care quality and children's success at school. In A. Reynolds & M. Wang (Eds.), *Early Childhood Learning: Programs for a New Century* (pp. 115–139). New York: Child Welfare League.

Vandell, D. L., Shumow, L., & Posner, J. (2005). After-school programs for low-income children: Differences in program quality. In J. L. Mahoney, R. W. Larson, & J. S. Eccles, *Organized activities as contexts of development: Extracurricular activities, after-school and community programs.* Mahwah, NJ: Lawrence Erlbaum Associates.

Vandello, J., & Cohen, D. (2003). Male honor and female fidelity: Implicit cultural scripts that perpetuate domestic violence. *Journal of Personality & Social Psychology, 84,* 997–1010.

Vandello, J., Cohen, D., Grandon, R., & Franiuk, R. (2009). Stand by your man: Indirect prescriptions for honorable violence and feminine loyalty in Canada, Chile, and the United States. *Journal of Cross-Cultural Psychology, 40,* 81–104.

Vandenbosch, L., & Eggermont, S. (2012). Maternal attachment and television viewing in adolescents' sexual socialization: Differential associations across gender. *Sex Roles, 66,* 38–52.

Vanderburg, R. (2006, October). Reviewing research on teaching writing based on Vygotsky's theories: What we can learn. *Reading & Writing Quarterly: Overcoming Learning Difficulties, 22,* 375–393.

VanEvra, J. (1990). *Television and child development.* Hillsdale, NJ: Erlbaum.

Vangelisti, A. (2006). Relationship dissolution: Antecedents, processes, and consequences. *Close relationships: Functions, forms and processes* (pp. 353–374). Hove, England: Psychology Press/Taylor & Francis (UK).

VanLaningham, J., Johnson, D., & Amato, P. (2001). Marital happiness, marital duration, and the U-shaped curve: Evidence from a five-wave panel study. *Social Forces, 78,* 1313–1341.

Vanlierde, A., Renier, L. & De Volder, A. G. (2008). Brain plasticity and multisensory experience in early blind individuals. In J. J. Rieser, D. H. Ashmead, F. F. Ebner, & A. L. Corn (Eds.), *Blindness and brain plasticity in navigation and object perception.* Mahwah, NJ: Lawrence Erlbaum Associates.

Vansteenkiste, M., Neyrinck, B., Niemiec, C., Soenens, B., De Witte, H., & Van den Broeck, A. (2007). On the relations among work value orientations, psychological need satisfaction and job outcomes: A self-determination theory approach. *Journal of Occupational and Organizational Psychology, 80,* 251–277.

Vanvuchelen, M., Roeyers, H., & De Weerdt, W. (2011). Development and initial validation of the Preschool Imitation and Praxis Scale (PIPS). *Research in Autism Spectrum Disorders, 5,* 463–473.

Vargha-Khadem, F., Carr, L. J., Isaacs, E., Brett, E., Adams, C., & Mishkin, M. (1997). Onset of speech after left hemispherectomy in a nine-year-old boy. *Brain, 120,* 159–182.

Vartanian, L. R. (2000). Revisiting the imaginary audience and personal fable constructs of adolescent egocentrism: a conceptual review. *Adolescence, 35,* 639–646.

Vasa, R. A., & Pine, D. S. (2006). Anxiety disorders. In C. A. Essau (Ed.), *Child and adolescent psychopathology: Theoretical and clinical implications.* New York: Routledge.

Vaughan, B. S., March, J. S., & Kratochvil, C. J. (2012). The evidence-based pharmacological treatment of paediatric ADHD. *International Journal of Neuropsychopharmacology, 15,* 27–39.

Vaughn, V., McKay, R. J., & Behrman, R. (1979). *Nelson textbook of pediatrics* (11th ed.). Philadelphia: Saunders.

Veatch, R. M. (1984). Brain death. In E. S. Shneidman (Ed.), *Death: Current perspectives* (3rd ed.). Palo Alto, CA: Mayfield.

Vecchiet, L. (2002). Muscle pain and aging. *Journal of Musculoskeletal Pain, 10,* 5–22.

Vecchiotti, S. (2003). Kindergarten: An overlooked educational policy priority. *Social Policy Report,* 3–19.

Vedantam, S. (2004, April 23). Antidepressants called unsafe for children: Four medications singled out in analysis of many studies. *The Washington Post,* A03.

Vedantam, S. (2006, December 20). Short mental workouts may slow decline of aging minds, study finds. *The Washington Post,* p. A1.

Veevers, J. E., & Mitchell, B. A. (1998). Intergenerational exchanges and perceptions of support within "boomerang kid" family environments. *International Journal of Aging & Human Development, 46,* 91–108.

Vélez, C. E., Wolchik, S. A., Tein, J., & Sandler, I. (2011). Protecting children from the consequences of divorce: A longitudinal study of the effects of parenting on children's coping processes. *Child Development, 82,* 244–257.

Vellutino, F. R. (1991). Introduction to three studies on reading acquisition: Convergent findings on theoretical foundations of code-oriented versus whole-language approaches to reading instruction. *Journal of Educational Psychology, 83,* 437–443.

Veneziano, R. (2003). The importance of paternal warmth. *Cross-Cultural Research: The Journal of Comparative Social Science, 37,* 265–281.

Veras, R. P., & Mattos, L. C. (2007). Audiology and aging: literature review and current horizons. *Revista Brasileira de Otorrinolaringologia (English Edition), 73,* 122–128.

Verbrugge, L. M. (1985). Gender and health: An update on hypotheses and evidence. *Journal of Health and Social Behavior, 26,* 156–182.

Vercellini, P., Zuliani, G., Rognoni, M., Trespidi, L., Oldani, S., & Cardinale, A. (1993). Pregnancy at forty and over: A case-control study. *European Journal of Obstetrics, Gynecology, & Reproductive Biology, 48,* 191–195.

Verdugo, R. R. (2011). The heavens may fall: School dropouts, the achievement gap, and statistical bias. *Education and Urban Society, 43,* 184–204.

Vereijken, C. M., Riksen-Walraven, J. M., & Kondo-Ikemura, K. (1997). Maternal sensitivity and infant attachment security in Japan: A longitudinal study. *International Journal of Behavioral Development, 21,* 35–49.

Verkerk, G., Pop, V., & Van Son, M., (2003). Prediction of depression in the postpartum period: A longitudinal follow-up study in high-risk and low-risk women. *Journal of Affective Disorders, 77,* 159–166.

Verkuyten, M. (2003). Positive and negative self-esteem among ethnic minority early adolescents: Social and cultural sources and threats. *Journal of Youth & Adolescence, 32,* 267–277.

Verma, J. (2004). Social values. *Psychology in India revisited: Developments in the discipline, Vol 3: Applied social and organisational psychology.* Thousand Oaks, CA: Sage Publications, Inc.

Vermandel, A., Weyler, J., De Wachter, S., & Wyndaele, J. (2008). Toilet training of healthy young toddlers: A randomized trial between a daytime wetting alarm and timed potty training. *Journal of Developmental & Behavioral Pediatrics, 29,* 191–196.

Vernon, J. A. (1990). Media stereotyping: A comparison of the way elderly women and men are portrayed on prime-time television. *Journal of Women and Aging, 2,* 55–68.

Verrity, P. (2007). *Violence and aggression around the globe.* Hauppauge, NY: Nova Science Publishers.

Vertes, R. (1986). A life-sustaining function for REM sleep: A theory. *Neuroscience & Biobehavioral Reviews, 10,* 371–376.

Vidaver, R. M., et al. (2000). Women subjects in NIH-Funded clinical research literature: Lack of progress in both representation and analysis by sex. *Journal of Women's Health Gender-Based Medicine, 9,* 495–504.

Vihman, M. M. (1991). Early syllables and the construction of phonology. In C. A. Ferguson, L. Menn, & C. Stoel-Gammon (Eds.), *Phonological development: Models, research, implications* (pp. 69–84). Hillsdale, NJ: Erlbaum.

Vilette, B. (2002). Do young children grasp the inverse relationship between addition and subtraction? Evidence against early arithmetic. *Cognitive Development, 17,* 1365–1383.

Vilhjalmsson, R., & Kristjansdottir, G. (2003). Gender differences in physical activity in older children and adolescents: The central role of organized sport. *Social Science Medicine, 56,* 363–374.

Viljoen, J., Elkovitch, N., & Ullman, D. (2008). Assessing risk for violence in adolescents. *Learning forensic assessment* (pp. 385–414). New York: Routledge/Taylor & Francis Group.

Villarosa, L. (2003, December 23). More teenagers say no to sex, and experts are sure why. *The New York Times,* pp. D6.

Vincent, J. A., Phillipson, C. R., & Downs, M. (2006). *The futures of old age.* Thousand Oaks, CA: Sage Publications.

Vincze, M. (1971). Examinations on the social contacts between infants and young children reared together. *Magyar Pszichologiai Szemle, 28,* 58–61.

Vingerhoets, A., Nyklicek, I., & Denollet, J. (Eds) (2008). *Emotion regulation: Conceptual and clinical issues.* New York: Springer Science + Business Media, 2008.

Vinik, J., Almas, A., & Grusec, J. (2011). Mothers' knowledge of what distresses and what comforts their children predicts children's coping, empathy, and prosocial behavior. *Parenting: Science and Practice, 11,* 56–71.

Vink, D., Aartsen, M., Comijs, H., Heymans, M., Penninx, B., Stek, M., et al. (2009). Onset of anxiety and depression in the aging population: Comparison of risk factors in a 9-year prospective study. *The American Journal of Geriatric Psychiatry, 17,* 642–652.

Vinovakis, M. A. (2005). *The birth of Head Start: Preschool education policies in the Kennedy and Johnson administrations.* Chicago: University of Chicago Press.

Virpillot, E. (1968). The development of scanning strategies and their relation to visual differentiation. *Journal of Experimental Child Psychology, 6,* 632–650.

Visscher, W. A., Bray, R. M., & Kroutil, L. A. (1999). Drug use and pregnancy. In R. M. Bray, M. E. Marsden, et al. (Eds.), *Drug use in metropolitan America.* Thousand Oaks, CA: Sage.

Vitaliano, P. P., Dougherty, C. M., & Siegler, I. C. (1994). Biopsychosocial risks for cardiovascular disease in spouse caregivers of persons with Alzheimer's disease. In R. P. Abeles, H. C. Gift, & M. G. Ory (Eds.), *Aging and quality of life.* New York: Springer.

Vitaro, F., & Pelletier, D. (1991). Assessment of children's social problem-solving skills in hypothetical and actual conflict situations. *Journal of Abnormal Child Psychology, 19,* 505–518.

Vizmanos, B., & Marti-Henneberg, C. (2000). Puberty begins with a characteristic subcutaneous body fat mass in each sex. *European Journal of Clinical Nutrition, 54,* 203–206.

Vogel, G. (1997, June 13). Why the rise in asthma cases? *Science, 276,* 1645.

Vohs, K. D., & Heatherton, T. (2004). Ego threats elicits different social comparison process among high and low self-esteem people: Implications for interpersonal perceptions. *Social Cognition, 22,* 168–191.

Völker, S. (2007). Infants' vocal engagement oriented towards mother versus stranger at 3 months and avoidant attachment behavior at 12 months. *International Journal of Behavioral Development, 31,* 88–95.

Volkow, N. D., Wang, G. J., Fowler, J. S., Logan, J., Gerasimov, M., Maynard, I., Ding, Y. S., Gatley, S. J., Gifford, A., & Granceschi, D. (2001). Therapeutic doses of oral methylphenidate significantly increase extracellular dopamine in the human brain. *Journal of Neuroscience, 21,* 1–5.

Volling, B. L., & Belsky, J. (1992). The contribution of mother–child and father–child relationships to the quality of sibling interaction: A longitudinal study. *Child Development, 63,* 1209–1222.

Vollrath, M. (2006). *Handbook of personality and health.* New York: John Wiley & Sons Ltd.

Vondra, J. I., & Barnett, D. (1999). Atypical attachment in infancy and early childhood among children at devel-

opmental risk. *Monographs of the Society for Research in Child Development, 64* (Serial No. 258).

Vondra, J., Shaw, D., Swearingen, L., Cohen, M., & Owens, E. (1999).Early relationship quality from home to school: A longitudinal study. *Early Education and Development, 10,* 163–190.

Voorpostel, M., & Blieszner, R. (2008). Intergenerational solidarity and support between adult siblings. *Journal of Marriage and Family, 70,* 157–167.

Votruba-Drzal, E., Coley, R. L., & Chase-Lansdale, L. (2004). Child care and low-income children's development: Direct and moderated effects. *Child Development, 75,* 396–412.

Vouloumanos, A., & Werker, J. (2007). Listening to language at birth: Evidence for a bias for speech in neonates. *Developmental Science, 10,* 159–164.

Vurpillot, E. (1968). The development of scanning strategies and their relation to visual differentiation. *Journal of Experimental Child Psychology, 6,* 632–650.

Vyas, S. (2004). Exploring bicultural identities of Asian high school students through the analytic window of a literature club. *Journal of Adolescent & Adult Literacy, 48,* 12–18.

Vygotsky, L. S. (1926/1997). *Educational psychology.* Delray Beach, FL: St. Lucie Press.

Vygotsky, L. S. (1930/1978). *Mind in society: The development of higher mental processes.* Cambridge, MA: Harvard University Press. (Original works published 1930, 1933, and 1935)

Vygotsky, L. S. (1979). *Mind in society: The development of higher mental processes.* Cambridge, MA: Harvard University Press. (Original works published 1930, 1933, and 1935)

Vygotsky, L. S. (1997). *Educational psychology.* Delray Beach, FL: St. Lucie Press. (Original work published 1926)

Wachs, T. (2002). Nutritional deficiencies as a biological context for development. In W. Hartup, W. Silbereisen, & K. Rainer (Eds.), *Growing points in developmental science: An introduction.* Philadelphia, PA: Psychology Press.

Wachs, T. D. (1992). *The nature of nurture.* Newbury Park, CA: Sage.

Wachs, T. D. (1993). The nature–nurture gap: What we have here is a failure to collaborate. In R. Plomin & G. E. McClearn (Eds.), *Nature, nurture, and psychology.* Washington, DC: American Psychological Association.

Wachs, T. D. (1996a). Environment and intelligence: Present status, future directions. In D. K. Detterman (Ed.), *Current Topics in Human Intelligence, Volume 5, The environment.* Norwood, NJ: Ablex Publishing.

Wachs, T. D. (1996b). Known and potential processes underlying developmental trajectories in childhood and adolescence. *Developmental Psychology, 32,* 796–801.

Wacker, J., Mueller, E. M., Hennig, J., & Stemmler, G. (2012). How to consistently link extraversion and intelligence to the catechol-O-methyltransferase (COMT) gene: On defining and measuring psychological phenotypes in neurogenetic research. *Journal of Personality and Social Psychology, 102,* 427–444.

Wade, N. (2001, October 4). Researchers say gene is linked to language. *The New York Times,* A1.

Wade, T., Tiggemann, M., Bulik, C., Fairburn, C., Wray, N., & Martin, N. (2008, February). Shared temperament risk factors for anorexia nervosa: A twin study. *Psychosomatic Medicine, 70*(2), 239–244.

Wagner, C., Greer, F., & The Section on Breastfeeding and Committee on Nutrition. (2008). Prevention of rickets and vitamin D deficiency in infants, children, and adolescents. *Pediatrics, 122,* 1142–1152.

Wagner, D. A. (1981). Culture and memory development. In H. C. Triandis & A. Heron (Eds.), *Handbook of cross-cultural psychology: Vol. 4: Developmental psychology.* Boston: Allyn & Bacon.

Wagner, H. J., Bollard, C. M., Vigouroux, S., Huls, M. H., Anderson, R., Prentice, H. G., Brenner, M. K., Heslop, H. E., & Rooney, C. M. (2004). A strategy for treatment of Epstein =Barr virus-positive Hodgkin's disease by targeting interleukin 12 to the tumor environment using tumor antigen-specific T Cells. *Cancer Gene Therapy, 2,* 81–91.

Wagner, R. K., & Sternberg, R. J. (1985). Alternate conceptions of intelligence and their implications for education. *Review of Educational Research, 54,* 179–223.

Wagner, R. K., & Sternberg, R. J. (1991). *Tacit knowledge inventory.* San Antonio, TX: The Psychological Corporation.

Wagner, W. G., Smith, D., & Norris, W. R. (1988). The pschological adjustment of enuretic children: A comparison of two types. *Journal of Pediatric Psychology, 13,* 33–38.

Wahlin, T. (2007). To know or not to know: A review of behaviour and suicidal ideation in preclinical Huntington's disease. *Patient Education and Counseling, 65,* 279–287.

Wahlsten, D., & Gottlieb, G. (1997). The invalid separation of effects of nature and nurture: Lessons from animal experimentation. In R. S. Sternberg & E. L. Grigorenko (Eds.), *Intelligence, heredity, and environment* (pp. 163–192). New York: Cambridge University Press.

Wainwright, J. L., Russell, S. T., & Pattterson, C. J. (2004). Psychosocial adjustment, school outcomes, and romantic relationships of adolescents with same-sex parents. *Child Development, 75,* 1886–1898.

Waite, S. J., Bromfield, C., & McShane, S. (2005). Successful for whom? A methodology to evaluate and inform inclusive activity in schools. *European Journal of Special Needs Education, 20,* 71–88.

Wake, M., Hardy, P., Canterford, L., Sawyer, M., & Carlin, J. (2007, July). Overweight, obesity and girth of Australian preschoolers: Prevalence and socio-economic correlates. *International Journal of Obesity, 31*(7), 1044–1051.

Wakefield, A., Murch, S., Anthony, A., Linnell, J., Casson, D., et al. (1998). Illeal-lymphoid-nodular hyperplasia, non-specific colitis, and pervasive developmental disorder in children. *The Lancet,*351, 637–641.

Wakefield, M., Reid, Y., Roberts, L., Mullins, R., & Gillies, P. (1998). Smoking and smoking cessation among men whose partners are pregnant: A qualitative study. *Social Science and Medicine, 47,* 657–664.

Wakeley, A., Rivera, S., & Langer, J. (2000). Can young infants add and subtract? *Child Development, 71,* 1525–1534.

Wakschlag, L. S., Leventhal, B. L., Pine, D. S., Pickett, K. E., & Carter, A. S. (2006). Elucidating early mechanisms of developmental psychopathology: The case of prenatal smoking and disruptive behavior. *Child Development, 77,* 893–906.

Walcott, D., Pratt, H., & Patel, D. (2003). Adolescents and eating disorders: Gender, racial, ethnic, sociocultural and socioeconomic issues. *Journal of Adolescent Research, 18,* 223–243.

Walden, T. A., & Baxter, A. (1989). The effect of context and age on social referencing. *Child Development, 60,* 1230–1240.

Walden, T. A., & Ogan, T. A. (1988). The development of social referencing. *Child Development, 59,* 1240–1249.

Walden, T., Kim, G., McCoy, C., & Karrass, J. (2007). Do you believe in magic? Infants' social looking during violations of expectations. *Developmental Science, 10,* 654–663.

Waldfogel, J. (2001). International policies toward parental leave and child care. *Caring for Infants and Toddlers, 11,* 99–111.

Waldholz, M. (2002, December 3). Genetic testing hits the doctor's office. *The Wall Street Journal,* D1, D8.

Waldholz, M. (2003, December 3). Genetic testing hits the doctor's office: New screens can predict odds of getting 1,004 diseases; getting pre-emptive surgery. *The Wall Street Journal*, p. B1.

Waldman, S. (2010, July 12). In plain English, he wants it to be official. *The Times-Union* (Albany, NY), A1.

Waldrop, D. P., & Kirkendall, A. M. (2009). Comfort measures: A qualitative study of nursing home-based end-of-life care. *Ournal of Palliative Medicine, 12*, 718–724.

Walker, A. J., & Pratt, C. C. (1991). Daughters' help to mothers: Intergenerational aid versus caregiving. *Journal of Marriage and the Family, 53*, 3–12.

Walker, A. J., Thompson, L., & Morgan, C. S. (1987). Two generations of mothers and daughters: Role position and interdependence. *Psychology of Women Quarterly, 11*, 195–208.

Walker, J., Anstey, K., & Lord, S. (2006, May). Psychological distress and visual functioning in relation to vision-related disability in older individuals with cataracts. *British Journal of Health Psychology, 11*, 303–317.

Walker, L. (1984). *The battered woman syndrome*. New York: Springer.

Walker, L. E. (1999). Psychology and domestic violence around the world. *American Psychologist, 54*, 21–29.

Walker, N. C., & O'Brien, B. (1999). The relationship between method of pain management during labor and birth outcomes. *Clinical Nursing Research, 8*, 119–134.

Walker, W. A., & Humphries, C. (2005). *The Harvard Medical School guide to healthy eating during pregnancy*. New York: McGraw-Hill.

Walker, W. A., & Humphries, C. (2007, September 17). Starting the good life in the womb. *Newsweek*, pp. 56–57.

Walker-Andrews, A. S. (1997). Infants' perception of expressive behaviors: Differentiation of multimodal information. *Psychological Bulletin, 121*, 437–456.

Walker-Andrews, A. S., & Dickson, L. R. (1997). Infants' understanding of affect. In S. Hala (Ed.), *The development of social cognition: Studies in developmental psychology* (pp. 161–186). Hove, England: Psychology Press/Erlbaum.

Walker-Andrews, A. S., & Lennon, E. (1991). Infants' discrimination of vocal expressions: Contributions of auditory and visual information. *Infant Behavior and Development, 14*, 131–142.

Wallace, I. F., Rose, S. A., McCarton, C. M., Kurtzberg, D., & Vaughan, H. G., Jr. (1995). Relations between infant neurobehavioral performance and cognitive outcome in very low birth weight preterm infants. *Journal of Developmental & Behavioral Pediatrics, 16*, 309–317.

Wallerstein, J. S., & Blakeslee, S. (1989). *Second chances*. New York: Ticknor & Fields.

Wallerstein, J. S., Lewis, J. M., & Blakeslee, S. (2000). *The unexpected legacy of divorce*. New York: Hyperion.

Wallerstein, J., & Resnikoff, D. (2005). Parental divorce and developmental progression: An inquiry into their relationship. In L. Gunsberg & P. Hymowitz, *A handbook of divorce and custody: Forensic, developmental, and clinical perspectives*. Hillsdale, NJ: Analytic Press, Inc.

Wallis, C. (1994, July 18). Life in overdrive. *Time*, pp. 42–50.

Wals, M., & Verhulst, F. (2005). Child and adolescent antecedents of adult mood disorders. *Current Opinion in Psychiatry, 18*, 15–19.

Walsh, B. T., & Devlin, M. J. (1998, May 29). Eating disorders: Progress and problems. *Science, 280*, 1387–1390.

Walster, H. E., & Walster, G. W. (1978). *Love*. Reading, MA: Addison-Wesley.

Walter, A. (1997). The evolutionary psychology of mate selection in Morocco: A multivariate analysis. *Human Nature, 8*, 113–137.

Walters, A., & Rye, D. (2009). Review of the relationship of restless legs syndrome and periodic limb movements in sleep to hypertension, heart disease, and stroke. *Sleep: Journal of Sleep and Sleep Disorders Research, 32*, 589–597.

Walters, E., & Gardner, H. (1986). The theory of multiple intelligences: Some issues and answers. In R. J. Sternberg & R. K. Wagner (Eds.), *Practical intelligence*. New York: Cambridge University Press.

Walther, V. N. (1997). Postpartum depression: A review for perinatal social workers. *Social Work in Health Care, 24*, 99–111.

Wang, C., He, Y., Liang, L., Zou, C., Hong, F., Dong, G., & Pei, J. (2011). Effects of short- and long-acting recombinant human growth hormone (PEG-rhGH) on left ventricular function in children with growth hormone deficiency. *Acta Paediatrica, 100*, 140–142.

Wang, L., Chyen, D., Lee, S., & Lowry, R. (2008, May). The association between body mass index in adolescence and obesity in adulthood. *Journal of Adolescent Health, 42*(5), 512–518.

Wang, M. (2007). Profiling retirees in the retirement transition and adjustment process: Examining the longitudinal change patterns of retirees' psychological well-being. *Journal of Applied Psychology, 92*, 455–474.

Wang, M., Lightsey, O., Pietruszka, T., Uruk, A., & Wells, A. (2007). Purpose in life and reasons for living as mediators of the relationship between stress, coping, and suicidal behavior. *The Journal of Positive Psychology, 2*, 195–204.

Wang, M. C., Peverly, S. T., & Catalano, R. (1987). Integrating special needs students in regular classes: Programming, implementation, and policy issues. *Advances in Special Education, 6*, 119–149.

Wang, M. C., Reynolds, M. C., & Walberg, H. J. (Eds.). (1996). *Handbook of special and remedial education: Research and practice* (2nd ed.). New York: Pergamon Press.

Wang, Q. (2001). Culture effects on adults' earliest childhood recollection and self-description: Implication for the relation between memory and the self. *Journal of Personality and Social Psychology, 81*, 220–233.

Wang, Q. (2004). The emergence of cultural self-constructs: Autobiographical memory and self-description in European American and Chinese children. *Developmental Psychology, 40*, 3–15.

Wang, Q. (2006, August). Culture and the development of self-knowledge. *Current Directions in Psychological Science, 15*, 182–187.

Wang, Q. (2008). Emotion knowledge and autobiographical memory across the preschool years: A cross-cultural longitudinal investigation. *Cognition, 108*, 117–135.

Wang, Q., Pomerantz, E., & Chen, H. (2007). The role of parents' control in early adolescents' psychological functioning: A longitudinal investigation in the United States and China. *Child Development, 78*, 1592–1610.

Wang, S., & Tamis-LeMonda, C. (2003). Do child-rearing values in Taiwan and the United States reflect cultural values of collectivism and individualism? *Journal of Cross-Cultural Psychology, 34*, 629–642.

Wang, S-H., Baillargeon, R., & Paterson, S. (2005). Detecting continuity violations in infancy: A new account and new evidence from covering and tube events. *Cognition, 95*, 129–173.

Wang, Z. W., Black, D., Andreasen, N. C., & Crowe, R. R. (1993). A linkage study of chromosome 11q in schizophrenia. *Archives of General Psychiatry, 50*, 212–216.

Wannamethee, S. G., Shaper, A. G., Walker, M., & Ebrahim, S. (1998). Lifestyle and 15-year survival free of heart attack, stroke, and diabetes in middle-aged British men. *Archives of Internal Medicine, 158*, 2433–2440.

Ward, R. A. (1984). *The aging experience: An introduction to social gerontology* (2nd ed.). New York: Harper & Row.

Ward, T. B., Finke, R. A., & Smith, S. M. (1995). *Creativity and the mind: Discovering the genius within*. New York: Plenum Press.

Ward, W. C., Kogan, N., & Pankove, E. (1972). Incentive effects in children's creativity. *Child Development, 43*, 669–677.

Wardle, F. (2007). Multiracial children in child development textbooks. *Early Childhood Education Journal, 35*, 253–259.

Wardle, J., Guthrie, C., & Sanderson, S. (2001). Food and activity preferences in children of lean and obese parents. *International Journal of Obesity & Related Metabolic Disorders, 25*, 971–977.

Warford, M. K. (2011). The zone of proximal teacher development. *Teaching and Teacher Education, 27*, 252–258.

Warin, J. (2000). The attainment of self-consistency through gender in young children. *Sex Roles, 42*, 209–231.

Warner, V., Weissman, M. M., Mufson, L., & Wickramaratne, P. J. (1999). Grandparents, parents, and grandchildren at high risk for depression: A three-generation study. *Journal of the American Academy of Child and Adolescent Psychiatry, 38*, 289–296.

Warnock, F., & Sandrin, D. (2004). Comprehensive description of newborn distress behavior in response to acute pain (newborn male circumcision). *Pain, 107*, 242–255.

Warren, C. W., Kann, L., Small, M. L., & Santelli, J. S. (1997). Age of initiating selected health-risk behaviors among high school students in the United States. *Journal of Adolescent Health, 21*, 225–231.

Warren, J. R. (2002). Reconsidering the relationship between student employment and academic outcomes: A new theory and better data. *Youth & Society, 33*, 366–370.

Warren, J. R., Lee, J. C., & Cataldi, E. F. (2004). Teenage employment and high school completion. In D. Conley & K. Albright (Eds.), *After the bell—Family background, public policy, and educational success*. London: Routledge.

Warrick, P. (1991, October 30). What the doctors have to say. *The Los Angeles Times*, p. E4.

Warriner, K., & Lavalle, D. (2008). The retirement experiences of elite female gymnasts: Self identity and the physical self. *Journal of Applied Sport Psychology, 20*, 301–317.

Warshak, R. A. (2000). Remarriage as a trigger of parental alienation syndrome. *American Journal of Family Therapy, 28*, 229–241.

Warshaw, R. (1988). *I never called it rape: The 'Ms.' report on recognizing, fighting, and surviving date and acquaintance rape*. New York: Harper & Row.

Wartella, E., Caplovitz, A., & Lee, J. (2004). From Baby Einstein to LeapFrog, from Dooms to the Sims, from instant messaging to internet chat rooms: Public interest in the role of interactive media in children's lives. *Social Policy Report, 18*(4), 7–8.

Warwick, P., & Maloch, B. (2003). Scaffolding speech and writing in the primary classroom: A consideration of work with literature and science pupil groups in the USA and UK. *Reading: Literacy & Language, 37*, 54–63.

Wass, H. (2004). A perspective on the current state of death education. *Death Studies, 28*, 289–308.

Wasserman, G., Factor-Litvak, P., & Liu, X. (2003). The relationship between blood lead, bone lead and child intelligence. *Child Neuropsychology, 9*, 22–34.

Wasserman, J., & Tulsky, D. (2005). A history of intelligence assessment. *Contemporary intellectual assessment: Theories, tests, and issues*. New York: Guilford Press.

Watanabe, H., Homae, F., & Taga, G. (2012). Activation and deactivation in response to visual stimulation in the occipital cortex of 6-month-old human infants. *Developmental Psychobiology, 54*, 1–15.

Waterhouse, J. M., & DeCoursey, P. J. (2004). Human circadian organization. In J. C. Dunlap & J. J. Loros (Eds.), *Chronobiology: Biological timekeeping*. Sunderland, MA: Sinauer Associates.

Waterland, R. A., & Jirtle, R. L. (2004). Early nutrition, epigenetic changes at transposons and imprinted genes, and enhanced susceptibility to adult chronic diseases. *Nutrition, 63–68.*

Waterman, A. (1982). Identity development from adolescence to adulthood: An extension of theory and a review of research. *Developmental Psychology, 18,* 341–358.

Waters, E. (1978). The reliability and stability of individual differences in infant–mother attachment. *Child Development, 49,* 483–494.

Waters, E., Hamilton, C. E., & Weinfield, N. S. (2000a). The stability of attachment security from infancy to adolescence and early adulthood: General introduction. *Child Develoment, 71,* 678–683.

Waters, E., Merrick, S., Treboux, D., Crowell, J., & Albersheim, L. (2000b). Attachment security in infancy and early adulthood: A 20-year longitudinal study. *Child Development, 71,* 684–689.

Waters, L., & Moore, K. (2002). Predicting self-esteem during unemployment: The effect of gender financial deprivation, alternate roles and social support. *Journal of Employment Counseling, 39,* 171–189.

Watkins, D., Dong, Q., & Xia, Y. (1997). Age and gender differences in the self-esteem of Chinese children. *Journal of Social Psychology, 137,* 374–379.

Watling, D., & Bourne, V. (2007, September). Linking children's neuropsychological processing of emotion with their knowledge of emotion expression regulation. *Laterality: Asymmetries of Body, Brain and Cognition, 12*(5), 381–396.

Watson, A. C., Nixon, C. L., Wilson, A., & Capage, L. (1999). Social interaction skills and theory of mind in young children. *Developmental Psychology, 35,* 386–391.

Watson, J. B. (1925). *Behaviorism.* New York: Norton.

Watson, J. B., & Rayner, R. (1920). Conditioned, emotional reactions. *Journal of Experimental Psychology, 3,* 1–14.

Watson, J. K. (2000). Theory of mind and pretend play in family context. (False belief). *Dissertation Abstracts International: Section B: The Sciences & Engineering, 60,* 3599.

Watt, N., & Kannampilly, A. (2009). 66-year-old to be oldest Briish woman to give birth. ABC News International. Retrieved from http://abcnews.go.com/International/story?id=7612856&page=1.

Watts-English, T., Fortson, B. L., Gibler, N., Hooper, S. R., & De Bellis, M. D. (2006). The psychobiologic of maltreatment in childhood. *Journal of Social Issues, 62,* 717–736.

Waugh, E., & Bulik, C. M. (1999). Offspring of women with eating disorders. *International Journal of Eating Disorders, 25,* 123–133.

Wayment, H., & Vierthaler, J. (2002). Attachment style and bereavement reactions. *Journal of Loss & Trauma, 7,* 129–149.

Weaver, A., & Dobson, P. (2004). Home and dry—some toilet training tips to give parents. *Journal of Family Care, 14,* 64, 66.

Webb, R. M., Lubinski, D., & Benbow, C. P. (2002). Mathematically facile adolescents with math/science aspirations: New perspectives on their educational and vocational development. *Journal of Educational Psychology, 94,* 785–794.

Weber, B. (2005, February 25.) From sidelines or in the rink, goalies are targets, even at 8. *New York Times,* p. B1, B8.

Weber, B. A., Roberts, B. L., Resnick, M., Deimling, G., Zauszniewski, J. A., Musil, C., & Yarandi, H. N. (2004). The effect of dyadic intervention on self-efficacy, social support and depression for men with prostate cancer. *Psycho-Oncology, 13,* 47–60.

Weber, K. S., Frankenberger, W., & Heilman, K. (1992). The effects of Ritalin on the academic achievement of children diagnosed with attention-deficit hyperactivity disorder. *Developmental Disabilities Bulletin, 20,* 49–68.

Webster, J., & Haight, B. (2002). *Critical advances in reminiscence work: From theory to application.* New York: Springer Publishing Co.

Webster, R. A., Hunter, M., & Keats, J. A. (1994). Peer and parental influences on adolescents' substance use: A path analysis. *International Journal of the Addictions, 29,* 647–657.

Wechler, H., Issac, L., Grodstein, T., & Sellers, D. (2000). *College binge drinking in the 1990s: a continuing problem: Results of the Harvard School of Public Health 1999 College Health Alcohol Study.* Cambridge, MA: Harvard University Press.

Wechsler, D. (1975). Intelligence defined and undefined. *American Psychologist, 30,* 135–139.

Wechsler, H., Issac, R., Grodstein, L., & Sellers, M. (2000). *College binge drinking in the 1990s: A continuing problem: Results of the Harvard School of Public Health 1999 College Health Alcohol Study.* Cambridge, MA: Harvard University.

Wechsler, H., Lee, J. E., Kuo, M., Seibring, M., Nelson, T. F., & Lee, H. (2002). *Trends in college binge drinking during a period of increased prevention efforts: Findings from 4 Harvard School of Public Health college alcohol study surveys, 1993–2001.*

Wechsler, H., & Nelson, T. F. (2001). Binge drinking and the American college student: What's five drinks. *Psychology of Addictive Behaviors, 15,* 287–291.

Wechsler, H., Rohman, M., & Solomon, R. (1981). Emotional problems and concerns of New England college students. *American Journal of Orthopsychiatry, 51,* 719.

Weed, K., Ryan, E. B., & Day, J. (1990). Metamemory and attributions as mediators of strategy use and recall. *Journal of Educational Psychology, 82,* 849–855.

Wegienka, G., Havstad, S., & Kelsey, J. (2006). Menopausal hormone therapy in a health maintenance organization before and after Women's Health Initiative hormone trials termination. *Journal of Women's Health, 15,* 369–378.

Wegman, M. E. (1993). Annual summary of vital statistics—1992. *Pediatrics, 92,* 743–754.

Wei, J., Hadjiiski, L. M., Sahiner, B., Chan, H. P., Ge, J., Roubidoux, M. A., Helvie, M. A., Zhour, C., Wu, Y.l T., Paramagul, C., & Zhang, Y. (2007). Computer-aided detection systems for breast masses: comparison of performances on full-field digital mammograms and digitized screen-film mammograms. *Academy of Radiology, 14,* 659–669.

Weichold, K., Silbereisen, R., & Schmitt-Rodermund, E. (2003). Short-term and long-term consequences of early versus late physical maturation in adolescents. In C. Hayward (Ed.), *Gender differences at puberty.* New York: Cambridge University Press.

Weigel, D. J., Devereux, P., Leight, G. K., & Ballard-Reisch, D. (1998). A longitudinal study of adolescents' perceptions of support and stress: Stability and change. *Journal of Adolescent Research, 13,* 158–177.

Weigel, D., Martin, S., & Bennett, K. (2006). Contributions of the home literacy environment to preschool-aged children's emerging literacy and language skills. *Early Child Development and Care [serial online], 176,* 357–378.

Weijerman, M., van Furth, A., Noordegraaf, A., van Wouwe, J., Broers, C., & Gemke, R. (2008). Prevalence, neonatal characteristics, and first-year mortality of Down syndrome: A national study. *The Journal of Pediatrics, 152,* 15–19.

Weinberg, M. K., & Tronick, E. Z. (1994). Beyond the face: an empirical study of infant affective configurations of facial, vocal, gestural, and regulatory behaviors. *Child Development, 65,* 1503–1515.

Weinberg, M. K., & Tronick, E. Z. (1996). Beyond the face: An empirical study of infant affective configurations of facial, vocal, gestural, and regulatory behaviors. *Child Development, 67,* 905–914.

Weinberg, R. A. (1989). Intelligence and IQ: Landmark issues and great debates. *American Psychologist, 44*(2), 98–104.

Weinberg, R. A. (1996). Commentary: If the natature-nurture war is over, why do we continue to battle? In D. K. Detterman, (Ed.), *Current Topics in Human Intelligence, Volume 5, The environment.* Norwood, NJ: Ablex Publishing.

Weinberg, R. A. (2004). The infant and the family in the twenty-first century. *Journal of the American Academy of Child & Adolescent Psychiatry, 43,* 115–116.

Weinberger, D. R. (2001, March 10). A brain too young for good judgment. *The New York Times,* p. D1.

Weindruch, R. (1996, January). Caloric restriction and aging. *Scientific American,* 46–52.

Weiner, B. (1985). *Human motivation.* New York: Springer-Verlag.

Weiner, B. (1994). Integrating social and personal theories of achievement striving. *Review of Educational Research, 64,* 557–573.

Weiner, B. (2007). Examining emotional diversity in the classroom: An attribution theorist considers the moral emotions.In P. A. Schutz & R Pekrun (Eds.), *Emotion in education.* San Diego: Elsevier Academic Press.

Weinfield, N. S., Sroufe, L. A., & Egeland, B. (2000). Attachment from infancy to early adulthood in a high-risk sample: Continuity, discontinuity, and their correlates. *Child Development, 71,* 695–702.

Weinstock, H., Berman, S., & Cates, W., Jr. (2004). Sexually transmitted diseases among American youth: Incidence and prevalence estimates, 2000. *Perspectives on Sexual and Reproductive Health , 36,* 182–191.

Weir, E. H. (1997, Summer). *Mount Holyoke College Vista,* pp. 1,4.

Weisinger, H. (1998, March 14). Tutored by television. *TV Guide,* 46–48.

Weiss, A. S. (1991). The measurement of self-actualization: The quest for the test may be as challenging as the search for the self. *Journal of Social Behavior and Personality, 6,* 265–290.

Weiss, J., Cen, S., Schuster, D., Unger, J., Johnson, C., Mouttapa, M., et al. (2006, June). Longitudinal effects of pro-tobacco and anti-tobacco messages on adolescent smoking susceptibility. *Nicotine & Tobacco Research, 8,* 455–465.

Weiss, M. R., Ebbeck, V., & Horn. T. S. (1997). Children's self-perceptions and sources of physical competence information: A cluster analysis. *Journal of Sport & Exercise Psychology, 19,* 52–70.

Weiss, R. (2003, September 2). Genes' sway over IQ may vary with class. *The Washington Post,* p. A1.

Weiss, R., & Raz, I. (2006, July). Focus on childhood fitness, not just fatness. *Lancet, 368,* 261–262.

Weisz, A., & Black, B. (2002). Gender and moral reasoning: African American youth respond to dating dilemmas. *Journal of Human Behavior in the Social Environment, 5,* 35–52.

Weitzman, E., Nelson, T., & Wechsler, H. (2003). Taking up binge drinking in college: The influences of person, social group, and environment. *Journal of Adolescent Health, 32,* 26–35.

Wellings, K., Collumbien, M., Slaymaker, E., Singh, S., Hodges, Z., Patel, D., et al. (2006, November). Sexual behaviour in context: A global perspective. *Lancet, 368*(9548), 1706–1738.

Wellman, H. M., Cross, D., & Watson, J. (2001). Meta-analysis of theory-of-mind development: The truth about false belief. *Child Development, 72,* 655–684.

Wellman, H., Fang, F., Liu, D., Zhu, L., & Liu, G. (2006, December). Scaling of theory-of-mind understandings in Chinese children. *Psychological Science, 17,* 1075–1081.

Wellman, H. M., & Gelman, S. A. (1992). Cognitive development: Foundational theories of core domains. *Annual Review of Psychology, 43,* 337–375.

Wellman, H., Lopez-Duran, S., LaBounty, J., & Hamilton, B. (2008). Infant attention to intentional action predicts preschool theory of mind. *Developmental Psychology, 44,* 618–623.

Wells, A. S., & Crain, R. L. (1994). Perpetuation theory and the long-term effects of school desegregation. *Review of Educational Research, 64,* 531–555.

Wells, B., Peppé, S., & Goulandris, N. (2004). Intonation development from five to thirteen. *Journal of Child Language, 31,* 749–778.

Wells, K. B., Golding, J. M., & Hough, R. L. (1989). Acculturation and the probability of use of services by Mexican-Americans. *Health Services Research, 24,* 237–257.

Wells, R., Lohman, D., & Marron, M. (2009). What factors are associated with grade acceleration? An analysis and comparison of two U.S. databases. *Journal of Advanced Academics, 20,* 248–273.

Welsh, T., Ray, M., Weeks, D., Dewey, D., & Elliott, D. (2009). Does Joe influence Fred's action? Not if Fred has autism spectrum disorder. *Brain Research, 1248,* 141–148.

Wenner, M. V. (1994). Depression, anxiety, and negative affectivity in elementary-aged learning disabled children. *Dissertation Abstracts International: Section B: the Sciences & Engineering.* Vol 54(9–B), 4938.

Werker, J., & Fennell, C. (2009). Infant speech perception and later language acquisition: Methodological underpinnings. *Infant pathways to language: Methods, models, and research disorders.* New York: Psychology Press.

Werker, J. F., Pons, F., Dietrich, C., Kajikawa, S., Fais, L., & Amano, S. (2007). Infant-directed speech supports phonetic category learning in English and Japanese. *Cognition, 103,* 1447–162.

Werner, E. E. (1972). Infants around the world: Cross-cultural studies of psychomotor development from birth to two years. *Journal of Cross-Cultural Psychology, 3,* 111–134.

Werner, E. E. (1993). Risk resilience, and recovery: Perspectives from the Kauai Longitudinal Study. *Development and Psychopathology, 5,* 503–515.

Werner, E. E. (1995). Resilience in development. *Current Directions in Psychological Science, 4,* 81–85.

Werner, E. E. (2005). What can we learn about resilience from large-scale longitudinal studies? In S. Goldstein, & R. B. Brooks (Eds.), *Handbook of resilience in children.* New York: Kluwer Academic/Plenum Publishers.

Werner, E., Myers, M., Fifer, W., Cheng, B., Fang, Y., Allen, R., et al. (2007). Prenatal predictors of infant temperament. *Developmental Psychobiology, 49,* 474–484.

Werner, E. E., & Smith, R. S. (1992). *Overcoming the odds: High-risk children from birth to adulthood.* Ithaca, NY: Cornell University Press.

Werner, E. E., & Smith, R. S. (2002). Journeys from childhood to midlife: Risk, resilience and recover. *Journal of Developmental & Behavioral Pediatrics, 23,* 456.

Werner, L. (2007). Issues in human auditory development. *Journal of Communication Disorders, 40,* 275–283.

Werner, L. A., & Marean, G. C. (1996). *Human auditory development.* Boulder, CO: Westview Press.

Werner, N. E., & Crick, N. R. (2004). Maladaptive peer relationships and the development of relational and physical aggression during middle childhood. *Social Development, 13,* 495–514.

Wertsch, J. (2008). From social interaction to higher psychological processes: A clarification and application of Vygotsky's theory. *Human Development, 51,* 66–79.

Wertsch, J. V. (1999). The zone of proximal development: Some conceptual issues. In P. Lloyd & C. Fernyhough (Eds.), *Lev Vygotsky: Critical assessments,* Vol. 3: *The zone of proximal development.* New York: Routledge.

Wertsch, J. V., & Tulviste, P. (1992). L. S. Vygotsky and contemporary developmental psychology. *Developmental Psychology, 28,* 548–557.

West, J. R., & Blake, C. A. (2005). Fetal alcohol syndrome: An assessment of the field. *Experimental Biology and Medicine, 230,* 354–356.

West, J., Romero, R., & Trinidad, D. (2007, August). Adolescent receptivity to tobacco marketing by racial/ethnic groups in California. *American Journal of Preventive Medicine, 33*(2), 121–123.

West, S. L., & O'Neal, K. K. (2004). Project D.A.R.E. outcome effectiveness revisited. *American Journal of Public Health, 94,* 1027–1029.

Westen, D. (1990). Psychoanalytic approaches to personality. In L. A. Previn (Ed.), *Handbook of personality: Theory and research.* New York: Guilford.

Westerhausen, R., Kreuder, F., Sequeira Sdos, S., Walter, C., Woerner, W., Wittling, R. A., Schweiger, E., & Wittling, W. (2004). Effects of handedness and gender on macro- and microstructure of the corpus callosum and its subregions: a combined high-resolution and diffusion-tensor MRI study. *Brain Research and Cognitive Brain Research, 21,* 418–426.

Westermann, G., Mareschal, D., Johnson, M. H., Sirois, S., Spratling, M. W., & Thomas, M. S. (2007). Neurosconstructivism. *Developmental Science, 10,* 75–83.

Wethington, E., Cooper, H., & Holmes, C. S. (1997). Turning points in midlife. In I. H. Gotlib & B. Wheaton (Eds.), *Stress and adversity over the life course: Trajectories and turning points* (pp. 215–231). New York: Cambridge University Press.

Wexler, B. (2006). *Brain and culture: Neurobiology, ideology, and social change.* Cambridge, MA: MIT Press.

Whalen, C. K., Jamner, L. D., Henker, B., Delfino, R. J., & Lozano, J. M. (2002). The ADHD spectrum and everyday life: Experience sampling of adolescent moods, activities, smoking, and drinking. *Child Development, 73,* 209–227.

Whalen, D., Levitt, A., & Goldstein, L. (2007). VOT in the babbling of French- and English-learning infants. *Journal of Phonetics, 35,* 341–352.

Whalen, J., & Begley, S. (2005, March 30). In England, girls are closing the gap with boys in math. *The Wall Street Journal,* p. A1.

Whaley, B. B., Parker, R. G. (2000). Expressing the experience of communicative disability: Metaphors of persons who stutter. *Communication Reports, 13,* 115–125.

Wheeldon, L. R. (1999). *Aspects of language production.* Philadelphia: Psychology Press.

Wheeler, G. (1998, March 13). The wake-up call we dare not ignore. *Science, 279,* 1611.

Wheeler, S., & Austin, J. (2001). The impact of early pregnancy loss. *American Journal of Maternal/Child Nursing, 26,* 154–159.

Whelan, T., & Lally, C. (2002). Paternal commitment and father's quality of life. *Journal of Family Studies, 8,* 181–196.

Whitaker, B. (2004, March 29). Employee of the century. *CBS Evening News.*

Whitaker, R. C., Wright, J. A., Pepe, M. S., Seidel, K. D., & Dietz, W. H. (1997, September 25). Predicting obesity in young adulthood from childhood and parental obesity. *The New England Journal of Medicine, 337,* 869–873.

Whitbourne, S. K. (1986). *Adult development* (2nd ed.). New York: Praeger.

Whitbourne, S. K. (1996). *The aging individual: Physical and psychological perspectives.* New York: Springer.

Whitbourne, S. K. (2001). *Adult development and aging: Biopsychosocial perspectives.* New York: Wiley.

Whitbourne, S., Jacobo, M., & Munoz-Ruiz, M. (1996). Adversity in the elderly. In R. S. Feldman (Ed.), *The psychology of adversity.* Amherst: University of Massachusetts Press.

Whitbourne, S. K., & Sneed, J. R. (2004). The paradox of well-being, identity processes, and stereotype threat: Ageism and its potential relationships to the self in later life. In T. Nelson (Ed.), *Ageism: Stereotyping and prejudice against older persons.* Cambridge, MA: MIT Press.

Whitbourne, S., Sneed, J., & Sayer, A. (2009). Psychosocial development from college through midlife: A 34-year sequential study. *Developmental Psychology, 45,* 1328–1340.

Whitbourne, S. K., & Wills, K. (1993). Psychological issues in institutional care of the aged. In S. B. Goldsmith (Ed.), *Long-term care.* Gaithersburg, MD: Aspen.

Whitbourne, S. K., Zuschlag, M. K., Elliot, L. B., & Waterman, A. S. (1992). Psychosocial development in adulthood: A 22–year sequential study. *Journal of Personality and Social Psychology, 63,* 260–271.

White, A., & Holmes, M. (2006). Patterns of mortality across 44 countries among men and women aged 15–44 years. *Journal of Men's Health & Gender, 3,* 139–151.

White, K. (2007). Hypnobirthing: The Mongan method. *Australian Journal of Clinical Hypnotherapy and Hypnosis, 28,* 12–24.

White, M., & White, G. (2006, August). Implicit and explicit occupational gender stereotypes. *Sex Roles, 55*(3), 259–266.

White, N. (2003). Changing conceptions: Young people's views of partnering and parenting. *Journal of Sociology, 39,* 149–164.

Whitebread, D., Coltman, P., Jameson, H., & Lander, R. (2009). Play, cognition and self-regulation: What exactly are children learning when they learn through play? *Educational and Child Psychology, 26,* 40–52.

Whitehurst, G. J., & Fischel, J. E. (2000). Reading and language impairments in conditions of poverty. In D. V. M. Bishop, & L. B. Leonard (Eds.), *Speech and language impairments in children: Causes, characteristics, intervention and outcome.* Philadelphia: Psychology Press/Taylor & Francis.

Whitelson, S. (1989, March). *Sex differences.* Paper presented at the annual meeting of the New York Academy of Science, New York.

Whiteman, M. C., Deary, I. J., Fowkes, F., & Gerry R. (2000). Personality and health: Cardiovascular disease. In S. E. Hampson (Ed.), *Advances in personality psychology, Vol. 1.* Philadelphia, PA: Psychology Press/Taylor & Francis.

Whiting, B. B. (1965). Sex identity conflict and physical violence: A comparative study. *American Anthropologist, 67,* 123–140.

Whiting, B. B., & Edwards, C. P. (1988). *Children of different worlds: The formation of social behavior.* Cambridge, MA: Harvard University Press.

Whiting, B. M., & Whinting, J. W. (1975). *Children of six countries: A psychological analysis.* Cambridge, MA: Harvard University Press.

Whiting, J., Simmons, L., Havens, J., Smith, D., & Oka, M. (2009). Intergenerational transmission of violence: The influence of self-appraisals, mental disorders and substance abuse. *Journal of Family Violence, 24,* 639–648.

Whorf, B. L. (1956). *Language, thought, and reality.* New York: Wiley.

Wickelgren, I. (1996, March 1). Is hippocampal cell death a myth? *Science, 271,* 1229–1230.

Wickelgren, W. A. (1999). Webs, cell assemblies, and chunking in neural nets: Introduction. *Canadian Journal of Experimental Psychology, 53,* 118–131.

Widaman, K. (2009). Phenylketonuria in children and mothers: Genes, environments, behavior. *Current Directions in Psychological Science, 18,* 48–52.

Wideman, M. V., & Singer, J. F. (1984). The role of psychological mechanisms in preparation for childbirth. *American Psychologist, 34,* 1357–1371.

Widom, C. S. (2000). Motivation and mechanisms in the "cycle of violence." In D. J. Hansen (Ed.), *Nebraska*

Symposium on Motivation Vol. 46, 1998: Motivation and child maltreatment (Current theory and research in motivation series). Lincoln, NE: University of Nebraska Press.

Wielgosz, A. T., & Nolan, R. P. (2000). Biobehavioral factors in the context of ischemic cardiovascular disease. *Journal of Psychosomatic Research, 48*, 339–345.

Wierson, M., & Forehand, R. (1994). Parent behavioral training for child noncompliance: Rationale, concepts, and effectiveness. *Current Directions in Psychological Science, 3*, 146–150.

Wigfield, A., & Eccles J. (2002). (Eds.). *Development of achievement motivation*. San Diego: Academic Press.

Wigfield, A., Galper, A., Denton, K., & Seefeldt, C. (1999). Teachers' beliefs about former Head Start and non–Head Start first-grade children's motivation, performance, and future educational prospects. *Journal of Educational Psychology, 91*, 98–104.

Wiggins, M., & Uwaydat, S. (2006, January). Age-related macular degeneration: Options for earlier detection and improved treatment. *The Journal of Family Practice, 55*, 22–27.

Wiik, K. A., Bernhardt, E., & Noack, T. (2009). A study of commitment and relationship quality in Sweden and Norway. *Journal of Marriage & the Family, 71*, 465–477.

Wilcox, A., Skjaerven, R., Buekens, P., & Kiely, J. (1995, March 1). Birth weight and perinatal mortality: A comparison of the United States and Norway. *Journal of the American Medical Association, 273*, 709–711.

Wilcox, H. C., Conner, K. R., & Caine, E. D. (2004). Association of alcohol and drug use disorders and completed suicide: An empirical review of cohort studies. *Drug & Alcohol Dependence, 76*, Special issue: Drug Abuse and Suicidal Behavior. pp. S11–S19.

Wilcox, M. D. (1992). Boomerang kids. *Kiplinger's Personal Finance Magazine, 46*, 83–86.

Wilcox, S., Castro, C. M., & King, A. C. (2006). Outcome expectations and physical activity participation in two samples of older women. *Journal of Health Psychology, 11*, 65–77.

Wilcox, S., Everson, K., Aragaki, A., Wassertheil-Smoller, S., Moulton, C., & Loevinger, B. (2003). The effects of widowhood on physical and mental health, health behaviors, and health outcomes: The Women's Health Initiative. *Health Psychology, 22*, 513–522.

Wilcox, T., Woods, R., Chapa, C., & McCurry, S. (2007). Multisensory exploration and object individuation in infancy. *Developmental Psychology, 43*, 479–495.

Wildberger, S. (2003, August). So you're having a baby. *Washingtonian, 85–86*, 88–90.

Wiley, S., Perkins, K., & Deaux, K. (2008). Through the looking glass: Ethnic and generational patterns of immigrant identity. *International Journal of Intercultural Relations, 32*, 385–398.

Wiley, T. L., Nondahl, D. M., Cruickshanks, K. J., & Tweed, T. S. (2005). Five-year changes in middle ear function for older adults. *Journal of the American Academy of Audiology, 16*, 129–139.

Wilfond, B., & Ross, L. (2009). From genetics to genomics: Ethics, policy, and parental decision-making. *Journal of Pediatric Psychology, 34*, 639–647.

Wilkes, S., Chinn, D., Murdoch, A., & Rubin, G. (2009). Epidemiology and management of infertility: A population-based study in UK primary care. *Family Practice, 26*, 269–274.

Wilkosz, M., Chen, J., Kennedy, C., & Rankin, S. (2011). Body dissatisfaction in California adolescents. *Journal of the American Academy of Nurse Practitioners, 23*, 101–109.

Willard, N. (2007). *Cyber-safe kids, cyber-savvy teens: Helping young people learn to use the Internet safely and responsibly*. San Francisco, CA: Jossey-Bass.

Williams, A., & Merten, M. (2009). Adolescents' online social networking following the death of a peer. *Journal of Adolescent Research, 24*, 67–90.

Williams, B. C. (1990). Immunization coverage among preschool children: The United States and selected European countries. *Pediatrics, 86*, 1052–1056.

Williams, C., Povey, R., & White, D. (2008). Predicting women's intentions to use pain relief medication during childbirth using the Theory of Planned Behaviour and Self-Efficacy Theory. *Journal of Reproductive and Infant Psychology, 26*, 168–179.

Williams, D., & Griffen, L. (1991). Elder abuse in the black family. In R. Hampton (Ed.), *Black family violence: Current research and theory*. Lexington, MA: Lexington Books.

Williams, H., & Monsma, E. (2007). Assessment of gross motor development. *Psychoeducational assessment of preschool children* (4th ed.). Mahwah, NJ: Lawrence Erlbaum Associates.

Williams, J., & Binnie, L. (2002). Children's concept of illness: An intervention to improve knowledge. *British Journal of Health Psychology, 7*, 129–148.

Williams, J., & Ross, L. (2007). Consequences of prenatal toxin exposure for mental health in children and adolescents: A systematic review. *European Child & Adolescent Psychiatry, 16*, 243–253.

Williams, J. M., & Currie, C. (2000). Self-esteem and physical development in early adolescence: Pubertal timing and body image. *Journal of Early Adolescence, 20*, 129–149.

Williams, K., & Dunne-Bryant, A. (2006, December). Divorce and adult psychological well-being: Clarifying the role of gender and child age. *Journal of Marriage and Family, 68*, 1178–1196.

Williams, R. B. (1993). Hostility and the heart. In D. Goleman & J. Gurin (Eds.), *Mind-body medicine*. Yonkers, NY: Consumer Reports Books.

Williams, R. B. (1996). Coronary-prone behaviors, hostility, and cardiovascular health: Implications for behavioral and pharmacological interventions. In K. Orth-Gomer & N. Schneiderman (Eds.), *Behavioral Medicine Approaches to Cardiovascular Disease Prevention*. Mahwah, NJ: Lawrence Erlbaum Associates.

Williams, R., Barefoot, J., & Schneiderman, N. (2003). Psychosocial risk factors for cardiovascular disease: More than one culprit at work. *JAMA: Journal of the American Medical Association, 290*, 2190–2192.

Williamson, G. M., & Schulz, R. (1993). Coping with specific stressors in Alzheimer's disease caregiving. *Gerontologist, 33*, 747–755.

Williamson, R., & Johnston, J.H. (1999). Challenging orthodoxy: An emerging agenda for middle level reform. *Middle School Journal, 12*, 10–17.

Willie, C., & Reddick, R. (2003). *A new look at black families* (5th ed.). Walnut Creek, CA: AltaMira Press.

Willis, S. (1996). Everyday problem solving. In J. E. Birren, K. W. Schaie, R. P. Abeles, M.Gatz, & T. A. Salthouse (Eds.), *Handbook of the psychology of aging* (4th ed.). San Diego: Academic Press.

Willis, S. L. (1985). Educational psychology of the older adult learner. In J. E. Birren & K. W. Schaie (Eds.), *Handbook of the psychology of aging* (2nd ed.). New York: Van Nostrand Reinhold.

Willis, S. L., Jay, G. M., Diehl, M., & Marsiske, M. (1992). Longitudinal change and prediction of everyday task competence in the elderly. *Research on Aging, 14*, 68–91.

Willis, S. L., & Nesselroade, C. S. (1990). Long-term effects of fluid ability training in old-old age. *Developmental Psychology, 26*, 905–910.

Willis, S., Tennstedt, S., Marsiske, M., Ball, K., Elias, J., Koepke, K., Morris, J., Rebok, G., Unverzagt, F., Stoddard, A., & Wright, E. (2006). Long-term effects of cognitive training on everyday functional outcomes

in older adults. *Journal of the American Medical Association, 296*, 2805–2814.

Willott, J., Chisolm, T., & Lister, J. (2001). Modulation of presbycusis: Current state and future directions. *Audiology & Neuro-Otology, 6*, 231–249.

Willoughby, M., Kupersmidt, J., Voegler-Lee, M., & Bryant, D. (2011). Contributions of hot and cool self-regulation to preschool disruptive behavior and academic achievement. *Developmental Neuropsychology, 36*, 162–180.

Willows, D. M., Kruk, R. S., & Corcos, E. (Eds.). (1993). *Visual processes in reading and reading disabilities*. Hillsdale, NJ: Erlbaum.

Willrich, M. (2011, January 21). Why parents fear the needle. *The New York Times*, Section A, pg. 2.

Wills, T., Resko, J., & Ainette, M. (2004). Smoking onset in adolescence: A person-centered analysis with time-varying predictors. *Health Psychology, 23*, 158–167.

Wills, T., Sargent, J., Stoolmiller, M., Gibbons, F., & Gerrard, M. (2008). Movie smoking exposure and smoking onset: A longitudinal study of mediation processes in a representative sample of U.S. adolescents. *Psychology of Addictive Behaviors, 22*, 269–277.

Wilmoth, J. R., Deegan, L. J., Lundström, & Horiuchi, S. (2000, September 29). Increase of maximum life-span in Sweden, 1861–1999. *Science, 289*, 2366–2368.

Wilmut, I. (1998). Cloning for medicine. *Scientific American*, 58–63.

Wilson, B., et al. (2002). Violence in children's television programming: Assessing the risks. *Journal of Communication, 52*, 5–35.

Wilson, B., & Gottman, J. (2002). Marital conflict, repair, and parenting. *Handbook of parenting: Vol. 4: Social conditions and applied parenting* (2nd ed., pp. 227–258). Mahwah, NJ: Lawrence Erlbaum Associates.

Wilson, G., Grilo, C., & Vitousek, K. (2007, April). Psychological Treatment of Eating Disorders. *American Psychologist, 62*(3), 199–216.

Wilson, M. A., Moore, P. S., Shennan, A., Lancashire, R. J., & MacArthur, C. (2011). Long-term effects of epidural analgesia in labor: A randomized controlled trial comparing high dose with two mobile techniques. *Birth: Issues in Perinatal Care, 38*, 105–110.

Wilson, M. N. (1989). Child development in the context of the black extended family. *American Psychologist, 44*, 380–385.

Wilson, R. (2004, December 3). Where the elite teach, it's still a man's world. *Chronicle of Higher Education, 51*, A8.

Wilson, R. S. (1983). The Louisville twin study: Developmental synchronies in behavior. *Child Development, 54*, 298–316.

Wilson, R., Beck, T., Bienias, J., & Bennett, D. (2007, February). Terminal cognitive decline: Accelerated loss of cognition in the last years of life. *Psychosomatic Medicine, 69*, 131–137.

Wilson, R., Beckett, L., & Bienias, J. (2003). Terminal decline in cognitive function. *Neurology, 60*, 1782–1787.

Wilson, S. L. (2003). Post-institutionalization: The effects of early deprivation on development of Romanian adoptees. *Child & Adolescent Social Work Journal, 20*, 473–483.

Wilson-Williams, L., Stephenson, R., Juvekar, S., & Andes, K. (2008). Domestic violence and contraceptive use in a rural Indian village. *Violence Against Women, 14*, 1181–1198.

Wimmer, H., & Gschaider, A. (2000). Children's understanding of belief: Why is it important to understand what happened? In P. Mitchell & K. J. Riggs (Eds.), *Children's reasoning and the mind*. Hove, England: Psychology Press/Taylor & Francis.

Wimmer, H., & Perner, J. (1983). Beliefs about beliefs: Representation and constrained function of wrong beliefs in young children's understanding of deception. *Cognition, 13,* 103–128.

Windle, M. (1994). A study of friendship characteristics and problem behaviors among middle adolescents. *Child Development, 65,* 1764–1777.

Wineburg, S. S. (1987). The self-fulfillment of the self-fulfilling prophecy. *Educational Researcher, 16,* 28–37.

Winefield, A. (2002). The psychology of unemployment. *Psychology at the turn of the millennium, vol. 2: Social, developmental, and clinical perspectives.* Florence, KY: Taylor & Frances/Routledge.

Wines, M. (2006, August 24). Africa adds to miserable ranks for child workers. *New York Times.,* p.D1.

Wing, L., & Potter, D. (2009) The epidemiology of autism spectrum disorders: Is the prevalence rising? In S. Goldstein, J. Naglieri, & S. Ozonoff (Eds), *Assessment of autism spectrum disorders.* New York: Guilford Press.

Winger, G., & Woods, J. H. (2004). *A handbook on drug and alcohol abuse: The biomedical aspects.* Oxford, England: Oxford University Press.

Wingert, P., & Brant, M. (2005, August 15). Reading your baby's mind. *Newsweek,* p. 32.

Wingert, P., & Kantrowitz, B. (1997, October 27). Why Andy couldn't read (Bright children who are also learning disabled). *Newsweek, 130,* p. 56.

Wingert, P., & Katrowitz, B. (2002, October 7). Young and depressed. *Newsweek,* pp. 53–61.

Wingert, P., & Kantrowitz, B. (2007, January 15). The new prime time. *Newsweek,* p. 38.

Wingfield, A., Tun, P. A., & McCoy, S. L. (2005). Hearing loss in older adulthood: What it is and how it interacts with cognitive performance. *Current Directions in Psychological Science, 14,* 144–147.

Wink, P., & Dillon, M. (2003). Religiousness, spirituality, and psychosocial functioning in late adulthood: Findings from a longitudinal study. *Psychology & Aging, 18,* 916–924.

Winn, R. L., & Newton, N. (1982). Sexuality in aging: A study of 106 cultures. *Archives of Sexual Behavior, 11,* 283–298.

Winner, E. (1986, August). Where pelicans kiss seals. *Psychology Today,* 24–35.

Winner, E. (1989). Development in the visual arts. In W. Damon (Ed.), *Child development today and tomorrow.* San Francisco: Jossey-Bass.

Winner, E. (1997). *Gifted children: Myths and realities.* New York: Basic Books.

Winner, E. (2000). The origins and ends of giftedness. *American Psychologist, 55,* 159–169.

Winner, E. (2006). Development in the arts: Drawing and music. *Handbook of child psychology: Vol 2, Cognition, perception, and language* (6th ed.). Hoboken, NJ: John Wiley & Sons Inc.

Winsler, A. (2003). Introduction to special issue: Vygotskian perspectives in early childhood education. *Early Education and Development, Special Issue, 14,* 253–269.

Winsler, A., De Leon, J., & Wallace, B. (2003). Private speech in preschool children: Developmental stability and change, across-task consistency, and relations with classroom behaviour. *Journal of Child Language, 30,* 583–608.

Winsler, A., Diaz, R. M., & Montero, I. (1997). The role of private speech in the transition from collaborative to independent task performance in young children. *Early Childhood Research Quarterly, 12,* 59–79.

Winsler, A., Feder, M., Way, E., & Manfra, L. (2006, July). Maternal beliefs concerning young children's private speech. *Infant and Child Development, 15,* 403–420.

Winsler, A., Hutchison, L. A., De Feyter, J. J., Manfra, L., Bleiker, C., Hartman, S. C., & Levitt, J. (2012). Child, family, and childcare predictors of delayed school entry and kindergarten retention among linguistically and ethnically diverse children. *Developmental Psychology.* Retrieved from http://www.ncbi.nlm.nih.gov/pubmed/22288368.

Winstead, B. A., (2005). Gender and psychopathology. In J. E. Maddux & B. A. Winstead (Eds.), *Psychopatholgoy: Foundations for a contemporary understanding.* Mahwah, NJ: Lawrence Erlbaum Associates.

Winter, G. (2001, August 24). Enticing third-world youth. *New York Times,* p. D1.

Winterich, J. (2003). Sex, menopause, and culture: Sexual orientation and the meaning of menopause for women's sex lives. *Gender & Society, 17,* 627–642.

Winters, K. C., Stinchfield, R. D., & Botzet, A. (2005). Pathways fo youth gambling problem severity. *Psychology of Addictive Behaviors, 19,* 104–107.

Winters, K., Botzet, A., Fahnhorst, T., Stinchfield, R., & Koskey, R. (2009). Adolescent substance abuse treatment: A review of evidence-based research. *Adolescent substance abuse: Evidence-based approaches to prevention and treatment.* New York: Springer Science + Business Media.

Wisborg, K., Kesmodel, U., Bech, B. H., Hedegaard, M., & Henriksen, T. B. (2003). Maternal consumption of coffee during pregnancy and still birth and infant death in first year of life: prospective study. *British Medical Journal, 326,* 420.

Wisdom, J., Rees, A., Riley, K., & Weis, T. (2007, April). Adolescents' perceptions of the gendered context of depression: "Tough" boys and objectified girls. *Journal of Mental Health Counseling, 29*(2), 144–162.

Wise, L., Adams-Campbell, L., Palmer, J., & Rosenberg, L. (2006, August). Leisure time physical activity in relation to depressive symptoms in the Black Women's Health Study. *Annals of Behavioral Medicine, 32,* 68–76.

Wise, P. M., Krajnak, K. M., & Kashon, M. L. (1996, July 5). Menopause: The aging of multiple pacemakers. *Science, 273,* 67–70.

Wisnia, S. (1994, June 27). On the right track. *The Washington Post,* p. D5.

Witelson, S. (1989, March). *Sex differences.* Paper presented at the annual meeting of the New York Academy of Science, New York.

Witkow, M., & Fuligni, A. (2007). Achievement goals and daily school experiences among adolescents with Asian, Latino, and European American backgrounds. *Journal of Educational Psychology, 99,* 584–596.

Witt, A., & Vinter, A. (2012). Artificial grammar learning in children: Abstraction of rules or sensitivity to perceptual features?. *Psychological Research/Psychologische Forschung, 76,* 97–110.

Witt, E. A., Donnellan, M., & Trzesniewski, K. H. (2011). Self-esteem, narcissism, and Machiavellianism: Implications for understanding antisocial behavior in adolescents and young adults. In C. T. Barry, P. K. Kerig, K. K. Stellwagen, & T. D. Barry (Eds.), *Narcissism and Machiavellianism in youth: Implications for the development of adaptive and maladaptive behavior.* Washington, DC: American Psychological Association.

Witt, S. D. (1997). Parental influence on children's socialization to gender roles. *Adolescence, 32,* 253–259.

Wodrich, D., & Tarbox, J. (2008). Psychoeducational implications of sex chromosome anomalies. *School Psychology Quarterly, 23,* 301–311.

Woelfle, J. F., Harz, K., & Roth, C. (2007). Modulation of circulating IGF-I and IGFBP-3 levels by hormonal regulators of energy homeostasis in obese children. *Experimental and Clinical Endocrinology Diabetes, 115,* 17–23.

Wohlwend, K. E. (2012). "Are you guys girls?": Boys, identity texts, and Disney Princess play. *Journal of Early Childhood Literacy, 12,* 3–23.

Woike, B., & Matic, D. (2004). Cognitive complexity in response to traumatic experiences. *Journal of Personality, 72,* 633–657.

Wolf, A. M., Gortmaker, S. L., Cheung, L., & Gray, H. M. (1993). Activity, inactivity, and obesity: Racial, ethnic, and age differences among schoolgirls. *American Journal of Public Health, 83,* 1625–1627.

Wolfe, M. S. (2006, May). Shutting down Alzheimer's. *Scientific American,* 73–79.

Wolfe, W. (2007, February 24). Late life love: Older couples find that love comes when they aren't looking for it and share the stories of their late-in-life romance. *The Star Tribune* (Minneapolis, MN), p. 1E.

Wolfe, W., Olson, C., & Kendall, A. (1998). Hunger and food insecurity in the elderly: Its nature and measurement. *Journal of Aging & Health, 10,* 327–350.

Wolff, P. H. (1963). Observations of the early development of smiling. In B. M. Foss (Ed.), *Determinants of infant behaviour* (Vol 4). London: Methuen.

Wolfner, G., Faust, D., & Dawes, R. M. (1993). The use of anatomically detailed dolls in sexual abuse evaluations: The state of the science. *Applied & Preventive Psychology, 2,* 1–11.

Wolfson, A. R., & Richards, M. (2011). Young adolescents: Struggles with insufficient sleep. In M. El-Sheikh (Eds.), *Sleep and development: Familial and sociocultural considerations.* New York: Oxford University Press.

Wolfson, C., Handfield-Jones, R., Glass, K. C., McClaren, J., et al. (1993). Adult children's perceptions of their responsibility to provide care for dependent elderly parents. *Gerontologist, 33,* 315–323.

Wolinsky, F., Wyrwich, K., & Babu, A. (2003). Age, aging, and the sense of control among older adults: A longitudinal reconsideration. *Journals of Gerontology: Series B: Psychological Sciences & Social Sciences, 58B,* S212–S220.

Wolitzky, D. L. (2011). Psychoanalytic theories of psychotherapy. In J. C. Norcross, G. R. VandenBos, & D. K. Freedheim (Eds.), *History of psychotherapy: Continuity and change* (2nd ed.). Washington, DC: American Psychological Association.

Women's Bureau, U.S. Department of Labor. (1998). *The median wages of women as a proportion of the wages that men receive.* Washington, DC: U.S. Government Printing Office.

Women's Bureau, U.S. Department of Labor. (2002). *Women's Bureau frequently asked questions.* Retrieved from http://www.dol.gov/wb/faq38.htm.

Wong, B. Y. L. (1996). *The ABCs of learning disabilities.* San Diego, CA: Academic Press.

Wong, C. A., Scavone, B. M., Peaceman, A. M., McCarthy, R. J., Sullivan, J. T., Diaz, N. T., Yaghmour, E., Marcus, R. L., Sherwani, S. S., Sproviero, M. T., Yilmaz, M., Patel, R., Robles, C., & Grouper, S. (2005, February 17). The risk of cesarean delivery with neuraxial analgesia given early versus late in labor. *New England Journal of Medicine, 352,* 655–665.

Wood, A. C., Saudino, K. J., Rogers, H., Asherson, P., & Kuntsi, J. (2007). Genetic influences on mechanically-assessed activity level in children. *Journal of Child Psychology and Psychiatry, 48,* 695–702.

Wood, D., Bruner, J. S., & Ross, G. (1976). The role of tutoring in problem solving. *Journal of Child Psychology & Psychiatry & Allied Disciplines, 17,* 89–100.

Wood, J. (1989). Theory and research concerning social comparisons of personal attributes. *Psychological Bulletin, 106,* 231–248.

Wood, K., Becker, J., & Thompson, J. (1996). Body image dissatisfaction in preadolescent children. *Journal of Applied Developmental Psychology, 17,* 85–100.

Wood, L., & Howley, A. (2012). Dividing at an early age: The hidden digital divide in Ohio elementary schools. *Learning, Media And Technology, 37,* 20–39.

Wood, R. (1997). Trends in multiple births, 1938–1995. *Population Trends, 87,* 29–35.

Wood, W., Wong, F. Y., & Chachere, J. G. (1991). Effects of media violence on viewers' aggression in unconstrained social interaction. *Psychological Bulletin, 109,* 371–383.

Woods, R. (2009). The use of aggression in primary school boys' decisions about inclusion in and exclusion from playground football games. *British Journal of Educational Psychology, 79,* 223–238.

Woolf, A., & Lesperance, L. (2003, September 22). What should we worry about. *Newsweek,* p. 72.

Woolfolk, A. E. (1993). *Educational psychology* (5th ed.). Needham Heights, MA: Allyn & Bacon.

Woolfolk, A. E. (1995). *Educational psychology* (6th ed.). Boston, MA: Allyn & Bacon.

Workman, L., & Reader, W. (2008). *Evolutionary psychology, an introduction: Second edition.* New York: Cambridge University Press.

World Bank. (2003). *Global development finance 2003—Striving for stability in development finance.* Washington, DC: World Bank.

World Bank. (2004). *World Development Indicators 2004 (WDI).* Washington, DC: World Bank.

World Conference on Education for All. (1990). *World declaration on education for all and framework for action to meet basic learning needs.* New York: Author.

The World Factbook. (2007, April 17). Estimates of infant mortality. Retrieved from https://www.cia.gov/cia/publications/factbook/rankorder/2091rank.html. World Factbook, (2009). *Estimates of infant mortality.* Retrieved from https://www.cia.gov/library/publications/the-world-factbook/rankorder/2091rank.html, 2009.

World Food Council. (1992). *The global state of hunger and malnutrition. 1992 report.* Table 2, p. 8. New York: Author.

World Food Programme. (2008). *Where we work: Korea.* Rome: United Nations World Food Programme.

World Food Summit. (2002). *The spectrum of malnutrition.* New York: United Nations.

World Health Organization. (1999). *Death rates from coronary heart disease.* Geneva: World Health Organization.

World Health Organization & Centers for Disease Control and Prevention. (1999). *Marketing of cigarettes overseas.* Geneva/Atlanta: Authors.

Worobey, J., & Bajda, V. M. (1989). Temperament ratings at 2 weeks, 2 months, and 1 year: Differential stability of activity and emotionality. *Developmental Psychology, 25,* 257–263.

Worrell, F., Szarko, J., & Gabelko, N. (2001). Multi-year persistence of nontraditional students in an academic talent development program. *Journal of Secondary Gifted Education, 12,* 80–89.

Wortman, C., & Silver, R. C. (1989). The myths of coping with loss. *Journal of Consulting and Clinical Psychology, 57,* 349–357.

Wortman, C. B., & Silver, R. C. (1990). Successful mastery of bereavement and widowhood: A life-course perspective. In P. B. Baltes & M. M. Baltes (Eds.), *Successful aging: Perspectives from the behavioral sciences.* Cambridge, England: Cambridge University Press.

Wright, J. C., Huston, A. C., Murphy, K. C., St. Peters, M., Piñon, M., Scantlin, R., et al. (2001). The relations of early television viewing to school readiness and vocabulary of children from low-income families: The early window project. *Child Development, 72,* 1347–1366.

Wright, J. C., Huston, A. C., Reitz, A. L., & Piemyat, S. (1994). Young children's perceptions of television reality: Determinants and developmental differences. *Developmental Psychology, 30,* 229–239.

Wright, J. C., Huston, A. C., Truglio, R., Fitch, M., Smith, E., & Piemyat, S. (1995). Occupational portrayals on television: Children's role schemata, career aspira-

tions, and perceptions of reality. *Child Development, 66,* 1706–1718.

Wright, M., Wintemute, G., & Claire, B. (2008). Gun suicide by young people in California: Descriptive epidemiology and gun ownership. *Journal of Adolescent Health, 43,* 619–622.

Wright, R. (1995, March 13). The biology of violence. *The New Yorker,* 68–77.

Wright, S. C., & Taylor, D. M. (1995). Identity and the language of the classroom: Investigation of the impact of heritage versus second language instruction on personal and collective self-esteem. *Journal of Educational Psychology, 87,* 241–252.

Wrosch, C., Bauer, I., & Scheier, M. (2005, December). Regret and quality of life across the adult life span: The Influence of disengagement and available future goals. *Psychology and Aging, 20,* 657–670.

Wu, C., & Chao, R. K. (2011). Intergenerational cultural dissonance in parent–adolescent relationships among Chinese and European Americans. *Developmental Psychology, 47,* 493–508.

Wu, C., Zhou, D., & Chen, W. (2003). A nested case-control study of Alzheimer's disease in Linxian, northern China. *Chinese Mental Health Journal, 17,* 84–88.

Wu, P., Hoven, C., Okezie, N., Fuller, C., & Cohen, P. (2007). Alcohol abuse and depression in children and adolescents. *Journal of Child & Adolescent Substance Abuse, 17*(2), 51–69.

Wu, P., Robinson, C., & Yang, C. (2002). Similarities and differences in mothers' parenting of preschoolers in China and the United States. *International Journal of Behavioral Development, 26,* 481–491.

Wu, Y., Tsou, K., Hsu, C., Fang, L., Yao, G., & Jeng, S. (2008). Brief report: Taiwanese infants' mental and motor development–6–24 months. *Journal of Pediatric Psychology, 33,* 102–108.

Wyer, R. (2004). The cognitive organization and use of general knowledge. In J. Jost & M. Banaji (Eds.), *Perspectivism in social psychology: The yin and yang of scientific progress.* Washington, DC: American Psychological Association.

Wygant, S. A. (1997). Moral reasoning about real-life dilemmas: Paradox in research using the defining issues test. *Personality and Social Psychology Bulletin, 23,* 1022–1033.

Wyman, P. A., Cowen, E. L., Work, W. C., Hoyt-Meyers, L., Magnus, K. B., & Fagen, D. B. (1999). Caregiving and developmental factors differentiating young at-risk urban children showing resilient versus stress-affected outcomes: A replication and extension. *Child Development, 70,* 645–659.

Wynn, K. (1992, August 27). Addition and subtraction by human infants. *Nature, 358,* 749–750.

Wynn, K. (1995). Infants possess a system of numerical knowledge. *Current Directions in Psychological Science, 4,* 172–177.

Wynn, K. (2000). Findings of addition and subtraction in infants are robust and consistent: Reply to Wakeley, Rivera, and Langer. *Child Development, 71,* 1535–1536.

Wyra, M., Lawson, M. J., & Hungi, N. (2007). The mnemonic keyword method: The effects of bidirectional retrieval training and of ability to image on foreign language vocabulary recall. *Learning and Instruction, 17,* 360–371.

Xiaohe, X., & Whyte, M. K. (1990). Love matches and arranged marriages: A Chinese replication. *Journal of Marriage and the Family, 52,* 709–722.

Xie, H., Cairns, B., & Cairns, R. (2005). The development of aggressive behaviors among girls: Measurement issues, social functions, and differential trajectories. *The development and treatment of girlhood aggression.* Mahwah, NJ: Lawrence Erlbaum Associates.

Xirasagar, S., Fu, J., Liu, J., Probst, J. C., & Lin, D. (2011). Neonatal outcomes for immigrant vs. native-born mothers in Taiwan: An epidemiological paradox. *Maternal and Child Health Journal, 15,* 269–279.

Yablo, P., & Field, N. (2007). The role of culture in altruism: Thailand and the United States. *Psychologia: An International Journal of Psychology in the Orient, 50,* 236–251.

Yagmurlu, B., & Sanson, A. (2009). Parenting and temperament as predictors of prosocial behaviour in Australian and Turkish Australian children. *Australian Journal of Psychology, 61,* 77–88.

Yamada, J., Stinson, J., Lamba, J., Dickson, A., McGrath, P., & Stevens, B. (2008). A review of systematic reviews on pain interventions in hospitalized infants. *Pain Research & Management, 13,* 413–420.

Yan, G., Zhang, K., & Zhao, Y. (2002). Psychological effect of doula labor on primigravidae. *Chinese Mental Health Journal, 16,* 157–158.

Yan, S., & Rettig, K. D. (2004). Korean American mothers' experiences in facilitating academic success for their adolescents. *Marriage & Family Review, 36,* 53–74.

Yan, Z., & Fischer, K. (2002). Always under construction: Dynamic variations in adult cognitive microdevelopment. *Human Development, 45,* 141–160.

Yancey, A. K., Grant, D., Kurosky, S., Kravitz-Wirtz, N., & Mistry, R. (2011). Role modeling, risk, and resilience in California adolescents. *Journal of Adolescent Health, 48,* 36–43.

Yang, C. D. (2006). *The infinite gift: How children learn and unlearn the languages of the world.* New York: Scribner.

Yang, R., & Blodgett, B. (2000). Effects of race and adolescent decision-making on status attainment and self-esteem. *Journal of Ethnic & Cultural Diversity in Social Work, 9,* 135–153.

Yang, S., & Rettig, K. D. (2004). Korean-American mothers' experiences in facilitating academic success for their adolescents. *Marriage & Family Review, 36,* 53–74.

Yang, Y. (2008). Social inequalities in happiness in the U.S. 1972–2004: An age-period-cohort analysis. *American Sociological Review, 73,* 204–226.

Yankee Group. (2001). *Teenage online activities.* Boston: Author.

Yankelovich, D. (1974, December). Turbulence in the working world: Angry workers, happy grads. *Psychology Today, 8,* 80–87.

Yardley, J. (2001, July 2). Child-death case in Texas raises penalty questions. *The New York Times,* p. A1.

Yarrow, L. (1990, September). Does my child have a problem? *Parents,* p. 72.

Yarrow, L. (1992, November). Giving birth: 72,000 moms tell all. *Parents,* pp. 148–159.

Yarrow, M. R., Scott, P. M., & Waxler, C. Z. (1973). Learning concern for others. *Developmental Psychology, 8,* 240–260.

Yato, Y., Kawai, M., Negayama, K., Sogon, S., Tomiwa, K., & Yamamoto, H. (2008). Infant responses to maternal still-face at 4 and 9 months. *Infant Behavior & Development, 31,* 570–577.

Ybarra, M. L., & Mitchell, K. J., (2004). Online aggressor/targets, aggressors, and targets: A comparison of associated youth characteristics. *Journal of Child Psychology and Psychiatry, 45,* 1308–1316.

Yecke, C. P. (2005). *Mayhem in the middle.* Washington, DC: Thomas B. Fordham Institute.

Yee, M., & Brown, R. (1994). The development of gender differentiation in young children. *British Journal of Social Psychology, 33,* 183–196.

Yell, M. L. (1995). The least restrictive environment mandate and the courts: Judicial activism or judicial restraint? *Exceptional Children, 61,* 578–581.

Yelland, G. W., Pollard, J., & Mercuri, A. (1993). The metalinguistic benefits of limited contact with a second language. *Applied Psycholinguistics, 14,* 423–444.

Yerkes, R. M. (1923). *A point scale for measuring mental ability. A 1923 revision.* Baltimore, MD: Warwick & York.

Head, D. (2005). Young people, sex and the media: the facts of life? *Journal of Family Studies, 11,* 326–327.

Yildiz, O. (2007). Vascular smooth muscle and endothelial functions in aging. *Annals of the New York Academy of Sciences, 1100,* 353–360.

Yim, I., Glynn, L., Schetter, C., Hobel, C., Chicz-DeMet, A., & Sandman, C. (2009). Risk of postpartum depressive symptoms with elevated corticotropin-releasing hormone in human pregnancy. *Archives of General Psychiatry, 66,* 162–169.

Yinger, J. (Ed.). (2004). *Helping children left behind: State aid and the pursuit of educational equity.* Cambridge, MA: MIT Press.

Yip, T. (2008). Everyday experiences of ethnic and racial identity among adolescents and young adults. *Handbook of race, racism, and the developing child.* Hoboken, NJ: John Wiley & Sons Inc.

Yip, T., Sellers, R. M., & Seaton, E. K. (2006). African American racial identity across the lifespan: Identity status, identity content, and depressive symptoms. *Child Development, 77,* 1504–1517.

Yllo, K. (1983). Using a feminist approach in quantitative research: A case study. In D. Finkelhor, R. J. Gelles, G. Hotaling, & M. A. Straus (Eds.), *The dark side of families.* Beverly Hills, CA: Sage.

Yllo, K., & Bograd, M. (Eds.). (1988). *Feminist perspectives on wife abuse.* Berkeley, CA: Sage.

York, E. (2008). Gender differences in the college and career aspirations of high school valedictorians. *Journal of Advanced Academics, 19,* 578–600.

Yoshikawa, H., & Hseuh, J. (2001). Child development and public policy: Toward a dynamic systems perspective. *Child Development, 72,* 1887–1903.

Yoshinaga-Itano, C. (2003). From screening to early identification and intervention: Discovering predictors to successful outcomes for children with significant hearing loss. *Journal of Deaf Studies & Deaf Education, 8,* 11–30.

Yost, M. (Ed.) (1999). *When love lasts forever.* Cleveland, OH: Pilgrim Press.

Young, D. (2011). "Gentle cesareans": Better in some respects, but fewer cesareans are better still. *Birth: Issues in Perinatal Care, 38,* 183–184.

Young, H., & Ferguson, L. (1979). Developmental changes through adolescence in the spontaneous nomination of reference groups as a function of decision context. *Journal of Youth and Adolescence, 8,* 239–252.

Young, S., Rhee, S., Stallings, M., Corley, R., & Hewitt, J. (2006, July). Genetic and environmental vulnerabilities underlying adolescent substance use and problem use: General or specific? *Behavior Genetics, 36,* 603–615.

Youniss, J. (1989). Parent–adolescent relationships. In W. Damon (Ed.), *Child development today and tomorrow.* San Francisco: Jossey-Bass.

Youniss, J., & Haynie, D. L. (1992). Friendship in adolescence. *Journal of Developmental and Behavioral Pediatrics, 13,* 59–66.

Yu, M., & Stiffman, A. (2007). Culture and environment as predictors of alcohol abuse/dependence symptoms in American Indian youths. *Addictive Behaviors, 32,* 2253–2259.

Yuill, N., & Perner, J. (1988). Intentionality and knowledge in children's judgments of actor's responsibility and recipient's emotional reaction. *Developmental Psychology, 24,* 358–365.

Zacchilli, T. L., & Valerio, C. Y. (2011). The knowledge and prevalence of cyberbullying in a college sample. *Journal of Scientific Psychology,* 11–23. Kemker, D. (2010, October 13). Science hero: Ameen Abdulrasool. Retrieved from http://www.myhero.com/go/hero.asp?hero=abdulrasool_06.

Zacks, R., & Hasher, L. (2002). Frequency processing: A twenty-five year perspective. In P. Sedlmeier (Ed.), *Frequency processing and cognition* (pp. 21–36). London: Oxford University Press.

Zafeiriou, D. I. (2004). Primitive reflexes and postural reactions in the neurodevelopmental examination. *Pediatric Neurology, 31,* 1–8.

Zagorsky, J. (2007). Do you have to be smart to be rich? The impact of IQ on wealth, income and financial distress. *Intelligence, 35,* 489–501.

Zahn-Waxler, C., & Polanichka, N. (2004). All things interpersonal: Socialization and female aggression. *Aggression, antisocial behavior, and violence among girls: A developmental perspective* (pp. 48–68). New York: Guilford Publications.

Zahn-Waxler, C., & Radke-Yarrow, M. (1990). The origins of empathic concern. *Motivation and Emotion, 14,* 107–130.

Zahn-Waxler, C., Robinson, J. L., & Emde, R. N. (1992). The development of empathy in twins. *Developmental Psychology, 28,* 1038–1047.

Zahn-Waxler, C., Shirtcliff, E., & Marceau, K. (2008). Disorders of childhood and adolescence: Gender and psychopathology. *Annual Review of Clinical Psychology, 4,* 275–303.

Zaidel, D. W. (1994). Worlds apart: Pictorial semantics in the left and right cerebral hemispheres. *Current Directions in Psychological Science, 3,* 5–8.

Zajonc, R. B. (2001). The family dynamics of intellectual development. *American Psychologist, 56,* 490–496.

Zalenski, R., & Raspa, R. (2006). Maslow's hierarchy of needs: A framework for achieving human potential in hospice. *Journal of Palliative Medicine, 9,* 1120–1127.

Zalsman, G., Levy, T., & Shoval, G. (2008). Interaction of child and family psychopathology leading to suicidal behavior. *Psychiatric Clinics of North America, 31,* 237–246.

Zalsman, G., Oquendo, M., Greenhill, L., Goldberg, P., Kamali, M., Martin, A., et al. (2006, October). Neurobiology of depression in children and adolescents. *Child and Adolescent Psychiatric Clinics of North America, 15,* 843–868.

Zampi, C., Fagioli, I., & Salzarulo, P. (2002). Time course of EEG background activity level before spontaneous awakening in infants. *Journal of Sleep Research, 11,* 283–287.

Zanardo, V., Nicolussi, S., Giacomin, C., Faggian, D., Favaro, F., & Plebani, M. (2001). Labor pain effects on colostral milk beta-endorphin concentrations of lactating mothers. *Biology of the Neonate, 79,* 87–90.

Zanjani, E. D., & Anderson, W. F. (1999, September 24). Prospects for in utero human gene therapy. *Science, 285,* 2084–2088.

Zaporozhets, A. V. (1965). The development of perception in the preschool child. *Monographs of the Society for Research in Child Development, 30,* 82–101.

Zarbatany, L., Hartmann, D. P., & Rankin, D. B. (1990). The psychological functions of preadolescent peer activities. *Child Development, 61,* 1067–1080.

Zarit, S. H., & Reid, J. D. (1994). Family caregiving and the older family. In C. B. Fisher & R. M. Lerner (Eds.), *Applied developmental psychology.* New York: McGraw-Hill.

Zauszniewski, J. A., & Martin, M. H. (1999). Developmental task achievement and learned resourcefulness in healthy older adults. *Archives of Psychiatric Nursing, 13,* 41–47.

Zautra, A. J., Reich, J. W., & Guarnaccia, C. A. (1990). Some everyday life consequences of disability and bereavement for older adults. *Journal of Personality and Social Psychology, 59,* 550–561.

Zeanah, C. (2009). The importance of early experiences: Clinical, research and policy perspectives. *Journal of Loss and Trauma, 14,* 266–279.

Zebrowitz, L., Luevano, V., Bronstad, P., & Aharon, I. (2009). Neural activation to babyfaced men matches activation to babies. *Social Neuroscience, 4,* 1–10.

Zeedyk, M., & Heimann, M. (2006). Imitation and socio-emotional processes: Implications for communicative development and interventions. *Infant and Child Development, 15,* 219–222.

Zeidner, M., Matthews, G., & Roberts, R. D. (2004). Emotional intelligence in the workplace: A critical review. *Applied Psychology: An International Review, 53,* 371–399.

Zelazo, N., Zelazo, P. R., Cohen, K., & Zelazo, P. D. (1993). Specificity of practice effects on elementary neuromotor patterns. *Developmental Psychology, 29,* 686–691.

Zelazo, P. D., Muller, U., Frye, D., & Marcovitch, S. (2003). The development of executive function in early childhood. *Monographs of the Society for Research in Child Development, 68.*

Zelazo, P. R. (1998). McGraw and the development of unaided walking. *Developmental Review, 18,* 449–471.

Zellner, D., Loaiza, S., Gonzalez, Z., Pita, J., Morales, J., Pecora, D., et al. (2006, April). Food selection changes under stress. *Physiology & Behavior, 87,* 789–793.

Zemach, I., Chang, S., & Teller, D. (2007). Infant color vision: Prediction of infants' spontaneous color preferences. *Vision Research, 47,* 1368–1381.

Zeman, J., Cassano, M., Perry-Parrish, C., & Stegall, S. (2006, April). Emotion regulation in children and adolescents. *Journal of Developmental & Behavioral Pediatrics, 27,* 155–168.

Zeng, Z. (2011). The myth of the glass ceiling: Evidence from a stock-flow analysis of authority attainment. *Social Science Research, 40,* 312–325.

Zernike, K., & Petersen, M. (2001, August 19). Schools' backing of behavior drugs comes under fire. *The New York Times, 1,* 28.

Zeskind, P. S., & Ramey, D. T. (1981). Preventing intellectual and interactional sequels of fetal malnutrition: A longitudinal, transactional, and synergistic approach to development. *Child Development, 52,* 213–218.

Zettergren, P. (2003). School adjustment in adolescence for previously rejected, average and popular children. *British Journal of Educational Psychology, 73,* 207–221.

Zevon, M., & Corn, B. (1990). Paper presented at the annual meeting of the American Psychological Association, Boston.

Zhai, F., Raver, C., & Jones, S. M. (2012). Academic performance of subsequent schools and impacts of early interventions: Evidence from a randomized controlled trial in head start settings. *Children and Youth Services Review, 34,* 946–954.

Zhang, L. (2008). Gender and racial gaps in earnings among recent college graduates. *Review of Higher Education: Journal of the Association for the Study of Higher Education, 32,* 51–72.

Zhang, L., & He, Y. (2011). Thinking styles and the Eriksonian stages. *Journal of Adult Development, 18,* 8–17.

Zhang, M., & Quintana, C. (2012). Scaffolding strategies for supporting middle school students' online inquiry processes. *Computers & Education, 58,* 181–196.

Zhang, Q., He, X., & Zhang, J. (2007). A comparative study on the classification of basic color terms by undergraduates from Yi nationality, Bai nationality and Naxi nationality. *Acta Psychologica Sinica, 39,* 18–26.

Zhang, Q., & Wang, Y. (2004). Trends in the association between obesity and socioeconomic status in U.S. adults: 1971 to 2000. *Obesity Research, 12,* 1622–1632.

Zhang, Y., Proenca, R., Maffel, M., Barone, M., Leopold, L., & Friedman, J. M. (1994). Positional cloning of the mouse obese gene and its human homologue. *Nature, 372,* 425–432.

Zhe, C., & Siegler, R. S. (2000). Across the great divide: Bridging the gap between understanding of toddlers' and older children's thinking. *Monographs of the Society for Research in Child Development, 65,* 2, Serial No. 261.

Zhou, B. F., Stamler, J., Dennis, B., Moag-Stahlberg, A., Okuda, N., Robertson, C., Zhao, L., Chan, Q., Elliot, P., & INTERMAP Research Group. (2003). Nutrient intakes of middle-aged me and women in China, Japan, United Kingdom, and United States in the late 1990s: The INTERMAP study. *Journal of Human Hypertension, 17,* 623–630.

Zhu, J., & Weiss, L. (2005). The Wechsler Scales. In D. P. Flanagan & P. L. Harrison (Eds.), *Contemporary intellectual assessment: Theories, tests, and issues.* New York: Guilford Press.

Zhul, J. L., Madsen, K. M., Vestergaard, M., Basso, O., & Olsen, J. (2005). Paternal age and preterm birth. *Epidemiology, 16,* 259–262.

Zigler, E. F. (1994, February). Early intervention to prevent juvenile delinquency. *Harvard Mental Health Newsletter,* 5–7.

Zigler, E. F., & Finn-Stevenson, M. (1995). The child care crisis: Implications for the growth and development of the nation's children. *Journal of Social Issues, 51,* 215–231.

Zigler, E. F., & Finn-Stevenson, M. (1999). Applied developmental psychology. In M. H. Bornstein & M. E. Lamb (Eds.), *Developmental psychology: An advanced textbook.* Mahwah, NJ: Erlbaum.

Zigler, E. F., & Gilman, E. (1998). The legacy of Jean Piaget. In G. A. Kimble & M. Wertheimer (Eds.), *Portraits of pioneers in psychology* (Vol. 3). Washington, DC: American Psychological Association.

Zigler, E. F., & Styfco, S. J. (1994). Head Start: Criticism in a constructive context. *American Psychologist, 49,* 127–132.

Zigler, E., & Styfco, S. (2004). Moving Head Start to the states: One experiment too many. *Applied Developmental Science, 8,* 51–55.

Zigler, E., Styfco, S. J., & Gilman, E. (1993). The national Head Start program for disadvantaged preschoolers. In E. Zigler & S. J. Styfco (Eds.), *Head Start and beyond:* *A national plan for extended childhood intervention* (pp. 1–41). New Haven, CT: Yale University Press.

Zillman, D. (1993). Mental control of angry aggression. In D. M. Wegner & J. W. Pennebaker (Eds.), *Handbook of mental control.* Englewood Cliffs, NJ: Prentice-Hall.

Zimbardo, P. (2007). *The Lucifer effect: Understanding how good people turn evil.* New York: Random House.

Zimmer, C. (2003, May 16). How the mind reads other minds. *Science, 300,* 1079–1080.

Zimmer-Gembeck, M. J., & Collins, W. A. (2003). Autonomy development during adolescence. In G. R. Adams & M. D. Berzonsky (Eds.), *Blackwell handbook of adolescence.* Malden, MA: Blackwell Publishing.

Zimmer-Gembeck, M. J., & Gallaty, K. J. (2006). Hanging out or hanging in? Young females' socioemotional functioning and the changing motives for dating and romance. In A. Columbus (Ed.), *Advances in psychology research, Vol 44.* Hauppauge, NY: Nova Science Publishers.

Zimmerman, B., & Schunk, D. (2003). Albert Bandura: The scholar and his contributions to educational psychology. *Educational psychology: A century of contributions.* Mahwah, NJ: Lawrence Erlbaum Associates.

Zimmerman, F., & Christakis, D. (2007). Associations between content types of early media exposure and subsequent attentional problems. *Pediatrics, 120,* 986–992.

Zimmerman, M. A., & Arunkumar, R. (1994). Resiliency research: Implications for schools and policy. *Social Policy Report, 8,* 1–18.

Zipke, M. (2007). The role of metalinguistic awareness in the reading comprehension of sixth and seventh graders. *Reading Psychology, 28,* 375–396.

Zirkel, S., & Cantor, N. (2004). 50 years after *Brown v. Board of Education*: The promise and challenge of multicultural education. *Journal of Social Issues, 60,* 1–15.

Zisook, S., & Shear, K. (2009). Grief and bereavement: What psychiatrists need to know. *World Psychiatry, 8,* 67–74.

Zito, J. (2002). Five burning questions. *Journal of Developmental & Behavioral Pediatrics, 23,* S23–S30.

Zito, J. M., Safer, D. J., dosReis, S., Gardner, J. F., Boles, M., & Lynch, F. (2000). Trends in prescribing of psychotropic medications to preschoolers. *Journal of the American Medical Association, 283,* 1025–1030.

Ziv, M., & Frye, D. (2003). The relation between desire and false belief in children's theory of mind: No satisfaction? *Developmental Psychology, 39,* 859–876.

Zmiri, P., Rubin, L., Akons, H., Zion, N., & Shaoul, R. (2011). The effect of day care attendance on infant and toddler's growth. *Acta Paediatrica, 100,* 266–270.

Zolotor, A., Theodore, A., Chang, J., Berkoff, M., & Runyan, D. (2008). Speak softly—and forget the stick corporal punishment and child physical abuse. *American Journal of Preventive Medicine, 35,* 364–369.

Zosh, J. M., Halberda, J., & Feigenson, L. (2011). Memory for multiple visual ensembles in infancy. *Journal of Experimental Psychology: General, 140.*

Zuckerman, G., & Shenfield, S. (2007, May). Child-adult interaction that creates a zone of proximal development. *Journal of Russian & East European Psychology, 45*(3), 43–69.

Zuckerman, M. (2003). Biological bases of personality. In T. Millon, & M. J. Lerner, (Eds.), *Handbook of psychology: Personality and social psychology* (Vol. 5). New York: John Wiley & Sons.

Zwelling, E. (2006). A challenging time in the history of Lamaze international: An interview with Francine Nichols. *Journal of Perinatal Education, 15,* 10–17.

Credits

Photo and Cartoons

Cover © olly/Fotolia

Chapter 1 Page 2 Hermien Lam/Catchlight Visual Services/Alamy; p. 3 67photo/Alamy; p. 6 Dinodia/AGE Fotostock; p. 8 Zurijeta/Shutterstock (bottom left); p. 8 Paul Matthew Photography/Shutterstock (center left); p. 8 Wealan Pollard/Alamy (center right); p. 8 Brian Summers/Glow Images (bottom right); p. 9 Lewis Wickes Hine/Corbis; p. 11 Scala/Art Resource, NY.

Chapter 2 Page 20 Judith Haeusler/Cultura Creative/Alamy; p. 21 Samantha Sais/REUTERS/Newscom; p. 23 Library of Congress Prints and Photographs Division [LC-USZ62-72266]; p. 25 Jon Erikson/The Image Works; p. 25 AP Images; p. 27 AF archive/Alamy; p. 30 Du Cane Medical Imaging Ltd./Science Source; p. 33 Judy Coleman Brinich; p. 33 NatUlrich/Shutterstock; p. 34 Nina Leen/Time & Life Pictures/Getty Images; p. 39 Bob Daemmrich/PhotoEdit (top); p. 39 BSIP SA/Alamy (bottom); p. 41 Mark Scheuern/Alamy; p. 42 Peter Arnold, Inc./Alamy; p. 45 Jeff Greenberg/PhotoEdit (left); p. 45 ZUMA Press, Inc./Alamy (right); p. 46 Ariel Skelley/Blend Images/Alamy (top); p. 46 MENDIL/BSIP/Alamy (bottom); p. 50 George Shelley/Corbis.

Chapter 3 Page 56 David M. Phillips/Science Source; p. 57 Profimedia.CZ a.s./Alamy; p. 58 Pascal Goetgheluck/Science Source; p. 60 Ken Love KRT/Newscom; p. 60 Alfred Pasieka/Science Source; p. 61 Pictorial Press Ltd/Alamy; p. 65 Omikron/Science Source; p. 66 Saturn Stills/Science Source; p. 71 © Michael Shaw/The New Yorker Collection/www.cartoonbank.com; p. 73 Loisjoy Thurstun/Bubbles Photolibrary/Alamy; p. 75 © J.B. Handelsman/The New Yorker Collection/www.cartoonbank.com; p. 78 Courtesy of Sandra Scarr, KinderCare Learning Centers, Inc., Alabama; p. 81 Dr. Yorgos Nikas/Science Source (left); p. 81 Petit Format/Science Source (center); p. 81 Neil Bromhall/Science Source (right); p. 82 Science Source; p. 83 © William Hamilton/The New Yorker Collection/www.cartoonbank.com.

Chapter 4 Page 94 Photobac/Shutterstock; p. 95 Photodisc/Thinkstock; p. 96 (top) Michael Newman/PhotoEdit; p. 96 (bottom) silverrobert/Fotolia; p. 100 Jiang Jin/Purestock/Alamy; p. 101 Peter Byron/Photoedit; p. 106 Chuck Nacke/Alamy; p. 110 Patricia Clifford; p. 112 Mark Thomas/Science Source; p. 116 Myrleen Ferguson/PhotoEdit; p. 117 Igor Stepovik/Shutterstock; p. 118 Tiffany M. Field, Ph.D.

Chapter 5 Page 124 OJO Images Ltd/Alamy; p. 125 FREE IMAGINATION/Agencja FREE/Alamy; p. 129 Christopher Futcher/E+/Getty Images; p. 129 (left) Mark Edward Atkinson/Tetra Images/Alamy; p. 129 (right) Radius Images/Alamy; p. 131 Science Photo Library/CMSP; p. 133 BlueMoon Stock/SuperStock; p. 133 Denise Hager/Catchlight Visual Services/Alamy; p. 133 (left) Gladskikh Tatiana/Shutterstock; p. 133 (right) Asia Images Group/Getty Images; p. 137 auremar/Fotolia; p. 139 Child Development Today and Tomorrow, ed., W. Damon, Jossey Bass. Copyright 1989 John Wiley & Sons, Inc.; p. 140 FancyVeerSet2/Alamy; p. 142 Karan Kapoor/Stone+/Getty Images; p. 143 Mark Richards/PhotoEdit; p. 144 Vitalinko/Fotolia; p. 145 maureen rigdon/Shutterstock; p. 146 Michelle D. Bridwell/PhotoEdit; p. 153 © Christopher Weyant/The New Yorker Collection/www.cartoonbank.com; p. 155 RaJi/Shutterstock; p. 156 Chris Priest/Science Photo Library/Science Source.

Chapter 6 Page 160 Goran Bogicevic/Shutterstock; p. 162 kalcutta/Fotolia; p. Tom Prettyman/PhotoEdit; p. 163 Farrell Grehan/Historical/Corbis; p. 166 George Doyle/Thinkstock; p. 167 Stevanne Auerbach; p. 168 Sandro Di Carlo Darsa/PhotoAlto/Alamy; p. 170 Marmaduke St. John/Alamy; p. 174 Exactostock/SuperStock; p. 175 Kevin Radford/SuperStock; p. 177 Orlando Sierra/AFP/Getty Images; p. 183 RIA Novosti/Alamy.

Chapter 7 Page 190 Cindy Charles/PhotoEdit; p. 191 Renee Jansoa/Fotolia; p. 194 David Sanders/Arizona Daily Star; p. 195 chuchi25/Fotolia; p. 197 dotshock/Shutterstock; p. 200 Carolyn Rovee Collier; p. 201 Monkey Business Images/Shutterstock; p. 202 Morgan Lane Photography/Shutterstock; p. 205 Gina Smith/Shutterstock; p. 206 Stanislav Fridkin/Shutterstock; p. 210 Mike Derer/AP Images; p. 211 Claudia Rehm/Westend61 GmbH/Alamy; p. 212 Courtesy of Mary Kriebel; p. 213 Darrin Jenkins/Alamy.

Chapter 8 Page 218 Maya Kruchankova/Shutterstock; p. 219 Kim Ruoff/Shutterstock; p. 222 Laura-Ann Petitto/Herbert Terrace; p. 223 Myrleen Pearson/PhotoEdit; p. 225 Boris Ryaposov/Shutterstock; p. 227 Golden Pixels LLC/Shutterstock; p. 230 Richard Wareham Fotografie/Alamy; p. 232 Johnny Greig/Alamy; p. 234 Karel Lorier/Alamy; p. 237 Bob Daemmrich/Alamy.

Chapter 9 Page 244 RimDream/Shutterstock; p. 245 Lauren Shear/Science Source; p. 247 Albert Harlingue/Roger-Viollet/The Image Works; p. 252 Wechsler Intelligence Scale for Children, Fourth Edition (WISC-IV). NCS Pearson, Inc. Reproduced with permission.; p. 252 Wavebreakmedia/Shutterstock; p. 256 Jupiterimages/Creatas/Thinkstock; p. 259 Bob Daemmrich/The Image Works; p. 260 Kevin R. Morris/Documentary Value/Corbis; p. 263 Elizabeth Crews Photography; p. 264 Christine Gonzalez; p. 265 Richard Hutchings/Science Source.

Chapter 10 Page 272 Henglein and Steets/Cultura/Getty Images; p. 273 Dave King/Dorling Kindersley, Ltd; p. 274 Phase4Photography/Shutterstock; p. 275 (top) Science Source; p. 275 (bottom) Daniel Grogan Photography; p. 277 Keith Brofsky/Brand X Pictures/PictureQuest; p. 279 Christina Kennedy/Alamy; p. 281 Visage/Stockbyte/Getty Images; p. 284 Courtesy Dr. Carroll Izard; p. 286 JazzBoo/Shutterstock; p. 287 Cristin Poirier; p. 288 Barbara Stitzer/PhotoEdit; p. 290 Suprijono Suharjoto/Fotolia; p. 291 Image supplied courtesy of Eric Nelson, Ph.D./National Institute of Mental Health, Mood and Anxiety Disorders Program; p. 292 JackF/Fotolia; p. 295 Lisa F. Young/Fotolia; p. 297 JackF/Fotolia; p. 299 Photodisc/Jupiter Images; p. 300 Myrleen Pearson/PhotoEdit.

Chapter 11 Page 304 Comstock Images/Getty Images; p. 305 Anders Sellin/Flickr/getty images; p. 307 (top) Stanete Alina/Fotolia; p. 307 (bottom) Thomas Northcut/Lifesize/Getty Images; p. 308 JLImages/Alamy; p. 309 Eric Raptosh Photography/Blend Images/Alamy; p. 311 Christopher Futcher/E+/Getty Images; p. 312 Chris Schmidt/Getty Images; p. 313 Siri Stafford/Digital Vision/Getty Images; p. 315 Jeff Greenberg/Alamy; p. 318 Lisa F. Young/Shutterstock; p. 320 Myrleen Pearson/PhotoEdit; p. 321 David Grossman/Alamy.

Chapter 12 Page 326 Andy Dean/Fotolia; p. 327 Ernest Prim/Fotolia; p. 329 Pavel L Photo and Video/Shutterstock.com; p. 330 (left) Melanie DeFazio/Fotolial; p. 330 (right) Science Source; p. 331 (left) Ocean/Corbis; p. 331 (right) Rob/Fotolia; p. 335; Janie Airey/The Agency Collection/Getty Images p. 336 Steve Skjold/Alamy; p. 337 DOONESBURY © (1997) Garry Trudeau. Used by permission of UNIVERSAL UCLICK. All rights reserved.; p. 338 Bill Aron/PhotoEdit; p. 342 Sandy L. Caron, Ph.D.; p. 342 Dynamic Graphics/Getty Images/Creatas/Thinkstock; p. 344 quavondo/E+/Getty Images.

Chapter 13 Page 350 Ocskay Bence/Shutterstock; p. 351 Tom-Hanisch/Fotolia; p. 353 (top) Michelle D. Bridwell/PhotoEdit; p. 353 (bottom) Caroline Woodham/Alamy; p. 355 Tony Freeman/PhotoEdit; p. 357 Charles Gupton/Stockbyte/Getty Images; p. 360 ZUMA Wire Service/Alamy; p. 362 Photo by Jerry Bauer. Courtesy of Harvard Graduate School of Education; p. 363 Jelani Quinn; p. 367 Catherine Ursillo/Science Source; p. 369 Courtesy of Albert Bandura; p. 370 Bill Aron/PhotoEdit; p. 371 David McNew/Getty Images; p. 374 Monkey Business/Fotolia.

Chapter 14 Page 380 Peathegee/Glow Images; p. 381 Mode Ian O'Leary/Mode Images/Alamy; p. 382 Morgan Lane Photography/Shutterstock; p. 383 Angela

Hampton Picture Library/Alamy; p. 385 © Bruce Eric Kaplan/The New Yorker Collection/www.cartoonbank.com; p. 386 Llike/Shutterstock; p. 388 Digital Vision/Thinkstock; p. 392 Jupiterimages/Comstock/Getty Images/Thinkstock; p. 393 micromonkey/Fotolia; p. 394 Bob Daemmrich/Alamy; p. 395 Angela Hampton Picture Library/Alamy; p. 398 photophonie/Fotolia; p. 399 Digital Vision/Thinkstock; p. 400 © Barbara Smaller/The New Yorker Collection/www.cartoonbank.com; p. 405 Phil Borden/PhotoEdit; p. 406 Robert Brenner/PhotoEdit; p. 408 (left) Photo Collection Alexander Alland, Sr./Historical/Corbis; p. 408 (right) Zhang Chaoqun/Xinhua/Photoshot/Newscom; p. 410 Creatas Images/Thinkstock.

Chapter 15 Page 418 Monkey Business Images/Shutterstock.com; p. 419 Brand X Pictures/Thinkstock; p. 422 (top) Smailhodzic/Shutterstock; p. 422 (bottom) © Bruce Eric Kaplan/The New Yorker Collection/www.cartoonbank.com; p. 425 © Bernard Schoenbaum/The New Yorker Collection/www.cartoonbank.com; p. 426 Image Source/Getty Images; p. 428 Gary S Chapman/Photographer's Choice RF/Getty Images; p. 430 Nick White/Digital Vision/Getty Images; p. 434 wavebreakmedia/Shutterstock; p. 440 IndiaPicture/Getty Images; p. 441 Monkey Business Images/Shutterstock; p. 443 David Bacon/Alamy; p. 445 H. Mark Weidman Photography/Alamy Limited.

Figures, Tables, and Excerpts

Chapter 1 Excerpt: Page 3: Louise Brown. Falco, M. (2012, July 3). Since IVF Began, 5 Million Babies Born. CNN News. Accessed online 7/3/12 http://www.10news.com/health/31243126/detail.html.

Chapter 2 Figure 2-1: Data from Bronfenbrenner, U., & Morris, P. (1998). The ecology of developmental processes. In W. Damon (Ed.), Handbook of child psychology (Vol. 1, 5th ed.). New York: Wiley; p. 33: Used with permission from Judy Coleman Brinich; p. 37 (EXCERPT) Hunt, M. (1993). The story of psychology. New York: Doubleday; Figure 2-4: Leyens, J. P., Camino, L., Parke, R. D., & Berkowitz, L. (1975). Effects of movie violence on aggression in a field setting as a function of group dominance and cohesion. *Journal of Personality and Social Psychology, 32*, 346–360.

Chapter 3 Figure 3-2: Martin & Park, 2009; Figure 3-5: Kimball, John W., Biology, 5th Ed., (c) 1983. Reprinted and electronically reproduced by permission of Pearson Education, Inc., Upper Saddle River, New Jersey; Figure 3-6: Celera Genomics: International Human Genome Sequencing Consortium, 2001; Table 3-1: Adapted from McGuffin, Riley, & Plomin, 2001; Figure 3-7: Based on Samet, DeMarini, & Malling, 2004, p. 971; Table 3-3: Human Genome Project, 2006, http://www.oml.gov/scl/techresources/Human_Genome/medicine/genetest.shtml. Figure 3-9: Based on Bouchard & McGue, 1981; Figure 3-10: Adapted from Tellegen et al., 1988; Table 3-4: Kagan, Arcus, & Snidman, 1993; Figure 3-11: Based on Gottesman, 1991; Figure 3-12: Based on Moore & Persaud, 2003; Figure 3-14: Reproductive Medicine Associates of New Jersey, 2002; Figure 3-15: Moore, 1974.

Chapter 4 Table 4-1: Apgar, 1953; Figure 4-2: The World Factbook, 2010; Figure 4-3: MacDorman & Mathews, 2009; Table 4-2: Adapted from Committee to Study the Prevention of Low Birthweight, 1985; p. 110: Patricia Clifford; Figure 4-4: International Cesarean Awareness Network, 2004; Figure 4-5: http://childstats.gov/2009; Table 4-3: "From Maternity to Parental Leave Policies: Women's Health, Employment and Child and Family Well-Being," by S. B. Kamerman, 2000 (Spring), *The Journal of the American Women's Medical Association*, p. 55, table 1; "Parental Leave Policies: An Essential Ingredient in Early Childhood Education and Care Policies, " by S. B. Kamerman, 2000, *Social Policy Report,* p. 14. Table 1.0; Table 4-6: Based on Eckerman & Oehler, 1992.

Chapter 5 Figure 5-2: National Center for Health Statistics, 2000; Figure 5-3: Cratty, B. Perceptual and Motor Development in Infants and Children, 3rd Ed., (c) 1986. Reprinted and electronically reproduced by permission of Pearson Education, Inc. Upper Saddle River, New Jersey; Figure 5-5: Fischer, K. W., & Rose, S. P. (1995). Concurrent cycles in the dynamic development of brain and behavior. Newsletter of the Society for Research in Child Development, p. 16; Figure 5-6: Source: Adapted from Frankenburg, W. K., Dodds, J., Archer, P., Shapiro, H., & Bresnick, B. (1992). The Denver II: A major revision and restandardization

of the Denver Developmental Screening Test. Pediatrics, 89, 91–97; Figure 5-7: Cratty, Braynt, Perceptual and Motor Development in Infants and Children, 2nd Ed., (c) 1979. Reproduced and Electronically reproduced by permission of Pearson Education, Inc. Upper Saddle River, New Jersey; Figure 5-8: Adapted from Cratty, 1979, p. 222; Figure 5-10: Based on Eveleth & Tanner, 1976; Figure 5-11: Adapted from Tanner, 1978; Figure 5-13: Based on data from Fantz, R. L. (1961). The origin of form perception. Scientific American, 72; Figure 5-15: Elkind, 1978; Figure 5-16: Data from UNICEF, Progress for Children, 2006, p. 12; Figure 5-17: National Center for Children in Poverty at the Joseph L. Mailman School of Public Health of Columbia University, 2010; Figure 5-18: Centers for Disease Control and Prevention, 2010; Figure 5-19: U.S. Department of Agriculture, 2011; Figure 5-20: Health R esources and Services Administration, 2008; Figure 5-21: Akinbami, 2011.

Chapter 6 Page 168 (Excerpt) Piaget, THE CONSTRUCTION OF REALITY IN THE CHILD, M. Cook, trans, Basic Books, (1954); p. 167 Printed with permission from Stevanne Auerbach. www.drtoy.com; Figure 6-8: Based on Dasen, Ngini, & Lavallée, 1979.

Chapter 7 Figure 7-3: Department for Education and Skills, England 2004; Figure 7-6: U.S. Drug Enforcement Administration, 2012.

Chapter 8 Figure 8-1: Adapted from Bornstein & Lamb, 1992a; Table 8-1: Adapted from R. Brown & C. Fraser, 1963; p. 225 (Excerpt): Schatz, M. (1994). A toddler's life. New York: Oxford University Press; Figure 8-3: Berko, J. (1958). The child's learning of English morphology. Word, 14, 150–177. Printed with permission of Jean Berko Gleason; Table 8-2: Based on Blount, 1982; Figure 8-4: Based on data from Gleason et al., 1991; Figure 8-5: B. Hart & Risley, 1995, p. 239; Figure 8-6: Printed by permission of Modern Language Association.

Chapter 9 Page 245 (Excerpt) Heward, W., Exceptional Children: an introductory survey of special education, 3rd Ed., (c) 1990. Reprinted and electronically reproduced by Pearson Education Inc., Upper Saddle River, New Jersey; Figure 9-3: Based on NCS Pearson, Inc., 1998; Figure 9-4: Based on data from Walters & Gardner, 1986; Table 9-2: Based on Bayley, N. 7 1993. *Bayley scales of infant development [BSID-II]* 2nd ed., San Antonio, TX: The Psychological Corporation; p. 264 (Box): Christine Gonzalez; p. 267 (Box): Murphy 2011.

Chapter 10 Table 10-1: E. Walters, 1963; Figure 10-2: Adapted from Bell & Ainsworth, 1972; Tomlinson-Keasey, 1985; Figure 10-5: Based on Kagan, Kearsley, & Zelazo, 1978; p. 287 (Box) Printed with permission from Christin Poirier; Figure 10-7: Based on Boehm & Campbell, 1995; Table 10-2: Thomas, Chess, & Birch, 1968.

Chapter 11 Figure 11-1: Based on data from Shavelson, Hubner, & Stanton, 1976; Table 11-1 Based on Marcia, 1980; Figure 11-2: U.S. Census Bureau, 2011; p. 320 Harter, S. (1990). Issues in the assessment of self-concept of children and adolescents. In A. LaGreca (Ed.), Through the eyes of a child. Boston: Allyn & Bacon.

Chapter 12 Figure 12-1: Morbidity and Mortality Weekly Report, 2008; p, 342 (Box) Sandra Caron; p. 344 (Extract) Gleick, E., Reed, S., & Schindehette, S. (1994, October 24). The baby trap. People Weekly, pp. 38–56; Figure 12-2: National Center for Chronic Disease Prevention and Health Promotion, 2011.

Chapter 13 Table 13-2: Based on Baumrind, 1971; Maccoby & Martin, 1983; Table 13-2: Based on Kohlberg, 1969; p. 363 (Box) Jelani Quinn; Figure 13-2: Based data from Center for Media and Public Affairs, 1995; Figure 13-3: United Nations Office on Drugs and Crime, 2011.

Chapter 14 Figure 14-1: Adapted from Farver, Kim, & Lee-Shin, 1995; p. 385 (Extract) Kotre, J., & Hall, E. (1990). Seasons of life. Boston: Little, Brown; Table 14-2: Based on Zarbatany, Hartmann, & Rankin, 1990; Figure 14-2: Based on Dodge, K. A. (1985). A social information processing model of social competence in children. In M. Perlmutter (Ed.), Minnesota Symposia on Child Psychology, 18, 77–126; Table 14-3: Based on Suitor et al., 2001; Figure 14-4: Based on Steinberg & Silverberg, 1986; Figure 14-5: Fuligni, Tseng, & Lam, 1999; Figure 14-6: PRIMEDIA/Roper National Youth Survey, 1999; Figure 14-7: Larson, Richards, Moneta, Holmbeck, & Duckett, 1996; Figure 14-8: Hofferth & Sandberg,

1998; Figure 14-9: U.S. Bureau of the Census, Statistical Abstract of the United States, 2011; Table 14-4: Shealy, C.N. (1995) From Boys Town to Oliver Twist . . . American Psychologist, 50, 565-580; Figure 14-10: U.S. Department of Health and Human Services, 2007; Figure 14-11: *Scientific American*, March 2002, p. 71.

Chapter 15 Figure 15-1: National Center for Education Statistics, 1997; Figure 15-2: Based on Tobin, Wu & Davidson, 1989; Figure 15-3: Based on Common Sense Media, 2011; Figure 15-4: Rideout et al., 2005; Figure 15-5: UNESCO, 2006; Figure 15-6: OECD (2005). Math performance of students around the world. Paris: Organisation for Economic Co-operation and Development; Figure 15-7: NAEP, 2003; Figure 15-8: PEW Research Center, 2008; Figure 15-9: Based on Phinney, 1990; Figure 15-10: National Center for Children in Poverty, 2006; Figure 15-1 Data from Smith, T.W. & Seokho, K., National Pride in Cross-national and Temporal Perspective, International Journal of Public Opinion Research, 18, Spring 2006, 127–136.

Name Index

A

Aalsma, M., 196
AAMR (American Association on Mental Retardation), 265
Abadie, V., 145
Aber, J. L., 48
Abramson, L., 293
Abramson, L. Y., 293
Abril, C., 432
ACIP, 103
Ackerman, B. P., 283, 290
Ackroyd, K., 289
Acocella, J., 11
Adams, G. R., 312
Adams, H. L., 338
Adams, M., 328
Adamson, L., 287
Adolphs, 291
Advocates for Youth, 345
Agrawal, A., 72
Aguirre, E., 422
Ahn, S., 407
Ahn, W., 289
Aikens, N., 444
Ainsworth, M. D. S., 275, 280
Ainsworth, S., 252
Aitchison, J., 220, 223, 225
Aitken, R. J., 80
Akhtar, S., 277
Akinbami, L. J., 155
Akmajian, A., 220
Aksan, N., 280, 287, 296
Akyol, A. K., 290
Albers, L., 111
Alberts, A., 195, 196
Alderfer, C., 260
Alexander, 445
Alexander, B., 101
Alexander, G., 329
Alexander, G. M., 117
Alfonso, V. C., 252
Alibeli, M., 6
Alipuria, L. L., 315
Allam, M., 145
Allen, B., 412
Allen, J., 395
Allen, L., 86
Allen, M., 409
Alley, A., 220
Allhusen, V., 422
Allison, A. C., 65
Allison, B., 312
Almas, A., 354
Almonte, J. L., 319
Aloise-Young, P. A., 396
Al-Owidha, A., 314
Alsop, 254
Altermatt, E., 386
Aly, H., 90
Amato, P., 405
American Academy of Pediatrics, 135, 207, 388, 411, 426
American Academy of Pediatrics Committee on Fetus and Newborn, 103
American College of Medical Genetics, 103
American Dietetic Association, 86

American Psychological Association, 51
Amitai, Y., 90
Ammerman, R. T., 410
Amsterlaw, J., 289
Anand, S., 425
Anders, Y., 420
Anderson, 429
Anderson, C. A., 16
Anderson, D., 426
Anderson, E., 406
Anderson, R. C., 238
Andrés-Pueyo, A., 40
Andrews, G., 385
Ängarne-Lindberg, T., 405
Ani, C., 150
Ansari, D., 131
Antonishak, J., 395
APA Reproductive Choice Working Group, 84
Apgar, V., 98
Apperly, I., 227
Apple, 434
Arafat, C., 426
Archer, J., 367, 374
Archer, P. W., 112
Arcus, D., 76
Arias, I., 412
Ariès, P., 11
Armitage, C. J., 151, 338
Armstrong, H. D., 316
Armstrong, J., 117
Armstrong, V., 14
Arnett, J., 7
Arnett, J. J., 402
Arnold, D. H., 231
Aro, H., 405
Aronson, E., 372
Aronson, J., 197, 198
Arredondo, E., 356, 439
Arsenault, L., 78
Arterberry, M., 143
Aschersleben, G., 136
Asendorpf, J., 307
Asher, S. R., 335, 389
Ashmead, D. H., 144
Aslin, R. N., 194, 223
Astheimer, L. B., 206
Atkins, S. M., 194
Atkinson, J., 117
Atkinson, R. C., 199
Audley-Piotrowski, S. R., 312
Augustyn, M., 427
Auinger, P., 431
Aujoulat, 389
Austin, J., 66
Axia, G., 146
Axinn, W. G., 339
Aydt, H., 330
Aylward, G. P., 258
Ayotte, V., 309
Ayoub, N. C., 101
Azuma, S. D., 88

B

Bacchus, L., 90
Bachman, H. J., 431
Bade, U., 298

Bader, A. P., 104
Badger, S., 402
Badner, J. A., 63
Badzakova-Trajkov, G., 239
Baer, J. S., 89
Bahrick, L., 147
Bahrick, L. E., 119
Bai, L., 384
Bailey, J. M., 72
Bairam, A., 87
Bajda, V. M., 297
Baker, J., 407
Baker, R. C., 362
Baker, S. A., 239
Bakermans-Kranenburg, M., 279
Balaiah, D., 342
Baldassaro, R., 370
Baldassarro, R., 16
Ballen, L., 101
Balthazart, J., 343
Bamaca, M., 443
Bandura, A., 27, 354, 368
Banti, S., 114
Baptista, T., 34
Bar, J. L., 77
Barber, S., 113
Barberá, E., 333
Barboza, G., 374
Barker, E., 292
Barlett, C., 16, 370
Barnard, W., 424
Barnes, H. V., 424
Barnett, R. C., 403
Baron-Cohen, S., 82, 331
Barone, D., 237
Barr, H. M., 89
Barr, R., 120
Barr, R. A., 224
Barr, R. G., 120
Bartel, V. B., 432
Bass, S., 408
Bates, J. E., 357
Bathurst, K., 403
Batson, C., 364
Bauer, P. J., 200, 201, 204
Bauman, K .E., 393
Baumeister, R. F., 319
Baumrind, D., 355, 356
Bayley, N., 257, 258
Bazargan, M., 48
Bazargan-Hejazi, 48
Beal, C. R., 132, 336
Bearce, K., 200
Bearer, 15
Bearman, P., 345
Beaulac-Baillargeon, L., 87
Becker, B., 395
Becker, J., 152
Begley, S., 102, 196
Behrman, R. E., 155, 408
Beland, K., 372
Belcher, J. R., 406
Belkin, L., 264
Bell, H., 384
Bell, K., 153
Bell, M., 200
Bell, S. M., 280
Belle, D., 404

Belluck, P., 357, 358
Belschak, F., 374
Belsky, J., 139, 422
Beltz, 331
Benbow, C. P., 267
Benelli, B., 227
Bengtson, V. L., 405
Benini, F., 146
Benjet, C., 411
Benson, E., 283
Benson, J. B., 206
Ben-Zeev, T., 197
Berenbaum, 331
Berends, M., 393
Bergen, H., 293
Bergenn, V. W., 130
Berger, L., 404
Bergin, C., 354
Bergman, A., 275
Bergman, N. J., 120
Bergmann, K. E., 106
Bergmann, R. L., 106
Berko, J., 225
Berkowitz, L., 44, 372
Berlin, L. J., 276
Berndt, T. J., 386
Bernier, A., 276
Bernstein, D. M., 210
Bernstein, N., 344
Bernstsen, D., 202
Bernt, F., 354
Berry, G. L., 426
Bertin, E., 287
Bertoncini, J., 223
Besag, V. E., 336
Bettencourt, B. A., 373
Bewley, S., 90
Bhanot, 440
Bhushan, B., 138
Bialystok, E., 239
Bickham, D. S., 426
Biddle, B. J., 436
Biehle, S. N., 328
Bierman, K., 424
Bierman, K. L., 389
Bigelow, A., 286
Binnie, L., 154
Birch, H. G., 297
Biro, F., 321
Bischof-Köhler, D., 307
Bissell, M., 409
Bjorklund, D. F., 34
Black, B., 363
Black, K., 401
Black, M., 406
Blake, C. A., 265
Blakemore, J., 331
Blau, G. M., 411
Block, J. S., 15
Blodgett, B., 321
Blom, I., 275
Blomqvist, Y., 108
Bloom, B., 154
Bloom, C., 204
Bloss, C. S., 69
Blount, B. G., 235
Bluemke, M., 16
Blum, D., 275

Blumenshine, P. M., 108
Boag, S., 25
Bober, S., 383
Boehm, 294
Bogle, K. A., 338
Bohn, A., 202
Boivin, 358
Bolle, 434
Bonanno, G., 9
Bond, B., 152
Bond, M. H., 239
Bonichini, S., 146
Bonke, B., 69
Bonnicksen, A., 84
Booth, A., 405
Booth, C., 278
Booth-LaForce, C., 277
Bootzin, R. R., 156
Bor, W., 371
Borland, M. V., 322
Bornstein, M., 330
Bornstein, M. H., 86, 221, 223, 224, 383
Bornstein, R. F., 23
Borowiecki, J., 152
Bos, H., 343
Boseovski, J. J., 210
Bosquet, M., 82
Boswell, M., 406
Bouchard, T. J., Jr., 73, 74
Boucher, N., 87
Boulton, 374
Bourgeois, N., 367
Bourne, V., 131, 132
Boutot, E., 104
Bower, B., 138
Bowker, 388
Bowlby, J., 275
Boyas, J., 345
Bracey, J., 443
Bracken, B., 266, 317
Brackett, M., 255
Braddick, O., 117
Bradlee, M., 153
Bradley, 447
Bradley, R., 15
Bradley, R. A., 101
Bradshaw, M., 75
Brady, S., 39
Brandhorst, A. R., 442
Branje, S., 399
Branta, C. F., 388
Branum, A., 108
Bray, G., 151
Breen, A., 338
Brehm, K., 264
Bremner, G., 112
Brewer, 445
Bridgett, D., 70
Brion, S., 49
Briones, 440
Brock, C., 438
Brock, J., 30
Brody, D., 139
Brody, N., 74
Bronfenbrenner, U., 31
Brooks-Gunn, J., 112, 150, 260, 424
Brown, 108, 289, 392, 447
Brown, B. B., 357, 392
Brown, E., 266
Brown, J., 333
Brown, J. S., 312
Brown, R., 223, 224
Brown, S., 88
Brown, S. P., 44
Brown, W. M., 88

Browne, K., 332
Brownell, C., 386
Brownell, C. A., 383
Bruck, M., 209, 210, 211
Bruckner, H., 345
Brueggeman, I., 101
Bruskas, D., 408
Bryant, J., 425
Bryant, J. A., 425
Bryden, P. J., 137
Bryk, 331
Bucciarelli, A., 9
Buchbinder, M., 103
Buckingham, R., 252
Buechner, J. S., 155
Buehler, C., 396
Bugental, D. B., 411
Buhrmester, D., 398
Buitelaar, J., 86
Bull, 289
Bullock, L., 89
Bumpus, M. F., 400
Bunch, K., 385
Bunge, A., 108
Burbach, J., 77
Burd, L., 89
Bureau of Labor Statistics, 420
Burgess, K. B., 392
Burkam, D. T., 433
Burks, V. S., 389
Burnett, P., 309
Burns, M., 383
Burock, D., 360
Burton, L., 82, 331, 444
Bushfield, S., 112
Bushman, B. J., 319
Buss, A. H., 73, 317
Buss, K. A., 284, 287
Bussey, K., 353
Byerley, W., 63
Byrd, C. M., 308
Byrd, D., 112
Byrd, R. S., 431
Byrne, B., 251

C

Cabrera, N., 420
Cacciatore, J., 112
Cadinu, M. R., 385
Cahill, K., 15
Cai, Y., 434
Cain, D., 422
Caine, E. D., 293
Caino, S., 130
Calarco, K., 89
Calhoun, F., 89
Caltran, G., 117
Calvert, S. L., 333
Camino, L., 44
Campbell, 294
Campbell, A., 330
Campbell, D., 101
Campbell, F. A., 308, 332
Campbell, J., 49
Campbell, K., 153
Campbell, S., 339
Campbell, W. K., 318, 319
Campos, J. J., 142, 146, 288
Camras, L., 284
Canals, J., 298
Candy, J., 330
Cannon, T., 77
Cannon, T. D., 77
Canterberry, M., 279
Cantor, N., 442
Capiluppi, C., 74
Caplan, L. J., 224

Capps, L. M., 289
Capranica, L., 152
Carbonneau, R., 278
Cardman, M., 435
Carey, S., 201
Carlson, S. M., 239
Carmody, D., 307
Carnegie Task Force, 345
Carney, J. V., 375
Carney, R. N., 203
Caron, A., 289
Caron, C., 155
Carpendale, J. I. M., 313, 360
Carpenter, M., 354
Carr, P., 197
Carrington, H., 285
Carswell, H., 383
Carter, R. T., 6
Carter-Saltzman, L., 74
Carver, L., 286, 288
Carver, L. J., 285, 286
Casalin, S., 296
Casasanto, D., 231, 232
Cashman, 440
Cashon, C., 41, 117, 192
Caspi, A., 78, 296
Cassidy, J., 276
Cauce, A., 75, 407
Cauffman, E., 367, 396
Cavallini, A., 142
Ceci, S., 210, 211
Ceci, S. J., 209, 211
Center for Media and Public Affairs, 369
Centers for Disease Control and Prevention, 104, 151, 152, 344
Chadha, 365
Chadwick, A., 382
Chaffin, M., 412
Chamberlain, P., 408
Champion, C., 355
Chandler, K. L., 266
Chang, S., 117
Chao, R. K., 399, 402
Chaplin, T., 293
Chapman, S. B., 213
Charles, G. T., 74
Chase-Landsdale, L., 422
Chasnoff, I. J., 88
Chau, 150
Chazan-Cohen, R., 424
Chee, C., 353
Chen, C., 14, 402
Chen, E., 332
Chen, J., 252, 357
Chen, S. X., 239
Chen, T., 357
Cherney, I., 329
Chertok, I., 89
Chess, S., 297, 298
Chick, C. F., 196
Chien, S., 117
Childers, J., 49
Chisholm, J., 372
Chiu, C., 231, 308
Chiu, M., 436
Chomsky, N., 230
Choy, C. M., 90
Christakis, D., 370, 427
Christine, J., 220
Christoff, K., 30
Chuang, S., 402
Ciani, A., 74
Ciarrochi, J., 338
Cicchetti, D., 412
Cillessen, A. N., 394

Cina, V., 66
Claire, B., 293
Clark, R., 278
Clarke-Stewart, K., 422
Claxton, L., 136
Clay, 428
Clearfield, M., 328
Closson, L., 395
Coats, E. J., 387
Cohen, L., 41, 117, 192
Cohen, L. B., 205
Cokley, K., 436
Colburne, K., 328
Colby, A., 360
Cole, C. F., 426
Cole, D. A., 312
Cole, M., 84
Cole, P., 367
Cole, P. M., 279
Cole, S. A., 276
Colella, D., 152
Coleman, S., 8
Colen, C., 344
Coles, 340
Coles, C., 88
Coley, R. L., 422
Coll, C., 315, 442
College Board, 435
Collins, A., 84
Collins, T. J., 279
Collins, W., 338
Collins, W. A., 400
Colom, R., 40
Colombo, J., 119
Coltrane, S., 328
Colwell, M., 383
Committee to Study Prevention of Low Birthweight, 109
Common Sense Media, 425
Compton, R., 131
Compton, S., 149
Condry, J., 328
Condry, S., 328
Conger, R., 356
Conner, K., 293
Conner, K. R., 293
Connolly, J. A., 338
Connor, C. M., 431
Conroy, S., 87
Consolacion, T., 343
Cook, E., 396
Cooper, H., 432
Corballis, M. C., 138
Corballis, P., 131
Corbett, M., 155
Corcoran, J., 344
Corcos, E., 148
Cordón, I. M., 201
Corenblum, B. B., 316
Cornew, L., 285
Cornish, K., 64
Cornock, 388
Cornwell, T., 151
Corsaro, W., 330
Corwyn, R., 15
Costello, E., 149
Costigan, K. A., 84
Côté, J., 25
Côté, J. E., 7
Cote, L., 223
Cotugo, G. G., 61
Courage, M. L., 200
Couture, G., 412
Couzin, J., 85
Cowan, N., 202
Cox, C., 83

Craig, C., 412
Cramer, M., 113
Cratty, B., 130, 136
Craven, R., 307
Crawford, D., 153
Crawford, M., 329
Crawley, A., 426
Crick, N., 367
Crick, N. R., 382
Crockenberg, S., 280
Crocker, 319
Crocker, J., 319
Crockett, L. J., 321
Croizet, J., 197
Cross, T., 266
Crossman, A., 211
Crouter, A. C., 400
Crowl, A., 407
Cuevas, K., 200
Curl, M. N., 100
Curley, J. P., 14
Curtis, D., 63
Cyna, A., 101

D

Daddis, C., 402
Dailard, C., 341
Daltabuit, M., 17
Dalton, T. C., 130
Damon, W., 386
Daniel, E., 315
Daniel, S., 293
Daniels, M., 74
Danner, F., 426
Danoff-Burg, 365
Dare, W. N., 90
Dariotis, J., 335
Darling, C. A., 341
Darrin Jenkins/Alamy, 213
Darroch, J. E., 341, 344
Das, A., 341
Dasen, P., 402
Daum, M. M., 136
Davenport, B., 367
Davidov, B. J., 443
Davidson, A. L., 396
Davidson, D. H., 423
Davidson, J. K., 341
Davidson, R. J., 285, 289
Davies, P. G., 197
Davies, P. T., 405
Davis, A., 64, 406
Davis, C., 198
Davis, C. L., 153
Davis, K., 428
Davis, L., 321
Davis, S. K., 255
Davis-Kean, P. E., 317
Davison, G. C., 343
Dawson, G., 286
Dean, R., 131
Dearing, E., 422
Deary, I., 249
Deater-Deckard, K., 15
DeCasper, 120
DeCasper, A., 82
DeCasper, A. J., 145
de Castro, B., 370
Deccache, 389
Decety, J., 354
De Clercq, A., 195
Declercq, E., 101
DeFrancisco, B., 200
De Gelder, B., 147
de Geus, E., 262
de Haan, M., 144

Dehaene-Lambertz, G., 230
DeHart, T., 320
de Jong, P. J., 318
Dekovic, M., 357
DeLamater, J. D., 341
De Leon, J., 226
DeLisi, L., 63
Delva, J., 153
Delville, 374
Demers, R. A., 220
Deng, C., 203
Denmark, F. L., 12
Dennis, J. G., 434
Dennis, T. A., 279, 308
Dent, A. L., 432
Department for Education and Skills, England, 196
DePaulo, 364
De Pauw, S. W., 70
Dernetz, V., 277
de Rosnay, M., 288
Derryberry, D., 296
Dervic, K., 293
Desjardins, R., 236
Desoete, A., 195, 214
de St. Aubin, E., 25
Dettmers, S., 432
DeVader, S. R., 106
Deveny, K., 330
Devlin, B., 74
deVries, M. W., 298
DeVries, R., 112
Dey, A. N., 154
Diamantopoulou, S., 319
Diamond, L., 343
Diaz, 113
Diego, M., 90, 99, 109, 146
Diener, M., 278
Dietz, W. H., 149
DiGiuseppe, R., 292
Dildy, G. A., 86
Dimino, J., 264
DiPietro, 87
DiPietro, J. A., 82, 84
Dishion, 441
Dishion, T., 401
Dissanayake, C., 307
Dittmann, M., 9
Dittmar, 428
Dittrich, R., 84
Dix, T., 288
Dixon, R. A., 12
Dixon, W. E., Jr., 231
Dmitrieva, J., 402
Dobson, V., 117
DocuTicker, 16
Dodge, K. A., 285, 357, 370, 389, 392
Dodson, C., 203
Dolan, 291
Dollar, J. M., 389
Domenech-Rodriguez, M., 407
Dominguez, H. D., 118
Domsch, H., 258
Donat, D., 211
Dondi, M., 117
Donleavy, G., 363
Donnellan, 318
Donnellan, M., 338
Donnellan, M. B., 312
Donnerstein, E., 370
Dorham, 441
Dornbusch, S., 357
Dornbusch, S. M., 393
Dougherty, M. R., 195, 290
Douglas, D., 413
Douglas-Hall, 150

Douglass, R., 150
Dove, H., 17
Dovidio, 445
Dowling, N., 428
Dowsett, C., 422
Doyle, R., 108
Dozier, M., 277
Drake, H. M., 211
Drew, L., 407
Driscoll, A. K., 321
Dromi, E., 223
Drouin, M., 339
Dryfoos, J. G., 402
Dubeau, D., 278
DuBois, D. L., 393
Dubois, J., 230
DuBreuil, S. C., 201
Duckett, E., 402, 403
Dudding, T. C., 97
Dudenhausen, J. W., 106
Duenwald, M., 83
Duerenberg, 129
Duerenberg-Yap, 129
Dumka, L., 6
Duncan, G. J., 112, 150, 260, 424
Dunkel, C. S., 314
Dunn, J., 322
Durant, J. E., 411
Durrant, R., 34
Dutta, T., 138
Dwairy, M., 357
D'Warte, J., 227
Dweck, C., 307
Dyer, S., 383
Dynda, A. M., 259
Dyson, A. H., 41
Dziurgot, T., 383

E

Eagly, A. H., 333
Earle, J., 341
East, P., 345
Easterbrooks, M., 278
Easton, J., 34
Ebbeck, V., 322
Eccles, J., 433
Eckerman, C. O., 120
Eckerman, G., 281
Edgerley, L., 113
Edison, S. C., 200
Edwards, C. P., 330, 335, 365, 383
Edwards, S., 32
Egeland, B., 277
Eggermont, S., 428
Eggum, 309
Eichstedt, J., 329, 330
Eid, M., 281
Eiden, R., 88
Eifert, G. H., 83
Eigsti, I., 412
Eikerman, C. O., 120
Eimas, P. D., 144
Einarson, A., 87
Eisbach, A. O., 289
Eisenberg, 291, 364
Eisenberg, N., 289, 290, 354, 355, 357, 389
Eisenbraun, K., 372
Eivers, A., 382
Elder, G. H., Jr., 312
Eley, T., 292
Elkana, O., 131
Elkind, D., 148, 195, 196, 424
Ellemers, N., 445
Elliot, E., 202
Elliott, K., 412

Ellis, 139
Ellis, B., 34
Ellis, L., 138, 307, 332
Ellis, S., 206
Ellison, C., 75
Ellman, L., 77
Elman, J., 30
Elmore, A., 406
Ely, R., 236
Endo, S., 281
Endocrine Society, 140
Engels, R., 391
Engh, T., 138
Engström, I., 16
Ennett, S. T., 393
Erdley, C. A., 386
Erikson, E. H., 25, 299, 312
Erlandsson, K., 108
Ertmer, D., 222
Ertmer, D. J., 144
Escott, D., 102
Eshel, N., 131
Espelage, D. L., 375
Espenschade, A., 135
Espinoza, G., 374
Estell, D. B., 336
Estudillo, A. G., 436
Ethier, L., 412
Evans, C., 112
Evans, G. W., 368, 383, 408, 410
Evans, J. J., 99
Eveleth, P., 139
Evenson, R., 90
Everett, K. D., 89

F

Fabes, R., 290, 330, 355
Fabes, R. A., 355, 373
Fagan, J., 258, 260
Fagan, M., 49
Falck-Ytter, 282
Falk, D., 236
Fane, B. A., 88
Fantz, R., 143
Farah, M., 237
Farmer, T. W., 395
Farroni, T., 118, 287
Farver, J. M., 368, 384, 385
Fasano, C., 255
Fawcett, A., 251
Feigenson, L., 200
Feiring, C., 277
Feldman, 394
Feldman, J., 213, 258
Feldman, J. F., 259
Feldman, R., 8, 108
Feldman, R. S., 290, 367, 387
Feldman, S. S., 400
Feldstein, S., 277
Fellmann, F., 66
Felson, R. B., 307
Feng, A., 49
Fenwick, J., 97
Fenwick, K., 144
Ferguson, D. L., 393
Ferguson, L., 396
Fergusson, D. M., 84
Fernald, A., 117, 144, 224, 289
Fernald, L., 150
Fernandez, L. C., 12
Fernández-Ballart, J. D., 298
Feshbach, S., 39
Festinger, L., 322
Fetchenhauer, D., 374
Fetterman, D. M., 428
Field, M. J., 155

Field, N., 365
Field, T., 9, 108, 109, 120, 146
Field, T. M., 120
Fifer, W. P., 145
Fine, M. A., 404, 405, 406
Finkelstein, D. I., 103
Finkelstein, Y., 88
Finn-Stevenson, M., 15, 149, 150
Fisch, S. M., 427
Fischer, A., 6
Fischer, K., 30
Fischer, K. W., 132
Fischer, N., 277
Fischer, T., 405
Fish, J. M., 8, 260
Fisher, C., 97
Fisher, C. B., 47, 51
Fiske, 441
Fitch, W., 230
Fitzgerald, D., 289
Fitzgerald, H., 46
Fitzgerald, P., 343
Flanagan, C., 405
Flanagan, D. P., 252
Flannery, D., 196
Flavell, J. H., 13
Fleer, M., 383
Fleischhaker, W., 63
Fletcher, 120
Fletcher, A. C., 375
Fletcher, R., 138
Flint, J., 75
Flom, R., 147, 286, 329
Floyd, R. G., 252
Flynn, E., 289
Foehr, 427, 428
Fogarty, R., 254
Fogel, A., 112, 286
Fok, M. S., 109
Food and Drug Administration, 346
Foote, A., 88
Ford, D. Y., 261
Ford, R. M., 289
Forrest, 394
Forsyth, 319
Foster, P., 128
Fowers, B. J., 443
Fowler, 228
Fraley, R. C., 277
Frankenburg, W. K., 134
Franko, D. L., 152
Fransen, M., 66
Fraser, C., 224
Frawley, T., 333
Frayling, T., 73
Frazier, L. M., 83
Frederickson, N., 436
Freeman, J. M., 111
Fremouw, W. J., 374
Freud, S., 343, 367
Frey, K. S., 372
Frick, J., 287
Frick, P. J., 375
Friederici, A., 287
Friedlander, L. J., 338
Friedman, 428
Friedman, D. E., 420, 424
Friedman, R., 442
Friedman, S., 113
Friedrich, M., 16
Friel, L. V., 407
Frierson, H. T., 308, 332
Frieze, I., 333
Friston, J. J., 282
Frith, C. D., 282
Fritz, C., 204

Fritz, J. J., 46
Froh, J., 292
Frye, D., 289
Fu, G., 361
Fujioka, T., 143
Fulcher, A., 101
Fuligni, A., 321, 399
Fuligni, A. J., 321, 400
Fuligni, A. S., 321
Furman, W., 338, 398, 401

G

Gabdois, 388
Gabelko, N., 267
Gage, J. D., 89
Gagné, M. H., 16, 411
Gagnon, S. G., 257
Galambos, N., 292
Galea, S., 9
Galinsky, E., 398
Gallagher, J. J., 266
Gallagher, K., 15
Gallaty, K. J., 338
Gallistel, C., 201
Gamino, J. F., 213
Gándara, 447
Gandour, J., 235
Gao, D., 153
Garabedian, M. J., 114
Garcia, C., 32, 447
Gardner, 289
Gardner, H., 138, 252, 253
Gardner, M. K., 254
Garrity, K., 120
Garry, M., 201
Gartstein, 298
Gaspar De Alba, M., 65
Gault, B., 432
Gavin, L. A., 401
Gazmarian, J. A., 90
Geary, D. C., 251
Geesey, 113
Gelles, R. J., 410, 411
Gelman, R., 201
Gelman, S., 154, 289
Gelman, S. A., 331
Gendall, P., 27
Genovese, J., 29
George, J. B. E., 152
Gerber, M., 239
Geronimus, A., 344
Gerressu, M., 341
Gershkoff-Stowe, L., 225
Gershoff, E., 357, 411
Gersten, R., 264
Gertler, P., 113
Gervain, J., 144
Gesell, A. L., 257
Geuze, R. H., 132
Ghetti, S., 203
Ghimire, D. J., 339
Ghule, M., 342
Giami, A., 345
Gibb, R., 131
Gibbons, F., 322
Gibbs, N., 86
Gibson, E. J., 142
Gifford-Smith, M., 386
Gilbert, L. A., 403
Gilbert, S., 293
Gilbert-MacLeod, C., 146
Giles-Sims, J., 357
Gillath, O., 279
Gillespie, N. A., 75
Gillham, J., 293
Gilligan, C., 313, 362

Gilmore, 201
Gingras, B., 254
Ginsberg, S., 195, 196
Ginsburg, K. R., 383
Giordano, P., 338
Gjelsvik, A., 155
Gleason, 236
Gleason, J., 236
Gleason, J. B., 236
Gleick, E., 344
Gleitman, L ., 232
Gleitman, L .R., 230
Glenberg, A. M., 426
Glick, 445
Gliga, T., 143
Glover, K., 329
Glynn, L. M., 13, 85
Goede, I., 399
Goetz, A., 34
Goggins, W., 102
Goldberg, A. B., 426
Goldberg, A. E., 231, 407
Goldfarb, Z., 103
Goldfield, G. S., 153
Goldin-Meadow, S., 222
Goldschmidt, L., 88
Goldsmith, L. T., 41
Goldstein, L., 221
Goldstein, T. R., 354
Goldston, D., 293
Goldweber, A., 367, 375
Goleman, D., 255
Golomb, C., 138
Golombok, S., 343, 407
González, 447
Good, C., 197
Goodman, 114
Goodman, G., 210
Goodman, G. S., 202, 210
Goodman, S. H., 87
Goodson, B. D., 422
Goodwin, M. H., 336
Gopnik, A., 281
Gormley, W. T., Jr., 424
Gottesman, I. I., 77
Gottfried, A., 403
Goulandris, N., 227
Gould, 249
Gould, M., 293
Gould, S. J., 115
Goyette-Ewing, M., 404
Grabe, S., 365
Gracia, 15
Graddol, D., 238
Grady, J., 70
Graham, L., 97
Graham, S., 46
Grall, T. S., 398
Grammer, J. K., 203
Granic, I., 401
Grant, A. M., 67
Grantham-McGregor, S., 150
Grattan, M. P., 132
Gray-Little, B., 321
Gredebäck, G., 283
Green, 434
Green, K., 314
Greenberg, J., 15, 421
Greenberger, E., 402
Greene, J. D., 360
Greene, K., 195
Greene, S., 406
Greenfield, D. B., 237
Greenwood, D. N., 151
Greenwood, J., 405
Gregory, K., 149

Gregory, S., 341
Grela, B., 225
Gresham, D., 290
Griffith, D. R., 88
Grigorenko, E. L., 74, 251
Groh, 7
Grønhøj, A., 401
Grosse, S. D., 67
Grossmann, T., 287
Gruber, A., 152
Grunau, 118
Grunbaum, J. A., 293
Grusec, J., 320, 354
Grusec, J. E., 27
Grych, J. H., 278
Guadalupe, K. L., 406
Guasti, M. T., 226
Guerra, N. F., 408
Guerrero, A., 436
Guerrini, L., 86
Guevara, M., 131
Guinote, 441
Guinsburg, R., 329
Gulcher, M., 407
Gullone, E., 290
Gullotta, T. P., 312, 411
Gump, L. S., 362
Gunter, B., 333
Guoliang, Y., 290
Gupta, A., 63
Gupta, R., 424
Gurewitsch, E. D., 84
Guricci, 129
Gurin, P., 442
Gurling, H., 86
Gustavsson, N. S., 48
Gutek, G. L., 421
Guthrie, C., 153
Gutman, 443
Guttmacher, Institute, 341, 344
Guttmann, J., 405
Guzman, R., 211

H

Haack, Y., 97
Hack, M., 108
Haddock, S., 403
Haeffel, J., 63
Hafdahl, A. R., 321
Hagen, J. W., 357
Hagerman, R., 64
Hagerman, R. J., 64
Hahn, E., 225
Haight, B. K., 142
Haith, M. M., 206
Halberda, J., 200
Halford, G., 385
Halgunseth, L. C., 407
Hall, E., 115, 305, 385
Hall, G. S., 12
Hall, J., 131
Halpern, D. F., 213
Hamilton, 344
Hamilton, B. E., 110
Hammer, C. S., 89
Hammer, T. J., 362
Hamon, R. R., 339
Han, W., 239
Hancox, 428
Hane, A., 277
Hankin, B. L., 293
Hannon, E., 144
Hannon, E. E., 234, 235
Hansen-Tift, A. M., 144, 220
Hanson, D. R., 77
Happ, 394

Harakeh, Z., 396
Harden, K., 261
Harder, J., 197
Harding, R., 99
Hare, M., 204
Hare, T., 131
Hargreaves, D., 152
Harlow, H. F., 275
Harnish, R. M., 220
Harper, D. A., 103
Harris, 13
Harris, J., 75
Harris, J. R., 321, 386
Harris, M., 139
Harris, R., 16, 370
Harrison, K., 152
Harrist, A., 279
Hart, B., 40, 236, 237
Hart, C. H., 285, 357
Hart, D., 360, 386
Hart, S., 285
Hart, S. L., 285
Hart, T. A., 343
Harter, S., 317, 320
Hartmann, D. P., 387
Hartmann, H., 86
Hartshorne, J., 236
Harvey, E., 403
Harvey, J. H., 404, 405, 406
Harwood, R. L., 357
Haslam, C., 89
Haslam, S., 445
Hastings, P. D., 354
Hastings, S., 254
Hattie, J., 138
Hatton, 261
Hau, K. T., 309, 322
Haugaard, J. J., 410
Hauser, M., 230
Haverkock, A., 298
Hawker, 374
Hawkins, A. O., 411
Hawkins-Rodgers, Y., 409
Hawley, 394
Hay, D., 382
Hayashi, 205
Hayden, R. G., 213
Hayes, S., 152
Hayne, H., 200, 201
Haynie, D. L., 374
Hazlett, H., 65
He, X., 232
He, Y., 25
Head, D., 427
Health eLine, 27
Heatherton, T., 322
Heaven, P., 338
Hedgepeth, E., 360
Heerey, E. A., 289
Heikkilä, K., 97
Heimann, M., 13, 120, 200, 201
Helmsen, J., 367
Hempel, 392
Heneghan, A., 113
Henig, 384
Henricsson, L., 319
Henriksen, 428
Henry, B., 375
Henry, K. L., 375
Henson, R., 396
Hernandez, 321
Hernández-Martinez, C., 298
Hernandez-Reif, M., 99, 109, 146, 286
Herrenkohl, T., 410
Herrenkohl, T. I., 16, 410
Herrmann, C. S., 132

Herrnstein, R. J., 74, 260
Hertenstein, M. J., 146, 288
Hertz-Pannier, L., 230
Heterelendy, F., 96
Hetherington, E., 406
Hetherington, E. M., 405
Heward, W. L., 245
Hewitt, B., 412
Hewlett, B., 278
Hewstone, M., 393
Heyes, C., 27
Heyman, R., 412
Hietala, J., 77
Higgins, D., 412
Higgins, D. A., 373
Higgins-D'Alessandro, 364
Higley, E., 277
Hill, N. E., 398
Hill, P. L., 196
Hill, S., 329
Hilliard, A., III, 198
Hindman, D. W., 48
Hine, D., 251
Hines, M., 88, 117
Hinshaw, S. P., 207
Hirsch, B. J., 393
Hirvonen, J., 77
Hiser, E., 132
Hitlin, S., 312
Hjelmstedt, A., 84
Hocutt, A. M., 264
Hoek, J., 27
Hoelterk, L. F., 339
Hoerr, S., 153
Hoersting, R. C., 317
Hoeve, M., 375
Hofer, M. A., 275
Hoff, E., 239
Hofferth, S., 404
Hofferth, S. L., 403, 404
Hoffman, 355
Hoffman, J., 339
Hoffman, L., 388
Holden, 374
Holden, G. W., 357
Holland, C., 258, 260
Hollenstein, T., 401
Hollich, G. J., 223
Hollingworth, H. L., 12
Hollingworth, L., 211
Holmbeck, G., 402
Holmes, D., 27
Holmes, D. L., 206
Holowaka, S., 131
Holt, L., 131
Holt, M. K., 375
Homae, F., 145, 223
Hong, S., 411
Hong, S. B., 421
Hooda, D., 356
Hooks, B., 14
Hooper, S. R., 65
Hoover-Dempsey, 434
Hopkins-Golightly, T., 99
Horn, A. R., 120
Horn, E., 345
Horn, T. S., 322
Hornor, 277
Horwitz, B. N., 74
Horwood, L., 84
Hossain, 89
Hotelling, B. A., 100
Hou, Y., 202
House, S. H., 130
Howe, M. J., 266
Howe, M. L., 200, 201

Howes, C., 398
Howes, O., 77
Howieson, N., 277
Howley, A., 428
Howsen, R. M., 322
Hoyme, H., 265
Hsu, C., 110
Hsu, V., 200
Hubel, D. H., 143
Huber, L., 445
Hubner, J. J., 310
Hudley, C., 393, 440
Huganir, 205
Hughes, J., 139
Hughes, P., 112
Hughes-Lynch, C. E., 264
Hughes-Scholes, C. H., 210
Hui, A., 322
Huijbregts, S., 8
Huiton, C. F., 67
Huizink, A., 86
Hulei, E., 357
Human Genome Project, 67, 68
Humenick, S. S., 100
Hummel, P., 146
Humphrey, N., 255
Humphries, C., 87
Humphry, R., 383
Hungi, N., 203
Hunnius, S., 284
Hunt, 439
Hunt, M., 37, 341
Hunter, J., 343
Hunter Smart, J. E., 388
Hurst, A., 73
Hust, S., 333
Huster, R. J., 132
Huston, A. C., 426
Hutchinson, D., 392
Hutton, P. H., 11
Huurre, T., 405
Hyde, 341
Hyde, J., 293, 365
Hyde, J. S., 341
Hyman, S. E., 63

I

Ialongo, N., 367
Ickovics, J., 86
Ijzendoorn, M., 279
Iles, J., 114
Illingworth, R. S., 133
Ingoldsby, B. B., 339
Ingraham, E., 101
Insel, B., 293
International Cesarean Awareness Network, 111
International Human Genome Sequencing Consortium, 58, 63
International Literacy Institute, 430
Inzlicht, M., 197
Ip, W., 102
Ireland, J. L., 374
Irving, M., 393, 440
Isaacs, K., 131
Isenberg, 434
Ishi-Kuntz, M., 407
Ispa, J. M., 407
Israel, E., 155
Iverson, P., 145
Izard, C., 424
Izard, C. E., 283, 290
Izard, J., 284
Izawa, C., 213

Jack, F., 201
Jackson, P. L., 354
Jacobs, S., 357
James, J., 140
James, W., 141
Janca, A., 9
Jang, K., 75
Jankowiak, W., 41
Jankowski, J., 213, 258
Jankowski, J. J., 259
Janssens, J. M. A. M., 357
Jared, D., 239
Jaswal, V., 203
Jelicic, H., 309
Jenkins, S., 317
Jensen, A. R., 74
Jensen, B., 321
Jensen, L., 316
Jeynes, W., 406
Ji, 87
Jia, F., 360
Jimenez, J., 211
Jimerson, S., 371
Jirtle, R. L., 73
Joe, S., 293
Joel, D., 82
Johnson, A. M., 342
Johnson, D., 155
Johnson, D. J., 423
Johnson, S., 286
Johnston, L., 153
Joiner, A., 41
Jokela, M., 237
Jolley, D. D., 130
Jones, B., 198
Jones, F., 120
Jones, H. E., 88, 120
Jones, M. H., 312
Jones, S. M., 424
Jones-Harden, B., 408
Jordan, A., 426
Jorgensen, G., 363
Josefsson, A., 111
Joseph, H., 293
Joshi, B., 342
Jost, 445
Joy, E. A., 90
Juby, H., 405
Jung, J., 144, 152
Junkkari, H., 405
Jurimae, T., 135
Juvonen, J., 374, 433

K

Kabir, A. A., 111
Kagan, J., 70, 76, 286, 296, 299
Kahana-Kalman, R., 287
Kail, R., 194, 195
Kaiser, L. L., 86
Kalb, C., 83, 154
Kaltiala-Heino, R., 139
Kamm, M. A., 97
Kan, P., 225
Kandler, C., 75
Kang, H., 436
Kantrowitz, E. J., 383
Kao, G., 321
Kapadia, S., 402
Kaplan, H., 17
Kaplan, S., 207
Kapur, S., 77
Karnilowicz, W., 399
Karniol, R., 333
Karp, S. M., 86
Karraker, K., 70

Karremans, J. C., 394
Kärtner, J., 9, 365
Kashima, Y., 307
Kassuba, T., 279
Kato, K., 15
Katulak, N., 255
Katzer, C., 374
Katzman, D., 339
Kaufman, J. C., 249
Kaufman, S., 249
Kaufmann, D., 357
Kauh, T., 335
Kautz, K. J., 207
Kawabata, Y., 382
Kayton, A., 103
Kazdin, A. E., 411
Kazura, K., 278
Kearsley, R., 286
Keast, D., 153
Keating, D., 14
Keck-Wherley, J., 64
Kecskes, I., 239
Keeler, G., 149
Keen, M., 136
Kelch-Oliver, K., 406
Keller, H., 307, 365
Kelley, K., 15
Kellman, P., 143
Kellogg, 138
Kellow, J., 198
Kelly, G., 340
Kelly, J., 278, 405
Kelly, M., 371
Kelly-Vance, L., 329
Kelly-Weeder, S., 83
Keltner, D., 289
Kemper, A. R., 103
Kennell, J. H., 104
Kerns, K., 278
Kerr, 319
Kerr, M., 391
Kershaw, T., 86
Kerstetter, D., 329
Kessler, T., 447
Khalkhali, S., 204
Khan, S., 138
Khatib, C., 41
Kidd, E., 225
Kiefer, S. M., 312
Kiel, E. J., 284, 287
Kieras, J., 289
Kiernan, M., 252
Kiesner, J., 385
Killen, M., 364
Kilner, J. M., 282
Kim, 114, 439
Kim, E., 411
Kim, J. K., 314
Kim, T. C., 25
Kim, Y. K., 385
Kimball, J. W., 63
Kinney, H. C., 85
Kinsey, A. C., 343
Kirby, D., 345
Kirby, J., 406
Kirchengast, S., 86
Kirsh, S. J., 39, 370
Kisilevsky, B., 145
Kitamura, C., 234
Kiuru, N., 392
Klebanov, P. K., 260
Klemencic, N., 155
Klier, C. M., 114
Kloep, M., 9
Klute, C., 392
Knafo, A., 401

Knickmeyer, R., 82, 331
Knight, 319, 407
Knight, G. P., 373
Knight, K. E., 375
Knorth, E., 409
Knowles, 346
Knowlton, B. J., 204
Knutson, J., 367
Kobayashi, J., 132
Kochanska, 279
Kochanska, G., 280, 287, 296, 329
Koehoorn, M., 139
Koenig, A., 412
Koenig, L. B., 75
Koffman, O., 345
Koglin, U., 367
Kohlberg, L., 333, 360, 361
Kohn, A., 432
Kohnert, K., 225
Kohut, 146
Kolata, G., 83
Kolb, B., 131, 384
Kontos, S., 398
Koren, G., 88
Koshmanova, T., 33
Kossowsky, J., 286
Kosunen, E., 139
Kotaska, A., 111
Kotler, J. A., 333
Kotre, J., 115, 305, 385
Kovelman, I., 239
Kozey, M., 251
Kraebel, K. S., 118
Kramer, M. S., 86
Kratochvil, C. J., 207
Krcmar, M., 195, 225
Kremen, W. S., 77
Krettenauer, T., 360
Kreutzer, J. C., 46
Kristjansdottir, G., 135
Kroger, J., 313, 314
Krohn, M. D., 375
Kronholz, J., 424
Krosnick, J. A., 425
Krowitz, A., 142
Kruk, R. S., 148
Krulewitch, L., 111
Kuczynski, L., 329
Kuhl, 235, 236
Kuhl, P., 144
Kuhl, P. K., 144, 221
Kuhn, D., 195
Kumar, A., 356
Kuo, L., 238
Kupersmidt, J. B., 392
Kuther, 364
Kuvalanka, K. A., 407
Kwan, L., 231
Kwon, K., 388

L

Lacerda, F., 201
Lacharite, C., 412
LaFreniere, P., 373
Laible, D., 298
Lall, M., 345
Lally, C., 278
Lam, 447
Lam, C., 234
Lam, M., 400
Lam, V., 330
Lamaze, F., 100
Lamb, M., 278
Lamb, M. E., 221, 279
Lamb, V. L., 423
Lambert, W. W., 372

Lamborn, 7
Lamkin, D., 204
Lamprecht, M., 317
Land, K. C., 423
Landgraff, C., 339
Landhuis, C., 153
Lane, D., 322
Lang, 447
Lang, A., 89
Langer, A., 142
Langille, D., 86
Langlois, J. H., 143
Lansford, J., 6, 405
Lansford, J. E., 389
Lansu, T. M., 394
Lantos, J. D., 103
La Prairie, 118
Lapsley, B., 196
Lapsley, D. K., 196
Larocque, M., 153
Larsen, K. E., 100
Larson, J., 371
Larson, R. W., 401, 402
Lau, M., 339
Laugharne, J., 9
Laursen, B., 391
Lavzer, J. I., 422
Lawlor, 428
Lawrence, W., 89
Lawson, K. R., 206
Lawson, M. J., 203
Leach, P., 422
Leadbetter, B., 292
Leaper, C., 236, 333
Lease, A., 388
Leathers, H. D., 128
Leavell, A., 278
Le Corre, M., 201
Lee, 433
Lee, B. R., 408
Lee, E., 336
Lee, M., 338
Lee, R. M., 321
Lee, V. E., 433
Leerkes, E., 280
Lee-Shin, Y., 384, 385
Legerstee, M., 120, 307
Lehman, D., 308
Lehman, M., 144
Leman, P., 330
Lemerise, E. A., 285
L'Engle, K., 333
Lenhart, A., 339
Leonard, L. B., 235
Leonard, T., 358
Lepage, J., 282
Lerner, 15
Lerner, J. V., 388
Lerner, R. M., 12, 47, 309, 317
Letendre, J., 373
Leung, A., 231
Leung, C., 399
LeVay, S., 343
Levin, J. R., 203
Levin, R., 341
Levine, R., 236
Levine, S. C., 329
Levitt, A., 221
Levy, T., 293
Lewis, J., 30
Lewis, M., 277, 283, 307, 329
Lewkowicz, D. J., 144, 147, 220
Lew-Williams, C., 223
Leyens, J. P., 43, 44
Li, 89, 155
Li, C., 292

Li, J., 48
Li, M., 34
Li, Q., 374
Liang, H., 292
Liblik, R., 135
Lichtenberg, P. A., 46
Lidz, J., 230
Liew, J., 289
Lightman, S. L., 99
Lin, H., 110
Lin, K., 225
Linder, 154
Lindsay, A., 153
Lindsey, E., 383
Linebarger, D. L., 427
Lines, P. M., 434
Ling, R., 339
Lipnevich, A. A., 252
Lipsitt, L. P., 145
Litovsky, R. Y., 144
Little, R. E., 109
Liu, H-M., 221
Liu, J., 110
Livingston, 445
Lluis-Font, J. M., 40
LoBue, V., 353
Lochman, J. E., 371
Lockhart, C., 357
Loehlin, J., 261
Loehlin, J. C., 358
Loewen, S., 30
Loftus, E. F., 201, 210
Logel, C., 197
Lohaus, A., 258
Lohman, D., 266
Lohman, D. F., 252
London, 211
London, B., 360
Longmore, M., 338
Lopez, G. F., 442
Lopez, M. F., 118
Lorenz, K., 99, 275, 367
Losonczy-Marshall, M., 329
Lothian, J., 100
Loui, 254
Love, A., 383
Love, J., 424
LoVullo, S., 27
Lu, M. C., 101
Lu, X., 315
Lubinski, D., 252, 267
Lucas, S. R., 393
Lucente, R. L., 312
Luke, 108
Luminet, 389
Luna, B., 131
Luong, G., 74
Lupien, S. P., 319
Lushnikova, I., 99
Lutenbacher, M., 86
Luthar, S., 395
Lutzker, J., 413
Luyten, P., 288
Lynam, D. R., 375
Lynch, M. E., 89
Lyndsay, 106
Lynn, R., 257
Lynskey, M., 72
Lyon, M. E., 293
Lyons, M. J., 77
Lyons, N. P., 362

M

Maas, C., 16, 410
Mabbott, D. J., 132

Maccoby, E. E., 355, 356
MacDonald, H., 276
MacDorman, 108
MacDorman, M., 101, 111
MacDorman, M. F., 112
MacEachron, A. E., 48
MacEvoy, J., 335
MacInnes, K., 155
MacKenzie, M. J., 411
MacPhee, M., 27, 46
Maier, M. F., 237
Maital, S., 223
Makariev, D., 298
Malla, A. K., 77
Maller, S., 260
Malling, H. V., 64, 65
Mallon, G. P., 343
Mameli, M., 84
Mandal, M., 138
Mandelman, S. D., 74
Mani, N., 9
Manlove, J., 345
Mann, C. C., 151
Mann, T., 48
Manning, M., 265
Manning, W., 338
Marceau, K., 292
March, J. S., 207
Marchant, M., 358
Marcia, J. E., 313, 314
Marcus, S., 293
Marentette, P. F., 222
Marin, M. M., 254
Marinova-Todd, S. H., 239
Markova, G., 120
Marks, A. K., 315, 442
Marlier, L., 145
Marquis, A., 118
Marron, M., 266
Marschik, P., 137
Marsh, H., 307, 309, 322
Marsh, H. W., 309, 322
Marsland, K., 423
Marti-Henneberg, C., 139
Martin, 261
Martin, C., 330
Martin, C. E., 343
Martin, C. L., 329, 330, 332, 333
Martin, G., 293
Martin, J. A., 59, 355, 356
Martin, L., 89
Martin, M. H., 25
Martin, S., 90
Martineau, J., 282
Martins, N., 39
Martiny, S. E., 447
Martorell, G. A., 411
Masalha, S., 8
Masataka, N., 144, 223, 224, 235
Masho, S. W., 112
Masling, J. M., 23
Massaro, A., 90
Masten, A., 296
Mathews, 108
Mathews, G., 331
Mathews, T. J., 101
Maton, K., 48
Matson, J., 27
Matsuda, Y., 234
Matsumoto, A., 132
Matsumoto, D., 9
Mattes, E., 87
Matthews, G., 254, 255
Mattison, R. E., 251
Mattson, S., 89
Mauritzson, U., 385

May, P. A., 89
Mayer, L., 406
Mayer, M. M., 137
Mayer, R. E., 192
Mayes, L., 88
Mayes, R., 207
Mayes, S., 251
Maynard, A., 195
Mayseless, O., 276
Mazzocco, M., 65
McAdams, D. P., 25
McAlister, A. R., 151
McBride-Chang, C., 436
McCabe, M., 412
McCardle, P., 239
McCartney, K., 422
McCarty, R., 136
McCord, J., 412
McCowan, L., 89
McCrae, R. R., 70, 296
McCrink, K., 194
McCullough, M. E., 49
McCutcheon-Rosegg, S., 101
McDonald, L., 29
McDonnell, L. M., 431
McDonough, L., 224
McDowell, D., 386
McDowell, M., 139
McElhaney, K., 395
McElwain, N., 277
McGadney-Douglass, B., 150
McGinn, D., 427
McGrew, K. S., 252
McGue, M., 74
McGuffin, P., 64
McGuire, J., 343
McHale, S., 335
McHale, S. M., 400
McKinney, R., 343
McKown, C., 308
McLean, K., 338
McLennan, 389
McLoyd, 411, 443
McLoyd, V., 444
McLoyd, V. C., 407
McMahon, S. D., 372
McMillan, M. M., 308, 332
McMurray, B., 223
McRae, K., 204, 291
McWilliams, N., 25
Mead, M., 441
Meade, C., 86
Mealey, L., 329
Meckstroth, E., 266
Meertens, R., 66
Meeus, W., 399
Mehta, C. M., 335
Meins, E., 276
Meisinger, E., 388
Melinder, A., 210
Melnyk, L., 211
Meltzoff, A., 281
Meltzoff, A. N., 28, 120, 239, 281
Melzer, D., 73
MeMarini, D. M., 64, 65
Menacker, F., 110
Mendoza, C., 266
Meng, Z., 284
Menlove, F. L., 27
Mennella, J., 145
Mercer, J. R., 261
Meritesacker, B., 298
Merkus, P. M., 155
Mertesacker, B., 298
Mervielde, I., 70
Mervis, J., 48

Messer, D., 426
Messer, S. B., 25
Messinger, D. S., 279
Mester, R., 293
Metzger, A., 70
Mezey, G., 90
Mezulis, A., 293
Miao, X., 203, 398
Michael, R. T., 341
Mickelson, K. D., 328
Miesnik, S., 111
Mikulincer, M., 276
Miles, R., 99, 107
Milevsky, A., 320
Miller, 30
Miller, C., 195
Miller, E. M., 50
Miller, J. L., 144
Miller, L., 87
Miller, L. E., 370
Miller, M., 207
Miller, N., 373
Miller, P. C., 357
Miller, R., 32
Miller-Perrin, C. L., 412
Milne, 428
Minagawa-Kawai, Y., 220
Minzenberg, M., 30
Mishna, F., 374
Misra, 365
Misri, S., 114
Mitchell, D., 119
Mitchell, P., 289
Mitchell, S., 9
Mittal, V., 77
Miyaki, K., 279
Mizuno, K., 145
Mizuta, I., 279
MMWR, 341
Modern Language Association, 238
Molina, J. C., 89, 118
Monahan, K., 396
Monastra, V., 77
Moneta, G., 383, 402
Monk, 291
Montague, D., 287
Montemayor, R., 312
Montgomery, 440
Moon, C., 119
Moon, M., 278
Moon, S. M., 266
Mooney, C., 104
Moore, G., 70, 299
Moore, K. L., 80, 85
Moore, L., 153
Moore, M. K., 120, 281
Morales, J. R., 408
Moran, K. C., 426
Moran, S., 252
Morano, M., 152
Morbidity and Mortality Weekly
    Report, 341
Morelli, G. A., 8
Morgan, B. E., 120
Morgenthaler, 156
Morice, A., 112
Morikawa, H., 224
Morris, 364
Morris, P., 31, 204
Morrison, F. J., 206, 431
Morrongiello, B., 144, 155
Mosher, 365
Moshman, D., 195
Mosleh, M., 360
Mossakowski, 447
Mottl-Santiago, J., 101

Mourad, N., 143
Moyle, J., 61
Mudar, R., 213
Muenchow, S., 423
Mulder, E., 86
Mulvey, K., 364
Mulvihill, 434
Mumme, D., 289
Munafò, M. R., 75
Munsters, J., 146
Murachver, T., 353
Murashima, M., 153
Murphy, 118, 267
Murphy, B., 389
Murphy, M., 65, 153
Murphy-Erby, Y., 345
Murray, C., 74, 260
Murray, G., 258, 286
Murray, J., 426
Murray, L., 286
Murray, S. J., 27
Murray-Close, D., 367
Musher-Eizenman, D. R., 370
Music, G., 278
Myers, R. H., 67

N

Nadel, S., 30
Nagda, B. A., 442
Nagle, R. J., 257
Nagy, E., 120
Nakagawa, M., 279
Nakato, E., 259, 284
Nangle, D. W., 386
Nanney, M., 153
Nansel, 374
Naoi, N., 234
Nash, A., 426
Nassif, A., 333
National Association for the
    Education of Young Children,
    420
National Center for Children in
    Poverty, 150, 151, 443, 444
National Center for Chronic
    Disease Prevention and Health
    Promotion, 344
National Center for Education
    Statistics, 421, 436
National Center for Health Statistics,
    111, 128
National Governors Association, 433
National Institute of Child Health
    and Human Development Early
    Child Care Research Network,
    422, 424
National Safety Council, 155
National Sleep Foundation, 428
Nazzi, T., 223
NCADC (National Coalition Against
    Domestic Violence), 16
NCB Now, 374
NCS Pearson, Inc., 251
Neal, T., 131
Negy, C., 321
Neiderhiser, J. M., 358
Neisser, U., 200
Nelson, C. A., 82, 144
Nelson, D. A., 357
Nelson, F., 48
Nelson, L., 402
Nelson, N., 328
Nelson, T., 291
Nesheim, S., 87
Newcombe, R., 202

Newman, 374
Newman, J., 431
Newsome, W., 371
Nguyen, S., 331
NICHD Early Child Care Research
    Network, 422
Nickerson, A., 412
Nicklas, T. A., 426
Nicolson, R., 251
Niederhofer, H., 82
Nielsen, M., 307
Nieto, S., 442
Nigg, J. T., 207
Nihart, M. A., 130
Nisbett, 262
Nisbett, R. E., 260
Noakes, M. A., 336
Noble, C. L., 131, 225
Noel, A., 431
Noonan, C., 155
Norgate, S., 72
Norman, R. M. G., 77
Norton, L., 341
Notaro, P., 154
Nyberg, F., 16
Nylen, K., 114
Nyqvist, K., 108

O
Oberg, G., 251
Oberlander, 87
Oberlander, S., 406
O'Connor, M., 90
OECD (Organization for Economic
    Cooperation and Development),
    435, 436
Oehler, J. M., 120
Ogbu, J., 436
Ogden, C. L., 128
O'Grady, W., 220, 223, 225
Oguz, V., 290
Okie, S., 153
Olafsen, 298
Olivardia, R., 152
Oliver, B., 49
Olness, K., 86
Olshansky, S., 64
Olson, 15
Olson, E., 101
Olson, R. K., 367
O'Malley, C., 289
O'Malley, P., 153
Ömeroglu, E., 255
Oretti, R. G., 114
Orlansky, M. D., 245
Ortiz, S. O., 259
Osher, 291
Osofsky, J., 410
Ostrager, B., 339
Ostrosky-Solis, F., 251
Ostrov, J., 367
O'Toole, 372
Ourgrin, D., 293
Outten, H., 321
Owens, E., 77
Oyserman, D., 442
Ozawa, M., 146, 405

P
Padilla-Walker, L., 278
Pagel, J. F., 156
Paige, R., 432
Paisley, T. S., 90
Panagiotides, H., 286
Pandey, S., 410
Panfile, T., 298

Papafragou, A., 232
Papini, D. R., 314
Papousek, 235
Papp, T., 239
Paquette, D., 278
Park, H. P., 239
Park, L. E., 319
Park, M. M., 59
Parke, R., 386
Parke, R. D., 44, 278, 328, 398, 407
Parker, S. T., 28
Parten, M. B., 383
Pascalis, O., 144, 258
Patil, R. R., 104
Patterson, C., 407
Patterson, C. J., 407
Patton, F., 315, 442
Patz, R. J., 410
Pauli-Pott, U., 298
Paulson, 432
Paulson, A., 436
Pavlov, I. P., 118
Paxton, J. M., 360
Paxton, S., 322
Payne, A., 382
Peach, J., 197
Pearson, B. Z., 239
Pearson, R. M., 99
Peay, H., 66
Peck, S., 277
Peckins, M. K., 370
Pecora, N., 426
Pedersen, N. L., 15
Pedersen, S., 336
Pelham, B., 320
Pellegrini, A. D., 384
Pellis, S., 384
Pellis, S. M., 384
Pellis, V. C., 384
Pellitteri, J., 255
Peltzer, K., 342
Pengpid, S., 342
Pennington, 407
Pennisi, E., 58
Penuel, W. R., 427
Pepler, D., 374
Pepler, D. J., 338
Peppé, S., 227
Pe-Pua, R., 399
Peretz, 254
Perez-Brena, N. J., 400
Perlmann, J., 9
Perlmann, R. Y., 236
Perrier, L., 97
Perrin, R. D., 412
Perrine, N. E., 396
Perry, T., 198
Persaud, T. V. N., 80
Persson, A., 370
Persson, G. E. B., 367
Peterman, K., 281
Petermann, F., 367
Peters, C., 48
Peterson, B. D., 83
Peterson, C., 202
Peterson, D. M., 313
Peterson, L., 412
Peterson, M., 152
Peterson, R. A., 44
Petit, G., 370
Petitto, 222
Petitto, L. A., 131, 222, 239
Petras, H., 367
Petrides, K., 436
Petrou, S., 108
Pettit, G. S., 357

PEW Research Center, 438
Phelan, P., 396
Philippot, P., 367
Phillips, K., 6
Phinney, 439
Phinney, J., 440
Phinney, J. S., 315, 320, 321, 393, 439
Phipps, M., 344
Piaget, J., 28, 352
Pick, A. D., 287
Pietromonaco, P. R., 151
Pillai, V., 344
Pillai Riddell, 146
Pine, K., 426
Pink, J., 252
Pinker, S., 225, 226, 231
Pipe, M., 202
Pittman, L., 406
Planinsec, J., 134
Plante, E., 236
Plomin, R., 49, 64, 265, 292
Plowman, L., 426
Pluess, M., 422
Plunkett, K., 9
Polanichka, N., 373
Polivka, B., 153
Polkinghorne, D. E., 41
Pollack, W., 338
Pollak, S., 131
Pollitt, E., 150
Polman, H., 370
Polyak, D., 275
Pomares, C. G., 145
Pomeroy, W. B., 343
Pompili, M., 293
Ponton, L. E., 340
Pop, V., 114
Pope, H., 152
Porges, S. W., 145
Porteous, 77
Porter, M., 111
Portes, A., 321
Posner, J., 422
Posner, M. I., 289
Poss, J., 30
Posthuma, D., 262
Poulin-Dubois, D., 288, 328, 329, 330
Poulton, 428
Poulton, R., 78
Powell, M., 210
Powell, M. B., 210
Prater, L., 436
Pratto, F., 336
Prezbindowski, A. K., 41
Price, D. W., 202
Price, R. J., Jr., 90
Priddis, L., 277
Prieler, M., 333
Primedia/Roper National Youth
    Survey, 401
Prince, M., 108
Prinz, W., 136
Prior, J., 139
Proctor, R., 309
Propper, C., 70, 299
Puchalski, M., 146
Puckering, C., 277
Pulkkinen, L., 375
Puri, S., 60
Putnick, D. L., 224
Pyszczynski, T., 15

Q
Quaid, L., 339
Quas, J., 210
Quinn, P., 143

Quintana, S., 308, 316
Quintana, S. M., 308

R
Raag, T., 330
Radwan, S., 252
Raeff, C., 399
Rafalovich, A., 207
Ragland, J., 30
Raikes, H., 424
Rainwater, L., 444
Raj, V., 200
Raman, L., 154
Ramani, G. B., 383
Ramaswamy, V., 354
Ramos, 87
Ramsay, D., 307
Ramsey-Rennels, J. L., 143
Ranganath, C., 30
Rankin, B., 421
Rankin, D. B., 387
Rankin, J., 322
Ransjö-Arvidson, A. B., 102
Rao, N., 332, 423
Rapee, R., 392
Rapin, I., 137
Ratanachu-Ek, S., 150
Rattenborg, K., 403
Rauch, S. L., 299
Raudsepp, L., 135
Raver, C., 424
Ray, E., 27
Ray, L., 75
Rayner, K., 212
Rayner, R., 118
Raz, S., 99
Razani, J., 260
Ready, 433
Reale, B., 111
Reddy, L. A., 382
Redsell, S. A., 103
Redshaw, M., 97
Reed, R. K., 101
Reed, S., 344
Rees, S., 99
Reese, E., 202
Reeve, J. M., 434
Rego, A., 211
Reifman, A., 260
Reis, S., 266
Reiss, D., 358
Reissland, N., 280
Rembiss, M., 34
Renzulli, J., 266
Rescorla, L., 220
Resnick, M. D., 401
Resnikoff, D., 405
Resta, R., 66
Rey, E., 33
Reyes, B., 345
Reyna, V. F., 195, 196, 290
Reznik, I., 293
Rhule, D., 17
Rice, M. L., 427
Richards, G., 251
Richards, M. H., 337, 402, 403
Richards, M. P. M., 139
Richardson, A., 293
Richardson, C. B., 364
Richardson, G., 88
Richardson, K., 72
Richert, A. J., 29
Richert, R., 40
Rick, S., 413
Ridder, E. M., 84
Rideout, 427, 428

Rideout, V., 425
Rideout, V. J., 426
Riemer, H., 32
Riley, B., 64
Riley, K., 232
Rimmele, U., 395
Rimpela, M., 139
Rinaldi, C., 389
Rinaldi, C. M., 336
Ripple, C., 154
Risley, T. R., 236, 237
Ritter, P., 322
Ritzen, E. M., 140
Rivas-Drake, D., 320
Rivera-Gaziola, M., 144
Rivero, 434
Rivers, C., 403
Robb, M., 40
Robbins, M. W., 410
Roberts, 427
Roberts, E., 84
Roberts, J., 296
Roberts, K. E., 343
Roberts, R., 321, 441
Roberts, R. D., 252, 254, 255
Robertson, W., 151
Robertson Blackmore, E., 112
Robins, R. W., 312, 318
Robinson, A., 424
Robinson, A. J., 258
Robinson, C., 357
Robinson, D. T., 434
Robinson, E., 227
Robinson, G. E., 73
Robinson, N. M., 266
Robinson, T., 426
Rochat, P., 286, 288, 306
Roche, T., 408, 409
Rodkin, P. C., 392
Rodriguez Martin, J., 128
Roeder, K., 74
Roelofs, J., 278
Roeyers, H., 195, 214
Rogan, J., 33
Rogers, S., 120
Rogosch, F., 412
Roll, S., 362
Romero, A., 321, 441
Ronald, A., 73
Rönkä, A., 375
Roopnarine, J., 278
Ropar, D., 289
Rosch, E., 232
Rose, A. J., 336, 389
Rose, R. J., 9
Rose, S., 207, 213, 258
Rose, S. A., 200, 259
Rose, S. P., 132
Rosen, K., 279
Rosen, S., 145
Rosenberg, M., 405
Rosenthal, G. E., 103
Rosenthal, M., 113
Rosenthal, S., 277
Ross, D., 368
Ross, I., 88
Ross, L., 67
Ross, S., 368
Roth, 139
Rothbart, M., 296
Rothbart, M. K., 289
Rothbaum, F., 279
Rothbaum, R., 90
Rotigel, J. V., 267
Rovee-Collier, C., 200
Rovee-Collier, C. K., 200

Rowland, C. F., 131, 225
Roy, E. A., 137
Rubin, D., 195
Rubin, K. H., 392
Ruble, D., 330, 332, 333
Ruble, D. N., 329
Ruda, M. A., 146
Rudd, L., 422
Rudman, 445
Rudy, D., 320, 407
Ruedy, N. E., 322
Ruff, H. A., 146, 206
Ruihe, H., 290
Ruiz-Casares, M., 404
Rumbaut, R., 321
Russell, S., 343
Russell, S. T., 321, 407
Rust, J., 333
Rustin, M., 41
Rutter, M., 15, 375
Ryan, A. M., 198, 392
Ryan, J. A., 86
Ryan, K. E., 198
Rydell, A., 319

S
Saar, M., 135
Sabatino, C., 406
Sadikaj, G., 153
Sadovsky, A., 289
Saeljoe, R., 385
Saewyc, E., 32
Saez, L., 239
Saffran, J. R., 223
Sagi-Schwartz, A., 279
Saiegh-Haddad, E., 227
Saini, M., 374
Salazar, M., 443
Salinas, M., 198
Salmivalli, 365
Salthouse, T., 252
Samet, J. H., 64, 65
Sampson, P. D., 89
Sanchez, 441
Sánchez, P., 443
Sandberg, J., 403, 404
Sandberg, J. F., 404
Sander, C., 99
Sanders, L. D., 206
Sanders, S., 153
Sanderson, S., 153
Sandler, H. M., 317
Sandman, C. A., 13, 85
Sandoval, J., 261
Sandrin, D., 146
Sang, B., 203
Santelli, J., 345
Santomero, A., 426
Sapolsky, R., 408
Sarsour, 406
Sato, Y., 146
Saulny, S., 9
Saults, J., 202
Saunders, J., 321
Sauzéon, H., 204
Savin-Williams, R. C., 338
Sawriker, 439
Sax, L., 207, 428
Saxon, T., 422
Scarr, S., 74, 78, 423
Schaal, B., 145
Schachner, A., 207, 234, 235
Schacter, E. P., 25
Schaeffer, C., 367
Schaller, M., 308
Schallert, D., 322

Scharfe, E., 283
Scharrer, E., 152
Schechter, D., 277
Schechter, T., 88
Scheepers, D., 446
Schemo, D. J., 266, 431, 436
Schempf, A. H., 88
Schenk, A. M., 374
Scherer, J., 144
Scherf, K. S., 131
Schick, K., 202
Schindehette, S., 344
Schipper, L., 34
Schirrer, J., 145
Schlaug, 254
Schmalz, D., 329
Schmidt, J., 436
Schmidt, M., 90
Scholte, R. H. J., 374
Schonert-Reichl, 354
Schoppe-Sullivan, S., 278, 298
Schore, A., 285, 289
Schork, N. J., 69
Schuetze, P., 88
Schultz, A. H., 115
Schultz, J., 312
Schunk, D., 354
Schutt, R. K., 39
Schutz, H., 322
Schwartz, 299, 440
Schwartz, C. E., 299
Schwartz, D., 343
Schwartz, I. M., 341
Schwartz, M., 153
Schwartz, O. S., 292
Schwartz, P., 195
Schwartz, S. H., 401
Schwartz, S. J., 7
Schwarz, B., 399
Schweinhart, L. J., 424
Schweitzer, M. E., 322
Scientific American, 413
Scotland, G. S., 102
Scott, P. M., 354
Scullin, M., 211
Sears, R. R., 266
Seaton, E. K., 315
Sebanc, A., 382
Seethaler, P. M., 252
Segal, N. L., 72
Segalowitz, S. J., 131, 137
Seibert, A., 278
Seitz, M., 15
Seligman, M., 293
Seligman, M. E. P., 389
Semerci, Ç., 360
Seokho, K., 446
Serbin, L., 328, 329, 330
Serry, M. D., 319
Servin, A., 329, 331
Shackelford, T., 34
Shad, M. U., 131
Shaffer, L., 338
Shah, V., 146
Shangguan, F., 252
Shankweiler, D., 251
Shapiro, J. R., 197, 445
Sharma, M., 60, 356
Shatz, 225
Shaunessy, E., 266
Shavelson, R., 310
Shaver, P. R., 276
Shavitt, S., 32
Shaw, D. S., 405
Shaw, M. L., 211
Shaywitz, B. A., 212

Shea, K. M., 109
Shealy, C. N., 409
Sheese, B., 298
Shepherd, J., 280
Sherman, S., 64
Shernoff, D., 436
Shi, B., 322
Shi, J., 252
Shi, L., 383
Shi, R., 118
Shi, X., 315
Shields, M. K., 408
Shiffrin, R. M., 199
Shih, 441
Shin, 440
Shiner, R., 296
Shirley, L., 330
Shirtcliff, E., 292
Shockey, E., 333
Shoval, G., 293
Shreeve, D. F., 277
Shreve, T., 321
Shuetze, P., 88
Shumow, L., 422
Shuster, T., 338
Sidanius, J., 336
Sidora-Arcoleo, K., 155
Sieber, J. E., 51
Siegel, L., 251
Siegel, S., 84
Siegler, R. S., 206, 213
Signorella, M., 333
Silenzio, V., 343
Silva, L., 320
Silva-Pereyra, J., 144
Silverberg, S., 399
Silverthorn, P., 375
Simcock, G., 200, 201
Simion, F., 117
Simmons, S. W., 102
Simms, K., 436
Simons, D. A., 411
Simons, L., 356
Simons, S. H., 118
Simpkins, S., 386
Simpson, J., 276
Simrock, G., 120
Singer, 88
Singh, S., 341, 344
Skårberg, K., 16
Skibbe, L. E., 431
Skinner, B. F., 26, 230
Skinner, J. D., 149
Slade, P., 102, 114
Slep, A. M., 412
Smedley, A., 8
Smedley, B. D., 8
Smeeding, T., 444
Smetana, 364
Smetana, J., 402
Smetana, J. G., 399, 401, 402
Smith, 88, 291
Smith, D., 428
Smith, G. C., 108
Smith, J., 358
Smith, J. S., 436
Smith, N., 120
Smith, P., 407
Smith, T. B., 320
Smith, T. W., 446
Smokowski, 443
Smutny, J., 266
Smuts, A. B., 357
Snidman, N., 70, 76
Snow, D., 222
Soderstrom, M., 234

Soenen, S., 84
Soken, N. H., 287
Soloman, S., 15
Solomon, S., 374
Sousa, C., 16, 410
Sousa, D. L., 211
Soussignan, R., 284
Southern Poverty Law Center, 447
Sowell, E. R., 131
Sparks, A., 338
Spear, L. P., 131
Spearman, C., 252
Spelke, 201
Spelke, E. S., 147
Spence, M., 82
Spencer, J., 345, 371, 372
Spencer, M. B., 393
Spencer, S. J., 197
Spencer, S. L., 197
Spiby, H., 102, 114
Spieker, S., 278
Spieker, S. J., 277
Spielman, D. A., 16
Spinrad, 291
Spinrad, T., 354, 355
Spinrad, T. L., 280, 289
Spjeldnes, S., 338
Sprang, G., 412
Sprenger, M., 203
Sroufe, L. A., 277
Stahl, S., 425
Stambaugh, T., 266
Stanton, J. C., 310
Stark, D. R., 424
Starr, R., 406
State, M., 63
Stattin, H., 391
Staub, E., 16
Stauss, K., 345
Steele, C., 197, 198
Steele, C. M., 197
Steenbergen-Hu, S., 266, 432
Stein, Z., 71
Steinberg, L., 357, 396, 399, 401
Steiner, J. E., 145
Steinmetz, S. K., 411
Stenberg, G., 288
Steri, A. O., 147
Stern, L., 149
Sternberg, J., 253, 254, 260
Sternberg, R., 252, 254
Sternberg, R. J., 246, 251
Stewart, L., 254
Stewart, M., 144
Stiffman, A., 32
Stifler, C. A., 280
Stifter, C. A., 389
Stipek, D., 431
Stock, P., 214
Stokes, 340
Stolberg, S. G., 112
Stone, D. H., 155
Stork, S., 153
Story, M., 153
Stotland, S., 153
Strasburger, V., 426
Straus, M. A., 410, 411, 412
Streissguth, A., 89
Striano, T., 286, 287, 288
Stright, A., 15
Strobel, A., 30
Stromswold, K., 230
Strough, J., 335
Stuart-Hamilton, I., 29
Styfco, S., 424
Suárez-Orozco, C., 321

Subotnik, R., 49
Suida-Robinson, T., 103
Suitor, J. J., 395, 396
Sullivan, M. W., 200, 283, 329
Suls, J. M., 307
Summers, J., 322
Sunderman, G., 432
Supple, A., 399
Sutfin, E. L., 407
Sutherland, R., 202
Swain, J. E., 285
Swanson, H., 239
Swanson, L. A., 235
Sweeney, J. A., 131
Sweet, M. A., 286
Swiatek, M., 266
Swingler, M. M., 286
Szaflarski, J. P., 131
Szarko, J., 267
Szkrybalo, J., 329

T
Taddio, A., 146
Taga, G., 223
Tajfel, 445, 447
Takahashi, K., 279
Taki, Y., 129
Tamis-LeMonda, C., 357, 420
Tan, H., 108
Tang, C., 102, 110
Tangney, J., 39
Tanner, E., 149, 150
Tanner, J., 139
Tanner, J. M., 130, 140
Tappan, M., 363
Tardif, T., 223
Tartleff-Dunn, S., 152
Tasker, F., 343
Tate, J. D., 393
Tatum, B., 321
Taylor, 108
Taylor, B., 422
Taylor, C. S., 388
Taylor, D. M., 407
Taylor, M. G., 331
Taylor, T. J., 232
Tellegen, A., 75
Teller, D., 117
Tenenbaum, H., 236
Tennen, H., 320
Terry, D., 112
Terzidou, V., 96
Tesoriero, 395
Tessor, A., 307
Theokas, C., 309
Théret, H., 282
Thøgersen, J., 401
Thomas, 205
Thomas, A., 297, 298
Thomas, H., 258
Thomas, R. B., 17
Thomas, R. M., 23
Thomas, T., 428
Thompson, D. M., 204
Thompson, J., 152
Thompson, R., 278
Thomson, A., 86
Thornberry, T. P., 375
Tibben, A., 67
Tibosch, M. M., 155
Tidhar, C., 426
Tiggemann, M., 152
Timmermans, S., 103
Tincani, M., 104
Tissaw, M., 120
Tobin, J. J., 423

Todd, B., 132
Todorova, I., 321
Tokoyawa, 443
Tolchinsky, L., 8
Tomasello, M., 34, 354
Tomasian, J., 387
Tomblin, J. B., 89
Tomlinson-Keasey, C., 280
Tongsong, T., 82
Topol, E. J., 69
Torelli, C. J., 32
Torvaldsen, S., 102
Toscano, J. C., 223
Towse, J., 202
Tracy, M., 408
Trainor, L., 120, 236
Trainor, L. J., 143
Trautwein, U., 432
Trawick-Smith, J., 383
Trehub, S. E., 143, 144
Trelease, J., 338
Tremblay, R. E., 367
Trepanier-Street, M., 421
Triche, 89
Tronick, E., 280
Tronick, E. Z., 17
Troop-Gordon, W., 336
Tropp, L., 393
Trzesniewski, K. H., 312, 318, 338
Tsang, J., 49
Tsao, F-M., 221
Tseng, V., 400
Tucker-Drob, E., 252
Tulsky, D., 247
Tulving, E., 204
Turati, C., 200
Turiel, C., 364
Turk, J., 64
Turkheimer, E., 261
Turnbull, D., 101
Turner, 445, 447
Turney, K., 321
Turton, P., 112
Tuvblad, C., 15
Twardosz, S., 413
Twenge, J. M., 318
Twomey, J., 67
Tynes, D. M., 200

U
Uchikoshi, Y., 426
Ueda, A., 145
Uher, R., 71
Ujiie, T., 279, 284
Ullman, M., 236
Ulutas, I., 255
Umaña-Taylor, 440
Umana-Taylor, A., 443
Umaña-Taylor, A. J., 400
Underwood, M., 52
UNESCO, 431
Ungar, L., 360
Unger, 439
Unger, R., 329
United Nations, 86, 98
United Nations Office on Drugs and Crime, 373
University of Akron, 17
Updegraff, K. A., 312, 400
Urquiza, A., 412
Urso, A., 146
U.S. Bureau of the Census, 238, 315, 316, 405, 406, 407, 438
U.S. Court of Federal Claims, 104
U.S. Department of Agriculture, 153

U.S. Department of Health and Human Services, 106, 410
U.S. Drug Enforcement Administration, 208
U.S. Secret Service, 372
Uylings, H., 13
Uzelac, S., 195

V
Vaccaro, B., 288
Vaillant, C. O., 300
Vaillant, G. E., 300
Vaillant-Molina, M., 119
Vaish, A., 286, 288, 354
Vaizey, C. J., 97
Valente, S. M., 343
Valenti, C., 143
Valerio, C. Y., 374
Valiente, C., 355, 357
Valles, N., 367
van Aken, M., 370
Van Balen, F., 60
Vande, 156
Vandell, D. L., 386, 422
Vandenbosch, L., 428
van der Mark, I., 289
van der Zwaag, B., 77
Vandewater, E. A., 426
van Erp, T. G. M., 77
van Gelderen, L., 343
van Goethem, A. A. J., 374
van Kleeck, A., 425
van Marle, K., 194
Van Schoiack-Edstrom, L., 372
van Soelen, I. C., 74
Van Son, M., 114
Van Tassel-Baska, J., 320
van Wesel, F., 6
van Wormer, K., 343
Vartanian, L. R., 196
Vaughan, B. S., 207
Vélez, C. E., 6, 405
Veneziano, R., 278
Verhaak, C. M., 155
Verhulst, S. J., 258
Verkerk, G., 114
Vernon, P., 75
Verrity, P., 373
Vignoles, 428
Vignoles, V. L., 447
Vilhjalmsson, R., 135
Villarosa, L., 344
Vinik, J., 354
Vinter, A., 226
Viswanathan, M., 239
Vitiello, V. E., 237
Vizmanos, B., 139
Vlahov, D., 9
Voelker, S., 307
Vohs, K. D., 322
Volker, S., 285
Vollebergh, W. M., 396
Vollmann, J., 84
von Hofsten, C., 201
Votruba-Drzal, E., 422
Vouloumanous, A., 145
Vurpillot, E., 206
Vyas, S., 442
Vygotsky, L. S., 32, 232, 252

W
Wacker, J., 262
Wade, N., 230
Wadsby, M., 405
Wahlin, T., 67
Wainwright, J. L., 407

Waismeyer, A., 281
Wakefield, 104
Wakschlag, L. S., 89
Walden, T., 120
Waldfogel, J., 112
Waldie, K. E., 239
Waldman, S., 443
Walk, R. D., 142
Walker, D., 99
Walker, S., 266
Walker, W. A., 87
Walker-Andrews, A., 287
Wallace, B., 226
Wallerstein, J., 405
Wallis, 433
Walters, E., 253, 276
Wang, M., 202
Wang, Q., 202, 307, 308
Wang, S., 357
Wang, W., 398
Wang, Y., 374
Ward, 428
Ward, A., 372
Ward, T., 34, 155
Wardle, F., 9
Wardle, J., 153
Warnock, F., 146
Warren, K., 89
Wartella, E., 40, 426
Wartella, E. A., 426
Washburn, J. J., 372
Wasserman, J., 247
Watanabe, H., 223
Waterlaw, R. A., 73
Waters, J. M., 9
Watling, D., 131
Watson, J. B., 25, 118
Watts-English, T., 413
Waugh, R., 279
Waxler, C. Z., 354
Webb, R. M., 267
Weber, B., 388
Weikart, D. P., 424
Weinberg, R. A., 47, 99
Weinfield, N. S., 277
Weinstein, J., 15
Weiss, L., 249
Weiss, M. R., 322
Weiss, R., 260
Weissman, D., 131
Weisz, A., 363
Weitzman, M., 431
Welkley, D. L., 406
Wellings, K., 342
Wellman, H., 289
Wells, B., 227

Wells, R., 266
Welner, 433
Welsh, T., 282
Werker, J., 145
Werker, J. F., 234, 235
Werner, E., 296
Wertheim, E., 322
Wessel, 434
West, J. R., 265
West, R. P., 358
Westerhausen, 331
Westerhausen, R. R., 132
Westermann, G., 132
Wexler, B., 14
Whalen, C. K., 207
Whalen, D., 221
Whalen, J., 196
Whaley, S., 90
Wheeler, K., 258, 260
Whelan, T., 278
Whitaker, R. C., 151
Whitbourne, S. K., 25
White, K., 101, 289
Whitebread, D., 383
Whiting, B. B., 330, 335, 365, 373
Whorf, B. L., 231
Widamam, K., 61
Widiger, T., 9
Widom, C. S., 412
Widström, A., 84
Wiers, R. W., 374
Wiesel, T. N., 143
Wigfield, A., 433
Wilcox, A. J., 109
Wilcox, H. C., 293
Wilcox, T., 147, 329
Wildberger, S., 86
Wilfond, B., 67
Wilkes, S., 83
Willford, J., 88
Willheim, E., 277
Williams, J., 88, 120, 154
Williams, L., 338
Williams, T., 321
Willoughby, M., 367
Willows, D. M., 148
Willrich, M., 104
Wills, 364
Wilson, A., 102
Wilson, B., 368
Wilson, B. J., 39
Wilson, P., 426
Wilson, S. L., 41
Winer, G., 154
Winger, G., 85
Winner, E., 354

Winsler, A., 226, 431
Winslow, E. B., 405
Winstead, 293
Wintemute, G., 293
Winters, K. C., 428
Wisborg, K., 90
Wisdom, J., 293
Wisner Fries, A., 131
Witt, A., 226
Witt, E. A., 338
Wohlwend, K. E., 330
Wood, A. C., 134
Wood, D., 289
Wood, D. N., 400
Wood, K., 152
Wood, L., 428
Wood, R., 59
Wood, W., 333
Woods, J. H., 85
Woods, R., 329, 388
World Factbook, 106, 107
Worobey, J., 297
Worrell, F., 267
Wright, J. C., 426, 427
Wright, M., 293
Wright, R., 50, 210
Wu, B., 402
Wu, C., 402
Wu, D. Y. H., 423
Wu, M., 110
Wu, P., 293, 357
Wurtele, S. K., 411
Wyer, R., 194
Wynn, K., 193, 194
Wyra, M., 203

X

Xie, H., 322
Xirasagar, S., 97

Y

Yablo, P., 365
Yamada, J., 146
Yancey, A. K., 292
Yang, C., 357
Yang, C. D., 231
Yang, R., 321
Yann, Z., 30
Yardley, J., 114
Yarrow, L., 102
Yarrow, M. R., 354
Yasui, 441
Yato, Y., 280
Yecke, C. P., 433
Yim, I., 114

Yinger, J., 431
Yoo, S. H., 9
Yoon, H., 405
Yoshikawa, H., 321
Young, D., 110
Young, H., 396
Young, K. R., 358
Yovsi, R. D., 307
Yu, H. C., 396
Yu, M., 32

Z

Zacchilli, T. L., 374
Zahn-Waxler, 291
Zahn-Waxler, C., 279, 292, 336, 373
Zakar, T., 96
Zalsman, G., 292, 293
Zaporozhets, A. V., 148
Zarbatany, L., 387
Zauszniewski, J. A., 25
Zebrowitz, L., 279
Zeedyk, M., 120
Zehnder, S., 333
Zeidner, M., 254, 255
Zelazo, P. D., 194
Zelazo, P. R., 286
Zemach, I., 117
Zerwas, S., 383
Zettergren, P., 395
Zevenbergen, A., 357
Zhai, F., 424
Zhang, J., 232
Zhang, L., 25
Zhang, Q., 232
Zhang, W., 399
Zhang, X., 89
Zhe, C., 213
Zheng, H., 423
Zheng, X., 357
Zhu, J., 108, 249
Zhu, X., 426
Zigler, E., 154, 266, 424
Zigler, E. F., 15
Zimmer, C., 289
Zimmer-Gembeck, M. J., 338, 400
Zimmerman, B., 354
Zimmerman, F., 370, 427
Zimmerman, M., 154
Zimmerman, R. R., 275
Zirkel, S., 442
Ziv, M., 289
Zosh, J. M., 200
Zuckerman, M., 74
Zuumbach, J., 16
Zwelling, E., 100

Subject Index

A

Abortions, 84
Abstract modeling, 354
Abstract thought, 175–177, 195
Abuse. *See* Child abuse; Domestic violence
Academics. *See* Education
Accommodation, in cognitive development, 29, 163
Acculturation, 439–440
Adaptation, in cognitive development, 28
Adolescence
  aggression and violence in, 351, 371–372, 373–375
  autonomy and independence in, 381, 399–402, 414
  brain growth in, 130–131
  bullying in, 373–375
  child development study of, 6
  cognitive development in, 28, 175–177, 192, 194–198, 215
  conformity and peer pressure in, 396
  dating in, 338–339
  depression in, 292–293, 343
  education of (*see* Education)
  egocentric thought in, 195–196, 215
  emotional development in, 274, 290–295
  emotional difficulties in, 292–295
  empathy in, 355
  employment and career choices in, 313, 315
  family relationship changes in, 381, 398–402, 414
  friend and peer influences in, 381, 391–396
  gender relations in, 336–339
  generation gap with parents in, 400–401
  identity development in, 300, 311–316, 319, 320–321, 322–323, 337–338, 398–402
  imaginary audiences in, 195
  information processing in, 194–198
  juvenile delinquency in, 351, 375
  masturbation in, 340–341
  metacognition in, 192, 195
  middle school transitions for, 432–433
  moral development in, 351, 355, 360–362, 364–365, 376–377
  online communication in, 374, 392, 394, 428–429
  parental conflicts in, 401–402
  personal fables in, 196
  personality development in, 300
  physical growth and development in, 129–131, 138–140, 311, 322, 337, 340
  popularity in, 394–396
  pregnancy during, 86, 108, 344–346
  puberty in, 138–140, 311, 322, 337, 340
  racial and ethnic self-awareness and identity development in, 308, 314–316, 320–321

self development in, 300, 308, 311–316, 319, 320–321, 322–323, 337–338, 398–402
sexting in, 339
sexuality and sexual behavior in, 339, 340–346, 364
social development in, 274, 290–295, 300, 336–339
substance use in, 131, 292, 293, 364, 375
suicide, suicide attempts and ideation in, 292, 293–295, 343, 373
television and media influences in, 427–429
virginity pledges in, 345
Adolescence (journal), 51
Adolescence (book) (Hall), 12
Adoption, 72–73
Age
  adolescent sexual intercourse initiation by, 341, 344
  age-graded influences, 9
  child development age ranges, 6–7 (*see also* Adolescence; Infancy and toddlerhood; Middle childhood; Preschool period)
  cognitive development stages based on, 28
  cross-sectional studies by, 49–50
  developmentally appropriate educational practice by, 424–425
  developmental scales of intelligence by, 257–258
  educational enrollment based on, 430–431
  generation gap, 400–401
  maturation rates and, 7
  mental age measurements of intelligence, 247–248
  prenatal development problems related to, 83, 86, 108
  sequential studies based on, 50
  small-for-gestational-age infants, 106
  survival and gestational age, 107–108
Aggression and violence
  adolescent, 351, 371–372, 373–375
  cognitive approaches to, 370–371
  cultural influences on, 372–373
  definition of, 366
  domestic (*see* Child abuse; Domestic violence)
  gender differences in, 367, 373
  genetic influences on, 367
  instrumental aggression as, 367
  juvenile delinquency and, 351, 375
  modeling, 368–370
  moral development relationship to, 371
  parenting style and response influencing, 372–373
  preschool period, 366–367, 368–371
  preventing children's, 16
  relational aggression as, 367

research on, 39–40, 42–44, 50, 53, 368–370
roots of, 367–373
school violence and bullying as, 371–372, 373–375
self-directed (*see* Suicide, suicide attempts and ideation)
social learning theory on, 368
television, movies, and video games influencing, 16, 39–40, 42–44, 368–370, 371
AIDS (acquired immune deficiency syndrome), 87
Ainsworth, Mary, 275–277, 279
Alcohol use. *See also* Substance use
  adolescent, 131, 364, 375
  fetal alcohol syndrome/effects from, 89, 265
  genetic influences on, 64, 77
  moral issues with, 364
  prenatal development impacted by, 83, 88–89, 90, 265
American Academy of Pediatrics
  on anesthesia for children, 146
  on autism and vaccines, 104
  on gender and sport participation, 135
  on importance of play, 383
  on postdelivery hospital stays, 103
  on spanking, 411
  on television exposure, 426
American College of Medical Genetics, 103
American College of Obstetricians and Gynecologists, 102
American Psychological Association
  abortion studies by, 84
  research-related ethical guidelines by, 50–52
  on restricting child-targeted advertising, 426
American Sign Language, 222, 235
Amnesia, 200
Amniocentesis, 57, 66, 67
Amusia, 254
Amygdala, 291, 299, 413
Androgens, 329, 331
Anoxia, 98–99
Antisocial personality disorders, 375
Anxiety
  bullying leading to, 374
  child abuse relationship to, 410
  divorce impacting, 405
  separation, 286
  stranger, 285–286
Apgar scale, 98–99
Archival research, 45
Arcuate fasciculus, 254
Ariès, Philippe, 11
Art, fine motor development via, 138, 139
Artificial insemination, 83, 84
Assimilation
  in cognitive development, 28–29, 163
  cultural, 439, 442
Associative play, 383, 384
Asthma, 154–155

Athletics. *See* Exercise and athletics
Attachment
  ambivalent, 276
  avoidant, 275–276
  cultural influences on, 277, 278–279
  disorganized-disoriented, 276
  father-child bonding as, 99, 277, 278
  imprinting and, 275
  mother-child bonding as, 99, 277, 278
  mutual regulation model of, 279–280
  producing, 277–280
  reactive attachment disorder, 277
  reciprocal socialization in, 280
  secure, 275, 276, 277, 279
  social development via, 99, 274–280, 298
  Strange Situation and patterns of, 275–277, 279
  temperament relationship to, 298
Attention
  ADHD lack of, 63, 64, 77, 207–208, 251, 375
  in cognitive development, 192, 204–208
  control of, 206
  planning abilities relationship to, 206–207
Attention deficit-hyperactivity disorder (ADHD)
  drugs prescribed for, 207, 208
  genetic influences on, 63, 64, 77
  information processing in, 207
  intelligence testing impacted by, 251
  juvenile delinquency relationship to, 375
Auditory perception. *See* Hearing or auditory perception
Auerbach, Stevanne, 167
Authoritarian parenting style, 355, 356
Authoritative parenting style, 319, 356–357
Autism
  cognitive neuroscience study of, 30
  genetic influences on, 77
  mirror neuron dysfunction and, 282
  social development difficulties in, 282, 289
  vaccines allegedly linked to, 104
Automatization, of information processing, 193
Autonomous cooperation stage of moral development, 353

B

Babbling, 221
Babies. *See* Infancy and toddlerhood
Bandura, Albert, 27, 35, 368
Bayley Scales of Infant Development, 257–258
Bed-wetting, 156
Behavioral genetics, 34, 63

Behavioral perspective
conditioning responses to stimuli in, 26–27, 118–119
theoretical basis of, 25–27, 35, 118–119
The Bell Curve (Herrnstein and Murray), 260–261
Berkeley Growth and Guidance Studies, 12
Bicultural identity, 315, 316, 439, 442–443
Bilingualism, 237–239, 442–443
Binet, Alfred, 11, 247
Bioecological approach, 31–32, 35
Biological perspective, 331–332, 334
Birth
anesthesia and pain-reducing drugs during, 102, 104
Apgar scale measurement system immediately after, 98–99
approaches to childbirth, 99–103, 121–122
attendants and participants in, 99–100, 101, 121–122
Bradley Method birthing for, 101
Cesarean delivery for, 109, 110–111
complications with, 106–114
development prior to (*see* Prenatal development)
fetal monitors used during, 111
hypnobirthing for, 101
labor leading to, 96–97, 104
Lamaze birthing techniques for, 100–101
low birth weights, 87, 89, 95, 106–109
midwives assisting at, 99–100, 101, 121–122
multiple, 59–60 (*see also* Twins)
newborn medical screening after, 98–99, 103
pain during, 102, 104
parental leave policies after, 112, 113
parent-child bonding after, 99 (*see also* Attachment)
physical appearance of neonates after, 96, 99
postdelivery hospital stays, 102–103
postmature, 109
postpartum depression after, 114
premature, 59, 86, 87, 95, 106–110
stillborn, 84, 106, 111
transition from fetus to neonate in, 98–99
Birth control, 90, 344, 345, 346
Birth defects, 85–90
Bisexuality, 342. *See also* Gays and lesbians
Blended families, 405–406
Bodily kinesthetic intelligence, 253
Body image, 151, 152, 342, 428
Bowlby, John, 275, 278, 279
Bradley Method birthing, 101
Brain development and function. *See also* Cognitive development
amygdala in, 291, 299, 413
arcuate fasciculus in, 254
child abuse impacting, 413
corpus callosum in, 331–332
emotional activation of, 291
face blindness impacted by, 395
fusiform gyrus in, 279
gender differences in, 331–332
hippocampus in, 204, 291, 299, 413
lateralization in, 131, 132

mirror neurons in, 282
myelin in, 82, 130–131, 134, 137
personality and temperament differences in, 299
physical growth and, 130–132
play and peer interaction relationship to, 384
prefrontal cortex in, 131, 291, 299, 384
prenatal, 82
sexual orientation differences in, 343
social development and, 279, 282, 291
Brain studies. *See* Neuroscience
Braxton-Hicks contractions, 96
Brazelton Neonatal Behavioral Assessment Scale, 98
Brinich, Judy Coleman, 33
Bronfenbrenner, Urie, 31–32, 35
Brown, Ivy, 106
Brown, Louise, 3–4, 9, 19
Bullying, 373–375

C

Caffeine, 90
Calder, James and Roberta, 121–122
Callan, Don, 53
Camacho, Luis, 274
Cantó, Sandra, 393
Canton, Sarah, 187–188
Careers in child development
child- and youth-care workers as, 409
child care director as, 33
children's toy advocate and author as, 167
clinical nurse specialist as, 110
diversity of specialists in, 7
licensed social worker as, 287
professional mediator as, 363
professor of family relations/human sexuality as, 342
reading resource teacher as, 212
special education teachers as, 264
variety of choices in, 18
Carlson, Jeff, 103
Caron, Sandra, 342
Carroll, Tracy, 420
Castro, Kaita, 115, 116, 117, 119
CAT (computerized axial tomography) scans, 42
Centers for Disease Control and Prevention, 104
Centration, 169–170
Cephalocaudal principle, 127
Cesarean delivery, 109, 110–111
Chen, Steven, 420
Chess, Stella, 297
Chicken pox, 87
Child abuse
children's aggression and violence relationship to, 16
cultural influences on, 411–412
cycle of violence in, 412
group or foster care due to, 408
memory of, 202
mental health issues related to, 408, 410, 412–413
physical abuse specifically, 410–412
prevalence of, 410
psychological abuse specifically, 412–413
spanking escalating into, 411

uninvolved parenting neglect as, 356
warning signs of, 410
Childbirth. *See* Birth
Child care centers, 273, 282, 421, 422–423
Child development
age ranges in, 6–7 (*see also* Adolescence; Age; Infancy and toddlerhood; Middle childhood; Preschool period)
careers in (*see* Careers in child development)
cognitive development in (*see* Cognitive development)
continuous *vs.* discontinuous change in, 12–13
critical and sensitive periods of, 12, 13–14, 85, 87
cultural, racial and ethnic influences on (*see* Culture; Ethnicity; Race)
definition and description of, 5
environmental influences in (*see* Environmental influences)
future of, 15
genetic factors in (*see* Genetics)
health issues in (*see* Mental health issues; Physical health)
history of, 10–12
individual differences in, 7
informed consumers of (*see* Informed consumerism)
intelligence studies in (*see* Intelligence)
key issues and themes of, 12–15
language development in (*see* Language development)
life-span approach to, 12, 14
moral development in (*see* Moral development)
nature and nurture perspectives on, 12, 14–15, 70–78, 260–262 (*see also* Environmental influences; Genetics; Heredity)
overview of, 3–4
personality development in (*see* Personality development)
physical development in (*see* Physical development)
plasticity of, 13–14
prenatal (*see* Pregnancy; Prenatal development)
research on (*see* Research)
scope of field of, 5–7
self development in (*see* Self development)
social development in (*see* Social development)
theoretical perspectives on (*see* Theoretical perspectives)
Child Development (journal), 51
Childhelp U.S.A., 410
Chiu, Sylvester, 338
Chomsky, Noam, 230
Chorionic villus sampling (CVS), 66, 67
Chromosomes, 58–59, 59–60
Circular reactions, 165–168
Circumcision, 145, 146
Classical conditioning, 26–27, 118, 119
Clifford, Patricia, 110
Cliques and crowds, 392
Cocaine, 88
Cognitive development. *See also* Brain development and function; Intelligence
abstract thought in, 175–177, 195

accommodation in, 29, 163
adaptation in, 28
adolescent, 28, 175–177, 192, 194–198, 215
assessment of theories on, 29, 30, 32, 33, 34, 35–36, 178–181, 185–186, 213–214
assimilation in, 28–29, 163
attention in, 192, 204–208
automatization in, 193
brain development and, 132
centration in, 169–170
child development study of, 5–6
circular reactions in, 165–168
cognitive neuroscience approaches to, 30, 42, 203–204, 205
cognitive perspective on, 27–30, 35, 333, 334, 370–371
concrete operational stage of, 163, 174–175
conservation in, 170–171, 173, 180–181
cultural differences in, 177, 180–181, 182–186, 202
definition of, 5
educational considerations of, 173, 177, 179, 184–185, 187–188, 196–198, 211–213, 420–425
egocentric thought in, 172, 195–196, 215
encoding, storage and retrieval in, 192–193
formal operational stage of, 163, 175–177
functionality in, 173
goal-directed behavior in, 166
identity knowledge in, 173
imitation in, 27, 166, 168, 180
infant and toddler, 28, 162, 163, 164–168, 178–180, 192, 193–194, 199–201, 204–206, 257, 258–259
information processing in, 29–30, 191–215, 252–254, 257, 258–259
intuitive thought in, 172–173
language development and, 169, 239 (*see also* Language development)
logical thought in, 174
memory processes in, 191–192, 199–204, 209–211, 257, 258
mental representations in, 168
metacognition in, 192, 195
middle childhood, 28, 174–175, 181, 194, 202–203
motor development and, 163, 164–168, 179
numerical and mathematical abilities and, 180, 193–194, 196–197, 201, 202
object permanence in, 166–167, 179–180
Piaget's theory of, 28–29, 35, 162–181
planning abilities in, 206–207
preoperational stage of, 163, 169–173
preschool period, 28, 168–173, 180, 201–202, 210–211, 384, 420–425
propositional thought in, 176
reversibility in, 174, 180
scaffolding in, 184–185
schemes in, 28, 163
sensorimotor stage of, 163, 164–168

social-cognitive learning theory on, 27
stages of, 163, 164–177, 179–181
symbolic function in, 169
transformation in, 171–172
Vygotsky's theory of, 32–33, 35, 182–186, 384
zone of proximal development in, 183–185
Cognitive perspective
on aggression and violence, 370–371
on gender differences, 333, 334
theoretical basis of, 27–30, 35
Cohort effects, 9, 49
Colvin, Johnetta, 404
Computer-based communication. See Online communication
Computerized axial tomography (CAT) scans, 42
Conception, 80. See also Fertilization
Connors, Ted, 393
Conservation, in cognitive development, 170–171, 173, 180–181
Constructive play, 383, 384
Contextual perspective, 31–33, 35
Continuous vs. discontinuous change, 12–13
Contraception, 90, 344, 345, 346
Conventional morality, 360, 361
Cooperative learning, 185
Cooperative play, 383, 384
Corker, Robert, 393
Corpus callosum, 331–332
Correlations
correlational research, 39–42
correlation coefficient, 40–41
naturalistic observations of, 41
Corticotropin-releasing hormone (CRH), 96
Critical thinking, 212–213
Cross-sectional research, 49–50
Crowell, Mindy, 273
Crystallized intelligence, 252
Culture. See also Ethnicity; Race; Socioeconomics
acculturation, 439–440
adolescent family relations influenced by, 399–400, 402
aggression and violence influenced by, 372–373
assimilation of, 439, 442
attachment influenced by, 277, 278–279
bicultural identity, 315, 316, 439, 442–443
bioecological approach to, 32
child abuse differences by, 411–412
child development consideration of, 8–9
cognitive development, cultural differences in, 177, 180–181, 182–186, 202
collectivist vs. individualist, 32, 307–308, 321, 399–400
cultural tools specific to, 185, 186
dating influenced by, 339
defining characteristics of, 8, 438, 441
discrimination, prejudice and stereotypes related to, 196–198, 251, 260, 314, 321, 393, 436–437, 440, 441, 444–447
educational influences of/ differences in, 197–198, 393,

423, 430, 431, 435–437, 438, 441–443
ethnographic research on, 41, 45
family structure differences by, 406, 407
friendships, peer relations and play influenced by, 384, 393, 394
gender, cultural approaches to, 330, 339
genetic influences on, 63, 76
integration of, 439
intelligence testing, cultural biases in, 251, 259–262
labor and delivery perceptions influenced by, 97
language development influenced by, 221, 223, 224, 235–236
marginalization of, 439
marital influence of, 6
memory influenced by, 202
mental health issues, cultural differences in, 292, 439–440
moral development influenced by, 357–358, 360–361, 365
multiculturalism, 438–447
national pride in, 446
online communication, access to varied by, 428–429
parenting styles, cultural differences in, 357–358, 372–373
personality development influenced by, 75, 76, 298
physical growth and development, cultural differences in, 127, 128, 129, 132, 135, 138–139, 150–151, 157
physical health, cultural differences in, 154, 155
preschool programs influenced by, 423
research diversity of, 46
self development influenced by, 32, 307–308, 314–316, 321, 438–441, 442–443
separation of, 439
sexuality influenced by, 341
socialcultural theory of, 32–33, 35, 182–186, 384
social development influenced by, 277, 278–279, 283, 298, 339, 384, 393, 394
sociocultural-graded influences, 9
Cyber-communications. See Online communication

D

Dalton, Troy, 207
DARE (Drug Abuse Resistance Education), 17
Darwin, Charles, 11, 34, 35
Dating, 338–339
Davis, Margot, 87
Deaf persons, language development in, 221, 222, 228, 235
Death
infant mortality rate, 86, 106, 107, 111–113
stillbirths, 84, 106, 111
suicide leading to, 292, 293–295, 343, 373, 412
Deferred imitation, 168
Depression
adolescent, 292–293, 343
bullying leading to, 374
child abuse relationship to, 412
divorce impacting, 405

gay and lesbian, 343
genetic influences on, 63, 77
maternal, 87, 112, 114
personality and temperament relationship to, 299
postpartum, 114
Depth perception, 142, 143
Developmental Psychology (journal), 46, 51
Diet and nutrition
cognitive development impacted by, 205
infant and toddler, 149, 205
malnutrition, 150–151
mother's, prenatal development and, 86, 90
MyPlate nutritional guidelines, 153
obesity relationship to, 151, 153
physical growth and development impacted by, 129, 139, 149–153
socioeconomic impacts on, 150–151, 443
Diethylstilbestrol (DES), 88
Discrimination, prejudice and stereotypes
definitions of, 444–445
gender, 60, 196–198, 328–331, 333, 337–338, 400, 430, 431
homosexual, 343, 407
racial, ethnic, cultural, 196–198, 251, 260, 314, 321, 393, 436–437, 440, 441, 444–447
social identity theory on, 445–447
social learning theory on, 445
sources or roots of, 445–447
Divorce, 402–403, 404–405
Dixon, Tamera, 95, 99, 106, 123
DNA (deoxyribonucleic acid), 58
Dodge, Kenneth, 370, 389
Domestic violence, 90. See also Child abuse
Dominance hierarchy, 336
Dominant traits, 61
Dopamine, 131
Dora the Explorer, 371, 420, 427
Doulas, 101
Down syndrome, 64, 86, 245, 265, 270
Drugs. See also Substance use
ADHD/ADD stimulant, 207, 208
adolescent use of, 292, 293
birth/delivery pain-reducing, 102, 104
DARE program effectiveness combating, 17
fertility, 59, 83, 88
prenatal development impacted by, 83, 87, 88, 90
vaccine, 103–104, 153
Durbin, Jackie, 338
Dyslexia, 251

E

Early childhood. See Infancy and toddlerhood; Preschool period
Education
academic achievement levels in, 435–437
academic disidentification in, 197–198
academic self-concept impacting, 309, 310, 322
access to public, 430
bilingualism approaches in, 237–239, 442–443
cognitive development considerations in, 173, 177, 179,

184–185, 187–188, 196–198, 211–213, 420–425
contextual perspectives on influence of, 31–32
cooperative learning in, 185
critical thinking taught in, 212–213
cultural influences/differences in, 197–198, 393, 423, 430, 431, 435–437, 438, 441–443
DARE program in, 17
developmentally appropriate educational practice, 424–425
elementary to middle school transition in, 432–433
enrollment timing for, 430–431
gender barriers in, 196–198, 430, 431
graduation rates in, 436
homeschooling as alternative, 434
homework in, 432
infant early learning capabilities, 117–119
information processing considerations in, 196–198, 211–213
intelligence relationship to, 15, 74, 247, 251–252, 254–255, 263–267
learning disabilities impacting, 251
least restrictive environment for, 263–264
legislation on, 264, 432
mainstreaming in, 263, 264
multicultural, 441–443
nature-nuture debating impacting approach to, 15, 74
prejudice combating strategies in, 447
preschool or early childhood, 420–425
Race to the Top program, 432
racial and ethnic barriers and differences in, 197–198, 393, 436–437
reading taught in, 211–212
reciprocal teaching in, 185
research influencing educational policy, 48
school violence and bullying, 371–372, 373–375
self development considerations in, 309, 310, 318–319, 321, 322
sex, 345
sociocultural aspects of, 430–437
socioeconomic impacts on, 425, 436–437, 443–444
trends in, 431–432
Education for All Handicapped Children Act, 264
EEG (electroencephalogram), 42
Egocentric thought, 172, 195–196, 215
Ehmke, Rachel, 373
Electroencephalogram (EEG), 42
Elkind, David, 424–425
Ellings, Lawson, 449
Embryos, 81–82, 85. See also Prenatal development
Embryoscopy, 67
Emilia, Reggio, 421
Emotions
adolescent, 274, 290–295
brain function and, 291
cultural influences on, 283
decoding other peoples', 286–287
difficulties with, in adolescents, 292–295

Emotions (*Continued*)
emotional development, 119–120, 274, 279–280, 283–295
emotional intelligence, 254–255
emotional self-regulation, 291–292, 367, 371
empathy as understanding of, 289, 290, 354–355
experiencing, 284–285
facial or nonverbal expressions relaying, 279–280, 283–287, 288
infant and toddler, 119–120, 274, 283–289, 354
infant social competence with, 119–120
instability of, 290–291
middle childhood period, 289–290
smiling expressing, 286
social referencing of, 287–288
stranger and separation anxiety triggering, 285–286
theory of mind on understanding, 288–289
vocal expressions relaying, 287
Empathy, 289, 290, 354–355
Employment and labor
child, 9, 11
dual working parents, 403, 420
self development relationship to, 305, 313, 315
Eng, Lee, 142
Enuresis, 156
Environmental influences
behavioral perspective on, 25–27, 35, 118–119
bioecological approach to, 31–32, 35
chronosystem of, 31, 32
cohort effects as, 9, 49
contextual perspective on, 31–33, 35
critical and sensitive periods of, 12, 13–14, 85, 87
cultural (*see* Culture)
evolutionary perspective on, 34, 35
exosystem of, 31
genetic interaction with, 12, 14–15, 64, 65, 70–78
intelligence impacted by, 14–15, 71, 73–74, 237, 260–262
macrosystem of, 31, 32
mesosystem of, 31
microsystem of, 31
nature-nurture perspective on, 12, 14–15, 70–78, 260–262
obesity impacted by, 151–153
personality and temperament impacted by, 70, 75, 76, 298–299
physical growth and development impacted by, 128, 129, 132, 135, 138–139, 150–151
prenatal development impacted by, 79, 84–90, 109
sexual orientation link to, 343
social (*see* Social development)
socioeconomic (*see* Socioeconomics)
Epidural anesthesia, 102
Episiotomies, 97
Erikson, Erik, psychosocial theory of, 24–25, 35, 299–300, 309, 312–313
Ethical issues. *See also* Moral development
genetics-related, 60, 67, 84
informed consent as, 51
pregnancy-related, 84

privacy as, 52
research-related, 50–52, 72
Ethnicity. *See also* Culture; Race
acculturation with dominant, 439–440
child abuse differences by, 411
child development consideration of, 8–9
definition and description of, 8
depression differences by, 292
discrimination, prejudice and stereotypes related to, 196–198, 251, 260, 314, 321, 393, 436–437, 440, 441, 444–447
educational differences by, 436–437
ethnic self-awareness and identity development, 308, 314–316, 320–321, 439–441
ethnic self-esteem impacts, 320–321
ethnographic research on, 41, 45
family structure differences by, 406, 407
friend and peer relations influenced by, 393
online communication access differences by, 428
physical growth and development differences by, 129
research diversity of, 46
sexuality differences by, 341
Ethnographic research, 41, 45
Evolutionary perspective, 34, 35
Exercise and athletics
friendships and popularity based on proficiency with, 388
gender and participation in, 135, 327, 388
obesity relationship to lack of, 153
physical growth and development relationship to, 134–136, 139
prenatal development impacted by, 90
Experimental research, 39, 42–46
Extroversion, 74

F

Face blindness, 395
Facebook.com, 392, 428
Facial expressions
emotional expression via, 279–280, 283–287, 288
smiling as, 286
Faison, Della, 449
Families. *See also* Fathers; Mothers
abuse in (*see* Child abuse; Domestic violence)
adolescent relationship changes with, 381, 398–402, 414
blended, 405–406
changing home environments of, 403
conflicts in, 401–402
contextual perspective on influence of, 31–32
culture of (*see* Culture; Ethnicity; Race)
divorce impacting, 402–403, 404–405
dual working parents in, 403, 420
family life in, 397–398
gay and lesbian-parented, 407
generation gap in, 400–401
multigenerational, 406
orphanages or group care in absence of, 408–409
poverty impacting, 405, 406, 407–408 (*see also* Poverty; Socioeconomics)

racial and ethnic differences in, 406, 407
self-care or home-alone children in, 404
siblings in, 398
single-parent, 398, 406
types and styles of, 402–409
Family and Medical Leave Act, 112
Fast mapping, 225
Fathers. *See also* Families
abuse by (*see* Child abuse; Domestic violence)
adolescent relationship changes with, 381, 398–402, 414
birth involvement of, 100–101
divorce of, 402–403, 404–405
father-child bonding or attachment, 99, 277, 278
gay, 407
gender identification with, 332, 343
parental leave policies for, 112, 113
parenting styles of (*see* Parenting styles)
prenatal environment impacts of, 89–90
step-, 405–406, 410
working, outside home, 403, 420
Fels Research Institute Study, 12
Fertilization
artificial insemination for, 83, 84
conception at time of, 80
fertility drugs for, 59, 83, 88
genetic combining from, 58–59
infertility and difficulties of, 83–84
in vitro fertilization, 3, 19, 83, 84
Fetal alcohol syndrome/effects (FAS/FAE), 89, 265
Fetal blood sampling, 67
Fetuses, 67, 81, 82, 85, 109–111. *See also* Birth; Prenatal development
Field, Tiffany, 118, 120
Films. *See* Television, movies, and video games
Fine motor development, 136–138, 139
Fluid intelligence, 252
FMRI (functional magnetic resonance imaging), 42
Follet, Michelle, 194
Food. *See* Diet and nutrition
Forensic developmental psychology, 209–211
Foster care, 408–409
Fragile X syndrome, 64
Freud, Sigmund, psychoanalytic theory of, 23–24, 25, 35, 275, 332, 334, 343, 355, 367
Friends and peers
adolescent influences of, 381, 391–396
aggression and violence influenced by, 351, 368, 372, 375
cliques and crowds among, 392
conformity and peer pressure among, 396
cultural influences of, 384, 393, 394
dominance hierarchy among, 336
gender segregation of, 335–336
infant sociability among, 273, 281–282
juvenile delinquency influenced by, 351, 375
middle childhood period, 385–387
morality and peer pressure, 351, 376–377
online social networking among, 392, 394, 428

popularity of, 387–389, 394–396
preschool period, 382–385
racial and ethnic segregation of, 393
reference groups among, 322–323, 392
self development influenced by, 312–313, 322–323
social comparison to, 322, 323–324, 392
social competence of, 387–389
social problem-solving among, 388–389
stages of friendship, 386–387
Functionality, in cognitive development, 173
Functional magnetic resonance imaging (fMRI), 42
Functional play, 383, 384
Fusiform gyrus, 279

G

Gamete intrafallopian transfer (GIFT), 83
Gametes, 58–59, 83
Gardner, Howard, 252, 253
Gays and lesbians
adolescent gender and social relations among, 337, 338
discrimination against, 343, 407
parenting by/families of, 407
sexual orientation of, 342–343
Gender
adolescent family relations influenced by, 400
adolescent gender relations, 336–339
aggression and violence differences by, 367, 373
athletic participation and, 135, 327, 388
biological perspective on, 331–332, 334
cognitive approaches to, 333, 334
cultural approaches to, 330, 339
dating and, 338–339
depression differences by, 292–293
discrimination, prejudice and stereotypes related to, 60, 196–198, 328–331, 333, 337–338, 400, 430, 431
educational barriers to achievement based on, 196–198, 430, 431
friendship segregation by, 335–336
gender constancy, 333
gender differences, 328–329, 331–334
gender identity, 329–331, 333, 343
gender roles, 328, 329
gross motor development differences by, 135–136
language development differences by, 132, 236, 336
moral development relationship to, 360, 362–363, 364, 365
parental gender identification, 332, 343
physical growth and development differences by, 127, 128, 130, 132, 134–135, 135–136, 138–140, 157, 388
physical health differences by, 155
popularity assessments by, 396
psychoanalytic perspective on, 332, 334
puberty-related differences in, 138–140

research diversity of, 46
self development differences by, 313, 321, 337–338
sexual biology and, 328, 331, 333
sexual double standard by, 341–342
sexual orientation and, 343
social learning approaches to, 332–333, 334
social relationships and, 335–339
societal and parental influences on, 328–334, 347
theoretical explanations of gender differences, 331–334
transgendered persons, 343
Generation gap, 400–401
Genetics. *See also* Heredity
aggression and violence roots in, 367
behavioral genetics study of, 34, 63
environment interaction with, 12, 14–15, 64, 65, 70–78
ethical issues related to, 60, 67, 84
evolutionary perspective on, 34, 35
genes and chromosomes in, 58–59, 59–60
genetic counseling and testing, 57, 66–69
genetic disorders, 57, 61–63, 63–66, 67–68, 103 (*see also specific disorders*)
genetic engineering, 30, 60, 83, 84
human genome mapping in, 63
intelligence impacted by, 14–15, 71, 73–74, 260–262
language development relationship to, 230–231
maturation in, 14
mental health issues linked to, 63, 64, 77–78
multiples births and, 59–60 (*see also* Twins)
nature-nurture perspective on, 12, 14–15, 70–78, 260–262
obesity impacted by, 73, 151–153
personality and temperament influenced by, 63, 70, 74–75, 76, 298–299
physical growth and development impacted by, 132
sex determination via, 59–60
sexual orientation link to, 343
trait determination via, 60–61, 62–63
transmission of genetic information, 61–63
X-linked genes in, 62
Genotypes, 61, 70–71
Gesell, Arnold, 257–258
Gifted children, 12, 48–49, 266–267
Gilligan, Carol, moral development approach of, 360, 362–363
Goal-directed behavior, 166
Gonorrhea, 87
Gonzales, Maria, 187–188
Gonzalez, Christine, 264
Grammar, 225–226, 226–227
Green, Christina-Taylor, 21, 54
Gross motor development, 133–136, 179
Growth. *See* Physical development

H

Habituation, 119, 258
Haglund, Karl, 305, 325
Hall, G. Stanley, 11–12
Handedness, right or left, 137–138

Harlow, Harry, 275
Hart, Sybil, 285
Haws, Andrea, 95
Head Start, 48, 424
Health. *See* Mental health issues; Physical health
Health insurance, 102–103, 113
Hearing or auditory perception
deafness as lack of, 221, 222, 228, 235
language development and, 144, 221, 222, 228, 235
physical growth and development of, 117, 128, 143–145, 148
Height, 126–130
Hemophilia, 62–63
Henry, Aldos, 396
Heredity
behavioral genetics study of, 34, 63
evolutionary perspective on, 34, 35
genetics as basis of (*see* Genetics)
mental health issues linked to, 63, 64, 77–78
nature-nurture perspective on, 12, 14–15, 70–78, 260–262
Herrnstein, Richard J., *The Bell Curve,* 260–261
Heteronomous morality, 352–353
Heterosexuality, 342–343
Hierarchical integration principle, 127
Hippocampus, 204, 291, 299, 413
Hollingworth, Leta Stetter, 12
Holophrases, 223
Homeschooling, 434
Homosexuality, 342–343. *See also* Gays and lesbians
Horowitz, Dana, 77
Howard, Leah and John, 57
Huntington's disease, 64, 66, 67
Hypnobirthing, 101

I

Identity. *See also* Self development
adolescent identity development, 300, 311–316, 319, 320–321, 322–323, 337–338, 398–402
bicultural, 315, 316, 439, 442–443
cognitive development and knowledge of, 173
collectivist, 32, 307–308, 321, 399–400
cultural influences on, 32, 307–308, 314–316, 321, 438–441, 442–443
Erikson on, 309, 312–313
evaluation of, 317–323
friend and peer influences on, 312–313, 322–323
gender, 329–331, 333, 343
identity achievement, 313
identity diffusion, 314
identity foreclosure, 313–314
individualist, 32, 308, 399
infant and toddler sense of, 306–307
Marcia on, 313–314
middle childhood period sense of, 305, 308–310, 317–320, 322, 323–324
moratorium on exploring, 313, 314
parenting styles impacting, 319–320, 323
physical development relationship to, 309, 310, 311, 322
preschool period sense of, 307–308, 367, 371
racial and ethnic, 308, 314–316, 320–321, 439–441

self-esteem development impacting, 317–321, 323, 337–338, 445–447
social comparison impacting, 322–323, 323–324
social identity theory on, 445–447
socioeconomic impacts on, 320–321
Imaginary audiences, 195
Imitation
abstract modeling as, 354
aggression and violence modeling as, 368–370
cognitive development and, 27, 166, 168, 180
deferred, 168
infant social development via, 119–120, 273, 281–282
linguistic, 220
moral development via, 354
social-cognitive learning theory on, 27, 354
social competence and, 119–120
Immanent justice, 353
Immigrants
acculturation of, 439–440
education in children of, 437
self-development in children of, 321
Immunizations, 103–104, 153
Imprinting, 275
Incipient cooperation stage of moral development, 353
Independence of systems principle, 127
Infancy and toddlerhood
Apgar scale measurement system in early, 98–99
attachment in, 99, 274–280, 298
attention in, 192, 204–206
baby biographies of, 11
birth before (*see* Birth)
brain growth in, 130
child care centers used in, 421
child development study of, 6
circular reactions in, 165–168
classical conditioning during, 118, 119
cognitive development in, 28, 162, 163, 164–168, 178–180, 192, 193–194, 199–201, 204–206, 257, 258–259
diet and nutrition in, 149, 205
emotional development in, 119–120, 274, 283–289, 354
empathy in, 289, 354
fine motor development in, 136
gender in, 328–329
gross motor development in, 133–134
habituation during, 119, 258
infant amnesia in, 200
infant mortality rate, 86, 106, 107, 111–113
information processing in, 192, 193–194, 199–201, 204–206, 257, 258–259
intelligence in, 256–259
language development in, 219, 220–224, 228, 234–236
learning capabilities in, 117–119
massage in, 99, 108, 146
maternal mental health impacting, 114
memory in, 192, 199–201, 257, 258
neonates or newborns as early, 96, 98–99, 103, 106–109, 115–121
operant conditioning during, 118–119
peer interaction in, 273, 281–282

personality development in, 296–300
physical appearance in, 96, 99
physical competence of newborns, 116
physical growth and development in, 125, 126–127, 130, 133–134, 136, 141–147
postmature infants, 109
premature or preterm infants, 59, 86, 87, 95, 106–110
reflexes in, 116, 146, 163, 165
self development in, 306–307
sensory capabilities in, 117, 141–147
separation anxiety in, 286
small-for-gestational-age infants, 106
smiling in, 286
social competence in, 119–121
social development in, 99, 119–121, 273–282, 283–289, 296–300, 301
social referencing in, 287–288
stranger anxiety in, 285–286
temperament in, 296–299
theory of mind on emotional understanding in, 288–289
vaccinations given in, 103–104
Infertility, 83–84
Information processing
adolescent, 194–198
applications of, 209–214
assessment of theory of, 213–214
attention in, 192, 204–208
automatization of, 193
in cognitive development, 29–30, 191–215, 252–254, 257, 258–259
cognitive neuroscience approaches to, 203–204, 205
control strategies improving, 203, 204
critical thinking use of, 212–213
cultural differences in, 202
educational considerations of, 196–198, 211–213
egocentric thought in, 195–196, 215
encoding, storage and retrieval in, 192–193, 199
forensic developmental psychology use of, 209–211
foundations of, 192–193
infant and toddler, 192, 193–194, 199–201, 204–206, 257, 258–259
intelligence theory based on, 252–254, 257, 258–259
memory in, 191–192, 199–204, 209–211, 257, 258
metacognition in, 192, 195
middle childhood, 194, 202–203
mnemonics for, 203, 204
numerical and mathematical abilities in, 193–194, 196–197, 201, 202
planning abilities in, 206–207
preschool period, 201–202, 210–211
reading use of, 211–212
scripted events in, 202
Informed consent, 51
Informed consumerism
adolescent suicide prevention as, 294–295
career selection as, 315
child development information assessments as, 16–17
critical evaluation of research as, 51

Informed consumerism (*Continued*)
early language development assessment as, 228
infant body and senses exercise as, 147
IQ test taking as, 267
labor strategies as, 104
memory control strategies as, 204
prejudice combating strategies as, 447
prenatal environment optimization as, 90
preschooler cognitive development promotion as, 173
preschooler moral behavior increases and aggression reduction as, 371
social competence increases as, 390
unwanted pregnancy prevention as, 346
Injuries, childhood, 155
Institute of Medicine, 104
Instrumental aggression, 367
Insurance, 102–103, 113
Integration
cultural, 439
hierarchical integration principle, 127
Intelligence. *See also* Cognitive development
alternative conceptions of, 252, 253
benchmarks of, 247–248
bodily kinesthetic, 253
controversies involving, 256–262
crystallized, 252
cultural biases in testing, 251, 259–262
definition of, 246–247, 257
determining individual strengths in, 246–255
developmental scales measuring, 257–258
education relationship to, 15, 74, 247, 251–252, 254–255, 263–267
emotional, 254–255
environmental influences on, 14–15, 71, 73–74, 237, 260–262
fairness in IQ testing, 249, 251–252, 269
fluid, 252
gifted or above-average, 12, 48–49, 266–267
infant and toddler, 256–259
information processing approach to, 252–254, 257, 258–259
intellectual disabilities, 265
intelligence quotients (IQs), 248–252
interpersonal, 253
intrapersonal, 253
learning disabilities and, 251
linguistic, 253
logical mathematical, 253
meaning of IQ scores, 251–252
measurements of, 247, 248–249, 250
mental age and, 247–248
musical, 253
naturalist, 253
nature-nurture debate on, 14–15, 71, 73–74, 260–262
reliability and validity of IQ tests, 249, 251
research on, 71, 73–74
socioeconomic impacts on, 237, 260–262
spatial, 253

take-at-home IQ tests, 261
triarchic theory of, 252–254
Interactionist approaches, to language development, 231
Internet usage. *See* Online communication
Interpersonal intelligence, 253
Intonation, 227
Intrapersonal intelligence, 253
Intuitive thought, 172–173
In vitro fertilization (IVF), 3, 19, 83, 84

J
Jacobs, Anne and Tim, 103
Juarez, Alma, 99–100
Juvenile delinquency, 351, 375

K
Kaiser Family Foundation, 427
Kaufman Assessment Battery for Children, Second Edition (KABC-II), 249
Kinsey, Alfred, 343
Klinefelter's syndrome, 65
Kohlberg, Lawrence, moral development approach of, 360–362
Kriebel, Mary, 212
Kwashiorkor, 150–151

L
Labor (birth-related), 96–97, 104
Labor (employment). *See* Employment and labor
Lamaze birthing techniques, 100–101
Language development
babbling in, 221
bilingualism in, 237–239, 442–443
brain growth impacting, 131, 132
characteristics of language, 220
children's conversations (with and to children), 234–239
cognitive development and, 169, 239
course of, 220–227
cultural influences on, 221, 223, 224, 235–236
deaf persons', 221, 222, 228, 235
expressive style of, 224
fast mapping in, 225
first sentences, 223–224
first words, 219, 222–223, 240, 242
fundamentals of, 220–224
gender differences in, 132, 236, 336
genetic influences on, 230–231
grammar in, 225–226, 226–227
hearing and auditory perception in, 144, 221, 222, 228, 235
holophrases in, 223
infant and toddler, 219, 220–224, 228, 234–236
interactionist approaches to, 231
intonation in, 227
language acquisition in, 230–231
language and thought relationship in, 169, 231–232
learning theory on, 230
linguistic comprehension *vs.* production in, 220, 221
linguistic intelligence and, 253
linguistic-relativity hypothesis on, 231
metalinguistic awareness in, 227
middle childhood, 226–228
morphemes in, 220

nativist approaches to, 230–231
origins of, 229–232
over- and underextension in, 224
phonology in, 220, 227
Piaget's theory of, 169, 226, 231–232
poverty relationship to, 236–237
pragmatics of, 226, 227
prelinguistic communication in, 220–222, 228
preschool period, 169, 225–226
private speech or self-talk in, 226, 228
referential style of, 224
research on, 49
self-control promotion via, 227–228
semantics in, 220
social speech in, 226
sounds to symbols, 220–224
syntax in, 225, 227
telegraphic speech in, 224
Vygotsky's theory of, 226, 232
Lanugo, 99
Latchkey children, 404
Lateralization, in brain development, 131, 132
Learning disabilities, 251
Learning theory and social learning theory
on aggression, 368
on gender, 332–333, 334
on imitation and modeling, 27, 354
on language development, 230
on moral development, 354
on prejudice, 445
on sexual orientation, 343
social-cognitive learning theory as, 27
Legal system
child witnesses in, 209–211
juvenile delinquency and, 351, 375
Leibowitz, Amy, 266
Lesbians. *See* Gays and lesbians
Levey, Lisa D'Annolfo, 358
Life-span approach, 12, 14
Linguistic-relativity hypothesis, 231
"Little Albert," 118
Lizzagara, Paco, 398–399
Locke, John, 11
Logical mathematical intelligence, 253
Logical thought, 174
Longitudinal research, 48–49
Lorenz, Konrad, 34, 35, 275, 367
Low birth weight infants, 87, 89, 95, 106–109
Lynch, Jared, 256

M
Mainstreaming, 263, 264
Malnutrition, 150–151
Marasmus, 150
Marcia, James, 313–314
Marcus, Cyril and Stewart, 73
Marginalization, cultural, 439
Marijuana, 88
Marques, Consuela, 285
Marriage
cultural influences on, 6
divorce ending, 402–403, 404–405
remarriage and blended families, 405–406
Marshall, Patrice, 269
Martell, Jim and Jason, 347
Massage, infant, 99, 108, 146
Masturbation, 340–341
Mathematical abilities. *See* Numerical and mathematical abilities

Maturation
age and maturation rates, 7
as genetic unfolding, 14
Maximally Discriminative Facial Movement Coding System (MAX), 283
McDougall, Roddy, 22
Measles, 103–104. *See also* Rubella (German measles)
Media. *See also* Online communication; Television, movies, and video games
adolescent influence of, 427–429
amount of time spent with, 425, 427
body image influenced by, 152, 342, 428
discrimination and prejudice fostered by, 445
gender influences of, 333
middle childhood influence of, 427–429
preschool influence of, 420, 425–427
Memory
accuracy of, 200–201, 202, 209–210
amnesia as lack of, 200
autobiographical, 202, 210
cognitive neuroscience approaches to, 203–204, 205
control strategies improving, 203, 204
cultural influences on, 202
duration of, 200–201
encoding, storage and retrieval of, 192–193, 199
explicit, 203–204
implicit, 203–204
infant and toddler, 192, 199–201, 257, 258
information processing approach to, 191–192, 199–204, 209–211, 257, 258
long-term, 199
metamemory, 203
middle childhood, 202–203
mnemonics for, 203, 204
preschool period, 201–202, 210–211
scripted events in, 202
sensory, 199
short-term or working, 199, 202
three-system approach to, 199
visual-recognition memory measurements, 257, 258
Mendel, Gregor, 60–61
Mensch, Diane, 102–103
Menstruation, 138–139
Mental health issues. *See also specific disorders*
adolescent, 292–295, 343, 373
attachment relationship to, 277
bullying impacting, 373–375
child abuse impacting, 408, 410, 412–413
cultural impacts on, 292, 439–440
divorce impacting, 405
environmental influences on, 77–78
gay and lesbian, 343
gender differences in, 292–293
genetic influences on, 63, 64, 77–78
information processing impacted by, 207
intelligence testing impacted by, 251
juvenile delinquency relationship to, 375
maternal, 87, 112, 114

personality and temperament relationship to, 299

prenatal development impacted by, 87

social development and, 282, 285–286, 289

Mental representations, 168

Merced, Anton, 311

Metacognition, 192, 195

Metalinguistic awareness, 227

Michaels, Kelly, 210

Michel, Tori, 344

Middle childhood

child development study of, 6

cognitive development in, 28, 174–175, 181, 194, 202–203

education in (*see* Education)

emotional development in, 289–290

empathy in, 290

family lives in, 398

fine motor development in, 137–138

friendships and peer relations in, 385–387

gender in, 327, 330, 335–336

gross motor development in, 135–136

information processing in, 194, 202–203

language development in, 226–228

memory in, 202–203

moral development in, 353, 360

personality development in, 300

physical growth and development in, 128–129, 135–136, 137–138, 148

physical health during, 153

self development in, 305, 308–310, 317–320, 322, 323–324

sensory development in, 148

siblings in, 398

social development in, 289–290, 300, 335–336

television and media influences in, 427–429

Midwives, 99–100, 101, 121–122

Mirror neurons, 282

Miscarriages, 84, 87, 89

Mitchell, Duncan, 395

Mnemonics, 203, 204

Montessori schools, 421

Moral development

abstract modeling in, 354

adolescent, 351, 355, 360–362, 364–365, 376–377

aggression and violence relationship to, 371

autonomous cooperation stage of, 353

conventional morality in, 360, 361

cultural influences on, 357–358, 360–361, 365

definition of, 352

effective parenting impacting, 355–358

empathy and, 354–355

gender relationship to, 360, 362–363, 364, 365

Gilligan's approach to, 360, 362–363

heteronomous morality stage of, 352–353

immanent justice beliefs in, 353

incipient cooperation stage of, 353

Kohlberg's approach to, 360–362

middle childhood period, 353, 360

moral behavior and reasoning disconnects in, 363–365

peer pressure impacting, 351, 376–377

Piaget's theory of, 352–353

postconventional morality in, 360, 361

preconventional morality in, 360, 361

preschool period, 352–355, 371

prosocial behavior and, 354, 359–365

research on, 49

social learning theory on, 354

theoretical approaches to, 352–354, 355, 360–363

Morphemes, 220

Mothers. *See also* Families

abuse by (*see* Child abuse; Domestic violence)

adolescent or teen, 86, 108, 344–346

adolescent relationship changes with, 381, 398–402, 414

age of, 83, 86, 108

diet and nutrition of, 86, 90

divorce of, 402–403, 404–405

gender identification with, 332, 343

health of, 87, 109

lesbian, 407

maternity leave policies for, 112, 113

mental health issues among, 87, 112, 114

mother-child bonding or attachment, 99, 277, 278

parenting styles of (*see* Parenting styles)

prenatal support of, 86

reproduction by (*see* Birth; Pregnancy; Prenatal development)

single-parenting by, 398, 406

step-, 405–406

substance use among, 83, 87, 88–89, 265

surrogate, 83, 84

working, outside home, 403, 420

Movies. *See* Television, movies, and video games

Mulford, Jared, 215

Muller, Karen and Lisa, 240

Multiculturalism, 438–447

Multigenerational families, 406

Mumps, 87, 104

Murray, Charles, *The Bell Curve,* 260–261

Music

amusia and tone deafness, 254

musical intelligence, 253

Mutual regulation model of attachment, 279–280

Myelin, 82, 130–131, 134, 137

MyPlate nutritional guidelines, 153

N

Narcissism, 319

National pride, 446

National Reading Panel, 212

National Research Council, 212

Nativist approaches, to language development, 230–231

Naturalistic observations, 41, 45

Naturalist intelligence, 253

Nature and nurture. *See also* Environmental influences; Genetics; Heredity

child development study of, 12, 14–15, 71–73

genetic and environmental interactions as, 70–78

intelligence influenced by, 14–15, 71, 73–74, 260–262

Neonates or newborns, 96, 98–99, 103, 106–109, 115–121. *See also* Infancy and toddlerhood

Neuroscience. *See also* Brain development and function

amusia/tone deafness studies in, 254

cognitive neuroscience approaches, 30, 42, 203–204, 205

computerized axial tomography (CAT) scans in, 42

electroencephalograms in, 42

emotional activation study in, 291

face blindness research in, 395

functional magnetic resonance imaging in, 42

psychophysiological research using, 42, 45

social development studies in, 279, 282

Neuroticism, 74

New York Longitudinal Study, 297

Nightmares or night terrors, 156

NMDA receptors, 205

No Child Left Behind Act, 432

Non-normative life events, 9

Nonorganic failure to thrive, 151

Nordstrom, Amber, 199

Numerical and mathematical abilities

academic achievement in, 435–436

cognitive development and, 180, 193–194, 196–197, 201, 202

educational gender barriers for, 196–197

logical mathematical intelligence, 253

Study of Mathematically Precocious Youth on, 267

Nutrition. *See* Diet and nutrition

O

Obesity

body image and, 151, 152

genetic influences on, 73, 151–153

physical growth and development relationship to, 139, 151–153

sedentary lifestyle leading to, 153, 426, 428

social influences on, 151–153

Object permanence, 166–167, 179–180

Obsessive-compulsive disorder (OCD), 64

Obstetricians, 101

Ogbu, John, 436–437

Online communication

adolescent use of, 374, 392, 394, 428–429

cyber-bullying as, 374

online social networks as, 392, 394, 428

preschool exposure to, 425–426

racial, ethnic and socioeconomic influences on, 428–429

Onlooker play, 383, 384

Operant conditioning, 26–27, 118–119

Orphanages, 408–409

Oxytocin, 96, 395

P

Pain

during birth, 102, 104

infants' sensitivity to, 145–146

Palermo, Lisa, 273, 281, 303

Palmer, Dave and Jessalyn, 157

Palmitate, 205

Pantagenes, Teddy, 434

Parallel play, 383, 384

Parent coaches, 358

Parenting styles

aggression influenced by, 372–373

authoritarian, 355, 356

authoritative, 319, 356–357

cultural differences in, 357–358, 372–373

moral development influenced by, 355–358

parent coaches addressing, 358

permissive, 355, 356

self-esteem impacted by, 319–320, 323

uninvolved, 356, 357

Parents. *See* Families; Fathers; Mothers; Parenting styles

Pavlov, Ivan, 118

Peers. *See* Friends and peers

Permissive parenting style, 355, 356

Personal fables, 196

Personality development

adolescent, 300

antisocial personality disorders, 375

child development study of, 6

culture influencing, 75, 76, 298

definition of, 6

environmental influences on, 70, 75, 76, 298–299

extroversion in, 74

genetic influences on, 63, 70, 74–75, 76, 298–299

infant and toddler, 296–300

middle childhood period, 300

neuroticism in, 74

preschool period, 299–300

psychoanalytic theory on, 23

psychosocial theory on, 299–300

temperament in, 70, 76, 134, 296–299

Pettigrew, Eric, 146–147

Phenotypes, 61, 71

Phenylketonuria (PKU), 61–62, 63–64

Phonology, 220, 227

Physical development

adolescent, 129–131, 138–140, 311, 322, 337, 340

body changes as, 126–130 (*see also* Puberty)

body image and, 151, 152, 342, 428

brain growth as, 130–132

child development study of, 5, 6

cultural differences in, 127, 128, 129, 132, 135, 138–139, 150–151, 157

definition of, 5

diet and nutrition impacting, 129, 139, 149–153

environmental influences on, 128, 129, 132, 135, 138–139, 150–151

exercise and athletics relationship to, 134–136, 139

fine motor development as, 136–138, 139

gender differences in, 127, 128, 130, 132, 134–135, 135–136, 138–140, 157, 388

gender relations impacted by, 337

gross motor development as, 133–136, 179

handedness, right or left, as, 137–138

height and weight changes, 126–130, 139, 151–153

Physical development (*Continued*)
  infant and toddler, 125, 126–127, 130, 133–134, 136, 141–147
  middle childhood, 128–129, 135–136, 137–138, 148
  physical appearance and genetics in, 60–61, 73
  physical appearance of neonates, 96, 99
  physical health impacting (*see* Physical health)
  prenatal, 80–82 (*see also* Prenatal development)
  preschool period, 126, 128, 130, 131, 133, 134–135, 136–137, 138, 139, 148
  principles of growth, 127
  puberty as, 138–140, 311, 322, 337, 340
  secular trends in, 139
  self development relationship to, 309, 310, 311, 322
  sensory development as, 117, 128, 141–148
  socioeconomic impacts on, 128, 129, 139, 150–151
Physical health
  abuse impacting (*see* Child abuse)
  asthma impacting, 154–155
  childhood health and wellness, 153–155
  cultural differences in, 154, 155
  diet and nutrition role in (*see* Diet and nutrition)
  exercise impacting (*see* Exercise and athletics)
  gender differences in, 155
  genetic disorders impacting, 57, 61–63, 63–66, 67–68, 103 (*see also* specific disorders)
  injuries impacting, 155
  insurance coverage of care for, 102–103, 113
  mother's, prenatal impacts of, 87, 109
  newborn screening of, 98–99, 103
  premature infant challenges with, 106–110
  socioeconomic impacts on, 154, 155, 443
  vaccinations and, 103–104, 153
Piaget, Jean
  background of, 162–163
  cognitive development theory of, 28–29, 35, 162–181
  language theories of, 169, 226, 231–232
  moral development theory of, 352–353
  neo-Piagetian theory, 29–30
Placentas, 81
Planning abilities, 206–207
Plasticity, 13–14, 131
Pluralistic society model, 442
Poirier, Christin, 287
Polio, 103
Polygenic traits, 62–63
Postconventional morality, 360, 361
Postpartum depression, 114
Poverty. *See also* Socioeconomics
  cost of, 443–444
  family life impacted by, 405, 406, 407–408
  intelligence impacted by, 237
  language development relationship to, 236–237

prenatal development impacted by, 85–86
  prevalence of, 443–444
Preconventional morality, 360, 361
Prefrontal cortex, 131, 291, 299, 384
Pregnancy
  abortion of, 84
  adolescent or teen, 86, 108, 344–346
  age during, 83, 86, 108
  birth control to prevent, 90, 344, 345, 346
  diet and nutrition impacting, 86, 90
  domestic violence during, 90
  environmental factors influencing, 79, 84–90, 109
  ethical issues related to, 84
  fertilization for, 3, 19, 58–59, 80, 83–84, 88
  maternal health impacting, 87, 109
  miscarriages of, 84, 87, 89
  parental leave policies after, 112, 113
  prenatal development during (*see* Prenatal development)
  prenatal support during, 86
  problems related to, 83–84, 84–90
  reproductive organs for, 80, 108
  surrogate, 83, 84
  threats to, 84–90
Prejudice. *See* Discrimination, prejudice and stereotypes
Premature or preterm infants, 59, 86, 87, 95, 106–110
Prenatal development. *See also* Pregnancy
  birth following (*see* Birth)
  critical and sensitive periods of, 13, 85, 87
  embryonic stage of, 81–82, 85
  environmental factors influencing, 79, 84–90, 109
  fathers' impact on, 89–90
  fertilization leading to, 3, 19, 58–59, 80, 83–84, 88
  fetal stage of, 81, 82, 85 (*see also* Fetuses)
  germinal stage of, 80–81
  maternal age impacting, 83, 86, 108
  maternal diet and nutrition impacting, 86, 90
  maternal health impacting, 87, 109
  maternal support during, 86
  postmature or lengthy, 109
  premature termination of (*see* Miscarriages; Premature or preterm infants)
  prenatal testing during, 57, 66–67
  reproductive organs for, 80, 108
  socioeconomic impacts on, 85–86, 108–109, 112–113
  stages of, 80–82
  substance use impacting, 83, 87, 88–89, 90, 265
  threats to, 84–90, 112–113
Preschool period
  aggression and violence in, 366–367, 368–371
  associative play in, 383, 384
  brain growth in, 130, 131
  child care centers used in, 421, 422–423
  child development study of, 6
  cognitive development in, 28, 168–173, 180, 201–202, 210–211, 384, 420–425

constructive play in, 383, 384
  cooperative play in, 383, 384
  education in, 420–425
  effectiveness of child care in, 422
  empathy in, 354–355
  family lives in, 398
  fine motor development in, 136–137, 138, 139
  friendships and peer relations in, 382–385
  functional play in, 383, 384
  gender in, 329–331, 333
  gross motor development in, 133, 134–135
  Head Start education in, 48, 424
  information processing in, 201–202, 210–211
  language development in, 169, 225–226
  memory in, 201–202, 210–211
  moral development in, 352–355, 371
  numerical and mathematical abilities in, 201
  onlooker play in, 383, 384
  parallel play in, 383, 384
  personality development in, 299–300
  physical growth and development in, 126, 128, 130, 131, 133, 134–135, 136–137, 138, 139, 148
  physical health during, 154, 155–156
  quality of child care in, 422–423
  self development in, 307–308, 367, 371
  sensory development in, 148
  social development in, 299–300, 420–425
  television and media influences in, 420, 425–427
  theory of mind in, 385
Privacy, 52
Private speech or self-talk, 226, 228
Propositional thought, 176
Prosocial behavior, 354, 359–365
Prosopagnosia, 395
Proximodistal principle, 127
Psamtik, 37, 50
Psychodynamic perspective
  psychoanalytic theory as, 23–24, 25, 35, 275, 332, 334, 343, 355, 367
  psychosocial theory as, 24–25, 35, 299–300, 309, 312–313
  theoretical basis of, 23–25, 35, 299
Psychological disorders. *See* Mental health issues
Psychophysiological research, 42, 45
Puberty, 138–140, 311, 322, 337, 340
Public policy, research used to improve, 48

Q

Qualitative research, 41
Quinn, Jelani, 363

R

Race. *See also* Culture; Ethnicity
  acculturation with dominant, 439–440
  child abuse differences by, 411
  child development consideration of, 8–9
  definition and description of, 8
  depression differences by, 292

discrimination, prejudice and stereotypes related to, 196–198, 251, 260, 314, 321, 393, 436–437, 440, 441, 444–447
  educational barriers to achievement based on, 197–198, 393, 436–437
  family structure differences by, 406, 407
  friend and peer relations influenced by, 393
  genetics of, 63
  online communication access differences by, 428
  physical growth and development differences by, 127, 129
  prenatal development and birth issues in relation to, 108–109, 111, 112–113
  racial differences in intelligence testing, 260–262
  racial self-awareness and identity development, 308, 314–316, 320–321, 439–441
  racial self-esteem impacts, 320–321
  research diversity of, 46
  sexuality differences by, 341
Race to the Top program, 432
Raven Progressive Matrices Test, 251
Reactive attachment disorder, 277
Reade, Jared, 432
Reading
  amount of time spent on, 425, 427
  dyslexia impacting, 251
  legislated requirements for, 432
  literacy rates, 431
  teaching, 211–212
Recessive traits, 61
Reciprocal socialization, 280
Reciprocal teaching, 185
Reference groups, 322–323, 392
Reflexes, infant, 116, 146, 163, 165
Relational aggression, 367
Reproduction. *See* Birth; Fertilization; Pregnancy; Prenatal development
Research
  abortion-related, 84
  aggression and violence-related, 39–40, 42–44, 50, 53, 368–370
  archival, 45
  case studies in, 41, 45
  control groups in, 42–43
  correlational, 39–42
  critical evaluation of, 51
  cross-sectional, 49–50
  developmental change measurements in, 47–50
  developmental questions identified and posed in, 37–38
  diversity of participants in, 46
  environmental, 71–73
  ethical issues in, 50–52, 72
  ethnographic, 41, 45
  experimental, 39, 42–46
  field studies in, 44–45
  genetic, 60–61, 71–73, 73–74, 75, 76
  hypotheses identified for, 38
  laboratory studies in, 45
  longitudinal, 48–49
  meta-analysis of multiple, 44
  naturalistic observations in, 41, 45
  nature-nurture, 71–73
  nonhuman, 72, 99, 275
  practice implications and applications of, 16, 48, 87, 185, 207, 358, 411

psychophysiological, 42, 45
public policy influenced by, 48
qualitative, 41
random assignment in, 43–44
research strategy selection for, 38–39
role of, 21–22
scientific method and, 37–45
sequential studies in, 50
setting selection for, 44–45
surveys in, 42, 45
theoretical perspectives influencing (*see* Theoretical perspectives)
theoretical *vs.* applied, 47
theories formulated for, 38
twin studies in, 60, 72–73, 73–74, 75, 281, 343
Respiratory distress syndrome, 106–107
Reversibility, 174, 180
Rimmele, Ulrike, 395
Rodriguez, Austin, 373
Rodriguez, Maddy, 256
Rosenblatt, Eli, 145
Ross, Elena, 301
Rousseau, Jean-Jacques, 11
Rubella (German measles), 87, 90, 103–104

S

Safer Choices program, 345
Scaffolding, 184–185
Schemes, cognitive development, 28, 163
Schizophrenia, 63, 64, 77
School age children. See Adolescence; Middle childhood
Schools. *See* Education
School violence and bullying, 371–372, 373–375
Science (journal), 51
Scripted events, 202
Second Step program, 372
Secular trends, 139
Self-care children, 404
Self development
adolescent, 300, 308, 311–316, 319, 320–321, 322–323, 337–338, 398–402
cognitive development and, 173
cultural influences on, 32, 307–308, 314–316, 321, 438–441, 442–443
education considerations of, 309, 310, 318–319, 321, 322
emotional self-awareness in, 288–289
emotional self-regulation as, 291–292, 367, 371
Erikson on, 309, 312–313
evaluation of self in, 317–323
friend and peer role in, 312–313, 322–323
gender differences in, 313, 321, 337–338
gender identity development as, 329–331, 333, 343
group membership boosting self-esteem in, 445–447
infant and toddler, 306–307
Marcia on, 313–314
middle childhood period, 305, 308–310, 317–320, 322, 323–324
morality as element of (*see* Moral development)
parenting styles impacting, 319–320, 323

physical development relationship to, 309, 310, 311, 322
preschool period, 307–308, 367, 371
psychological moratorium from, 313, 314
race and ethnicity impacting self-esteem in, 320–321
racial and ethnic self-awareness and identity development as, 308, 314–316, 439–441
self-control and language promotion as, 227–228
self-esteem development as, 317–321, 323, 337–338, 445–447
social comparison impacting, 322–323, 323–324
social identity theory on, 445–447
socioeconomic impacts on, 320–321
Semantics, 220
Senses
hearing or auditory perception as, 117, 128, 143–145, 148, 221, 222, 228, 235
infant sensory capabilities, 117, 141–147
middle childhood, 148
multimodal perception of, 146–147, 259
physical growth and development of, 117, 128, 141–148
preschool period, 148
sensorimotor stage of cognitive development, 163, 164–168
sensory memory, 199
sight or vision, 117, 142–143, 144, 148, 257, 258–259
smell as, 117, 145
stimulation of, 147
taste as, 117, 145
touch as, 117, 145–146 (*see also* Massage, infant)
Separation, cultural, 439
Separation anxiety, 286
Sesame Street, 371, 420, 426–427
Sex, biological
gender and, 328, 331, 333 (*see also* Gender)
genetic determination of, 59–60
genetic engineering of, 60, 83, 84
Sexting, 339
Sexuality
abstinence from, 345, 346
adolescent, 339, 340–346, 364
becoming sexual, 340–342
bisexuality, 342
cultural influences on, 341
double standard of, 341–342
heterosexuality, 342–343
homosexuality, 342–343 (*see also* Gays and lesbians)
masturbation as, 340–341
moral issues with, 364
psychoanalytic theory on, 23–24
puberty as start of sexual maturation, 138–140, 311, 322, 337, 340
racial and ethnic differences in, 341
sexual intercourse as, 341–342
sexual orientation of, 342–343
teen pregnancy and, 86, 108, 344–346
virginity pledges to refrain from premarital, 345
Sexually transmitted diseases, 87, 345
Sheehan, Elissa, 25, 26

Sickle-cell anemia, 64–65
Sight or vision, 117, 142–143, 144, 148, 257, 258–259
Single-parent families, 398, 406
Skandera, Daniel, 245, 270
Skinner, B. F., 26, 35
Sleep
challenges with, 156
divorce impacting, 405
enuresis or bed-wetting during, 156
infant states of arousal and, 120
nightmares or night terrors during, 156
television and media usage impacting, 428
Small-for-gestational-age infants, 106
Smallpox, 103
Smell, 117, 145
Smiling, 286
Social development
adolescent, 274, 290–295, 300, 336–339
attachment in, 99, 274–280, 298
autism and difficulties of, 282, 289
child care settings impacting, 273, 282
child development study of, 6
cohort effects on, 9, 49
cultural influences on, 277, 278–279, 283, 298, 339, 384, 393, 394
dating and, 338–339
definition of, 6
emotional development and, 119–120, 274, 279–280, 283–295
family as source of (*see* Families; Fathers; Mothers)
friends and peers as source of, 273, 281–282, 382–390, 391–396 (*see also* Friends and peers)
gender and social relationships in, 335–339
infant and toddler, 99, 119–121, 273–282, 283–289, 296–300, 301
interpersonal intelligence role in, 253
language development relationship to, 226, 234–239
middle childhood, 289–290, 300, 335–336
nature-nurture perspective on, 12, 14–15, 75
online social networking for, 392, 394, 428
personality development as, 6, 23, 63, 70, 74–75, 76, 134, 296–300, 375
preschool period, 299–300, 420–425
prosocial behavior and, 354, 359–365
psychosocial theory on, 24–25, 35, 299–300, 309, 312–313
roots of sociability in, 274–282
smiling and social smiling in, 286
social comparison impacting, 322–323, 323–324, 392
social competence as, 119–121, 387–389, 390
socialcultural theory of, 32–33, 35, 182–186, 384
social identity theory on, 445–447
social learning theory on, 27, 332–333, 334, 354, 368, 445
social problem-solving as, 388–389
social referencing in, 287–288

sociocultural-graded influences on, 9 (*see also* Culture)
stranger and separation anxiety in, 285–286
Social identity theory, 445–447
Social learning theory
on aggression, 368
on gender differences, 332–333, 334
on imitation and modeling, 27, 354
on moral development, 354
on prejudice, 445
social-cognitive learning theory as, 27
theoretical basis of, 27
Society for Research in Child Development, 50
Socioeconomics
computer access impacted by, 428–429
cost of poverty and low socioeconomic status, 443–444
dietary and nutritional impacts of, 150–151, 443
divorce impacting, 405
educational impacts of, 425, 436–437, 443–444
employment impacting (*see* Employment and labor)
family life impacted by, 405, 406, 407–408
intelligence impacted by, 237, 260–262
language development relationship to, 236–237
physical growth and development impacted by, 128, 129, 139, 150–151
physical health impacted by, 154, 155, 443
prenatal development and birth impacted by, 85–86, 108–109, 112–113
self development and self-esteem impacted by, 320–321
single-parent family's, 406
Sonoembryology, 67
Spanking, 411
Spatial intelligence, 253
Sports. See Exercise and athletics
Spousal abuse, 90. See also Child abuse
Stanford-Binet Intelligence Scales, Fifth Edition (SB5), 248
Stanford Studies of Gifted Children, 12
Stereotypes. See Discrimination, prejudice and stereotypes
Sternberg, Robert, 252–254
Stillbirths, 84, 106, 111
Stoddard, Jake, 323–324
StopBullying.gov website, 374
Stranger anxiety, 285–286
Strange Situation, 275–277, 279
Substance use. See also Alcohol use; Drugs; Tobacco use
adolescent, 131, 292, 293, 364, 375
DARE program effectiveness combating, 17
genetic influences on, 64, 77
moral issues with, 364
prenatal development impacted by, 83, 87, 88–89, 90, 265
Suicide, suicide attempts and ideation
adolescent, 292, 293–295, 343, 373
bullying leading to, 373
child abuse leading to, 412

Suicide, suicide attempts and ideation
    (*Continued*)
  gay and lesbian, 343
  prevention of, 294–295
Surrogacy, 83, 84
Survey research, 42, 45
Symbolic function, 169
Syntax, 225, 227
Syphilis, 87
System of Multicultural Pluralistic
    Assessment (SOMPA), 251, 261

T
Taste, 117, 145
Tauton, Leanne, 292
Tay-Sachs disease, 65
Teenagers. *See* Adolescence
Telegraphic speech, 224
Television, movies, and video games
  adolescent influence of, 427–429
  aggression and viewed aggression
    correlation, 16, 39–40, 42–44,
    368–370, 371
  amount of time spent on, 425, 427
  body image influenced by, 152, 428
  controlling exposure to, 426
  discrimination and prejudice
    fostered by, 445
  Dora the Explorer on, 371, 420, 427
  gender influences of, 333
  middle childhood influence of,
    427–429
  preschool influence of, 420,
    425–427
  sedentary lifestyle associated with
    watching, 153, 426, 428
  Sesame Street on, 371, 420,
    426–427
Temperament
  attachment relationship to, 298
  categorization of, 297–298
  consequences of, 298
  cultural influences on, 298
  genetic and environmental
    influences on, 70, 76, 298–299
  infant behavior reflecting, 296–299
  physical growth and development
    reflective of, 134
Teratogens, 85–90
Terman, Lewis, 48–49
Terzic, Arif, 191, 217
Tessel, Melindah and Jermain, 91
Texting, 339, 391, 427
Thalidomide, 88

Theoretical perspectives
  assessments of, 25, 27, 29, 30, 32,
    33, 34, 35–36, 178–181,
    185–186, 213–214, 353
  behavioral perspective as, 25–27,
    35, 118–119
  bioecological approach as, 31–32,
    35
  biological perspective as, 331–332,
    334
  classical conditioning as, 26–27,
    118, 119
  cognitive neuroscience approaches
    as, 30, 42, 203–204, 205
  cognitive perspective as, 27–30, 35,
    333, 334, 370–371
  contextual perspective as,
    31–33, 35
  evolutionary perspective as, 34, 35
  Gilligan's approach as, 360,
    362–363
  information processing approach as,
    29–30, 191–215, 252–254, 257,
    258–259
  interactionist approaches as, 231
  Kohlberg's approach as, 360–362
  learning theory as, 27, 230,
    332–333, 334, 343, 354, 368, 445
  Marcia's theory as, 313–314
  nativist approaches as, 230–231
  operant conditioning as, 26–27,
    118–119
  Piaget's theory as, 28–29, 35,
    162–181, 226, 231–232, 352–353
  psychoanalytic perspective as,
    23–24, 25, 35, 275, 332, 334,
    343, 355, 367
  psychodynamic perspective as,
    23–25, 35, 299
  psychosocial theory as, 24–25, 35,
    299–300, 309, 312–313
  research on (*see* Research)
  socialcultural theory as, 32–33, 35,
    182–186, 384
  social identity theory as, 445–447
  social learning theory as, 27,
    332–333, 334, 354, 368, 445
  theories, defined, 22
  theory of mind as, 288–289, 385
  triarchic theory of intelligence as,
    252–254
  Vygotsky's theory as, 32–33, 35,
    182–186, 226, 232, 252, 384
Thomas, Alexander, 297

Tobacco use, 88–89, 90. *See also*
    Substance use
Toddlerhood. *See* Infancy and
    toddlerhood
Touch, 117, 145–146. *See also*
    Massage, infant
Toussaint, Antoine, 269
Traits
  dominant, 61
  genetic development of, 60–61,
    62–63
  personality (*see* Personality
    development)
  physical, 73 (*see also* Physical
    development)
  polygenic, 62–63
  recessive, 61
Transformation, in cognitive
    development, 171–172
Transgendered persons, 343
Treatments, experimental research on,
    42–43
Triarchic theory of intelligence,
    252–254
Twins
  genetics of, 59–60
  infant sociability among, 281
  intelligence of, 73–74
  mental health issues among, 77
  physical growth and development
    in, 134
  premature births among, 108
  research on, 60, 72–73, 73–74, 75,
    281, 343
  sexual orientation of, 343

U
Ultrasound sonography, 66, 67
Umbilical cords, 81, 97
Uninvolved parenting style, 356, 357
United Nations High Commission for
    Human Rights, 383
U.S. Department of Agriculture,
    MyPlate nutritional guidelines, 153
U.S. Department of Education, 48

V
Vaccinations, 103–104, 153
Vernix, 99
Video games. *See* Television, movies,
    and video games
Violence. *See* Aggression and
    violence; Child abuse; Domestic
    violence

Virginity pledges, 345
Vision, 117, 142–143, 144, 148, 257,
    258–259
Visual-recognition memory
    measurements, 257, 258
Vocal expressions, 287. *See also*
    Language development
Vygotsky, Lev Semenovich
  intelligence theories of, 252
  language theories of, 226, 232
  socialcultural and cognitive
    development theory of, 32–33,
    35, 182–186, 384

W
Watson, John B., 26, 35
Web-based communication. *See*
    Online communication
Wechsler Intelligence Scale for
    Children-Fourth Edition
    (WISC-IV), 249, 250
Weight
  excessive/obesity, 73, 139,
    151–153, 426, 428
  low birth, 87, 89, 95, 106–109
  physical growth and development
    changing, 126–130, 139,
    151–153
Whorf, Benjamin Lee, 231
Wilder, Marcia, 414
Women
  child development contributions
    of, 12
  as mothers (*see* Mothers)
  reproduction in (*see* Birth;
    Fertilization; Pregnancy; Prenatal
    development)
Work. *See* Employment and labor
World Health Organization, 433

X
X-linked genes, 62

Y
Yates, Andrea, 114

Z
Zone of proximal development (ZPD),
    183–185
Zygote intrafallopian transfer (ZIFT),
    83
Zygotes, 58, 59, 80–81, 83. *See also*
    Prenatal development